United States Secretary of Labor

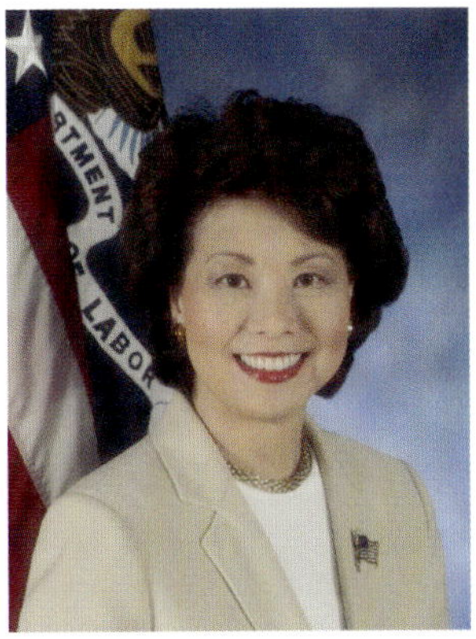

The key to a comfortable retirement is planning well in advance. Yet a recent survey indicates that with the "Baby Boom" generation approaching retirement age, less than half of Americans have calculated how much they will need to save for retirement.

To help Americans prepare for retirement, the U.S. Department of Labor has developed this book: *Taking the Mystery Out of Retirement Planning*. The information contained here is valuable to everyone, but it is specifically designed to help those who are about a decade from retirement.

Americans are living longer, healthier, and more active lives than ever before. Ideally, retirement years are a time for pursuing other interests, travel, perhaps volunteering in the community or even starting a new career.

To ensure a financially secure retirement, it is critical to make the right choices years ahead. Start on the path to retirement security ***today*** so you can have the retirement you have dreamed of.

Sincerely,

Elaine L. Chao

TAKING THE MYSTERY OUT OF RETIREMENT PLANNING

TABLE OF CONTENTS

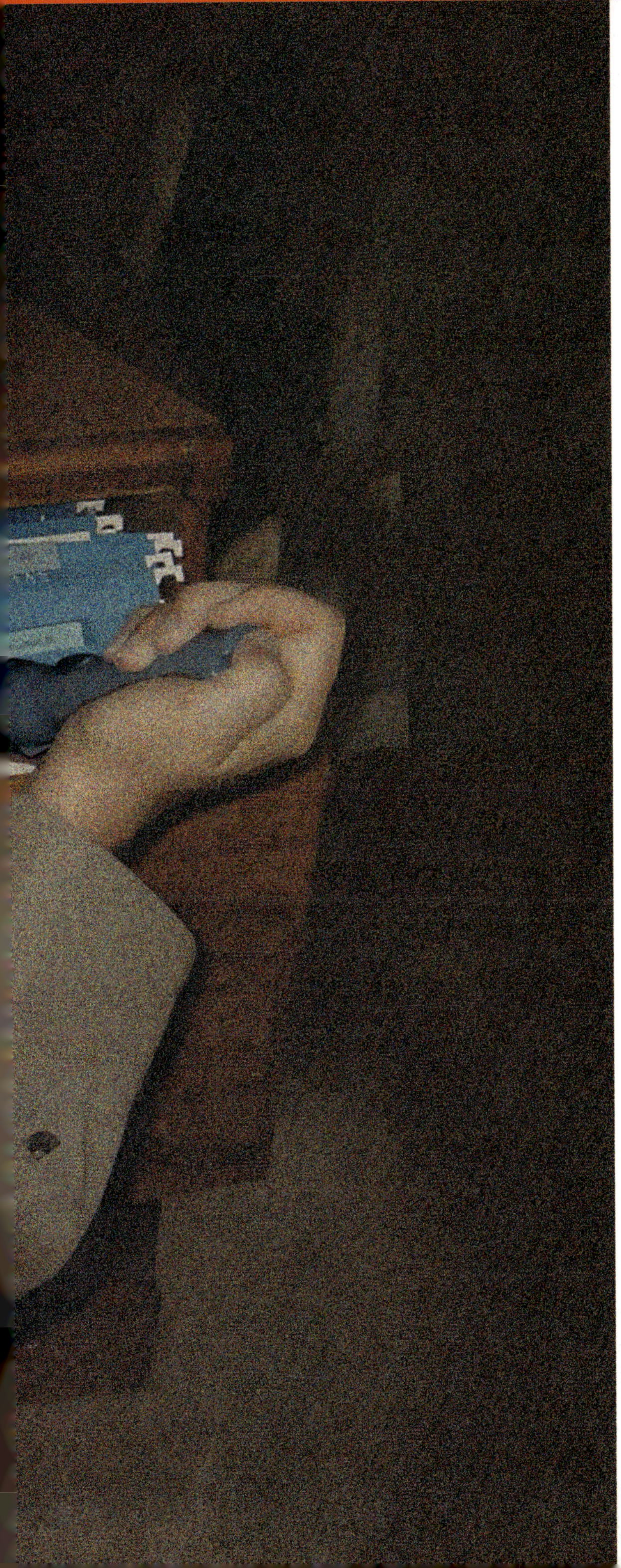

PLANNING FOR A LIFETIME

It's not going to be your parents' retirement—rewarded at 65 with a gold watch, a guaranteed pension, and health insurance for life. For many Americans, retiring in this new century is a mystery. Earlier generations of workers could rely on employer-provided pensions, but now many workers will need to rely on their own work-related and personal savings plus Social Security benefits. These savings have to last longer because Americans are living longer, often into their eighties and nineties.

If you are one of those people who want to plan – and are about 10 years from the day you retire – this booklet is for you. Today's (and tomorrow's) retirees may well have a new kind of retirement. With a longer and healthier life span, bikes, boats, planes, and RVs may be part of your life, because you are more likely than previous generations to be an active older American.

Opportunities to take courses, start a new career, and become a volunteer can make your future an adventure. A longer life, however, will also mean more medical care, some of which will not be covered by the federal Medicare program.

The whole retirement scene has changed and many American workers find it a mystery. In fact, a 2006 survey by the Employee Benefit Research Institute (EBRI) suggests that only 42 percent of Americans have tried to calculate how much they need to save for retirement. In this booklet, each chapter will give you clues on how to take control of your finances so that when you retire, you have the time and money to do what you've always wanted. For some, it's simply being with friends and family. For others, it's starting a new hobby or craft. And for some, it's starting a new life.

Whether you are 10 years from retirement or have a different timeframe – or even if you are retired – this booklet will help you to unravel the financial mysteries of life after work and to discover changes you can make for a financially secure future.

Time on Your Side

Getting started today will help you put time on your side. To help, *Taking the Mystery Out of Retirement Planning* offers a simplified, bottom-line approach to figuring out just how much you may need when you retire. The worksheets in this booklet will provide a guesstimate. Regard them as a starting point.

Each chapter in this booklet asks you to chart a different part of your financial life – your savings and your expenses – and helps you project future costs and savings well into your retirement years. Of course, no one has a crystal ball, and life has a way of throwing changes our way. But getting time on your side now, before you retire, means you will not be awake at 3 a.m. worrying about, instead of planning for, the future.

How to Use This Booklet: Simply read it to get familiar with retirement issues. Better yet, fill out the worksheets to figure the dollar amounts of what you have, how much it will grow in 10 years, and how much you may need to last over a 30-year period. Remember these amounts are only estimates, and you will want to update them from time to time.

Take your time. You may want to tackle one or two chapters, fill out the worksheets provided and then spend some time gathering the documents and information you will want to keep. Whether you approach the booklet chapter by chapter or all at once, keep going. Don't get stuck on details – guessing is okay, and you can always come back later with more accurate numbers and information.

This booklet uses three time periods in charting your retirement savings. The starting point is today, when you are about 56 years old and plan to work approximately 10 years more. This is a good time to take stock of where you are in terms of retirement savings and set financial goals you would like to achieve in the 10-year period you plan to work.

The second point in time is the day you retire, when you are about 65 to 66 years old. That period between now and then is an important one. In those (approximately 10) years, you will have time to put more of your paycheck to work in a retirement account. It will grow, not only from your additional savings, but also from the "miracle of compounding," the world's greatest math discovery, according to everyone's favorite genius, Albert Einstein. This is the result of earnings from interest and from investments continually increasing the base amount.

Finally, the third time period used in this booklet is the approximately 30-year span you hope to enjoy retirement. It is the time period experts suggest you plan for, based on the average 65-year old American male living 17 more years and the average 65-year old female living 20 more years. These are only averages, so planning for 30 years will help you avoid outliving your income.

As you read through this booklet, keep an eye on the Timeline for Retirement that follows. Some of the terms, like "catch-up" retirement contributions beginning at age 50, may be new to you. The timeline offers some milestone opportunities to make changes so you can have the kind of retirement you want. The time to start is today.

CLUE 1

Timeline For Retirement:

AT AGE 50 Begin making catch-up contributions, an extra amount that those over 50 can add, to 401(k) and other retirement accounts.

AT 59 1/2 No more tax penalties on early withdrawals from retirement accounts, but leaving money in means more time for it to grow.

AT 62 The minimum age to receive Social Security benefits, but delaying means a bigger monthly benefit.

AT 65 Eligible for Medicare.

AT 66 Eligible for full Social Security benefits if born between 1943 and 1954.

AT 70 1/2 Start taking minimum withdrawals from most retirement accounts by this age; otherwise, you may be charged heavy tax penalties in the future.

Chapter 1

TRACKING DOWN TODAY'S MONEY

This chapter will help you shine a light on the mystery of where you will find the money to support yourself in retirement. Many people don't have a clear idea of how much money they actually have, so it's hard to know how much they might be able to count on when they no longer work. Finding out what part of today's money can go toward retirement simply means adding up the value of all your current assets. In this case, "assets" are cash, investments, and anything of value you can exchange for cash, like your house, savings bonds, or even fine jewelry. This figure will be your first important clue.

Recording these amounts could be a pleasant surprise. You don't want to count emergency money and savings for your children's education or a big trip – only money that you are not going to touch for at least 10 years. For purposes of the following worksheet, you also don't want to include any future Social Security benefits and guaranteed pensions because these items are future income, not current assets (and they will be included later). Money in work-related retirement plans, like 401(k) plans, is counted, however, and you will want to include amounts from current and former jobs. In fact, these assets will probably be at the top of your "today's money" list that follows.

More Than You Think

Tracking your money in retirement plans should be fairly easy. If you didn't roll over your retirement plan balance when you changed jobs into a new retirement plan account or into an IRA, or if you didn't take your account balance as cash, you may discover some forgotten retirement assets you have. This is a good time to think about keeping your money with fewer, rather than more, quality financial institutions so it is easier to manage.

Recording current and old retirement account amounts on Worksheet A, Today's Money (see page 8), is important for a couple of reasons. First, locating any old account could take time. The longer it's "lost," the harder it will be to find. Second, understanding your current financial standing should automatically start you thinking about how to make your money grow.

Quit Worrying, Start Planning

Remember you're facing a retirement that's probably going to be longer than your parents' and will involve more uncertainties. This new kind of retirement probably means there are many American workers worrying about, instead of planning for, the future.

You can choose to stop worrying and start figuring. Not only will you come up with facts to work with, the chances are good you might change the way you save. The 2006 EBRI survey also found that 51 percent of people who tried to figure out their financial futures ended up changing their retirement savings plans.

If you are a married woman: In preparing for retirement, women face the very real possibility of spending part of their retirement years without the support of a husband – most likely through widowhood. The loss of a spouse can sometimes mean the loss or reduction of benefits that can place women in financial jeopardy. For that reason, women will need to focus on their financial resources as a single person as well as half of a couple.

For purposes of the following worksheets, consider filling them out as a couple and as a single person. Consider what happens to your Social Security and to retirement benefits if your spouse dies or you divorce. Know what assets you can count on. Check Social Security benefit documents, retirement plan documents, and wills. Remember that wills are important, but they may not provide the protection desired. Depending on the way assets are titled or the terms of a will, the money women believe they can count on may not be passed to the surviving spouse.

"51 percent of people who tried to figure out their financial futures ended up changing their retirement savings plan."

When filling out the worksheets that follow, remember to include your spouse's assets if you're married. Like all of the worksheets in this booklet, be prepared to redo this first one. A raise and changes in your investments, for example, will affect the numbers on Worksheet A. To make it easy, extra worksheets are included at the back of this booklet.

ABOUT WORKSHEET A (PAGE 8):

TODAY'S MONEY

Here you will write down money you have today that you plan to use when you retire in about 10 years (do not add Social Security and traditional pensions at this stage; they will be figured in later on). The first money source, the balance on your current retirement plan account at work (a 401(k)

MUTUAL
FUND

plan, for instance), should be easy to find. If you don't have a recent statement, ask the benefits department at work.

If you rolled over accounts from former jobs into an IRA, then read your statement or call the financial institution holding this account. In addition, get statements from all your bank or mutual fund IRA accounts, Keogh retirement savings, Simplified Employee Pension-IRAs (SEP-IRAs), and Savings Incentive Match Plans for Employees of Small Employers (SIMPLE) plans.

Personal savings and investments are next as possible retirement resources. They could be in a savings or checking account at a bank or credit union or in a brokerage account. The assets in these accounts may include cash, U.S. savings bonds, certificates of deposit, stock and bond mutual funds, and individual stocks and bonds.

To get a dollar amount for your home equity, subtract the current mortgage balance from the current market value of your house. Also subtract the amount you owe on home equity loans or lines of credit (enter it as a negative amount on the worksheet). The bank holding the mortgage can provide the amount of your remaining mortgage balance. An appraiser or real estate professional can give you an estimate of the value of your house in the current market, or you can check on the Internet recent sales in your neighborhood (real estate values can change, however, so check your home's value from time to time).

Be realistic about how much of your home equity might be available for retirement. Remember that you will always need housing, and that condo fees, real estate taxes, maintenance and repairs, and rent tend to go up.

Other assets could be valuable collections or the cash value of life insurance. Keep in mind that the actual value of items like houses, boats, and collections can be determined only when real buyers make real offers.

"Be realistic about how much of your home equity might be available for retirement...you will always need housing."

WORKSHEET A

TODAY'S MONEY

Instructions: Record amounts for yourself and for your spouse in columns 1 and 2. Add up the money across each row for you and your spouse and write the total in column 3. Then add all the numbers down column 3 and write the total in column 3 at the bottom.

	1 You	2 Spouse	3 Total
Work-related retirement savings			
401(k) or 403(b)			
Keogh			
SEP-IRA			
SIMPLE IRA			
Other			
IRAs (traditional)			
IRAs (Roth)			
Other			
Home equity			
Market value of home			
Mortgage and liens (enter as negative amount)			
Personal savings and investments			
Other assets (collections, etc.)			
TOTAL ASSETS			

Chapter 2

TRACKING DOWN FUTURE MONEY-AT RETIREMENT

Now that you know from Chapter 1 how much money you have today, you can estimate how much that money could be worth – because it will probably grow – in the 10 years between now and retirement. The worksheets will help you project a 10-year total, which will help you estimate a 30-year total. Yes, it's just a guesstimate, because the further in the future you plan, the more that can happen. But the totals give you some idea of how much you may have for your retirement years.*

In addition, the worksheets in this chapter will let you see how much your money can grow by investing it in different ways. In fact, you will be able to assign different rates of return to different types of savings and to see how your decisions can impact the growth of your money over the next 10 years. Rates of return are simply the amount your money earns over a certain period.

How your money increases over time will depend on the nature of your investments, the rates of return, and other factors, such as the economy. One kind of investment, for instance, is a bond, which is often referred to as a "fixed income" investment because the interest rate is fixed. As an example, if you owned a bond with an original value of $10,000 and you got a 5 percent return (or yield) on your investment, your original investment would increase to $16,289 in 10 years.

Digging Deeper

You will probably want to dig deeper by assigning different rates of return to different pots of money – workplace savings accounts, IRAs, bank savings accounts -- you have put aside for retirement. Let's say you have $2,000 in a checking account that you never use. Your rate of return, in this case, with interest compounded monthly, will be low, maybe 1 percent. But your money is safe. Then let's say you've invested in a stock mutual fund for 15 years using your retirement plan account and you get a return of 11 percent. Investments in securities can bring a higher rate of return than simple interest because prices of securities often rise and gains are compounded. Of course, security prices can fall, as we saw with stocks in 2000 and 2001. The tradeoff for aiming for higher returns is taking on more risk, including the risk of losing money. Keep this in mind in selecting rates of return for the worksheets that follow.

In the example above, with some money invested in stocks and some in a safer, interest-bearing account, you are already doing what the experts recommend. You are practicing "asset allocation" by putting your money in different types of products that earn different rates of return. Financial planners highly recommend this technique as a way to spread risk. A general allocation is to have some money in "cash," such as a savings, checking, or money market account with

*People who are retired may want to skip the worksheets in this chapter and focus on the information about ways to grow your money.

AND AFTER

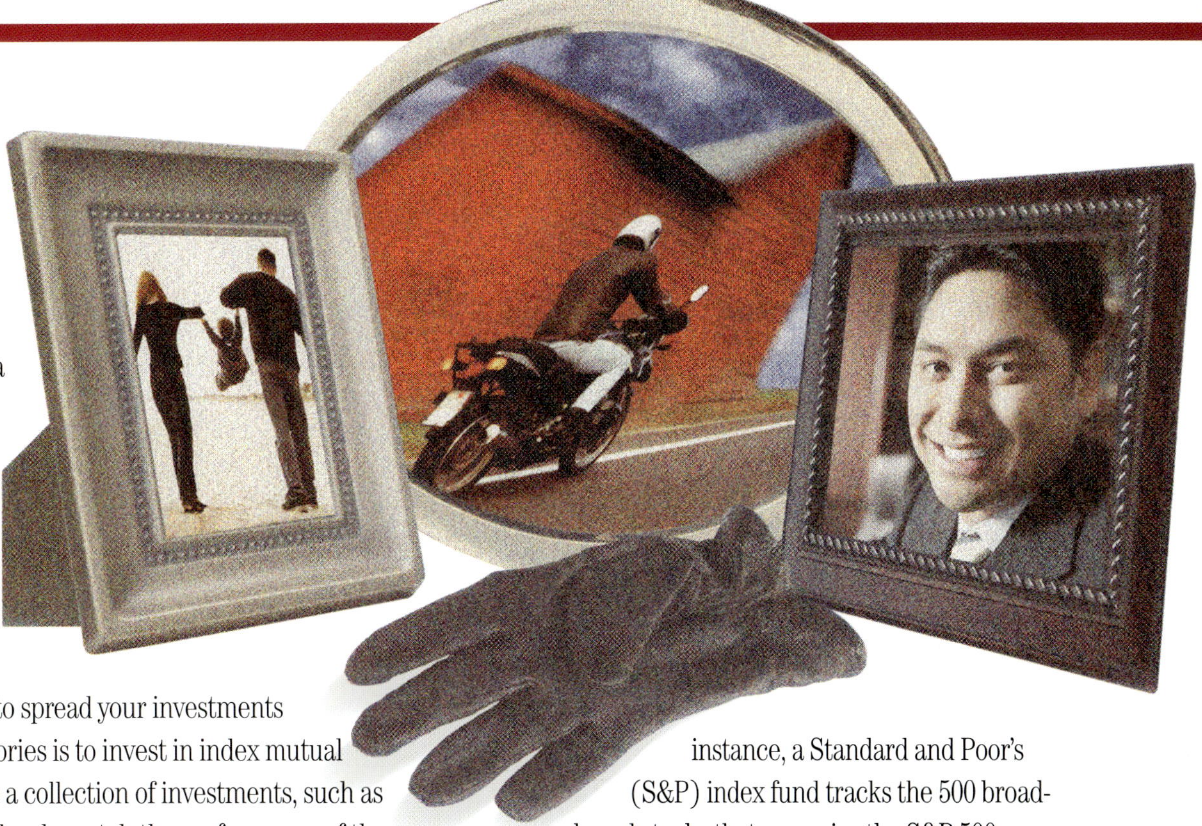

little or no risk; some money in bonds, with a little more risk but paying more interest; and some money in stocks, with more risk but a likely higher return, especially in the long run.

Another way to spread your investments among different categories is to invest in index mutual funds. Index funds are a collection of investments, such as bonds or stocks, that closely match the performance of the major holdings for that category of investment. For instance, a Standard and Poor's (S&P) index fund tracks the 500 broad-based stocks that comprise the S&P 500 Index. A bond index fund would track the performance of major bond holdings in that index. In this way, your investment is following the financial market for that particular category.

"Experts recommend that you spread your money among a range of investments so that your money is diversified."

Experts recommend that you spread your money among a range of investments so that your money is "diversified." In addition, most experts add that you should not only invest *among* categories but *within* each major category as well. For instance, your risk of losing money is less if you buy shares in several mutual funds investing in various types of assets (such as large company stocks, small company stocks and bonds). Even investing in just one mutual fund will help you to diversify compared to investing in individual securities on your own, since mutual funds, by their nature, allow you to invest in a collection of stocks, bonds, etc.

Financial planners believe that diversifying your investments helps reduce risk as markets move up and down. For example, in 1980 when some certificates of deposit (CDs) were paying 12 percent, stocks were barely

CLUE 2

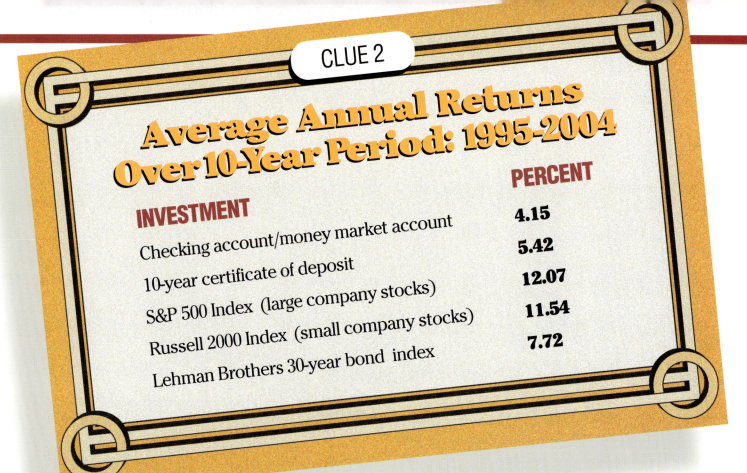

Average Annual Returns Over 10-Year Period: 1995-2004

INVESTMENT	PERCENT
Checking account/money market account	4.15
10-year certificate of deposit	5.42
S&P 500 Index (large company stocks)	12.07
Russell 2000 Index (small company stocks)	11.54
Lehman Brothers 30-year bond index	7.72

holding their own; but in 1999 most stock prices were rising fast, and CDs were paying 5 percent. You will see sample rates of return for some common places to put your money in the box above.

Too much money in one type of investment is always a bad idea and puts your money at risk. For example, many American workers are holding a lot of their employers' stock in their retirement accounts. This ties both your current paycheck and your retirement savings to one employer's success . . . or failure. This can be risky.

ABOUT WORKSHEETS B (PAGE 12) AND C (PAGE 14):

YOUR MONEY AND NEW SAVINGS

One quick way to estimate how much money you could have by your first year of retirement is to multiply your total retirement assets from Worksheet A, Chapter 1, by 1.629 (the factor equal to a 5 percent rate of return for 10 years). The result shows how much you will have if your money grows at 5 percent in that 10-year period. For example:

$100,000.00 (total from Worksheet A)
x 1.629
$162,900.00

The 5 percent return, by the way, is used to keep things simple: remember investment returns go up and down and cannot be guaranteed.

But digging deeper may mean coming up with your own numbers, and the worksheets that follow let you do just that. To keep it simple, the worksheets give you a choice of rates of return – 3, 5, and 7 percent – and include multiplication factors for each of these rates. **(Instructions continue on pg.13)**

WORKSHEET B

YOUR MONEY-10 YEARS FROM TODAY

Asset Growth Factors for Three Selected Rates of Return

1.344 for 3% 1.629 for 5% 1.967 for 7%

Work-related retirement savings	1 **Current $ value** (from Worksheet A, Column 3)	2 **Asset growth factor** (rate of return)	3 **Asset value in 10 years** (Column 1 x Column 2)
401(k) or 403(b)			
Keogh			
SEP-IRA			
SIMPLE IRA			
Other			
IRAs (traditional)			
IRAs (Roth)			
Other			
Home equity			
Market value of home			
Mortgage and liens (enter as negative amount)			
Personal savings and investments			
Other assets (collections, etc.)			
TOTAL ASSETS			

They are lower than the 8 to 10 percent returns often used before the stock market fell in 2000. Whether you're an optimist or a pessimist about interest and rates of return, being conservative in your estimates is safer; better to have extra money than too little.

Worksheet B, *Your Money - 10 Years from Today* will let you take your current retirement saving sources and then figure out how much they might grow over 10 years, depending on how the money is invested.

In Worksheet B, you will be able to transfer the dollar amounts for your income sources directly from column 3 of Worksheet A, starting with 401(k) and 403(b) plans. Then multiply each of these results by an asset growth (rate of return) factor you'll see at the top of Worksheet B. Write the total in Column 3.

The rate you choose depends on what you've done with your retirement savings. If they're all in fixed income investments, your rate is predetermined. If they're in mutual funds, you'll need to do some research to figure out past rates of return as a guide for estimates for the future. Retirement plan statements should indicate past rates of return. But remember, for investments, past performance never guarantees future results.

Like Worksheet A, Social Security benefits and pensions are not included since you most likely won't receive these sources of income until retirement. There will be more later in the publication about how waiting to receive Social Security (and pension) benefits will mean a bigger check.

Estimating a rate of return on your home will depend on the real estate market in your community. Figure a low estimate for this and for any personal property in which the value depends on how much a buyer would pay. Also consider any mortgage or liens you have on the home since those would be repaid from any cash you would obtain on the sale of the home.

If you have other investments, such as annuities, put them in the "Other assets" row of Worksheet B. In addition to these sources, include any money you can count on receiving in the next 10 years – for example, an inheritance – and enter its estimated lump-sum value.

As an example of a possible calculation, suppose you have $10,000 in a traditional IRA, and you believe it will earn 5 percent over the next 10 years. Your calculation would look like this:

$10,000.00	(amount in an IRA)
x 1.629	(rate of return factor for 5%)
$16,290.00	(savings in 10 years)

When you have finished Worksheet B, go on to Worksheet C, *New Savings Between Now and Retirement*. This worksheet will allow you to take any additional workplace and personal savings you can expect to add between now and retirement and determine how much they will grow to at the time of your retirement.

You can enter any estimated periodic contributions (such as to your 401(k) or IRA) between now and retirement in the first column. Remember that you are only estimating the rate of return on this money over a period of years and that you will need to review your estimate from time to time.

Multiply these amounts by the savings growth factor for the rate of return you select from the top of Worksheet C. As with

WORKSHEET C

NEW SAVINGS BETWEEN NOW AND RETIREMENT

Savings Growth Factors for Three Selected Rates of Return

139.741 for 3% 155.282 for 5% 173.085 for 7%

	1 Estimated monthly savings amount	2 Savings growth factor	3 Value of savings in 10 years (Column 1 x Column 2)
Work-related retirement savings			
401(k) or 403(b)			
Keogh			
SEP-IRA			
SIMPLE IRA			
Other			
IRAs (traditional)			
IRAs (Roth)			
Other			
Home equity			
Market value of home			
Mortgage and liens (enter as positive amount)			
Personal savings and investments			
Other assets (collections, etc.)			
TOTAL ASSETS			

Worksheets A and B, three different rates of return have been selected but based upon the nature of your investments, you may want to use a different rate of return. Enter the results in the third column.

As an example, if you save $100 a month in a workplace 401(k) plan, and if you believe that investment will earn 5 percent per year, the calculation would look like this:

$100.00	(savings each month)
x 155.282	(rate of return factor for 5%)
$15,528.20	(savings in 10 years)

You are making great progress in tracking down your retirement assets and solving the first half of your retirement mystery. Now move on to Worksheet D, *Monthly Income Over a 30-Year Retirement,* to take all of your anticipated assets from Worksheets B and C and convert them to a monthly income that you can use later to compare with your anticipated monthly expenses in retirement.

In this worksheet, we now add Social Security and pension benefits since it deals with income you can rely on during retirement.

You can fill in the box in Column 3 for Social Security benefits by using information readily available from your Social Security Administration (SSA) statement. You should be getting a SSA statement every year with information about your own benefit.

If you have a fixed pension from work, the amount for Worksheet D is based on your pay at the end of your career. Your employer, union, or pension plan administrator can give you details about the amount and start date of your pension, and whether you will get your pension in a lump sum or fixed monthly checks (see discussion in Chapter 5 describing these options to help you choose). If you receive your benefit as a lump sum, put that amount in Column 1. If you receive it as a fixed monthly benefit, fill in only Column 3.

If you were in a traditional pension plan that was abandoned for some reason, like your employer going out of business, you will still receive some (or all) of your pension benefits since these plans are federally insured. Information about your plan and benefits may be available from the Pension Benefit Guaranty Corporation. (See Chapter 6 for PBGC contact information.)

For those assets you tracked down for Worksheets B and C, take the totals for each source, such as your 401(k) plan, from both worksheets, add them together and enter them in Column 1. Select an income conversion factor representing the rate of return you expect to earn on those assets in the future and enter it in Column 2. Multiply Column 1 by Column 2 and enter the result in Column 3. Remember, this calculation is a guesstimate, since things that impact your income, such as your tax status, will vary.

When you add up all of the numbers in Column 3, you will have a monthly income for the 30 years of your retirement. This fixed monthly income is used to simplify the calculations. Realize that it takes into account the continued growth of your assets while you are withdrawing money to live on.

Also keep in mind that while the worksheet includes your home equity, you may need to live in your home for some time or use some of the assets from its sale to purchase another home or pay for rent, so it may not provide immediate income.

Here is an example of the Worksheet D calculation:

$50,000.00	(401(k) account balance)
x 0.005368	(income conversion factor for 5%)
$268.40	(per month)

WORKSHEET D

MONTHLY INCOME OVER A 30-YEAR RETIREMENT

Income Conversion Factors for Assumed Rates of Interest

0.004216 for 3% 0.005368 for 5% 0.006653 for 7%

	1 Accumulated assets (Column 3 from Worksheet B plus Column 3 from Worksheet C)	2 Income conversion factor	3 Monthly income beginning at retirement (Column 1 x Column 2)
Social Security			
Work-Related Retirement Savings			
Pension benefits			
401(k) or 403(b)			
Keogh			
SEP-IRA			
SIMPLE IRA			
Other			
IRAs (traditional)			
IRAs (Roth)			
Home equity			
Market value of home			
Mortgage and liens (enter as negative amount)			
Personal savings and investments			
Other assets (collections, etc.)			
TOTAL ASSETS			

Chapter 3

TRACKING DOWN FUTURE EXPENSES

This chapter will start you on the road toward a realistic look at your expenses in retirement and how they will be affected by inflation. These numbers are important clues to your retirement mystery.

You will be looking at your expenses today and estimating how they will change over time and, specifically, during two other time periods: the day you retire 10 years from now and over the approximate 30-year span of your retirement. In doing so, you will have some idea of whether the money you have saved will be enough to last. You will also have a chance to look at your spending patterns and decide how they could change over time. After all, you can't control inflation over this stretch of time, but you certainly can control what you spend.

Your expenses will likely change as you grow older. Early on, you will spend less on work-related things like transportation and clothing. Maybe you'll spend more on traveling, hobbies, or other things you have always wanted to do. As you age, it is likely that more of your budget will go toward medical expenses, which you will read about soon. Retired people may find that recording their expenses will alter future spending patterns.

ABOUT WORKSHEET E (PAGE 19):

MONTHLY EXPENSES TODAY

First add up current monthly expenses in Worksheet E (*Monthly Expenses Today*). Then in Worksheet F, *Monthly Expenses in 10 Years*, take those totals and adjust them for inflation to estimate your expenses during your first year of retirement. Chapter 4 will look at those expenses over a 30-year retirement and how you will be spending the income you just calculated. If you want a quick estimate of how much monthly income you'll need to cover expenses in retirement, figure on at least 70 percent of your preretirement income. Many experts are now increasing that figure to 80 or 90 percent.

Avoid getting stuck on the details and giving up because you don't have exact records of your spending. If you don't know the exact amount you pay for car insurance, for example, use a guesstimate until you can look it up. You can always come back with more accurate numbers.

Don't include things like college tuition that are one-time costs. If monthly bills for one item vary, like your heating bill, get a year's worth, add them up, and divide that total by 12 for an average monthly expense. If you get a bill four times a year, add up a year's worth and divide by 12 for an average monthly cost. Remember to include your spouse's expenses if you're married and the expenses of anyone financially dependent on you.

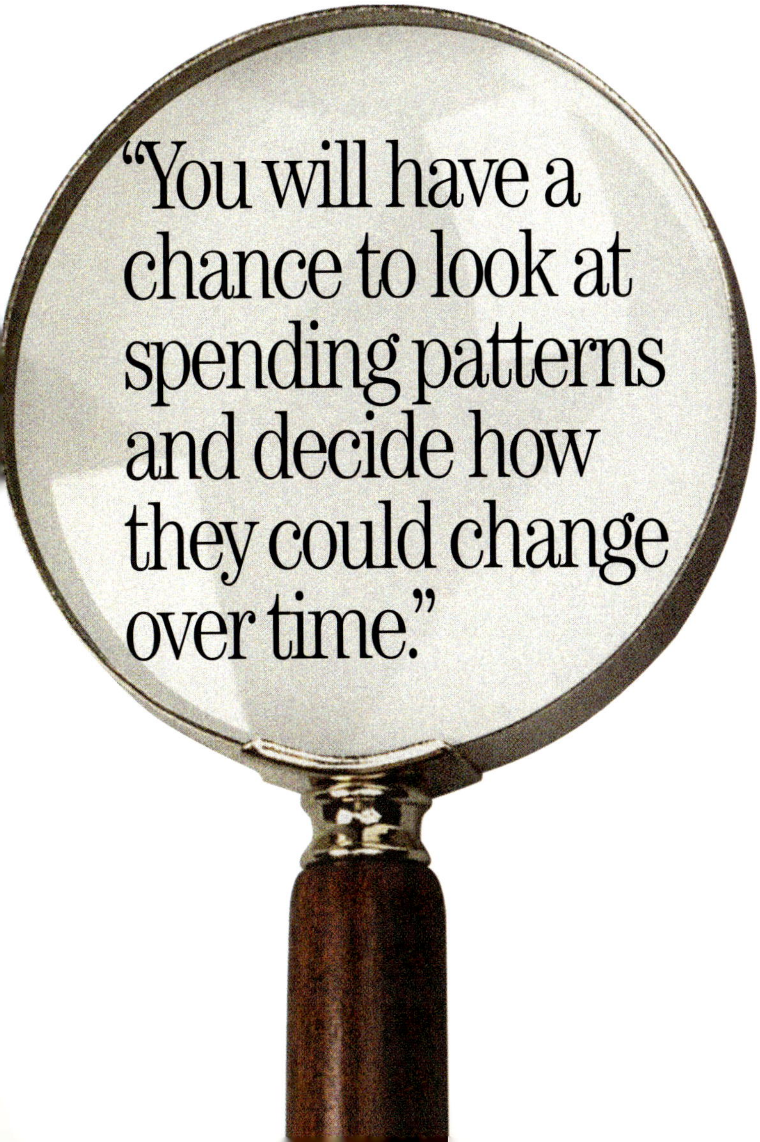

"You will have a chance to look at spending patterns and decide how they could change over time."

Inflation and Your Future

Inflation, in its simplest terms, means that dollar for dollar your money will not buy as much next year as it does this year. This means inflation is a major factor in determining how much money you will need in retirement since, to cover inflation's impact, you will need more money every year. In other words, if your money is not earning more than the rate of inflation, you will lose part of your nest egg's buying power.

You can't know and can't control future inflation. The only accurate inflation rates are from the past, and they vary widely. In 1980, overall prices went up a whopping 13.5 percent; in 2002, they went up only 1.6 percent. Looking at the past shows how rates may vary widely. Worksheet F uses the factor for a 3.5 percent rise in prices for the next 10 years. But these are estimates, and remember, we've gotten used to low inflation overall—with a few glaring exceptions—over the last decade.

Facing Down Rising Costs

One exception to low inflation rates is medical costs, which have risen faster than inflation over the last 20 years, and which some experts think will rise about 7 percent a year over the coming years. If you have, or your family history includes, a serious medical condition like heart

WORKSHEET E

MONTHLY EXPENSES TODAY

	1 Monthly Amount
Housing	
Mortgage (Including condo fees)	
Rent	
Maintenance	
Food (at home)	
Utilities	
Electricity	
Heat	
Internet/cable	
Phones	
Water/sewer	
Clothing	
Taxes	
Real estate	
Income (state and federal)	
Other property taxes	
Insurance	
House	
Life	
Car	
Disability	
Long-term care	

	Monthly Amount[1]
Loans	
Car	
Credit card	
Other	
Workplace retirement and personal savings	
Personal Care	
Hair cut	
Dry cleaning	
Gym	
Other	
Transportation	
Car repairs and maintenance	
Gas	
Parking	
Public transportation	
Health Care	
Health insurance	
Doctor visits	
Hospital	
Medicine	
Over-the-counter medicine	

	Monthly Amount[1]
Health Care (continued)	
Dental	
Vision	
Noncovered items	
Travel/vacations	
Entertainment	
Eating out	
Hobbies	
Movies/theater	
Charitable contributions	
Other	
Gifts	
Membership dues	
Pet-related costs	
TOTAL ESTIMATED MONTHLY EXPENSES (other than health)	
TOTAL ESTIMATED MONTHLY EXPENSES (health)	

disease, you will probably spend more on health care than you ever imagined. In fact, the consulting firm of Hewitt Associates estimates that, on average, 20 percent of retiree income will be spent on health care.

While Medicare is a great benefit to persons 65 and older, it does not cover all medical costs – deductibles, copayments, and long-term care, for example. Medicare Part A covers hospital care only. Medicare Part B, an additional insurance you will be offered when you become 65, covers doctors' services, outpatient hospital care, and things like physical and occupational therapy and some home health care. The current cost of Medicare Part B is about $88.50 per month, and it goes up every year. In addition to Medicare Parts A and B, many retirees buy Medigap policies for uncovered services like dental and vision care and drugs. Depending upon where you live and the policy you choose, you can pay $55 to $300 a month. In 1999, Medicare, private insurance, and/or Medicaid paid for only about 65 percent of retirees' overall health care expenses.

An additional feature is the Medicare prescription drug program (Medicare Part D). Those who become eligible for Medicare Part A and/or Part B can join a prescription drug plan offered in their area. By paying a small premium – around $37 a month in 2006 – those who join can get prescription drugs at a lower cost. (The *Resources* section on page 42 includes publications about this program.)

If you are thinking about retiring early, you may have to buy health insurance until Medicare kicks in at age 65 if your employer does not cover health care for retirees. You should know that employer-provided health benefits for retirees might not be guaranteed, and could be reduced or eliminated by your former employer under some circumstances.

Where Will You Live When You Retire?

Make planning for your future housing needs one of your first priorities since where you live in retirement affects not only your income, but also your emotional, social, and physical well being. It is an important part of your overall retirement strategy. While the cost of owning a home hasn't gone up as much as health care, it is high in many regions. Home heating and cooling costs are rising fast too. Maintenance, condo fees, real estate taxes, and insurance are other costs affected by inflation.

As you age, you may want to look into other types of housing. Independent living facilities, designed for reasonably healthy older people, often require a hefty down payment, say $200,000, and then a monthly fee of about $2,000. Saving for nursing home care, which in 2005 averaged $203 a day for a private room, also might make you feel more financially secure, given that at least 40 percent of today's 65-year-old Americans will spend some time in the future in a nursing home.

With medical and housing costs such a big part of a retirement budget, it's no surprise that products and services have been developed to help plan for and manage these costs. Rising health care costs, in particular, could consume all the money saved for retirement. One of the more recent products developed is long-term care insurance, which can protect retirees' assets by paying for medical care in a nursing home and sometimes in your own home. Premiums vary by the features you choose,

own home. Premiums vary by the features you choose, such as the amount of the daily benefit paid and protection against inflation. The typical annual premiums for a 60-year old can be as high as $2,500 a year. Buying such a policy at a later age means higher premiums. If you're considering a policy, get some advice, because long-term care insurance is a new product and some policyholders may find the coverage isn't what they need.

"On average, 20 percent of retiree income will be spent on health care."

To cope with these future expenses, some preretirees are starting special health care savings funds at work, separate from their retirement savings. One example is a new type of account, a health savings account (HSA), which is designed to help certain employees save for future qualified medical and retiree health expenses on a tax-free basis. Essentially, an HSA is a savings account into which you can deposit money for future use. If you belong to a health plan with a deductible of at least $1,000 (for individual coverage) or $2,000 (for family coverage), you may be able to set up an HSA. Individuals who don't belong to a workplace health plan can sign up for HSAs with some banks, insurance companies, and other approved entities.

These accounts can receive contributions from you, your employer, or even a family member on your behalf. You can use the funds from an HSA to help offset future medical costs, and the money in your account can be carried over from year to year. In addition, this type of account is portable; it stays with you as you move from one employer to another or if you leave the work force. To learn more about health savings account criteria, see the *Resources* section.

WORKSHEET F

MONTHLY EXPENSES IN 10 YEARS

(First year of retirement)

	1 Total monthly expenses now (from monthly expenses column in Worksheet E)	2 10-year inflation factor of 1.4106 (3.5%) (except for health care)	3 Total expenses in 10 years adjusted for inflation (Columns 1x2)
Housing			
Mortgage (Including condo fees) Rent Maintenance			
Food (at home)			
Utilities			
Electricity Heat Internet/cable Phones Water/sewer			
Clothing			
Taxes			
Real estate Income (state and federal) Other property taxes			
Insurance			
House Life Car Disability Long-term care			

	1 Total monthly expenses now (from monthly expenses column in Worksheet E)	2 10-year inflation factor of 1.4106 (3.5%) (except for health care)	3 Total expenses in 10 years adjusted for inflation (Columns 1x2)	
Loans				
Car Credit card Other				
Workplace retirement and personal savings				
Personal Care				
Hair cut Dry cleaning Gym Other				
Transportation				
Car repairs and maintenance Gas Parking Public transportation				
Health Care	For a	7% inflation factor, use	1.9672	
Health insurance Medicare Part B Medicare Part D Medigap Doctor visits Hospital Medicine Over-the-counter medicine				

WORKSHEET F CONTINUED

MONTHLY EXPENSES IN 10 YEARS

(First year of retirement)

	1 Total monthly expenses now (from monthly expenses column in Worksheet E)	2 10-year inflation factor of 1.4106 (3.5%) (except for health care)	3 Total expenses in 10 years adjusted for inflation (Columns 1x2)
Health Care (continued)			
Dental Vision Noncovered items			
Travel/vacations			
Entertainment			
Eating out Hobbies Movies/theater			
Charitable contributions			
Other			
Gifts Membership dues Pet-related costs			
TOTAL MONTHLY EXPENSES ADJUSTED FOR 10 YEARS INFLATION (other than health)			
TOTAL MONTHLY EXPENSES ADJUSTED FOR 10 YEARS INFLATION (health)			

ABOUT WORKSHEET F (PAGE 23):

MONTHLY EXPENSES IN 10 YEARS

This worksheet will show you how inflation can increase your total expenses in your first year of retirement.

You will notice that Worksheet F has room for some new types of health-related expenses many retirees are likely to incur in retirement.

Here is an example of the calculations you will do in Worksheet F:

$200.00 (amount spent on food each month today)
x 1.4106 (inflation factor of 3.5%)

$282.12 (cost of the same food basket in 10 years)

"If you want
a quick estimate,
figure on at least
80-90 percent of your
preretirement
income to cover
expenses."

Note that for many mortgages and some loans, your payments have taken into account the rate of inflation. If you have a fixed mortgage or loan, you will not need to do the calculation for this item. However, your mortgage expenses may change after retirement if you decide to sell your home and purchase something smaller or move to a region with lower housing costs.

The worksheets in this booklet don't account for savings during retirement in order to simplify the calculations. However, you may find or put aside additional savings in retirement. For example, since your home mortgage will be paid at some point, this may be one place where money will be freed up. You may want to use that money (or other funds) as savings during retirement, whether to add to your nest egg for unexpected retirement emergencies or to plan for inflated expenses later in your retirement. But remember, it is easier to save now than it will be in retirement.

Chapter 4

COMPARING INCOME AND EXPENSES

Now you will compare your income with your expenses during retirement and see if they match up. This is the number you've been working toward as you've investigated your assets and income, then expenses, and finally, figured the effects of time on your money. By the end of Chapter 4, you will discover whether you need to save more for retirement and, if so, how much more...and you will learn how to grow your savings over time.

Few people will have exactly the amount of money they will need in retirement. Most will get a negative figure – a gap – when they do the math. If this is your situation, this chapter can help you figure how much more to save each month over the next 10 years until you retire. After you come up with your totals, be sure to read on to find out the difference a year can make and the five ways to close the gap and boost your savings. Where will you find additional savings? Here are some suggestions for active workers and retirees alike.

You probably know by now the easiest way to watch your nest egg grow is to make the maximum contribution to your workplace savings plan through payroll deductions. If you are 50 or over, you will have the chance to add even more to your savings through catch-up contributions, ranging from $500 to $5,000, depending on the type of retirement plan you have. And you are reducing your taxes. If there's no retirement plan at work, you can add annual contributions to any IRA accounts you have.

Join the Club

Most people haven't thought about how long their savings will last in retirement or how much inflation will increase over time.

Worksheet G is where all your prior work comes together. Building on the clues uncovered in the earlier worksheets, Worksheet G compares your anticipated income and expenses over the 30 years of your retirement. Making the comparison in dollars valued at the time of your retirement, this worksheet takes into account that while you will have a fixed monthly income, your expenses will increase due to inflation.

At the beginning of retirement, most people's monthly income likely will exceed their expenses; but after a decade or so, expenses begin to exceed the monthly income. Realizing this now will allow you to save and invest any extra income in the early years of retirement so that it will

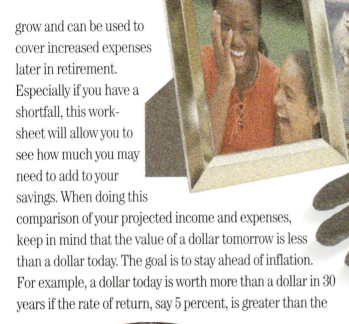

grow and can be used to cover increased expenses later in retirement. Especially if you have a shortfall, this worksheet will allow you to see how much you may need to add to your savings. When doing this comparison of your projected income and expenses, keep in mind that the value of a dollar tomorrow is less than a dollar today. The goal is to stay ahead of inflation. For example, a dollar today is worth more than a dollar in 30 years if the rate of return, say 5 percent, is greater than the inflation rate, say 3.5 percent. The worksheet addresses the impact of inflation by converting your anticipated cash flows into a constant dollar value at the time of your retirement.

"Few people will have exactly the amount of money they will need in retirement."

ABOUT WORKSHEET G (PAGE 29):

COMPARING PROJECTED INCOME AND EXPENSES

Start Worksheet G by taking the total monthly income calculated in Worksheet D and multiply it by a value adjustment factor you select from Clue 3 (page 31). Select the rate of return with a 0 percent inflation rate. Then multiply this result by 360 – the number of months in a 30-year retirement. Enter that amount in Column 4 of Worksheet G.

WORKSHEET G

COMPARING PROJECTED INCOME AND EXPENSES- ARE YOU PREPARED?

	1 **At retirement**	2 **Inflation adjusted value factor** (see Clue 3)	3 **Value at retirement for one month** (Column 1 x Column 2)
Total projected income Worksheet D, col 3 total, page 16			
Total projected expenses Worksheet F, col 3 total, page 25 **H**ealth **O**ther than health			
Projected value of income less expenses Subtract line 2 from line 1			

Next move on to expenses in row 2, taking the total monthly expenses calculated in Worksheet F. For expenses other than health, go to Clue 3 (page 31) to select an inflation adjustment value factor. Use the 3.5 percent inflation rate (used in Worksheet F) or select another that you believe will reflect inflation over the 30 years of your retirement. For health, use the 7 percent inflation rate used previously or select another rate. Multiply this result by 360 and enter it in column 4. Subtract the total value of projected expenses ("other than health" and "health") over 30 years of retirement in Column 4 from the corresponding total value of your projected income (Column 4).

Here is an example of how this works:

Projected value of income:

$1,400.00/month
x 0.5174 (5% rate of return, 0% inflation)
x 360 (months in 30 years)

$260,769.60

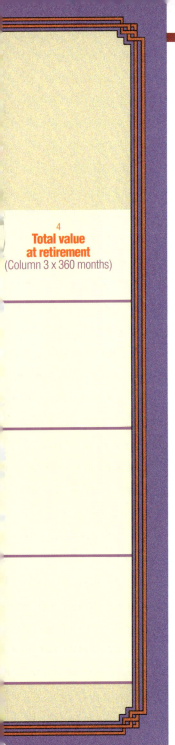

4
Total value at retirement
(Column 3 x 360 months)

Projected value of expenses:

Health expenses	Other than health expenses
\$200.00 /month	\$700.00 /month
x 1.3691 (5% rate of return, 7% inflation)	x 0.8054 (5% rate of return, 3.5% inflation)
x 360 (months in 30 years)	x 360 (months in 30 years)
\$98,575.20	\$202,960.80

Total projected value of expenses:
\$301,536.00

\$260,769.60 (value of income over 30 years)
-\$301,536.00 (value of expenses over 30 years)
-\$ 40,766.40 (shortfall)

"As you set aside more money, the combination of savings and earnings will help close the gap."

CLUE 3

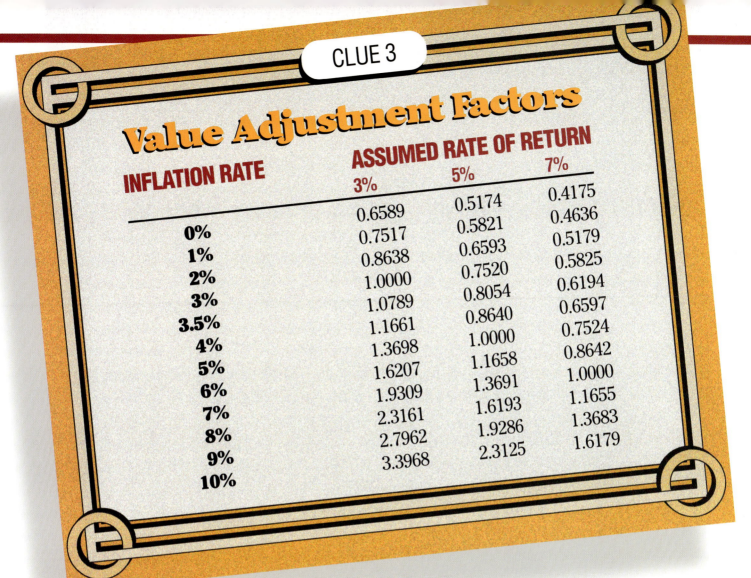

Value Adjustment Factors

INFLATION RATE	ASSUMED RATE OF RETURN 3%	5%	7%
0%	0.6589	0.5174	0.4175
1%	0.7517	0.5821	0.4636
2%	0.8638	0.6593	0.5179
3%	1.0000	0.7520	0.5825
3.5%	1.0789	0.8054	0.6194
4%	1.1661	0.8640	0.6597
5%	1.3698	1.0000	0.7524
6%	1.6207	1.1658	0.8642
7%	1.9309	1.3691	1.0000
8%	2.3161	1.6193	1.1655
9%	2.7962	1.9286	1.3683
10%	3.3968	2.3125	1.6179

If the result is negative, don't worry. Just about everyone will need to make up a shortfall in savings. Remember, also, that it is difficult to project inflation rates, especially for health care, that far in the future. It is better, however, to have a rough idea of where you stand than have no guesstimate at all.

The good news is that time is on your side. Remember the effect of interest compounding and how it can work to make your money grow in 10 years. Each year, as you set aside more money, the combination of savings and earnings will help close the gap. Worksheet H lets you figure out how much you need to start to save today to make up the gap between projected income and expenses. Multiply the gap from Worksheet G by an additional savings factor you select from the top of Worksheet H, based on the rate of return you think you will earn.

For example:

$40,766.40 (gap from Worksheet G example above)
x 0.00644 (5% rate of return)

$262.54 /month to close the gap

Socking away that amount of money over the next 10 years, while getting a rate of return you're comfortable with, should go a long way toward matching up income and expenses over 30 years of retirement.

The good news is that you don't have to save the total amount of any gap between what you have and what you need. Each year the amount you invest will grow, and the growth of your savings lessens the amount you need to save.

WORKSHEET H

ADDITIONAL SAVINGS NEEDED BEFORE RETIREMENT (IN 10 YEARS)

Additional savings factors:

0.00716 for 3% 0.00644 for 5% 0.00578 for 7%

Gap between projected total value of expenses and projected total value of income (from Worksheet G)	1 $
Additional savings factor	2
Additional monthly savings needed (multiply line 1 x line 2)	3 $

Five Ways to Close the Gap

Where will you find additional savings? Here are some suggestions for active workers and retirees alike.

Number 1 - Work your contributions at work

Without exception, retirement planners advise contributing the maximum to your retirement plan, especially if your employer contributes, too. If your contributions are made by salary deduction, saving is easier to do and may seem almost painless. And contributing more means postponing, or "deferring," taxes until you withdraw the money at retirement. Then you may be in a lower tax bracket.

Catch-up provisions for some retirement plans allow you to contribute extra amounts if you're over 50. Information about 401(k) catch-up contributions is available from your retirement plan administrator or on the Internet. If your plan has a catch-up provision, act on it now.

Number 2 - Work longer, retire later

Staying employed as long as possible benefits your retirement finances in several ways. Having an income gives your retirement savings more time to grow. A regular income could mean more regular savings. If you work for a company that provides health insurance, you won't have to fully pay for a policy yourself.

You don't have to stay at your same job if there are other opportunities. Maybe you want a new career, one that ties in to your personal interests. Longer life spans and better

CLUE 4

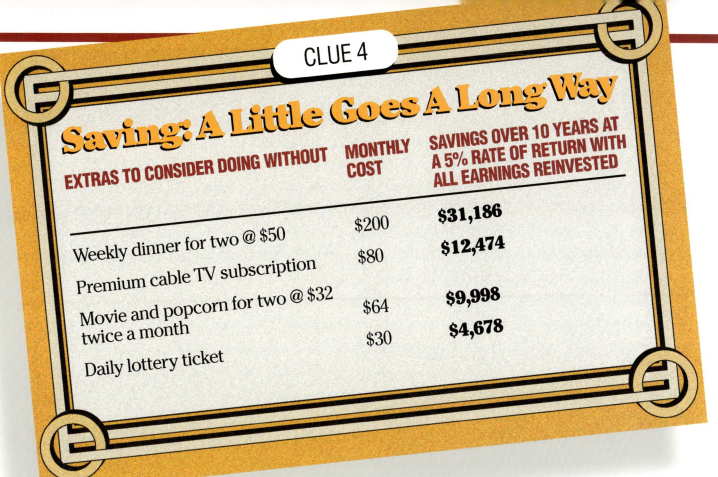

Saving: A Little Goes A Long Way

EXTRAS TO CONSIDER DOING WITHOUT	MONTHLY COST	SAVINGS OVER 10 YEARS AT A 5% RATE OF RETURN WITH ALL EARNINGS REINVESTED
Weekly dinner for two @ $50	$200	**$31,186**
Premium cable TV subscription	$80	**$12,474**
Movie and popcorn for two @ $32 twice a month	$64	**$9,998**
Daily lottery ticket	$30	**$4,678**

health mean many older people have the energy and enthusiasm employers are looking for, not to mention the skills and experience. Many people find the social benefits of working as important as the financial ones.

Number 3 - Cut expenses, big and little

Moving to a region with lower housing and living costs or moving to a smaller home can help narrow the savings gap. Another option is staying in your community but downsizing to a smaller place like a condo or apartment. The same factors that drove up the value of your current house, however, will also have driven up overall housing costs, including real estate taxes. Housing is a major part of everyone's budget so think carefully about where you want to be and whether you can afford it. Keep in mind, however, that moving includes its own financial expenses and means leaving friends and your community.

Financial planners say that preretirement years are the wrong time to take on large debts, including home equity loans and high interest credit card debt. Buying a new car, boat, or vacation home is not wise if you need to save. Investing that $400 a month (an average 5-year car loan payment) and getting a 5 percent return would put more than $27,000 in your retirement account. Consider keeping your old car or buying a used one.

Preretirement is also the wrong time to give or "loan" large sums of money to your children and grandchildren. Their earning power is usually far better than yours. Now is the time to take care of your finances so you don't have to ask others to bear the financial burden for your care later on.

Number 4 - Social Security, now or later?

The amount of your monthly Social Security benefit goes up the older you are when you start receiving it. For example, a 61-year-old man earning $60,000 in 2004 and eligible for his early Social Security benefit at 62 would receive an additional $1,000 a year by waiting 1 year, until he is 63, to collect his benefits. On the other hand, retirees who are seriously ill, who need the money immediately, or who feel comfortable investing their monthly checks may choose not to wait.

For example, a worker turning 62 in 2005 would have a full retirement age of 66 under Social Security. At full retirement, that person's benefit will be $1,281. If, however, that person starts to receive benefits at age 62, his/her

monthly benefit would be reduced to $960. By waiting until age 70, that same worker's monthly benefit would be $1,690.

As a general rule, early retirement will give you about the same total Social Security benefits over your lifetime, but in smaller amounts to take into account the longer period you will be receiving them.

If you delay retirement beyond the full Social Security retirement age, you can earn retirement credits, increasing Social Security by a certain percentage (depending on date of birth) until you reach age 70.

Regardless of the age you start receiving Social Security benefits, remember to sign up for Medicare at age 65.

Number 5 - Put your money where the returns are

Educate yourself about investing and consider paying a professional to help you choose the right place for your money. Financial experts say too many people keep too much money in the wrong kinds of accounts, for example checking accounts, savings accounts, and money market funds, which typically have low interest or return rates. Review the discussion in Chapter 2 about asset allocation and diversification of investments.

Adding $200 a month, or $2,400 a year over 10 years, to a starting retirement savings balance of $40,000 would more than double your money, assuming a 5 percent rate of return and all earnings reinvested.

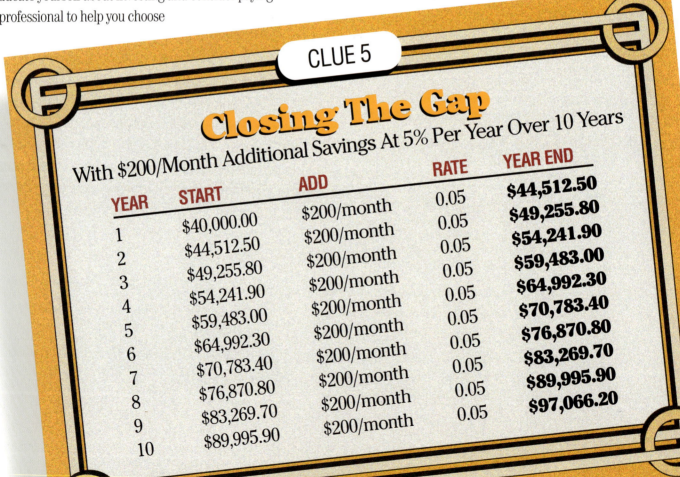

CLUE 5

Closing The Gap

With $200/Month Additional Savings At 5% Per Year Over 10 Years

YEAR	START	ADD	RATE	YEAR END
1	$40,000.00	$200/month	0.05	**$44,512.50**
2	$44,512.50	$200/month	0.05	**$49,255.80**
3	$49,255.80	$200/month	0.05	**$54,241.90**
4	$54,241.90	$200/month	0.05	**$59,483.00**
5	$59,483.00	$200/month	0.05	**$64,992.30**
6	$64,992.30	$200/month	0.05	**$70,783.40**
7	$70,783.40	$200/month	0.05	**$76,870.80**
8	$76,870.80	$200/month	0.05	**$83,269.70**
9	$83,269.70	$200/month	0.05	**$89,995.90**
10	$89,995.90	$200/month	0.05	**$97,066.20**

Chapter 5

MAKING YOUR MONEY LAST

The point of all the calculations you have done in this booklet is to make sure your income will last a lifetime. If doing the worksheets has uncovered a gap between your retirement income and expenses, you probably will be changing some financial habits over the next 10 years. The only part of your retirement mystery that remains is deciding how you are going to make your retirement income last as long as you do. You will need a strategy.

Solving your retirement mystery has revealed that more saving (especially for medical costs), more investing, and less spending will boost your confidence and your financial bottom line as you near the end of your working life.

For now, you will probably need to focus on adding to your nest egg and investing it wisely. Take into account that you will also have income taxes to pay. Take the short tax quiz in this chapter to find out about minimizing your taxes in retirement.

You may also want to take a look at financial products and services that could help build some financial security into your retirement. But first, a word of caution. Because you're growing a nest egg, you may start hearing from people offering their own strategies for managing your retirement money. These people may be relatives and friends. You will also hear from strangers in phone calls, letters, and emails. Some may offer to double your money at no risk. Think long and hard about involving them in your financial affairs, unless they're qualified financial professionals and can be objective. Retirees are frequently targets for scams. Don't give out any personal information to strangers. Don't be a courtesy victim. Con artists will not hesitate to exploit your good manners. Save courtesy for friends and family members, not potential swindlers!

It's A Big Deal

"Having a strategy" may sound like retirement is a battle or a complicated business opportunity. You may be thinking, "What's the big deal? I'll just withdraw money when I need to pay bills." Your parents may have done fine by simply cashing their monthly Social Security and pension checks to

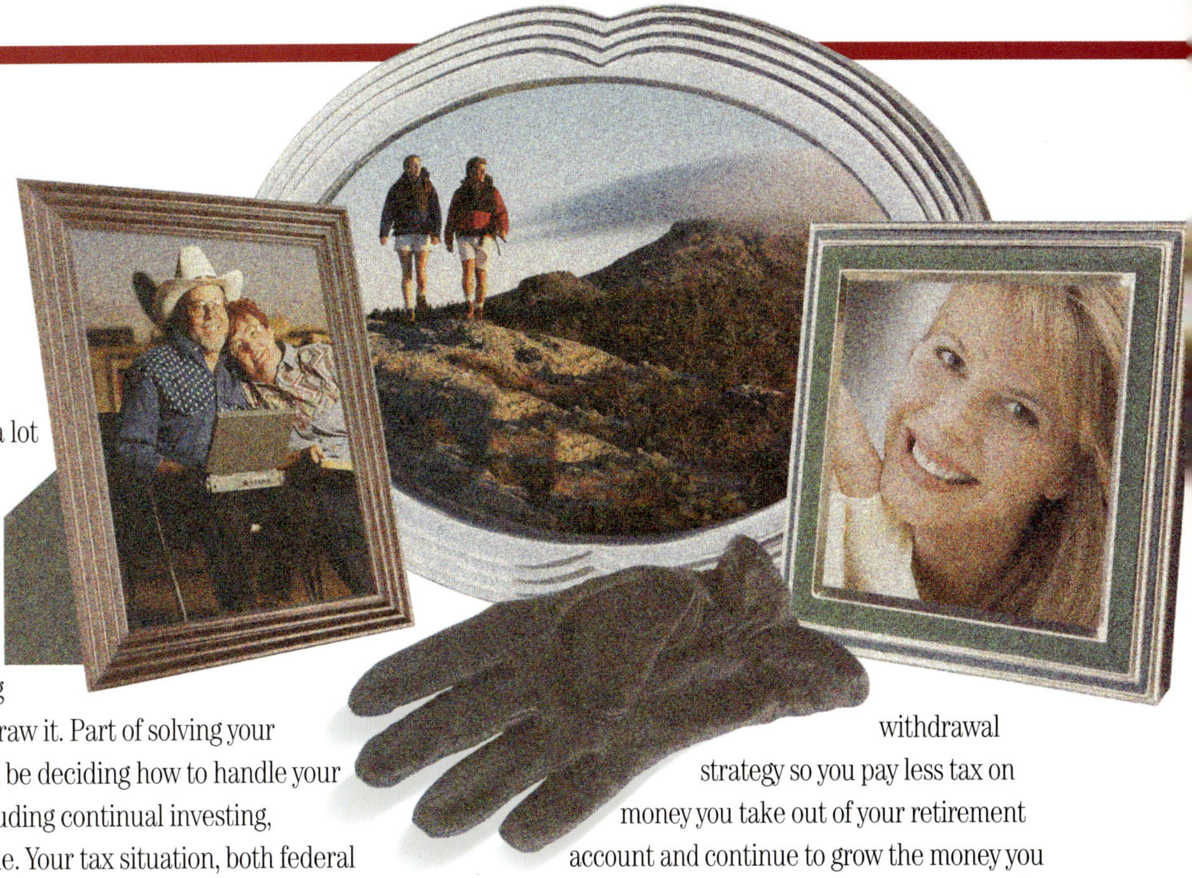

live on. Their taxes on this income most likely were a lot simpler and a lot easier to do.

In today's world, keep in mind that the money you have saved and invested will be earning income until you withdraw it. Part of solving your retirement mystery will be deciding how to handle your retirement money, including continual investing, throughout your lifetime. Your tax situation, both federal and state, may not be so clear. You need to plan a withdrawal strategy so you pay less tax on money you take out of your retirement account and continue to grow the money you leave in. A qualified tax adviser can help here.

"Part of solving your retirement mystery is deciding how to handle your retirement money."

Getting Your Retirement Benefits

You may need to decide whether to take your pension or your retirement plan benefit in a lump sum or in an annuity. You can find out about your retirement plan payout options by reading your plan documents. Or you can contact the plan administrator directly for information about what your plan offers.

If you are in a traditional pension plan, your benefit is paid in the form of an annuity – that is, through periodic payments, typically monthly, for an extended period, usually your lifetime. If you select an option that provides for a survivor benefit for your spouse, note that your monthly benefit will be reduced. The survivor benefit is typically 50 percent of the retiree's benefit, but some plans provide for other options, such as 75 percent.

If you are in a defined contribution plan, such as a 401(k) plan, you do not automatically get your benefit as an annuity. Your retirement benefit can be taken as a lump sum paid entirely at the time of your retirement or, as in some plans, through periodic payments over a short period of time, such as 3 or 5 years. Your plan may provide an annuity option or you may choose to buy an annuity with all or part of your lump sum benefit. If you choose to take your benefit in a lump sum, be sure to put it in a tax-deferred account, such as an IRA, within 60 days to avoid paying high income taxes (the highest tax being 35 percent as of 2006) on the amount. You will then have to decide how to invest what could be the most money you've ever accumulated and make sure it lasts for the 30 years of your retirement.

If you choose an annuity, make sure you realize the risks and rewards. An annuity provides a steady stream of income that lasts throughout your lifetime and can provide adjustments for inflation. This is helpful especially in the early years of retirement when there may be the temptation to spend the excess income instead of saving it to make sure it is there in 20 to 30 years. Keep in mind that if you die sooner than expected, however, the insurance company may keep the remaining balance unless you have opted for a survivor benefit. That is why annuities are usually not recommended for those with a shortened life span. Annuities come in many varieties. If you are purchasing one, choose an insurance company with a good credit rating and track record. Be sure you know what you're buying – there are costs involved in ending the contract. The more you learn upfront, the better.

You can also buy an annuity with money from other assets such as an inheritance or the sale of your house. Like other annuities, you will receive a monthly check for a defined period or for life. The tax treatment of these payouts will be different, however. Like any investment, review the terms of the annuity before you purchase it. For example, will the amount paid vary based on investment returns or is it fixed, what will you pay in related fees, etc.

Another way to make your money last is to obtain a reverse mortgage – essentially a bank loan based on the amount of the equity in your home. It can provide you with a monthly check, but at a cost. You are spending down the value of your home. If you can keep your house in good repair so the bank sees value in the loan, this is a way to supplement your income and not have to leave your home. When you or your heirs sell the house, however, the loan has to be repaid. Talk with the bank about any taxes due on these payments, and make your family aware of your reverse mortgage.

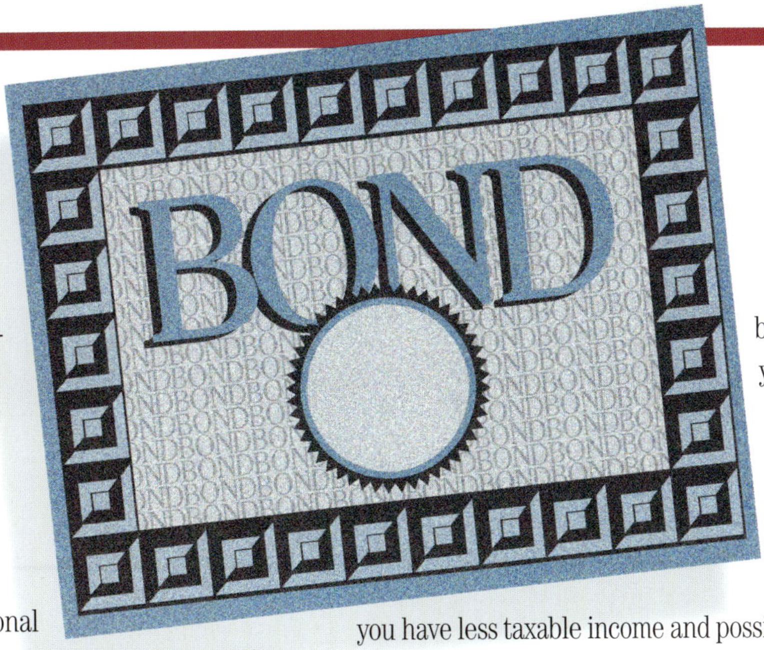
BOND

Also, remember long-term care insurance can help you plan for increased health care costs in your later years.

Withdrawals: Which Pot?

You probably have some personal savings included in your retirement nest egg that you've already paid taxes on. A Roth IRA, for example, is a good place to leave money you've invested for growth because the withdrawals are not taxed. Retirement experts say you usually should withdraw from this pot of money earlier in retirement when you may be in a higher income tax bracket. Withdraw your taxable retirement plan money (such as your 401(k) or other workplace savings plan) later, when you have less taxable income and possibly higher deductions due to medical expenses.

Be aware, however, that the IRS requires you to start withdrawing tax-deferred money from retirement accounts when you turn 70 1/2 years of age. (This is a milestone on the *Retirement Timeline* at the beginning of this booklet.) By doing so, you will avoid tax penalties. These withdrawals are called "minimum required distributions," and the formula for determining the amount can be complicated. You may want to consult a tax expert for help.

"Experts say you need to continue investing and diversifying your assets throughout your life."

Can You Beat It?

As you're withdrawing money to pay your bills in retirement, you should be trying to grow your remaining money to at least keep up with inflation. Of course, it's better to beat inflation. Experts say you need to continue investing and diversifying your assets throughout your life. Keeping your money in accounts paying guaranteed interest rates will keep it safe, but not from inflation. Inflation is a major threat to your financial future, so make it a consideration in your investment decisions.

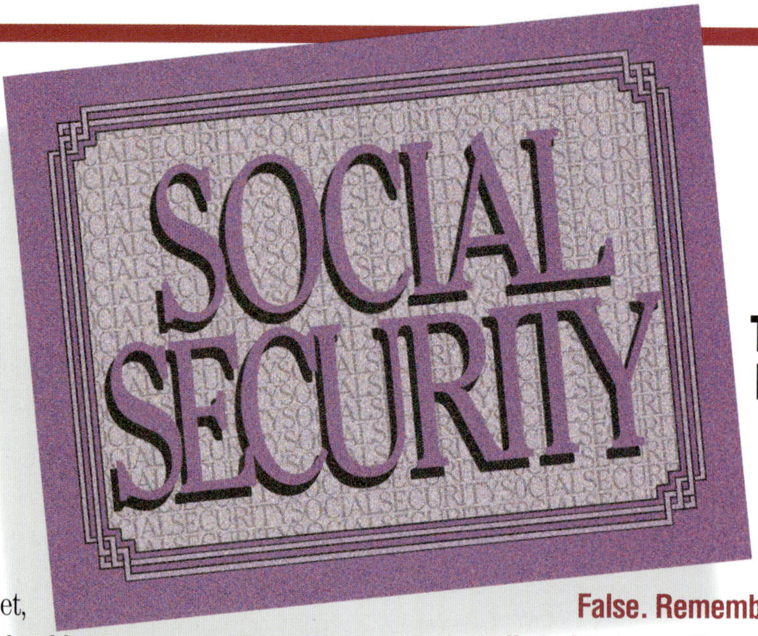

Going It Alone Vs. Getting Help

With a lot of study and regular attention to changes in tax laws, the economy, the stock market, and your money, you may be able to come up with a strategy to minimize taxes and maximize income. There's even software to help.

There's another road, too. You can hire someone to develop your strategy and manage your money for you. Especially during the later years of your retirement, you may want to seek the help of a professional, when you may have less interest, energy, and ability to keep your strategy on target.

Good money managers, and the companies they work for and with, are required by law to be clear and open about their fees and charges and whether they are paid by commissions or for the sales of financial products, such as annuities and mutual funds. Be sure to ask questions, get references, and avoid anyone who guarantees performance on returns. This way you can make an informed decision. After all, it is your money you are putting in their hands.

Taxes & Retirement– True or False?

Income taxes go away when you're retired. True or False?

False. Remember all that pretax money you contributed to your retirement plan? When you withdraw it at retirement, you pay income taxes.

Social Security benefits are not sheltered from taxes. True or False?

True. A portion of your Social Security benefits is included in your taxable income if, for example, in 2006 you have taxable income and Social Security benefits of more than $25,000 for a single person and $32,000 for a couple.

There are no tax consequences if you don't start to withdraw your pretax savings at age 70 1/2. True or False?

False. There is a 50 percent tax penalty on amounts that the IRS requires to be taken out after age 70 1/2 and that are not withdrawn when required. In tax terms, these are called "minimum required distributions."

A Few Words About Scams

As you plan your retirement, don't let fear, desperation, or the need to catch up financially push you into any hasty investment decisions. In all legitimate investments, higher returns are accompanied by higher risks – risks you may well not want to take as you near retirement. Be wary of anyone who claims they can sell you a product that offers great reward without great risk -- a sure sign of a scam. Here are a few points to keep in mind when you make any financial decision:

Recognize that anyone can claim to be a "financial consultant" or "investment counselor." That person may not have the special training, expertise, or credentials necessary to back up the claim, however. Ask about licensing and professional designations and check them out with securities regulators and any trade groups in which they claim membership.

Understand your investments and never be afraid to ask questions. Good financial professionals are never pushy, and they never dismiss your concerns.

Don't let embarrassment or fear keep you from reporting suspected investment fraud or abuse. Contact the securities agency in your state as soon as you suspect a problem or believe you have been dealt with unfairly.

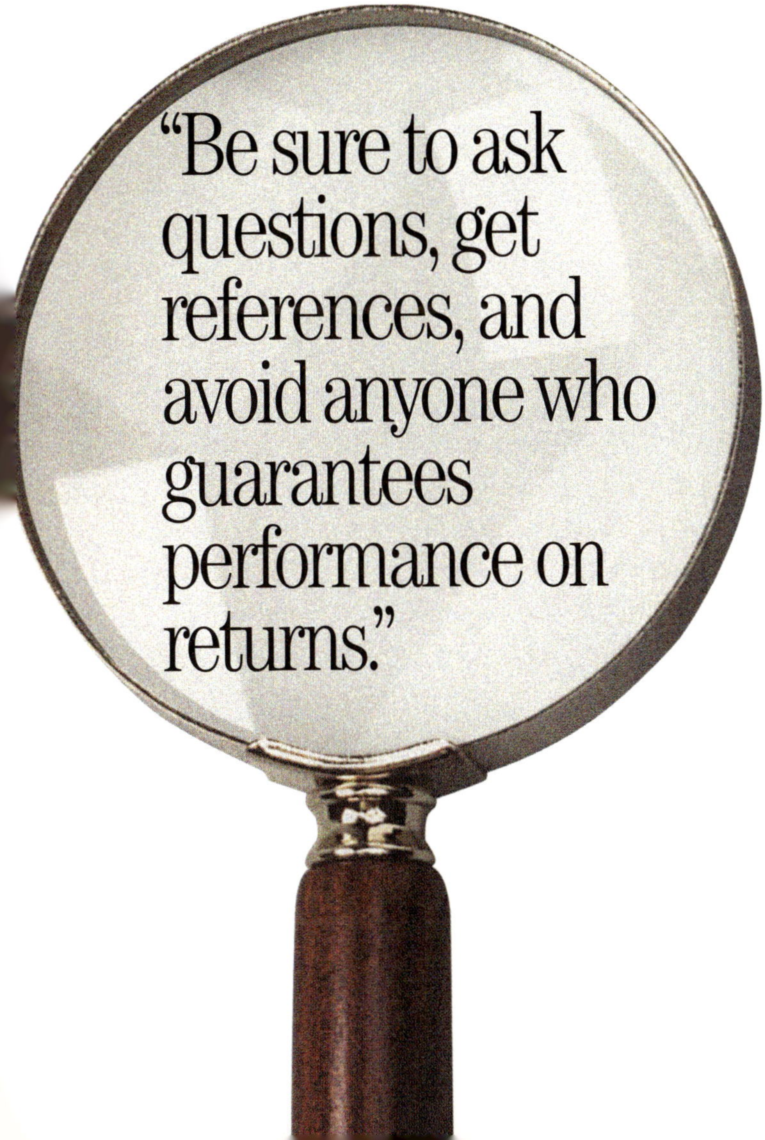
"Be sure to ask questions, get references, and avoid anyone who guarantees performance on returns."

Never judge a person's integrity by how they sound or how they appear. The most successful con artists sound extremely professional and have the ability to make even the flimsiest investment seem as safe as putting money in the bank.

Monitor your investments. Ask tough questions and insist on speedy and satisfactory answers. Make sure you get regular written and oral reports. Look for signs of excessive or unauthorized trading of your funds when you receive statements, and do not be swayed by assurances that this kind of practice is routine.

Above all, become an informed investor. In investing, as in life, if it sounds too good to be true, it probably is.

Now that you have tracked down all the clues pertinent to your retirement mystery, you've almost solved the case. In the next chapter, you will find several resources to turn to for more information. Take advantage of them.

Chapter 6
Tracking Down Help for Retirement

Like a black and white TV, retirement used to have high contrast and few choices: One day you were working and the next day you weren't. One day you lived on a paycheck and the next day on pension and Social Security checks. Your income was fixed and retirement was no mystery.

You have the power to put some color, maybe even gold, in your retirement. It mostly means putting into action a plan to close the income-expense gap and manage your money smartly now and during your later years. You won't be alone. In the next 25 years, one in five Americans will be over 65. That's a lot of people today who will need to work on a clear and realistic retirement plan during the next 10 years. Make sure you're one of them so your retirement wishes come true.

In the following list of resources, you will find ways to discover more clues about retiring gradually and maybe working longer, paying attention to your assets and income, saving and investing, planning for increased expenses, including medical costs, and developing a withdrawal strategy. The information available on the Web sites listed is rich in detail and wide in scope. But remember to protect your privacy by not giving out personal information, such as your Social Security number, telephone, or address, unless you know whom you're dealing with.

In fact, helping American workers succeed in a new kind of retirement has become the focus for a number of government agencies and organizations. Businesses selling products and services like annuities, long-term care insurance, and income management services are another source of information. To reach all these sources, use the Internet, your telephone, and the public library.

Periodically look back over the worksheets you have done and fill them out again as your finances change. Chart your progress through the next 10 years until retirement . . . and beyond. Get time on your side and get going.

RESOURCES

This publication is presented by:

U.S. Department of Labor
Employee Benefits Security Administration
200 Constitution Ave., N.W., Washington, DC 20210
Web site: http://www.dol.gov/ebsa
Toll-free publication request line: 1-866-444-EBSA (3272)

North American Securities Administrators Association, Inc.
750 First St., N.E., Suite 1140, Washington, DC 20002
Web site: http://www.nasaa.org
(202) 737-0900

The Actuarial Foundation
475 North Martingale Rd., #600, Schaumburg, IL 60173
Web site: http://www.actuarialfoundation.org
(847) 706-3535

"Chart your progress through the next 10 years until retirement."

The following Web sites, booklets, pamphlets, and other references are available from the organizations above and others that focus on retirement and savings issues.

Retirement Savings Calculators:

(Note: The Department of Labor does not endorse one specific Web site over another.)

http://cgi.money.cnn.com/tools

http://www.kiplinger.com/personalfinance/tools/

http://www.choosetosave.org

http://www.wiser.heinz.org
(special site for women and retirement)

Retirement Planning and General Retirement Issues:

http://www.dol.gov/ebsa
Savings Fitness . . .
A Guide to Your Money and Your Financial Future

Top 10 Ways to Prepare for Retirement

Women and Retirement Savings

What You Should Know About Your Retirement Plan

Request copies by calling 1-866-444-EBSA (3272)

http://www.ssa.gov
The Social Security Administration Web site has online resources to help calculate your retirement benefits, and to learn about survivor benefits and Medicare. Two publications you may want to view or order:
Understanding the Benefits

What Every Woman Should Know

http://www.aarp.org
The AARP offers a wealth of information, including a fact sheet on reverse mortgages and a section on "Money and Work."
Future Focus: Your Guide to Financial Planning for Retirement

Phone: 1-888-OUR-AARP (1-888-687-2277)

http://www.pbgc.gov
For those employees who may have worked for a company with a traditional defined benefit (DB) pension, the Pension Benefit Guaranty Corporation can assist in locating any money still in your account. Those with DB plans will also find these two booklets useful:
Your Guaranteed Pension

Finding a Lost Pension

Phone: 1-800 400-7242

http://www.nefe.org
Browse the Web site of the National Endowment for Financial Education (and especially the "Multimedia Access" section) for a wealth of preretirement information. Also view the following publication:
Guidebook to Help Late Savers Prepare for Retirement

Saving and Investing:

http://www.consumerfed.org
In addition to consumer fact sheets and studies, the Consumer Federation of America's Web site offers a free savings brochure, *6 Steps to Six-Figure Savings*
Phone: (202)387-6121

http://www.sec.gov
The Securities and Exchange Commission Web site offers a menu of online "Investor Information" topics for consumer reference. View "Invest Wisely: An Introduction to Mutual Funds" and dozens of other titles.

http://www.mymoney.gov
This Web site is sponsored by the Financial Literacy and Education Commission, U.S. Department of the Treasury, and has among its offerings the *My Money Tool Kit*. You can order a copy online.

http://www.irs.gov/pub/irs-pdf/p590.pdf
The Internal Revenue Service's *Individual Retirement Arrangements* is one of several guides to retirement plans that the agency offers.

http://www.pueblo.gsa.gov
The Federal Citizen Information Center Web site is your portal to government information from car insurance to retirement savings. You can also order a free copy of the *Consumer Information Catalog* at this site.

http://www.360financialliteracy.org
A recent addition to the Internet is this site sponsored by the American Institute of Certified Public Accountants. The Web pages view finances throughout life – from childhood to college, career, and retirement and estate planning.

Getting Help:

www.nasaa.org/investor_education/
This site alerts readers to the latest money scams and to any disciplinary rulings against individual financial advisers. The Web site also includes a section on investor education, including this publication:
Protecting Your Finances: How to Avoid Investment Frauds and Scams.

http://www.cfp.net/learn
The Certified Financial Planner Board of Standards Web site lets you look up a certified financial planner near you. The organization also distributes a free "Financial Planning Resource Kit." 1-888-237-6275

http://www.napfa.org
This is the site for the National Association of Personal Financial Advisors, an organization of fee-only comprehensive financial professionals. The Web site also includes retirement planning information. 1-800-366-2732

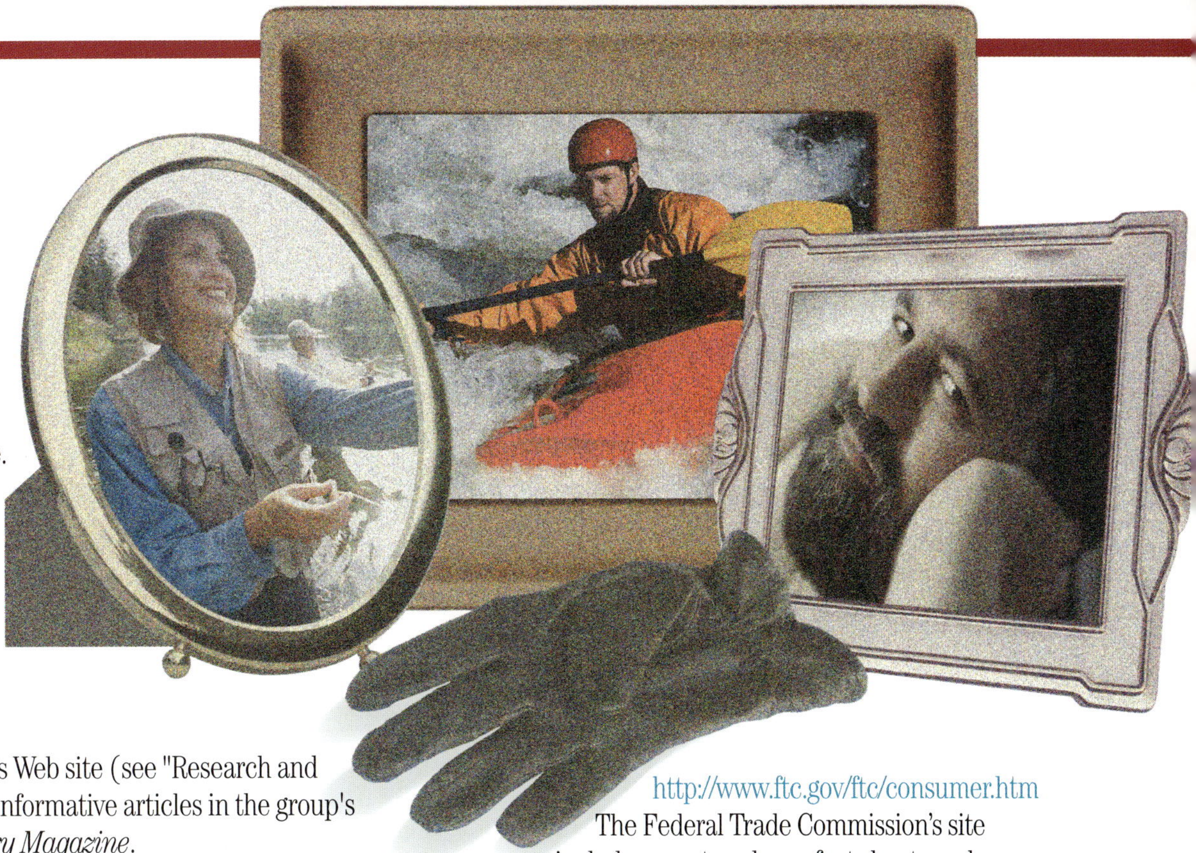

http://www.actuarialfoundation.org/

View the following two publications on this site.

Seven Life-Defining Financial Decisions

Making Your Money Last for a Lifetime: Why You Need to Know About Annuities

www.soa.org

The Society of Actuaries Web site (see "Research and Publications") links to informative articles in the group's publication, *The Actuary Magazine*.

http://www.ftc.gov/ftc/consumer.htm

The Federal Trade Commission's site includes over two dozen fact sheets and brochures warning consumers about scam investments. View *Reverse Mortgages: Get the Facts before Cashing in On Your Home's Equity and others.*

http://www.aoa.gov/eldfam/eldfam.asp

Topics from money to housing are included at this Administration on Aging "Elders & Families" site.

http://www.medicare.gov

http://www.ssa.gov/prescriptionhelp/

The Centers for Medicare and Medicaid Services (U.S. Department of Health and Human Services) site is your first and most reliable resource for information on Medicare. It includes information on billing, appeals, long-term care, and links to information on the prescription drug program. Start with these two publications:

Medicare & You 2006

Medicare Prescription Drug Coverage: How to Join

"Get time on your side and get going."

WORKSHEETS FOR THE FUTURE

You have seen the following worksheets before. They appear on some of the preceding pages. This additional collection will prove useful:

It will help you redo some or all of your calculations from time to time.

If you get a raise and add it to your savings, that's an ideal time to update Worksheet A.

Its abbreviated instructions will provide an extra level of understanding.

Do you plan to pay off a mortgage between now and retirement? This will also affect your worksheet calculations.

And each time you add more to savings, you close any gap between the money you have and the money you will need for retirement. (Worksheet H)

Saving copies of all the worksheets will clarify the progress you are making toward your retirement goals.

These lighter colored versions will also make it easier to make extra copies as needed. So if you anticipate needing more than one extra set, why not make it now?

And don't forget to use your trusty number 2 pencil. Remember, the reward for completing this information should be a happy retirement future rather than a beautifully drafted plan. Done well, it will be as considered and accurate as it is erased and dog-eared. Accomplishing such a goal will require that each mystery be solved a clue at a time.

If all this sounds a little daunting, please don't forget our generous time frame – 10 years if we start now. Even devoting just one hour a month will allow more than enough attention to develop your successful strategy.

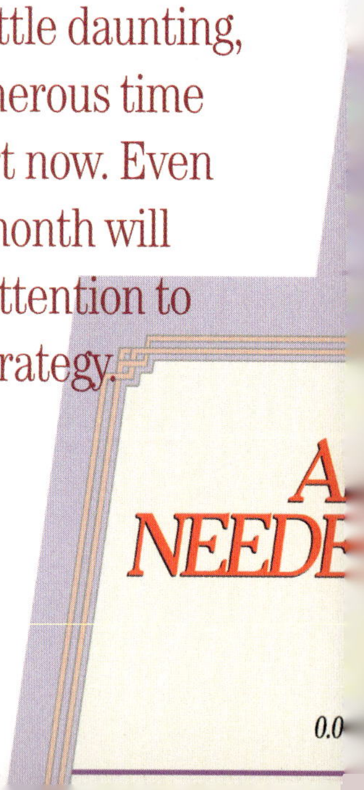

WORKSHEET A
TODAY'S MONEY
WORKSHEET B
YOUR MONEY-
10 YEARS FROM TODAY
WORKSHEET C
NEW SAVINGS BETWEEN
WORKSHEET D
MONTHLY INCOME OVER
A 30-YEAR R
Income Conversion Factors f
0.004216 for 3%
WORKSHEET E
MONTHLY EXPENSES
TODAY
WORKSHEET F
MONTHLY EXPENSES IN 10 YEARS
WORKSHEET G
COMPARING PROJECTED INCOME
AND EXPENSES-
ARE YOU PREPARED?
2
Inflation adjusted
value factor
(see Clue 3)
3
Value in dollars
at retirement
for one month
(Column 1 x Column 2)
4
Total value of
in dollars
at retirement
(Column 3 x 360 months)
IRAs
IRAs
Othe
Hom
Mort
(ente
Pers
WORKSHEET H
DITIONAL SAVINGS
BEFORE RETIREMENT
(IN 10 YEARS)
Additional savings factors:
for 3%
0.00644 for 5%
0.00578 for 7%

INSTRUCTIONS FOR WORKSHEET A

TODAY'S MONEY

Worksheet A lets you shine some light on the money you will have to support yourself (and your spouse, if you have one) in retirement.

Write down in this worksheet only the money you have today that you plan to use when you retire. Include the balance on your 401(k) plan, Keogh, SEP-IRA, and SIMPLE plans in the spaces provided. The next rows include savings in IRAs (both traditional and Roth), savings accounts in a bank, and the market value of your home.

Enter mortgage and other liens as a negative amount, then go on to add any other personal savings and investments you have, including the cash value of life insurance and any valuable collections you may have.

Don't add balances from your Social Security statements and from a traditional pension plan, if you have one – save that for Worksheet D.

INSTRUCTIONS FOR WORKSHEET B

YOUR MONEY- 10 YEARS FROM TODAY

This worksheet takes the total from Worksheet A and projects it into the future – specifically, to the day you retire. How much money will you have?

By choosing a savings growth factor for a 3, 5, or 7 percent rate of return, you can take current retirement saving sources and project earnings on each of them during the next 10 years. You will be able to transfer the dollar amounts for your income sources directly from Column 3 of Worksheet A. Multiply that number by the savings growth factor you choose and enter the new number in Column 3.

Like Worksheet A, Social Security benefits and traditional pensions are not included since you won't receive these sources of income until retirement.

INSTRUCTIONS FOR WORKSHEET C

NEW SAVINGS BETWEEN NOW AND RETIREMENT

You may well have additional workplace and personal savings to add to your earnings between now and retirement. Worksheet C lets you calculate potential growth using a savings growth factor representing 3, 5, or 7 percent rates of return, depending on how much you believe each of the worksheet items will increase in value between now and the day you retire in 10 years.

To get 10-year totals, multiply the amount you believe you will add monthly to IRAs, 401(k)s and other savings instruments by the growth factor you select. The result: the value of your new savings in 10 years.

WORKSHEET A
TODAY'S MONEY

Instructions: Record amounts for yourself and for your spouse in columns 1 and 2. Add up the money across each row for you and your spouse and write the total in column 3. Then add all the numbers down column 3 and write the total in column 3 at the bottom.

	1 You	2 Spouse	3 Total
Work-related retirement savings			
401(k) or 403(b)			
Keogh			
SEP-IRA			
SIMPLE IRA			
Other			
IRAs (traditional)			
IRAs (Roth)			
Other			
Home equity			
Market value of home			
Mortgage and liens (enter as negative amount)			
Personal savings and investments			
Other assets (collections, etc.)			
TOTAL ASSETS			

WORKSHEET B

YOUR MONEY–10 YEARS FROM TODAY

Asset Growth Factors for Three Selected Rates of Return

1.344 for 3% 1.629 for 5% 1.967 for 7%

	1 **Current $ value** (from Worksheet A, Column 3)	2 **Asset growth factor** (rate of return)	3 **Asset value in 10 years** (Column 1 x Column 2)
Work-related retirement savings			
401(k) or 403(b)			
Keogh			
SEP-IRA			
SIMPLE IRA			
Other			
IRAs (traditional)			
IRAs (Roth)			
Other			
Home equity			
Market value of home			
Mortgage and liens (enter as negative amount)			
Personal savings and investments			
Other assets (collections, etc.)			
TOTAL ASSETS			

WORKSHEET C

NEW SAVINGS BETWEEN NOW AND RETIREMENT

Savings Growth Factors for Three Selected Rates of Return

139.741 for 3%   155.282 for 5%   173.085 for 7%

	1 Estimated monthly savings amount	2 Savings growth factor	3 Value of savings in 10 years (Column 1 x Column 2)
Work-related retirement savings			
401(k) or 403(b)			
Keogh			
SEP-IRA			
SIMPLE IRA			
Other			
IRAs (traditional)			
IRAs (Roth)			
Other			
Home equity			
Market value of home			
Mortgage and liens (enter as positive amount)			
Personal savings and investments			
Other assets (collections, etc.)			
TOTAL ASSETS			

INSTRUCTIONS FOR WORKSHEET D

MONTHLY INCOME OVER A 30-YEAR RETIREMENT

Worksheet D takes your earnings and savings over a lifetime and projects a monthly income – the amount you will have to live on – during a 30-year retirement period. Unlike previous worksheets, this one adds the amount of your Social Security benefit and any payout from a traditional pension plan.

If you have a fixed pension (rather than, or in addition to, a 401(k)-type plan), your pension plan administrator or union can give you the approximate amount of your pension and tell you whether you can receive it as a lump sum or as fixed monthly payments. If it is a lump sum, enter that amount in Column 1 of the worksheet; if you receive it as a fixed monthly benefit, fill in only Column 3.

For other assets, those you tracked down in Worksheets B and C, add the totals for each item from both worksheets and enter the total in Column 1 of this worksheet. Then select an income conversion factor representing a 3, 5, or 7 percent rate of return and enter it in Column 2. Multiply Column 1 by Column 2 and enter the result in Column 3. Remember, this is a guesstimate of your monthly income for the 30 years of retirement since things that impact your income will vary.

WORKSHEET D

MONTHLY INCOME OVER A 30-YEAR RETIREMENT

Income Conversion Factors for Assumed Rates of Interest

0.004216 for 3% 0.005368 for 5% 0.006653 for 7%

	1 **Accumulated assets** (Column 3 from Worksheet B plus Column 3 from Worksheet C)	2 **Income conversion factor**	3 **Monthly income beginning at retirement** (Column 1 x Column 2)
Social Security			
Work-Related Retirement Savings			
Pension benefits			
401(k) or 403(b)			
Keogh			
SEP-IRA			
SIMPLE IRA			
Other			
IRAs (traditional)			
IRAs (Roth)			
Home equity			
Market value of home			
Mortgage and liens (enter as negative amount)			
Personal savings and investments			
Other assets (collections, etc.)			
TOTAL ASSETS			

INSTRUCTIONS FOR WORKSHEET E

MONTHLY EXPENSES TODAY

Now that you know what your savings and investments are, the next step is to move on to today's expenses. Worksheet E helps you calculate what you spend today.

Some monthly expenses are easy to figure. Others, like a heating bill, may not remain the same from month to month and will require a calculation of your average monthly bill over a year's time. Still other bills may arrive only quarterly. While you may want to guesstimate some of these bills the first time you fill in the worksheets, you will probably want to add more accurate figures later.

If you are married, include your spouse's expenses; in addition, if anyone is financially dependent on you, add in those expenses, too.

WORKSHEET E

MONTHLY EXPENSES TODAY

	1 Monthly Amount
Housing	
Mortgage (Including condo fees)	
Rent	
Maintenance	
Food (at home)	
Utilities	
Electricity	
Heat	
Internet/cable	
Phones	
Water/sewer	
Clothing	
Taxes	
Real estate	
Income (state and federal)	
Other property taxes	
Insurance	
House	
Life	
Car	
Disability	
Long-term care	

	[1] Monthly Amount
Loans	
Car	
Credit card	
Other	
Workplace retirement and personal savings	
Personal Care	
Hair cut	
Dry cleaning	
Gym	
Other	
Transportation	
Car repairs and maintenance	
Gas	
Parking	
Public transportation	
Health Care	
Health insurance	
Doctor visits	
Hospital	
Medicine	
Over-the-counter medicine	

	[1] Monthly Amount
Health Care (continued)	
Dental	
Vision	
Noncovered items	
Travel/vacations	
Entertainment	
Eating out	
Hobbies	
Movies/theater	
Charitable contributions	
Other	
Gifts	
Membership dues	
Pet-related costs	
TOTAL ESTIMATED MONTHLY EXPENSES (other than health)	
TOTAL ESTIMATED MONTHLY EXPENSES (health)	

WORKSHEET F

MONTHLY EXPENSES IN 10 YEARS

(First year of retirement)

	1 Total monthly expenses now (from monthly expenses column in Worksheet E)	2 10-year inflation factor of 1.4106 (3.5%) (except for health care)	3 Total expenses in 10 years adjusted for inflation (Columns 1x2)
Housing			
Mortgage (Including condo fees)			
Rent			
Maintenance			
Food (at home)			
Utilities			
Electricity			
Heat			
Internet/cable			
Phones			
Water/sewer			
Clothing			
Taxes			
Real estate			
Income (state and federal)			
Other property taxes			
Insurance			
House			
Life			
Car			
Disability			
Long-term care			

	1 Total monthly expenses now (from monthly expenses column in Worksheet E)	2 10-year inflation factor of 1.4106 (3.5%) (except for health care)	3 Total expenses in 10 years adjusted for inflation (Columns 1x2)
Loans			
Car Credit card Other			
Workplace retirement and personal savings			
Personal Care			
Hair cut Dry cleaning Gym Other			
Transportation			
Car repairs and maintenance Gas Parking Public transportation			
Health Care	For a	7% inflation factor, use	1.9672
Health insurance Medicare Part B Medicare Part D Medigap Doctor visits Hospital Medicine Over-the-counter medicine			

WORKSHEET F CONTINUED

MONTHLY EXPENSES IN 10 YEARS

(First year of retirement)

	1 Total monthly expenses now (from monthly expenses column in Worksheet E)	2 10-year inflation factor of 1.4106 (3.5%) (except for health care)	3 Total expenses in 10 years adjusted for inflation (Columns 1x2)
Health Care (continued)			
Dental Vision Noncovered items			
Travel/vacations			
Entertainment			
Eating out Hobbies Movies/theater			
Charitable contributions			
Other			
Gifts Membership dues Pet-related costs			
TOTAL MONTHLY EXPENSES ADJUSTED FOR 10 YEARS INFLATION (other than health)			
TOTAL MONTHLY EXPENSES ADJUSTED FOR 10 YEARS INFLATION (health)			

INSTRUCTIONS FOR WORKSHEET F

MONTHLY EXPENSES IN 10 YEARS

Inflation will increase your expenses, even in the 10 years between now and retirement. Worksheet F helps you calculate how much inflation might affect each of the items in the expenses you recorded in Worksheet E. In addition, it includes room for some new types of health-related expenses many retirees are likely to incur in retirement. This chart assumes an inflation rate of 3.5 percent for items other than health-related expenses and assumes a 7 percent inflation rate for health expenses.

Note: Many mortgage and some loan payments have already taken into account the rate of inflation. If you have a fixed mortgage or loan, you will not need to do the calculation for this item.

WORKSHEET G

COMPARING PROJECTED INCOME AND EXPENSES-ARE YOU PREPARED?

	1 At retirement	2 Inflation adjusted value factor (see Clue 3)	3 Value at retirement for one month (Column 1 x Column 2)
Total projected income Worksheet D, col 3 total			
Total projected expenses Worksheet F, col 3 total **H**ealth **O**ther than health			
Projected value of income less expenses Subtract line 2 from line 1			

4
Total value at retirement
lumn 3 x 360 months)

INSTRUCTIONS FOR WORKSHEET G

COMPARING PROJECTED INCOME AND EXPENSES

This worksheet compares your anticipated income and expenses over the 30 years of your retirement and will reflect any shortfall between the two.

Use the total monthly income calculated in Worksheet D and multiply it by a value adjustment factor you select from Clue 3 on page 31. Select the rate of return with a 0 percent inflation rate. Then multiply this result by 360 months and enter that amount in Column 4 of Worksheet G. This is your total projected income.

Next, record the total monthly expenses calculated in Worksheet F. For expenses other than health, choose an inflation adjustment value factor from Clue 3 on page 31. Use the 3.5 percent inflation rate (used in Worksheet F) or select another that you believe will reflect inflation over the 30 years of your retirement.

For health, use a 7 percent inflation rate or select another rate. Multiply this result by 360 months and enter it in Column 4. Now subtract the total value of projected expenses ("other than health" and "health") over 30 years of retirement in Column 4 from the corresponding total value of your projected income (also in Column 4). The result is the projected value of income less expenses.

WORKSHEET H

ADDITIONAL SAVINGS NEEDED BEFORE RETIREMENT (IN 10 YEARS)

Additional savings factors:

0.00716 for 3% 0.00644 for 5% 0.00578 for 7%

Gap between projected total value of expenses and projected total value of income (from Worksheet G)	1 $
Additional savings factor	2
Additional monthly savings needed (multiply line 1 x line 2)	3 $

GPO U.S. GOVERNMENT PRINTING OFFICE:2006–326-784

CCH®

PENSION AND EMPLOYEE BENEFITS

CODE • ERISA • REGULATIONS

As of January 1, 2007
Committee Reports

CCH Editorial Staff Publication

Wolters Kluwer
Law & Business

Portfolio Managing Editor . . . . Jan Gerstein
Editor . . . . Elizabeth Pope
Production Editor . . . . Lauren Miller

Compiled from

CCH PENSION PLAN GUIDE

As of January 1, 2007

ISBN 13: 978-0-8080-1574-1

ISBN 10: 0-8080-1574-5

4025 W. Peterson Ave.
Chicago, IL 60646-6085
1 800 248-3248
hr.cch.com

Wolters Kluwer
Law & Business

Printed in the United States of America

ABOUT THIS EDITION

This edition of "Pension and Employee Benefits—Code • ERISA • Regulations" is specially designed to give those involved in the employee benefit plan field instant briefcase and desktop access to selected Internal Revenue Code and ERISA provisions and to corresponding regulatory authority.

Contents—Two-Volume Edition

Volumes 1 and 2 contain the following:

1. The provisions of the Internal Revenue Code (IRC) and regulations dealing with pension plans, profit-sharing and stock bonus plans, deferred compensation, and related employee benefits. Coverage includes all recent law changes, including those made by the Pension Protection Act of 2006 (P.L. 109-280), the Tax Relief and Health Care Act of 2006 (P.L. 109-432), and the Tax Increase Prevention and Reconciliation Act of 2005 (P.L. 109-222). Also included are new 2006 final regulations regarding Roth 401(k) plans, comparability rules for employer contributions to health savings accounts, and standards for electronically-delivered benefit plan notices, elections and consents.

2. The provisions of the Employee Retirement Income Security Act of 1974 (ERISA) and the final or temporary regulations thereunder, including 2006 EBSA final regulations on the termination of abandoned individual account plans and PBGC final regulations on premium penalty waivers. Recent law changes, including those made by the Pension Protection Act of 2006 (P.L. 109-280) and the Deficit Reduction Act of 2005 (P.L. 109-171) have also been reflected.

3. Regulations that have been proposed under the IRC and ERISA, but have not yet been adopted. Some of the proposed IRS regulations may be relied upon by taxpayers until final guidance is issued. Proposed regulation preambles are also included.

4. Relevant non-IRC/non-ERISA provisions of the Pension Protection Act of 2006, the Bankruptcy Abuse Prevention and Consumer Protection Act of 2005, the Katrina Emergency Tax Relief Act of 2005, the Economic Growth and Tax Relief Reconciliation Act of 2001, the IRS Restructuring and Reform Act of 1998, the Small Business Job Protection Act of 1996, the Health Insurance Portability and Accountability Act of 1996, the GATT (General Agreement on Tariffs and Trade), the Omnibus Budget Reconciliation Act of 1993, the Unemployment Compensation Amendments of 1992, the Revenue Reconciliation Act of 1990, the Omnibus Budget Reconciliation Act of 1989, the Technical and Miscellaneous Revenue Act of 1988, the Omnibus Budget Reconciliation Act of 1987, the Single-Employer Pension Plan Amendments Act of 1986, the Tax Reform Act of 1986, and earlier laws.

Contents—Optional Preambles Volume

In addition to the basic two-volume edition described above, a volume containing official IRS and DOL preambles to final and temporary regulations is also available. The preambles provide introductory material issued with each set of regulations that helps explain their purpose and content.

Contents—Optional Committee Reports Volume

In addition to the basic two-volume edition described above, a volume containing selected committee reports relating to legislation affecting pensions and employee benefits enacted since the passage of ERISA is also available. Readers may search by Code or ERISA section, or by public law number, to find the relevant legislative history.

Finding Devices

Convenient finding lists lead the reader to the materials mentioned above.

Topical Indexes reflect all matters covered in all editions.

This publication is compiled from the CCH Pension Plan Guide and CCH Employee Benefits Management, as of January 1, 2007.

January 2007

Table of Contents

Finding List
Committee Reports by Internal Revenue Code Section

Listed below is the location of all Committee Report excerpts associated with a particular section of the Internal Revenue Code.

Subtitle A—Income Taxes

Code Sec.		Par. (¶)
1042	Sales of stock to employee stock ownership plans or certain cooperatives	13,382.10
1372	Partnership rules to apply for fringe benefit purposes	13,463.10
1400M	Definitions	13,473.020
1400P	Housing tax benefits	13,474.020
1400Q	Special rules for use of retirement funds	13,475.020; 13,475.022; 13,475.024; 13,475.026
1402	Definitions	13,480.09

Subtitle B—Estate and Gift Taxes

2039	Annuities	13,500.06; 13,500.062; 13,500.065; 13,500.07; 13,500.08; 13,500.09

Subtitle C—Employment Taxes

3121	Definitions	13,530.07; 13,530.075; 13,530.08; 13,530.085; 13,530.09; 13,530.10
3306	Definitions	13,540.06; 13,540.07; 13,540.08; 13,540.09
3401	Definitions	13,550.078; 13,550.08; 13,550.09
3405	Special rules for pensions, annuities, and certain other deferred income	13,566.095; 13,566.10

Subtitle D—Miscellaneous Excise Taxes

4965	Excise tax on certain tax-exempt entities entering into prohibited tax shelter transactions	13,598.05
4971	Taxes on failure to meet minimum funding standards	13,600.07; 13,600.08; 13,600.09; 13,600.10
4972	Tax on nondeductible contributions to qualified employer plans	13,610.025; 13,610.03; 13,610.04; 13,610.05; 13,610.06; 13,610.08; 13,610.083; 13,610.085; 13,610.089; 13,610.09; 13,610.10
4973	Tax on excess contributions to individual retirement accounts, certain section 403(b) contracts, and certain individual retirement annuities	13,620.05; 13,620.08; 13,620.095; 13,620.10
4975	Tax on prohibited transactions	13,640.018; 13,640.02; 13,640.03; 13,640.04; 13,640.06; 13,640.07; 13,640.08; 13,640.09; 13,640.10
4977	Tax on certain fringe benefits provided by an employer	13,648D.10
4978	Tax on certain dispositions by employee stock ownership plans and certain cooperatives	13,648F.10
4978B	Tax on disposition of employer securities to which section 133 applied	13,648I.10; 13,648I.17
4979	Tax on certain excess contributions	13,648J.09; 13,648J.10
4980	Tax on reversion of qualified plan assets to employer	13,648P.08; 13,648P.095; 13,648P.10
4980B	Failure to satisfy continuation coverage requirements of group health plans	13,648W.07; 13,648W.08; 13,648W.09; 13,648W.095; 13,648W.10
4980F	Failure of applicable plans reducing benefit accruals to satisfy notice requirements	13,648W-75.045; 13,648W-75.05
4980G	Failure of employer to make comparable health savings account contributions	13,648W-92.085

Subtitle F—Procedure and Administration

6039I	Returns and records with respect to employer-owned life insurance contracts	13,678.50
6047	Information relating to certain trusts and annuity plans	13,690.05; 13,690.08; 13,690.09
6050U	Charges or payments for qualified long-term care insurance contracts under combined arrangements	13,706.50
6057	Annual registration, etc.	13,730.095; 13,730.10
6058	Information required in connection with certain plans of deferred compensation	13,740.10
6059	Periodic report of actuary	13,750.10; 13,750A.10
6109	Identifying numbers	13,780.09
6652	Failure to file certain information returns, registration statements, etc.	13,800.06; 13,800.07; 13,800.08; 13,800.085
6693	Failure to provide reports on individual retirement accounts or annuities; Penalties relating to designated nondeductible contributions	13,850.09; 13,850.095; 13,850.10
7476	Declaratory judgments relating to qualification of certain retirement plans	13,910.09; 13,910.10
7701	Definitions	13,920.085; 13,920.09; 13,920.10
7702B	Treatment of qualified long-term care insurance	13,945.90
7802	Internal Revenue Service Oversight Board	13,950.10; 13,950.15

Subtitle K—Group Health Plan Requirements

9812	Parity in the application of certain limits to mental health benefits	13,968U-8.045; 13,968U-8.05; 13,968U-8.10

Finding List
Committee Reports by ERISA Section

Listed below is the location of all Committee Report excerpts associated with a particular section of the Employee Retirement Income Security Act of 1974.

Title I: Protection of Employee Benefit Rights

Act Sec.		Par. (¶)
414	Effective date	14,840.10
501	Criminal penalties	14,910.10
502	Civil enforcement	14,920.081; 14,920.083; 14,920.085; 14,920.09; 14,920.095; 14,920.10
503	Claims procedure	14,930.10
504	Investigative authority	14,940.10
505	Regulations	14,950.10
506	Coordination and responsibility of agencies enforcing Employee Retirement Income Security Act and related federal laws	14,960.085; 14,960.09; 14,960.10
507	Administration	14,970.10
508	Appropriations	14,980.10
510	Interference with rights protected under Act	15,000.09; 15,000.10
511	Coercive interference	15,010.09; 15,010.10
512	Advisory council	15,020.10
513	Research, studies, and annual report	15,030.10
514	Effect on other laws	15,040.075; 15,040.08; 15,040.085; 15,040.09; 15,040.10
515	Delinquent contributions	15,043.10
601	Plans must provide continuation coverage to certain individuals	15,045.10
602	Continuation coverage	15,045F.098; 15,045F.099; 15,045F.10
607	Definitions and special rules	15,046F.10
609	Additional standards for group health plans	15,046M.098; 15,046M.10
711	Standards relating to benefits for mothers and newborns	15,050J.10
712	Parity in the application of certain limits to mental health benefits	15,050K.045; 15,050K.05; 15,050K.10

Title II: Amendments to the Internal Revenue Code Relating to Retirement Plans

[Note: Title II amendments to the Internal Revenue Code, encompassing ERISA Secs. 1011—2008, are incorporated in place in the Internal Revenue Code provisions in Volume I.]

1012	Minimum vesting standards	15,060.10
1032	Duties of Secretary of Health, Education, and Welfare	15,070.10

Title III: Jurisdiction, Administration, Enforcement; Joint Pension Task Force, Etc.

3001	Procedures in connection with the issuance of certain determination letters by the Secretary of the Treasury	15,110.08; 15,110.10
3002	Procedures with respect to continued compliance with requirements relating to participation, vesting, and funding standards	15,120.10
3003	Procedures in connection with prohibited transactions	15,130.10
3004	Coordination between the Department of the Treasury and the Department of Labor	15,140.10
3021	Establishment	15,150.10
3022	Duties	15,160.09; 15,160.10
3031	Congressional study	15,170.10
3032	Protection for employees under federal procurement, construction, and research contracts and grants	15,180.10
3041	Establishment of Joint Board for the Enrollment of Actuaries	15,210.10
3042	Enrollment by Joint Board	15,220.10

Title IV: Plan Termination Insurance

4001	Definitions	15,310.07; 15,310.09; 15,310.095; 15,310.10
4002	Pension Benefit Guaranty Corporation	15,320.07; 15,320.08; 15,320.09; 15,320.10
4003	Investigatory authority; cooperation with other agencies; civil actions	15,330.09; 15,330.095; 15,330.10
4004	[Repealed]	15,340.10
4005	Establishment of Pension Benefit Guaranty funds	15,350.07; 15,350.09; 15,350.10
4006	Premium rates	15,360.07; 15,360.075; 15,360.08; 15,360.085; 15,360.09; 15,360.10
4007	Payment of premiums	15,370.07; 15,370.08; 15,370.09
4008	Report by the corporation	15,380.10
4009	Portability assistance	15,390.10
4010	Authority to require certain information	15,395.09; 15,395.10
4011	Notice to participants	15,400.09; 15,400.10
4021	Plans covered	15,410.09; 15,410.10
4022	Single-employer plan benefits guaranteed	15,420.08; 15,420.09; 15,420.095; 15,420.10; 15,420.20
4022A	Multiemployer plan benefits guaranteed	15,429H.05; 15,429H.10
4022B	Aggregate limit on benefits guaranteed	15,429L.10
4023	Plan fiduciaries	15,430.095; 15,430.10
4041	Termination of single-employer plans	15,440.075; 15,440.08; 15,440.085; 15,440.09; 15,440.10
4041A	Termination of multiemployer plans	15,449F.10
4042	Institution of termination proceedings by the corporation	15,450.075; 15,450.08; 15,450.085; 15,450.095; 15,450.10

Public Law–Committee Report Locator Table

Listed below is the location of all Committee Report excerpts associated with a particular Public Law number. Public Law numbers are presented in chronological order.

P.L. No.	Name	Enactment Date	Paragraph
91-172	Tax Reform Act of 1969	December 30, 1969	**11,190.10; 11,190.15**
92-580	[None designated]	October 27, 1972	**13,500.09**
93-406	Employee Retirement Income Security Act of 1974	September 2, 1974	**11,190.05; 11,330.05; 11,330.08; 11,330.10; 11,700.10; 11,750.10; 11,800A.10; 11,850.10; 12,050.10; 12,100.10; 12,150.11; 12,200.10; 12,250.10; 12,300.10; 12,350.10; 12,350.15; 12,400.10; 13,600.10; 13,610.10; 13,620.10; 13,640.10; 13,730.10; 13,750.10; 13,750A.10; 13,910.10; 13,920.10; 13,950.10; 13,950.15; 14,120.10; 14,130.10; 14,130.15; 14,140.10; 14,210.10; 14,220.10; 14,230.10; 14,240.10; 14,250.10; 14,260.10; 14,270.10; 14,280.10; 14,290.10; 14,300.10; 14,310.10; 14,410.10; 14,420.10; 14,430.10; 14,440.10; 14,450.10; 14,450.15; 14,460.10; 14,470.10; 14,480.10; 14,490.10; 14,500.10; 14,510.10; 14,610.10; 14,620.10; 14,620.15; 14,620.20; 14,620.25; 14,620.30; 14,620.35; 14,620.40; 14,630.10; 14,630.15; 14,640.10; 14,650.10; 14,660.10; 14,710.10; 14,720.10; 14,730.10; 14,740.10; 14,750.10; 14,760.10; 14,770.10; 14,780.10; 14,790.10; 14,800.10; 14,810.10; 14,820.10; 14,830.10; 14,840.10; 14,910.10; 14,920.10; 14,930.10; 14,940.10; 14,950.10; 14,960.10; 14,970.10; 14,980.10; 15,000.10; 15,010.10; 15,020.10; 15,030.10; 15,040.10; 15,060.10; 15,070.10; 15,110.10; 15,120.10; 15,130.10; 15,140.10; 15,150.10; 15,160.10; 15,170.10; 15,180.10; 15,210.10; 15,220.10; 15,320.10; 15,330.10; 15,340.10; 15,350.10; 15,360.10; 15,370.09; 15,390.10; 15,410.10; 15,420.10; 15,430.10; 15,440.10; 15,450.10; 15,460.10; 15,470.10; 15,480.10; 15,490.10; 15,500.10; 15,510.10; 15,610.10; 15,620.10; 15,630.10; 15,640.10; 15,650.10; 15,661.10; 15,662.10; 15,720.10**
94-267	IRC of 1954—Employee Retirement	April 15, 1976	**11,700.09; 11,750.09; 11,800.09; 11,850.09**
94-455	Tax Reform Act of 1976	October 4, 1976	**11,260.09; 11,270.09; 11,283.10; 11,330.04; 11,700.08; 11,750.08; 11,800.08; 11,800A.09; 11,850.08; 12,400.09; 13,120.09; 13,140.09; 13,160.09; 13,500.08; 13,780.09; 15,160.09; 15,320.09**
95-30	Tax Reduction and Simplification Act of 1977	May 23, 1977	**11,270.08**
95-216	Social Security Amendments of 1977	December 20, 1977	**15,420.20**
95-458	Excise Tax—Trucks, Buses, etc.	October 13, 1978	**11,750.07; 11,800.07**
95-600	Revenue Act of 1978	November 6, 1978	**11,270.07; 11,288A.10; 11,289.10; 11,290.09; 11,330.03; 11,700.06; 11,700.07; 11,750.06; 11,800.06; 11,850.07; 12,050.09; 12,100.09; 12,130.10; 12,400.08; 13,153.10; 13,500.07; 13,540.09; 13,550.09; 13,620.095; 13,640.09; 13,740.10; 13,910.09; 13,920.09**
96-222	Technical Corrections Act of 1979	April 1, 1980	**11,270.065; 11,288A.097; 11,330.025; 11,700.059; 11,750.055; 11,800.055; 11,850.065; 12,050.08; 12,130.09; 12,400.075; 13,153.09; 13,500.065; 13,530.10; 13,540.08; 13,550.08; 13,620.08; 13,640.08; 13,850.10**

P.L. No.	Name	Enactment Date	Paragraph
96-364	Multiemployer Pension Plan Amendments Act of 1980	September 26, 1980	**11,700.057; 11,850.063; 12,200.09; 12,250.085; 12,250.09; 12,350.085; 12,600.10; 12,650.10; 12,700.10; 12,750.10; 12,800.10; 12,850.10; 13,600.09; 14,130.093; 14,130.095; 14,230.095; 14,410.09; 14,430.095; 14,610.09; 14,620.095; 14,730.09; 14,730.095; 14,920.095; 15,043.10; 15,310.10; 15,320.08; 15,350.09; 15,360.09; 15,429H.10; 15,429L.10; 15,430.095; 15,449F.10; 15,510.095; 15,640.08; 15,650.095; 15,663.10; 15,664.10; 15,665.10; 15,667.10; 15,669.10; 15,670.10; 15,671.10; 15,673.10; 15,674.10; 15,675.10; 15,676.10; 15,679.10; 15,680.10; 15,681.10; 15,682.10; 15,684.10; 15,685.10; 15,686.10; 15,688.10; 15,689.10; 15,690.10; 15,691.10; 15,692.10; 15,696.10; 15,700.10; 15,701.10; 15,702.10; 15,703.10; 15,704.10; 15,706.10; 15,708.10; 15,709.10; 15,710.10; 15,712.10; 15,713.10; 15,714.10; 15,715.10; 15,716.10; 15,717.10; 15,718.10; 15,720.09; 15,720.091**
96-603	Private Foundation Returns	December 28, 1980	**11,899A.05**
96-605	Miscellaneous Revenue Act of 1980	December 28, 1980	**12,350.09; 12,400.07**
96-608	Taxation—Individuals Living Abroad	December 28, 1980	**11,750.05**
97-34	Economic Recovery Tax Act of 1981	August 13, 1981	**11,190.045; 11,240.09; 11,283.095; 11,330.02; 11,750.047; 11,850.062; 12,050.075; 12,050.077; 12,100.085; 13,124.10; 13,500.062; 13,610.09**
97-37	Former Prisoners of War Benefits Act of 1981	August 14, 1981	**11,355.10**
97-248	Tax Equity and Fiscal Responsibility Act of 1982	September 3, 1982	**11,190.043; 11,190.044; 11,230.09; 12,050.07; 12,100.08; 12,350.075; 12,400.06; 12,500.10; 13,500.06; 13,540.07; 13,566.10; 13,610.089; 13,690.09; 13,800.085**
97-354	Subchapter S Act	October 19, 1982	**13,463.10**
97-448	Technical Corrections Act of 1982	January 12, 1983	**11,190.042; 11,240.07; 11,283.09; 11,330.017; 12,130.08; 13,124.09**
97-473	Periodic Payments Settlement Act of 1982	January 14, 1983	**11,260.07; 14,130.092; 15,040.09**
98-21	Social Security Act Amendments of 1983	April 20, 1983	**11,950.09; 12,000.09; 13,530.09; 13,540.06**
98-369	Tax Reform Act of 1984	July 18, 1984	**11,100.10; 11,190.040; 11,230.085; 11,240.05; 11,250.10; 11,288A.095; 11,289M.10; 11,330.016; 11,358F.10; 11,700.05; 11,750.045; 11,850.061; 12,050.065; 12,350.07; 12,400.05; 12,500.09; 12,900.10; 12,950.10; 13,124.085; 13,132.085; 13,150.09; 13,193.10; 13,648D.10; 13,920.085; 15,676.09; 15,684.09; 15,686.09; 15,704.09; 15,720.087**
98-397	Retirement Equity Act of 1984	August 23, 1984	**11,190.041; 11,750.043; 12,150.10; 12,200.085; 12,350.065; 12,550.10; 13,730.095; 13,800.08; 14,250.09; 14,420.09; 14,430.09; 14,440.09; 14,450.09; 14,460.095; 15,040.085**
98-473	Continuing Appropriations, 1985—Comprehensive Crime Control Act of 1984	October 12, 1984	**14,810.09; 14,960.09**
99-44	Recordkeeping Repeal Act	May 24, 1985	**11,355.095**
99-272	Consolidated Omnibus Budget Reconciliation Act	April 7, 1986	**11,280.09; 11,289M.095; 11,300.09; 11,750.042; 11,850.06; 12,250.08; 14,440.085; 14,655.10; 15,045.10; 15,310.095; 15,360.085; 15,429H.05; 15,440.09; 15,450.095; 15,520.10; 15,620.09; 15,661.09; 15,662L.10; 15,662R.10**
99-514	Tax Reform Act of 1986	October 22, 1986	**11,190.039; 11,282.10; 11,289.095; 11,289H.10; 11,289M.09; 11,300.085; 11,358P.10; 11,700.048; 11,750.041; 11,800.053; 11,850.058; 12,050.063; 12,130.07; 12,150.095; 12,200.08; 12,350.06; 12,400.048; 12,500.085; 12,550.095; 12,900.095; 13,153.085; 13,610.085; 13,648P.10; 14,420.07; 14,430.085; 14,450.085; 15,045F.10; 15,720.085**
100-202	Long-Term Continuing Appropriations Act	December 22, 1987	**14,130.09**

P.L. No.	Name	Enactment Date	Paragraph
100-203	Omnibus Budget Reconciliation Act of 1987	December 22, 1987	11,330.015; 11,700.046; 12,200.075; 12,250.075; 13,530.085; 14,210.095; 14,230.09; 14,240.07; 14,440.08; 14,620.09; 14,640.095; 14,657.10; 14,730.085; 14,770.095; 14,830.08; 14,920.09; 15,110.08; 15,310.07; 15,350.07; 15,360.08; 15,370.08; 15,420.095; 15,440.085; 15,450.085; 15,470.095; 15,520.09; 15,620.08; 15,640.07; 15,661.08; 15,662.09; 15,662U.10
100-647	Technical and Miscellaneous Revenue Act of 1988	November 10, 1988	11,190.038; 11,230.08; 11,282.095; 11,283.085; 11,288A.09; 11,289.09; 11,289H.095; 11,289M.085; 11,300.08; 11,330.014; 11,358P.095; 11,700.045; 11,750.040; 11,800.051; 11,850.056; 12,050.061; 12,130.065; 12,150.09; 12,300.095; 12,350.055; 12,400.046; 12,500.083; 13,124.08; 13,153.08; 13,530.08; 13,550.078; 13,566.095; 13,610.083; 13,648J.10; 13,648P.095; 13,648W.10; 13,850.095
101-239	Omnibus Budget Reconciliation Act of 1989	December 19, 1989	11,300.075; 11,330.013; 11,700.043; 11,750.038; 11,850.055; 12,050.059; 12,130.063; 12,200.073; 12,250.073; 12,350.053; 12,400.045; 13,153.078; 13,382.10; 13,648I.17; 13,648W.095; 13,690.08
101-508	Omnibus Budget Reconciliation Act of 1990	November 5, 1990	11,190.037; 11,230.075; 11,283.80; 11,289.085; 11,300.07; 13,030.10; 13,640.07; 13,648I.10; 13,648P.08
102-89	Rural Telephone Cooperative Association Amendments, ERISA Act Amendments of 1991	September 14, 1991	14,130.085
102-318	Unemployment Compensation Amendments of 1992	July 3, 1992	11,190.031; 11,190.036; 11,700.042; 11,750.036; 11,800.045; 11,850.054; 12,050.058; 12,200.063; 12,350.051; 12,400.044
102-486	Comprehensive National Energy Policy Act of 1992	October 24, 1992	11,289M.08; 13,160.085
103-66	Omnibus Budget Reconciliation Act of 1993	August 10, 1993	11,289.08; 11,289M.075; 11,300.065; 11,700.04; 12,050.057; 13,193.085; 13,327.095; 13,648W.09; 15,040.08; 15,046M.10
103-465	General Agreement on Tariffs and Trade (GATT); Retirement Protection Act	December 8, 1994	11,700.038; 11,850.052; 12,250.07; 12,250.071; 12,550.09; 13,030.095; 13,610.08; 14,430.084; 14,620.07; 14,620.08; 15,310.09; 15,330.095; 15,360.075; 15,395.10; 15,400.10; 15,420.09; 15,440.08; 15,450.08; 15,460.095; 15,530.08
104-188	Small Business Job Protection Act	August 10, 1996	11,190.034; 11,250.09; 11,260.065; 11,282.094; 11,289.075; 11,290.08; 11,330.011; 11,700.036; 11,750.034; 11,800.049; 11,850.050; 12,050.056; 12,200.071; 12,350.05; 12,550.08; 13,150.08; 13,153.076; 13,160.084; 13,312.03; 13,313.03; 13,480.09; 13,530.07; 13,530.075; 13,600.08; 13,640.06; 13,648F.10; 13,648W.07; 13,690.05; 13,800.07; 13,850.09; 14,210.090; 14,430.083; 14,450.084; 14,710.095; 14,740.095; 14,780.098; 15,045F.098
104-191	Health Insurance Portability and Accountability Act	August 21, 1996	11,190.035; 11,250.095; 11,280.08; 11,288A.08; 11,300.06; 13,160.083; 13,314.10; 13,648W.08; 14,920.085; 14,960.085; 15,045F.099; 15,046F.10
104-193	Personal Responsibility and Work Opportunity Reconciliation Act	August 22, 1996	15,046M.098
104-204	Mental Health Parity Act of 1996	September 26, 1996	13,968U-8.10; 15,050J.10; 15,050K.10
105-34	Taxpayer Relief Act	August 5, 1997	11,190.033; 11,330.010; 11,700.034; 11,750.032; 12,050.047; 12,050.052; 12,097.10; 12,200.069; 12,250.068; 13,610.06; 13,620.05; 13,640.03; 13,640.04; 14,210.080; 14,220.07; 14,240.096; 14,430.081; 14,460.09; 14,620.088; 14,770.093; 14,780.096; 14,920.083
105-206	IRS Restructuring and Reform Act of 1998	July 22, 1998	11,190.032; 12,050.049; 12,097.08
106-170	Ticket to Work and Work Incentives Improvement Act	December 17, 1999	11,289.07; 13,030.08

P.L. No.	Name	Enactment Date	Paragraph
107-16	Economic Growth and Tax Relief Reconciliation Act	June 7, 2001	**11,109.50; 11,118.50; 11,289.06; 11,289M.07; 11,330.005; 11,700.022; 11,700.024; 11,700.025; 11,700.026; 11,700.028; 11,700.032; 11,750.024; 11,750.026; 11,750.028; 11,750.03; 11,799A.048; 11,799A.049; 11,799A.50; 11,850.042; 11,850.044; 11,850.046; 11,850.048; 12,050.035; 12,050.04; 12,050.045; 12,130.06; 12,200.04; 12,200.05; 12,200.06; 12,250.03; 12,250.05; 12,350.04; 12,400.02; 12,400.03; 12,400.04; 12,500.08; 13,153.02; 13,153.03; 13,153.04; 13,153.05; 13,153.06; 13,153.07; 13,610.04; 13,610.05; 13,648W-75.05; 14,140.08; 14,430.077; 14,430.079; 14,440.04; 14,620.084; 14,620.086; 14,740.093; 14,780.094**
108-218	Pension Funding Equity Act of 2004	April 10, 2004	**12,250.025; 13,030.07; 14,210.075; 15,686.08; 15,689.09**
108-311	Working Families Tax Relief Act of 2004	October 4, 2004	**11,700.021; 11,750.022; 12,050.033; 12,400.017; 13,610.03; 13,968U-8.05**
108-357	American Jobs Creation Act of 2004	October 22, 2004	**11,190.030; 12,145.10; 13,100.05; 13,100.06; 13,130.08; 13,640.02; 15,050K.05**
109-135	Gulf Opportunity Zone Act of 2005	December 21, 2005	**11,295.08; 11,750.021; 12,145.09; 12,400.015; 13,473.020; 13,474.020; 13,475.020; 13,475.022; 13,475.024; 13,475.026**
109-222	Tax Increase Prevention and Reconciliation Act of 2005	May 17, 2006	**12,097.07; 13,598.05**
109-280	Pension Protection Act of 2006	August 17, 2006	**11,109.45; 11,190.029; 11,250.085; 11,330.004; 11,700.02; 11,750.19; 11,800.043; 11,850.039; 12,050.031; 12,097.06; 12,145.08; 12,200.035; 12,250.023; 12,350.038; 12,400.013; 12,550.07; 12,850.09, 12,950.09; 13,030.06; 13,151L.50; 13,151M.50; 13,151N.50; 13,151O.50; 13,153.018; 13,160.081; 13,600.07; 13,610.025; 13,640.018; 13,648J.09; 13,648W-75.045; 13,678.50; 13,706.50; 13,800.06; 13,945.90; 14,130.08; 14,210.07; 14,230.085; 14,240.065; 14,250.08; 14,430.075; 14,440.038; 14,450.083; 14,460.085; 14,500.09; 14,610.08; 14,620.082; 14,630.09; 14,640.09; 14,650.09; 14,655.09; 14,657.09; 14,660.09; 14,740.091; 14,780.092; 14,820.09; 14,920.081; 15,000.09; 15,010.09; 15,040.075; 15,320.07; 15,330.09; 15,360.07; 15,370.07; 15,380.10; 15,395.09; 15,400.09; 15,410.09; 15,420.08; 15,440.075; 15,450.075; 15,460.09; 15,470.09; 15,530.07; 15,669.09; 15,675.09; 15,676.08; 15,689.08; 15,696.09; 15,713.09**
109-432	Tax Relief and Health Care Act of 2006	December 20, 2006	**11,280.075; 11,335.085; 12,050.029; 13,648W-92.085; 13,968U-8.045; 15,050K.045**

Internal Revenue Code Committee Reports

[Code Sec. 21]

[¶ 11,100.10]

Committee Report on P.L. 98-369 (Tax Reform Act of 1984)

[House Committee Report]

Explanation of Provision

Under the bill, the personal income tax credits—the dependent care credit, credit for elderly and disabled, residential energy credit and political contribution credit—will be allowable against tax before all other credits. Next the foreign tax credit, credit for clinical testing of certain drugs, and fuel production credit will be allowable against tax under the conditions of present law.

The business income tax credits—the investment tax credit (both the regular and the energy credits), targeted jobs credit, alcohol fuels credit, and ESOP credit—will be combined into one general business credit. This credit will be allowable against 100 percent of the first $25,000 of tax liability and 85 percent of the remaining tax liability. Tax liability generally means the income tax imposed reduced by other nonrefundable credits. The credit will be used on a FIFO basis with a 3-year carryback and 15-year carryforward period. The research activities credit will continue to be allowed against 100 percent of a taxpayer's tax liability.

Effective Date

The provision will be effective for taxable years beginning after 1983. Credits earned in pre-1984 years will continue to be carried to post-1983 years under the substantive rules (apart from the tax liability limitations) under which they were earned. Likewise, credits earned in post-1983 years may be carried back to pre-1984 years, subject to the new tax liability limitation rules imposed by the bill.

[Code Sec. 25B]

[¶ 11,109.45]

Committee Report on P.L. 109-280 (Pension Protection Act of 2006)

[Joint Committee on Taxation Report]

The provision makes the saver's credit permanent.

The provision also provides that an individual may direct that the amount of any refund attributable to the saver's credit be directly deposited by the Federal government into an applicable retirement plan, meaning an IRA, qualified retirement plan, section 403(b) annuity, or governmental section 457 plan designated by the individual (if the plan or other arrangement agrees to accept such direct deposits). In the case of a joint return, each spouse is entitled to designate an applicable retirement plan with respect to payments attributable to such spouse. The provision does not change the rules relating to the tax treatment of contributions to such plans or other arrangements.

Effective Date

The extension of the saver's credit is effective on enactment. The provision relating to direct deposit of refunds relating to the saver's credit is effective for taxable years beginning after December 31, 2006. (In addition, another provision of bill, described below, provides for indexing of the income limits on the saver's credit.)

For the Committee Report on P.L. 109-280 relating to additional IRA contributions for certain employees, see ¶ 11,330.004.

[¶ 11,109.50]

Committee Report on P.L. 107-16 (Economic Growth and Tax Relief Reconciliation Act)

[Senate Committee Report]

The bill provides a temporary nonrefundable tax credit for contributions made by eligible taxpayers to a qualified plan. The maximum annual contribution eligible for the credit is $2,000. The credit rate depends on the adjusted gross income ("AGI") of the taxpayer. Only joint returns with AGI of $50,000 or less, head of household returns of $37,500 or less, and single returns of $25,000 or less are eligible for the credit. The AGI limits applicable to single taxpayers apply to married taxpayers filing separate returns. The credit is in addition to any deduction or exclusion that would otherwise apply with respect to the contribution. The credit offsets minimum tax liability as well as regular tax liability. The credit is available to individuals who are 18 or over, other than individuals who are full-time students or claimed as a dependent on another taxpayer's return.

The credit is available with respect to elective contributions to a section 401(k) plan, section 403(b) annuity, or eligible deferred compensation arrangement of a State or local government (a "sec. 457 plan"), SIMPLE, or SEP, contributions to a traditional or Roth IRA, and voluntary after-tax employee contributions to a qualified retirement plan. The present-law rules governing such contributions continue to apply.

The amount of any contribution eligible for the credit is reduced by taxable distributions received by the taxpayer and his or her spouse from any savings arrangement described above or any other qualified retirement plan during the taxable year for which the credit is claimed, the two taxable years prior to the year the credit is claimed, and during the period after the end of the taxable year and prior to the due date for filing the taxpayer's return for the year. In the case of a distribution from a Roth IRA, this rule applies to any such distributions, whether or not taxable.

The credit rates based on AGI are as follows.

Joint filers	*Heads of households*	*All other filers*	*Credit rate (percent)*
$0-$30,000	$0-$22,500	$0-$15,000	50
$30,000-$32,500	$22,500-$24,375	$15,000-$16,250	20
$32,500-$50,000	$24,375-$37,500	$16,250-$25,000	10
Over $50,000	Over $37,500	Over $25,000	0

Effective Date

The provision is effective for taxable years beginning after December 31, 2001, and before January 1, 2007.

[Conference Committee Report]

The conference agreement follows the Senate amendment.

[Code Sec. 45E]

[¶ 11,118.50]

Committee Report on P.L. 107-16 (Economic Growth and Tax Relief Reconciliation Act)

[Senate Committee Report]

The bill provides a nonrefundable income tax credit for 50 percent of the administrative and retirement-education expenses for any small business that adopts a new qualified defined benefit or defined contribution plan (including a section 401(k) plan), SIMPLE plan, or simplified employee pension ("SEP"). The credit applies to 50 percent of the first $1,000 in administrative and retirement-education expenses for the plan for each of the first three years of the plan.

The credit is available to an employer that did not employ, in the preceding year, more than 100 employees with compensation in excess of $5,000. In order for an employer to be eligible for the credit, the plan must cover at least one nonhighly compensated employee. In addition, if the credit is for the cost of a payroll deduction IRA arrangement, the arrangement must be made available to all employees of the employer who have worked with the employer for at least three months.

The credit is a general business credit.[1] The 50 percent of qualifying expenses that are effectively offset by the tax credit are not deductible; the other 50 percent of the qualifying expenses (and other expenses) are deductible to the extent permitted under present law.

Effective Date

The credit is effective with respect to costs paid or incurred in taxable years beginning after December 31, 2001, with respect to plans established after such date.

[Conference Committee Report]

The conference agreement follows the Senate amendment.

[1] The credit cannot be carried back to years before the effective date.

[Code Sec. 72]

[¶ 11,190.029]

Committee Report on P.L. 109-280 (Pension Protection Act of 2006)

[Joint Committee on Taxation Report]

[Treatment of distributions to individuals called to active duty for at least 179 days]

Under the provision, the 10-percent early withdrawal tax does not apply to a qualified reservist distribution. A qualified reservist distribution is a distribution (1) from an IRA or attributable to elective deferrals under a 401(k) plan, 403(b) annuity, or certain similar arrangements, (2) made to an individual who (by reason of being a member of a reserve component as defined in section 101 of title 37 of the U.S. Code) was ordered or called to active duty for a period in excess of 179 days or for an indefinite period, and (3) that is made during the period beginning on the date of such order or call to duty and ending at the close of the active duty period. A 401(k) plan or 403(b) annuity does not violate the distribution restrictions applicable to such plans by reason of making a qualified reservist distribution.

An individual who receives a qualified reservist distribution may, at any time during the two-year period beginning on the day after the end of the active duty period, make one or more contributions to an IRA of such individual in an aggregate amount not to exceed the amount of such distribution. The dollar limitations otherwise applicable to contributions to IRAs do not apply to any contribution made pursuant to the provision. No deduction is allowed for any contribution made under the provision.

This provision applies to individuals ordered or called to active duty after September 11, 2001, and before December 31, 2007. The two-year period for making recontributions of qualified reservist distributions does not end before the date that is two years after the date of enactment.

Effective Date

The provision applies to distributions after September 11, 2001. If refund or credit of any overpayment of tax resulting from the provision would be prevented at any time before the close of the one-year period beginning on the date of the enactment by the operation of any law or rule of law (including res judicata), such refund or credit may nevertheless be made or allowed if claim therefor is filed before the close of such period.

[Inapplicability of 10-percent additional tax on early distributions of pension plans of public safety employees]

Under the provision, the 10-percent early withdrawal tax does not apply to distributions from a governmental defined benefit pension plan to a qualified public safety employee who separates from service after age 50. A qualified public safety employee is an employee of a State or political subdivision of a State if the employee provides police protection, firefighting services, or emergency medical services for any area within the jurisdiction of such State or political subdivision.

Effective Date

The provision is effective for distributions made after the date of enactment.

[Tax treatment of combined annuity or life insurance contracts with a long-term care insurance feature]

For the Committee Report on P.L. 109-280 on combined annuities with a long-term care feature, see ¶ 13,706.50.

[¶ 11,190.030]

Committee Report on P.L. 108-357 (American Jobs Creation Act of 2004)

[Senate Amendment]

The Senate amendment modifies the present-law rules under which certain contributions and earnings that have not been previously taxed are treated as basis (under sec. 72). Under the Senate amendment, employee or employer contributions are not included in basis if: (1) the employee was a nonresident alien at the time the services were performed with respect to which the contribution was made; (2) the contribution is with respect to compensation for labor or personal services from sources without the United States; and (3) the contribution was not subject to income tax under the laws of the United States or any foreign country.

The Senate amendment authorizes the Secretary of the Treasury to issue regulations to carry out the purposes of the Senate amendment, including regulations treating contributions as not subject to income tax under the laws of any foreign country under appropriate circumstances.

[Conference Agreement]

The conference agreement follows the Senate amendment with modifications.

Under the conference agreement, employee or employer contributions are not included in basis (under sec. 72) if: (1) the employee was a nonresident alien at the time the services were performed with respect to which the contribution was made; (2) the contribution is with respect to compensation for labor or personal services from sources without the United States; and (3) the contribution was not subject to income tax (and would have been subject to income tax if paid as cash compensation when the services were rendered) under the laws of the United States or any foreign country.

Additionally, earnings on employer or employee contributions are not included in basis if: (1) the earnings are paid or accrued with respect to any employer or employee contributions which were made with respect to compensation for labor or personal services; (2) the employee was a nonresident alien at the time the earnings were paid or accrued; and (3) the earnings were not subject to income tax under the laws of the United States or any foreign country.

The conference agreement does not change the rules applicable to calculation of basis with respect to contributions or earnings while an employee is a U.S. resident.

There is no inference that this conference agreement applies in any case to create tax jurisdiction with respect to wages, fees, and salaries otherwise exempt under section 893. Similarly, there is no inference that the conference agreement applies where contrary to an agreement of the United States that has been validly authorized by Congress (or in the case of a treaty, ratified by the Senate), and which provides an exemption for income.

Most U.S. tax treaties specifically address the taxation of pension distributions. The U.S. Model treaty provides for exclusive residence-based taxation of pension distributions to the extent such distributions were not previously included in taxable income in the other country. For purposes of the U.S. Model treaty, the United States treats any amount that has increased the recipient's basis (as defined in section 72) as having been previously included in taxable income. The following example illustrates how the conference agreement could affect the amount of a distribution that may be taxed by the United States pursuant to a tax treaty.

Assume the following facts. A, a nonresident alien individual, performs services outside the United States, in A's country of residence, country Z. A's employer makes contributions on behalf of A to a pension plan established in country Z. For U.S. tax purposes, no portion of the contributions or earnings are included in A's income (and would not be included in income if the amounts were paid as cash compensation when the services were performed) because such amounts relate to services performed without the United States.[951] Later in time, A retires and becomes a permanent resident of the United States.

Under the conference agreement, the employer contributions to the pension plan would not be taken into account in determining A's basis if A was not subject to income tax on the contributions by a foreign country and the contributions would have been subject to tax by a foreign country if the contributions had been paid to A as cash compensation when the services were performed. Thus, in those circumstances, A would be subject to U.S. tax on the distribution of all of the contributions, as such distributions are made. However, if the contributions would not have been subject to tax in the foreign country if they had been paid to A as cash compensation when the services were performed, under the conference agreement, the contributions would be included in A's basis. Earnings that accrued while A was a nonresident alien would not result in basis if not taxed under U.S. or foreign law. Earnings that accrued while A was a permanent resident of the United States would be subject to present-law rules. This result generally is consistent with the treatment of pension distributions under the U.S. Model treaty.

The conference agreement authorizes the Secretary of the Treasury to issue regulations to carry out the purposes of the conference agreement, including regulations treating contributions as not subject to income tax under the laws of any foreign country under appropriate circumstances. For example, Treasury could provide that foreign income tax that was merely nominal would not satisfy the "subject to income tax" requirement.

The conference agreement also changes the rules for determining basis in property received in connection for the performance of services in the case of an individual who was a nonresident alien at the time of the performance of services, if the property is treated as income from sources outside the United States. In that case, the individual's basis in the property does not include any amount that was not subject to income tax (and would have been subject to income tax if paid as cash compensation when the services were performed) under the laws of the United States or any foreign country.

Effective Date

The conference agreement is effective for distributions occurring on or after the date of enactment. No inference is intended that the earnings subject to the conference agreement are included in basis under present law.

[¶ 11,190.031]

Committee Report on P.L. 102-318 (Unemployment Compensation Amendments of 1992)

For Committee Report on P.L. 102-318, dealing with rollovers and withholding on nonperiodic pension distributions, see ¶ 11,750.036.

[951] Sec. 872.

[¶ 11,190.032]

Committee Reports on P.L. 105-206 (IRS Restructuring and Reform Act of 1998)

[Senate Committee Report]

Waiver of early withdrawal tax for IRS levies on employer-sponsored retirement plans or IRAs.—The provision provides an exception from the 10-percent early withdrawal tax for amounts withdrawn from any employer-sponsored retirement plan or an IRA that are subject to a levy by the IRS. The exception applies only if the plan or IRA is levied; it does not apply, for example, if the taxpayer withdraws funds to pay taxes in the absence of a levy, in order to release a levy on other interests, or in any other situation not addressed by the express statutory exceptions to the 10-percent early withdrawal tax.

Effective Date.

The provision is effective for withdrawals after the date of enactment.

Senate Amendment.—Mr. MOYNIHAN.—* * * Mr. President, it was with these challenges in mind that Senator Kerrey and I offered this amendment to briefly delay some of the effective dates in the Finance Committee's IRS Restructuring legislation in order to allow time for the Y2K conversion to be completed. This amendment has been drafted based on Commissioner Rossotti's recommendations, and has been modified after consultations with the Majority.

The amendment would delay the effective date on a list of provisions from date of enactment until after the century date change.* * *

[Conference Committee Report]

Conference Agreement.

The conference agreement follows the Senate amendment, with a modification to the effective date. The provision is effective for distributions after December 31, 1999.

[¶ 11,190.033]

Committee Reports on P.L. 105-34 (Taxpayer Relief Act)

[House Committee Report]

Penalty-free withdrawals from IRAs for higher education expenses.—The bill provides that the 10-percent early withdrawal tax does not apply to distributions from IRAs (including American Dream IRAs added by the bill) if the taxpayer uses the amounts to pay qualified higher education expenses (including those related to graduate level courses) of the taxpayer, the taxpayer's spouse, or any child, or grandchild of the individual or the individual's spouse.

The penalty-free withdrawal is available for "qualified higher education expenses," meaning tuition, fees, books, supplies, equipment required for enrollment or attendance, and room and board at a post-secondary educational institution (defined by reference to sec 481 of the Higher Education Act of 1965). Qualified higher education expenses are reduced by any amount excludable from gross income under section 135 relating to the redemption of a qualified U.S. savings bond and certain scholarships and veterans benefits.

Effective date

The provision is effective for distributions after December 31, 1997, with respect to expenses paid after such date for education furnished in academic periods beginning after such date.

[Senate Committee Report]

Individual retirement arrangements.—

In general.—The bill * * * (3) provides an exception from the early withdrawal tax for withdrawals for first-time home purchase (up to $10,000) and long-term unemployed individuals, * * *

Modifications to early withdrawal tax.—The bill provides that the 10-percent early withdrawal tax does not apply to withdrawals from an IRA (including an IRA Plus) for (1) up to $10,000 of first-time homebuyer expenses and (2) distributions for long-term unemployed individuals.

Under the bill, qualified first-time homebuyer distributions are withdrawals of up to $10,000 during the individual's lifetime that are used within 120 days to pay costs (including reasonable settlement, financing, or other closing costs) of acquiring, constructing, or reconstructing the principal residence of a first-time homebuyer who is the individual, the individual's spouse, or a child, grandchild, or ancestor of the individual or individual's spouse. A first-time homebuyer is an individual who has not had an ownership interest in a principal residence during the 2-year period ending on the date of acquisition of the principal residence to which the withdrawal relates. The bill requires that the spouse of the individual also meet this requirement as of the date the contract is entered into or construction commences. The date of acquisition is the date the individual enters into a binding contract to purchase a principal residence or begins construction or reconstruction of such a residence. Principal residence is defined as under the provisions relating to the rollover of gain on the sale of a principal residence.

Under the bill, any amount withdrawn for the purchase of a principal residence is required to be used within 120 days of the date of withdrawal. The 10-percent additional income tax on early withdrawals is imposed with respect to any amount not so used. If the 120-day rule cannot be satisfied due to a delay in the acquisition of the residence, the taxpayer may recontribute all or part of the amount withdrawn to an IRA Plus prior to the end of the 120-day period without adverse tax consequences.

Under the bill, the 10-percent early withdrawal tax does not apply to distributions to an individual after separation form employment if the individual has received unemployment compensation for 12 consecutive weeks under any Federal or State unemployment compensation law and the distribution is made during any taxable year during which the unemployment compensation is paid or the succeeding taxable year. This exception does not apply to any distribution made after the individual has been employed for at least 60 days after the separation of employment. To the extent provided in regulations, the provision applies to a self-employed individual if, under Federal or State law, the individual would have received unemployment compensation but for the fact the individual was self employed.

* * *

Effective date

The provision is effective for taxable years beginning after December 31, 1997.

[¶ 11,190.034]

Committee Reports on P.L. 104-188 (Small Business Job Protection Act)

Other Tax Technical Corrections

[House Committee Report]

[*IRA penalty-free withdrawals*]

Penalty-free withdrawals from IRAs for higher education expenses.—The bill provides that the 10-percent early withdrawal tax does not apply to distributions from IRAs (including American Dream IRAs added by the bill) if the taxpayer uses the amounts to pay qualified higher education expenses (including those related to graduate level courses) of the taxpayer, the taxpayer's spouse, or any child, or grandchild of the individual or the individual's spouse.

The penalty-free withdrawal is available for "qualified higher education expenses," meaning tuition, fees, books, supplies, equipment required for enrollment or attendance, and room and board at a post-secondary educational institution (defined by reference to sec 481 of the Higher Education Act of 1965). Qualified higher education expenses are reduced by any amount excludable from gross income under section 135 relating to the redemption of a qualified U.S. savings bond and certain scholarships and veterans benefits.

Effective date

The provision is effective for distributions after December 31, 1997, with respect to expenses paid after such date for education furnished in academic periods beginning after such date.

Unrecovered investment in annuity contract

The bill modifies the definition of the unrecovered investment in the contract, in the case of a contract with a refund feature, so that the entire investment in the contract can be recovered tax-free.

Effective Date

The provision is effective as if enacted in the Tax Reform Act of 1986.

[Conference Committee Report]

Senate Amendment

The Senate Amendment follows the House bill.

Conference Agreement

The conference agreement follows the House bill and the Senate amendment* * *.

Simplified Distribution Rules

[House Committee Report]

Recovery of basis

* * *

The bill provides that basis recovery on payments from qualified plans generally is determined under a method similar to the present-law simplified alternative method provided by the IRS. The portion of each annuity payment that represents a return of basis equals to [sic] the employee's total basis as of the annuity starting date, divided by the number of anticipated payments under the following table:

Age	Number of Payments:
Not more than 55	360
56-60	310
61-65	260
66-70	210
More than 70	160

* * *

Effective Date

* * *

Recovery of basis

The provision is effective with respect to annuity starting dates beginning 90 days after the date of enactment.

* * *

[Conference Committee Report]

* * *

Senate Amendment

The Senate amendment is the same as the House bill.

Recovery of basis

The conference agreement follows the House bill and the Senate amendment.

* * *

Miscellaneous Pension Simplification

Managers' Amendment to H.R. 3448

Church pension plan simplification

* * *

Investment in contract rules not applicable to foreign missionaries.—The amendment would provide that, in the case of foreign missionaries, amounts contributed to a plan by the employer are investment in the contract even though the amounts, if paid directly to the employee would have been excludable under section 911.

Effective Date

The amendment would be effective for years beginning after December 31, 1996.

[Conference Committee Report]

The conference agreement follows the Senate amendment with technical modifications.

[¶ 11,190.035]

Committee Reports on P.L. 104-191 (Health Insurance Portability and Accountability Act)

IRA Distributions to Unemployed

[Joint Committee on Taxation Report]

Penalty-free IRA distributions

The proposal would provide that distributions from an individual retirement arrangement ("IRA") for medical expenses in excess of 7.5 percent of adjusted gross income ("AGI") would not be subject to the 10-percent tax on early withdrawals. In addition, the 10-percent tax would not apply to distributions for medical insurance (without regard to the 7.5 percent floor) if the individual has received unemployment compensation under Federal or State law for at least 12 weeks.

The proposal is similar to a provision in the Balanced Budget Act of 1995.

Effective Date

The proposal would be effective for taxable years beginning after December 31, 1996.

[Conference Committee Report]

The conference agreement follows the Senate amendment, with the modification that the exception ceases to apply if the individual has been reemployed for at least 60 days.

[¶ 11,190.036]

Committee Report on P.L. 102-318 (Unemployment Compensation Amendments of 1992)

For Committee Report on P.L. 102-318, dealing with rollovers and withholding on nonperiodic pension distributions, see ¶ 11,750.036.

[¶ 11,190.037]

Committee Reports on P.L. 101-508 (Omnibus Budget Reconciliation Act of 1990)

[House Committee Report]

[*Employee benefits: group-term life insurance*]

The bill provides that, for purposes of the group-term life insurance rules, a key employee includes any former employee (rather than just a retired employee) if the employee was a key employee when he separated from service. This change relates to provisions that were repealed when section 89 was enacted in the Tax Reform Act of 1986. With the repeal of section 89, these provisions are again operative. The change conforms the definition of key employee to the definition of employee generally under the group-term life insurance rules.

The provision applies to employees who separate from service after the date of enactment.

[Conference Committee Report]

The conference agreement contains the tax technical correction provisions of H.R. 5822 as reported by the House Ways and Means Committee.

[¶ 11,190.038]

Committee Reports on P.L. 100-647 (Technical and Miscellaneous Revenue Act of 1988)

[Senate Committee Report]

Deferred Annuity Contracts

The rule under which certain contracts will not be treated as annuity contracts was intended to apply for purposes of the Federal income taxation of the policyholder, but was not intended to extend to the tax treatment of the insurance company. Accordingly, the bill would clarify that the treatment of annuity contracts held by nonnatural persons applies generally for purposes of subtitle A of Title I of the Code, other than subchapter L.

The bill also provides that, with respect to the exception to the rule regarding treatment of annuity contracts held by nonnatural persons for an annuity that is purchased by an employer upon termination of a qualified plan, the exception applies to an annuity that is held until all amounts are distributed to the employee for whom such contract was puchased or to the employee's beneficiary.

The bill modifies the definition of an immediate annuity contract to prevent the structuring of a contract that appears to be an immediate annuity contract, but that is in substance a deferred annuity. Accordingly, the bill provides that an annuity is an immediate annuity only if the annuity provides for a series of substantially equal periodic payments (to be made not less frequently than annually) during the annuity period. An annuity will not be treated as failing to satisfy this requirement if it is an annuity payable over the joint lives of 2 or more individuals and the amounts paid to a survivor after the death of the first annuitant are less than the amounts paid during the joint lives of the annuitants.

[Senate Committee Report]

Tax Treatment of Distributions

Basis recovery rules.—The bill provides that if employee contributions (and the income attributable thereto) under a defined benefit plan are credited to a separate account that generally is treated as a defined contribution plan (sec. 414(k)), then such separate account is also treated as a defined contribution plan for purposes of the basis recovery rules. The bill clarifies that this separate contract treatment applies without regard to whether the distribution is received as an annuity.

The bill repeals the special basis recovery rules that apply in the case of a plan substantially all of the contributions to which are employee contributions.

The bill clarifies that transfers from one contract (as defined under sec. 72) to another contract are to be treated as consisting of a pro rata amount of income and basis in the same manner as if the transfer had been a distribution prior to the annuity starting date. This rule applies to transfers in any form, such as plan divisions, mergers, etc.

The bill provides that the effective date of the provision allowing a deduction in the last taxable year of the annuitant for unrecovered basis is effective for individuals whose annuity starting date is after July 1, 1986. Thus, in the case of an individual whose annuity starting date is after July 1, 1986, and before January 1, 1987, the rule limiting the amount of basis recovered does not apply, but the rule providing a deduction at death for unrecovered basis does apply. This rule is provided because it would be unfair to deny individuals who lost the benefit of the 3-year basis recovery rule the benefit of the deduction for unrecovered basis at death.

The bill provides a special rule with respect to plans maintained by a State that, on May 5, 1986, provided for withdrawls by the employee of employee contributions (other than as an annuity). In the case of such plans, the modifications in the basis recovery rules for distributions prior to the annuity starting date apply only to the extent that the amount distributed exceeds the employee's basis as of December 31, 1986. In addition, amounts received (other than as an annuity) before or with the first annuity payment are treated as having been recovered before the annuity starting date.

[Senate Committee Report]

Early retirement exception

The bill modifies the early retirement exception to apply in any case in which an employee receives a distribution on account of separation from service after attainment of age 55, rather than requiring an early retirement under the plan. The intent of this provision is to eliminate what is considered a requirement that has little substantive effect, but could require plan amendment.

The modified early retirement exception continues to apply if the employee returns to work for the same employer (or for a different employer) as long as the employee did, in fact, separate from service before the plan distribution. Of course, any short-term separation is to be closely scrutinized to determine if it is a bona fide, indefinite separation from service that would qualify for this exception to the early withdrawal tax.

As under present law, this exception does not apply to IRA distributions.

Exception for distributions from ESOPs

The bill modifies the ESOP exception to the additional income tax on early withdrawals to provide that the exception is available to the extent that a distribution from an ESOP is attributable to assets that have been invested, at all times, in employer securities (as defined in sec. 409(l)) that satisfy the requirements of sections 409 and 401(a)(28) for the 5-year period immediately preceding the plan year in which the distribution occurs. Employer securities that are transferred to an ESOP from another plan are also eligible for the exception to the early withdrawal tax as long as the holding period requirement is satisfied with respect to such employer securities taking into account the time such employer securities were held in the other plan.

For example, assume that employer securities that were transferred from a profit-sharing plan are held in an ESOP for the 1-plan year period immediately preceding the plan year in which the distribution is made. If the profit-sharing plan met the requirement of sections 401(a)(28) and 409 with respect to the employer securities for the 4-plan year period immediately prior to the transfer to the ESOP, then the holding period requirement is satisfied. On the other hand, if the profit-sharing plan did not satisfy sections 401(a)(28) and 409 with respect to transferred securities, the holding period requirement would not be satisfied and the exception to the early withdrawal tax does not apply to the transferred amounts. The bill clarifies that the employer securities are not required to be subject to the requirements of sections 401(a)(28) and 409 prior to the time those requirements are effective (i.e., stock acquired after December 31, 1986, in the case of sec. 401(a)(28)).

These changes are designed to ensure that the ESOP exception only applies with respect to employer securities that are subject to the section 401(a)(28) and section 409 rules applicable to ESOPs.

Under the bill, an ESOP includes both an ESOP described in section 4975(e)(7) and a tax-credit ESOP (within the meaning of sec. 409).

Exceptions not applicable to IRAs

Because the rules relating to qualified domestic relations orders do not apply to IRAs, the bill clarifies that the exception to the early withdrawal tax in the case of distributions pursuant to a qualified domestic relations order does not apply to IRA distributions. This is consistent with the pre-Act law applicable to IRAs.

Deferred annuity contracts

The bill clarifies that the substantially equal payment exception and the recapture tax for distributions in violation of the substantially equal payment exception are not limited to distributions to employees under an employer-maintained pension plan. Rather, the exception and recapture tax apply to all distributions under a deferred annuity whether or not received by an individual with respect to the individual's status as an employee.

Further, the bill clarifies that the additional income tax applicable to early withdrawal from a deferred annuity (sec. 72(q) does not apply if a distribution is otherwise subject to the early withdrawal rules for qualified plans (sec. 72(t)), whether or not an exception to the additional income tax on early withdrawals from a qualified plan applies under section 72(t)(2).

The bill modifies the effective date of the provision relating to the additional income tax on early withdrawals under deferred annuity so that the changes in the early withdrawal tax do not apply to any distribution under an annuity contract if (1) as of March 1, 1986, payments were being made under such contract pursuant to a written election providing a specific schedule for the distribution of the taxpayer's interest in such contract, and (2) such distribution is made pursuant to such written election.

Substantially equal payment exception

The bill provides that the substantially equal payment exception is available only if the beneficiary whose life or life expectancy is taken into account in determining whether the exception is satisfied is a designated beneficiary of the individual. For this purpose, rules similar to those applicable under section 401(a)(9) are to apply.

Qualified voluntary employee contributions

In order to prevent the imposition of two 10-percent early withdrawal taxes on distributions attributable to QVECs, the bill repeals the 10-percent early withdrawal tax applicable only to QVECs. Thus, distributions from QVECs are treated as distributions from a qualified plan for purposes of the 10-percent additional income tax on early withdrawals and are eligible for any of the applicable exceptions otherwise available for distributions from qualified plans.

Tax-sheltered annuities

The bill provides that the distribution restrictions added by the Act with respect to tax-sheltered annuities are effective for years beginning after December 31, 1988, but only with respect to distributions from such tax-sheltered annuities that are attributable to assets that were not held as of the close of the last year beginning before January 1, 1989. Thus, the new rules apply to contributions made in years beginning after December 31, 1988, and to earnings on those contributions and on amounts held as of the last year beginning before January 1, 1989.

Involuntary cashouts under a qualified plan

The bill clarifies that the additional income tax on early withdrawals under a qualified plan is to apply in the case of an involuntary cashout under section 411(a)(11) or 417(e). Of course, the early withdrawal tax does not apply if the amount of the benefit paid to an employee is rolled over to another qualified plan or an IRA.

[¶ 11,190.039]

Committee Reports on P.L. 99-514 (Tax Reform Act of 1986)

[House Committee Report]

Basis recovery rules

* * *

With respect to amounts received after the annuity starting date, the special three-year basis recovery rule is eliminated. Thus, an employee must include in income a portion of each payment made on or after the employee's annuity starting date.

The bill provides that in computing the portion of each payment that may be excluded from income, the employee's expected total return is to be determined as of the date of the payment. The bill limits the total amount that an employee may exclude from income to the total amount of the employee's contribution. In addition, if an employee's benefits cease prior to the date the employee's total contributions have been recovered, the amount of unrecovered contributions is allowed as a deduction to the annuitant for his last taxable year. For purposes of the provisions of present law relating to net operating losses, the deduction is treated as related to a trade or business of the employee.

Constructive receipt under a tax-sheltered annuity

Under the bill, an owner of a tax-sheltered annuity is subject to tax only when benefits are actually received.

[Senate Committee Report]

10-year averaging and pre-1974 capital gains treatment

The bill generally repeals 10-year forward averaging, phases out pre-1974 capital gains treatment over a 6-year period, and makes 5-year forward averaging (calculated in the same manner as 10-year averaging under present law) available for one lump-sum distribution received by an individual on or after attainment of age 59 1/2.

Under the bill, individuals are permitted to make a one-time election with respect to a single lump sum received on or after the individual attains age 59 1/2 to use 5-year forward averaging. In addition, the bill provides a special transition rule under which any participant who attains age 50 by January 1, 1986, is permitted to make one election with respect to a single lump-sum distribution to use 5-year forward averaging (under the new tax rates) or 10-year averaging (under current tax rates), without regard to the requirement of attainment of age 59 1/2. An election under the special transition rule to use income averaging on a lump sum received prior to age 59 1/2 eliminates the availability of an election after age 59 1/2 under the general rule.

The bill also provides a special transition rule under which individuals who have attained age 50 by January 1, 1986, may elect capital gains treatment with respect to a lump-sum distribution, without regard to the six-year phase-out of capital gains treatment.

Finally, the bills does not modify the present-law rules governing the availability of net unrealized appreciation on employer securities.

Basis recovery rules

Overview.—The bill modifies the basis recovery rules applicable to distributions from plans in which there are after-tax employee contributions by (1) eliminating the 3-year basis recovery rule for distributions in annuity form after the annuity starting date, and (2) requiring, with respect to distributions prior to the annuity starting date, that after-tax employee contributions be recovered on a pro-rata basis. The bill also provides rules governing the recovery of basis on distributions from an IRA to which the individual has made nondeductible contributions.

Pre-annuity starting date distributions.—The bill modifies the basis recovery rules for pre-annuity starting date distributions to provide for the pro rata recovery of employee contributions. Thus, with respect to a pre-annuity starting date distribution, a participant is entitled to exclude that portion of the payment that bears the same ratio to the total payment as the participant's after-tax employee contributions (and amounts treated as after-tax employee contributions) bears to the total value of the participant's accrued benefit (or account balance) under the plan as of the date of distribution or as of such other time as the Secretary may prescribe. The Secretary is authorized to prescribe appropriate rules for estimating the amounts referred to in the prior sentence where precise calculation would be unjustifiably burdensome.

If an employee is only partially vested in the portion of his benefits attributable to employer contributions (for example, in the case of a plan with a graded vesting schedule), the portion of employee's accrued benefit that has not yet vested is not taken into account in determining the total value of the participant's accrued benefit.

Post-annuity starting date distributions.—With respect to amounts received in the form of an annuity after the annuity starting date, the special 3-year basis recovery rule is eliminated. Thus, an employee must include in income a portion of each payment made on or after the employee's annuity starting date.

The bill limits the total amount that an employee may exclude from income to the total amount of the employee's contribution. In addition, if an employee's benefits cease prior to the date the employee's total contributions have been recovered, the amount of unrecovered contributions is allowed as a deduction to the annuitant for his last taxable year. For purposes of the provisions of present law relating to net operating losses, the deduction is treated as related to a trade or business of the employee.

As under present law, with respect to distributions that are not received in the form of an annuity and that are paid after the annuity starting date, the amount is deemed to be attributable first to income on the contract.

Effective Dates

The provisions relating to the taxation of lump-sum distributions are effective for distributions made after December 31, 1986.

The provisions relating to the basis recovery rules for amounts received before a participant's annuity starting date are generally effective for distributions made after December 31, 1986, but do not apply to employee contributions made prior to January 1, 1987 to the extent that, on May 5, 1986, such contributions were available for distribution under a plan before separation from service. Thus, except in the case of plans in which substantially all contributions are employee contributions, withdrawals made after the effective date, but prior to an individual's annuity starting date, are to be treated as made first from pre-1987 employee contributions that were available for in-service withdrawal. After all such contributions have been recovered, any subsequent distributions are taxed under the new pro-rata basis recovery rules of the bill.

The repeal of the special 3-year basis recovery rule generally is effective with respect to any individual whose annuity starting date is after [July 1, 1986].

[Conference Committee Report]

Constructive receipt under a tax-sheltered annuity

The conference agreement follows the House bill and the Senate amendment.

10-year averaging and pre-1974 capital gains treatment

The conference agreement follows the Senate amendment. Under the conference agreement, if an individual who has attained age 50 by January 1, 1986, elects, pursuant to the transition rule, to retain the capital gains character of the pre-1974 portion of a lump sum distribution, the capital gains portion is taxed at a rate of 20 percent. The 20 percent rate applies to all taxpayers, regardless of the maximum effective capital gains rate under present law.

Basis recovery rules

Pre-annuity starting date

The conference agreement generally follows the Senate amendment. However, under the conference agreement, employee contributions to a defined contribution plan or a separate account of a defined benefit plan (and the income attributable thereto) are treated as a separate contract for purposes of section 72 and application of the pro-rata rule. Thus, under the conference agreement, if an employee withdraws employee contributions from such a plan or account, then for tax purposes, the distribution will be considered to be part nontaxable, i.e., a return of employee contributions, and part taxable, i.e., a distribution of earnings on those contributions. The distribution will not, however, be considered to be attributable to employer contributions. If an employee withdraws all amounts attributable to employee contributions and such amount is less than the employee's contributions, the employee may recognize a loss.

Post-annuity starting date

The conference agreement follows the House bill and the Senate amendment, except that it extends the separate contract rule to post-annuity starting date distributions.

Rollovers

The conference agreement modifies the rules relating to rollovers of partial distributions. Under the conference agreement, partial distributions may be rolled over only if the distribution is due to the death of the employee, is on account of the employee's separation from service (including the separation from service of a self-employed individual) or is made after the employee has become disabled. The requirement that a partial distribution not be one of a series of periodic payments is eliminated.

Under a special rule, a distribution in satisfaction of the diversification requirements applicable under the agreement to employee stock ownership plans may be rolled over even if the distribution does not otherwise qualify for rollover treatment.

The conference agreement contains a special rule permitting amounts deposited in certain financially distressed financial institutions to be rolled over into an IRA or qualified plan notwithstanding that the rollover does not occur within 60 days of the date of the original distribution to the employee. Under this rule, the 60-day period does not include periods while the deposit is frozen. In addition, the individual has a minimum 10 days after the release of the funds to complete the rollover.

[House Committee Report]

The bill modifies the exception to the income inclusion rule by reducing the $50,000 limit on a loan by the [excess of the highest outstanding balance of loans from the plan during the 1-year period ending on the day before the date the loan is made over the outstanding balance of loans from the plan on the date the loan is made.]

In addition, the extended repayment period permitted for purchase or improvement of a principal residence of the participant. Plan loans to improve an existing principal residence, to purchase a second home, and to finance the purchase of a home or home improvements for other members of the employee's family are subject to the 5-year repayment rule.

The bill also requires that a plan loan be amortized in level payments, made not less frequently than quarterly, over the term of the loan.

* * *

Effective Date

The provisions would be effective for amounts received as a loan after December 31, [1986]. Any renegotiation, extension, renewal, or revision after December 31, [1986], of an existing loan is treated as a new loan on the date of such renegotiation, etc.

[Conference Committee Report]

The conference agreement follows the House bill, with modifications and clarifications as described below.

The conference agreement follows the House bill with respect to the reduction of the $50,000 limit on loans, with a clarification. Under the conference agreement, a loan, when added to the outstanding balance of all other loans from the plan, cannot exceed $50,000 reduced by the excess of the highest outstanding balance of loans from the plan during the 1-year period ending on the day before the date the loan is made over the outstanding balance of loans from the plan on the date the loan is made.

For example, a participant with a vested benefit of $200,000 borrows $30,000 from a plan on January 1. On November 1, the participant wants to borrow an additional amount without triggering a taxable distribution. At that time, the outstanding balance on the first loan is $20,000. The maximum amount the participant can borrow is [$20,000, i.e., $50,000 – $20,000 – ($30,000 – $20,000).]

The conference agreement follows the House bill with respect to the principal residence exception to the 5-year repayment rule and the level amortization rule. The conferees intend tha the level amortization requirement does not apply to a period when the employee is on a leave of absence without pay for up to 1 year. In addition, the requirement does not preclude repayment or acceleration of the loan prior to the end of the commitment period. Thus, for example, the provision does not preclude a plan from requiring full repayment upon termination of employment.

The provisions are generally effective with respect to loans made after December 31, 1986. Any renegotiation, extension, renewal, or revision after December 31, 1986, of an existing loan is treated as a new loan on the date of such renegotiation, etc.

Under the conference agreement, the deduction of interest on all loans from a qualified plan or tax-sheltered annuity is subject to the general limits on deductibility of interest contained in the conference agreement. In addition, effective with respect to loans made, renegotiated, extended, renewed, or revised after December 31, 1986, no deduction is allowed with respect to interest paid on (1) loans secured with elective deferrals under a qualified cash or deferred arrangement or tax-sheltered annuity, and (2) any loan to a key employee (even if the interest on such loans is otherwise deductible under the general interest provisions of the agreement). Effective for interest paid after December 31, 1986, no basis is allowed with respect to any interest paid on a loan from a qualified plan or tax-sheltered annuity.

[House Committee Report]

Explanation of Provisions

Under the bill, if any annuity contract is held by a person who is not a natural person (such as a corporation), then the contract is not treated as an annuity contract for Federal income tax purposes and the income on the contract for any taxable year is treated as ordinary income received or accrued by the owner of the contract during the taxable year.

In the case of a contract the nominal owner of which is a person who is not a natural person (e.g., a corporation or a trust), but the beneficial owner of which is a natural person, the contract is treated as held by a natural person. Thus, if a group annuity contract is held by a corporation as agent for natural persons who are the beneficial owners of the contract, the contract is treated as an annuity contract for Federal income tax purposes. However, the committee intends that, if an employer is the nominal owner of an annuity contract, the beneficial owners of which are employees, the contract will be treated as held by the employer. The committee intends this rule because it is concerned that the Internal Revenue Service would have difficulty monitoring compliance with the general rule that a deferred annuity is not available on a tax-favored basis, to fund nonqualified deferred compensation.

Income on the contract means the excess of (1) the sum of the net surrender value of the contract at the end of the taxable year and any amounts distributed under the contract for all years, over (2) the investment in the contract, i.e., the aggregate amount of premiums paid under the contract minus policyholder dividends or the aggregate amounts received under the contract that have not been included in income. The Secretary is authorized to substitute fair market value for net surrender value in appropriate cases, if necessary to prevent avoidance of the otherwise required income inclusion.

The provision does not apply to any annuity contract that is acquired by the estate of a decedent by reason of the death of the decedent, is held under a qualified plan (sec. 401(a) or 403(a)), as a tax-sheltered annuity (sec. 403(b)) or under an IRA, or is a qualified funding asset for purposes of a structured settlement agreement (sec. 130).

[Conference Committee Report]

Income on the contract

The conference agreement follows the House bill and the Senate amendment with modifications. Under the conference agreement, the exceptions to the tax treatment of annuity contracts held by nonnatural persons is expanded in three respects.

First, an exception is provided for an annuity which constitutes a qualified funding asset (as defined in sec. 130(d), but without regard to whether there is a qualified assignment). Thus, an exception is provided for (1) qualified funding assets purchased by structured settlement companies, and (2) annuity contracts (which otherwise meet the definition of a qualified funding asset) purchased and held directly by a property or casualty insurance company to fund periodic payments for damages.

Second, the conference agreement provides an exception in the case of a deferred annuity that (1) is purchased by an employer upon the termination of a qualified plan and (2) is held by the employer until the employee separates from service with the employer.

Third, an exception is provided for an immediate annuity, which is defined as an annuity (1) which is purchased with a single premium or annuity consideration, and (2) the annuity starting date of which commences no later than 1 year from the date of purchase of the annuity.

The provision is effective for contributions to annuity contracts after February 28, 1986.

[¶ 11,190.040]

Committee Reports on P.L. 98-369 (Tax Reform Act of 1984)

[Senate Committee Report]

Present Law

Cash withdrawals prior to the annuity starting date are includible in gross income to the extent that the cash value of the contract (determined immediately before the amount is received and without regard to any surrender charge) exceeds the investment in the contract. A penalty tax of 5 percent is imposed on the amount of any such distribution that is includible in income, to the extent that the amount is allocable to an investment made within 10 years of the distribution. The penalty is not imposed if the distribution is made after the contractholder attains age 59 ½, when the contractholder becomes disabled, upon the death of the contractholder or as a payment under an annuity for life or at least 5 years. No income is recognized to the recipient of an annuity on the death of the contractholder. However, since the recipient has the same investment in the contract as the deceased contractholder, the recipient is subject to income tax on the income accumulated in the contract prior to death when it is distributed from the contract.

Explanation of Provision

Penalty on premature distributions

The bill generally retains the present-law provisions for annuity contracts. However, the 5-percent penalty on premature distributions will apply to any amount distributed to the taxpayer, without regard to whether the distribution is allocable to an investment made within 10 years, unless the taxpayer owner has attained age 59 ½. This is consistent with a general objective of the bill to encourage the use of annuities as retirement savings as opposed to short-term savings.

Distribution in event of annuity holder's death

If the owner of any annuity contract dies before the annuity starting date, the specific distribution rules would apply, depending on decedent's beneficiary with respect to the contract. For these purposes, the "beneficiary" is the person who becomes the new owner of the annuity contract. First, if there is a nonspousal beneficiary, the income in the annuity contract generally will have to be distributed within 5 years after the death of the owner. Second, if the decedent's spouse is the beneficiary, the annuity contract may be continued (together with deferral of tax on the accrued and future income under the contract) until distribution to or the death of the spouse. Thus, a spousal beneficiary steps into the shoes of the decedent owner. Third, if the beneficiary is a minor child, the contract can be continued until the child reaches age 21, after which distribution of the income must be made within 5 years. Fourth, if the beneficiary is a handicapped individual, the contract can be continued until that individual reaches age 21, and then distribution must occur within 5 years, or an annuity for the beneficiary must be commenced covering any period (including the life of the handicapped individual). If, for example, a husband's interest in an annuity contract passes to his wife on his death and to their minor child on her death (both prior to the annuity starting date), the contract can be continued until the child reaches age 26, even if that date is more than 5 years after the wife's death. As with some present-law annuity provisions, to the extent that the terms used refer to individuals (e.g., death, spouse, or age), the provisions are intended to apply only to individual owners of annuity contracts.

This amendment will not apply to amounts received under contracts issued under qualified plans or IRAs. For this purpose, qualified plans are plans that have received employer contributions that were deductible from gross income when made.

Effective Date

These amendments to the annuity rules shall apply to contracts issued after the day which is six months after the date of enactment.

[Conference Committee Report]

The conference agreement follows generally the Senate amendment, but with some modifications to the rules for the treatment of annuity contracts in the event of the contractholder's death. These modified rules generally conform to those applicable to qualified pension plans and IRAs.

To be treated as an annuity contract, the contract must provide that, if the contractholder dies on or after the annuity starting date and before the entire interest in the contract has been distributed, the remaining portion of such interest will be distributed at least as rapidly as the method of distribution in effect. If the contractholder dies before the annuity starting date, generally, the entire interest must be distributed within 5 years after the date of death of the contractholder, or must be annuitized for some period (including the life of a designated beneficiary) within 1 year after that date. If there is a spousal beneficiary upon the contractholder's death, the contract (including deferral of income tax) may be continued in the name of the spouse as the contractholder.

As under both the House bill and the Senate amendment, the new provisions will be effective for contracts issued more than 6 months after enactment. For these purposes, an annuity contract issued in exchange for another will be considered a new contract subject to the new penalty and distribution-at-death rules. The grandfather provisions granted in TEFRA for amounts invested in or credited to investments in annuity contracts prior to August 13, 1982, continue in effect for purposes of applying the distribution of income-first rules applicable to annuity contracts.

The conference agreement also adopts a technical correction to the TEFRA annuity provisions which allows any investment in a multiple premium annuity contract (issued prior to the effective date of the new penalty provisions) to be treated as having been made on January 1 of the year of investment. This technical correction is intended to simplify the accounting requirements of the 10-year-aging rule in TEFRA for the penalty on early distributions from annuity contracts.

[Senate Committee Report]

Explanation of Provisions

Under the bill, in the case of any qualified pension or annuity plan, tax-sheltered annuity, or government plan in which substantially all of the accrued benefits are derived from employee contributions, the amounts contributed by the employee generally are treated as if the amounts have been contributed to the purchase of a tax-deferred annuity. Thus, the first amounts withdrawn from such a plan are treated as coming out of earnings in the employee's account. In addition, if an employee receives (directly or indirectly) any amount as a loan under the plan, the bill treats the amount of the loan as a withdrawal from the plan.

The committee expects that, in determining whether substantially all of the accrued benefits are derived from employee contributions, the Secretary may take into account such factors as the extent to which (1) employer contributions have not been made under a profit-sharing plan because of the employer's lack of profits, (2) benefits attributable to employer contributions have been distributed (so long as the plan continues to provide for the accrual of significant employer-provided benefits), and (3) the investment experience of the employee-contribution accounts invested at the employee's direction is greater during a particular year than the experience on assets attributable to employer contributions.

Effective Dates

The provisions are effective with respect to any amount received by an employee 90 days or more after the date of enactment. The provisions relating to loans under the plan are effective with respect to any loans received by an employee after the 90th day after the date of enactment. For purposes of determining whether an employee receives a loan after the effective date, a demand loan that is outstanding on the effective date is treated as giving rise to a new loan on that date.

[Conference Committee Report]

The conference agreement generally follows the Senate amendment with two exceptions. First, the conference agreement defines a plan in which substantially all of the contributions are employee contributions as a plan with respect to which more than 85 percent of the total contributions during a representative period (such as 5 years as determined under Treasury regulations) are employee contributions. Of course, if less than 85 percent of the total contributions for all years during which the plan is in existence are employee contributions, then the plan is not a plan in which substantially all of the contributions are employee contributions.

In addition, under the conference agreement, in the case of the Federal Government or an instrumentality of the Federal Government, the 85 percent test is to be applied by aggregating all plans maintained by the Federal Government or such instrumentality. This aggregation rule applies only to those plans that are actively administered by the Federal Government or the instrumentality. For example, if a plan of the Federal Government was administered by a commercial financial institution, it would not be aggregated for purposes of applying the 85 percent test.

Of course, the conferees intend that amounts which are contributed to a qualified cash or deferred arrangement pursuant to an employee's election to defer are not treated as employee contributions to the extent that the amounts are not currently includible in gross income (sec. 402(a)(8)).

In the case of a pre-existing thrift or savings feature to an employer-funded defined benefit arrangement, the conferees intend that the 85 percent test is applied by aggregating the thrift or savings feature with the defined benefit arrangement. This aggregation rule applies only if the employer has consistently treated the 2 features as a single plan, as by consistently filing for (and receiving) one determination letter and filing one annual return covering both features. Voluntary employee contributions to a qualified defined benefit pension plan are not treated as a separate defined contribution plan merely because they are taken into account as contributions to a defined contribution plan in applying the overall limits on contributions and benefits.

[¶ 11,190.041]

Committee Report on P.L. 98-397 (Retirement Equity Act of 1984)

[House Committee Report]

Where an annuity is transferred, or a beneficial interest in a trust is transferred or created, incident to divorce or separation, the transferee will be entitled to the usual annuity treatment, including recovery of the transferor's investment in the contract (under sec. 72), or the usual treatment as the beneficiary of a trust (by reason of sec. 682), notwithstanding that the annuity payments or payments by the trust qualify as alimony or otherwise discharge a support obligation.

* * *

Effective Date

The provision applies (1) to transfers after the date of enactment of the bill, and (2) to transfers after December 31, 1983, and on or before the date of enactment of the bill if both parties elect. However, it will not apply to transfers after the date of enactment pursuant to instruments in effect before that date unless both parties elect to have the provision apply.

[¶ 11,190.042]

Conference Committee Report on P.L. 97-448 (Technical Corrections Act of 1982)

Present law.—Under income tax rules (sec. 72(p)) added by the Tax Equity and Fiscal Responsibility Act of 1982 (TEFRA), a loan made to an employee under an employer's tax qualified pension, profit-sharing, or stock bonus plan, or tax sheltered annuity program, generally is treated as a distribution from the plan unless certain requirements are met. All or a portion of the amount treated as distributed may be includible in gross income. Under the Act, a loan to an employee which is required to be repaid within 5 years generally is not treated as a taxable distribution when made if that loan, when added to the employee's outstanding loan balance under all plans of the employer, does not exceed the lesser of (1) one-half of the employee's vested plan benefits, or (2) $50,000 but in no event less than $10,000.

The income tax provisions relating to plan loans generally apply to loans made from tax-qualified plans of private employers or from government plans after August 13, 1982. Amounts borrowed by an employee on or before that date generally are not treated as taxable distributions. However, if a loan outstanding on August 13, 1982, is thereafter renegotiated, those amounts subject to the renegotiation are treated as if borrowed on the date of the renegotiation and may be treated as taxable distributions.

House bill.—No provision.

Senate amendment.—No provision.

House amendment.—Under the amendment if (1) a taxpayer borrows from a governmental plan after August 13, 1982, and before January 1, 1983, and (2) under the applicable State law the loan requires the renegotiation of all outstanding prior loans made to the taxpayer from the plan, then the required renegotiation will not be considered a renegotiation under the income tax rules for plan loans. Thus, the amount of the prior outstanding loan balance of the employee under the plan will not be treated as a taxable distribution on account of the required renegotiation. The amendment will apply, however, only if the required renegotiaion does not extend the duration of, or change the interest rate on, any outstanding prior loan from the plan.

The additional amount which is borrowed by the taxpayer after August 13, 1982, and before January 1, 1983, is taken into account under the income tax rules as a loan made on the date on which the amount is borrowed. The additional amount that is borrowed may, therefore, be treated as a distribution at the time it is borrowed.

Conference agreement.—The conference agreement generally follows the House amendment except that it provides that the special rule concerning renegotiations only applies to renegotiations made between August 13, 1982, and September 3, 1982 (the date of enactment of TEFRA). Additionally, the agreement provides that, in the case of a renegotiation which extends the duration of the loan, the special rule only applies if this extension is eliminated by April 1, 1983. For example, if a renegotiation on August 20, 1982, extended the duration of the loan, the special rule would be available if, as a result of a further renegotiation, the duration of the outstanding balance of the loan on August 13, 1982 was reduced to the period applicable on August 13, 1982. Of course, a further renegotiation which is limited to reducing the duration of the loan would not be treated as a new loan under the Code.

The agreement does not change the income tax treatment of a loan that would be treated as a distribution notwithstanding the special rule concerning renegotiations.

[¶ 11,190.043]

Committee Report on P.L. 97-248 (Tax Equity and Fiscal Responsibility Act of 1982)

[Senate Amendment]

The Senate amendment provides that amounts received before the annuity starting date will be treated first as withdrawals of income earned on investments to the extent of such income, the remainder being treated as a return of capital. Likewise, loans under the contract, or amounts received upon assignment or pledging of the contract, will be treated as amounts received under the contract. These provisions apply as of July 1, 1982, but do not apply to income amounts allocable to investments made before July 2, 1982, to endowment or life insurance contracts (except to the extent prescribed in regulations), or to contracts purchased under qualified pension plans.

In addition, the Senate amendment imposes a penalty on certain distributions from an annuity contract. The penalty will be equal to 10 percent of the amount includible in income, to the extent the amount is allocable to an investment made within 10 years of the receipt. However, the penalty will not apply to a distribution that is (1) made on or after the policyholder reaches age 59 ½; (2) made to a beneficiary on or after death of the policyholder; (3) attributable to the policyholder becoming disabled; (4) a payment under an annuity for life or at least 5 years; (5) from a qualified pension plan; or (6) allocable to an investment before July 2, 1982.

The penalty only applies to distributions made after December 31, 1982.

Conference agreement.—The conference agreement generally follows the Senate amendment, but reduces the amount of the penalty to 5 percent and changes the effective date for the provisions to August 13, 1982 (except that the penalty still applies to distributions made after December 31, 1982).

Also, under the conference agreement, a replacement contract obtained in a tax-free exchange of contracts succeeds to the status of the surrendered contract for purposes of the new provisions. Such exchanges are subject to the new provisions in this Act for information reporting on pension plans and commercial annuity contracts. * * *

[¶ 11,190.044]

Committee Report on P.L. 97-248 (Tax Equity and Fiscal Responsibility Act of 1982)

For Committee Report on P.L. 97-248, relating to loans from plans, see ¶ 12,400.06.

[¶ 11,190.045]

Committee Report on P.L. 97-34 (Economic Recovery Tax Act of 1981)

For Committee Reports on P.L. 97-34, Sec. 311, relating to individual retirement plans and taxation of distributions of voluntary employee distributions, see ¶ 11,330.02.

For Committee Report on P.L. 97-34, Sec. 312, relating to self-employed retirement plans, see ¶ 11,850.062.

[¶ 11,190.05]

Committee Report on P.L. 93-406 (Employee Retirement Income Security Act of 1974)

[Conference Committee Explanation]

Premature distributions.—The conference substitute increases the tax on premature distributions to 10 percent of the amount of the premature distribution (instead of 10 percent of the marginal regular tax on the premature distribution, as under present law).

Withdrawing of voluntary contributions by owner-employees.—The conference substitute allows an owner-employee to withdraw his own voluntary contributions to an H.R. 10-plan before retirement without penalty. It also contains a technical amendment which repeals the "stacking" rules of section 72(m)(1) (i.e., the rules which determine the order in which different categories of income are deemed to be distributed). The conferees intend that distributions from an H.R. 10-plan to an owner-employee be treated first as repayments of any excess contributions made on his behalf, and second as withdrawals of voluntary contributions.

Effective dates

In general, the amendments with respect to H.R. 10-plans are to apply to taxable years beginning after December 31, 1973. The rule with respect to the $100,000 contribution base limitation is to apply to taxable years beginning after December 31, 1975, or, if earlier, the first year in which contributions under the plan exceed the deductible contribution limits of present law. The rules facilitating the use of defined benefit plans for the self-employed are to apply to taxable years beginning after December 31, 1975. The rules with respect to excess contributions are to apply to contributions made in taxable years beginning after December 31, 1975, and the rules with respect to premature distributions are to apply to distributions made in taxable years beginning after December 31, 1975.

The rule permitting withdrawal of voluntary contributions by owner-employees is to apply to taxable years ending after the date of enactment [September 2, 1974].

[¶ 11,190.10]

Committee Report on P.L. 91-172 (Tax Reform Act of 1969)

[House General Explanation]

The bill provides that the ordinary income portion of qualified lump-sum distributions received in one taxable year of the employee are to be eligible for the limitation of tax rule in sec. 72(n)(2) of the code, presently limited to lump-sum pension distributions to self-employed taxpayers under H.R. 10 plans. This rule, in effect, provides a special 5-year "forward" averaging of the lump-sum payment by limiting the tax to 5 times the increase in tax which would result from including 20 percent of the net lump-sum distribution (i.e., excluding employee contributions) in gross income in the year received. Employees (or their beneficiaries), other than section 401(c)(1) employees, receiving such lump-sum distributions are to be eligible to use the special 5-year forward averaging method only on the ordinary income amount so distributed or paid on account of separation from service or death. Self-employed individuals will continue to be eligible for the special 5-year averaging only on distributions received on account of death or disability (as defined in sec. 72(m)(7)), or received after the age of 59 ½.

In addition to being eligible under the bill for the special 5-year forward averaging on the ordinary income part of a lump-sum pension distribution, an employee (other than a sec. 401(c)(1) employee) is to be allowed to recompute the tax paid on the ordinary income portion of the distribution at the end of 5 taxable years (including the year of the distribution) by including 20 percent of the ordinary income amount in the gross income in each of the 5 years, and determining if the tax he would have paid, had he received the amount ratably over the 5 years, would have resulted in a lower tax liability than he previously paid under the special 5-year averaging rule. If the recomputed tax is less than that actually paid, the taxpayer will be entitled to a refund of the overpayment. This provision will benefit retirees whose average income in subsequent years is lower than in the year of receipt. If the taxpayer dies before the fifth taxable year, the recomputation of tax liability will be made by adding 20 percent of the ordinary income amount of the distribution in each of the taxable years the decedent lived of the 5-year period (other than the taxable year ending with his death), and multiplying the average of the increase in tax so computed by five. If this is less than the tax actually paid his estate will receive the refund.

[¶ 11,190.15]

Committee Report on P.L. 91-172 (Tax Reform Act of 1969)

[House Technical Explanation]

Subsection (b) of section 515 of the bill amends section 72(n) of the code (relating to treatment of certain distributions with respect to contributions by self-employed individuals). As amended, section 72(n) includes provisions which limit the amount of tax attributable to the ordinary income portion of a distribution or payment from a qualified plan, where within 1 taxable year of the distributee or payee the total amount payable to him is distributed or paid.

Application of subsection

Subparagraph (A) of new section 72(n)(1) of the code, as amended by section 515(b)(1) of the bill, provides that subsection (n) of section 72 is to apply to amounts distributed to a distributee (in the case of an employee's trust described in sec. 401(a) of the code which is exempt from tax under sec. 501(a) of the code) or paid to a payee (in the case of an annuity plan described in sec. 403(a)), if the total distributions or amounts payable to the distributee or payee with respect to an employee (including a self-employed individual who is an employee within the meaning of sec. 401(c)(1) of the code) are paid to the distributee or payee within one of his taxable years, but only to the extent that section 402(a)(2) or section 403(a)(2) does not apply to such amounts. Under those sections, a portion of such a distribution or payment may be considered to be capital gain.

Distributions to which applicable

Subparagraph (B) of new section 72(n)(1) of the code provides that subsection (n) of section 72 is to apply only to distributions or amounts paid (1) on account of the employee's death whether before or after retirement, (2) in the case of an employee other than a self-employed individual (who is treated as under section 401(c)(1)), on account of his separation from the service, or (3) with respect to a self-employed individual, after he has attained the age of 59 ½ years or after he has become disabled (within the meaning of sec. 72(n)(7)).

Minimum period of service

Subparagraph (C) of new section 72(n)(1) of the code provides that subsection (n) of section 72 is to apply to a distribution from or under a trust or annuity plan to an employee only if he has been a participant in such plan for 5 or more years before such distribution.

Amounts subject to penalty

Subparagraph (D) of new section 72(n)(1) of the code continues the rule of existing law that subsection (n) of section 72 is not to apply to certain amounts includible in gross income as a penalty under subsection (m)(5) of section 72.

[Code Sec. 79]

[¶ 11,230.075]

Committee Reports on P.L. 101-508 (Omnibus Budget Reconciliation Act of 1990)

[House Committee Report]

[*Employee benefits: group-term life insurance*]

The bill provides that, for purposes of the group-term life insurance rules, a key employee includes any former employee (rather than just a retired employee) if the employee was a key employee when he separated from service. This change relates to provisions that were repealed when section 89 was enacted in the Tax Reform Act of 1986. With the repeal of section 89, these provisions are again operative. The change conforms the definition of key employee to the definition of employee generally under the group-term life insurance rules.

The provision applies to employees who separate from service after the date of enactment.

[Conference Committee Report]

The conference agreement contains the tax technical correction provisions of H.R. 5822 as reported by the House Ways and Means Committee.

[¶ 11,230.08]

Committee Reports on P.L. 100-647 (Technical and Miscellaneous Revenue Act of 1988)

[Conference Committee Report]

Valuation of group-term life insurance

* * *

House Bill

The cost of group-term life insurance under the table prescribed by the Secretary is to reflect the age of the insured without any special rules for individuals older than age 63. Thus, the prescribed tables are to be revised to include rates for age brackets over age 64.

The provision applies to group-term life insurance provided after December 31, 1988.

* * *

Conference Agreement

The conference agreement follows the House bill * * *.

See also ¶ 11,249H.10 for Committee Reports on P.L. 99-514.

[¶ 11,230.085]

Committee Reports on P.L. 98-369 (Tax Reform Act of 1984)

[Senate Committee Report]

Group Term Life for Employees

The cost of group term life insurance purchased by an employer for an employee for a taxable year is included in the employee's gross income to the extent that the cost is greater than the sum of the cost of $50,000 of life insurance plus any contribution made by an employee to the cost of the insurance. Among the exceptions to this rule is one that applies to terminated employees who have reached retirement age or are disabled. As a result, an employer may provide group-term life insurance for these two groups of former employees in amounts greater than $50,000 without any portion of the costs being included in their gross income.

If a group-term life insurance plan maintained by an employer discriminates in favor of any key employee, the exclusion for the cost of the first $50,000 of this insurance is not available. In that event the full cost of the group-term life insurance for any key employee is included in the gross income of the employee (based on the uniform cost table).

The cost of an employee's share of group life insurance is determined on the basis of uniform premiums, computed with respect to 5-year age brackets. In the case of an employee who has attained age 64, the cost does not exceed the cost for a 63-year old individual.

Explanation of Provision

The bill effects three changes in the present-law treatment of group life insurance. First, the $50,000 limitation on the amount of group life insurance that may be provided tax-free to employees also will apply to retired as well as active employees.[1] The amendments do not alter the cost tables under present law, however, so a retired employee's benefit will be computed at the age 63 cost.

Second, the nondiscrimination rules will be applied to plans covering retired employees. Thus, the cost of group-term coverage that is provided to retiring key employees will not be subject to any exclusion from gross income if the plan is found to be discriminatory. For purposes of determining whether a plan is discriminatory, insurance coverage for retired employees would be tested separately from insurance for active employees. The committee believes that this separate treatment of retired and active employees is appropriate because employers often provide lower group-term benefits to retirees. This reduction in benefits under a plan generally reflects a retired employee's reduced need for insurance coverage to replace his or her earning potential. Third, under the bill, if a plan fails to qualify for the exclusion because it is discriminatory, then the employees and retirees will have to include in income the actual cost of their insurance benefit rather than the table cost prescribed by the Treasury.

Unless a plan is discriminatory, under the bill's provisions, a retired employee's benefit will be computed on the basis of the uniform cost tables. At age 65 the cost is presently $1.17 per thousand of excess insurance. Thus, a retiree age 65 who receives $100,000 of group-term coverage would recognize $702 of income which would have a maximum tax effect of $351. By contrast, the rate schedules of one major company set the premium for $100,000 of individual term coverage for a 65-year old male in excess of $3,000 per year.

Finally, the bill provides a specific exception to the application of section 83 so that the cost of the group-term life insurance coverage will be included in the income of a retired employee for the year in which the coverage is received, whether or not the benefit of retirement coverage vests upon retirement.

Effective Date

In general, the amendments made by this section shall apply to taxable years that begin after December 31, 1983.

The amendments made by this section do not apply to any group-term life insurance plan in existence on January 1, 1984 or to any group-term life insurance plan of the employer (or successor employer) which is a comparable successor to an existing plan, with respect to an individual who retires under the plan and who attained age 55 on or before January 1, 1984. Generally, the term employer may be interpreted broadly to allow employee transfers between comparable plans offered by an affiliated group. Also, for these purposes a successor employer refers to a situation in which an employer assumes the group-term insurance obligations of another employer because of a business merger or acquisition, but does not refer to a new employer when an individual covered by a plan changes jobs and becomes covered by the new employer's group-term insurance plan.

The provision for nonapplication of the new provisions will not itself apply to any plan which is discriminatory after March 15, 1987, with respect to any individual retiring after that date. For purposes of whether a plan meets the nondiscrimination requirements, coverage provided to employees who retired on or before March 15, 1987, will not be taken into account.

[Conference Committee Report]

The conference agreement generally follows the Senate amendment. By adopting the Senate amendment, including the clarification of when the group-term life insurance benefit for a retired employee is included in income, the conferees do not intend to affect in any way the determination of whether the form of the benefit received by an employee upon retirement constitutes group-term life insurance for purposes of section 79.

However, the conference agreement does modify the nonapplicability provision for existing plans. That is, the new provisions will not apply to any group-term life insurance plan in existence on January 1, 1984 (or to any comparable successor plan), but only with respect to those individuals who retire under the plan, who were employed during 1983 by the employer having the plan, and who attained age 55 on or before January 1, 1984.

The new provisions do not apply to any employees who retired before January 1, 1984. Also, the nonapplication provision will not apply to any plan that is discriminatory after December 31, 1986, with respect to any individual retiring after that date.

[¶ 11,230.09]

Committee Report on P.L. 97-248 (Tax Equity and Fiscal Responsibility Act of 1982)

For Committee Reports on P.L. 97-248, relating to group term life insurance, see ¶ 12,400.06.

[Code Sec. 83]

[¶ 11,240.05]

Committee Report on P.L. 98-369 (Tax Reform Act of 1984)

For the Committee Report on P.L. 98-369, relating to group-term insurance for employees, see ¶ 11,230.085.

[¶ 11,240.07]

House Committee Report on P.L. 97-448 (Technical Corrections Act of 1982)

Present law

ERTA provided that if stock received by a taxpayer is subject to the "insider" trading restriction of section 16(b) of the Securities Exchange Act of 1934, the time the income with respect to that stock is taken into account under section 83 is postponed.

Explanation of provision

The bill clarifies that the new rules apply to transfers after December 31, 1981, without regard to the recipient's taxable year.

The bill corrects the name of the Securities Exchange Act of 1934 as referred to in the Code.

Effective date

The provision applies to transfers after December 31, 1981.

---

[1] The bill would not apply the limitation to those who have terminated employment because of a disability.

[¶ 11,240.09]

Committee Report on P.L. 97-34 (Economic Recovery Tax Act of 1981)

[House Committee Report]

Under the provision, a taxpayer who receives stock subject to the application of section 16(b) of the Securities and Exchange Act of 1934 will be treated as being subject to a substantial risk of forfeiture for the 6-month period during which that section applies. Thus, the employee will include in income, and the employer may deduct, at the time the restriction lapses, the difference between the value of the stock at that time and the amount paid for the stock (if any).

A similar rule is applicable if the stock is subject to restriction by reason of the need to comply with the "Pooling-of-Interests Accounting" rules set forth in Accounting Series Release Numbered 130 ((10/5/72) 37 FR 20937; 17 CFR 211.130) and Accounting Series Release Numbered 135 ((1/18/73) 38 FR 1734; CFR 211.135).

The provision will apply to taxable years ending after June 30, 1969.

However, for taxable years beginning before January 1, 1982, the provision will apply only if the person receiving the property elects, in accordance with Treasury regulations, to have the provision apply.

[Code Sec. 101]

[¶ 11,250.085]

Committee Report on P.L. 109-280 (Pension Protection Act of 2006)

For the Committee Report on P.L. 109-280 on the tax treatment of company-owned life insurance, see ¶ 13,678.50.

[¶ 11,250.09]

Committee Report on P.L. 104-188 (Small Business Job Protection Act)

Simplified Distribution Rules

[House Committee Report]

$5,000 exclusion for employer-provided death benefits

* * *

The bill repeals the $5,000 exclusion for employer-provided death benefits.

* * *

Effective Date

* * *

$5,000 exclusion for employer-provided death benefits.—The provision applies with respect to decedents dying after date of enactment.

* * *

[Conference Committee Report]

* * *

Senate Amendment

The Senate amendment is the same as the House bill.

Exclusion of $5,000 for employer-provided death benefits.—The conference agreement follows the House bill and the Senate amendment.

* * *

[¶ 11,250.095]

Committee Report on P.L. 104-191 (Health Insurance Portability and Accountability Act)

Accelerated Death Benefits

[House Committee Report]

Treatment of accelerated death benefits by recipients

The bill provides an exclusion from gross income as an amount paid by reason of the death of an insured for (1) amounts received under a life insurance contract and (2) amount received for the sale or assignment of a life insurance contract to a qualified viatical settlement provider, provided that the insured under the life insurance contract is either terminally ill or chronically ill.[13]

The provision does not apply in the case of an amount paid to any taxpayer other than the insured, if such taxpayer has an insurable interest by reason of the insured being a director, officer or employee of the taxpayer, or by reason of the insured being financially interested in any trade or business carried on by the taxpayer.

A terminally ill individual is defined as one who has been certified by a physician as having an illness or physical condition that reasonably can be expected to result in death within 24 months of the date of certification. A physician is defined for this purpose in the same manner as under the long-term care insurance rules of the bill.[14]

A chronically ill individual is defined under the long-term care provisions of the bill.[15] In the case of amounts received with respect to a chronically ill individual (but not amounts received by reason of the individual being terminally ill), the $175 per day ($63,875 annual) limitation on excludable benefits that applies for per diem type long-term care insurance contracts also limits amounts that are excludable with respect to such contracts under this provision. The payor of a payment with respect to an individual who is chronically ill is required to report to the IRS the aggregate amount of such benefits paid to any individual during any calendar year, and the name, address and taxpayer identification number of such individual. A copy of the report must be provided to the payee by January 31 following the year of payment, showing the name of the payer and the aggregate amount of such benefits paid to the individual during the calendar year. Failure to file the report or provide the copy to the payee is subject to the generally applicable penalties for failure to file similar information reports.

A qualified viatical settlement provider is any person that regularly purchases or takes assignments of life insurance contracts on the lives of the terminally ill individuals and either: (1) is licensed for such purposes in the State in which the insured resides; or (2) if the person is not required to be licensed by that State, meets the requirements of the sections 8 and 9 of the Viatical Settlements Model Act (issued by the National Association of Insurance Commissioners (NAIC)), and also meets the section of the NAIC Viatical Settlements Model Regulation relating to standards for evaluation of reasonable payments, including discount rates, in determining amounts paid by the viatical settlement provider.

Effective Date

The provision applies to amounts received after December 31, 1996.

[Conference Committee Report]

Senate Amendment

The Senate amendment is the same as the House bill, except that, in the case of a chronically ill insured, while the Senate amendment does provide that the exclusion for amounts received under a life insurance contract applies if the amount is received under a rider or other provision of the contract that is treated as a long-term care insurance contract under section 7702B (as added by the bill), the Senate amendment does not include the explicit language of the House bill requiring that the amount be treated as a payment for long-term care services under section 7702B.

Conference Agreement

The conference agreement follows the House bill and the Senate amendment, with technical modifications and clarifications.

The conference agreement provides that the amount paid for the sale or assignment of any portion of the death benefit under a life insurance contract on the life of a terminally or chronically ill individual to a viatical settlement provider is excludable by the recipient as an amount paid under the contract by reason of the death of the insured. For example, the sale or assignment of a life insurance contract that has a rider providing for long-term care insurance, payments under which rider are funded by and reduce the death benefit, is considered the sale or assignment of the death benefit. Sale or assignment of a stand-alone rider providing for long-term care insurance (where payments under the rider are not funded by reductions in the death benefit), however, is not considered the sale or assignment of the death benefit.

The conference agreement provides that a viatical settlement provider is any person regularly engaged in the trade or business of purchasing or taking assignments of life insurance contracts on the lives of insured individuals who are terminally ill or chronically ill, so long as the viatical settlement provider meets certain requirements. The viatical settlement provider must either (1) be licensed, in the State where the insured resides, to engage in such transactions with terminally ill individuals (if the insured is terminally ill) or with chronically ill individuals (if the insured is chronically ill), or (2) if such licensing with respect

[13] The exclusion for amounts received under a life insurance contract on the life of an insured who is chronically ill applies if the amount is received under a rider or other provision of the contract that is treated as a long-term care insurance contract under section 7702B (as added by the bill), and the amount is excludable as a payment for long-term care services under section 7702B.

[14] A physician is defined for these purposes as in section 1861(r)(1) of the Social Security Act, which provides that a physician means a doctor of medicine or osteopathy legally authorized to practice medicine and surgery by the State in which he performs such function or action (including a physician within the meaning of section 1101(a)(7) of that Act). Section 1101(a)(7) of that Act provides that the term physician includes osteopathic practitioners within the scope of their practice as defined by State law.

[15] Thus, a chronically ill individual is one who has been certified within the previous 12 months by a licensed health care practitioner as (1) being unable to perform (without substantial assistance) at least 2 activities of daily living for at least 90 days due to a loss of functional capacity, (2) having a similar level of disability as determined by the Secretary of the Treasury in consultation with the Secretary of Health and Human Services, or (3) requiring substantial supervision to protect such individual from threats to health and safety due to severe cognitive impairment. Activities of daily living are eating, toileting, transferring, bathing, dressing and continence. Nothing in the bill requires the contract to take into account all of the activities of daily living.

to the insured individual is not required in the State, meet other requirements depending on whether the insured is terminally or chronically ill. If the insured is terminally ill, the viatical settlement provider must meet the requirements of sections 8 and 9 of the Viatical Settlements Model Act, relating to disclosure and general rules (issued by the National Association of Insurance Commissioner (NAIC)), and also meet the section of the NAIC Viatical Settlements Model Regulation relating to standards for evaluation of reasonable payments, including discount rates, in determining amounts paid by the viatical settlement provider. If the insured is chronically ill, the viatical settlement provider must meet requirements similar to those of sections 8 and 9 of the NAIC Viatical Settlements Model Act, and also must meet the standards, if any, promulgated by the NAIC for evaluating the reasonableness of amounts paid in viatical settlement transactions with chronically ill individuals.

The conference agreement clarifies the rules for chronically ill insureds so that the tax treatment of payments with respect to chronically ill individuals is reasonably similar under the long-term care rules of the bill and under this provision. In the case of a chronically ill individual, the exclusion under this provision with respect to amounts paid under a life insurance contract and amounts paid in a sale or assignment to a viatical settlement provider applies if the payment received is for costs incurred by the payee (not compensated by insurance or otherwise) for qualified long-term care services (as defined under the long-term care rules of the bill) for the insured person for the period, and two other requirements (similar to requirements applicable to long-term care insurance contracts under the bill) are met. The first requirement is that under the terms of the contract giving rise to the payment, the payment is not a payment or reimbursement of expenses reimbursable under Medicare (except where Medicare is a secondary payor under the arrangement, or the arrangement provides for per diem or other periodic payments without regard to expenses for qualified long-term care services). The conference agreement provides that no provision of law shall be construed or applied so as to prohibit the offering of such a contract giving rise to such a payment on the basis that the contract coordinates its payments with those provided under Medicare. The second requirement is that the arrangement complies with those consumer protection provisions applicable under the bill to long-term care insurance contracts and issuers that are specified in Treasury regulations. It is intended that such guidance incorporate rules similar to those of section 6F (relating to right to return, permitting the payee 30 days to rescind the arrangement) of the NAIC Long-Term Care Insurance Model Act, and section 13 (relating to requirements for application, requiring that the payee be asked if he or she already has long-term care insurance, Medicaid, or similar coverage) of the NAIC Long-Term Care Insurance Model Regulations. If the NAIC or the State in which the policyholder resides issues standards relating to chronically ill individuals, then the analogous requirements under Treasury regulations cease to apply.

An individual who meets the definition of a terminally ill individual is not treated as chronically ill, for purposes of this provision.

Payments made on a per diem or other periodic basis, without regard to expenses incurred for qualified long-term care services, are nevertheless excludable under this provision, subject to the dollar cap on excludable benefits that applies for amounts that are excludable under per diem type long-term care insurance contracts. The conference agreement modifies the calculation of the dollar cap applicable to aggregate payments under per diem type long-term care insurance contracts and amounts received with respect to a chronically ill individual pursuant to a life insurance contract.[17] The amount of the dollar cap with respect to the aggregate amount received under per diem type long-term care insurance contracts and this provision with respect to any one chronically ill individual (who is not terminally ill) is $175 per day ($63,875 annually) (indexed), reduced by the amount of reimbursements and payments received by anyone for the cost of qualified long-term care services for the chronically ill individual. If more than one payee receives payments with respect to any one chronically ill individual, the amount of the dollar cap is utilized first by the chronically ill person, and any remaining amount is allocated in accordance with Treasury regulations. If payments under such contracts exceed the dollar cap, then the excess is excludable only to the extent of actual costs incurred for long-term care services. Amounts in excess of the dollar cap, with respect to which no actual costs (in excess of the dollar cap) were incurred for long-term care services, are fully includable in income without regard to rules relating to return of basis under Code section 72. The conference agreement modifies the reporting requirement for payors of amounts excludable under the provision. Thus, in addition to the reporting requirements of the House bill, a payor is required to report the name, address, and taxpayer identification number of the chronically ill individual on account of whose condition such amounts are paid, and whether the contract under which the amount is paid is a per diem-type contract.

[¶ 11,250.10]

Committee Report on P.L. 98-369 (Tax Reform Act of 1984)

[House Committee Report]

The transfer of a life insurance contract to a spouse incident to a divorce or separation generally will no longer result in the proceeds of the policy later being includible income, since the policy will have a carryover basis and therefore the transfer for value rules (sec. 101(a)(2)) will not apply. Also, the transfer of an installment obligation will not trigger gain and the transfer of investment credit property will not result in recapture if the property continues to be used in the trade or business.

Effective Date

The provision applies (1) to transfers after the date of enactment of the bill, and (2) to transfers after December 31, 1983, and on or before the date of enactment of the bill if both parties elect. However, it will not apply to transfers after the date of enactment pursuant to instruments in effect before that date unless both parties elect to have the provision apply.

[Code Sec. 104]

[¶ 11,260.065]

Committee Reports on 104-188 (Small Business Job Protection Act)

Revenue Offsets

[House Committee Report]

Modify exclusion for personal injury or sickness damages

Include in income all punitive damages.—The bill provides that the exclusion from gross income does not apply to any punitive damages received on account of personal injury or sickness whether or not related to a physical injury or physical sickness. Under the bill, present law continues to apply to punitive damages received in a wrongful death action if the applicable State law (as in effect on September 13, 1995 without regard to subsequent modification) provides, or has been construed to provide by a court decision issued on or before such date, that only punitive damages may be awarded in a wrongful death action. The Committee intends no inference as to the application of the exclusion to punitive damages prior to the effective date of the bill in connection with a case involving a physical injury or physical sickness.

Include in income damage recoveries for nonphysical injuries.—The bill provides that the exclusion from gross income only applies to damages received on account of a personal physical injury or physical sickness. If an action has its origin in a physical injury or physical sickness, then all damages (other than punitive damages) that flow therefrom are treated as payments received on account of physical injury or physical sickness whether or not the recipient of the damages is the injured party. For example, damages (other than punitive damages) received by an individual on account of a claim for loss of consortium due to the physical injury or physical sickness of such individual's spouse are excludable from gross income. In addition, damages (other than punitive damages) received on account of a claim of wrongful death continue to be excludable from taxable income as under present law.

The bill also specifically provides that emotional distress is not considered a physical injury or physical sickness.[24] Thus, the exclusion from gross income does not apply to any damages received (other than for medical expenses as discussed below) based on a claim of employment discrimination or injury to reputation accompanied by a claim of emotional distress. Because all damages received on account of physical injury or physical sickness are excludable from gross income, the exclusion from gross income applies to any damages received based on a claim of emotional distress that is attributable to a physical injury or physical sickness. In addition, the exclusion from gross income specifically applies to the amount of damages received that is not in excess of the amount paid for medical care attributable to emotional distress.

The Committee intends no inference as to the application of the exclusion to damages prior to the effective date of the bill in connection with a case not involving a physical injury or physical sickness.

Effective Date

The provisions generally are effective with respect to amounts received after June 30, 1996. The provisions do not apply to amounts received under a written binding agreement, court decree, or mediation award in effect on (or issued on or before) September 13, 1995.

[Conference Committee Report]

Senate Amendment

Include in income all punitive damages.—The Senate amendment is the same as the House bill.

Conference Agreement

Include in income all punitive damages.—The conference agreement follows the House bill and the Senate amendment.

Include in income damage recoveries for nonphysical injuries.—The conference agreement follows the House bill.

---

[17] See item C, above. *[Editor's Note: See Committee Reports at ¶ 11,280.08.]*

[24] The Committee intends that the term emotional distress includes physical symptoms (e.g., insomnia, headaches, stomach disorders) which may result from such emotional distress.

Effective Date

The provision generally are effective with respect to amounts received after date of enactment. The provisions do not apply to amounts received under a written binding agreement, court decree, or mediation award in effect on (or issued on or before) September 13, 1995.

[¶ 11,260.07]

Committee Report on 97-473 (Periodic Payments Settlement Act of 1982)

[House Committee Report]

Explanation of Provisions

The bill specifically provides that the Code section 104 exclusion from gross income of damages for personal injuries or sickness applies whether the damages are paid as lump sums or as periodic payments. This provision is intended to codify, rather than change, present law. Thus, the periodic payments as personal injury damages are still excludable from income only if the recipient taxpayer is not in constructive receipt of or does not have the current economic benefit of the sum required to produce the periodic payments. See Rev. Rul. 79-220 and Rev. Rul. 77-230.

The bill also adds a new section to the Code providing that, under certain circumstances, any amount received for agreeing to undertake an assignment of a liability to make periodic payments as personal injury damages is not included in gross income. Specifically, any amount so received will not be included in gross income to the extent it is used to purchase an annuity or an obligation of the United States if the annuity or obligation is designated (under regulations prescribed by the Secretary) to fund the periodic payments and the purchase is made within 60 days before or after the date of the assignment. For example, if an assignee receives a $100X for assuming the liability and only $98X is necessary to purchase an annuity or United States' obligation to fund the required periodic payments, the assignee must report $2X as ordinary income. Likewise, this provision only applies when there is an assignment of a liability to make periodic payments as personal injury damages as the assignee assumes the liability from a person who was a party to the suit or agreement that determined the damages and if (1) the periodic payments are fixed and determinable as to amount and time of payment; (2) the periodic payments cannot be accelerated, deferred, increased, or decreased by the recipient; (3) the assignee is subject to the same rights and liabilities of the person who assigned the liability; and (4) the periodic payments are excludable by the recipient as damages for personal injuries or sickness (sec. 104(a)(2)). Thus, an assignment by either the person originally liable (the tortfeasor) or by that person's insurance company generally would be covered by the new provision.

Finally, the new section added by the bill requires that the assignee's basis in the annuity contract (i.e., the investment in the contract for purposes of Code sec. 72) or the United States' obligation be reduced by amounts that were excluded from gross income under the new provision. Thus, under the example above, if the assignee purchases an annuity for the amount necessary to fund the periodic payments ($98X), the basis of the annuity will be reduced by $98X under the new provision. Also, any gain recognized on the disposition of either will be ordinary income. Although the assignee will have to include any amounts disbursed from the annuity or United States' obligation in gross income, the assignee will also be entitled to deduct the full amount when it is periodically paid as personal injury damages.

Effective Date

The provisions of the bill will be effective for taxable years ending after [1982].

[Conference Committee Report]

House bill

The House bill excludes from gross income damage payments for injuries or sickness whether paid as lump sums or as periodic payments.

Furthermore, under certain circumstances, an amount received for agreeing to undertake an assignment of liability to make periodic payments of personal injury damages is not included in gross income. Specifically, any amount so received will not be included in gross income to the extent it is used to purchase an annuity contract issued by a company licensed to do business as an insurance company under the laws of any State or an obligation of the United States. It is intended that the definition of a "qualified funding asset," meaning an annuity contract designed to satisfy a "qualified assignment," encompass an annuity policy the payments from which end upon the death of a measuring life, i.e., an annuity with a life contingency.

The provision is effective for taxable years ending after 1982.

Senate amendment

The Senate amendment is similar to the House bill except that if an annuity contract is used to fund periodic payments, it must be issued by a life insurance company.

Conference agreement

The conference agreement follows the House bill.

The conferees wish to emphasize that, as a result of this legislation, no negative inference should be drawn as to the appropriate tax treatment of such transactions under present law and administrative rulings.

[¶ 11,260.09]

Committee Report on P. L. 94-455 (Tax Reform Act of 1976)

Present law

Present law excludes from gross income amounts received as a pension, annuity, or similar allowance for personal injuries or sickness resulting from active service in the armed forces of any country, as well as similar amounts received by disabled members of the National Oceanic and Atmospheric Administration (NOAA, formerly called the Coast and Geodetic Survey), the Public Health Service, or the Foreign Service (sec. 104(a)(4)). (Under present regulations (Reg. sec. 1.105—4(a)(3)(i)(a)), the portion of a disability pension received by a retired member of the armed forces which is in excess of the amount excludable under section 104(a)(4) is excluded as sick pay under a wage continuation plan subject to the limits of section 105(d) if such pay is received before the member reaches retirement age.) In addition, payments of benefits under any law administered by the Veterans' Administration are excludable from gross income (section 3101(a) of Title 38 of the United States Code). Thus, disability benefits administered by the Veterans' Administration are exempt from tax under present law.

General reasons for change

Your committee is concerned with two somewhat conflicting aspects of the exclusion of disability payments from gross income: on the one hand, the abuse of the exclusion in certain instances, particularly by retiring members of the armed forces, and on the other hand, the expectation and reliance of present members of the affected government services, especially the armed forces, on the government benefits available to them when they entered government employment or enlisted in or were drafted into the military.

Criticism of the exclusion of armed forces disability pensions from income focuses on a number of cases involving the disability retirement of military personnel. In many cases, armed forces personnel have been classified as disabled for military service shortly before they would have become eligible for retirement principally to obtain the benefits of the special tax exclusion on the disability portion of their retirement pay. In most of these cases the individuals, having retired from the military, earn income from other employment while receiving tax-free "disability" payments from the military. Your committee questions the equity of allowing retired military personnel to exclude the payments which they receive as tax-exempt disability income when they are able to earn substantial amounts of income from civilian work, despite disabilities such as high blood pressure, arthritis, etc.

However, in order to provide benefits to any present personnel who may have joined or continued in the government or armed services in reliance on possible tax benefits from this provision, your committee believes any changes in the tax treatment of military disability payments should affect only future members of the armed forces NOAA, Public Health Service and Foreign Service.

Explanation of provisions

Your committee's bill eliminates the exclusion of disability payments from income for those covered under section 104(a)(4), that is, members of the armed forces of any country, NOAA, the Public Health Service and the Foreign Service. This change applies only prospectively to persons who join these government services after September 24, 1975. Specific exceptions continue the exclusion in certain cases for future disability payments for injuries and sickness resulting from active service in the armed forces of the United States.

At all times, Veterans' Administration disability payments will continue to be excluded from gross income. In addition, even if a future serviceman who retires does not receive his disability benefits from the Veterans' Administration, he will still be allowed to exclude from his gross income an amount equal to the benefits he could receive from the Veterans' Administration. Otherwise, future members of the armed forces will be allowed to exclude military disability retirement payments from their gross income only if the payments are directly related to "combat injuries." A combat-related injury is defined as an injury or sickness which is incurred as a result of any one of the following activities: (1) as a direct result of armed conflict; (2) while engaged in extra-hazardous service, even if not directly engaged in combat; (3) under conditions simulating war including maneuvers or training; or which is (4) caused by an instrumentality of war, such as weapons. This definition of combat-related injuries is meant to cover an injury or sickness attributable to the special dangers associated with armed conflict or preparation or training for armed conflict.

All persons who were members of the armed forces of any country (or military reserve unit), the National Oceanic and Atmospheric Administration, the Public Health Service and the Foreign Service as of September 24, 1975, or who as of that date were subject to a written binding commitment to enter these Government services or were retirees from these services receiving disability retirement payments which are excluded from their gross income under present law, will continue to exclude such payments from gross income under the committee's decision. In addition, disability benefits administered by the Veterans' Administration will continue to be exempt from tax, as under present law.

Effective date

This provision is to apply to members of the armed forces of any country, the National Oceanic and Atmospheric Administration, the Public Health Service and the Foreign Service who joined these services after September 24, 1975. * * *.—**House Ways and Means Committee Report.**

* * * Present law contains no special provision for disability payments to civilian government employees resulting from acts of terrorism. The committee amendment allows disability payments for injuries to civilian government employees resulting from acts of terrorism the same exclusion as combat-related injuries which are provided for in a separate amendment. The amendment applies to taxable years beginning after December 31, 1976. * * *.— **Senate Finance Committee Report.**

* * * The Conference agreement follows the House bill. (The Conference agreement also includes [the] separate Senate provision regarding the exclusion for disability payments for injuries to civilian government employees resulting from acts of terrorism[.])

The Conference agreement also includes a clarifying technical amendment applicable to partially disabled individuals who were retired on disability before January 1, 1976, and were entitled to a sick pay exclusion on December 31, 1975. For purposes of the section 72 annuity exclusion, such an individual's annuity starting date shall not be deemed to occur before the beginning of the taxable year in which taxpayer attains age 65, or before the beginning of an earlier taxable year for which the taxpayer makes an irrevocable election not to seek the benefits of the sick pay exclusion for such year and all subsequent years. * * *.—**Conference Committee Report.**

[Code Sec. 105]

[¶ 11,270.065]

Committee Report on P. L. 96-222 (Technical Corrections Act of 1979)

[Senate Committee Report]

Sec. 103(a)(13)(B)— Nondiscrimination requirement.

The 1978 Act was not clear as to whether the group in whose favor discrimination as to eligibility for participation was prohibited consists of all highly compensated individuals employed by an employer or of only those who are plan participants.

The bill clarifies that the nondiscrimination rule regarding eligibility for self-insured medical reimbursment plans takes into account all highly compensated individuals employed by the employer.

This provision applies to payments made after December 31, 1979.

Sec. 103(a)(13)(C)— Excess reimbursements.

Under the 1978 Act, the discrimination tests for measuring the amount of reimbursements under a particular benefit are not the same as the tests for determining whether that particular benefit is discriminatory.

The bill conforms the rules for measuring excess reimbursements under a self-insured medical reimbursement plan to the rules prohibiting discrimination in favor of highly compensated individuals under such plans.

This provision applies to payments made after December 31, 1979.

Sec. 103(a)(13)(D)— Effective date.

Under the rules provided by the Revenue Act of 1978 for medical reimbursement plans, excess reimbursements made during a plan year are includable in the gross income of a highly compensated individual for the taxable year in which (or with which) the plan year ends.

Because the rules apply for taxable years beginning after December 31, 1979, excess reimbursements made during 1979, in a plan year beginning after January 1, 1979, and ending after December 31, 1979, will be includable in the 1980 gross income of a highly compensated individual whose taxable year is the calendar year.

The bill provides that the medical reimbursement plan rules apply only to reimbursements paid after December 31, 1979. Under the bill, reimbursements made before January 1, 1980 will not be taken into account under the rules for medical reimbursement plans for any purpose. (Under the House bill, payments made during 1979, in a plan year ending in 1980, would be excludible from gross income but would be taken into account in determining whether the plan met the nondiscrimination rules for the plan year.)

This provision is effective as if it had been included in section 366 of the 1978 Act.

[¶ 11,270.07]

Committee Reports on P. L. 95-600 (Revenue Act of 1978)

Sec. 366— Medical reimbursement plans.

[Senate Committee Report]

* * * Under the bill, nondiscrimination standards will be provided for uninsured medical reimbursement plans provided by employers for employees. The bill will prohibit discrimination in favor of certain employees who are officers, shareholders, or highly compensated. All (or a portion) of benefits paid under a discriminatory plan to employees in whose favor discrimination is prohibited would be included in the gross income of those employees.

Under the bill, a medical reimbursement plan is any plan or arrangement under which an employer reimburses an employee for health or accident expenses incurred by the employee (or a dependent of the employee). The bill applies only to an uninsured medical reimbursement plan, that is, a plan (or a portion of a plan) under which benefits are not provided by a licensed insurance company. Because underwriting considerations generally preclude or effectively limit abuses in insured plans, the committee does not regard the bill as a precedent for the treatment of insured health or accident plans.

Coverage.—Under the bill, a medical reimbursement plan will not qualify for favorable tax treatment unless it meets breadth-of-coverage requirements similar to requirements that are applicable to qualified pension plans.

Operation.—Under the bill, excludible treatment of reimbursements for key employees is reduced (or eliminated) if the benefits covered by the plan discriminate in favor of key employees. This test is applied to benefits subject to reimbursement under the plan rather than the actual benefit payments or claims under the plan. Under the bill, a plan is discriminatory if it provides greater benefits for key employees than other employees. For example, a plan would be discriminatory if benefits thereunder are in proportion to employee compensation. No advance determination by the Internal Revenue Service as to the tax status of a plan is required.

Key employees.—Under the bill, the status of an employee as an officer or shareholder will be determined on the basis of the employee's officer status or stock ownership during the year. However, under the bill, the level of an employee's compensation will be determined on the basis of the employee's compensation for the previous year. For a new employer, the compensation level of an employee for the first and second year of operation would be determined on the basis of the employee's actual rate of compensation during the first year of the employer's operation. Medical reimbursement benefits are not taken into account in the determining the level of compensation.

Special rules.—Also, in applying the breadth-of-coverage rules and the nondiscriminatory operation rules, benefits provided for an employee under Medicare or other Federal or state law providing for health or accident benefits may be offset against the benefits provided under a medical reimbursement plan.

Treatment of key employees.—If a plan fails the breadth-of-coverage rules or the nondiscriminatory rule for a year, then all or a portion of the amount reimbursed to key employees covered by the plan during that year would be includible in their income. Where a benefit is available only to key employees, the includible portion for each key employee is the amount reimbursed to the employee with respect to benefits not available to a broad cross-section of employees. In a case of discriminatory coverage, the includible portion for each key employee is determined by multiplying the amount reimbursed to the employee during the year by a fraction, the numerator of which is the amount reimbursed to key employees under the plan for the year and the denominator of which is the total amount reimbursed under the plan to all employees of the employer for that year.

The medical reimbursement plan rules apply for taxable years beginning after December 31, 1979.

[Conference Committee Report]

* * * The conference agreement generally follows the Senate amendment.

Under the conference agreement, an employee who qualifies for benefits under a medical reimbursement plan on the date of enactment of the Act and who is not employed by the employer after that date, would not be considered in testing a plan for prohibited discrimination. Also, under the conference agreement, employees whose customary weekly employment is for less than 35 hours would be considered part-time and employees whose customary annual employment is for less than 9 months would be considered seasonal.

In addition, the conference agreement provides that amounts reimbursed under a medical reimbursement plan would not be subject to withholding tax or social security tax.

Although no advance rulings from the Internal Revenue Service would be required, the conferees expect that in a typical case, advance rulings will be available. The conferees also expect that a determination by the Service that a plan is discriminatory will not be applied retroactively where the plan has made reasonable efforts to comply with tax discrimination rules.

The conference agreement authorizes the Secretary of the Treasury to prescribe necessary regulations. The conferees expect that these regulations will provide that reimbursement for diagnostic procedures (medical examinations, X-rays, etc.) need not be considered by an employer to be a part of a medical reimbursement plan. However, this exception is to apply only for diagnostic procedures performed at a facility which provides no services other than medical services and ancillary services and applies to travel expenses only to the extent such expenses are ordinary and necessary.

Under the conference agreement, an employer's plan will not violate the discrimination rules merely because benefits under the plan are offset by benefits paid under a self-insured or insured plan of the employer or another employer, or by benefits paid under Medicare or other Federal or State law.

Under the conference agreement, if a self-insured medical reimbursement plan is included in a "cafeteria plan", the medical reimbursement plan rules would determine the status of a benefit as a taxable or nontaxable fringe benefit and the cafeteria plan rules would determine whether an employee would be taxed as though he elected all available taxable benefits (including taxable benefits under a discriminatory medical reimbursement plan). The conference agreement applies to claims filed and paid in taxable years beginning after December 31, 1979.

Sec. 701(c)—Exclusion computation clarified.

[House Committee Report (H.R. 6715)]

To eliminate any ambiguity, the sick pay exclusion is restructured to specify that the $5,200 maximum exclusion is to be applied separately to each spouse and that the $15,000 adjusted gross income limit is to be applied to their combined adjusted gross income. The provision applies to taxable years beginning after December 31, 1975.

[¶ 11,270.08]

Committee Report on P.L. 95-30 (Tax Reduction and Simplification Act of 1977)

Present law

Under present law, the revisions in the sick pay provision made by the Tax Reform Act of 1976 apply to taxable years beginning after December 31, 1975. The 1976 Act repealed the prior sick pay provision and substituted a new disability income exclusion of $100 a week, which is available only to taxpayers under age 65 who have retired on disability as permanently and totally disabled. The maximum amount excludable is reduced dollar-for-dollar for adjusted gross income (including disability income) in excess of $15,000. Thus, a taxpayer who receives $5,200 in disability income and $15,000 (or more) in other income, which together equal $20,200 (or more), is not entitled to any exclusion.

The 1976 Act also provided that, upon reaching age 65, the taxpayer can begin to recover his or her investment in an annuity arrangement under section 72. A special rule allows certain permanently and totally disabled retirees who determine that they will not be able to claim any (or little) sick pay exclusion to benefit from the section 72 exclusion before age 65. Under this rule, in order to claim the section 72 annuity exclusion, the taxpayer must make an irrevocable election not to seek the benefits of the disability income exclusion for that year and all subsequent years.

The 1976 Act also provided several transitional rules. One of the transitional rules allows taxpayers who retired on disability before January 1, 1976, and who were entitled to a sick pay exclusion on December 31, 1975, also to benefit from the section 72 annuity exclusion before age 65, if they make an irrevocable election not to claim the disability income exclusion.

Reasons for change

Although the Tax Reform Act of 1976 did not become law until October 4, 1976, the revisions in the sick pay exclusion were made applicable back to January 1, 1976. Even though the House version of the tax reform bill, which passed on December 4, 1975, changed the sick pay provision prospectively (by applying the revisions to taxable years beginning after December 31, 1975), most of the taxpayers affected by the change were not aware of it. Consequently, many taxpayers were surprised to learn, at the end of 1976 or early in 1977, that the sick pay exclusion was not available for 1976. For many of these taxpayers this change meant a large and unexpected final tax payment with their 1976 returns. For many taxpayers retired on disability pensions, such a large unanticipated cash payment represented a serious hardship. The committee believes that individual taxpayers should be given more advance warning when a change of this magnitude is made.

Explanation of provision

The bill generally changes the effective date of the sick pay exclusion made by the Tax Reform Act of 1976 from taxable years beginning after December 31, 1975, to taxable years beginning after December 31, 1976.

However, some taxpayers already relied on the changes made by the 1976 Act when they filed their tax returns. Other taxpayers may prefer to file returns under the new provision.

Among those who have already filed, some have begun to recover their contributions to a pension plan, either because they made one of the irrevocable elections provided by the 1976 Act for claiming the section 72 annuity exclusion, or because they reached age 65 during 1976 and, believing the prior sick pay exclusion unavailable, had begun to recover their investment in their annuity contracts under section 72. If the effective date of the provision were changed and no other amendment provided, such a taxpayer would be required to "undo" the election or recovery of contributions and file an amended return.

To avoid this problem and to assist those taxpayers who prefer the tax treatment provided in Tax Reform Act changes to the tax treatment under the old sick pay provision, the committee amendment permits taxpayers under age 65 who have already made elections or would like to elect the section 72 exclusion on their 1976 tax returns, as well as those taxpayers age 65 and older who simply claimed the annuity exclusion because they believed the new disability exclusion unavailable, to benefit from the annuity exclusion, "as if" the Tax Reform Act disability income exclusion still applied to 1976, if they wish. Those who wish to change their "irrevocable" elections or to undo their recoveries of contributions for 1976 are also permitted to do so by the committee amendment.

Thus, taxpayers who make (or have made) an "irrevocable election" on their 1976 tax returns still may begin to recover the investments in their annuity contracts in 1976. If these taxpayers wish to claim the old sick pay exclusion in 1976, they must revoke these elections and file amended returns. Taxpayers who revoke these elections may then elect to begin recovering their annuity costs in 1977 or a subsequent year.

Taxpayers who reached age 65 before January 1, 1977, were too old to claim the new disability exclusion for 1976 and could begin in 1976 to recover their contributions to their annuity arrangements in accordance with the provisions of the Tax Reform Act of 1976. Under the committee amendment, these taxpayers may (if they have not reached mandatory retirement age) elect to claim the old sick pay exclusion for 1976 and file amended returns. They would then start to recover the contributions to their annuities in their taxable years beginning in 1977, when the new provision becomes generally effective.

Taxpayers who reached an initial or minimum retirement age before January 1, 1977, were under age 65 on December 31, 1976, and erroneously began recovering their annuity contributions without making irrevocable elections may make their elections for 1976 retroactively. In that event, they still may recover their annuity contributions in 1976 unless the election is subsequently revoked. Alternatively, by filing amended returns, these taxpayers may claim the old sick pay exclusion in 1976.

A taxpayer electing to claim the old sick pay exclusion for 1976 may be liable for an additional tax if the amount of that exclusion is less than the amount excludable under section 72.

A taxpayer who makes an election for 1976 to recover his or her contributions to an annuity arrangement, in accordance with the 1976 Act rules, may revoke that election at any time before the expiration of the statute of limitations for the 1976 tax return. However, under the committee amendment, the statute of limitations is then automatically extended (if necessary) to be sure that the Service will have at least one year after the revocation to examine the return and determine whether this revocation results in an increase in tax liability for 1976. In effect, this means that the statute of limitations will not be extended if the revocation occurs within 2 years after the filing of the 1976 return. In general, the statute of limitations will be extended only if the revocation is made during the third year. If the statute of limitations is extended for this reason, then it will be extended only for purposes of determining a deficiency attributable to the revocation; that is, this extension will not open up the statute of limitations as to any other issues on the 1976 tax return.

The Internal Revenue Service has already printed and distributed the Federal income tax forms and instructions for 1976. Both the forms and instructions are based on the law as amended by the Tax Reform Act of 1976. The Service believes that for most taxpayers who wish to have the old sick pay rules continued for 1976, the only feasible method of administering a change in the effective date will be to have taxpayers file amended returns for 1976 and claim refunds. However, in those instances where the change in tax treatment (from cost recovery under sec. 72 to sick pay exclusion under sec. 105(d)) has no tax consequences for 1976, the Service may advise taxpayers that they can simply restore to the annuity basis (or "cost") on their returns for 1977, the amounts that would have otherwise been excluded as sick pay (under sec. 105(d)) during tax year 1976, and begin to recover their contributions in tax year 1977; in this way, these taxpayers will not have to file amended returns for 1976. Another group that should file amended returns—but with increased tax liabilities rather than claims for refunds—are those taxpayers for whom the old sick pay exclusion (under sec. 105(d)) provides a lesser tax benefit for 1976 than cost recovery (under sec. 72), but who nevertheless wish to use the old rules for 1976 because that course in their cases is expected ultimately to provide greater aggregate tax benefits.

The Service anticipates that this provision will increase the number of individual amended returns for 1976 by about 1 million more than the approximately 900,000 amended returns filed in a normal year. The Service estimates that processing the extra amended returns will cost about $6 million.

Effective date

The provision generally changes the effective date of the sick pay changes made by the Tax Reform Act of 1976 from taxable years beginning after December 31, 1975, to taxable years beginning after December 31, 1976. This change is effective on October 4, 1976 (the date of enactment of the Tax Reform Act of 1976).—**Senate Finance Committee Report.**

[¶ 11,270.09]

Committee Reports on P.L. 94-455 (Tax Reform Act of 1976)

Present law

Under present law, gross income does not include amounts received under wage continuation plans when an employee is "absent from work" on account of personal injuries or sickness. The payments that are received when an employee is absent from work are generally referred to as "sick pay" (under sec. 105(d)).

The proportion of salary covered by the wage continuation payments and any hospitalization of the taxpayer determines whether or not there is a waiting period before the exclusion applies. If the sick pay is more than 75 percent of the regular weekly rate, the waiting period before the exclusion is available is 30 days whether or not the taxpayer is hospitalized during the period. If the rate of sick pay is 75 percent or less of the regular weekly rate and the taxpayer is not hospitalized during the period, the waiting period is 7 days. If the sick pay is 75 percent or less of the regular weekly rate and the taxpayer was hospitalized for at least 1 day during the period, there is no waiting period and the sick pay exclusion applies immediately. In no case may the amount of "sick pay" exceed $75 a week for the first 30 days and $100 a week after the first 30 days.

During the period that a retired employee is entitled to the sick pay exclusion, he may not recover any of his contributions toward any annuity under section 72. [Reg. § 1.72-15(b) and (c)(2).]

General reasons for change

Section 105(d) which provides the exclusion for "sick pay" is extremely complex. The provision's complexity requires a separate 28-line tax form which is sufficiently difficult that many taxpayers must obtain professional assistance in order to complete it and avail themselves of the exclusion. Your committee believes that elimination of the complexity in this area is imperative.

In addition, the present sick pay provision causes some inequities in the tax treatment of sick employees compared to working ones and the treatment of lower-income taxpayers compared to those with higher incomes. Excluding sick pay payments (received in lieu of wages) from income when an employee is absent from work, while taxing the same payments if made as wages while he is at work, is not justified. A working employee generally incurs some costs of earning income not incurred by a sick employee who stays at home. The latter may incur additional medical expenses on account of his sickness; but he may deduct such expenses as medical expenses if they exceed the percentage of income limitations.

Under present law, low- and middle-income taxpayers receive on a percentage basis less benefit from the sick pay exclusion than do taxpayers in higher marginal tax brackets because of the progressivity of tax rates. As a result, more than 60 percent of the benefits from this provision currently goes to taxpayers with adjusted gross incomes (including sick pay) over $20,000. Taxpayers who receive no sick pay, of course, receive no benefit at all. Your committee believes that the exclusion allowed section 105 should not have a regressive effect and that the provision should be amended to direct a fairer share of its tax benefits to low- and middle-income taxpayers.

Explanation of provision

Your committee's bill repeals the present sick pay exclusion and substitutes a maximum annual exclusion of $100 a week ($5,200 a year) for taxpayers under age 65 who have retired on disability and are permanently and totally disabled. For this purpose, permanently and totally disabled means unable to engage in any substantial gainful activity by reason of any medically determinable physical or mental impairment which can be expected to result in death or which has lasted or can be expected to last for a continuous period of not less than 12 months. Your committee has indicated that it expects that proof of disability must be substantiated by the taxpayer's employer who is to certify this status under procedures approved in advance by the Internal Revenue Service. The Service may also issue regulations requiring the taxpayer to provide proof from time to time that he is still disabled. (After age 65, taxpayers will be eligible for the revised elderly credit.)

The maximum amount excludable is to be reduced on a dollar-for-dollar basis by the taxpayer's adjusted gross income (including disability income) in excess of $15,000. Thus, if a taxpayer receives $5,200 in disability income and $15,000 (or more) in other income which together equal $20,200 (or more), he would not be entitled to any exclusion of his disability payments.

In order to claim this exclusion, a taxpayer who is married at the close of a taxable year must file a joint return with his or her spouse, unless they have lived apart at all times during that year.

Your committee's bill provides that after a taxpayer has reached age 65, he can begin to recover his investment in an annuity contract (if any) by deeming the employee's investment in the contract for the purpose of section 72 to be zero until the beginning of the taxable year in which he attains age 65 or until the beginning of an earlier taxable year for which the taxpayer makes an irrevocable election not to seek the benefits of the sick pay exclusion for that year or subsequent years. This provision enables taxpayers who decide they will not be able to claim any sick pay exclusion to benefit from the section 72 exclusion before age 65.

The bill also provides a transitional rule allowing persons who, before January 1, 1976, retire on disability or who were entitled to retire on disability, and on January 1, 1976, were permanently and totally disabled (though they may not have been permanently and totally disabled on their retirement date) to claim a sick pay exclusion if they otherwise qualify.

The new rules will apply both to civilians and to military personnel. However, Veterans' Administration payments remain completely exempt from tax. * * *.—**House Ways and Means Committee Report.**

[Code Sec. 106]

[¶ 11,280.075]

Committee Report on P.L. 109-432 (Tax Relief and Health Care Act of 2006)

For the Committee Report on P.L. 109-432 on Health Savings Accounts, see ¶ 11,335.085.

[¶ 11,280.08]

Committee Reports on P.L. 104-191 (Health Insurance Portability and Accountability Act)

Long-Term Care Services and Contracts

[House Committee Report]

Treatment of long-term care insurance

Exclusion of long-term care proceeds.—A long-term care insurance contract generally is treated as an accident and health insurance contract. Amounts (other than policyholder dividends or premium refunds) received under a long-term care insurance contract generally are excludable as amounts received for personal injuries and sickness, subject to a cap of $175 per day, or $63,875 annually, on per diem contracts only. If the aggregate payments under all per diem contracts with respect to any one insured exceed $175 per day, then the excess is not excludable from gross income. The dollar cap is indexed by the medical care cost component of the consumer price index.

* * *

Definition of long-term care insurance contract.—A long-term care insurance contract is defined as any insurance contract that provides only coverage of qualified long-term care services and that meets other requirements. The other requirements are that (1) the contract is guaranteed renewable, (2) the contract does not provide for a cash surrender value or other money that can be paid, assigned, pledged or borrowed, (3) refunds (other than refunds on the death of the insured or complete surrender or cancellation of the contract) and dividends under the contract may be used only to reduce future premiums or increase future benefits, and (4) the contract generally does not pay or reimburse expenses reimbursable under Medicare (except where Medicare is a secondary payor, or the contract makes per diem or other periodic payments without regard to expenses).

A contract does not fail to be treated as a long-term care insurance contract solely because it provides for payments on a per diem or other periodic basis without regard to expenses incurred during the period.

Medicare duplication rules.—The bill provides that no provision of law shall be construed or applied so as to prohibit the offering of a long-term care insurance contract on the basis that the contract coordinates its benefits with those provided under Medicare. Thus, long-term care insurance contracts are not subject to the rules requiring duplication of Medicare benefits.

Definition of qualified long-term care services.—Qualified long-term care services means necessary diagnostic, preventive, therapeutic, curing, treating, mitigating and rehabilitative services, and maintenance or personal care services that are required by a chronically ill individual and that are provided pursuant to a plan of care prescribed by a licensed health care practitioner.

A chronically ill individual is one who has been certified within the previous 12 months by a licensed health care practitioner as (1) being unable to perform (without substantial assistance) at least 2 activities of daily living for at least 90 days[6] due to a loss of functional capacity, (2) having a similar level of disability as determined by the Secretary of the Treasury in consultation with the Secretary of Health and Human Services, or (3) requiring substantial supervision to protect such individual from threats to health and safety due to severe cognitive impairment. Activities of daily living are eating, toileting, transferring, bathing, dressing and continence.[7]

It is intended that an individual who is physically able but has a cognitive impairment such as Alzheimer's disease or another form of irreversible loss of mental capacity be treated similarly to an individual who is unable to perform (without substantial assistance) at least 2 activities of daily living. Because of the concern that eligibility for the medical expense deduction not be diagnosis-driven, the provision requires the cognitive impairment to be severe. It is intended that severe cognitive impairment mean a deterioration or loss in intellectual capacity that is measured by clinical evidence and standardized tests which reliably measure impairment in: (1) short- or long-term memory; (2) orientation to people, places or time; and (3) deductive or abstract reasoning. In addition, it is intended that such deterioration or loss place the individual in jeopardy of harming self or others and therefore require substantial supervision by another individual.

A licensed health care practitioner is a physician (as defined in sec. 1861(r)(1) of the Social Security Act) and any registered professional nurse, licensed social worker, or other individual who meets such requirements as may be prescribed by the Secretary of the Treasury.

---

[6] The 90-day period is not a waiting period. Thus, for example, an individual can be certified as chronically ill if the licensed health care practitioner certifies that the individual will be unable to perform at least 2 activities of daily living for at least 90 days.

[7] Nothing in the bill requires the contract to take into account all of the activities of daily living. For example, a contract could require that an individual be unable to perform (without substantial assistance) 2 out of any 5 such activities, or for another example, 3 out of the 6 activities.

* * *

Deduction for long-term care insurance of self-employed individuals.—The present-law 30 percent deduction for health insurance expenses of self-employed individuals is phased up to 50 percent under the bill. Because the bill treats payments of eligible long-term care insurance premiums in the same manner as medical insurance premiums, the self-employed health insurance deduction applies to eligible long-term care insurance premiums under the bill.

Long-term care riders on life insurance contracts.—In the case of long-term care insurance coverage provided by a rider on or as part of a life insurance contract, the requirements applicable to long-term care insurance contracts apply as if the portion of the contract providing such coverage were a separate contract. The term "portion" means only the terms and benefits that are in addition to the terms and benefits under the life insurance contract without regard to long-term care coverage. As a result, if the applicable requirements are met by the long-term care portion of the contract, amounts received under the contract as provided by the rider are treated in the same manner as long-term insurance benefits, whether or not the payment of such amounts causes a reduction in the contract's death benefit or cash surrender value. The guideline premium limitation applicable under section 7702(c)(2) is increased by the sum of charges (but not premium payments) against the life insurance contract's cash surrender value, the imposition of which reduces premiums paid for the contract (within the meaning of sec. 7702(f)(1)). In addition, it is anticipated that Treasury regulations will provide for appropriate reduction in premiums paid (within the meaning of sec. 7702(f)(1)) to reflect the payment of benefits under the rider that reduce the cash surrender value of the life insurance contract. A similar rule should apply in the case of a contract governed by section 101(f) and in the case of the payments under a rider that are excludable under section 101(g) of the Code (as added by this bill).

Health care continuation rules.—The health care continuation rules do not apply to coverage under a long-term care insurance contract.

Inclusion of excess long-term care benefits.—In general, the bill provides that the maximum annual amount of long-term care benefits under a per diem type contract that is excludable from income with respect to an insured who is chronically ill (not including amounts received by reason of the individual being terminally ill)[10] cannot exceed the equivalent of $175 per day for each day the individual is chronically ill. Thus, for per diem type contracts, the maximum annual exclusion for long-term care benefits with respect to any chronically ill individual (not including amounts received by reason of the individual being terminally ill) is $63,875 (for 1997). If payments under such contracts exceed the dollar limit, then the excess is excludable only to the extent the individual has incurred actual costs for long-term care services. If the insured is not the same as the holder of the contract, the insured may assign some or all of this limit to the contract holder at the time and manner prescribed by the Secretary.

This $175 per day limit is indexed for inflation after 1997 for increases in the medical care component of the consumer price index. The Treasury Secretary, in consultation with the Secretary of Health and Human Services, is directed to develop a more appropriate index, to be applied in lieu of the foregoing. Such an alternative might appropriately be based on increases in skilled nursing facility and home health care costs. It is intended that the Treasury Secretary annually publish the indexed amount of the limit as early in the year as it can be calculated.

* * *

Effective Date

The provisions defining long-term care insurance contracts and qualified long-term care services apply to contracts issued after December 31, 1996. Any contract issued before January 1, 1997, that met the long-term care insurance requirements in the State in which the policy was sitused at the time it was issued is treated as a long-term care insurance contract, and services provided under or reimbursed by the contract are treated as qualified long-term care services.

A contract providing for long-term care insurance may be exchanged for a long-term care insurance contract (or the former cancelled and the proceeds reinvested in the latter within 60 days) tax free between the date of enactment and January 1, 1998. Taxable gain would be recognized to the extent money or other property is received in the exchange.

The issuance or conformance of a rider to a life insurance contract providing long-term care insurance coverage is not treated as a modification or a material change for purposes of applying sections 101(f), 7702 and 7702A of the Code.

* * *

The provisions relating to the maximum exclusion for certain long-term care benefits and reporting are effective for taxable years beginning after December 31, 1996.

* * *

[Joint Committee on Taxation Report]

* * *

Life insurance company reserves.—In determining reserves for insurance company tax purposes, the proposal would provide that the Federal income tax reserve method applicable for a long-term care insurance contract issued after December 31, 1996, would be the method prescribed by the National Association of Insurance Commissioners (or, if no reserve method has been so prescribed, a method consistent with the tax reserve method for life insurance, annuity or noncancellable accident and health insurance contracts, whichever is most appropriate). The method currently prescribed by the NAIC for long-term care insurance contracts is the one-year full preliminary term method. As under present law, however, in no event could the tax reserve for a contract as of any time exceed the amount which would be taken into account with respect to the contract as of such time in determining statutory reserves.

* * *

[Conference Committee Report]

The conference agreement generally follows the House bill, except as follows.

Chronically ill individual.—The conference agreement provides that, for purposes of determining whether an individual is chronically ill, the number of activities of daily living that are taken into account under the contract may not be less than five. For example, a contract could require that an individual be unable to perform (without substantial assistance) two out of any five of the activities listed in the bill. By contrast, a contract does not meet this requirement if it required that an individual be unable to perform two out of any four of the activities listed in the bill.

In addition, the conference agreement modifies the second test for whether an individual is chronically ill (i.e., that the individual has a level of disability similar to an individual who is unable to perform (without substantial assistance) at least two activities of daily living). Under the conference agreement, this test is met if the individual has been certified within the previous 12 months by a licensed health care practitioner as having a similar level of disability, as determined under regulations prescribed by the Secretary in consultation with the Secretary of Health and Human Services.

Health care continuation rules.—The health care continuation rules do not apply to coverage under a plan, substantially all of the coverage under which is for qualified long-term care services.

State-maintained plans.—The conference agreement modifies the definition of a qualified long-term care insurance contract. Under the conference agreement, an arrangement is treated as a qualified long-term care insurance contract if an individual receives coverage for qualified long-term care services under a State long-term care plan, and the terms of the arrangement would satisfy the requirements for a long-term care insurance contract under the provision, were the arrangement an insurance contract. For this purpose, a State long-term care plan is any plan established and maintained by a State (or instrumentality of such State) under which only employees (and former employees, including retirees) of a State or of a political subdivision or instrumentality of the State, and their relatives, and their spouses and spouses' relatives, may receive coverage only for qualified long-term care services. Relative is defined as under section 152(a)(1)-(8). No inference is intended with respect to the tax consequences of such arrangements under present law.

Inclusions of excess long-term care benefits.—The conference agreement modifies the calculation of the dollar cap applicable to aggregate payments under per diem type long-term care insurance contracts and amounts received with respect to a chronically ill individual pursuant to a life insurance contract.[12] The amount of the dollar cap with respect to any one chronically ill individual (who is not terminally ill) is $175 per day ($63,875 annually, as indexed), reduced by the amount of reimbursements and payments received by anyone for the cost of qualified long-term care services for the chronically ill individual. If more than one payee receives payments with respect to any one chronically ill individual, then everyone receiving periodic payments with respect to the same insured is treated as one person for purposes of the dollar cap. The amount of the dollar cap is utilized first by the chronically ill person, and any remaining amount is allocated in accordance with Treasury regulations. If payments under such contracts exceed the dollar cap, then the excess is excludable only to the extent of actual costs (in excess of the dollar cap) incurred for long-term care services. Amounts in excess of the dollar cap, with respect to which no actual costs were incurred for long-term care services, are fully includable in income without regard to rules relating to return of basis under Code section 72.

The managers of the bill wish to clarify that, although the legislation imposes a daily (or equivalent) dollar cap on the amount of excludable benefits under certain types of long-term care insurance in certain circumstances, this limitation is not intended to suggest a preference or otherwise convey or facilitate a competitive advantage to one type of long-term care insurance compared to another type of long-term care insurance.

---

[10] Terminally ill is defined as under the provision of the bill relating to accelerated death benefits. In general, under that provision, an individual is considered to be terminally ill if he or she is certified as having an illness or physical condition that reasonably can be expected to result in death within 24 months of the date of the certification.

[12] See item D, below. *[Editor's Note: See Committee Reports at ¶11,250.095 and ¶13,314.10.—CCH]*

The Chairmen of the House Committee on Ways and Means and the Senate Finance Committee shall jointly request that the NAIC, in consultation with representatives of the insurance industry and consumer organizations, develop and conduct a study to determine the marketing and other effects, if any, of the dollar limit on excludable long-term care benefits under certain types of long-term care insurance contracts under the bill. Such Chairmen are to request that the NAIC, if it agrees to such request, shall submit the results of its study to the such Committees by no later than two years after agreeing to the request.

* * *

A grandfather rule is provided under the conference agreement in the case of a per diem type contract issued to a policyholder on or before July 31, 1996. Under the grandfather rule, the amount of the dollar cap with respect to such a per diem contract is calculated without any reduction for reimbursements for qualified long-term care services under any other contract issued with respect to the same insured on or before July 31, 1996. The other provisions of the dollar cap are not affected by the grandfather rule. The grandfather rule ceases to apply as of the time that any of the contracts issued on or before July 31, 1996, with respect to the insured are exchanged, or benefits are increased.

Life insurance company reserves.—The conference agreement includes the Senate amendment provision with respect to life insurance reserves. Thus, under the conference agreement, in determining reserves for insurance company tax purposes, the Senate amendment provides that the Federal income tax reserve method applicable for a long-term care insurance contract is the method prescribed by the NAIC (or, if no reserve method has been so prescribed, a method consistent with the tax reserve method for life insurance, annuity or noncancellable accident and health insurance contracts, whichever is most appropriate). As under present law, in no event may the tax reserve for a contract as of any time exceed the amount which would be taken into account with respect to the contract as of such time in determining statutory reserves.

* * *

Effective Date

* * * The conference agreement provides that the provision relating to life insurance company reserves is effective for contracts issued after December 31, 1997.

[¶ 11,280.09]

Committee Reports on P.L. 99-272 (Consolidated Omnibus Budget Reconciliation Act)

Senate Committee Report

* * *. Under the bill, any highly compensated individual covered by any insured or self-insured group health plan would be denied the income exclusion for employer contributions to the plan (sec. 106) if that plan, or any other group health plan maintained by the employer, fails to provide qualified beneficiaries a continuation coverage election.

The bill defines a highly compensated individual as any employee who is among the five highest-paid officers, a 10-percent shareholder, or among the 25-percent highest-paid employees.

* * *

Under the bill, no employer will be permitted to deduct contributions to any insured or self insured group health plan (sec. 106) if that plan or any other group health plan maintained by the employer fails to provide qualified beneficiaries a continuation coverage election.

See also, the Committee Reports at ¶ 11,300.09.

* * *

[Code Sec. 119]

[¶ 11,282.094]

Committee Reports on P.L. 104-188 (Small Business Job Protection Act)

Small Business Provisons

[Managers' Amendment to H.R. 3448]

Employee housing for certain medical research institutions

The amendment would allow certain medical research institutions ("academic health centers") that engage in basic and clinical research, have a regular faculty and teach a curriculum in basic and clinical research to students in attendance at the institution to be treated as an "educational institution" for purposes of Code section 119(d).

Effective Date

The amendment would be effective for taxable years beginning after December 31, 1995.

[Conference Committee Report]

The conference agreement follows the Senate amendment, with a further modification that treats as "educational institutions" for purposes of Code section 119(d) certain entities ("university systems") organized under State law composed of public institutions described in Code section 170(b)(1)(A)(ii). The conferees intend that, for purposes of the present-law requirement of Code section 119(d)(3)(A) that the employee housing be provided on (or in the proximity of) a campus of the employer, a campus of one of the component educational institutions of a university system should be considered to be a campus of the university system.

[¶ 11,282.095]

Committee Reports on P.L. 100-647 (Technical and Miscellaneous Revenue Act of 1988)

[Senate Committee Report]

Tax Treatment of Qualified Campus Lodging

If the appraised value of qualified campus lodging is determined as of the close of the calendar year in which the taxable year begins, the 5-percent ceiling on the value of use of such lodging may not be known until after the beginning of the rental period and thus after the rent for the lodging has been established. The result may be that the rent chosen is below the 5-percent ceiling which may give rise to income for the individual using the lodging.

The bill modifies the date on which the appraised value is determined in the case of a rental period not greater than 1 year. In such case, the appraised value may be determined at any time during the calendar year in which the rental period begins.

[¶ 11,282.10]

Committee Reports on P.L. 99-514 (Tax Reform Act of 1986)

[Senate Committee Report]

Explanation of Provision

The bill provides that for Federal tax purposes, the fair market value of use (on an annualized basis) of qualified campus lodging furnished by, or on behalf of, an educational institution (within the meaning of sec. 170(b)(1)(A)(ii))[1] shall be treated as not greater than five percent of the appraised value for the lodging, but only if under rules prescribed by the Secretary an independent appraisal of the fair market value is obtained by a qualified appraiser. Thus, the appraiser must be qualified to make appraisals of housing, and the appraisal cannot be made by the employer institution or any officer, trustee, or employee thereof.

The committee does not intend that a new appraisal must be obtained each year. However, the committee intends that the appraisal must be reviewed annually, in a manner prescribed by the Secretary, but that such review should not impose undue cost on the educational institution.

Accordingly, under the safe-harbor valuation rule of the bill, if the rent paid for qualified campus lodging is equal to or exceeds on an annualized basis five percent of the value determined by such an appraisal, no amount is included, on account of such housing, in the employee's gross income for income tax purposes or in the wage or benefit base for social security and other employment tax purposes.

The provision applies to lodging furnished to any employee of the educational institution (or to the employee's spouse or dependents), including nonfaculty employees, for use as a residence, if the employer-furnished lodging is located on a campus of, or in the proximity of, the educational institution.

If no appraisal is obtained that meets the requirements of the provision, then the fair rental value for tax purposes is to be determined in the manner as would be done absent a special rule, taking into account all the relevant facts and circumstances. This does not preclude a taxpayer whose appraisal is found defective from subsequently obtaining a qualified appraisal and using the safe-harbor rule. For purposes of applying the first sentence of this paragraph to determine the fair rental value of campus lodging, the average of the rentals paid by individuals (other than employees or students of the educational institution) during such year for lodging provided by the educational institution that is comparable to the campus lodging provided to the employee is to be considered the fair rental value.

The new provision relating to qualified campus lodging does not affect the applicability of section 119(a) to lodging that qualifies for the exclusion in section 119(a).

Effective Date

The provision applies for taxable years or periods beginning after December 31, 1985.

---

[1] An educational organization is described in sec. 170(b)(1)(A)(ii) "if its primary function is the presentation of formal instruction and it normally maintains a regular faculty and curriculum and normally has a regularly enrolled body of pupils or students in attendance at the place where its educational activities are regularly carried on. The term includes institutions such as primary, secondary, preparatory, or high schools, and colleges and universities," and includes both public and private schools (Treas. Reg. sec. 1.170A-9(b)(1)).

For prior taxable years, it is intended (1) that the IRS is to follow the safe-harbor valuation rule of the bill as if in effect for those years (except with respect to any amount of value of campus lodging that was treated by the taxpayer as wages or included in income when furnished), and (2) that the value of the property as assessed by State or local tax authorities for State or local property tax purposes is to be treated as if it were the value determined by a qualified appraisal.

[Conference Committee Report]

The conference agreement generally follows the Senate amendment (including the directive to the IRS with respect to prior taxable years).

[Code Sec. 120]

[¶ 11,283.80]

Committee Report on P.L. 101-508 (Omnibus Budget Reconciliation Act of 1990)

[Senate Committee Report]

[*Employer-provided group legal services*]

The bill extends the exclusion for employer-provided group legal services and the tax exemption for qualified group legal services organizations through taxable years beginning before January 1, 1992. The special rule limiting the exclusion in the case of taxable years beginning in 1990 is repealed.

Effective Date

The provision is effective for taxable years beginning after September 30, 1990.

[Conference Committee Report]

The conference agreement follows the Senate amendment.

[¶ 11,283.085]

Committee Report on P.L. 100-647 (Technical and Miscellaneous Revenue Act of 1988)

[Senate Committee Report]

Extension of exclusion for employer-provided group legal plan. Under the provision, the exclusion for group legal services and the section 501(c)(2) exemption would be restored retroactively to the date of expiration and would be extended so that they would expire for taxable years ending after December 31, 1988. However, under the provision, the exclusion of the premium value of any insurance-type protection against legal expenses for any individual in a taxable year would be limited to $70. This limit would apply to the premium value of a plan (whether insured or self-insured) but not to the reimbursements or services provided under the plan.

In addition, under the provision, the provision under a tax-exempt trust of group legal services benefits that are in excess of the $70 limit and taxable solely for that reason would not cause the trust to lose its tax-exempt status.

Also, for taxable years ending before January 1, 1989, the provision under a cafeteria plan of a group legal services benefit that is taxable solely because of the $70 cap would be considered the provision of a qualified benefit (sec. 125(e)) and thus would not disqualify the cafeteria plan.

The provision would be effective as of the date of the expiration of the exclusion and exemption [December 31, 1987].

[¶ 11,283.09]

House Committee Report on P.L. 97-448 (Technical Corrections Act of 1982)

Explanation of provision

The bill clarifies that the section 501(c)(20) exemption provision, as well as the exclusion provision relating to group legal service plans, will terminate after 1984.

Effective date

The provision is effective on the date of enactment of the bill.

[¶ 11,283.095]

Committee Report on P.L. 97-34 (Economic Recovery Tax Act of 1981)

[Conference Committee Report]

Senate amendment

Employer contributions to, and benefits provided under, a qualified group legal services plan are excluded from an employee's income. This income exclusion expires December 31, 1981.

Under the Senate amendment, the income exclusion for qualified group legal services plans is extended through December 31, 1984.

Conference agreement

The conference agreement follows the Senate amendment.

[¶ 11,283.10]

Committee Reports on P.L. 94-455 (Tax Reform Act of 1976)

Present law

Prepaid group legal services plans are a recent, innovative means of providing legal services. Because of the relative novelty of these fringe benefit plans and the variety of their design, the tax treatment of the employer contributions on behalf of the employee and of the benefits received by the employee under such plans has not yet been clearly established.

However, depending on the structure of the plan, it appears that the employee will be required to include in his income either (1) his share of the amounts contributed by his employer to the group legal services plan or (2) the value of legal services or reimbursement of expenses for legal services received under the employer-funded plan, or both. (If plans are funded with contributions which are partially taxable and partially tax-free to the employee, the employee may be required to include any benefits in income to the extent the contributions for the plan constitute amounts not previously included in the employee's income.)

Amounts contributed by the employer for an employee to a group legal services plan or the value of services or reimbursements if provided directly by the employer to the employee under a plan are deductible by the employer as ordinary and necessary business expenses, if they meet the usual standards for trade or business deductions.

Reasons for change

The committee believes that it is appropriate to provide a tax incentive to promote prepaid legal services plans. Within the last 3 years, the American Bar Association and many State bar associations have endorsed the creation of this type of arrangement as a means of making legal services more generally available. Several unions have already established prepaid group legal services plans which are supported entirely or in part by employer contributions.

The committee believes that excluding such employer contributions from the employees' income will promote interest in such plans and increase the access to legal services for many taxpayers by encouraging employers to offer and employees to seek such plans as a fringe benefit.

The committee believes a tax incentive, which would increase the availability of legal services, is especially helpful to middle-income taxpayers who at present may be the most under-represented economic group in terms of legal services. Lower-income persons have access to publicly-supported legal aid services, while taxpayers with higher incomes can generally afford their own legal expenses.

The committee believes that providing favorable tax treatment for group prepaid legal services plans (which has some similarity to the tax treatment provided for accident and health plans) will grant taxpayers some relief from the high cost of legal fees and will promote the adoption and implementation of such plans by many employers and employees.

In order to insure that the tax law encourages only those plans which may be considered nondiscriminatory employee fringe benefits, the committee believes it necessary to adopt rules which will prohibit discrimination and minimize the possibility of abuse of the tax incentive by those taxpayers who might create such plans to channel otherwise taxable compensation through a plan providing a tax-fee fringe benefit.

Explanation of provision

The committee amendment excludes from an employee's income amounts contributed by an employer to a qualified group legal services plan for employees (or their spouses or dependents) as well as any services received by an employee or any amounts paid to an employee under such a plan as reimbursement for legal services for the employee, his spouse, or his dependents. The exclusion does not apply to direct reimbursements made by the employer to the employee. There is no corresponding provision in the House bill.

In order to be a qualified plan under which employees are entitled to the tax-free benefits provided by the amendment, a group legal services plan must fulfill several requirements with regard to its provisions, the employer, and the covered employees. These requirements are designed to insure that the tax-free fringe benefits are provided on a nondiscriminatory basis and that the possibility of tax abuse through the misuse of such plans is minimized.

A qualified group legal services plan must be a separate written plan of an employer for the exclusive benefit of his employees or their spouses or dependents. The plan must supply the employees, their spouses, and dependents with specified benefits consisting of personal (i.e., nonbusiness) legal services through prepayment of, or provision in advance for, all or part of an employee's, his spouse's, or his dependents' legal fees. Benefits must be set forth so that the employees understand what legal services are covered by the plan.

The amendment also provides that amounts contributed by employers under a plan may be paid only (1) to insurance companies, (2) to trusts (exempt under new sec. 501(c)(20), described below), (3) as prepayments to providers of legal services under the plan, or (4) to a combination of the three permissible types of payment arrangements.

In order to be a qualified plan, a group legal services plan must also meet requirements with respect to nondiscrimination in contributions or benefits and in eligibility for enrollment.

The committee amendment requires that the contributions paid by an employer and the benefits provided under a plan may not discriminate in favor of employees who are officers, shareholders, self-employed individuals, or highly-compensated. The plan must benefit employees who qualify under a classification which the employer sets up and which the Service determines does not discriminate in favor of employees who are officers, shareholders, self-employed individuals, or highly compensated. However, in determining whether the classification is discriminatory the employer may exclude from the calculations those employees who are members of a collective bargaining unit if there is evidence that group legal services plan benefits were the subject of good faith bargaining between representatives of that group and the employer.

A limit is placed on the proportion of the amounts contributed under the plan which can be for employees who own more than 5 percent of the stock or of the capital or profits interest in the employer corporation or unincorporated trade or business. The aggregate of the contributions for those employees and their spouses and dependents must not be more than 25 percent of the total contributions.

Under the amendment, in order to be treated as a qualified group of legal services plan, the plan must notify the Internal Revenue Service that it is applying for recognition of this qualified status. If the plan fails to notify the Service by the time prescribed in Treasury regulations, then the plan cannot be regarded as a qualified plan for any period before it in fact gave notice. For example, if the Treasury regulations provide that a plan is required to notify the Service before the end of the first plan year in order to be treated as a qualified plan from the beginning of the first plan year, and the organization does not file its notice until half way through the second plan year, then (1) the organization is not qualified for its first plan year, and (2) the organization is not qualified for that part of the second plan year preceding the date on which the notice finally was filed. However, if the notice was filed on the last day of the first plan year, then the organization would be qualified from the first day of that first plan year. (Recognizing that existing plans are to be covered by this provision and that there may be a delay in the final publication of these notification regulations, the amendment also provides that this initial notice is to be considered timely if it is given at any time through the 90th day after the publication of the first final Treasury Regulations on this point.)

Furthermore, several additional special rules and definitions are to apply to qualified group legal services plans.

An individual who is an employee within the meaning of section 401(c)(1) of the Code is, for purposes of these group legal services provisions, an "employee" and also is a "self-employed individual". This means that, in general, the term "self-employed individual" means, and the term "employee" includes, individuals who have earned income for a taxable year, as well as individuals who would have earned income except that their trades or businesses did not have net profits for a taxable year.

An individual who owns the entire interest in an unincorporated trade or business is treated as his own employer. A partnership is considered the employer of each partner who is an employee of the partnership. Under a special rule for the allocation of contributions, the Treasury Department's regulations must provide that allocations of amounts contributed under the plan shall take into account the expected relative utilization of benefits to be provided under the plan from those contributions or plan assets and the manner in which any premium charge (or retainer or other price) for the plan was developed.

The term "dependent" has the meaning given to it under section 152. Therefore, the plan may cover an individual whose relationship to the employee is listed in section 152, if the employee provides over half of the support for that individual for the calendar year in which the employee's taxable year begins. Since the plan must be for the exclusive benefit of employees and their spouses and dependents, the plan is not to cover any other persons.

For determining stock ownership in corporations, the amendment adopts the attribution rules provided under subsection (d) and (e) of section 1563 (without regard to sec. 1563(e)(3)(C)). The Treasury Department is to issue regulations for determining ownership interests in unincorporated trades or businesses, such as partnerships or proprietorships, following the principles governing the attribution of stock ownership.

The amendment also provides that a trust created or organized in the United States, whose exclusive function is to form part of a qualified group legal services plan under section 120, is to be exempt from income tax (new sec. 501(c)(20)). Such a trust shall be subject to the rules governing organizations exempt under section 501(c), including the taxation of any unrelated business income. * * *.—**Senate Finance Committee.**

Supplemental Report

* * * The conference agreement follows the Senate amendment, except that it applies prospectively only for five taxable years beginning after December 31, 1976, and ending before January 1, 1982. The conference agreement also requires a study of the provision by the Departments of the Treasury and of Labor, with final reports to be submitted to the House Committee on Ways and Means and to the Senate Committee on Finance not later than December 31, 1980. * * *.—**Conference Committee Report.**

[Code Sec. 125]

[¶ 11,288A.08]

Committee Report on P.L. 104-191 (Health Insurance Portability and Accountability Act)

[House Committee Report]

* * *

Exclusion for employer-provided long-term care coverage.—A plan of an employer providing coverage under a long-term care insurance contract generally is treated as an accident and health plan. Employer-provided coverage under a long-term care insurance contract is not, however, excludable by an employee if provided through a cafeteria plan; similarly, expenses for long-term care services cannot be reimbursed under an FSA.[5]

* * *

[¶ 11,288A.09]

Committee Report on P.L. 100-647 (Technical and Miscellaneous Revenue Act of 1988)

[House Committee Report]

Dependent care expenses under cafeteria plan

Under the bill, with respect to any cafeteria plan participant who, prior to January 1, 1988, elected dependent care assistance for a taxable year beginning after 1987, for the plan year of the election such dependent care assistance is not to fail to be a qualified benefit merely because it is includible in the participant's income due to the provision in the Revenue Act of 1987 regarding overnight camp expenses.

Definition of active participant for IRA deduction

The Act provided that Federal judges are to be treated as active participants, thereby subjecting such judges (and their spouses) to the phaseout of the IRA deduction. The Third Circuit decision does not affect the impact of this provision of the Act. However, to clarify further the Act's provision, the bill provides that Federal judges are to be considered active participants in a plan established for its employees by the United States. Therefore, for example, if a married Federal judge filing a joint return has AGI of $50,000 in a taxable year, neither the judge nor the judge's spouse may deduct any contributions to an IRA for such year.

[¶ 11,288A.095]

Committee Report on P.L. 98-369 (Tax Reform Act of 1984)

[House Committee Report]

Cafeteria Plans

The bill amends the definition of cafeteria plans for purposes of Code section 125 to provide that such plans may offer employees choices only among cash or those fringe benefits (other than scholarships or fellowships, educational assistance, vanpooling, and those benefits excludable under provisions of the bill) that are excludable from gross income under a specific section of the Internal Revenue Code.

For this purpose, group-term life insurance that is includible in income only because the amount of the insurance exceeds $50,000 or because the insurance is on the life of the employee's spouse or children is treated as a nontaxable benefit. With respect to vacation days offered under a cafeteria plan, vacation days which cannot be used or cashed out in a later calendar or plan year also are to be treated as a nontaxable benefit. However, vacation days which may be used or cashed out in a later year are to be treated as deferred compensation which may not be offered under a cafeteria plan.

[Conference agreement]

The conference agreement follows the House bill provisions on cafeteria plans, and adopts several additional provisions.

First, the conference agreement amends the cafeteria plan rules to provide that if, for a plan year, more than 25 percent of the total nontaxable benefits are provided to employees who are key employees with respect to the plan for such year (as determined under the rules of section 416(i)(1)), such key employees will be taxed as though they received all available taxable benefits under the plan. Generally, in determining the portion of the total nontaxable benefits that is provided to key employees, coverage under a plan (e.g., an accident or health

[5] The bill does not otherwise modify the requirements relating to FSAs. An FSA is defined as a benefit program providing employees with coverage under which specified incurred expenses may be reimbursed (subject to maximums and other reasonable conditions), and the maximum amount of reimbursement that is reasonably available to a participant is less than 500 percent of the value of the coverage.

plan) and not actual expense reimbursements under such a plan are to be counted.

Second, the conference agreement applies certain reporting requirements with respect to cafeteria plans. Under regulations prescribed by the Secretary of the Treasury, each employer that maintains a cafeteria plan during a taxable year beginning after December 31, 1984, will be required to file a return for such year showing the number of employees of the employer, the number of employees participating in the plan, the total cost of the plan for the taxable year, and specified employer identification information. Based on these general returns, the Secretary is to require a select and statistically significant group of employers to file additional information returns with respect to their cafeteria plans. These additional returns will contain such information as the Secretary may require. Examples of such information include a breakdown of the above information by salary range and type of benefit provided, as well as information which may be necessary to allow Treasury to develop a plan to insure that the requirements of the cafeteria plan rules (such as nondiscrimination and maximum percentage of benefits to key employees) are adequately enforced.

Third, the conference agreement provides both general and special transition relief, with respect to the proposed Treasury regulations on cafeteria plans, for cafeteria plans and "flexible spending arrangements" in existence on February 10, 1984. (A "flexible spending arrangement" consists of a benefit of a type to which a statutory exclusion may be applied, such as an accident or health plan under sections 105 and 106, with respect to which an employee is assured of receiving, in cash or some other benefit, amounts available for expense reimbursement without regard to whether the employee incurs the covered expenses.) The general relief rule provides that a plan will not fail to be a cafeteria plan merely because of a failure to satisfy the rules relating to cafeteria plans under the proposed Treasury regulations and that a flexible spending arrangement will not fail the requirements of the applicable statutory exclusions merely because of a failure to satisfy the rules relating to such exclusions under these regulations. This general relief is provided until the earlier of January 1, 1985, or the effective date of any modification of the plan or arrangement to provide additional benefits if such modification becomes effective after February 10, 1984. The conference agreement does not prevent the application of the proposed Treasury regulations after the earlier of such dates.

Thus, for example, if on February 10, 1984, a flexible spending arrangement failed to satisfy the rules relating to accident or health plans under the proposed Treasury regulations and thereafter continues to fail such rules because such arrangement provides for the cash-out or carryover of unused amounts at the end of the plan year, such arrangement will be treated as qualifying as an accident or health plan until the earlier of the two dates provided above.

The general transition rule is applicable to both benefit bank flexible spending arrangements and zero balance reimbursement account (ZEBRA) type flexible spending arrangements. Under a benefit bank arrangement, the employee generally allocates a specified amount of dollars to a reimbursement account for specified benefits, e.g., medical, legal, and dependent care, at the beginning of the plan year. As expenses are incurred during the year, the employee is entitled to reimbursement of these expenses from the account. For example, if an employee with $500 allocated to his account incurred medical expenses of $250, he could be reimbursed for these expenses from the account. At the end of the year, he would receive the remaining $250 in cash. In contrast, under the ZEBRA-type arrangement, amounts generally are not specifically allocated to an account before the beginning of the year, but instead amounts are allocated only after an expense is incurred.

The conference agreement also provides special transition relief with respect to the rules contained in the proposed regulations relating to the statutory nontaxable benefits. This relief provision provides that a flexible spending arrangement in existence under a cafeteria plan on February 10, 1984, will not fail to be a nontaxable benefit under the applicable exclusions merely because a participant will receive amounts available but unused for expense reimbursement. An arrangement will qualify for the special relief only if, under the arrangement, the employee must fix the amount of contributions to be made on his or her behalf before the beginning of the applicable period of coverage and taxable cash is not available before the end of such period or, if earlier, at the termination of employment. In lieu of distributing taxable cash to a participant at the end of the applicable period of coverage, it would also be permissible for the unused amounts to be carried over to the succeeding year. Further, an arrangement could permit a participant to terminate contributions during the period of coverage or to change the rate or amount of contributions during the period of coverage on account of certain changes in family status or change in employment status from full-time to part-time, or vice versa. The conferees intend that this special transition relief will be available to arrangements that, on February 10, 1984, and thereafter, failed to satisfy these restrictions if such arrangements are modified, before January 1, 1985, to comply with such restrictions. The special relief under this rule is for benefits provided before the earlier of July 1, 1985, or the effective date of any modification of the arrangement to provide additional benefits if such modification becomes effective after February 10, 1984. The conference agreement does not prevent the application of the proposed Treasury regulations after the earlier of the applicable dates.

Cafeteria plans and flexible spending arrangements that were not in existence on February 10, 1984, generally do not qualify for either the general or the special transition rules under the conference agreement. Thus, the conference agreement does not prevent the current application of the proposed Treasury regulations to such plans and arrangements. However, plans that were not actually in existence as of February 10, 1984, but with respect to which substantial implementation costs has been incurred by the employer by such date are to be treated as having been in existence on such date. The conferees intend that if an employer has incurred, as of February 10, 1984, either more than $15,000 of implementation costs or more than one-half of the total costs of implementing a cafeteria plan, the transition rules are to be available with respect to the cafeteria plan. In making this determination, total implementation costs are the costs of designing and installing computer programs for operation of the plan and the costs of printing cafeteria plan brochures for employees. Costs associated with more than one plan of the same employer are to be allocated among the plans on the basis of the number of participants in the plans.

Finally, the conference agreement provides that the Secretary of Health and Human Services, in cooperation with the Secretary of the Treasury, is to submit a report to the House Committee on Ways and Means and the Senate Committee on Finance on the effect of cafeteria plans on the containment of health costs. This report is to be submitted by April 1, 1985. The study is to examine the impact which the use of cafeteria plans (including flexible spending arrangements) has on the containment of health care costs and to recommend what modifications might be desirable with respect to the cafeteria plan rules to optimize the potential to reduce medical costs while balancing against other health care policy goals. Included within the study should be an analysis of the advisability of establishing Federal guidelines relative to the type of medical plans that can qualify for cafeteria plan treatment in a manner similar to that applicable to qualified pensions plans and the advisability of adding additional benefits to cafeteria plans. In this regard, the conferees intend to examine, before January 1, 1986, the operation of the nondiscrimination rules and the forfeitability requirements with respect to cafeteria plans, and the effect of such provisions on the Federal tax base and on health cost containment.

[¶ 11,288A.097]

Committee Report on P.L. 96-222 (Technical Corrections Act of 1979)

[Senate Committee Report]

Sec. 101(a)(6)(A)— Participation standards. Prior to the Revenue Act of 1978, if a cafeteria plan was in existence on June 27, 1974, a participant in the plan was taxable only to the extent the participant elected taxable benefits under the plan. The 1978 Act made this favorable tax treatment applicable to all cafeteria plans meeting certain nondiscrimination standards, including a standard regarding the maximum number of years of employment which may be required as a condition of plan participation.

The committee believes that the use of the term "service requirement" in the cafeteria plan participation eligibility rules might lead taxpayers to believe that hours of service must be counted as they are under the qualified retirement plan participation rules (Code Sec. 410(a)).

The bill makes it clear that the cafeteria plan participation standard is based on years of employment rather than years or hours of service. The committee expects that the Treasury Department will prescribe by regulation what constitutes a year of employment.

This provision applies for plan years beginning after December 31, 1978.

Sec. 101(a)(6)(B)— Effective date.

Under the cafeteria plan rules added by the Revenue Act of 1978, amounts required to be included in income by a highly-compensated participant because the plan does not satisfy nondiscrimination standards will be treated as received or accrued in the participant's taxable year in which the plan ends. The cafeteria plan rules are effective for taxable years beginning after December 31, 1978.

Because the cafeteria plan rules apply to participants' taxable years beginning after December 31, 1978, amounts contributed during 1978 under a cafeteria plan which has a fiscal plan year and which does not satisfy the new nondiscrimination rules might have to be included in income by certain participants in 1979. Thus, in certain cases, the cafeteria plan rules apply retroactively.

The committee does not believe that the cafeteria plan rules should cause amounts contributed in 1978 under a cafeteria plan which was in existence on June 27, 1974, to be included in income. In addition, the committee believes that cafeteria plans in existence on June 27, 1974, should not have to be amended retroactively to comply with the new rules contained in the Revenue Act of 1978.

The bill makes the cafeteria plan provisions of the Revenue Act of 1978 effective for plan years, rather than for participants' taxable years, beginning after December 31, 1978. Thus, highly compensated participants in fiscal year plans will not have income solely because of the new cafeteria plan rules until 1980. In addition, to comply with the cafeteria plan rules, amendments to plans will not have to be effective before the beginning of the first plan year after 1978.

This provision is effective as if it had been included in the Revenue Act of 1978 as enacted.

[¶ 11,288A.10]

Committee Report on P.L. 95-600 (Revenue Act of 1978)

Sec. 134— Cafeteria plans. **Senate Committee Report.**— *General.*—Under the bill, generally, employer contributions under a written cafeteria plan which permits employees to elect between taxable and nontaxable benefits are excluded from the gross income of an employee to the extent that nontaxable benefits are elected. For this purpose, nontaxable benefits include group-term life insurance up to $50,000 coverage, disability benefits, accident and health benefits, and group legal services to the extent such benefits are excludable from gross income, but do not include deferred compensation.

The bill limits plan participation to individuals who are employees. In this regard, the committee intends that a plan may include former employees as participants and may provide benefits for beneficiaries of participants.

Under the bill, in the case of a highly compensated employee (an employee who is an officer, a more-than-5-percent shareholder, or within the highest paid group of all employees, or an employee who is a spouse or dependent of such an individual), amounts contributed under a cafeteria plan will be included in gross income for the taxable year in which the plan year ends, to the extent the individual could have elected taxable benefits unless the plan meets specified antidiscrimination standards with respect to coverage and eligibility for participation in the plan and with respect to contributions or benefits.

Coverage and eligibility.—A cafeteria plan will be considered to meet the coverage standards of the bill if it benefits a classification of employees found by the Secretary of the Treasury not to discriminate in favor of highly compensated employees. The plan will meet the eligibility standards of the bill if it (1) does not require an employee to complete more than three consecutive years of employment in order to become eligible to participate, and (2) allows an employee who is otherwise eligible to participate to enter the plan as a participant not later than the first day of the first plan year beginning after the date the employee completes three consecutive years of employment.

Contributions or benefits.—The bill provides that a cafeteria plan must not discriminate as to contributions or benefits in favor of highly compensated employees. A plan will not be discriminatory if total benefits and nontaxable benefits attributable to highly compensated employees, measured as a percentage of compensation, are not significantly greater than total benefits and nontaxable benefits attributable to other employees (measured on the same basis), provided the plan is not otherwise discriminatory under the standards of the bill.

In the case of a cafeteria plan which provides health benefits, the bill provides that the plan will not be treated as discriminatory if: (1) contributions on behalf of each participant include an amount which equals either 100 percent of the cost of health benefit coverage under the plan of the majority of highly compensated participants who are similarly situated (e.g., same family size), or are at least equal to 75 percent of the cost of the most expensive health benefit coverage elected by any similarly situated plan participant, and (2) the other contributions or benefits provided by the plan bear a uniform relationship to the compensation of plan participants. Of course, the committee intends that a cafeteria plan will not be considered to be discriminatory where the other contributions or benefits provided (or total contributions or benefits in the case of a plan which does not provide health benefits) for a highly compensated employee are a lower percentage of that employee's compensation than the plan provides for employees who are not highly compensated.

Under the bill, a plan is considered to meet all discrimination tests if it is maintained under an agreement which the Secretary of the Treasury finds to be a collective bargaining agreement between employee representatives and one or more employers.

In testing a cafeteria plan for discriminatory coverage of employees and discriminatory contributions or benefits, the bill provides that all employees who are employed by a commonly controlled group of businesses are treated as if they were employed by a single employer. The rules for aggregating employees of businesses under common control are the same as the rules which are used in testing tax-qualified pension plans for discrimination (sec. 414(b) and (c)). The committee intends that, where an employer maintains two or more cafeteria plans, the employer may choose to have the plans considered as a single plan for purposes of the discrimination tests.

The amendment is effective for taxable years beginning after December 31, 1978.

[Code Sec. 127]

[¶ 11,289.06]

Committee Report on P.L. 107-16 (Economic Growth and Tax Relief Reconciliation Act)

[Exclusion of employer-provided educational assistance]

[Senate Committee Report]

The provision extends the exclusion for employer-provided educational assistance to graduate education and makes the exclusion (as applied to both undergraduate and graduate education) permanent.

Effective date

The provision is effective with respect to courses beginning after December 31, 2001.

[Conference Committee Report]

The conference agreement follows the Senate amendment.

[¶ 11,289.07]

Committee Report on P.L. 106-170 (Ticket to Work and Work Incentives Improvement Act)

[Employer-provided educational assistance]

[Conference Committee Report]

The conference agreement provides that the present-law exclusion for employer-provided educational assistance is extended through December 31, 2001.

Effective date

The provision is effective with respect to courses beginning after May 31, 2000, and before January 1, 2002.

[¶ 11,289.075]

Committee Reports on P.L. 104-188 (Small Business Job Protection Act)

Extension of Certain Expiring Provisions

[House Committee Report]

Employer-provided educational assistance

The bill extends the exclusion for employer-provided educational assistance for taxable years beginning after December 31, 1994, and before January 1, 1997. In years beginning after December 31, 1995, the exclusion would not apply with respect to graduatelevel courses.

To the extent employers have previously filed Forms W-2 reporting the amount of educational assistance provided as taxable wages, present Treasury regulations would require the employer to file Forms W-2c (i.e., corrected Forms W-2) with the Internal Revenue Service.[2] It is intended that employers would also be required to provide copies of Form W-2c to affected employees.

The Secretary is directed to establish expedited procedures for the refund of any overpayment of employment taxes paid on excludable educational assistance provided in 1995 and 1996, including procedures for waiving the requirement that an employer obtain an employee's signature if the employer demonstrates to the satisfaction of the Secretary that any refund collected by the employer on behalf of the employee will be paid to the employee.

Because the exclusion is extended, no interest and penalties should be imposed if an employer failed to withhold income and employment taxes on excludable educational assistance or failed to report such educational assistance. Further, it is intended that the Secretary establish expedited procedures for refunding any interest and penalties relating to educational assistance previously paid.

Effective date

The provision is effective with respect to taxable years beginning after December 31, 1994, and before January 1, 1997, and the restriction of the exclusion to undergraduate education is effective for taxable years beginning after December 31, 1995.

[Conference Committee Report]

The conference agreement follows the House bill, with the following modifications. The exclusion expires with respect to courses beginning after May 31, 1997. The exclusion for graduate courses applies in 1995. In 1996, the exclusion for graduate courses does not apply to courses beginning after June 30, 1996.

[¶ 11,289.08]

Committee Reports on P.L. 103-66 (Omnibus Budget Reconciliation Act of 1993)

[*Employer-provided educational assistance*]

[Senate Committee Report]

The bill retroactively extends the exclusion for employer-provided educational assistance for 24 months (through June 30, 1994). In the case of a taxable year beginning in 1994, only amounts paid before July 1, 1994, by the employer for educational assistance for the employee can be taken into account in determining the amount excludable under section 127 for the taxable year.

The committee understands that the expiration of the exclusion and the retroactive extension creates a number of administrative problems for employers and employees because some employers and employees treated educational assistance provided between July 1, 1992, and December 31, 1992, as excludable from income, while some treated it as taxable income. If educational assistance provided during such period was treated as taxable, then the employee would be

[2] Treasury regulation section 31.6051-1(c).

entitled to a refund of excess taxes paid. The committee intends that the Secretary will use his existing authority to the fullest extent possible to alleviate any administrative problems and to facilitate the recoupment of excess taxes paid in the simplest way possible.

The bill also clarifies the rule under which educational assistance that does not satisfy section 127 may be excluded from income if and only if it meets the requirements of a working condition fringe benefit.

Effective date

The extension of the exclusion is effective for taxable years ending after June 30, 1992. The clarification to the working condition fringe benefit rule is effective for taxable years beginning after December 31, 1988.

[Conference Committee Report]

The conference agreement follows the Senate amendment, except that the exclusion for employer-provided educational assistance is extended retroactively and through December 31, 1994.

The conferees intend that the Secretary will use his existing authority to the fullest extent possible to alleviate any administrative problems that may result from the expiration and retroactive extension of the exclusion and to facilitate in the simplest way possible the recoupment of excess taxes paid with respect to educational assistance provided in the last half of 1992.

Effective date

The conference agreement follows the Senate amendment.

[¶ 11,289.085]

Committee Reports on P.L. 101-508 (Omnibus Budget Reconciliation Act of 1990)

[Senate Committee Report]

[*Employer-provided educational assistance*]

The bill extends the exclusion for employer-provided educational assistance benefits through taxable years beginning before January 1, 1992. The special rule limiting the exclusion in the case of a taxable year beginning in 1990 is repealed. In addition, the rule restricting the availability of the exclusion with respect to graduate level courses is repealed.

Effective date

Effective for taxable years beginning after September 30, 1990.

[Conference Committee Report]

The conference agreement follows the Senate amendment.

[¶ 11,289.09]

Committee Reports on P.L. 100-647 (Technical and Miscellaneous Revenue Act of 1988)

[House Committee Report]

The exclusion for educational assistance is restored retroactively to the date of expiration and is extended so that it expires for taxable years beginning after December 31, 1990.

However, the prior-law limit of $5,250 is reduced to $1,500. In addition, the exclusion does not apply to any payment for, or the provision of any benefits with respect to, any graduate level courses of a kind normally taken by an individual pursuing a program leading to a law, business, medical, or similar advanced academic or professional degree. For this purpose, the phrase "graduate-level course" means a course taken by an individual who (1) has received a bachelor's degree (or the equivalent thereof), or (2) is receiving credit toward a more advanced degree.

Neither the limit nor the graduate education rule applies to graduate teaching or research assistants who receive tuition reduction under section 117(d).

In addition, the bill clarifies the definition of education ineligible for the exclusion—i.e., education involving sports, games, or hobbies. Under this clarification, education with respect to a subject commonly considered a sport, game, or hobby, such as photography or gardening, is ineligible for the exclusion unless such education (1) has a reasonable relationship to an activity maintained by the employee for profit; (2) has a reasonable relationship to the business of the employer; or (3) is required as part of a degree program. Of course, education meeting these criteria may fail to be eligible for the exclusion for other reasons (such as the graduate education rule described above).

Effective Date

The provision generally is effective on the date of enactment. The amendments with respect to the $1,500 limit and graduate education apply to taxable years beginning after December 31, 1988. The amendment with respect to hobbies is considered a retroactive clarification of prior law.

[Conference Committee Report]

* * *

Senate Amendment

Extension.—The section 127 exclusion is restored retroactively to the date of expiration and is extended so that it expires for taxable years beginning after December 31, 1988.

Graduate-level education.—The Senate amendment is the same as the House bill, except that the present law rules relating to benefits provided to graduate teaching and research assistants are retained. In other words, the Senate amendment permits amounts paid to graduate teaching and research assistants to be excluded from income under either the tuition reduction provision of section 117(d) or the educational assistance program provision of section 127.

Sports, games, and hobbies.—The Senate amendment is the same as the House bill.

Single trust.—It was unclear under prior law whether the prohibition on providing employees with a choice between nontaxable educational assistance benefits under section 127 and other remuneration includible in gross income prohibited the provision of taxable and nontaxable educational assistance benefits from a single trust. The Senate amendment [by means of legislative history] clarifies the prior-law rules so that it is permissible to pay taxable and nontaxable educational assistance benefits from the same trust.

Effective date

Senate amendment provisions are generally effective as of the date of expiration of the exclusion. The provisions with respect to hobbies and employee choice are considered to be retroactive clarifications of prior law.

Conference Agreement

Extension.—The conference agreement follows the Senate amendment.

Graduate-level education.—The conference agreement follows the House bill, except that the provision is effective for taxable years beginning after December 31, 1987. In addition, the conference agreement makes permanent the rule permitting tuition reduction benefits paid to graduate teaching and research to be excluded from income under section 117(d) (subject to the compensation limit of section 117(c)).

Sports, games, and hobbies.—The conference agreement follows the House bill * * *.

Single trust.—The conference agreement follows the Senate amendment.

[¶ 11,289.095]

Committee Reports on P.L. 99-514 (Tax Reform Act of 1986)

[House Committee Report]

Explanation of Provision

The bill extends the educational assistance and group legal services exclusions for two years. Thus, these exclusions are scheduled to expire for taxable years beginning after December 31, 1987 and ending after December 31, 1987, respectively.

Effective Date

The provisions are effective upon enactment.

[Senate Committee Report]

Explanation of Provision

* * *

Increased cap on educational assistance

In addition, the bill increases the cap on annual excludable educational assistance benefits to $5,250 from $5,000. * * *

Effective Date

The provisions are effective (1) in the case of educational assistance benefits, for taxable years beginning after December 31, 1985, and (2) in the case of group legal services benefits and the tax exemption for qualified group legal services organizations, for taxable years ending after December 31, 1985.

* * *

[Conference Committee Report]

* * *

The conference agreement follows the House bill with respect to extending for two years, rather than making permanent, the educational assistance and group legal services exclusions and the tax-exempt status of group legal services organizations. The agreement follows the Senate amendment raising the cap on annual excludable educational assistance benefits from $5,000 to $5,250, but does not adopt the Senate amendment indexing this cap. * * *

The conference agreement modifies the transition rule for group legal services benefits provided under a cafeteria plan. Under the modified transition rule, an employee will be permitted to revoke an election to take cash or a qualified benefit other than group legal services and to make a new election to take group legal services instead. Such revocation and new election must be made no later than 60 days after the date of enactment and may relate to any period after December 31, 1985. This transition rule is limited to cafeteria plans that, prior to the date of conference action, did not allow employees to elect group legal services benefits with respect to a period after December 31, 1985.

[¶ 11,289.10]

Committee Report on P.L. 95-600 (Revenue Act of 1978)

Sec. 164— Educational assistance plans.

[Senate Committee Report]

General.—The provision excludes from an employee's gross income amounts paid for expenses incurred by the employer for educational assistance to the employee if such amounts are paid or such expenses are incurred pursuant to a program which meets certain requirements. In the case of education paid for, or furnished by, an individual's employer under such a program, the provision eliminates the need to distinguish job-related educational expenses from personal educational expenses for income tax purposes.[1]

Excludible benefits.—The educational benefits which may be excluded from income are those furnished by an employer only to employees. The types of educational assistance which may be furnished are not restricted. The employer may provide educational assistance to the employee directly or the employer may reimburse the employee for the latter's expenses. Under the bill, an employee can exclude from income tuition, fees, and similar payments, as well as the cost of books, supplies, and equipment paid for, or provided by, his employer; however, the employee cannot exclude tools or supplies which the employer provides and which the employee may retain after completion of the course of instruction. Meals, lodging, or transportation also may not be excluded under this section. There is no restriction as to who may furnish the educational assistance. Such assistance may be furnished by an educational institution or any other party. Also, the employer, alone or in conjunction with other employers, may furnish the education directly to the employees. The education which may be furnished is not limited to job-related courses nor to courses which are part of a degree program. However, the exclusion does not apply to educational assistance furnished for courses involving sports, games, or hobbies, except where the education provided involves the business of the employer.

For a program to qualify under this provision, the employees must not be able to choose taxable benefits in lieu of the educational benefits.

A taxpayer may not claim any deduction, for example, a business expense deduction, nor may he claim any credit with respect to any amount which is excluded from his income under this provision. Thus, no double tax benefit can be obtained.

An employer educational assistance program is not required to be funded nor to be approved in advance by the Internal Revenue Service.

Nondiscrimination requirements.—In order to be a qualified program, an educational assistance program also must meet requirements with respect to nondiscrimination in contributions or benefits and in eligibility for enrollment. The bill requires that a program must benefit employees who qualify under a classification set up by the employer and found by the Secretary not to be discriminatory in favor of employees who are officers, shareholders, self-employed individuals, highly compensated, or their dependents. The program must be available to a broad class of employees rather than to a particular individual. However, employees may be excluded from a program if they are members of a collective bargaining unit and there is evidence that educational assistance benefits were the subject of good faith bargaining between the unit and the employer or employers offering the program.

The bill specifically provides that a program shall not be considered discriminatory merely because it is utilized to a greater degree by one class of employees than by another class or because successful completion of a course, or attaining a particular course grade, is required for, or considered in, determining the availability of benefits.

Reasonable notification of the availability and terms of the program must be provided to eligible employees.

Operation.—Under the bill, the exclusion does not apply if the program discriminates in favor of certain employees. A program is discriminatory if more than 5 percent of the benefits can be paid to shareholders, officers, highly compensated employees, self-employed individuals, or dependents of any of these groups.

Special rules.—An individual who qualifies as an employee within the definition in section 401(c)(1) of the Code is also an employee for purposes of these provisions. Thus, in general, the term "self-employed individual" means, and the term "employee" includes, individuals who have earned income for a taxable year, as well as individuals who would have earned income except that their trades or businesses did not have net profits for a taxable year.

An individual who owns the entire interest in an unincorporated trade or business is treated as his own employer. A partnership is considered the employer of each partner who is also an employee of the partnership.

For determining stock ownership in corporations, the bill adopts the attribution rules provided under subsection (d) and (e) of section 1563 (without regard to sec. 1563(e)(3)(C)). The Treasury Department is to issue regulations for determining ownership interests in unincorporated trade or businesses, such as partnerships or proprietorships, following the principles governing the attribution of stock ownership.

The bill also provides that amounts excluded from income as educational assistance are not to be treated as wages subject to withholding of income nor as wages subject to employment taxes.

There is no comparable provision in the House bill.

The bill applies to taxable years beginning after December 31, 1978.

[Conference Committee Report]

The conference agreement follows the Senate amendment except that the provision is temporary. The exclusion applies to taxable years beginning after December 31, 1978, and ending before January 1, 1984.

[Code Sec. 129]

[¶ 11,289H.095]

Committee Report on P.L. 100-647 (Technical and Miscellaneous Revenue Act of 1988)

[Senate Committee Report]

$5,000 Limit on Dependent Care Assistance Exclusion

Under the bill, the $5,000 (or $2,500) limit generally applies to the amount of dependent care services that is covered by a dependent care assistance program and that is received by a taxpayer during a taxable year, even if the taxpayer does not receive payment from the employer for any expenses paid or incurred by the taxpayer in connection with such services until a subsequent taxable year.

For example, assume that in 1988, unmarried employee A, whose taxable year is the calendar year, incurred $6,000 of dependent care expenses (which he paid); in 1989, the figure was $5,000. During this period, A's only employer, B, maintained a dependent care assistance program that satisfied the requirements of section 129. Pursuant to the program, B is to reimburse A for all his dependent care expenses. However, during 1988, B only made $3,000 of payments. During 1989, an additional $8,000 of payments were made.

Under the bill, the $5,000 limit on dependent care services covered by a program is exceeded in 1988 by $1,000. This $1,000 excess is includible in A's income for 1988 with respect to the dependent care assistance program. In 1989, A only receives $5,000 worth of dependent care services covered by a dependent care assistance program. This equals the limit with respect to A. Thus, for 1989, A has no includible amount attributable to the receipt of dependent care services covered by the dependent care assistance program.

These provisions for applying the $5,000 (or $2,500) limit are intended to conform to the manner in which employers maintain their records and thus are intended to facilitate administration of the limit. In addition, in comparison to applying the limit on a cash basis, these provisions prevent avoidance of the limit by, for example, delaying the date of payment. The provisions can also prevent inappropriate application of the limit, such as in instances in which payment at the end of one year is inavoidably delayed into a second year for which a full $5,000 will be paid for current expenses.

These provisions with respect to the $5,000 limit generally apply to taxable years beginning after December 31, 1987, with 2 modifications. First, a taxpayer may elect to have the provisions apply to taxable years beginning after December 31, 1986. The election may be made by a taxpayer by filing an income tax return in a manner consistent with these provisions for any taxable year beginning before January 1, 1988.

The second modification applies to any taxpayer who does not make the election described above. Such taxpayers are subject to the following transition rule. Any dependent care services covered by a dependent care assistance program that are received by the taxpayer in a taxable year beginning in 1987 are to be treated as provided in the taxpayer's first taxable year beginning after December 31, 1987, if the employer payment for such services is not received in the year in which the services are received.

For example, assume the same facts as in the above example, except that the years involved are 1987 and 1988, rather than 1988 and 1989. Assume further that C does not make the election described above. In 1987, C only received $3,000 in employer payments and thus, under the rules in effect prior to the bill provision, has no inclusion in 1987 attributable to those payments. In 1988, when the bill provision first applies to C, C only receives $5,000 worth of dependent care

[1] However, such a distinction still would have to be made in situations where the education is not excluded under this provision.

services covered by a dependent care assistance program. Thus, without regard to the special transition rule, C would have no inclusion attributable to services received in 1988.

Because C did not make the election, however, the special transition rule applies to her. Under this rule, the first step is to determine the amount of covered services received by C in 1987 for which no payment is made by D during 1987. In this example, such amount is $3,000. This amount of services is then considered to have been received by C in 1988. Thus, the total covered services C is considered to receive in 1988 is increased from $5,000 to $8,000, a total that is $3,000 over the limit. Thus, for 1988, C has $3,000 includible in her income attributable to the receipt of dependent care services covered by the dependent care assistance program.

Under the bill, the reporting requirement applicable to the employer with respect to dependent care assistance is modified to conform to the changes with respect to the $5,000 (or $2,500) limit. Thus, the bill requires that the amount reported with respect to an employee be the amount *incurred* for dependent care assistance with respect to such employee. In addition, the bill requires that such reporting be made to the IRS, in addition to the employee, on the Form W-2.

These provisions apply with respect to calendar years after 1987. However, a taxpayer may elect to have the provision relating to the amount reported apply to calendar year 1987. This election may be made by a taxpayer by providing reports in a manner consistent with such provision for calendar year 1987. For taxpayers who do not make this election, a rule similar to the rule aplicable to the $5,000 (or $2,500) limit applies. Thus, any amount incurred for dependent care assistance in 1987 are to be treated as incurred in 1988 if the employer payment for such services is not made in 1987.

[¶ 11,289H.10]

Committee Reports on P.L. 99-514 (Tax Reform Act of 1986)

[House Committee Report]

Explanation of Provision

Under the bill, the exclusion for dependent care assistance benefits is limited to $5,000 a year ($2,500 in the case of a married individual filing a separate return). In the case of a married couple filing a joint return, the $5,000 limit applies with respect to the couple in order to effectuate the committee's intent to coordinate the limit on the exclusion with the limit on the amount of child care expenses eligible for the child care credit.

The bill provides a special rule for determining the value of child care in a facility on the employer's premises (on-site facility). Under this rule, the value of the benefit is measured by the value of services provided to employees who actually use the facility.

Effective Date

The provision is effective for taxable years beginning after December 31, 1985.

[Conference Committee Report]

* * *

The conference agreement follows the House bill with respect to the limit on the exclusion for dependent care assistance, effective for taxable years beginning after December 31, 1986.

[Code Sec. 132]

[¶ 11,289M.07]

Committee Report on P.L. 107-16 (Economic Growth and Tax Relief Reconciliation Act)

[House Committee Report]

[Treatment of employer-provided retirement advice]

Qualified retirement planning services provided to an employee and his or her spouse by an employer maintaining a qualified plan are excludable from income and wages. The exclusion does not apply with respect to highly compensated employees unless the services are available on substantially the same terms to each member of the group of employees normally provided education and information regarding the employer's qualified plan. "Qualified retirement planning services" are retirement planning advice and information. The exclusion is not limited to information regarding the qualified plan, and, thus, for example, applies to advice and information regarding retirement income planning for an individual and his or her spouse and how the employer's plan fits into the individual's overall retirement income plan. On the other hand, the exclusion does not apply to services that may be related to retirement planning, such as tax preparation, accounting, legal or brokerage services.

It is intended that the provision will clarify the treatment of retirement advice provided in a nondiscriminatory manner. It is intended that the Secretary, in determining the application of the exclusion to highly compensated employees, may permit employers to take into consideration employee circumstances other than compensation and position in providing advice to classifications of employees. Thus, for example, the Secretary may permit employers to limit certain advice to individuals nearing retirement age under the plan.

Effective Date

The provision is effective with respect to years beginning after December 31, 2001.

[Conference Committee Report]

Senate Amendment

The Senate amendment is the same as the House bill.

Conference Agreement

The conference agreement follows the House bill and the Senate amendment.

[¶ 11,289M.075]

Committee Reports on P.L. 103-66 (Omnibus Budget Reconciliation Act of 1993)

For Committee Reports on P.L. 103-66, Sec. 13101, relating to employer-provided educational assistance, see ¶ 11,289.08.

[¶ 11,289M.08]

Committee Reports on P.L. 102-486 (Comprehensive National Energy Policy Act of 1992)

1. Employer-provided transportation benefits

* * *

House Bill

Under the House bill, gross income and wages (for both income and payroll tax purposes) does not include qualified transportation fringe benefits. In general, a qualified transportation fringe is (1) transportation in a commuter highway vehicle if such transportation is in connection with travel between the employee's residence and place of employment, (2) a transit pass, or (3) qualified parking. Cash reimbursements made by the employer for such expenses under a bona fide reimbursement arrangement also qualify for the exclusion.

The maximum amount of qualified parking that is excludable from an employee's gross income is $160 per month (regardless of the total value of the parking). Other qualified transportation fringes are excludable from gross income to the extent that the aggregate value of the benefits does not exceed $60 per month (regardless of the total value of the benefits). The $60 and $160 limits are indexed for inflation, rounded down to the next whole dollar.

A commuter highway vehicle is a highway vehicle with the capacity to seat at least 6 adults (not including the driver) and at least 80 percent of the mileage use of which is for transporting employees between their residences and their place of employment using at least one-half of the adult seating capacity of the vehicle (not including the driver). Transportation furnished in a commuter highway vehicle operated by or for the employer is considered provided by the employer.

A transit pass includes any pass, token, farecard, voucher, or similar item entitling a person to transportation on mass transit facilities (whether publicly or privately owned). Types of transit facilities that may qualify for the exclusion include, for example, rail, bus, and ferry.

Qualified parking is parking provided to an employee on or near the business premises of the employer, or on or near a location from which the employee commutes to work by mass transit, in a commuter highway vehicle, or by carpool. As under present law, the exclusion does not apply to any parking facility or space located on property owned or leased by the employee for residential purposes.

Effective date

The provision applies to benefits provided by the employer on or after January 1, 1993.

Senate Amendment

The Senate amendment is generally the same as the House bill, except that the parking cap is $145 per month, rather than $160 per month. In addition, the $60 and $145 limits are indexed for inflation in $5 increments.

Under the Senate amendment, cash reimbursements for transit passes do not qualify for the transit exclusion if vouchers that are exchangeable only for transit passes are readily available to the employer.

Effective date

Same as the House bill.

Conference Agreement

The conference agreement follows the Senate amendment, except that the parking cap is $155 per month.

[¶ 11,289M.085]

Committee Report on P.L. 100-647 (Technical and Miscellaneous Revenue Act of 1988)

[House Committee Report]

Under the bill, the transportation of cargo by air and the transportation of passengers by air is treated as the same service for purposes of section 132(b). Thus, an employee performing services in the air cargo line of business may receive air travel (including air travel under reciprocal agreements with other airlines) as a no-additional-cost service.

Effective Date

This proposal would be effective for transportation provided on or after January 1, 1988. The effective date of the provision is not intended to create any inference with respect to the law prior to 1988.

[¶ 11,289M.09]

Committee Reports on P.L. 99-514 (Tax Reform Act of 1986)

[Senate Committee Report]

a. Clarification of line of business requirement

Explanation of Provision

The bill clarifies that a leased section of a department store which, in connection with the offering of beautician services, customarily makes sales of beauty aids in the ordinary course of business is to be treated as engaged in over-the-counter sales of property, and thus is to be treated as a part of the line of business of the person operating the store. The committee intends that this treatment is to be available without requiring that a specific percentage of the beauty salon's revenue must be earned through the sale of such beauty products because beauty salons have traditionally occupied such leased sections (even though the bulk of their revenue is attributable to performing services rather than selling property.) This is contrasted with businesses (such as insurance companies) that have not traditionally occupied such leased sections.

b. Definition of dependent children

Explanation of Provision

The bill defines dependent child to mean any child of the employee (1) who is a dependent of the employee, or (2) both of whose parents are deceased and who has not attained age 25.

c. Clarification of cross-reference

Explanation of Provision

To clarify the mechanics of the cross-reference in Code section 132(f), the bill adds the words "for use by such employee" in section 132(a)(2). Accordingly, the qualified employee discount exclusion applies in certain circumstances where the price at which property or services are provided to the employee by the employer for use by such employee (or the spouse or dependent children or parents of the employee) is less than the price to nonemployee customers.

d. Cross-reference in definition of customer

Explanation of Provision

The bill provides that this exception to the definition of customers also applies for purposes of section 132(c)(2)(A), defining the term "gross profit percentage."

e. Excise tax on certain fringe benefits

Explanation of Provision

The bill clarifies that, in the case of an agricultural cooperative incorporated in 1964, the grandfather rule, requiring that employees in all lines of business of an employer be eligible for employee discounts, is applied without taking into account employees of an employer that became a member of a controlled group including the agricultural cooperative during July of 1980.

f. Applicability of section 132(a)(1) exclusion to certain pre-divestiture retired telephone employees

Explanation of Provision

The provision applies an intended transitional rule under which the fair market value of free telephone service provided to employees of the Bell System who had retired prior to divestiture of the system on January 1, 1984 is excluded from income and wages of such pre-divestiture retired employees. The exclusion pursuant to the provision does not apply to the furnishing of any property or to the furnishing of any type of service that was not furnished to such retirees as of January 1, 1984.

The provision applies in the case of an employee who, prior to January 1, 1984, separated from the service (by reason of retirement or disability) of an entity subject to the modified final judgment (as defined in Code sec. 559(c)(4)). The provision does not apply to any employee who separated from such service on or after January 1, 1984. No inference is intended from adoption of this transitional rule as to the interpretation of the no-additional-cost service exclusion in any other circumstances.

Under the provision, all entities subject to the modified final judgment are treated as a single employer in the same line of business for purposes of determining whether telephone service provided to the employee is a no-additional-cost service. Also, payment by an entity subject to the modified final judgment of all or part of the cost of local telephone service provided to the employee by a person other than an entity subject to the modified final judgment (including rebate of the amount paid by the employee for the service and payment to the person providing the service) is treated as telephone service provided to the employee by such single employer for purposes of determining whether the telephone service is a no-additional-cost service.

For purposes of this provision, the term "employee" has the meaning given to such term in Code section 132(f). Except as otherwise provided in this provision, the general requirements for the Code section 132(a)(1) exclusion apply; e.g., the exclusion applies to officers, owners, or highly compensated employees only if the no-additional-cost service is available to employees on a nondiscriminatory basis.

g. Cafeteria plans

Explanation of Provision

Under the bill, the definition of permissible cafeteria plan benefits is clarified. The effect of the provision, which changes the reference in section 125 from nontaxable benefits to qualified benefits is to (1) eliminate any possible implication that a taxable benefit provided through a cafeteria plan is nontaxable, and (2) clarify that certain taxable benefits, as permitted under Treasury regulations, can be provided in a cafeteria plan.

The bill makes two changes to the transition relief provided to certain cafeteria plans under section 531(b) of the Tax Reform Act of 1984. The first change provides that a cafeteria plan, in existence on February 10, 1984, maintained pursuant to one or more collective bargaining agreements between employee representatives and one or more employers will be granted relief under the transition rules until the expiration of the last collective bargaining agreement relating to the cafeteria plan. When a collective bargaining agreement terminates is determined without regard to any extension of the agreement agreed to after July 18, 1984. Also, if a cafeteria plan is amended to conform with either the requirements of the Act or the requirements of any cafeteria plan regulations, the amendment is not treated as a termination of the agreement.

Second, the bill provides that a cafeteria plan which suspended a type or amount of benefit after February 10, 1984, and subsequently reactivated the benefit is eligible for transition relief under either the general or special transition relief provision.

h. Clarification of de minimis fringe benefits

Explanation of Provision

The committee clarifies that the de minimis fringe benefit exclusion includes tokens, vouchers, and reimbursements to cover the costs of commuting by public transit, as long as the amount of such reimbursement, etc., provided by the employer does not exceed $15 a month ($180 a year). The value of all such transit benefits (including any discounts on passes) furnished to the same individual are aggregated for purposes of determining whether the $15 limit is reached.

i. Transitional rules for treatment of certain reductions in tuition

Explanation of Provision

Under the bill, for purposes of testing whether a tuition reduction program is nondiscriminatory, a special rule applies to a certain plan. A plan is treated as nondiscriminatory if (1) the plan meets the nondiscrimination requirement (as added by the bill) on the day on which eligibility to participate in the plan closed, (2) at all times thereafter, the tuition reductions available under the plan are available on substantially the same terms to all employees eligible to participate in the plan, and (3) the eligibility to participate in the plan closed on June 30, 1972, or December 31, 1975. Of course, the conditions for eligibility cannot be altered after the eligibility closed.

In addition, in the case of an employer who maintains plans to which the special rule applies, employees not included in the plan who are included in a unit of employees covered by an agreement that the Secretary of the Treasury finds to be a collective bargaining agreement between employee representatives and one or more employers, if there is evidence that such benefits were the subject of good faith bargaining are excluded from consideration. For purposes of testing plans not subject to this special rule, employees covered by plans subject to this special rule are disregarded in all respects.

[House Committee Report]

* * *

The bill provides that any tuition reduction provided with respect to a full-time course of education furnished at the graduate level before July 1, 1988, is not included in gross income if (1) the reduction would not have been included in income under Treasury Regulations in effect on July 18, 1984, and (2) the reduction is provided with respect to a student who was accepted for admission to such course of education before July 1, 1984, and began the course of education before June 30, 1985.

h. Working condition fringe

Explanation of Provision

The committee clarifies the application of the product testing provision for purposes of the working condition fringe exclusion in the case of automobile testing. As described above, the product testing exclusion rule does not apply unless the employer imposes limitations on the employee's use of the item that significantly reduce the value of any personal benefit to the employee. The committee intends that this particular requirement is satisfied if the employer charges the employee a reasonable amount for any personal use of the automobile; thus, the product testing exclusion rule applies in such a case if all the other requirements for the rule are met.

An employer is treated as having imposed a sufficient charge for any personal benefit to an employee from the use of an evaluation product if the charge exceeds the cost to the employer in making the product available to employees.

The committee also clarifies the exception to the working condition fringe benefit rule for full-time automobile salesmen. This exception is not intended to be restricted to employees who have the formal job title of salesperson. Rather, the term is intended to apply to full-time employees of an automobile dealer who are automobile floor salespersons; to automobile salesmanagers; or to other employees who, as an integral part of their employment, regularly perform the functions of a floor salesperson or salesmanager, directly engage in the promotion and negotiation of sales to customers, and derive a significant part of their compensation from such activity. This provision, however, does not apply to owners of large automobile dealerships who do not customarily engage in significant sales activities.

[Conference Committee Report]

Fringe benefit provisions

The conference agreement follows the Senate amendment with the following exceptions:

a. Working condition fringe.—The conference agreement adopts the clarification in the legislative history of the House bill that the application of the product testing provision for purposes of the working condition fringe benefit exclusion in the case of automobile testing is not violated if the employer charges the employee a reasonable amount for any personal use of the automobile as long as all of the other requirements are satisfied.

b. Automobile salesmen.—The conference agreement adopts the clarification in the legislative history of the House bill relating to the working condition fringe benefit rule for full-time automobile salesmen.

c. De minimis fringe.—The conference agreement adopts the provision in the legislative history of the Senate bill clarifying the applicability of the de minimis fringe benefit exclusion to the provision of public transit passes.

d. Qualified tuition reduction.—The conference agreement adopts the House bill provision relating to an exception to the rules relating to qualified tuition reductions for certain students.

[¶ 11,289M.095]

Committee Report on P.L. 99-272 (Consolidated Omnibus Budget Reconciliation Act)

[House Committee Report on H.R. 3838]

[I]f an individual performed services for a qualified air transportation organization and the services are performed primarily for persons engaged in providing air transportation and are of the kind that would qualify the individual for no-additional-cost services in the form of air transportation, then the qualified air transportation organization is treated as engaged in the line of business of air transportation with respect to that individual.

An organization is considered a qualified air transportation organization if (1) the organization was in existence on September 12, 1984, (2) the organization either (a) is described in section 501(c)(6) of the Code and membership of the organization is limited to entities engaged in the transportation by air of individuals or property for compensation or hire or (b) is a corporation all the stock of which is owned entirely by entities engaged in the transportation by air of individuals or property for compensation or hire, and (3) if the organization is operated in furtherance of the activities of its members or owners.

The committee also clarifies that employees of airline subsidiaries that engage in activities (such as providing food services on airline flights or providing ticketing and reservation services) normally engaged in directly by the air carrier are considered in the same line of business for purposes of the no-additional-cost service rule. These transition rules are intended to provide relief in the case of activities that had, at one time, been provided directly by an air carrier and which were spun off into a separate company. The committee does not intend the provision to apply to travel agencies or other organizations that have never been directly related to an air carrier.

[Senate Committee Report]

The bill amends section 132(f) to provide that any use of commercial air transportation by a parent of an employee is treated as use by the employee, effective January 1, 1985. For purposes of this rule, the term employee does not include an individual who is an employee solely by reason of section 132(f)(1)(B).

The bill provides a special rule applicable if (1) a corporation that is predominantly engaged in airline-related services is a member of an affiliated group (within the meaning of sec. 1504(a)) another member of which operates an airline and (2) employees of the first corporation who are directly engaged in providing airline-related services are entitled to no-additional-cost services with respect to air transportation provided by such other member. If this rule applies, the first corporation is treated as engaged in the air transportation line of business of the affiliate which operates the airline, for purposes of determining whether the employees who are directly engaged in providing airline-related services are eligible for the no-additional-cost service exclusion in section 132(a)(1). This provision is effective January 1, 1985.

The term "airline-related services" means any of the following services provided in connection with commercial air transportation: (i) catering; (ii) baggage handling; (iii) ticketing and reservation; (iv) flight planning and weather analysis; (v) restaurants located at an airport and gift shops located at an airport; and (vi) such other similar services provided to airlines as may be prescribed by Treasury regulations. (Flight planning and weather analysis generally means activities such as the provision of computerized and specialized flight plans, the provision of weather information to airlines and notams (notices to airmen), and the provision of computer packages related to those services.) The Treasury may include in category (vi) as similar services only services that directly benefit airlines, and cannot include in category (vi) services (whether or not furnished at airports) that are for the convenience of airline passengers, such as hotels, car rentals, and magazine publishing.

The bill also provides a transitional rule for persons employed, as of September 12, 1984, by an airline affiliate under certain circumstances. The transitional rule applies to an individual if, as of September 12, 1984, all of the following conditions are met:

(1) The individual was an employee (within the meaning of sec. 132, including sec. 132(f)) of one member of an affiliated group (as defined in sec. 1504), referred to as the "first corporation," and was eligible for no-additional-cost services in the form of air transportation provided by another member of the affiliated group, referred to as the "second corporation";

(2) at least 50 percent of the individuals performing service for the first corporation were or had been employees of, or had previously performed services for, the second corporation; and

(3) the primary business of the affiliated group was commercial air transportation of passengers.

If all three conditions are met, the first corporation is treated as engaged in the same air transportation line of business as the second corporation for purposes of applying paragraphs (1) and (2) of Code section 132(a), with respect to no-additional-cost services and qualified employee discounts provided for such individuals by the second corporation, and an individual of the second corporation who is performing services for the first corporation is also treated as an employee of the first corporation.

This provision applies to certain benefits provided after December 31, 1984. The intended beneficiaries of the provision are employees of Pan American World Services, Inc. who meet the requirements of the provision.

[Conference Committee Report]

The Conference agreement follows the Senate amendment, with a modification to reflect the House airline affiliate technical corrections provision (in H.R. 3838).

[¶ 11,289M.10]

Committee Reports on P.L. 98-369 (Tax Reform Act of 1984)

Explanation of Provisions

Overview

Under the bill, certain fringe benefits provided by an employer are excluded from the recipient employee's gross income for Federal income tax purposes and from the wage base (and, if applicable, the benefit base) for purposes of income tax withholding, FICA, FUTA, and RRTA.

The excluded fringe benefits are those benefits that qualify under one of the following five categories as defined in the bill: (1) a no-additional-cost service, (2) a qualified employee discount, (3) a working condition fringe, (4) a *de minimis* fringe, and (5) a qualified tuition reduction. Special rules apply with respect to certain parking or eating facilities provided to employees, on-premises athletic facilities, and demonstration use of an employer-provided car by auto salespersons. Some of the exclusions under the bill apply to benefits provided to the spouse and dependent children of a current employee, to former employees who separated from service because of retirement or disability (and their spouses and dependent children), and to the widow(er) of a deceased employee (and the dependent children of deceased employees).

In the case of a no-additional-cost service, a qualified employee discount, employee parking or eating facilities, or a qualified tuition reduction, the exclusion applies with respect to benefits provided to officers, owners, or highly compensated employees only if the benefit is made available to employees on a basis which does not discriminate in favor of officers, owners, or highly compensated employees.

Any fringe benefit that does not qualify for exclusion under the bill (for example, free or discounted goods or services which are limited to corporate officers) and that is not excluded under another statutory fringe benefit provision of the Code is taxable to the recipient under Code sections 61 and 83, and is includible in wages for employment tax purposes, at the excess of its fair market value over any amount paid by the employee for the benefit.

The provisions of the bill generally take effect on January 1, 1984, except that the tuition reduction exclusion applies with respect to education furnished after June 30, 1984.

No-additional-cost Service

General rule

Under this category, the entire value of any no-additional-cost service provided by an employer to an employee for the use of the employee (or of the employee's spouse or dependent children) is excluded for income and employment tax purposes. However, the exclusion applies only if the service is available to employees on a nondiscriminatory basis (see description below of the nondiscrimination rules of the bill). The exclusion applies whether the service is provided directly for no charge or at a reduced price or whether the benefit is provided through a cash rebate of all or part of the amount paid for the service.

To qualify under this exclusion, the employer must incur no substantial additional cost in providing the service to the employee, computed without regard to any amounts paid by the employee for the service. For this purpose, the term cost includes any revenue forgone because the service is furnished to the employee rather than to a nonemployee.[3] In addition, the service provided to the employee must be of the type which the employer offers for sale to nonemployee customers in the ordinary course of the line of business of the employer in which the employee is performing services.

Generally, situations in which the employers incur no additional cost in providing services to employees are those in which the employees receive, at no substantial additional cost to the employer, the benefit of excess capacity which otherwise would have remained unused because nonemployee customers would not have purchased it. Thus, employers that furnish airline, railroad, or subway seats or hotel rooms to employees working in those lines of business in such a way that nonemployee customers are not displaced, and telephone companies that provide telephone service to employees within existing capacity, incur no substantial additional cost in the provision of these services to employees, as this term is used in the bill.[4]

Line of business limitation

To be excluded under this category, a service must be the same type of service which is sold to the public in the ordinary course of the line of business of the employer in which the employee works. (Thus, types of services most of the employer's production of which are provided or sold to the employer's employees do not qualify for this exclusion.) For purposes of this limitation, a single employer is treated as consisting of more than one line of business if, after aggregating businesses under common control (see "definition of employer," below), the products or services the employer sells to nonemployees customers fall into more than one industry group.

In providing guidance as to the treatment of an employer as consisting of separate lines of business for this purpose, Treasury regulations may take into account the business segments into which corporations divide themselves for financial reporting purposes. Also, Treasury regulations may refer to the Standard Industrial Classifications used for other governmental purposes.

Under this limitation, for example, an employer which provides airline services and hotel services to the general public is considered to consist of two separate lines of business. As a consequence, the employees of the airline business of the employer may not exclude the value of free hotel rooms provided by the hotel business of the employer, and vice versa. The purpose of the line of business limitation is to avoid, to the extent possible, the competitive imbalances and inequities which would result from giving the employees of a conglomerate or other large employer with several lines of business a greater variety of tax-free benefits than could be given to the employees of a small employer with only one line of business. Thus, small businesses will not be disadvantaged in their ability to compete with large businesses providing the same goods or services, and employees of small business[es] will not be disadvantaged, in comparison to employees of multifaceted businesses, in terms of receiving tax-free economic benefits.

If an employee provides services that directly benefit more than one line of business of the employer, then the individual is treated as performing services in all such lines of business. Thus, for example, the chief executive officer, payroll department employees, and similar "headquarters" employees may exclude the value of no-additional-cost services provided by either the airline or hotel lines of business of the employer if they provide services which directly benefit both those lines of business.

Reciprocal arrangements

Under the bill, the employees of one employer are allowed the no-additional-cost service exclusion for services provided by an unrelated employer (i.e., another employer not under common control) only if the services provided to the employee are the same type of services as provided to nonemployee customers by both the line of business (of the first employer) in which the employee works and the line of business (of the other employer) in which the services are provided to the employee. In addition, both employers must be parties to a written reciprocal agreement under which the employees of each such line of business may receive the service from the other employer,[5] and neither employer may incur any substantial additional cost (including forgone revenue or payments to the other employer) in providing such service or pursuant to such agreement.

The criteria for determining whether two unrelated employers are providing the same type of service are the same as described above (under "line of business limitation") for determining the composition of the distinct lines of business comprised by a single employer. Thus, for example, the exclusion is available if two unrelated airlines provide free standby flights to each other's airline employees, but is not available to a hotel's employees if they receive free standby flights from an airline line of business (whether the airline is operated by the employees' employer or another employer).

Definition of employee

The bill provides that, with respect to a line of business of an employer, the term employee means (1) an individual who is currently employed by the employer in that line of business; (2) an individual who separated from service with the employer in that line of business by reason of retirement or disability; and (3) a widow or widower of an individual who died while employed by the employer in that line of business or of an individual who had separated from service with the employer in that line of business by reason of retirement or disability. The bill also provides that any use (e.g., of a standby airline flight) by the spouse or a dependent child of the employee (as so defined) is to be treated as use by the employee.[6] These definitions are relevant both for purposes of eligibility for the exclusion under the bill and for purposes of defining nonemployee customers.

Examples

As an illustration of the no-additional-cost service category of excludable benefits, assume that a corporation which operates an airline as its only line of business provides all of its employees (and their spouses and dependent children) with free travel, on the same terms to all employees, as stand-by passengers on the employer airline if the space taken on the flight has not been sold to the public shortly before departure time. In such a case, the entire fair market value of the free travel is excluded under the no-additional-cost service rule in the bill. This conclusion follows because the service provided by the employer to its employees who work in the employer's airline line of business is the same as that sold to the general public (airline flights), the service is provided at no substantial additional cost to the employer (the seat would have been unsold to nonemployees if the employee had not taken the trip),[7] and the eligibility terms satisfy the nondiscrimination rules of the bill since all employees are eligible for the benefit on the same terms.

This exclusion also applies where employees of the airline line of business of an employer receive free stand-by flights from the airline line of business of another employer through a written reciprocal agreement, if the benefit to the employee would have been excluded under this provision of the bill had it been provided in the same manner by the employee's employer. Thus, for example, the free flights furnished by the other employer must be available to the employees of the first employer on the same nondiscriminatory basis as required for the exclusion when furnished by the first employer, and neither employer may incur any substantial cost (including forgone revenue or any payment from one employer to the other) in providing the service or pursuant to the agreement.

Another example of a no-additional-cost service is the provision of utility services to the employees of the utility where there is excess capacity, such as the provision by a telephone company of free or reduced-cost telephone service to its employees.[8] Because the phone lines, switching capacity, and other overhead already exist, the telephone calls which employees may make without charge or at a reduced price impose no substantial additional cost on the employer. Thus, assuming the telephone service is provided to employees on a nondiscriminatory

[3] For the purpose of determining whether any revenue is forgone, it shall be assumed by the Treasury Department that the employee would not have purchased the service unless it were available to the employee at a below-market price.

[4] The employer does incur substantial additional cost (and hence the exclusion is not available) if a substantial amount of time is spent by employees in providing a service for other employees, as contrasted with the no-additional-cost situation in which the services provided to the employee (e.g., the in-flight services provided to an airline employee traveling on a standby basis) are merely incidental to services provided to nonemployee customers.

[5] Because businesses under common control are considered to be one employer (see "definition of employer," below), employees of one such commonly controlled business are eligible for the exclusion without need for a written agreement with the other commonly controlled business(es); however, the same-line-of-business test still applies in such cases.

[6] For this purpose, dependent child means any child (as defined in Code sec. 151(e)(3)) of the employee who is a dependent of the employee or both of whose parents have died. A child of divorced, etc., parents to whom section 152(e) applies is treated as a dependent of both parents.

[7] Neither the provision of meals and refreshments to a passenger, nor any extra fuel consumption attributable to the weight of an additional passenger, is considered a substantial additional cost.

[8] Local telephone service and long-distance telephone service are to be considered the same line of business.

basis, the requirements of this exclusion category are met, and the value of the service is excluded from gross income and wages.

Under the bill, the exclusion for no-additional-cost service is not available, for example, to employees in the hotel line of business of a corporation for receipt of free stand-by travel on an airline operated by the same corporation, or to employees of a consumer goods manufacturer who travel for personal purposes on a company plane (even if the plane is otherwise making a trip on company business). In each of these cases, even assuming that there were no substantial additional cost to the employer in providing the service on a space-available basis, the service is not the same type generally provided to the general public in the specific line of business of the employer in which the employee-recipient works. Accordingly, the requirements of the no-additional-cost exclusion are not satisfied.

Qualified Employee Discount

General rule

Under the bill, certain employee discounts[9] allowed from the selling price of qualified goods or services of the employer are excluded for income and employment tax purposes, but only if the discounts are available to employees on a nondiscriminatory basis (see description below of the nondiscrimination rules of the bill). The exclusion applies whether the qualified employee discount is provided through a reduction in price or through a cash rebate from a third party.

The exclusion is not available for discounts on any personal property (tangible or intangible) of a kind commonly held for investment or for discounts on any real property. Thus, for example, the exclusion does not apply to discounts on any employee purchases of securities, gold coins, residential or commercial real estate, or interests in mineral-producing property (regardless of whether a particular purchase is made for investment purposes). This limitation is provided because the committee does not believe that favorable tax treatment should be provided when noncash compensation is provided in the form of property which the employee could typically sell at close to the same price at which the employer sells the property to its nonemployee customers. Under the discount exclusion of the bill, an employee of a brokerage house may purchase stock and receive an excludable discount on a commission (subject to the 20-percent limitation discussed below for discounts on services). However, any discount allowed on the price of the stock itself is not eligible for the discount exclusion.

Line of business limitation

To qualify under this exclusion, the goods or services on which the discount is available must be those which are offered for sale by the employer to nonemployee customers in the ordinary course of the employer's line of business in which the employee works. (Thus, types of goods or services most of the employer's production of which are provided or sold to the employer's employees do not qualify for this exclusion.) The rules for treatment of a single employer as consisting of more than one line of business are the same as those described above in connection with the exclusion for a no-additional-cost service. However, the discount exclusion is not available for goods or services provided by another employer, whether or not a reciprocal agreement exists, except where commonly controlled businesses are treated as one employer (see "definition of employer," below).

For example, merchandise held for sale in the retail department store line of business of a firm is eligible for the discount exclusion if purchased at a discount by an employee of the firm who works in that line of business. Similarly, an employee who works for a manufacturer assembling appliances is eligible for the discount exclusion if the employee purchases the assembled appliances from the manufacturer-employer at a discount.

On the other hand, if an employee works for a company that consists of more than one line of business, such as a company consisting of a retail department store business, a hotel business, and an electrical component manufacturing business, an employee is eligible for the discount exclusion only for merchandise or services offered to customers in the ordinary course of business in the particular line of business in which the employee works. This is the case regardless of whether the employer makes discounts available to the employees in the other two lines of business. Thus, in this example, employees of the hotel business or of the electrical component manufacturing business are not eligible for the discount exclusion if these employees purchase merchandise at a discount from the employer's department store. However, employees of units of the employer that provide repair, or financing services with respect to, or that sell by catalog, retail merchandise are considered as providing services in the retail merchandise line of business and hence are eligible for excludable discounts on merchandise items.

A grandfather rule under the bill relaxes the line of business limitation in certain existing situations. If (1) on October 5, 1983, the employees of one member ("the first member") of an affiliated group (as defined in section 1504) were entitled to employee discounts at retail department stores operated by another member ("the second member") of the affiliated group, and (2) in the year for which the income and employment tax determination is being made, most of the sales of the affiliated group are attributable to the operation of retail department stores, then, for purposes of the exclusion for qualified employee discounts, the first member of the affiliated group is to be treated as engaged in the same line of business as the second member (the operator of the department stores). Thus, the employees of the first member may exclude qualified discounts received at the retail department stores operated by the second member. This rule does not operate in the reverse direction, however; that is, the employees of the department stores may not exclude any discounts received on property or services offered by the other member of the affiliated group, whether or not such discounts were allowed on October 5, 1983.

Definition of employee

The bill provides that, with respect to a line of business of an employer, the term employee means (1) an individual who is currently employed by the employer in that line of business; (2) an individual who separated from service with the employer in that line of business by reason of retirement or disability; and (3) a widow or widower of an individual who died while employed by the employer in that line of business or of an individual who had separated from service with the employer in that line of business by reason of retirement or disability. The bill also provides that any use (e.g., of discounted goods) by the spouse or a dependent child of the employee (as defined) is to be treated as use by the employee.[10] These definitions are relevant both for purposes of eligibility for the exclusion under the bill and for purposes of defining nonemployee customers.

Amount of exclusion

General rule.—Under the bill, an employee discount is excluded only up to a specified limit. In the case of merchandise, the excludable amount of the discount is limited to the selling price of the merchandise, multiplied by the employer's gross profit percentage. The discount exclusion for a service may not exceed 20 percent of the selling price, regardless of the actual gross profit percentage.

Merchandise.—In the case of merchandise, the excludable amount of the discount may not exceed the selling price of the merchandise, multiplied by the employer's gross profit percentage. For this purpose, the employer's gross profit percentage for a period means the excess of the aggregate sales price for the period of merchandise sold by the employer in the relevant line of business over the aggregate cost of such merchandise to the employer, then divided by the aggregate sales price.

For example, if total sales of such merchandise during a year were $1,000,000 and the employer's cost for the merchandise was $600,000, then the gross profit percentage for the year is 40 percent ($1,000,000 minus $600,000 equals 40 percent of $1,000,000). Thus, an employee discount with respect to such merchandise is excluded from income to the extent it does not exceed 40 percent of the selling price of the merchandise to nonemployee customers. If in this case the discount allowed to the employee exceeds 40 percent (for example, 50 percent), the excess discount on a purchase (10 percent in the example) is included in the employee's gross income.[11]

For the purposes of determining the employer's profit percentage, cost is to be computed by the employer in the same manner as it is for computing the employer's Federal income tax liability, under the inventory rules in Code section 471 and the regulations thereunder. Thus, for example, a retailer is to use the "retail method" of pricing inventories under Treas. Reg. sec. 1.471-8 in computing cost for purposes of the gross profit percentage discount limitation if that is the method used by the employer to value inventories for income tax purposes.

The bill provides that an employer may compute the gross profit percentage on the basis of all merchandise held for sale to customers (including employee customers) in the employer's line of business in which the employee works. As an alternative, the employer may select any reasonable classification of such merchandise for the computation. For example, a retail department store business may compute a gross profit percentage for the store business as a whole, or may compute different gross profit percentages for different departments or types of merchandise (high markup items versus low markup items), provided such classifications are made on a reasonable basis. Under either computation method, the determination of the gross profit percentage is to be made on the basis of the employer's experience during a representative period, such as the prior year.

Services.—The discount exclusion for a service is limited to 20 percent of the selling price of the service; there is no profit percentage limitation. The selling price is the price at which the service is provided in the ordinary course of business to customers who are not employees.[12]

Selling price.—Regulations under section 61 for the valuation of nonexcluded discounts provided to employees are to provide that if, in a line of business, a discounted price is, in effect, the price at which a product or service is offered to the public because a discount is regularly provided by the employer in the

---

[9] The term "employee discount" is defined in the bill as the amount by which the price at which the good or service is provided to the employee by the employer is less than the price at which such good or service is being offered by the employer to customers who are not employees.

[10] For this purpose, dependent child means any child (as defined in Code sec. 151(e)(3)) of the employee who is a dependent of the employee or both of whose parents have died. A child of divorced, etc., parents to whom section 152(e) applies is treated as a dependent of both parents.

[11] This result occurs because the amount included in gross income as gross income attributable to a discount sale, under section 61, is the difference between fair market value and the price the employee pays for the merchandise. Since the fair market value of merchandise when sold to employees is the price at which the merchandise is being offered by the employer to customers who are not employees, the 50-percent discount in the example is included in gross income. Under the bill, a discount of 40 percent is excluded from gross income. The net result is that 10 percent of the selling price is included in the employee's gross income.

[12] For purposes of this provision, an insurance policy is considered a service. Thus, an exclusion is allowed for up to 20 percent of the price of the policy. This exclusion does not apply to loans given by financial institutions to their employees at a discounted rate of interest.

ordinary course of business through arrangements negotiated with large groups of consumers (e.g., to all members of professional associations) and substantial sales are made at a discount under these agreements, then the fair market value of the discounted products or services is to be measured by reference to the regularly discounted group selling price. In such a case, the regularly discounted group selling price also is to be used to compute the limit on the exclusion for qualified employee discounts on services, for example, so that an employee includes amounts in income on a purchase of services at a discount only to the extent that the price charged to the employee was less than 80 percent of the discounted group selling price.

Leased sections of department stores

In cases in which a department store leases floor space to another employer (such as a cosmetics firm), and employees of the lessee engage in over-the-counter sales of merchandise which appear to the public to be made by department store employees, then, for purposes of the exclusion in the bill for qualified employee discounts, the leased section is treated as part of the line of business of the employer operating the department store, and the employees of the lessee who are in the leased section are treated as employees of the department store. Thus, even if such individuals selling cosmetics on the department store floor are actually employees of the cosmetic company rather than of the store, they are considered employees of the department store for purposes of the exclusion for qualified employee discounts. Accordingly, if these individuals in the leased section receive from the store a qualified discount on their purchases of goods in the store other than cosmetics, the amount of the discount (subject to the profit percentage limitation) is excluded from income. (Of course, the exclusion is not available to other employees of the cosmetics firm who do not engage in over-the-counter sales in the leased section of the store.) Likewise, because the cosmetic section itself is considered part of the department store line of business, any qualified discount allowed to department store employees by the cosmetics firm to purchase cosmetics in the leased section is excluded (subject to the profit percentage limitation).

Working Condition Fringe

General rules

Under the bill, the fair market value of any property or services provided to an employee of the employer is excluded for income and employment tax purposes to the extent that the costs of the property or services would be deductible as ordinary and necessary business expenses (under Code secs. 162 or 167) if the employee had paid for such property or services. The nondiscrimination rules applicable to certain other provisions of Title V of the bill do not apply as a condition fringe, except for employee parking (as described below).

Examples

By way of illustration, the value of use by an employee of a company car or airplane for business purposes is excluded as a working condition fringe. (However, use of a company car or plane for personal purposes is not excludable. Merely incidental personal use of a company car, such as a small detour for a personal errand, might qualify for exclusion as a de minimis fringe.) As another example, assume the employer subscribes to business periodicals for an employee (e.g., a brokerage house buys a financial publication for its brokers). In that case, the fair market value of the subscriptions is an excluded working condition fringe, since the expense could have been deducted as a business expense if the employee had directly paid for the subscription.

Examples of other benefits excluded as working condition fringes are those provided by an employer primarily for the safety of its employees, if such safety precautions are considered ordinary and necessary business expenses. For example, if for security reasons the U.S. Government or a private business provides a bodyguard or car and driver to an employee, the value of the bodyguard or use of the car and driver is treated as a working condition fringe and hence is not includible in income of the employee. Other examples of excluded working condition fringes are employer expenditures for on-the-job training or travel by an employee if such expenditures meet the present-law requirements for deductibility under section 162.

In contrast, assume that an employer agrees to pay the real estate broker's commission on the sale of an employee's house to assist the employee in moving to another job site for the employer. The payment of the commission by the employer is not excludable as a working condition fringe, because direct payment of the commission expense by the employee would not be deductible by the employee as a section 162 business expense.[13]

The fair market value of the use of consumer goods which are manufactured for sale to nonemployee customers and which are provided to employees for product testing and evaluation outside the employer's office is excluded as a working condition fringe only if (1) consumer testing and evaluation of the product is an ordinary and necessary business expense of the employer, (2) business reasons necessitate that the testing and evaluation be performed off-premises by employees (i.e., the testing and evaluation cannot be carried out adequately in the employer's office or in laboratory testing facilities), (3) the item is furnished to the employee for purposes of testing and evaluation, (4) the item is made available to the employee for no longer than necessary to test and evaluate its performance, and the item must be returned to the employer at completion of the testing and evaluation period, (5) the employer imposes limitations on the employee's use of the item which significantly reduce the value of any personal benefit to the employee, and (6) the employee must submit detailed reports to the employer on the testing and evaluation. The fifth requirement above is satisfied, for example, if (i) the employer places limitations on the employee's ability to select among different models or varieties of the consumer product which is furnished for testing and evaluation purposes, (ii) the employer's policy provides for the employee, in appropriate cases, to purchase or lease at his or her own expense the same type of item as that being tested (so that personal use by the employee's family will be limited), and (iii) the employer requires that members of the employee's family generally cannot use the item. If products are furnished under a testing and evaluation program only to officers, owners, or highly compensated employees, this fact may be considered in a determination of whether the goods are furnished for testing and evaluation purposes or for compensation purposes, unless the employer can show a business reason for the classification of employees to whom the products are furnished (e.g., that automobiles are furnished for testing and evaluation by an automobile manufacturing company to its design engineers and supervisory mechanics.)

Employee parking

Under a special rule in the bill, the fair market value of free or reduced-cost parking provided to an employee on or near the business premises of the employer is excludable as a working condition fringe. For officers, owners, or highly compensated employees, however, this exclusion applies only if such parking is available on a nondiscriminatory basis (see description below of the nondiscrimination rules of the bill).

Demonstration use by auto salespersons

Under a special rule, the fair market value of any use of an employer-provided automobile by an automobile salesperson in the geographic sales area in which the dealer's sales office is located is an excludable working condition fringe if (1) such use of the car is provided primarily for the purpose of facilitating the salesperson's performance of services for the employer, and (2) there are substantial restrictions on the personal use of the car by the salesperson. For example, if an auto salesperson is required to have a car available for showing to customers during working hours, is required to drive the make of car which the auto dealer sells, is limited in the amount of miles he or she may drive the auto, may not store personal possessions in the auto, and is prohibited from using the car for vacation trips, then use of the car in the sales area qualifies for the exclusion under the bill.

De Minimis Fringe

General rules

Under the bill, if the fair market value of any property or a service that otherwise would be a fringe benefit includible in gross income is so small that accounting for the property or service would be unreasonable or administratively impracticable, the value is excluded for income and employment tax purposes. The nondiscrimination rules applicable to certain other provisions of the bill do not apply as a condition for exclusion of property or a service as a de minimis fringe, except for subsidized eating facilities (as described below).

In determining whether the de minimis exlusion applies, the fair market values of all property or services provided to an individual during a calendar year are to be aggregated, *except* for (1) property or services that are excluded from taxation under another specific statutory exclusion provision of the Code, as amended by this bill (such as health benefits or qualified employee discounts) and (2) any nonexcluded property or service provided for the employee that (without regard to the aggregation rule) does not qualify as a de minimis fringe because the value of the individual item is too large.

To illustrate, benefits which generally are excluded from income and employment taxes as de minimis fringes (without regard to the aggregation rule) include the typing of personal letters by a company secretary, occasional personal use of the company copying machine, monthly transit passes provided at a discount not exceeding $15, occasional company cocktail parties or picnics for employees, occasional supper money or taxi fare because of overtime work, traditional holiday gifts of property with a low fair market value, occasional theatre or sporting event tickets, and coffee and doughnuts furnished to employees.

Subsidized eating facilities

If an employer provides and operates an eating facility for its employees on or near the employer's business premises and if revenue derived from the facility normally equals or exceeds the direct operating costs of the facility, the excess of the value of the meals over the fees charged to employees is excluded under the bill if the nondiscrimination rules (see description below) are satisfied. (Free meals provided on an employer's premises to employees for the convenience of the employer are excludable from income to the extent provided by present-law section 119, which is not amended by this bill.) While the benefits provided to a particular employee who eats regularly at such a facility may not qualify as a de minimis fringe absent this rule, the recordkeeping difficulties involved in identifying which employees ate which meals on particular days, as well as the values and costs for each such meal, led the committee to conclude that a general exclusion should be provided for subsidized eating facilities as defined in the bill.

* * *

[13] A portion of this amount might be deductible, however, as a moving expense under Code section 217.

Athletic Facilities

In general, the fair market value of any on-premises athletic facility provided and operated by an employer for its employees, where substantially all the use of the facility is by employees of the employer (or their spouses or dependent children[14]), is excluded under the bill for income and employment tax purposes. The athletic facility need not be in the same location as the business premises of the employer, but must be located on premises of the employer and may not be a facility for residential use. Examples of athletic facilities are swimming pools, gyms, tennis courts, and golf courses.

The exclusion for certain employer-provided athletic facilities does not apply to the providing of memberships in a country club or similar facility unless the facility itself is owned and operated by the employer and satisfies the employee-use and other requirements for the exclusion. Thus where no exclusion is available under this provision, the fair market value of such country club membership is includible in the income of the employee who is provided with membership, and is deductible to the extent permitted by present-law sections 162 and 274.

A nondiscrimination requirement is not provided in the bill as a condition for this exclusion, because present law (Code sec. 274) denies a deduction to the employer for costs attributable to a facility which is primarily for the benefit of officers, owners, or highly compensated employees.

Nondiscrimination Rules

To qualify under the bill for the exclusions for no-additional-cost services, qualified employee discounts, employee parking or eating facilities, or qualified tuition reductions, the benefit must be available on substantially the same terms to each member of a group of employees which is defined under a reasonable classification set up by the employer that does not discriminate in favor of officers, owners, or highly compensated employees (the "highly compensated group"). If the availability of the fringe benefit does not satisfy this nondiscrimination test, the exclusion applies only to those employees (if any) who receive the benefit and who are not members of the highly compensated group. For example, if an employer offers a 20-percent discount (which otherwise satisfies the requirements for a qualified employee discount) to rank-and-file employees and a 35-percent discount to the highly compensated group, the entire value of the 35-percent discount (not just the excess over 20 percent) is includible in gross income and wages of the members of the highly compensated group who make purchases at a discount.

The determination of whether a particular classification is reasonable depends on the facts and circumstances involved. A classification that, on its face, makes benefits available only to officers, owners, or highly compensated employees is per se discriminatory, and no exclusion is available to the highly compensated group members for the value of such benefits. On the other hand, an employer could establish a classification that is based on certain appropriate factors, such as seniority, full-time vs. part-time employment, or job description, provided that the effect of the classification is nondiscriminatory. Under a special rule, availability of a tuition reduction benefit only to those employees of an education organization who are faculty members is not a discriminatory classification. A determination that a classification is reasonable for purposes of applying the nondiscrimination rules of this bill is not to be taken as an indicator as to whether or not the classification is reasonable for purposes of applying other nondiscrimination rules in the Code, such as the rules in section 401(a)(4) for qualified plans.

Thus, for example, if an employer makes free or reduced-cost parking available to all its employees according to seniority or on a "first-come, first-served" basis, and if those employees who obtain parking constitute a fair cross-section of all employees, then the fair market value of the parking provided is excluded under the bill. A preferential assignment to highly compensated group members of parking space when made for legitimate business reasons (such as a need to use their cars for sales trips or plant inspections during the work day) does not itself violate the nondiscrimination rule, provided that any remaining parking spaces are available to employees on a nondiscriminatory basis. Further, in a situation where parking space is made available on a nondiscriminatory basis, the assignment of particular locations within the parking facility does not have to be made on a nondiscriminatory basis. On the other hand, if an employer provides free or reduced-cost parking only to highly compensated employees without legitimate business reasons, the fair market value of the parking is not excluded for those highly compensated employees.

Another example of a fringe benefit which the nondiscrimination requirement applies is the provision by retail stores of discounts to employees and their families. Suppose that a store makes this benefit available only to executives and salespersons, but not to employees in other categories, such as clerical and maintenance. To determine whether such a classification would be discriminatory in this particular case, all employees of the store would be divided into categories according to their level of compensation. If the number of the most highly compensated employees to whom the benefit is available, as a proportion of all employees in that category, were not substantially higher than the corresponding proportions for the remaining categories of employees, then the classification would not be considered to be one that discriminated in favor of the highly compensated.

For purposes of the nondiscrimination rule, the determination of which employees are highly compensated would depend on the facts and circumstances of the case, but could rely on Treasury Department guidelines. Examples of such guidelines could be that employees with compensation above, for example, a specific percentile in the employer's compensation distribution or above, for example, a specific annual rate, or both, are to be treated as highly compensated. Such guidelines could vary by industry and could reflect unique characteristics of particular employers or particular industry categories of employment. The committee intends that, insofar as practicable, the Internal Revenue Service is to issue advance determinations as to whether the nondiscrimination requirements of the bill are met in the case of employers, such as nonprofit organizations, to which similar requirements in other sections of the Code have not frequently been applied.

The nondiscrimination rules do not apply to a working condition fringe (other than parking) or a de minimis fringe (other than subsidized eating facilities). For example, if an employer for valid business reasons makes a bodyguard available only to its executives, the working fringe exclusion applies even though the availability of the benefit would not satisfy the nondiscrimination rules of the bill.

Other Rules

Definition of employer

For purposes of new Code section 132, all employees of all corporations that are members of a controlled group of corporations (within the meaning of Code sec. 44(b)), all employees of all trades or businesses (whether or not incorporated) under common control (sec. 414(c)), or all employees of an affiliated service group (sec. 414(m)) are treated as employed by a single employer. Consequently, if a chain of retail hardware stores separately incorporates each hardware store as a wholly owned subsidiary of one corporation, the employees of one subsidiary may receive qualified employee discounts from stores operated by the other subsidiaries (since all such hardware stores are in the same line of business). Similarly, the nondiscrimination rules are applied under the bill by aggregating related employers, but without aggregating related employees in different lines of business (as defined above in the descriptions of the exclusions for no-additional-cost services and qualified employee discounts).

Under the bill, the aggregation of commonly controlled, etc., employers does not change the other requirements for exclusion. For example, if a controlled group of corporations consists of two corporations whose products are in different industry groups, they are not considered as consisting of a single line of business even though treated as one employer. Thus, for example, a qualified employee discount received from a related employer is excludable only if that employer is engaged in the same line of business as that in which the employee works.

Nonapplicability to certain fringe benefits

A benefit is not excludable under new Code section 132 (except pursuant to the exclusion for de minimis benefits) if another section of the Internal Revenue Code provides rules for the tax treatment of that general type of benefit. For example, the fair market value of day care services provided to an employee is excludable only pursuant to the provisions of Code section 129. If in a particular situation such services do not qualify for exclusion under section 129 (e.g., because the nondiscrimination requirements of that section are not met), no exclusion is available under the bill (other than the de minimis exclusion).

Correspondingly, the provisions of section 132 do not modify any present-law statutory exclusions (except to the extent that the bill modifies the definition of cafeteria plans under sec. 125). For example, Code section 119 excludes from the gross income of an employee the value of meals furnished on the employer's business premises for the convenience of the employer. Under Treasury regulations, meals provided free of charge are treated as furnished for the employer's convenience if the meals are furnished for a substantial noncompensatory business reason of the employer. For example, on-premises meals satisfy this requirement if furnished so that the employee is available for emergency calls during meal periods, if employees are restricted to a short meal period which precludes eating out, or if there are insufficient eating facilities in the vicinity (Treas. Reg. sec. 1.119-1(a)). The bill does not affect the present-law exclusion provisions of section 119.

Cafeteria Plans

The bill amends the definition of cafeteria plans for purposes of Code section 125 to provide that such plans may offer employees choices only among cash or those fringe benefits (other than scholarships or fellowships, educational assistance, vanpooling, and those benefits excludable under provisions of the bill) that are excludable from gross income under a specific section of the Internal Revenue Code.

For this purpose, group-term life insurance that is includible in income only because the amount of the insurance exceeds $50,000 or because the insurance is on the life of the employee's spouse or children is treated as a nontaxable benefit. With respect to vacation days offered under a cafeteria plan, vacation days which cannot be used or cashed out in a later calendar or plan year also are to be treated as a nontaxable benefit. However, vacation days which may be used or cashed out in a later year are to be treated as deferred compensation which may not be offered under a cafeteria plan.

---

[14] See note 6, *supra*.

Treasury Regulations

Treasury regulations are to be issued to implement the provisions of this bill. Such regulations must be consistent with the language of the bill and with the legislative history (as reflected, in part, in the committee reports on the bill). Thus, any example of a fringe benefit which the reports state is excluded under the bill from income and wages must be so treated in the regulations.

Any fringe benefit that does not qualify for exclusion under the bill (for example, free or discounted goods or services that are made available by the employer only to corporate officers) or under another specific statutory fringe benefit provision is includible in gross income (under Code sections 61 and 83) for income tax purposes, and subject to income tax withholding, FICA, and FUTA, at the excess of its fair market value over any amount paid by the employee for the benefit. For purposes of assisting both taxpayers and the IRS, the Treasury is to issue regulations setting forth appropriate and helpful rules for the valuation of taxable fringe benefits, and coordinating the applications of sections 61 and 83.

The committee notes that noncash remuneration generally is already subject to FICA, FUTA, and income tax withholding under present law. It is intended that, in the absence of a specific statutory provision to the contrary, the regulations under these provisions are to be revised to make clear that remuneration for employment should not be exempt from these employment taxes merely because the remuneration is paid in the form of property or services rather than cash. Since the statutory term "remuneration" is to be interpreted broadly to include compensation for services which have been performed, noncash benefits (such as allowances for meals when the employee is not away from home overnight) which are not excluded under the provisions of this bill or other statutory provisions are to be subject to these employment taxes. This broad interpretation of remuneration is especially important in the case of FICA, for which withholding is generally the only collection method available. In providing guidance to employers concerning the time at which noncash remuneration is considered to be paid by the employer and thus subject to employment taxes, the regulations are to allow sufficient flexibility to minimize administrative problems which employers may have in complying with the law.

The committee understands that under established practices in certain industries, employers may make available to employees damaged, distressed, or returned goods at a price which equals or exceeds the fair market value of such items but which may be less than the cost to the employer of the items before being damaged, etc. In such situations, no amount is to be includible in the employee's income where the purchase price paid by the employee equals or exceeds the fair market value of the item.

Under existing Code provisions and section 61 regulations benefits to military personnel such as subsistence, housing, and uniform allowances are excludable from income (see Treas. Reg. sec. 1.61-2(b)). This bill does not make any change in existing excludable military benefits. Thus, for example, the value of discounts at military commissaries is to be considered as provision of subsistence under existing regulations and fully excludable without regard to the bill.

Effective Date

The provisions of the bill generally take effect on January 1, 1984, except that the exclusion for qualified tuition reductions (sec. 503 of the bill) applies with respect to education furnished after June 30, 1984.

* * *

Explanation of Provisions

Moratorium on fringe benefit regulations generally

The bill extends the legislative moratorium on issuance of fringe benefits regulations through December 31, 1985.

Under the bill, the Treasury Department (Internal Revenue Service) is prohibited from issuing prior to January 1, 1986 final regulations, under Code section 61, relating to the income tax treatment of nonstatutory fringe benefits. In addition, no regulations relating to the treatment of nonstatutory fringe benefits under section 61 are to be proposed which would be effective prior to January 1, 1986.

Although the provision of the bill relates only to the issuance of regulations, it is the intent of the Congress that the Treasury Department (Internal Revenue Service) will not in any significant way alter, or deviate from, the historical income-tax treatment of traditional nonstatutory fringe benefits through the issuance of revenue rulings or revenue procedures, etc. The bill does not prevent the Treasury or Revenue Service from continuing to study the question of the appropriate tax treatment of nonstatutory fringe benefits.

Faculty housing

Under the bill, the extended legislative moratorium is applied to prohibit the issuance of income tax regulations providing for the inclusion in gross income of the excess of the fair market value of qualified campus lodging over the greater of the operating costs paid in furnishing the lodging or the rent received. The term qualified campus lodging means lodging furnished by an educational institution (within the meaning of sec. 170(b)(1)(A)(ii))[2] to any employee of the educational institution (or to the employee's spouse or dependents), including non-faculty employees. The bill applies only if the employer-furnished lodging is located on a campus of, or in close proximity to, the educational institution. Under the bill, the moratorium does not apply with respect to any amount of the value of lodging if such amount was treated as wages or included in income when furnished.

Effective Date

The general extension of the legislative moratorium is effective on enactment. The application of the extended moratorium with respect to qualified campus lodging applies with respect to lodging furnished after December 31, 1983 and before January 1, 1986.

* * *

[Conference Committee Report]

* * *

General rules

The conference agreement follows the House bill, with modifications to the effective date and certain provisions as described below. Thus, under the conference agreement, the general legislative moratorium on regulations that expired December 31, 1983 is not extended. Instead, the conference agreement sets forth statutory provisions under which (1) certain fringe benefits provided by an employer are excluded from the recipient employee's gross income for Federal income tax purposes and from the wage base (and, if applicable, the benefit base) for purposes of income tax withholding. FICA, FUTA, and RRTA, and (2) any fringe benefit that does not qualify for exclusion under the bill and that is not excluded under another statutory fringe benefit provision of the Code is includible in gross income for income tax purposes, and in wages for employment tax purposes, at the excess of its fair market value over any amount paid by the employee for the beneifit. The latter rule is confirmed by clarifying amendments to Code sections 61(a), 3121(a), 3306(b), and 3401(a) and section 209 of the Social Security Act.

The conferees intend that Treasury regulations are to be issued to implement the statutory fringe benefit provisions of the bill. Such regulations are to be consistent with the language of the bill in the legislative history as reflected in House Report No. 98-432 (Pt. 2) and this Statement of Managers. Thus, for example, as stated in the report of the Ways and Means Committee, the bill does not modify the existing rules under which benefits to military personnel, such as subsistence, housing, and uniform allowances, are excludable from gross income.

The conference agreement adds a rule giving the Treasury Department regulatory authority to provide the time and manner for collection (or payment) by an employer of employment taxes on noncash fringe benefits. To the maximum extent practicable, such regulations may provide for collection (or payment) of FICA taxes under sections 3101 and 3111 with respect to noncash fringe benefits in a calendar quarter not later than the time for collection (or payment) of such taxes on cash wages paid on the last day of that quarter. The regulations may provide similar rules for other employment taxes.

Exclusions

No-additional-cost-services; qualified employee discounts

The conference agreement provides an additional, elective grandfather rule which in certain circumstances relaxes the line of business limitation requirement for the exclusion for qualified employee discounts and (to the extent described below) for the exclusion for no-additional-cost services.

Under this grandfather rule, if all the following requirements are met, the exclusion for qualified employee discounts (if otherwise available) extends to the providing by an employer of discounts on goods or services in a particular line of business to an employee who works in a different line of business of the employer than that line of business in which such goods or services on which the discount is available are offered for sale by the employer.

(1) On and after January 1, 1984, the employer offers such discounts on goods or services in that particular line of business to substantially all its employees in all of its lines of business which existed on January 1, 1984;

(2) The employee works in a line of business of the employer which was a line of business of the employer on January 1, 1984; and

(3) The employer timely elects the applicability of this grandfather rule.

This grandfather rule also applies, if requirements of the same nature are met, with respect to no-additional-cost services which are provided by an employer to an employee notwithstanding that the service is not the same type of service sold to the public in the line of business of the employer in which the employee works, except that this grandfather rule does not apply with respect to no-additional-cost services provided to the employee by a person other than an employer of the employee (i.e., pursuant to a reciprocal agreement between employers).

Thus, where all these requirements are met, all employees of any line of business of the employer which was in existence on January 1, 1984 are treated,

[2] An educational organization is described in sec. 170(b)(1)(A)(ii) "if its primary function is the presentation of formal instruction and it normally maintains a regular faculty and curriculum and normally has a regularly enrolled body of pupils or students in attendance at the place where its educational activities are regularly carried on. The term includes institutions such as primary, secondary, preparatory, or high schools, and colleges and universities," and includes both public and private schools (Treas. Reg. sec. 1.170A-9(b)(1)).

for purposes of new Code sections 132(a)(1) and 132(a)(2) but not for purposes of new Code section 132(g)(2), as employees of the particular line of business (which was in existence on January 1, 1984) in which such goods or services are offered for sale by the employer.

This additional grandfather rule applies on a calendar year basis. If elected, the rule applies to the first calendar year following the year of election and to all subsequent years unless revoked by the employer. A revocation must be made prior to the beginning of the calendar year to which the grandfather rule is not to apply. The election is to be made in the manner prescribed by Treasury regulations. For purposes of the grandfather rule, all members of the same affiliated group of corporations (as defined in sec. 1504) are treated as one corporation.

Under the conference agreement, an employer making the election is subject to an excess fringe benefit excise tax for any calendar year as to which the grandfather rule election is in effect if the aggregate fair market value of all excludable no-additional-cost service benefits and qualified employee discount benefits (whether or not excludable only pursuant to the grandfather rule) provided by the employer during the calendar year to all its employees exceeds one percent of the total of all taxable compensation paid to all employees of the employer for the year. This computation takes into account all employees in all lines of business of the employer, including lines of business as to which the elected grandfather rule does not apply (e.g., where the line of business did not exist on January 1, 1984). The rate of the new excise tax is 30 percent of the excess described in the preceding sentences. The amount of tax is not deductible by the employer.

In addition, the conference agreement modifies the grandfather rule in the House bill to provide a revised definition of an affiliated group for such purposes.

Working condition fringe

The following modifications are made by the conference agreement with respect to working condition fringes:

(1) The nondiscrimination requirement in the House bill for the exclusion (as a working condition fringe) of employee parking provided on or near the business premises of the employer is deleted;

(2) The availability of the exclusion of qualified auto demonstration use (as a working condition fringe) is limited to full-time auto salespersons. The exclusion is not available to any other persons, such as part-time auto salespersons, mechanics, the dealer's bookkeeper, etc.; and

(3) The availability of the working condition fringe exclusion for certain consumer product testing and evaluation as described in the report of the Ways and Means Committee is clarified by providing that gross income does not include personal use of such consumer goods provided to an employee primarily for such product testing and evaluation which does not qualify under the requirements in such report to the extent that the employee pays or reimburses the employer for such personal use.

De minimis fringe

In lieu of the aggregation rule in the House bill, the conference agreement provides that the frequency with which similar fringe benefits (otherwise excludable as de minimis fringes) are provided by the employer to its employees is to be taken into account, among other relevant factors, in determining whether the fair market value of the property or service is so small that accounting for the property or service would be unreasonable or administratively impracticable. Under this rule, where an employer exercises sufficient control and imposes significant restrictions over personal use of a copying machine such that substantially all (at least 85 percent) of the use of the machine can be shown to be for business purposes, the employer may treat as a de minimis fringe any personal use of the machine by a particular employee which might occur.

Nondiscrimination requirements

As stated above, the conference agreement deletes the nondiscrimination requirement for the exclusion of employee parking as a working condition fringe.

Faculty housing

The conference agreement generally follows the Senate amendment in imposing a moratorium on the issuance of income tax regulations providing for the inclusion in gross income of the excess of the fair market value of qualified campus lodging over the greater of the operating costs paid in furnishing the lodging or the rent received. This moratorium with respect to qualified campus lodging applies only with respect to lodging furnished after December 31, 1983 and before January 1, 1986. No inference is intended by imposition of a moratorium for such period as to the proper income tax treatment of faculty housing furnished prior to 1984 or after 1985.

Effective date

Under the conference agreement, the provisions are effective beginning January 1, 1985, except that the moratorium with respect to qualified campus lodging applies only with respect to lodging furnished after December 31, 1983 and before January 1, 1986.

* * *

Cafeteria plans

Present law

The cafeteria plan rules of the Code provide that a participant in a nondiscriminatory cafeteria plan will not be treated as having received a taxable benefit offered under the plan solely because the participant has the opportunity, before the benefit becomes available to the participant, to choose among the taxable and nontaxable benefits offered under the plan. The term "taxable benefit" includes cash, property, and other benefits that are currently taxable to the participant upon receipt. "Nontaxable benefit" includes any benefit that is not currently taxable to the participant upon receipt (e.g., group-term life insurance up to $50,000, coverage under an accident or health plan, and coverage under a dependent care assistance program).

Present law does not permit a cafeteria plan to offer either vanpooling or any benefit that defers the receipt of compensation, with the exception of the opportunity for participants to make elective contributions under a qualified cash or deferred arrangement.

The cafeteria plan rules generally do not affect whether any particular benefit offered under the plan is a taxable or nontaxable benefit. Thus, a benefit that is nontaxable under the Internal Revenue Code when offered separately is a nontaxable benefit under a cafeteria plan only if the rules providing for the exclusion of the benefit from gross income continue to be satisfied when the benefit is provided under the cafeteria plan.

On February 10, 1984, the Internal Revenue Service issued a news release (IR-84-22), which stated that so-called "flexible spending arrangements" offered as part of cafeteria plans do not provide employees with nontaxable benefits under the Code because, under such arrangements, employees are assured of receiving the benefit of what they would have received had not covered expenses been incurred.

In May 1984, the Internal Revenue Service issued proposed regulations with respect to the cafeteria plan rules and the statutory rules governing the exclusion of benefits from gross income. These proposed regulations state that an otherwise nontaxable benefit will be nontaxable if offered in a cafeteria plan only if it continues to satisfy the provisions governing its exclusion from gross income. Accordingly, the proposed regulations state that employer contributions with respect to an accident or health plan, a qualified group legal services plan, or a dependent care assistance program are not excluded from a participant's gross income under the Internal Revenue Code to the extent that the participant is assured of receiving benefits under the plan without regard to whether he or she incurs covered expenses.

* * *

Conference agreement

The conference agreement follows the House bill provisions on cafeteria plans, and adopts several additional provisions.

First, the conference agreement amends the cafeteria plan rules to provide that if, for a plan year, more than 25 percent of the total nontaxable benefits are provided to employees who are key employees with respect to the plan for such year (as determined under the rules of section 416(i)(1)), such key employees will be taxed as though they received all available taxable benefits under the plan. Generally, in determining the portion of the total nontaxable benefits that is provided to key employees, coverage under a plan (e.g., an accident or health plan) and not actual expense reimbursements under such a plan are to be counted.

Second, the conference agreement applies certain reporting requirements with respect to cafeteria plans. Under regulations prescribed by the Secretary of the Treasury, each employer that maintains a cafeteria plan during a taxable year beginning after December 31, 1984, will be required to file a return for such year showing the number of employees of the employer, the number of employees participating in the plan, the total cost of the plan for the taxable year, and specified employer identification information. Based on these general returns, the Secretary is to require a select and statistically significant group of employers to file additional information returns with respect to their cafeteria plans. These additional returns will contain such information as the Secretary may require. Examples of such information include a breakdown of the above information by salary range and type of benefit provided, as well as information which may be necessary to allow Treasury to develop a plan to insure that the requirements of the cafeteria plan rules (such as nondiscrimination and maximum percentage of benefits to key employees) are adequately enforced.

Third, the conference agreement provides both general and special transition relief, with respect to the proposed Treasury regulations on cafeteria plans, for cafeteria plans and "flexible spending arrangements" in existence on February 10, 1984. (A "flexible spending arrangement" consists of a benefit of a type to which a statutory exclusion may be applied, such as an accident or health plan under sections 105 and 106, with respect to which an employee is assured of receiving, in cash or some other benefit, amounts available for expense reimbursement without regard to whether the employee incurs the covered expenses.) The general relief rule provides that a plan will not fail to be a cafeteria plan merely because of a failure to satisfy the rules relating to cafeteria plans under the proposed Treasury regulations and that a flexible spending arrangement will not fail the requirements of the applicable statutory exclusions merely because of a failure to satisfy the rules relating to such exclusions under these regulations.

This general relief is provided until the earlier of January 1, 1985, or the effective date of any modification of the plan or arrangement to provide additional benefits if such modification becomes effective after February 10, 1984. The conference agreement does not prevent the application of the proposed Treasury regulations after the earlier of such dates.

Thus, for example, if on February 10, 1984, a flexible spending arrangement failed to satisfy the rules relating to accident or health plans under the proposed Treasury regulations and thereafter continues to fail such rules because such arrangement provides for the cash-out or carryover of unused amounts at the end of the plan year, such arrangment will be treated as qualifying as an accident or health plan until the earlier of the two dates provided above.

The general transition rule is applicable to both benefit bank flexible spending arrangements and zero balance reimbursement account (ZEBRA) type flexible spending arrangements. Under a benefit bank arrangement, the employee generally allocates a specified amount of dollars to a reimbursement account for specified benefits, e.g. medical, legal, and dependent care, at the beginning of the plan year. As expenses are incurred during the year, the employee is entitled to reimbursement of these expenses from the account. For example, if an employee with $500 allocated to his account incurred medical expenses of $250 he could be reimbursed for these expenses from the account. At the end of the year, he would receive the remaining $250 in cash. In contrast, under the ZEBRA-type arrangement, amounts generally are not specifically allocated to an account before the beginning of the year, but instead amounts are allocated only after an expense is incurred.

The conference agreement also provides special transition relief with respect to the rules contained in the proposed regulations relating to the statutory nontaxable benefits. This relief provision provides that a flexible spending arrangement in existence under a cafeteria plan on February 10, 1984, will not fail to be a nontaxable benefit under the applicable exclusions merely because a participant will receive amounts available but unused for expense reimbursement. An arrangement will qualify for the special relief only if, under the arrangement, the employee must fix the amount of contributions to be made on his or her behalf before the beginning of the applicable period of coverage and taxable cash is not available before the end of such period or, if earlier, at the termination of employment. In lieu of distributing taxable cash to a participant at the end of the applicable period of coverage, it would also be permissible for the unused amounts to be carried over to the succeeding year. Further, an arrangement could permit a participant to terminate contributions during the period of coverage or to change the rate or amount of contributions during the period of coverage on account of certain changes in family status or change in employment status from full-time to part-time, or vice versa. The conferees intend that this special transition relief will be available to arrangements that, on February 10, 1984, and thereafter, failed to satisfy these restrictions if such arrangments are modified, before January 1, 1985, to comply with such restrictions. The special relief under this rule is for benefits provided before the earlier of July 1, 1985, or the effective date of any modification of the arrangement to provide additional benefits if such modification becomes effective after February 10, 1984. The conference agreement does not prevent the application of the proposed Treasury regulations after the earlier of the applicable dates.

Cafeteria plans and flexible spending arrangments that were not in existence on February 10, 1984, generally do not qualify for either the general or the special transition rules under the conference agreement. Thus, the conference agreement does not prevent the current application of the proposed Treasury regulations to such plans and arrangements. However, plans that were not actually in existence as of February 10, 1984, but with respect to which substantial implementation costs have been incurred by the employer by such date are to be treated as having been in existence on such date. The conferees intend that if an employer has incurred, as of February 10, 1984, either more than $15,000 of implementation costs or more than one-half of the total costs of implementing a cafeteria plan, the transition rules are to be available with respect to the cafeteria plan. In making this determination, total implementation costs are the costs of designing and installing computer programs for operation of the plan and the costs of printing cafeteria plan brochures for employees. Costs associated with more than one plan of the same employer are to be allocated among the plans on the basis of the number of participants in the plans.

Finally, the conference agreement provides that the Secretary of Health and Human Services, in cooperation with the Secretary of the Treasury, is to submit a report to the House Committee on Ways and Means and the Senate Committee on Finance on the effect of cafeteria plans on the containment of health costs. This report is to be submitted by April 1, 1985. The study is to examine the impact which the use of cafeteria plans (including flexible spending arrangements) has on the containment of health care costs and to recommend what modifications might be desirable with respect to the cafeteria plan rules to optimize the potential to reduce medical costs while balancing against other health care policy goals. Included within the study should be an analysis of the advisability of establishing Federal guidelines relative to the type of medical plans that can qualify for cafeteria plan treatment in a manner similar to that applicable to qualified pensions plans and the advisability of adding additional benefits to cafeteria plans. In this regard, the conferees intend to examine, before January 1, 1986, the operation of the nondiscrimination rules and the forfeitability requirements with respect to cafeteria plans, and the effect of such provisions on the Federal tax base and on health cost containment.

[Code Sec. 151]

[¶ 11,290.08]

Committee Report on P.L. 104-188 (Small Business Job Protection Act)

Revenue Offsets

[Managers' Amendment to H.R. 3448]

Apply mathematical or clerical error procedures for dependency exemptions and filing status when correct TINs not provided

If an individual fails to provide a correct TIN for a dependent, the IRS would be authorized to deny the dependency exemption. Such a change would also have indirect consequences for other tax benefits currently conditioned on being able to claim a dependency exemption (e.g., head of household filing status and the dependent care credit). In addition, the failure to provide a correct TIN for a dependent would be treated as a mathematical or clerical error and thus any notification that the taxpayer owes additional tax because of that failure would not be treated as a notice of deficiency.

Effective Date

The amendment would be effective for tax returns for which the due date (without regard to extensions) is 30 days or more after the date of enactment. For taxable years beginning in 1995, no requirement to obtain a TIN would apply in the case of dependents born after October 31, 1995. For taxable years beginning in 1996, no requirement to obtain a TIN would apply in the case of dependents born after November 30, 1996.

[Conference Committee Report]

The conference agreement follows the Senate amendment.

[¶ 11,290.09]

Committee Report on P.L. 95-600 (Revenue Act of 1978)

Sec. 102—Increased personal exemptions

[Conference Committee Report]

House bill

Under present law, the amount of the personal exemption is $750 for the taxpayer, his or her spouse, and each dependent whose gross income is less than $750 (unless the dependent is the taxpayer's child and is either under age 19 or a student). An additional exemption is provided for a taxpayer who is blind or age 65 or over. Present law also provides a general tax credit, which is the larger of $35 per exemption or 2 percent of the first $9,000 of taxable income (in excess of the zero bracket amount), with a maximum credit of $180. The credit is scheduled to expire at the end of 1978.

The House bill provides a permanent increase in the personal exemption from $750 to $1,000, and increases the gross income limit for a dependent from $750 to $1,000. The general tax credit is allowed to expire at the end of 1978. The increase in the personal exemption is effective for taxable years beginning after December 31, 1978. The general tax credit will no longer apply for taxable years ending after December 31, 1978.

Senate amendment

The Senate amendment is the same as the House bill.

Conference agreement

The conference agreement follows the House bill and Senate amendment.

[Code Sec. 152]

[¶ 11,295.08]

Committee Report on P.L. 109-135 (Gulf Opportunity Zone Act of 2005)

[Joint Committee on Taxation]

Technical Corrections

[Amendment Related to the Working Families Tax Relief Act of 2004 (P.L. 108-311)]

Uniform definition of child (Act Secs. 201, 203 and 207).—The provision makes conforming amendments, consistent with those enacted with respect to various other provisions, for purposes of health savings accounts, the dependent care credit, and dependent care assistance programs. Under the conforming amendments, an individual may qualify as a dependent for these limited purposes without regard to whether the individual has gross income that exceeds an otherwise applicable gross income limitation or is married and files a joint return. In addition, such an individual who is treated as a dependent under these conforming amendment provisions is not subject to the general rule that a dependent of a taxpayer shall be treated as having no dependents for the taxable year of such individual beginning in such calendar year.

The provision clarifies Code section 152(e) to permit a divorced or legally separated custodial parent to waive, by written declaration, his or her right to claim a child as a dependent for purposes of the dependency exemption and child credit (but not with respect to other childrelated tax benefits). By means of the waiver, the noncustodial parent is granted the right to claim the child as a dependent for these purposes. The provision clarifies that the waiver rules under the uniform definition of qualifying child operate as under prior law.

[Code Sec. 162]

[¶ 11,300.06]

Committee Reports on P.L. 104-191 (Health Insurance Portability and Accountability Act)

Health Insurance Costs for Self-Employed Individuals.

[Conference Committee Report]

The conference agreement increases the deduction for health insurance of self-employed individuals as follows: the deduction would be 40 percent in 1997; 45 percent in 1998 through 2002, 50 percent in 2003; 60 percent in 2004, 70 percent in 2005; and 80 percent in 2006 and thereafter.

The conference agreement also provides that payments for personal injury or sickness through and arrangements having the effect of accident or health insurance (and that are not merely reimbursement arrangements) are excludable from income. In order for the exclusion to apply, the arrangement must be insurance (e.g., there must be adequate risk shifting). This provision equalizes the treatment of payments under commercial insurance and arrangements other than commercial insurance that have the effect of insurance. Under this provision, a self-employed individual who receives payments from such an arrangement could exclude the payments from income.

Effective Date

The provision is effective for taxable years beginning after December 31, 1996. No inference is intended with respect to the excludability of payments under arrangements having the effect of accident or health insurance under present law.

[¶ 11,300.065]

Committee Reports on P.L. 103-66 (Omnibus Budget Reconciliation Act of 1993)

[*Self-employed individuals—Health insurance deduction*]

The 25-percent deduction is extended retroactively from July 1, 1992, through December 31, 1993. In addition, the bill provides that the determination of whether a self-employed individual or his or her spouse are eligible for employer-paid health benefits is made on a monthly basis.

Effective Date

The provision is effective for taxable years ending after June 30, 1992.

[*Noncomplying group health plans*]

[Conference Committee Report]

In general, the conference agreement disallows employer deductions for any amounts paid or incurred in connection with a group health plan (including amounts reimbursed through a voluntary employees' beneficiary association (VEBA)) if the plan fails to reimburse hospitals for inpatient services provided in the state of New York at the same rate that licensed commercial insurers are required to reimburse hospitals for inpatient services for individuals not covered by a group health plan. For purposes of this provision, a licensed commercial insurer is a commercial insurer licensed to do business in the state of New York and authorized to write accident and health insurance, and whose policies provide inpatient hospital coverage on an expense incurred basis. Blue Cross and Blue Shield is not a licensed commercial insurer for this purpose.

If a group health plan provides inpatient hospital services through a health maintenance organization (HMO); the conference agreement disallows employer deductions in connection with the plan if the plan fails to reimburse hospitals for inpatient services at the same rate (without regard to exempt individuals) that HMOs are required to reimburse hospitals for individuals not covered by a group health plan.

If a group health plan provides coverage for inpatient hospital services through a Blue Cross and Blue Shield corporation, the conference agreement disallows employer deductions in connection with the plan if the plan fails to reimburse hospitals for inpatient services at the same rate that such corporations are required to reimburse hospitals for individuals not covered by a group health plan.

The deduction disallowance does not apply to any group health plan which is not required under the laws of the state of New York (determined without regard to this provision or other provisions of Federal law) to reimburse for hospital services at the rates described above. Thus, self-insured plans are not subject to the deduction disallowance with respect to the 11 percent surcharge imposed on commercial insurers through March 31, 1993. Similarly, the deduction disallowance does not apply to self-insured plans that do not provide for reimbursement directly to hospitals on an expense incurred basis. The deduction denial also does not apply to payments by self-insured plans exempt from New York's all-payer reimbursement system because of agreements in effect on May 1, 1985.

No inference is intended as to whether any provision of the New York all-payer hospital reimbursement system is preempted by ERISA.

Effective Date

The provision is effective with respect to inpatient hospital services provided to participants after February 2, 1993, and on or before May 12, 1995.

[¶ 11,300.07]

Committee Reports on P.L. 101-508 (Omnibus Budget Reconciliation Act of 1993)

[Senate Committee Report]

[Deduction for health insurance costs of self-employed individuals]

The bill extends the 25-percent deduction for health insurance costs of self-employed individuals through taxable years beginning before January 1, 1992. The special rule prorating the deduction for taxable years beginning in 1990 is repealed.

Effective Date

The provision is effective for taxable years beginning after September 30, 1990.

[Conference Committee Report]

The conference agreement follows the Senate Amendment.

[¶ 11,300.075]

Committee Reports on P.L. 101-239 (Omnibus Budget Reconciliation Act of 1989)

[House Committee Report]

Health care continuation coverage

Covered employees.—Under the bill, the definition of covered employee includes any individual who is (or was) provided coverage under a group health plan by virtue of the performance of services by the individual for 1 or more persons maintaining the plan. Thus, the term "covered employee" can include an individual by virtue of the individual's performance of services as, for example, an independent contractor for a third party or as a partner for his or her partnership.

Pursuant to this provision, for purposes of the health care continuation rules, references to employer or employee in the statute are considered to include persons receiving or performing services other than in an employer-employee relationship. In addition, persons receiving services are subject to the employer aggregation rules of section 414(t) and the employee leasing rules of section 414(n) to the same extent as if such persons were employers with respect to the service performer.

The changes made by this provision are mandated by national health policy concerns, are limited solely to the health care continuation rules, and are not intended to alter or change in any manner the current statutory and common law relationship between an individual and the person for whom the individual performs services.

This provision applies to plan years beginning after December 31, 1989.

New coverage.—The bill provides that continuation coverage is not terminated upon the coverage of the qualified beneficiary under the group health plan of another employer if such plan contains any exclusion or limitation with respect to any preexisting condition of the qualified beneficiary. The committee intends that the notices required to be provided to qualified beneficiaries regarding their rights under the continuation coverage rules include a description of the rules relating to preexisting conditions.

This provision is intended to carry out the purpose of the health care continuation rules, which was to reduce the extent to which certain events, such as the loss of one's job, could create a significant gap in health coverage. Such a gap in coverage occurs when the new employer group health coverage excludes or limits coverage for a preexisting condition that is covered by the continuation coverage.

This provision generally applies to plan years beginning after December 31, 1989. The provision also applies to individuals who elected continuation coverage after December 31, 1988, and before September 15, 1989, and paid for such coverage in accordance with the continuation coverage rules before September 15, 1989.

Payment of premiums.—The bill clarifies that a plan may not require the payment of any premium before the day which is 45 days after the day on which the qualified beneficiary made the initial election for continuation coverage. This delayed due date for the initial premium does not prevent the collection of a premium for the period of delay. The provision is effective for plan years beginning after December 31, 1989.

Definition of qualifying event.—The provision provides an optional rule under which an employer (or, in the case of a multiemployer group health plan, the plan) may elect to treat the loss of coverage as the qualifying event. If such an election is made, the notice and election requirements, as well as the maximum period for continuation coverage, is measured from the date coverage is lost, rather than from the date of the event.

The provisions apply to plan years beginning on or after January 1, 1990.

Notice.—Two special notice rules are provided for multiemployer plans. Under the first rule, a multiemployer plan may extend both the 30-day and the 14-day notice period. This facilitates compliance for plans that rely on the employer's contribution reports to determine whether a qualifying event has occurred but do not require those reports to be filed monthly.

In many of the industries that have multiemployer plans, employment patterns are quite fluid. A construction worker, for example, might work for one contractor one week, another the next, and a third employer the following week. Some longshore workers may work for several different employers in the course of a single day. Thus, an individual employer may not know whether or not a qualifying event has occurred that results in a loss of coverage, because the employer does not know whether the participant has gone to work for another covered employer.

Under the second rule, a multiemployer plan may relieve contributing employers of the obligation to provide the plan with notice that certain qualifying events have occurred.

These changes are merely intended to facilitate compliance with the notice rules. However, there is no intent to diminish the right of qualified beneficiaries in any way, and it is intended that the notice provisions be interpreted and applied in such a manner to ensure that qualified beneficiaries do not lose any coverage as a result of the notice rules.

The provisions apply to plan years beginning on or after January 1, 1990.

[Conference Committee Report]

The conference agreement follows the House bill with the following modifications:

* * *

(2) *Continuation health care coverage rules.*—The conference agreement also makes modifications to the continuation coverage rules in the case of individuals who are entitled to Medicare coverage. The conferees intend that if a covered employee has a qualifying event that results in 18 months of continuation coverage and the covered employee becomes entitled to Medicare coverage before the expiration of the 18 months, a qualified beneficiary (other than the covered employee) who is at that time covered under the group health plan is entitled to continuation coverage for a total of 36 months from the date of the original qualifying event. Thus, this rule is the same as if, for example, a reduction in hours were followed by the death of the employee. Failure to comply with this rule is not a good faith interpretation of the continuation coverage rules.

The conference agreement adopts the provision in the Ways and Means Committee bill regarding termination of continuation coverage in the case of preexisting conditions, with a modification to the effective date.

[¶ 11,300.08]

Committee Reports on P.L. 100-647 (Technical and Miscellaneous Revenue Act of 1988)

[Senate Committee Report]

Deductibility of Health Insurance Costs

The bill clarifies that, consistent with the Congressional intent reflected in the Statement of Managers, the amount deductible under section 162(m) is not taken into account in computing net earnings from self-employment (sec. 1402(a)) or for purposes of the Social Security Act. Therefore, the amounts deductible under section 162(m) do not reduce the income base for purposes of the self-employed individual's social security tax or for purposes of benefit credit under the Social Security Act.

Under the bill, the deduction under section 162(m) is limited to the earned income derived by the taxpayer from the trade or business with respect to which the plan providing the health insurance is established.

[¶ 11,300.085]

Committee Reports on P.L. 99-514 (Tax Reform Act of 1986)

[Senate Committee Report]

Explanation of Provision

The bill provides a deduction for 25 percent of the amounts paid for health insurance for a taxable year on behalf of a self-employed individual and the individual's spouse and dependents. This deduction is allowable in calculating adjusted gross income. A self-employed individual means an individual who has earned income for the taxable year (sec. 401(c)(1)). However, under the bill, no deduction is allowable to the extent the deduction exceeds the self-employed individual's net earnings from self employment (sec. 1402(a)) for the taxable year. In addition, no deduction is allowable for any taxable year for which the self-employed individual is eligible to participate (on a subsidized basis) in a health plan of an employer of the self-employed individual or such individual's spouse.

* * *

Under the bill, the amount allowable as a deduction for health coverage for a self-employed individual is not also taken into account for purposes of determining the amount of any medical deduction to which the self-employed individual is entitled. Thus, such amounts deductible under this provision are not treated as medical expenses of the individual for purposes of determining whether the 10 percent of adjusted gross income threshold for the itemized medical expense deduction (sec. 213(a)) is met.

Finally, the bill provides that the amount deductible under this provision is not taken into account in computing net earnings from self-employment (sec. 1402(a)). Therefore, the amounts deductible under this provision do not reduce the income base for the self-employed individual's social security tax.

The bill directs the Secretary of the Treasury to provide guidance to self-employed individuals to whom this deduction applies with respect to the nondiscrimination requirements applicable to insured accident or health plans.

Effective date

The provisions are effective for tax years beginning after December 31, 1986.

[Conference Committee Report]

The conference agreement follows the Senate amendment, except as outlined below. First, the deduction is reduced from 50 percent of the amounts paid for health insurance to 25 percent of such amounts.

In addition, the conference agreement deletes the requirement that coverage be provided for all employees in all unincorporated trades or businesses with respect to which the self-employed individual is a 5-percent owner. Instead, the deduction is allowed only if the coverage is provided under one or more plans meeting the applicable nondiscrimination requirements, as if the coverage were employer-provided. The conference agreement also limits the deduction to the taxpayer's earned income for the taxable year. The provision allowing this deduction does not apply to any taxable year beginning after December 31, 1989.

[¶ 11,300.09]

Committee Reports on P.L. 99-272 (Consolidated Omnibus Budget Reconciliation Act)

[House Committee Report]

***. Under [the bill], employers sponsoring group health plans must extend an option for continued participation in the plan to spouses and dependent children previously covered under the plan if coverage was lost because of a change in family status.

This option would be offered during a period beginning when the individual would otherise lose coverage and ending not earlier than 60 days after the individual is notified of his or her continuation of coverage rights. "Qualified beneficiaries" (i.e., individuals who fall into the three categories described above) could elect continuation of group coverage on their own behalf.... [E]vidence of insurability [would not be required] and the coverage provided would generally be identical in scope to that provided to similarly situated spouses and dependent children who had not undergone a change in family status. ***. A qualified beneficiary who was a covered dependent child would lose coverage as soon as the person no longer met the group health plan's definition of a dependent child.

Various notice requirements are imposed on the group health plan in order to assure that individuals understand their continuation rights under the bill. In addition, the covered employee would be required to notify the administrator of the group health plan of any change in family status and the employer must notify the administrator in the case of the death of the covered employee.

The bill authorizes the Secretary of the Treasury to prescribe rules defining the appropriate continuation coverage for qualified beneficiaries under a plan terminated in connection with a plant closing. The committee intends that continuation coverage be required notwithstanding the plant closing if the employer continues to maintain any other health plan. The required continuation coverage generally would be that coverage in effect immediately prior to the closing. However, the regulations are to include rules precluding an employer from reducing or eliminating coverage in anticipation of the plant closing.

* * *

The bill generally defines qualified beneficiaries to include the spouse and dependent children of an employee entitled to coverage under the terms of the group health plan. In addition, the covered employee is a qualified beneficiary entitled to elect continuation coverage upon termination of employment.

However, the provision intends to extend prior coverage rather than create new classes of covered employees. Thus, no employee, spouse, or child will be considered a qualified beneficiary unless, on the date before the qualifying event, that individual was a beneficiary under the plan. Thus, for example, no employee who had opted not to be covered by a contributory group health plan could elect continuation coverage upon termination of employment. Similarly, if a covered employee had elected not to receive dependent coverage, no spouse or child subsequently is entitled to elect continuation coverage upon the occurrence of a qualifying event.

If there are multiple "qualifying events," the status of an individual as a qualified beneficiary is determined on the day before the occurrence of the earliest qualifying event. For example, if a covered participant terminates employment without electing continuation coverage, no beneficiary could subsequently elect continuation coverage, e.g., upon the participant's death.

If there are multiple "qualified beneficiaries," only one election generally is required. Where the covered employee terminates employment, for example, no spouse or child would receive continuation coverage unless the employee elects to continue coverage. Similarly, upon the employee's death, divorce, or becoming eligible for Medicare, continuation coverage is to be provided only if the spouse so elects. In that instance, the spouse effectively decides whether coverage will be continued for the children.

The only exceptions to this rule occur where the child is the only qualified beneficiary (e.g., where the spouse is not entitled to coverage under the plan, or with respect to children attaining majority).

* * *

[Senate Committee Report]

*** Under the bill, generally effective for plan years beginning after June 30, 1986, no deduction is permitted for employer contributions to any group health plan if that plan or any other plan of the employer fails to provide qualified beneficiaries a continuation coverage election. The election must be provided for previously covered family members of deceased, divorced, or Medicare-eligible workers, employees who have separated from service (and their dependents), and certain children who would otherwise lose coverage under the terms of the plan upon attainment of majority.

In addition, no income exclusion is permitted under the bill for any highly compensated individual if the plan in which the individual participates or any other group health plan maintained by the employer fails to provide continuation coverage.

Under the bill, all qualified beneficiaries who would otherwise lose coverage as a result of a qualifying event must have the right to elect, within the 60-day period beginning on the date of the qualifying event, to continue coverage. Qualifying events include (1) the death of the covered employee; (2) the separation from service of the covered employee (whether voluntary or involuntary); (3) the divorce or legal separation of the covered employee from the employee's spouse; (4) the covered employee's commencement of Medicare coverage; or (5) the cessation of dependent child coverage under the terms of the plan (e.g., upon attainment of majority).

*** The committee intends that the employer should be required to provide notice of the election to all covered employees no later than the date on which the employee becomes entitled to coverage under the plan.

In addition, a qualified beneficiary must, under the bill, elect continuation coverage no later than 60 days after the date of the qualifying event. Provided the qualified beneficiary elects to continue coverage within the 60-day period, the continuation coverage must be effective as of the date of the qualifying event

In general, the continuation coverage for which a qualified beneficiary must be offered an election is coverage identical to the coverage provided immediately before the qualifying event. For example, if, under the plan, the covered employee had the right to select among several levels of coverage, the qualified beneficiary generally would be entitled to continue whatever level of coverage the employee had selected for the beneficiary prior to the qualifying event.

[Conference Committee Report]

Covered Employers.—The conference agreement generally follows the House bill and the Senate amendment, by amending ERISA, the Code, and the Public Health Service Act. Under the agreement, the changes to the Code and ERISA do not apply to churches, Federal, State and local governments, and small employers. Small employers are defined as those with fewer than 20 employees. In addition, the amendments to the Public Health Service Act apply only with respect to State and local governments (other than those with fewer than 20 employees).

To avoid the issuance of duplicate and perhaps inconsistent regulations, the conferees authorized the Secretary of Labor to promulgate regulations implementing the disclosure and reporting requirements, and the Secretary of Treasury to issue regulations defining required coverage, deductions, and income inclusion. The Secretary of Health and Human Services is to issue regulations regarding the requirement that State and local governments provide continuation coverage for qualified beneficiaries. The conferees intend that any regulations issued by the Secretary of Health and Human Services will conform (in terms of actual requirements) with those regulations issued by the Secretary of Treasury and Labor. Under the agreement, enforcement of the requirements imposed through the Public Health Service Act will be through suits for equitable relief filed by qualified beneficiaries. Of course, as under present law, all affected agencies will have the opportunity to comment before regulations are issued.

Sanctions for Noncompliance.—Any regulations issued pursuant to these changes are to be effective after the date of issuance. However, pending the promulgation of regulations, employers are required to operate in good faith compliance with a reasonable interpretation of these substantive rules, notice requirements, etc.

The conference agreement generally follows H.R. 3500 and the Senate amendment except that the only sanction imposed on covered State and local governments under the Public Health Service Act are suits for equitable relief.

Qualified Beneficiaries.—The conference agreement generally follows the House bill and the Senate amendment except that no continuation coverage is required for terminated employees if the termination occurs by reason of the employee's gross misconduct.

Type of Benefit Coverage.—The conference agreement generally follows the House bill with a modification so that the type of benefit coverage is identical, as of the time the coverage is being provided, to the coverage provided under the plan to similarly situated beneficiaries under the plan with regard to whom a qualifying event has not occurred.

Duration of Coverage.—The conference agreement generally follows Title IX of the Senate amendment, requiring that continuation coverage provided to widows, divorced spouses, spouses of Medicare-eligible employees, and dependent children who become ineligible for coverage under the plan be provided for 3 years, while coverage for terminated employees and employees with reduced hours must be provided for 16 months. The agreement provides that the coverage period begins with the date of the qualifying event. As under the House bill and Title IX of the Senate amendment, no coverage need be provided after (1) failure to make timely payment under the plan, (2) the qualified beneficiary is covered under another group health plan as a result of employment, reemployment, or remarriage, and (3) the qualified beneficiary becomes entitled to Medicare benefits. In addition, as under the House bill and Title VII of the Senate amendment, no coverage need be provided after the employer ceases to maintain any group health plan.

Cost of Coverage.—The conference agreement generally follows Title VII of the Senate amendment. For a self-insured plan the conferees agreed that the "applicable" premium for any year generally is equal to a reasonable estimate of the cost of providing coverage for such period for a similarly situated beneficiary. The cost is to be determined on an actuarial basis and takes into account such factors as the Secretary may prescribe in regulations. Alternately, unless there has been a significant change affecting a self-insured plan (e.g., a modification of covered benefits, a significant change in the number or composition of the covered workforce, etc.), the employer may elect to use as the applicable premium, the cost for a similarly situated beneficiary for the preceding year, adjusted to reflect cost-of-living increases as measured by the GNP deflator.

In general, similarly situated individuals are those individuals defined by the plan (consistent with Treasury regulations) to be similarly situated and with respect to which no qualifying event has occurred. The Secretary of the Treasury is to define similarly situated individuals by taking into account the plan under which the coverage is provided (e.g., high or low option), the type of coverage (single or family coverage) and, if appropriate, regional differences in health costs. The conferees do not intend that similarly situated mean medically identical (for example, all employees with heart problems); nor do the conferees intend that plans can define similarly situated beneficiaries by reference to classifications that are in violation of Title VII of the Equal Pay Act.

In addition, the conferees intend that Treasury regulations defining a plan should preclude an employer from grouping employees to inappropriately increase the cost of continuation coverage for qualified beneficiaries who are rank-and-file employees (or their beneficiaries).

Notice Requirements.—The conference agreement generally follows the House bill. Thus, notice of the option to continue health coverage must be provided in the summary plan description. In addition, in the event of an employee's death, separation from service, or Medicare eligibility, the employer is required to notify the plan administrator within 30 days of the qualifying event who will in turn notify the qualified beneficiary within 14 days.

In the event of other qualifying events (e.g., divorce, legal separation, or the child's becoming ineligible) the employee or qualified beneficiary affected by that event is required to notify the plan administrator. Unless the qualified beneficiary is the party providing notice, the plan administrator is in turn required to notify the qualified beneficiary. The election period begins not later than the later of (1) the date on which coverage terminates, or (2) the date on which the qualified beneficiary receives notice of the right to elect continuation coverage. Any election by a qualified beneficiary is considered an election by other qualified beneficiaries who would otherwise lose coverage by reason of the same qualifying event.

The conferees intend that the Secretary of Labor will issue regulations defining what notice will be adequate for this provision. The conferees intend that notice by mail to the qualified beneficiary's last known address is to be adequate; however, mere posting is not to be adequate. In addition, in applying these requirements to multi-employer plans, the conferees intend that the Secretary of Labor should take into account the special problems faced by those plans.

Conversion Option.—The conference agreement generally follows the House bill and Title IX of the Senate amendment. Under the agreement, a qualified beneficiary must be offered a conversion option from any plan (including a self-insured plan) only if such an option is otherwise available under the plan to other participants.

Effective Date

These provisions are effective for plan years beginning after June 30, 1986. In the case of a group health plan maintained pursuant to one or more collective bargaining agreements, the bill does not apply to plan years beginning before the later of (1) the date the last of the collective bargaining agreements terminate, or (2) January 1, 1987.

[Code Sec. 219]

[¶ 11,330.004]

Committee Report on P.L. 109-280 (Pension Protection Act of 2006)

[Joint Committee on Taxation Report]

[Additional IRA contributions for certain employees]

Under the provision, an applicable individual may elect to make additional IRA contributions of up to $3,000 per year for 2006-2009. An applicable individual must have been a participant in a section 401(k) plan under which the employer matched at least 50 percent of the employee's contributions to the plan with stock of the employer. In addition, in a taxable year preceding the taxable year of an additional contribution: (1) the employer (or any controlling corporation of the employer) must have been a debtor in a bankruptcy case, and (2) the employer or any other person must have been subject to an indictment or conviction resulting from business transactions related to the bankruptcy. The individual must also have been a participant in the section 401(k) plan on the date six months before the bankruptcy case was filed. An applicable individual who elects to make these additional IRA contributions is not permitted to make IRA catch-up contributions that apply to individuals age 50 and older.

Effective Date

The provision is effective for taxable years beginning after December 31, 2006, and before January 1, 2010.

* * *

[Inflation indexing of gross income limitations on certain retirement savings incentives]

The bill indexes the income limits applicable to the saver's credit beginning in 2007. (Another provision of the bill, described above, permanently extends the saver's credit.) Indexed amounts are rounded to the nearest multiple of $500. Under the indexed income limits, as under present law, the income limits for single taxpayers is one-half that for married taxpayers filing a joint return and the limits for heads of household are three-fourths that for married taxpayers filing a joint return.

The bill also indexes the income limits for IRA contributions beginning in 2007. The indexing applies to the income limits for deductible contributions for active participants in an employer-sponsored plan,[185] the income limits for deductible contributions if the individual is not an active participant but the individual's spouse is, and the income limits for Roth IRA contributions. Indexed amounts are rounded to the nearest multiple of $1,000. The provision does not affect the phase-out ranges under present law. Thus, for example, in the case of an active participant in an employer-sponsored plan, the phase-out range is $20,000 in the case of a married taxpayer filing a joint return and $10,000 in the case of an individual taxpayer.

Effective Date

The provision is effective for taxable years beginning after December 31, 2006.

[Direct deposit of tax refunds in an IRA]

The Secretary is directed to develop forms under which all or a portion of a taxpayer's refund may be deposited in an IRA of the taxpayer (or the spouse of the taxpayer in the case of a joint return). The provision does not modify the rules relating to IRAs, including the rules relating to timing and deductibility of contributions.

Effective Date

The form required by the provision is to be available for taxable years beginning after December 31, 2006.

[¶ 11,330.005]

Committee Reports on P.L. 107-16 (Economic Growth and Tax Relief Reconciliation Act)

[Senate Committee Report]

[Individual retirement arrangements]

Increase in annual contribution limits.—The provision increases the maximum annual dollar contribution limit for IRA contributions from $2,000 to $2,500 for 2002 through 2005, $3,000 for 2006 and 2007, $3,500 for 2008 and 2009, $4,000 for 2010, and $5,000 for 2011. After 2011, the limit is adjusted annually for inflation in $500 increments.

Additional catch-up contributions.—The bill provides that individuals who have attained age 50 may make additional catch-up IRA contributions. The otherwise maximum contribution limit (before application of the AGI phase-out limits) for an individual who has attained age 50 before the end of the taxable year is increased by $500 for 2002 through 2005, $1000 for 2006 through 2009, $1,500 for 2010, and $2,000 for 2011 and thereafter.

* * *

Effective Date

The provision is generally effective for taxable years beginning after December 31, 2001.

* * *

[Conference Committee Report]

Increase in annual contribution limits

The conference agreement increases the maximum annual dollar contribution limit for IRA contributions from $2,000 to $3,000 for 2002 through 2004, $4,000 for 2005 through 2007, and $5,000 for 2008. After 2008, the limit is adjusted annually for inflation in $500 increments.

Additional catch-up contributions

The conference agreement provides that individuals who have attained age 50 may make additional catch-up IRA contributions. The otherwise maximum contribution limit (before application of the AGI phase-out limits) for an individual who has attained age 50 before the end of the taxable year is increased by $500 for 2002 through 2005, and $1,000 for 2006 and thereafter.

* * *

[¶ 11,330.010]

Committee Reports on P.L. 105-34 (Taxpayer Relief Act)

For Committee Report on P.L. 105-34, dealing with Roth IRAs, see ¶ 12,097.10.

[Senate Committee Report]

Individual retirement arrangements.—

In general.—The bill (1) increases the AGI phase-out limits for deductible IRAs, (2) provides that an individual is not considered an active participant in an IRA merely because the individual's spouse is an active participant, * * *

Increase income phase-out ranges for deductible IRAs.—The bill increases the AGI phase-out range for deductible IRA contributions as follows:

[In thousands of dollars]

	Phase-Out Range	
Taxable years beginning in:	*Single Taxpayers*	*Joint Returns*
1998 and 1999	$30,000—$40,000	$50,000—$60,000
2000 and 2001	$35,000—$45,000	$60,000—$70,000
2002 and 2003	$40,000—$50,000	$70,000—$80,000
2004 and thereafter	$50,000—$60,000	$80,000—$100,000

[185] Under the bill, for 2007, the lower end of the income phase out for active participants filing a joint return is $80,000 as adjusted to reflect inflation.

Active participant rule.—The bill provides that an individual is not considered an active participant in an employer-sponsored plan merely because the individual's spouse is an active participant.

* * *

Effective Date

The provision is effective for taxable years beginning after December 31, 1997.

Conference Committee Report

The conference agreement follows the Senate amendment, with modifications.

Under the conference agreement, as under the Senate amendment, an individual is not considered an active participant in an employer-sponsored retirement plan merely because the individual's spouse is an active participant. However, under the conference agreement, the maximum deductible IRA contribution for an individual who is not an active participant, but whose spouse is, is phased out for taxpayers with AGI between $150,000 and $160,000.

Under the conference agreement, the deductible IRA income phase-out limits are increased as follows:

Joint Returns

Taxable years beginning in:	*Phase-out range*
1998	$50,000 – $60,000
1999	$51,000 – $61,000
2000	$52,000 – $62,000
2001	$53,000 – $63,000
2002	$54,000 – $64,000
2003	$60,000 – $70,000
2004	$65,000 – $75,000
2005	$70,000 – $80,000
2006	$75,000 – $85,000
2007 and thereafter	$80,000 – $100,000

Single Taxpayers

Taxable years beginning in:	*Phase-out range*
1998	$30,000 – $40,000
1999	$31,000 – $41,000
2000	$32,000 – $42,000
2001	$33,000 – $43,000
2002	$34,000 – $44,000
2003	$40,000 – $50,000
2004	$45,000 – $55,000
2005 and thereafter	$50,000 – $60,000

The following examples illustrate the income phase-out rules.

Example 1.—Suppose for a year W is an active participant in an employer-sponsored retirement plan, and W's husband, H, is not. Further assume that the combined AGI of H and W for the year is $200,000. Neither W nor H is entitled to make deductible contributions to an IRA for the year.

Example 2.—Same as example 1, except that the combined AGI of W and H is $125,000. H can make deductible contributions to an IRA. However, a deductible contribution could not be made for W.

[¶ 11,330.011]

Committee Reports on P.L. 104-188 (Small Business Job Protection Act)

Increased Access to Retirement Savings

[Senate Committee Report]

Spousal IRAs

The bill modifies the present-law rules relating to deductible IRAs by permitting deductible IRA contributions of up to $2,000 to be made for each spouse (including, for example. a homemaker who does not work outside the home) if the combined compensation of both spouses is at least equal to the contributed amount

Effective Date

The provision is effective for taxable years beginning after December 31, 1996.

[Conference Committee Report]

The conference agreement follows the Senate amendment.

For Committee Report on P.L. 102-318, dealing with rollovers and withholding on nonperiodic pension distributions, see ¶ 11,750.036.

[¶ 11,330.013]

Committee Report on P.L. 101-239 (Omnibus Budget Reconciliation Act of 1989)

[Conference Committee Report]

The conference agreement follows the House bill with the following modifications:

* * *

(5) *Definition of compensation for IRAs.*—The conference agreement provides that the definition of compensation for purposes of the deduction limits for individual retirement accounts (IRAs) includes earned income that is not subject to self-employment tax (SECA) because of the religious beliefs of the individual, effective for contributions after the date of enactment.

[¶ 11,330.014]

Committee Report on P.L. 100-647 (Technical and Miscellaneous Revenue Act of 1988)

[Senate Committee Report]

IRA deduction limit.—Present law creates an unintended incentive for married couples to file separate returns. If one spouse is an active participant and the other spouse is not, the couple can increase their IRA deduction limit under certain circumstances by filing separate returns.

In order to eliminate this incentive for a married couple living together, the bill provides that, for purposes of determining whether an IRA contribution is deductible for a taxable year, if the couple lives together at any time during the year, the active participant status of both spouses is taken into account for purposes of calculating the IRA deduction limit. If the spouses file separate returns, the applicable dollar amount is $0 and only the AGI of the spouse making the IRA contribution is taken into account.

Also under the bill, a taxpayer is not considered married for a year if the taxpayer and the taxpayer's spouse (1) did not live together at any time during the taxable year, and (2) did not file a joint return for the taxable year. A taxpayer meeting these requirements for a taxable year is treated as an unmarried individual for the taxable year. Accordingly, for purposes of determining the taxpayer's deduction limit, only the taxpayer's AGI and status as an active participant is taken into account, and the applicable dollar amount is $25,000.

These provisions apply to contributions for taxable years beginning after December 31, 1987, except that a taxpayer may elect to have the provisions apply to contributions for taxable years beginning after December 31, 1986. The election may be made by treating IRA contributions in a manner consistent with these provisions on the taxpayer's income tax return for any taxable year beginning before January 1, 1988.

[¶ 11,330.015]

Committee Report on P.L. 100-203 (Omnibus Budget Reconciliation Act of 1987)

[House Committee Report]

In a recent Tax Court decision (*Porter v. Commissioner,* 88 TC [548, Dec. 43,751]), it was held that Article III judges are not employees of the United States and, therefore, are not active participants in a plan established for its employees by the United States. Whether or not an individual is an employee is also relevant for other purposes under the Code, such as for the exclusion of certain benefits from income and the eligibility for certain deductions.

The committee believes that judges should not be permitted to make deductible IRA contributions on a basis more favorable than other individuals. Further, the committee finds it appropriate to clarify that judges are treated as employees for purposes of the Code so that they are eligible for certain benefits (such as the exclusion from income for employer-provided health benefits).

The decision in *Porter v. Commissioner* would be overturned, and judges would be treated as employees for purposes of the Code and as active participants for purposes of the IRA deduction limit.

Effective date

This provision would be effective for years beginning after December 31, 1987.

See ¶ 12,050.063 for Committee Reports on P.L. 99-514.

[¶ 11,330.016]

Committee Reports on P.L. 98-369 (Tax Reform Act of 1984)

[Senate Committee Report]

Reasons for Change

The committee has learned that the annual IRA reports are not being filed in the time and manner that is desired. When reports are filed, the information concerning contributions made during the course of a year is stated as a single total and does not distinguish between contributions that may have been made for different years. As a result of these shortcomings, the committee decided to reaffirm the Secretary's authority in present law to require reporting as to each year for which contributions are made and to increase the penalty for failure to file in the manner and by the time required.

Additionally, the committee is concerned that the ability of taxpayers to make contributions between the time (without extensions) prescribed for filing the return for the taxable year and that time with extensions impedes the Secretary's ability to monitor deductions for these contributions.

Explanation of Provision

Section 408(i) which requires that the trustee of an IRA make required reports is amended to require that the report show both the total amount contributed each year and the taxable years to which the contributions relate.

Section 408 is also amended to require that all contributions relating to a taxable year must be made no later than the due date (without extensions) for filing the return for the taxable year. For most taxpayers, this date is April 15.

The penalty for failure to provide reports on individual retirement accounts and annuities is increased from $10 to $50 for each failure.

[Conference Committee Report]

The conference agreement follows the Senate amendment, except that the provision is effective for contributions made after December 31, 1984. The conferees wish to clarify that the trustee may require that the owner of the IRA certify as to which year a contribution relates and that, except in unusual circumstances, the trustee may rely on that certification.

The date by which this report must be provided to the Internal Revenue Service and the periods to which the report relates are to be specified by the Secretary in regulations. The conferees intend that generally trustees will be required to report only once a year on the cumulative total of contributions relating to a particular taxable year. The Secretary may, however, provide for more frequent reporting if he determines that it is appropriate to do so. As to the date by which the report must be provided to the Internal Revenue Service, the Secretary could, for example, require reporting by the end of May on all IRA contributions relating to the taxable year with respect to which the individual's tax return was due on the preceding April 15.

[Senate Committee Report]

* * *

[The] provision repeals the special rules for alimony and treats all taxable alimony received by a divorced spouse as compensation for purposes of the IRA deduction limit.

Effective Date

The provision applies for taxable years beginning after December 31, 1984.

[¶ 11,330.017]

Committee Report on P.L. 97-448 (Technical Corrections Act of 1982)

Present law

ERTA generally allows individuals an annual deduction for contributions to an individual retirement account, annuity, or bond (IRA) limited to the lesser of $2,000 ($2,250 for a spousal IRA) or 100 percent of compensation. In lieu of the deduction for IRA contributions, an employee is allowed a deduction (subject to the IRA limit) for qualified voluntary employee contributions to an employer's retirement plan. Accumulated deductible employee contributions under an employer's plan generally are subject to IRA-type rules.

Explanation of provision

The bill clarifies the rules for spousal IRAs to insure that an employee is not denied a deduction for contributions to an IRA for the benefit of a spouse having no compensation merely because the employee is also allowed a deduction for employer contributions to an IRA which qualifies as a simplified employee pension (SEP). In addition, the bill makes it clear that a deduction is allowable for IRA contributions for the benefit of a spouse who has no compensation and who has not attained age 70 ½ before the close of the taxable year, even if the spouse having compensation is age 70 ½ or older.

The bill deletes simplified employee pension from the definition of qualified employer plan. (Except for the limit on contributions, SEPs are generally subject to the tax rules applicable to IRAs.)

The bill clarifies the rules allowing a deduction for individual retirement savings by providing that, for a self-employed individual, compensation includes net earnings from self-employment reduced by any amount allowable as a deduction to the individual for contributions made on behalf of the individual to a tax-qualified plan (an "H.R. 10" plan or "Keogh" plan). In addition, the bill clarifies that compensation, for this purpose, does not include pension and annuity payments or other deferred compensation.

The bill clarifies the rule allowing a deduction for certain voluntary employee contributions made to a qualified employer or government plan after the close of the taxable year by providing that such contributions must be made on account of that taxable year.

The bill clarifies that a 10-percent additional income tax is imposed on early withdrawals (generally, before age 59 ½) of accumulated deductible employee contributions from either the plan to which the contributions were made or from a plan to which the accumulated contributions were rolled over or otherwise transferred.

The bill revises the rules relating to lump-sum distributions and rollover amounts under qualified plans and tax-sheltered annuity programs to clarify that partial (as well as total) distributions of accumulated deductible employee contributions are eligible for tax-free rollover treatment.

The bill clarifies that accumulated deductible employee contributions payable to a beneficiary of a deceased employee under a tax-qualified plan are eligible for the estate tax exclusion only if any lump-sum distribution also payable to the beneficiary under the plan is eligible for the exclusion.

The bill clarifies that an owner-employee (a sole proprietor, or a partner whose partnership interest exceeds 10 percent) is permitted to make deductible employee contributions to a tax-qualified plan (an "H.R. 10" plan or "Keogh" plan) notwithstanding the rules which may preclude nondeductible employee contributions by the owner-employee.

The bill clarifies effective date provisions for the estate and gift tax provisions relating to individual retirement savings.

Effective date

The provisions apply to taxable years beginning after December 31, 1981.

[¶ 11,330.02]

Committee Reports on P.L. 97-34 (Economic Recovery Tax Act of 1981)

Sec. 311— Retirement savings— Senate Committee Report.—In the case of an individual who is not an active participant in a qualified plan, tax-sheltered annuity program, or government plan (*i.e.,* one who is currently eligible to make deductible IRA contributions), the present annual contribution limit is raised to the lesser of $2,000 ($2,250 for a spousal IRA) or 100 percent of compensation.

In the case of an employee who is an active participant in a plan (*i.e.,* one who is not currently eligible for an IRA deduction), a deduction is allowed to an individual for retirement savings limited to the lesser of $1,500 ($1,625 for a spousal IRA) or 100 percent of compensation. In the case of a plan participant, a deduction is allowed for contributions to an IRA or for qualified voluntary contributions by (or on behalf of) the employee to the plan. An employee can allocate deductible contributions to all plans in which he participates, so long as the total amount deducted does not exceed the lesser of $1,500 or 100 percent of compensation. An employee for whom an employer contributes under a SEP is considered an active plan participant and is allowed a deduction for his own IRA contributions (under the limits applicable to active plan participants) as well as a deduction for employer contributions to the SEP (limited under the SEP rules on the basis of contributions by, and compensation from, each separate employer). (For applicable limits under a SEP, see 2. Retirement plan deduction for self-employed individuals, *Explanation of Provisions, Increased contribution limit.*)

The requirement that contributions to a spousal IRA be equally divided between spouses is deleted, but annual contributions for either spouse cannot exceed $2,000 ($1,500 for an active participant) for a year.

A participant's contributions to a qualified plan, a tax-sheltered annuity program, or a government plan are qualified voluntary contributions if (1) the contributions are not mandatory, (2) deductible employee contributions are accepted under the plan, and (3) the participant does not designate the contribution as nondeductible.

An employee is allowed the deduction for qualified voluntary contributions only if the plan has made provision for the acceptance of deductible employee contributions. Rules are provided under which (1) a plan may permit participants to make or revise their designations for a year retroactively and (2) a plan may permit certain contributions made after the close of a calendar year to be treated as if made on the last day of the year. The bill continues the present law requirement that the opportunity to make voluntary contributions must be reasonably available to a nondiscriminatory group of employees. This availability standard will apply to the aggregate of deductible and nondeductible voluntary contributions and to the deductible voluntary contributions alone. If the eligibility standard is satisfied, the committee intends that the limit on the amount of voluntary contributions permitted under qualified plans of an employer is not to be less than the deductible limit provided by the bill for qualified voluntary employee contributions.

Accumulated deductible employee contributions (*i.e.,* net qualified voluntary contributions adjusted for income, gain, loss, and expense) are subject to the same tax treatment accorded amounts held in an IRA, with certain exceptions. All distributions of accumulated deductible employee contributions are includible in gross income, except for tax-free rollovers to an IRA or to another plan where the rollover amount will be held as accumulated deductible employee contributions. Distributions of accumulated deductible employee contributions may be made without penalty after age 59 ½ or in the event of disability or death. Other distributions of accumulated deductible employee contributions are subject to the same 10-percent additional income tax that applies to early withdrawals from an IRA.

A distribution of accumulated deductible employee contributions from a qualified plan may be transferred under the rollover rules to an IRA or to another qualified plan if the plan administrator of the other plan (1) treats the amount transferred as accumulated deductible employee contributions, and (2) permits such transfers on a nondiscriminatory basis. Of course, the amount transferred would not be taken into account under the limits on the amount of voluntary employee contributions under qualified plans. Such a rollover may be made without regard to whether the distribution is included in lump-sum distribution or a distribution on account of termination of the plan, and without regard to whether the distribution constitutes a total distribution of the accumulated deductible employee contributions under the distributing plan. In addition, if a distribution of accumulated deductible employee contributions from a qualified plan is rolled over tax-free to an IRA, a total distribution from the IRA which is attributable only to a rollover from a qualified plan may be rolled over to a plan under which the distribution will be treated as accumulated deductible employee contributions, etc. Similar rules are provided for tax-sheltered annuities.

The IRA rules requiring that distributions commence not later than the taxable year in which the individual attains age 70 ½ and that distributions be made within a prescribed time after the individual's death do not apply to accumulated deductible employee contributions unless rolled over to an IRA. If accumulated deductible employee contributions are applied toward the purchase of life insurance, the amount so applied is treated as a distribution to which the usual tax rules for distributions apply. In addition, if an employee borrows from or against such accumulated contributions, the amount of the loan or security interest is treated as distributed.

A plan which accepts deductible employee contributions is not required to hold assets purchased with such contributions (or income and gain therefrom) apart from the plan's other assets. Where these assets are not segregated from other plan assets, the committee expects that an employee's accumulated deductible contributions will be adjusted for income, etc. under the plan at least annually. In applying certain IRA rules to deductible employee contributions, the committee does not intend to imply that it would be appropriate to apply such rules to other plan contributions or benefits.

The bill does not change the usual vesting rules for qualified plans, under which a participant's accrued benefit derived from accumulated deductible employee contributions is nonforfeitable at all times. Under the bill, deductible employee contributions and deductible IRA contributions (other than employer contributions to a SEP) are not taken into account for purposes of the limitations on contributions and benefits for qualified plans and tax-sheltered annuities.

Accumulated deductible employee contributions do not qualify under the bill for 10-year forward income averaging long-term capital gain treatment, deferred recognition of gain on employer securities, or the income tax death benefit exclusion for certain benefits under qualified plans. For purposes of the estate tax and gift tax exclusions for qualified plans and certain tax-sheltered annuities, as well as for purposes of the income tax treatment of annuities, accumulated deductible employee contributions are treated as a benefit derived from employer contributions.

An employer is not required to withhold income tax on an employee's voluntary contributions to a plan if it is reasonable to believe that the employee will be entitled to a deduction for the contributions.

Treasury regulations are to provide rules under which the plan administrator of a plan accepting deductible employee contributions is to provide reports to the Treasury and to plan participants.

A clarifying amendment is made with regard to the income tax treatment of the proceeds of a retirement bond purchased with a rollover contribution.

Effective Dates

These provisions generally are effective for taxable years beginning after December 31, 1981. The amendments to the estate tax and gift tax rules apply to the estates of decedents dying and to transfers made after such date. The amendment relating to redeemed retirement bonds applies to taxable years beginning after December 31, 1974.

Joint Explanatory Statement of the Committee of Conference.—House bill.—In the case of an individual who is not an active participant in an employer-sponsored plan, the annual contribution limit is raised from the lesser of $1,500 or 15 percent of compensation to the lesser of $2,000 or 100 percent of compensation. The limit for a spousal IRA is increased from $1,750 to $2,250, and the present-law requirement that contributions under a spousal IRA be equally divided between the spouses is deleted.

In the case of an employee who is an active participant in a plan, a deduction is allowed for contributions to an IRA or for voluntary contributions to the plan. The voluntary contributions and earnings thereon under a plan are subject to IRA-type rules, except that (1) distributions starting at age 70 ½ are not mandated and (2) rollovers may be made to an IRA with regard to the present law rule limiting rollovers to one per year.

Under the House bill, benefits under a qualified plan (including deductible employee contributions and earnings thereon) are taxed only when paid to the employee or a beneficiary and are not taxed if merely made available. Of course, as under present law, if benefits are paid with respect to an employee to a creditor of the employee, a child of the employee, etc., the benefits paid would be treated as if paid to the employee.

Under present law, individuals generally may self-direct IRA investments or investments under an account in a qualified plan. Under the House bill, amounts invested in collectibles (antiques, art, gems, stamps, etc.) under an IRA or a self-directed account in a qualified plan are treated as distributions for income tax purposes.

Under the House bill, the proceeds of a redeemed U.S. retirement bond which is distributed under a qualified bond purchase plan may be rolled over, tax-free, to an IRA. U.S. retirement bonds purchased for an employee may be redeemed only after the employee attains age 59 ½, dies or becomes disabled. Also, the bill clarifies the treatment of IRA retirement bonds acquired in a tax-free rollover.

Senate amendment

The Senate amendment is generally the same as the House bill, except that (1) active plan participants are allowed a deduction for contributions to an IRA or for qualified voluntary contributions to a plan limited annually to the lesser of $1,500 ($1,625 for a spousal IRA) or 100 percent of compensation for the year, and (2) a surviving or divorced spouse may deduct at least $1,125 annually for life for contributions to a spousal IRA established by the individual's former spouse at least 5 years before the death or divorce.

In addition, the Senate amendment does not include provisions relating to investments in collectibles under IRAs or self-directed accounts in qualified plans or to rollovers of the redemption proceeds of U.S. retirement bonds. Also, voluntary contributions and earnings thereon are taxed only if paid, but other plan benefits are taxed if paid or made available.

The Senate amendment requires that Treasury provide the Congress (before June 30, 1982) a study of the tax incentives for individual retirement savings.

Conference agreement

The conference agreement follows the House bill, except that a divorced spouse is allowed a deduction for contributions to a spousal IRA established by the individual's former spouse at least 5 years before the divorce if the former spouse contributed to the IRA under the spousal IRA rules for at least three of the five years preceding the divorce. If these requirements are met, the limit on the divorced spouse's IRA contributions for a year is not less than the lesser of (1) $1,125 or (2) the sum of the divorced spouse's compensation and alimony includible in gross income. [No Committee Report was issued in the House on the version of the bill adopted. Most of the material in the Senate Committee Report is applicable.]

For Committee Report on P.L. 97-34, Sec. 312, relating to self-employed retirement plans, see ¶ 11,850.062.

[¶ 11,330.025]

Senate Committee Report on P.L. 96-222 (Technical Corrections Act of 1979)

Sec. 101(a)(10)(D)—Contributions after age 70 ½.

The Revenue Act of 1978 created a new type of individual retirement plan, known as a simplified employee pension. Under the rules for simplified employee pensions, an employer may be obligated to contribute to the individual retirement account or annuity of an employee who has attained age 70 ½. Under the usual rules for individual retirement accounts and annuities, such a contribution is includible in the gross income of the employee but the contribution is not deductible by the employee and is considered an excess IRA contribution.

Contributions by a corporation, a sole proprietorship, or a partnership to a tax-qualified pension plan on behalf of an individual who has attained age 70 ½ are deductible (within limits) under present law. The nondeductibility of employer contributions to the simplified employee pension of an employee who has attained age 70 ½ is an unintended barrier to the establishment of simplified employee pensions.

The bill allows an employee who has attained age 70 ½ to deduct employer contributions to the employee's individual retirement account or annuity if the account or annuity is a simplified employee pension.

This provision applies for taxable years beginning after December 31, 1978. This is the same effective date as was provided for simplified employee pensions under the Revenue Act of 1978.

[¶ 11,330.03]

Committee Reports on P.L. 95-600 (Revenue Act of 1978)

Sec. 152(e)—Simplified employee pensions—The Senate Committee Report on Sec. 152 is at ¶ 12,050.09.

Sec. 156(c)—Rollovers of tax sheltered annuities—The Conference Committee Report on Sec. 156 is at ¶ 11,800.06.

Sec. 157(a)—Extended time for contributions.

House Committee Report.—The committee bill extends the date by which an individual can make deductible contributions to an IRA for a taxable year. Under the amendment, such contributions will be deductible for the year if made on or before the date prescribed by law for filing the individual's Federal income tax return for the year (including extensions). As under present law, the individual would be permitted to establish an IRA on the same date on which he or she made the contribution, so the extension of the time for making a contribution to an IRA would apply to plan establishment as well as to contributions.

The amendments made by this section apply to taxable years beginning after December 31, 1977.

Sec. 157(b)—Correction of excess contributions.

House Committee Report 95-1739.—The committee bill would allow an individual a deduction from gross income for a taxable year where he corrects a previous excess contribution to an IRA by contributing less than his maximum deduction allowable for the year. The maximum deduction allowed by the amendment would be the amount of the undercontribution. For example, if an individual were entitled to make a contribution of $1,000 for 1978 and 1979, an excess contribution of $400 for 1978 could be corrected by making a contribution of only $600 for 1979 ($400 less than the individual's maximum permissible contribution) and the individual would be entitled to a $1,000 deduction for 1978 and for 1979.

If the individual erroneously took a deduction in a previous year for any part of the excess contribution and the period for assessing a deficiency for the previous year has expired, the amount allowed as a deduction under the amendment would be correspondingly reduced.

The committee bill provides a transitional rule with respect to amounts of excess contributions made up by undercontributions for years prior to 1978. The rule would allow a one-time catch-up deduction from gross income for those amounts for 1978 rather than requiring amended returns to be filed for each year of undercontribution. For example, if an individual entitled to make a $1,500 contribution for 1978 had made an excess contribution of $800 for 1976, and $300 for 1977, he could correct both excess contributions (totaling $1,100) by making only a $400 contribution for 1978 and would be entitled to a $1,500 deduction for that year.

The amendments made by this section will apply to taxable years beginning after December 31, 1975.

Sec. 157(c)—Withdrawal of excess contributions—The House Committee Report on Sec. 157(c) is at ¶ 12,050.09.

[¶ 11,330.04]

Committee Reports on P.L. 94-455 (Tax Reform Act of 1976)

Present law

Under present law, an individual who is covered by a governmental plan is not allowed to make tax-deductible contributions to an individual retirement account (IRA).

Reasons for change

The rule prohibiting contributions to IRAs by a participant in a governmental plan denies IRA deductions to members of the National Guard and Armed Forces Reserves because they are covered by the U.S. military retirement plan. Generally, under this plan, members of the Reserves or Guard who serve for less than 20 years are not entitled to benefits. Consequently, many members of the Reserves or Guard are denied individual retirement account deductions even though they will not obtain benefits under the Government's plan.

Explanation of provisions

The committee amendment allows individual retirement account deductions for a year by a member of the Armed Forces Reserves or National Guard (who is otherwise eligible for the deduction) if his service for the year, excluding active duty for training, is less than 90 days. The House bill did not include a comparable provision.

Effective date

The amendment would apply for taxable years beginning after December 31, 1975.

House bill

No provision.

Senate amendment

Under present law an active participant in a governmental plan in a taxable year is not allowed a deduction for a contribution to an individual retirement account (IRA) for that year.

For taxable years beginning after 1975, the Senate amendment extends the deduction for contributions to an IRA to a person who would be eligible for an IRA but for membership in a volunteer fire department or in a governmental plan for volunteer firemen.

Conference agreement

The conference agreement follows the Senate amendment, but limits the deduction to firefighters who have not accrued an annual benefit in excess of $1,800 (when expressed as a single life annuity payable at age 65) under a firefighter's plan.

[¶ 11,330.05]

Committee Report on P.L. 93-406 (Employee Retirement Income Security Act of 1974)

[Conference Committee Explanation]

Deductions for contributions to IRA's.—Under the conference substitute, the maximum annual deduction is to be $1,500, or 15 percent of compensation, whichever is less. Consequently, the percentage limitation for contributions to individual retirement accounts is the same as the percentage limitation for contributions to H.R. 10 plans (although the H.R. 10 plan has a $7,500 limitation on the amount which may be set aside in order to provide an incentive for the self-employed to establish qualified plans which will also benefit their employees).

The deduction is to be available to any individual who is not an active participant in a qualified or government plan, or a section 403(b) contract (available to employees of certain types of tax-exempt organizations) and is to be available whether or not the taxpayer itemizes his other deductions. The individual may himself make payments into such an account or this may be done by his employer or his union. If both husband and wife are eligible, each can make contributions to his or her own individual retirement account.

* * *

[¶ 11,330.08]

Committee Report on P.L. 93-406 (Employee Retirement Income Security Act of 1974)

[House Ways and Means Committee Explanation]

If an employee is given the option to elect not to be covered by a qualified, etc., plan and he so elects, generally he will not be treated as being an active participant in the plan for purposes of the retirement savings deduction. For example, if an employer offers a qualified plan that requires matching employee contributions, but the employee elects not to participate in the plan, he is not to be considered as an active participant in the plan. However, where an employee who opts out of a qualified plan can elect later to become an active participant in it and can receive benefits for all prior years (for which he opted out) upon payment of, *e.g.,* all mandatory contributions plus interest for the prior periods, the employee is to be treated as being an active participant in the plan for the prior years with respect to which he pays the required amount and accrues benefits.

Otherwise, an individual could receive a retirement savings deduction for a number of years and also, at his own discretion, later become covered by a qualified plan for the same years.

[¶ 11,330.10]

Committee Report on P.L. 93-406 (Employee Retirement Income Security Act of 1974)

[Conference Committee Explanation]

Requirements for an IRA.—Under the conference substitute, the assets of an individual retirement account may be invested in a trusteed or custodial account with a bank, savings and loan, or credit union, or in an annuity contract, or in a qualified retirement bond.

In addition, the substitute allows a retirement savings deduction for amounts paid under certain life insurance endowment contracts (which will be treated as individual retirement annuities) to the extent the amounts paid are properly allocable to retirement savings. However, only the retirement saving element in the contract, and not the part of the premium used to purchase life insurance, is to be deductible. For example, if a premium of $1,000 were paid under a qualified endowment contract, and $200 of this amount were allocable (under regulations) to the cost of the life insurance element, and $800 to the retirement savings aspect of the contract, the $800 would be allowed as a retirement savings deduction (if the individual were eligible for a deduction of this amount).

[Code Sec. 223]

[¶ 11,335.085]

Committee Report on P.L. 109-432 (Tax Relief and Health Care Act of 2006)

[Joint Committee on Taxation Report]

[Provisions relating to health savings accounts]

Allow rollovers from health FSAs and HRAs into HSAs for a limited time

The provision allows certain amounts in a health FSA or HRA to be distributed from the health FSA or HRA and contributed through a direct transfer to an HSA without violating the otherwise applicable requirements for such arrangements. The amount that can be distributed from a health FSA or HRA and contributed to an HSA may not exceed an amount equal to the lesser of (1) the balance in the health FSA or HRA as of September 21, 2006 or (2) the balance in the health FSA or HRA as of the date of the distribution. The balance in the health FSA or HRA as of any date is determined on a cash basis (i.e., expenses incurred that have not been reimbursed as of the date the determination is made are not taken into account). Amounts contributed to an HSA under the provision are excludable from gross income and wages for employment tax purposes, are not taken into account in applying the maximum deduction limitation for other HSA contributions, and are not deductible. Contributions must be made directly to the HSA before January 1, 2012. The provision is limited to one distribution with respect to each health FSA or HRA of the individual.

The provision is designed to assist individuals in transferring from another type of health plan to a high deductible health plan. Thus, if an individual for whom a contribution is made under the provision does not remain an eligible individual during the testing period, the amount of the contribution is includible in gross income of the individual. An exception applies if the employee ceases to be an eligible individual by reason of death or disability. The testing period is the period beginning with the month of the contribution and ending on the last day of the 12th month following such month. The amount is includible for the taxable year of the first day during the testing period that the individual is not an eligible individual. A 10-percent additional tax also applies to the amount includible.

A modified comparability rule applies with respect to contributions under the provision. If the employer makes available to any employee the ability to make contributions to the HSA from distributions from a health FSA or HRA under the provision, all employees who are covered under a high deductible plan of the employer must be allowed to make such distributions and contributions. The present-law excise tax applies if this requirement is not met.

For example, suppose the balance in a health FSA as of September 21, 2006, is $2,000 and the balance in the account as January 1, 2008 is $3,000. Under the provision, a health FSA will not be considered to violate applicable rules if, as of January 1, 2008, an amount not to exceed $2,000 is distributed from the health FSA and contributed to an HSA of the individual. The $2,000 distribution would not be includible in income, and the subsequent contribution would not be deductible and would not count against the annual maximum tax deductible contribution that can be made to the HSA. If the individual ceases to be an eligible individual as of June 1, 2008, the $2,000 contribution amount is included in gross income and subject to a 10- percent additional tax. If instead the distribution and contribution are made as of June 30, 2008, when the balance in the health FSA is $1,500, the amount of the distribution and contribution is limited to $1,500.

The present law rule that an individual is not an eligible individual if the individual has coverage under a general purpose health FSA or HRA continues to apply. Thus, for example, if the health FSA or HRA from which the contribution is made is a general purpose health FSA or HRA and the individual remains eligible under such arrangement after the distribution and contribution, the individual is not an eligible individual.

Certain FSA coverage treated as disregarded coverage

The provision provides that, for taxable years beginning after December 31, 2006, in certain cases, coverage under a health flexible spending arrangement ("FSA") during the period immediately following the end of a plan year during which unused benefits or contributions remaining at the end of such plan year may be paid or reimbursed to plan participants for qualified expenses is disregarded coverage. Such coverage is disregarded if (1) the balance in the health FSA at the end of the plan year is zero, or (2) in accordance with rules prescribed by the Secretary of Treasury, the entire remaining balance in the health FSA at the end of the plan year is contributed to an HSA as provided under another provision of the bill.[77]

Thus, for example, if as of December 31, 2006, a participant's health FSA balance is zero, coverage under the health FSA during the period from January 1, 2007, until March 15, 2007 (i.e., the "grace period") is disregarded in determining if tax deductible contributions can be made to an HSA for that period. Similarly, if the entire balance in an individual's health FSA as of December 31, 2006, is distributed and contributed to an HSA (as under another provision of the bill) coverage during the health FSA grace period is disregarded.

It is intended that the Secretary will provide guidance under the provision with respect to the timing of health FSA distributions contributed to an HSA in order to facilitate such rollovers and the establishment of HSAs in connection with high deductible plans. For example, it is intended that the Secretary would provide rules under which coverage is disregarded if, before the end of a year, an individual elects high deductible plan coverage and to contribute any remaining FSA balance to an HSA in accordance with the provision even if the trustee-to-trustee transfer cannot be completed until the following plan year. Similar rules apply for the general provision allowing amounts from a health FSA or HRA to be contributed to an HSA in order to facilitate such contributions at the beginning of an employee's first year of HSA eligibility.

The provision does not modify the permitted health FSA grace period allowed under existing Treasury guidance.

Repeal of annual plan deductible limitation on HSA contribution limitation

The provision modifies the limit on the annual deductible contributions that can be made to an HSA so that the maximum deductible contribution is not limited to the annual deductible under the high deductible health plan. Thus, under the provision, the maximum aggregate annual contribution that can be made to an HSA is $2,850 (for 2007) in the case of self-only coverage and $5,650 (for 2007) in the case of family coverage.

Earlier indexing of cost of living adjustments

Under the provision, in the case of adjustments made for any taxable year beginning after 2007, the Consumer Price Index for a calendar year is determined as of the close of the 12-month period ending on March 31 of the calendar year (rather than August 31 as under present law) for the purpose of making cost-of-living adjustments for the HSA dollar amounts that are indexed for inflation (i.e., the contribution limits and the high-deductible health plan requirements). The provision also requires the Secretary of Treasury to publish the adjusted amounts for a year no later than June 1 of the preceding calendar year.

Allow full contribution for months preceding month that taxpayer is an eligible individual

In general, the provision allows individuals who become covered under a high deductible plan in a month other than January to make the full deductible HSA contribution for the year. Under the provision, an individual who is an eligible individual during the last month of a taxable year is treated as having been an eligible individual during every month during the taxable year for purposes of computing the amount that may be contributed to the HSA for the year. Thus, such individual is allowed to make contributions for months before the individual was enrolled in a high deductible health plan. For the months preceding the last month of the taxable year that the individual is treated as an eligible individual solely by reason of the provision, the individual is treated as having been enrolled in the same high deductible health plan in which the individual was enrolled during the last month of the taxable year.

If an individual makes contributions under the provision and does not remain an eligible individual during the testing period, the amount of the contributions attributable to months preceding the month in which the individual was an eligible individual which could not have been made but for the provision are includible in gross income. An exception applies if the employee ceases to be an eligible individual by reason of death or disability. The testing period is the period beginning with the last month of the taxable year and ending on the last day of the 12th month following such month. The amount is includible for the taxable year of the first day during the testing period that the individual is not an eligible individual. A 10-percent additional tax also applies to the amount includible.

---

[77] The amount that can be contributed is limited to the balance in the health FSA as of September 21, 2006.

For example, suppose individual "A" enrolls in high deductible plan "H" in December of 2007 and is otherwise an eligible individual in that month. A was not an eligible individual in any other month in 2007. A may make HSA contributions as if she had been enrolled in plan H for all of 2007. If A ceases to be an eligible individual (e.g., if she ceases to be covered under the high deductible health plan) in June 2008, an amount equal to the HSA deduction attributable to treating A as an eligible individual for January through November 2007 is included in income in 2008. In addition, a 10-percent additional tax applies to the amount includible.

Modify employer comparable contribution requirements for contributions made to nonhighly compensated employees

The provision provides an exception to the comparable contribution requirements which allows employers to make larger HSA contributions for nonhighly compensated employees than for highly compensated employees. Highly compensated employees are defined as under section 414(q) and include any employee who was (1) a five-percent owner at any time during the year or the preceding year; or (2) for the preceding year, (A) had compensation from the employer in excess of $100,000[78] (for 2007) and (B) if elected by the employer, was in the group consisting of the top-20 percent of employees when ranked based on compensation. Nonhighly compensated employees are employees not included in the definition of highly compensated employee under section 414(q).

The comparable contribution rules continue to apply to the contributions made to nonhighly compensated employees so that the employer must make available comparable contributions on behalf of all nonhighly compensated employees with comparable coverage during the same period.

For example, an employer is permitted to make a $1,000 contribution to the HSA of each nonhighly compensated employee for a year without making contributions to the HSA of each highly compensated employee.

One-time rollovers from IRAs into HSAs

The provision allows a one-time contribution to an HSA of amounts distributed from an individual retirement arrangement ("IRA"). The contribution must be made in a direct trustee-to-trustee transfer. Amounts distributed from an IRA under the provision are not includible in income to the extent that the distribution would otherwise be includible in income. In addition, such distributions are not subject to the 10-percent additional tax on early distributions.

In determining the extent to which amounts distributed from the IRA would otherwise be includible in income, the aggregate amount distributed from the IRA is treated as includible in income to the extent of the aggregate amount which would have been includible if all amounts were distributed from all IRAs of the same type (i.e., in the case of a traditional IRA, there is no pro-rata distribution of basis). As under present law, this rule is applied separately to Roth IRAs and other IRAs.

The amount that can be distributed from the IRA and contributed to an HSA is limited to the otherwise maximum deductible contribution amount to the HSA computed on the basis of the type of coverage under the high deductible health plan at the time of the contribution. The amount that can otherwise be contributed to the HSA for the year of the contribution from the IRA is reduced by the amount contributed from the IRA. No deduction is allowed for the amount contributed from an IRA to an HSA.

Under the provision, only one distribution and contribution may be made during the lifetime of the individual, except that if a distribution and contribution are made during a month in which an individual has self-only coverage as of the first day of the month, an additional distribution and contribution may be made during a subsequent month within the taxable year in which the individual has family coverage. The limit applies to the combination of both contributions.

If the individual does not remain an eligible individual during the testing period, the amount of the distribution and contribution is includible in gross income of the individual. An exception applies if the employee ceases to be an eligible individual by reason of death or disability. The testing period is the period beginning with the month of the contribution and ending on the last day of the 12th month following such month. The amount is includible for the taxable year of the first day during the testing period that the individual is not an eligible individual. A 10-percent additional tax also applies to the amount includible.

The provision does not apply to simplified employee pensions ("SEPs") or to SIMPLE retirement accounts.

Effective Date

The provision allowing rollovers from health FSAs and HRAs into HSAs is effective for distributions and contributions on or after the date of enactment and before January 1, 2012. The provision disregarding certain FSA coverage is effective after the date of enactment with respect to coverage for taxable years beginning after December 31, 2006. The provision repealing the annual plan limitation on the HSA contribution limitation is effective for taxable years beginning after December 31, 2006. The provision relating to cost-of-living adjustments is effective for adjustments made for taxable years beginning after 2007. The provision allowing contributions for months preceding the month that the taxpayer is an eligible individual is effective for taxable years beginning after December 31, 2006. The provision modifying the comparability rule is effective for taxable years beginning after December 31, 2006. The provision allowing one-time rollovers from an IRA into an HSA is effective for taxable years beginning after December 31, 2006.

[Code Sec. 274]

[¶ 11,355.095]

Committee Reports on P.L. 99-44 (Recordkeeping Repeal Act)

[Conference Committee Report]

1. REPEAL OF "CONTEMPORANEOUS" REQUIREMENT

House bill

The House bill repeals the word "contemporaneous," effective as if it had never been enacted.

Senate amendment

The Senate amendment is the same as the House bill.

Conference agreement

The conference agreement follows the House bill and the Senate amendment.

2. ALTERNATE SUBSTANTIATION METHOD

House bill

The House bill provides that, as an alternative to maintaining adequate records, taxpayers may substantiate deductions and credits under section 274(d) by sufficient written evidence corroborating their own statement.

The committee report also specifies that certain information concerning mileage and business use of vehicles, as well as similar information concerning business use of other listed property, must be requested on tax returns.

The House bill is effective on January 1, 1986. For 1985, the substantiation rules in effect prior to the 1984 Act would apply.

Senate amendment

The Senate amendment is similar to the House bill in that it provides for an alternate substantiation method. However, the Senate amendment does not require that the evidence must be written in order to qualify as sufficient under the alternate substantiation standard. The Senate amendment is effective January 1, 1985.

The Senate amendment does not specifically require that questions regarding the business use of automobiles and other listed property be asked on tax returns.

Conference agreement

Substantiation standards—In general

The conference agreement generally follows the Senate amendment as to the substantiation standards under section 274(d). Thus, section 274(d) is amended to require that a taxpayer must have adequate records or sufficient evidence corroborating the taxpayer's own statement to support credits or deductions for expenditures subject to the section 274(d) substantiation rules. As under pre-1984 Act law, section 274(d) as amended by the bill requires the taxpayer to substantiate (1) the amount of the expense or item subject to section 274(d), (2) the time and place of the travel, entertainment, amusement, recreation, or use of the facility or property, or the date and description of the gift, (3) the business purpose of the expense or other item, and (4) the business relationship to the taxpayer of persons entertained, using the facility or property, or receiving the gift.

The conferees believe that a taxpayer's uncorroborated statement as to the business use of an automobile or other listed property does not alone have sufficient probative value to warrant consideration by the Internal Revenue Service or the courts. Consequently, the conferees adopt for this purpose the standard of prior law applicable to travel away from home and business entertainment (sec. 274(d)) that requires taxpayers to provide either adequate records or sufficient evidence corroborating their own statements in order to support a deduction or credit under section 274(d). The more general substantiation standards applicable under section 162,[1] which have been interpreted to permit in certain circumstances uncorroborated statements by taxpayers to support business deductions not subject to section 274(d) or other special rules, are to have no application to deductions or credits with respect to local travel, computers, and other listed property first required (under this bill) to meet the section 274(d) substantiation standards beginning January 1, 1986, just as they are to have no application with respect to expenditures with respect to travel away from home, etc., which continue to be subject to section 274(d) substantiation standards.

The conference agreement does not include the provision of the House bill that would require that the sufficient evidence corroborating the taxpayer's own

[78] This amount is indexed for inflation.

[1] Under general tax law principles, the courts have held that a taxpayer bears the burden of proving both the eligibility of any expenditure claimed as a deduction or credit and also the amount of any such eligible expenditure including the expenses of using a car in the taxpayer's trade or business. See, e.g., *Interstate Transit Lines v. Comm'r,* 319 U.S. 590, 593 (1943) [43-1 USTC ¶ 9486]; *Comm'r v. Heininger,* 320 U.S. 467 (1943) [44-1 USTC ¶ 9109]; *Gaines v. Comm'r* 35 T.C.M. 1415 (1976) [CCH Dec. 34,048(M)].

statement be written. The conferees believe that oral evidence corroborating the taxpayer's own statement, such as oral testimony from a disinterested, unrelated party describing the taxpayer's activities, may be of sufficient probative value that it should not be automatically excluded from consideration under section 274(d).

The conferees emphasize, however, that different types of evidence have different degrees of probative value. The conferees believe that oral evidence alone has considerably less probative value than written evidence. In addition, the conferees believe that the probative value of written evidence is greater the closer in time it relates to the expenditure. Thus, written evidence arising at or near the time of the expenditure, absent unusual circumstances, has much more probative value than evidence created years later, such as written evidence first prepared for audit or court.

The conferees specifically approve the types of substantiation that were required under prior law, and consider the longstanding Treasury regulations on recordkeeping issued under section 274(d)[2] prior to the 1984 Act to reflect accurately their intent as to the substantiation that taxpayers are required to maintain.[3] While taxpayers may choose to keep logs on the use of their automobiles, and while such evidence generally has more probative value than evidence developed later, the Treasury is specifically prohibited from requiring that taxpayers keep daily contemporaneous logs of their use of automobiles.

Although the conferees intend that the principles of these regulations fully apply to deductions and credits claimed for local travel and the use of other listed property under section 274(d), the conferees also recognize that these principles will need to be carefully applied to local travel and listed property not previously subject to section 274(d). This will need to be done because the nature of making these expenditures generally differs from the nature of making the types of expenditures that had been required to meet the section 274(d) substantiation standards prior to the 1984 Act, such as travel away from home and business meals. For example, deductions associated with local travel may be for annual amounts for items such as depreciation and insurance, rather than a series of discrete expenditures for meals or hotels. Also, expenses for travel away from home often involve a third party, such as an airline, train, or hotel, that provides a receipt for the taxpayer of the date and amount of the expenditure and the destination or location. Similarly, expenses for business meals generally occur in restaurants, which provide a similar receipt. While these receipts do not, of course, encompass all of the elements of the substantiation requirements under section 274(d),[4] they do aid taxpayers in their recordkeeping. Similar third party involvement generally is not available for local travel or the use of computers. Similarly, expenses for travel away from home or for business meals do not generally occur with the same frequency as individual local travel trips. Because the bill repeals the 1984 Act requirement of contemporaneous records, taxpayers are not required to maintain trip-by-trip logs and records encompassing each element of the substantiation standards of section 274(d) to justify a deduction or credit.

Consequently, the conferees recognize that some adjustment generally will need to be made in order to apply these principles to the specific factual circumstances surrounding expenditures for local travel and use of listed property not previously subject to section 274(d) rules. The conferees believe that the courts and the Treasury can make these required adjustments without sacrificing these principles, and without reverting to the section 162 standards (including the *Cohan*[5] rule), which the conferees have determined are inadequate and unacceptable for purposes of section 274(d). In several cases previously decided under section 274(d), it is not clear that the courts had rejected the *Cohan* rule; the conferees believe that the courts must clearly and explicitly reject the *Cohan* rule for expenditures required to meet the substantiation requirements of section 274(d).

Written policy statements

The conferees intend that the two types of written policy statements satisfying the conditions described below, if initiated and kept by an employer to implement a policy of no personal use (or no personal use except for commuting) of a vehicle provided by the employer, qualify as sufficient evidence corroborating the taxpayer's own statement[6] and therefore will satisfy the employer's substantiation requirements under section 274(d). Therefore, the employee need not keep a separate set of records for purposes of the employer's substantiation requirements under section 274(d) with respect to use of a vehicle satisfying these written policy statement rules. A written policy statement adopted by a governmental unit as to employee use of its vehicles would be eligible for these exceptions to the section 274(d) substantiation rules. Thus, a resolution of a city council or a provision of state law or the state constitution would qualify as a written policy statement, so long as the conditions described below are met.

The first type of written policy statement that will satisfy the employer's substantiation requirements under section 274(d) is a policy that prohibits personal use by the employee. In order to be eligible for this special rule, all of the following conditions must be met—

(1) The vehicle is owned or leased by the employer and is provided to one or more employees for use in connection with the employer's trade or business;

(2) When the vehicle is not being used for such business purposes, it is kept on the employer's business premises (or temporarily located elsewhere, e.g., for repair);

(3) Under the employer's written policy, no employee may use the vehicle for personal purposes, other than de minimis personal use (such as a stop for lunch between two business deliveries);

(4) The employer reasonably believes that no employee uses the vehicle, other than de minimis use, for any personal purpose;

(5) No employee using the vehicle lives at the employer's business premises; and

(6) There must be evidence that would enable the Internal Revenue Service to determine whether the use of the vehicle met the five preceding conditions.

The second type of written policy statement that will satisfy the employer's substantiation requirements under section 274(d) is a policy that prohibits personal use by the employee, except for commuting. In order to be eligible for this rule, all of the following conditions must be met—

(1) The vehicle is owned or leased by the employer and is provided to one or more employees for use in connection with the employer's trade or business and is used in the employer's trade or business;

(2) For bona fide noncompensatory business reasons, the employer requires the employee to commute to and/or from work in the vehicle;

(3) The employer establishes a written policy under which the employee may not use the vehicle for personal purposes, other than commuting or de minimis personal use (such as a stop for a personal errand between a business delivery and the employee's home);

(4) The employer reasonably believes that, except for de minimis use, the employee does not use the vehicle for any personal purpose other than commuting;

(5) The employer accounts for the commuting use by including an appropriate amount (specified in Treasury regulations) in the employee's gross income;[7] and

(6) There must be evidence that would enable the Internal Revenue Service to determine whether the use of the vehicle met the five preceding conditions.

This second type of written policy statement is not available if the employee using the vehicle for commuting is an officer or one-percent owner of the employer.[8]

Tax return questions

The conference agreement generally follows the House bill [for the House Committee Report on tax return questions, see page 31] as to information to be requested on tax returns about business use of vehicles and other listed property.

The conferees want to ensure that taxpayers claim only the deductions and credits to which they are entitled, but without being unduly burdened by unnecessarily complex recordkeeping requirements. At the same time, the conferees believe that taxpayers should provide sufficient information on their returns so that the Internal Revenue Service can make a preliminary evaluation of the appropriateness of the taxpayer's claimed deductions. Previously, the Internal Revenue Service found it difficult to make such a preliminary evaluation without auditing the taxpayer, which can also be a significant burden on the taxpayer.

---

[2] See Treas. Reg. sec. 1.274-5.

[3] Prior law provided that adequate records or sufficient evidence may take the following forms:

a. Account books
b. Diaries
c. Logs
d. Documentary evidence (receipts, paid bills)
e. Trip sheets
f. Expense reports
g. Statements of witnesses
h. If the employee is required to make an adequate accounting to the employer and the reimbursement equals expenses, the employee is not required to report the expenses and reimbursement on his or her tax return. (A reimbursement would equal expenses where the reimbursement is determined pursuant to data on the type of automobile and its availability for personal purposes, and on a reasonable allocation of local operating and fixed costs.)

The conferees expect the Internal Revenue Service and the courts to continue to weigh carefully the probative value of these as well as all other, forms of evidence. The Service and the courts continue to have the ability to discount or reject totally evidence that has limited or no probative value (such as documents actually created much later than they purport to have been created). As noted above, section 274(d) requires that the records or evidence (whatever their particular form) must substantiate not just the amount of the expense, but also the time and place of the travel, entertainment, amusement, recreation, or use of the facility or property, or the date and description of the gift; the business purpose of the expense or other item; and the business relationship to the taxpayer of persons entertained, using the facility or property, or receiving the gift.

[4] For example, the third party is not in a position to record the business purpose of the trip or meal; the taxpayer must provide that information, which is required under the section 274(d) substantiation rules.

[5] *Cohan v. Commissioner,* 39 F.2d 540, 544 (2d Cir. 1930) [2 USTC ¶ 489].

[6] The substance of these two special rules was set forth in the temporary Treasury regulations repealed by the bill. The conferees intend that these rules, as described in this report, be reinstated in the new regulations required by the bill.

[7] Of course, if in fact the employee uses the vehicle for personal purposes in violation of the particular type of written policy statement, then the employee has additional gross income.

[8] This restriction, which makes this rule inapplicable to officers or one-percent owners, applies for substantiation purposes under the conference agreement. The treatment of commuting use of vehicles by such persons for valuation purposes is to be determined separately under Treasury regulations. No inference is intended, on the basis of the exclusion of officers and one-percent owners from eligibility under this substantiation rule, as to the treatment of commuting use of vehicles by such persons under valuation rules prescribed by Treasury regulations.

Therefore, the conferees intend that individual taxpayers (whether employees or self-employed) claiming deductions or credits for business use of an automobile or other listed property subject to the substantiation standards of section 274(d) are to provide on their returns the substance of the information (generally on appropriate existing tax forms) called for by all the questions as set forth in the House report on the bill.[9] Corporate taxpayers, as well as all other taxpayers and entities, claiming such deductions or credits also are to be asked to supply such information on the forms or schedules they are required to file.

The conferees have carefully considered the fact that furnishing additional tax return information, although involving only a limited number of questions, requires some additional effort by taxpayers. However, the conferees note that computations involved with respect to vehicles (such as mileage and percentage of business use) normally would be made by taxpayers in the process of determining the proper amount of deductions and credits to claim, and that other information can be obtained through "yes" or "no" questions. Accordingly, to achieve better compliance and more accurate computations, the conference agreement directs the Internal Revenue Service to obtain this information on appropriate tax forms or schedules, notwithstanding any otherwise applicable paperwork reduction considerations.

The conferees intend that employees give this return information to their employers with respect to employer-provided vehicles. Generally, the employer would report this information on its tax return, since the employer is claiming the tax deductions or credits for use of the vehicle. An employer which provides more than five cars to its employees, however, would not have to include all this information on the employer's return; instead, such an employer must obtain this information from its employees, must so indicate on its return, and must retain the information received. The Internal Revenue Service could then examine on audit the information that the employees had provided to the employer. An employer may rely on such a statement from its employee (unless the employer knows or has reason to know it is false) to determine the credits and deductions to which the employer is entitled and to determine the amount, if any, which must be included in [the] employee's income and wages by the employer because of the employee's commuting or other personal use of the employer-provided car.

Effective dates

The modification to the substantiation standards of section 274(d) that provides that taxpayers must substantiate deductions or credits subject to that provision by adequate records or sufficient evidence corroborating their own statement is effective January 1, 1985.

Use of listed property that was not subject to section 274(d) substantiation rules prior to the 1984 Act (such as local travel in an automobile or use of computers) is subject to the section 274(d) substantiation requirements effective January 1, 1986.[10] For 1985, use of such listed property is not subject to the special substantiation standards under section 274(d).

The tax return information (described above) must be requested on returns for taxable years beginning in 1985 (i.e., in the case of most individuals, returns which must be filed by April 15, 1986.)

[House Committee Report]

Information Required on Return

The committee wants to ensure that taxpayers claim only the deductions to which they are entitled without being unduly burdened by complex recordkeeping requirements. The committee also believes that taxpayers should provide sufficient information on their returns so that the Internal Revenue Service can make a preliminary evaluation of the appropriateness of the taxpayer's claimed deductions. Previously, the Internal Revenue Service found it difficult to make this sort of preliminary evaluation without auditing the taxpayer, which can also be a significant burden on the taxpayer. Therefore, the committee believes that taxpayers should all answer a few short questions on their returns if they claim the tax benefits for the business use of an automobile.

The committee believes that taxpayers will not be significantly burdened by responding to a few questions, most of them requiring a yes or no response. The committee directs that the following questions appear on the tax return, to be answered by taxpayers claiming credits or deductions for the business use of an automobile:

1. Total number of miles driven during the year: __ miles.
2. Percentage of personal use claimed: . . %.
3. Was the vehicle used for commuting? Yes . . No . . . If Yes, the distance normally commuted: . miles.
4. Was the vehicle available for personal use in off duty hours? Yes . . No . . .
5. Is another vehicle available for personal use? Yes . . No . . .
6. I have adequate records or sufficient written evidence to justify these deductions: Yes . . No . . * * *.

The committee notes that the requirement that these questions be included on the tax forms does not appear in the bill because the Internal Revenue Code does not generally specify the format or specific content of forms. The Internal Revenue Code does not need to be amended to provide the authority to require these questions, since that authority already exists in sections 6001 and 6011.

The committee intends that employees who claim deductions or credits for business use of their own can be asked these questions on Form 2106 (relating to employee business expenses); some of this information is already required to be provided on that form. Unincorporated taxpayers who claim these credits or deductions on either Schedules C or F (or on some other form) will be asked these questions on that form. Corporate taxpayers, as well as all other taxpayers and entities, will be asked these questions on the forms they are required to file.

The committee intends that employees give this information to their employers if the employer provided the car. Generally, the employer would put this information on its tax return, since the employer is claiming the tax benefits of the use of the car. Employers who provide more than 5 cars to employees, however, would not have to include this information on the employer's return; the Internal Revenue Service could examine on audit the information that the employees provide to the employer. The employer would have to indicate on his return that he has received this information from the employees. The employer can rely on the employee's statement (unless the employer has reason to know it is false) to determine the credits and deductions to which the employer is entitled and to determine the amount of income, if any, the employer must include in the employee's income because of the employer's personal use of the employer's car.

The committee intends that similar questions be asked on the tax return about other listed property, such as yachts, airplanes, and computers. For computers, for example, the following questions should be asked:

1. Percentage of personal used claimed: . . %.
2. Was the computer located at your . . place of business or . . your home or . . both? If both, what percentage of the year was it at home: . %.
3. Do you have records or written evidence to justify these deductions? Yes . . No . . .

[Conference Committee Report]

House bill

The House bill repeals all Treasury regulations (temporary or proposed) issued prior to the enactment of this House bill that carry out the amendments made by section 179(b) of the Tax Reform Act of 1984. Thus, such regulations issued to implement the changes to section 274(d) made by that Act, particularly the inclusion in that section of the word "contemporaneous," are revoked.[11] In addition, any regulations relating to the return preparer provision and the special negligence penalty (described above) are revoked.[12] These revoked regulations are to have no force and effect whatsoever.

Senate amendment

The Senate amendment is the same as the House bill.

Conference agreement

The conference agreement follows the House bill and the Senate amendment. Thus, the conference agreement provides that regulations issued to carry out the amendments made by paragraphs (1)(C), (2), and (3) of section 179(b) of the 1984 Act shall have no force and effect.

[Conference Committee Report]

House bill

Substantiation rules

The House bill exempts from the section 274(d) substantiation rules (as modified by the bill) any vehicle that, by reason of its nature, is not likely to be

9 In the case of a vehicle, the information required to be requested on the tax return relates to mileage (total, business, commuting, and other personal), percentage of business use, date placed in service, use of other vehicles and after-work use, whether the taxpayer has evidence to support the business use claimed on the return, and whether or not the evidence is written. In the case of other listed property subject to the section 274(d) rules, information should be requested in connection with appropriate tax forms or schedules as to type of property (e.g., yacht, computer, airplane, etc.), percentage of business use, whether the taxpayer has written [*sic*] evidence to support the business use claimed on the return, and whether or not the evidence is written. Under the conference agreement, the Internal Revenue Service is not required to request on returns the specific question relating to computers set forth as question 2 on page 10 of the committee report on the House bill.

10 This January 1, 1986 effective date applies only to the extent that use of listed property was first made subject to the substantiation standards of section 274(d) by the 1984 Act. Deductions for expenses or items that were subject to the section 274(d) substantiation standards prior to the 1984 Act (such as use of an automobile for travel away from home or use of a yacht that is an entertainment, recreation, or amusement facility) remain subject to the section 274(d) substantiation standards for all taxable years ending after December 31, 1962.

11 Also, the provisions of the temporary regulations that prohibit an employer from including the entire value of the use of an automobile in the income of certain employees are revoked. Thus, an employer is permitted to charge the entire value of an employer-provided car to an employee as income and wages (for income tax, FICA, FUTA, and RRTA withholding purposes). The employer may then reimburse the employee for business use of the car, or the employee may claim a deduction on the employee's income tax return for the business use of the car.

12 The bill only revokes such regulation (issued prior to enactment) carrying out such amendments made by sections 179(b)(1)(C), (2), and (3) of the 1984 Act. Thus, the bill does not revoke any other regulations, such as regulations issued under sections 61 and 132 (relating to valuation).

used more than a de minimis amount for personal purposes. This provision is effective for taxable years beginning after December 31, 1985; thus, for 1985 the pre-1984 Act substantiation rules continue to apply with respect to such vehicles.

The committee report on the House bill lists the following vehicles as examples of vehicles exempted under the bill from the section 274(d) substantiation rules: (a) clearly marked police and fire vehicles (as described in the report); (b) delivery trucks with seating only for the driver, or only for the driver plus a folding jump seat; (c) flatbed trucks; (d) any vehicle designed to carry cargo with a loaded gross vehicle weight over 14,000 pounds; (e) passenger buses used as such with a capacity of at least 20 passengers; (f) ambulances used as such or hearses used as such; (g) bucket trucks ("cherry pickers"); (h) cranes and derricks; (i) forklifts; (j) cement mixers; (k) dump trucks (including garbage trucks); (l) refrigerated trucks; (m) tractors; and (n) combines.

The report on the House bill also states that the committee recognizes that it may not have developed an exhaustive list of vehicles not susceptible to personal use. Therefore, the report states, the committee intends that the Internal Revenue Service is to expand this list through either regulations or revenue rulings to include any vehicles not included in the listing in the report that are appropriate for listing because by their nature it is highly unlikely that they will be used more than a very minimal amount for personal purposes.

The report also states that the committee did not generally exempt from the section 274(d) substantiation rules all pickup trucks and vans, because these vehicles can easily be used for personal purposes. Some taxpayers purchase these vehicles as substitutes for passenger sedans, and use them predominantly (or entirely) for personal purposes. On the other hand, however, the committee report recognized that this is not applicable to all vans. For example, a van that has only a front bench for seating, in which permanent shelving[13] has been installed, that constantly carries merchandise, and that has been specially painted with advertising or the company's name, is a vehicle not susceptible to personal use.

Income inclusion

The committee report on the House bill states that it is appropriate for Treasury regulations to provide that under certain conditions all use by an employee of any employer-provided vehicle that is exempted under the House bill from the section 274(d) substantiation rules (see above) is excluded, as a working condition fringe benefit (sec. 132(a)(3)),[14] from the employee's gross income, and from wages (and, where appropriate, from the benefit base) for purposes of FICA, FUTA, and RRTA taxes. Such exclusions pursuant to Treasury regulations are to be effective as of January 1, 1985.

Senate amendment

Substantiation rules

The Senate amendment provides that the following vehicles are exempt from the section 274(d) substantiation rules (as modified by the amendment), and that any commuting or other personal use of such exempted vehicles is excluded from the user's gross income, and from wages (and, where appropriate, from the benefit base) for purposes of FICA, FUTA, and RRTA taxes, effective January 1, 1985:

(a) Vehicles required to be used as an integral part of the trade or business of an individual or of the employer (such as calling on customers or clients, making deliveries, or visiting job sites), so long as use in the trade or business is at least 75 percent of the vehicle's total use;

(b) Vehicles used by an employee from commuting, where the commuting is for a bona fide business purpose, where the employer does not permit the employee to make other personal use of the vehicle (other than de minimis use), and where use in the trade or business of the employer is at least 75 percent of total use; and

(c) Vehicles used by a governmental unit for police or other law enforcement purposes and vehicles used as an ambulance.

Income inclusion

The Senate amendment provides that any commuting or other personal use of such exempted vehicles (described above) is excluded from the user's gross income, and from wages (and, where appropriate, from the benefit base) for purposes of FICA, FUTA, and RRTA taxes, effective January 1, 1985.

ITC and depreciation caps

The Senate amendment provides that police and law enforcement vehicles and ambulances placed in service after June 18, 1984 are exempt from the investment tax credit and depreciation limitations set forth in section 280F.

[Conference Agreement]

The conference agreement follows the House bill, with the following modifications.

The conferees intend that school buses (as defined in Code section 4221(d)(7)(C)), qualified specialized utility repair trucks, and qualified moving vans, in addition to the list above (items (a) through (n) in the description of the House bill), are also to be examples of vehicles that, by reason of their nature, are not likely to be used more than a de minimis amount for personal purposes.

The term "qualified specialized utility repair trucks" means trucks (not including vans or pickup trucks) specifically designed and used to carry heavy tools, testing equipment, or parts where (1) the shelves, racks, or other permanent interior construction which has been installed to carry and store such heavy items is such that it is unlikely that the truck will be used more than a very minimal amount for personal purposes[15] and (2) the employer requires the employee to drive the truck home in order to be able to respond in emergency situations for purposes of restoring or maintaining electricity, gas, telephone, water, sewer, or steam utility services.

The term "qualified moving vans" means vans used by professional moving companies in the trade or business of moving household or business goods where no personal use of the van is allowed other than for travel to and from a move site (or for de minimis use), where personal use for travel to and from a move site is an irregular practice (i.e., not more than five times a month on average), and where personal use is limited to situations in which it is more convenient to the employer, because of the location of the employee's residence, for the van not to be returned to the employer's business location.

Also, the conferees agreed that the Treasury Department has authority to issue regulations exempting from the section 274(d) substantiation rules, and from inclusion in income and wages, officially authorized uses of unmarked vehicles by law enforcement officers. To qualify for this exemption, the personal use must be authorized by the Federal, State, county, or local governmental agency or department that owns or leases the vehicle and employs the officer, and must be for law-enforcement functions such as undercover work or reporting directly from home to a stakeout or surveillance site, or to an emergency situation. Use of an unmarked vehicle for vacation or recreation trips cannot qualify as an authorized use. The term "law enforcement officer" means an individual who is employed on a full-time basis by a governmental unit that is responsible for the prevention or investigation of crime involving injury to persons or property, who is authorized by law to carry firearms and execute search warrants and also to make arrests (other than merely a citizen arrest), and who regularly carries firearms (except when it is not possible to do this because of the requirements of undercover work). The term "law enforcement officer" does not include Internal Revenue Service special agents.

The conference agreement also provides that if, for example, a municipal government ordinance requires that police officers driving clearly marked police cars who are on duty at all times must take the vehicle home when the employee is not on his or her regular shift, and prohibits any personal use (except for this commuting use) of the vehicle outside the city (i.e., outside the limit of the officer's arrest powers), then all use of the vehicle could be considered in such regulations as an excludable working condition fringe.

[¶ 11,355.10]

Committee Report on P.L. 97-37 (Former Prisoners of War Benefits Act of 1981)

[Conference Committee Report]

Senate amendment

Present law generally disallows deductions for business gifts to the extent that the cost of all gifts to the same individual during the taxable year exceeds $25. This general rule does not apply, however, to items costing $100 or less which are awarded to an employee by reason of length of service or for safety achievement.

The Senate amendment increases the ceiling on the deductibility of employee awards, and expands the purposes for which they may be given. The amendment allows employee awards for length of service, productivity, or safety achievement, and increases the ceiling from $100 to $400 per item. The amendment also allows a deduction for such awards to the extent that the item is awarded as part of a permanent, written plan or program that does not discriminate in favor of officers, shareholders, or highly compensated employees as to eligibility or benefits. A deduction is allowed for such plan awards only if the average cost of all awards under the plan during the taxable year does not exceed $400. However, no deduction may be claimed under such an award plan or program to the extent the cost of an item exceeds $1,600. The amendment is effective for taxable years ending after the date of enactment.

Conference agreement

The conference agreement follows the Senate amendment.

---

[13] It is intended that this shelving fill most of the cargo area.

[14] Absent such a special exclusion, commuting use (or other personal use) by an employee of an employer-provided vehicle could not qualify as a working condition fringe benefit because the costs of commuting to and from work (or of other personal use of a vehicle) are nondeductible pursuant to Code section 262. See, e.g., *Fausner v. Comm'r*, 413 U.S. 838 (1973) [73-2 USTC ¶ 9515].

[15] An example of this would be permanent shelving that fills most of the cargo area.

[Code Sec. 280F]

[¶ 11,358F.10]

Committee Report on P.L. 98-369 (Tax Reform Act of 1984)

[Conference Committee Report]

House bill

The limits on the amount of investment tax credit and annual depreciation deductions that may be claimed with respect to an automobile are reduced as follows under the House bill: (1) the investment tax credit is limited to $675; (2) depreciation in the first taxable year the automobile is placed in service is limited to $3,600; and (3) depreciation in any subsequent taxable year is limited to $5,400. For years after 1985, the reduced limits are indexed for inflation, as measured by the percentage growth of the automobile component of the Consumer Price Index for All Urban Consumers between October of the preceding year and October, 1984. Adjustments for inflation are otherwise determined as under present law. The committee report states that the committee intends that the Secretary of the Treasury prescribe all limits adjusted for inflation.

The reduced limits are generally effective for property placed in service or leased by the taxpayer after April 2, 1985. However, property acquired by the taxpayer pursuant to a binding contract in effect on April 1, 1985, and at all times thereafter, is not subject to the reduced limits if it is placed in service before August 1, 1985; and property of which the taxpayer is the lessee pursuant to a binding contract in effect on April 1, 1985, and [at] all times thereafter, is not subject to the reduced limits if the taxpayer first uses the property under the lease before August 1, 1985.

Senate amendment

No provision.

Conference agreement

The conference agreement follows the House bill, with three modifications: (1) depreciation in the first taxable year is limited to $3,200; (2) depreciation in any subsequent taxable year is limited to $4,800; and (3) the reduced limits on the investment credit and depreciation are not indexed for inflation until 1989. For automobiles placed in service in any year after 1988, the reduced limits are adjusted for the percentage increase of the automobile component of the Consumer Price Index for All Urban Consumers between October of the preceding year and October 1987. The conferees made these changes to the House bill to ensure that the conference agreement is revenue neutral.

[Code Sec. 280G]

[¶ 11,358P.095]

Committee Report on P.L. 100-647 (Technical and Miscellaneous Revenue Act of 1988)

[Senate Committee Report]

* * *

Under present law, a corporation could fail to qualify for the shareholder approval exception if it has nonvoting preferred stock that is publicly traded, even if all common stock of the corporation is not publicly traded. In some cases, an interest in preferred stock is more in the nature of debt than equity. The purpose of the golden parachute provisions is to protect equity shareholders whose interest in the corporation could be impaired by parachute payments to disqualified individuals. No protection is necessary in the case of nonvoting preferred stock if the preferred shareholders receive the redemption or liquidation value to which they are entitled.

Thus, the bill provides that, for purposes of the shareholder approval requirements, the term "stock" does not include any stock (1) that is not entitled to vote, (2) that is limited and preferred as to dividends and does not participate in corporate growth to any significant extent, (3) that has redemption and liquidation rights which do not exceed the issue price of such stock (except for a reasonable redemption or liquidation premium), (4) that is not convertible into another class of stock, and (5) the rights of which are not adversely affected by the parachute payments.

The bill addresses several issues that arise in the application of the shareholder approval requirements for a corporation the stock of which is not publicly traded by expanding the Secretary's regulatory authority under the golden parachute provisions. It is expected that regulations will address these issues, particularly the application of the shareholder approval requirements in the case of shareholders that are not individuals (i.e., the shareholders are partnerships, corporations, or other nonindividual entities), and to what extent nonvoting interests in the entity shareholder have the right to affect the approval of that shareholder. In general, it is anticipated that the normal voting rights of the entity shareholder will determine whether or not the entity shareholder approves the parachute payments. For example, limited partners with no right to vote on partnership issues generally would not be entitled to vote with respect to the partnership shareholder's approval of a parachute payment.

The bill specifically authorizes the Secretary to prescribe regulations addressing the application of the shareholder approval requirements to entity shareholders that hold de minimis amounts of stock in the corporation. Of course, shareholder approval would still be required if the corporation constituted a substantial portion of the assets of the entity shareholder.

For purposes of the small business exception, the bill provides that "small business corporation" is defined as in section 1361(b) but without regard to paragraph (1)(C) thereof (relating to nonresident aliens). In the golden parachute context, the effect of the use of the small business corporation definition was to treat domestic corporations less favorably to the extent they were owned by foreign persons rather than U.S. persons. Because less favorable treatment was accorded to these corporations solely because they were owned by foreign persons (as contrasted to U.S. corporations whose shareholders were not taxable by the United States), this golden parachute provision discriminated against foreign persons and would have violated certain U.S. treaties.

[¶ 11,358P.10]

Committee Reports on P.L. 99-514 (Tax Reform Act of 1986)

[Senate Committee Report]

4. Corporate Provisions

* * *

l. Golden parachutes * * *

Present Law

Under present law (sec. 280G), no deduction is allowed for "excess parachute payments" and a nondeductible 20-percent excise tax is imposed on the recipient of any excess parachute payment.

* * *

Explanation of Provisions

Exemption for certain corporations

In general.—Under the bill, the term parachute payment does not include any payment made to (or for the benefit of) a disqualified individual (1) with respect to a corporation that was, immediately before the change in control, a small business corporation or (2) with respect to a corporation no stock of which was, immediately before the change in control, readily tradable on an established securities market, or otherwise, provided shareholder approval was obtained with respect to the payment to a disqualified individual.

Small business corporation.—A corporation qualifies as a small business corporation if the corporation does not (1) have more than 35 shareholders, (2) have a shareholder who is not an individual (other than an estate or a qualifying trust), (3) have a nonresident alien as a shareholder, and (4) have more than one class of stock.

Corporation with no readily tradable securities.—The Secretary of the Treasury may, by regulations, provide that a corporation fails to meet the requirement that it have no stock that is readily tradable if a substantial portion of the assets of any entity consists (either directly or indirectly) of stock in the corporation and interests in the entity are readily tradable on an established securities market, or otherwise. For example, if a publicly traded corporation sells the stock of a 70 percent subsidiary and the assets of the subsidiary constitute a substantial portion of the assets of the parent, the committee intends that the exemption for a corporation with no readily tradable securities will not be available with respect to payments to disqualified individuals on account of the change in ownership or control of the subsidiary.

The committee is also concerned that, absent specific rules, a taxpayer might utilize the exemption for shareholder approval to avoid the golden parachute provisions by creating tiers of entities. Such avoidance is possible if the gross value of the entity-shareholder's interest in the corporation constitutes a substantial portion of such entity's assets. The committee contemplates that, in such cases, the Secretary will adopt regulations requiring approval of the owners of the entity rather than the approval of the entity itself. Of course, such shareholder approval may be obtained only if the entity shareholder also has no stock that is readily tradable. On the other hand, if the entity's interest in the corporation constitutes less than substantial portion of its assets, approval of the compensation arrangement by the authorized officer of the entity is sufficient because, under present law, the golden parachute provisions do not apply to the sale of less than a substantial portion of the assets of a corporation (in this case, the entity).

The shareholder approval requirements are met with respect to any payment if (1) the payment is approved by a separate vote of the shareholders who, immediately before the change in ownership or control, hold more than 75 percent of the voting power of all outstanding stock of the corporation and (2) adequate disclosure was made to all shareholders of the material facts concerning payments that, absent this exemption, would be parachute payments.

The committee intends that adequate disclosure to shareholders will include full and truthful disclosure of the material facts and such additional information as may be necessary to make the disclosure not materially misleading. Further, the committee intends that an omitted fact will be considered material if there is a substantial likelihood that a reasonable shareholder would consider it important.

A disqualified individual who is to receive payments that would be parachute payments (absent shareholder approval) and who is a shareholder is removed from the shareholder base against which the shareholder approval test is applied. A shareholder who is related (under the principles of sec. 318) to the disqualified individual described in the preceding sentence is also removed from the shareholder base. If all shareholders are disqualified individuals or related to disqualified individuals, then disqualified individuals are not removed from the shareholder base.

Reasonable compensation

In the case of any payment made on account of a change in ownership or control, the amount treated as a parachute payment will not include the portion of such payment that the taxpayer establishes by clear and convincing evidence is reasonable compensation for personal services to be rendered on or after the date of the change in ownership or control. Moreover, such payments are not taken into account in determining whether the threshold (i.e., 3 times the base amount) contained in the definition of parachute payments is exceeded.

The committee intends that reasonable compensation for services to be rendered may include, under certain circumstances, payments to an individual as damages for a breach of contract. For example, if an employer fires an employee before the end of a contract term, the amount the employee collects as damages for salary and other compensation may be treated as reasonable compensation for services to be rendered if (1) the damages do not exceed the compensation the individual would have received if the individual continued to perform services for the employer; (2) the individual demonstrates, by clear and convincing evidence, that the payments were received because an offer to work was made and rejected; and (3) any damages were reduced by mitigation. On the other hand, if damages are collected for a failure to make severance payments, damages collected would not be for personal services to be rendered because the individual does not have to demonstrate a willingness to work and reduce damages by mitigation.

The committee intends that evidence that amounts paid to a disqualified individual for services to be rendered that are not significantly greater than amounts of compensation (other than compensation contingent on a change in ownership or control or termination of employment) paid to the disqualified individual in prior years or customarily paid to similarly situated employees by the employer or by comparable employers will normally serve as clear and convincing evidence of reasonable compensation for such services.

The amount treated as an excess parachute payment is reduced by the portion of the payment that the taxpayer establishes by clear and convincing evidence is reasonable compensation for personal services actually rendered before the change in control. For purposes of this provision, reasonable compensation for services performed before the date of change is first offset against the base amount.

Exemption for payments under qualified plans

Under the bill, the term parachute payment does not include any payment from or under a qualified pension, profit-sharing, or stock bonus plan (sec. 401(a)), a qualified annuity plan (sec. 403(a)), or a simplified employee pension (sec. 408(k)). Moreover, such payments from or under a qualified plan are not taken into account in determining whether the threshold for excess parachute payments is exceeded.

Treatment of affiliated groups

The bill provides that, except as otherwise provided in regulations, all members of an affiliated group of corporations (sec. 1504) shall be treated as a single corporation for purposes of the golden parachute provisions. Any person who is an officer or highly compensated individual with respect to any member of the affiliated group is treated as an officer or highly compensated individual of such single corporation. Notwithstanding the general definition of an affiliated group of corporations, for purposes of this provision, an affiliated group of corporations also includes the following:

(1) Tax-exempt corporations;

(2) Insurance companies;

(3) Foreign corporations (unless the disqualified individual is employed by a foreign corporation that is acquired by another foreign corporation, neither of which is subject to tax in the U.S.);

(4) Corporation with respect to which a possession tax credit election (sec. 936) is in effect for the taxable year);

(5) Regulated investment companies and real estate investment trusts; and

(6) A DISC or former DISC.

Definition of highly compensated individual

Under the bill, the term highly compensated individual is defined to include only an employee (or a former employee) who is among the highest-paid one percent of individuals performing services for the corporation or for any corporation that is a member of an affiliated group or the 250 highest paid individuals who perform services for a corporation or for each member of an affiliated group.

Excluded amounts

Under the bill, amounts that are not treated as parachute payments are not taken into account in determining whether the threshold contained in the definition of parachute payments is exceeded. This provision applies to (1) payments made with respect to a small business corporation or a corporation that satisfies the shareholder approval requirements; (2) payments that are reasonable compensation for personal services to be rendered on or after the date of the change of control; and (3) payments from or under a qualified plan.

Securities laws violation

The bill limits the treatment of payments made pursuant to an agreement that violates securities laws as parachute payments only to violations of generally enforced securities laws or regulations. Further, the Internal Revenue Service is to bear the burden of proof with respect to the occurrence of a securities law violation.

Effective date

The provisions are effective as if enacted in DEFRA. For example, amounts paid before the date of enactment under an agreement otherwise subject to the golden parachute provisions may be exempt from such provisions under the small business corporation exception, the shareholder approval exception, the exception for payments from or under a qualified plan, or exceptions for payments of reasonable compensation for services to be rendered. In addition, shareholder approval could be obtained after the date of enactment with respect to prior transactions.

Further, the committee intends that a contract is not treated as amended in a significant, relevant respect under certain circumstances. For example, if a nonqualified stock bonus plan is amended to prevent the forfeiture of previously granted but unvested shares in the event of the termination of the plan following a merger, consolidation, or sale, such an amendment is not treated as amending the plan in a significant, relevant respect. This rule applies provided that participants in the plan are entitled to no grandfathered parachute benefits that have the effect of compensating them for the possible forfeiture of shares in the event of a merger, consolidation, or sale of the corporation. Under the plan, if the company terminates the plan, the vesting of previously granted shares would continue as if the plan had not been terminated. If the company is sold, however, the plan could be terminated without allowing previously granted shares to continue to vest. Under this situation, participants are not entitled to benefits that are contingent on a change in ownership or control. Instead, the plan amendment merely prevents the possible forfeiture of benefits that could occur only in the event of the merger, consolidation, or sale of the corporation. On the other hand, whether an award made after June 14, 1984, under the plan constitutes a parachute payment will depend on the facts and circumstances at the time the award is made.

* * *

[Conference Committee Report]

* * *

The conference agreement follows the Senate amendment . . . .

The conference agreement is not intended, with respect to the golden parachute provision relating to the adoption of the affiliated group rules, to create an inference with respect to the definition of a change in control.

[Code Sec. 401]

[¶ 11,700.02]

Committee Report on P.L. 109-280 (Pension Protection Act of 2006)

[Joint Committee on Taxation Report]

[Increasing participation through automatic enrollment arrangements]

In general

Under the provision, a 401(k) plan that contains an automatic enrollment feature that satisfies certain requirements (a "qualified automatic enrollment feature") is treated as meeting the ADP test with respect to elective deferrals and the ACP test with respect to matching contributions. In addition, a plan consisting solely of contributions made pursuant to a qualified automatic enrollment feature is not subject to the top-heavy rules.

A qualified automatic enrollment feature must meet certain requirements with respect to: (1) automatic deferral; (2) matching or nonelective contributions; and (3) notice to employees.

Automatic deferral/amount of elective contributions

A qualified automatic enrollment feature must provide that, unless an employee elects otherwise, the employee is treated as making an election to make elective deferrals equal to a stated percentage of compensation not in excess of 10 percent and at least equal to: three percent of compensation for the first year the deemed election applies to the participant; four percent during the second year; five percent during the third year; and six percent during the fourth year and thereafter. The stated percentage must be applied uniformly to all eligible employees.

Eligible employees mean all employees eligible to participate in the arrangement, other than employees eligible to participate in the arrangement immediately before the date on which the arrangement became a qualified automatic contribution arrangement with an election in effect (either to participate at a certain percentage or not to participate).

Matching or nonelective contribution requirement

Contributions

An automatic enrollment feature satisfies the contribution requirement if the employer either (1) satisfies a matching contribution requirement or (2) makes a nonelective contribution to a defined contribution plan of at least three percent of an employee's compensation on behalf of each nonhighly compensated employee who is eligible to participate in the automatic enrollment feature. A plan generally satisfies the matching contribution requirement if, under the arrangement: (1) the employer makes a matching contribution on behalf of each nonhighly compensated employee that is equal to 100 percent of the employee's elective deferrals as do not exceed one percent of compensation and 50 percent of the employee's elective deferrals as exceeds one percent but does not exceed six percent of compensation and (2) the rate of match with respect to any elective deferrals for highly compensated employees is not greater than the rate of match for nonhighly compensated employees. It is intended that the provision apply to section 403(b) annuities.

A plan including an automatic enrollment feature that provides for matching contributions is deemed to satisfy the ACP test if, in addition to meeting the safe harbor contribution requirements applicable to the qualified automatic enrollment feature: (1) matching contributions are not provided with respect to elective deferrals in excess of six percent of compensation, (2) the rate of matching contribution does not increase as the rate of an employee's elective deferrals increases, and (3) the rate of matching contribution with respect to any rate of elective deferral of a highly compensated employee is no greater than the rate of matching contribution with respect to the same rate of deferral of a nonhighly compensated employee.

Vesting

Any matching or other employer contributions taken into account in determining whether the requirements for a qualified automatic enrollment feature are satisfied must vest at least as rapidly as under two-year cliff vesting. That is, employees with at least two years of service must be 100 percent vested with respect to such contributions.

Withdrawal restrictions

Under the provision, any matching or other employer contributions taken into account in determining whether the requirements for a qualified automatic enrollment feature are satisfied are subject to the withdrawal rules applicable to elective contributions.

Notice requirement

Under a notice requirement, each employee eligible to participate in the arrangement must receive notice of the arrangement which is sufficiently accurate and comprehensive to apprise the employee of such rights and obligations and is written in a manner calculated to be understood by the average employee to whom the arrangement applies. The notice must explain: (1) the employee's right under the arrangement to elect not to have elective contributions made on the employee's behalf or to elect to have contributions made in a different amount; and (2) how contributions made under the automatic enrollment arrangement will be invested in the absence of any investment election by the employee. The employee must be given a reasonable period of time after receipt of the notice and before the first election contribution is to be made to make an election with respect to contributions and investments.

Application to tax-sheltered annuities

The new safe harbor rules for automatic contribution plans apply with respect to matching contributions under a section 403(b) annuity through the operation of section 403(b)(12).

Corrective distributions

The provision includes rules under which erroneous automatic contributions may be distributed from the plan no later than 90 days after the date of the first elective contribution with respect to the employee under the arrangement. The amount that is treated as an erroneous contribution is limited to the amount of automatic contributions made during the 90-day period that the employee elects to treat as an erroneous contribution. It is intended that distributions of such amounts are generally treated as a payment of compensation, rather than as a contribution to and then a distribution from the plan. The 10-percent early withdrawal tax does not apply to distributions of erroneous automatic contributions. In addition, it is intended that such contributions are not taken into account for purposes of applying the nondiscrimination rules, or the limit on elective deferrals. Similarly, it is intended that distributions of such contributions are not subject to the otherwise applicable withdrawal restrictions. The rules for corrective distributions apply to distributions from (1) qualified pension plans under Code section 401(a), (2) plans under which amounts are contributed by an individual's employer for Code section 403(b) annuity contract and (3) governmental eligible deferred compensation plans under Code section 457(b).

The corrective distribution rules are not limited to arrangements meeting the requirements of a qualified enrollment feature.

Excess contributions

In the case of an eligible automatic contribution arrangement, the excise tax on excess contributions does not apply to any excess contributions or excess aggregate contributions which, together with income allocable to the contributions, are distributed or forfeited (if forfeitable) within six months after the close of the plan year. Additionally, any excess contributions or excess aggregate contributions (and any income allocable thereto) that are distributed within the period required to avoid application of the excise tax are treated as earned and received by the recipient in the taxable year in which the distribution is made (regardless of the amount distributed), and the income allocable to excess contributions or excess aggregate contributions that must be distributed is determined through the end of the year for which the contributions were made.

Preemption of State law

The provision preempts any State law that would directly or indirectly prohibit or restrict the inclusion in a plan of an automatic contribution arrangement. The Labor Secretary may establish minimum standards for such arrangements in order for preemption to apply. An automatic contribution arrangement is an arrangement: (1) under which a participant may elect to have the plan sponsor make payments as contributions under the plan on behalf of the participant, or to the participant directly in cash, (2) under which a participant is treated as having elected to have the plan sponsor make such contributions in an amount equal to a uniform percentage of compensation provided under the plan until the participant specifically elects not to have such contributions made (or elects to have contributions made at a different percentage), and (3) under which contributions are invested in accordance with regulations issued by the Secretary of Labor relating to default investments as provided under the bill. The State preemption rules under the bill are not limited to arrangements that meet the requirements of a qualified enrollment feature.

A plan administrator must provide notice to each participant to whom the automatic contribution arrangement applies. If the notice requirement is not satisfied, an ERISA penalty of $1,100 per day applies.

Effective Date

The provision is effective for years beginning after December 31, 2007. The preemption of conflicting State regulations is effective on the date of enactment. No inference is intended as to the effect of conflicting State regulations prior to date of enactment.

[Distributions during working retirement]

Under the provision, for purposes of the definition of pension plan under ERISA, a distribution from a plan, fund, or program is not treated as made in a form other than retirement income or as a distribution prior to termination of covered employment solely because the distribution is made to an employee who has attained age 62 and who is not separated from employment at the time of such distribution.

In addition, under the Code, a pension plan does not fail to be a qualified retirement plan solely because the plan provides that a distribution may be made to an employee who has attained age 62 and who is not separated from employment at the time of the distribution.

Effective Date

The provision is effective for distributions in plan years beginning after December 31, 2006.

[Defined contribution plans required to provide employees with freedom to invest their plan assets]

In general

Under the provision, in order to satisfy the plan qualification requirements of the Code and the vesting requirements of ERISA, certain defined contribution plans are required to provide diversification rights with respect to amounts invested in employer securities. Such a plan is required to permit applicable individuals to direct that the portion of the individual's account held in employer securities be invested in alternative investments. An applicable individual includes: (1) any plan participant; and (2) any beneficiary who has an account under the plan with respect to which the beneficiary is entitled to exercise the rights of a participant. The time when the diversification requirements apply depends on the type of contributions invested in employer securities.

Plans subject to requirements

The diversification requirements generally apply to an "applicable defined contribution plan,"[245] which means a defined contribution plan holding publicly-traded employer securities (i.e., securities issued by the employer or a member

[245] Under ERISA, the diversification requirements apply to an "applicable individual account plan.".

of the employer's controlled group of corporations[246] that are readily tradable on an established securities market).

For this purpose, a plan holding employer securities that are not publicly traded is generally treated as holding publicly-traded employer securities if the employer (or any member of the employer's controlled group of corporations) has issued a class of stock that is a publicly-traded employer security. This treatment does not apply if neither the employer nor any parent corporation[247] of the employer has issued any publicly-traded security or any special class of stock that grants particular rights to, or bears particular risks for, the holder or the issuer with respect to any member of the employer's controlled group that has issued any publicly-traded employer security. For example, a controlled group that generally consists of corporations that have not issued publicly-traded securities may include a member that has issued publicly-traded stock (the "publicly-traded member"). In the case of a plan maintained by an employer that is another member of the controlled group, the diversification requirements do not apply to the plan, provided that neither the employer nor a parent corporation of the employer has issued any publicly-traded security or any special class of stock that grants particular rights to, or bears particular risks for, the holder or issuer with respect to the member that has issued publicly-traded stock. The Secretary of the Treasury has the authority to provide other exceptions in regulations. For example, an exception may be appropriate if no stock of the employer maintaining the plan (including stock held in the plan) is publicly traded, but a member of the employer's controlled group has issued a small amount of publicly-traded stock.

The diversification requirements do not apply to an ESOP that: (1) does not hold contributions (or earnings thereon) that are subject to the special nondiscrimination tests that apply to elective deferrals, employee after-tax contributions, and matching contributions; and (2) is a separate plan from any other qualified retirement plan of the employer. Accordingly, an ESOP that holds elective deferrals, employee contributions, employer matching contributions, or nonelective employer contributions used to satisfy the special nondiscrimination tests (including the safe harbor methods of satisfying the tests) is subject to the diversification requirements under the Provision. The diversification rights applicable under the provision are broader than those applicable under the Code's present-law ESOP diversification rules. Thus, an ESOP that is subject to the new requirements is excepted from the present-law rules.[248]

The new diversification requirements also do not apply to a one-participant retirement plan. For purposes of the Code, a one-participant retirement plan is a plan that: (1) on the first day of the plan year, either covered only one individual (or the individual and his or her spouse) and the individual owned 100 percent of the plan sponsor (i.e., the employer maintaining the plan), whether or not incorporated, or covered only one or more partners (or partners and their spouses) in the plan sponsor; (2) meets the minimum coverage requirements without being combined with any other plan of the business that covers employees of the business; (3) does not provide benefits to anyone except the individuals and partners (and spouses) described in (1); (4) does not cover a business that is a member of an affiliated service group, a controlled group of corporations, or a group of corporations under common control; and (5) does not cover a business that uses the services of leased employees.[249] It is intended that, for this purpose, a "partner" includes an owner of a business that is treated as a partnership for tax purposes. In addition, it includes a two-percent shareholder of an S corporation.[250]

Elective deferrals and after-tax employee contributions

In the case of amounts attributable to elective deferrals under a qualified cash or deferred arrangement and employee after-tax contributions that are invested in employer securities, any applicable individual must be permitted to direct that such amounts be invested in alternative investments.

Other contributions

In the case of amounts attributable to contributions other than elective deferrals and after-tax employees contributions (i.e., nonelective employer contributions and employer matching contributions) that are invested in employer securities, an applicable individual who is a participant with three years of service,[251] a beneficiary of such a participant, or a beneficiary of a deceased participant must be permitted to direct that such amounts be invested in alternative investments.

A transition rule applies to amounts attributable to these other contributions that are invested in employer securities acquired before the first plan year for which the new diversification requirements apply. Under the transition rule, for the first three years for which the new diversification requirements apply to the plan, the applicable percentage of such amounts is subject to diversification as shown in Table 1, below. The applicable percentage applies separately to each class of employer security in an applicable individual's account. The transition rule does not apply to plan participants who have three years of service and who have attained age 55 by the beginning of the first plan year beginning after December 31, 2005.

Table 1.—Applicable Percentage for Employer Securities Held on Effective Date

Plan year for which diversification applies:	Applicable percentage:
First year	33 percent
Second year	66 percent
Third year	100 percent

The application of the transition rule is illustrated by the following example. Suppose that the account of a participant with at least three years of service held 120 shares of employer common stock contributed as matching contributions before the diversification requirements became effective. In the first year for which diversification applies, 33 percent (i.e., 40 shares) of that stock is subject to the diversification requirements. In the second year for which diversification applies, a total of 66 percent of 120 shares of stock (i.e., 79 shares, or an additional 39 shares) is subject to the diversification requirements. In the third year for which diversification applies, 100 percent of the stock, or all 120 shares, is subject to the diversification requirements. In addition, in each year, employer stock in the account attributable to elective deferrals and employee after-tax contributions is fully subject to the diversification requirements, as is any new stock contributed to the account.

Rules relating to the election of investment alternatives

A plan subject to the diversification requirements is required to give applicable individuals a choice of at least three investment options, other than employer securities, each of which is diversified and has materially different risk and return characteristics. It is intended that other investment options generally offered by the plan also must be available to applicable individuals.

A plan does not fail to meet the diversification requirements merely because the plan limits the times when divestment and reinvestment can be made to periodic, reasonable opportunities that occur at least quarterly. It is intended that applicable individuals generally be given the opportunity to make investment changes with respect to employer securities on the same basis as the opportunity to make other investment changes, except in unusual circumstances. Thus, in general, applicable individuals must be given the opportunity to request changes with respect to investments in employer securities with the same frequency as the opportunity to make other investment changes and that such changes are implemented in the same timeframe as other investment changes, unless circumstances require different treatment.

Except as provided in regulations, a plan may not impose restrictions or conditions with respect to the investment of employer securities that are not imposed on the investment of other plan assets (other than restrictions or conditions imposed by reason of the application of securities laws). For example, such a restriction or condition includes a provision under which a participant who divests his or her account of employer securities receives less favorable treatment (such as a lower rate of employer contributions) than a participant whose account remains invested in employer securities. On the other hand, such a restriction does not include the imposition of fees with respect to other investment options under the plan, merely because fees are not imposed with respect to investments in employer securities.

Effective Date

The provision is effective for plan years beginning after December 31, 2006.

In the case of a plan maintained pursuant to one or more collective bargaining agreements, the provision is effective for plan years beginning after the earlier of (1) the later of December 31, 2007, or the date on which the last of such collective bargaining agreements terminates (determined without regard to any extension thereof after the date of enactment), or (2) December 31, 2008.

A special effective date applies with respect to employer matching and nonelective contributions (and earnings thereon) that are invested in employer securities that, as of September 17, 2003: (1) consist of preferred stock; and (2) are held within an ESOP, under the terms of which the value of the preferred stock is subject to a guaranteed minimum. Under the special rule, the diversification requirements apply to such preferred stock for plan years beginning after the earlier of (1) December 31, 2007; or (2) the first date as of which the actual value of the preferred stock equals or exceeds the guaranteed minimum. When the new diversification requirements become effective for the plan under the special

[246] For this purpose, "controlled group of corporations" has the same meaning as under section 1563(a), except that, in applying that section, 50 percent is substituted for 80 percent.

[247] For this purpose, "parent corporation" has the same meaning as under section 424(e), i.e., any corporation (other than the employer) in an unbroken chain of corporations ending with the employer if each corporation other than the employer owns stock possessing at least 50 percent of the total combined voting power of all classes of stock with voting rights or at least 50 percent of the total value of shares of all classes of stock in one of the other corporations in the chain.

[248] An ESOP will not be treated as failing to be designed to invest primarily in qualifying employer securities merely because the plan provides diversification rights as required under the provision or greater diversification rights than required under the provision.

[249] For purposes of ERISA, a one-participant retirement plan is defined as under the provision of ERISA that requires advance notice of a blackout period to be provided to participants and beneficiaries affected by the blackout period, as discussed below.

[250] Under section 1372, a two-percent shareholder of an S corporation is treated as a partner for fringe benefit purposes.

[251] Years of service is defined as under the rules relating to vesting (sec. 411(a)).

rule, the applicable percentage of employer securities held on the effective date that is subject to diversification is determined without regard to the special rule.

[Updating of employee plans compliance resolution system]

The provision clarifies that the Secretary has the full authority to establish and implement EPCRS (or any successor program) and any other employee plans correction policies, including the authority to waive income, excise or other taxes to ensure that any tax, penalty or sanction is not excessive and bears a reasonable relationship to the nature, extent and severity of the failure.

Under the provision, the Secretary of the Treasury is directed to continue to update and improve EPCRS (or any successor program), giving special attention to (1) increasing the awareness and knowledge of small employers concerning the availability and use of EPCRS, (2) taking into account special concerns and circumstances that small employers face with respect to compliance and correction of compliance failures, (3) extending the duration of the self-correction period under SCP for significant compliance failures, (4) expanding the availability to correct insignificant compliance failures under SCP during audit, and (5) assuring that any tax, penalty, or sanction that is imposed by reason of a compliance failure is not excessive and bears a reasonable relationship to the nature, extent, and severity of the failure.

Effective Date

The provision is effective on the date of enactment.

[Extension to all governmental plans of moratorium on application of certain nondiscrimination rules]

The provision exempts all governmental plans from the nondiscrimination and minimum participation rules. The provision also treats all governmental cash or deferred arrangements as meeting the participation and nondiscrimination requirements applicable to a qualified cash or deferred arrangement.

Effective Date

The provision is effective for any year beginning after the date of enactment.

[Rule for church plans which self-annuitize]

The bill provides that annuity payments provided with respect to any account maintained for a participant or beneficiary under a qualified church plan does not fail to meet the minimum distribution rules merely because the payments are not made under an annuity contract purchased from an insurance company if such payments would not fail such requirements if provided with respect to a retirement income account described in section 403(b)(9).

For purposes of the provision, a qualified church plan means any money purchase plan described in section 401(a) which (1) is a church plan (as defined in section 414(e)) with respect to which the election provided by section 410(d) has not been made, and (2) was in existence on April 17, 2002.

Effective Date

The provision is effective for years beginning after the date of enactment. No inference is intended from the provision with respect to the proper application of the minimum distribution rules to church plans before the effective date.

[Application of minimum distribution rules to governmental plans]

The provision directs the Secretary of the Treasury to issue regulations under which a governmental plan is treated as complying with the minimum distribution requirements, for all years to which such requirements apply, if the plan complies with a reasonable, good faith interpretation of the statutory requirements. It is intended that the regulations apply for periods before the date of enactment.

Effective Date

The provision is effective on the date of enactment.

[Modifications of rules governing hardships and unforeseen financial emergencies]

The provision directs the Secretary of the Treasury to revise the rules for determining whether a participant has had a hardship or unforeseeable emergency to provide that if an event would constitute a hardship or unforeseeable emergency under the plan if it occurred with respect to the participant's spouse or dependent, such event shall, to the extent permitted under the plan, constitute a hardship or unforeseeable emergency if it occurs with respect to a beneficiary under the plan. The provision requires that the revised rules be issued within 180 days after the date of enactment.

Effective Date

The provision is effective on the date of enactment.

[¶ 11,700.021]

Committee Report on P.L. 108-311 (Working Families Tax Relief Act of 2004)

[Conference Agreement]

Defined contribution plans.—The Small Business Job Protection Act of 1996 amended section 401(a)(26) (generally requiring that a qualified retirement plan benefit the lesser of 50 employees or 40 percent of the employer's workforce) so that it no longer applies to defined contribution plans. Section 401(a)(26)(C) (which treats employees as benefiting in certain circumstances) was not repealed even though it relates only to defined contribution plans. The provision repeals section 401(a)(26)(C).

[¶ 11,700.022]

Committee Report on P.L. 107-16 (Economic Growth and Tax Relief Reconciliation Act)

[House Committee Report]

Repeal of multiple use test

The provision repeals the multiple use test.

Effective Date

The provision is effective for years beginning after December 31, 2001.

[Conference Committee Report]

Senate Amendment

The Senate amendment is the same as the House bill.

Conference Agreement

The conference agreement follows the House bill and the Senate amendment.

[¶ 11,700.024]

Committee Report on P.L. 107-16 (Economic Growth and Tax Relief Reconciliation Act)

[Senate Committee Report]

Rollovers of mandatory distributions

The provision makes a direct rollover the default option for involuntary distributions that exceed $1,000 and that are eligible rollover distributions from qualified retirement plans. The distribution must be rolled over automatically to a designated IRA, unless the participant affirmatively elects to have the distribution transferred to a different IRA or a qualified plan or to receive it directly.

The written explanation provided by the plan administrator is required to explain that an automatic direct rollover will be made unless the participant elects otherwise. The plan administrator is also required to notify the participant in writing (as part of the general written explanation or separately) that the distribution may be transferred without cost to another IRA.

The provision amends the fiduciary rules of ERISA so that, in the case of an automatic direct rollover, the participant is treated as exercising control over the assets in the IRA upon the earlier of (1) the rollover of any portion of the assets to another IRA, or (2) one year after the automatic rollover.

The provision directs the Secretary of Labor to issue safe harbors under which the designation of an institution and investment of funds in accordance with the provision are deemed to satisfy the requirements of section 404(a) of ERISA. In addition, the provision authorizes and directs the Secretary of the Treasury and the Secretary of Labor to give consideration to providing special relief with respect to the use of low-cost individual retirement plans for purposes of the provision and for other uses that promote the preservation of tax-qualified retirement assets for retirement income purposes.

Effective Date

The provision applies to distributions that occur after the Department of Labor has adopted final regulations implementing the provision.

[Conference Committee Report]

The conference agreement follows the Senate amendment, with modifications. The conference agreement directs the Secretary of Labor to adopt final regulations implementing the conference agreement not later than three years after the date of enactment.

[¶ 11,700.025]

Committee Report on P.L. 107-16 (Economic Growth and Tax Relief Reconciliation Act)

[Conference Committee Report]

401(k) plans and definition of individual account plan

House Bill

The House bill modifies the effective date of the rule excluding certain elective deferrals (and earnings thereon) from the definition of individual account plan by providing that the rule does not apply to any elective deferral used to acquire an interest in the income or gain from employer securities or employer real property acquired (1) before January 1, 1999, or (2) after such date pursuant to a written contract which was binding on such date and at all times thereafter.

Effective Date

The House bill is effective as if included in the section of the Taxpayer Relief Act of 1997 that contained the rule excluding certain elective deferrals (and earnings thereon).

Senate Amendment

The Senate amendment is the same as the House bill.

Conference Agreement

The conference agreement follows the House bill and the Senate amendment.

[¶ 11,700.026]

Committee Reports on P.L. 107-16 (Economic Growth and Tax Relief Reconciliation Act)

[House Committee Report]

Distributions upon severance of employment

The provision modifies the distribution restrictions applicable to section 401(k) plans, section 403(b) annuities, and section 457 plans to provide that distribution may occur upon severance from employment rather than separation from service. In addition, the provisions for distribution from a section 401(k) plan based upon a corporation's disposition of its assets or a subsidiary are repealed; this special rule is no longer necessary under the provision.

Effective Date

The provision is effective for distributions after December 31, 2001, regardless of when the severance of employment occurred.

[Conference Committee Report]

Senate Amendment

The Senate amendment is the same as the House bill.

Conference Agreement

The conference agreement follows the House bill and the Senate amendment.

The conferees intend that a plan may provide that certain specified types of severance from employment do not constitute distributable events. For example, a plan could provide that a severance from employment is not a distributable event if it would not have constituted a "separation from service" under the law in effect prior to a specified date. Also, if a plan describes distributable events by reference to section 401(k)(2), the plan may be amended to restrict distributable events to fewer than all events that constitute a severance from employment. Thus, for example, if a plan sponsor had employees who experienced a severance from employment in the past that the "same desk rule" prevented from being treated as a distributable event, the plan sponsor would have the option of providing in the plan that such severance from employment would, or would not, be treated as a distributable event under the plan.

The conferees intend that, as under current law, if there is a transfer of plan assets and liabilities relating to any portion of an employee's benefit under a plan of the employee's former employer to a plan being maintained or created by the employee's new employer (other than a rollover or elective transfer), then that employee has not experienced a severance from employment with the employer maintaining the plan that covers the employee.

[¶ 11,700.028]

Committee Report on P.L. 107-16 (Economic Growth and Tax Relief Reconciliation Act)

[Conference Committee Report]

Life expectancy tables

Conference Agreement

The conference agreement directs the Treasury to revise the life expectancy tables under the applicable regulations to reflect current life expectancy.

Effective Date

The conference agreement is effective on the date of enactment.

[¶ 11,700.032]

Committee Reports on P.L. 107-16 (Economic Growth and Tax Relief Reconciliation Act)

[House Committee Report]

Increase in benefit and contribution limits

Compensation limitation.—The provision increases the limit on compensation that may be taken into account under a plan to $200,000. This amount is indexed in $5,000 increments.

* * *

Effective Date

The provision is effective for years beginning after December 31, 2001.

[Conference Committee Report]

* * *

Compensation limitation.—The conference agreement follows the House bill.

* * *

Effective Date

The conference agreement generally is effective for years beginning after December 31, 2001. The provisions relating to defined benefit plans are effective for years ending after December 31, 2001.

[¶ 11,700.034]

Committee Reports on P.L. 105-34 (Taxpayer Relief Act)

[Senate Committee Report (Code and Related Non-Code Provisions)]

Modification of prohibition on assignment or alienation.—The bill permits a participant's benefit in a qualified plan to be reduced to satisfy liabilities of the participant to the plan due to (1) the participant being convicted of committing a crime involving the plan, (2) a civil judgment (or consent order or decree) entered by a court in an action brought in connection with a violation of the fiduciary provisions of ERISA, or (3) a settlement agreement between the Secretary of Labor or the Pension Benefit Guaranty Corporation and the participant in connection with a violation of the fiduciary provisions of ERISA. The court order establishing such liability must require that the participant's benefit in the plan be applied to satisfy the liability. If the participant is married at the time his or her benefit under the plan is offset to satisfy the liability, spousal consent to such offset is required unless the spouse is also required to pay an amount to the plan in the judgment, order, decree or settlement or the judgment, order, decree or settlement provides a 50-percent survivor annuity for the spouse. The bill will make the corresponding changes to ERISA.

Effective Date

The provision is effective for judgments, orders, and degrees issued, and settlement agreements entered into, on or after the date of enactment.

[Conference Committee Report]

The conference agreement follows the Senate amendment. The conference agreement clarifies that an offset is includible in income on the date of the offset.

[Senate Committee Report (Related Non-Code Provision)]

Plans not disqualified merely by accepting rollover contributions.—The bill clarifies the circumstances under which a qualified plan could accept rollover contributions without jeopardizing its qualified status. Under the provision, if the trustee of the plan making the distribution notifies the recipient plan that the distributing plan is intended to be a qualified plan, the plan receiving the rollover will not be disqualified if the distributing plan was not in fact a qualified plan.

Effective Date

The provision is effective for rollover contributions made after December 31, 1997.

[Conference Committee Report]

The conference agreement follows the Senate amendment, as modified. Under the conference agreement, the Secretary of the Treasury is directed to clarify that, under its regulations protecting plans from disqualification because they receive invalid rollover contributions, it is not necessary for a distributing plan to have a determination letter in order for the administrator of the receiving plan to reasonably conclude that a contribution is a valid rollover.

[House Committee Report]

Cash or deferred arrangements for irrigation and drainage entities.—Under the bill, mutual irrigation or ditch companies and districts organized under the laws of a State as a municipal corporation for the purpose of irrigation, water conservation or drainage (or a national association of such organizations) are permitted to maintain qualified cash or deferred arrangements, even if the company or district is a State or local government organization.

Effective Date

The provision is effective with respect to years beginning after December 31, 1997.

[¶ 11,700.036]

Committee Report on P.L. 104-188 (Small Business Job Protection Act)

Simplified Distribution Rules

[House Committee Report]

Required distributions

* * *

The bill modifies the rule that requires all participants in qualified plans to commence distributions by age 70-1/2 without regard to whether the participant is still employed by the employer and generally replaces it with the rule in effect prior to the tax Reform Act of 1986. Under the bill, distributions generally are required to begin by April 1 of the calendar year following the later of first, the calendar year in which the employee attains age 70-1/2 or second, the calendar year in which the employee retires. However, in the case of a 5-percent owner of the employer, distributions are required to begin no later than the April 1 of the calendar year following the year in which the 5-percent owner attains age 70-1/2.

In addition, in the case of an employee (other than a 5-percent owner) who retires in a calendar year after attaining age 70-1/2, the bill generally requires the employee's accrued benefit to be actuarially increased to take into account the period after age 70-1/2 in which the employee was not receiving benefits under the plan. Thus, under the bill, the employee's accrued benefit is required to reflect the value of benefits that the employee would have received if the employee had retired at age 70-1/2 and had begun receiving benefits at that time.

The actuarial adjustment rule and the rule requiring 5-percent owners to begin distributions after attainment of age 70-1/2 does not apply, under the bill, in the case of a governmental plan or church plan.

Effective Date

* * *

Required distributions.—The provision is effective for years beginning after December 31, 1996. Under the provision, the Committee intends that a plan (or annuity contract) could permit, but would not be required to permit participants who have already begun to receive distributions but do not have to under the provision, to stop receiving distributions until such distributions are required under the provision.

[Conference Committee Report]

* * *

Senate Amendment

The Senate amendment is the same as the House bill.

Required distributions.—The conference agreement follows the House bill and the Senate amendment. The conferees intend that the actuarial adjustment rule does not apply in the case of a defined contribution plan.

Increased Access to Retirement Savings

[Senate Committee Report]

SIMPLE 401(k) plans

* * *

In general, under the bill, a cash or deferred arrangement (i.e., 401(k) plan), will be deemed to satisfy the special nondiscrimination tests applicable to employee elective deferrals and employer matching contributions if the plan satisfies the contribution requirements applicable to SIMPLE plans. In addition, the plan is not subject to the top-heavy rules for any year for which this safe harbor is satisfied. The plan is subject to the other qualified plan rules.

The safe harbor is satisfied if, for the year, the employer does not maintain another qualified plan and (1) employee's elective deferrals are limited to no more than $6,000, (2) the employer matches employees' elective deferrals up to 3 percent of compensation (or, alternatively, makes a 2 percent of compensation nonelective contribution on behalf of all eligible employees with at least $5,000 in compensation), and (3) no other contributions are made to the arrangement. Contributions under the safe harbor have to be 100 percent vested. The employer cannot reduce the matching percentage below 3 percent of compensation.

* * *

Effective Date

The provisions relating to SIMPLE plans are effective for years beginning after December 31, 1996.

[Conference Committee Report]

Conference Agreement

The conference agreement follows the Senate amendment.

Increased Access to Retirement Savings

[Senate Committee Report]

Tax-exempt organizations eligible under section 401(k)

The bill allows tax-exempt organizations (including, for this purpose, Indian tribal governments, a subdivision of an Indian tribal government, an agency or instrumentality of an Indian tribal government or subdivision thereof, or a corporation chartered under Federal, State, or tribal law which is owned in whole or in part by any of such entities) to maintain qualified cash or deferred arrangements. The bill retains the present-law prohibition against the maintenance of cash or deferred arrangements by State and local governments, except to the extent it may apply to Indian tribal governments.

Effective Date.—The provision is effective for plan years beginning after December 31, 1996. The Committee intends no inference with respect to whether Indian tribal governments are permitted to maintain qualified cash or deferred arrangements under present law.

[Conference Committee Report]

The conference agreement follows the Senate amendment. Thus, under the conference agreement, no inference is intended with respect to whether Indian tribal governments are permitted to maintain qualified cash or deferred arrangements under present law.

Nondiscrimination Provisions

[House Committee Report]

Modification of additional participation requirements

The bill provides that the minimum participation rule applies only to defined benefit pension plans. In addition, the bill provides that a defined benefit pension plan does not satisfy the rule unless it benefits no fewer than the lesser of (1) 50 employees or (2) the greater of (a) 40 percent of all employees of the employer or (b) 2 employees (1 employee if there is only 1 employee).

The bill provides that the requirement that a line of business has at least 50 employees does not apply in determining whether a plan satisfies the minimum participation rule on a separate line of business basis.

Effective Date

The provision is effective for years beginning after December 31, 1996.

[Conference Committee Report]

Senate Amendment

The Senate amendment is the same as the House bill.

Conference Agreement

The conference agreement follows the House bill and the Senate amendment.

Nondiscrimination Provisions

[House Committee Report]

Rules for qualified cash or deferred arrangements and matching contributions

Prior-year data.—The bill modifies the special nondiscrimination tests applicable to elective deferrals and employer matching and after-tax employee contributions to provide that the maximum permitted actual deferral percentage (and actual contribution percentage) for highly compensated employees for the year is determined by reference to the actual deferral percentage (and actual contribution percentage) for nonhighly compensated employees for the preceding, rather than the current, year. A special rule applies for the first plan year.

Alternatively, under the bill, an employer is allowed to elect to use the current year actual deferral percentage (and actual contribution percentage). Such an election can be revoked only as provided by the Secretary.

Safe harbor for cash or deferred arrangements.—The bill provides that a cash or deferred arrangement satisfies the special nondiscrimination tests if the plan satisfies one of two contribution requirements and satisfies a notice requirement.

A plan satisfies the contribution requirements under the safe harbor rule for qualified cash or deferred arrangements if the plan either first, satisfies a matching contribution requirement or second, the employer makes a nonelective contribution to a defined contribution plan of at least 3 percent of an employee's compensation on behalf of each nonhighly compensated employee who is eligible to participate in the arrangement without regard to whether the employee makes elective contributions under the arrangement.

A plan satisfies the matching contribution requirement if, under the arrangement: first, the employer makes a matching contribution on behalf of each nonhighly compensated employee that is equal to (a) 100 percent of the employee's elective contributions up to 3 percent of compensation and (b) 50 percent of the employee's elective contributions from 3 to 5 percent of compensation, and second, the rate of match with respect to any elective contribution for highly compensated employees is not greater than the rate of match for nonhighly compensated employees.

Alternatively, if the rate of matching contribution with respect to any rate of elective contribution requirement is not equal to the percentages described in the preceding paragraph, the matching contribution requirement will be deemed to be satisfied if first, the rate of an employer's matching contribution does not increase as an employee's rate of elective contribution increases and second, the aggregate amount of matching contributions at such rate of elective contribution at least equals the aggregate amount of matching contributions that would be made if matching contributions satisfied the above percentage requirements. For example, the alternative test will be satisfied if an employer matches 125 percent of an employee's elective contributions up to the first 3 percent of compensation, 25 percent of elective deferrals from 3 to 4 percent of compensation, and provides no match thereafter. However, the alternative test will not be satisfied if an employer matches 80 percent of an employee's elective contributions up to the first 5 percent of compensation. The former example satisfies the alternative test because the employer match does not increase and the aggregate amount of matching contributions at any rate of elective contribution is at least equal to the aggregate amount of matching contributions required under the general safe harbor rule.

Employer matching and nonelective contributions used to satisfy the contribution requirements of the safe harbor rules are required to be nonforfeitable and are subject to the restrictions on withdrawals that apply to an employee's elective deferrals under a qualified cash or deferred arrangement (sec. 401(k)(2)(B) and (C)). It is intended that employer matching and nonelective contributions used to satisfy the contribution requirements of the safe harbor rules can be used to satisfy other qualified retirement plan nondiscrimination rules (except the special nondiscrimination test applicable to employer matching contributions (the ACP test)). So, for example, a cross-tested defined contribution plan that includes a qualified cash or deferred arrangement can consider such employer matching and nonelective contributions in testing.[10]

The notice requirement is satisfied if each employee eligible to participate in the arrangement is given written notice, within a reasonable period before any year, of the employee's rights and obligations under the arrangement.

Alternative method of satisfying special nondiscrimination test for matching contributions.—The bill provides a safe harbor method of satisfying the special nondiscrimination test applicable to employer matching contributions (the ACP test). Under this safe harbor, a plan is treated as meeting the special nondiscrimination test if first, the plan meets the contribution and notice requirements applicable under the safe harbor method of satisfying the special nondiscrimination requirement for qualified cash or deferred arrangements, and second, the plan satisfies a special limitation on matching contributions.

The limitation on matching contributions is satisfied if: first, the employer matching contributions on behalf of any employee may not be made with respect to employee contributions or elective deferrals in excess of 6 percent of compensation; second, the rate of an employer's matching contribution does not increase as the rate of an employee's contributions or elective deferrals increases; and third, the matching contribution with respect to any highly compensated employee at any rate of employee contribution or elective deferral is not greater than that with respect to an employee who is not highly compensated.

Any after-tax employee contributions made under the qualified cash or deferred arrangement will continue to be tested under the ACP test. Employer matching and nonelective contributions used to satisfy the safe harbor rules for qualified cash or deferred arrangements cannot be considered in calculating such test. However, employer matching and nonelective contributions in excess of the amount required to satisfy the safe harbor rules for qualified cash or deferred arrangements can be taken into account in calculating such test.

Distribution of excess contributions and excess aggregate contributions.—The bill provides that the total amount of excess contributions (and excess aggregate contributions) is determined as under present law, but the distribution of excess contributions (and excess aggregate contributions) are required to be made on the basis of the amount of contribution by, or on behalf of, each highly compensated employee. Thus, excess contributions (and excess aggregate contributions) are deemed attributable first to those highly compensated employees who have the greatest dollar amount of elective deferrals.

Effective Date

The provisions relating to use of prior-year data and the distribution of excess contributions and excess aggregate contributions are effective for years beginning after December 31, 1996. The provisions providing for a safe harbor for qualified cash or deferred arrangements and the alternative method of satisfying the special nondiscrimination test for matching contributions are effective for years beginning after December 31, 1998.

[Conference Committee Report]

Senate Amendment

The Senate amendment is the same as the House bill.

Conference Agreement

The conference agreement follows the House bill and the Senate amendment.

Miscellaneous Pension Simplification

[House Committee Report]

Plans covering self-employed individuals

The bill eliminates the special aggregation rules that apply to plans maintained by self-employed individuals that do not apply to other qualified plans.

Effective Date

The provision is effective for years beginning after December 31, 1996.

[Conference Committee Report]

Senate Amendment

The Senate amendment is the same as the House bill.

Conference Agreement

The conference agreement follows the House bill and the Senate amendment.

Miscellaneous Pension Simplification

[House Committee Report]

Distributions under rural cooperative plans

The bill provides that a rural cooperative plan that includes a cash or deferred arrangement may permit distributions to plan participants after the attainment of age 59½ or on account of hardship. In addition, the definition of a rural cooperative is expanded to include certain public utility districts and a national association of rural cooperatives.

Effective Date.—The provision generally is effective for distributions after the date of enactment. The modifications to the definition of a rural cooperative apply to plan years beginning after December 31, 1996.

[Conference Committee Report]

Senate Amendment

The Senate amendment is the same as the House bill.

Conference Agreement

The conference agreement follows the House bill and the Senate amendment.

Miscellaneous Pension Simplification

[House Committee Report]

Uniform retirement age

[10] The Committee intends that if two plans which include qualified cash or deferred arrangements are treated as one plan for purposes of the nondiscrimination and coverage rules, such qualified cash or deferred arrangements will be treated as one qualified cash or deferred arrangement for purposes of the safe harbor rules. In such a case, unless both qualified cash or deferred arrangements satisfied the safe harbor, both qualified cash or deferred arrangements tested together will have to satisfy the ADP and ACP tests.

The bill provides that for purposes of the general nondiscrimination rules (sec. 401(a)(4)) the Social Security retirement age (as defined in sec. 415) is a uniform retirement age and that subsidized early retirement benefits and joint and survivor annuities are not treated as not being available to employees on the same terms merely because they are based on an employee's Social Security retirement age (as defined in sec. 415).

Effective Date

The provision is effective for years beginning after December 31, 1996.

[Conference Committee Report]

Senate Amendment

The Senate amendment is the same as the House bill.

Conference Agreement

The conference agreement follows the House bill and the Senate amendment.

Miscellaneous Pension Simplification

[Managers' Amendment to H.R. 3448]

Alternative nondiscrimination rules for early participation plans

Under the amendment, for purposes of the ADP test, a section 401(k) plan could elect to ignore employees (other than highly compensated employees) eligible to participate before they have completed 1 year of service and reached age 21, provided the plan separately satisfies the minimum coverage rules of section 410(b) taking into account only those employees who have not completed 1 year of service or are under age 21. Instead of applying two separate ADP tests, such a plan could apply a single ADP test that compares the ADP for all highly compensated employees who are eligible to make elective contributions with the ADP for those nonhighly compensated employees who are eligible to make elective contributions and who have completed one year of service and reached age 21. A similar rule would apply for purposes of the ACP test.

Effective Date

The amendment would be effective for plan years beginning after December 31, 1998.

[Conference Committee Report]

The conference agreement follows the Senate amendment.

[¶ 11,700.038]

Committee Report on P.L. 103-465 (General Agreement on Tariffs and Trade (GATT), Retirement Protection Act)

[House Committee Report]

Rounding rules for cost-of-living adjustments

The provision provides that (1) the dollar limit on benefits under a defined benefit pension plan is indexed in $5,000 increments, (2) the dollar limit on annual additions under a defined contribution plan is indexed in $5,000 increments, (3) the limit on elective deferrals is indexed in $500 increments, and (4) the minimum compensation limit for SEP participation is indexed in $50 increments. In addition, the provision provides that the cost-of-living adjustment with respect to any calendar year is based on the increase in the applicable index as of the close of the calendar quarter ending September 30 of the preceding calendar year so that the adjusted dollar limits would be available before the beginning of the calendar year to which they apply. No limit is reduced below the limit in effect for plan years beginning in 1994.

Effective date

The provision is effective for years beginning after December 31, 1994.

Prohibition on benefit increases where plan sponsor is in bankruptcy

The bill amends the Code and ERISA to prohibit an employer in bankruptcy from adopting an amendment to an underfunded plan that increases benefits unless the benefit increase does not become effective until after the effective date of the employer's plan of reorganization. The prohibition does not apply to amendments that (1) provide reasonable, de minimis increases in liabilities for employees of the debtor, (2) repeal an amendment made within the first 2 ½ months of plan year that would reduce accruals for that plan year, as permitted under section 302(c)(8) of ERISA, or (3) are needed to meet the qualification requirements contained in the Code.

Effective date

The provision is effective with respect to plan amendments adopted on or after December 8, 1994.

[¶ 11,700.04]

Committee Reports on P.L. 103-66 (Omnibus Budget Reconciliation Act of 1993)

[*Compensation for retirement plan purposes*]

[Senate Committee Report]

Under the bill, the limit on compensation taken into account under a qualified plan (sec. 401(a)(17)) is reduced to $150,000. This limit is indexed for cost-of-living adjustments in increments of $10,000. Corresponding changes are also made to other provisions (secs. 404(l), 408(k)(3)(C), (6)(D)(ii), and (8), and 505(b)(7)) that take into account the section 401(a)(17) limit.

Effective date

The provision is generally effective for benefits accruing in plan years beginning after December 31, 1993. Special transition rules apply in the case of governmental plans and plans maintained pursuant to a collective bargaining agreement.

In the case of an eligible participant in a plan maintained by a State or local government, the limit on compensation taken into account is the greater of the limit under the proposal and the compensation allowed to be taken into account under the plan as in effect on July 1, 1993. For purposes of this rule, an eligible participant is an individual who first became a participant in the plan during a plan year beginning before the first plan year beginning after the earlier of: (1) the plan year in which the plan is amended to reflect the proposal, or (2) December 31, 1995. This special rule does not apply unless the plan is amended to incorporate the dollar limit in effect under section 401(a)(17) by reference, effective with respect to persons other than eligible participants for benefits accruing in plan years beginning after December 31, 1995 (or earlier if the plan amendment so provides).

In the case of a plan maintained pursuant to one or more collective bargaining agreements ratified before the date of enactment, the provision does not apply to contributions or benefits accruing under such agreements in plan years beginning before the earlier of (1) the latest of (a) January 1, 1994, (b) the date on which the last of such collective bargaining agreements terminates (without regard to any extension or modification on or after the date of enactment), or (c) in the case of a plan maintained pursuant to collective bargaining under the Railway Labor Act, the date of execution of an extension or replacement of the last of such collective bargaining agreements in effect on the date of enactment, or (2) January 1, 1997.

[Conference Committee Report]

The conference agreement follows the Senate amendment.

[¶ 11,700.042]

Committee Report on P.L.102-318 (Unemployment Compensation Amendments of 1992)

Committee Report on Unemployment Compensation Amendments of 1992 (P.L. 102-318), dealing with rollovers and withholding on nonperiodic pension distributions, see ¶ 11,750.036.

[¶ 11,700.043]

Committee Reports on P.L. 101-239 (Omnibus Budget Reconciliation Act of 1989)

[Senate Committee Report]

Requirement that medical benefits be incidental or subordinate.—Under the provision, the medical benefits described in section 401(h) are considered subordinate to the retirement benefits only if the aggregate of actual contributions (made after the date on which the plan first includes such medical benefits) to provide such medical benefits and any life insurance protection does not exceed 25 percent of the aggregate contributions actually made after such date (rather than the cost related to benefit accruals) other than contributions to fund past service credits. This rule does not apply to a transfer of excess assets permitted under the temporary rule described above.

Under this rule, for example, if a section 401(h) retiree medical benefits plan was established at a time when the plan was fully funded (as determined under section 412), the employer is precluded from making contributions to fund the section 401(h) account unless and until the plan falls below the full funding limit. This is because the permissible level of contributions is measured by actual contributions to the pension plan after the date the retiree medical benefits plan is established.

Internal Revenue Service General Counsel Memorandum, 39785, issued on April 3, 1989, is rejected to the extent it concludes that contributions to a section 401(h) account may be based on plan costs rather than actual contributions to the plan.

No inference is intended as to whether a contribution to a section 401(h) account prior to the effective date of this proposal met the requirement that the medical benefits be subordinate to the retirement benefits of the plan where the determination as to whether such requirement was met was based on plan costs rather than on actual contributions to the plan.

Effective date

The proposal relating to the subordination requirement (i.e., the 25-percent rule) for purposes of determining the permissible contribution to a section 401(h) account is effective with respect to contributions paid to the plan after October 3, 1989.

[Conference Committee Report]

The conference agreement follows the Senate amendment, except that the provision does not apply to contributions made to a section 401(h) account on or before December 31, 1989, if (1) before October 3, 1989, the employer requested a private letter ruling or determination letter with respect to the qualification of the plan containing the section 401(h) account or the deductibility of contributions to the account, (2) the request sets forth that the method by which the plan meets the subordination requirement is based upon cost rather than upon actual contributions, (3) the method under which such contributions are to be determined is permissible under section 401(h) as interpreted by General Counsel Memorandum 39785, and (4) on or before October 3, 1989, the Internal Revenue Service issued a private letter ruling, determination letter, or other letter providing that the plan including the account is qualified under section 401(a) or that the contributions to the account are deductible, or acknowledging that the account would not adversely affect the qualified status of the particular plan, contingent on all phases of the plan being approved.

[House Committee Report]

Security rules for underfunded plans.—The bill clarifies that, in determining the amount of security that must be provided, the increase in current liability attributable to the plan amendment and all plan amendments after December 22, 1987, are taken into account. Thus, for example, an employer cannot avoid the security requirement by adopting a series of plan amendments, each one of which separately results in an increase in current liability that is below the $10 million threshold but which together increase current liability by more than the $10 million threshold.

The bill provides that the security provision does not apply to plans that are not subject to the minimum funding requirements. Thus, for example, the provision does not apply to church or governmental plans.

The bill conforms the ERISA provision to the Code provision by clarifying that the Secretary of the Treasury has regulatory authority with respect to partial release of the security.

The bill provides that a contributing sponsor that is required to provide security is required to notify the PBGC of the plan amendment. This change conforms the statutory provisions to the legislative history. The PBGC may assess a penalty, payable to the PBGC, of up to $1,000 for each day the required notice is not provided. This penalty is consistent with the penalty added by the Act for the failure to provide certain other information to the PBGC. Under the bill, as under the Act, the penalty is to reflect the materiality of the failure to provide the required information.

With respect to the special effective date for collectively bargained plans, the bill provides that extensions, amendments, or modifications of the bargaining agreement on or after December 22, 1987, are disregarded.

The bill also extends the $1,000 penalty, described above, to failures to notify the PBGC of the failure to make required contributions.

[¶ 11,700.045]

Committee Reports on P.L. 100-647 (Technical and Miscellaneous Revenue Act of 1988)

[Senate Committee Report]

The bill clarifies that, for purposes of the special nondiscrimination test, the elective deferrals of eligible highly compensated employees, rather than all highly compensated employees, are taken into account. Under prior law, highly compensated employees were defined by reference to eligible employees. However, the new uniform definition of highly compensated employees does not refer to eligible employees and, therefore, the clarification is necessary to obtain a result consistent with prior law.

The bill provides that, for purposes of determining whether matching contributions may be used to satisfy the special nondiscrimination test for elective deferrals and for purposes of the vesting rules (sec. 411), a matching contribution is not treated as forfeitable merely because the matching contribution is forfeited because the contribution to which it relates is an excess deferral (sec. 402(g)(2)(A)), an excess contribution (sec. 401(k)(8)(B)), or an excess aggregate contribution (sec. 401(m)(6)(B)). The bill clarifies that excess contributions distributed (or treated as distributed) by the end of the plan year following the year the excess contributions arose are not subject to the excise tax on excess distributions (sec. 4980A).

* * *

The bill reconciles the statutory provision and the intent of Congress articulated in the Statement of Managers by providing that the prohibition on conditioning benefits on elective deferrals is not limited to employer-provided benefits. Thus, for example, a plan may not provide that voluntary after-tax employee contributions may not be made until an employee makes a specified amount of elective deferrals under a qualified cash or deferred arrangement.

The bill modifies the grandfather rule applicable to section 401(k) plans maintained by governmental employers. Under the bill, the prohibition on section 401(k) plans does not apply to (1) an employer that is a State or local government or political subdivision thereof, or agency or instrumentality thereof, if the employer adopted a section 401(k) plan before May 6, 1986, and (2) an employer that is a tax-exempt governmental unit other than a governmental unit described in (1) (e.g., the Tennessee Valley Authority), if the employer adopted a section 401(k) plan before July 2, 1986. Because the grandfather rule in the bill applies to the employer and not merely the plan, an employer that satisfies the conditions of the grandfather may adopt a new section 401(k) plan.

Because the identity of the employer is more likely to change in the case of tax-exempt employers that are not governmental entities (such as through a merger of unrelated tax-exempt organizations), the bill limits this expansion of the grandfather rule to tax-exempt governmental units.

In addition, if an employer maintained a section 401(k) plan before July 2, 1986, and the employer subsequently became a tax-exempt organization, the grandfather rule for tax-exempt organizations is considered to be satisfied.

* * *

As originally enacted, the exception to the withdrawal restrictions for certain sales of assets or subsidiaries does not encompass other transactions that have the effect of sales of assets or subsidiaries. The bill expands the exception to include certain dispositions of assets or subsidiaries other than sales and clarifies that the exception only applies if the transferor corporation continues to maintain the plan after the disposition. Thus, the bill provides that distributions can be made from a qualified cash or deferred arrangement on the (1) disposition by a corporation of substantially all of the assets (within the meaning of sec. 409(d)(2)) used by such corporation if the employee continues employment with the transferee corporation and the transferor corporation continues to maintain the plan, or (2) disposition by a corporation of the corporation's interest in a subsidiary (within the meaning of sec. 409(d)(3)) if the employee continues employment with the subsidiary and the transferor corporation continues to maintain the plan.

The bill incorporates statutorily the requirement that a distribution must be a total distribution in order for the exceptions for dispositions of assets or subsidiaries or for termination of a plan to apply. Under the bill, with respect to distributions after March 31, 1988, these exceptions only apply if the distribution is a "lump sum distribution." For this purpose, "lump sum distribution" means a lump-sum distribution under the income averaging rules (sec. 402(e)(4)), but without regard to (1) the required events (such as attainment of age 59 ½) for eligibility for income averaging, (2) the election requirement, and (3) the minimum period of plan participation requirement. Thus, for this purpose, a distribution can constitute a lump-sum distribution even though, for example, the employee receives the distribution prior to age 59 ½, has already elected lump-sum treatment for a prior distribution, or has not been a participant in the plan for at least 5 years.

The bill also provides that with respect to distributions after October 16, 1987, the exception to the withdrawal restrictions for the termination of the plan is conditioned on the employer not establishing or maintaining another defined contribution plan for a reasonable period established by the Secretary.

[Conference Committee Report]

* * *

Conference Agreement

The conference agreement follows the Senate amendment with the following modifications.

With respect to the provisions permitting distributions from a section 401(k) plan following termination of the plan, the conference agreement clarifies that, as under proposed Treasury regulations, a distribution may be made notwithstanding the fact that the employer maintains an employee stock ownership plan (ESOP) (as defined in section 4975(e)(7) of the Code) after the termination.

[Senate Committee Report]

Line of business

Under the bill, the Secretary may permit, under appropriate circumstances, the minimum participation rule to be applied separately to separate lines of business, as defined under section 414(r) without regard to section 414(r)(7). Thus, for this purpose, separate operating units are not considered to be separate lines of business.

In determining whether to permit this separate testing, the Secretary is to consider whether the separate lines of business are related. For example, a football team and a manufacturing business are totally unrelated, so that it may be appropriate to allow separate testing in such circumstances.

Sanction

The bill modifies the sanction applicable to a plan that ceases to be qualified based on a failure to satisfy either the minimum participation rule or the coverage rules. Under the bill, if a plan is not qualified and one of the reasons is the failure to satisfy the minimum participation rule or the coverage rules (either directly or indirectly through the application of sec. 401(a)(4)), any highly compensated employee is to include in income such employee's vested accrued benefit (other than such employee's investment in the contract). (This modification does not affect the application of the general rules of sec. 402(b)(1) regarding issues other than the amount includible in the year of disqualification, such as the application of sec. 72 to distributions from the disqualified plan.)

In addition, if a plan is not qualified solely because it does not satisfy either the minimum participation rule or the coverage rule (either directly or indirectly through the application of sec. 401(a)(4)) or both, the bill provides that there is to be no inclusion in income by reason of such failure to qualify with respect to any employee who was not a highly compensated employee at any time during the trust year in which the plan became disqualified or during any prior year for which service was creditable to such employee under the plan (or a predecessor plan). For purposes of determining whether an employee was a highly compensated employee in any year, the definition of highly compensated employee applicable with respect to such year for purposes of the coverage rules is to apply.

Except for these changes, the sanctions applicable under present law, including the rules regarding the disallowance of an employer's deduction for contributions to a disqualified plan, continue to apply.

These modifications of the sanctions for disqualification are intended to fulfill the intent of the Act with respect to (1) ensuring that the disqualification sanction is adequate with respect to highly compensated employees, and (2) reducing the sanction with respect to nonhighly compensated employees in appropriate circumstances.

Applicability of affiliated service group and employee leasing rules

In order to prevent avoidance of the minimum participation rule, the bill provides that the affiliated service group rules (sec. 414(m)) and the employee leasing rules (sec. 414(n)) apply for purposes of the minimum participation rule. The bill further clarifies that the Secretary's general regulatory authority to prevent avoidance of certain requirements (sec. 414(o)) applies to the minimum participation rule.

Special transition rule

Under the bill, the special transition rule applicable in the case of certain dispositions or acquisitions of a business (sec. 410(b)(6)(C)) is to apply to the minimum participation rule. This is intended to prevent the minimum participation rule from disrupting business transactions by allowing a grace period following certain transactions for the new entities to comply with the minimum participation rule.

Reversion tax and interest rate

With respect to the rule under present law regarding the exemption from the reversion tax in the case of the termination or merger of certain plans not satisfying the minimum participation rule, the interest rate required to be used in determining the accrued benefit of any highly compensated employee and the corresponding reversion to the employer will in may cases understate the value of the employee's accrued benefit and thus represent an inappropriate reduction in the employee's accrued benefit. In order to avoid this result, the bill modifies the rule referred to above in several respects.

First, the bill clarifies that for purposes of determining the amount to be distributed from a plan to an employee, the value of an employee's accrued benefit is not to be affected by this transitional rule regarding the minimum participation rule. Thus, for this purpose, the accrued benefit is to be determined under the interest rate used by the plan, if otherwise permissible under the Code.

Second, the bill provides a rule regarding the permissible interest rate to be used for certain purposes. The interest rate rule applies in the case of a termination, asset transfer, or asset distribution with respect to a plan that would have failed to satisfy the requirements of the minimum participation rule had the effective date of such rule been August 16, 1986.

If the interest rate rule applies to a plan, the interest rate used in determing an "eligible amount" is to be no less than the highest of:

(1) the rate in effect under the plan on August 16, 1986, or if on August 16, 1986, the rate is determined under a formula (or other method), the rate determined under such formula (or other method);

(2) the highest rate applicable under the plan at any time after August 15, 1986, and before the termination, transfer, or distribution in calculating the present value of the accrued benefit of a nonhighly compensated employee under the plan (or any other plan used in determining whether the plan meets the requirements of sec. 401). For this purpose, if at any time during this period the rate is determined under a formula (or other method), the rate considered to be used during any such period is the rate that would be determined under the formula (or other method) if such formula (or other method) were in effect on the date of termination, transfer, or distribution; or

(3) 5 percent.

For purposes of (1) above, the rate is to be determined without regard to any amendment adopted after August 16, 1986, even if such amendment is effective retroactively to apply on August 16, 1986. For purposes of (2) above, the rate is to be determined without regard to any amendment adopted after October 26, 1987, even if such amendment is effective retroactively to apply on August 16, 1986. If more than one rate (or formula or method) applies under a plan, such as different rates applying to benefits of different value, the rate applicable under the plan for purposes of (1) and (2) above is the highest of the different rates.

(No inference is intended, based on (2) above, that within a plan (or plans aggregated for purposes of section 410) a higher interest rate may be used in determining the present value of the accrued benefit of a nonhighly compensated employee than is used with respect to any highly compensated employee.)

The term "eligible amount" means the amount that with respect to a highly compensated employee:

(1) may be rolled over under the applicable rules (sec. 402(a)(5));

(2) is eligible for income averaging (sec. 402(e)(1)) or grandfathered capital gains treatment; or

(3) may be transferred to another plan without inclusion in income.

In addition, if an annuity contract purchased after August 16, 1986, is distributed to a highly compensated employee by a plan to which the interest rate rule applies in connection with a termination of or distribution from such plan, the annuity contract is included in the employee's income to the extent of the excess of the purchase price of such contract over the present value of the employee's accrued benefit (or portion thereof) with respect to which the contract is being distributed. For this purpose, the present value of the accrued benefit is to be determined by using the lowest interest rate permitted in determining an eligible amount under the rules described above. The bill also provides that the excess that is includible in income under the above rule is to be disregarded for purposes of the early withdrawal tax (sec. 72(t)) and the excess distribution tax (sec. 4980A).

In the case of a termination if a distribution from a plan to which the interest rate rule applies, the excess (if any) of (1) the amount distributed to a highly compensated employee by reason of the termination or distribution over (2) the amount determined by using the lowest interest rate permitted in determining an eligible amount, also is disregarded for purposes of the early withdrawal tax and the excess distribution tax.

Former employees

It is further intended that for purposes of the minimum participation rule, former employees generally are to be tested separately under rules similar to those applicable for purposes of the coverage rules.

[Senate Committee Report]

Further, the bill provides that, notwithstanding any other provision of law, a plan or contract is permitted (except as provided in regulations prescribed by the Secretary) to incorporate by reference the uniform benefit commencement date and the required distribution rules for qualified plans (sec. 401(a)(9)).

It is further intended that an employee who has not retired from an employer prior to 1989, but has attained age 70 ½ prior to 1989, is considered to have attained age 70 ½ in 1989 for purposes of determining the new uniform benefit commencement date with respect to a plan maintained by the employer.

[Senate Committee Report]

The bill clarifies that generally it is only employer-provided contributions and benefits that are taken into account in determining whether the contributions or benefits with respect to compensation above and below the integration level satisfy the integration rules.

To fulfill Congressional intent to conform certain qualified plan rules to the social security system, the bill modifies the definition of "covered compensation," so that the references to age 65 are replaced by references to social security retirement age (sec. 415(b)(8)), which can be age 65, 66, or 67, depending on the date of birth of the employee.

The bill also clarifies that "average annual compensation" means the participant's highest average annual compensation for any period of at least 3 consecutive years (or, if shorter, the participant's full period of service). Thus, defined benefit plans providing benefits based on career average compensation are not prevented from integrating.

[Senate Committee Report]

Under the bill, in the case of a plan that is intended to be a money purchase pension plan or a profit-sharing plan, a trust forming part of such plan will not be qualified unless the plan designates such intent at such time and in such manner as the Secretary may prescribe. Of course, a plan amendment is not required to comply with this rule until such time as plan amendments generally are required under the Act (Act sec. 1140). Prior to such time, the Secretary may require designation in a different manner.

[House Committee Report]

The bill provides that, in the case of a governmental plan, the required beginning date is the later of (1) the required beginning date under the normal rule or (2) April 1 of the calendar year following the calendar year in which the employee retires.

Effective Date

The provision is effective as if included in the Tax Reform Act of 1986 (i.e., generally for years beginning after December 31, 1988).

[Conference Committee Report]

* * *

Conference Agreement

The conference agreement follows the House bill, except that the provision also applies to church employees. For this purpose, the term "church" has the meaning given such term by section 3121(w)(3)(A), including a qualified church controlled organization (as defined in section 3121(w)(3)(B)).

[Senate Committee Report]

Under present law, a pension plan is not a taxqualified plan unless it benefits no fewer than the lesser of (1) 50 employees of the employer, or (2) 40 percent of all employees of the employer. Under the provision, a plan maintained by a governmental employer for police or firefighters, which is structured generally to take into account the early retirement ages of such employees, would satisfy the minimum participation rule if the plan satisfied the rule taking into account only the employees of the employer who are police or firefighters. Similarly, police or firefighters would not be taken into account in applying the minimum participation rule to coverage of employees of the employer who are not police or firefighters.

The provision would be effective as if included in the Tax Reform Act of 1986.

[House Committee Report]

Explanation of Provision

The bill provides that the minimum participation rule does not apply to any governmental plan (within the meaning of sec. 414(d)) with respect to employees who were participants in the plan on July 14, 1988.

Effective Date

The provision is effective upon enactment.

[Conference Committee Report]

* * *

Conference Agreement

The conference agreement follows the Senate amendment with respect to the application of the minimum participation rule to qualified safety employees, with a clarification that the provision is effective as if included in section 1112(b) of the Reform Act, and the Treasury study.

The conference agreement follows the House bill with respect to governmental plans, with the modification that the provision only applies to plan years beginning before January 1, 1993. The provision is effective as if included in section 1112(b) of the Reform Act.

[Senate Committee Report]

Cash or Deferred Arrangements

In general

The bill provides that income on excess deferrals is includible in gross income in the year distributed, rather than in the year of the deferral. To prevent individuals from electing to make excess deferrals in order to defer current taxation of income, the bill requires, as a condition of qualification, that a plan that has a cash or deferred arrangement provide that elective deferrals under the arrangement and all other plans, contracts, or arrangments of the employer maintaining the plan for a calendar year may not exceed the limitation on elective deferrals in effect for taxable years beginning in such calendar year. A similar restriction is required to be included in a simplified employee pension (SEP) (sec. 408(k)), tax-sheltered annuity contract (sec. 403(b)), or section 501(c)(18) plan that permits elective deferrals. The bill provides that, for purposes of the required plan provision, the limit on elective deferrals need not be explicitly set forth, but can be incorporated by reference.

The provision is generally effective with respect to plan years beginning after December 31, 1987. A delayed effective date applies in the case of certain plans maintained pursuant to a collective bargaining agreement with respect to contributions made pursuant to the bargaining agreement.

Treatment of excess deferrals

Under the bill, income on excess deferrals distributed before the applicable April 15 date, including income earned during and after the year to which the deferral relates, is includible in income in the year distributed, rather than in the year to which the deferral relates. The bill clarifies that any distribution of less than the entire amount of excess deferrals plus income attributable to such deferrals is treated as a pro rata distribution of excess deferrals and income.

The bill clarifies that excess deferrals (and income on such deferrals) distributed by the applicable April 15 are not subject to the 15-percent tax on excess distributions (sec. 4980A).

[Joint Committee Explanation of Senate Consensus Amendment]

Under the Tax Reform Act of 1986, a qualified retirement plan must cover at least the lesser of (1) 50 employees, or (2) 40 percent of the employees of the employer (sec. 401(a)(26)). Federal law requires government contractors to provide certain employees specified retirement benefits or make a specified level of contributions to retirement plans. In some cases where these requirements apply, such as the construction industry, individuals change employers frequently. In order to provide the specified benefits and address the problem of frequent job changes, some employers have established a multiple employer plan covering the affected employees, while maintaining other qualified retirement plans for employees not subject to the Federal requirements. The provision would require the Treasury Department to perfom a study of the effects of the new minimum participation rule on arrangements of this type. The study should consider (1) the Federal requirements with respect to employee benefits for employees of government contractors, (2) whether a special minimum participation rule should apply to multiple employer plans where such Federal requirements apply, and (3) ways in which the plans of employers subject to such requirements could be modified to satisfy the minimum participation rule.

The study would be required to be completed by September 1, 1989.

[Explanation of House Committee Amendment to H.R. 4333]

The House bill provides that the minimum participation rule does not apply to any governmental plan with respect to employees who were participants in the plan on July 14, 1988.

[Conference Committee Report]

* * *

Conference Agreement

The conference agreement follows the House bill with respect to governmental plans, with the modification that the provision only applies to plan years beginning before January 1, 1993. The provision is effective as if included in section 1112(b) of the Reform Act.

[House Committee Report]

Under the bill, rural telephone cooperatives are permitted to maintain section 401(k) plans on the same basis as rural electric cooperatives.

Effective Date

The provision is effective for years beginning after the date of enactment.

[¶ 11,700.046]

Committee Report on P.L. 100-203 (Omnibus Budget Reconciliation Act of 1987)

[House Committee Report]

The conference agreement generally follows the Finance Committee amendment, with certain modifications. Under the conference agreement, if a plan amendment increasing current liability is adopted, the contributing sponsor and members of the controlled group of the contributing sponsor must provide security in favor of the plan (e.g., a bond) equal to the excess of (1) the lesser of (i) the amount by which the plan's assets are less than 60 percent of current liability, taking into account the benefit increase and the unfunded current liability attributable to prior plan amendments, or (ii) the amount of the benefit increase, over (2) $10 million. The employer must notify the PBGC of the benefit increase before it is effective. As under the Finance Committee amendment, current liability is calculated by disregarding the unamortized portion of unfunded old liability.

[¶ 11,700.048]

Committee Reports on P.L. 99-514 (Tax Reform Act of 1986)

[House Bill]

The House bill revises the manner in which a pension plan may be integrated with social security. Pursuant to regulations to be issued by the Secretary of the Treasury, the maximum amount of social security benefits that may be taken into account by an employer for any year of service with such employer may not exceed 1/40 of the total social security benefits permitted to be taken into account. Thus, the bill precludes an employer from taking into account benefits attributable to OASDI contributions of former employers of an employee.

Under a flat-benefit excess plan, the full 37 ½ percent excess amount (reduced for integrated ancillary benefits) could be applied only to an employee who had 40 years of service with the employer upon retirement at age 65. If an employee only had 20 years of service with the employer, the maximum excess benefit at age 65 would be 16.75 percent (37 ½ multiplied by 20/40, the ratio of 20 years of service to 40), assuming that the plan has no integrated ancillary benefits.

For an offset plan, the full 83 ⅓ percent offset (reduced for integrated ancillary benefits) could be applied only to an employee who retired at age 65 with 40 years of service with the employer. Thus, if an employee retired at age 65 with 30 years of service with the employer, the maximum offset would be 62.5 percent (83 ⅓ multiplied by 30/40, the ratio of 30 years of service to 40), assuming the plan has no integrated ancillary benefits.

The bill generally would not have a significant effect on unit benefit plans because such plans will automatically reduce the social security benefit taken into account under the plan for employees retiring with less than 37 ½ years of service due to the reduced number of years taken into account under the unit benefit formula for such employees. Furthermore, the bill generally would not affect the integration of defined contribution plans integrated with OASDI benefits (except to the extent such plans are determined to be nondiscriminatory on the basis of benefits). Also, the committee anticipates that similar rules would apply to the integration of other employer-provided benefits under Federal, State, or foreign law.

The provision applies to plan years beginning after December 31, 1986.

[Senate Amendment]

In general

The Senate amendment provides that a plan is not to be considered discriminatory merely because the contributions and benefits of (or on behalf of) employees under the plan favor highly compensated employees if the plan meets the new requirements of the bill relating to the integration of contributions or benefits.

Permitted disparity in defined contribution plans

In general.—Under the Senate amendment, a defined contribution plan meets the disparity limits for integrated plans only if the excess contribution percentage under the plan does not exceed the base contribution percentage by an amount specified in the bill. The bill provides that the excess contribution percentage is not to exceed the lessor of (1) 200 percent of the base contribution percentage, or (2) the sum of the base contribution percentage and the rate of the tax imposed on employers under the Federal Insurance Contributions Act (5.7 percent for 1986) as of the beginning of the plan year.

For example, under the Senate amendment, if a defined contribution plan provided for contributions of 10 percent of pay on compensation in excess of the taxable wage base, then the plan is required to provide contributions of at least 5 percent of pay on compensation up to the taxable wage base in order to satisfy the integration rules for defined contribution plans. Alternatively, if the plans provided contributions of 10 percent of pay on compensation up to the taxable wage base, then the contributions for compensation in excess of the taxable wage base are limited to 15.7 percent because the permitted disparity cannot be greater than the OASDI tax rate (i.e., 5.7 percent in 1986).

Contributions to a plan that are subject to the nondiscrimination rules in section 401(k) or 401(m) (or, in the case of simplified employer pensions, sec. 408(k)(6)) may not rely on these integration requirements, but rather must satisfy the separate nondiscrimination rules under such other provisions.

Excess contribution percentage.—Under the Senate amendment, the excess contribution percentage is the percentage of remuneration that is contributed under the plan with respect to that portion of remuneration in excess of the compensation level specified under the plan for the year.

Base contribution percentage.—The Senate amendment provides that the base contribution percentage is the percentage of remuneration contributed under the plan with respect to that portion of remuneration not in excess of the compensation level specified under the plan for the year.

Under the Senate amendment, the compensation level refers to the dollar amount of remuneration specified under the plan as the compensation level for the year. The compensation level specified in the plan may not exceed the contributions or benefit base under the Social Security Act (i.e., the taxable wage base) in effect at the beginning of the plan year ($42,000 for plan years beginning in 1986). In addition, an employer may not set a lower compensation level if such level discriminates in favor of highly compensated employees.

Remuneration.—Remuneration is defined as total compensation, or basic or regular compensation, whichever is used in determining contributions or benefits under the plan. With respect to a self-employed individual, the Senate amendment provides that compensation includes the individual's earned income. The self-employed individual's basic or regular rate of compensation is equal to the portion of the individual's earned income that bears the same ratio to his earned income as the regular or basic compensation of employees under the plan bears to the total compensation of such employees.

Permitted disparity in defined benefit pension plans

In general

Under the Senate amendment, a defined benefit pension plan meets the requirement for integrated plans only if it meets the requirements for integrated offset plans or those for integrated excess plans. Under a special limitation provided by the Senate amendment, a defined benefit pension plan will not fail to meet the nondiscrimination rules (sec. 401(a)(4)) merely because it limits benefits by reference to the final pay of a participant.

Excess plans

In general.—A defined benefit pension plan meets the disparity limits for integrated excess plans if (1) the excess benefit percentage does not exceed 200 percent of the base benefit percentage, and (2) any optional form of benefit, preretirement benefit, actuarial factor, or other benefit or feature provided by the plan with respect to remuneration in excess of the compensation level specified by the plan for the year is provided with respect to remuneration that is not in excess of that level.

Benefit percentages.—Under the rules for integration of defined benefit pension plans as excess plans, the excess and base benefit percentages are to be computed in the same manner as those percentages are to be computed for defined contribution plans, except that the computation is to be based on benefits rather than contributions. Thus, the term the "excess benefit percentage" refers to the benefits provided under the plan (expressed as a percentage of remuneration) with respect to that portion of remuneration in excess of the compensation level specified in the plan. The base benefit percentage refers to the benefits provided under the plan (expressed as a percentage of remuneration) with respect to that portion of remuneration not in excess of the compensation level specified in the plan.

For purposes of the rules relating to defined benefit excess plans, the terms "compensation level" and "remuneration" have the same meanings as for purposes of the rules relating to defined contribution plans.

Offset plans

In general.—A defined benefit pension plan meets the requirements for integrated offset plans if it provides that a participant's accrued benefit derived from employer contributions (sec. 411(c)(1)) may not be reduced by reason of the offset by more than 50 percent of the benefit that would have accrued without regard to the reduction. The bill provides that a defined benefit pension plan is an offset plan if each participant's normal retirement benefit derived from employer contributions (sec. 411) is reduced (offset) by a dollar amount specified by the plan and if the same dollar amount of reduction is applicable to all plan participants. The Secretary is directed to prescribe rules for "normalizing" benefits, though not necessarily in the manner described in Rev. Rul. 81-202, and to prevent discriminatory modifications in the amount of the dollar offset from year to year.

Example.—Under an offset plan, the offset may never reduce a participant's accrued benefit by more than 50 percent, and may accrue no faster than the rate at which the participant's benefit under the plan would accrue without regard to the offset. For example, assume that a plan provides for a normal retirement benefit of 50 percent of final pay, less $20,000. The plan provides that the participant's accrued benefit is to accrue under the fractional accrual rule of section 411(b). Normal retirement age under the plan is age 65. Assume that a participant commences working for the employer and becomes a participant in the plan at age 40. Upon the date that the participant has completed 5 years of service with the employer, the participant has an accrued benefit (without regard to the dollar offset) of 5/25ths of 50 percent of final pay (or 10 percent of final pay). At that time, the value of the offset "accrued" to the participant may not exceed the lesser of (a) 5/25ths of $20,000 ($4,000), or (b) one-half of the participant's accrued benefit (determined without regard to the offset) to date.

Multiple plans

The bill provides rules that apply to a plan that benefits a highly compensated employee who participates in 2 or more plans maintained by the employer that would be considered discriminatory but for the integration rules. In such a case, the integration rules are to be applied to each of the plans by taking into account the total contributions and benefits for such highly compensated employee under all of such plans of the employer.

Benefits limited by reference to final pay

The bill provides that a defined benefit pension plan (including an offset or excess plan) is not to be considered discriminatory merely because it provides that the employer-provided accrued retirement benefit for any participant under the plan is not to exceed the excess (if any) of (1) the participant's final pay with the employer, over (2) the employer-provided retirement benefit, created under Federal law, that is attributable to the participant's service with the employer. The

Secretary shall prescribe rules for "normalizing" accrued benefits for purposes of this rule. Also, this limit may not be applied to reduce minimum benefits under the top-heavy rules.

Under the bill, for purposes of determining the final-pay limit that may be imposed by an integrated defined benefit pension plan, a participant's final pay is the total compensation paid to the participant by the employer during the participant's highest year of compensation ending with or within the 5-year period ending with the year in which the participant separated from service with the employer.

Effective date

The provisions are effective with respect to benefits accrued in plan years beginning after December 31, 1988.

A special effective date applies to plans maintained pursuant to a collective bargaining agreement. Under this special rule, in the case of a plan maintained pursuant to a collective bargaining agreement between employee representatives and one or more employers ratified before March 1, 1986, the amendments are not effective for plan years beginning before the earlier of (1) the later of (i) January 1, 1989, or (ii) the date on which the last of the collective bargaining agreements terminates, or (2) January 1, 1991. Extensions or renegotiations of the collective bargaining agreements, if ratified after February 28, 1986, are disregarded.

[Conference Agreement]

In general

The conference agreement generally follows both the House bill and the Senate amendment with the following modifications: (1) the deemed accrual period for social security benefits in the House bill is reduced from 40 years to 35 years and is applied for purposes of integrating offset plans, flat excess plans, and unit benefit excess plans; (2) in order to limit the extent to which an employer may increase, relative to the present law integration rules, the disparity between benefits accruing with respect to compensation above and below the integration level, additional limits on such disparity are applied; and (3) the uniform definition of compensation under new section 414(s) is applied.

The additional limits added by the agreement on the permitted disparity are a simplified form of the present-law integration rules, modified to eliminate the need for offset plans to determine an employee's actual lifetime social security benefit, provide for parity between offset plans and excess plans, provide uniform rules for both final average excess plans and career average excess plans, and eliminate the adjustments for integrated ancillary benefits (except for early retirement benefits).

The conferees recognize that some plans that satisfy both the present-law integration rules and the rules adopted in the House bill and the Senate amendment may not satisfy the additional limits added by the agreement. Similarly, the conferees realize that for some other plans the additional limits will permit a greater disparity in benefits above and below the integration level than that permitted under present law. However, the conferees have determined that, in attempting to limit the disparity permitted under the new rules to approximately the levels permitted under present law, the goals of simplifying the integration rules, providing consistent rules for different types of plans, and updating the rules to reflect the current social security system justify the simplified approach adopted under the agreement.

Permitted disparity in defined contribution plans

Under the agreement, a defined contribution plan meets the disparity limits for integrated plans only if the excess contribution percentage (i.e., the contribution with respect to compensation over the integration level, expressed as a percentage of compensation) does not exceed the base contribution percentage (i.e., the contribution with respect to compensation up to the integration level, expressed as a percentage of such compensation) by more than the lesser of (i) the base contribution percentage, or (ii) the greater of 5.7 percentage points or the percentage equal to the portion of the rate of tax in effect under section 3111(a) attributable to old-age insurance as of the beginning of the plan year.

The conferees understand that for 1986 the rate of tax attributable to old-age insurance is less than 5 percent. The conferees expect that the Social Security Administration will advise the Secretary when such rate becomes greater than 5.7 percent and, thereafter, will determine the amount of such rate and advise the Secretary for timely publication.

As under the Senate amendment, a plan must specify the applicable integration level for a year. The maximum integration level permitted for a year, however, is the OASDI contribution and benefit base under social security (taxable wage base) in effect at the beginning of the year ($42,000 for plan years beginning in 1986). The Secretary may develop such rules as are necessary to prevent an employer from selecting a lower integration level that discriminates in favor of highly compensated employees. Also, contributions subject to the nondiscrimination rules of section 401(k), 401(m), or 408(k)(6) may not rely on the integration rules to satisfy such rules. Finally, the agreement does not modify any other requirements currently applicable to integrated defined contribution plans, including, for example, the requirement that an integrated profitsharing or stock bonus plan provide benefits only upon retirement, death, or other separation from service.

Permitted disparity in defined benefit pension plans

In general

The agreement provides both ratio limits and percentage point limits on the maximum disparity permitted under a defined benefit excess plan and on the maximum offset permitted under a defined benefit offset plan. The ratio limits are the same as the limits adopted in the Senate amendment. The percentage point limits are a simplified form of the present-law integration rules.

Excess plans

In general.—The agreement provides that the excess benefit percentage (i.e., benefits provided with respect to compensation in excess of the applicable integration level, expressed as a percentage of compensation) under a defined benefit excess plan may not exceed the base benefit percentage (i.e., benefits provided with respect to compensation not in excess of such integration level, expressed as a percentage of such compensation) by more than the maximum excess allowance.

Maximum excess allowance.—In the case of an excess plan, the maximum excess allowance with respect to benefits attributable to any year of service taken into account under the plan is the lesser of (i) the base benefit percentage, or (ii) 3/4 of a percentage point. The maximum excess allowance for such a plan with respect to total benefits is the lesser of (i) the base benefit percentage, or (ii) 3/4 of a percentage point times the participant's years of service (not in excess of 35) taken into account under the plan.

These limits apply to excess plans that base benefits on final average compensation as well as excess plans that base benefits on career average compensation. Under the conference agreement, an integrated final pay plan may not base plan benefits on less than 3 years of service (or for a participant's full period of service, if less).

A year is treated as taken into account under a plan for purposes of applying the maximum excess allowance if benefits are treated as accruing on behalf of the participant for such year. Thus, for example, an excess plan that provides for the accrual of benefits over a participant's years of participation is to be treated as taking only years of participation into account.

This maximum excess allowance applies to both a flat-benefit final pay plan and a unit benefit final pay plan. For example, assume a flat-benefit plan with a benefit formula providing a retirement benefit for any participant retiring at age 65 with at least 15 years of service equal to 20 percent of the participant's final average compensation not in excess of the applicable integration level. Assume further that the plan provides for the accrual of the retirement benefit under the fractional rule of section 411(b). In order to satisfy the new integration rules with respect to a participant retiring at age 65 with 20 years of participation, the plan may not provide a benefit in excess of 35 percent of compensation over the integration level. If this participant had 35 years of participation at age 65, the plan would be precluded from providing a benefit with respect to final average compensation over the integration level in excess of 40 percent of such compensation. If an employee with 10 years of participation in this plan separated from service at age 50, such employee's accrued benefit would be 8 percent of his final average compensation up to the applicable integration level plus up to 15.5 percent of his final average compensation over the integration level.

Reductions of the 3/4 percent factor.—The Secretary is directed to prescribe regulations requiring the reduction of the 3/4 percent factor in the maximum excess allowance for plans (both final average and career average plans) using integration levels in excess of covered compensation. The conferees direct the Secretary to provide for such reductions on the basis of brackets of integration levels in excess of covered compensation. Such reductions and brackets should correspond to the comparable reductions and brackets for offset plans. The Secretary is not authorized, however, to provide for an increase in the 3/4 factor for plans using integration levels lower than covered compensation.

The term "covered compensation" has the same meaning as under present law, i.e., with respect to an employee, the average of the taxable wage bases in effect for each year during the 35-year period ending with the year the employee attains age 65, assuming no increase in such wage base for years after the current year and before the employee actually attains age 65.

The conferees intend that the reductions for higher integration levels will reflect the decreasing percentages of compensation replaced by the employer-provided PIA under social security as compensation increases above covered compensation. The Secretary is directed to consult with the Social Security Administration in developing the prescribed reductions.

Optional forms of benefits and other features.—The agreement follows the requirement in the Senate amendment that any optional form of benefit, preretirement benefit, actuarial factor, and other factor or feature under the plan provided with respect to compensation above the integration level also be provided with respect to compensation below the integration level. Thus, for example, if a lump sum distribution option, calculated using particular actuarial assumptions, is available with respect to benefits relating to compensation above the integration level, the same lump sum option must be available on an equivalent basis with respect to benefits based on compensation up to the integration level.

Multiple integration levels.—The Secretary is directed to provide rules under which an excess plan may use 2 or more integration levels. The permitted disparity with respect to each such integration level should be based on the percentages of compensation up to each such level replaced by the employer-provided portion of PIA under social security.

Offset plans

The agreement provides that in the case of a defined benefit offset plan, a participant's accrued benefit may not be reduced by reason of the offset by more than the maximum offset allowance for such participant. The maximum offset allowance with respect to a participant for any year of service taken into account under the plan is the lesser of (i) 50 percent of the benefit that would have accrued without regard to the offset reduction, or (ii) 3/4 percent of the participant's final average compensation times the participant's years of service with the employer (not in excess of 35) taken into account under the plan. For purposes of this allowance, a participant's final average compensation is to be calculated by disregarding compensation in any year over the taxable wage base for such year.

The Secretary is directed to reduce the 3/4 factor under the maximum offset allowance for participants with final average compensation in excess of covered compensation. Such reductions are to be based on the decreasing percentages of compensation replaced by the employer-provided PIA under social security as compensation increases above covered compensation. The Secretary is directed to consult with the Social Security Administration in developing such prescribed reductions. In addition, the reductions applicable to the 3/4 factor for offset plans should correspond to the reductions applicable to the 3/4 factor for excess plans using integration levels in excess of covered compensation. Finally, the conferees direct the Secretary to publish annually a table setting forth the appropriate offset factors for brackets of final average compensation in excess of covered compensation.

The term "offset plan" means any defined benefit plan under which the employer-provided benefit for each participant is reduced by an amount specified in the plan not in excess of the maximum offset allowance for such participant. In addition, an offset plan must base benefits on average annual compensation for at least the lesser of (1) a 3-year period or (2) the total number of the participant's years of service. Such term does not include a qualified plan merely because the benefits under such plan are reduced by benefits under another qualified plan. An offset plan may reduce participants' benefits by less than the maximum offset allowance so long as the offset amount or formula is specified in the plan, does not discriminate in favor of highly compensated employees, and is not otherwise inconsistent with the purposes of the integration rules.

Reductions for early retirement benefits

Under the conference agreement, the Secretary is also directed to reduce the 3/4 percent factor in the maximum excess allowance and maximum offset allowance for plans providing for unreduced benefits (other than for disability, as defined under the Social Security Act) commencing before the social security retirement age (as defined in section 415). As under current law, the 3/4 factor is to be reduced by 1/15 for each of the first five years that the benefit commencement date precedes the social security retirement age (currently age 65), and by an additional 1/30 for each of the next five years that the benefit commencement date precedes the social security retirement age. If the benefit commencement date is earlier than 10 years before the social security retirement age, the factor is to be actuarially reduced for each such additional year. Also, as under current law, the determination of whether early retirement benefits require an adjustment is based on a comparison of the benefit actually provided under the plan at the early retirement age with the benefit that would be provided under a plan at such age that has the maximum disparity permitted under the integration rules (calculated by applying the 1/15, 1/30 adjustment).

Multiple integrated plans

The agreement directs the Secretary to develop rules to prevent excessive use of the disparity permitted under this subsection with respect to any employee through the integration of more than one qualified plan. Such rules are to limit to 100 percent the sum of the percentages, calculated separately for each plan with overlapping coverage, of the maximum benefit disparity actually used in each plan.

Benefits limited by reference to final pay

The agreement adopts the Senate amendment rule permitting a defined benefit plan to limit the employer-provided accrued retirement benefit under the plan for any participant to the excess of the participant's final pay with the employer over the employer-provided PIA actually provided for such participant under social security and attributable to service by the participant with the employer. This limit is applied to the participant's accrued retirement benefit (disregarding ancillaries) under the defined benefit plan. Similarly, the limit is applied by taking into account only the worker's benefit (PIA) under social security, disregarding auxiliary benefits (spousal, survivor, children's, and disability benefits). The agreement clarifies that for purposes of determining the portion of the employer-provided PIA under social security for a participant that is attributable to service with the employer, such PIA is treated as accruing ratably over 35 years. However, the conferees do not intend that the limit also be prorated. Finally, as under the Senate amendment, this limit may not be applied either to reduce minimum benefits under the topheavy rules or to reduce accrued benefits within the meaning of section 411(d)(6).

Effective date

The new integration rules apply with respect to benefits accruing in plan years beginning after December 31, 1988. A special effective date applies with respect to benefits accruing under a plan maintained pursuant to a collective bargaining agreement.

[Senate Committee Report]

Explanation of Provision

The bill creates uniform rules for foreitures under any defined contribution plan. The bill permits, but does not require, forfeitures to be reallocated to other participants. Thus, forfeitures arising in any defined contribution plan (including a money purchase pension plan) can be either (1) reallocated to the accounts of other participants in a nondiscriminatory fashion, or (2) used to reduce future employer contributions or administrative costs.

Effective Date

The provision is effective for years beginning after December 31, 1985.

[Conference Committee Report]

Conference Agreement

The conference agreement follows the House bill and Senate amendment.

[Senate Committee Report]

Explanation of Provision

Under the bill, an employer's contribution to a profit-sharing plan is not limited to the employer's current or accumulated profits. This provision applies without regard to whether the employer is tax-exempt.

[Conference Committee Report]

Conference Agreement

The conference agreement follows the Senate amendment, except that the provision is effective for plan years beginning after December 31, 1985. The conferees also intend that the Secretary may require defined contribution plans to contain provisions specifying whether they are pension plans or discretionary contribution plans.

[Senate Committee Report]

Explanation of Provision

Under the bill, members of fishing boat crews (described in sec. 3121(b)(20)) are treated as self-employed individuals for purposes of the rules relating to qualified pension, profit-sharing, or stock bonus plans.

Effective Date

The provision is effective for taxable years beginning after December 31, 1986.

[Conference Committee Report]

The conference agreement follows the Senate amendment, effective for taxable years beginning after December 31, 1986.

[Senate Committee Report]

The Senate amendment eliminates the pass-through voting requirements of present law in the case of employer securities issued by certain newspapers whose stock is not readily traded and also permits ESOPs established by such employers to acquire nonvoting common stock in certain cases.

[Conference Committee Report]

The conference agreement follows the Senate amendment. The conference agreement clarifies that the special rules for newspapers apply to employers (determined without regard to the controlled group rules) whose stock is not publicly traded and a substantial portion of whose business consists of publishing a newspaper for general circulation on a regular basis.

[House Committee Report]

Diversification of investments

In general

The bill requires an ESOP to offer a partial diversification election to participants who meet certain age and participation requirements (qualified employees). Under the bill, a qualified employee must be entitled annually during any diversification election period occurring within the employee's qualified election period direct diversification of up to 25 percent of the participant's account balance (50 percent after attainment of age 60). To the extent that a participant elects to diversify a portion of the account balance, the bill requires an ESOP to offer at least three investment options not inconsistent with regulations prescribed by the Secretary and to complete the diversification within a specified period.

Under the bill, distribution to the participant within 90 days after the close of the annual diversification election period of an amount not to exceed the maximum amount for which a participant elected diversification is deemed to satisfy the diversification requirement.

Qualified election period; qualified employees

Each ESOP must provide an annual diversification election period for the 90-day period following the close of the ESOP plan year. Thus, within 90 days after the end of a plan year, an ESOP must permit an election by those qualified employees who become or remain eligible to make a diversification election during the plan year. Under the bill, any employee who has attained at least age 55 and completed at least 10 years of participation in the ESOP is a qualified employee. Any qualified employee is permitted to make a diversification election during any diversification election period occurring within that employee's qualified election period.

A qualified employee's qualified election period generally begins with the plan year following the plan year during which the qualified employee attains age 55 and ends with the fifth succeeding plan year. If, however, the employee has not completed 10 years of participation in the ESOP by the end of the plan year in which the employee attains age 55, the qualified election period begins with the plan year following the year in which he completes 10 years of participation and ends with the plan year following the year in which he attains age 60.

For example, in the case of an ESOP using the calendar year as the plan year, a participant who completes 10 years of participation before attaining age 55 and who attains age 55 in 1990, becomes a qualified employee in the 90-day election period beginning January 1, 1991. That participant will remain eligible to direct diversification during the annual election periods in 1992, 1993, 1994, 1995 and 1996.

Amount eligible for diversification

Under the bill, for any participant who has attained age 55 (but not age 60) and completed 10 years of participation in the plan, the amount of a participant's account balance subject to the diversification election at the end of the plan year is 25 percent of the participant's account balance at the end of the year reduced by amounts previously diversified. For any participant who has attained age 60 and completed 10 years of participation, the amount eligible for diversification at the end of the plan year is 50 percent of the participant's account balance at the end of the year, minus amounts previously diversified. Because these rules permit diversification not to exceed a cumulative amount, the scope of each year's election depends, in part, on prior elections.

The committee intends the Secretary of the Treasury to issue regulations providing that no separate diversification election be provided for de minimis amounts. In addition, in no event will amounts previously diversified be required to be reinvested in employer securities due to decreases in the value of the account balance.

These rules are illustrated by the following example:

Assume a participant with 10 years of participation in an ESOP attains age 55 during the 1986 plan year and that the ESOP uses a calendar plan year. During the 90-day period beginning on January 1, 1987, and ending on March 31, 1987, the participant may direct the trustee to diversify up to 25 percent of the participant's account balance. If the participant elects to direct diversification of the maximum amount—25 percent—the only amounts for which the participant may elect diversification during the 1988, 1989, 1990, and 1991 election periods are amounts attributable to increases in the participant's account balance, whether attributable to growth or additional employer contributions. However, pursuant to regulations to be issued by the Secretary of the Treasury, no diversification election is required for de minimis amounts.

From January 1, 1992 to March 31, 1992, the participant must be given the opportunity to direct diversification of up to 33- 1/3 percent of the remaining account balance (bringing the total amount subject to the diversification election to a cumulative 50 percent of the participant's account balance at the end of the 1991 plan year). Whether or not this participant directed diversification in 1992, no further diversification election is required to be provided to the participant.

Alternatively, if the participant did not elect diversification during the 1987 election period, a similar election would be available during the 1988, 1989, 1990, and 1991 election periods. In each year, the participant could elect to direct diversification with respect to that portion of the account balance that, when aggregated with prior amounts for which diversification was elected, did not exceed 25 percent of the account balance at the end of that year.

If the participant did not elect diversification during the 1987-1991 election periods, a final election would be available in 1992 (i.e., the first election period following the plan year in which the participant attains age 60) to direct diversification of up to 50 percent of the participant's account balance.

Implementation of diversification

No later than 90 days after the close of the election period, the plan trustee(s) must complete diversification pursuant to participant elections. The trustee(s) may satisfy this requirement (1) by distributing to the participant an amount equal to the amount for which the participant elected diversification, or (2) by substituting for the amount of the employer securities for which the participant elects diversification, an equivalent amount of other assets, in accordance with the participant's investment direction. The ESOP must offer at least three investment options (not inconsistent with regulations prescribed by the Secretary) that may, but need not, include an option to permit full self-direction.

Whether or not the trustees must actually sell employer securities to satisfy the diversification elections depends, in part, on the extent to which the ESOP is invested in employer securities. Provided the amount of total trust assets invested in other than employer securities is greater than the total amount for which diversification is elected, it may be possible to complete diversification (without disposing of employer securities) by allocating alternative assets to electing participants' accounts or by disposing of such alternative assets and reinvesting the proceeds in the investments directed by participants.

In addition, under the bill, a participant who receives a distribution of securities in satisfaction of a diversification election is permitted to roll over the distribution into another qualified plan or IRA.

* * *

Independent appraiser

Under the bill, the valuation of employer securities contributed to or purchased by an ESOP must be determined by an independent appraiser (within the meaning of section 170(a)(1)). The appraiser's name must be reported to the Internal Revenue Service.

[Conference Committee Report]

Diversification of investments

The conference agreement follows the House bill, except that the effective date of the diversification requirements is delayed for one year. Thus, the diversification rules are effective with respect to [stock] acquired [after] December 31, 1986.

Under the conference agreement, as under the House bill, a "qualified employee" is entitled annually during the participant's "qualified election period" to direct diversification of up to 25 percent of the participant's account balance (50 percent after attainment of age 60). Any employee who has attained age 55 and completed 10 years of participation is a qualified employee. An employee is entitled to an election in each year within the qualified election period.

In meeting the diversification requirements, it is not intended that plan sponsors offer employer securities as one of the diversification options. As under the House bill, the diversification requirement can be met by a distribution of the portion of the account balance for which diversification was elected, or cash in lieu thereof. If, under this rule, stock is distributed in satisfaction of the diversification requirement, the usual put option rules apply. Amounts which are distributed in satisfaction of the diversification requirement may be rolled over to an IRA or to another qualified plan. The diversification requirement is satisfied if an employer provides the option to transfer the portion of the account balance for which diversification is elected into a plan which provides for employee-directed investment and in which the required diversification options are available.

* * *

Independent appraiser

The conference agreement follows the House bill, except that valuation by an independent appraiser is not required in the case of employer securities which are readily tradable on an established securities market. The requirement is effective with respect to stock acquired after December 31, 1986.

Cash or Deferred Plans

[House Committee Report]

Modification of nondiscrimination tests

In addition, the bill alters the special nondiscrimination tests applicable to qualified cash or deferred arrangements so that the actual deferral percentage under a cash or deferred arrangement by highly compensated employees for a plan year may not exceed either (1) 125 percent of the actual deferral percentage of all nonhighly compensated employees eligible to defer under the arrangement, or (2) the lesser of 200 percent of the actual deferral percentage of all eligible nonhighly compensated employees or the actual deferral percentage for all eligible nonhighly compensated employees plus two percentage points.

Under the bill, if a highly compensated employee participates in more than one qualified cash or deferred arrangement of an employer, the employee's actual deferral percentage for purposes of testing each arrangement under the special nondiscrimination tests is to be determined by aggregating the employee's elective deferrals under all of the arrangements of the employer.

In addition, the bill authorizes the Secretary of the Treasury to prescribe regulations relating to the extent to which elective deferrals under a cash or deferred arrangement of an employer are, or may be, aggregated with certain other types of contributions (e.g., employer matching contributions, nonelective contributions, and employee contributions) for purposes of applying the special nondiscrimination tests. Further, the bill authorizes regulations limiting the multiple use of the second or alternative part of the special nondiscrimination tests.

If the special nondiscrimination rules are not satisfied for any year, the bill provides that the qualified cash or deferred arrangement will not be disqualified if the excess contributions (plus income allocable to the excess contributions) are distributed before the close of the following plan year. Distribution of the excess contributions may be made notwithstanding any other provision of law and the amount distributed is not subject to the additional income tax on early withdrawals.

Excess contributions

Under the bill, excess contributions mean, with respect to any plan year, the excess of the aggregate amount of elective deferrals paid to the cash or deferred arrangement and allocated to the accounts of highly compensated employees over the maximum amount of elective deferrals that could be allocated to the accounts of highly compensated employees without violating the nondiscrimination requirements applicable to the arrangement. To determine the amount of excess contributions and the employees to whom the excess contributions are to be distributed, the bill provides that the elective deferrals of highly compensated employees are reduced in the order of their actual deferral percentages beginning with those highly compensated employees with the highest actual deferral percentages. The excess contributions are to be distributed to those highly compensated employees for whom a reduction is made under the preceding sentence in order to satisfy the special nondiscrimination tests.

For example, assume that the elective deferrals by the three highly compensated employees—A, B, and C—of employer X as of the close of the 1987 plan year are 10 percent, 8 percent, and 6 percent of compensation, respectively. Assume further that the actual deferral percentage limit on elective deferrals for the highly compensated employees in the qualified cash or deferred arrangement for the 1987 plan year is 7 percent.

The following method is to be utilized to determine the amount of excess contributions and the employees to whom the excess contributions are to be distributed. The elective deferrals by the highly compensated employees with the highest deferral ratios are treated as excess contributions to the extent that reducing such deferrals is necessary to bring the arrangement into compliance with the special nondiscrimination test. In this example, in order to reduce the actual deferral percentage for the highly compensated employees to 7 percent, it is necessary, first, to reduce the elective deferrals of employee A from 10 percent to 8 percent and, second, to reduce the elective deferrals of employees A and B from 8 percent to 7.5 percent. Thus, elective deferrals in excess of 7.5 percent are to be treated as excess contributions.

Excise tax on excess contributions

Under the bill, a penalty tax is imposed on the employer making excess contributions to a qualified cash or deferred arrangement (sec. 4979). The tax is equal to 10 percent of the excess contributions under the arrangement for the plan year ending in the taxable year. However, the tax does not apply to any excess contributions that, together with income allocable to the excess contributions, are distributed no later than 2 ½ months after the close of the plan year to which the excess contributions relate.

Excess contributions (plus income) distributed within the applicable 2 ½ month period are to be treated as received and earned by the employee in the employee's taxable year in which the excess contributions, but for the employee's deferral election, would have been received as cash. For purposes of this rule, the first elective deferrals for the plan year will be treated as the excess contributions. If the excess contributions (plus income) are distributed after the 2 ½ month period and before the close of the subsequent plan year, such amounts are to be included in the employee's income in the taxable year of distribution (rather than in a prior taxable year). In this case, the employer will be subject to the 10-percent excise tax on excess contributions.

Other restrictions

The bill imposes several additional restrictions on qualified cash or deferred arrangements. First, no withdrawals generally are permitted under a qualified cash or deferred arrangement prior to death, disability, separation from service, or bona fide plan termination or (except in the case of a pre-ERISA money purchase pension plan) the attainment of age 59 ½. However, a cash or deferred arrangement (other than a pre-ERISA money purchase pension plan) may permit hardship withdrawals from elective deferrals (but not income on the elective deferrals). Present law standards relating to what constitutes a hardship continue to apply.

In addition, the bill provides that a qualified cash or deferred arrangement cannot require, as a condition of participation in the arrangement, that an employee complete a period of service with the employer (or employers) maintaining the plan in excess of one year of service.

Under the bill, an employer generally may not condition, either directly or indirectly, contributions and benefits (other than matching contributions in the plan of which that arrangement is a part) upon an employee's elective deferrals. For example, an employer may not require an employee to make contributions under a cash or deferred arrangement as a condition of participating in a defined benefit pension plan. Similarly, elective deferrals under a qualified cash or deferred arrangement may not be used to ensure that another plan, when combined with the cash or deferred arrangement, satisfies the usual coverage or nondiscrimination requirements (secs. 410(b) and 401(a)(4)). In addition, under the bill, a floor offset defined benefit pension plan may not provide for offsets attributable to elective deferrals under a qualified cash or deferred arrangement.

The bill provides that qualified cash or deferred arrangements are not available to employees of tax-exempt organizations or governmental entities. However, this restriction does not apply to a plan maintained by a rural electric cooperative (defined in sec. 457(d)(9)(B)), a national association of such cooperatives, or a plan maintained by the Tennessee Valley Authority.

The bill provides that, in the case of employer contributions (including elective deferrals under a qualified cash or deferred arrangement) that satisfy the immediate vesting and withdrawal restrictions applicable to elective deferrals under a qualified cash or deferred arrangement, the determination of whether the plan to which the contributions are made is a profit-sharing plan is to be made without regard to whether the employer has current or accumulated profits. This is the case even if the plan does not contain a qualified cash or deferred arrangement.

[Senate Committee Report]

Explanation of Provisions

Limit on elective deferrals

In general

Under the bill, the maximum amount that an employee can elect to defer for any taxable year under all cash or deferred arrangements in which the employee participates is limited to $7,000. The $7,000 cap is adjusted for inflation by reference to percentage increases in the social security wage base at the same time and in the same manner as the indexing of dollar limits on benefits under section 415.

Whether or not an employee has deferred more than $7,000 a year is determined without regard to any community property laws. In addition, the $7,000 limit is coordinated with elective deferrals under simplified employee pensions (SEPs). In addition, the benefits under an unfunded deferred compensation plan of a State or local government (sec. 457) and a plan described in section 501(c)(18) are coordinated with the limits on elective deferrals under a qualified cash or deferred arrangement or a SEP. Moreover, for purposes of determining an individual's cap on elective deferrals for a year, the $7,000 cap (as indexed) is reduced by the amount of the individual's contributions to a tax-sheltered annuity contract to the extent that the contributions are made pursuant to a salary reduction agreement.

Unlike the overall limits on annual additions, which apply separately to amounts accumulated under plans of unrelated employers, this $7,000 cap limits all elective deferrals by an employee under all cash or deferred arrangements, SEPs, and sec. 501(c)(18) plans in which the employee participates. In addition, the $7,000 cap applies on the basis of the employee's taxable year, rather than the plan's limitation year.

Because, under the bill, the $7,000 limit applies only to elective deferrals, each employer may make additional contributions on behalf of any employee to the extent that such contributions, when aggregated with elective deferrals made by the employee under that employer's plan during the limitation year, do not exceed the overall limit (generally the lesser of 25 percent of compensation or $30,000).

Treatment of excess deferrals

If, in any taxable year, the total amount of elective deferrals contributed on behalf of an employee to all qualified cash or deferred arrangements and SEPs in which the employee participates exceeds $7,000, then the amount in excess of $7,000 (the excess deferrals) is included in the employee's gross income for the year to which the excess deferrals relate. In addition, with respect to any excess deferrals, no later than the first March 1 after the close of the employee's taxable year, the employee may allocate the excess deferrals among the arrangements in which the employee participates and may notify the administrator of each plan of the portion of the excess deferrals allocated to it. Under the bill, not later than the first April 15 after the close of the employee's taxable year, each plan may distribute to the employee the amount of the excess deferrals (plus income attributable to the excess) allocated to the plan. This distribution of excess deferrals may be made notwithstanding any other provision of law.

The committee intends that, to ease the administrative burden on employees and employers and the IRS, the arrangements maintained by any single employer may preclude an employee from making elective deferrals under such arrangements for a taxable year in excess of $7,000. To the extent that excess deferrals are made to arrangements of an employer, all amounts contributed in excess of the annual cap shall be treated as after-tax employee contributions.

The amounts of excess deferrals distributed to an employee (plus the income thereon) are included in the employee's gross income for the year to which the excess deferrals relate. Thus, the amounts distributed are treated as if they had not been contributed to the qualified cash or deferred arrangement and are not subject to any additional income taxes for early withdrawals. However, such excess deferrals are taken into account in applying the special nondiscrimination tests to the elective deferrals. The committee intends that the Secretary may require the recalculation of the actual deferral percentages after the distribution of excess deferrals in certain cases.

Excess deferrals that are not distributed by the applicable April 15 date are not treated as after-tax employee contributions upon subsequent distribution even though such deferrals were included in the employee's income. In addition, undistributed excess deferrals are treated as elective deferrals subject to the special nondiscrimination test.

The following example illustrates the application of the elective deferral limitation. Assume that, in 1987, employee A (whose taxable year is the calendar year) electively defers $5,000 under employer X's qualified cash or deferred arrangement and $3,000 under employer Y's qualified cash or deferred arrangement. For 1987, employee A may exclude from gross income only $7,000 of the total $8,000 of elective deferrals. The $1,000 excess deferral may be withdrawn from X's plan or Y's plan, or partially from both plans. A can request that $750 (plus income allocable to $750) be distributed from X's plan and that $250 (plus income allocable to $250) be distributed from Y's plan.

If the $1,000 of excess deferrals (plus income allocable to the $1,000) is distributed by April 15, 1988, A is required to include the excess (plus income) in gross income for 1987. The amount distributed would not then be included in gross income again in 1988. Further, A would not be subject to the [10]-percent additional income tax on withdrawals prior to age 59 ½.

Finally, employers X and Y are required, except to the extent provided by regulations, to take the distributed amounts into account when they test their qualified cash or deferred arrangements under the nondiscrimination tests for the year to which the excess relates.

If either of the plans fails to make the requested distribution by April 15, 1988, then the excess deferrals are to remain in the qualified cash or deferred arrangement, subject to the general withdrawal restrictions applicable to such arrangements. In addition, notwithstanding that A included the excess deferrals in gross income for 1987, A will not be treated as having any investment in the contract on account of the excess deferrals that were not distributed. Thus, the full amount of the excess deferrals not distributed will again be included in income when actually distributed from the arrangement. Further, the undistributed excess deferrals will be taken into account as elective deferrals in applying the special nondiscrimination tests applicable to the cash or deferred arrangement.

* * *

Excess contributions

If the special nondiscrimination rules are not satisfied for any year, the bill provides that the cash or deferred arrangement will not be disqualified if the excess contributions (plus income allocable to such contributions) are distributed before the close of the following plan year. Such distribution may be made notwithstanding any other provision of law and is not subject to the additional tax on early distributions.

Under the bill, excess contributions mean, with respect to any plan year, the excess of (1) the aggregate amount of elective deferrals paid to the cash or deferred arrangement and allocated to the accounts of highly compensated employees, over (2) the maximum amount of elective deferrals that could be allocated to the accounts of highly compensated employees without violating the nondiscrimination requirements applicable to the arrangement. The bill provides that excess contributions are required to be distributed in a manner which ensures that the special nondiscrimination test will be satisfied. To determine the amount of excess contributions and the employees to whom the excess contributions are to be distributed, the bill provides that the elective deferrals of highly compensated employees are reduced in the order of their actual deferral percentages beginning with those highly compensated employees with the highest actual deferral percentages. The excess contributions are to be distributed to those highly compensated employees for whom a reduction is made under the preceding sentence in order to satisfy the special nondiscrimination tests.

For example, assume that the elective deferrals by the three highly compensated employees—A, B, and C—of employer X as of the close of the 1987 plan year are 10 percent, 8 percent, and 6 percent of compensation, respectively. Assume further that the actual deferral percentage limit on elective deferrals for the highly compensataed employees in the qualified cash or deferred arrangement for the 1987 plan year is 7 percent.

The following method is to be utilized to determine the amount of excess contributions and the employees to whom the excess contributions are to be distributed. The elective deferrals by the highly compensated employees with the highest deferral ratios are treated as excess contributions to the extent that reducing such deferrals is necessary to bring arrangement into compliance with the special nondiscrimination test. In this example, in order to reduce the actual deferral percentage for the highly compensated employees to 7 percent, it is necessary, first, to reduce the elective deferrals of employee A from 10 percent to 8 percent and, second, to reduce the elective deferrals of employees A and B from 8 percent to 7.5 percent. Thus, elective deferrals in excess of 7.5 percent are to be treated as excess contributions.

* * *

Excise tax on excess contributions

Under the bill, and excise tax is imposed on the employer making excess contributions to a qualified cash or deferred arrangement (sec. 4979). The tax is equal to 10 percent of the excess contributions under the arrangement for the plan year ending in the taxable year. However, the tax does not apply to any excess contributions that, together with income allocable to the excess contributions, are distributed no later than 2 ½ months after the close of the plan year to which the excess contributions relate.

Excess contributions (plus income) distributed within the applicable 2 ½ month period are to be treated as received and earned by the employee in the employee's taxable year in which the excess contributions, but for the employee's deferral election, would have been received as cash. Under the bill, the first elective deferrals for the plan year will be treated as the excess contributions. If the excess contributions (plus income) are distributed after the 2 ½ month period and before the close of the subsequent plan year, such amounts are to be included in the employee's income in the taxable year of distribution (rather than in a prior taxable year). If the distribution is not made within the 2 ½ month period, the employer will be subject to the 10-percent excise tax on excess contributions.

Other restrictions

The bill modifies certain present-law restrictions and imposes several additional restrictions on qualified cash or deferred arrangements. First, the bill provides that distributions may be made to a participant in a qualified cash or deferred arrangement on account of the sale of a subsidiary or termination of the plan of which the arrangement is a part. Under the bill, the exception for distributions upon the sale of a subsidiary is available with respect to a participant who has not separated from service with the subsidiary.

The bill limits hardship withdrawals under a qualified cash or deferred arrangement to the amount of an employee's elective deferrals. Hardship withdrawals are not permitted from income on any contributions or from employer matching or nonelective employer contributions taken into account for purposes of the special nondiscrimination test and, as under present law, are not permitted from a pre-ERISA money purchase pension plan. Present-law standards relating to the definition of a hardship continue to apply.

In addition, the bill provides that a qualified cash or deferred arrangement cannot require, as a condition of participation in the arrangement, that an employee complete a period of service with the employer (or employers) maintaining the plan in excess of one year of service.

Under the bill, an employer generally may not condition, either directly or indirectly, contributions and benefits (other than matching contributions) upon an employee's elective deferrals. For example, if an employee's participation in a defined benefit pension plan depends upon whether the employee makes deferrals under a cash or deferred arrangement, then the arrangement is not a qualified cash or deferred arrangement. Similarly, elective deferrals under a qualified cash or deferred arrangement may not be used to ensure that another plan, when combined with the cash or deferred arrangement, satisfies the usual coverage or nondiscrimination requirements (secs. 410(b) and 401(a)(4)). In addition, under the bill, a floor offset defined benefit pension plan may not provide for offsets attributable to elective deferrals under a qualified cash or deferred arrangement.

The bill provides that qualified cash or deferred arrangements are not available to employees of State or local governments [and tax-exempt organizations].

[Conference Committee Report]

Limit on elective deferrals

The conference agreement is the same as the Senate amendment except that the method of indexing the $7,000 limit on annual elective deferrals is the same method that applies for purposes of adjusting the dollar limits on benefits under section 415. Therefore, the limits are adjusted for percentage increases in the Consumer Price Index (CPI), beginning in 1988.

In addition, as under the Senate amendment, the conference agreement provides that elective deferrals in excess of the annual limit are treated as elective deferrals for purposes of applying the special nondiscrimination requirements for qualified cash or deferred arrangements, except to the extent provided under rules prescribed by the Secretary. The Secretary is to prescribe rules preventing use of this rule to increase artificially the actual deferral percentage of the nonhighly compensated employees.

To the extent that an excess deferral is distributed by the first April 15 following the close of the taxable year in which the excess deferral was made, the excess deferral is not treated as an annual addition for purposes of the overall limits on contributions and benefits (sec. 415).

Similarly, excess deferrals distributed by the required date are not subject to the additional income tax on early withdrawals from qualified plans. In addition, the conferees intend that a plan distributing excess deferrals is not to be required to obtain the consent of the participant or the consent of the participant's spouse with respect to the distribution of excess deferrals. Further, a distribution of excess deferrals is not to be treated as violating an outstanding qualified domestic relations order (within the meaning of sec. 414(p)).

The provision is effective for years beginning after December 31, 1986.

Further, the provisions do not apply to elective deferrals of an employee made during 1987 and attributable to services performed during 1986 under a qualified cash or deferred arrangement if, under the terms of the arrangement in effect on August 16, 1986, (1) the employee's election to make the elective deferrals is made before January 1, 1987, and (2) the employer identifies the amount of the elective deferral before January 1, 1987.

Special limitation for investment in employer securities

The conference agreement does not adopt the provision in the Senate amendement allowing an additional $2,500 in annual elective deferrals in the case of amount invested in employer securities.

Nondiscrimination requirements

The conference agreement follows the House bill with certain modifications.

Definition of highly compensated employees

The conference agreement modifies the definition of highly compensated employees to which the nondiscrimination requirements apply and provides that this uniform definition applies generally for purposes of nondiscrimination requirements for qualified plans and employee benefit programs. In addition, the conference agreement adopts the provision in the Senate amendment providing a special definition of highly compensated employees for purposes of the special nondiscrimination requirements of qualified cash or deferred arrangement and in the case of a certain company.

Special nondiscrimination requirements

The conference agreement follows the House bill with respect to the special nondiscrimination tests applicable to qualified cash or deferred arrangements.

In addition, the conference agreement provides that, for purposes of applying the special nondiscrimination requirements, under rules prescribed by the Secretary, employer matching contributions that meet the vesting and withdrawal restrictions for elective deferrals under a qualified cash or deferred arrangement and qualified nonelective contributions may be taken into account. Qualified nonelective contributions are defined to mean employer contributions (other than matching contributions) with respect to which (1) the employee may not elect to have the contributions paid to the employee in cash in lieu of being contributed to the plan and (2) the vesting and distribution restrictions applicable to qualified cash or deferred arrangements are satisfied.

Excess contributions

The conference agreement follows the House bill and the Senate amendment with respect to the treatment of excess contributions (i.e., contributions to highly compensated employees that violate the special nondiscrimination requirements applicable to qualified cash or deferred arrangements). The conference agreement modifies the rules for determining the amount of income attributable to excess contributions. Under the conference agreement, the amount of income attributable to excess contributions is that portion of the income on the participant's account balance for the year that bears the same ratio as the excess contributions bear to the total account balance.

For purposes of determining the year in which the excess contributions are includible in income, the excess contributions are treated as the first contributions made for a year.

In addition, the conferees intend that the Secretary will prescribe rules relating to the coordination of an employee's excess deferrals (i.e., amounts in excess of the annual limit on elective deferrals) and the excess contributions and that, generally, the excess deferrals are to be calculated and distributed first and then the excess contributions are to be allocated among the highly compensated employees and distributed.

Under the conference agreement, the provision in the Senate amendment under which excess contributions that are distributed to a highly compensated employee are not subject to the additional income tax on early withdrawals from qualified plans is adopted. In addition, the conferees intend that a plan is not required to obtain the consent of the participant or the participant and spouse to distribute an excess contribution.

The conference agreement provides that a plan can distribute excess deferrals and excess contributions without regard to the terms of the plan or any other law until the first plan year for which plan amendments are required.

Effective dates

The provisions generally are effective for years beginning after December 31, 1986.

A special effective date applies to plans maintained pursuant to a collective bargaining agreement. Under this special rule, in the case of a plan maintained pursuant to a collective bargaining agreement between employee representatives and one or more employers ratified before March 1, 1986, the amendments are not effective, with respect to employees covered by the agreement, for plan years beginning before the earlier of (1) January 1, 1989, or (2) the date on which the last of the collective bargaining agreement terminates (determined without regard to any extensions in the collective bargaining agreement).

The rule relating to aggregation of a highly compensated employee's benefit under more than one qualified cash or deferred arrangement and the rules relating to the treatment of excess contributions are effective for plan years beginning after December 31, 1986.

Other restrictions

The conference agreement adopts the following provisions with respect to qualified cash or deferred arrangements:

Hardship withdrawals.—The conference agreement follows the House bill and the Senate amendment which limits hardship withdrawals from a qualified cash or deferred arrangement to the amount of an employee's elective deferrals. Therefore, hardship withdrawals are not permitted from amounts attributable to income on elective deferrals.

Under the conference agreement, employer matching contributions and nonelective contributions (to the extent taken into account for purposes of the special nondiscrimination test), and income on such matching or nonelective contributions may not be distributed on account of hardship.

The provision is effective for years beginning after December 31, 1988.

A special effective date applies to plans maintained pursuant to a collective bargaining agreement. Under this special rule, with respect to employees covered under a plan maintained pursuant to a collective bargaining agreement between employee representatives and one or more employers ratified before March 1, 1986, the amendments are not effective, with respect to employees subject to the agreement, for plan years beginning before the earlier of (1) the later of January 1, 1989, or the date on which the last of the collective bargaining agreement terminates (determined without regard to any extensions in the collective bargaining agreement), or (2) January 1, 1991.

Withdrawals on account of plan termination, etc.—The conference agreement generally follows the Senate amendment with respect to the provision permitting distributions from a qualified cash or deferred arrangement upon (1) plan termination without the establishment of a successor plan; (2) the date of the sale by a corporation of substantially all of the assets used by the corporation in a trade or business if the employee continues employment with the corporation acquiring the assets; or (3) the date of the sale by a corporation of the corporation's interest in a subsidiary if the employee continues employment with the subsidiary. Under the conference agreement, a distribution upon any of the 3 events described above is permitted only if it constitutes a total distribution of the employee's balance to the credit in the cash or deferred arrangement.

The provision is effective for distributions occurring after December 31, 1984.

Conditioning other benefits on elective deferrals.—The conference agreement follows the House bill and the Senate amendment with respect to the rule that a qualified cash or deferred arrangement cannot condition, either directly or indirectly, contributions and benefits (other than matching contributions in the plan of which the arrangement is a part) upon an employee's elective deferrals.

In addition, the conference agreement adopts the provision in the House bill and the Senate amendment that any elective deferrals under a qualified cash or deferred arrangement may not be taken into account for purposes of determining whether another plan meets the coverage requirements (sec. 410(b)) or the general nondiscrimination rules (sec. 401(a)(4)) or other qualification rules. This provision does not apply for purposes of applying the average benefit percentage requirement under the coverage requirements (but does apply for purposes of the present-law classification requirement that is part of the average benefit test).

The conferees clarify that the provision relating to conditioning other benefits on elective deferrals applies in the situation in which a plan provides that voluntary after-tax employee contributions may not be made until an employee makes a minimum amount of elective deferrals under a qualified cash or deferred arrangement. The conferees also clarify that this provision precludes the use of elective deferrals to satisfy the minimum contribution required on behalf of nonkey employees in a top-heavy plan.

Further, the conference agreement follows the Senate amendment with respect to qualified offset arrangements with a clarification of the definition of an employer for purposes of the provision.

The provisions are effective for years beginning after December 31, 1988.

A special effective date applies to plans maintained pursuant to a collective bargaining agreement. Under this special rule, with respect to employees covered under a plan maintained pursuant to a collective bargaining agreement between employee representatives and one or more employers ratified before March 1, 1986, the amendments are not effective, with respect to employees subject to the agreement, for plan years beginning before the earlier of (1) the later of January 1, 1989, or the date on which the last of the collective bargaining agreement terminates (determined without regard to any extensions in the collective bargaining agreement), or (2) January 1, 1991.

Eligibility to participate.—The conference agreement follows the House bill and the Senate amendment with respect to the provision that a qualified cash or deferred arrangement cannot require, as a condition of participation in the arrangement, that an employee complete a period of service greater than 1 year with the employer maintaining the plan, effective for years beginning after December 31, 1988.

A special effective date applies to plans maintained pursuant to a collective bargaining agreement. Under this special rule, in the case of a plan maintained pursuant to a collective bargaining agreement between employee representatives and one or more employers ratified before March 1, 1986, the amendments are not effective, with respect to employees covered by the agreement, for years beginning before the earlier of (1) the later of January 1, 1989, or the date on which the last of the collective bargaining agreement terminates (determined without regard to any extensions in the collective bargaining agreement), or (2) January 1, 1991.

Tax-exempt and State and local employers.—Under the conference agreement, the provision in the House bill prohibiting tax-exempt organizations and State and local governments (or a political subdivision of a State or local government) from establishing qualified cash or deferred arrangements is adopted.

The conference agreement provides that this provision does not apply to plans adopted before (1) May 6, 1986, in the case of an arrangement maintained by a State or local government (or political subdivision of a State or local government), or (2) July 2, 1986, in the case of an arrangement maintained by a tax-exempt organization. The grandfather treatment is limited to the employers who adopted the plan before the dates specified above. However, the grandfather treatment is not limited to employees (or classes of employees) covered by the plan as of the date the grandfather treatment is provided.

The provision is effective for years beginning after December 31, 1986. However, in the case of a plan maintained by a State or local government that was adopted before May 6, 1986 (and is, therefore, eligible for the grandfather rule), the following provisions in the conference agreement applicable to qualified cash or deferred arrangements do not apply until years beginning after December 31, 1988: (1) the modification of the special nondiscrimination tests, (2) the new definition of highly compensated employees, (3) the new definition of compensation, and (4) the rule aggregating highly compensated employees.

Definition of compensation

The conference agreement adopts a uniform definition of compensation for purposes of applying the special nondiscrimination requirements, effective for years beginning after December 31, 1988.

[Senate Committee Report]

f. Discrimination standards applicable to cash or deferred arrangements

Explanation of Provision

Under the bill, if an employee participates in more than one cash-or-deferred arrangement of an employer, all such cash-or-deferred arrangements are treated as one arrangement for purposes of determining the employee's actual deferral percentage. Thus, an employee's actual deferral percentage taken into account for purposes of applying the special deferral percentage tests under any plan of the employer is the sum of the elective deferrals for that employee under each plan of the employer which provides a cash-or-deferred arrangement, divided by the participant's compensation from the employer.

In addition, the bill clarifies that a plan which includes an otherwise qualified cash-or-deferred arrangement that satisfies the special tests provided by section 401(k)(3) will be treated as satisfying the general nondiscrimination test of section 401(a)(4) with respect to the elective deferrals.

[Conference Committee Report]

The conference agreement follows the Senate amendment * * *.

[¶ 11,700.05]

Committee Reports on P.L. 98-369 (Tax Reform Act of 1984)

[Conference Committee Report]

Standards for cash-or-deferred arrangements

Present law

Under present law, a cash-or-deferred arrangement is subject to special tests under which the amount that highly compensated employees can elect to defer (and exclude from current gross income) depends upon the level of deferrals by other employees. These special tests do not permit employer-provided social security benefits to be taken into account. However, proposed Treasury regulations permit a cash-or-deferred arrangement to satisfy the general nondiscrimination standards applicable to qualified plans in lieu of the special tests. The general nondiscrimination rules permit employer-provided social security benefits to be taken into account.

House bill

Under the House bill, a cash-or-deferred arrangement is not a qualified cash-or-deferred arrangement unless the special tests applicable to such an arrangement are satisfied. If an arrangement fails to satisfy the special tests, amounts deferred are not excluded from gross income, but the plan of which the arrangement is a part is not to be disqualified if it meets the usual rules for qualification, including the general nondiscrimination requirements.

* * *

The provision is effective for plan years beginning after December 31, 1984.

* * *

Conference agreement

The conference agreement generally follows the House bill, with two amendments. First, the conference agreement provides that the deferral percentage taken into account for purposes of applying the special deferral percentage tests is the sum of the deferral percentages for an employee under each cash or deferred arrangement in which the employee participates.

Second, under the conference agreement, the provision does not apply to a cash or deferred arrangement maintained, on June 8, 1984, by a State government and with respect to which a determination letter had been issued on December 6, 1982. The conferees intend that no inference is to be drawn from this effective date provision with respect to the issue of whether a State government may maintain a profit-sharing plan.

In addition, the conferees intend that the agreement does not change the rule contained in proposed Treasury regulations: nonelective contributions by the employer to a cash or deferred arrangement may be taken into account in applying the special deferral percentage tests. Such contributions may be taken into account only if the contributions (1) are nonforfeitable when made and (2) satisfy the withdrawal restrictions applicable to elective deferrals under a qualified cash or deferred arrangement.

[House Committee Report]

* * *

Explanation of Provision

The provision revises the tax-qualification rules to permit a qualified money purchase pension plan which was in existence on June 27, 1974, and which provided for a salary reduction arrangement on that date, to continue the arrangement after 1979. However, this revision to the tax-qualification rules will apply only to those money purchase pension plans under which employer and employee contributions may not exceed the limits (e.g., the percentage of pay) provided under the plan's contribution formula on June 27, 1974.

In addition, for plan years beginning after 1983, a salary reduction arrangement under a money purchase pension plan must meet the special tax-qualification rules for cash or deferred arrangements added by the 1978 Revenue Act with respect to employee eligibility to participate in the arrangement and to prohibited discrimination in favor of employees who are officers, shareholders, or highly compensated. These rules presently apply to cash or deferred arrangements under qualified profit-sharing or stock bonus plans.

The provisions of the bill apply to salary reduction arrangements under money purchase pension plans of taxable employers and tax-exempt organizations.

Effective Date

The bill will apply for plan years beginning after the date of enactment. The rules in effect prior to ERISA will apply for plan years beginning after December 31, 1979, and before the date of enactment.

[House Committee Report]

Explanation of Provision

In applying the overall limits on contributions and benefits under qualified pension plans, the bill provides that any contributions allocated to an individual medical benefit account (sec. 401(h)(2)) of an employee under a qualified defined benefit plan is to be treated as an annual addition under a qualified defined contribution plan. Accordingly, the amount allocated for a year would be included, together with employer contributions and reallocated forfeitures, in determining whether the defined benefit plan and any defined contribution plan of the employer meet the separate limits and the combined limits provided with respect to such plans. To the extent provided by Treasury regulations, an amount allocated to a medical benefit account under a defined benefit plan before the effective date of the provision could be reallocated to the individual medical benefit account of a participant without inclusion in the annual addition.

The bill provides that an account is an individual medical benefit account if it is established for a participant in a defined benefit plan, all medical benefits permitted to be paid under the plan with respect to the participant, the participant's spouse, or their dependents are payable solely from the account, and the account may be used for no other participant.

Under the bill, a defined benefit plan that provides medical benefits for retired employees is required to maintain an individual medical benefit account for any plan participant who [at any time during the plan year or any preceding plan year during which contributions were made on behalf of such employee] is a 5-percent owner (as defined in sec. 416(i)(1)(B)(i)). Of course, the medical benefits provided under a qualified defined benefit plan are required to meet nondiscrimination standards.

Effective Date

The provision applies to years beginning after March 31, 1984.

See also ¶ 11,900.085 for the committee report on the repeal of the bond purchase provisions.

See also ¶ 11,330.016 for the Committee Report on annual returns for IRAs.

The Committee Reports on P.L. 97-284 are at ¶ 12,400.06.

The Committee Reports on P.L. 97-34, Secs. 331—339, relating to employee stock ownership plans, are at ¶ 11,117.10.

[¶ 11,700.057]

Committee Report on P.L. 96-364 (Multiemployer Pension Plan Amendments Act of 1980)

The Senate Committee Report on P.L. 96-364 (Secs. 208(e) and 410(b)) is at ¶ 14,730.095.

[¶ 11,700.059]

Committee Report on P.L. 96-222 (Technical Corrections Act of 1979)

The Senate Committee Report on P.L. 96-222 (Sec. 101(a)(7)(L)) is at ¶ 12,130.09.

[¶ 11,700.06]

Committee Report on P.L. 95-600 (Revenue Act of 1978)

[Senate Committee Report]

The committee's bill adds new provisions to the Code * * * to permit employers to establish tax-qualified cash or deferred profit-sharing plans (or stock bonus plans). In addition, it provides a transitional rule to permit plans in existence on June 27, 1974, to rely on certain pre-1972 revenue rulings until plan years beginning in 1980.

The bill provides that a participant in a qualified cash or deferred arrangement will not have to include in income any employer contribution to the plan merely because he could have elected to receive such amount in cash instead. For the cash or deferred arrangement to be a tax-qualified plan, it must satisfy the normal pension plan qualification rules. In addition, it must satisfy the following requirements: (1) it must not permit the distribution of amounts attributable to employer contributions merely because of the completion of a stated period of plan participation or the passage of a fixed period of time (unlike profit-sharing plans in general, where distributions may be made in the third calendar year following the calendar year of the employer's contribution), and (2) all amounts contributed by the employer pursuant to an employee's election must be nonforfeitable at all times.

Special nondiscrimination rules are provided for these arrangements in lieu of the normal rules to test for discrimination as to actual plan participation or as to contributions to the plan. Under these rules, a cash or deferred arrangement will meet these nondiscrimination requirements for qualification for a plan year if (1) the actual deferral percentage for the highest paid one-third of all participants does not exceed the deferral percentage for the other eligible employees by more than 50 percent, or (2) the actual deferral percentage for the highest paid one-third of all participants does not exceed the actual deferral percentage of the other eligible employees by more than three percentage points. (If this latter test is used, the actual deferral percentage for the highest paid one-third cannot exceed the actual deferral percentage of all other eligible employees by more than 150 percent. Paid one-third of all participants, only amounts considered as compensation under the provisions of the plan are taken into account. Therefore, the plan would have to have participation by employees in the lower paid group in order to obtain any deferral for the highest paid one-third.)

The House bill, which was designed as a temporary solution, would have permitted new cash or deferred arrangements to be tax-qualified if they satisfied the law with respect to cash or deferred arrangements as it was administered before January 1, 1972.

The amendment is effective for taxable years beginning after December 31, 1979, however, a transitional rule is provided for those cash or deferred arrangements in existence on January 27, 1974 under which their qualified status for plan years beginning before January 1, 1980 shall be determined in a manner consistent with Rev. Rul. 56-497 (1956-2 C.B. 284), Rev. Rul. 63-180 (1963-2 C.B. 189), and Rev. Rul. 68-89, (1968-1 C.B. 402).

[¶ 11,700.07]

Committee Report on P.L. 95-600 (Revenue Act of 1978)

The Senate Committee Reports on Secs. 141(f) and 143(a) are reproduced at ¶ 12,130.10. The Senate Committee Report on Sec. 152 is reproduced at ¶ 12,050.09.

[¶ 11,700.08]

Committee Report on P.L. 94-455 (Tax Reform Act of 1976)

Permanent plan.—The committee amendment also makes clear that an ESOP which satisfies the investment tax credit rules does not fail to be a permanent program merely because employer contributions are not made for a year if the additional investment tax credit is not available for the year (for reasons other than the employer's failure to make the contribution).— **Senate Finance Committee Report.**

* * *

The committee amendment clarifies present law by providing that a segregated asset account can be used as an investment medium for assets of a qualified pension, profit-sharing, or annuity plan even though the account is held as a reserve under a contract which does not require the holder of the account to provide for the payment of annuities. The committee amendment also permits assets of a qualified plan to be held in a segregated asset account instead of a trust. The amendment does not in any way modify the requirements of title I of the Employee Retirement Income Security Act which requires certain pension plan assets to be held in a trust.

The House bill contains no comparable provision.

Effective Date

The committee amendment applies for taxable years beginning after December 31, 1975.—**Senate Finance Committee Report.**

[¶ 11,700.09]

Committee Report on P.L. 94-267 (IRC of 1954—Employee Retirement)

[House Committee Report]

The Report of the House Committee on P.L. 94-267 is reproduced at ¶ 11,750.09.

[¶ 11,700.10]

Committee Report on P.L. 93-406 (Employee Retirement Income Security Act of 1974)

[Conference Committee Explanation]

Joint and survivor annuities.—Under the conference substitute, when a plan provides for a retirement benefit in the form of an annuity, and the participant has been married for the one-year period ending on the annuity starting date, the plan must provide for a joint and survivor annuity. The survivor annuity must be not less than half of the annuity payable to the participant during the joint lives of the participant and his spouse.

In the case of an employee who retires, or who attains the normal retirement age, the joint and survivor provision is to apply unless the employee elected otherwise.

In the case of an employee who is eligible to retire prior to the normal retirement age under the plan, and who does not retire, the joint and survivor provisions need not be applicable under the plan, unless the employee made an affirmative election. Moreover, the plan need not make this option available until the employee is within 10 years of normal retirement age. (Of course, a plan may provide that a joint and survivor annuity is to be the only form of benefit payable under the plan, and in this case, no election need be provided.)

These rules should help to avoid the situation where an employee who had not yet retired might have his own retirement benefit reduced as a result of inaction on his part and should also help to prevent adverse selection as against the plan.

The employee is to be afforded a reasonable opportunity, in accordance with regulations, to exercise his election out of, (or before normal retirement age, possibly into) the joint and survivor provision before the annuity starting date (or before he becomes eligible for early retirement). The employee is to be supplied with a written explanation of the joint and survivor provision, explained in layman's language, as well as the practical (dollar and cents) effect on him (and his or her spouse) of making an election either to take or not to take the provision. At the same time, regulations in this area should take cognizance of the practical difficulties which certain industries (particularly those having multiemployer plans) may have in contacting all of their participants.

To prevent adverse selection the plan may provide that any election, or revocation of an election, is not to become effective if the participant dies within some period of time (not in excess of two years) of the election or revocation (except in the case of accidental death where the accident which causes death occurs after the election).

* * *

Alienation.—Under the conference substitute, a plan must provide that benefits under the plan may not be assigned or alienated. However, the plan may provide that after a benefit is in pay status, there may be a voluntary revocable assignment (not to exceed 10 percent of any benefit payment) by an employee which is not for purposes of defraying the administrative costs of the plan. For purposes of this rule, a garnishment or levy is not to be considered a voluntary assignment. Vested benefits may be used as collateral for reasonable loans from a plan, where the fiduciary requirements of the law are not violated.[4]

* * *

Social Security benefits of terminated participants.—The conference substitute codifies the current administrative practice which provides that qualified plans may not use increases in social security benefits or wage base levels to reduce employee plan benefits that are already in pay status. A similar protection is also extended against reductions in plan benefits where social security benefit levels (or wage base levels) are increased after the individuals concerned are separated from service prior to retirement. This requirement also applies to plans covered

[4] This rule will not apply to irrevocable assignments made before the date of enactment and the plan provision required under this rule need not be adopted prior to January 1, 1976 (so long as the plan complies with the substance of this rule after enactment).

under title I (even if the plan is not qualified). A similar principle will apply in the case of an individual receiving disability benefits under social security and also under an employer plan.

* * *

Payment of benefits.—Under the conference substitute, a plan is generally required to commence benefit payments (unless the participant otherwise elects) not later than the 60th day after the close of the plan year in which the latest of the following events occurs:

(1) the participant attains age 65 (or any earlier normal retirement age specified under the plan),

(2) ten years have elapsed from the time the participant commenced participation in the plan, or

(3) the participant terminates his service with the employer.

Also, if the plan permits an employee who has not separated from service to receive a subsidized early retirement benefit if he meets certain age and service requirements, the plan must also permit an employee who fulfills the service requirement, but separates from service before he meets the age requirement, to receive benefit payments, on an actuarially reduced basis, when the separated employee meets the age requirement. For example, if the plan provides a benefit of $100 a month at age 65, or at age 55 for employees with 30 years of service who are still employed on their 55th birthday, then an employee who separates from service at age 50 with 30 years service, would have the right to draw down an actuarially reduced benefit (perhaps $50 a month) at age 55. The actuarial adjustments are to be made in accordance with regulations to be prescribed by the Secretary of the Treasury, or his delegate.

* * *

Comparability of plans having different vesting provisions under the antidiscrimination rules.—The conference substitute provides that highly mobile employees, such as engineers, are permitted to trade off high benefits which might be available under one retirement plan of their employer for their right to participate in another plan with lower benefits, but more rapid vesting.

* * *

Defined benefit limits for proprietorships, partnerships, and subchapter S corporations.—The substitute authorizes Treasury regulations to allow self-employed persons and shareholder-employees in effect to translate the 15-percent/$7,500 limitations on contributions into approximately equivalent limitations on benefits which individuals can receive under a defined benefit plan. In this respect, the substitute contains a table (based on certain interest and mortality rates) which will serve as a guideline for regulations. The Treasury Department may, by regulations, modify this table from time to time for years beginning after December 31, 1977, to take account of changes in interest and mortality rates which occur after 1973.

The conference substitute also contains technical rules to prevent an individual from obtaining unintended high benefit accruals late in his career merely by establishing a "token plan" early in his career.

A plan which covers owner-employees is not permitted to use the defined benefit provisions unless it provides benefits for all participants on a nonintegrated basis (i.e., without taking social security benefits into account).

[*Retroactive changes.*]—Under the substitute, retroactive plan amendments which correct a plan that does not meet the requirements for tax qualification are allowed to cure a new plan or to cure an amendment to an existing plan. Such retroactive changes can be made within the time for filing the employer's tax return for the year in which the plan was put into effect or in which the amendment was adopted (or such later time as is designated by the Secretary of the Treasury).

[Code Sec. 402]

[¶ 11,750.19]

Committee Report on P.L. 109-280 (Pension Protection Act of 2006)

[Joint Committee on Taxation Report]

[Rollover of after-tax amounts in annuity contracts]

The provision allows after-tax contributions to be rolled over from a qualified retirement plan to another qualified retirement plan (either a defined contribution or a defined benefit plan) or to a tax-sheltered annuity. As under present law, the rollover must be a direct rollover, and the plan to which the rollover is made must separately account for after-tax contributions (and earnings thereon).

Effective Date

The provision is effective for taxable years beginning after December 31, 2006.

[Rollovers by nonspouse beneficiaries]

The provision provides that benefits of a beneficiary other than a surviving spouse may be transferred directly to an IRA. The IRA is treated as an inherited IRA of the nonspouse beneficiary. Thus, for example, distributions from the inherited IRA are subject to the distribution rules applicable to beneficiaries. The provision applies to amounts payable to a beneficiary under a qualified retirement plan, governmental section 457 plan, or a tax-sheltered annuity. To the extent provided by the Secretary, the provision applies to benefits payable to a trust maintained for a designated beneficiary to the same extent it applies to the beneficiary.

Effective Date

The provision is effective for distributions after December 31, 2006.

[Tax-free distributions from governmental retirement plans for premiums for health and long-term care insurance for public safety officers]

The bill provides that certain pension distributions from an eligible retirement plan used to pay for qualified health insurance premiums are excludible from income, up to a maximum exclusion of $3,000 annually. An eligible retirement plan includes a governmental qualified retirement or annuity plan, 403(b) annuity, or 457 plan. The exclusion applies with respect to eligible retired public safety officers who make an election to have qualified health insurance premiums deducted from amounts distributed from an eligible retirement plan and paid directly to the insurer. An eligible retired public safety officer is an individual who, by reason of disability or attainment of normal retirement age, is separated from service as a public safety officer[199] with the employer who maintains the eligible retirement plan from which pension distributions are made.

Qualified health insurance premiums include premiums for accident or health insurance or qualified long-term care insurance contracts covering the taxpayer, the taxpayer's spouse, and the taxpayer's dependents. The qualified health insurance premiums do not have to be for a plan sponsored by the employer; however, the exclusion does not apply to premiums paid by the employee and reimbursed with pension distributions. Amounts excluded from income under the provision are not taken into account in determining the itemized deduction for medical expenses under section 213 or the deduction for health insurance of self-employed individuals under section 162.

Effective Date

The provision is effective for distributions in taxable years beginning after December 31, 2006.

[¶ 11,750.021]

Committee Report on P.L. 109-135 (Gulf Opportunity Zone Act of 2005)

[Joint Committee on Taxation]

Technical Corrections

[Amendment Related to the Economic Growth and Tax Relief Reconciliation Act of 2001 (P.L. 107-16)]

Option to treat elective deferral as after-tax Roth contributions (Act sec. 617).—A special rule allows employees with at least 15 years of service with certain organizations to make additional elective deferrals to a tax-deferred annuity, subject to an annual and cumulative limit. The cumulative limit is $15,000, reduced by any additional pretax elective deferrals made for preceding years. For taxable years beginning after 2005, plans may allow employees to designate pretax elective deferrals as Roth contributions. Under the provision, the $15,000 cumulative limit is reduced also by designated Roth contributions made for preceding years.

[¶ 11,750.022]

Committee Report on P.L. 108-311 (Working Families Tax Relief Act of 2004)

[Conference Agreement]

Rollovers among various types of retirement plans.—Section 641 of EGTRRA expanded the rollover rules to allow rollovers among various types of tax-favored retirement plans. The provision makes a conforming change to the cross-reference to the rollovers rules in the Code provision relating to qualified retirement annuities.

---

[199] The term "public safety officer" has the same meaning as under section 1204(8)(A) of the Omnibus Crime Control and Safe Streets Act of 1986.

[¶ 11,750.024]

Committee Report on P.L. 107-16 (Economic Growth and Tax Relief Reconciliation Act)

[Conference Committee Report]

Waiver of 60-day rollover period

[Conference Agreement]

The conference agreement provides that the Secretary may waive the 60-day rollover period if the failure to waive such requirement would be against equity or good conscience, including cases of casualty, disaster, or other events beyond the reasonable control of the individual subject to such requirement. For example, the Secretary may issue guidance that includes objective standards for a waiver of the 60-day rollover period, such as waiving the rule due to military service in a combat zone or during a Presidentially declared disaster (both of which are provided for under present law), or for a period during which the participant has received payment in the form of a check, but has not cashed the check, or for errors committed by a financial institution, or in cases of inability to complete a rollover due to death, disability, hospitalization, incarceration, restrictions imposed by a foreign country, or postal error.

Effective Date

The conference agreement applies to distributions made after December 31, 2001.

[¶ 11,750.026]

Committee Report on P.L. 107-16 (Economic Growth and Tax Relief Reconciliation Act)

[House Committee Report]

Rollovers

In general.—The provision provides that eligible rollover distributions from qualified retirement plans, section 403(b) annuities, and governmental section 457 plans generally could be rolled over to any of such plans or arrangements.[1]

Similarly, distributions from an IRA generally are permitted to be rolled over into a qualified plan, section 403(b) annuity, or governmental section 457 plan. The direct rollover and withholding rules are extended to distributions from a governmental section 457 plan, and such plans are required to provide the written notification regarding eligible rollover distributions.[2]

The rollover notice (with respect to all plans) is required to include a description of the provisions under which distributions from the plan to which the distribution is rolled over may be subject to restrictions and tax consequences different than those applicable to distributions from the distributing plan. Qualified plans, section 403(b) annuities, and section 457 plans would not be required to accept rollovers.

Some special rules apply in certain cases. A distribution from a qualified plan is not eligible for capital gains or averaging treatment if there was a rollover to the plan that would not have been permitted under present law. Thus, in order to preserve capital gains and averaging treatment for a qualified plan distribution that is rolled over, the rollover would have to be made to a "conduit IRA" as under present law, and then rolled back into a qualified plan. Amounts distributed from a section 457 plan are subject to the early withdrawal tax to the extent the distribution consists of amounts attributable to rollovers from another type of plan. Section 457 plans are required to separately account for such amounts.

Rollover of after-tax contributions.—The provision provides that employee after-tax contributions may be rolled over into another qualified plan or a traditional IRA. In the case of a rollover from a qualified plan to another qualified plan, the rollover is permitted to be accomplished only through a direct rollover. In addition, a qualified plan would not be permitted to accept rollovers of after-tax contributions unless the plan provides separate accounting for such contributions (and earnings thereon). After-tax contributions (including nondeductible contributions to an IRA) would not be permitted to be rolled over from an IRA into a qualified plan, tax-sheltered annuity, or section 457 plan.

In the case of a distribution from a traditional IRA that is rolled over into an eligible rollover plan that is not an IRA, the distribution is attributed first to amounts other than after-tax contributions.

Expansion of spousal rollovers.—The provision provides that surviving spouses may roll over distributions to a qualified plan, section 403(b) annuity, or governmental section 457 plan in which the surviving spouse participates.

Treasury regulations.—The Secretary is directed to prescribe rules necessary to carry out the provision. Such rules may include, for example, reporting requirements and mechanisms to address mistakes relating to rollovers. It is anticipated that the IRS would develop forms to assist individuals who roll over after-tax contributions to an IRA in keeping track of such contributions. Such forms could, for example, expand Form 8606—Nondeductible IRAs, to include information regarding after-tax contributions.

Effective Date

The provision is effective for distributions made after December 31, 2001. It is intended that the Secretary will revise the safe harbor rollover notice that plans may use to satisfy the rollover requirements. No penalty is imposed on a plan for a failure to provide the information required under the provision with respect to any distribution made before the date that is 90 days after the date the Secretary issues a new safe harbor rollover notice, if the plan administrator makes a reasonable attempt to comply with such notice requirement. For example, the provision requires that the rollover notice include a description of the provisions under which distributions from the eligible retirement plan receiving the distribution may be subject to restrictions and tax consequences which are different from those applicable to distributions from the plan making the distribution. A plan is treated as making a reasonable good faith effort to comply with this requirement if the notice states that distributions from the plan to which the rollover is made may be subject to different restrictions and tax consequences than those that apply to distributions from the plan from which the rollover is made.

[Conference Committee Report]

The conference agreement follows the House bill, with the following modification. Hardship distributions from governmental section 457 plans are not considered eligible rollover distributions.

[¶ 11,750.028]

Committee Report on P.L. 107-16 (Economic Growth and Tax Relief Reconciliation Act)

[House Committee Report]

Hardship distributions

The Secretary of the Treasury is directed to revise the applicable regulations to reduce from 12 months to 6 months the period during which an employee must be prohibited from making elective contributions and employee contributions in order for a distribution to be deemed necessary to satisfy an immediate and heavy financial need. The revised regulations are to be effective for years beginning after December 31, 2001.

In addition, any distribution made upon hardship of an employee is not an eligible rollover distribution. Thus, such distributions may not be rolled over, and are subject to the withholding rules applicable to distributions that are not eligible rollover distributions. The provision does not modify the rules under which hardship distributions may be made. For example, as under present law, hardship distributions of qualified employer matching contributions are only permitted under the rules applicable to elective deferrals.

The provision is intended to clarify that all assets distributed as a hardship withdrawal, including assets attributable to employee elective deferrals and those attributable to employer matching or nonelective contributions, are ineligible for rollover. This rule is intended to apply to all hardship distributions from any tax qualified plan, including those made pursuant to standards set forth in section 401(k)(2)(B)(i)(IV) (which are applicable to section 401(k) plans and section 403(b) annuities) and to those treated as hardship distributions under any profit-sharing plan (whether or not in accordance with the standards set forth in section 401(k)(2)(B)(i)(IV)). For this purpose, a distribution that could be made either under the hardship provisions of a plan or under other provisions of the plan (such as provisions permitting in-service withdrawal of assets attributable to employer matching or nonelective contributions after a fixed period of years) could be treated as made upon hardship of the employee if the plan treats it that way. For example, if a plan makes an in-service distribution that consists of assets attributable to both elective deferrals (in circumstances where those assets could be distributed only upon hardship) and employer matching or nonelective contributions (which could be distributed in nonhardship circumstances under the plan), the plan is permitted to treat the distribution in its entirety as made upon hardship of the employee.

Effective Date

The provision directing the Secretary to revise the rules relating to safe harbor hardship distributions is effective on the date of enactment. The provision providing that hardship distributions are not eligible rollover distributions is effective for distributions made after December 31, 2001. The Secretary has the authority to issue transitional guidance with respect to the provision providing that hardship distributions are not eligible rollover distributions to provide sufficient time for plans to implement the new rule.

---

[1] Hardship distributions from governmental section 457 plans would be considered eligible rollover distributions.

[2] The elective withholding rules applicable to distributions from qualified plans and section 403(b) annuities that are not eligible rollover distributions are also extended to distributions from governmental section 457 plans. Thus, periodic distributions from governmental section 457 plans that are not eligible rollover distributions are subject to withholding as if the distribution were wages and nonperiodic distributions from such plans that are not eligible rollover distributions are subject to withholding at a 10-percent rate. In either case, the individual may elect not to have withholding apply.

[Conference Committee Report]

Senate Amendment

The Senate amendment is the same as the House bill.

Conference Agreement

The conference agreement follows the House bill and the Senate amendment.

[¶ 11,750.03]

Committee Report on P.L. 107-16 (Economic Growth and Tax Relief Reconciliation Act)

[House Committee Report]

Increase in elective deferral limits

Elective deferral limitations.—The provision increases the dollar limit on annual elective deferrals under section 401(k) plans, section 403(b) annuities and salary reduction SEPs to $11,000 in 2002. In 2003 and thereafter, the limits are increased in $1,000 annual increments until the limits reach $15,000 in 2006, with indexing in $500 increments thereafter. The provision increases the maximum annual elective deferrals that may be made to a SIMPLE plan to $7,000 in 2002. In 2003 and thereafter, the SIMPLE plan deferral limit is increased in $1,000 annual increments until the limit reaches $10,000 in 2005. Beginning after 2005, the $10,000 dollar limit is indexed in $500 increments.

* * *

Effective Date

The provision is effective for years beginning after December 31, 2001.

[Conference Committee Report]

Elective deferral limitations.—The conference agreement follows the House bill.

* * *

Effective Date

The conference agreement generally is effective for years beginning after December 31, 2001. The provisions relating to defined benefit plans are effective for years ending after December 31, 2001.

[¶ 11,750.032]

Committee Reports on P.L. 105-34 (Taxpayer Relief Act)

[Senate Committee Report]

Matching contributions of self-employed individuals not treated as elective deferrals.—The bill provides that matching contributions for self-employed individuals are treated the same as matching contributions for employees, i.e., they are not treated as elective contributions and are not subject to the elective contribution limit.

Effective Date

The provision is effective for years beginning after December 31, 1997.

[Conference Committee Report]

The conference agreement follows the Senate amendment, and clarifies that the provision does not apply to qualified matching contributions that are treated as elective contributions for purposes of satisfying the ADP test.

Effective Date

Same as the Senate amendment, except that the conference agreement provides that the provision is effective for years beginning after December 31, 1996, in the case of SIMPLE retirement plans.

[¶ 11,750.034]

Committee Report on P.L. 104-188 (Small Business Job Protection Act)

Simplified Distribution Rules

[Senate Committee Report]

Lump-sum distributions

The bill repeals 5-year averaging for lump-sum distributions from qualified plans. Thus, the bill repeals the separate tax paid on a lump-sum distribution and also repeals the deduction from gross income for taxpayers who elect to pay the separate tax on a lump-sum distribution. The bill preserves the transition rules adopted in the Tax Reform Act of 1986 (i.e., 10-year averaging and capital gains treatment for the pre-1974 portion of the lump-sum distribution), but not 5-year averaging, with respect to lump-sum distributions to individuals eligible for such transition rules.

* * *

Effective Date

Lump-sum distributions.—The provision is effective for taxable years beginning after December 31, 1999

* * *

[Conference Committee Report]

Lump-sum distributions.—The conference agreement follows the Senate amendment.

* * *

Miscellaneous Pension Simplification

[House Committee Report]

Modifications of section 403(b)

Multiple salary reduction agreements permitted.—The bill provides that for participants in a tax-sheltered annuity plan, the frequency that a salary reduction agreement may be entered into, the compensation to which such agreement applies, and the ability to revoke such agreement shall be determined under the rules applicable to qualified cash or deferred arrangements.

Effective Date

The provision is effective for taxable years beginning after December 31, 1995.

[Conference Committee Report]

Senate Amendment

The Senate amendment is the same as the House bill.

Conference Agreement

The conference agreement follows the House bill and the Senate amendment.

[¶ 11,750.036]

Committee Report on P.L. 102-318 (Unemployment Compensation Amendments of 1992)

[Conference Committee Report]

* * *

3. ROLLOVER AND WITHHOLDING ON NONPERIODIC PENSION DISTRIBUTIONS

Present law

Distributions from tax-qualified pension plans (sec. 401(a)), qualified annuity plan (sec. 403(a)), and tax-sheltered annuities (sec. 403(b)) generally are included in gross income in the year paid or distributed under the rules relating to the taxation of annuities. A total or partial distribution of the balance to the credit of an employee may, under certain circumstances, be rolled over tax free to another plan or annuity or to an individual retirement arrangement (IRA).

For purposes of the rule denying rollover treatment in the case of certain periodic payments, payments made before, with, or after the commencement of the periodic payments are not treated as part of the series of periodic payments.

Income tax withholding on pension distributions is required unless the payee elects not to have withholding apply. If no election is made, tax is withheld from nonperiodic payments at a 10-percent rate, unless the payments are part of a qualified total distribution, in which case tables published by the Internal Revenue Service are used to determine the withholding rate. A qualified total distribution generally is a payment within one year of the entire interest in a plan.

House bill

No provision.

Senate amendment

Under the Senate amendment, any part of the taxable portion of a distribution from a qualified pension or annuity plan or a tax-sheltered annuity (other than a minimum required distribution) can be rolled over tax free to an IRA or another qualified plan or annuity, unless the distribution is one of a series of substantially equal payments made (1) over the life (or joint life expectancies) of the participant and his or her beneficiary, or (2) over a specified period of 10 years or more.

For purposes of the rule denying rollover treatment in the case of certain periodic payments, a single-sum payment that is not substantially equal to the periodic payments that is made before, with, or after the commencement of the periodic payments is not treated as one of the series of periodic payments. For example, if an employee receives 30 percent of his or her accrued benefit in the form of single-sum distribution upon retirement with the balance payable in annuity form, the amount of the single-sum distribution can be rolled over.

A qualified retirement or annuity plan must permit participants to elect to have any distribution that is eligible for rollover treatment transferred directly to an eligible transferee plan specified by the participant.

Withholding is imposed at a rate of 20 percent on any distribution that is eligible to be rolled over but that is not transferred directly to an eligible transferee plan. Payees cannot elect to forego withholding with respect to such distributions.

Plan amendments required under the provision do not have to be made before the first plan year beginning on or after January 1, 1994, if the plan is operated in accordance with the provision and the amendment applies retroactively.

Effective date: The provision is effective for distributions after December 31, 1992.

Conference agreement

The conference agreement follows the Senate amendment, with modifications.

The conference agreement provides that the plan administrator must provide a written explanation to a recipient of his or her distribution options (including the direct trustee-to-trustee transfer option) within a reasonable period of time before making an eligible rollover distribution. The Secretary of the Treasury is directed to develop a model notice.

The administrator may require that a recipient electing a direct trustee-to-trustee transfer provide adequate information in a timely manner regarding the eligible retirement plan to which the transfer is to be made. The transferor plan and its administrator will not be subject to penalties or liability because of reasonable reliance on such information provided by a recipient, and is not required to independently verify such information. As under the Senate amendment and present law, a qualified retirement plan is not required to accept a direct trustee-to-trustee transfer.

The direct trustee-to-trustee transfer option is considered a distribution option, so that spousal consent and other similar participant and beneficiary protection rules apply. Because a direct transfer generally is considered a distribution from the transferor plan, rights and options available under the transferor plan need not be preserved under the transferee plan.

The conference agreement clarifies that the explicit exclusion from gross income of amounts transferred in a direct trustee-to-trustee transfer in accordance with the provision is not intended to affect the treatment of direct transfers under other provisions of the Code.

Under the conference agreement, in the case of section 403(b) tax-sheltered annuity plans maintained by state and local governments which are prohibited under State law from making direct trustee-to-trustee transfers, the provisions relating to trustee-to-trustee transfers and withholding do not apply to distributions before the earlier of (1) January 1, 1994, or (2) 90 days after the date on which the State law is amended to permit such transfers.

[¶ 11,750.038]

Committee Report on P.L. 101-239 (Omnibus Budget Reconciliation Act of 1989)

[House Committee Report]

One-time election for elective deferrals

The provision clarifies the regulatory authority in the exception to the definition of elective deferrals (sec. 402(g)(3)) to provide that a contribution is not treated as an elective deferral if, under the salary reduction agreement, the contribution is made pursuant to (1) a one-time irrevocable election made by the employee at the time of initial eligibility to participate in the agreement or (2) a similar arrangement involving a one-time irrevocable election specified in regulations. As under present law, the regulatory authority does not apply to arrangements other than tax-sheltered annuities.

For the Committee Reports on P.L. 101-239, relating to ESOPs, see ¶ 12,130.063

[¶ 11,750.040]

Committee Reports on P.L. 100-647 (Technical and Miscellaneous Revenue Act of 1988)

[Senate Committee Report]

The bill repeals the provisions of the 1986 Act relating to rollovers of partial distributions, other than the rule permitting distributions made to satisfy the diversification requirements to be rolled over. Thus, under the bill, as under the law prior to the 1986 Act, a partial distribution may be rolled over only if (1) the distribution equals at least 50 percent of the balance to the credit of the employee in the plan (determined immediately before such distribution and without aggregating plans of the same type), (2) with respect to distributions after March 31, 1988, the distribution is not one of a series of periodic payments, and (3) the employee elects rollover treatment (in accordance with regulations). The bill reinstates the pre-1986 Act requirements because the provisions in the Act, particularly the rule aggregating plans of the same type, unduly restricted the situations in which partial distributions could be rolled over. In addition, the bill provides that a partial distribution may be rolled over only if the distribution is made (1) on account of the employee's death, (2) on account of the employee's separation from service, or (3) after the employee has become disabled (within the meaning of sec. 72(m)(7)).

It is intended that, for purposes of the rule denying rollover treatment in the case of a distribution that is part of a series of periodic payments, the mere fact that payments to an employee are made in more than one taxable year does not automatically mean that they constitute a series of periodic payments. For example, it is not uncommon for an employer to make a lump-sum distribution to an employee in one taxable year and discover a calculation error in the following taxable year that requires another distribution to the employee. It is further intended, under these circumstances, that the first distribution is to be treated as a lump-sum distribution (as under present law) and the second distribution is to be treated as a partial distribution eligible for rollover treatment. The partial distribution rollover rules were originally enacted because of employer errors in calculating the lump-sum distributions to which employees are entitled and it is expected that the Secretary's interpretation of the rules will be consistent with this intent.

The bill retains the rule permitting rollover of a distribution made to satisfy the diversification requirements (sec. 401(a)(28)) if an employee elects such treatment and provides that if amounts are rolled over pursuant to these rules an employee is not prohibited from electing income averaging for a subsequent lump-sum distribution.

The bill clarifies that the special rule for frozen deposits applies only to amounts that are frozen within 60 days of the date that the amounts are distributed from the plan.

[Senate Committee Report]

The bill deletes the IRA rollover restriction under which certain distributions from IRAs with respect to 5-percent owners are not treated as rollover distributions for purposes of the IRA rules. This provision is effective for rollover distributions made in taxable years beginning after December 31, 1986. Thus, the bill clarifies that, as is the case with other taxpayers, 5-percent owners may roll over a qualified plan distribution into an IRA and subsequently roll the amount distributed from the IRA into another qualified plan. Different rules for 5-percent owners and ot TAXPAYERS ARE NO LONGER NECESSARY UNDER THE ACT BECAUSE ALL DISTRIBUTIONS FROM QUALIFIED PLANS ARE GENERALLY SUBJECT TO THE EARLY WITHDRAWAL TAX FORMERLY APPLICABLE ONLY TO DISTRIBUTIONS TO 5-PERCENT OWNERS.

[Senate Committee Report]

Under the bill, the election to waive net unrealized appreciation treatment with respect to a lump-sum distribution is to be made on the tax return on which the distribution is required to be included in gross income if the special treatment is waived. This change is designed to give taxpayers more time to determine whether or not they should make the election. An election to waive the special treatment of net unrealized appreciation does not preclude an election for income averaging.

[Senate Committee Report]

The bill clarifies that a 5-year averaging election may be made by an individual, trust, or estate for a lump-sum distribution received with respect to an employee who had attained age 59 ½. In addition, the bill provides that an income averaging election or election of long-term capital gains treatment under the special transition rules may be made by any individual, trust, or estate with respect to an employee who had attained age 50 by January 1, 1986.

The bill also clarifies that, for purposes of 5-year income averaging, the phaseout of the 15-percent bracket applies.

Further, under the bill, the election under the special transition rule of 10-year averaging (under the prior-law tax rates) is to take into account the prior-law zero bracket amount. This change is needed to preserve the prior-law treatment for persons who elect the grandfather rule.

The bill clarifies that a capital gains election made under either of the special transition rules is treated as an income averaging election (within the meaning of sec. 402(e)(4)(B)) for all purposes under the Code (including, for example, sec. 4980A relating to the 15-percent tax on excess distributions).

[Senate Committee Report]

Early retirement exception

The bill modifies the early retirement exception to apply in any case in which an employee receives a distribution on account of separation from service after attainment of age 55, rather than requiring an early retirement under the plan. The intent of this provision is to eliminate what is considered a requirement that has little substantive effect, but could require plan amendment.

The modified early retirement exception continues to apply if the employee returns to work for the same employer (or for a different employer) as long as the employee did, in fact, separate from service before the plan distribution. Of course, any short-term separation is to be closely scrutinized to determine if it is a bona fide, indefinite separation from service that would qualify for this exception to the early withdrawal tax.

As under present law, this exception does not apply to IRA distributions.

Exception for distributions from ESOPs

The bill modifies the ESOP exception to the additional income tax on early withdrawals to provide that the exception is available to the extent that a distribution from an ESOP is attributable to assets that have been invested, at all times, in employer securities (as defined in sec. 409(l)) that satisfy the requirements of sections 409 and 401(a)(28) for the 5-year period immediately preceding the plan year in which the distribution occurs. Employer securities that are transferred to an ESOP from another plan are also eligible for the exception to the early withdrawal tax as long as the holding period requirement is satisfied with respect to such employer securities taking into account the time such employer securities were held in the other plan.

For example, assume that employer securities that were transferred from a profit-sharing plan are held in an ESOP for the 1-plan year period immediately preceding the plan year in which the distribution is made. If the profit-sharing plan met the requirements of sections 401(a)(28) and 409 with respect to the employer securities for the 4-plan year period immediately prior to the transfer to the ESOP, then the holding period requirement is satisfied. On the other hand, if the profit-sharing plan did not satisfy sections 401(a)(28) and 409 with respect to the transferred securities, the holding period requirement would not be satisfied and the exception to the early withdrawal tax does not apply to the transferred amounts. The bill clarifies that the employer securities are not required to be subject to the requirements of sections 401(a)(28) and 409 prior to the time those requirements are effective (i.e., stock acquired after December 31, 1986, in the case of sec. 401(a)(28)).

These changes are designed to ensure that the ESOP exception only applies with respect to employer securities that are subject to the section 401(a)(28) and section 409 rules applicable to ESOPs.

Under the bill, an ESOP includes both an ESOP described in section 4975(e)(7) and a tax-credit ESOP (within the meaning of sec. 409).

Exceptions not applicable to IRAs

Because the rules relating to qualified domestic relations orders do not apply to IRAs, the bill clarifies that the exception to the early withdrawal tax in the case of distributions pursuant to a qualified domestic relations order does not apply to IRA distributions. This is consistent with the pre-Act law applicable to IRAs.

Deferred annuity contracts

The bill clarifies that the substantially equal payment exception and the recapture tax for distributions in violation of the substantially equal payment exception are not limited to distributions to employees under an employer-maintained pension plan. Rather, the exception and recapture tax apply to all distributions under a deferred annuity whether or not received by an individual with respect to the individual's status as an employee.

Further, the bill clarifies that the additional income tax applicable to early withdrawal from a deferred annuity (sec. 72(q)) does not apply if a distribution is otherwise subject to the early withdrawal rules for qualified plans (sec. 72(t)), whether or not an exception to the additional income tax on early withdrawals from a qualified plan applies under section 72(t)(2).

The bill modifies the effective date of the provision relating to the additional income tax on early withdrawals under a deferred annuity so that the changes in the early withdrawal tax do not apply to any distribution under an annuity contract if (1) as of March 1, 1986, payments were being made under such contract pursuant to a written election providing a specific schedule for the distribution of the taxpayer's interest in such contract, and (2) such distribution is made pursuant to such written election.

Substantially equal payment exception

The bill provides that the substantially equal payment exception is available only if the beneficiary whose life or life expectancy is taken into account in determining whether the exception is satisfied is a designated beneficiary of the individual. For this purpose, rules similar to those applicable under section 401(a)(9) are to apply.

Qualified voluntary employee contributions

In order to prevent the imposition of two 10-percent early withdrawal taxes on distributions attributable to QVECs, the bill repeals the 10-percent early withdrawal tax applicable only to QVECs. Thus, distributions from QVECs are treated as distributions from a qualified plan for purposes of the 10-percent additional income tax on early withdrawals and are eligible for any of the applicable exceptions otherwise available for distributions from qualified plans.

Tax-sheltered annuities

The bill provides that the distribution restrictions added by the Act with respect to tax-sheltered annuities are effective for years beginning after December 31, 1988, but only with respect to distributions from such tax-sheltered annuities that are attributable to assets that were not held as of the close of the last year beginning before January 1, 1989. Thus, the new rules apply to contributions made in years beginning after December 31, 1988, and to earnings on those contributions and on amounts held as of the last year beginning before January 1, 1989.

Involuntary cashouts under a qualified plan

The bill clarifies that the additional income tax on early withdrawals under a qualified plan is to apply in the case of an involuntary cashout under section 411(a)(11) or 417(e). Of course, the early withdrawal tax does not apply if the amount of the benefit paid to an employee is rolled over to another qualified plan or an IRA.

[Conference Committee Report]

* * *

Conference Agreement

The conference agreement makes income averaging available with respect to distributions to an alternate payee who is a spouse or former spouse of the employee. In particular, the conference agreement provides that if a distribution of the balance of the credit to the employee would constitute a lump-sum distribution, then a distribution of the balance of the credit to the alternate payee constitutes a lump-sum distribution. In determining whether the distribution consists of the balance to the credit of the alternate payee, only the interest of the alternate payee is taken into account.

The provision is effective for taxable years ending after December 31, 1984.

[¶ 11,750.041]

Committee Reports on P.L. 99-514 (Tax Reform Act of 1986)

[Senate Committee Report]

Lump-sum distributions

The bill conforms the rules relating to the taxation of lump-sum distributions to the break-in-service rules. Under the bill, in determining whether any distribution payable on account of separation from service is a lump sum distribution, the balance to the credit of the employee is determined without taking into account any increase in vesting that could occur if the employee is reemployed by the employer.

Under the bill, however, if the employee is reemployed by the employer before the occurrence of five consecutive one-year breaks in service and the nonforfeitable interest of the employee in the amount of the pre-break accrued benefit is thereby increased, then the reduction in tax attributable to the treatment of the distribution as a lump-sum distribution is to be recaptured as provided by Treasury regulations. Such a reduction in tax could occur on account of an election to use 10-year forward averaging with respect to a lump-sum distribution, the special treatment of net unrealized appreciation of employer securities (Code sec. 402(e)(4)(J)), or long-term capital gains treatment for a portion of a lump-sum distribution. In addition, if such a recapture is made, the participant's previous lump sum distribution election is not taken into account in determining whether the employer is eligible to make another election.

[Conference Committee Report]

* * *

The conference agreement follows the Senate amendment * * *.

[Senate Committee Report]

* * *

Rollovers

The bill provides that, in determining whether a distribution to an employee on account of separation from service is eligible to be rolled over to another plan or to an IRA, the balance to the credit of the employee is determined without regard to any increased vesting that may occur if the employee returns to service with the employer. However, if (1) the employee excluded the distribution from income on account of a rollover, (2) the employee returns to service with the employer before incurring five consecutive one-year breaks in service and (3) the vested percentage of benefits accrued before the separation from service is increased, then any subsequent distributions to the employee from the plan in which the increased vesting occurs are not eligible for 10-year income averaging or capital gains treatment.

The rule denying eligibility for 10-year forward averaging or capital gains treatment on subsequent distributions does not apply if the distribution that was rolled over was made without the consent of the participant (e.g., the amount distributed did not exceed $3,500).

* * *

[Conference Committee Report]

The Retirement Equity Act of 1984

The conference agreement follows the Senate amendment * * *.

[Senate Committee Report]

Notice of Rollover Treatment

* * *

Explanation of Provision

The bill makes it clear that a plan administrator is to provide notice when making any distribution eligible for rollover treatment. Thus, for example, notice is to be provided when a distribution eligible for rollover treatment pursuant to the partial rollover rules is made.

[Conference Committee Report]

The conference agreement follows the Senate amendment * * *.

[Senate Committee Report]

* * *

Qualifying rollover distributions

The bill clarifies that the distribution of the entire balance to the credit of an employee in a qualified plan may be treated as a distribution eligible for rollover under the partial distribution rollover rules, so long as such distribution does not constitute a "qualified total distribution." Thus, a total distribution that is not made on account of plan termination, is not eligible for lump sum treatment and does not consist of accumulated deductible employee contributions, would be eligible for rollover under the partial distribution rollover rules.

The bill clarifies that accumulated deductible employee contributions (within the meaning of sec. 72(o)(5)) are not taken into account for purposes of calculating the balance to the credit of an employee under the partial distribution rollover rules. In addition, the bill clarifies that a self-employed individual is generally treated as an employee for purposes of the rules governing the tax treatment of distributions, including the rules relating to rollover distributions.

The bill provides that the rules relating to rollovers in the case of a surviving spouse of an employee who received distributions after the employee's death apply to permit rollovers to an IRA but not to another qualified plan. Also, the bill clarifies that partial distributions are to be rolled over within 60 days of the distribution to be eligible for rollover under the partial distribution rollover rules.

[Conference Committee Report]

The conference agreement follows the Senate amendment * * *.

[Senate Committee Report]

Rollovers

The bill provides that distributions after December 31, 1983, but before July 18, 1984, may not be rolled over to a qualified plan if any part of the distribution is attributable to contributions made on behalf of an owner-employee. In addition, distributions made after July 18, 1984, but before the enactment of this bill, may not be rolled over to a qualified plan if any part of the distribution is a benefit attributable to contributions made on behalf of an employee while a key employee (but only if the individual is a key employee on account of status as a 5-percent owner) in a top-heavy plan.

See, however, the provisions of the bill relating to the extension of the additional income tax to all participants under tax-favored retirement arrangements. For years beginning on or after the effective date of those provisions, the restrictions on rollovers are repealed as deadwood because the additional tax on early withdrawals would apply to distributions from any plan without regard to the recipient's status as a 5-percent owner with respect to the plan making the distribution.

[Conference Committee Report]

The conference agreement follows the Senate amendment * * *.

[Senate Committee Report]

b. Treatment of distributions if substantially all contributions are employee contributions

* * *

Explanation of Provision

Under the bill, a plan is defined as one in which substantially all of the contributions are employee contributions if 85 percent or more of the total contributions during a representative period are employee contributions. Also, the bill provides that the 5-percent additional income tax on premature distributions from annuity contracts does not apply to distributions from a plan substantially all of the contributions of which are derived from employee contributions.

The bill clarifies that deductible employee contributions are not taken into account as employee contributions for purposes of testing whether 85 percent or more of the total contributions to a plan during a representative period are employee contributions.

* * *

[Conference Committee Report]

The conference agreement follows the Senate amendment * * *.

[¶ 11,750.042]

Committee Report on P.L. 99-272 (Consolidated Omnibus Budget Reconciliation Act)

[Conference Committee Report]

Under the conference agreement, a participant or beneficiary who receives distributions from a termination trust is, subject to certain requirements, permitted to roll over the distributions to an IRA * * *.

For the Committee Report on P.L. 99-514, dealing with the SEP deduction converted to exclusion from income, see ¶ 12,050.063.

[¶ 11,750.043]

Committee Report on P.L. 98-397 (Retirement Equity Act of 1984)

[Senate Committee Report]

Under the bill, when the administrator of a qualified plan makes a qualifying rollover distribution, the administrator is to provide notice to the recipient that (1) the distribution will not be taxed currently to the extent transferred to another qualified pension plan or an IRA, and (2) the transfer must be made within 60 days of receipt in order to qualify for this tax-free rollover treatment. In the case of a series of distributions that may constitute a lump sum distribution, the committee intends that this notice will explain that the 60-day period does not begin to run until the last distribution is made. In addition, this notice is to provide a written explanation of the 10-year income averaging and capital gains provisions if applicable.

The committee intends that the Secretary of the Treasury will provide an officially approved notice that plan administrators may use to satisfy this notice requirement.

The committee recognizes that, under certain circumstances, it may be difficult for a plan administrator to determine whether a particular distribution is a qualifying rollover distribution. Thus, your committee intends that a plan administrator satisfies the notice requirement if notice is provided with every payment from or under the plan so long as the notice, in addition to satisfying the other requirements, includes a statement describing how a recipient may determine whether the particular distribution is a qualifying rollover distribution.

[¶ 11,750.045]

Committee Reports on P. L. 98-369 (Tax Reform Act of 1984)

[Senate Committee Report]

Qualifying rollover distributions

Under the bill, distributions of less than the balance to the credit of an employee under a qualified pension or annuity plan, or tax-sheltered annuity contract may be rolled over, tax-free, by the employee (or the surviving spouse of the employee) to an IRA. A rollover of a partial distribution is permitted only if (1) the distribution equals at least 50 percent of the balance to the credit of the employee, determined immediately before the distribution, (2) the distribution is not one of a series of periodic payments, and (3) the employee elects tax-free rollover treatment at the time and in the manner prescribed by the Secretary of the Treasury. For purposes of determining whether a distribution is at least 50 percent of the balance to the credit of the employee under a qualified pension plan or a tax-sheltered annuity contract, amounts credited under similar other qualified pension plans or tax-sheltered annuity contracts of the same employer are not aggregated.

As under present law, the rollover of a partial distribution must be made within 60 days after the date of distribution. If the employee or surviving spouse of the employee elects partial distribution rollover treatment, no portion of the distribution may be rolled over to another qualified pension plan or a tax-sheltered annuity. In addition, no special treatment is accorded to net unrealized appreciation of employer securities. Any subsequent distribution from the same plan (or any other plan of the employer required to be aggregated for the lump sum distribution rules) is not eligible for the special 10-year income averaging or long-term capital gain treatment accorded lump sum distributions. Similarly, if an employee elects partial distribution rollover treatment under a tax-sheltered annuity, a subsequent distribution under any other tax-sheltered annuity of the same employer is not eligible for long-term capital gains treatment.

In the case of a rollover of a partial distribution, the maximum amount rolled over may not exceed the portion of the distribution includible in gross income. Also, amounts in IRAs may not be rolled over to a qualified pension plan or to a tax-sheltered annuity contract if the balance in the IRA consists, in part, of a rollover of a partial distribution.

[House Committee Report]

The bill amends the rules relating to qualifying rollover distributions to provide that a rollover to a qualified pension, etc., plan is not permitted if any part of the distribution of a benefit is attributable to contributions made on behalf of the employee while a key employee in a top-heavy plan. The rule is necessary because of special restrictions that apply to these benefits. If a distribution to a self-employed individual is not attributable to contributions made while the individual was a key employee in a top-heavy plan, however, a rollover to a qualified pension, etc., plan or a qualified annuity plan is permitted.

Also, see ¶ 11,900.085 for the committee report on the repeal of the bond purchase provisions.

[¶ 11,750.047]

Committee Reports on P. L. 97-34 (Economic Recovery Tax Act of 1981)

For Committee Reports on P. L. 97-34, Sec. 311, relating to individual retirement plans and taxation of distributions of voluntary employee distributions, see ¶ 11,330.02.

[¶ 11,750.05]

Committee Report on P. L. 96-608 (Taxation—Individuals Living Abroad)

[Senate Committee Report]

Present law

An employee who receives a lump sum distribution from a tax-qualified pension, profit-sharing, or stock bonus plan may defer tax on the distribution by rolling over the proceeds (net of any employee contributions) within 60 days of receipt (1) to an IRA (an individual retirement account, annuity, or bond), or (2) to another employer-sponsored qualified pension, etc., plan.[1] The rollover rule also applies to the spouse of an employee who receives a lump sum distribution on account of the employee's death. A lump sum distribution from a qualified plan is eligible for favorable income tax treatment (e.g., 10-year income-averaging) if no portion of the distribution is rolled over.

A lump sum distribution must be a distribution of the balance to the credit of an employee under a qualified pension, etc., plan, made within one taxable year of the recipient. Generally, the distribution must have been made on account of death or separation from service, or after the employee attains age 59 ½. If an employer maintains more than one qualified plan of the same type, the plans are aggregated for the purpose of determining whether the balance to the credit of an employee has been distributed. Under the aggregation rules, all pension plans (defined benefit and money purchase) maintained by the employer are treated as a single plan, all profit-sharing plans maintained by the employer are treated as a single plan, and all stock bonus plans maintained by the employer are treated as a single plan.

Reasons for change

The committee believes that the present lump sum distribution rollover rules are too restrictive.

Explanation of provision

This provision would allow an employee who receives a total distribution from a money purchase pension plan (which is otherwise eligible for tax-free rollover treatment) to roll over the distribution to an IRA or to another qualified plan where the employer also maintains a defined benefit pension plan covering the employee even though a total distribution is not made from the defined benefit plan in the same taxable year. The provision also would apply to the spouse of an employee if the spouse receives such a total distribution on account of the employee's death.

If the recipient rolls over a total distribution from a money purchase pension plan and, in a subsequent taxable year, receives a total distribution from a defined benefit pension plan maintained by the employer, the later plan distribution could be rolled over tax free (if it otherwise meets the requirements for a tax-free rollover) but otherwise would not be eligible for the favorable income tax treatment accorded lump sum distributions.

Effective date

Generally, this provision would apply to payments made in taxable years beginning after December 31, 1978. In the case of such payments made before January 1, 1981, the period for making a rollover would not expire before December 31, 1980.

Revenue effect

It is estimated that this provision would reduce budget receipts by less than $5 million annually.

[¶ 11,750.055]

Senate Committee Report on P. L. 96-222 (Technical Corrections Act of 1979)

Sec. 101(a)(14)(C)—Surviving spouse's rollover.

Under present law, a surviving spouse who receives a lump sum death benefit distribution from a tax-qualified plan is permitted to make a rollover of the distribution to an IRA. Rollovers, however, are not permitted for complete distributions to surviving spouses upon termination of tax qualified retirement plans.

The Revenue Act of 1978, as enacted, did not make clear that a distribution to a surviving spouse upon plan termination is eligible for rollover treatment.

The bill clarifies that a lump sum distribution from, or complete distribution upon termination of, a qualified plan which is paid to the surviving spouse of a deceased plan participant, and which is attributable to the participant, is eligible for rollover treatment.

This provision applies to distributions completed after December 31, 1978, in taxable years ending after that date.

Sec. 101(a)(14)(D)— Five year participation requirement.

Under present law, generally an individual who receives a lump sum distribution from a tax-qualified retirement plan is eligible to roll over all or a portion of the distribution without regard to the individual's years of participation under the plan.

However, prior to the Revenue Act of 1978, an individual was required to be a participant in a tax-qualified retirement plan for five years in order to qualify for a rollover to an IRA (or to another tax-qualified retirement plan) of a lump sum distribution from the plan. The 1978 Act eliminated this five-year requirement for taxable years beginning after December 31, 1977, and permitted individuals denied the opportunity for a rollover during 1978, because of the five-year requirement, to complete their rollovers at any time before January 1, 1979.

The committee believes that individuals denied the opportunity for a rollover during 1978 because of the five-year requirement were not given sufficient time after enactment of the Act to complete a rollover.

The bill permits individuals denied rollover treatment of distributions from tax-qualified retirement plans during 1978, solely because of the five-year plan participation requirement, to make such rollovers until the end of 1980.

This amendment would apply to payments made in taxable years beginning after December 31, 1977.

[¶ 11,750.06]

Committee Report on P. L. 95-600 (Revenue Act of 1978)

Sec. 101(d)—Widening of tax brackets—House Committee Report.

The provision includes a technical amendment to the income averaging provisions relating to the addition of the zero bracket amount to base period income for years before the adoption of the zero bracket system (i.e., pre-1977). The amendment specifies that the zero bracket amount increase of the base period income is not to be the new zero bracket amount in this bill but is to remain at the existing level (i.e., $3,200 for joint returns, $2,200 for single individuals and single heads of household and $1,600 for married individuals filing separately).

Sec. 135(b)—Cash or deferred arrangements. The Senate Committee Report on Sec. 135 is at ¶ 11,700.06.

Sec. 157(f)—Rollover of proceeds from sale of property—House Committee Report.

The committee bill would permit the recipient of a lump sum distribution from a qualified plan or a complete distribution upon termination of a qualified plan, which consists in whole or in part of property other than cash to receive tax-free rollover treatment by contributing the proceeds from the *bona fide* sale of the property rather than the property itself to an IRA or to another qualified plan within 60 days from the date of the distribution.

For example, assume that on September 1, 1980, an individual receives a lump-sum distribution consisting of $50,000 in cash and $50,000 worth of Corporation A stock (valued as of September 1, 1978). Assume further than [that] on September 30, 1980, the individual sells all of the stock for $60,000. His rollover contribution (to be completed within 60 days of the September 1, 1980 distribution date) would be $110,000 ($50,000 of cash, plus the $60,000 worth of proceeds received on the sale of the stock). If the individual made a full $110,000 rollover, no gain would be recognized on the sale of the stock. (This is the same result which would have occurred if the property had been rolled over on September 29—the day before the sale).

The same rule would apply in the case of a loss on the sale of the stock. If, on September 30, 1980, the individual sold the Corporation A stock for $40,000, then his maximum rollover contribution would be $90,000, and if the rollover were completed within the 60-day rollover period, no loss would be recognized on the sale of the stock.

[1] A rollover to a plan is not permitted if any part of the lump-sum distribution represents contributions made while the employee was self-employed.

If the employee rolls over less than the full amount of his distribution under the rules as set forth above, then the following rules will apply.

Generally, under present law (and under the committee bill) where an employee receives a distribution of property from a qualified plan, and this distribution is not rolled over, then the employee is required to treat the fair market value of the property as ordinary income, and the amount taken into income becomes the employee's basis in the property.[1] Gain or loss subsequently realized on the sale of the stock is generally treated as capital gain or loss.

These same principles apply where there is a partial rollover of the proceeds of the sale of property, except that it will generally be necessary to allocate the retained proceeds between the ordinary income and capital gains portion of the retained amount. For purposes of these rules, the amount of ordinary income is determined by multiplying the fair market value of the property on the date of distribution by a fraction, the numerator of which is the amount of proceeds retained, and the denominator of which is the total proceeds of the sale. The amount of capital gain or loss is determined by multiplying the difference between the fair market value of the property on the date of sale, and the fair market value on the date of distribution by this same fraction (retained proceeds over total proceeds).

In some cases, where the individual receives both cash and property, or several pieces of property, it will be necessary to determine the extent to which the individual has rolled over cash (or proceeds from the sale of one piece of property as opposed to another) and to what extent he has rolled over proceeds. The committee bill permits the individual to make an election in this regard (not later than the date for filing his tax return for the year in question) by filing a written designation with the IRS. Once made, this designation is irrevocable. If no designation is made, the rollover amount is to be allocated pro rata between the cash distribution received from the plan and the value of any property received (determined as of the date of the distribution).

Thus, in the case of a partial rollover involving proceeds from the sale of property, the rollover amount will be tax free (until it is distributed from the IRA, at which point it will be treated as ordinary income) and the retained portion will be taxed partly as ordinary income, and partly as capital gain or loss, in accordance with the computation outlined above.

For example, assume that on September 1, 1980, an individual employed by Corporation B receives a lump-sum distribution consisting of $50,000 in cash and $50,000 worth of Corporation A stock (valued as of September 1, 1980). Assume further that on September 30, 1980, that individual sells all of the stock for its then fair market value of $60,000. His maximum rollover contribution (to be completed within 60 days of the September 1, 1980, distribution date) would be $110,000 ($50,000 of cash, plus the $60,000 of proceeds received on the sale of the stock). As discussed above, if the individual made a full $110,000 rollover, no gain would be recognized on the sale of the stock. But, assume that the individual makes a rollover of only $80,000. He now may designate irrevocably on his tax return for the year of the rollover the extent to which he has rolled over cash from the plan and the extent to which he has rolled over proceeds from the sale of the stock.[2] Assume the individual designates the rollover as $30,000 of cash from the plan and $50,000 of proceeds. He then will have retained $20,000 ($50,000 - $30,000) of cash from the plan and $10,000 ($60,000 - $50,000) of proceeds, and will be taxed as follows:

Ordinary income	
Cash	$20,000
Proceeds (5/6 × $10,000)	8,333
Total	$28,333
Gain from sale or exchange of capital asset:	
Proceeds (1/6 × $10,000)	$1,667

All of the foregoing discussion assumes that the employee had made no contributions to the plan. If the employee had made contributions to the plan, the committee bill would permit the employee to designate (by the due date for filing his tax return) which portion of the lump-sum distribution was attributable to his own contributions, and which portion of the money and property distributed was attributable to his employer's contributions to the plan. If the employee fails to make this designation, then each item of money or property received will be treated as being attributable pro rata, based on the proportion of total employee to employer contributions to the plan.

The amendments made by this section will apply to qualifying rollover distributions completed after December 31, 1978, in taxable years ending after December 31, 1978.

Conference Committee Report

The only clarification made by the conferees concerns the portion of money or other property to be treated as attributable to the employee contributions where property received in the distribution is sold and a partial rollover of the distribution is made. The conferees have agreed that employee contributions should come first from the ordinary income portion of the amount of the distribution retained.

Sec. 157(g)—Rollover by surviving spouse—House Committee Report.

Under the committee bill, if an individual participating in a qualified plan dies and his or her spouse receives a distribution from the plan which qualifies as a lump sum distribution, the spouse could, within 60 days of the date of the distribution, make a tax-free rollover contribution to an IRA of the assets distributed from the qualified plan.

The amendments made by this section will apply to lump sum distributions completed after December 31, 1978 in taxable years ending after such date.

Sec. 157(h)—Removal of five-year requirement— House Committee Report.

The committee bill would remove the requirement that an individual must participate in the qualified plan from which he or she receives a lump sum distribution for 5 or more years in order to be eligible for a tax-free rollover of the distribution to an IRA or to another qualified plan. For individuals who received lump sum distributions in a taxable year beginning in 1978, but who could not engage in a tax-free rollover because of the five-year participation rule, the amendment extends the time period for making such rollovers until December 31, 1978.

The committee bill also would reduce the limitation on rollovers between IRAs which allows only one such rollover every three years. Thus, an individual would be allowed to make rollover contributions of amounts from one IRA to another once each year.

The amendments made by this section will apply to taxable years beginning after December 31, 1977.

[¶ 11,750.07]

Committee Report on P.L. 95-458 (Excise Tax—Trucks, Buses, etc.)

[Senate Committee Report]

I. Summary.— * * 4. Partial rollovers of lump-sum distribution.*—Under present law, an individual who is eligible to make a tax-free rollover contribution of amounts distributed from a qualified retirement plan is required to contribute the entire amount of the distribution to an IRA or to another qualified plan. The committee amendment allows an individual to make a rollover contribution of any portion of the distribution. In addition, the amendment provides a special "makeup" rule for individuals who, prior to enactment of the bill, attempted to make a rollover contribution but failed to transfer the entire amount of the distribution. Such persons are allowed to make a rollover contribution of any portion of the distribution to an IRA or to a qualified retirement plan on or before December 31, 1978 or 60 days after enactment of the amendment, whichever is later.

II. General Statement.— * * D. Partial Rollovers of Lump Sum Distributions (sec. 4 of the bill and sec. 402 of the Code).—Present law.*—Under present law, a lump-sum distribution from a qualified retirement plan or a complete distribution upon termination of such plan is not includible in a plan participant's gross income if he or she makes a rollover contribution to an IRA (an individual retirement account, an individual retirement annuity, or a retirement bond) or to another qualified retirement plan within 60 days of the date of the distribution (sec. 402(a) of the code). For a contribution to qualify as a rollover contribution, the individual must contribute to the IRA or to the other qualified plan the amount of money plus all of the assets received from the qualified plan, except for an amount allocable to previous employee contributions to the qualified plan.

An employee who fails to contribute the required amount is taxed on the entire distribution from the qualified plan in the year received. (If the distribution qualifies as a lump-sum distribution, the individual may elect special 10-year income averaging.) Also under present law, assets contributed to an IRA in a nonqualified rollover constitute an excess contribution to the IRA. Accordingly, (1) a 6-percent excise tax is imposed for each year for which the excess remains (sec. 4973), (2) the excess contribution and the earnings thereon are included in gross income when distributed from the IRA (sec. 408(d)), and (3) the excess contribution and earnings thereon generally are subject to a 10-percent penalty tax if distributed before age 59 ½ (sec. 408(f)).

Reasons for change

The committee understands that the requirement that a rollover contribution must contain the entire amount of money and other property distributed has caused problems for plan participants who receive lump-sum distributions from qualified retirement plans. If the recipient or his or her employer makes an error in determining the amount of the rollover contribution, the rollover is disqualified, and the recipient is subject to severe tax penalties. In addition, the committee understands that persons receiving distributions of property other than money frequently have trouble finding an IRA trustee to accept the property as part of a rollover. As a result, such individuals are unable under present law to save any portion of the distribution for retirement needs on a tax-deferred basis.

Explanation of provision

The provision permits a plan participant who receives a lump-sum distribution from a qualified retirement plan or a complete distribution upon termination of a qualified retirement plan to make a rollover contribution of all or a portion of the

[1] There is a limited exception to this rule under certain circumstances where the employee receives a lump-[sum] distribution of stock in his employer. In this case, the employee is generally not required to recognize income based on appreciation in the value of the stock which occurred after the stock was contributed to the plan. Of course, when the stock is sold, the employee will recognize capital gain or loss.

[2] The property must actually be sold for such a designation to be available.

distribution (less the amount allocable to employee contributions) to an IRA or to another qualified plan. If the individual makes a rollover contribution of less than the full distribution eligible for rollover treatment, the amount retained will be taxed in the year of receipt as ordinary personal service income and will not be eligible for special 10-year income averaging.

In addition, the provision permits special "makeup" rollovers for individuals who, prior to enactment of the bill, received a lump-sum distribution and attempted to comply with the present-law rule which requires a rollover contribution to contain all the property distributed. Such individuals would have until the later of December 31, 1978 or the 60th day after the date of enactment of the bill to make a qualified rollover contribution of all or a portion of the property received in a lump-sum distribution. For purposes of this special makeup rollover only, an individual may contribute money in lieu of property received in the distribution to the extent the money transferred does not exceed the fair market value of the retained property on the date of distribution (or at any time within 60 days thereafter).

Effective date

The amendments made by this provision would apply with respect to taxable years beginning after December 31, 1974 (the effective date for establishment of IRA's pursuant to the Pension Reform Act of 1974).

Revenue effect

The provision is estimated to have a negligible impact on budget receipts.

Remarks of Congressman Corman of California during the House debate on September 12, 1978.—The fourth section of the bill is a Senate provision which would allow tax-free treatment for any portion of a lump-sum distribution from a qualified retirement plan which is deposited in an individual retirement account or another qualifying plan. There is also a special makeup rule for individuals who previously attempted to make a rollover deposit but failed to transfer the required amount.

In addition to various technical amendments, an amendment is made which is necessary to this Senate amendment to extend the relief provided by the bill to plans funded by annuity contracts. A similar makeup rule would apply to individuals who previously attempted to roll over distributions from annuity plans, but failed to transfer the entire amount of the distribution. (September 12, 1978 Congressional Record H 9514).

[¶ 11,750.08]

Committee Report on P.L. 94-455 (Tax Reform Act of 1976)

Senate amendment

Under present law, the part of a lump-sum distribution earned before 1974 is treated as capital gain and the post-1973 part is taxed, if the taxpayer elects, as ordinary income in a "separate basket", with 10-year income averaging. If the election is not made, the post-1973 part of the distribution is taxed as ordinary income under the usual rules.

Under the Senate amendment a taxpayer may irrevocably elect to treat all of a lump sum distribution as if it were earned after 1973 so that it will be taxed as ordinary income in a separate basket, with 10-year income averaging. The election applies to distributions made after 1975 in taxable years beginning after 1975.

Conference agreement

The conference agreement follows the Senate amendment. **Conference Committee Report.**

[¶ 11,750.09]

Committee Report on P.L. 94-267 (IRC of 1954—Employee Retirement)

[House Committee Report]

I. Summary.—Under the bill, tax-free rollover treatment is to be available to an employee who receives a payment on account of a termination of his employer's retirement plan or an account of a complete discontinuance of contributions under such a plan. This treatment is also to be made available in certain situations involving sales of subsidiaries and divisions of corporations. The payment from the plan generally must be reinvested by the employee in a qualified plan or individual retirement account within 60 days.

This provision is to apply with respect to payments made to an employee on or after July 4, 1974.

II. Explanation of the Bill.— Present law.—Under the present law,[1] an employee who receives a lump sum distribution from a qualified pension, profit-sharing, stock bonus, or annuity plan may generally contribute (roll over), on a tax-free basis, the portion of the distribution not consisting of employee contributions, to another such plan or to an individual retirement account, individual retirement annuity, or individual retirement bond (referred to collectively as an "IRA"). If the contribution satisfies certain requirements, the plan distribution will generally not be taxed to the employee until a subsequent distribution by the other plan or IRA. Tax-free rollovers are also permitted from an IRA to a plan under these rules if the IRA assets were derived solely from a qualified plan.

To qualify as a tax-free rollover, the same property (other than money) distributed by the plan or IRA must be contributed to the other plan or IRA within 60 days after it is received.

A distribution from a qualified plan is not accorded tax-free rollover treatment unless it is a lump-sum distribution. Thus, for example, it must be made within one taxable year of the recipient, it must consist of the balance to the credit of the employee under the plan, the employee must have been a planned participant for 5 or more taxable years, and the distribution must be made on account of the employee's separation from service[2] or death, or after the employee has attained age 59 ½ or (in the case of a self-employed individual) became disabled.

General reasons for change.—It has been brought to your committee's attention that in a significant number of cases employers terminate plans and distribute their assets even though the employees continue to work for the same employers. This may happen, for example, when an employer is acquired by another corporation and becomes a subsidiary of that other corporation. Your committee has concluded that, in such a case, an employee who wishes to recommit those funds to some sort of tax-qualified retirement vehicle (e.g., tax-qualified pension plan or IRA) or to a profit-sharing or stock bonus plan should be permitted to do so on the same basis as an employee under present law whose distribution qualifies as a lump sum distribution. This tax-free rollover treatment is to apply to a distribution which would be a lump sum distribution but for the fact that it is made on account of a termination of the plan or a complete discontinuance of contributions under the plan. This treatment is also to be made available in certain situations involving sales of subsidiaries and divisions of corporations.

Your committee has concluded that such a rule would have been included in the Employee Retirement Income Security Act of 1974 (ERISA) if the issue had been presented during the legislative consideration of that Act. As a result, this bill makes the rule retroactive so as to achieve as nearly as practical the results that would have been achieved had the rule been enacted as part of ERISA.

Explanation of provision

Under the bill, a distribution of the balance to the credit of an employee under a pension, etc., plan which is paid to the employee within one taxable year, on account of the termination of the plan or the complete discontinuance of contributions under the plan, is to be eligible for tax-free rollover treatment.

Because in some cases it may be difficult to fix the date when a complete discontinuance of contributions occurs, the bill provides that for this purpose a complete discontinuance of contributions is deemed to occur at the time the administrator of the plan notifies the Internal Revenue Service that all contributions under the plan have been completely discontinued.[3]

For this purpose, if an employee if a subsidiary corporation or a corporation which is a member of a controlled group of corporations receives a distribution from the plan of the parent corporation or another member of the controlled group in connection with the liquidation, sale, or other means of terminating the parent-subsidiary or controlled group relationship, the distribution could be treated as if it were made on account of the termination of the plan and could be eligible for tax-free rollover treatment.

Similarly, under the bill, if a corporation sells to another corporation the assets it uses in a trade or business (e.g., what is usually described as a branch or division) and the employees of the seller become employees of the buyer, then a distribution from the seller's plan to those employees could be eligible for tax-free rollover treatment.

Your committee understands that there may be some circumstances to which this bill literally applies, where under present law the employee is already entitled to lump sum distribution (the 10-year "separate basket" treatment provided under ERISA (sec. 402(e) of the Code)) or rollover treatment. This bill is not intended to withdraw lump sum distribution treatment in any case where it is provided under present law.

Effective date

The new rules are to apply to distributions made to employees on or after July 4, 1974 (60 days before the date of the enactment of ERISA, under which tax-free rollover treatment became available).

Special rules are provided for termination distributions which have taken place or will take place before enactment of this bill, in order to make it possible for such a distribution to qualify for tax-free rollover treatment. Under these special rules, the 60-day period within which a qualified distribution under the new rules must be rolled over is not to expire before December 31, 1976.[4] This is done in order to provide sufficient time for the Internal Revenue Service to publish the necessary instructions and for the Service and others to publicize for the tax-free rollover treatment provided by the bill.

An employee who received a plan termination distribution of property (other than money) in this transition period may have recognized that the distribution

---

[1] Sections 402(a)(5), 403(a)(4), 408(d)(3), and 409(b)(3)(C) of the Internal Revenue Code of 1954.

[2] The "separation-from-service" alternative does not apply to self-employed individuals.

[3] Further, the plan is to be considered as having been terminated no later than the date that notice is sent, for purposes of section 411(d)(3), which requires the vesting of all funded benefits when there has been a complete discontinuance of contributions under a plan that does not come under the new ERISA funding rules of section 412.

[4] This extension of the 60-day rule also applies to distributions made after the bill's enactment and before November 2, 1976.

did not qualify for tax-free rollover treatment under present law and may have sold or exchanged the property. In such a case, (1) the sale or exchange itself generally would have been a taxable event and (2) the same-property rule described above (under *Present law*) would prevent this relief provision of the bill from applying. In order to avoid such frustration of the purposes of this retroactive element of this provision, the bill provides that where the property distributed was sold or exchanged during the period ending with the date of the enactment of this bill), the rules are satisfied if the proceeds of the sale (less any employee contributions) are rolled over. Further, the bill provides for nonrecognition of gain or loss on the sale or exchange if such proceeds are rolled over.

Under the bill, the time for rolling over a distribution does not expire before December 31, 1976. To accommodate taxpayers who have already paid tax on distributions, the bill permits the rollover to be made in two stages. Under this two-stage approach, the amount required to be rolled over by December 31, 1976, would be reduced by the tax imposed on the distribution. At the election of the taxpayer, the remaining portion of the distribution would be considered to be rolled over by December 31, 1976, if, within 30 days after the Internal Revenue Service allows a credit or a refund on account of the rollover, the taxpayer rolls over the amount of that refund or credit.

In order to protect against situations where a taxpayer improperly fails to make the second-stage contribution, the bill provides that the period of limitations on assessment of a deficiency (e.g., of income tax or of chapter 43 excise tax) on account of that failure is not to expire before 3 years from the date the taxpayer notifies the Internal Revenue Service whether the second-stage contribution has been timely made. The bill also authorizes the assessment of a deficiency before the expiration of such 3-year period.

In the usual case, where the Service sends the taxpayer a tax refund check, the refund would be considered allowed when the check is sent. For this purpose, under Treasury regulations, the tax imposed on a taxpayer's distribution is to be the excess of the tax imposed on his or her income, including the distribution, over the tax imposed on his or her income excluding the distribution.

[¶ 11,750.10]

Committee Report on P.L. 93-406 (Employee Retirement Income Security Act of 1974)

[Conference Committee Explanation]

General rule.—Both the House bill and the Senate amendment treat the post-1973 taxable portion of a lump-sum distribution from a qualified pension, profit-sharing or stock bonus plan as ordinary income taxed under an averaging device which treats it as if it were received evenly over a period of years. Under the House bill, this special averaging treatment provides the treatment which would be applicable if the amount were spread over a period of 10 years, while the Senate amendment provides the treatment which would be applicable if it were spread over 15 years. Both the House and Senate versions treat the portion of the payment attributable to the pre-1974 period as long-term capital gain.

The conference substitute accepts the 10-year averaging period provided under the House bill. Both the House bill and the Senate amendment compute the ordinary income portion under the same general type of averaging device and this same general procedure is used in the conference substitute. The ordinary income portion is to be computed without regard to the taxpayer's other income (i.e., in effect it is taxed entirely separately as if this were the only income received by the individual). The tax rate schedule to be used in this separate-treatment approach is the schedule provided in the Code for unmarried individuals (whether or not the taxpayer is married). If the plan participant has service both before 1974 and after 1973, the amount attributed to the post-1973 service is the total taxable distribution times a fraction, the numerator of which is calendar years of active participation after 1973 and the denominator of which is total years of active participation. It is understood that the Treasury Department will provide regulations for allocating fractions of years for plan participants who have both pre-1974 and post-1973 value in lump-sum distributions.

The taxable portion of a distribution is to be the portion of the distribution attributable to employer contributions and to income earned on the account. The portion of the distribution representing the employee's contributions remains nontaxable.

Definition of a lump-sum distribution.—The House bill would change the requirements used in determining what qualifies as a lump-sum distribution. The Senate amendment makes no changes in the existing rules on this subject. The conferees have accepted the new House rules.

Under existing law, a distribution generally is treated as a lump-sum distribution if it clears the employee's balance in a single trust, even though there are other trusts in that plan and even though the employee receiving the distribution is a participant in several plans maintained by the same employer. The conference substitute retains the requirement that an employee's entire account be distributed. For this purpose, however, all trusts which are part of a plan are to be treated as a single trust. Furthermore, for this purpose all plans of a given category (the categories are pension plans, profit-sharing plans, and stock bonus plans) maintained by an employer are to be treated as a single plan.

The conference substitute also follows the House bill in permitting a distribution to an employee (common-law definition of an employee) after he attains age 59 ½ to be treated as a lump-sum distribution entitled to the special averaging and partial capital gain treatment, even though the recipient has not left his employment. Under present law, the age 59 ½ rule applies only to self-employed persons. This change from existing law is a part of the effort to eliminate to the extent feasible the distinctions between taxation of lump-sum distributions to regular employees and to the self-employed, as discussed below.

Multiple lump-sum distributions in one taxable year.—The House bill requires that a taxpayer who wishes to use the special averaging and capital gains treatment described above for one lump-sum distribution must use that treatment for the aggregate of the lump-sum distributions he receives in the same taxable year. The Senate amendment and existing law contain no comparable provision. The conference substitute accepts the House rule.

Aggregation of distributions over six years.—Both the House bill and the Senate amendment require that the lump-sum distributions received by an individual during a taxable year be aggregated with all lump-sum distributions to that recipient during his five prior taxable years, but only for purposes of determining the tax brackets in which the income is to be taxed. However, the House bill limits this five-year "lookback" rule to lump-sum distributions made after 1973. No similar provision is contained in the Senate amendment.

The conferees accepted this rule enunciated in both the House and the Senate versions and also accepted the House bill restriction limiting the lookback aggregation to distributions made after 1973.

Treatment of distributions of annuity contracts.—Both the House bill and the Senate amendment provide that a distribution of an annuity contract is to remain nontaxable, but must be included in the six-year aggregation computation described above in order to determine the tax bracket rates on a taxable lump-sum distribution. The House bill provides the annuity contract is to be included in the aggregation computation at its fair market value, while the Senate amendment fixes the value as the cash surrender value as of the time of the distribution.

The conference substitute, as in both the House and Senate versions, includes an annuity contract distribution within the aggregation computation, but continues to treat the annuity contract distribution itself as nontaxable.

The conference substitute provides that the value of an annuity contract for the purposes of the aggregation rule referred to above is to be its current actuarial value. Normally this will be sufficiently close to the cash surrender value of the annuity so that, under Treasury regulations, the cash surrender value (disregarding any loan on the policy) would be treated as the "current actuarial value". However, if the cash surrender value is artificially reduced, Treasury regulations may provide for a simplified method of determining the cash surrender value the annuity would normally carry. If the annuity contract has no cash surrender value, its current actuarial value is to be the present value of the payments anticipated under the annuity contract, computed with regard to the life expectancy of the recipient (and the life expectancy of the recipients' spouse, unless the recipient elects not to take the annuity as a joint and survivor annuity). The present value of these anticipated payments is to be determined under tables to be issued by the Treasury Department.

Recipients eligible for lump-sum distributions.— The House bill provides that the only recipients of lump-sum distributions who may elect the special averaging treatment are individuals, estates, and trusts. The Senate amendment (and present law) place no restrictions on who may use the special averaging treatment. The conference substitute generally accepts the restrictions of the House bill, but with modifications in the case of lump-sum distributions to trusts.

Under the conference substitute, a lump-sum distribution may be made to multiple trusts, but, if this occurs, the tax paid on account of the distribution is to be the tax payable as if the entire distribution were made to one recipient, with the tax liability apportioned among the multiple trusts in accordance with the relative amounts received by each.

In cases of distributions to individuals and estates (in which instances an entire lump-sum distribution must be made to one recipient) the recipient is to make an election as to whether to claim the special averaging treatment. (The personal representative of the employee is to make the election if distributions are made to multiple trusts). This election is of significance because, as discussed below, only one election may be made with respect to an employee who has attained age 59 ½.

As under the House bill, the conference substitute provides that an employee must generally be regarded as the recipient, for purposes of the requirement of aggregation of all lump-sum distributions in a period of six taxable years, even if he or she causes the distribution to be made to a trust, if the employee retains such an interest in the trust as would require his taxation as the substantial owner of the trust under the present tax rules, even if the grantor of the trust is technically the employer or plan.[1]

In the House bill, a trust would be allowed to elect the special averaging treatment only if (1) the use of the trust would not affect the includibility of the distribution in the employee's gross estate, and (2) the trust would be sole

[1] If the lump-sum distribution is made to a recipient other than a trust during the employee's lifetime, it is intended that the usual assignment-of-income and constructive receipt rules are to apply to determine whether the employee is to be liable for the tax upon the distribution.

recipient of the entire balance to the credit of the employee. These provisions were not adopted by the conferees.

As indicated above, attainment of age 59 ½ is made a criterion of eligibility for a regular employee (as well as for a self-employed person, as under present law) for the special averaging lump-sum treatment under the conference substitute. It was not considered necessary, however, to specify that a beneficiary is entitled to the special averaging and partial capital gain treatment for a distribution on account of the death of an employee *after* his retirement (as well as before).[2]

Number of elections.—The House bill allows the special averaging treatment to be elected freely until the employee attains age 59 ½, after which time only one election may be made with respect to that employee. The Senate amendment does not have an election procedure. As in the case under present law, the Senate version makes the treatment mandatory for lump-sum distributions and does not limit the number of times this special treatment may be used.

The conferees followed the House bill in allowing only one election with respect to an employee after he has attained age 59 ½. Thus, if an employee has made one election after attaining age 59 ½, he may not thereafter obtain the special averaging treatment for another distribution. As under present law, however, an employee, or his beneficiary, who is barred from the special averaging treatment by an earlier election may nevertheless gain the partial capital gain treatment for pre-1974 value if the distribution is made on account of the employee's death or separation from service. In addition, such an employee who receives a distribution because of attaining age 59 ½ may also receive the partial capital gains treatment although he is barred from the special averaging for the ordinary income portion.

A recipient who elects this special averaging treatment may still elect the usual income averaging provided under sec. 1301.[3] A taxpayer who surrenders an annuity may use the normal 5-year income averaging and also may use the special averaging for lump-sum distributions.

Lump-sum distributions to the self-employed.— Under the House bill, the same 10-year ordinary income averaging may be elected for distributions on account of plan participation by self-employed persons as may be elected on account of the participation of regular employees. (Under present law, lump-sum distributions to self-employed persons are taxed under special 5-year averaging provisions.) There is no comparable Senate provision.

The conferees accepted the House provision eliminating the distinction of treatment between regular employees and the self-employed in this respect. If they elect the special averaging treatment, self-employed persons are also entitled to capital gain taxation on the pre-1974 value of their lump-sum distributions.

Computation of tax in lump-sum distribution.—It is recognized that the computation of tax due on a lump-sum distribution with an annuity lump-sum distribution, as reflected in the reports of the House Ways and Means Committee and the Senate Finance Committee, is incorrect in that it subtracts the entire minimum distribution allowance from the amount of the annuity, instead of subtracting only that portion of the minimum distribution allowance that is proportionate to the amount of the annuity distribution as compared with the total distribution. This incorrectly increases the tax on the taxable distribution because it minimizes the tax attributable to the annuity distribution. The less the tax attributable to the annuity distribution, the larger is the tax attributable to the taxable distribution.

The correct computation is as follows:

First example.—On December 31, 1975, A terminates his services and receives a lump-sum distribution of $65,000 from a qualified plan. The distribution includes employer securities with a fair market value of $25,000 and a basis of $10,000. A has been participating in the plan since January 1, 1966. The plan is noncontributory. A is married; both A and his wife are 50. Their only other income is A's salary of $15,000 and his salary from a second job ($5,000). Their itemized deductions are $3,000. Their average base period income (for purposes of regular income averaging) from the preceding four years (1971 through 1974) is $14,000.

The tax on the portion of the distribution which is not treated as a long-term capital gain is computed as follows:

Net distribution ($65,000 total distribution less $15,000 unrealized appreciation on employer securities)	$50,000
Less: Minimum distribution allowance: 50 percent of first $20,000	$10,000
Reduced by: 20 percent of net distributions in excess of $20,000	6,000
	4,000
Distribution less allowance	46,000

The tax on 1/10th of the distribution less allowance computed from the tax rate schedule for single taxpayers is $816.00.

Multiply this amount by 10: $8,160.00.

Then, multiply by the fraction,

$$\frac{\text{Years of participation in plan after 1973}}{\text{Total years of participation}} = \frac{2}{10} = 0.2$$

which yields $1,632.00.

Thus, the tax on the ordinary income portion of the distribution is $1,632.00.

The amount of the distribution taxed as a long-term capital gain is the amount of the net distribution multiplied by the fraction,

$$\frac{\text{Years of participation before 1974}}{\text{Total years of participation}} = \frac{8}{10} = 0.8$$

Net distribution	$50,000
Capital gains element	40,000

The capital gains element is taxed along with other income (exclusive of the ordinary income element) in the normal way. The tax on the taxable income of $35,500 ($15,000 salary from first job, plus $5,000 from second job, plus $40,000 capital gains element of lump-sum distribution, less $20,000 capital gains exclusion, less $3,000 itemized deductions, less two $750 personal exemptions) is calculated using the tax rate schedule for married taxpayers filing joint returns. In this case the alternative tax on capital gains is not available, but the regular-five-year income averaging provisions are.

Ordinary tax	$10,130.00
Tax—Using regular income averaging[1]	8,828.00

[1] As indicated above, average base period income is $14,000.

Selecting the tax computation method which yields the smallest amount of tax, A uses the regular five-year income averaging method and has a tax of $8,828.00.

Finally, A combines the tax on the capital gains portion of the distribution and his salary, with the tax on the ordinary income portion of the distribution:

Tax on salary and capital gains portion of distribution	$8,828.00
Tax on ordinary income portion of distribution	1,632.00
Total 1975 income tax	10,460.00

A's basis in the employer securities is $10,000.

Second example.—On December 31, 1976, A receives a distribution from a qualified plan with respect to his second job. In this case the distribution is a nontransferable annuity contract, the value of which is $6,000; and a cash distribution of $4,000 financed solely by the employer. A had participated in the plan since January 1, 1967. Mr. and Mrs. A's only other income in 1976 is A's salary of $25,000 and interest of $3,000 on the $40,000 cash received in the prior lump-sum distribution. They have itemized deductions of $2,100. Mr. and Mrs. A's 1976 tax is computed as follows:

First, compute the tax on the portion of the distribution which is not treated as a long-term capital gain and which is taxed separately.

Step 1:

1976 cash distribution	$4,000
1976 annuity contract	6,000
Prior year net distributions	50,000
Total	60,000
Less: Minimum distribution allowance: 50 percent of first $20,000	$10,000
Reduced by: 20 percent of net distribution in excess of $20,000	8,000
Total	2,000
	58,000

Ten times the tax on one-tenth of $58,000 (from the rate schedule for single taxpayers) is $10,680.

[2] Thus, no change in present law is intended by the deletion of references to this in sections 402(a)(2) and 403(a)(2)(A)(iii) of the code.

[3] H. Rept. 93-807, p. 150, which indicates that a common-law employee who uses the special averaging provided under present law may nevertheless also use the regular five-year income averaging for his other income and capital gain, is incorrect. Under the conference substitute, however, both types of income averaging may be used concurrently by both regular employees and the self-employed.

Step 2:

1976 annuity		$6,000
Minimum distribution allowance from step 1	$2,000	
Portion of minimum distribution allowance attributable to annuity distribution		

$$\frac{\$6,000}{60,000} \times \$2,000 = \$200 \quad \ldots \quad 200$$

Remainder	5,800

Ten times the tax on one-tenth of $5,800 (from the rate schedule for single taxpayers) is $820.

Step 3: $10,680.00 – $820 = $9,860

Step 4:

Determine ordinary income and capital gains elements of A's distribution and his prior year distribution. The ordinary income element of A's latest distribution is determined by multiplying the cash distribution of $4,000 by:

$$\frac{\text{Years of participation in plan after 1973} = 3/10 = 0.3}{\text{Total years of participation}}$$

Thus, A's ordinary income element is $1,200. $10,000 of Mr. A's prior distribution of $50,000 was ordinary income.

Thus, the tax on the ordinary income element is the fraction of the tax from Step No. 3 which the ordinary income elements of the 1976 and prior year distributions bear to the entire distributions.

$$\frac{\$1,200 + \$10,000}{\$4,000 + \$50,000} \times \$9,860 = \$2,045.04$$

Step 5:

The tax on the ordinary income element of A's 1975 distribution from their 1975 income tax income return was $1,632.00. Subtracting that from the tax calculated in Step No. 4 yields the tax on the ordinary income element of A's latest distribution:

$2,045.04 – $1,632.00 = $413.04

Second, compute the tax on all other income, including the capital gains portion of the distribution.

Step 6:

In Step No. 4, the ordinary income element of the distribution was calculated as $1,200. Therefore, the long-term capital gains element is:

$4,000.00 – $1,200 = $2,800.00

Step 7:

The capital gains element is taxed along with other income in the regular manner.

Capital gains element	$2,800
Less: 50 percent of net long-term capital gain	1,400
Total	1,400
Salary	25,000
Interest	3,000
Adjusted gross income	29,400
Less: Itemized deductions	2,100
Less: Personal exemptions (2 × $750)	1,500
Taxable income	25,800

The tax on $25,800 is calculated using the tax rate schedule for married taxpayers filing joint returns. In this case, neither the alternative tax on capital gains nor the regular five-year income averaging provision is available.

Ordinary tax	$6,308.00

Third, A combines the tax on the capital gains portion of the distribution and his other income, with the tax on the ordinary income portion of the distribution.

Step 8:

Tax on capital gains portion of distribution and on other income	$6,308.00
Tax on ordinary income portion of distribution	413.04
Total 1976 income tax	6,721.04

If in the examples above, A has attained age 59 ½, he may elect to treat only one of the distributions as a lump-sum distribution qualifying for ten-year averaging. In computing the tax liability on the distribution which he elects to qualify for ten-year averaging, A will not aggregate any distribution (except in the case of a distribution of an annuity contract) made after attaining age 59 ½ which is not treated as a lump-sum distribution for purposes of the ten-year averaging.

[Code Sec. 402A]

[¶ 11,799A.048]

Committee Report on P.L. 107-16 (Economic Growth and Tax Relief Reconciliation Act)

[House Committee Report]

Transfer of benefits from TSAs or 457 plans

A participant in a State or local governmental plan is not required to include in gross income a direct trustee-to-trustee transfer to a governmental defined benefit plan from a section 403(b) annuity or a section 457 plan if the transferred amount is used (1) to purchase permissive service credits under the plan, or (2) to repay contributions and earnings with respect to an amount previously refunded under a forfeiture of service credit under the plan (or another plan maintained by a State or local government employer within the same State).

Effective Date

The provision is effective for transfers after December 31, 2001.

[Conference Committee Report]

Senate Amendment

The Senate amendment is the same as the House bill.

Conference Agreement

The conference agreement follows the House bill and the Senate amendment.

[¶ 11,799A.049]

Committee Report on P.L. 107-16 (Economic Growth and Tax Relief Reconciliation Act)

[House Committee Report]

Contribution limits for tax-sheltered annuities

Conforming limits on tax-sheltered annuities.—The provision repeals the exclusion allowance applicable to contributions to tax-sheltered annuities. Thus, such annuities are subject to the limits applicable to tax-qualified plans.

The provision also directs the Secretary of the Treasury to revise the regulations relating to the exclusion allowance under section 403(b)(2) to render void the requirement that contributions to a defined benefit plan be treated as previously excluded amounts for purposes of the exclusion allowance. For taxable years beginning after December 31, 1999, the regulatory provisions regarding the exclusion allowance are to be applied as if the requirement that contributions to a defined benefit plan be treated as previously excluded amounts for purposes of the exclusion allowance were void.

* * *

Effective Date

The provision generally is effective for years beginning after December 31, 2001. The provision regarding the regulations under section 403(b)(2) is effective on the date of enactment.

[Conference Committee Report]

The conference agreement follows the House bill, with the following modifications.

With respect to the increase in the defined contribution plan limit, the conferees intend that the Secretary of the Treasury will use the Secretary's existing authority to address situations where qualified nonelective contributions are targeted to certain participants with lower compensation in order to increase the average deferral percentage of nonhighly compensated employees.

For taxable years beginning after December 31, 1999, a plan may disregard the requirement that contributions to a defined benefit plan be treated as previously excluded amounts for purposes of the exclusion allowance.

[¶ 11,799A.50]

Committee Report on P.L. 107-16 (Economic Growth and Tax Relief Reconciliation Act)

[Senate Committee Report]

Option to treat elective deferrals as after-tax contributions

A section 401(k) plan or a section 403(b) annuity is permitted to include a "Roth contribution program" that permits a participant to elect to have all or a portion of the participant's elective deferrals under the plan treated as Roth contributions. Roth contributions are elective deferrals that the participant designates (at such time and in such manner as the Secretary may prescribe)[1] as not excludable from the participant's gross income.

The annual dollar limitation on a participant's Roth contributions is the section 402(g) annual limitation on elective deferrals, reduced by the participant's elective deferrals that the participant does not designate as Roth contributions. Roth contributions are treated as any other elective deferral for purposes of nonforfeitability requirements and distribution restrictions.[2] Under a section 401(k) plan, Roth contributions also are treated as any other elective deferral for purposes of the special nondiscrimination requirements.[3]

The plan is required to establish a separate account, and maintain separate recordkeeping, for a participant's Roth contributions (and earnings allocable thereto). A qualified distribution from a participant's Roth contribution account is not includible in the participant's gross income. A qualified distribution is a distribution that is made after the end of a specified nonexclusion period and that is (1) made on or after the date on which the participant attains age 59 ½, (2) made to a beneficiary (or to the estate of the participant) on or after the death of the participant, or (3) attributable to the participant being disabled.[4] The nonexclusion period is the 5-year-taxable period beginning with the earlier of (1) the first taxable year for which the participant made a Roth contribution to any Roth contribution account established for the participant under the plan, or (2) if the participant has made a rollover contribution to the Roth contribution account that is the source of the distribution from a Roth contribution account established for the participant under another plan, the first taxable year for which the participant made a Roth contribution to the previously established account.

A distribution from a Roth contribution account that is a corrective distribution of an elective deferral (and income allocable thereto) that exceeds the section 402(g) annual limit on elective deferrals or a corrective distribution of an excess contribution under the special nondiscrimination rules (pursuant to sec. 401(k)(8) (and income allocable thereto) is not a qualified distribution. In addition, the treatment of excess Roth contributions is similar to the treatment of excess deferrals attributable to non-Roth contributions. If excess Roth contributions (including earnings thereon) are distributed no later than the April 15th following the taxable year, then the Roth contributions are not includible in gross income as a result of the distribution, because such contributions are includible in gross income when made. Earnings on such excess Roth contributions are treated the same as earnings on excess deferrals distributed no later than April 15th, i.e., they are includible in income when distributed. If excess Roth contributions are not distributed no later than the applicable April 15th, then such contributions (and earnings thereon) are taxable when distributed. Thus, as is the case with excess elective deferrals that are not distributed by the applicable April 15th, the contributions are includible in income in the year when made and again when distributed from the plan. Earnings on such contributions are taxable when received.

A participant is permitted to roll over a distribution from a Roth contribution account only to another Roth contribution account or a Roth IRA of the participant.

The Secretary of the Treasury is directed to require the plan administrator of each section 401(k) plan or section 403(b) annuity that permits participants to make Roth contributions to make such returns and reports regarding Roth contributions to the Secretary, plan participants and beneficiaries, and other persons that the Secretary may designate.

Effective Date

The provision is effective for taxable years beginning after December 31, 2003.

[Conference Committee Report]

Senate Amendment

The Senate amendment is the same as the House bill, except that the Senate amendment refers to designated plus contributions as "Roth contributions."

Effective Date

The Senate amendment is effective for taxable years beginning after December 31, 2003.

Conference Agreement

The conference agreement follows the Senate amendment, with a modification of the effective date.

Effective Date

The conference agreement is effective for taxable years beginning after December 31, 2005.

[Code Sec. 403]

[¶ 11,800.043]

Committee Report on P.L. 109-280 (Pension Protection Act of 2006)

For the Committee Report on P.L. 109-280 on the purchase of permissive service credit, see ¶ 12,400.013. For the Committee Report on P.L. 109-280 on the modification of rules governing hardships and unforeseen financial emergencies, see ¶ 11,700.02.

[¶ 11,800.045]

Committee Report on P.L. 102-318 (Unemployment Compensation Amendments of 1992)

For Committee Report on Unemployment Compensation Amendments of 1992 (P.L. 102-318), dealing with rollovers and withholding on nonperiodic pension distributions, see ¶ 11,750.036.

[¶ 11,800.049]

Committee Report P.L. 104-188 (Small Business Job Protection Act)

Miscellaneous Pension Simplification

[House Committee Report]

Modifications of section 403(b)

Application of elective deferral limit.—Under the bill, each tax-sheltered annuity contract, not the tax-sheltered annuity plan, must provide that elective deferrals made under the contract may not exceed the annual limit on elective deferrals. The Committee intends that the contract terms be given effect in order for this requirement to be satisfied. Thus, for example, if the annuity contract issuer takes no steps to ensure that deferrals under the contract do not exceed the applicable limit, then the contract will not be treated as satisfying section 403(b). The provision is intended to make clear that the exclusion of elective deferrals from gross income by employees who have not exceeded the annual limit on elective deferrals will not be affected to the extent other employees exceed the annual limit. However, if the occurrence of an uncorrected elective deferral made by an employee is attributable to reasonable error, the contract will not fail to satisfy section 403(b), and only the portion of the elective deferral in excess of the annual limit would be includible in gross income.

Effective Date

The provision is effective for years beginning after December 31, 1995, except that an annuity contract is not required to meet any change in any requirement by reason of the provision before the 90th day after the date of enactment.

[Conference Committee Report]

Senate Amendment

The Senate amendment is the same as the House bill.

Conference Agreement

The conference agreement follows the House bill and the Senate amendment.

[¶ 11,800.051]

Committee Reports on P.L. 100-647 (Technical and Miscellaneous Revenue Act of 1988)

[Senate Committee Report]

Tax-Sheltered Annuities

The Act does not specify how years of service are to be determined for purposes of the catch-up rule. The bill provides that, for this purpose, years of service are defined as in section 403(b). This definition will provide consistency with the way years of service are generally calculated under the rules relating to tax-sheltered annuities.

It is recognized that it may be difficult for employers to calculate whether an individual's lifetime elective deferrals exceed the individual's lifetime limit for

[1] It is intended that the Secretary generally will not permit retroactive designations of elective deferrals as Roth contributions.

[2] Similarly, Roth contributions to a section 403(b) annuity are treated the same as other salary reduction contributions to the annuity (except that Roth contributions would be includible in income).

[3] It is intended that the Secretary will provide ordering rules regarding the return of excess contributions under the special nondiscrimination rules (pursuant to sec. 401(k)(8)) in the event a participant makes both regular elective deferrals and Roth contributions. It is intended that such rules will generally permit a plan to allow participants to designate which contributions would be returned first or to permit the plan to specify which contributions will be returned first.

[4] A qualified special purpose distribution, as defined under the rules relating to Roth IRAs, does not qualify as a tax-free distribution from a Roth contribution account.

purposes of the catch-up rule because employers may not have records for prior years with respect to the portion of contributions to tax-sheltered annuities that were elective deferrals. Accordingly, under the bill, for purposes of calculating an individual's lifetime elective deferrals under the catch-up rule, elective deferrals for prior years are to be determined in the manner prescribed by the Secretary. Under this provision, it is expected that the Secretary will provide administrable methods that employers can use to calculate elective deferrals for prior years.

The bill conforms the statutory language to the legislative history by providing that contributions to a tax-sheltered annuity are not considered elective deferrals if the contributions are made pursuant to a one-time irrevocable election made by the employee at the time of initial eligibility to participate in the annuity or are made pursuant to a similar arrangement specified in regulations. The bill does not change the definition of salary reduction agreement for purposes of section 3121(a)(5)(D). This amendment also does not affect the definition of elective deferrals other than with respect to tax-sheltered annuities.

[Senate Committee Report]

The Tax Reform Act of 1986 generally applied the qualified pension plan coverage and nondiscrimination rules to the nonelective and matching contributions or benefits of tax-sheltered annuity programs, generally effective for plan years beginning after December 31, 1988. The provision would modify three nondiscrimination rules in the following manner: (1) student employees who are not taken into account for employment tax purposes may be disregarded; (2) adjunct professors and other part-time employees could be disregarded if they normally work less than 20 hours per weeks; and (3) the nondiscrimination tests could be applied by testing at the level of the institution that maintains the plan, as long as the institution functions as, and has been historically recognized as, a separate employer. The provision also would clarify that the special rules applicable to multiple employer pension plans (sec. 413(c)) for purposes of determining whether certain rules are required to be satisfied on an employer-by-employer or on an aggregate basis are applicable to multiple employer tax-sheltered annuity programs. In addition, for plan years beginning before January 1, 1992, the nondiscrimination rules could be applied by testing with respect to a statistically valid sample of employees.

The provision would be effective as if included in the Tax Reform Act of 1986.

[Conference Committee Report]

* * *

Conference Agreement

The conference agreement follows the Senate amendment, with the clarification that the provision is effective as if included in section 1120(b) of the Reform Act. The conferees intend that the institution maintaining the plan is generally to be interpreted as not including any employer (or portion thereof) that may not maintain a section 403(b) annuity program.

[¶ 11,800.053]
Committee Reports on P.L. 99-514 (Tax Reform Act of 1986)

[House Committee Report]

Elective Contributions Under Tax-Sheltered Annuities

Limit on elective deferrals

Under the bill, the maximum amount that an employee can elect to defer for any taxable year under all tax-sheltered annuities in which the employee participates is limited to $7,000 [The Conference Bill raises the amount for tax-sheltered 403(b) annuities]. Whether or not an employee has deferred more than $7,000 a year is determined without regard to any community property laws. In addition, the $7,000 limit is coordinated with elective 401(k) deferrals and the annual deduction limit for IRA contributions.

Unlike the overall limits on annual additions, which apply separately to amounts accumulated under plans of different employers, this $7,000 cap limits all elective deferrals by an employee. Thus, the $7,000 limit applies to aggregate deferrals made under all tax-sheltered annuity programs and cash or deferred arrangements in which the employee participates. [The Conference Bill clarifies the definition of elective deferrals.]

Because this $7,000 limit applies only to elective deferrals, each employer may make additional contributions on behalf of any employee to the extent that such contributions, when aggregated with elective deferrals made by the employee under the employer's tax-sheltered annuity during the limitation year, do not exceed the exclusion allowance or the overall limits on contributions and benefits.

If, in any taxable year, the total amount of elective deferrals contributed on behalf of an employee to any tax-sheltered annuities and qualified cash or deferred arrangements in which the employee participates exceeds $7,000, then the amount in excess of $7,000 (the excess deferrals) [is] included in the employee's gross income for the year. In addition, with respect to any excess deferrals, by March 1, after the close of the employee's taxable year, the employee may allocate the excess deferrals among the tax-sheltered annuities in which the employee participates and notify the administrator of each program of the portion of the excess deferrals allocated to it. Further, not later than April 15 after the close of the employee's taxable year, each program is to distribute to the employee the amount of the excess deferrals (plus income attributable to the excess) allocated to the plan. This distribution of excess deferrals may be made notwithstanding any other provision of law.

The committee intends that the tax-sheltered annuities maintained by any single employer should preclude an employee from making elective deferrals under the program for any taxable year in excess of $7,000.

The amount of excess deferrals distributed to any employee (plus the income on the excess deferrals) [is] included in the employee's income for the year to which the excess deferrals relate. However, the amounts are treated as if they had not been contributed to the tax-sheltered annuity program and, therefore, are not subject to any additional income taxes for early withdrawals.

Excess deferrals that are not distributed by the applicable April 15 date are not treated as employee contributions upon subsequent distribution even though such deferrals had been included in the employee's income.

Special catch-up election

Finally, the bill provides an exception to the $7,000 annual limit (but not to the otherwise applicable exclusion allowance (sec. 403(b)) or the overall limit on contributions and benefits (sec. 415) in the case of employees of an educational organization, a hospital, a home health service agency, or a church, convention or association of churches. Under this exception, any eligible employee who had completed 15 years of service with the employer would be permitted to make an additional salary reduction contribution under the following conditions:

(1) In no year can the additional contributions be more than $3,000;

(2) An aggregate limit of $15,000 applies to the total amount of contributions that, in any year, exceed $7,000; and

(3) In no event can this exception be used if an individual's lifetime elective deferrals exceed the individual's lifetime limit.

The lifetime limit on elective deferrals for an individual, solely for purposes of the special catch-up rule, is $5,000 multiplied by the number of years of service that the individual performed with the employer.

Effective Dates

The provisions generally are effective for years beginning after December 31, [1986]. A special effective date is provided in the case of a tax-sheltered annuity program maintained pursuant to one or more collective bargaining agreements ratified before [March 1, 1986], between employee representatives and one or more employers. Under this special rule, the provisions do not apply to contributions made under such an agreement in taxable years beginning before the earlier of (1) the date on which the last of the collective bargaining agreements terminates or (2) January 1, [1989].

[Conference Committee Report]

Elective Contributions Under Tax-Sheltered Annuities

Limit on elective deferrals

The conference agreements follows the House bill, except that the annual limit on elective deferrals uder a tax-sheltered annuity is increased to $9,500. The $9,500 limit applies until the cost-of-living adjustments to the annual limit on elective deferrals under a qualified cash or deferred arrangement raise that limit from $7,000 to $9,500, at which time the limit on elective deferrals under a tax-sheltered annuity is also indexed in the same manner as the indexing of the annual limit for elective deferrals under a qualified cash or deferred arrangement.

The conference agreement clarifies the definition of elective deferrals to which the annual limit applies. In the case of an employer that allows employees a one-time election to participate in a contributory defined benefit pension plan with a single mandatory contribution rate or a tax-sheltered annuity program with elective deferrals, neither the election of an employee to participate in the defined benefit plan nor the employee contributions made to the defined benefit plan are to be treated as elective deferrals for purposes of the annual limit. Similarly, if an employee is required to contribute a fixed percentage of compensation to a tax-sheltered annuity as a condition of employment, the contributions are not treated as elective deferrals. This is considered elective deferrals if the employer and employee enter into temporary employment contracts. The conferees do not intend these examples to constitute the only situations in which contributions are not treated as elective deferrals. The conferees direct the Secretary to provide guidance to employers on other contributions that are not to be treated as elective deferrals.

Special catch-up election

The conference agreement follows the House bill and extends the special catch-up election to employees of health and welfare service agencies.

Effective dates

The provisions are effective for taxable years beginning after December 31, 1986.

A special effective date applies to plans maintained pursuant to a collective bargaining agreement. Under this special rule, with respect to employees covered under a plan maintained pursuant to a collective bargaining agreement between employee representatives and one or more employers ratified before March 1, 1986, the amendments are not effective for plan years beginning before the earlier of (1) January 1, 1989, or (2) the date on which the last of the collective bargaining agreement[s] terminates (determined without regard to any extensions in the collective bargaining agreement).

[House Committee Report]

Tax-sheltered annuities

In general

The bill generally applies the coverage and nondiscrimination rules of present law (secs. 410(b) and 401(a)(4)) to tax-sheltered annuity programs (other than those maintained for church employees). Under the bill, the coverage and nondiscrimination rules apply to any tax-sheltered annuity programs to which the sponsoring employer makes contributions. To the extent the program permits elective employee deferrals, a special coverage and nondiscrimination rule applies to those elective deferrals.

Employer contributions

If an employer makes contributions to a tax-sheltered annuity program, the bill requires that the program must satisfy the coverage and nondiscrimination rules of present law (secs. 410(b) and 401(a)(4)).

Nondiscriminatory coverage

These rules require that a tax-sheltered annuity program cover employees in general rather than merely the employer's highly compensated employees. * * *

Elective deferrals

The bill provides a special coverage and nondiscrimination rule applicable to tax-sheltered annuity programs that permit elective deferrals. If the employer makes nonelective contributions under a program, the special rule applies only to the elective deferrals and the general nondiscrimination rules described above apply to the nonelective contributions. If, however, the employer maintains a tax-sheltered annuity program that permits only elective deferrals (i.e., no nonelective contributions are made), only the special rule for elective deferrals applies.

Under the bill, a tax-sheltered annuity program that permits elective deferrals will be considered discriminatory with respect to those deferrals unless the opportunity to make elective deferrals is made available to all employees of the entity sponsoring the tax-sheltered annuity program. To ensure that the opportunity to make elective deferrals is available to all employees, the bill provides that the employer generally is not to require any minimum dollar amount (or percentage of compensation) as a condition of participation. However, because the contribution must be sufficient to make purchase of the annuity contract practicable, the bill authorizes the Secretary of the Treasury to issue regulations permitting an employer to establish a reasonable de minimis threshold. * * *

Under the bill, elective deferrals under a tax-sheltered annuity program consist of those employer contributions made by reason of a salary reduction agreement, whether evidenced by a written instrument or otherwise (sec. 3121(a)(5)(D)), to the extent those contributions are excludable from the employee's gross income. In applying the special test for deferrals, no employees of the entity sponsoring the tax-sheltered annuity program (other than nonresident aliens with no U.S.-source earned income) may be excluded from consideration. For example, the qualified plan rules permitting the exclusion of certain employees based upon age and service and coverage under collective bargaining agreements do not apply.

As under present law, the new coverage and nondiscrimination rules generally apply with respect to the "employer" as defined in section 414(b), (c), (m), and (o). In addition, the present-law rules relating to leased employees continue to apply (sec. 414(n)). However, the rules relating to elective deferrals will apply, pursuant to Treasury regulations, with respect to the entity of the employer sponsoring the tax-sheltered annuity program. For example, in determining whether a tax-sheltered annuity program offered by a State university permits all employees the opportunity to make elective deferrals, the relevant workforce includes all employees of the State university, not all employees of the State.

Employers subject to the nondiscrimination rule

In general, all employers eligible to sponsor a tax-sheltered annuity program are subject to the nondiscrimination rules added by the bill. However, these rules do not apply to tax-sheltered annuity programs maintained for church employees.

For purposes of this exclusion, the term "church" is defined to include only a church described in section 501(c)(3) or a qualified church-controlled organization. These terms generally have the same meaning as they do for purposes of exclusion from the SECA and FICA taxes (sec. 1402 and 3121). Accordingly, for purposes of this provision, the term church includes (1) a convention or association of churches, and (2) an elementary or secondary school that is controlled, operated, or principally supported by a church or by a convention or association of churches.

Similarly, the term qualified church-controlled organization means any church-controlled tax-exempt organization described in section 501(c)(3) other than an organization that both (1) offers goods, services, or facilities for sale (other than on an incidental basis) to the general public (e.g., to individuals who are not members of the church), other than goods, services, or facilities that are sold at a nominal charge which is substantially less than the cost of providing such goods, services, or facilities, and also (2) normally receives more than 25 percent of its support from either (a) governmental sources, or (b) receipts from admissions, sales of merchandise, performance of services, or furnishing of facilities in activities that are not unrelated trades or businesses, or from (a) and (b) combined.

A tax-sheltered annuity program of an otherwise qualified church organization will be subject to the coverage and nondiscrimination rules only if both conditions (1) and (2) in the preceding paragraph exist. Thus, these rules generally will not apply to the typical seminary, religious retreat center, or burial society, regardless of its funding sources, because it does not offer goods, services, or facilities for sale to the general public. Similarly, the rules do not apply to a church-run orphanage or old-age home, even if it is open to the general public, if not more than 25 percent of its support was derived from the receipts of admissions, sales of merchandise, performance of services, or furnishing of facilities (in other than unrelated trades or businesses) or from governmental sources. The committee specifically intends that the coverage and nondiscrimination rules will apply to church-run universities (other than religious seminaries) and hospitals if both conditions (1) and (2) exist.

Auxiliary organizations of a church (including youth groups, women's auxiliaries, etc.) generally would satisfy neither of the conditions, and thus the coverage and nondiscrimination rules will not apply. Similarly, these rules generally will not apply to tax-sheltered annuity programs maintained by church pension boards or fund-raising organizations.

Effective Date

These nondiscrimination rules generally apply for years beginning after December 31, [1988].

* * *

[Conference Committee Report]

In general

The conference agreement generally follows the House bill, subject to the following modifications.

If an employer provides nonelective or matching contributions or benefits under a tax-sheltered annuity program, the conference agreement requires that such employer contributions or benefits satisfy the new coverage and nondiscrimination rules applicable to qualified plans, as modified or added pursuant to the conference agreement * * *, rather than the coverage and nondiscrimination rules applicable to qualified plans under present law.

Except as otherwise noted below, these rules apply in the same manner to tax-sheltered annuity programs as they do to qualified plans. Thus, the full array of rules relating to nondiscrimination apply (such as, for example, the limit on the amount of compensation that may be taken into account, the special nondiscrimination rule applicable to matching contributions, the employee leasing rules, and the minimum participation rules).

Integration

As with respect to qualified plans, employers maintaining tax-sheltered annuity programs generally may integrate contributions or benefits under the new integration rules for purposes of the average benefits test (sec. 410(b)), for establishing comparability between programs (or between a program and a plan), and for satisfying the benefits test within a plan (sec. 401(a)(4)). However, under the rules prescribed by the Secretary, there is no permitted disparity under the new integration rules for employees who are not covered by social security.

Permissive aggregation

If a tax-sheltered annuity program, standing alone, fails to satisfy the percentage test, the ratio test, or the classification test, the employer may elect to treat the tax-sheltered annuity program and a qualified plan or another tax-sheltered annuity program as a single plan solely for purposes of demonstrating that the tax-sheltered annuity program satisfies the coverage requirements. If a tax-sheltered annuity program is aggregated with another tax-sheltered annuity or with a qualified plan for purposes of satisfying the coverage rules, the aggregated arrangements must provide contributions or benefits that do not discriminate in favor of highly compensated employees (secs. 401(a)(4) and 401(m)).

The requirement that such aggregated arrangements provide comparable contributions or benefits generally applies in the same manner to tax-sheltered annuity programs as it does to qualified plans. Thus, the principles of Rev. Rul. 81-202, as modified in the ways described in [¶ 602] are to apply. However, the conferees intend that the Secretary is to prescribe rules applicable to tax-sheltered annuities that reduce the administrative burden of applying Rev.Rul. 81-202. For example, the Secretary might permit, under appropriate circumstances, testing less frequently than annually.

In applying the average benefit percentage component of the average benefits test to a tax-sheltered annuity program, an employer may at its election include all qualified plans in determining the average benefit percentages.

As under the House bill, a tax-sheltered annuity program may not be aggregated with a qualified plan for purposes of determining whether the qualified plan satisfies the applicable coverage and nondiscrimination rules, including the average benefits test.

Excludable employees

The categories of employees that are excluded in applying the coverage rules to tax-sheltered annuities are the same as those that are excluded in applying the rules to qualified plans, except that, in addition, an employer is to exclude from consideration students who normally work less than 20 hours per week. This additional category of excludable employees is treated in the same manner as the category of employees who do not meet the service requirements for qualified plans. Thus, for example, the 20-hour requirement only applies if the employer excludes all students normally working less than 20 hours per week.

Elective deferrals

The conference agreement follows the House bill, except that in applying the nondiscriminatory coverage rule applicable to elective deferrals under a tax-sheltered annuity program, the employer is to exclude from consideration students who normally work fewer than 20 hours per week, as discussed above. The conference agreement also clarifies that, in applying the average benefits test, elective deferrals under a tax-sheltered annuity are to be disregarded.

The conference agreement also clarifies the definition of an elective deferral. If an employee has a one-time election to participate in a program that requires an employee contribution, such contribution will not be considered an elective deferral to the extent that the employee is not permitted subsequently to modify the election in any manner. In addition, the Secretary is authorized to prescribe additional instances in which employer contributions to a plan will not be considered elective despite the existence of limited rights of election by the employee.

Employers subject to the nondiscrimination rule

The conference agreement follows the House bill. In addition, the conference agreement provides that for purposes of the nondiscrimination rules applicable to tax-sheltered annuity programs, the general rules regarding aggregation of employers and testing on a line of business or operating unit basis shall apply under the rules prescribed by the Secretary. The Secretary may provide for a narrower definition of employer for purposes of the rules applicable to elective deferrals.

Effective date

The application of the nondiscrimination rules to tax-sheltered annuity programs is effective for plan years beginning after December 31, 1988.

[House Committee Report]

Before-death and after-death distribution rules

The bill clarifies the required beginning date for distributions from or under qualified plans, tax-sheltered annuities, and IRAs and extends to tax-sheltered annuities the distribution rules applicable to qualified plans. As noted above, under current law, in the case of a 5-percent owner, distributions from a qualified plan must commence no later than April 1 of the calendar year following the year in which the 5-percent owner attains age 70 ½. The bill clarifies that an individual is considered to be a 5-percent owner for a calendar year if the individual was a 5-percent owner (within the meaning of section 416(i)(1)(B)) at any time during the plan year ending in the calendar year in which the individual attains age 70 ½, or during any of the four preceding plan years. The bill also clarifies that if an employee becomes a 5-percent owner in a plan year subsequent to the plan year in which the employee attained age 70 ½, the required beginning date is April 1 of the calendar year following the calendar year in which ends the plan year that the employee becomes a 5-percent owner.

The bill clarifies that distributions from IRAs are to commence no later than April 1 of the calendar year following the year in which the owner of the IRA attains age 70 ½, without regard to whether the owner has retired. In addition, the bill clarifies that distributions from IRAs are subject to the incidental death benefit rules applicable to qualified plans.

Under the bill, the required beginning date and the general before-death and after-death distribution rules applicable to qualified plans also apply to amounts held under tax-sheltered annuity contracts (including custodial accounts held by regulated investment companies and to retirement income accounts provided by churches, etc.) The qualified plan distribution rules extended to tax-sheltered annuities by the bill would apply only to benefits accrued under the contract after the June 30 or December 31, next following the issuance of Treasury regulations under the qualified plan distribution rules. With respect to the majority of tax-sheltered annuities and accounts, which are structured as defined contribution plans, contributions and earnings thereon would be treated as benefit accruals for purposes of this rule. The bill also codifies the requirement that distributions from a tax-sheltered annuity satisfy the incidental death benefits rule. As a result of the amendments to section 403(b) made by the bill, if a tax-sheltered annuity fails to satisfy the distribution requirements (in form or in operation), then the amounts held under the contract are to be included in the employee's gross income (sec. 403(c)).

[Senate Committee Report]

* * *

The bill clarifies that distributions from IRAs are to commence no later than April 1 of the calendar year following the year in which the owner of the IRA attains age 70 ½, without regard to whether the owner has retired. In addition, the bill clarifies that distributions from IRAs are subject to the incidental death benefit rules applicable to qualified plans.

The bill repeals the exception to the required distribution rules applicable to amounts held by an ESOP, which are subject to the 84-month rule of Code Section 409(a). Instead, the bill provides an exception to the 84-month rule for amounts required to be distributed under the required distribution rules for qualified plans.

Further, the bill provides that amounts required to be distributed from a qualified plan or IRA under the required distribution rules are not eligible for rollover treatment. This rule ensures that an individual will not be able to circumvent the required distribution rules by taking a required distribution at year's end and rolling over that distribution before or after the beginning of the next year. This restriction would apply only to the amounts required to be distributed. Thus, individuals would not be prevented from rolling over those distributions that (1) exceed the minimum required distribution, or (2) occur during a year in which no minimum distribution is required. For this purpose, the first amounts distributed to an individual during a taxable year are treated as amounts required to be distributed.

[Conference Committee Report]

* * *

The conference agreement follows the Senate amendment with the following exceptions.

a. Tax-sheltered annuities.—The provision in the House bill requiring that distributions commence under a tax-sheltered annuity no later than when the employee attains age 70 ½ is adopted.

* * *

For committee reports on P.L. 98-369, see ¶ 11,750.045.

[¶ 11,800.055]

Committee Report on P.L. 96-222 (Technical Corrections Act of 1979)

[Senate Committee Report]

Prior to the Revenue Act of 1978, recipients of distributions under a tax-sheltered annuity purchased by certain employers which are tax-exempt organizations or public schools were not eligible to defer tax on those distributions by rolling the distributions over to an individual retirement plan (an individual retirement account or annuity, or a retirement bond). The Act permits the recipient of a lump-sum distribution from a tax-sheltered annuity to defer tax on the distribution by rolling it over within 60 days of receipt to an IRA or to another tax-sheltered annuity. Due to a clerical error, as enacted, the rollover provision applies to distributions or transfers made after December 31, 1978, in taxable years beginning after that date.

The conferees on the Revenue Act of 1978 intended that the tax-sheltered annuity rollover provisions would be available for lump sum distributions received after December 31, 1977. To carry out the original intent of the conferees, the committee believes it is necessary to provide an extended rollover period for recipients of distributions in 1978 who could not have satisfied the requirement that amounts distributed must be rolled over within 60 days of receipt.

The bill makes the tax-sheltered annuity rollover provisions effective for distributions or transfers made after December 31, 1977, in taxable years beginning after that date. In addition, the bill provides that the recipient of a qualifying distribution in 1978 will have until December 31, 1980, to complete a rollover to either an IRA or another tax-sheltered annuity. Upon completion of the rollover, the recipient of a qualifying distribution in 1978 will be able to amend his or her 1978 income tax return to take into account the portion of the distribution originally included in income which is no longer subject to tax because of the rollover.

The bill also makes a clerical amendment to Code sections 403(b)(1) and 4973(c)(1) by inserting "409(b)(3)(C)" in lieu of "409(d)(3)(C)".

This provision is effective as if it had been included in the Revenue Act of 1978 as enacted.

[¶ 11,800.06]

Committee Report on P.L. 95-600 (Revenue Act of 1978)

Sec. 154—Custodial accounts for regulated investment company stock.

[Senate Committee Report]

The bill permits stock of a regulated investment company to qualify under the tax-sheltered annuity rules if the stock cannot be distributed before the employee retires, dies, separates from service, becomes disabled, attains age 59 ½, or encounters financial hardship, such as unusual medical expenses.

The amendment applies for taxable years beginning after December 31, 1978.

Sec. 156—Rollovers of tax-sheltered annuities—Conference Committee Report.

***Senate amendment* * * ***

The Senate amendment permits recipients of a "lump-sum distribution" from a tax-sheltered annuity to defer tax on the distribution by rolling it over within 60 days of receipt to an individual retirement arrangement or to another tax-sheltered annuity. This provision will apply to distributions or transfers made after December 31, [1978], in taxable years beginning after that date.

Conference agreement

The conference agreement follows the Senate amendment but makes technical changes to coordinate the Senate amendment with the technical changes to the individual retirement account provisions made by another provision of the bill. Thus, under the conference agreement, the recipient of a lump-sum distribution from an annuity contract described in section 403(b)(1) or a custodial account which meets the requirements of section 403(b)(7) will be eligible to completely or partially roll over the otherwise taxable portion of such distribution to an individual retirement plan. Subsequently, the amount rolled over to the individual retirement plan plus earnings, could be rolled over to another annuity contract or custodial account, but could not be rolled into a tax-qualified retirement plan.

Sec. 157(g)(2)—Rollover by surviving spouse. The House Committee Report on Sec. 157(g) is at ¶ 11,750.06.

[¶ 11,800.07]

Committee Report on P.L. 95-458 (Excise Tax—Trucks, Buses, etc.)

The Report of the Senate Finance Committee on P.L. 95-458 is reproduced at ¶ 11,750.07.

[¶ 11,800.08]

Committee Report on P.L. 94-455 (Tax Reform Act of 1976)

The amendment would permit an investment in stock on a closed-end investment company to qualify for treatment as a tax-sheltered annuity by deleting the provision in present law that limits qualifying investments in regulated investment companies to investments in those which only issue redeemable stock.

Effective date

This amendment would apply to taxable years beginning after December 31, 1975.—Senate Finance Committee Report.

[¶ 11,800.09]

Committee Report on P.L. 94-267 (IRC of 1954—Employee Retirement)

The Report of the House Committee on P.L. 94-267 is reproduced at ¶ 11,750.09.

[¶ 11,800A.09]

Committee Report on P.L. 94-455 (Tax Reform Act of 1976)

[Senate Committee Report]

Present law

Under present law, in general, an employee's contributions to a tax qualified retirement plan maintained by his employer are not tax deductible. In the case of a salary reduction plan, or a cash and deferred profit-sharing plan, however, the Internal Revenue Service has permitted employees to exclude from income certain amounts contributed by their employers to the plan, even where the source of these amounts is the employee's agreement to take salary or bonus reductions, or forego salary increases.

On December 6, 1972, the Service issued proposed regulations which would have changed this result in the case of salary reduction plans, and which called into question the continued viability of the treatment of cash and deferred profit-sharing plans.

In order to allow time for congressional study of these areas, section 2006 of the Employee Retirement Income Security Act of 1974 (ERISA) provided for a temporary freeze of the status quo. Under ERISA, contributions to plans in existence on June 27, 1974, are governed under the law as it was applied prior to January 1, 1972 and this treatment is to continue at least through December 31, 1976, or (if later) until regulations are issued in final form in this area, which would change the pre-1972 administration of the law. Section 2006 of ERISA provides that these regulations, if issued, are not to be retroactive for purposes of the social security taxes or the Federal withholding taxes, and are not to be retroactive prior to January 1, 1977, for Federal income tax purposes.

In the case of plans not in existence on June 27, 1974, contributions made on a salary reduction basis, or made, at the employee's option, to a cash and deferred profit-sharing plan, are treated as employee contributions (until January 1, 1977, or until new regulations are prescribed in this area). This was intended to prevent a situation where a new plan might begin in reliance on pre-1972 law while Congress has not yet determined what the law should be in the future.

Also to be covered under these principles are so-called "cafeteria plans," under which the employees may have a choice between certain fringe benefits, some of which would constitute taxable income to the employee, whereas other forms of benefit might not. Thus, cafteria plans in existence on June 27, 1974, also are governed under the pre-1972 law until at least January 1, 1977. However, in the case of new plans, the value of any benefits selected under a cafeteria plan are to be includable in income until at least January 1, 1977 (or, if later, until new regulations in this area have been promulgated). In general, the same rules to be applied in determining whether or not a salary reduction plan was in existence on June 27, 1974, are also to be applied to cafeteria plans. Of course, minor plan amendments (such as changing the plan to allow cash payments to cover cases of breakage, i.e., where two alternative benefits available under the cafeteria plan do not have exactly the same value) would not cause an existing plan to be classified as a new plan for purposes of these rules.

Reasons for change

The committee believes it is not possible to study adequately the questions involved in order to enact permanent legislation regarding salary reduction and cash and deferred profit-sharing plans prior to the January 1, 1977 end of the temporary freeze of the status quo provided for in section 2006 of ERISA. The committee therefore decided to extend the time for the congressional review of the treatment of these plans.

Explanation of provision

In order to allow additional time for congressional study of these areas, the committee amendment would extend the temporary freeze from January 1, 1977, until January 1, 1979.

The committee amendment is effective on the date of enactment of the Act.

[Conference Committee Report]

House bill

No provision.

Senate amendment

On December 6, 1972, the IRS issued proposed regulations which would have changed the tax treatment of salary reduction, cafeteria, and cash or deferred profit-sharing plans. In order to allow time for congressional study of these areas, section 2006 of ERISA provided for a temporary freeze of the status quo until December 31, 1976. Under the Senate amendment the temporary freeze of the status quo (under which plans established before June 27, 1974, are governed by the law in effect prior to the 1972 proposed regulations) would be extended until January 1, 1978.

Conference agreement

The conference agreement follows the Senate amendment.

[¶ 11,800A.10]

Committee Report on P.L. 93-406 (Employee Retirement Income Security Act of 1974

[Conference Committee Explanation]

Under present law, in general, an employee's contributions to a qualified retirement plan maintained by his employer are not tax deductible. In the case of a salary reduction plan, or a cash or deferred profit-sharing plan, however, the Internal Revenue Service has permitted employees to exclude from income certain amounts contributed by their employers to the plan, even where the source of these amounts is the employee's agreement to take salary or bonus reductions, or forego salary increases.

On December 6, 1972, the Service issued proposed regulations which would have changed this result in the case of salary reduction plans, and which called into question the continued viability of the treatment of cash and deferred profit-sharing plans.

In order to allow time for congressional study of these areas, the conference substitute provides for a temporary freeze of the status quo. Thus, contributions to plans in existence on June 27, 1974, are to be governed under the law as it was applied prior to January 1, 1972. This treatment is to continue at least through December 31, 1976, or (if later) until regulations are issued in final form in this area, which would change the pre-1972 administration of the law. These regulations, if issued, are not to be retroactive for purposes of the social security taxes or the Federal withholding taxes, and are not to be retroactive prior to January 1, 1977, for Federal income tax purposes.

In the case of plans not in existence on June 27, 1974, contributions made on a salary reduction basis, or made, at the employee's option, to a cash or deferred profit-sharing plan, are to be treated as employee contributions (until January 1, 1977, or until new regulations are prescribed in this area). This will prevent a situation where a new plan might begin in reliance on pre-1972 law while Congress has not yet determined what the law should be in the future.

Generally a plan will be treated as having been established on June 27, 1974, if the plan had been reduced to writing and had been adopted and approved by the directors on or before that date, even if contributions had not yet been made to the plan on a salary reduction basis.[1] New participants may, of course, be added to an existing plan in the normal course of business.

Also to be covered under these principles are so-called cafeteria plans, under which the employees may have a choice between certain fringe benefits, some of which would constitute taxable income to the employee, whereas other forms of benefit might not. Thus, existing cafeteria plans also are to be governed under pre-1972 law until at least January 1, 1977. However, in the case of new plans, the value of any benefits selected under a cafeteria plan are [sic] to be includable in income until at least January 1, 1977 (or, if later, until new regulations in this area have been promulgated). In general, the same rules to be applied in determining whether or not a salary reduction plan was in existence on June 27, 1974, are also to be applied to cafeteria plans. Of course, minor plan amendments (such as changing the plan to allow cash payments to cover cases of breakage, i.e., where two alternative benefits available under the cafeteria plan do not have exactly the same value) would not cause an existing plan to be classified as a new plan for purposes of these rules.

The conferees agree with the statements in the Ways and Means Committee report (No. 93-807) to the effect that there should be no inferences drawn from this action as to whether or not the pre-1972 application of the law is, or is not, correct, or as to whether new regulations in this area should, or should not, be issued, or as to what these regulations, if any, should provide.

[Code Sec. 404]

[¶ 11,850.039]

Committee Report on P.L. 109-280 (Pension Protection Act of 2006)

[Joint Committee on Taxation Report]

Single-employer defined benefit pension plans

General deduction limit

Under the bill, for taxable years beginning in 2006 and 2007, in the case of contributions to a single-employer defined benefit plan, the maximum deductible amount is not less than the excess (if any) of (1) 150 percent of the plan's current liability, over (2) the value of plan assets.

For taxable years beginning after 2007, in the case of contributions to a single-employer defined benefit pension plan, the maximum deductible amount is equal to the greater of: (1) the excess (if any) of the sum of the plan's funding target, the plan's target normal cost, and a cushion amount for a plan year, over the value of plan assets (as determined under the minimum funding rules[160]); and (2) the minimum required contribution for the plan year.[161]

However, in the case of a plan that is not in at-risk status, the first amount above is not less than the excess (if any) of the sum of the plan's funding target and target normal cost, determined as if the plan was in at-risk status, over the value of plan assets.

The cushion amount for a plan year is the sum of (1) 50 percent of the plan's funding target for the plan year; and (2) the amount by which the plan's funding target would increase if determined by taking into account increases in participants' compensation for future years or, if the plan does not base benefits attributable to past service on compensation, increases in benefits that are expected to occur in succeeding plans year, determined on the basis of average annual benefit increases over the previous six years.[162] For this purpose, the dollar limits on benefits and on compensation apply, but, in the case of a plan that is covered by the PBGC insurance program, increases in the compensation limit (under sec. 401(a)(17)) that are expected to occur in succeeding plan years may be taken into account.[163] The rules relating to projecting compensation for future years are intended solely to enable employers to reduce volatility in pension contributions; the rules are not intended to create any inference that employees have any protected interest with respect to such projected increases.

Overall deduction limit

Under the bill, in applying the overall deduction limit to contributions to one or more defined benefit pension plans and one or more defined contribution plans for years beginning after December 31, 2007, single-employer defined benefit pension plans that are covered by the PBGC insurance program are not taken into account. Thus, the deduction for contributions to a defined benefit pension plan or a defined contribution plan is not affected by the overall deduction limit merely because employees are covered by both plans if the defined benefit plan is covered by the PBGC insurance program (i.e., the separate deduction limits for contributions to defined contribution plans and defined benefit pension plans apply). In addition, in applying the overall deduction limit, the amount necessary to meet the minimum funding requirement with respect to a single-employer defined benefit pension plan that is not covered by the PBGC insurance program is treated as not less than the plan's funding shortfall (as determined under the minimum funding rules).

Multiemployer defined benefit pension plans

General deduction limit

Under the bill, for taxable years beginning after 2005, in the case of contributions to a multiemployer defined benefit pension plan, the maximum deductible amount is not less than the excess (if any) of (1) 140 percent of the plan's current liability, over (2) the value of plan assets.

Overall deduction limit

Under the bill, for taxable years beginning after December 31, 2005, in applying the overall deduction limit to contributions to one or more defined benefit pension plans and one or more defined contribution plans, multiemployer plans are not taken into account. Thus, the deduction for contributions to a defined benefit pension plan or a defined contribution plan is not affected by the overall deduction limit merely because employees are covered by both plans if either plan is a multiemployer plan (i.e., the separate deduction limits for contributions to defined contribution plans and defined benefit pension plans apply).

Effective Date

The effective dates of the provisions regarding deductions are described above under each provision.

Updating deduction rules for combination of plans

Under the bill, the overall limit on employer deductions for contributions to combinations of defined benefit and defined contribution plans applies to contributions to one or more defined contribution plans only to the extent that such contributions exceed six percent of compensation otherwise paid or accrued during the taxable year to the beneficiaries under the plans. As under present law, for purposes of determining the excise tax on nondeductible contributions, matching contributions to a defined contribution plan that are nondeductible solely because of the overall deduction limit are disregarded.

Effective Date

The provision is effective for contributions for taxable years beginning after December 31, 2005.

[¶ 11,850.042]

Committee Report on P.L. 107-16 (Economic Growth and Tax Relief Reconciliation Act)

[House Committee Report]

Deductions for ESOP dividends

In addition to the deductions permitted under present law for dividends paid with respect to employer securities that are held by an ESOP, an employer is entitled to deduct dividends that, at the election of plan participants or their beneficiaries, are (1) payable in cash directly to plan participants or beneficiaries, (2) paid to the plan and subsequently distributed to the participants or beneficiaries in cash no later than 90 days after the close of the plan year in which the dividends are paid to the plan, or (3) paid to the plan and reinvested in qualifying employer securities.

The provision permits the Secretary to disallow the deduction for any ESOP dividend if the Secretary determines that the dividend constitutes, in substance, the avoidance or evasion of taxation.

Effective Date

The provision is effective for taxable years beginning after December 31, 2001.

[Conference Committee Report]

Senate Amendment

In addition to the deductions permitted under present law for dividends paid with respect to employer securities that are held by an ESOP, an employer is entitled to deduct the applicable percentage of dividends that, at the election of plan participants or their beneficiaries, are (1) payable in cash directly to plan participants or beneficiaries, (2) paid to the plan and subsequently distributed to the participants or beneficiaries in cash no later than 90 days after the close of the plan year in which the dividends are paid to the plan, or (3) paid to the plan and reinvested in qualifying employer securities. The applicable percentage is 25 percent for 2002 through 2004, 50 percent for 2005 through 2007, 75 percent for 2008 through 2010 and 100 percent for 2011 and thereafter.

---

[1] Where shareholder approval is required for formal adoption of the plan, such shareholder approval must also have occurred by June 27, 1974.

[160] In determining the maximum deductible amount, the value of plan assets is not reduced by any pre-funding balance or funding standard account carryover balance.

[161] The bill retains the present-law rule, under which, in the case of a single-employer plan covered by the PBGC that terminates during the year, the maximum deductible amount is generally not less than the amount needed to make the plan assets sufficient to fund benefit liabilities as defined for purposes of the PBGC termination insurance program.

[162] In determining the cushion amount for a plan with 100 or fewer participants, a plan's funding target does not include the liability attributable to benefit increases for highly compensated employees resulting from a plan amendment that is made or becomes effective, whichever is later, within the last two years.

[163] Expected increases in the limitations on benefits under section 415, however, may not be taken into account.

Conference Agreement

The conference agreement follows the House bill. The provision of the conference agreement that authorizes the Secretary to disallow the deduction for any ESOP dividend if the Secretary determines that the dividend constitutes, in substance, the avoidance or evasion of taxation includes authority to disallow a deduction of unreasonable dividends. For purposes of the section 404(k)(2)(A)(iii) reinvested dividends, a dividend paid on common stock that is primarily and regularly traded on an established securities market would be reasonable. In addition, for this purpose in the case of employers with no common stock (determined on a controlled group basis) that is primarily and regularly traded on an established securities market, the reasonableness of a dividend is determined by comparing the dividend rate on stock held by the ESOP with the dividend rate for common stock of comparable corporations whose stock is primarily and regularly traded on an established securities market. Whether a corporation is comparable is determined by comparing relevant corporate characteristics such as industry, corporate size, earnings, debt-equity structure and dividend history.

[¶ 11,850.044]

Committee Report on P.L. 107-16 (Economic Growth and Tax Relief Reconciliation Act)

[Senate Committee Report]

Deduction of unfunded current liability

Deduction for contributions to fund termination liability.—The special rule allowing a deduction for unfunded current liability generally is extended to all defined benefit pension plans, i.e., the provision applies to multiemployer plans and plans with 100 or fewer participants. The special rule does not apply to plans not covered by the PBGC termination insurance program.[1]

The provision also modifies the special rule by providing that the deduction is for up to 100 percent of unfunded termination liability, determined as if the plan terminated at the end of the plan year. In the case of a plan with less than 100 participants for the plan year, termination liability does not include the liability attributable to benefit increases for highly compensated employees resulting from a plan amendment which was made or became effective, whichever is later, within the last two years.

Effective Date

The provision is effective for plan years beginning after December 31, 2001.

[Conference Committee Report]

Senate Amendment

* * *

Effective Date

The Senate amendment is effective for plan years beginning after December 31, 2001.

Conference Agreement

The conference agreement follows the Senate amendment, with modifications.

* * *

With respect to the special rule allowing a deduction for unfunded current liability, the modification of the rule to provide that the deduction is for up to 100 percent of unfunded termination liability is applicable only for a plan that terminates within the plan year.

[¶ 11,850.046]

Committee Report on P.L. 107-16 (Economic Growth and Tax Relief Reconciliation Act)

[Senate Committee Report]

Definition of compensation for deduction purposes

Under the provision, the definition of compensation for purposes of the deduction rules includes salary reduction amounts treated as compensation under section 415. In addition, the annual limitation on the amount of deductible contributions to a profit-sharing or stock bonus plan is increased from 15 percent to 25 percent of compensation of the employees covered by the plan for the year. Also, except to the extent provided in regulations, a money purchase pension plan is treated like a profit-sharing or stock bonus plan for purposes of the deduction rules.

Effective Date

The provision is effective for years beginning after December 31, 2001.

[Conference Committee Report]

The conference agreement follows the Senate amendment.

[¶ 11,850.048]

Committee Report on P.L. 107-16 (Economic Growth and Tax Relief Reconciliation Act)

[House Committee Report]

Deduction limits and elective deferrals

Under the provision, elective deferral contributions are not subject to the deduction limits, and the application of a deduction limitation to any other employer contribution to a qualified retirement plan does not take into account elective deferral contributions.

Effective Date

The provision is effective for years beginning after December 31, 2001.

[Conference Committee Report]

The conference agreement follows the House bill.

[¶ 11,850.050]

Committee Report on P.L. 104-188 (Small Business Job Protection Act)

Miscellaneous Pension Simplification

[Managers' Amendment to H.R. 3448]

Church pension plan simplification

Special rules for chaplains and self-employed ministers.—The amendment would allow self-employed ministers to participate in a church plan. For purposes of the definition of a church plan, a self-employed minister would be treated as his or her own employer and as if the employer were a tax-exempt organization under section 501(c)(3). The earned income of the self-employed minister would be treated as his or her compensation. Self-employed ministers would be able to deduct their contributions.

In addition, ministers employed by an organization other than a church would be treated as if employed by a church. Thus, such ministers could also participate in a church plan. The amendment would provide that if a minister is employed by an employer that is not eligible to maintain a church plan, the minister would not be taken into account by that employer in applying nondiscrimination rules.

The amendment would permit retirement income accounts to be established for self-employed ministers.

* * *

Effective Date

The amendment would be effective for years beginning after December 31, 1996.

[Conference Committee Report]

The conference agreement follows the Senate amendment with technical modifications.

[¶ 11,850.052]

Committee Report on P.L. 103-465 (General Agreement on Tariffs and Trade (GATT); Retirement Protection Act)

[House Committee Report]

ERISA citations

The bill provides that the references to ERISA in Code section 404(g) are to ERISA as in effect on the date of enactment [December 8, 1994] of the bill.

Effective date

The provision is effective on the date of enactment [December 8, 1994].

[1] The PBGC termination insurance program does not cover plans of professional service employers that have fewer than 25 participants.

[¶ 11,850.054]

Committee Report on P.L. 102-318 (Unemployment Compensation Amendments of 1992)

For Committee Report on Unemployment Compensation Amendments of 1992 (P.L. 102-318), dealing with rollovers and withholding on nonperiodic pension distributions, see ¶ 11,750.036.

[¶ 11,850.055]

Committee Report on P.L. 101-239 (Omnibus Budget Reconciliation Act of 1989)

[House Committee Report]

Deduction for payments relating to standard terminations

The deduction rule relating to employer liability payments treated as contributions to qualified plans is amended to clarify that the rule applies in the case of standard terminations, effective for payments made after January 1, 1986, in taxable years ending after that date.

[¶ 11,850.056]

Committee Reports on P.L. 100-647 (Technical and Miscellaneous Revenue Act of 1988)

[Senate Committee Report]

Under the bill, increases in the $200,000 limit on includible compensation may not be taken into account before they occur in determining the deduction limit for contributions to a qualified plan. Similarly, such increases may not be taken into account before they occur in calculating the full funding limitation (as determined under sec. 412).

Further, the bill makes it clear that the $200,000 cap on includible compensation does not apply, under present law, in the case of an employer's deduction for benefits provided under a nonqualified deferred compensation plan.

[Senate Committee Report]

To take into account SEPs that are maintained on the basis of the employer's taxable year, the bill provides that, in the case of such SEPs, the 15 percent of compensation limitation applies to compensation paid during the employer's taxable year.

[Senate Committee Report]

Aggregation of All Defined Benefit Plans

The bill clarifies that the aggregation of all defined benefit plans only applies for purposes of determining whether a plan has more than 100 participants. Thus, the aggregation rule does not require that all defined benefit plans of the employer be aggregated for purposes of determining whether the plan has unfunded current liability.

The bill deletes the language that specifies that assets are not reduced by the credit balance in the funding standard account for purposes of calculating unfunded current liability under the deduction rule. This language is no longer necessary because, under the bill, unfunded current liability is calculated without such a reduction, except for purposes of the new minimum funding rules or as provided by the Secretary (see above). It is intended that the Secretary will not provide for such a reduction for purposes of this deduction rule.

For purposes of the overall deduction limit, the bill provides that, in the case of a defined benefit plan (other than a multiemployer plan) with more than 100 participants, the amount necessary to satisfy the minimum funding standard is not less than the unfunded current liability of the plan. This change conforms the overall deduction limit to the rule permitting deductions up to unfunded current liability.

[¶ 11,850.058]

Committee Reports on P.L. 99-514 (Tax Reform Act of 1986)

[Conference Committee Report]

Present Law

In general

The contributions of an employer to a qualified plan are deductible in the year for which the contributions are paid, within limits. No deduction is allowed, however, for a contribution that is not an ordinary and necessary business expense or an expense for the production of income. The deduction limits applicable to an employer's contribution depend on the type of plan to which the contribution is made and may depend on whether an employee covered by the plan is also covered by another plan of the employer. Under the Code, if a contribution for a year exceeds the deduction limits, then the excess generally may be deducted in succeeding years as a carryover. Deductions are not allowed with respect to contributions or benefits in excess of the overall limits on contributions or benefits.

Profit-sharing and stock bonus plans

In the case of a qualified profit-sharing or stock bonus plan, employer contributions for a year not in excess of 15 percent of the aggregate compensation of covered employees are generally deductible for the year paid. Under the Code, if employer contributions for a group of employees for a particular year exceed the deduction limits, then the excess may be carried over and deducted in later years. On the other hand, if the contribution for a particular year is lower than the deduction limit, then the unused limitation may be carried over and used in later years. In the case of a limitation carryover, the amount deducted in a later year is not to exceed 25 percent of the aggregate compensation of employees covered by the plan during that year.

Defined benefit pension plans

In general

Employer contributions under a defined benefit pension plan are required to meet a minimum funding standard. The deduction allowed by the Code for an employer's contribution to a defined benefit pension plan is limited to the greatest of the following amounts:

(1) The amount necessary to meet the minimum funding standard for plan years ending with or within the taxable year.

(2) The level amount (or percentage of compensation) necessary to provide for the remaining unfunded cost of the past and current service credits of all employees under the plan over the remaining future service of each employee. Under the Code, however, if the remaining unfunded cost with respect to any three individuals is more than 50 percent of the cost for all employees, then the cost attributable to each of those employees is spread over at least five taxable years.

(3) An amount equal to the normal cost of the plan plus, if past service or certain other credits are provided, an amount necessary to amortize those credits in equal annual payments over 10 years. Generally, this rule permits contributions in excess of the contributions required by the minimum funding standard.

Certain excess contributions

The minimum funding standard includes provisions (the full funding limitation) designed to eliminate the requirement that additional employer contributions be made for a period during which it is fully funded. The funding standard, however, does not prohibit employers from making contributions in excess of the full funding limitation.

Employer contributions in excess of the deduction limits provided by the Code are not currently deductible. A deduction carryover is generally allowed, however, for employer contributions to a qualified plan in excess of the deductible limits.

A pension, profit-sharing, or stock bonus plan does not meet the requirements of the Code for qualified status unless it is for the exclusive benefit of employees and their beneficiaries. Under some circumstances, employer contributions in excess of the level for which a deduction is allowed may indicate that the plan is not being maintained for the exclusive benefit of employees.

Money purchase pension plans

Employer contributions to a money purchase plan are generally deductible under the same rules that apply to defined benefit pension plans. Under a qualified money purchase pension plan, the amount required under the minimum funding standard is the contribution rate specified by the plan.

Combination of pension and other plans

If an employer maintains a pension plan (defined benefit or money purchase) and either a profit-sharing or a stock bonus plan for the same employee for the same year, then the employer's deduction for contributions for that year is generally limited to the greater of the contribution necessary to meet the minimum funding requirements of the pension plan for the year or 25 percent of the aggregate compensation of employees covered by the plans for the year. Deduction and limitation carryovers are provided.

House Bill

The House bill repeals the limit carryforward applicable to profit-sharing and stock bonus plans, extends the combined plan deduction limit to a combination of a defined benefit and a money purchase pension plan, requires that certain social security taxes be taken into account in applying the 15 percent and 25 percent of compensation deduction limits, and imposes a 10-percent excise tax on nondeductible contributions to qualified plans.

The provisions of the House bill relating to deduction limits generally apply to employer taxable years beginning after December 31, 1985. However, certain unused pre-1986 limit carryforwards are not affected by the provision generally repealing limit carryforwards.

Senate Amendment

The Senate amendment is the same as the House bill except that (1) the Senate amendment does not require that certain social security taxes be taken into account in applying the 15 percent and 25 percent of compensation deduction limits, and (2) the Senate amendment does not impose an excise tax on nondeductible contributions to qualified plans. The Senate amendment also clarifies that a fully insured plan (sec. 412(i)) is treated as a defined benefit pension plan for purposes of the combined plan deduction limit.

The Senate amendment is effective for employer taxable years beginning after December 31, 1986.

Conference Agreement

In general

The conference agreement generally follows the Senate amendment with modifications. The conference agreement adopts the House bill applying a 10-percent excise tax to nondeductible employer contributions. The conferees clarify that, with respect to an employer that is exempt from tax, the 10-percent excise tax is to apply to contributions that would, if the employer were not exempt, be nondeductible. The conference agreement also imposes a limit of $200,000 on the amount of compensation that may be taken into account in computing deductions for plan contributions. The limit is to be adjusted for cost-of-living increases at the time and in the manner provided for adjusting the overall limits on annual benefits under a qualified defined benefit pension plan (sec. 415(d)).

Fully insured plans

The conference agreement includes a technical modification relating to fully insured plans which provides that the annual premium payments are deemed to be the amount required to meet the minimum funding requirements in the case of a fully insured plan.

Effective date

The provisions are effective for taxable years beginning after December 31, 1986.

[¶ 11,850.06]

Committee Report on P.L. 99-272 (Consolidated Omnibus Budget Reconciliation Act)

Conference Committee Report

The conference agreement provides rules as to the deductibility of payments to the PBGC and the termination trust.

[¶ 11,850.061]

Committee Reports on P.L. 98-369 (Tax Reform Act of 1984)

[Senate Committee Report]

The bill permits a deduction for dividends paid on stock held by an ESOP (including a tax credit ESOP), provided the dividends are either paid out currently to employees or used to repay an ESOP loan. Dividends may either be paid directly to plan participants by the corporation or may be paid to the plan and distributed to participants no later than 60 days [90 days, in Conference bill—CCH] after the close of the plan year in which paid.

* * *

Because such dividends are deductible to the employer corporation, they do not qualify for the partial exclusion from income otherwise permitted under Code section 116.

Effective Date

The provisions of the bill are generally effective for years beginning after December 31, 1984.

[Conference Committee Report]

The conference agreement generally follows the Senate amendment. The deduction for dividends paid with respect to stock held in an ESOP will be permitted only if the dividends are paid out currently to employees.

[House Committee Report]

The bill provides that, for purposes of determining the maximum allowable deduction of a self-employed individual for contributions to a qualified plan, the earned income of the self-employed individual is determined without regard to the deductions allowable for contributions to a qualified pension, etc., plan.

The bill amends the effective date of the repeal of the special deduction rules for defined contribution H.R. 10 plans to clarify that the rules do not apply to a qualified defined benefit H.R. 10 plan.

The bill amends the limit on deductions by employees for employer contributions to SEPs to conform with the dollar limit on annual additions to qualified defined contribution plans. Accordingly, the bill raises the dollar limit on employee deductions to $30,000.

The bill also repeals the following provisions relating to self-employed individuals:

(1) the rule relating to the return of excess contributions made on behalf of a self-employed individual prior to the due date of the annual return;

(2) the special limit on contributions by an employer on behalf of an owner-employee to pay premiums or other consideration for an annuity, endowment, or life insurance contract on the life of the owner-employee issued under an H.R. 10 plan;

(3) certain special deduction rules applicable to plans benefiting self-employed individuals or shareholder-employees; and

(4) the special limitation applicable to certain level premium annuity contracts under plans benefiting owner-employees.

Also, see ¶ 13,155.09 for committee reports on extended vacation pay plans.

[¶ 11,850.062]

Committee Report on P.L. 97-34 (Economic Recovery Tax Act of 1981)

[House Committee Report]

Increased contribution limit; excess contributions.—In general, the bill increases the deduction limit for employer contributions to defined contribution H.R. 10 plans, defined contribution plans maintained by subchapter S corporations, and SEPs to $15,000. The 15-percent limit on contributions is not changed. In addition, the bill provides that if an excess contribution is made, the six-percent excise tax on the excess contribution will not apply if the excess, together with any net income attributable to it, is withdrawn from the plan on or before the date for filing the return for the taxable year (including extensions). This rule corresponds to a rule for excess contributions made to IRAs.

For defined benefit H.R. 10 or subchapter S corporation plans, the compensation taken into account in determining permitted annual benefit accruals is increased to $100,000. The bill continues the requirement of present law under which an increase in the compensation taken into account to determine benefit accruals under a plan is treated as starting a new period of plan participation.

Increase in includible compensation.—Under the bill, the maximum amount of compensation which may be used to determine contributions in an H.R. 10 or subchapter S plan, or a SEP is increased from $100,000 to $200,000. However, if annual compensation in excess of $100,000 is taken into account under the plan, the rate of employer contributions for a plan participant who is a common-law employee cannot be less than the equivalent of 7 ½ percent of that participant's compensation. Of course, as under present law, the amount actually contributed to a particular plan for a participant will be less if the plan is integrated with social security. Also, contributions or benefits under another qualified plan of the employer may be taken into account for the purpose of determining whether the 7 ½-percent minimum is met.

Employee borrowing.—The bill extends all partners the present law rule under which a loan from an H.R. 10 plan, or the use of an interest in the plan as security for a loan, is treated as a distribution.

Plan termination distributions.—The bill provides that the present-law rule which precludes future contributions to an H.R. 10 plan for an owner-employee after certain distributions are made to the owner-employee will not apply with respect to a distribution made on account of plan termination.

Effective dates

These provisions generally are effective for taxable years beginning after December 31, 1981. However, the bill provides a transitional rule for a loan outstanding on December 31, 1981, to a partner who is not an owner-employee. Such a loan will not be treated as a distribution from the plan unless renegotiated, extended, renewed or revised after that date.

[Conference Committee Report]

House bill

The deduction limit for employer contributions to a defined contribution Keogh plan, to a defined contribution plan maintained by a subchapter S corporation, or to a simplified employee pension (SEP) is increased from $7,500 to $15,000. The 15-percent limit on contributions is not changed. To provide a similar increase in the level of benefits permitted under a defined benefit Keogh or subchapter S corporation plan, the compensation taken into account in determining permitted annual benefit accruals is increased from $50,000 to $100,000.

The bill also increases the amount of compensation which may be taken into account to determine contributions to a Keogh plan, to a subchapter S plan, or to a SEP. Under the bill, the includible compensation limit is increased from $100,000 to $200,000. However, if annual compensation in excess of $100,000 is taken into account the rate of employer contributions for a plan participant who is a common-law employee cannot be less than the equivalent of 7 ½ percent of that participant's compensation.

The House bill also extends to all partners the present-law rule under which a loan from a Keogh plan to an owner-employee or his use of an interest in the plan as security for a loan is treated as a distribution.

In addition, the House bill permits (1) the penalty-free correction of an excess contribution to a Keogh plan if the excess is withdrawn before the return filing due date and (2) early withdrawals from a terminated Keogh plan by an owner-employee without regard to the 5-year ban on Keogh plan contributions for the owner-employee.

Senate amendment

The Senate amendment generally follows the House bill except that it contains no provision relating to excess contributions to Keogh plans or distributions made on account of the termination of a Keogh plan.

Conference agreement

The conference agreement follows the House bill.

[¶ 11,850.063]

Committee Report on P.L. 96-364 (Multiemployer Pension Plan Amendments Act of 1980)

[Senate Committee Report]

Deductibility of employer liability payments

Present law

Under present law, an employer is allowed a deduction for a contribution to a qualified pension plan for its employees. The deduction is allowed (within limits) in the taxable year for which the contribution is made.[1] Payments of employer liability under the termination insurance program are treated as employer contributions.[2]

Reasons for Change

The Committees have determined that the payment of withdrawal liability by an employer should be treated as a contribution to the plan by the employer without regard to the usual limitation on employer deductions for contributions to a tax qualified plan.

Explanation of Provision

The bill generally allows a deduction for amounts paid by a taxpayer under the employer withdrawal liability provisions of the termination insurance program without regard to the usual limitations on employer deductions for contributions to a tax qualified plan.

Under the bill, for employer tax deduction purposes, withdrawal liability payments are treated as employer contributions to the plan. Thus, the deduction of total plan contributions, including withdrawal liability payments, is subject to the full funding limitation. In addition, withdrawal liability payments are deductible only if paid for a taxable year which ends with or within a taxable year of the plan for which the plan is qualified. Of course, an employer's total contribution to the plan, including withdrawal liability payments, must be ordinary and necessary business expenses of the employer to be deductible. Special rules are provided which allow a deduction for employer liability payments to a taxpayer whose liability for the payments arises out of the liability of an employer who is a member of the same control group of companies that includes the taxpayer.

Effective Date

This provision of the bill is effective upon enactment.

[¶ 11,850.065]

Committee Report on P.L. 96-222 (Technical Corrections Act of 1979)

[Senate Committee Report]

Sec. 101(a)(5)—Title insurance company plans.

Prior to the Revenue Act of 1978, section 404(a)(5) of the Code provided that where an employer deferred payment of compensation to an employee pursuant to a nonqualified plan, the employer could deduct the compensation only in the year in which the compensation was includible in the employee's gross income. If the payment was not made pursuant to a qualified plan, but pursuant to a "method of employer contributions or compensation [having] the effect of a stock bonus, pension, profit-sharing, or annuity plan, *or similar plan* deferring the receipt of compensation . . . ," the deduction-timing limitations of section 404(a) were also applicable (italics added).

Section 133 of the 1978 Act added a new Code Section 404(d) which extends the deduction-timing limitation of section 404(a) to payments of deferred compensation made to independent contractors. Section 133 of the 1978 Act also amended section 404(b) by changing the words "or similar plan" to read "or other plan." These amendments apply to deductions for taxable years beginning after December 31, 1978.

The Lawyers' Title Guaranty Fund (the Fund) is an unincorporated business trust whose members consist of almost 6,000 Florida lawyers. The Fund issues title insurance policies on the basis of title examinations made by the lawyer-members. Under the agreement between the lawyers and the Fund, the payment by the Fund to lawyer-members on account of their issuance of title policies is deferred for 7 years, the period of adverse possession under Florida law. One of the principal reasons for this deferral of payment is that retention of these amounts due for commissions serves to provide a more adequate financial base to provide security to policyholders. In *Lawyers' Title Guaranty Fund v. United States*, 508 F. 2d 1 (5th Cir. 1975), the court held that the obligations of the Fund to lawyer-members were deductible by the Fund as ordinary and necessary business expenses in the year of the issuance of the policy. This decision was accepted by the Internal Revenue Service in Rev. Rul. 77-266, 1977-2 C.B. 236.

Nonetheless, the changes made by the 1978 Act would disallow any deduction for amounts due to lawyer-members of the Fund until the amounts are made available to lawyer-members after the 7-year period of limitations in Florida. The resulting tax on these amounts would decrease the necessary reserves of the Fund since it is not possible to increase the premium rates of title insurance to the home buyers for policies sold during 1979. This could adversely affect the security of the home buyers.

Accordingly, the committee believes that it is appropriate to delay the effective date of the change made by the 1978 Act in this case for one year until taxable years beginning after December 31, 1979. This one-year delay will provide the Fund adequate time to restructure their handling of the commissions on title insurance.

The bill provides that the changes made by section 133 of the Revenue Act of 1978 are to apply to taxable years beginning after December 31, 1979, in the case of a qualified title insurance company plan. A qualified title insurance company plan is a plan which defers the payment of amounts credited by a qualified title insurance company to separate accounts for members of the company in consideration of their issuance of policies of title insurance and under which no part of the credited amounts is payable to or withdrawable by the members until after the period for the adverse possession of real property under applicable State law. A qualified title insurance company is defined to mean an unincorporated title insurance company organized as a business trust which is engaged in the business of providing title insurance coverage on interest in and liens upon real property obtained by clients of the members of the company and which is subject to tax under section 831 of the Internal Revenue Code of 1954.

This amendment is effective as if it were included in the Revenue Act of 1978.

Sec. 101(a)(10)(E) and (f)—Coordination rules.

The Revenue Act of 1978 created a new type of individual retirement plan, known as a simplified employee pension. Under the Act, if an employer maintains a defined contribution H.R. 10 plan for a self-employed individual and contributes to a simplified employee pension for that individual, the limitations on the employer's deduction for the contribution to the H.R. 10 plan is reduced by the deduction allowed for the contribution to the simplified employee pension so that the limitation on the total deductible amount set aside for that individual is not increased.

The rules for simplified employee plans do not provide for coordination with the rules for defined benefit plans of self-employed individuals or with rules for plans covering shareholder-employees of subchapter S corporations.

Under the bill, the limitation on the amount that may be set aside tax free in a defined contribution plan by a subchapter S corporation on behalf of a shareholder-employee is reduced by the amount deducted by the employer for contributions to the simplified employee pension of that employee. Also, the bill does not allow an employer who maintains a defined benefit plan for self-employed individuals or shareholder-employees to contribute to simplified employee pensions.

This provision applies to taxable years beginning after December 31, 1978. This is the same effective date as was provided by the Revenue Act of 1978 for simplified employee pensions.

[¶ 11,850.07]

Committee Report on P.L. 95-600 (Revenue Act of 1978)

Sec. 133—Deferred compensation to independent contractors.

[House Committee Report]

The bill adds a new provision (sec. 404(d)) which denies a deduction for deferred compensation provided under a nonqualified plan to non-employee participants, including cash-basis corporations, until that compensation is includible in the gross income of the participants. This rule is not intended to apply to normal year-end compensation accruals to unrelated persons which are paid within a reasonable time after the close of the taxable year.

The bill clarifies current law by providing that a method of compensation or employer contributions having the effect of a plan deferring the receipt of compensation does not have to be similar to a stock bonus, pension, profit-sharing, or annuity plan to be subject to the deferred compensation deduction-timing rules (sec. 404). Under the bill, amounts of compensation deferred under an unemployment contract or year-end bonuses declared by a corporate board of directors, but not paid within a reasonable period of time after the close of the taxable year, would be subject to the deduction-timing rules of sec. 404 to the extent that another Code provision (e.g., sec. 267(a)(2)) does not operate to deny the deduction.

The amendments made by this section will apply to deductions for taxable years beginning after December 31, 1978.

Sec. 141(f)(9)—Qualifications for ESOPs. The Senate Committee Report is at ¶ 12,130.12.

1 See Code sec. 404(a)(1)(A) and Prop. Treas. Reg. § 1.404(a)-14.

2 See Code sec. 404(g).

Sec. 152(f)—Simplified pension plans. The Senate Committee Report is at ¶ 12,050.09.

[¶ 11,850.08]

Committee Report on P.L. 94-455 (Tax Reform Act of 1976)

Under the committee amendment, the allowable annual addition to a self-employed individual's account under a defined contribution plan is not less than the minimum amount deductible under the $750 and 100-percent-of-earned-income rules, provided that the taxpayer's adjusted gross income for the taxable year does not exceed $15,000. The $15,000 limit insures that the provision is limited to its intended beneficiaries—low- and moderate-income taxpayers.

The House bill does not include a comparable provision.

Effective Date

The committee amendment applies to taxable years beginning after December 31, 1975.—**Senate Committee Report.**

[¶ 11,850.09]

Committee Report on P.L. 94-267 (IRC of 1954—Employee Retirement)

The Report of the House Committee on H.R. 12725 (P.L. 94-267) is reproduced at ¶ 11,750.09.

[¶ 11,850.10]

Committee Report on P.L. 93-406 (Employee Retirement Income Security Act of 1974)

[Conference Committee Explanation]

Maximum deduction limitation.—The substitute generally provides that deductions are to be allowed to the extent of contributions required to meet the minimum funding standards. In addition, the present "5 percent" method allowing deductions of not in excess of 5 percent of the annual compensation of covered employees is repealed. Also, the "normal cost" method allowing deductions for normal cost, plus 10 percent of unfunded past service cost is to be amended to allow deductions for contributions of normal cost, plus amortization over 10 years. Further, deductible limits are to be determined under the funding method and actuarial assumptions used for the minimum funding rules.

Generally, under the substitute, the maximum deduction is to be limited to the required contribution where a plan is subject to the full funding limitation. However, a special election is available under the substitute with regard to deductions if a plan becomes fully funded as a result of an amendment that decreases plan liabilities (benefits payable under the plan). This election is available only with respect to plan amendments that are negotiated through the collective bargaining process. Under this election, the maximum amount deductible generally will be normal cost under the plan less the amount needed to amortize over 10 years (principal plus interest) the decrease in plan liabilities as a result of the plan amendment. However, if a plan is fully funded without regard to the collectively bargained decrease in liabilities, no deduction is to be allowed. If a plan elects this provision, the amounts deductible in future years for contributions to the plan will be decreased (pursuant to regulations) by the amount required for a 10-year amortization of the collectively bargained decrease in liabilities.

A special rule is provided with respect to plans of regulated public utilities doing business in 40 States and furnishing certain telephone or other communications services which are rate regulated. (This rule also applies to plans of other companies which are members of a controlled group that includes such a public utility doing business in 40 States.) Under this provision, if the Secretary of the Treasury finds that the plan is a collectively bargained plan, the rules described above for deductions where there have been decreases in liabilities on account of plan amendments would apply to decreases in plan liabilities as a result of an increase in benefits under Title II of the Social Security Act.

* * *

Specific contributions limits on proprietorships, partnerships, or subchapter S corporations.—The conference substitute increases the maximum deductible contributions on behalf of self-employed persons to the lesser of 15 percent of earned income or $7,500. The same change is made as to excludable contributions on behalf of subchapter S corporation shareholder-employees. In applying the percentage limitations, not more than $100,000 of earned income may be taken into account. Self-employed persons (but not shareholder-employees) are permitted to set aside up to $750 a year out of earned income, without regard to the percentage limitations.

* * *

Rules for certain negotiated plans.—Under the bill as passed by the House, special rules were provided for welfare and benefit plans established before 1954 as a result of an agreement between a union and the government during a period of government operation of the major part of the productive facilities of the industry in which the employer is engaged. The special provisions enable these types of plans to establish two separate trusts—one for the payment of welfare benefits and a second for the payment of retirement benefits. In order to facilitate the restructuring of a welfare and pension plan into two separate plans the bill as passed by the House provides special rules for self-employed individuals who were treated as participants under the plan. The bill as passed by the Senate did not contain provisions pertaining to this manner [sic]. The conference substitute accepts the House provision without amendment.

[Code Sec. 404A]

[¶ 11,899A.05]

Committee Report on P.L. 96-603 (Private Foundation Returns)

[Senate Committee Report]

Explanation of provision

In general

The bill permits employers to elect a special set of provisions relating to deductions (and adjustments to earnings and profits) for qualified foreign plans. A "qualified foreign plan" means any written plan of an employer for deferring the receipt of compensation with respect to which the election has been made, but only if two requirements are met. First, the plan must be for the exclusive benefit of the employer's employees or their beneficiaries. Second, 90 percent or more of the amounts taken into account for the taxable year under the plan must be attributable to services (i) performed by nonresident aliens, (ii) the compensation for which is not subject to Federal income tax under the Code (as modified by applicable treaties). A plan is written to the extent it is defined by plan instruments, an applicable statute, or both. The bill does not apply to plans for independent contractors.

Under the bill, amounts paid or accrued by an employer under such a plan are not allowable as a deduction under Code sections 162, 212, or 404, but if they satisfy the conditions of Code section 162, they are allowable as a deduction under the bill for the taxable year for which the amounts are properly taken into account under the bill.

Certain provisions of the bill apply only to funded plans, while others apply only to reserve plans. Other provisions apply to both types. A qualified foreign plan is subject under the bill to the provisions relating to funded plans unless the taxpayer elects to be subject to the provisions for reserve plans.

That Committee intends that, for taxable years beginning after December 31, 1980 (and prior years to the extent the taxpayer elects retroactive effectiveness of the provisions), the taxpayer may claim a deduction for deferred compensation only pursuant to the terms of the bill, to the extent permitted for contributions to qualified plans, or to the extent permitted under section 404(a)(5). However, the Committee also intends that, for prior years, no inference should be drawn from the enactment of legislation as to the deductibility of contributions to foreign deferred compensation plans.

Funded plans

Generally, in the case of a funded plan contributions are properly taken into account for the taxable year in which paid. However, a provision similar to that available to domestic plans permits in some cases delay in payment of the contribution up to the time the return for the year is filed.

A contribution will be taken into account only if it is paid to a trust (or the equivalent of a trust) for the exclusive benefit of employees or their beneficiaries, for a retirement annuity, or directly to a participant or beneficiary.

In the case of a defined benefit plan, limitations to prevent distortion of income or the allowable foreign tax credit are placed on the amount deductible in any year which are similar to the limits imposed on domestic plans, except that aspects of the domestic limitations which relate to the minimum funding requirements are omitted because the funding rules do not apply to qualified foreign plans. Deductions for contributions to profit sharing plans are also subject to limitations similar to those imposed on domestic plans. Where more than one type of deferred compensation plan is maintained, the general rule limiting deductions for contributions to 25 percent of other compensation is also applicable. If the contributions paid in any year (reduced by certain amounts not allowable as deductions under the bill) exceed the foregoing limitations, a carryforward of the excess is permitted.

Reserve plans

In the case of an unfunded reserve plan, the amount properly taken into account for the taxable year is the reasonable addition for that year to a reserve for the taxpayer's liability under the plan. All benefits paid under the plan are to be charged to the reserve. In the case of a plan which is or has been a qualified reserve plan, an amount equal to the portion of any decrease for the taxable year in the reserve which is not attributable to the payment of benefits is to be included in gross income. The reserve must be decreased to the extent that it exceeds the taxpayer's liability properly taken into account.

The addition to the reserve is computed by discounting the accrued vested liabilities of the employer under the plan by an interest rate which is intended to approximate the amount which the employer could reasonably be expected to earn on funds invested in its business. The bill prescribes a formula for determining the permissible interest rate to be used in discounting the employer's liabilities under the plan in order to compute the amount allowable as an addition to the reserve for the year. The taxpayer may select a discount rate which is no more than 20 percent above, and not more than 20 percent below, the average rate of interest for long term corporate bonds in the appropriate foreign country for a 15-year period prior to the year of the adjustment to the reserve. Once a discount rate within this permissible rate has been selected by the taxpayer for the plan, that rate shall remain in effect for the plan until the first year for which the rate is no longer within the permissible range. If in any year the rate selected by the taxpayer ceases to fall within the permissible range, the taxpayer shall select a new rate of interest which is within the permissible range applicable for that year.

Unless otherwise required or permitted by the Treasury, the reserve for the taxpayer's liability is to be determined under the unit credit method modified to reflect the following requirements. First, an item shall be taken into account for a taxable year only if there is no substantial risk that the rights of the employee will be forfeited, and the item meets such additional requirements as the Treasury may by regulations prescribe as necessary or appropriate to ensure that the liability will be satisfied. Second, any increase or decrease to the reserve on account of the adoption of the plan or a plan amendment, experience gains and losses, any change in plan assumptions, and changes in the interest rate is to be amortized over a 10-year period. Other factors prescribed by regulations must also be amortized over the 10-year period. These could include, for example, adjustments in the reserve resulting from changes in levels of compensation on which benefits depend, or the vesting in one year of a benefit which was accrued in a prior year.

Consistency with foreign law

In the case of any qualified foreign plan, whether funded or reserve, the amount allowed as a deduction under the bill for any taxable year is equal to the lesser of (i) the cumulative U.S. amount, or (ii) the cumulative foreign amount, reduced in either case by the aggregate amount determined under the bill for all prior taxable years. "Cumulative U.S. amount" means the aggregate amount determined with respect to the plan under this provision for the taxable year and for all prior taxable years to which the bill applies. (This determination is to be made, however, for each taxable year without regard to the limitation imposed by this provision.) "Cumulative foreign amount" means the aggregate amount allowed as a deduction under the appropriate foreign tax laws for the taxable year and all prior taxable years to which this provision applies. If the deduction under the foreign tax law is later adjusted, the taxpayer is to notify the Treasury of the adjustment on or before the date prescribed by regulations, and the Treasury will redetermine the amount of the U.S. tax for the year or years affected. (In any such case, rules similar to the rules of Code section 905(c) will apply. See the discussion below under the heading "Foreign tax credit redeterminations.")

In determining the earnings and profits and accumulated profits of any corporation with respect to a qualified foreign plan, the principles of this limitation are generally to apply. However, the deduction allowed in computing the earnings and profits or the accumulated profits of any foreign corporation with respect to a qualified foreign plan is not in any event to exceed the amount allowed as a deduction under the appropriate tax laws for such taxable year. This additional limitation is imposed in response to the possibilities for distortion of a taxpayer's indirect foreign tax credit which are presented by the present annual system for determining the amount of the foreign taxes paid by a subsidiary which are attributable to dividends paid to its U.S. shareholders. The effective rate of foreign tax paid by a foreign subsidiary determined with reference to U.S. accounting rules may fluctuate significantly from year to year for a variety of reasons, including, in particular, differences between the U.S. accounting rules for computing the foreign subsidiaries earnings and profits or accumulated profits and the accounting rules used by the foreign government in imposing the tax. The interaction of these foreign rate fluctuations and the annual rules for computing the indirect foreign tax credit permit substantial distortions of the taxpayer's deemed paid foreign tax credit as compared with the effective tax rate of the subsidiary over a period of years. For example, dividends might be repatriated only in high effective tax rate years of the subsidiary (measured under U.S. accounting rules), yielding a deemed paid credit higher than the long term effective rate of the subsidiary. Conversely, dividends might be repatriated through years in which the subsidiary has no accumulated profits according to U.S. accounting rules, with the result that the taxes paid by the subsidiary for the year are lost. This potential for distortion might be eliminated if the indirect credit were computed with reference to the subsidiary's accumulated foreign taxes and undistributed accumulated profits for all years. Until and unless such a change [is] so made, however, it was determined that no carryforward of any amount which is disallowed for a year because the foreign deduction of the subsidiary for the year exceeded the U.S. deduction for the year will be permitted to a future year where it would increase the amount allowable under U.S. rules over the amount of the foreign deduction for the later year. (The impact of this limitation is that such an excess is permanently lost.)

Other limitations

The bill further provides that, except as provided in Code section 404(a)(5), no deduction will be allowed under the bill for any item to the extent it is attributable to services (i) performed by a citizen or resident of the United States who is an officer, shareholder, or highly compensated, or (ii) performed in the United States the compensation for which is subject to Federal income tax under the Code (as modified by applicable treaties).

No deduction is allowed under the bill with respect to any plan for any taxable year unless the taxpayer furnishes to the Treasury (i) a statement from the foreign tax authorities specifying the amount of the deduction allowed in computing taxable income under foreign law for the year with respect to the plan, (ii) if the return under foreign tax law shows the deduction for plan contributions or reserves as a separate, identifiable item, a copy of the foreign tax return for the taxable year, or (iii) such other statement, return, or other evidence as the Treasury prescribes by regulation as being sufficient to establish the amount of the deduction under foreign law.

Actuarial assumptions must be reasonable in the aggregate. Also, in the case of a reserve plan, rates of interest used for actuarial computations are to be the appropriate market interest rates for borrowing money in the appropriate country, as determined under regulations prescribed by the Treasury. No deduction is allowable for any amount to the extent that it would cause the fair market value of the plan's assets to exceed the accrued liability (including normal cost) under the plan. Any change in the method (but not the actuarial assumptions) used to determine the amount allowed as a deduction is to be treated as a change in accounting method under Code section 446(e). Thus, such a change would require the permission of the Treasury and could give rise to an adjustment to income (Code section 481). In applying section 481 with respect to any such election, the period for taking into account any increase or decrease in accumulated profits, earnings and profits or taxable income resulting from the application of section 481(a)(2) shall be the year for which the election is made and the nine succeeding years.

Foreign tax credit redeterminations

The allowance of deductions under the bill depends, in part, on the allowance of deductions under foreign law. The bill provides that when there is a change in deductions allowed under foreign law the taxpayer will be required to notify the Treasury of this change. This requirement parallels existing rules requiring notification if foreign taxes when paid differ from amounts claimed as credits by the taxpayer. The bill also clarifies enforcement of the provisions which require the taxpayer to notify the Treasury of changes in its foreign income tax liabilities.

The bill provides that interest may be assessed and collected on the tax due resulting from a redetermination if the taxpayer has failed to notify the Treasury (on or before the date prescribed by regulations for giving such notice) of the foreign tax change, unless it is shown that such failure is due to reasonable cause and not due to willful neglect. The interest may be assessed and collected, however, only from the time of the refund of foreign income tax or any adjustments affecting deductions allowable under the bill or the time of any other adjustment to foreign income tax paid or accrued. Moreover, if the failure is not excusable, an additional penalty is to be assessed of 5 percent of the deficiency attributable to the redetermination for each month (or fraction of a month) during which the failure continues, not to exceed 25 percent.

Foreign trusts

The bill would make it clear that in the case of a contribution to a foreign trust subject to the special deduction rules, the corporation making the contributions is not treated as the owner of part of the trust merely because the trust has or acquires U.S. beneficiaries.

Effective date

The amendments made by this provision are generally applicable to employer contributions or accruals by U.S. taxpayers and from subsidiaries of such taxpayers for taxable years after December 31, 1980. In addition, a taxpayer may elect to have the amendments apply retroactively. A retroactive election only applies to funded plans maintained by foreign branches of the taxpayer, but it applies to both funded plans or reserve plans maintained by foreign subsidiaries of the taxpayer. In the case of retroactive application to foreign subsidiaries, the legislation would apply to all dividends distributed out of accumulated profits and earnings and profits earned by such subsidiaries after December 31, 1971 and included in the taxpayer's income in its open period. Any retroactive election can only be revoked with the consent of the IRS. Any retroactive election shall apply to all open years of the taxpayer after December 31, 1971 (other than any open years which precede a closed year of the taxpayer).

[Code Sec. 406]

[¶ 11,950.09]

Committee Report on P.L. 98-21 (Social Security Act Amendments of 1983)

[House Committee Report]

Under present law (sec. 406), if U.S. citizens are employed by a domestic cororation's foreign subsidiary and the domestic parent corporation has entered into an agreement to pay FICA tax for the U.S. citizens employed by its foreign subsidiary, then such U.S. citizens can be included in the qualified pension, profit-sharing, stock bonus, and so forth, plan of the domestic parent corporation.

Your Committee recognizes that the rational of present law section 406 is that it should be possible to provide coverage under qualified pension, profit-sharing, stock bonus, etc., plans to the same extent that social security coverage can be extended. In view of the provision of the Committee bill that allows the extension of social security coverage to resident aliens employed by a foreign affiliate of an American employer, your Committee concluded that a corresponding change should be made in the treatment of coverage under qualified pension, profit-sharing, stock bonus, etc., plans.

The Committee bill provides that, if the requirements of present law are otherwise satisfied, coverage under a qualified pension, profit-sharing, stock bonus, etc., plan of an american employer can be extended to resident aliens, as well as U.S. citizens. Thus, an American employer can treat U.S. citizens and resident aliens employed by a foreign affiliate as its own employees, for purposes of extending coverage under a qualified pension, profit-sharing, stock bonus, etc., plan. A conforming amendment is made to section 407, relating to the treatment of certain employees of domestic subsidiaries operating primarily abroad as employees of the domestic parent corporation.

The bill will apply to American employers who enter into agreements to pay FICA tax after the date of enactment, and to American employers who modify agreements previously entered into after the date of enactment. At the election of any American employer, the provision will apply to an agreement to pay FICA tax entered into on or before the date of enactment. The conforming change to section 407 will apply to any plan established after the date of enactment; or, at the election of a domestic parent corporation, to any plan established on or before the date of enactment.

[Code Sec. 407]

[¶ 12,000.09]

Committee Report on P.L. 98-21 (Social Security Act Amendments of 1983)

Committee Report on P.L. 98-21, is at ¶ 11,950.09.

[Code Sec. 408]

[¶ 12,050.029]

Committee Report on P.L. 109-432 (Tax Relief and Health Care Act of 2006)

For the Committee Report on P.L. 109-432 on Health Savings Accounts, see ¶ 11,335.085.

[¶ 12,050.031]

Committee Report on P.L. 109-280 (Pension Protection Act of 2006)

[Joint Committee on Taxation Report]

Qualified charitable distributions from IRAs

The provision provides an exclusion from gross income for otherwise taxable IRA distributions from a traditional or a Roth IRA in the case of qualified charitable distributions.[299] The exclusion may not exceed $100,000 per taxpayer per taxable year. Special rules apply in determining the amount of an IRA distribution that is otherwise taxable. The present-law rules regarding taxation of IRA distributions and the deduction of charitable contributions continue to apply to distributions from an IRA that are not qualified charitable distributions. Qualified charitable distributions are taken into account for purposes of the minimum distribution rules applicable to traditional IRAs to the same extent the distribution would have been taken into account under such rules had the distribution not been directly distributed under the provision. An IRA does not fail to qualify as an IRA merely because qualified charitable distributions have been made from the IRA. It is intended that the Secretary will prescribe rules under which IRA owners are deemed to elect out of withholding if they designate that a distribution is intended to be a qualified charitable distribution.

A qualified charitable distribution is any distribution from an IRA directly by the IRA trustee to an organization described in section 170(b)(1)(A) (other than an organization described in section 509(a)(3) or a donor advised fund (as defined in section 4966(d)(2)). Distributions are eligible for the exclusion only if made on or after the date the IRA owner attains age 70-1/2.

The exclusion applies only if a charitable contribution deduction for the entire distribution otherwise would be allowable (under present law), determined without regard to the generally applicable percentage limitations. Thus, for example, if the deductible amount is reduced because of a benefit received in exchange, or if a deduction is not allowable because the donor did not obtain sufficient substantiation, the exclusion is not available with respect to any part of the IRA distribution.

If the IRA owner has any IRA that includes nondeductible contributions, a special rule applies in determining the portion of a distribution that is includible in gross income (but for the provision) and thus is eligible for qualified charitable distribution treatment. Under the special rule, the distribution is treated as consisting of income first, up to the aggregate amount that would be includible in gross income (but for the provision) if the aggregate balance of all IRAs having the same owner were distributed during the same year. In determining the amount of subsequent IRA distributions includible in income, proper adjustments are to be made to reflect the amount treated as a qualified charitable distribution under the special rule.

Distributions that are excluded from gross income by reason of the provision are not taken into account in determining the deduction for charitable contributions under section 170.

Qualified charitable distribution examples

The following examples illustrate the determination of the portion of an IRA distribution that is a qualified charitable distribution. In each example, it is assumed that the requirements for qualified charitable distribution treatment are otherwise met (e.g., the applicable age requirement and the requirement that contributions are otherwise deductible) and that no other IRA distributions occur during the year.

Example 1.—Individual A has a traditional IRA with a balance of $100,000, consisting solely of deductible contributions and earnings. Individual A has no other IRA. The entire IRA balance is distributed in a distribution to an organization described in section 170(b)(1)(A) (other than an organization described in section 509(a)(3) or a donor advised fund). Under present law, the entire distribution of $100,000 would be includible in Individual A's income. Accordingly, under the provision, the entire distribution of $100,000 is a qualified charitable distribution. As a result, no amount is included in Individual A's income as a result of the distribution and the distribution is not taken into account in determining the amount of Individual A's charitable deduction for the year.

Example 2.—Individual B has a traditional IRA with a balance of $100,000, consisting of $20,000 of nondeductible contributions and $80,000 of deductible contributions and earnings. Individual B has no other IRA. In a distribution to an organization described in section 170(b)(1)(A) (other than an organization described in section 509(a)(3) or a donor advised fund), $80,000 is distributed from the IRA. Under present law, a portion of the distribution from the IRA would be treated as a nontaxable return of nondeductible contributions. The nontaxable portion of the distribution would be $16,000, determined by multiplying the amount of the distribution ($80,000) by the ratio of the nondeductible contributions to the account balance ($20,000/$100,000). Accordingly, under present law, $64,000 of the distribution ($80,000 minus $16,000) would be includible in Individual B's income.

Under the provision, notwithstanding the present-law tax treatment of IRA distributions, the distribution is treated as consisting of income first, up to the total amount that would be includible in gross income (but for the provision) if all amounts were distributed from all IRAs otherwise taken into account in determining the amount of IRA distributions. The total amount that would be includible in income if all amounts were distributed from the IRA is $80,000. Accordingly, under the provision, the entire $80,000 distributed to the charitable organization is treated as includible in income (before application of the provision) and is a qualified charitable distribution. As a result, no amount is included in Individual B's income as a result of the distribution and the distribution is not taken into account in determining the amount of Individual B's charitable deduction for the year. In addition, for purposes of determining the tax treatment of other distributions from the IRA, $20,000 of the amount remaining in the IRA is treated as Individual B's nondeductible contributions (i.e., not subject to tax upon distribution).

Split-interest trust filing requirements

The provision increases the penalty on split-interest trusts for failure to file a return and for failure to include any of the information required to be shown on such return and to show the correct information. The penalty is $20 for each day the failure continues up to $10,000 for any one return. In the case of a split-interest trust with gross income in excess of $250,000, the penalty is $100 for each day the failure continues up to a maximum of $50,000. In addition, if a person (meaning any officer, director, trustee, employee, or other individual who is under a duty to file the return or include required information)[300] knowingly failed to file the return or include required information, then that person is personally liable for such a penalty, which would be imposed in addition to the penalty that is paid by the organization. Information regarding beneficiaries that are not charitable organizations as described in section 170(c) is exempt from the requirement to make information publicly available. In addition, the provision repeals the present-law exception to the filing requirement for split-interest trusts that are required in a taxable year to distribute all net income currently to beneficiaries. Such exception remains available to trusts other than split-interest trusts that are otherwise subject to the filing requirement.

Effective Date

The provision relating to qualified charitable distributions is effective for distributions made in taxable years beginning after December 31, 2005, and taxable years beginning before January 1, 2008. The provision relating to information returns of split-interest trusts is effective for returns for taxable years beginning after December 31, 2006.

[¶ 12,050.033]

Committee Reports on P.L. 108-311 (Working Families Tax Relief Act of 2004)

[Conference Agreement]

SIMPLE plan contributions for domestic or similar workers.—Section 637 of EGTRRA provides an exception to the application of the excise tax on nondeductible retirement plan contributions in the case of contributions to a SIMPLE IRA or SIMPLE section 401(k) plan that are nondeductible solely because they are not made in connection with a trade or business of the employer (e.g., contributions on behalf of a domestic worker). Section 637 of EGTRRA did not specifically modify the present-law requirement that compensation for purposes of determin-

[299] The provision does not apply to distributions from employer-sponsored retirements plans, including SIMPLE IRAs and simplified employee pensions ("SEPs").

[300] Sec. 6652(c)(4)(C).

ing contributions to a SIMPLE plan must be wages subject to income tax withholding, even though wages paid to domestic workers are not subject to income tax withholding. The provision revises the definition of compensation for purposes of determining contributions to a SIMPLE plan to include wages paid to domestic workers, even though such amounts are not subject to income tax withholding.

[¶ 12,050.035]

Committee Reports on P.L. 107-16 (Economic Growth and Tax Relief Reconciliation Act)

[House Committee Report]

Definition of compensation

The provision amends the definition of compensation for purposes of all qualified plans and IRAs (including SIMPLE arrangements) to include an individual's net earnings that would be subject to SECA taxes but for the fact that the individual is covered by a religious exemption.

Effective Date

The provision is effective for taxable years beginning after December 31, 2001.

[Conference Committee Report]

* * *

The conference agreement follows the House bill.

* * *

[¶ 12,050.04]

Committee Reports on P.L. 107-16 (Economic Growth and Tax Relief Reconciliation Act)

[House Committee Report]

Elective deferral limitations

* * *

The provision increases the dollar limit on annual elective deferrals under section 401(k) plans, section 403(b) annuities and salary reduction SEPs to $11,000 in 2002. In 2003 and thereafter, the limits are increased in $1,000 annual increments until the limits reach $15,000 in 2006, with indexing in $500 increments thereafter. The provision increases the maximum annual elective deferrals that may be made to a SIMPLE plan to $7,000 in 2002. In 2003 and thereafter, the SIMPLE plan deferral limit is increased in $1,000 annual increments until the limit reaches $10,000 in 2005. Beginning after 2005, the $10,000 dollar limit is indexed in $500 increments.

* * *

Effective Date

The provision is effective for years beginning after December 31, 2001.

[Conference Committee Report]

Elective deferral limitations.—The conference agreement follows the House bill.

* * *

Effective Date

The conference agreement generally is effective for years beginning after December 31, 2001. The provisions relating to defined benefit plans are effective for years ending after December 31, 2001.

[¶ 12,050.045]

Committee Reports on P.L. 107-16 (Economic Growth and Tax Relief Reconciliation Act)

For Committee Report on P.L. 107-16, dealing with IRA contributions, see ¶ 11,330.005.

Deemed IRAs under employer plans.—The bill provides that, if an eligible retirement plan permits employees to make voluntary employee contributions to a separate account or annuity that (1) is established under the plan, and (2) meets the requirements applicable to either traditional IRAs or Roth IRAs, then the separate account or annuity is deemed a traditional IRA or a Roth IRA, as applicable, for all purposes of the Code. For example, the reporting requirements applicable to IRAs apply. The deemed IRA, and contributions thereto, are not subject to the Code rules pertaining to the eligible retirement plan. In addition, the deemed IRA, and contributions thereto, are not taken into account in applying such rules to any other contributions under the plan. The deemed IRA, and contributions thereto, are subject to the exclusive benefit and fiduciary rules of ERISA to the extent otherwise applicable to the plan, and are not subject to the ERISA reporting and disclosure, participation, vesting, funding, and enforcement requirements applicable to the eligible retirement plan. An eligible retirement plan is a qualified plan (Sec. 401(a)), tax-sheltered annuity (Sec. 403(b)), or a governmental section 457 plan.

* * *

Effective Date

The provision relating to deemed IRAs under employer plans is effective for plan years beginning after December 31, 2002.

* * *

[Conference Committee Report]

* * *

Deemed IRAs under employer plans.—The conference agreement follows the Senate amendment.

* * *

Effective Date

The conference agreement is generally effective for taxable years beginning after December 31, 2001. The provision relating to deemed IRAs under employer plans is effective for years beginning after December 31, 2002.

[¶ 12,050.047]

Committee Reports on P.L. 105-34 (Taxpayer Relief Act)

For Committee Report on P.L. 105-34, dealing with Roth IRAs, see ¶ 12,097.10.

For Committee Reports on P.L. 105-34, dealing with matching contributions of self-employed individuals, see ¶ 11,750.032.

[¶ 12,050.049]

Committee Reports on P.L. 105-206 (IRS Restructuring and Reform Act of 1998)

[Senate Committee Report]

Application of requirements for SIMPLE IRAs in the case of mergers and acquisitions.—The bill conforms the treatment applicable to SIMPLE IRAs upon acquisition, disposition or similar transaction for purposes of (1) the 100 employee limit, (2) the exclusive plan requirement, and (3) the coverage rules for participation. In the event of such a transaction, the employer will be treated as an eligible employer and the arrangement will be treated as a qualified salary reduction arrangement for the year of the transaction and the two following years, provided rules similar to the rules of section 410(b)(6)(C)(i)(II) are satisfied and the arrangement would satisfy the requirements to be a qualified salary reduction arrangement after the transaction if the trade or business that maintained the arrangement prior to the transaction had remained a separate employer.

Effective Date

The provision is effective as if included in the Small Business Job Protection Act of 1996.

[Conference Committee Report]

Conference Agreement

The conference agreement follows the Senate amendment * * *.—

[Senate Committee Report]

Treatment of Indian tribal governments under section 403(b).—The bill clarifies that an employee participating in a 403(b)(7) custodial account of the Indian tribal government may roll over amounts from such account to a section 401(k) plan maintained by the Indian tribal government.

Effective Date

The provision is effective as if included in the Small Business Job Protection Act of 1996.—

[Conference Committee Report]

Conference Agreement

The conference agreement follows the Senate amendment * * *.—

[¶ 12,050.052]

Committee Reports on P.L. 105-34 (Taxpayer Relief Act)

[House Committee Report]

Maximum dollar limitation for SIMPLE IRAs.—The bill provides that in the case of a SIMPLE IRA, the $2,000 maximum limitation applicable to IRAs is increased to the limitations in effect for contributions made under a qualified salary reduction arrangement. This includes employee elective contributions and required employer contributions.

Effective date

This provision is effective for tax years beginning after December 31, 1996.

[House Committee Report]

Application of exclusive plan requirement for SIMPLE IRAs to noncollectively bargained employees.—The bill provides that an employer who maintains a plan for collectively bargained employees is permitted to maintain a SIMPLE IRA for noncollectively bargained employees.

Effective date

This provision is effective for tax years beginning after December 31, 1996.

[House Committee Report]

Application of exclusive plan requirement for SIMPLE IRAs in the case of mergers and acquisitions.—The bill provides that if an employer maintains a qualified plan and a SIMPLE IRA in the same year due to an acquisition, disposition or similar transaction the SIMPLE IRA is treated as a qualified salary reduction arrangement for the year of the transaction and the following calendar year.

Effective date

This provision is effective for tax years beginning after December 31, 1996.

[House Committee Report]

Reporting requirements for SIMPLE IRAs.—The bill conforms the time for providing reports for SIMPLE IRAs to that for IRA reports generally. Thus, the bill would provide that the report required to be furnished to the individual under a SIMPLE IRA would be provided within 31 days after each calendar year.

Effective date

This provision is effective for tax years beginning after December 31, 1996.

[¶ 12,050.056]

Committee Report on P.L. 104-188 (Small Business Job Protection Act)

Increased Access to Retirement Savings

[Senate Committee Report]

Establish SIMPLE retirement plans for small employers

In general

The bill creates a simplified retirement plan for small business called the savings incentive match plan for employees ("SIMPLE") retirement plan. SIMPLE plans can be adopted by employers who employed 100 or fewer employees earning at least $5,000 in compensation for the preceding year and who do not maintain another employer-sponsored retirement plan. A SIMPLE plan can be either an IRA for each employee or part of a qualified cash or deferred arrangement ("401(k) plan"). If established in IRA form, a SIMPLE plan is not subject to the nondiscrimination rules generally applicable to qualified plans (including the top-heavy rules) and simplified reporting requirements apply. Within limits, contributions to a SIMPLE plan are not taxable until withdrawn.

A SIMPLE plan can also be adopted as part of a 401(k) plan. In that case, the plan does not have to satisfy the special nondiscrimination tests applicable to 401(k) plans and is not subject to the top-heavy rules. The other qualified plan rules continue to apply.

SIMPLE retirement plans in IRA form

In general.—A SIMPLE retirement plan allows employees to make elective contributions to an IRA. Employee contributions have to be expressed as a percentage of the employee's compensation, and cannot exceed $6,000 per year. The $6,000 dollar limit is indexed for inflation in $500 increments.

Under the bill, the employer is required to satisfy one of two contribution formulas. Under the matching contribution formula, the employer generally is required to match employee elective contributions on a dollar-for-dollar basis up to 3 percent of the employee's compensation. Under a special rule, the employer could elect a lower percentage matching contribution for all employees (but not less than 1 percent of each employee's compensation). In order for the employer to lower the matching percentage for any year, the employer has to notify employees of the applicable match within a reasonable time before the 60-day election period for the year (described below). In addition, a lower percentage cannot be elected for more than 2 out of any 5 years.

Alternatively, for any year, an employer is permitted to elect, in lieu of making matching contributions, to make a 2 percent of compensation nonelective contribution on behalf of each eligible employee with at least $5,000 in compensation for such year. If such an election were made, the employer has to notify eligible employees of the change within a reasonable period before the 60-day election period for the year (described below). No contributions other than employee elective contributions and required employer matching contributions (or, alternatively, required employer nonelective contributions) can be made to a SIMPLE account.

Only employers who employed 100 or fewer employees earning at least $5,000 in compensation for the preceding year and who do not currently maintain a qualified plan can establish SIMPLE retirement accounts for their employees. Under a special rule, employers are given a 2-year grace period to maintain a SIMPLE plan once they are no longer eligible.

Each employee of the employer who received at least $5,000 in compensation from the employer during any 2 prior years and who is reasonably expected to receive at least $5,000 in compensation during the year must be eligible to participate in the SIMPLE plan. Nonresident aliens and employees covered under a collective bargaining agreement do not have to be eligible to participate in the SIMPLE plan. Self-employed individuals can participate in a SIMPLE plan.

All contributions to an employee's SIMPLE account have to be fully vested.

Distributions from a SIMPLE plan generally are taxed as under the rules relating to IRAs, except that an increased early withdrawal tax (25 percent) applies to distributions within the first 2 years the employee first participates in the SIMPLE plan.

Tax treatment of SIMPLE accounts contributions and distributions.—Contributions to a SIMPLE account generally are deductible by the employer. In the case of matching contributions, the employer will be allowed a deduction for a year only if the contributions are made by the due date (including extensions) for the employer's tax return. Contributions to a SIMPLE account are excludable from the employee's income. SIMPLE accounts, like IRAs, are not subject to tax. Distributions from a SIMPLE retirement account generally are taxed under the rules applicable to IRAs. Thus, they are includible in income when withdrawn. Tax-free rollovers can be made from one SIMPLE account to another. A SIMPLE account can be rolled over to an IRA on a tax-free basis after a two-year period has expired since the individual first participated in the SIMPLE plan. To the extent an employee is no longer participating in a SIMPLE plan (e.g., the employee has terminated employment), the employee's SIMPLE account will be treated as an IRA.

Early withdrawals from a SIMPLE account generally are be subject to the 10-percent early withdrawal tax applicable to IRAs. However, withdrawals of contributions during the 2-year period beginning on the date the employee first participated in the SIMPLE plan are subject to a 25-percent early withdrawal tax (rather than 10 percent).

Employer matching or nonelective contributions to a SIMPLE account are not treated as wages for employment tax purposes.

Administrative requirements.—Each eligible employee can elect, within the 60-day period before the beginning of any year (or the 60-day period before first becoming eligible to participate), to participate in the SIMPLE plan (i.e., to make elective deferrals), and to modify any previous elections regarding the amount of contributions. An employer is required to contribute employees' elective deferrals to the employee's SIMPLE account within 30 days after the end of the month to which the contributions relate. Employees must be allowed to terminate participation in the SIMPLE plan at any time during the year (i.e., to stop making contributions). The plan can provide that an employee who terminates participation cannot resume participation until the following year. A plan can permit (but is not required to permit) an individual to make other changes to his or her salary reduction contribution election during the year (e.g., reduce contributions). An employer is permitted to designate a SIMPLE account trustee to which contributions on behalf of eligible employees are made.

The bill also amend parts 1 and 4, Subtitle B, Title 1 of ERISA so that only simplified reporting requirements apply to SIMPLE plans and so that the employer (and any other plan fiduciary) will not be subject to fiduciary liability resulting from the employee (or beneficiary) exercising control over the assets in the SIMPLE account. For this purpose an employee (or beneficiary) will be treated as exercising control over the assets in his or her account upon the earlier of (1) an affirmative election with respect to the initial investment of any contributions, (2) a rollover contribution (including a trustee-to-trustee transfer) to another SIMPLE account or IRA, or (3) one year after the SIMPLE account is established. The Committee intends that once an employee (or beneficiary) is treated as exercising control over his or her SIMPLE account, the relief from fiduciary liability would extend to the period prior to when the employee (or beneficiary) was deemed to exercise control.

Reporting requirements

Trustee requirements.—The trustee of a SIMPLE account is required each year to prepare, and provide to the employer maintaining the SIMPLE plan, a summary description containing the following basic information about the plan; the name and address of the employer and the trustee; the requirements for eligibility; the benefits provided under the plan; the time and method of making salary reduction elections; and the procedures for and effects of, withdrawals (including rollovers) from the SIMPLE account. At least once a year, the trustee is also required to furnish an account statement to each individual maintaining a SIMPLE account. In addition, the trustee is required to file an annual report with the Secretary. A trustee who fails to provide any of such reports or descriptions will be subject to a penalty of $50 per day until such failure is corrected, unless the failure is due to reasonable cause.

Employer reports.—The employer maintaining a SIMPLE plan is required to notify each employee of the employee's opportunity to make salary reduction contributions under the plan as well as the contribution alternative chosen by the employer immediately before the employee becomes eligible to make such election. This notice must include a copy of the summary description prepared by the trustee. An employer who fails to provide such notice will be subject to a penalty of $30 per day on which such failure continues, unless the failure is due to reasonable cause.

Definitions

For purposes of the rules relating to SIMPLE plans, compensation means compensation required to be reported by the employer on Form W-2, plus any elective deferrals of the employee. In the case of a self-employed individual, compensation means net earnings from self-employment. The $150,000 compensation limit (sec. 401(a)(17)) applies only for purposes of the 2 percent of compensation nonelective contribution formula. The term employer includes the employer and related employers. Related employers includes trades or businesses under common control (whether incorporated or not), controlled groups of corporations, and affiliated service groups. In addition, the leased employee rules apply.

For purposes of the rule prohibiting an employer from establishing a SIMPLE plan, if the employer has another qualified plan, an employer is treated as maintaining a qualified plan if the employer (or a predecessor employer) maintained a qualified plan with respect to which contributions were made, or benefits were accrued, with respect to service for any year in the period beginning with the year the SIMPLE plan became effective and ending with the year for which the determination is being made. A qualified plan includes a qualified retirement plan, a qualified annuity plan, a governmental plan, a tax-sheltered annuity, and a simplified employee pension.

* * *

Repeal of SARSEPs

Under the bill, the present-law rules permitting SARSEPs no longer apply after December 31, 1996, unless the SARSEP was established before January 1, 1997. Consequently, an employer is not permitted to establish a SARSEP after December 31, 1996. SARSEPs established before January 1, 1997, can continue to receive contributions under present-law rules, and new employees of the employer hired after December 31, 1996, can participate in the SARSEP in accordance with such rules

Effective Date

The provisions relating to SIMPLE plans are effective for years beginning after December 31, 1996.

[Conference Committee Report]

Conference Agreement

The conference agreement follows the Senate amendment.

Miscellaneous Pension Simplification

[House Committee Report]

Uniform penalty provisions for certain pension reporting requirements

The bill incorporates into the general penalty structure the penalties for failure to provide information reports relating to pension payments to the IRS and to recipients.

Effective Date

The provision is effective with respect to returns and statements the due date for which is after December 31, 1996.

[Conference Committee Report]

Senate Amendment

The Senate amendment is the same as the House bill.

Conference Agreement

The conference agreement follows the House bill and the Senate amendment.

[¶ 12,050.057]

Committee Report on P.L. 103-66 (Omnibus Budget Reconciliation Act of 1993)

For Committee Reports on Omnibus Budget Reconciliation Act of 1993 (P.L. 103-66), relating to compensation for retirement plan purposes, see ¶ 11,700.04.

[¶ 12,050.058]

Committee Report on P.L. 102-318 (Unemployment Compensation Amendments of 1992)

For Committee Report on Unemployment Compensation Amendments of 1992 (P.L. 102-318), dealing with rollovers and withholding on nonperiodic pension distributions, see ¶ 11,750.036.

[¶ 12,050.059]

Committee Report on P.L. 101-239 (Omnibus Budget Reconciliation Act of 1989)

For the Committee Reports on Omnibus Budget Reconciliation Act of 1989 (P.L. 101-239), relating to the transfer of IRA interests as part of a divorce, see ¶ 12,350.053.

[¶ 12,050.061]

Committee Reports on P.L. 100-647 (Technical and Miscellaneous Revenue Act of 1988)

[Senate Committee Report]

Under the bill, for purposes of applying the special IRA rules of section 72, the value of the contract (calculated after adding back distributions that are made during the year), income on the contract, and investment in the contract are computed as of the close of the calendar year in which the taxable year begins (rather than the calendar year with or within which the taxable year ends). The provision is intended to facilitate computations with respect to taxpayers with fiscal year taxable years.

[Senate Committee Report]

* * *

The bill amends the rules relating to distributions of excess contributions to take into account the fact that nondeductible contributions may be made to an IRA. The bill permits any IRA contributions to be distributed without income or excise tax consequences prior to the due date (including extensions) for filing the individual's income tax return for the year the contributions are made. Thus, under the bill, the normal rules for the taxation of IRA distributions do not apply to a distribution of any contributions to an IRA if (1) the distribution is received on or before the due date (including extensions) for the individual's return for the taxable year for which the contributions were made, (2) no deduction is allowed under section 219 with respect to the contributions, and (3) the distribution is accompanied by the amount of net income attributable to the contributions. As under present law, net income on the contributions are deemed to have been earned and receivable in the taxable year in which the contributions were made.

* * *

[Senate Committee Report]

* * *

The bill clarifies that certain IRA contributions not in excess of $2,250 may be withdrawn by providing that, for purposes of the rule relating to return of excess contributions after the due date of the individual's return for the year for which the contributions were made, the amount allowable as a deduction under section 219 is computed without regard to the AGI phaseout for active participants (sec. 219(g)).

[Senate Committee Report]

The bill clarifies that a distribution from a qualified plan and corresponding contribution to an IRA that results in any portion of a distribution being excluded from gross income under the rollover provisions is treated as a rollover distribution for purposes of the IRA rollover provisions.

[Conference Committee Report]

* * *

The conference agreement follows the Senate amendment * * *.

* * *

Rollover contributions to IRAs.—Code Sec. 402(a)(5)(F), as amended by TRA '86 and effective for tax years beginning after 1986, is amended by the Act to make it clear that the transfer to an IRA of an amount distributed by a qualified plan is a "rollover contribution" under Code Sec. 408(d)(3) only if the transfer causes some part of the distribution to be excluded from gross income under

Code Sec. 402(a)(5)(A). Before this amendment, Sec. 402(a)(5)(F) could have been construed to treat the transfer to an IRA as a rollover contribution even if it did not cause an exclusion from gross income (e.g., when the transfer was outside the 60-day time limit). The amendment is generally effective for years beginning after 1986. However, in the case of a plan maintained pursuant to one or more collective bargaining agreements ratified before March 1, 1986, it does not apply to distributions to individuals covered by such agreements in plan years beginning before the earlier of (1) the later of (A) January 1, 1989, or (B) the date on which the last of such collective bargaining agreements terminates (determined without regard to any extension thereof after February 28, 1986), or (2) January 1, 1991.

[Senate Committee Report]

The bill clarifies that, for purposes of the rules relating to SEPs (other than sec. 408(k)(2)(C)), the uniform definition of compensation (sec. 414(s)) applies. The bill also clarifies that, for purposes of applying the 125-percent test to a salary reduction SEP, compensation does not include compensation in excess of $200,000, indexed for increases in the cost of living. For 1988, the indexed limit is $208,940.

The bill clarifies that, in determining whether the employer maintaining a salary reduction SEP had more than 25 employees in the prior taxable year, only employees who were eligible to participate in the SEP (or would have been required to be eligible to participate if a SEP were maintained) are taken into account. This rule is consistent with the eligibility rules for SEPs, that is, individuals who are not required to be eligible to participate in the SEP may be disregarded in determining whether the 25-employee rule is satisfied.

The bill adds provisions designed to ensure that excess contributions to a salary reduction SEP are distributed. These rules are different from the rules relating to excess deferrals in cash or deferred arrangements because, in the case of a SEP, the employer may not force an employee to take a distribution of excess deferrals because the SEP contributions are held in an IRA which the employee controls.

The bill specifically authorizes the Secretary to prescribe appropriate rules, including rules requiring that the excess contributions (plus income) be distributed, reporting requirements, and rules providing that contributions to a SEP (plus income) may not be withdrawn until a determination that the special nondiscrimination test has been satisfied is made. In addition, the bill provides that, until such a determination has been made, any transfer or distribution from a SEP of salary reduction contributions (or income on such contributions) is subject to tax in accordance with section 72 and to the early withdrawal tax (sec. 72(t)(1)), regardless of whether an exception to the tax would otherwise be available.

Consistent with the inclusion of SEP contributions that are made pursuant to a salary reduction agreement for purposes of FICA (sec. 3121(a)(5) and FUTA (sec. 3306(b)(5)), the bill would include such contributions for purposes of determining benefits under the Social Security Act.

[Senate Committee Report]

To conform to the conversion of the SEP deduction to an exclusion, the bill provides that, for purposes of section 408(d)(4), (5) and section 4973, an amount excludable from income under section 402(h) is treated as an amount allowable as a deduction under section 219. In addition, the bill amends the definition of wages for withholding tax purposes (sec. 3401(a)(12)(C)) to provide that contributions to a SEP are not considered wages if it is reasonable to believe that the contributions will be excludable from income (rather than deductible).

[Joint Committee Explanation of Senate Consensus Amendment]

Under the provision, coins issued under the laws of any State would not be treated as collectibles for purposes of the IRA prohibition on investments in collectibles, as long as the coins are held by a person independent of the IRA owner. The provision would be effective for State coins acquired by an IRA after the date of enactment.

[¶ 12,050.063]

Committee Reports on P.L. 99-514 (Tax Reform Act of 1986)

[Senate Committee Report]

Nondeductible contributions permitted to IRAs

* * *

A designated nondeductible contribution is any contribution to an IRA for a taxable year that does not exceed the nondeductible limit and that the individual designates as a nondeductible contribution. The designation may be made or revoked up to the due date for filing the individual's tax return for the year.

The committee intends that the individual's designation of nondeductible contributions will be made to the trustee or issuer accepting the IRA contributions at the time of such contribution. This rule is provided to aid the trustee or issuer in maintaining records relating to the characterization of IRA contributions as nondeductible contributions, income on nondeductible contributions, and other amounts. The designation is also intended to assist the trustee or issuer in complying with reporting requirements applicable to IRAs. With respect to the annual reporting requirements of present law, the committee expects that the financial institution, when reporting contributions to an IRA to the Internal Revenue Service, will specify whether the contribution is a designated nondeductible contribution.

The trustee or issuer may specify a uniform date by which a designation must be made. For example, the trustee or issuer could require a designation at the time a contribution is made or, alternatively, could specify a uniform date (such as April 15) for designations.

Under the bill, any amount paid, distributed, or transferred from an IRA that has received designated nondeductible IRA contributions is treated as part nondeductible contributions and as part earnings on such nondeductible contributions, based on the fair market value of the IRA at the time of distribution.

* * *

For purposes of determining the fair market value of an IRA, the committee intends that the Secretary may permit the use of an annual, quarterly, or monthly valuation date in situations in which the value of the IRA on the date of distribution or transfer is not readily ascertainable. Under such circumstances, a prior valuation date similar to the valuation date permitted to be used for purposes of distributions from or under a qualified plan could be used.

In general, any amount paid or distributed that is a return of nondeductible contributions is treated as a nontaxable return of basis. If the individual rolls over to another IRA all or any part of the amount paid or distributed, the amount rolled over is treated as attributable to the nondeductible contributions in the same proportion as the amount paid or distributed was a return of nondeductible contributions.

The committee intends that the trustee or issuer of an IRA will provide a statement to an individual (with a copy to the IRA) when an amount is paid or distributed from an IRA specifying the portion of any distribution that is a return of nondeductible contributions. In addition, the committee intends that a copy of this statement is to be supplied to the trustee or issuer of an IRA to which a rollover contribution is made so that the character of the amounts rolled over is retained. Similarly, at any time a trustee-to-trustee transfer of IRA funds is made, any information relating to the character of the amounts transferred is to be supplied to the IRA and to the new trustee or issuer. This statement is required in addition to, and not in lieu of, the annual reporting requirement of present law.

Annual IRA contributions that exceed either the deductible limit or the nondeductible limit (whichever applies) are treated as excess contributions that are subject to an annual 6 percent excise tax (sec. 4973). Under the bill, if contributions in a later taxable year are less than the deductible or nondeductible limit for the taxable year, then the excess contributions for the earlier year may be applied against the limit for the current taxable year. Thus, under the bill, excess nondeductible contributions from a prior year could be recharacterized as deductible contributions for the current year if the individual is no longer an active participant. Similarly, excess deductible contributions could be recharacterized as nondeductible contributions.

[Conference Committee Report]

Nondeductible contributions permitted to IRAs

As under the Senate amendment, the conference agreement permits individuals to make designated nondeductible IRA contributions to the extent that deductible contributions are not allowed. Thus, an individual may make nondeductible contributions to the extent of the excess of (1) the lesser of $2,000 or 100 percent of compensation over (2) the IRA deduction limit with respect to the individual. The nondeductible IRA limit is $2,250, in the case of a spousal IRA.

In addition, the conference agreement permits a taxpayer to elect to treat deductible IRA contributions as nondeductible. An individual might make such an election, for example, if the individual had no taxable income for the year after taking into account other deductions.

Under the conference agreement, a designated nondeductible contribution means any contribution to an IRA for a taxable year that is designated as a nondeductible contribution in the manner prescribed by the Secretary. The designation is to be made on the individual's tax return for the taxable year to which the designation relates. Designated nondeductible contributions may be made up to the due date of the individual's tax return for the taxable year (without extensions).

An individual who files an amended return for a taxable year may change the designation of IRA contributions from deductible to nondeductible or vice versa. Such an amended return is to be treated as a return filed for the taxable year to which the return relates. Of course, under the usual rules, any increased tax liability that the individual may owe as a result of such a change in designation is to accompany the amended return.

An individual who makes a designated nondeductible contribution to an IRA for a taxable year or who receives a distribution from an IRA during a taxable year is required to provide such information as the Secretary may prescribe on the individual's tax return for the taxable year and, to the extent required, for succeeding taxable years. The information that may be required includes, but is not limited to (1) the amount of designated nondeductible contributions for the taxable year, (2) the aggregate amount of designated nondeductible contributions for all preceding taxable years which have not previously been withdrawn, (3) the aggregate balance of all IRAs of the individual as of the close of the calendar year with or within which the taxable year ends, and (4) the amount of distributions from IRAs during the taxable year.

If the required information is not provided on the individual's tax return for a taxable year, then all IRA contributions are presumed to have been deductible and, therefore, are taxable upon withdrawal from the IRA. The taxpayer can rebut this presumption with satisfactory evidence that the contributions were nondeductible.

Amounts withdrawn from an IRA during a taxable year are includible in income for the taxable year under rules similar to the rules applicable to qualified plans under section 72. Under special rules applicable to IRAs for purposes of section 72, (1) all IRAs of an individual are treated as one contract, (2) all distributions during a taxable year are treated as one distribution, (3) the value of the contract (calculated after adding back distributions during the year), income on the contract, and investment in the contract is computed as of the close of the calendar year with or within which the taxable year ends, and (4) the aggregate amount of withdrawals excludable from income for all taxable years shall not exceed the taxpayer's investment in the contract for all taxable years. The conference agreement provides that, if an individual withdraws an amount from an IRA during a taxable year and the individual has previously made both deductible and nondeductible IRA contributions, then the amount includible in income for the taxable year is the portion of the amount withdrawn which bears the same ratio to the amount withdrawn for the taxable year as the individual's aggregate nondeductible IRA contributions bear to the aggregate balance of all IRAs of the individual (including rollover IRAs and SEPs).

In the case of a withdrawal from an IRA, for purposes of the rules relating to withholding on pensions, annuities, and certain other deferred income, the payor is to assume that the amount withdrawn is includible in income.

For example, assume that (1) an individual makes a $2,000 IRA contribution for the individual's 1987 tax year, $1,500 of which is deductible, (2) no withdrawls are made from the IRA during the taxable year, (3) the account balance at the end of the taxable year is $2,200, and (4) no prior IRA contributions have been made. The individual is required to report all such information on the individual's 1987 tax return. For 1988, assume (1) the individual makes a $2,000 IRA contribution to another IRA account, none of which is deductible, (2) no withdrawals are made from the IRA during the taxable year, and (3) the aggregate account balance at the end of the taxable year for both IRAs is $4,600. In the individual's 1989 taxable year, no IRA contributions are made and $1,000 is withdrawn from the IRA to which the individual contributed during the 1987 taxable year. At the end of the 1989 taxable year, the aggregate account balance of both IRAs is $4,000. The $1,000 withdrawn from an IRA during the 1989 tax year is treated as partially a return of nondeductible contributions, calculated as the percentage of $1,000 that the total nondeductible contributions ($500 plus $2,000) is of the total account balance ($4,000) at the end of the taxable year plus distributions during the year ($1,000). Thus, 2,500/5,000 or ½ of the $1,000 withdrawal is treated as a return of nondeductible contributions (and, therefore, is not taxable).

Under the conference agreement, an individual who overstates the amount of designated nondeductible contributions made for any taxable year is subject to a $100 penalty for each such overstatement unless the individual can demonstrate that the overstatement was due to reasonable cause.

The trustee of an IRA is required to report certain information to the Secretary and to the individuals for whom an IRA is maintained for each calendar year. This information is to include (1) contributions made to the IRA during the calendar year, (2) distributions from the IRA occurring during the calendar year, and (3) the aggregate account balance as of the end of the calendar year. This information is required to be reported by the January 31 following the end of the calendar year. In the case of a failure to report the required information, as under present law, the penalty for the failure is $25 for each day during which the failure occurs, but the total amount imposed on any person for a failure to report is not to exceed $15,000.

The provisions are effective for contributions and distributions in taxable years beginning after December 31, 1986.

[Senate Committee Report]

Explanation of Provisions

In general

The bill revises the qualification requirements relating to SEPs to permit employees to elect to have SEP contributions made on their behalf or to receive the contributions in cash. In addition, the bill makes miscellaneous changes to the SEP requirements to decrease the administrative burden of maintaining a SEP.

Salary reduction SEPs

Under the bill, employees who participate in a SEP would be permitted to elect to have contributions made to the SEP or to receive the contributions in cash. If an employee elects to have contributions made on the employee's behalf to the SEP, the contribution is not treated as having been distributed or made available to the employee. In addition, the contribution is not treated as an employee contribution merely because the SEP provides the employee with such an election. Therefore, under the bill, an employee is not required to include in income currently the amounts an employee elects to have contributed to the SEP. Elective deferrals under a SEP are to be treated like elective deferrals under a qualified cash or deferred arrangement and, thus, are subject to the $7,000 (indexed) cap on elective deferrals.

Consistent with the rules applicable to elective deferrals under a qualified cash or deferred arrangement or tax-sheltered annuity under present law, elective deferrals under a SEP are not excludable from the definition of wages for employment tax purposes.

The bill provides that the election to have amounts contributed to a SEP or received in cash is available only if at least 50 percent of the employees of the employer elect to have amounts contributed to the SEP and is available only in a taxable year in which the employer maintaining the SEP has 25 or fewer employees [at anytime during the prior taxable year].

* * *

SEP deduction converted to exclusion from income

Under the bill, the amounts contributed to a SEP by an employer on behalf of an employee and the elective deferrals under a SEP are excludable from gross income, rather than deductible as under present law.

In addition, the bill (1) modifies the rules relating to maintaining a SEP on a calendar year basis, and (2) prescribes rules for maintaining a SEP on a taxable year basis. In the case of a SEP maintained on a calendar year basis, contributions made in a calendar year are deductible for the taxable year with which or within which the calendar year ends, and the contributions are treated as made on the last day of the calendar year if the contributions are made by the due date (plus extensions) of the employer's tax return.

In the case of a SEP maintained on a taxable year basis, contributions are deductible for the taxable year and contributions are treated as made on the last day of the taxable year if the contributions are made by the due date of the employer's tax return for the taxable year, plus any extensions of the due date to which the employer is entitled.

Participation requirements

Under the bill, the participation requirements for SEPs are modified to require that an employer make contributions for a year on behalf of each employee who (1) has attained age 21,* (2) has performed services for the employer during at least 3 of the immediately preceding 5 years, and (3) received at least $300 in compensation from the employer for the year. Thus, the bill adds a de minimis exception to the requirement that contributions must be made on behalf of all employees. In addition, the bill provides that this 100-percent participation requirement applies separately to elective arrangements and, for purposes of such elective arrangements, an individual who is eligible is deemed to receive an employer contribution. If nonelective SEP contributions are made for any employee, nonelective contributions must be made for all employees satisfying participation requirements. Similarly, if any employee is eligible to make elective SEP deferrals, all employees satisfying the participation requirements must be eligible to make elective SEP deferrals.

Wage-based contribution limitation for SEPs

Under the bill, the $200,000 limit on compensation taken into account and the $300 de minimis threshold would be indexed at the same time and in the same manner as the dollar limits on benefits under a defined benefit pension plan (sec. 415(d)). As a result, these amounts will be indexed by reference to percentage changes in the social security taxable wage base.

Definition of computation period

The bill permits an employer to elect to use a computation period other than the calendar year for purposes of determining contributions to a SEP. Under the bill, a permissible computation period (other than a calendar year) will include an employer's taxable year, subject to any terms and conditions that the Secretary of the Treasury may prescribe.

Integration rules

The bill eliminates the current rules under which nonelective SEP contributions may be combined with employer OASDI contributions for purposes of the applicable nondiscrimination. In place of these rules, the bill permits nonelective SEP contributions to be tested for nondiscrimination under the new rules for qualified defined contribution plans permitting a limited disparity between the contribution percentages applicable to compensation below and compensation above the social security wage base.

Effective Date

The provisions are effective for years beginning after December 31, 1986.

* Age 25 is reduced to age 21 under the provisions of the bill making technical corrections to the retirement Equity Act of 1984.

[Conference Committee Report]

The conference agreement follows the Senate amendment with two modifications of the special nondiscrimination test applicable to salary reduction SEPs.

Under the first modification, the deferral percentage for each highly compensated employee cannot exceed the average deferral percentage for all other nonhighly compensated eligible employees by more than 12 percent.

Under the second modification, the exception from the rule of constructive receipt is limited to employers that did not have more than 25 employees at any time during the prior taxable year.

The provisions apply for taxable years beginning after December 31, 1986.

[Senate Committee Report]

[SEPs] Maximum age requirement

* * *

The bill reduces from 25 to 21 the maximum age requirement that a SEP may impose as a condition of plan participation. Thus, a SEP may not require, as a condition of participation, attainment of an age greater than 21 or the performance of service during more than three of the immediately preceding five calendar years (whichever occurs later).

[Conference Committee Report]

* * *

The conference agreement follows the Senate amendment except as follows:

a. Simplified employee pensions.—The provision in the Senate amendment relating to participation requirements under simplified employee pensions is effective for plan years beginning after the date of enactment.

[¶ 12,050.065]

Committee Reports on P.L. 98-369 (Tax Reform Act of 1984)

[Conference Committee Report]

* * *

Before-death distribution rules

* * *

Under the conference agreement, a trust is not a qualified trust unless the plan of which it is a part provides that the entire interest of the employee will be distributed no later than the required commencement date. Alternatively, the entire interest is to be distributed, beginning no later than the required commencement date, over (1) the life of the employer, (2) the lives of the employee and a designated beneficiary, (3) a period not extending beyond the life expectancy of the employee, or (4) a period not extending beyond the life expectancy of the employee and a designated beneficiary.

Under the conference agreement, the required commencement date is April 1 of the calendar year following the year in which (1) the employee attains age 70 ½ or (2) the employee retires, whichever is later. If an employee is a 5-percent owner (as defined in section 416) with respect to the plan year ending in the calendar year in which the employee attains age 70 ½, the employee's entire interest is to be distributed no later than April 1 of the calendar year following such plan year even though the employee has not retired. In the case of employer securities that may not be distributed on account of the 84-month holding period of section 409A(d), the rule applicable to 5-percent owners does not apply with respect to such securities until the applicable holding period expires.

Of course, the conferees intend that an individual who is subject to the 70 ½ distribution requirement on the effective date of the conference agreement will not be treated as failing to meet the 70 ½ distribution requirement merely because the individual would have been required to begin payments if the rules had been effective in earlier years. The distribution requirement with respect to such an individual commences on April 1 of the year following the first year for which the provision is effective, based on the individual's age in that year.

For purposes of the before-death distribution rules, the conferees intend that an employee's "entire interest" does not include ancillary benefits (such as lump sum death benefits) that are, in no event, available to the employee.

The conferees intend that, in implementing these before-death distribution rules, Treasury regulations will require that distributions over any of the permissible periods are to satisfy a minimum distribution rule similar to the rules under present law, except that the participant's life expectancy may be recalculated no more frequently than annually. Similarly, if payments are made over the joint life expectancy of the employee and the employee's spouse, such joint life expectancy may be recalculated no more frequently than annually. The conferees intend that, in the case of payments made over the joint life expectancy of the employee and a nonspouse beneficiary, Treasury regulations will provide a method of recalculation under the minimum distribution rule that takes into consideration the change in life expectancy of the employee, but not the change in life expectancy of the nonspouse beneficiary.

Distributions over any of the permissible periods from or under a defined benefit pension plan are deemed to satisfy the minimum distribution rule if the plan makes substantially nonincreasing annual payments over any of these periods. The conferees intend, however, that regulations will permit defined benefit pension plan distributions to increase under certain circumstances. For example, certain cost-of-living increases in an employee's annual payments, cash refunds of employee contributions upon an employee's death, an increase in annual benefit payments to the employee upon the death of the employee's beneficiary, and increases based on investment experience generally could be permitted. In no event, however, may increasing payments be permitted if the effect of the increase is circumvention of the minimum distribution rules.

Under a defined contribution plan, the minimum distribution rule is satisfied if the payments are subject to an irrevocable payout schedule that satisfies the minimum distribution rule. In addition, a defined benefit pension plan or a defined contribution plan may satisfy the minimum distribution rule by distributing an immediate annuity contract that provides for payments that satisfy the minimum distribution rule (e.g., provides for substantially nonincreasing annual payments).

The conferees intend that, as under present law, plan distributions, including distributions under annuity contracts distributed by a qualified plan, are required to meet the incidental benefit rule. For example, if a plan provides for a before-death distribution of an immediate annuity contract to the employee and a beneficiary, then the present value of the payments projected to be paid to the employee are to be more than 50 percent of the present value of the payments projected to be paid to the employee and the beneficiary. As under present law, distributions in accordance with the rules relating to qualified joint and surviving annuities will satisfy the incidental benefit rule.

After-death distribution rules

The conference agreement provides rules that apply in the case of an employee's death before the employee's entire interest has been distributed. In the case in which distributions have commenced to the employee before death, the conference agreement provides that the remaining portion of the employee's interest is to be distributed at least as rapidly as under the method of distribution in effect prior to death. For example, if an employee elected to receive benefits in the form of equal annual installments for a term of 20 years (which did not extend beyond the life expectancy of the employee) and the employee died after benefits had been paid for 10 years, the remaining interest of the employee could be distributed in equal annual installments over a term not exceeding 10 years. Of course, the beneficiary could elect to accelerate payments of the remaining interest.

In the case in which distributions have not commenced to the employee before the employee's death, the conference agreement provides that the entire interest of the employee is to be distributed within 5 years after the death of the employee. Under the conference agreement, two exceptions apply to this 5-year distribution rule.

The first exception provides that the 5-year rule does not apply if (1) any portion of the employee's interest is payable to (or for the benefit of) a designated beneficiary, (2) the portion of the employee's interest to which the beneficiary is entitled will be distributed over the life of the beneficiary (or over a period not extending beyond the life expectancy of the beneficiary), and (3) the distributions commence no later than 1 year after the date of the employee's death. The conferees intend that this exception applies only if amounts are paid to the beneficiary under rules that satisfy the minimum distribution rule applicable to before-death distributions. Recalculation of life expectancy is not permitted under this provision.

The Secretary may, under regulations, provide exceptions to the 1-year rule under appropriate circumstances (e.g., if a beneficiary cannot be located). The conferees intend, however, that the regulations could require that catch-up distributions be made with respect to amounts deferred under such exceptions.

The second exception applies if the designated beneficiary is the surviving spouse of the employee. Under this provision, the 5-year rule does not apply if (1) the portion of employee's interest to which the surviving spouse is entitled will be distributed over the life of the surviving spouse (or over a period not extending beyond the life expectancy of the surviving spouse), and (2) the distributions commence no later than the date on which the employee would have attained age 70 ½. If the surviving spouse dies before payments are required to commence, then the 5-year rule is to be applied as if the surviving spouse were the employee. The conferees intend that payments to the surviving spouse will satisfy the exception to the 5-year distribution requirement if payments are made pursuant to a qualified joint and survivor annuity.

For purposes of the after-death distribution rules, the conference agreement provides that any amount paid to a child is treated as if it had been paid to the surviving spouse of an employee if the amount becomes payable to the surviving spouse when the child reaches the age of majority (or such other event as may be specified in Treasury regulations).

Under the conference agreement, similar rules are provided for after-death distributions from or under an individual retirement account or annuity. In addition, under the conference agreement, the rules applicable to after-death distributions under an annuity contract are to apply to a custodial account that is treated as a tax-sheltered annuity contract (sec. 403(b)(7)).

[Senate Committee Report]

Distributions prior to age 59 ½

Under the bill, the 10-percent penalty tax on premature distributions applies only to a participant to the extent that the distribution is attributable to years in which the participant was a 5-percent owner (as defined in section 416 of the Code) without regard to whether the plan was top heavy for such years.

[Senate Committee Report]

Effective Dates

The provision repeals the amendments to Code sec. 401(a)(9) that were enacted by section 242(a) of TEFRA and applied to plan years beginning after December 31, 1983. The new provisions generally are effective for plan years beginning after December 31, 1984. In the case of a governmental plan (as defined in section 414(d)), the new distribution rules are effective for plan years beginning after December 31, 1986. In the case of plans maintained pursuant to one or more collective bargaining agreements, the new rules do not apply to years beginning before the earlier of (1) January 1, 1988, or (2) the date on which the last of the collective bargaining agreements relating to the plan terminates. Employee designations made before January 1, 1984, in accordance with section 242(b)(2) of TEFRA remain effective. Thus, if an employee made a proper designation before January 1, 1984, such designation continues to be effective and a plan that makes a distribution in accordance with such designation does not fail to satisfy these new rules.

[House Committee Report]

The bill revises the definition of a key employee to include any employee, rather than any participant in an employer plan, who has the requisite relationship to the employer. An employee includes a former employee who must be considered under the five-year lookback rule. In addition, the bill provides that, for purposes of determining the ten employees owning the largest interests in the employer, (1) only employees with annual pay in excess of the dollar limit for the year on annual additions to qualified defined contribution plans ($30,000 for 1984) are taken into account as key employees and (2) if two employees have the same interest in the employer, the employee with greater annual compensation is treated as having a larger interest. Further, the bill clarifies that the determination of the amount of an employee's interest in an employer for purposes of determining the top-ten owners, 5-percent owners, or 1-percent owners is determined without regard to the aggregation rules of sections 414(b), (c), or (m).

Under the bill, the requirement that the employer make a minimum contribution on behalf of each participant who is not a key employee applies to a SEP if the SEP arrangement is top-heavy.

The bill clarifies that distributions under a terminated plan are taken into account under the 5-year lookback rule in determining the top heavy status of plans maintained by an employer.

The bill provides that the $200,000 limit on compensation taken into account under SEPs will be adjusted for inflation at the same time and in the same manner as the adjustments to the overall dollar limit on annual additions under a qualified defined contribution plan. In addition, the bill clarifies that no adjustment will be made to the $200,000 limit on compensation taken into account under the rules for top-heavy plans until adjustments are made to the overall dollar limits on contributions and benefits.

[House Committee Report]

The bill clarifies that the provision applies with respect to individuals dying after December 31, 1983.

[House Committee Report]

The bill provides that, if an employer does not maintain an integrated plan at any time during the taxable year, OASDI contributions may be taken into account as contributions by the employer to an employee's simplified employee pension (SEP). This rule applies, however, only if OASDI contributions are taken into account with respect to each employee maintaining a SEP.

See also ¶ 12,050.065 for the Committee Reports on before-death and after death distribution rules enacted by the Act.

[¶ 12,050.07]

Committee Report on P.L. 97-248 (Tax Equity and Fiscal Responsibility Act of 1982)

Under the bill, a distribution from an IRA is not includable in the recipient's gross income to the extent that the participant makes a rollover contribution to another eligible retirement plan within 60 days of the receipt of the distribution.

If the recipient makes a rollover contribution of less than the full amount of the distribution, the amount retained will be taxed in the year of receipt as ordinary income.

Effective Date

The bill applies to distributions made after December 31, 1982.—**Senate Finance Committee Report.**

See also the Committee Reports at ¶ 12,400.06.

[¶ 12,050.075]

House Committee Report on P.L. 97-34 (Economic Recovery Tax Act of 1981)

[House Committee Report]

Under the bill, an amount in an IRA or in an individually-directed account in a qualified plan which is used to acquire a collectible would be treated as if distributed in the taxable year of the acquisition. The usual income tax rules for distributions from an IRA or from a qualified plan apply.

A "collectible" is defined in the bill as any work of art, rug, antique, metal, gem, stamp, coin, alcoholic beverage, or any other item of tangible personal property specified by the Secretary.

Although the bill changes the tax treatment of the acquisition of collectibles under individually-directed accounts, it does not modify the tax-qualification standards of the Code for pension, profit-sharing, or stock bonus plans or the nontax rules of ERISA.

For example, the tax qualification of a pension plan would not be adversely affected merely because an amount was treated as distributed to a participant under this provision at a time when the plan is not permitted to make a distribution to the participant.

The committee expects that Treasury regulations will provide for appropriate adjustments that will avoid double taxation of benefits under a plan where the collectible is not actually distributed.

The provision is effective for property acquired after December 31, 1981, in taxable years ending after that date.

[¶ 12,050.077]

Committee Reports on P.L. 97-34 (Economic Recovery Tax Act of 1981)

For Committee Reports on P.L. 97-34, Sec. 311, relating to individual retirement plans, see ¶ 11,330.02.

For Committee Report on P.L. 97-34, Sec. 312, relating to self-employed retirement plans, see ¶ 11,850.062.

[¶ 12,050.08]

Committee Report on P.L. 96-222 (Technical Corrections Act of 1979)

[Senate Finance Committee Report]

Sec. 101(a)(10)(A)—SEP participation.

The Revenue Act of 1978 created a new type of individual retirement plan, known as a simplified employee pension. Employer contributions to simplified employee pensions must not discriminate in favor of employees who are officers, shareholders, or highly compensated. In testing employer contributions for discrimination, certain employees who are included in a collective bargaining unit or who are nonresident aliens may be excluded from consideration. However, the simplified employee pension rules may have required employers to include these employees in the group of employees who are entitled to share in employer contributions to simplified employee pensions.

The requirement that certain collective bargaining unit employees or nonresident aliens share in employer contributions to simplified employee pensions even though these employees can be excluded from consideration in testing whether simplified employee pensions are discriminatory is inconsistent with the purpose of the simplified employee pension provisions and with the corresponding provisions of the Internal Revenue Code relating to tax-qualified pension plans.

The bill permits certain employees who are included in a collective bargaining unit or who are nonresident aliens to be excluded from the group of employees who are entitled to share in employer contributions to simplified employee pensions.

The provision applies to taxable years beginning after December 31, 1978. This is the same effective date as was provided by the Revenue Act of 1978 with respect to simplified employee pensions.

Sec. 101(a)(10)(C)—SEP excess contributions.

The rules relating to individual retirement accounts and annuities permit the withdrawal of an excess contribution (other than a rollover contribution) without the usual 10 percent additional income tax on early distributions to the extent no deduction was allowed for the contribution. The early distribution tax applies, however, if the amount contributed for the year exceeds $1,750 and the excess is not withdrawn by the time for filing the tax return for the year of the excess contribution (including extensions). Under present law, deductible contributions to individual retirement accounts and annuities may not exceed $1,750, except in the case of a simplified employee pension where contributions up to $7,500 may be deductible. No dollar limitation applies to an excess rollover contribution. Consequently, if an excess contribution is made by an employer to an individual retirement account or annuity of an employee under the simplified employee pension rules and the amount of the contribution is greater than $1,750, the 10 percent additional income tax could apply if the excess is not withdrawn in time.

The $1,750 limit of present law is not appropriate for employer contributions to simplified employee pensions because up to $7,500 of such contributions for a taxable year may be deductible.

The bill permits an individual to withdraw excess employer contributions to a simplified employee pension free of the 10-percent additional income tax where the withdrawal does not exceed the amount of the employer contribution or $7,500 whichever is less. The bill does not affect the treatment of contributions other than excess employer contributions.

This provision applies for taxable years beginning after December 31, 1978. This is the same effective date as was provided for simplified employee pensions under the Revenue Act of 1978.

Sec. 101(a)(10)(F)—Coordination rules for H.R. 10 and tax-option corporation plans.—The Committee report on Sec. 101(a)(10)(F) is at ¶ 11,850.065.

Sec. 101(a)(10)(G)—SEP social security integration barred.

Under present law, employer contributions to the individual retirement accounts or annuities of employees can qualify as employer contributions to the simplified employee pensions of employees if an employer contribution is made to the individual retirement account or annuity of each employee who is entitled to a contribution.[1] Although the employer's contributions must generally bear a uniform relationship to the total compensation of each employee, these contributions can be integrated with the Social Security system. Under the integration rules, which are generally similar to the rules for integrated H.R. 10 plans, if certain requirements are met, the employer contribution on behalf of an employee is reduced by the amount of Social Security tax to be imposed on the employer with respect to the employee's wages. As under an integrated H.R. 10 plan, contributions for owner-employees are reduced by the amount of the self-employment tax imposed on the individual's earnings and, in the case of a self-employed individual other than an owner-employee, by an amount equal to the Social Security tax which would have been imposed if the individual's earnings from self-employment were wages.

Under the 1978 Act, it is not clear whether an employer could make integrated contributions to the simplified employee pension of an employee while maintaining an integrated qualified pension, profit-sharing, or stock bonus plan for the same employee (possibly reducing the employee's benefits twice with respect to the same benefits or contributions considered to be provided by the employer under Social Security).

The bill clarifies present law by providing that an employer may not make integrated contributions to simplified employee pensions for a year in which the employer maintains an integrated pension, etc., plan. Although it is possible to design rules which would permit partial integration of a simplified employee pension where a partially integrated pension, etc. plan is maintained, the committee believes that the complexity of the rules for partial integration would be inconsistent with the committee's intent in providing for simplified employee pensions. The House bill did not include any similar provision.

The amendment applies for taxable years beginning after December 31, 1978. This is the same effective date as was provided by the Revenue Act of 1978 for simplified employee pensions.

[¶ 12,050.09]

Committee Report on P.L. 95-600 (Revenue Act of 1978)

Sec. 152—Simplified employee pensions—Senate Committee Report.

If an employee establishes and maintains an individual retirement account or an individual retirement annuity which meets the requirements of the bill, the limitation of deductions for contributions to the account is increased to the lesser of $7,500 or 15 percent of the employee's earned income for amounts contributed by his or her employer to the account or annuity. The limits on employee contributions to an account or annuity are not changed by the bill. For example, if the employer contribution to an employee's account is less than the usual limit on deductible contributions by the employee for a year, the employee could make additional contributions that year to make up the difference. On the other hand, the employee could not make additional deductible contributions to the account for a year in which the employer contributions exceed the usual limits. In the case of an employee who is an officer or shareholder, or in the case of an owner-employee, the deduction limit is reduced if Social Security taxes are treated as employer contributions. (See additional requirements, below.)

The employee's deduction for amounts contributed by his or her employer to an individual retirement account or individual retirement annuity would be allowed even though the employee is an active participant in a qualified plan, a governmental plan, or a tax-sheltered annuity. However, make-up contributions would not be allowed.

Additional requirements.—Under the bill, the expanded deduction limits apply to an employee's individual retirement account or annuity only if employer contributions to it are made under a written formula followed by the employer and if the account or annuity is maintained solely by the employee. The formula is required to provide nondiscriminatory contributions for a calendar year for each employee who has attained age 25 and has performed service for the employer during any part of 3 of the immediately preceding 5 calendar years. The employer contributions provided under the formula must not discriminate in favor of any employee who is an officer, shareholder, or highly compensated. However, for purposes of testing whether the employer's contributions benefit the requisite employees, employees covered by a collective bargaining agreement and nonresident aliens may be excluded from consideration if those employees could be excluded from consideration under similar rules applicable to qualified pension plans.

Under the bill, employer contributions are generally considered to be discriminatory unless they bear a uniform relationship to the first $100,000 of each employee's total compensation. The employer's formula may, however, provide that employer contributions for each employee are reduced by the amount of the employer's share of Social Security tax. In the case of contributions on behalf of a sole proprietor or a partner who is an owner-employee (within the meaning of the H.R. 10 plan rules), the reduction for an owner-employee is the amount of self-employment tax imposed on that individual. In any case, the employer's formula must specify the method for allocating contributions to each covered employee.

Other IRA rules.—The bill makes no change in the present IRA rules realting to distributions, early or late withdrawals, loans, or self-dealing.

Reporting requirement.—The bill authorizes the Secretary to require such reports as may be required to carry out the purposes of the provisions. The committee expects that these requirements will be minimal.

The amendment applies for taxable years beginning after December 31, 1978.

Secs. 156(c)(1) and (c)(3)—Tax Sheltered annuity rollover. The Conference Committee Report on Sec. 156 is at ¶ 11,800.06.

Sec. 157(c)—Withdrawal of excess contributions—House Committee Report.

The committee bill would allow an individual who has made a total contribution for a year which does not exceed $1,750 to an IRA, all or part of which is an excess contribution, and who does not correct the excess contribution prior to the due date for filing his or her tax return for the year, later to withdraw the excess contributed for the year without (1) incurring a 10-percent premature distribution penalty tax, and (2) being required to include the amount withdrawn in gross income.[1] (In order to avoid administrative and computational problems, the taxpayer is not required to withdraw any earnings attributable to the excess contribution; if such earnings were withdrawn they would be subject to tax, as under present law.) The amendment would apply only to the extent that a deduction was not allowed for the amount of the excess contribution withdrawn. (A deduction would be treated as not having been allowed if the taxpayer did not claim the deduction, or if IRS disallowed the deduction upon audit. If a deduction was claimed and allowed for a year which the statute of limitations is not closed, a taxpayer could come under these provisions by filing an amended return for the year for which the excess contribution was made.)

The committee bill provides a transitional rule for excess contributions to IRAs for taxable years beginning before January 1, 1978. For such excess contributions, the provisions of the amendment would apply without regard to the $1,750 limitation. Thus, an individual could withdraw all such excess contributions, regardless of amount, to the extent deductions were not previously allowed for the excess contributions.

The committee bill also allows an individual to withdraw an excess contribution (regardless of the amount) made with respect to a rollover contribution (including an attempted rollover contribution) in any case in which the excess contribution occurred because the individual making the contribution reasonably relied on erroneous information required to be supplied by the plan, trust, or institution making the distribution which was the subject of the rollover.

The committee bill applies to distributions from IRAs in taxable years beginning after December 31, 1975. Thus, under the bill, the IRS is to refund to taxpayers all penalties and income taxes based on distributions from IRAs after that date which corrected previous excess contributions.

The amendments made by this section will apply to distributions from IRAs in taxable years beginning after December 31, 1975.

Sec. 157(d)—Flexible premium payments—House Committee Report.

The committee bill would require that an annuity contract provide for the flexible payment of premiums in order to qualify as an individual retirement annuity.

The committee bill provides a transitional rule under which the exchange before January 1, 1981, of any fixed premium individual retirement annuity issued on or before the effective date of the amendment for a flexible premium annuity contract would, at the election of the individual, be treated as a nontaxable exchange.

The amendment made by this section will apply to contracts issued or exchanged after the date of its enactment.

Sec. 157(e)—Clarification of dollar limitation—House Committee Report.

---

[1] Each employee who has (1) attained age 25 and (2) performed service for the employer during any 3 of the immediately preceding 5 calendar years must be entitled to a contribution.

[1] As under present law, the 6-percent excess contribution tax would not apply to the year of withdrawal.

The committee bill would modify the definitions of an individual retirement annuity and a retirement bond to make it clear that the maximum dollar limitation for deductible contributions to a spousal IRA is $1,750.

The amendments made by this section will apply to taxable years beginning after December 31, 1976.

Sec. 157(g)(3)—Rollover by surviving spouse—The House Committee Report on Sec. 157 is at ¶ 11,750.06.

Sec. 157(h)(3)—Removal of five-year requirement. The House Committee Report on Sec. 157(h) is at ¶ 11,750.06.

[¶ 12,050.10]

Committee Report on P.L. 93-406 (Employee Retirement Income Security Act of 1974)

[Conference Committee Explanation]

Requirements for an IRA.—Under the conference substitute, the total amounts payable under qualified endowment contracts cannot be greater than $1,500 per year. However, an individual may contribute (and deduct) the difference between his maximum allowable retirement savings deduction and the retirement savings element under an endowment contract through another funding medium (such as a trusteed bank account). Under the conference substitute the insurance companies are to provide (before the close of the year) every individual who has purchased a qualified endowment contract with a statement as to the portion of the premiums which is deductible and the portion which is not deductible, as well as any other information required under regulations. A similar statement must be furnished to the Internal Revenue Service.

Insurance contracts are restricted to endowment contracts in order to provide a substantial savings element. The endowment contract also must be issued by a life insurance company qualified to sell insurance in the jurisdiction where the contract is sold (and may include no insurance element other than life insurance). In addition, the contract must mature no later than the taxable year in which the individual attains age 70 ½. The conferees intend that for an endowment contract to qualify, the premiums payable under the contract (for any given maturity value) are not to increase over the life of the contract, the cash surrender value of the contract at the maturity date is to be not less than the death benefit payable under the contract at any time, and the death benefit at some point during the life of the contract must exceed the greater of the cash value or the sum of the premiums paid under the contract.

Distributions from qualified endowment contracts are to be taxable as ordinary income to the extent allocable to retirement savings, and are to be taxed as life insurance proceeds to the extent allocable to life insurance. When a contract has matured, the full value of the contract will constitute retirement savings and all amounts payable under a matured contract are to be taxed as ordinary income to the recipient (whether or not he is the individual who made contributions to the account and whether or not that individual is alive at the time the payments are made from the account).

Under the conference substitute, the assets of an individual retirement account may not be commingled with other property, except in a common trust fund or investment fund (i.e., a group trust), solely for the purposes of diversifying investments, under rules similar to those established in Rev. Rul. 56-267, 1956-1 C.B. 206. Also, following Rev. Rul. 56-267, the conferees intend that, solely for purposes of diversification of investments, the assets of qualified individual retirement accounts may be pooled with the assets of qualified section 401(a) trusts, without adversely affecting the tax-qualification of either the individual retirement accounts or the section 401(a) trusts. The conferees intend that the group trust itself will be entitled to exemption from tax under the Internal Revenue Code in accordance with the rules of Rev. Rul. 56-267.

The conferees intend that this legislation with respect to individual retirement accounts is not to limit in any way the application of the Federal securities laws to individual retirement accounts or the application to them of the laws relating to common trusts or investment funds maintained by any institution. As a result, the Securities and Exchange Commission will have the authority to act on the issues arising with respect to individual retirement accounts independently of this legislation.

The conferees understand that the Internal Revenue Service anticipates developing a prototype individual retirement account which would include a full disclosure of all the material elements governing the retirement savings deduction. This prototype plan would qualify under the requirements for an individual retirement account. Other plans would be required to seek prior approval from the Internal Revenue Service and the conferees expect that one of the requirements for approval would be a disclosure statement of all the material elements governing the retirement savings deduction. The conferees also expect the Internal Revenue Service to develop a pamphlet which sets forth the restrictions and limitations with regard to the individual retirement accounts, including, for example, the penalties for premature distributions, the fact that the account is not eligible for estate and gift tax advantages or the lump-sum distribution rules that qualified plans are entitled to. It is the hope of the conferees that such pamphlet would receive wide distribution so that individuals would be fully informed on the restrictions and limitations of such an account. Also, in accordance with regulations to be prescribed by the Secretary of Treasury or his delegate, there is to be disclosure of such matters as load factors for insurance contracts and earnings factors for individual retirement accounts. These required disclosures are to be made in layman's language, and civil penalties are imposed under the substitute for failure to adequately disclose.

Requirements for an IRA annuity.—Under the conference substitute, retirement savings may also be invested in annuity contracts. This may be an individual annuity contract, or a joint and survivor contract for the benefit of the individual and his spouse. The annual premium for the contract is not to exceed $1,500, and the contract is to be nontransferable and is not to be used as security for a loan. Also, distributions from the account must begin by the end of the year in which the individual attains age 70 ½.

Employer and union-sponsored IRA's.—Under the substitute, employers and labor unions (and other employee associations) are to be able to establish individual retirement accounts for their employees or members. There is no requirement that the accounts must be established on a nondiscriminatory basis (since any employee not covered under an employer-sponsored account could establish his own account) but, of course, if the employer also maintains a qualified plan, he cannot satisfy the coverage requirements with respect to that plan by taking into account the fact that employees not covered under the plan are covered by individual retirement accounts. Even if the contributions are made by the employer, these amounts constitute income to the employee, and are subject to FICA and FUTA taxes. However, employer contributions are not to be subject to withholding for income tax purposes if it is reasonable for the employer to believe that the employee will be entitled to receive a deduction for the contribution.

Taxation of distributions—in general.—Generally, the individual is to have a zero basis in his individual retirement account and the proceeds are to be fully taxable when distributed. These distributions are not to be eligible for capital gains treatment, or the special averaging rules applicable to lump-sum distributions from qualified plans (although the general averaging rules of sec. 1301 are to be available). Also, the amounts in individual retirement accounts are not to be excluded from tax for purposes of estate and gift tax.

Premature distributions.—In the event of a premature distribution (or deemed distribution) from the account before the individual attains age 59 ½, the individual's tax on this amount is to be increased by 10 percent of the total distribution (except in the case of death or disability, or distributions of excess contributions made within the time for filing the individual's tax return for the year in which the excess contributions occur).

If an individual borrows money from an individual account (or from a group trust in which the account assets were invested) the entire account of the individual is disqualified, earnings on the account are no longer tax-exempt, and the participant is then to be taxed as if he had received a distribution of the fair market value of all the assets in his account. (If he borrows money, using his interest in the account as security, the portion used as security is to be treated as a distribution.) A similar result (i.e., deemed distribution of the entire account) would follow if the individual borrowed money from the insurance company issuing an annuity or endowment contract, or otherwise used the contract as security for a loan. Clearly, if the assets of the account were invested in such a way as to provide for the direct and immediate benefit of the participant (for example, if the account were used for a downpayment on the house where he lived) then the entire account would be deemed to be distributed. Of course, in the case of any deemed distribution from an individual retirement account, the amount of the distribution would not be includible in income a second time in a later year when the amount was actually distributed. (Questions of the order in which income is distributed where only part of the account is disqualified are to be determined under regulations.)

An individual may invest directly in an endowment contract but does not receive a deduction for the part of the premium which is allocable to life insurance protection. Thus, where the assets of an individual retirement account are invested in a qualifying endowment contract for the participant, this transaction is to be treated as an automatic rollover by the account, and only the amount of the assets which are allocable to the purchase of life insurance protection under the endowment contract are to be deemed to be distributed to the participant. This amount would be includible in income by the participant, but would not be subject to the 10 percent tax on premature distributions.

* * *

Tax-free rollovers to facilitate pension transfers.—To facilitate portability of pensions—or their transfer with the employee as he changes jobs—the conference substitute provides that money or property may be distributed from a tax-qualified plan or from an individual retirement account to the plan participant, on a tax-free basis, if the same money or property is reinvested by the participant within 60 days in a qualifying individual retirement account.

In the case of distributions from a qualified plan, the distribution must be a lump-sum distribution (see Part X, Lump-Sum distributions) to qualify as a tax-free rollover.

Amounts received from a qualified plan may also be transfered to another qualified plan through the medium of an individual retirement account (with the consent of the individual's new employer) but in this case the conduit retirement account must consist of nothing but assets transferred from a qualified plan (and the earnings on this amount) to prevent a situation where retirement savings might indirectly obtain tax advantages not intended. (These qualified plan distributions may also be reinvested directly in the qualified plan of the individual's new employer on a tax-free basis, if the reinvestment occurs within 60 days after the individual receives the distribution.) However, an individual may have one individual retirement account for transferred savings from a qualified plan and another which represents a normal individual account set aside. For similar reasons, if the individual retirement account contains assets transferred from an H.R. 10 plan, on behalf of a self-employed person, no rollover is permitted from that retirement account to a qualified corporate plan.

Also, in the case of rollovers from a qualified plan, the amount contributed to the individual retirement account is to be the amount received, less the amount contributed to the plan by the individual as an employee contribution. (This is because the employee must always have a zero basis is his individual retirement account.)

Under the committee substitute, rollovers are permitted to and from qualifying investments in individual retirement bonds (discussed below) on the same basis as investments in other types of individual retirement accounts and annuities. At age 70 ½, the individual must cash in his bonds (since the proceeds of the bonds will be deemed to be distributed in full) but the assets may be rolled over into an investment which will satisfy the age 70 ½ payment requirements.

Tax-free rollovers between individual retirement accounts may occur only once every three years.

* * *

Other rules.—The conference substitute provides that the proceeds of individual retirement accounts, etc., are to constitute retirement income for purposes of the retirement income credit. The substitute also includes the provisions of the Senate amendment that if a retirement account or annuity is transferred pursuant to a divorce settlement, the transfer is not to be taxable.

Effective Date

The deduction for retirement savings is to be available for taxable years beginning after December 31, 1974. The tax-free rollover of assets between qualified plans applies to transfers after the date of enactment [September 2, 1974].

[Code Sec. 408A]

[¶ 12,097.06]

Committee Report on P.L. 109-280 (Pension Protection Act of 2006)

[Joint Committee on Taxation Report]

The provision allows distributions from tax-qualified retirement plans, tax-sheltered annuities, and governmental 457 plans to be rolled over directly from such plan into a Roth IRA, subject to the present law rules that apply to rollovers from a traditional IRA into a Roth IRA. For example, a rollover from a tax-qualified retirement plan into a Roth IRA is includible in gross income (except to the extent it represents a return of after-tax contributions), and the 10-percent early distribution tax does not apply. Similarly, an individual with AGI of $100,000 or more could not roll over amounts from a tax-qualified retirement plan directly into a Roth IRA.

Effective Date

The provision is effective for distributions made after December 31, 2007.

[¶ 12,097.07]

Committee Reports on P.L. 109-222 (Tax Increase Prevention and Reconciliation Act of 2005).

[Conference Committee Report]

Present Law

There are two general types of individual retirement arrangements ("IRAs"): traditional IRAs and Roth IRAs. The total amount that an individual may contribute to one or more IRAs for a year is generally limited to the lesser of: (1) a dollar amount ($4,000 for 2006); and (2) the amount of the individual's compensation that is includible in gross income for the year. In the case of an individual who has attained age 50 before the end of the year, the dollar amount is increased by an additional amount ($1,000 for 2006). In the case of a married couple, contributions can be made up to the dollar limit for each spouse if the combined compensation of the spouses that is includible in gross income is at least equal to the contributed amount. IRA contributions in excess of the applicable limit are generally subject to an excise tax of six percent per year until withdrawn.

Contributions to a traditional IRA may or may not be deductible. The extent to which contributions to a traditional IRA are deductible depends on whether or not the individual (or the individual's spouse) is an active participant in an employer-sponsored retirement plan and the taxpayer's AGI. An individual may deduct his or her contributions to a traditional IRA if neither the individual nor the individual's spouse is an active participant in an employer-sponsored retirement plan. If an individual or the individual's spouse is an active participant in an employer-sponsored retirement plan, the deduction is phased out for taxpayers with AGI over certain levels. To the extent an individual does not or cannot make deductible contributions, the individual may make nondeductible contributions to a traditional IRA, subject to the maximum contribution limit. Distributions from a traditional IRA are includible in gross income to the extent not attributable to a return of nondeductible contributions.

Individuals with adjusted gross income ("AGI") below certain levels may make contributions to a Roth IRA (up to the maximum IRA contribution limit). The maximum Roth IRA contribution is phased out between $150,000 to $160,000 of AGI in the case of married taxpayers filing a joint return and between $95,000 to $105,000 in the case of all other returns (except a separate return of a married individual).[541] Contributions to a Roth IRA are not deductible. Qualified distributions from a Roth IRA are excludable from gross income. Distributions from a Roth IRA that are not qualified distributions are includible in gross income to the extent attributable to earnings. In general, a qualified distribution is a distribution that is made on or after the individual attains age , death, or disability or which is a qualified special purpose distribution. A distribution is not a qualified distribution if it is made within the five-taxable year period beginning with the taxable year for which an individual first made a contribution to a Roth IRA.

A taxpayer with AGI of $100,000 or less may convert all or a portion of a traditional IRA to a Roth IRA.[542] The amount converted is treated as a distribution from the traditional IRA for income tax purposes, except that the 10-percent additional tax on early withdrawals does not apply.

In the case of a distribution from a Roth IRA that is not a qualified distribution, certain ordering rules apply in determining the amount of the distribution that is includible in income. For this purpose, a distribution that is not a qualified distribution is treated as made in the following order: (1) regular Roth IRA contributions; (2) conversion contributions (on a first in, first out basis); and (3) earnings. To the extent a distribution is treated as made from a conversion contribution, it is treated as made first from the portion, if any, of the conversion contribution that was required to be included in income as a result of the conversion.

Includible amounts withdrawn from a traditional IRA or a Roth IRA before attainment of age , death, or disability are subject to an additional 10-percent early withdrawal tax, unless an exception applies.

House Bill

No provision.

Senate Amendment

No provision.

Conference Agreement

The conference agreement eliminates the income limits on conversions of traditional IRAs to Roth IRAs.[543] Thus, taxpayers may make such conversions without regard to their AGI.

For conversions occurring in 2010, unless a taxpayer elects otherwise, the amount includible in gross income as a result of the conversion is included ratably in 2011 and 2012. That is, unless a taxpayer elects otherwise, none of the amount includible in gross income as a result of a conversion occurring in 2010 is included in income in 2010, and half of the income resulting from the conversion is includible in gross income in 2011 and half in 2012. However, income inclusion is accelerated if converted amounts are distributed before 2012.[544] In that case, the amount included in income in the year of the distribution is increased by the amount distributed, and the amount included in income in 2012 (or 2011 and 2012 in the case of a distribution in 2010) is the lesser of: (1) half of the amount includible in income as a result of the conversion; and (2) the remaining portion of such amount not already included in income. The following example illustrates the application of the accelerated inclusion rule.

Example.—Taxpayer A has a traditional IRA with a value of $100, consisting of deductible contributions and earnings. A does not have a Roth IRA. A converts the traditional IRA to a Roth IRA in 2010, and, as a result of the conversion, $100 is includible in gross income. Unless A elects otherwise, $50 of the income resulting from the conversion is included in income in 2011 and $50 in 2012. Later in 2010, A takes a $20 distribution, which is not a qualified distribution and all of which, under the ordering rules, is attributable to amounts includible in gross income as a result of the conversion. Under the accelerated inclusion rule, $20 is included in income in 2010. The amount included in income in 2011 is the lesser of (1) $50 (half of the income resulting from the conversion) or (2) $70 (the remaining income from the conversion), or $50. The amount included in income in 2012 is the lesser of (1) $50 (half of the income resulting from the conversion) or (2) $30 (the remaining income from the conversion, i.e., $100 - $70 ($20 included in income in 2010 and $50 included in income in 2011)), or $30.

Effective Date

The provision is effective for taxable years beginning after December 31, 2009.

---

[541] In the case of a married taxpayer filing a separate return, the phaseout range is $0 to $10,000 of AGI.

[542] Married taxpayers filing a separate return may not convert amounts in a traditional IRA into a Roth IRA.

[543] Under the conference agreement, married taxpayers filing a separate return may convert amounts in a traditional IRA into a Roth IRA.

[544] Whether a distribution consists of converted amounts is determined under the present-law ordering rules.

[¶ 12,097.08]

Committee Reports on P.L. 105-206 (IRS Restructuring and Reform Act of 1998)

[Senate Committee Report]

Conversions of IRAs into Roth IRAs.—

Distributions of converted amounts

Distributions before the end of the 4-year spread

The bill modifies the rules relating to conversions of IRAs into Roth IRAs in order to prevent taxpayers from receiving premature distributions from a Roth conversion IRA while retaining the benefits of 4-year income averaging. In the case of conversions to which the 4-year income inclusion rule applies, income inclusion will be accelerated with respect to any amounts withdrawn before the final year of inclusion. Under this rule, a taxpayer that withdraws converted amounts prior to the last year of the 4-year spread will be required to include in income the amount otherwise includible under the 4-year rule, plus the lesser of (1) the taxable amount of the withdrawal, or (2) the remaining taxable amount of the conversion (i.e., the taxable amount of the conversion not included in income under the 4-year rule in the current or a prior taxable year). In subsequent years (assuming no such further withdrawals), the amount includible in income under the 4-year will be the lesser of (1) the amount otherwise required under the 4-year rule (determined without regard to the withdrawal) or (2) the remaining taxable amount of the conversion.

Under the bill, application of the 4-year spread will be elective. The election will be made in the time and manner prescribed by the Secretary. If no election is made, the 4-year rule will be deemed to be elected. An election, or deemed election, with respect to the 4-year spread cannot be changed after the due date for the return for the first year of the income inclusion (including extensions).

The following example illustrates the application of these rules.

Example: Taxpayer A has a nondeductible IRA with a value of $100 (and no other IRAs). The $100 consists of $75 of contributions and $25 of earnings. A converts the IRA into a Roth IRA in 1998 and elects the 4-year spread. As a result of the conversion, $25 is includible in income ratably over 4 years ($6.25 per year). The 10-percent early withdrawal tax does not apply to the conversion. At the beginning of 1999, the value of the account is $110, and A makes a withdrawal of $10. Under the proposal, the withdrawal would be treated as attributable entirely to amounts that were includible in income due to the conversion. In the year of withdrawal, $16.25 would be includible in income (the $6.25 includible in the year of withdrawal under the 4-year rule, plus $10 ($10 is less than the remaining taxable amount of $12.50 ($25-$12.50)). In the next year, $2.50 would be includible in income under the 4-year rule. No amount would be includible in income in year 4 due to the conversion.

Application of early withdrawal tax to converted amounts

The bill modifies the rules relating to conversions to prevent taxpayers from receiving premature distributions (i.e., within 5 years) while retaining the benefit of the nonpayment of the early withdrawal tax. Under the bill, if converted amounts are withdrawn within the 5-year period beginning with the year of the conversion, then, to the extent attributable to amounts that were includible in income due to the conversion, the amount withdrawn will be subject to the 10-percent early withdrawal tax.[63]

Applying this rule to the example above, the $10 withdrawal would be subject to the 10-percent early withdrawal tax (unless as exception applies).

Application of 5-year holding period

The bill will also eliminate the special rule under which a separate 5-year holding period begins for purposes of determining whether a distribution of amounts attributable to a conversion is a qualified distribution; thus, the 5-year holding rule for Roth IRAs will begin with the year for which a contribution is first made to a Roth IRA. A subsequent conversion will not start the running of a new 5-year period.

Ordering rules

Ordering rules will apply to determine what amounts are withdrawn in the event a Roth IRA contains both conversion amounts (possibly from different years) and other contributions. Under these rules, regular Roth IRA contributions will be deemed to be withdrawn first, then converted amounts (starting with the amounts first converted). Withdrawals of converted amounts will be treated as coming first from converted amounts that were includible in income. As under present law, earnings will be treated as withdrawn after contributions. For purposes of these rules, all Roth IRAs, whether or not maintained in separate accounts, will be considered a single Roth IRA.

Corrections

In order to assist individuals who erroneously convert IRAs into Roth IRAs or otherwise wish to change the nature of an IRA contribution, contributions to an IRA (and earnings thereon) may be transferred in a trustee-to-trustee transfer from any IRA to another IRA by the due date for the taxpayer's return for the year of the contribution (including extensions). Any such transferred contributions will be treated as if contributed to the transferee IRA (and not to the transferor IRA). Trustee-to-trustee transfers include transfers between IRA trustees as well as IRA custodians, apply to transfers from and to IRA accounts and annuities, and apply to transfers between IRA accounts and annuities with the same trustee or custodian.

Effect of death on 4-year spread

Under the bill, in general, any amounts remaining to be included in income as a result of a 1998 conversion will be includible in income on the final return of the taxpayer. If the surviving spouse is the sole beneficiary of the Roth IRA, the spouse may continue the deferral by including the remaining amounts in his or her income over the remainder of the 4-year period.

Calculation of AGI limit for conversions

The bill clarifies the determination of AGI for purposes of applying the $100,000 AGI limit on IRA conversions into Roth IRAs. Under the bill, the conversion amount (to the extent otherwise includible in AGI) is subtracted from AGI as determined under the rules relating to IRAs (sec. 219) for the year of distribution. Thus, for example, the AGI- based phase out of the exemption from the disallowance for passive activity losses from rental real estate activities (sec. 469(i)(3)) would be applied taking into account the amount of the conversion that is includible in AGI, and then the amount of the conversion would be subtracted from AGI in determining whether a taxpayer is eligible to convert an IRA into a Roth IRA.

Effective Date

The provision is effective as if included in the 1997 Act, i.e., for taxable years beginning after December 31, 1997.—

[Conference Committee Report]

Conference Agreement

The conference agreement follows the Senate amendment, with the following modifications, additions, and deletions. * * *

Savings and Investment Incentives of the 1997 Act

Conversion of IRAs into Roth IRAs

The conferees wish to clarify that for purposes of determining the $100,000 adjusted gross income ("AGI") limit on IRA conversions to Roth IRAs, the conversion amount is not taken into account. Thus, for this purpose, AGI (and all AGI-based phaseouts) are to be determined without taking into account the conversion amount. For purposes of computing taxable income, the conversion amount (to the extent otherwise includible in AGI) is to be taken into account in computing the AGI-based phaseout amounts. The conferees wish to clarify that the language of the Senate Finance committee report (appearing in connection with section 6005(b) of the Senate amendment) relating to calculation of AGI limit for conversions is superseded.* * *.—

[Senate Committee Report]

*Contribution limit to Roth IRAs.—*The bill clarifies the intent of the Act that an individual may contribute up to $2,000 a year to all the individual's IRAs. Thus, for example, suppose an individual is not eligible to make deductible IRA contributions because of the phase-out limits, and is eligible to make a $1,000 Roth IRA contribution. The individual could contribute $1,000 to the Roth IRA and $1,000 to a nondeductible IRA.

Effective Date

The provision is effective as if included in the 1997 Act, i.e., for taxable years beginning after December 31, 1997.—

[Conference Committee Report]

Conference Agreement

The conference agreement follows the Senate amendment * * *.—

*Exclusion of minimum required distributions from AGI for Roth IRA conversions.—*The proposal would modify the definition of AGI to exclude required minimum distributions from the taxpayer's AGI solely for purposes of determining eligibility to convert from an IRA to a Roth IRA. As under present law, the required minimum distribution would not be eligible for conversion and would be includible in gross income.

Effective Date

The proposal would be effective for taxable years beginning after December 31, 2004.—

Conference Agreement

The conference agreement follows the Senate amendment.

[63] The otherwise available exceptions to the early withdrawal tax, e.g., for distributions after age 59-1/2, would apply.

Effective Date

Same as Senate amendment.—

[¶ 12,097.10]

Committee Reports on P.L. 105-34 (Taxpayer Relief Act)

[Senate Committee Report]

Individual retirement arrangements.—

In general.—The bill * * * (4) replaces present-law nondeductible IRAs with a new IRA called the IRA Plus. All individuals may make nondeductible contributions of up to $2,000 annually to an IRA Plus. No income limitations apply to IRA Plus accounts; however, the $2,000 maximum contribution limit is reduced to the extent an individual makes deductible contributions to an IRA. An IRA Plus is an IRA which is designated at the time of establishment as an IRA Plus in the manner prescribed by the Secretary. Qualified distributions from an IRA Plus are not includible in income.

* * *

IRA Plus accounts

Contributions to IRA Plus accounts.—The maximum annual contribution that may be made to an IRA Plus is the lesser of $2,000 (reduced by deductible IRA contributions) or the individual's compensation for the year. As under the present-law rules relating to deductible IRAs, a contribution of up to $2,000 for each spouse may be made to an IRA Plus provided the combined compensation of the spouses is at least equal to the contributed amount.

Contributions to an IRA Plus may be made even after the individual for whom the account is maintained has attained age 70-1/2.

Taxation of distributions.—Qualified distributions from an IRA Plus are not includible in gross income, nor subject to the additional 10-percent tax on early withdrawals. A qualified distribution is a distribution that (1) is made after the 5-taxable year period beginning with the first taxable year in which the individual made a contribution to an IRA Plus, and (2) which is (a) made on or after the date on which the individual attains age 59-1/2, (b) made to a beneficiary (or to the individual's estate) on or after the death of the individual, (c) attributable to the individual's being disabled, or (d) a qualified special purpose distribution. Qualified special purpose distributions are distributions that are exempt from the 10-percent early withdrawal tax because they are for first-time homebuyer expenses or long-term unemployed individuals.

Distributions from an IRA Plus that are not qualified distributions are includible in income to the extent attributable to earnings, and subject to the 10-percent early withdrawal tax (unless an exception applies). The same exceptions to the early withdrawal tax that apply to IRAs apply to IRA Plus accounts.

An ordering rule applies for purposes of determining what portion of a distribution that is not a qualified distribution is includible in income. Under the ordering rule, distributions from an IRA Plus are treated as made from contributions first, and all an individual's IRA Plus accounts are treated as a single IRA Plus. Thus, no portion of a distribution from an IRA Plus is treated as attributable to earnings (and therefore includible in gross income) until the total of all distributions from all the individual's IRA Plus accounts exceeds the amount of contributions.

Distributions from an IRA Plus may be rolled over tax free to another IRA Plus.

Conversions of an IRA to an IRA Plus.—All or any part of amounts in a present-law deductible or nondeductible IRA may be converted into an IRA Plus. If the conversion is made before January 1, 1999, the amount that would have been includible in gross income if the individual had withdrawn the converted amounts is included in gross income ratably over the 4-taxable year period beginning with the taxable year in which the conversion is made. The early withdrawal tax does not apply to such conversions.

A conversion of an IRA into an IRA Plus can be made in a variety of different ways and without taking a distribution. For example, an individual may make a conversion simply by notifying the IRA trustee. Or, an individual may make the conversion in connection with a change in IRA trustees through a rollover or a trustee-to-trustee transfer. If a part of an IRA balance is converted into an IRA Plus, the IRA Plus amounts may have to be held separately.

Effective date

The provision is effective for taxable years beginning after December 31, 1997.

Conference Committee Report

The conference agreement follows the Senate amendment, with modifications. Under the conference agreement, the new IRA is called the "Roth IRA" rather than the IRA Plus. The maximum contribution that can be made to a Roth IRA is phased out for individuals with AGI between $95,000 and $110,000 and for joint filers with AGI between $150,000 and $160,000. Under the conference agreement, distributions to long-term unemployed individuals do not qualify as special purpose distributions. Thus, only first-time homebuyer expenses (as defined under the Senate amendment) qualify as special purpose distributions.

Under the conference agreement, only taxpayers with AGI of less than $100,000 are eligible to roll over or convert an IRA into a Roth IRA.

The conference agreement retains present-law nondeductible IRAs. Thus, an individual who cannot (or does not) make contributions to a deductible IRA or a Roth IRA can make contributions to a nondeductible IRA. In no case can contributions to all an individual's IRAs for a taxable year exceed $2,000.

[Code Sec. 409]

[¶ 12,100.08]

Committee Report on P.L. 97-248 (Tax Equity and Fiscal Responsibility Act of 1982)

For Committee Report on P.L. 97-248, relating to partial rollovers, see ¶ 12,050.07.

[¶ 12,100.085]

Committee Reports on P.L. 97-34 (Economic Recovery Tax Act of 1981)

For Committee Reports on P.L. 97-34, Sec. 311, relating to individual retirement plans, see ¶ 11,330.02.

[¶ 12,100.09]

Committee Reports on P.L. 95-600 (Revenue Act of 1978)

The Conference Community Report on Sec. 156, tax-sheltered annuity rollovers, is at ¶ 11,800.06. The House Committee Report on Sec. 157(e), clarification of dollar, is at ¶ 12,050.09.

[¶ 12,100.10]

Committee Report on P.L. 93-406 (Employee Retirement Income Security Act of 1974)

[Conference Committee Explanation]

Qualified retirement bonds.—Deductible employee savings may be invested in a special retirement bond to be issued by the Federal Government. Generally, the rules governing retirement bonds are closely comparable to the rules governing other forms of qualifying individual retirement savings. Thus, the bonds may be cashed prior to age 59 ½, but, except in the case of a rollover, the individual is generally to be subject to a 10 percent penalty tax (unless the bonds are cashed due to death or disability). However, the bond may be redeemed within 12 months of its purchase without penalty (and without payment of interest) and in this case the individual is not to be entitled to a deduction for the contribution.

The bonds are to cease to bear interest when the individual attains age 70 ½, and the proceeds of the bonds are to be deemed to be distributed in that year (whether or not the bonds are actually cashed in). However, as discussed above, the individual may roll the proceeds over into another qualifying form of individual retirement investment.

[¶ 12,130.06]

Committee Reports on P.L. 107-16 (Economic Growth and Tax Relief Reconciliation Act)

[House Committee Report]

Prohibited allocations of stock in S corporation ESOP

In general

Under the provision, if there is a nonallocation year with respect to an ESOP maintained by an S corporation: (1) the amount allocated in a prohibited allocation to an individual who is a disqualified person is treated as distributed to such individual (i.e., the value of the prohibited allocation is includible in the gross income of the individual receiving the prohibited allocation); (2) an excise tax is imposed on the S corporation equal to 50 percent of the amount involved in a prohibited allocation; and (3) an excise tax is imposed on the S corporation with respect to any synthetic equity owned by a disqualified person.[1]

It is intended that the provision will limit the establishment of ESOPs by S corporations to those that provide broad-based employee coverage and that benefit rank-and-file employees as well as highly compensated employees and historical owners.

Definition of nonallocation year

A nonallocation year means any plan year of an ESOP holding shares in an S corporation if, at any time during the plan year, disqualified persons own at least 50 percent of the number of outstanding shares of the S corporation.

A person is a disqualified person if the person is either (1) a member of a "deemed 20-percent shareholder group" or (2) a "deemed 10-percent shareholder." A person is a member of a "deemed 20-percent shareholder group" if the aggregate number of deemed-owned shares of the person and his or her family members is at least 20 percent of the number of deemed-owned shares of stock in

[1] The plan is not disqualified merely because an excise tax is imposed under the provision.

the S corporation.[2] A person is a deemed 10-percent shareholder if the person is not a member of a deemed 20-percent shareholder group and the number of the person's deemed-owned shares is at least 10 percent of the number of deemed-owned shares of stock of the corporation.

In general, "deemed-owned shares" means: (1) stock allocated to the account of an individual under the ESOP, and (2) an individual's share of unallocated stock held by the ESOP. An individual's share of unallocated stock held by an ESOP is determined in the same manner as the most recent allocation of stock under the terms of the plan.

For purposes of determining whether there is a nonallocation year, ownership of stock generally is attributed under the rules of section 318,[3] except that: (1) the family attribution rules are modified to include certain other family members, as described below, (2) option attribution would not apply (but instead special rules relating to synthetic equity described below would apply), and (3) "deemed-owned shares" held by the ESOP are treated as held by the individual with respect to whom they are deemed owned.

Under the provision, family members of an individual include (1) the spouse[4] of the individual, (2) an ancestor or lineal descendant of the individual or his or her spouse, (3) a sibling of the individual (or the individual's spouse) and any lineal descendant of the brother or sister, and (4) the spouse of any person described in (2) or (3).

The provision contains special rules applicable to synthetic equity interests. Except to the extent provided in regulations, the stock on which a synthetic equity interest is based are treated as outstanding stock of the S corporation and as deemed-owned shares of the person holding the synthetic equity interest if such treatment would result in the treatment of any person as a disqualified person or the treatment of any year as a nonallocation year. Thus, for example, disqualified persons for a year include those individuals who are disqualified persons under the general rule (i.e., treating only those shares held by the ESOP as deemed-owned shares) and those individuals who are disqualified individuals if synthetic equity interests are treated as deemed-owned shares.

"Synthetic equity" means any stock option, warrant, restricted stock, deferred issuance stock right, or similar interest that gives the holder the right to acquire or receive stock of the S corporation in the future. Except to the extent provided in regulations, synthetic equity also includes a stock appreciation right, phantom stock unit, or similar right to a future cash payment based on the value of such stock or appreciation in such value.[5]

Ownership of synthetic equity is attributed in the same manner as stock is attributed under the provision (as described above). In addition, ownership of synthetic equity is attributed under the rules of section 318(a)(2) and (3) in the same manner as stock.

Definition of prohibited allocation

An ESOP of an S corporation is required to provide that no portion of the assets of the plan attributable to (or allocable in lieu of) S corporation stock may, during a nonallocation year, accrue (or be allocated directly or indirectly under any qualified plan of the S corporation) for the benefit of a disqualified person. A "prohibited allocation" refers to violations of this provision. A prohibited allocation occurs, for example, if income on S corporation stock held by an ESOP is allocated to the account of an individual who is a disqualified person.

Application of excise tax

In the case of a prohibited allocation, the S corporation is liable for an excise tax equal to 50 percent of the amount of the allocation. For example, if S corporation stock is allocated in a prohibited allocation, the excise tax would equal to 50 percent of the fair market value of such stock.

A special rule would apply in the case of the first nonallocation year, regardless of whether there is a prohibited allocation. In that year, the excise tax also would apply to the fair market value of the deemed-owned shares of any disqualified person held by the ESOP, even though those shares are not allocated to the disqualified person in that year.

As mentioned above, the S corporation also is liable for an excise tax with respect to any synthetic equity interest owned by any disqualified person in a nonallocation year. The excise tax is 50 percent of the value of the shares on which synthetic equity is based.

Treasury regulations

The Treasury Department is given the authority to prescribe such regulations as may be necessary to carry out the purposes of the provision.

Effective Date

The provision generally is effective with respect to plan years beginning after December 31, 2004. In the case of an ESOP established after March 14, 2001, or an ESOP established on or before such date if the employer maintaining the plan was not an S corporation on such date, the provision is effective with respect to plan years ending after March 14, 2001.

[Conference Committee Report]

The conference agreement follows the House bill. The conference agreement authorizes the Secretary to determine, by regulation or other guidance of general applicability, that a nonallocation year occurs in any case in which the principal purpose of the ownership structure of an S corporation constitutes, in substance, an avoidance or evasion of the prohibited allocation rules. For example, this might apply if more than 10 independent businesses are combined in an S corporation owned by an ESOP in order to take advantage of the income tax treatment of S corporations owned by an ESOP.

[¶ 12,130.063]

Committee Reports on P.L. 101-239 (Omnibus Budget Reconciliation Act of 1989)

[House Committee Report]

Interest exclusion for ESOP loans.—Under the provision, the partial interest exclusion applies with respect to a securities acquistion loan only if, immediately after the acquisition and, in general, at all times thereafter, the ESOP owns at least 30 percent of each class of outstanding stock of the corporation which issued the employer securities, or 30 percent of the total value of all outstanding stock of the corporation. The partial interest exclusion does not apply to interest allocable to any period during which the ESOP does not meet this 30-percent ownership threshold. For example, assume that the 30-percent requirement is met for the first 6 months of a year, but not the second 6 months. Interest allocable to the first 6 months is eligible for the interest exclusion, but interest allocable to the second 6 months is not.

The Secretary is authorized to provide that limited failures to meet the 30-percent threshold will not result in the loss of the partial interest exclusion, if the failure is corrected within 90 days of the date on which the failure occurred. The Secretary is authorized to extend this period for an additional 90 days. It is recognized that in some circumstances there will be periods of time when the ESOP may, for legitmate reasons, temporarily fall below the threshold, for example, if there is a reorganization of the company, and the new employer's securities are being substituted for the former employer's securities. The committee intends, however, that the authority of the Secretary is to be exercised only in limited circumstances and in such a manner as to prevent avoidance of the 30-percent ownership requirement.

The provision also expressly overrides Revenue Ruling 89-76. Under the provision, a loan is not treated as a securities acquisition loan and, therefore, the partial interest exclusion is not available (1) if the loan was originated by a lender other than a qualified lender, or (2) for any period after the loan is first held by a person other than a qualified lender.

Dividends paid deduction.—Under the provision, the 30-percent ownership requirement that applies to the partial interest exclusion also applies to the deduction for dividends paid on employer securities held by an ESOP. Thus, the dividends paid deduction is applicable only during periods that the ESOP owns at least 30 percent of each outstanding class of stock of the corporation issuing the employer securities held by the ESOP or 30 percent of the total value of all outstanding stock of the corporation. In addition, the dividend deduction is limited to dividends on stock acquired with a securities acquisition loan. These restrictions apply regardless of whether dividends are paid out currently to plan participants or are used to repay an acquisition loan.

As under the provision relating to the partial interest exclusion, the Secretary has the authority to provide that temporary failures to meet the 30-percent requirement will not result in a loss of the dividend deduction. As is the case with the partial interest exclusion, this authority is to be interpreted narrowly to prevent avoidance of the 30-percent ownership rule.

Under the provision, dividends may be used to repay an acquisition loan only if those dividends are paid with respect to employer securities acquired with that loan. Also, for example, if an exempt loan is repaid, the dividend deduction does not apply if the dividends on the employer securities acquired with the loan are used to repay another loan used to acquire other employer securities. The committee believes that this restriction is consistent with the original intent of the provision, as reflected in the legislative history that accompanied the enactment of the dividend deduction for dividends used to repay a loan. However, no inference is intended with respect to the scope of the dividend deduction prior to the effective date of the provision. In addition, no inference is intended with respect to the permissible sources of payments on exempt loans under Title I of the Employee Retirement Income Security Act of 1974 (ERISA).

Dividends on allocated as well as unallocated employer securities may be used to repay the loan used to acquire the securities on which the dividends are paid. However, as under present law, if dividends on allocated shares are so used, employer securities with a fair market value of not less than the amount of such dividends are to be allocated to the participant's account for the year for which the dividends would otherwise have been allocated to the participant's account.

---

[2] A family member of a member of a "deemed 20-percent shareholder group" with deemed owned shares is also treated as a disqualified person.

[3] These attribution rules also apply to stock treated as owned by reason of the ownership of synthetic equity.

[4] As under section 318, an individual's spouse is not treated as a member of the individual's family if the spouses are legally separated.

[5] The provisions relating to synthetic equity do not modify the rules relating to S corporations, e.g., the circumstances in which options or similar interests are treated as creating a second class of stock.

Under the provision, (1) the employer maintaining, or the plan administrator of, an ESOP that acquires stock in a transaction to which section 133 applies or holds stock to which section 404(k) applies, and (2) any person making or holding a loan to which section 133 applies, is required to make such returns and reports as the Secretary may require. Such returns and reports shall be made to the Secretary or to such other persons as the Secretary may prescribe. For example, the Secretary is authorized to require an employer to notify each qualified lender if the ESOP fails to satisfy the 30-percent ownership requirement and the period of time such failure exists.

Deferral of gain on certain sales of stock to an ESOP.—Under the provision, the deferral of recognition of gain on the sale of employer securities to an ESOP is available only if, in addition to the present-law requirements, the taxpayer holds the securities for at least 3 years before the sale of the stock to the ESOP. The committee intends that the rules relating to holding periods of property (sec. 1223) apply in determining whether the 3-year holding period requirement is satisfied.

Limits on contributions and benefits under an ESOP.—The special rule permitting an increase in the dollar limitation on annual additions in the case of contributions to an ESOP is repealed.

Payment of estate tax liability by an ESOP.—The provision permitting the assumption of estate tax liability by an ESOP is repealed.

Estate tax deduction for sales to an ESOP.—The provision permitting an estate tax deduction for proceeds of certain sales of employer securities to an ESOP is repealed.

Relief from net operasting loss provisions.—The provision providing that employer securities acquired by certain ESOPs are not counted in determining whether an ownership change has occurred for purposes of the net operating loss rules is repealed.

Effective Dates

Interest exclusion for ESOP loans.—The modifications of the partial interest exclusion apply to loans made after July 10, 1989, including (except as provided below) loans made after July 10, 1989, to refinance loans made on or before July 10, 1989. The provision does not apply to any loan pursuant to a written binding commitment in effect on July 10, 1989, and at all times thereafter before such loan is made. This exception applies only to the extent that the proceeds of such loan are used to acquire employer securities pursuant to a written binding contract (or a tender offer registered with the Securities and Exchange Commission) in effect on July 10, 1989, and at all times thereafter before such securities are acquired.

The committee intends that this grandfather rule also applies to a loan pursuant to a written binding commitment in effect on July 10, 1989, and at all times thereafter before such loan is made, to the extent that the loan is used to replace or refinance a loan the proceeds of which were used to acquire employer securities for the ESOP on or before June 10, 1989. Such a grandfathered loan may be refinanced without loss of the grandfather if the requirements described below relating to refinancings are satisfied, other than the requirement that the original lender be a qualified lender.

The modifications also do not apply to any loan made on or before July 10, 1992, pursuant to a written agreement entered into on or before July 10, 1989, which agreement evidences the intent of the borrower on a periodic basis to enter into immediate allocation securities acquisition loans (sec. 133(b)(1)(B)). This provision applies only if one or more immediate allocation securities acquisition loans were made to the borrower on or before July 10, 1989.

In addition, the modifications of the partial interest exclusion do not apply to loans made to refinance loans made on or before July 10, 1989, or to loans made to refinance loans made after July 10, 1989, and that are grandfathered under the rules described above if (1) the outstanding principal of the loan is not increased by the refinancing, (2) the original lender was a lender that qualifies for the interest exclusion under section 133, and (3) the term of the loan does not extend beyond the later of (a) the last day of the term of the original securities acquisition loan or (b) the last day of the 7-year period beginning on the date the original securities acquisition loan was made. Under the 7-year rule, for example, the original loan could be for a term of 3 years, and the refinanced loan could extend the loan for no more than an additional 4 years without the loss of the partial interest exclusion. It is intended that a grandfathered loan will not lose the benefit of the grandfather merely because the interest rate on the loan is adjusted periodically by an independent (e.g., unrelated to the ESOP, its trustee or the sponsor of the ESOP) remarketing and interest-setting agent, or when the debt is remarketed in a manner consistent with the provisions of the bill.

The committee intends that the refinancing rules described above also apply in the case of a securities acquisition loan that consists of a loan to the employer with a corresponding loan to the ESOP (a "back-to-back" or "mirror" loan) (see sec. 133(b)(3)), if the loan is restructured so that the loan is directly from the financial institution to the ESOP with a guarantee from the employer rather than a loan from the employer.

With respect to the grandfather rule for certain loans made after July 10, 1989, the existence of a written binding loan commitment can be demonstrated, for example, by a combination of documentation by the lender, written communications by the borrower or the borrower's agent (e.g., an investment banker or a broker), and documentation of the borrower showing that the loan was approved by the lender and that the offer to make the loan was received by the borrower. Such documentation must include the principal terms of the loan, such as the principal amount, interest rate or spread, and maturity of the loan. Of course, a loan made pursuant to such a written binding commitment does not quality under the grandfather rule unless the proceeds of the loan are used to acquire employer securities pursuant to a written binding contract (or a tender offer registered with the Securities and Exchange Commission) in effect on July 10, 1989, and at all times thereafter before such securities are acquired.

Dividends paid deduction.—The modifications of the dividend deduction apply to dividends paid on employer securities acquired by an ESOP after July 10, 1989, except to the extent the dividends are paid on employer securities acquired with a loan that meets the requirements for the grandfather from the modifications of section 133 (whether or not the loan actually qualifies under section 133) is grandfathered from the modification to section 133. Employer securities are not considered to have been acquired by an ESOP on or before July 10, 1989, where, for example, the securities were acquired by a qualified plan on or before July 10, 1989, but the plan was not an ESOP until after July 10, 1989.

In some situations, an ESOP may hold employer securities that are convertible preferred stock. If the dividends on such employer securities are grandfathered from the modifications to the dividend deduction, the grandfather will not cease to apply merely because such securities are converted after July 10, 1989, (in accordance with applicable Code provisions) into common stock that constitutes employer securities.

Deferral of gain on certain sales of stock to an ESOP.—The modification of the deferral of gain provision (sec. 1042) applies to sales to an ESOP after July 10, 1989.

Limits on contributions and benefits under an ESOP.—The repeal of the special limit on contributions to an ESOP is effective for years beginning after July 12, 1989.

Payment of estate tax liability by an ESOP.—The repeal of the provision permitting the assumption of estate tax liability by an ESOP applies to estates of decedents dying after July 12, 1989.

Estate tax deduction for sales to an ESOP.—The repeal of the estate tax deduction for sales of employer securities to an ESOP applies to estates of decedents dying after July 12, 1989.

Relief from net operating loss provisions.—The repeal of the special net operating loss rule relating to acquisitions of employer securities by an ESOP applies to acquisitions after July 12, 1989, other than acquisitions pursuant to a binding written contract in effect on July 12, 1989, and at all times thereafter before such acquisition.

[Senate Committee Report]

The provision limits the circumstances in which the partial interest exclusion applies. In general under the provision the partial interest exclusion does not apply to a securities acquisition loan unless (1) immediately after the acquisition of the securities acquired with the loan the ESOP owns at least 30 percent of each class of outstanding stock of the corporation issuing the employer securities or 30 percent of the total value of all outstanding stock of the corporation, (2) the term of the loan does not exceed 15 years, and (3) each participant is entitled to direct the plan as to the manner in which shares allocated to the participant's account that were acquired with a section 133 loan are to be voted. These requirements apply to transfers of stock with respect to an immediate allocation loan as well as other types of securities acquisition loans. The requirement that the term of the loan does not override other requirements relating to ESOPs, such as the rules under section 4975.

The 30-percent requirement is designed to ensure that the ESOP holds a substantial percentage of the company's stock. After the sale of the stock to the ESOP, the ESOP must generally hold the employer securities for at least 3 years. An excise tax is imposed on the employer sponsoring the ESOP if, within 3 years after the acquisition of the employer securities with a loan to which section 133 applies, the ESOP disposes of employer securities and the total number of employer securities held by the ESOP is less than the total number held after the acquisition or the value of the employer securities held by the plan after the disposition is less than 30 percent of the value of the outstanding securities. The excise tax does not apply to certain distributions, such as distributions to plan participants and distributions with respect to certain corporate reorganizations.

An excise tax is also imposed if the ESOP disposes of the employer securities before the securities are allocated to accounts of participants and the proceeds from such disposition are not so allocated.

The amount of each excise tax is 10 percent of the amount realized on the disposition. The excise tax rules are similar to those that apply in situations where there has been a sale of stock to an ESOP that entitles the seller to defer recognition of gain on the sale (sec. 1042) or an estate tax deduction (sec. 2057).

The voting requirements of the provision apply to all shares acquired with the loan to which the partial interest exclusion applies. This requirement applies to all issues and applies regardless of whether the employer has a registration-type class of securities. In addition, if the shares are convertible preferred stock, the participants must be entitled to direct the voting of such stock as if the preferred stock had the voting rights of the common stock of the employer having the greatest voting power.

Effective Date

The provision would generally be effective with respect to loans made after June 6, 1989, including (except as provided below) loans made after June 6, 1989, to refinance loans made on or before June 6, 1989. The provision would not apply to any loan (1) pursuant to a binding written commitment to make a securities acquisition loan in effect on June 6, 1989, and at all times thereafter before the loan is made, (2) the proceeds of which are used to acquire employer securities pursuant to a written binding contract (or tender offer registered with the Securities and Exchange Commission) in effect on June 6, 1989, and at all times thereafter before such securities are acquired, (3) to the extent made to finance the acquisition of employer securities by an ESOP pursuant to one or more collective bargaining agreements between employee representatives and one or more employers which was agreed to on or before June 6, 1989, and ratified before such date or within a reasonable period thereafter and which agreement sets forth the material terms of the acquisition (which requirement may be met if the agreement sets forth the material terms of the ESOP), or (4) with respect to which a filing was made with an agency of the United States on or before June 6, 1989, which specified the aggregate principal amount of the loan or debt obligations, and (a) such filing specifies that the loan is intended to be a securities acquisition loan (as defined in sec. 133) and is for registration required to permit the offering of such loan, or (b) such filing is for approval required in order for the ESOP to acquire more than a certain percentage of the stock of the employer. The grandfather in item (4) relates only to governmental filings required in order for the ESOP debt to be issued or the employer securities to be acquired by the ESOP and, thus, for example, does not apply to requests for a determination letter from the Internal Revenue Service that the ESOP is a qualified plan.

In addition, the provision would not apply to loans made after June 6, 1989, to refinance loans made on or before such date (or to refinance loans described in the preceding paragraph), if (1) such refinanced loan meets the requirements of section 133 (as in effect before the amendments made by the provision[),] (2) the outstanding principal amount of the loan is not increased, and (3) the term of such loan does not extend beyond the later of (a) the last day of the term of the original securities acquisition loan, or (b) the last day of the 7-year period beginning on the date the original securities acquisition loan was made.

The refinancing rules described above also apply in the case of a securities acquisition loan that consists of a loan to the employer with a corresponding loan to the ESOP (a "back-to-back" or "mirror" loan) (see sec. 133(b)(3)), if the loan is restructured so that the loan is directly from the financial institution to the ESOP with a guarantee from the employer rather than a loan from the employer.

The committee understands that ESOP loan transactions are not identical, and that the course of events leading up to the conclusion of a transaction differs from case to case. Thus, with respect to the grandfather rule for loans made pursuant to a written binding commitment, the committee recognizes that whether there is a written binding loan commitment depends on all the facts and circumstances and that the existence of such a commitment can be demonstrated in a variety of ways.

It is not necessary that the final loan documents be executed by the parties in order to demonstrate the existence of a written binding loan commitment. The existence of such a commitment can be demonstrated, for example, by any combination of documents which include some or all of documentation of the lender, written communications by the borrower or the borrower's agent (e.g., an investment banker or a broker), and documentation of the borrower showing that the loan was approved by the lender and that the offer to make the loan was received by the borrower. No one particular document is necessary to qualify for the grandfather.

The documentation would have to include the principal terms of the loan, such as the principal amount, interest rate or spread or formula pursuant to which the interest rate will be set, and maturity of the loan. It is intended that the grandfather will not fail to be met if the loan commitment is for a specified amount and the borrower borrows less than the full amount. In addition, the grandfather will not fail to be met merely because the interest rate is to be set in accordance with rates prevailing at the time the loan is made, or because the only modification in the loan terms is a reduction in the interest rate that occurs before the loan is made. The grandfather will also not fail to be met merely because a loan commitment that met the conditions of the grandfather had an expiration date and the commitment was extended before the expiration date without change in the material terms of the commitment.

The written binding commitment grandfather applies to all types of securities acquisition loans. Thus, for example, immediate allocation loans, as well as other types of securities acquisition loans, would be grandfathered under the provision if a binding written commitment to make a securities acquisition loan existed on June 6, 1989, and at all times thereafter before the loan is made.

[Conference Committee Report]

Partial interest exclusion for ESOP loans.—The conference agreement follows the House bill and the Senate amendment, with modifications. Under the conference agreement, the partial interest exclusion is not available unless the ESOP owns more than 50 percent of (1) each class of outstanding stock of the corporation issuing the employer securities, or (2) the total value of all outstanding stock of the corporation. The amount of stock of the corporation held by the ESOP is determined as under the House bill. Thus, options held by the ESOP are not counted toward the 50-percent requirement.

As under the House bill, the partial interest exclusion does not apply to interest allocable to any period during which the ESOP does not meet the more than 50 percent requirement. In addition, the House bill provision relating to reporting requirements is included. The provisions of the Senate bill relating to voting rights, the 15-year limitation on the term of the securities acquisition loans, and excise taxes also apply. The conference agreement does not adopt the provision of the House bill that overrides Revenue Ruling 89-76. Under the conference agreement, the more than 50 percent requirement may be satisfied by counting all stock in any ESOP maintained by the employer (or other member of the employer's controlled group).

As under the Senate amendment, it is intended that during the period the excise tax relating to securities to which section 2057 applied is in effect, any disposition of employer securities will be treated as having been made in the following order: first, from securities described in section 4978A(d)(1); second, from securities described in section 4978A(d)(2); third, from section 133 securities acquired during the 3-year period ending on the date of such disposition, beginning with the securities first so acquired; fourth, from section 133 securities acquired before such 3-year period unless such securities (or proceeds from the disposition) have been allocated to accounts of participants or beneficiaries; fifth, from securities described in section 4978A(d)(3); and last from securities described in section 4978A(d)(4).

The provision is generally effective for loans made after July 10, 1989. In addition, the conference agreement adopts the transition rules of both the House bill and the Senate amendment. Thus, under the conference agreement, the provision does not apply to a loan made after July 10, 1989, (1) if the loan is made pursuant to a written binding commitment in effect on July 10, 1989, to the extent the proceeds of such loan are used to acquire employer securities pursuant to a written binding contract (or tender offer) in effect on July 10, 1989; (2) the loan is an immediate allocation securities acquisition loan made on or before July 10, 1992, pursuant to a written agreement entered into on or before July 10, 1989, and certain requirements are satisfied; (3) if the loan is made pursuant to a written binding commitment in effect on June 6, 1989, or to the extent that the proceeds of the loan are used to acquire employer securities pursuant to a written binding contract (or tender offer) in effect on June 6, 1989; (4) to the extent the loan is used to acquire employer securities pursuant to a collective bargaining agreement setting forth the material terms of the ESOP (or referencing an existing ESOP) which was agreed to on or before June 6, 1989, by one or more employers and employee representatives (and ratified on or before such date or within a reasonable period thereafter); or (5) with respect to which certain governmental filings were made on or before June 6, 1989. As under the Senate amendment, the grandfather with respect to certain governmental filings relates only to governmental filings required in order for the ESOP debt to be issued or for a certain percentage of the corporation's stock to be acquired by the ESOP and, thus, for example, the rule is not satisfied by a request for a determination letter from the Internal Revenue Service that the ESOP is a qualified plan.

A special effective date applies to loans not otherwise grandfathered under the provision with respect to a plan that does not satisfy the more than 50 percent requirement of the provision, but would have satisfied the provisions of the House bill and the Senate amendment. Under the provision, the more than 50 percent requirement does not apply in the case of a loan made after July 10, 1989, if (1) the requirements of the provision are satisfied by substituting at least 30 percent for more than 50 percent and (2) the loan is made (a) on or before November 17, 1989, (b) the loan is made after November 17, 1989, pursuant to a binding written commitment in effect on November 17, 1989, or (c) to the extent that the proceeds of the loan are used to acquire employer securities pursuant to a written binding contract (or tender offer) in effect on November 17, 1989.

In addition, the provision does not apply to a loan made after July 10, 1989, to refinance securities acquisition loans (determined without regard to sec. 133(b)(2)) made on or before such date or to refinance loans grandfathered under the provision if (1) such refinancing loan meets the requirements of section 133 (as in effect before the amendment made by the provision, (2) the outstanding principal amount of the loan is not increased, and (3) the term of such loan does not extend beyond the later of (a) the last day of the term of the original securities acquisition loan, or (b) the last day of the 7-year period beginning on the date the original securities acquisition loan was made. These refinancing rules apply in the case of a securities acquisition loan that consists of a loan to the employer with a corresponding loan to the ESOP (a back-to-back or mirror loan) (see sec. 133(b)(3)), if the loan is restructured so that the loan is directly from the financial institution to the ESOP with a guarantee from the employer rather than a loan from the employer. The refinancing rules also apply to a series of refinancings. The conference agreement does not contain the provision of the House bill requiring that the original lender must have been a qualified lender.

The conferees intend that the written binding commitment rule apply to the extent that a loan made pursuant to a written binding commitment that otherwise satisfies the requirements of the grandfather rule is used to replace or refinance a loan the proceeds of which were used to acquire employer securities before the applicable grandfather date. Such a grandfathered loan may be refinanced without loss of the grandfather if the requirements relating to refinancings are otherwise met.

The conferees understand that ESOP loan transactions are not identical, and that the course of events leading up to the conclusion of a transaction differs from case to case. Thus, with respect to the grandfather rules for loans made pursuant to a written binding commitment, the conferees recognize that whether there is a written binding loan commitment depends on all the facts and circumstances and that the existence of such a commitment can be demonstrated in a variety of ways.

It is not necessary that the final loan documents be executed by the parties in order to demonstrate the existence of a written binding loan commitment. The existence of such a commitment can be demonstrated, for example, by any combination of documents which include some or all of documentation of the lender, written communications by the borrower or the borrower's agent (e.g., an investment banker or broker), and documentation of the borrower showing that the loan was approved by the lender and that the offer to make the loan was received by the borrower. No one particular document is necessary to qualify for the grandfather.

The documentation would have to include the principal terms of the loan, such as the principal amount, interest rate or spread or formula pursuant to which the interest rate will be set, and maturity of the loan. It is intended that the grandfather will not fail to be met if the loan commitment is for a specified amount and the borrower borrows less than the full amount. In addition, the grandfather will not fail to be met merely because the interest rate is to be set in accordance with rates prevailing at the time the loan is made, or because the only modification in the loan terms is a reduction in the interest rate that occurs before the loan is made. The grandfather will also not fail to be met merely because a loan commitment that met the conditions of the grandfather had an expiration date and the commitment was extended before the expiration date without change in the material terms of the commitment.

The written binding commitment grandfather rules apply to all types of securities acquisition loans. Thus, for example, immediate allocation loans, as well as other types of securities acquisition loans, would be grandfathered under the provision if a binding written commitment to make a securities acquisition loan existed on June 6, 1989, and at all times thereafter before the loan is made. Of course, such loans may also qualify under the special rule for immediate allocation loans.

The conferees also intend that a grandfathered loan will not lose the benefit of the grandfather merely because the interest rate on the loan is adjusted periodically by an independent (e.g., unrelated to the ESOP, its trustee or the sponsor of the ESOP) remarketing and interest-setting agent, or when the debt is remarketed.

In general, the rules for determining whether a written binding commitment exists are the same under all the ESOP grandfather rules. However, for purposes of the June 6, 1989, binding commitment rule only, a loan is treated as being made pursuant to a written binding commitment in effect on June 6, 1989, if the loan would have met the conditions necessary to satisfy the June 6, 1989, binding commitment transition rule, except for the fact that the commitment lapsed after June 6, 1989, provided that the loan was closed on or before November 17, 1989, on substantially the same terms as contained in the original written commitment.

Dividends paid deduction.—The conference agreement follows the Senate amendment, except that the conference agreement includes the provision in the House bill that dividends may be used to repay an acquisition loan only if the dividends are on employer securities acquired with the loan. The effective date of the provision is the same as the House bill, except that August 4, 1989, is substituted for July 10, 1989. Thus, the provision is effective for securities acquired by the ESOP after August 4, 1989, other than securities acquired with the proceeds of a loan made pursuant to a written binding commitment in effect on August 4, 1989, to the extent the proceeds of such loan are used to acquire employer securities pursuant to a written binding contract (or tender offer) in effect on August 4, 1989. Employer securities are not considered to have been acquired by an ESOP on or before August 4, 1989, for example, if the securities were acquired by a qualified plan on or before August 4, 1989, but the plan was not an ESOP until after August 4, 1989.

As under present law, a loan does not have to qualify as a securities acquisition loan under section 133 in order for the dividend deduction to apply to dividends used to repay the loan.

As under the House bill, no inference is intended as to the scope of the dividend deduction prior to the effective date of the provision. In addition, no inference is intended with respect to the permissible sources of payments on exempt loans under Title I of the Employee Retirement Income Security Act of 1974.

Deferral of gain on certain sales of stock to an ESOP.—The conference agreement follows the House bill.

Limits on contributions and benefits under an ESOP.—The conference agreement follows the House bill.

Payment of estate tax liability by an ESOP.—The conference agreement follows the House bill.

Estate tax deduction for sales to an ESOP.—The conference agreement follows the House bill, with the modification that the provision applies to estates of decedents dying after the date of enactment.

Relief from net operating loss provisions.—The conference agreement follows the House bill.

Committee Reports on P.L. 100-647 (Technical and Miscellaneous Revenue Act of 1988)

[Senate Committee Report]

Estate Tax Deduction for Sales to ESOP

The bill conforms the nonallocation rules applicable to sales under section 2057 to the nonallocation rules applicable to sales under section 1042 (relating to nonrecognition treatment for certain sales of stock to an ESOP). With respect to the rule prohibiting allocation or accrual of benefits under a plan attributable to securities acquired in a qualified sale (or assets in lieu of such securities), the bill clarifies that the nonallocation period is the period beginning on the date of the sale and ending on the later of (1) the date that is 10 years after the date of sale or (2) the date of the plan allocation attributable to the final payment of acquisition indebtedness incurred in connection with such sale.

The bill also provides that individuals who are ineligible to receive an allocation of securities (or other assets) solely because they are lineal descendants of the decedent can receive an allocation of the securities acquired in a qualified sale provided that the total amount of such securities (or assets in lieu thereof) allocated to all such lineal descendants is not more than 5 percent of all employer securities acquired in the decedent's qualified sale.

Finally, the bill clarifies that, in the case of a plan that fails to comply with the nonallocation rules, the statutory period for the assessment of the excise tax imposed with respect to such failure (sec. 4979A) is extended.

Voting Rights for Employer Stock

Present law

* * * all ESOPs are required to pass through certain voting rights to plan participants. The circumstances under which participants are entitled to exercise voting rights depend on whether the employer has a registration-type class of securities. The Act provides that these voting requirements may be satisfied if the plan permits each participant 1 vote with respect to the issue in question and the plan trustee votes the shares held by the plan in the proportion determined by the votes of participants.

Explanation of provision

The bill conforms the 1-vote-per-participant rule to the legislative history by providing that it applies only where the employer does not have a registration-type class of securities.

Sales of Stock to an ESOP

In order to conform the statute to Congressional intent, the bill clarifies that the nonallocation period is the period beginning on the date of the sale and ending on the later of (1) the date that is 10 years after the date of sale or (2) the date of the plan allocation attributable to the final payment of acquisition indebtedness incurred in connection with such sale.

In some situations, the rules for determining whether an individual is a 25 percent shareholder may be more favorable under the Act than under prior law. The provision of the Act, however, is effective prospectively only. The bill provides that, for purposes of determining whether an individual is a 25-percent shareholder with respect to sales occurring before October 22, 1986, in taxable years beginning after July 18, 1984, all allocated securities held by qualified plans may be treated as outstanding with respect to the individual if securities allocated to the individual under the qualified plans are treated as securities owned by the individual. This rule applies consistently to all individuals with respect to any sales to which section 1042 applies.

The bill provides that the excise tax on certain distributions (sec. 4978) does not apply to employer securities which are required to be disposed of pursuant to the new diversification rules.

[Senate Committee Report]

ESOP Diversification Rules

In order to conform to Congressional intent, the bill clarifies that a qualified participant's qualified election period generally begins with the plan year during which the participant attains age 55 and ends with the fifth succeeding plan year. If, however, the participant has not completed 10 years of plan participation by the end of the plan year in which the participant attains age 55, the qualified election period begins with the plan year in which the participant competes 10 years of plan participation and ends with the fifth succeeding plan year.

For example, in the case of an ESOP using the calendar year as the plan year, a participant who completes 10 years of plan participation before attaining age 55 and who attains age 55 in 1990, becomes a qualified participant in the plan year beginning January 1, 1990. That participant is eligible to direct diversification during the 90-day election period beginning January 1, 1991, and remains eligible to direct diversification during the annual election periods in 1992, 1993, 1994, 1995, and 1996.

Similarly, if the participant completes 10 years of participation in 1990 when the participant is 58, the participant becomes a qualified participant in the plan year beginning January 1, 1990. The participant is eligible to direct diversification during the election periods in 1991, 1992, 1993, 1994, 1995, and 1996,

Under the bill, the qualified election period of any participant does not begin before the first plan year beginning after December 31, 1986. Thus, for example, under the bill, if a participant in a calendar year ESOP attained age 55 and had 10 years of plan participation in 1986, the participant is eligible to make a diversification election during the election periods in 1988, 1989, 1990, 1991, 1992, and 1993.

The committee understands that some plans already may have provided for diversification elections in 1988, whereas some plans may not have done so pending the enactment of this bill or the issuance of guidance by the Secretary. Accordingly, the bill provides flexibility with respect to diversification elections required under the bill in 1988. Accordingly, in the case of an individual who first became a qualified participant during the first plan year beginning after December 31, 1986, the employer may satisfy the diversification requirements by providing the first diversification election to the individual during the election period either with respect to the first plan year beginning after December 31, 1986, or the first plan year beginning after December 31, 1987.

The bill also clarifies that diversification is to be completed no later than 90 days after the close of the election period, regardless of the method used to implement diversification elections. Thus, diversification is to be completed within the 90-day period regardless of whether diversification is implemented by means of distribution, transfer to another qualified plan which offers the requisite investment options, or reinvestment of employer securities in other assets.

Distributions From Tax-Credit ESOPs

The bill clarifies that the exception to the 84-month rule for distributions on termination of a tax-credit ESOP is effective with respect to distributions (rather than plan terminations) occurring after December 31, 1984. This exception is available without regard to whether the employer established a successor plan, including an ESOP. The meaning of "termination" and "distribution" for purposes of this rule are to be construed liberally to implement the purposes of the exception, and are not intended to affect the meaning of termination and distribution for other purposes. Thus, for example, a transfer from a tax-credit ESOP to another qualified plan is to be treated as a distribution for purposes of the exception. Of course, any distribution or transfer must comply with any applicable qualification rules. For example, this exception to the 84-month rule does not override the rule requiring consent to distributions if the participant's vested benefits exceed $3,500 (sec. 411(a)(11)).

In order to coordinate the 84-month rule with the new diversification rules, the bill provides that the 84-month rule does not apply to the extent that a distribution is made to satisfy the diversification requirement. This exception to the 84-month rule applies only to the extent that the diversification requirement cannot be satisfied by distributing employer securities that have already met the 84-month rule.

Timing of ESOP Distributions

Under the special distribution rule applicable to ESOPs, the bill provides that, in the case of a separation from service for reasons other than separation on or after normal retirement age, death, or disability, distributions are not required to begin if the participant returns to service with the employer prior to the time distribution is otherwise to begin under the rule.

The special ESOP distribution rules create a conflict with the rules added by the Retirement Equity Act of 1984, which provide that benefits in excess of certain amounts cannot be distributed without the consent of the participant (sec. 411(a)(11)), and that, in certain cases, benefits must be paid in the form of a joint and survivor annuity (secs. 401(a)(11) and 417). The bill provides that the provisions of sections 411(a)(11), 401(a)(11) and 417 are controlling. Thus, for example, distribution to a participant cannot commence under the special ESOP rules unless the applicable consent requirements of sections 411(a)(11), 401(a)(11), and 417 are satisfied.

Voting Rights for Employer Stock

The bill incorporates in the statute the provision in the Statement of Managers that the exception to the voting rules applies to an employer (determined without regard to the controlled group rules) whose business consists of publishing a newspaper for general circulation on a regular basis. Thus, the exception does not apply to members of the controlled group that do not meet this requirement.

The bill replaces the term "not publicly traded" in section 401(a)(22) with the term "not readily tradable on an established market" to conform to the term used in section 409. This change is not intended as a substantive change in the rules of section 401(a)(22).

Right to Demand Securities From ESOP

To coordinate with the new diversification rules, the bill provides that a participant does not have the right to demand that benefits be paid in the form of employer securities with respect to the portion of the participant's account that the participant elected to diversify.

Sales of Stock to an ESOP

The bill provides that the excise tax on certain distributions (sec. 4978) does not apply to employer securities which are required to be disposed of pursuant to the new diversification rules.

Partial Exclusion of Interest Earned on ESOPs

In general

The bill clarifies the availability of the partial interest exclusion in the case of refinancings of the various types of securities acquisition loans.

Back-to-back loans

The bill provides that, with respect to back-to-back loans the terms of which are not substantially similar, if the total commitment period of the loan is extended beyond 7 years, the partial exclusion will be available, but for the first 7 years of the loan only. This 7-year period begins as of the date of the original loan. The provision is effective with respect to a loan used to acquire employer securities after July 18, 1984, and a loan made after July 18, 1984, that is used (or is a part of a series of loans used) to refinance a loan that (1) was used to acquire employer securities after July 18, 1984, and (2) met the requirements of section 133 (other than subsection (b)(2) thereof) as in effect at the time the loan was made.

Immediate allocation loans

The bill provides that, with respect to immediate allocation loans, if the total commitment period is extended beyond 7 years, the partial interest exclusion will be available, but for the first 7 years of the loan only. This 7-year period begins as of the date of the original loan. This provision is effective as if included in the Act.

Refinancings

The bill provides that a loan to an ESOP (other than an immediate allocation loan or a back-to-back loan that has terms that are not substantially similar) after July 18, 1984, that is used (or is part of a series of loans used) to refinance a loan will qualify as a securities acquisition loan provided that (1) the original loan met the requirements of section 133 (other than subsection (b)(2) thereof) as in effect on the date of the loan, or, if later, July 19, 1984; and (2) the original loan was used to acquire employer securities after May 23, 1984. Immediate allocation loans and back-to-back loans that have terms that are not substantially similar are described above.

Under the bill, if a securities acquisition loan (other than an immediate allocation loan or a back-to-back loan that has terms that are not substantially similar) is refinanced and as a result the total commitment period exceeds the greater of the original commitment period or 7 years, then the partial exclusion continues to apply, but only during the first 7 years of the commitment period (measured from the date of the original loan) or the original commitment period, whichever is greater. For example, if an otherwise qualified securities acquisition loan to an ESOP with an original commitment period of 5 years is refinanced and the commitment period is extended for 2 years (for a total commitment period of 7 years), the partial exclusion would apply during the entire 7 years of the loan.

Under the bill, as under the Act, if the terms of the back-to-back loans are no longer substantially similar as a result of the refinancing, the partial exclusion is available only during the first 7 years of the loan.

Dividends Paid Deduction

The bill provides that, with respect to dividends used to make payments on a loan described in section 404(a)(9), the dividend deduction is available with respect to dividends on both unallocated and allocated ESOP securities. However, dividends on allocated ESOP securities may be used to make payments on such a loan only if the account to which the dividend would have been allocated is allocated employer securities with a fair market value not less than the amount of the dividend that would have been allocated. In addition, such allocation is required to be made in the year the dividend would otherwise have been allocated.

The bill also provides that use of dividends to repay an acquisition loan in accordance with section 404(k) does not violate the prohibited transaction rules of section 4975(d)(3).

[¶ 12,130.07]

Committee Reports on P.L. 99-514 (Tax Reform Act of 1986)

[Senate Committee Report]

Explanation of Provisions

Overview

Under the bill, additional requirements are provided for any ESOP (within the meaning of sec. 4975(e)(7) or sec. 409). These additional qualification requirements (1) permit distributions upon termination of an ESOP, (2) modify the distribution and put option requirements, and (3) modify the special limits on allocations of contributions to an ESOP to conform the definition of highly compensated employee to the new definition provided for qualified plans generally.

Distributions upon plan termination

The bill amends the tax credit ESOP distribution provisions to permit certain distributions upon plan termination. Thus, the 84-month rule generally will not apply with respect to distributions made on account of the termination of a tax-credit ESOP.

Distribution and put option requirements

Timing of distribution

The bill modifies the rules relating to the timing and form of required distributions. Under the bill, an ESOP is to permit distributions to employees who separate from service before normal retirement age. Unless an employee otherwise elects in writing, the payment of benefits under an ESOP must begin no later than one year after the later of the plan year (1) in which the participant terminates employment due to retirement, disability, or death, or (2) which is the fifth plan year following the participant's separation from service (provided the participant does not return to service with the employer prior to that time).

The bill provides an exception to the general rule on availability of a distribution in the case in which any portion of a participant's account balance is attributable to securities for which any portion of an acquisition indebtedness related to such securities is outstanding. Therefore, if a portion of a participant's account balance includes employer securities which were acquired in connection with a loan that has not been fully repaid, the exception applies. Under this exception, distributions are not required to be made available to a participant under the general rule until the plan year following the plan year in which the loan is fully repaid.

The rules added by the bill are intended as an acceleration of the otherwise applicable benefit commencement date. Accordingly, if the general rules (sec. 401(a)(14) require the commencement of distributions at an earlier date, those general rules override this special ESOP rule.

Form of distribution

The bill generally retains the present-law requirement that a participant in an ESOP who is entitled to a distribution under the plan must be provided the right to demand that the distribution be made in the form of employer securities rather than in cash and the present-law requirement that a participant who receives a distribution of employer securities from a tax credit ESOP or a leveraged ESOP must be given a put option with respect to distributed employer securities that are not readily tradable. However, the bill modifies the permissible periods over which the employer may pay the option price to the participant. The modifications contained in the bill apply with respect to all ESOP distributions, not merely the accelerated distributions added by the bill.

Unless the plan provides that a participant may elect a longer distribution period, the plan is to provide distributions over a period not longer than 5 years. The bill extends this distribution period if the participant's account balance exceeds $500,000 by one year (up to 5 additional years) for each $100,000 (or fraction thereof) by which the account balance exceeds $500,000. These dollar amounts are indexed at the same time and in the same manner as the dollar limits on benefits under a defined benefit pension plan (sec. 415(d)).

In the case of a total distribution of employer securities to a participant that are put to the employer, the bill provides that the employer must pay the option price to the participant in substantially equal annual payments over a period not exceeding 5 years and beginning not more than 30 days after the exercise of the put option. The employer is not required to provide security with respect to such installment payments, but is required to credit a reasonable rate of interest with respect to the outstanding balance under such installment payments of the option price. A total distribution means the distribution within one taxable year of the recipient of the account balance under the plan.

In the case of a put option exercised as part of an installment distribution, the employer is required to pay the option price within 30 days after the exercise of the option.

Extension of put option requirements to stock bonus plans

Under the bill, distributions of nonreadily tradable securities of an employer from a stock bonus plan are subject to the put option requirements applicable to ESOPs.

Modification of limitations on annual additions for ESOPs

Under the bill, the definition of an employee who is subject to the one-third allocation limit for purposes of the special limitation on annual additions for ESOPs (sec. 415(c)(6)) is modified to conform to the new definition of highly compensated employee added under the bill for purposes of qualified pension profit-sharing, or stock bonus plans, and for purposes of employee benefit plans.

* * *

Effective Dates

The provision permitting distributions upon plan termination generally is effective for termination distributions made after December 31, 1984.

The distribution and payment requirements are effective with respect to distributions attributable to stock acquired after the date of enactment. The extension of the put option requirement to stock bonus plans is effective for distributions attributable to stock acquired after the date of enactment. The modified definition of highly compensated employees is effective for years beginning after December 31, 1986.

[Conference Committee Report]

Changes in qualification requirements relating to ESOPs

Vesting

* * * Of course, ESOPs are subject to the vesting provisions applicable to all qualified plans under the conference agreement.

Nondiscrimination rules

* * * Of course, ESOPs are subject to the provisions in the conference agreement generally applicable to all qualified plans, including, for example, the coverage and minimum participation requirements and the limit on includible compensation.

* * *

Timing of distributions

The conference agreement follows the Senate amendment.

Put option requirements

The conference agreement follows the Senate amendment, except that security is required if the employer defers payment of the option price.* * *

Extension of put option requirements to stock bonus plans

The conference agreement follows the Senate amendment.

Modification of limitations on annual additions to ESOPs

The conference agreement follows the Senate amendment.

* * *

The conferees intend that, for purposes of the rule permitting distributions from a tax credit ESOP on termination of the plan, a termination includes a partial termination of such a plan as to the employees of a particular subsidiary or operating trade or business in situations where such employees no longer have a significant relationship with the sponsor of the plan.

[House Committee Report]

Diversification of investments

In general

The bill requires an ESOP to offer a partial diversification election to participants who meet certain age and participation requirements (qualified employees). Under the bill, a qualified employee must be entitled annually during any diversification election period occuring within the employee's qualified election period direct diversification of up to 25 percent of the participant's account balance (50 percent after attainment of age 60). To the extent that a participant elects to diversify a portion of the account balance, the bill requires an ESOP to offer at least three investment options not inconsistent with regulations prescribed by the Secretary and to complete the diversification within a specified period.

Under the bill, distribution to the participant within 90 days after the close of the annual diversification election period of an amount not to exceed the maximum amount for which a participant elected diversification is deemed to satisfy the diversification requirement.

Qualified election period; qualified employees

Each ESOP must provide an annual diversification election period for the 90-day period following the close of the ESOP plan year. Thus, within 90 days after the end of a plan year, an ESOP must permit an election by those qualified employees who become or remain eligible to make a diversification election during the plan year. Under the bill, any employee who has attained at least age 55 and completed at least 10 years of participation in the ESOP is a qualified employee. Any qualified employee is permitted to make a diversification election during any diversification election period occurring within that employee's qualified election period.

A qualified employee's qualified election period generally begins with the plan year following the plan year during which the qualified employee attains age 55 and ends with the fifth succeeding plan year. If, however, the employee has not completed 10 years of participation in the ESOP by the end of the plan year in which the employee attains age 55, the qualified election period begins with the plan year following the year in which he completes 10 years of participation and ends with the plan year following the year in which he attains age 60.

For example, in the case of an ESOP using the calendar year as the plan year, a participant who completes 10 years of participation before attaining age 55 and who attains age 55 in 1990, becomes a qualified employee in the 90-day election period beginning January 1, 1991. That participant will remain eligible to direct diversification during the annual election periods in 1992, 1993, 1994, 1995 and 1996.

Amount eligible for diversification

Under the bill, for any participant who has attained age 55 (but not age 60) and completed 10 years of participation in the plan, the amount of a participant's account balance subject to the diversification election at the end of the plan year is 25 percent of the participant's account balance at the end of the year reduced by amounts previously diversified. For any participant who has attained age 60 and completed 10 years of participation, the amount eligible for diversification at the end of the plan year is 50 percent of the participant's account balance at the end of the year, minus amounts previously diversified. Because these rules permit diversification not to exceed a cumulative amount, the scope of each year's election depends, in part, on prior elections.

The committee intends the Secretary of the Treasury to issue regulations providing that no separate diversification election be provided for de minimis amounts. In addition, in no event will amounts previously diversified be required to be reinvested in employer securities due to decreases in the value of the account balance.

These rules are illustrated by the following example:

Assume a participant with 10 years of participation in an ESOP attains age 55 during the 1986 plan year and that the ESOP uses a calendar plan year. During the 90-day period beginning on January 1, 1987, and ending on March 31, 1987, the participant may direct the trustee to diversify up to 25 percent of the participant's account balance. If the participant elects to direct diversification of the maximum amount—25 percent—the only amounts for which the participant may elect diversification during the 1988, 1989, 1990, and 1991 election periods are amounts attributable to increases in the participant's account balance, whether attributable to growth or additional employer contributions. However, pursuant to regulations to be issued by the Secretary of the Treasury, no diversification election is required for de minimis amounts.

From January 1, 1992 to March 31, 1992, the participant must be given the opportunity to direct diversification of up to 33 ⅓ percent of the remaining account balance (bringing the total amount subject to the diversification election to a cumulative 50 percent of the participant's account balance at the end of the 1991 plan year). Whether or not this participant directed diversification in 1992, no further diversification election is required to be provided to the participant.

Alternatively, if the participant did not elect diversification during the 1987 election period, a similar election would be available during the 1988, 1989, 1990, and 1991 election periods. In each year, the participant could elect to direct diversification with respect to that portion of the account balance that, when aggregated with prior amounts for which diversification was elected, did not exceed 25 percent of the account balance at the end of that year.

If the participant did not elect diversification during the 1987-1991 election periods, a final election would be available in 1992 (i.e., the first election period following the plan year in which the participant attains age 60) to direct diversification of up to 50 percent of the participant's account balance.

Implementation of diversification

No later than 90 days after the close of the election period, the plan trustee(s) must complete diversification pursuant to participant elections. The trustee(s) may satisfy this requirement (1) by distributing to the participant an amount equal to the amount for which the participant elected diversification, or (2) by substituting for the amount of the employer securities for which the participant elects diversification, an equivalent amount of other assets, in accordance with the participant's investment direction. The ESOP must offer at least three investment options (not inconsistent with regulations prescribed by the Secretary) that may, but need not, include an option to permit full self-direction.

Whether or not the trustees must actually sell employer securities to satisfy the diversification elections depends, in part, on the extent to which the ESOP is invested in employer securities. Provided the amount of total trust assets invested in other than employer securities is greater than the total amount for which diversification is elected, it may be possible to complete diversification (without disposing of employer securities) by allocating alternative assets to electing participants' accounts or by disposing of such alternative assets and reinvesting the proceeds in the investments directed by participants.

In addition, under the bill, a participant who receives a distribution of securities in satisfaction of a diversification election is permitted to roll over the distribution into another qualified plan or IRA.

* * *

Independent appraiser

Under the bill, the valuation of employer securities contributed to or purchased by an ESOP must be determined by an independent appraiser (within the meaning of section 170(a)(1)). The appraiser's name must be reported to the Internal Revenue Service.

[Conference Committee Report]

Diversification of investments

The conference agreement follows the House bill, except that the effective date of the diversification requirements is delayed for one year. Thus, the diversification rules are effective with respect to [stock] acquired [after] December 31, 1986.

Under the conference agreement, as under the House bill, a "qualified employee" is entitled annually during the participant's "qualified election period" to direct diversification of up to 25 percent of the participant's account balance (50 percent after attainment of age 60). Any employee who has attained age 55 and completed 10 years of participation is a qualified employee. An employee is entitled to an election in each year within the qualified election period.

In meeting the diversification requirements, it is not intended that plan sponsors offer employer securities as one of the diversification options. As under the House bill, the diversification requirement can be met by a distribution of the portion of the account balance for which diversification was elected, or cash in lieu thereof. If under this rule, stock is distributed in satisfaction of the diversification requirement, the usual put option rules apply. Amounts which are distributed in satisfaction of the diversification requirement may be rolled over to an IRA or to another qualified plan. The diversification requirement is satisfied if an employer provides the option to transfer the portion of the account balance for which diversification is elected into a plan which provides for employee-directed investment and in which the required diversification options are available.

* * *

Independent appraiser

The conference agreement follows the House bill, except that valuation by an independent appraiser is not required in the case of employer securities which are readily tradable on an established securities market. The requirement is effective with respect to stock acquired after December 31, 1986.

[Senate Committee Report]

Explanation of Provisions

Qualified securities; qualified replacement property

The bill makes several clarifying changes to the definition of qualified securities and qualified replacement property.

With respect to qualified securities, the bill makes it clear that stock of a corporation with no readily tradable stock outstanding may be eligible for nonrecognition treatment whether or not the corporation or any member of the controlled group has outstanding any readily tradable debt securities. The bill also clarifies that the nonrecognition provision applies only if the gain on the sale would otherwise have been long-term capital gain. For example, the sale of securities that had been held for less than six months, and the sale of securities which otherwise would be treated as ordinary income (e.g., by reason of the collapsible corporation provisions) will be ineligible for nonrecognition treatment under this provision.

With respect to qualified replacement property, the bill makes it clear that securities issued by a government or political subdivision may not be treated as replacement property.

Qualified replacement property is limited under the bill to securities issued by a domestic operating corporation other than the corporation that issued the securities involved in the nonrecognition transaction. The bill generally defines a domestic operating corporation as a corporation substantially all the assets of which were, at the time the securities were purchased, used in the active conduct of a trade or business.

If (1) the corporation issuing the qualified replacement property owns stock representing control of one or more other corporations, or (2) one or more other corporations own stock representing control of the corporation issuing the qualified replacement property, then all such corporations will be treated as one corporation for purposes of determining whether the corporation is a domestic operating corporation and for purposes of determining whether the corporation that issued the qualified replacement property also issued the qualified securities. For purposes of this provision, control means control within the meaning of section 304(c), except that in testing control for this purpose, qualified replacement property of the electing taxpayer attributable to that sale is disregarded. Thus, the stock of a start-up company will constitute qualified replacement property, notwithstanding the fact that the start-up company and the corporation that issued the securities involved in the nonrecognition transaction are treated as the same corporation under section 304(c).

The bill also clarifies that the stock of a bank or thrift institution will not be ineligible to be treated as qualified replacement property solely because the institution has passive income in excess of 25 percent of its gross receipts for the preceding year.

Finally, the bill clarifies that, in the case of the death of an individual who sold qualified securities to an ESOP, the executor of the individual's estate may invest the proceeds (within 12 months after the date of the sale) in qualified replacement property pursuant to an election under section 1042. The executor similarly could designate as qualified replacement property any property acquired by the decedent for which a statement of purchase has not been filed. The estate's basis in the qualified replacement property is to be determined under the general principles applicable under section 1042. A beneficiary who receives the qualified replacement property from the estate has a basis in the property equal to that of the executor's in the property, rather than the fair market value of the property on the date that the beneficiary acquires it.

Further, the bill provides an extended replacement period for sellers who had acquired replacement property that, pursuant to this bill, will no longer be considered qualified replacement property. Under the bill, if a security was acquired by a taxpayer prior to [January 1, 1987], and such security no longer constitutes qualifying replacement property, the period of time for the purchase of qualified replacement property is extended to [January 1, 1987]. Of course, this extension does not increase the amount of gain for which nonrecognition treatment may be claimed.

Thirty-percent test

Under the bill, it is clarified that the ESOP or eligible worker-owned cooperative must hold, immediately after the sale, at least 30 percent of the total number of shares of all classes of stock (other than preferred stock described in section 1504(a)(4)) or 30 percent of the total value of all stock of the corporation that issued the qualified securities. With respect to sales after [after May 6, 1986], in taxable years ending after that date, 30-percent ownership by the employee organization is to be tested after application of the ownership attribution rules of Code section 318(a)(4).

The requirement that the plan hold 30 percent of outstanding stock (after application of sec. 318(a)(4)) is effective for sales of securities after July 18, 1984.

Exclusive benefit

The bill makes several clarifying changes to the requirement that the employee organization be maintained for the exclusive benefit of employees. First, the bill clarifies that no portion of the assets attributable to qualified securities with respect to which a nonrecognition election is made (sec. 1042 securities) may be allocated to (1) a taxpayer seeking nonrecognition treatment, (2) any person who is related to that taxpayer in one of the ways described in Code section 267(b), or (3) any other person who owns (after application of the attribution rules of Code section 318(a)) more than 25 percent (by number) of (a) any class of outstanding stock of the corporation that issued such qualified securities, or (b) any class of stock of certain related corporations.

In addition, the bill makes it clear that this restriction applies to prohibit any direct or indirect accrual of benefits under all qualified plans of an employer or an allocation of assets attributable to the qualified securities involved in the nonrecognition transaction. Thus, for example, an ESOP in which the taxpayer seeking nonrecognition treatment participates could not allocate to the taxpayer's account any assets attributable to the securities involved in the nonrecognition transaction. Nor could the employer make an allocation of other assets to the taxpayer under the ESOP without making additional allocations to other participants sufficient separately to satisfy the nondiscrimination requirements of Code section 401(a).

The bill clarifies that an individual is to be treated as a 25-percent shareholder only if the individual is a 25-percent shareholder (1) at any time during the one-year period ending on the date of the sale of section 1042 securities to an ESOP, or (2) on the dates upon which any section 1042 securities sold to the ESOP are allocated. In the case of an individual who satisfies the condition described at (1), the individual will continue to be treated as a 25-percent shareholder until all of the qualified securities acquired pursuant to the sale are allocated. In the case of an individual who does not satisfy the condition described at (1), but meets the condition described at (2), the individual will be treated as a 25-percent shareholder only with respect to those section 1042 securities allocated on the date or dates that the individual is a 25-percent shareholder.

The bill also provides that, for purposes of determining whether an individual owns more than 25 percent of the outstanding stock of the corporation which issued the employer securities, all allocated securities held by an ESOP are treated as securities owned by the ESOP participant to whom the securities are allocated. The treatment of shares held by an ESOP as held by a shareholder for purposes of applying the 25-percent test applies to sales of qualified securities after enactment.

The bill also provides that individuals who would be ineligible to receive an allocation of qualified securities *solely* because they are lineal descendants of other individuals who are ineligible to receive allocations of section 1042 securities may receive an allocation of the section 1042 securities provided that the total amount of such securities allocated to all such lineal descendants is not more than 5 percent of all section 1042 securities.

Disqualification

The bill also provides that an ESOP that acquires section 1042 securities is required to comply with the restriction on the allocation of securities to the sellers, family members, and 25-percent shareholders (sec. 409(n)). The sanction for failure to comply with the restriction would be disqualification of the plan with respect to those participants who received prohibited allocations. Thus, failure to comply results in income inclusion for those participants of the value of their prohibited allocations on the date of such allocations. However, violation of the restriction does not cause disqualification of the plan if the violation occurred more than ten years after all of the section 1042 securities acquired in the transaction had been allocated.

Under the bill, if there is a prohibited allocation by an ESOP or an eligible worker-owned cooperative of employer securities acquired in a section 1042 transaction, then a 50-percent excise tax is imposed on the amount involved in the prohibited allocation. A prohibited allocation means (1) any allocation of employer securities acquired in a qualified sale if the provisions of section 409(n), relating to prohibitions on allocations to certain individuals, are violated and (2) any benefit accruing to a person in violation of the provisions of section 409(n). The liability for this excise tax is to be paid by the employer who maintains an ESOP or by the eligible worker-owned cooperative.

Eligible taxpayers

Generally, effective for sales after March 28, 1985, the bill limits the class of taxpayers eligible to elect nonrecognition treatment under this provision by making the election unavailable to any subchapter C corporation. However, a subchapter C corporation may elect nonrecognition treatment with respect to certain sales made no later than July 1, 1985, provided the sales otherwise satisfy the requirements of this provision and are made pursuant to a binding contract in effect on March 28, 1985, and at all times thereafter. The bill provides an exception to the March 28, 1985, date for 2 transactions.

* * *

Disposition of qualified replacement property

The bill also clarifies the coordination of the provision's requirement that gain be recognized upon disposition of any qualified replacement property with other rules providing nonrecognition treatment. Effective for dispositions made after the date of enactment, the bill overrides all other provisions permitting nonrecognition and requires that gain realized upon the disposition of qualified replacement property be recognized at that time. The bill exempts from the rule that gain is to be recognized upon the disposition of qualified replacement property: (1) dispositions at death; (2) dispositions by gift; (3) certain exchanges required in the event of a reorganization provided the corporation involved in the reorganization is not controlled by the taxpayer holding qualified replacement property; and (4) subsequent sales of the qualified replacement property to an ESOP, pursuant to a transaction governed by section 1042.

The amount of gain required to be recognized upon the disposition of qualified replacement property is limited to the amount not recognized pursuant to the election provided by this provision by reason of the acquisition of such replacement property. Any gain in excess of that amount continues to be eligible for any otherwise applicable nonrecognition treatment.

To ensure that this rule is not avoided through the use of controlled corporations, the bill provides special rules for corporations controlled by the taxpayer seeking nonrecognition treatment. If the taxpayer owns stock representing control (within the meaning of section 304(c)) of the corporation issuing the qualified replacement property, the taxpayer shall be treated as having disposed of such qualified replacement property when the corporation disposes of a substantial portion of its assets other than in the ordinary course of its trade or business.

b. Deduction for dividends paid on ESOP stock * * *

Explanation of Provision

The bill makes it clear that dividends paid on any employer stock held by the ESOP and allocated as of the date of distribution to a participant's account may be deducted under this provision, including those dividends paid on employer stock that is not considered to be qualified employer securities within the meaning of section 4091(l). No deduction is permitted, however, with respect to employer stock held in a suspense account (as of the date of distribution) under an ESOP. The bill clarifies that a deduction is permitted for dividends paid on stock which is allocated to participants' accounts as of the date of distribution of such dividends. The bill also makes it clear that current distributions of dividends paid on employer stock allocated to a participant's account under an ESOP will not be considered disqualifying distributions.

The bill clarifies that a corporation will be allowed a deduction for dividends paid on stock held by an ESOP whether such dividends are passed through to beneficiaries of plan participants or to the plan participants themselves. In addition, effective for dividends paid after the date of the bill's enactment, the bill makes it clear that employer deductions for dividends paid on employer stock held by an ESOP are to be permitted only in the year in which the dividend is paid or distributed to the participant beneficiary. Thus, where the employer pays such dividends directly to participants in accordance with plan provisions, a deduction would be permitted in the year paid. However, where the employer pays such dividends to the ESOP for redistribution to participants no later than 90 days after the close of the plan year, a deduction would be permitted in the employer's taxable year in which the dividend is distributed from the ESOP to the participants. The bill clarifies that dividends paid on employer stock held by an ESOP are treated as paid under a contract separate from the contract under which the stock is held. However, the provision is inapplicable to dividends paid before January 1, 1986, if the employer deducted such dividends in the taxable year they were paid to the ESOP and filed a return for that taxable year before the date of enactment.

The bill clarifies that, although the dividends for which the Act allows a deduction are generally to be treated as distributions under the plan, they are to be fully taxable. Thus, these distributions are not to be treated as distributions of net employee contributions. The provision is inapplicable to dividends paid before January 1, 1986, which a taxpayer treated as the nontaxable return of employee contributions for purposes of a return filed before the date of enactment.

Further, the bill empowers the Treasury to disallow deductions for dividends paid on stock held by an ESOP, if the dividend constitutes, in substance, the avoidance of taxation. Thus, for example, if amounts paid by an employer, and treated for tax purposes as 404(k) dividends, are the payment of unreasonable compensation, such payments would not qualify for treatment as section 404(k) dividends.

c. Partial exclusion of interest earned on ESOP loans * * *

Explanation of Provision

The bill (1) clarifies the interaction of the partial interest exclusion with other provisions affecting tax-exempt income, and (2) clarifies the meaning of the term "securities acquisition loan."

Interaction with other provisions.—The bill makes it clear that for purposes of section 291(e), relating to certain tax preference items, (1) interest on an obligation eligible for the partial exclusion of section 133 will not be treated as exempt from tax, * * *

In addition, the bill clarifies the coordination of the partial exclusion with the installment payment provisions (sec. 483) and the original issue discount rules (secs. 1271 through 1275). The bill makes it clear that, in testing the adequacy of the stated interest rate for purposes of section 483 and sections 1271 through 1275, the applicable Federal rate will be adjusted as appropriate to reflect the partial interest exclusion. In addition, the bill clarifies that the below market interest rate rules (sec. 7872) do not apply to a loan between a sponsoring employer and an ESOP, provided that the interest rate payable on such loan is no less than the interest rate payable by the employer on a corresponding section 133 loan.

Securities acquisition loan.—The bill would clarify the definition of the term "securities acquisition loan" in several respects. First, the bill would make it clear that the refinancing of a loan to an ESOP after the effective date of section 133 will qualify as a securities acquisition loan, provided that the repayment period of the original loan is not extended, and the refinanced loan otherwise satisfies the requirements of section 133. Thus, for example, loans used to acquire employer securities after July 18, 1984, qualify for such refinancing notwithstanding that the original loan would not have qualified as a securities acquisition loan under section 133. For example, if a purchase money obligation was utilized to acquire employer securities after July 18, 1984, the refinancing of such loan is permitted to qualify under section 133.

The bill also clarifies that the requirement that a loan from a sponsoring corporation to an ESOP be made on terms "substantially similar" to those applicable to the loan between a commercial lender and the sponsoring corporation does not preclude repayment of the sponsoring corporation's loan to the ESOP more rapidly than the repayment of the loan from the commercial lender to the sponsoring corporation, provided that the allocations of stock within the ESOP do not result in discrimination in favor of highly compensated employees. The terms of such loans are to be negotiated between the plan's sponsor and the lender; however, the repayment period of the loan from the commercial lender could not be more than 7 years unless the repayment terms of the two loans are substantially similar.

The bill would also clarify that, although a securities acquisition loan may not originate with any member of the controlled group, it may be held by a member of the controlled group. However, during any such time that a securities acquisition loan is held by a member of the controlled group, any interest received with respect to such loan during such period would not qualify for the exclusion provided under section 133.

6. Voting Rights

* * *

Explanation of Provision

The bill modifies the voting rights requirements applicable to nonregistration type employer securities held by an ESOP by (1) mandating that voting rights be passed through to participants with respect to certain enumerated issues; and (2) accommodating the one man-one vote philosophy of certain types of ESOPs and EWOCs.

First, the bill would require, with respect to certain issues specified in the bill, that a trustee permit participants to direct the vote under employer securities allocated to the participants' accounts, regardless of whether the issue was required (by law or charter) to be decided by more than a majority vote of the outstanding common shares voted. The issues on which the pass-through of voting rights would be required include merger or consolidation, recapitalization, reclassification, liquidation, dissolution, or sale of substantially all of the assets of a trade or business of the corporation, and to the extent provided by regulations, other similar issues.

Second, the bill would permit the trustee of an ESOP or EWOC, the by-laws or terms of which required that the interests in the ESOP or EWOC be governed on a one vote per participant basis, to vote the employer securities in a manner that reflected the one man-one vote philosophy. Under this alternative, each ESOP or EWOC participant would be entitled to cast one vote on an issue. The trustee would then be required to vote the employer securities held by the ESOP or EWOC in proportion to the results of the votes cast on the issue by the participants.

The requirements relating to one vote per participant are effective on the date of enactment. The requirements relating to pass-through voting are effective after December 31, 1986 for securities acquired after December 31, 1979.

[*Prohibited Allocations*]

Under the bill, certain penalties apply if any portion of the assets attributable to employer securities acquired in a qualified sale accrue or are allocated for the benefit of (1) a decedent whose estate makes such a sale, (2) any person who is related to the decedent in one of the ways described in section 267(b), or (3) any other person who owns (after application of the attribution rules of sec. 318(a)) more than (a) 25 percent (by number) of any class of outstanding stock of the corporation (or certain related corporations) that issued such qualified securities, or (b) more than 25 percent of the total value of any class of outstanding stock of the corporation or of certain related corporations.

In addition, the bill makes it clear that this restriction applies to penalize any direct or indirect accrual of benefits under any qualified plan of the employer or an allocation of assets under the plan attributable to the securities involved in the qualified sale. Thus, for example, an ESOP in which the decedent has an interest should not allocate to the decedent's account any assets attributable to the securities involved in the sale. Nor should the employer make an allocation under the plan of other assets to the decedent in order to make up for the failure to allocate the securities involved in the qualified sale.

The bill clarifies that an individual is to be treated as a 25-percent shareholder only if the individual is a 25-percent shareholder (1) at any time during the one-year period ending on the date of a qualified sale to an ESOP, or (2) on the date upon which any of the securities sold to the ESOP in a qualified sale are allocated. In the case of an individual who satisfies the condition described at (1), the individual will continue to be treated as a 25-percent shareholder until all of the securities acquired pursuant to the qualified sale are allocated. In the case of an individual who does not satisfy the condition described at (1), but meets the condition described at (2), the individual will be treated as a 25-percent shareholder only with respect to those securities allocated on the date or dates that the individual is a 25-percent shareholder.

The bill also provides that, for purposes of determining whether an individual owns more than 25 percent of the outstanding stock of the corporation which issued the employer securities, all allocated securities held by an ESOP are treated as securities owned by the ESOP participant to whom the securities are allocated. The treatment of shares held by an ESOP as held by a shareholder for purposes of applying the 25-percent test applies to qualified sales after the date of enactment.

Under the bill, individuals who would be ineligible to receive an allocation of securities *solely* because they are lineal descendants of the decedent may receive an allocation of the securities acquired in the qualified sale provided that the total amount of such securities allocated to all such lineal descendants is not more than 5 percent of all employer securities acquired in the qualified sale.

The bill would also provide that an ESOP that acquires securities in a qualified sale is required to provide that the restriction on the allocation of securities to the sellers, family members, and 25-percent shareholders will be satisfied. The sanction for failure to comply with the restriction would be disqualification of the plan with respect to those participants who received prohibited allocations. Thus, failure to conply would result in income inclusion for those participants of the value of their prohibited allocations as of the date of such allocations. However, violation of the restriction would not cause disqualification of the plan if the violation occurred more than 10 years after all of the securities acquired in the qualified sale had been allocated.

* * *

[*Tax on Prohibited Allocations*]

* * *

Under the bill, if there is a prohibited allocation by an ESOP or an eligible worker-owned cooperative of employer securities acquired in a section 1042 transaction, then a 50 percent excise tax is imposed on the amount involved in the prohibited allocation. A prohibited allocation means (1) any allocation of employer securities acquired in a qualified sale if the provisions of section 409(n), relating to prohibitions on allocations to certain individuals, are violated and (2) any benefit accruing to a person in violation of the provisions of section 409(n). The liability for this excise tax is to be paid by the employer who maintains an ESOP or by the eligible worker-owned cooperative.

* * *

[Conference Committee Report]

Welfare benefit plan provisions

The conference agreement follows the Senate amendment * * *

[House Committee Report]

Explanation of Provision

The bill makes several changes to clarify the applicability of these provisions and the coordination with the provisions governing the installment payment of estate taxes under section 6166. First, the bill makes it clear, that, with respect to the estates of individuals dying after September 27, 1985, only executors of those estates eligible to make deferred payments of estate taxes may be relieved of estate tax liability under this provision. In addition, under the bill, the transfer of employer securities to an ESOP or to an eligible worker-owned cooperative will not be treated as a disposition or withdrawal which triggers acceleration of the remaining unpaid tax.

The bill makes it clear that, after the transfer, the ongoing eligibility of the estate and the ESOP or cooperative to make installment payments applicable to their respective interests is to be tested separately. Thus, with respect to the estate's remaining interest (if any), cumulative dispositions and withdrawals of amounts up to 50 percent of the estate's remaining interest would be permitted without requiring acceleration of the remaining unpaid tax. Similarly, with respect to an ESOP or cooperative, cumulative dispositions and withdrawals of up to 50 percent of the interest transferred to such organization would be permitted without requiring acceleration. In addition, under the bill, a distribution made by an ESOP to participants on account of death, retirement after attainment of age 59 ½, disability, or any separation from service resulting in an one-year break in service will not be treated as a disposition requiring acceleration of any unpaid tax and will not be taken into account in determining whether any subsequent disposition triggers acceleration.

The bill also makes it clear that no executor will be relieved of estate tax liability with respect to employer securities transferred to an eligible worker-owned cooperative unless the cooperative guarantees the payment of any estate tax or interest by surety bond or other means as required by the Secretary of the Treasury.

* * *

[Senate Committee Report]

[Same as House Committee Report.]

[Conference Committee Report]

[The conference agreement follows the House bill and the Senate amendment with respect to common provisions.]

* * *

[Senate Committee Report]

[*Reduction of Accrued Benefit*]

* * *

The bill provides that an ESOP will not be treated as violating the rule preventing reductions in accrued benefits merely because the plan sponsor eliminates or retains the discretion to eliminate a lump-sum option or an installment payout option with respect to a nondiscriminatory class of employees. Similarly, an employer could retain discretion to limit the option of the plan participants to elect a stock distribution in cases in which the employer becomes substantially employee-owned, or the plan ceases to be an ESOP or a stock bonus plan. In addition, an employer would be permitted to eliminate a required cash distribution option in cases in which the employer securities become readily tradable or to require a cash distribution in cases in which stock in the plan is sold in connection with a sale of substantially all of the company.

An ESOP sponsor is permitted the flexibility to amend the plan to change distribution and payment options under the plan provided any such amendments are within the permissible parameters of the distribution and payment requirements of present law.

[Conference Committee Report]

The conference agreement follows the Senate amendment * * *

[¶ 12,130.08]

Committee Report on P.L. 97-448 (Technical Corrections Act of 1982)

The bill adds provisions relating to regulated public utilities which conform the rules for the payroll-based tax credit for ESOP contributions to the rules for the investment-based tax credit for ESOP contributions. These rules limit the normalization requirements to compensation paid which is subject to ratemaking.

The bill clarifies that the tax-qualified status of an ESOP is not affected merely because employer contributions are determined solely by reference to the payroll-based tax credit allowable to the employer for the contributions.

The bill clarifies that certain cash distribution provisions, if provided under a tax credit ESOP of an employer whose stock generally is required to be held only by employees, will not affect the plan's status either under the qualified plan rules or those additional rules applicable to tax credit ESOPs.

The bill clarifies the rules permitting a distribution to a participant under a tax credit ESOP in the event of the participant's transfer from one employer to another incident to a sale of assets by the former employer to the new employer.

Effective date

The provisions generally apply to compensation paid or accrued after December 31, 1982.

[¶ 12,130.09]

Committee Report on P.L. 96-222 (Technical Corrections Act of 1979)

[Senate Committee Report]

Sec. 101(a)(7)(B)—Effective dates.

The bill clarifies the operation of the effective date provision of section 141 of the Revenue Act of 1978, which made changes in the law governing tax credit employee stock ownership plans and employee stock ownership plans. The general effective date is retained. Thus, the tax credit employee stock ownership plan changes in the 1978 Act generally apply with respect to qualified investment for taxable years beginning after December 31, 1978. In addition, special effective date provisions apply to the tax credit employee stock ownership plan provisions of the Act relating to (1) voting rights, (2) the right of a tax credit employee stock ownership plan to distribute cash in lieu of employer securities (subject to the right of a participant to demand a distribution in the form of employer securities), and (3) put option requirements.

The voting right provision applies to plans to which the new tax credit employee stock ownership plan provisions generally apply beginning with the first day of such application. A tax credit employee stock ownership plan is required to follow the new voting rights pass-through rules with respect to all employer securities held by it if additional employer securities were acquired by the tax credit employee stock ownership plan on account of qualified investment made in a taxable year beginning after December 31, 1978.

The right of a tax credit employee stock ownership plan to distribute cash in lieu of employer securities (subject to the right of a participant to demand a distribution in the form of employer securities) applies to tax credit employee stock ownership plan distributions after December 31, 1978, provided that the new tax credit employee stock ownership plan rules have become applicable to the plan.

The tax credit employee stock ownership plan put option requirements apply to employer securities which are not readily tradable on an established market and which are acquired by the tax credit employee stock ownership plan after December 31, 1978, on account of a qualified investment made after that date. Your committee deleted the House-passed provision which provided that the employer is permitted to elect to have the 1978 Act put option rules in the Act apply to all employer securities held by the tax credit employee stock ownership plan which are not readily tradable on an established market. The House-passed provision provided that the election could be revoked only with the consent of the Secretary. Your committee deleted the House-passed provision, which allows an employer to elect to have the new put option rules apply to all employer securities held by a tax credit employee stock ownership plan which are not readily tradable on an established market, because it understands that the Secretary of the Treasury has existing authority to allow the election and the revocation of the election of the 1978 Act put option rules with respect to employer securities held by a tax credit employee stock ownership plan.

The bill as passed by the House also allows taxpayers to elect irrevocably to accelerate the general effective date by a year. In such a case, the tax credit employee stock ownership plan changes would apply with respect to qualified investment for taxable years beginning after December 31, 1977. The committee amended this provision to require that, with respect to a tax credit employee stock ownership plan in existence on December 31, 1978, if such an election is made, contributions for the year of the election would have to be allocated under the pre-1978 Act rules. The committee was concerned that an election by a tax credit employee stock ownership plan in existence on December 31, 1978, to have the 1978 Act tax credit employee stock ownership plan rules apply one year early would allow an employer to change the allocation formula, with the result that some employees covered by the tax credit employee stock ownership plan who would have been entitled to an allocation of employer securities to their accounts under the pre-1978 Act tax credit employee stock ownership plan rules would be denied the allocation because of the retroactive election of the 1978 Act tax credit employee stock ownership plan rules.

The bill also would provide effective dates for the changes made by the 1978 Act relating to employee stock ownership plans. These changes concern (1) voting rights, (2) put option requirements, and (3) the right of an employee stock ownership plan to distribute cash in lieu of employer securities (subject to the right of a participant to demand a distribution in the form of employer securities).

Under the bill, in the case of qualifying employer securities acquired by an employer stock ownership plan after December 31, 1979, the plan is required (1) to pass through voting rights to plan participants on such securities, under certain circumstances, and (2) to give participants put options on qualifying employer securities which are not readily tradable on an established market. The committee expects that, under regulations prescribed by the Secretary of the Treasury, an employee stock ownership plan could treat qualifying employer securities acquired by it prior to January 1, 1980, under the new voting rights and put option provisions, but is not required to do so.

The right of an employee stock ownership plan to distribute cash in lieu of employer securities (subject to the right of a participant to demand a distribution in the form of employer securities) applies to distributions made after December

31, 1978. (Under the House-passed bill the effective date for such cash distributions from employee stock ownership plans was December 31, 1979.)

The amendment made by this section is effective as if it had been included in section 141 of the Revenue Act of 1978.

Sec. 101(a)(7)(D)—Tax-free contributions to TRASOPs

Generally, under present law, no gain or loss would be recognized by a corporation which makes a required contribution to a tax credit ownership plan of employer securities issued by a related corporation.

For technical reasons, this rule, as enacted by the Revenue Act of 1978, did not apply to all required contributions of such employer securities to a tax credit employee stock ownership plan.

The bill provides that no gain or loss is recognized by an employer on the required transfer of employer securities to a tax credit employee stock ownership plan which it maintains.

The amendment is effective with respect to qualified investment for taxable years beginning after December 31, 1978.

Sec. 101(a)(7)(E)—Cash distributions.

Under present law, employee stock ownership plans are required to meet certain rules also applicable to tax credit employee stock ownership plans. These rules relate to the pass-through of voting rights to participants and to participants' rights to demand employer securities.

Under the Revenue Act of 1978, it was not clear whether an employee stock ownership plan which meets these rules may distribute cash in lieu of employer securities to a participant entitled to a distribution from the plan.

The bill clarifies that, like a tax credit employee stock ownership plan, an employee stock ownership plan may (subject to a participant's right to require a distribution in the form of employer securities) distribute cash in lieu of employer securities to a participant entitled to a distribution from the plan.

This provision is effective with respect to distributions made after December 31, 1978.

Sec. 101(a)(7)(F)—Matched contributions to remain 84 months.

Under present law, employer securities allocated to a participant's account under a tax credit employee stock ownership plan cannot be distributed from that account for an 84-month period. Prior to the Revenue Act of 1978, this rule applied to securities contributed by the employer attributable to the additional one percent investment tax credit and to securities attributable to matched employer and employee contributions under the additional one-half percent investment tax credit rules.

Under the Revenue Act of 1978, it is unclear whether the rule applies to securities attributable to matched employer and employee contributions.

The bill clarifies that the rule requiring matched employer and employee contributions to a tax credit employee stock ownership plan to remain in the plan for an 84-month period is still applicable. This is consistent with the provisions of the 1978 Act which continue the pre-1978 Act rule that employer contributions to a tax credit employee stock ownership plan may be made for the taxable year in which the additional investment tax credit is allowed regardless of when timely matching employee contributions are made.

This provision is effective with respect to qualified investment for taxable years beginning after December 31, 1978.

Sec. 101(a)(7)(I)—First TRASOP year.

While the Revenue Act of 1978 relieved tax credit employee stock ownership plans of the requirement that a tax-qualified plan be established by the close of the first taxable year for which an employer maintaining the plan claims a deduction or credit for a plan contribution, the 1978 Act was not clear as to the date by which a tax credit stock ownership plan does have to be established for the first year of its existence.

Under the bill a tax credit employee stock ownership plan does not have to be established by the close of the first taxable year for which the employer maintaining the plan claims an additional investment tax credit with respect to the plan. However, in order for the tax credit employee stock ownership plan to be tax-qualified for the first year of its existence as required under present law, it must be established by the income tax filing deadline (including extensions) for the first taxable year for which the employer maintaining the plan claims an additional investment tax credit with respect to the plan.

The amendment made by this section is effective as if it had been included in section 141 of the Revenue Act of 1978.

Sec. 101(a)(7)(J)—"Employer securities."

Under present law, in the case of a tax credit employee stock ownership plan, the only types of employer securities which may be acquired and held by the plan are (1) common stock of the corporation which is readily tradable on an established securities market and (2) noncallable preferred stock of the issuing corporation which is readily convertible into such common stock. The shares acquired by a tax credit employee stock ownership plan, other than shares which are readily tradable on an established securities market, must have a combination of (1) voting rights equivalent to rights possessed by shareholders of the class of common stock of the issuing corporation having the greatest voting rights and (2) dividend rights equivalent to rights possessed by shareholders of that class of stock of the issuing corporation having the greatest dividend rights.

The committee believes that a technical correction to the definition of qualifying employer securities with respect to tax credit employee stock ownership plans and employee stock ownership plans is necessary to make it clear (1) that where an employer contributes securities which are not readily tradable on an established securities market, the securities must have a combination of voting power and dividend rights equal to or in excess of the greatest voting power and dividend rights of any classes of common stock of the corporation; (2) that preferred stock convertible to such common stock which is not readily tradable could be contributed; and (3) that noncallable preferred stock would include stock which could be called provided that the holder of the stock could receive other employer securities either by conversion or in exchange for the securities surrendered pursuant to the call.

The bill makes three changes to the definition of employer securities which are applicable to both tax credit employee stock ownership plans and employee stock ownership plans.

First, the bill makes it clear that where the employer does not have a class of common stock which is readily tradable on an established market, the employer can contribute stock having a combination of voting power and dividend rights at least equal to the greatest voting power and dividend rights of any classes of common stock of the corporation.

Second, the bill makes it clear that the definition of employer securities includes preferred stock which is convertible into such common stock which is not readily tradable.

Third, the bill provides that, under regulations to be issued by the Secretary, preferred stock is to be treated as noncallable if, after the call, the holder of the securities has a reasonable opportunity to convert the securities to common stock. The committee also intends that preferred stock will be treated as noncallable if, pursuant to the call the holder of the securities receives solely employer securities in exchange for the securities.

These changes to the definition of employer securities for the purpose of employee stock ownership plans, as well as the Technical Corrections Act provision which conforms the definition of qualifying employer securities for the purpose of employee stock ownership plans to the definition of employer securities for the purpose of tax credit employee stock ownership plans, are intended to make no change in the status of qualifying employer securities contributed to employee stock ownership plans before December 31, 1979, the general effective date of the 1978 Act changes affecting employee stock ownership plans.

Under the House bill, the definition of employer securities with respect to an employee stock ownership plan is the same as the definition of employer securities with respect to tax credit employee stock ownership plan.

The amendment made by this section is effective as if it had been included in section 141 of the Revenue Act of 1978.

Sec. 101(a)(7)(L)—Nomenclature.

Under the Revenue Act of 1978, the type of plan previously referred to as a TRASOP (or investment tax credit ESOP) was designated as an ESOP. The type of plan previously referred to as an ESOP or leveraged ESOP was designated as a leveraged employee stock ownership plan.

The committee has determined that the names given the respective tax-qualified employee stock ownership vehicles by the 1978 Act do not adequately describe the types of plans involved. Accordingly, the committee has decided to give each of these plans a new name which it considers more appropriate.

Under the bill, an investment tax credit ESOP or ESOP (as defined in the 1978 Act) is renamed "tax credit employee stock ownership plan," (commonly referred to as a TRASOP). Under the bill, a leveraged employee stock ownership plan is renamed "employee stock ownership plan" (commonly referred to as an ESOP).

The amendment made by this section is effective as if it had been included in section 141 of the Revenue Act of 1978.

[¶ 12,130.10]

Committee Reports on P.L. 95-600 (Revenue Act of 1978)

[Senate Committee Report]

General.—The bill (1) makes several amendments to the TRASOP and ESOP provisions of the present law, (2) makes the TRASOP provisions, as amended, part of the Code for the first time, and (3) makes the TRASOP provisions permanent by repealing the present law December 31, 1980, expiration date.

Qualification requirements for TRASOPs.— Under the bill, all TRASOPs are required to be tax-qualified plans. This represents a departure from the present law provision for non-qualified TRASOPs which meet certain specified statutory standards. The committee expects that the regulations which generally apply to tax-qualified plans will henceforth also apply to TRASOPs, and that the Treasury Department will not write separate regulations regarding the application of the tax-qualification standards to TRASOPs, except where TRASOPs are distinguished from other qualified plans by statute.

Under the bill, a TRASOP may be treated as tax-qualified from its effective date even though the TRASOP is not actually established until the date for filing the employer's tax return for its taxable year (including extensions).

Allocation of TRASOP contributions.—Because under the bill, TRASOPs are subject to the same qualification requirements generally applicable to tax-qualified plans, employer contributions to a TRASOP for a plan year generally are not required to be allocated to those plan participants who are not employed on the last day of the plan year, except to the extent that a failure to allocate contributions to such employees would result in prohibited discrimination. As under present law, the allocation of employer TRASOP contributions for a year must be made in proportion to total compensation of all participants sharing in the allocation for the plan year, taking into account only the first $100,000 of compensation for an employee. As under present law, a TRASOP is not permitted to integrate with Social Security.

Provisions relating to employer securities.— Under the bill, if an ESOP or TRASOP holds employer stock issued by a corporation whose stock is "publicly traded", the plan must provide that the stock is to be voted by the plan participants. In addition, the stock must provide for voting and dividend rights equivalent to the rights possessed by shareholders of the highest class of stock of the issuing corporation which is "readily available" on a public market. Shares of stock will not be deemed to be "readily available" if in a particular year there are only occasional sales of this stock on a national or regional securities exchange or quoted on NASDAQ. If an ESOP or TRASOP holds employer stock issued by a corporation which is closely-held, the plan must provide that the plan participants will be entitled to vote the stock with respect to corporate issues which must by law (or charter) be decided by more than a majority vote of common shareholders (such as a merger, acquisition, consolidation, or sale of all or substantially all of a corporation's assets).

In addition, the bill requires the Treasury Department to conduct a 1-year study and to prepare a report to the committee with respect to the extent to which voting rights and different forms of financial disclosure should be given to participants in ESOPs and TRASOPs which hold employer stock issued by closely-held corporations, and with respect to the resale rights which should be available to a participant (or beneficiary) who receives a distribution of employer stock from an ESOP, a TRASOP stock bonus plan. In conducting its study the Treasury Department is expected to consult with the Department of Labor, congressional staffs, and representatives of private businesses.

The bill provides that in the case of an ESOP under which the borrowing of funds from a third party is permitted for the purpose of acquiring employer securities, and in the case of a TRASOP, the only types of employer securities which may be acquired and held by the plan are common stock of the issuing corporation and preferred stock of the issuing corporation which is readily convertible into its common stock.

The bill modifies the definition of employer securities for purposes of the TRASOP provisions by applying a 50-percent test in lieu of the present law 80-percent test in determining whether corporations are members of the same parent-subsidiary controlled group of corporations. The bill does not disturb the present law rule under which an 80-percent test is applied in the TRASOP employer securities definition in determining whether corporations are members of the same brother-sister controlled group.

The bill provides that in a case where a parent corporation and a subsidiary corporation (including a second tier subsidiary) are members of an affiliated group of corporations, the subsidiary corporation will not recognize gain or loss on a contribution to a TRASOP maintained by it of stock in the parent corporation.

Minimum tax.—The bill provides that in any case where an employer claims additional investment tax credit as a result of a TRASOP contribution, the additional credit will not result in the imposition of additional minimum tax on the employer. The bill makes no change in the present law provision which increases the base for computing the minimum tax for each dollar of investment tax credit (other than investment tax credit attributable to TRASOP contributions).

Timing of TRASOP contributions.—The bill requires that an employer maintaining a TRASOP make its TRASOP contribution for the year in which the investment giving rise to the additional investment tax credit is made, although the credit may not actually be used until a later taxable year. This represents a change in the present law rule permitting the making of TRASOP contributions when the credit is used rather than for the taxable year in which the investment is made. The committee believes that individuals employed by the employer during the year a qualified investment is made should be permitted to share in the growth of the company attributable to the investment.

Special rule for contributions attributable to one-half percent TRASOP credit.—With respect to the employer TRASOP contribution, attributable to an extra one-half percent of additional investment tax credit for a year, the bill requires an employer to make such contributions to the extent that matching employee contributions are made. The employer is allowed to claim the credit with respect to such employer TRASOP contributions in the year for which the contributions are matched by employee contributions. This could result in an amount of investment tax credit being contributed to a TRASOP for a year which exceeds 1 ½ percent of the qualified investment for the year. An employee is given a two-year period beginning with the close of the employer's taxable year for which the investment to which the credit relates was made to make his or her matching employee contributions.

Deduction of TRASOP contributions.—In any case where the credit for a TRASOP contribution expires, a deduction is allowed for the amount of the expired credit in the year in which the credit expires.

Prohibition of withdrawal of TRASOP contributions on recapture.—The bill repeals the present law rule which permits an employer to withdraw from a TRASOP a contribution attributable to additional investment tax credit which is recaptured. Under the bill, TRASOP contribution made with respect to a particular qualified investment may not be withdrawn if all or a portion of the credit is later recaptured due to an early disposition of the property the purchase of which gave rise to the credit. The bill does not change the present law provision which permits the employer to either (1) deduct the amount of the contribution attributable to the recaptured additional investment tax credit for the taxable year in which the recapture occurs, or (2) apply the amount of the contribution attributable to the recaptured additional investment tax credit against its obligation for a future TRASOP contribution.

Distributions from ESOPs and TRASOPs.— Under the bill, a participant in an ESOP or a TRASOP who is entitled to a distribution under the plan is given the right to demand that the distribution be made in the form of employer securities rather than in cash. Subject to a participant's right to demand a distribution of employer securities, the plan may elect to distribute the participant's interest to him in cash, in employer securities, or partially in cash and partially in employer securities. The committee feels that each participant (or beneficiary) must be advised in writing of the right to require a stock distribution before the ESOP or TRASOP may actually elect to distribute cash.

Put option on ESOP or TRASOP stock.—Under the bill, any participant (or beneficiary) who receives a distribution of employer stock attributable to an ESOP loan or an additional investment tax credit must be given a "put option" on the employer stock distributed to him or her, provided that this employer stock is not publicly traded or is subject to a trading limitation when distributed, as these terms are defined in the Treasury regulations issued on September 2, 1977. The put option which a participant (or beneficiary) receives on shares of employer stock distributed from an ESOP or TRASOP should have the following terms:

1. Upon receipt of the employer stock, the distributee must have up to six months to require that the employer repurchase this stock, at its fair market value. Although the obligation to repurchase stock under the put option would apply to the employer, not the ESOP or the TRASOP, it is permissible for the ESOP or TRASOP to actually make the purchase in lieu of the employer. If the distributee does not exercise the put option within the six-month period, the option will temporarily lapse.

2. After the close of the employer's taxable year in which the temporary lapse of a distributee's put option occurs, and following a determination of the value of the employee stock (determined in accordance with Treasury regulations) as of the end of that taxable year, the employer will notify each distributee who did not exercise the initial put option in the preceding year of the value of the employer stock. Each such distributee will then have up to three months to require that the employer repurchase his or her shares of employer stock. If the distributee does not exercise this put option, then the employer stock will not be subject to a put option in the future.

3. At the option of the party repurchasing employer stock under the put option, such stock may be repurchased on an installment basis over a period of five years. If the distributee agrees, the repur chase period may be extended to a period of ten years. As security for the installment repurchase, the seller must at least be given a promissory note, the full payment of which could be required by the seller if the repurchaser defaults in the payments of a scheduled installment payment. In addition, if the term of the installment obligation exceeds five years, the employee must be given adequate security for the outstanding amount of the note.

4. Because a distributee might wish to contribute the ESOP or TRASOP distribution to an IRA in a "tax-free" rollover and because the contribution would have to be made before expiration of the first six-month put option period, under the bill, the IRA trustee must be able to exercise the same put option as the actual distributee.

Certain distributions from tax-qualified plans.—Under the bill, the amount of a distribution which is a death benefit distribution from a qualified plan which is eligible to be treated as a lump sum distribution is excludible from the estate of the deceased plan participant only in situations where the recipient of the distribution agrees in writing not to elect to treat the distribution as a lump sum distribution eligible for special favorable income tax treatment.

The bill changes the present law rules that an employer who receives a distribution of employer securities from a qualified plan must always contribute the employer securities to an IRA in order for the contribution to qualify as a tax-free rollover contribution to an IRA. The bill permits an employee who receives employer securities, as part of a lump sum distribution from a qualified plan or as part of a complete distribution upon termination of a qualified plan, to receive tax-free rollover treatment by contributing the proceeds from the sale of the stock rather than the stock itself to an IRA with 60 days from the date of the distribution.

* * * In addition, the modification to the ESOP and TRASOP rules under the bill generally are effective after December 31, 1978.

[Conference Committee Report]

The conference agreement follows the Senate amendment except that (1) the TRASOP provisions are not made permanent, but rather, the expiration date of those provisions is extended for three years until December 31, 1983, * * *.

[Code Sec. 409A]

[¶ 12,145.08]

Committee Report on P.L. 109-280 (Pension Protection Act of 2006)

[Joint Committee on Taxation Report]

Under the provision, if during any restricted period in which a defined benefit pension plan of an employer is in at-risk status,[54] assets are set aside (directly or indirectly) in a trust (or other arrangement as determined by the Secretary of the Treasury), or transferred to such a trust or other arrangement, for purposes of paying deferred compensation of an applicable covered employee, such transferred assets are treated as property transferred in connection with the performance of services (whether or not such assets are available to satisfy the claims of general creditors) under Code section 83. The rule does not apply in the case of assets that are set aside before the defined benefit pension plan is in at-risk status.

If a nonqualified deferred compensation plan of an employer provides that assets will be restricted to the provision of benefits under the plan in connection with a restricted period (or other similar financial measure determined by the Secretary of Treasury) of any defined benefit pension plan of the employer, or assets are so restricted, such assets are treated as property transferred in connection with the performance of services (whether or not such assets are available to satisfy the claims of general creditors) under Code section 83.

A restricted period is (1) any period in which a single-employer defined benefit pension plan of an employer is in at risk-status, (2) any period in which the employer is in bankruptcy, and (3) the period that begins six months before and ends six months after the date any defined benefit pension plan of the employer is terminated in an involuntary or distress termination. The provision does not apply with respect to assets set aside before a restricted period.

In general, applicable covered employees include the chief executive officer (or individual acting in such capacity), the four highest compensated officers for the taxable year (other than the chief executive officer), and individuals subject to section 16(a) of the Securities Exchange Act of 1934. An applicable covered employee includes any (1) covered employee of a plan sponsor; (2) covered employee of a member of a controlled group which includes the plan sponsor; and (3) former employee who was a covered employee at the time of termination of employment with the plan sponsor or a member of a controlled group which includes the plan sponsor.

A nonqualified deferred compensation plan is any plan that provides for the deferral of compensation other than a qualified employer plan or any bona fide vacation leave, sick leave, compensatory time, disability pay, or death benefit plan. A qualified employer plan means a qualified retirement plan, tax-deferred annuity, simplified employee pension, and SIMPLE.[55] A qualified governmental excess benefit arrangement (sec. 415(m)) is a qualified employer plan. An eligible deferred compensation plan (sec. 457(b)) is also a qualified employer plan under the provision. The term plan includes any agreement or arrangement, including an agreement or arrangement that includes one person.

Any subsequent increases in the value of, or any earnings with respect to, transferred or restricted assets are treated as additional transfers of property. Interest at the underpayment rate plus one percentage point is imposed on the underpayments that would have occurred had the amounts been includible in income for the taxable year in which first deferred or, if later, the first taxable year not subject to a substantial risk of forfeiture. The amount required to be included in income is also subject to an additional 20-percent tax.

Under the provision, if an employer provides directly or indirectly for the payment of any Federal, State or local income taxes with respect to any compensation required to be included in income under the provision, interest is imposed on the amount of such payment in the same manner as if the payment were part of the deferred compensation to which it related. As under present law, such payment is included in income; in addition, under the provision, such payment is subject to a 20 percent additional tax. The payment is also nondeductible by the employer.

Effective date

The provision is effective for transfers or other reservations of assets after date of enactment.

[¶ 12,145.09]

Committee Report on P.L. 109-135 (Gulf Opportunity Zone Act of 2005)

[Joint Committee on Taxation]

Technical Corrections

[Amendments Related to the American Jobs Creation Act of 2004 (P.L. 108-357)]

Nonqualified deferred compensation plans (Act sec. 885).—The provision clarifies that the additional tax and interest under the nonqualified deferred compensation provision of the Act are not treated as payments of regular tax for alternative minimum tax purposes. The provision also clarifies that the application of the rule providing that certain additional deferrals must be for a period of not less than five years is not limited to the first payment for which deferral is made. The provision also clarifies that Treasury Department guidance providing a limited period during which plans can conform to the requirements applies to plans adopted before January 1, 2005. The provision also clarifies that the effective date of the funding provisions relating to offshore trusts and financial triggers is January 1, 2005. Thus, for example, amounts set aside in an offshore trust before such date for the purpose of paying deferred compensation and plans providing for the restriction of assets in connection with a change in the employer's financial health are subject to the funding provisions on January 1, 2005. Under the provision, not later than 90 days after the date of enactment of this provision, the Secretary of the Treasury shall issue guidance under which a nonqualified deferred compensation plan which is in violation of the requirements of the funding provisions relating to offshore trusts and financial triggers will be treated as not violating such requirements if the plan comes into conformance with such requirements during a limited period as specified by the Secretary in guidance. For example, trusts or assets set aside outside of the United States that would otherwise result in income inclusion and interest under the provision as of January 1, 2005, may be modified to come into conformance with the provision during the limited period of time as specified by the Secretary.

[¶ 12,145.10]

Committee Reports on P.L. 108-357 (American Jobs Creation Act of 2004)

[House Committee Report]

Present Law

In general

The determination of when amounts deferred under a nonqualified deferred compensation arrangement are includible in the gross income of the individual earning the compensation depends on the facts and circumstances of the arrangement. A variety of tax principles and Code provisions may be relevant in making this determination, including the doctrine of constructive receipt, the economic benefit doctrine,[448] the provisions of section 83 relating generally to transfers of property in connection with the performance of services, and provisions relating specifically to nonexempt employee trusts (sec. 402(b)) and nonqualified annuities (sec. 403(c)).

In general, the time for income inclusion of nonqualified deferred compensation depends on whether the arrangement is unfunded or funded. If the arrangement is unfunded, then the compensation is generally includible in income when it is actually or constructively received. If the arrangement is funded, then income is includible for the year in which the individual's rights are transferable or not subject to a substantial risk of forfeiture.

Nonqualified deferred compensation is generally subject to social security and Medicare taxes when the compensation is earned (i.e., when services are performed), unless the nonqualified deferred compensation is subject to a substantial risk of forfeiture. If nonqualified deferred compensation is subject to a substantial risk of forfeiture, it is subject to social security and Medicare tax when the risk of forfeiture is removed (i.e., when the right to the nonqualified deferred compensation vests). Amounts deferred under a nonaccount balance plan that are not reasonably ascertainable are not required to be taken into account as wages subject to social security and Medicare taxes until the first date that such amounts are reasonably ascertainable. Social security and Medicare tax treatment is not affected by whether the arrangement is funded or unfunded, which is relevant in determining when amounts are includible in income (and subject to income tax withholding).

In general, an arrangement is considered funded if there has been a transfer of property under section 83. Under that section, a transfer of property occurs when a person acquires a beneficial ownership interest in such property. The term "property" is defined very broadly for purposes of section 83.[449] Property includes real and personal property other than money or an unfunded and unsecured promise to pay money in the future. Property also includes a beneficial interest in assets (including money) that are transferred or set aside from claims of the creditors of the transferor, for example, in a trust or escrow account. Accordingly, if, in connection with the performance of services, vested contributions are made to a trust on an individual's behalf and the trust assets may be

---

[54] At-risk status is defined as under the provision relating to funding rules for single-employer defined benefit pension plans and applies if a plan's funding target attainment percentage for the preceding year was less than 60 percent.

[55] A qualified employer plan also includes a section 501(c)(18) trust.

[448] See, e.g., *Sproull* v. *Commissioner,* 16 T.C. 244 (1951), aff'd per curiam, 194 F.2d 541 (6th Cir. 1952); Rev. Rul. 60-31, 1960-1 C.B. 174.

[449] Treas. Reg. sec. 1.83-3(e). This definition in part reflects previous IRS rulings on nonqualified deferred compensation.

used solely to provide future payments to the individual, the payment of the contributions to the trust constitutes a transfer of property to the individual that is taxable under section 83. On the other hand, deferred amounts are generally not includible in income if nonqualified deferred compensation is payable from general corporate funds that are subject to the claims of general creditors, as such amounts are treated as unfunded and unsecured promises to pay money or property in the future.

As discussed above, if the arrangement is unfunded, then the compensation is generally includible in income when it is actually or constructively received under section 451.[450] Income is constructively received when it is credited to an individual's account, set apart, or otherwise made available so that it may be drawn on at any time. Income is not constructively received if the taxpayer's control of its receipt is subject to substantial limitations or restrictions. A requirement to relinquish a valuable right in order to make withdrawals is generally treated as a substantial limitation or restriction.

Rabbi trusts

* * *

Arrangements have developed in an effort to provide employees with security for nonqualified deferred compensation, while still allowing deferral of income inclusion. A "rabbi trust" is a trust or other fund established by the employer to hold assets from which nonqualified deferred compensation payments will be made. The trust or fund is generally irrevocable and does not permit the employer to use the assets for purposes other than to provide nonqualified deferred compensation, except that the terms of the trust or fund provide that the assets are subject to the claims of the employer's creditors in the case of insolvency or bankruptcy.

As discussed above, for purposes of section 83, property includes a beneficial interest in assets set aside from the claims of creditors, such as in a trust or fund, but does not include an unfunded and unsecured promise to pay money in the future. In the case of a rabbi trust, terms providing that the assets are subject to the claims of creditors of the employer in the case of insolvency or bankruptcy have been the basis for the conclusion that the creation of a rabbi trust does not cause the related nonqualified deferred compensation arrangement to be funded for income tax purposes.[451] As a result, no amount is included in income by reason of the rabbi trust; generally income inclusion occurs as payments are made from the trust.

The IRS has issued guidance setting forth model rabbi trust provisions.[452] Revenue Procedure 92-64 provides a safe harbor for taxpayers who adopt and maintain grantor trusts in connection with unfunded deferred compensation arrangements. The model trust language requires that the trust provide that all assets of the trust are subject to the claims of the general creditors of the company in the event of the company's insolvency or bankruptcy.

Since the concept of rabbi trusts was developed, arrangements have developed which attempt to protect the assets from creditors despite the terms of the trust. Arrangements also have developed which attempt to allow deferred amounts to be available to individuals, while still purporting to meet the safe harbor requirements set forth by the IRS.

Reasons for Change

The Committee is aware of the popular use of deferred compensation arrangements by executives to defer current taxation of substantial amounts of income. The Committee believes that many nonqualified deferred compensation arrangements have developed which allow improper deferral of income. Executives often use arrangements that allow deferral of income, but also provide security of future payment and control over amounts deferred. For example, nonqualified deferred compensation arrangements often contain provisions that allow participants to receive distributions upon request, subject to forfeiture of a minimal amount (i.e., a "haircut" provision).

The Committee is aware that since the concept of a rabbi trust was developed, techniques have been used that attempt to protect the assets from creditors despite the terms of the trust. For example, the trust or fund may be located in a foreign jurisdiction, making it difficult or impossible for creditors to reach the assets.

While the general tax principles governing deferred compensation are well established, the determination whether a particular arrangement effectively allows deferral of income is generally made on a facts and circumstances basis. There is limited specific guidance with respect to common deferral arrangements. The Committee believes that it is appropriate to provide specific rules regarding whether deferral of income inclusion should be permitted.

The Committee believes that certain arrangements that allow participants inappropriate levels of control or access to amounts deferred should not result in deferral of income inclusion. The Committee also believes that certain arrangements, such as offshore trusts, which effectively protect assets from creditors, should be treated as funded and not result in deferral of income inclusion.[453]

Explanation of Provision

Under the provision, all amounts deferred under a nonqualified deferred compensation plan[454] for all taxable years are currently includible in gross income to the extent not subject to a substantial risk of forfeiture[455] and not previously included in gross income, unless certain requirements are satisfied. If the requirements of the provision are not satisfied, in addition to current income inclusion, interest at the underpayment rate plus one percentage point is imposed on the underpayments that would have occurred had the compensation been includible in income when first deferred, or if later, when not subject to a substantial risk of forfeiture. Actual or notional earnings on amounts deferred are also subject to the provision.

Under the provision, distributions from a nonqualified deferred compensation plan may be allowed only upon separation from service (as determined by the Secretary), death, a specified time (or pursuant to a fixed schedule), change in control in a corporation (to the extent provided by the Secretary), occurrence of an unforeseeable emergency, or if the participant becomes disabled. A nonqualified deferred compensation plan may not allow distributions other than upon the permissible distribution events and may not permit acceleration of a distribution, except as provided in regulations by the Secretary.

In the case of a specified employee, distributions upon separation from service may not be made earlier than six months after the date of the separation from service. Specified employees are key employees[456] of publicly-traded corporations.

Amounts payable at a specified time or pursuant to a fixed schedule must be specified under the plan at the time of deferral. Amounts payable upon the occurrence of an event are not treated as amounts payable at a specified time. For example, amounts payable when an individual attains age 65 are payable at a specified time, while amounts payable when an individual's child begins college are payable upon the occurrence of an event.

Distributions upon a change in the ownership or effective control of a corporation, or in the ownership of a substantial portion of the assets of a corporation, may only be made to the extent provided by the Secretary. It is intended that the Secretary use a similar, but more restrictive, definition of change in control as is used for purposes of the golden parachute provisions of section 280G consistent with the purposes of the provision. The provision requires the Secretary to issue guidance defining change of control within 90 days after the date of enactment.

An unforeseeable emergency is defined as a severe financial hardship to the participant resulting from a sudden and unexpected illness or accident of the participant, the participant's spouse, or a dependent (as defined in 152(a)) of the participant; loss of the participant's property due to casualty; or other similar extraordinary and unforeseeable circumstances arising as a result of events beyond the control of the participant. The amount of the distribution must be limited to the amount needed to satisfy the emergency plus taxes reasonably anticipated as a result of the distribution. Distributions may not be allowed to the extent that the hardship may be relieved through reimbursement or compensation by insurance or otherwise, or by liquidation of the participant's assets (to the extent such liquidation would not itself cause a severe financial hardship).

A participant is considered disabled if he or she (i) is unable to engage in any substantial gainful activity by reason of any medically determinable physical or mental impairment which can be expected to result in death or can be expected to last for a continuous period of not less than 12 months; or (ii) is, by reason on any medically determinable physical or mental impairment which can be expected to result in death or can be expected to last for a continuous period of not less than 12 months, receiving income replacement benefits for a period of not less than three months under an accident and health plan covering employees of the participant's employer.

As previously discussed, except as provided in regulations by the Secretary, no accelerations of distributions may be allowed. For example, changes in the form of a distribution from an annuity to a lump sum are not permitted. The provision provides the Secretary authority to provide, through regulations, limited exceptions to the general rule that no accelerations can be permitted. It is intended that exceptions be provided only in limited cases where the accelerated distribution is required for reasons beyond the control of the participant. For example, it is anticipated that an exception could be provided in order to comply with Federal conflict of interest requirements or court-approved settlements.

The provision requires that the plan must provide that compensation for services performed during a taxable year may be deferred at the participant's election only if the election to defer is made no later than the close of the preceding taxable year, or at such other time as provided in Treasury regulations.

---

[450] Treas. Reg. secs. 1.451-1 and 1.451-2.

[451] This conclusion was first provided in a 1980 private ruling issued by the IRS with respect to an arrangement covering a rabbi; hence the popular name "rabbi trust." Priv. Ltr. Rul. 8113107 (Dec. 31, 1980).

[452] Rev. Proc. 92-64, 1992-2 C.B. 422, modified in part by Notice 2000-56, 2000-2 C.B. 393.

[453] The staff of the Joint Committee on Taxation made recommendations similar to the new provision in the report on their investigation of Enron Corporation, which detailed how executives deferred millions of dollars in Federal income taxes through nonqualified deferred compensation arrangements. See Joint Committee on Taxation, Report of Investigation of Enron Corporation and Related Entities Regarding Federal Tax and Compensation Issues, and Policy Recommendations (JCS-3-03), February 2003.

[454] A plan includes an agreement or arrangement, including an agreement or arrangement that includes one person.

[455] As under section 83, the rights of a person to compensation are subject to a substantial risk of forfeiture if the person's rights to such compensation are conditioned upon the performance of substantial services by any individual.

[456] Key employees are defined in section 416(i) and generally include officers having annual compensation greater than $130,000 (adjusted for inflation and limited to 50 employees), five percent owners, and one percent owners having annual compensation from the employer greater than $150,000.

For example, it is expected that Treasury regulations provide that, in appropriate circumstances, elections to defer incentive bonuses earned over a period of several years may be made after the beginning of the service period, as long as such elections may in no event be made later than 12 months before the earliest date on which such incentive bonus is initially payable. The Secretary may consider other factors in determining the appropriate election period, such as when the amount of the bonus payment is determinable. It is expected that Treasury regulations will not permit any election to defer any bonus or other compensation if the timing of such election would be inconsistent with the purposes of the provision. Under the provision, in the first year that an employee becomes eligible for participation in a nonqualified deferred compensation plan, the election may be made within 30 days after the date that the employee is initially eligible.

The time and form of distributions must be specified at the time of initial deferral. A plan could specify the time and form of payments that are to be made as a result of a distribution event (e.g., a plan could specify that payments upon separation of service will be paid in lump sum within 30 days of separation from service) or could allow participants to elect the time and form of payment at the time of the initial deferral election. If a plan allows participants to elect the time and form of payment, such election is subject to the rules regarding initial deferral elections under the provision.

Under the provision, a plan may allow changes in the time and form of distributions subject to certain requirements. A nonqualified deferred compensation plan may allow a subsequent election to delay the timing or form of distributions only if: (1) the plan requires that such election cannot be effective for at least 12 months after the date on which the election is made; (2) except in the case of elections relating to distributions on account of death, disability or unforeseeable emergency, the plan requires that the additional deferral with respect to which such election is made is for a period of not less than five years from the date such payment would otherwise have been made; and (3) the plan requires that an election related to a distribution to be made upon a specified time may not be made less than 12 months prior to the date of the first scheduled payment. It is expected that in limited cases, the Secretary shall issue guidance, consistent with the purposes of the provision, regarding to what extent elections to change a stream of payments are permissible.

If impermissible distributions or elections are made, or if the nonqualified deferred compensation plan allows impermissible distributions or elections, all amounts deferred under the plan (including amounts deferred in prior years) are currently includible in income to the extent not subject to a substantial risk of forfeiture and not previously included in income. In addition, interest at the underpayment rate plus one percentage point is imposed on the underpayments that would have occurred had the compensation been includible in income when first deferred, or if later, when not subject to a substantial risk of forfeiture.

Under the provision, in the case of assets set aside (directly or indirectly) in a trust (or other arrangement determined by the Secretary) for purposes of paying nonqualified deferred compensation, such assets are treated as property transferred in connection with the performance of services under section 83 (whether or not such assets are available to satisfy the claims of general creditors) at the time set aside if such assets are located outside of the United States or at the time transferred if such assets are subsequently transferred outside of the United States. Any subsequent increases in the value of, or any earnings with respect to, such assets are treated as additional transfers of property. Interest at the underpayment rate plus one percentage point is imposed on the underpayments that would have occurred had the amounts been includible in income for the taxable year in which first deferred or, if later, the first taxable year not subject to a substantial risk of forfeiture. It is expected that the Secretary shall provide rules for identifying the deferrals to which assets set aside are attributable, for situations in which assets equal to less than the full amount of deferrals are set aside. The Secretary has authority to exempt arrangements from the provision if the arrangements do not result in an improper deferral of U.S. tax and will not result in assets being effectively beyond the reach of creditors.

Under the provision, a transfer of property in connection with the performance of services under section 83 also occurs with respect to compensation deferred under a nonqualified deferred compensation plan if the plan provides that upon a change in the employer's financial health, assets will be restricted to the payment of nonqualified deferred compensation. The transfer of property occurs as of the earlier of when the assets are so restricted or when the plan provides that assets will be restricted. It is intended that the transfer of property occurs to the extent that assets are restricted or will be restricted with respect to such compensation. For example, in the case of a plan that provides that upon a change in the employer's financial health, a trust will become funded to the extent of all deferrals, all amounts deferred under the plan are treated as property transferred under section 83. If a plan provides that deferrals of certain individuals will be funded upon a change in financial health, the transfer of property would occur with respect to compensation deferred by such individuals. Any subsequent increases in the value of, or any earnings with respect to, such assets are treated as additional transfers of property. Interest at the underpayment rate plus one percentage point is imposed on the underpayments that would have occurred had the amounts been includible in income for the taxable year in which first deferred or, if later, the first taxable year not subject to a substantial risk of forfeiture.

A nonqualified deferred compensation plan is any plan that provides for the deferral of compensation other than a qualified employer plan or any bona fide vacation leave, sick leave, compensatory time, disability pay, or death benefit plan. A qualified employer plan means a qualified retirement plan, tax-deferred annuity, simplified employee pension, and SIMPLE.[457] A governmental eligible deferred compensation plan (sec. 457) is also a qualified employer plan under the provision.[458] Plans subject to section 457, other than governmental eligible deferred compensation plans, are subject to both the requirements of section 457 and the provision. For example, in addition to the requirements of the provision, an eligible deferred compensation plan of a tax-exempt employer would still be required to meet the applicable dollar limits under section 457.

Interest imposed under the provision is treated as interest on an underpayment of tax. Income (whether actual or notional) attributable to nonqualified deferred compensation is treated as additional deferred compensation and is subject to the provision. The provision is not intended to prevent the inclusion of amounts in gross income under any provision or rule of law earlier than the time provided in the provision. Any amount included in gross income under the provision shall not be required to be included in gross income under any provision of law later than the time provided in the provision. The provision does not affect the rules regarding the timing of an employer's deduction for nonqualified deferred compensation.

The provision requires annual reporting to the Internal Revenue Service of amounts deferred. Such amounts are required to be reported on an individual's Form W-2 for the year deferred even if the amount is not currently includible in income for that taxable year. Under the provision, the Secretary is authorized, through regulations, to establish a minimum amount of deferrals below which the reporting requirement does not apply. The Secretary may also provide that the reporting requirement does not apply with respect to amounts of deferrals that are not reasonably ascertainable. It is intended that the exception for amounts not reasonable ascertainable only apply to nonaccount balance plans and that amounts be required to be reported when they first become reasonably ascertainable.[459]

The provision provides the Secretary authority to prescribe regulations as are necessary to carry out the purposes of provision, including regulations: (1) providing for the determination of amounts of deferral in the case of defined benefit plans; (2) relating to changes in the ownership and control of a corporation or assets of a corporation; (3) exempting from the provisions providing for transfers of property arrangements that will not result in an improper deferral of U.S. tax and will not result in assets being effectively beyond the reach of creditors; (4) defining financial health; and (5) disregarding a substantial risk of forfeiture.

It is intended that substantial risk of forfeitures may not be used to manipulate the timing of income inclusion. It is intended that substantial risks of forfeiture should be disregarded in cases in which they are illusory or are used inconsistent with the purposes of the provision. For example, if an executive is effectively able to control the acceleration of the lapse of a substantial risk of forfeiture, such risk of forfeiture should be disregarded and income inclusion should not be postponed on account of such restriction.— **House Committee Report (H.R. REP. NO. 108-548, pt. 1)**

[Conference Committee Report]

In general

The conference agreement follows the House bill with the following modifications. Under the conference agreement, all amounts deferred under a nonqualified deferred compensation plan[807] for all taxable years are currently includible in gross income to the extent not subject to a substantial risk of forfeiture[808] and not previously included in gross income, unless certain requirements are satisfied.[809] If the requirements of the provision are not satisfied, in addition to current income inclusion, interest at the underpayment rate plus one percentage point is imposed on the underpayments that would have occurred had the compensation been includible in income when first deferred, or if later, when not subject to a substantial risk of forfeiture. The amount required to be included in income is also subject to a 20-percent additional tax.[810]

Current income inclusion, interest, and the additional tax apply only with respect to the participants with respect to whom the requirements of the provision are not met. For example, suppose a plan covering all executives of an employer (including those subject to section 16(a) of the Securities and Exchange Act of 1934) allows distributions to individuals subject to section 16(a) upon a distribution event that is not permitted under the provision. The individuals subject to section 16(a), rather than all participants of the plan, would be

[457] A qualified employer plan also includes a section 501(c)(18) trust.

[458] A governmental deferred compensation plan that is not an eligible deferred compensation plan is not a qualified employer plan.

[459] It is intended that the exception be similar to that under Treas. Reg. sec. 31.3121(v)(2)-1(e)(4).

[807] A plan includes an agreement or arrangement, including an agreement or arrangement that includes one person. Amounts deferred also include actual or notional earnings.

[808] As under section 83, the rights of a person to compensation are subject to a substantial risk of forfeiture if the person's rights to such compensation are conditioned upon the performance of substantial services by any individual.

[809] It is intended that Treasury regulations will provide guidance regarding when an amount is deferred. It is intended that timing of an election to defer is not determinative of when the deferral is made.

[810] These consequences apply under the provision to amounts deferred after the effective date of the provision.

required to include amounts deferred in income and would be subject to interest and the 20-percent additional tax.

Permissible distributions

In general

Under the provision, distributions from a nonqualified deferred compensation plan may be allowed only upon separation from service (as determined by the Secretary), death, a specified time (or pursuant to a fixed schedule), change in control of a corporation (to the extent provided by the Secretary), occurrence of an unforeseeable emergency, or if the participant becomes disabled. A nonqualified deferred compensation plan may not allow distributions other than upon the permissible distribution events and, except as provided in regulations by the Secretary, may not permit acceleration of a distribution.

Separation from service

In the case of a specified employee who separates from service, distributions may not be made earlier than six months after the date of the separation from service or upon death. Specified employees are key employees[811] of publicly-traded corporations.

Specified time

Amounts payable at a specified time or pursuant to a fixed schedule must be specified under the plan at the time of deferral. Amounts payable upon the occurrence of an event are not treated as amounts payable at a specified time. For example, amounts payable when an individual attains age 65 are payable at a specified time, while amounts payable when an individual's child begins college are payable upon the occurrence of an event.

Change in control

Distributions upon a change in the ownership or effective control of a corporation, or in the ownership of a substantial portion of the assets of a corporation, may only be made to the extent provided by the Secretary. It is intended that the Secretary use a similar, but more restrictive, definition of change in control as is used for purposes of the golden parachute provisions of section 280G consistent with the purposes of the provision. The provision requires the Secretary to issue guidance defining change of control within 90 days after the date of enactment.

Unforeseeable emergency

An unforeseeable emergency is defined as a severe financial hardship to the participant: (1) resulting from an illness or accident of the participant, the participant's spouse, or a dependent (as defined in sec. 152(a)); (2) loss of the participant's property due to casualty; or (3) other similar extraordinary and unforeseeable circumstances arising as a result of events beyond the control of the participant. The amount of the distribution must be limited to the amount needed to satisfy the emergency plus taxes reasonably anticipated as a result of the distribution. Distributions may not be allowed to the extent that the hardship may be relieved through reimbursement or compensation by insurance or otherwise, or by liquidation of the participant's assets (to the extent such liquidation would not itself cause a severe financial hardship).

Disability

A participant is considered disabled if he or she (1) is unable to engage in any substantial gainful activity by reason of any medically determinable physical or mental impairment which can be expected to result in death or can be expected to last for a continuous period of not less than 12 months; or (2) is, by reason of any medically determinable physical or mental impairment which can be expected to result in death or can be expected to last for a continuous period of not less than 12 months, receiving income replacement benefits for a period of not less than three months under an accident and health plan covering employees of the participant's employer.

Prohibition on acceleration of distributions

As mentioned above, except as provided in regulations by the Secretary, no accelerations of distributions may be allowed. In general, changes in the form of distribution that accelerate payments are subject to the rule prohibiting acceleration of distributions. However, it is intended that the rule against accelerations is not violated merely because a plan provides a choice between cash and taxable property if the timing and amount of income inclusion is the same regardless of the medium of distribution. For example, the choice between a fully taxable annuity contract and a lump-sum payment may be permitted. It is also intended that the Secretary provide rules under which the choice between different forms of actuarially equivalent life annuity payments is permitted.

It is intended that the Secretary will provide other, limited, exceptions to the prohibition on accelerated distributions, such as when the accelerated distribution is required for reasons beyond the control of the participant and the distribution is not elective. For example, it is anticipated that an exception could be provided if a distribution is needed in order to comply with Federal conflict of interest requirements or a court-approved settlement incident to divorce. It is intended that Treasury regulations provide that a plan would not violate the prohibition on accelerations by providing that withholding of an employee's share of employment taxes will be made from the employee's interest in the nonqualified deferred compensation plan. It is also intended that Treasury regulations provide that a plan would not violate the prohibition on accelerations by providing for a distribution to a participant to pay income taxes due upon a vesting event subject to section 457(f), provided that such amount is not more than an amount equal to the income tax withholding that would have been remitted by the employer if there had been a payment of wages equal to the income includible by the participant under section 457(f). It is also intended that Treasury regulations provide that a plan would not violate the prohibition on accelerations by providing for automatic distributions of minimal interests in a deferred compensation plan upon permissible distribution events for purposes of administrative convenience. For example, a plan could provide that upon separation from service of a participant, account balances less than $10,000 will be automatically distributed (except in the case of specified employees).

Requirements with respect to elections

The provision requires that a plan must provide that compensation for services performed during a taxable year may be deferred at the participant's election only if the election to defer is made no later than the close of the preceding taxable year, or at such other time as provided in Treasury regulations.[812] In the case of any performance-based compensation based on services performed over a period of at least 12 months, such election may be made no later than six months before the end of the service period. It is not intended that the provision override the constructive receipt doctrine, as constructive receipt rules continue to apply. It is intended that the term "performance-based compensation" will be defined by the Secretary to include compensation to the extent that an amount is: (1) variable and contingent on the satisfaction of preestablished organizational or individual performance criteria and (2) not readily ascertainable at the time of the election. For the purposes of the provision, it is intended that performance-based compensation may be required to meet certain requirements similar to those under section 162(m), but would not be required to meet all requirements under that section. For example, it is expected that the Secretary will provide that performance criteria would be considered preestablished if it is established in writing no later than 90 days after the commencement of the service period, but the requirement of determination by the compensation committee of the board of directors would not be required. It is expected that the Secretary will issue guidance providing coordination rules, as appropriate, regarding the timing of elections in the case when the fiscal year of the employer and the taxable year of the individual are different. It is expected that Treasury regulations will not permit any election to defer any bonus or other compensation if the timing of such election would be inconsistent with the purposes of the provision.

The time and form of distributions must be specified at the time of initial deferral. A plan could specify the time and form of payments that are to be made as a result of a distribution event (e.g., a plan could specify that payments upon separation of service will be paid in lump sum within 30 days of separation from service) or could allow participants to elect the time and form of payment at the time of the initial deferral election. If a plan allows participants to elect the time and form of payment, such election is subject to the rules regarding initial deferral elections under the provision. It is intended that multiple payout events are permissible. For example, a participant could elect to receive 25 percent of their account balance at age 50 and the remaining 75 percent at age 60. A plan could also allow participants to elect different forms of payment for different permissible distribution events. For example, a participant could elect to receive a lump-sum distribution upon disability, but an annuity at age 65.

Under the provision, a plan may allow changes in the time and form of distributions subject to certain requirements. A nonqualified deferred compensation plan may allow a subsequent election to delay the timing or form of distributions only if: (1) the plan requires that such election cannot be effective for at least 12 months after the date on which the election is made; (2) except in the case of elections relating to distributions on account of death, disability or unforeseeable emergency, the plan requires that the additional deferral with respect to which such election is made is for a period of not less than five years from the date such payment would otherwise have been made; and (3) the plan requires that an election related to a distribution to be made upon a specified time may not be made less than 12 months prior to the date of the first scheduled payment. It is expected that in limited cases, the Secretary will issue guidance, consistent with the purposes of the provision, regarding to what extent elections to change a stream of payments are permissible. The Secretary may issue regulations regarding elections with respect to payments under nonelective, supplemental retirement plans.

Foreign trusts

Under the provision, in the case of assets set aside (directly or indirectly) in a trust (or other arrangement determined by the Secretary) for purposes of paying nonqualified deferred compensation, such assets are treated as property transferred in connection with the performance of services under section 83 (whether or not such assets are available to satisfy the claims of general creditors) at the time set aside if such assets (or trust or other arrangement) are located outside of the United States or at the time transferred if such assets (or trust or other arrangement) are subsequently transferred outside of the United States. Any subsequent increases in the value of, or any earnings with respect to, such assets are treated as additional transfers of property. Interest at the underpayment rate

[811] Key employees are defined in section 416(i) and generally include officers having annual compensation greater than $130,000 (adjusted for inflation and limited to 50 employees), five percent owners, and one percent owners having annual compensation from the employer greater than $150,000.

[812] Under the provision, in the first year that an employee becomes eligible for participation in a nonqualified deferred compensation plan, the election may be made within 30 days after the date that the employee is initially eligible.

plus one percentage point is imposed on the underpayments that would have occurred had the amounts set aside been includible in income for the taxable year in which first deferred or, if later, the first taxable year not subject to a substantial risk of forfeiture. The amount required to be included in income is also subject to an additional 20-percent tax.

It is expected that the Secretary will provide rules for identifying the deferrals to which assets set aside are attributable, for situations in which assets equal to less than the full amount of deferrals are set aside. The provision does not apply to assets located in a foreign jurisdiction if substantially all of the services to which the nonqualified deferred compensation relates are performed in such foreign jurisdiction. The provision is specifically intended to apply to foreign trusts and arrangements that effectively shield from the claims of general creditors any assets intended to satisfy nonqualified deferred compensation arrangements. The Secretary has authority to exempt arrangements from the provision if the arrangements do not result in an improper deferral of U.S. tax and will not result in assets being effectively beyond the reach of creditors.

Triggers upon financial health

Under the provision, a transfer of property in connection with the performance of services under section 83 also occurs with respect to compensation deferred under a nonqualified deferred compensation plan if the plan provides that upon a change in the employer's financial health, assets will be restricted to the payment of nonqualified deferred compensation. An amount is treated as restricted even if the assets are available to satisfy the claims of general creditors. For example, the provision applies in the case of a plan that provides that upon a change in financial health, assets will be transferred to a rabbi trust.

The transfer of property occurs as of the earlier of when the assets are so restricted or when the plan provides that assets will be restricted. It is intended that the transfer of property occurs to the extent that assets are restricted or will be restricted with respect to such compensation. For example, in the case of a plan that provides that upon a change in the employer's financial health, a trust will become funded to the extent of all deferrals, all amounts deferred under the plan are treated as property transferred under section 83. If a plan provides that deferrals of certain individuals will be funded upon a change in financial health, the transfer of property would occur with respect to compensation deferred by such individuals. The provision is not intended to apply when assets are restricted for a reason other than change in financial health (e.g., upon a change in control) or if assets are periodically restricted under a structured schedule and scheduled restrictions happen to coincide with a change in financial status. Any subsequent increases in the value of, or any earnings with respect to, restricted assets are treated as additional transfers of property. Interest at the underpayment rate plus one percentage point is imposed on the underpayments that would have occurred had the amounts been includible in income for the taxable year in which first deferred or, if later, the first taxable year not subject to a substantial risk of forfeiture. The amount required to be included in income is also subject to an additional 20-percent tax.

Definition of nonqualified deferred compensation plan

A nonqualified deferred compensation plan is any plan that provides for the deferral of compensation other than a qualified employer plan or any bona fide vacation leave, sick leave, compensatory time, disability pay, or death benefit plan.[813] A qualified employer plan means a qualified retirement plan, tax-deferred annuity, simplified employee pension, and SIMPLE.[814] A qualified governmental excess benefit arrangement (sec. 415(m)) is a qualified employer plan. An eligible deferred compensation plan (sec. 457(b)) is also a qualified employer plan under the provision. A tax-exempt or governmental deferred compensation plan that is not an eligible deferred compensation plan is not a qualified employer plan. The application of the provision is not limited to arrangements between an employer and employee.

For purposes of the provision, it is not intended that the term "nonqualified deferred compensation plan" include an arrangement taxable under section 83 providing for the grant of an option on employer stock with an exercise price that is not less than the fair market value of the underlying stock on the date of grant if such arrangement does not include a deferral feature other than the feature that the option holder has the right to exercise the option in the future. The provision is not intended to change the tax treatment of incentive stock options meeting the requirements of 422 or options granted under an employee stock purchase plan meeting the requirements of section 423.

It is intended that the provision does not apply to annual bonuses or other annual compensation amounts paid within 2 ½ months after the close of the taxable year in which the relevant services required for payment have been performed.

Other rules

Interest imposed under the provision is treated as interest on an underpayment of tax. Income (whether actual or notional) attributable to nonqualified deferred compensation is treated as additional deferred compensation and is subject to the provision. The provision is not intended to prevent the inclusion of amounts in gross income under any provision or rule of law earlier than the time provided in the provision. Any amount included in gross income under the provision is not be required to be included in gross income under any provision of law later than the time provided in the provision. The provision does not affect the rules regarding the timing of an employer's deduction for nonqualified deferred compensation.

Treasury regulations

The provision provides the Secretary authority to prescribe regulations as are necessary to carry out the purposes of provision, including regulations: (1) providing for the determination of amounts of deferral in the case of defined benefit plans; (2) relating to changes in the ownership and control of a corporation or assets of a corporation; (3) exempting from the provisions providing for transfers of property arrangements that will not result in an improper deferral of U.S. tax and will not result in assets being effectively beyond the reach of creditors; (4) defining financial health; and (5) disregarding a substantial risk of forfeiture. It is intended that substantial risk of forfeitures may not be used to manipulate the timing of income inclusion. It is intended that substantial risks of forfeiture should be disregarded in cases in which they are illusory or are used in a manner inconsistent with the purposes of the provision. For example, if an executive is effectively able to control the acceleration of the lapse of a substantial risk of forfeiture, such risk of forfeiture should be disregarded and income inclusion should not be postponed on account of such restriction. The Secretary may also address in regulations issues relating to stock appreciation rights.

Aggregation rules

Under the provision, except as provided by the Secretary, employer aggregation rules apply. It is intended that the Secretary issue guidance providing aggregation rules as are necessary to carry out the purposes of the provision. For example, it is intended that aggregation rules would apply in the case of separation from service so that the separation from service from one entity within a controlled group, but continued service for another entity within the group, would not be a permissible distribution event. It is also intended that aggregation rules would not apply in the case of change in control so that the change in control of one member of a controlled group would not be a permissible distribution event for participants of a deferred compensation plan of another member of the group.

Reporting requirements

Amounts required to be included in income under the provision are subject to reporting and Federal income tax withholding requirements. Amounts required to be includible in income are required to be reported on an individual's Form W-2 (or Form 1099) for the year includible in income.

The provision also requires annual reporting to the Internal Revenue Service of amounts deferred. Such amounts are required to be reported on an individual's Form W-2 (or Form 1099) for the year deferred even if the amount is not currently includible in income for that taxable year. It is expected that annual reporting of annual amounts deferred will provide the IRS greater information regarding such arrangements for enforcement purposes. It is intended that the information reported would provide an indication of what arrangements should be examined and challenged. Under the provision, the Secretary is authorized, through regulations, to establish a minimum amount of deferrals below which the reporting requirement does not apply. The Secretary may also provide that the reporting requirement does not apply with respect to amounts of deferrals that are not reasonably ascertainable. It is intended that the exception for amounts not reasonable ascertainable only apply to nonaccount balance plans and that amounts be required to be reported when they first become reasonably ascertainable.[815]

Effective Date

The provision is effective for amounts deferred in taxable years beginning after December 31, 2004. Earnings on amounts deferred before the effective date are subject to the provision to the extent that such amounts deferred are subject to the provision.

Amounts deferred in taxable years beginning before January 1, 2005, are subject to the provision if the plan under which the deferral is made is materially modified after October 3, 2004. The addition of any benefit, right or feature is a material modification. The exercise or reduction of an existing benefit, right, or feature is not a material modification. For example, an amendment to a plan on November 1, 2004, to add a provision that distributions may be allowed upon request if participants are required to forfeit 10 percent of the amount of the distribution (i.e., a "haircut") would be a material modification to the plan so that the rules of the provision would apply to the plan. Similarly, accelerating vesting under a plan after October 3, 2004, would be a material modification. A change in the plan administrator would not be a material modification. As another example, amending a plan to remove a distribution provision (e.g., to remove a "haircut") would not be considered a material modification.

Operating under the terms of a deferred compensation arrangement that complies with current law and is not materially modified after October 3, 2004, with respect to amounts deferred before January 1, 2005, is permissible, as such amounts would not be subject to the requirements of the provision. For example, subsequent deferrals with respect to amounts deferred before January 1, 2005,

---

[813] The provision does not apply to a plan meeting the requirements of section 457(e)(12) if the plan was in existence as of May 1, 2004, was providing nonelective deferred compensation described in section 457(e)(12) on such date, and is established or maintained by an organization incorporated on July 2, 1974. If the plan has a material change in the class of individuals eligible to participate in the plan after May 1, 2004, the provision applies to compensation provided under the plan after the date of such change.

[814] A qualified employer plan also includes a section 501(c)(18) trust.

[815] It is intended that the exception be similar to that under Treas. Reg. sec. 31.3121(v)(2)-1(e)(4).

under a plan that is not materially modified after October 3, 2004, would be subject to present law and would not be subject to the provision.[816] No inference is intended that all deferrals before the effective date are permissible under present law. It is expected that the IRS will challenge pre-effective date deferral arrangements that do not comply with present law.

For purposes of the effective date, an amount is considered deferred before January 1, 2005, if the amount is earned and vested before such date. To the extent there is no material modification after October 3, 2004, present law applies with respect to vested rights.

No later than 60 days after the date of enactment, the Secretary shall issue guidance providing a limited period of time during which a nonqualified deferred compensation plan adopted before December 31, 2004, may, without violating the requirements of the provision relating to distributions, accelerations, and elections be amended (1) to provide that a participant may terminate participation in the plan, or cancel an outstanding deferral election with respect to amounts deferred after December 31, 2004, if such amounts are includible in income of the participant as earned, or if later, when not subject to a substantial risk of forfeiture, and (2) to conform with the provision with respect to amounts deferred after December 31, 2004. It is expected that the Secretary may provide exceptions to certain requirements of the provision during the transition period (e.g., the rules regarding timing of elections) for plans coming into compliance with the provision. Moreover, it is expected that the Secretary will provide a reasonable time, during the transition period but after the issuance of guidance, for plans to be amended and approved by the appropriate parties in accordance with this provision.—**Conference Committee Report (H.R. CONF. REP. NO. 108-755)**

[Code Sec. 410]

[¶ 12,150.09]

Committee Report on P.L. 100-647 (Technical and Miscellaneous Revenue Act of 1988)

[Senate Committee Report]

* * *

The bill incorporates in the statute the provision in the Statement of Managers that a plan maintained by an employer that has no nonhighly compensated employees for a year is considered to satisfy the coverage requirements for such year. As is so with respect to the coverage rules generally, this rule is to apply separately with respect to former employees under rules prescribed by the Secretary. This rule is not intended to apply for other purposes, such as nondiscrimination rules applicable to section 401(k) plans.

In addition, it is intended that the Secretary is to exercise his authority with respect to the application of the coverage rules to former employees to except, in appropriate cases, retiree benefit increases from the general rule of separate testing.

[¶ 12,150.095]

Committee Reports on P.L. 99-514 (Tax Reform Act of 1986)

Minimum Coverage Requirements

[Senate Committee Report]

[The "percentage," "reasonable classification," and "alternative reasonable classification tests" referred to below are included for informational purposes only. These tests have been changed as discussed in the Conference Committee Report below.]

* * *

Employees benefiting under the plan

For purposes of [(a) the] percentage test, (b) the reasonable classification test, and (c) the alternative reasonable classification test, an employee, generally, will be treated as benefiting under the plan only if the employee is a participant in the plan. However, in the case of a cash or deferred arrangement or the portion of a defined contribution plan to which employee contributions and employer matching contributions are made, an employee will be treated as benefiting under the plan if the employee is eligible to make contributions to the plan.

Aggregation of plans and comparability

As under present law, for purposes of applying the percentage test or the reasonable classification test, more than one plan may be designated as a unit and tested as a single entity, if the plans so designated provide benefits that do not discriminate in favor of highly compensated employees. Also, for purposes of satisfying the alternative reasonable classification test, two or more comparable plans may be aggregated for purposes of determining whether the plans together satisfy the classification test of present law.

Under the bill, the comparability analysis contained in Rev. Rul. 81-202 is to be modified to substitute the new integration rules for the integration rules of current law. The committee encourages the Secretary of the Treasury to issue revised and simplified guidelines for comparability analysis.

Excludable employees

For purposes of determining whether a plan (a) benefits 80 percent of all employees, (b) benefits a reasonable classification of employees, or (c) satisfies the alternative reasonable classification test, the bill generally permits the employer to exclude from consideration certain classes of employees.

Minimum age and service.—If a plan (a) prescribes minimum age or service requirements as a condition of participation, and (b) excludes all employees who do not satisfy such requirements, then the employer may disregard such employees in applying the percentage test (as under present law), and in applying the reasonable classification test. For purposes of applying the alternative reasonable classification test, the employer may take into account all employees, or alternatively, may exclude those employees who have not satisfied the minimum age and service requirements that are the lowest such age or service requirements for any plans taken into account in applying the test. The lowest age and service used need not be the age and service requirements under the same plan.

The bill provides that employees who are not excluded from consideration in applying the alternative reasonable classification test because they are covered under a separate plan, but who could have been excluded had the employer used other minimum age or service requirements in such other plan, may be excluded from consideration if the coverage of such employees, tested separately, satisfies the coverage and nondiscrimination rules.

Collective bargaining agreement.—As under present law, for purposes of applying the percentage test and the reasonable classification test to a plan, the employer may exclude from consideration employees not included in the plan who are included in a unit of employees covered by a collective bargaining agreement.

For purposes of the alternative reasonable classification test, all employees included in a unit of employees covered by a collective bargaining agreement are disregarded, regardless of whether any of those individuals are covered by any of the plans being tested, except for purposes of determining whether an alternative plan satisfies the requirements of section 410(b)(1)(B) as in effect immediately before the enactment of the Tax Reform Act of 1986.

Miscellaneous.—As under present law, nonresident aliens with no United States source income may be disregarded for purposes of applying the coverage rules. Similarly, in the case of a collective bargaining agreement covering a unit of airline pilots, employees not covered by the agreement may be disregarded.

* * *

Special rules for certain dispositions and acquisitions

The bill contains special transition rules for certain dispositions or acquisitions of a business. Under the bill, if a person becomes or ceases to be a member of a controlled group or affiliated service group, the coverage rules will be deemed satisfied during the transition period (as defined in the bill), provided that (1) the coverage rules were satisfied immediately before the acquisition or disposition, and (2) the coverage under the plan does not change significantly during the transition period (other than by reason of the acquisition or disposition). The transition period is defined under the bill as the period beginning on the date of the acquisition or disposition and ending on the last day of the first plan year beginning after the transition.

Effective Date

The provision generally is effective for plan years beginning after December 31, 1988.

A special effective date applies to plans maintained pursuant to a collective bargaining agreement. Under this special rule, in the case of a plan maintained pursuant to a collective bargaining agreement between employee representatives and one or more employers ratified before March 1, 1986, the amendments are not effective for plan years beginning before the earlier of (1) the later of (i) January 1, 1989, or (ii) the date on which the last of the collective bargaining agreements terminates, or (2) January 1, 1991. Extensions or renegotiations of the collective bargaining agreement, if ratified after February 28, 1986, are disregarded.

[Conference Committee Report]

Overview

With respect to the coverage rules applicable to qualified plans, the conference agreement follows the Senate amendment, except as outlined below.

General coverage rules

Under the conference agreement, a plan is not qualified unless the plan satisfies at least one of the following requirements:

(1) the plan benefits at least 70 percent of all nonhighly compensated employees (referred to herein as the "percentage test");

[816] There is no inference that all subsequent deferral elections under plans that are not materially modified are permissible under present law.

(2) the plan benefits a percentage of nonhighly compensated employees which is at least 70 percent of the percentage of highly compensated employees benefiting under the plan (referred to herein as the "ratio test"); or

(3) the plan meets the average benefits test.

An employer that has no nonhighly compensated employees in its workforce is considered to pass the coverage test.

Average benefits test

A plan meets the average benefits test if (1) the plan benefits such employees as qualify under a classification set up by the employer and found by the Secretary not to be discriminatory in favor of highly compensated employees ("classification test"); and (2) the average benefit percentage for nonhighly compensated employees of the employer is at least 70 percent of the average benefit percentage for highly compensated employees of the employer.

Classification test.—For purposes of the average benefits test, the conferees intend that the classification test is generally to be based on the present-law section 410(b)(1)(B) (as modified judicially and administratively in the future). However, it is to be applied using the new definitions of highly compensated employees and excludable employees.

Thus, the test is to be applied on the basis of the facts and circumstances of each case, including the difference between the coverage percentages of the highly compensated employees and the other employees, the percentage of total employees covered, and the difference between the compensation of the covered employees and the compensation of the excluded employees. Nevertheless, the conferees expect that the Secretary will consider providing an objective safe harbor based on these and other relevant factors to facilitate compliance with the test.

Average benefit percentage.—The term "average benefit percentage" means, with respect to any group of employees, the average of the benefit percentages calculated separately with respect to each employee in such group. The term "benefit percentage" means the employer-provided contributions (including forfeitures) or benefits of an employee under all qualified plans of the employer, expressed as a percentage of such employee's compensation. If benefit percentages are determined on the basis of employer-provided contributions, all employer-provided benefits must be converted into contributions for testing purposes. Similarly, if benefit percentages are determined on the basis of employer-provided benefits, all employer-provided contributions are to be converted into benefits. In determining the amount of contributions or benefits, the approach of Rev. Rul. 81-202 is to be the sole rule applicable, as modified in the manner described below. Thus, in the case of benefits testing, the benefit percentages are determined based on projected benefits.

The conferees further intend that the rules of Rev. Rul. 81-202 be modified in several respects, both for purposes of the average benefit percentage test and for purposes of determining whether 2 or more plans that are treated as a single plan under the percentage test, ratio test, or classification test discriminate in favor of highly compensated employees (sec. 401(a)(4)). First, Rev. Rul. 81-202 is to be modified to reflect the new limits contained in the conference agreement on the extent to which a plan may be integrated. Also, the new limitation on the amount of compensation that may be taken into account and the new definition of compensation applies under Rev. Rul. 81-202 as they apply for all nondiscrimination rules.

Rev. Rul. 81-202 is also to be modified to take into account other significant plan features. For example, determinations under Rev. Rul. 81-202 are to take into account the rate at which benefits actually accrue and, in appropriate cases, may take into account the existence of different plan options such as loans or lump-sum distributions that are available to highly compensated participants, but not to a proportionate number of nonhighly compensated participants. Moreover, the conferees clarify that under Rev. Rul. 81-202 the same actuarial assumptions are to be used in valuing different benefits or contributions. In appropriate circumstances, Rev. Rul. 81-202 may also be modified to take into account reasonable salary projections. The Secretary may also, in circumstances justifying special scrutiny, consider requiring a certificate of comparability from an enrolled actuary.

Finally, the conferees do not intend to restrict the authority of the Secretary to modify, as appropriate, aspects of Rev. Rul. 81-202 not discussed above. Also, the conferees do not intend that application of the rules of Rev. Rul. 81-202 to the average benefit percentage test be interpreted as requiring that an averaging approach be adopted for purposes of applying these rules to multiple plans being tested as a single plan under section 401(a)(4).

For purposes of determining benefit percentages, all pre-tax contributions or benefits provided under a qualified plan are considered employer-provided and must be taken into account, including, for example, elective contributions under a qualified cash or deferred arrangement. In no case may an employer disregard any qualified plan in determining benefit percentages, even if such qualified plan satisfies the percentage test or ratio test standing alone. Contributions or benefits under other types of plans or programs (such as SEPs or tax-sheltered annuity programs (sec. 403(b)) are not taken into account.

After the benefit percentage of each employee is determined in the manner described above, the average for the two groups (highly compensated employees and nonhighly compensated employees) is then to be determined by averaging the individual benefit percentages of each employee (including employees not covered by any plan) in a manner similar to the computation of the actual deferral percentage of a group of employees under a qualified cash or deferred arrangement.

Period of computing percentage.—The conference agreement provides that each employee's benefit percentage is to be computed, at the election of the employer, on the basis of contributions or benefits for (a) the current plan year, or (b) a period of consecutive plan years (not in excess of 3 years) ending with the current plan year. As under the Senate amendment, the period of consecutive plan years chosen by the employer is to be uniformly applied in computing each employee's benefit percentage, and may not be changed without the consent of the Secretary.

In addition, the conferees clarify that the fact that a failure to meet the new coverage tests was due to unforeseen circumstances does not affect application of the tests.

Employees benefiting under the plan

The conference agreement follows the Senate amendment. The conference agreement also clarifies that, for purposes of the average benefit percentage component of the average benefits test, it is actual benefits, not eligibility, that is taken into account. As under current law, this is also true for purposes of establishing comparability between plans.

Aggregation of plans and comparability

The conference agreement follows the Senate amendment, except that Rev. Rul. 81-202 is to be modified in the manner described above.

Excludable employees

For purposes of (a) the percentage test, (b) the ratio test, and (c) the average benefits test, the conference agreement generally follows the Senate amendment, with the following exceptions.

Minimum age and service.—The rules applicable under the Senate amendment to the percentage and reasonable classification tests apply to the percentage, ratio and classification tests. The rules applicable to the alternative reasonable classification test apply to the average benefits test (other than the classification test).

The conference agreement reflects the Senate amendment rule permitting employees who do not meet the age 21 and one year of service requirements to be tested separately. However, under the conference agreement, such separate testing is permissible even if such employees are not covered by a separate plan. Under the agreement, an employer may elect to test all such excludable employees separately. Alternatively, an employer may elect to test one group of excludable employees separately without testing all excludable employees separately if such group is defined in a nondiscriminatory manner solely by reference to the age or service requirements. For example, an employer may elect to test separately all employees excludable solely on the grounds that they do not have one year of service, but not include in such testing group employees excluded under the age rule. Also, the employer may test separately a group of employees who would pass an age or service requirement that is less restrictive than the age 21 or one year of service requirement. For example, an employer could test separately all employees excludable solely on the grounds that they are not age 21, but who are at least 18.

Collective bargaining agreement.—For purposes of applying (a) the percentage test, (b) the ratio test, or (c) the average benefits test to qualified plan coverage of employees who are not included in a unit of employees covered by a collective bargaining agreement, all employees covered by such an agreement are disregarded. However, in applying the same tests to employees covered by any such agreement, an employee may not be disregarded based on the fact that such employee is not covered under the collective bargaining agreement.

* * *

Special rules for certain dispositions and acquisitions

The conference agreement follows the Senate amendment.

Former employees

Under rules prescribed by the Secretary, the coverage rules are to apply separately to former employees. The conferees intend that for this purpose rules similar to those applicable to employee benefits may be applied.* * *

Sanction

The conference agreement modifies the sanction applicable to a plan that fails to qualify due solely to a failure to satisfy the new coverage rules. Under the agreement, nonhighly compensated employees are not taxable on amounts contributed to or earned by the trust merely because a plan fails to satisfy the coverage requirements. Highly compensated employees, on the other hand, are taxable on the value of their vested accrued benefit attributable to employer contributions and income on any contributions to the extent such amounts have not previously been taxed to the employee. Except for these two charges, the sanctions applicable under current law are not modified. Thus, as under present law, in appropriate circumstances, apply lesser sanctions than those authorized.

Minimum Participation Rule

[Senate Committee Report]

Explanation of Provision

Under the bill, a plan is not a qualified plan unless it benefits no fewer than the lesser of (a) 50 employees or (b) 40 percent or more of all employees of the employer. The requirement may not be satisfied by aggregating comparable plans. In the case of a cash or deferred arrangement or the portion of a defined contribution plan to which employee contributions or employer matching contributions are made, an employee wil be treated as benefiting under the plan if the employee is eligible to make contributions to the plan.

The bill generally provides that, for purposes of applying the minimum participation rules, the same categories of employees may be disregarded for purposes of applying the general coverage rules. In the case of a plan covering only employees included in a unit of employees covered by a collective bargaining agreement, all employees not included in such unit may be disregarded for purposes of satisfying the minimum participation rule.

Effective Date

The provisions are generally effective for plan years beginning after December 31, 1968.

A special effective date applies to plans maintained pursuant to a collective bargaining agreement. Under this special rule, in the case of a plan maintained pursuant to a collective bargaining agreement between employee representatives and one or more employers ratified before March 1, 1986, the amendments are not effective for plan years beginning the earlier of (1) the later of (i) January 1, 1989, or (ii) the date on which the last of the collective bargaining agreements terminates, or (2) January 1, 1991. Extensions or renegotiations of the collective bargaining agreement, if ratified after February 28, 1986, are disregarded.

[Conference Committee Report]

The conference agreement follows the Senate amendment with the following modifications and clarifications.

First, the minimum participation rule generally does not apply to a multiemployer plan. However, this exemption does not appply to a multiemployer plan that covers any professional (e.g., doctor, lawyer, or investment banker). In addition, the special rule in the Senate amendment regarding plans covering only employees included in a unit of employees covered by a collective bargaining agreement also does not apply to a plan that covers any professional. No inference is intended from these rules that a plan covering a professional may be a multiemployer plan.

Second, the conference agreement provides that, under regulations prescribed by the Secretary, any separate benefit structure, any separate trust, or any separate arrangement with respect to a defined benefit plan may be treated as a separate plan for purposes of applying the minimum participation rule. Thus, for example, a plan that provides two different formulas for calculating participants' benefits or contributions may be treated as at least two plans. Also, if defined benefit plan assets are payable from more than one source, such as from more than one trust, each source of assets may be considered a separate plan. If any particular person or persons have any priority (under the terms of the plan or by arrangement outside of the plan) with respect to a source of assets for defined benefits, such as a right to some or all of a possible reversion, such person or persons may be considered the sole participant or participants with respect to that "plan."

In general, it is the intent of the conferees to define "plan" in such a way as to carry out the purposes of the minimum participation rule. Thus, if there is a single defined benefit structure and a single source of assets, there may be more than one plan for purposes of this rule if, under all the facts and circumstances (including those outside of the plan), the arrangement has an effect similar to providing a plan or account to a group of employees that would not satisfy the minimum participation rule. For example, a group of employees might agree to provide each one of them with investment authority with regard to a separate pool of assets held with respect to the defined benefit structure. If such employees may be compensated in any manner, inside or outside the plan, by reference to the results of their investments, each part of the pool of assets may be considered a separate plan benefiting the participant controlling the investment thereof.

In addition, "plan" is to be defined so as to preclude the use of structures such as defined benefit plan-defined contribution plan combinations (with benefit offsets) to avoid the rule.

If any plan, as specially defined herein, fails to satisfy the minimum participation rule, the entire plan (as otherwise defined) fails to satisfy the qualification standard (sec. 401(a)). Also, except to the extent provided in regulations, a plan will not satisfy this rule for a year unless it satisfies it on each day of the year.

The conferees also clarify how the minimum participation rules apply with respect to coverage of employees who could be excluded under the age or service rules from participation in a qualified plan. Generally, the rule is to apply as if the only employees of the employer were the excludable employees who may be tested separately under the coverage tests. However, all employees of the employer must be taken into account if any highly compensated employee is covered as an excludable employee for more than one year. Also, if any excludable employee is covered under a defined benefit pension plan, all employees of the employer are to be taken into account in applying the minimum participation rule to such plan, except where (1) the benefits provided under such coverage are comparable (or less than comparable) to the coverage of nonexcludable employees; and (2) the plan covering such excludable employees would satisfy the minimum participation rule (taking into account all employees of the employer) but for the fact that such plan has a different defined benefit structure from the plan covering the nonexcludable employees. Thus, payments with respect to defined benefits provided to excludable employees must come from the same source as payments with respect to defined benefits provided to nonexcludable employees. All employees of the employer are to be taken into account if only the excludable employees are covered by a defined benefit plan.

If excludable employees may be tested separately under the rules described above, such employees may be disregarded in applying the minimum participation rule to other employees.

The Secretary may exempt from the application of this rule two limited situations. The Secretary may, under appropriate conditions, exempt a plan that benefits no employee who is or ever has been a highly compensated employee with respect to service being credited under the plan, provided that such plan is not necessary for another plan or plans to satisfy the applicable coverage rules (sec. 410(b)).

The Secretary may, under appropriate conditions, also exempt a plan that may not be terminated on account of the provisions of the Single Employer Pension Plan Amendment Act (SEPPAA) because it is underfunded. However, such exemption may not apply unless benefit accruals cease, the plan obtains a letter of insufficiency for each plan year of exemption, and the plan eliminates, under rules prescribed by the Secretary, any different benefit structure or separate arrangement (as described above).

Further, the conference agreement provides that if (i) a plan is in existence on August 16, 1986, (ii) the plan would fail to meet the requirements of the minimum participation rule if such rule were in effect on August 16, 1986, and (iii) there is no transfer of assets to or liabilities from the plan, or merger or spinoff involving the plan, after August 16, 1986, such plan may be terminated and the 10-percent excise tax on the reversion of assets (*See* Part D.3., below) is not imposed on any employer reversion from such plan. Such termination and reversion are permissible even though the terminating plan relies on another plan that is not terminated for qualification. In determining the amount of any such employer reversion, the present value of the accrued benefit of any individual who is a highly compensated employee, is to be determined by using an interest rate that is equal to the maximum interest rate that may be used for purposes of calculating a participant's accrued benefit under section 411(a)(11)(B). * * * The Secretary is to prescribe rules preventing avoidance of this interest rate rule through distributions prior to or in lieu of a reversion.

[¶ 12,150.10]

Committee Report on P.L. 98-397 (Retirement Equity Act of 1984)

[Senate Committee Report]

Maximum age conditions.—The bill provides that a pension plan may not require, as a condition of participation, completion of more than one year of service or attainment of an age greater than 21 (whichever occurs later).[1] The reduction in the maximum participation age further limits the extent of backloading of benefit accruals.

Under the bill, a plan is not permitted to ignore, for purposes of the minimum vesting requirements, an employee's years of service completed after the employee has attained age 18.

[¶ 12,150.11]

Committee Report on P.L. 93-406 (Employee Retirement Income Security Act of 1974)

[Conference Committee Explanation]

Plans subject to the provisions.—Under title I of the conference substitute (the labor law provisions) the new participation and coverage rules are to be enforced by the Secretary of Labor when participants bring violations to his attention or when cases come to his attention which initially were under consideration by the Secretary of Treasury on which he has previously initiated action. The rules are to apply to employee pension benefit plans of employers or employee organizations established in or affecting interstate commerce. Under this title II (the tax law provisions), the participation and coverage rules are to be administered by the Secretary of the Treasury or his delegate, and the rules apply to tax-qualified pension, profit-sharing, and stock bonus plans.[1]

---

[1] In addition, the bill changes the maximum age requirement under a plan maintained exclusively for the benefit of employees of certain tax-exempt educational organizations (sec. 410(a)(1)(B)(ii) of the Code) from 30 to 26.

[1] The division of administrative responsibility between Labor and Treasury is discussed in Part XII, below "General Provisions Relating to Jurisdiction, Administration, Enforcement: Joint Pension Task

Exceptions to coverage.—The participation and coverage requirements of title I (the labor law provisions) do not apply to governmental plans (including Railroad Retirement Act plans), church plans (except those electing coverage), plans maintained solely to comply with workmen's unemployment, disability, or compensation laws, plans maintained outside the United States primarily for the benefit of nonresident aliens, employee welfare plans, excess plans (which provide for benefits or contributions in excess of those allowable for tax-qualified plans), unfunded deferred compensation arrangements, plans established by labor organizations (those referred to in sec. 501(c)(5) of the Internal Revenue Code) which do not provide for employer contributions after the date of enactment, and fraternal or other plans of organizations (described in sec. 501(c)(8), 501(c)(9)) which do not receive employer contributions, or trusts described in 501(c)(18) of the Internal Revenue Code. Title I does not apply to buy-out agreements involving retiring or deceased partners (under sec. 736 of the Internal Revenue Code). In addition, title I does not apply to employer or union-sponsored individual retirement accounts (see "Employee Savings for Retirement").

The participation requirements of title II apply only to plans which qualify for certain tax deferral privileges by meeting the standards as to participation and other matters set forth in the Internal Revenue laws. However, governmental plans and church plans which do not elect to come under the new provisions will nevertheless be treated as qualified for purposes of the tax deferral privileges for the employees, if they meet the requirements of present law. Also the rules do not apply to plans of labor organizations (described in sec. 501(c)(5)) or fraternal or other organizations (described in sec. 501(c)(8) or (9)) which do not provide for employer contributions.

Exemption for church plans.—As indicated above, both title I and title II exempt church plans from the participation and coverage requirements of the conference substitute (although title II requires these plans to comply with present law in order to be qualified). This exemption does not apply to a plan which is primarily for the benefit of employees engaged in an unrelated trade or business, or (except as noted below) to a multiemployer plan unless all of the participating employers are churches or conventions or associations of churches (rather than merely church-related agencies). However, a multiemployer plan which was in existence on January 1, 1974, and which covers church-related agencies (such as schools and hospitals) is to be treated as a church plan for purposes of the exemption (even though it continues to cover those agencies) for plan years beginning before January 1, 1983, but not for subsequent plan years.

A church plan may make an irrevocable election to be covered under title I and title II (in a form and manner to be prescribed in regulations). A plan which makes this election is to be covered under the bill for purposes of the new participation, vesting, funding and form of benefit rules, as well as the fiduciary and disclosure rules and will also be covered under the plan termination insurance provisions.

General rule as to participation.—Generally, under title I and title II of the conference substitute, an employee cannot be excluded from a plan on account of age or service if he is at least 25 years old and has had at least one year of service. However, if the plan provides full and immediate vesting for all participants, it may require employees to be age 25, with 3 years of service, in order to participate. As an alternative, any plan which is maintained exclusively for employees of a governmental or tax-exempt educational organization which provides full and immediate vesting for all participants may have a participation requirement of age 30, with 1 year of service.

Maximum age requirement.—Under the conference substitute, in general, a plan may not exclude an employee because he is too old. However, because of cost factors, it was decided that in a defined benefit plan it would be appropriate to permit the exclusion of an employee who is within 5 years of attaining normal retirement age under the plan (or older) when he is first employed. (These employees would be counted as part of the employer's work force, however, for purposes of determining whether or not his plan satisfied the breadth-of-coverage requirements.) Of course, if a plan defines normal retirement age as the later of age 65, or the tenth anniversary of the employee's participation in the plan, the plan could not impose a maximum age requirement (because no employee would be within 5 years of normal retirement age when first employed). A "target benefit" plan, as defined in Treasury regulations, could also impose a maximum age requirement (even though it is not a defined benefit plan), because in many respects the pattern of costs and benefits of target benefit plans closely resembles the pattern of costs and benefits of defined benefit plans.

Year of service defined.—Under the conference substitute, in general, for purposes of the participation requirements, the term "year of service" means a 12-month period during which the employee has worked at least 1,000 hours. This 12-month period is measured from the date when the employee enters service. Thus, the employee has fulfilled his 1,000-hour-requirement if he has 1,000 hours of work by the first anniversary date of his employment. Under the substitute, the employee (if age 25 or older) would then be admitted to the plan within 6 months or his anniversary date of employment or by the beginning of the first plan year following his first anniversary date, whichever occurred earlier. (Of course, this does not mean that an employee would have to be admitted to the plan if he were lawfully excluded for reasons other than age or service.)

The plan would not be required to admit the employee if he had "separated from the service" before the otherwise applicable admission date. In general, "separated from the service" means the employee was discharged or quit; it does not mean temporary absence due to vacation, sickness, strike, seasonal layoff, etc.

If the employee did not complete 1,000 hours of service by his first anniversary date, but is still employed, he would start over toward meeting his 1,000 hour requirement. For this purpose, the plan could provide (on a consistent basis) that the relevant 12-month period is either (a) the year between his first anniversary date and his second anniversary date, or (b) the first plan year which began after the individual was first employed. For example, assume the plan is on a calendar year basis, and that an employee begins work on July 1, 1976. Between July 1, 1976, and June 30, 1977, the employee has less than 1,000 hours of service. The plan could provide that the employee would be tested the second time for purposes of participation based on the year from July 1, 1977 through June 30, 1978, or based on the year from January 1, 1977 through December 31, 1977 (but not January 1, 1978 through December 31, 1978).

The regulations with respect to "year of service" are to be written by the Secretary of Labor for purposes of participation and vesting. The term "hour of service" will also be defined in Labor Department regulations.

For purposes of participation (and vesting), in the case of any maritime industry (as defined in Labor Department regulations), 125 days of service are to be treated as the equivalent of 1,000 hours of service, but this rule will not apply to other industries.

Seasonal and part-time workers.—In general, the 1,000 hour standard is to apply for purposes of determining whether or not an employee may be excluded from the plan as a seasonal or part-time employee (replacing the 5-month year, 20-hour week standard now in the Internal Revenue Code). However, in the case of seasonal industries where the customary period of employment is less than 1,000 hours, the term "year of service" is to be determined in accordance with Labor Department regulations.

Breaks in service.—Under the conference substitute, a 1-year break in service occurs in any calendar year, plan year, or other consecutive 12-month period designated by the plan on a consistent basis (and not prohibited under Labor Department regulations) in which the employee has 500 hours of service or less.

The general rule is that all service with the employer (pre-break and post-break) is to be taken into account for purposes of determining whether the employee has met the participation requirements. However, if an employee has a 1-year break in service, the plan may require a 1-year waiting period before reentry, at which point the employee's pre-break and post-break service are [sic] to be aggregated, and the employee is to receive full credit for the waiting period service. For example, if the plan is on a calendar year basis, and an employee who has a 1-year break in service reenters employment on November 1, 1976, works 200 hours in 1976, and 1700 hours by November 1, 1977, the employee under this provision would be considered as reentering the plan for 1977. As a result, his pre-break and post-break service would be aggregated, and he would advance for year on the vesting schedule for 1977. He would also accrue benefits for that year. (Other rules with respect to break-in-service are explained below in connection with vesting and benefit accrual.)

In the case of a plan which has a 3-year service requirement for participation (because the plan provides 100 percent immediate vesting), the plan may provide that employees who have a 1-year break in service before completing their 3-year service requirement must start over toward fulfilling that requirement after the break in service.

Eligibility—collective-bargaining units, air pilots.—Title II of the conference substitute provides that employees who are under a collective bargaining agreement can be excluded for purposes of the breadth-of-coverage requirements (coverage for 70 percent of all employees or 80 percent of all eligible employees if at least 70 percent of all employees are eligible to benefit under the plan, or coverage on a nondiscriminatory basis), if the employees are excluded from the plan and there is evidence that retirement benefits have been the subject of good-faith bargaining. However, if the union employees are covered under the plan, benefits or contributions must be provided for them on a nondiscriminatory basis.

Title II of the substitute provides another exception to the breadth-of-coverage rule. It provides that air pilots represented in accordance with the Railway Labor Act may bargain separately for tax-qualified employee plan benefits, without including other workers within the industry (but only in the case of a plan which covers no employees other than air pilots). In addition, the conferees intend that the joint congressional pension task force study group, created under this legislation, study this area to see whether a similar rule should be applied to other unions or professional groups in the future.

Nonresident aliens.—Title II of the conference substitute provides that employees who are nonresident aliens with no United States income from the employer in question are to be excluded for purposes of applying the breadth-of-coverage requirements and for purposes of applying the antidiscrimination rules (whether or not they are covered under the plan).

* * *

(Footnote Continued)

Force, Etc." Except where otherwise noted, the regulations with respect to participation, vesting and funding are to be written by the Secretary of the Treasury or his delegate.

H.R. 10 plans.—In general, the provisions of present law which allow a 3-year service requirement for participation (but do not allow the plan to impose an age requirement), and require 100 percent immediate vesting, would continue to govern owner-employee H.R. 10 plans (those for sole proprietors and 10 percent owners and their employees). However, certain provisions of this bill, such as the rules with respect to year of service and breaks in service are also to apply for purposes of the H.R. 10 plans.

* * *

Year of service defined.—In general, under the conference substitute, the rules with respect to "year of service", seasonal and part-time employees, etc., are the same for purposes of the vesting schedule as they are for purposes of participation (i.e., generally 1,000 hours of service except for seasonal industries, where the customary work year is less than 1,000 hours). However, the relevant year for purposes of applying the vesting schedule may be any 12-month period provided under the plan (plan year, calendar year, etc.) regardless of the anniversary date of the participant's employment (even though the anniversary date is the measuring point for purposes of the participation requirements for an employee's first year).

For purposes of benefit accrual, in general, the plan may use any definition of the term "year of service" which the plan applies on a reasonable and consistent basis (subject to Department of Labor regulations). (Of course, the "year" for benefit accrual purposes cannot exceed the customary work year for the industry involved.) However, the plan must accrue benefits for less than full time service on at least a pro rata basis. For example, if a plan requires 2,000 hours of service for a full benefit accrual (50 weeks of 40 hours each) then the plan would have to accrue at least 75 percent of a full benefit for a participant with 1,500 hours of service. Generally, a plan would not be required to accrue any benefit for years in which the participant had less than 1,000 hours of service. In the case of industries or occupations where the customary year is less than 1,000 hours (for example, the tuna fishing industry, or the winter season employees of a ski lodge), the rules with respect to benefit accrual would be determined under Department of Labor regulations. As previously indicated a special rule is provided for the maritime industries.

[Code Sec. 411]

[¶ 12,200.035]

Committee Report on P.L. 109-280 (Pension Protection Act of 2006)

[Joint Committee on Taxation Report]

[Benefit accrual standards]

Age discrimination rules in general

Under the provision, a plan is not treated as violating the prohibition on age discrimination under ERISA, the Code, and ADEA if a participant's accrued benefit,[154] as determined as of any date under the terms of the plan would be equal to or greater than that of any similarly situated, younger individual who is or could be a participant. For this purpose, an individual is similarly situated to a participant if the individual and the participant are (and always have been) identical in every respect (including period of service, compensation, position, date of hire, work history, and any other respect) except for age. Under the provision, the comparison of benefits for older and younger participants applies to all possible participants under all possible dates under the plan, in the same manner as the present-law application of the backloading and accrual rules.

In addition, in determining a participant's accrued benefit for this purpose, the subsidized portion of any early retirement benefit or any retirement type subsidy is disregarded. In some cases the value of an early retirement subsidy may be difficult to determine; it is therefore intended that a reasonable approximation of such value may be used for this purpose. In calculating the accrued benefit, the benefit may, under the terms of the plan, be calculated as an annuity payable at normal retirement age, the balance of a hypothetical account, or the current value of the accumulated percentage of the employee's final average compensation. That is, the age discrimination rules may be applied on the basis of the balance of the a hypothetical account or the current value of the accumulated percentage of the employee's final average compensation, but only if the plan terms provide the accrued benefit in such form. The provision is intended to apply to hybrid plans, including pension equity plans.

The provision makes it clear that a plan is not treated as age discriminatory solely because the plan provides offsets of benefits under the plan to the extent such offsets are allowable in applying the requirements under section 401(a) of the Code. It is intended that such offsets also comply with ERISA and the ADEA.

A plan is not treated as failing to meet the age discrimination requirements solely because the plan provides a disparity in contributions and benefits with respect to which the requirements of section 401(l) of the Code are met.

A plan is not treated as failing to meet the age discrimination requirements solely because the plan provides for indexing of accrued benefits under the plan. Except in the case of any benefit provided in the form of a variable annuity, this rule does not apply with respect to any indexing which results in an accrued benefit less than the accrued benefit determined without regard to such indexing. Indexing for this purpose means, with respect to an accrued benefit, the periodic adjustment of the accrued benefit by means of the application of a recognized investment index or methodology. Under the provision, in no event may indexing be reduced or cease because of age.

Rules for applicable defined benefit plans

In general

Under the provision, an applicable defined benefit plan fails to satisfy the age discrimination rules unless the plan meets certain requirements with respect to interest credits and, in the case of a conversion, certain additional requirements. Applicable defined benefit plans must also satisfy certain vesting requirements.

Interest requirement

A plan satisfies the interest requirement if the terms of the plan provide that any interest credit (or equivalent amount) for any plan year is at a rate that is not less than zero and is not greater than a market rate of return. A plan does not fail to meet the interest requirement merely because the plan provides for a reasonable minimum guaranteed rate of return or for a rate or return that is equal to the greater of a fixed or variable rate of return. An interest credit (or an equivalent amount) of less than zero cannot result in the account balance or similar amount being less than the aggregate amount of contributions credited to the account. The Secretary of the Treasury may provide rules governing the calculation of a market rate of return and for permissible methods of crediting interest to the account (including fixed or variable interest rates) resulting in effective rates of return that meet the requirements of the provision.

If the interest credit rate (or equivalent amount) is a variable rate, the plan must provide that, upon termination of the plan, the rate of interest used to determine accrued benefits under the plan is equal to the average of the rates of interest used under the plan during the five-year period ending on the termination date.

Conversion rules

Under the provision, special rules apply if an amendment to a defined benefit plan is adopted which would have the effect of converting the plan into an applicable defined benefit plan (an "applicable plan amendment").[155] If an applicable plan amendment is adopted after June 29, 2005, the plan fails to satisfy the age discrimination rules unless the plan provides that the accrued benefit of any individual who was a participant immediately before the adoption of the amendment is not less than the sum of (1) the participant's accrued benefit for years of service before the effective date of the amendment, determined under the terms of the plan as in effect before the amendment; plus (2) the participant's accrued benefit for years of service after the effective date of the amendment, determined under the terms of the plan as in effect after the terms of the amendment.

For purposes of determining the amount in (1) above, the plan must credit the accumulation account or similar amount with the amount of any early retirement benefit or retirement-type subsidy for the plan year in which the participant retires if, as of such time, the participant has met the age, years of service, and other requirements under the plan for entitlement to such benefit or subsidy.

Vesting rules

The provision amends the ERISA and Code rules relating to vesting to provide that an applicable defined benefit plan must provide that each employee who has completed at least three years of serves has a nonforfeitable right to 100 percent of the employee's accrued benefit derived from employer contributions.

Minimum present value rules

The provision provides that an applicable defined benefit plan is not treated as failing to meet the minimum present value rules[156] solely because of the present value of the accrued benefit (or any portion thereof) of any participant is, under the terms of the plan, equal to the amount expressed as the balance in the hypothetical account or as an accumulated percentage of the participant's final average compensation.

Rules on plan termination

The provision provides rules for making determinations of benefits upon termination of an applicable defined benefit plan. Such a plan must provide that, upon plan termination, (1) if the interest credit rate (or equivalent amount) under the plan is a variable rate, the rate of interest used to determine accrued benefits under the plan shall be equal to the average of the rates of interest used under the plan during the five-year period ending on the termination date and (2) the interest rate and mortality table used to determine the amount of any benefit under the plan payable in the form of an annuity payable at normal retirement age

[154] For purposes of this rule, the accrued benefit means such benefit accrued to date.

[155] If the benefits under two or more defined benefit plans established by an employer are coordinated in such a manner as to have the effect of the adoption of an applicable plan amendment, the sponsor of the defined benefit plan or plans providing for the coordination is treated as having adopted an applicable plan amendment as of the date the coordination begins. In addition, the Secretary of Treasury is directed to issue regulations to prevent the avoidance of the requirements with respect to an applicable plan amendment through the use of two or more plan amendments rather than a single amendment.

[156] ERISA sec. 205(g), Code sec. 417(e). A plan complying with the provision also does not violate certain rules relating to vesting (ERISA sec. 203(a)(2) and Code sec. 411(a)(2)) and the determination of the accrued benefit (in the case of a plan which does not provide for employee contributions) (ERISA sec. 204(c) and Code sec. 411(c)).

is the rate and table specified under the plan for such purposes as of the termination date. For purposes of (2), if the rate of interest is a variable rate, then the rate is the average of such rates during the five-year period ending on the termination date.

Definition of applicable defined benefit plan

An applicable defined benefit plan is a defined benefit plan under which the accrued benefit (or any portion thereof) is calculated as the balance of a hypothetical account maintained for the participant or as an accumulated percentage of the participant's final average compensation. The Secretary of the Treasury is to provide rules which include in the definition of an applicable defined benefit plan any defined benefit plan (or portion of such a plan) which has an effect similar to an applicable defined benefit plan.

No inference

Nothing in the provision is to be construed to infer the treatment of applicable defined benefit plans or conversions to such plans under the rules in ERISA, ADEA and the Code prohibiting age discrimination[157] as in effect before the provision is effective. In addition, no inference is to be drawn with respect to the application of the minimum benefit rules to applicable defined benefit plans before the provision is effective.

Regulations relating to mergers and acquisitions

The Secretary of the Treasury is directed to prescribe regulations for the application of the provisions relating to applicable defined benefit plans in cases where the conversion of a plan to a cash balance or similar plan is made with respect to a group of employees who become employees by reason of a merger, acquisition, or similar treatment. The regulations are to be issued not later than 12 months after the date of enactment.

Effective Date

In general, the provision is effective for periods beginning on or after June 29, 2005.

The provision relating to the minimum value rules is effective for distributions after the date of enactment.

In the case of a plan in existence on June 29, 2005, the interest credit and vesting requirements for an applicable defined benefit plan generally apply to years beginning after December 31, 2007, except that the plan sponsor may elect to have such requirements apply for any period after June 29, 2005, and before the first plan year beginning after December 31, 2007. In the case of a plan maintained pursuant to one or more collective bargaining agreements, a delayed effective date applies with respect to the interest credit and vesting requirements for an applicable defined benefit plan.

The provision relating to conversions of plans applies to plan amendments adopted after and taking effect after June 29, 2005, except that a plan sponsor may elect to have such amendments apply to plan amendments adopted before and taking affect after such date.

The direction to the Secretary of the Treasury to issue regulations relating to mergers and acquisitions is effective on the date of enactment.

[Faster vesting of employer nonelective contributions]

The provision applies the present-law vesting schedule for matching contributions to all employer contributions to defined contribution plans.

The provision does not apply to any employee until the employee has an hour of service after the effective date. In applying the new vesting schedule, service before the effective date is taken into account.

Effective Date

The provision is generally effective for contributions for plan years beginning after December 31, 2006.

In the case of a plan maintained pursuant to one or more collective bargaining agreements, the provision is not effective for contributions (including allocations of forfeitures) for plan years beginning before the earlier of (1) the later of the date on which the last of such collective bargaining agreements terminates (determined without regard to any extension thereof on or after the date of enactment) or January 1, 2007, or (2) January 1, 2009.

In the case of an employee stock ownership plan ("ESOP") which on September 26, 2005, had outstanding a loan incurred for the purpose of acquiring qualifying employer securities, the provision does not apply to any plan year beginning before the earlier of (1) the date on which the loan is fully repaid, or (2) the date on which the loan was, as of September 26, 2005, scheduled to be fully repaid.

[Provisions relating to plan amendments]

A plan amendment made pursuant to the changes made by the bill or regulations issued thereunder, may be retroactively effective and will not violate the anticutback rule, if, in addition to meeting the other applicable requirements, the amendment is made on or before the last day of the first plan year beginning on or after January 1, 2009 (2011 in the case of a governmental plan).

A plan amendment will not be considered to be pursuant to the bill (or applicable regulations) if it has an effective date before the effective date of the provision under the bill (or regulations) to which it relates. Similarly, the provision does not provide relief from the anticutback rule for periods prior to the effective date of the relevant provision (or regulations) or the plan amendment. The Secretary of the Treasury is authorized to provide exceptions to the relief from the prohibition on reductions in accrued benefits. It is intended that the Secretary will not permit inappropriate reductions in contributions or benefits that are not directly related to the provisions under the bill.

Effective Date

The provision is effective on the date of enactment.

[¶ 12,200.04]

Committee Report on P.L. 107-16 (Economic Growth and Tax Relief Reconciliation Act)

[House Committee Report]

Employer may disregard rollover for purposes of cash-out rules

For purposes of the cash-out rule, a plan is permitted to provide that the present value of a participant's nonforfeitable accrued benefit is determined without regard to the portion of such benefit that is attributable to rollover contributions (and any earnings allocable thereto).

Effective Date

The provision is effective for distributions after December 31, 2001.

[Conference Committee Report]

Senate Amendment

The Senate amendment is the same as the House bill.

Conference Agreement

The conference agreement follows the House bill and the Senate amendment.

[¶ 12,200.05]

Committee Report on P.L. 107-16 (Economic Growth and Tax Relief Reconciliation Act)

[House Committee Report]

Treatment of forms of distribution

A defined contribution plan to which benefits are transferred would not be treated as reducing a participant's or beneficiary's accrued benefit even though it does not provide all of the forms of distribution previously available under the transferor plan if (1) the plan receives from another defined contribution plan a direct transfer of the participant's or beneficiary's benefit accrued under the transferor plan, or the plan results from a merger or other transaction that has the effect of a direct transfer (including consolidations of benefits attributable to different employers within a multiple employer plan), (2) the terms of both the transferor plan and the transferee plan authorize the transfer, (3) the transfer occurs pursuant to a voluntary election by the participant or beneficiary that is made after the participant or beneficiary received a notice describing the consequences of making the election, and (4) the transferee plan allows the participant or beneficiary to receive distribution of his or her benefit under the transferee plan in the form of a single sum distribution. The bill does not modify the rules relating to survivor annuities under section 417. Thus, as under present law, a plan that is a transferee of a plan subject to the joint and survivor rules is also subject to those rules.

Except to the extent provided by the Secretary of the Treasury in regulations, a defined contribution plan is not treated as reducing a participant's accrued benefit if (1) a plan amendment eliminates a form of distribution previously available under the plan, (2) a single sum distribution is available to the participant at the same time or times as the form of distribution eliminated by the amendment, and (3) the single sum distribution is based on the same or greater portion of the participant's accrued benefit as the form of distribution eliminated by the amendment.

Furthermore, the provision directs the Secretary of the Treasury to provide by regulations that the prohibitions against eliminating or reducing an early retirement benefit, a retirement-type subsidy, or an optional form of benefit do not apply to plan amendments that eliminate or reduce early retirement benefits, retirement-type subsidies, and optional forms of benefit that create significant burdens and complexities for a plan and its participants, but only if such an amendment does not adversely affect the rights of any participant in more than a de minimis manner.

---

[157] ERISA sec. 204(b)(1)(H), ADEA sec. 4(i)(1), and Code sec. 411(b)(1)(H).

It is intended that the factors to be considered in determining whether an amendment has more than a de minimis adverse effect on any participant would include (1) all of the participant's early retirement benefits, retirement-type subsidies, and optional forms of benefits that are reduced or eliminated by the amendment, (2) the extent to which early retirement benefits, retirement-type subsidies, and optional forms of benefit in effect with respect to a participant after the amendment effective date provide rights that are comparable to the rights that are reduced or eliminated by the plan amendment, (3) the number of years before the participant attains normal retirement age under the plan (or early retirement age, as applicable), (4) the size of the participant's benefit that is affected by the plan amendment, in relation to the amount of the participant's compensation, and (5) the number of years before the plan amendment is effective.

This provision of the bill does not affect the rules relating to involuntary cash outs (sec. 411(a)(11)) or survivor annuity requirements (sec. 417). Accordingly, if a participant is entitled to protections of the joint and survivor rules, those protections may not be eliminated. The intent of the provision authorizing regulations is solely to permit the elimination of early retirement benefits, retirement-type subsidies, or optional forms of benefit that have no more than a de minimis effect on any participant but create disproportionate burdens and complexities for a plan and its participants.

For example, assume the following. Employer A acquires employer B and merges B's defined benefit plan into A's defined benefit plan. The defined benefit plan maintained by B before the merger provides an early retirement subsidy for individuals age 55 with a specified number of years of service. E1 and E2 are were [sic] employees of B and who transfer to A in connection with the merger. E1 is 25 years old and has compensation of $40,000. The present value of E1's early retirement subsidy under B's plan is $75. E2 is 50 years old and also has compensation of $40,000. The present value of E2's early retirement subsidy under B's plan is $10,000.

Assume that A's plan has an early retirement subsidy for individuals who have attained age 50 with a specified number of years of service, but the subsidy is not the same as under B's plan. Under A's plan, the present value of E2's early retirement subsidy is $9,500. Maintenance of both subsidies would create burdens for the plan and complexities for the plan and its participants.

Treasury regulations could permit E1's early retirement subsidy under B's plan to be eliminated entirely (i.e., even if A's plan did not have an early retirement subsidy). Taking into account all relevant factors, including the value of the benefit, E1's compensation, and the number of years until E1 would be eligible to receive the subsidy, the subsidy is de minimis. Treasury regulations could permit E2's early retirement subsidy under B's plan to be eliminated as to be replaced by the subsidy under A's plan, because the difference in the subsidies is de minimis. However, A's subsidy could not be entirely eliminated.

The Secretary is directed to issue, not later than December 31, 2003, final regulations under section 411(d)(6), including regulations required under the provision.

Effective Date

The provision is effective for years beginning after December 31, 2001, except that the direction to the Secretary is effective on the date of enactment.

[Conference Committee Report]

The conference agreement follows the House bill.

[¶ 12,200.06]

Committee Report on P.L. 107-16 (Economic Growth and Tax Relief Reconciliation Act)

[House Committee Report]

Faster vesting of employer matching contributions

The provision applies faster vesting schedules to employer matching contributions. Under the provision, employer matching contributions are required to vest at least as rapidly as under one of the following two alternative minimum vesting schedules. A plan satisfies the first schedule if a participant acquires a nonforfeitable right to 100 percent of employer matching contributions upon the completion of three years of service. A plan satisfies the second schedule if a participant has a nonforfeitable right to 20 percent of employer matching contributions for each year of service beginning with the participant's second year of service and ending with 100 percent after six years of service.

Effective Date

The provision is effective for contributions for plan years beginning after December 31, 2001, with a delayed effective date for plans maintained pursuant to a collective bargaining agreement. The provision does not apply to any employee until the employee has an hour of service after the effective date. In applying the new vesting schedule, service before the effective date is taken into account.

[Conference Committee Report]

Senate Amendment

The Senate amendment is the same as the House bill.

Conference Agreement

The conference agreement follows the House bill and the Senate amendment.

[¶ 12,200.063]

Committee Report on P.L. 102-318 (Unemployment Compensation Amendments of 1992)

For Committee Report on Unemployment Compensation Amendments of 1992 (P.L. 102-318), dealing with rollovers and withholding on nonperiodic pension distributions, see ¶ 11,750.036.

[¶ 12,200.069]

Committee Reports on P.L. 105-34 (Taxpayer Relief Act)

[House Committee Report (Code and Related Non-Code Provisions)]

Cash out of certain accrued benefits.—The bill increases the limit on involuntary cash-outs to $5,000 from $3,500. The $5,000 amount is adjusted annually for inflation beginning after 1997 (in $50 increments).

Effective Date

The provision is effective for plan years beginning on and after the date of enactment.

[Conference Committee Report]

Senate Amendment

The Senate amendment is the same as the House bill, except the Senate amendment also makes a corresponding change to title I of ERISA and provides that the $5,000 amount is adjusted for inflation beginning after 1997 in $50 increments.

Conference Agreement

The conference agreement follows the House bill and the Senate amendment, except that the conference agreement does not increase the $5,000 limit for inflation.

[¶ 12,200.071]

Committee Report on P.L. 104-188 (Small Business Job Protection Act)

Miscellaneous Pension Simplification

[House Committee Report]

Special vesting rule for multiemployer plans eliminated

The bill conforms the vesting rules for multiemployer plans to the rules applicable to other qualified plans.

Effective Date

The provision is effective for plan years beginning on or after the earlier of (1) the later of January 1, 1997, or the date on which the last of the collective bargaining agreements pursuant to which the plan is maintained terminates, or (2) January 1, 1999, with respect to participants with an hour of service after the effective date.

[Conference Committee Report]

Senate Amendment

The Senate amendment is the same as the House bill.

Conference Agreement

The conference agreement follows the House bill and the Senate amendment.

[¶ 12,200.073]

Committee Reports on P.L. 101-239 (Omnibus Budget Reconciliation Act of 1989)

[House Committee Report]

Under the bill, normal retirement age is defined to mean the later of (1) age 65, or (2) the 5th anniversary of the time a plan participant commenced participation in the plan.

[House Committee Report]

Vesting standards

The repeal of class-year vesting was not intended to adversely affect the vesting status of any participant. To fulfill this intent, the bill provides a special rule applicable to plans that after October 22, 1986, used class-year vesting. Whether a plan falls within this category is to be determined without regard to any amendment adopted after October 22, 1986, eliminating class-year vesting.

Plans that fall within the above category are to apply a special rule to any employee that has an hour of service (1) before the adoption of any amendment eliminating class-year vesting, and (2) on or after the first day of the first plan year for which the repeal of class-year vesting is applicable to such employee with respect to the plan. Under this special rule, for the year described in (2) above and any subsequent year, the employee's nonforfeitable right to the employee's accrued benefit derived from employer contributions is to be determined under the class-year vesting schedule that was eliminated if such schedule would yield a larger nonforfeitable right than the new vesting schedule.

In addition, the bill clarifies that a matching contribution is not treated as forfeitable merely because the contribution is forfeitable if the contribution it matches is an excess contribution (sec. 401(k)(8)(B)), an excess deferral (sec. 402(g)(2)(A)), or an excess aggregate contribution (sec. 401(m)(6)(B)).

[Conference Committee Report]

The conference agreement follows the House bill with the following modifications:

* * *

(1) *Repeal of class-year vesting.*—The repeal of class-year vesting was not intended to adversely affect the vesting status of plan participants. The bill contains a special vesting rule to fulfill this intent. The rule applies to any employee who (a) has an hour of service before the adoption of any amendment eliminating class-year vesting, and (b) has an hour of service on or after the first day of the first year for which the repeal of class-year year vesting is applicable to such employee. Under the conference agreement, this special rule is further limited to employees who have not incurred a 5-year break in service immediately before performing the hour of service described in (b). The conference agreement also provides that compliance with this special vesting rule will not result in a violation of the minimum participation rule.

[House Committee Report]

Interest on accumulated contributions.—There has been some uncertainty as to the effect of the Pension Protection Act interest rate rules for employee contributions, and the proper method for determining the accrued benefit derived from employee contributions. In addition, the present-law rules for determining an employee's accrued benefit produce inconsistencies in some cases. In order to resolve these issues, the bill modifies the rules relating to the accrued benefit derived from employee contributions.

The bill provides that, in calculating an employee's accumulated contributions, interest on mandatory contributions is credited (1) for the period up to the date for which the determination is being made at the rate determined under the present-law rules, and (2) for the period beginning with the determination date and ending on the date on which the employee attains normal retirement age, at the interest rate used under the plan in calculating the present value of accrued benefits (sec. 417(e)(3)). The conversion of the employee's contributions (plus interest) to an annuity is calculated using the interest rate used under the plan in determining the present value of accrued benefits (sec. 417(e)(3)).

The bill also eliminates the present-law limitation on the accrued benefit derived from employee contributions.

Some employers may have already amended their plans to conform to the interest rate rule of the Pension Protection Act, or may have adopted a new plan that conforms to such rule. If such plans are amended to conform to the bill, in some cases this might be considered a prohibited reduction in accrued benefits (sec. 411(d)(6)). Accordingly, the bill provides a transition rule that permits such plans to be amended to conform to the new rules without violating the reduction in accrued benefit rules.

[¶ 12,200.075]

Committee Report on P.L. 100-203 (Omnibus Budget Reconciliation Act of 1987)

[Conference Committee Report]

Under the [Labor and Human Resources Committee amendment], the 5-percent rate is replaced by a rate equal to 120 percent of the mid-term applicable Federal rate (AFR) (as in effect for the first [month] of the plan year). The Secretary of the Treasury does not have the authority to alter this rate. The provision is effective on the date of enactment.

The conference agreement follows the Labor and Human Resources Committee amendment, effective for years beginning after December 31, 1987.

[¶ 12,200.08]

Committee Reports on P.L. 99-514 (Tax Reform Act of 1986)

[Senate Committee Report]

Explanation of Provision

In general

The bill provides that a plan is not a qualified plan (except in the case of a multiemployer plan), unless a participant's employer-provided benefit vest[s] at least as rapidly as under one of 2 alternative minimum vesting schedules.

A plan satisfies the first schedule if a participant has a nonforfeitable right to 100 percent of the participant's accrued benefit derived from employer contributions upon the participant's completion of 5 years of service. A plan satisfies the second alternative schedule if a participant has a nonforfeitable right to at least 20 percent of the participant's accrued benefit derived from employer contributions after 3 years of service, 40 percent at the end of 4 years of service, 60 percent at the end of 5 years of service, 80 percent at the end of 6 years of service, and 100 percent at the end of 7 years of service.

Top-heavy plans

The provisions of the bill relating to vesting do not alter the requirements applicable to plans that become top heavy. Thus, a plan that becomes top heavy is required to satisfy one of the two alternative vesting schedules applicable under present law to top-heavy plans.

Class year plans

Under the bill, a plan with class year vesting will not meet the qualification standards of the Code unless, under the plan's vesting schedule, a participant's total accrued benefit becomes nonforfeitable at least as rapidly as under one of the two alternative vesting schedules specified in the bill.

Changes in vesting schedule

Under the bill, if a plan's vesting schedule is modified by plan amendment, the plan will not be qualified unless each participant with no less than 3 years of service is permitted to elect, within a reasonable period after the adoption of the amendment, to have the nonforfeitable percentage of the participant's accrued benefit computed without regard to the amendment.

Multiemployer plans

As an exception to the general vesting requirements, the bill requires that, in the case of a multiemployer plan, a participant's accrued benefit derived from employer contributions be 100 percent vested no later than upon the participant's completion of 10 years of service.

Effective Date

The provisions are generally applicable for plan years beginning after December 31, 1988, with [respect] to participants who perform at least one hour of service in a plan year to which the new provision applies.

A special effective date applies to plans maintained pursuant to a collective bargaining agreement. Under this special rule, in the case of a plan maintained pursuant to a collective bargaining agreement between employee representatives and one or more employers ratified before March 1, 1986, the amendments are not effective for plan years beginning before the earlier of (1) the later of (i) January 1, 1989, or (ii) the date on which the last of the collective bargaining agreements terminates, or (2) January 1, 1991. Extensions or renegotiations of the collective bargaining agreement, if ratified after February 28, 1986, are disregarded.

[Conference Committee Report]

The conference agreement follows the Senate amendment. In addition, the conference agreement modifies the rule permitting an employer to condition participation in a plan on 3 years of service. Under the conference agreement a plan may require, as a condition of participation, that an employee complete a period of service with the employer of no more than two years. A plan that requires that an employee complete more than one year of service as a condition of participation must also provide that each participant in the plan has a nonforfeitable right to 100 percent of the accrued benefit under the plan when the benefit is accrued.

In addition, the conference agreement limits the special rule for multiemployer plans to employees covered by a collective bargaining agreement.

Also, benefits that become vested due to the provisions are to be immediately guaranteed by the PBGC (without regard to the phase-in rule).

The conference agreement also modifies the effective date so that the provision applies to all employees who have one hour of service after the effective date. This revised effective date also applies to the conference agreement modification regarding years of service required for participation.

In addition, the conference agreement limits the delayed effective date for plans maintained pursuant to a collective bargaining agreement to employees covered by such agreements.

[Senate Committee Report]

Withdrawal of mandatory contributions

* * *

Explanation of Provision

Class-year vesting

The bill generally conforms the break-in-service rules applicable to class-year plans to the break-in-service rules provided for other types of plans. Under the bill, a class-year plan generally is to provide that 100 percent of each participating employee's right to benefits derived from employer contributions for a plan year (the contribution year) is to be nonforfeitable as of the close of the fifth plan year of service (whether or not consecutive) with the employer following the contribution year. A plan year is a plan year of service with the employer if the participant has not separated from service with the employer as of the close of the year.

The bill provides that, if a participant incurs five consecutive one-year breaks in service before the completion of five plan years of service with respect to a contribution year, then the plan may provide that the participant forfeits any right to or derived from the employer contributions for the contribution year.

The provision is effective for contributions made for plan years beginning after the date of enactment, except that the provision is not effective with respect to a collectively bargained plan until the applicable effective date of the Act for that plan.

* * *

[Conference Committee Report]

The conference agreement follows the Senate amendment * * *.

[Senate Committee Report]

Cash Out of Certain Accrued Benefits

* * *

Explanation of Provision

The bill clarifies that, for purposes [of] determining whether a participant's benefit exceeds $3,500, the nonvested portion of the participant's accrued benefit is to be disregarded.

The bill would also permit the distribution from an employee stock ownership plan (ESOP) of dividends that are deductible by the employer under section 404(k), without the consent of the participant, or the participant and the participant's spouse even where the present value of the participant's benefit exceeds $3,500.

[¶ 12,200.085]

Committee Reports on P.L. 98-397 (Retirement Equity Act of 1984)

[Senate Committee Report]

Break in service rules.—The bill provides that, in the case of a nonvested participant, years of service with the employer or employers maintaining the plan before any period of consecutive 1-year breaks in service are required to be taken into account after a break in service unless the number of consecutive 1-year breaks in service equals or exceeds the greater of (1) 5 years or (2) the aggregate number of years of service before the consecutive 1-year breaks in service. * * * This "rule of parity" is applicable for participation and vesting purposes.

For example, if a nonvested participant with 3 years of service under a plan terminates employment and incurs 4 consecutive 1-year breaks in service, the plan generally is not permitted to disregard the participant's 3 years of service for either participation or vesting purposes upon the participant's resumption of employment with the employer. On the other hand, if the participant incurs 5 consecutive 1-year breaks in service under this example, the plan could disregard the years of service prior to the break in service.

In addition, the bill provides that, in the case of a participant in a defined contribution plan or in a defined benefit pension plan funded solely by insurance contracts, years of service after a break in service are counted for purposes of determining the vested percentage of the participant's accrued benefit derived from employer contributions before the break in service unless the participant incurs at least 5 consecutive 1-year breaks in service. Under the Bill, a conforming change is made to the rules relating to the cash out of accrued benefits.

[Senate Committee Report]

[The bill provides, as under present law that] if any years of service are not required to be taken into account by reason of a period of breaks in service under [the parity] rule, then those years of service are not required to be taken into account * * * if there is a subsequent break in service.

[Senate Committee Report]

Maternity or paternity leave.—Under the bill, for purposes of determining whether a break in service has occurred for participation and vesting purposes, an individual is deemed to have completed hours of service during certain periods of absence from work. This rule applies to an individual who is absent from work (1) by reason of the pregnancy of the individual, (2) by reason of the birth of a child of the individual, (3) by reason of the placement of a child in connection with the adoption of the child by the individual, or (4) for purposes of caring for the child during the period immediately following the birth or placement for adoption.

The committee intends that an individual will qualify for this maternity or paternity leave credit if a child is placed with the individual for a trial period prior to adoption. No credit need be given, however, merely by reason of the placement of a child in a foster home.

During the period of absence, the individual is treated as having completed (1) the number of hours that normally would have been credited but for the absence, or (2) if the normal work hours are unknown, eight hours of service for each normal workday during the leave (whether or not approved). The total number of hours of service required to be treated as completed under the bill is 501 hours.

The hours of service required to be credited under the bill must be credited only (1) in the year in which the absence begins for one of the permitted reasons if the crediting is necessary to prevent a break in service in that year, or (2) in the following year. For example, an individual who completes at least 501 hours during a year before leaving employment by reason of pregnancy or who is otherwise entitled to credit for up to 501 hours during the year is entitled to credit of up to 501 hours in the next year, because such credit is not needed in the year in which the absence begins.

Under the bill, an individual is not entitled to credit for maternity or paternity leave unless the absence from work is for one of the permitted reasons. For example, suppose that an individual was absent from work on account of a layoff, gave birth to a child two years after the layoff began, and was not recalled to work. Under these circumstances, the individual is not entitled to credit for maternity or paternity leave because the absence from work was not for one of the permitted reasons. On the other hand, if the employer had recalled the individual immediately prior to the birth of the child, the individual would be entitled to credit for maternity or paternity leave.

An employer may require, as a condition of providing credit for the hours required under this rule, that the individual certify to the employer that the leave was taken for the permitted reasons. This certification could be required to include, for example, a statement from a doctor that the leave was taken by reason of the birth of a child of the individual. In addition, the employer may require that the individual supply information relating to the number of normal workdays for which there was an absence. The committee intends that credit will not be denied for failure to supply any required information if the plan administrator has access to the relevant information without regard to whether the participant submits it.

Under the bill, hours credited under these rules for maternity or paternity leave are not required to be taken into account for purposes of determining a participant's year of participation under the benefit accrual rules.

The bill provides that, if the present value of an accrued benefit exceeds $3,500, then the benefit is not to be considered nonforfeitable if the plan provides that the present value of the benefit can be immediately distributed without the consent of the participant (and, if applicable, the participant's spouse). Under the bill, the interest rate to be used in determining whether the present value of a benefit exceeds $3,500 is not to be greater than the interest rate that would be used (as of the date of the distribution) by the Pension Benefit Guaranty Corporation (PBGC) for purposes of determining the present value of a lump sum distribution upon termination of the plan. The committee intends that the PBGC rate in effect at the beginning of the plan year may be used throughout the plan year if the plan so provides.

[¶ 12,200.09]

Committee Report on P.L. 96-364 (Multiemployer Pension Plan Amendments Act of 1980)

[Senate Committee Report]

Minimum vesting requirements

Present law

Under present law, benefits under a plan which are vested may be forfeited only (1) in the case of death, (2) where benefits are suspended upon reemployment, (3) in the case of certain retroactive plan amendments which reduce benefits, or (4) in the case of certain withdrawals of mandatory employee contributions. Also, under present law, with certain very limited exceptions, all of a participant's years of service with an employer must be taken into account for vesting purposes.

Reason for change

The changes made under the reorganization provisions and the provisions relating to the definition of multiemployer plan require conforming changes in the ERISA rules relating to vesting.

Explanation of provisions

In general.—The bill provides for additional circumstances under which vested benefits under a multiemployer plan, which are nonforfeitable under present law, could be forfeited. The bill provides that certain of a participant's years of service with an employer, currently taken into account for vesting purposes, could be disregarded in the case of a multiemployer plan. In addition, the bill conforms the vesting provisions of ERISA to changes in other parts of the bill.

Cessation of contributions under a multiemployer plan.—Under the bill, a multiemployer plan does not fail to meet the vesting requirements of ERISA merely because the plan provides for the forfeiture of accrued benefits attributable to service with a participant's employer before the employer is required to contribute to the plan in the event that the employer ceases making contributions to the plan.

Reduction and suspension of benefits.—Under the bill, a multiemployer plan does not fail to meet the vesting requirements of ERISA merely because benefits payments under the plan, other than basic benefits, are suspended in the event of plan insolvency.

Authority to disregard service after withdrawal or plan termination.—Under the bill, if an employer completely withdraws from a multiemployer plan, a participant's years of service with the employer completed after the withdrawal would not be required to be taken into account in determining the participant's vested percentage in the accrued benefits under the plan. This rule applies to certain partial withdrawals involving the decertification of the employee representative only to the extent permitted in regulations prescribed by the Secretary of the Treasury.

Also, under the bill, if a multiemployer plan terminates for purposes of termination insurance, an employee's years of service completed after the date of termination are not required to be taken into account in determining a participant's vested percentage in his accrued benefits under the plan.

Effective Date

This provision of the bill applies on the date of enactment.

[¶ 12,200.10]

Committee Report on P.L. 93-406 (Employee Retirement Income Security Act of 1974)

[Conference Committee Explanation]

Plans subject to the provisions; exceptions from coverage; exemption for church plans.—The rules in these areas are the same as the corresponding rules discussed above under Participation and Coverage.

General rules.—Under the conference substitute[1] plans must provide full and immediate vesting in benefits derived from employee contributions.

With respect to employer contributions, the plan (except class year plans) must meet one of three alternative standards. Two of those, the 5-to 15-year graded standard and the 10-year/100-percent standard are the same as provided in the House bill (and briefly described above). The third standard under the conference substitute is a modification of the House-bill "rule of 45". As under the House rule, under the modified rule of 45, an employee with 5 or more years of covered service must be at least 50 percent vested when the sum of his age and years of covered service total 45, and there must be provision for at least 10 percent additional vesting for each year of covered service thereafter. Unlike the House bill, however, each employee with 10 years of covered service (regardless of his age) must be at least 50 percent vested and there must be provision for 10 percent additional vesting for each year of service thereafter.

In addition, all plans would have to meet the requirement of present law that an employee must be 100 percent vested in his accrued benefit when he attains the normal or stated retirement age (or actually retires).

Service credited for vesting purposes.—Generally, under the conference substitute, once an employee becomes eligible to participate in a pension plan, all his years of service with an employer (including pre-participation service, and service performed before the effective day of the Act) are to be taken into account for purposes of determining his place on the vesting schedule. However, the plan may ignore periods for which the employee declined to make mandatory contributions, and periods for which the employer did not maintain the plan or a predecessor plan, as defined in Treasury regulations (i.e., if the plan provides past service credits for purposes of benefit accrual, it must also provide past service credits for purposes of participation and vesting).

Generally, the plan may also ignore service performed before the age 22; however, if a plan elects to use the rule of 45, service before age 22 may be ignored only if the employee was not a participant in the plan during the years before age 22.

The plan may also exclude part-time or seasonal service (i.e., generally years when the employee had less than 1,000 hours of service).

Also, if the employee has had a "break in service", his service performed prior to the break may be ignored to the extent permitted under the "break in service" rules (discussed below).

Service performed prior to January 1, 1971, may be ignored by the plan, unless (and until) the employee has at least 3 years of service after December 31, 1970.

* * *

Breaks in service.—Under the conference substitute, a 1-year break in service occurs in any calendar year, plan year, or other consecutive 12-month period designated by the plan and applied on a consistent basis (and not prohibited under Labor Department regulations) in which the employee has no more than 500 hours of service. For example, if the plan is on a calendar year basis, and the employee works 1,000 hours in 1976, 501 hours in 1977, 501 hours in 1978, and 1,000 hours or more in 1979, the employee would not have a break in service (although the plan would not be required to accrue benefits or give vesting schedule credit for 1977 or 1978).

The rules with respect to breaks in service for vesting and benefit accrual purposes may be summarized as follows:

(1) If an employee has a 1-year break in service, the plan may require (for administrative reasons) a 1-year waiting period before his pre-break and post-break service must be aggregated under the plan. However, once the employee has completed this waiting period, he must receive credit for that year (for purposes of vesting and accrued benefit).

(2) In the case of an individual account plan (including a plan funded solely by individual insurance contracts, as well as a "target benefit plan") if any employee has a 1-year break in service, his vesting percentage in pre-break benefit accruals does not have to be increased as a result of post-break service.

(3) Subject to rules (1) and (2), once an employee has achieved any percentage of vesting, then all of his pre-break and post-break service must be aggregated for all purposes.

(4) For all nonvested employees (and subject to rules (1) and (2)), the employee would not lose credits for pre-break service until his period of absence equaled his years of covered service. Under this "rule of parity," for example, if a nonvested employee had three years of service with the employer, and then had a break in service of 2 years, he could return, and after fulfilling his 1-year reentry requirement, he would have 4 years of covered service, because his pre-break and post-break service would be aggregated.[2]

For years beginning prior to the effective date of the vesting provisions, a plan may apply the break-in-service rules provided under the plan, as in effect from time to time. However, no plan amendment made after January 1, 1974, may provide for break-in-service rules which are less beneficial to any employee than the rules in effect under the plan on that date, unless the amendment complies with the break-in-service rules established under this bill.

The principles of some of the rules outlined above may be illustrated as follows: For example, assume a plan is on a calendar year basis, and an employee with a 1-year break in service reenters employment on November 1, 1976, works 200 hours in 1976, and 1,700 hours by November 1, 1977. In this case, the employee would be eligible to reenter the plan on November 1, 1977, his pre-break and post-break service would be aggregated, he would advance one year on the vesting schedule for 1977, and he would also accrue benefits for 1977. On the other hand, if the employee reentered employment on March 1, 1976, worked 1,700 hours before December 31, 1976, and was not separated from service by March 1, 1977, he would be eligible to reenter the plan on March 1, 1977, advance one year on the vesting schedule for his 1976 service, and the plan would have to provide at least a partial benefit accrual for 1976.

Predecessor employer.—The rules concerning service with a predecessor employer are the same for purposes of vesting and benefit accrual as the rules for purposes of participation, discussed above.

Multiemployer plans.—Under the conference substitute, service with any employer, for any year in which the employer is a member of the plan, is to be counted for purposes of vesting as if all employers who are parties to the plan were a single employer.

Permitted forfeitures of vested rights.—Under the conference substitute, except as outlined below, an employee's rights, once vested, are not to be forfeitable for any reason. An employee's rights to benefits attributable to his own contributions may never be forfeited.

(1) The plan may provide that an employee's vested rights to benefits attributable to employer contributions may be forfeited on account of the employee's death (unless a "joint and survivor" annuity is to be provided).

(2) Also, the plan may provide that payment of benefits attributable to employer contributions may be suspended for any period in which the employee is reemployed by the same employer under whose plan the benefits are being paid (in the case of a single employer plan). In the case of a multiemployer plan, however, a suspension of benefit payments is permitted when the employee is employed in the same industry, in the same trade or craft and also in the same geographical area covered under the contract, as was the case immediately

---

[1] Unless otherwise indicated, the rules with respect to vesting appear in both title I and title II of the conference substitute. Unless otherwise indicated, the regulations with respect to vesting are to be written by the Secretary of the Treasury, or his delegate.

[2] Also, in the case of a defined benefit plan, the employee would have at least 3 years of accrued benefits under the plan (2 years of accrued benefits due to his pre-break participation and 1 year of benefits accrued with respect to the 1 year reentry period).

before he retired. Regulations with respect to the suspension of benefits are to be prescribed by the Department of Labor.

(3) A plan amendment may reduce an employee's vested or nonvested accrued benefit attributable to employer contributions, but only for the current year, and only if the amendment is adopted within 2 ½ months from the close of the plan year in question (without regard to any extensions). In the case of a multiemployer plan, the retroactive amendment may effect [sic] the current year, and the two immediately preceding years (thus, a multiemployer plan amendment adopted by December 31, 1978, could effect [sic] plan benefits for 1976, if the plan was on a calendar year). However, no plan amendment which reduces accrued benefits is permitted unless the Secretary of Labor has 90 days prior notice of the proposed amendment, and approves it (or fails to disapprove it). No such approval is to be granted, except to prevent substantial economic hardship, including a serious danger that the plan will be terminated unless the amendment is allowed. In addition, it must be found that the economic hardship cannot be overcome by means of funding variance. Subject to these rules, no plan amendment may retroactively reduce the accrued benefit of any participant (whether or not that benefit is vested).

(4) A plan may provide that an employee's rights to benefits from employer contributions may be forfeited where the employee is less than 50 percent vested in these benefits and withdraws all or any part of his own mandatory contributions to the plan. However, the plan must also provide a "buy back" rule, i.e., that the employee's forfeited benefits will be fully restored if the employee repays the withdrawn contributions (with interest of 5-percent per annum, compounded annually) to the plan.

In the case of a plan which does not provide for mandatory contributions after the date of enactment [September 2, 1974], the plan may provide, in this case, that the employee will forfeit a proportionate part of his pre-date-of-enactment accrued benefits derived from employer contributions even if he is 50 percent or more vested in these benefits. Also, the plan is not required to have a "buy back" clause with respect to the withdrawal of preenactment contributions. Additional regulations in this area are to be prescribed by the Secretary of the Treasury, or his delegate.

(5) A plan may provide for the "cash out" of an employee's accrued benefit. In other words, the plan may pay out, in a lump sum, the entire value of an employee's vested accrued benefit. (However, portability is available to the employee because other provisions of the bill permit the employee to reinvest in an individual retirement account on a tax-sheltered basis.) If the plan does make such a cash-out, then the plan would not be required to vest the employee in his accrued benefits which are not vested at the time he separates from the service, if the employee is later reemployed. However, the employee's pre-break service would have to be taken into account for all other purposes, subject to the break-in-service rules, e.g., for purposes of his place on the vesting schedule.)

A cash-out could be made from the plan without the employee's consent only if the payment (a) was made due to the termination of the employee's participation in the plan, (b) constituted the value of the employee's entire interest in the plan, and (c) did not exceed an amount (to be prescribed in regulations by the Secretary of the Treasury or his delegate), based on the reasonable administrative needs of the plan, and, in any event, not in excess of $1,750 (with respect to the value of the benefit attributable to the employer's contributions). Despite the foregoing provisions, generally, the conferees prefer that all amounts contributed for retirement purposes be retained and used for those purposes. Thus, a plan could provide for no cash-out, or the employee's collective bargaining unit might wish to bargain for such a provision.

A higher cash-out could be made with the employee's consent. However, even these voluntary cash-outs could only be made if the employee terminated his participation in the plan, or under other circumstances to be prescribed in regulations.

Moreover, the plan must provide, in all cases (except where a distribution equal to the value of the full accrued benefit is made), that all accrued benefits must be fully restored (except to the extent provided under the break-in-service rules) if the employee repays the amount of the cash-out, with interest. Repayment of an involuntary cash-out would have to be allowed under the plan at any time after the employee reentered employment under the plan, and repayment of voluntary cash-outs would have to be allowed under circumstances to be prescribed in regulations. However, an individual account plan would not be required to permit repayment after the employee had a one year break in service.

Accrued benefit.—Under the conference substitute, the term "accrued benefit" refers to pension or retirement benefits. The term does not apply to ancillary benefits, such as payment of medical expenses (or insurance premiums for such expenses), or disability benefits which do not exceed the normal retirement benefit payable at age 65 to an employee with comparable service under the plan, or to life insurance benefits payable as a lump sum.

Also, the accrued benefit does not include the value of the right to receive early retirement benefits, or the value of social security supplements or other benefits under the plan which are not continued for any employee after he has attained normal retirement age. However, an accrued benefit may not be reduced on account of increasing age or service (except to the extent of social security supplements or their equivalents).

In the case of a plan other than a defined benefit plan, the accrued benefit is to be the balance in the employee's individual account.

In the case of a defined benefit plan, the accrued benefit is to be determined under the plan, subject to certain requirements. In general, the accrued benefit is to be defined in terms of the benefit payable at normal retirement age. Normal retirement age generally is to be the age specified under the plan. However, it may not be later than age 65 or the tenth anniversary of the time the participant commenced participation, whichever last occurs. No actuarial adjustment of the accrued benefit would be required, however, if an employer voluntarily postponed his own retirement. For example, if the plan provided a benefit of $400 a month payable at age 65, this same $400 a month benefit (with no upward adjustment) could also be paid by the plan to an individual who voluntarily retired at age 68.

Each defined benefit plan is to be required to satisfy one of three accrued benefit tests (which limit the extent of "back-loading" permitted under the plan).

The three percent test.—Under this alternative each participant must accrue, for each year of participation, at least 3 percent of the benefit which is payable under the plan to a participant who begins participation at the earliest possible entry age and serves continuously until age 65, or normal retirement age under the plan, whichever is earlier. This test is to be applied on a cumulative basis (i.e., any amount of "front loading" is permitted). Also, in the case of a plan amendment, the test would be cumulative. For example, assume that a plan provided a flat benefit of $200 a month payable at age 65 during the first 10 years of an individual's participation, then [was] amended to provide a flat benefit of $400 a month; the participant's accrued benefit at the end of his 11th year of participation would equal $132 (3 percent of $400, times 11 years of service.)

In addition, if a plan elects this alternative, and if the plan provides a given benefit to a person who is employed when he attains retirement age, who has a given amount of service, then any employee who has that amount of service, even though he leaves before retirement age, would be entitled to this same benefit when he reaches retirement age. For example, if the plan is based on compensation and provides a 40 percent of salary benefit for an employee who served at least 20 years and is still employed at age 65, then the plan must provide that an employee who served 20 years from age 35 to age 55 would be entitled to that same 40 percent of compensation benefit (beginning at normal retirement age or age 65).

133 ⅓ percent test.—Under this alternative, the plan is to qualify if the accrual rate for any participant for any later year is not more than 133 ⅓ percent of his accrual rate for the current year. Thus, (unlike the House bill) the conference substitute permits an unlimited amount of "front loading" under this test. The accrual rate can be based on either a dollar or percentage rate. In applying these rules, a plan amendment in effect for the current year is to be treated as though it were in effect for all plan years. (For example, if a plan provides a one percent rate of accrual for all participants in 1976, and is amended to provide a 2 percent rate of accrual for all participants in 1977, the plan will meet this test, even though 2 is more than 1 ⅓ times 1). Also, if the plan has a scheduled increase in the rate of accruals, which will not be in effect for any participant until future years, this scheduled increase will not be taken into account for purposes of the backloading rules until it actually takes effect. Also, in applying the 133 ⅓ percent test, social security benefits and all other factors used to compute benefits under the plan will be treated as remaining constant, at current year levels, for all future years.

Pro rata rule.—As a third alternative, the conference substitute contains a modified version of the rule contained in the Senate amendment. Under this test, for purposes of determining the accrued benefit, the retirement benefit is to be computed as though the employee continued to earn the same rate of compensation annually that he had earned during the years which would have been taken into account under the plan (but not in excess of 10), had the employee retired on the date in question. This amount is then to be multiplied by a fraction, the numerator of which is the employee's total years of active participation in the plan up to the date when the computation is being made, and the denominator of which is the total number of years of active participation he would have had if he continued his employment until normal retirement age. This test is cumulative in the sense that unlimited front loading is permitted. For purposes of this test social security benefits and all other relevant factors used to compute benefits shall be treated as remaining constant at current year levels for all future years. Also for purposes of this rule the term "normal retirement age" would be defined as set forth above, and the test would apply only to the benefit payable at, or after, normal retirement age (i.e., it would not take account of subsidized early retirement (to the extent such a benefit does not exceed the benefit payable at normal retirement age) and social security supplements).[3]

---

[3] For example, assume a social security offset plan providing a benefit equal to 2 percent of high-3 years compensation per year of service with the employer, minus 30 percent of the primary social security benefit, with a normal retirement age of 65. Assume also an employee who began employment at age 25, and terminated employment at age 45, 100 percent vested, with high-3 years pay of $19,000, $20,000, and $21,000. At the time the employee separates from service the primary social security benefit payable to him at age 65 (under the social security law as [sic] effect when he terminates) would be $6,000 if he continued to work with the employer at his same annual rate of compensation until normal retirement age. His accrued benefit under the plan would equal $7,100. (If the employee had remained in service until age 65, he would have 40 years service, times 2 percent per year (80 percent), times $20,000 average high-3 years compensation ($16,000), minus 30 percent of the $6,000 primary social security benefit payable to the employee at age 65 under then current law ($16,000 minus $1,800 equals $14,200) times 20/40ths (20 years of service over 40 total years from age 25 to age 65) equals $7,100.)

In the case of a plan amendment, the rule would work as follows. Assume an individual begins participation at age 25 in a plan which provides 1 percent of high-three-years pay during his first 10 years of service. In the 11th year the plan amends to provide 2 percent of pay for all future years of service. The employee separates from service at the end of the 11th year (and is 100 percent vested). His accrued benefit would equal 19.25 percent of average high-three-years pay (10 (years of participation) times 1 percent per

A plan is not to be treated as failing to meet the tests solely because the accrual of benefits under the plan does not become effective until the employee has two continuous years of service, measured from the anniversary date of employment.

In the case of a plan funded exclusively through the purchase of insurance contracts, the accrued benefit is to be the cash surrender value of the contract (determined as though the funding requirements with respect to the plan had been fully satisfied).

In the case of a variable annuity plan, the accrued benefit is to be determined in accordance with regulations to be prescribed by the Secretary of the Treasury or his delegate.

Benefits accrued in the past.—Generally, the vesting rules of the conference substitute are to apply to all accrued benefits, including those which accrued before the effective date of the provisions (subject, however, to the break-in-service rules discussed above). However, many plans now in existence have no accrued benefit formula for the past, thus making it impossible in these cases to determine what the employee is vested in. To deal with this situation, the conference substitute provides that the accrued benefit under a plan for years prior to the effective date of the vesting provisions for any participant is to be not less than the greater of (1) the accrued benefit under the provisions of the plan (as in effect from time to time), or (2) an accrued benefit which is not less than one-half of the benefit which would have accrued under one of the three back-loading tests described above.

The plan may choose which of the 3 standards it wishes to apply for the past (subject to the antidiscrimination rules); however, the same standard must be applied to all the plan's participants on a consistent basis. The plan is not required to choose, for the past, the same test which it applies in the future.

Changes in vesting schedule.—The conference substitute provides that if, at any time in the future, the plan changes its vesting schedule, the vesting percentage for each participant in his accrued benefit accumulated to the date when the plan amendment is adopted (or the date the amendment becomes effective, if later) cannot be reduced as a result of the amendment. In addition, as a further protection for long service employees, any participant with at least 5 years of service may elect to remain under the pre-amendment vesting schedule with respect to all of his benefits accrued both before and after the plan amendment.

Allocations between employee and employer contributions.—The House bill and the Senate amendment are quite similar in the rules they apply in allocating contributions between those made by the employee and the employer and the conference substitute follows the House bill as to technical matters in the case of this provision. In addition, the substitute makes a clarifying amendment which provides (in the case of a defined benefit plan), that the accrued benefit attributable to employee contributions can never be less than the sum of those contributions (computed without interest). This assures that the employee will at least be vested in his own contributions to the plan, on a dollar-for-dollar basis. (Thus, for example, in the case of an individual insurance contract, employer contributions to the plan must at least absorb the load factor, but, of course, payment of the load factor by the employer would not cause the plan to be treated as a plan which was not funded solely through the purchase of insurance contracts.

Discrimination.—Under the conference substitute the rules of the House bill are adopted with respect to the relationship of the minimum vesting standards of the bill to the antidiscrimination rules of present law (sec. 401(a)(4) of the Internal Revenue Code). In general, a plan which meets the vesting requirements provided in this substitute is not to be considered as discriminatory, insofar as its vesting provisions are concerned, unless there is a pattern of abuse under the plan (such as the firing of employees before their accrued benefits vest) or there has been (or there is reason to believe there will be) an accrual of benefits or forfeitures tending to discriminate in favor of employees who are officers, shareholders or who are highly compensated.

In the past, however, the law in this area has been administered on a case-by-case basis, without uniform results in fact situations of a similar nature. As a result, except in cases where actual misuse of the plan occurs in operation, the Internal Revenue Service is directed not to require a vesting schedule more stringent than 40 percent vesting after 4 years of employment with 5 percent additional vesting for each of the next 2 years, and 10 percent additional vesting for each of the following five years. Also, this more rapid vesting would generally not be required except in a case where the rate of likely turnover for officers, shareholders, or highly compensated employees was substantially less (perhaps as much as 50 percent less) than the rate of likely turnover for rank-and-file employees. Of course, where there is a pattern of firing employees to avoid vesting, the limitations described above would not apply. Also, it generally is not intended that any plan (or successor plan of a now existing plan) which is presently under a more rapid vesting schedule should be permitted to cut back its vesting schedule as a result of this statement.

In addition, the conferees have directed the joint pension task force study group to examine problems of the interrelationship of the vesting and the antidiscrimination rules carefully. The conferees also expect the Treasury or the Internal Revenue Service to supply information with respect to patterns of benefit loss for different categories of plans (as designated by the task force) under the minimum vesting schedules prescribed under this legislation, and such other information as the task force study group may require. In other words, the experimental rules outlined above (40 percent vesting after 4 years, etc.) are intended to apply only until the responsible congressional committees can review the situation after receiving the report of the task force study group. [See 1974 Pension Reform Act Sec. 3022 at CCH ¶ 79,261.]

Moreover, the conferees intend that the antidiscrimination rules of present law in areas other than the vesting schedule are not to be changed. Thus, the present antidiscrimination rules with respect to coverage, and with respect to contributions and benefits are to remain in effect. Also, the antidiscrimination rules may be applied with respect to benefit accruals.

The conference substitute contains a technical rule to be applied in the case of target benefit plans (and other defined contribution plans), which provides that regulations may establish reasonable earnings assumptions and other factors for these plans in order to prevent discrimination.

Plan termination.—Under the conference substitute, as under present law, all accrued benefits in a qualified pension plan must become fully vested (in accordance with the rules of the bill concerning allocation of assets upon plan termination and to the extent then funded) in the event of a plan termination, or the complete discontinuance of contributions under the pension plan. Under the substitute, this rule is no longer to apply to cases where employers have not made contributions to plans covered under the funding requirements of the bill, because the bill reaches this problem by imposing an excise tax on underfunding. However, the rule of full immediate vesting is still to apply in the case of a termination, or partial termination of a plan, and in the case of the discontinuance of contributions to plans which are not subject to the new funding requirements (e.g., profit-sharing plans, church plans, and government plans). Also, the substitute contains a provision to make clear that the vesting requirements under the bill are not intended to operate to overturn rules which require that, in the event of plan termination, the benefits under the plan are not be distributed in a manner that discriminates in favor of officers, shareholders, or highly compensated employees.

Class year plans.—Under the substitute, the minimum vesting requirements are satisfied in the case of a class year plan if the plan provides for 100 percent vesting of the benefits derived from employer contributions within 5 years after the end of the plan year for which the contributions were made. Also, under the substitute forfeitures with respect to employer contributions would be permitted on a class-year-by-class-year basis, for any year for which the employee withdraws his own mandatory contributions to the plan, if he is less than 50 percent vested with respect to that year. For purposes of these rules, withdrawals will be applied to the earliest year for which the employee has made contributions which have not yet been withdrawn.

Recordkeeping requirements.—Under the conference substitute, in the case of a single employer plan, the employee, once each year, is to be entitled to request his plan administrator to furnish a statement as to his vesting and accrued benefit status. A similar statement is to be supplied automatically when a vested employee terminates his coverage under the plan. In the case of multiemployer plans, the recordkeeping and information supplying duties are to be performed by the plan administrator and, to the maximum extent practicable (in light of their different circumstances), multiemployer plans are to meet the same standards in this area as single employer plans (in accordance with regulations to be prescribed by the Secretary of Labor or his delegate).

[Code Sec. 412]

[¶ 12,250.023]

Committee Report on P.L. 109-280 (Pension Protection Act of 2006)

[Joint Committee on Taxation Report]

[Minimum funding standards for single-employer defined benefit pension plans]

Interest rate required for plan years beginning in 2006 and 2007

For plan years beginning after December 31, 2005, and before January 1, 2008, the provision applies the present-law funding rules, with an extension of the interest rate applicable in determining current liability for plan years beginning in 2004 and 2005. Thus, in determining current liability for funding purposes for plan years beginning in 2006 and 2007, the interest rate used must be within the permissible range (90 to 100 percent) of the weighted average of the rates of interest on amounts invested conservatively in long-term investment-grade corporate bonds during the four-year period ending on the last day before the plan year begins.

Funding rules for plan years beginning after 2007 - in general

For plan years beginning after December 31, 2007, in the case of single-employer defined benefit plans, the provision repeals the present-law funding rules (including the requirement that a funding standard account be maintained) and provides a new set of rules for determining minimum required contribu-

(Footnote Continued)

year, 30 (years of projected participation) times 2 percent per year, times 11/40ths (11 years of participation over 40 total years between age 25 and age 65)).

tions.[23] Under the provision, the minimum required contribution to a single-employer defined benefit pension plan for a plan year generally depends on a comparison of the value of the plan's assets with the plan's funding target and target normal cost. As described in more detail below, under the provision, credit balances generated under present law are carried over (into a "funding standard carryover balance") and generally may be used in certain circumstances to reduce otherwise required minimum contributions. In addition, as described more fully below, contributions in excess of the minimum contributions required under the provision for plan years beginning after 2007 generally are credited to a prefunding balance that may be used in certain circumstances to reduce otherwise required minimum contributions. To facilitate the use of such balances to reduce minimum required contributions, while avoiding use of such balances for more than one purpose, in some circumstances the value of plan assets is reduced by the prefunding balance and/or the funding standard carryover balance.

The minimum required contribution for a plan year, based on the value of plan assets (reduced by any prefunding balance and funding standard carryover balance) compared to the funding target, is shown in the following table:

If:	The minimum required contribution is:
the value of plan assets (reduced by any prefunding balance and funding standard carryover balance) is less than the funding target,	the sum of: (1) target normal cost; (2) any shortfall amortization charge; and (3) any waiver amortization charge.
the value of plan assets (reduced by any prefunding balance and funding standard carryover balance) equals or exceeds the funding target,	the target normal cost, reduced (but not below zero) by the excess of (1) the value of plan assets (reduced by any prefunding balance and funding standard carryover balance), over (2) the funding target.

Under the provision, a plan's funding target is the present value of all benefits accrued or earned as of the beginning of the plan year. A plan's target normal cost for a plan year is the present value of benefits expected to accrue or be earned during the plan year. A shortfall amortization charge is generally the sum of the amounts required to amortize any shortfall amortization bases for the plan year and the six preceding plan years. A shortfall amortization base is generally required to be established for a plan year if the plan has a funding shortfall for a plan year.[24] A shortfall amortization base may be positive or negative, i.e., an offsetting amortization base is established for gains. In general, a plan has a funding shortfall if the plan's funding target for the year exceeds the value of the plan's assets (reduced by any prefunding balance and funding standard carryover balance). A waiver amortization charge is the amount required to amortize a waived funding deficiency.

The provision specifies the interest rates and mortality table that must be used in determining a plan's target normal cost and funding target, as well as certain other actuarial assumptions, including special assumptions ("at-risk" assumptions) for a plan in at-risk status. A plan is in at-risk status for a year if the value of the plan's assets (reduced by any prefunding and funding standard carryover balances) for the preceding year was less than (1) 80 percent of the plan's funding target determined without regard to the at-risk assumptions, and (2) 70 percent of the plan's funding target determined using the at-risk assumptions. Under a transition rule, instead of 80 percent, the following percentages apply: 65 percent for 2008, 70 percent for 2009, and 75 percent for 2010.

Target normal cost

Under the provision, the minimum required contribution for a plan year generally includes the plan's target normal cost for the plan year. A plan's target normal cost is the present value of all benefits expected to accrue or be earned under the plan during the plan year (the "current" year). For this purpose, an increase in any benefit attributable to services performed in a preceding year by reason of a compensation increase during the current year is treated as having accrued during the current year.

If the value of a plan's assets (reduced by any funding standard carryover balance and prefunding balance) exceeds the plan's funding target for a plan year, the minimum required contribution for the plan year is target normal cost reduced by such excess (but not below zero).

Funding target and shortfall amortization charges

In general

If the value of a plan's assets (reduced by any funding standard carryover balance and prefunding balance) is less than the plan's funding target for a plan year, so that the plan has a funding shortfall,[25] the minimum required contribution is generally increased by a shortfall amortization charge. As discussed more fully below, the shortfall amortization charge is the aggregate total (not less than zero) of the shortfall amortization installments for the plan year with respect to any shortfall amortization bases for the plan year and the six preceding plan years.

Funding target

A plan's funding target for a plan year is the present value of all benefits accrued or earned under the plan as of the beginning of the plan year. For this purpose, all benefits (including early retirement or similar benefits) are taken into account. Benefits accruing in the plan year are not taken into account in determining the plan's funding target, regardless of whether the valuation date for the plan year is later than the first day of the plan year.[26]

Shortfall amortization charge

The shortfall amortization charge for a plan year is the aggregate total (not less than zero) of the shortfall amortization installments for the plan year with respect to any shortfall amortization bases for that plan year and the six preceding plan years. The shortfall amortization installments with respect to a shortfall amortization base for a plan year are the amounts necessary to amortize the shortfall amortization base in level annual installments over the seven-plan-year period beginning with the plan year. The shortfall amortization installment with respect to a shortfall amortization base for any plan year in the seven-year period is the annual installment determined for that year for that shortfall amortization base. Shortfall amortization installments are determined using the appropriate segment interest rates (discussed below).

Shortfall amortization base and phase-in of funding target

A shortfall amortization base is determined for a plan year based on the plan's funding shortfall for the plan year. The funding shortfall is the amount (if any) by which the plan's funding target for the year exceeds the value of the plan's assets (reduced by any funding standard carryover balance and prefunding balance).

The shortfall amortization base for a plan year is (1) the plan's funding shortfall, minus (2) the present value, determined using the segment interest rates (discussed below), of the aggregate total of the shortfall amortization installments and waiver amortization installments that have been determined for the plan year and any succeeding plan year with respect to any shortfall amortization bases and waiver amortization bases for preceding plan years.

A shortfall amortization base may be positive or negative, depending on whether the present value of remaining installments with respect to prior year amortization bases is more or less than the plan's funding shortfall. In either case, the shortfall amortization base is amortized over seven years. Shortfall amortization installments for a particular plan year with respect to positive and negative shortfall amortization bases are netted in determining the shortfall amortization charge for the plan year, but the resulting shortfall amortization charge cannot be less than zero. Thus, negative amortization installments may not offset waiver amortization installments or normal cost.

Under a special rule, a shortfall amortization base does not have to be established for a plan year if the value of a plan's assets (reduced by any prefunding balance, but only if the employer elects to use any portion of the prefunding balance to reduce required contributions for the year) is at least equal to the plan's funding target for the plan year. For purposes of the special rule, a transition rule applies for plan years beginning after 2007 and before 2011. The transition rule does not apply to a plan that (1) is not in effect for 2007, or (2) is subject to the present-law deficit reduction contribution rules for 2007 (i.e., a plan covering more than 100 participants and with a funded current liability below the applicable threshold).

Under the transition rule, a shortfall amortization base does not have to be established for a plan year during the transition period if the value of plan assets (reduced by any prefunding balance, but only if the employer elects to use the prefunding balance to reduce required contributions for the year) for the plan year is at least equal to the applicable percentage of the plan's funding target for the year. The applicable percentage is 92 percent for 2008, 94 percent for 2009, and 96 percent for 2010. However, the transition rule does not apply to a plan for any plan year after 2008 unless, for each preceding plan year after 2007, the plan's shortfall amortization base was zero (i.e., the plan was eligible for the special rule each preceding year).

Early deemed amortization of funding shortfalls for preceding years

If a plan's funding shortfall for a plan year is zero (i.e., the value of the plan's assets, reduced by any funding standard carryover balance and prefunding

[23] A delayed effective date applies to certain plans as discussed in Items C, D and E below. Changes to the funding rules for multiemployer plans are discussed in Title II below. Governmental plans and church plans continue to be exempt from the funding rules to the extent provided under present law.

[24] Under a special rule, discussed below, a shortfall amortization base does not have to be established if the value of a plan's assets (reduced by any prefunding balance, but only if the employer elects to use any portion of the prefunding balance to reduce required contributions for the year) is at least equal to the plan's funding target for the plan year.

[25] Under a special rule, in determining a plan's funding shortfall, the value of plan assets is not reduced by any funding standard carryover balance or prefunding balance if, with respect to the funding standard carryover balance or prefunding balance, there is in effect for the year a binding written with the Pension Benefit Guaranty Corporation which provides that such balance is not available to reduce the minimum required contribution for the plan year.

[26] Benefits accruing during the plan year are taken into account in determining normal cost for the plan year.

balance, is at least equal to the plan's funding target for the year), any shortfall amortization bases for preceding plan years are eliminated. That is, for purposes of determining any shortfall amortization charges for that year and succeeding years, the shortfall amortization bases for all preceding years (and all shortfall amortization installments determined with respect to such bases) are reduced to zero.

Waiver amortization charges

The provision retains the present-law rules under which the Secretary of the Treasury may waive all or a portion of the contributions required under the minimum funding standard for a plan year (referred to as a "waived funding deficiency").[27] If a plan has a waived funding deficiency for any of the five preceding plan years, the minimum required contribution for the plan year is increased by the waiver amortization charge for the plan year.

The waiver amortization charge for a plan year is the aggregate total of the waiver amortization installments for the plan year with respect to any waiver amortization bases for the five preceding plan years. The waiver amortization installments with respect to a waiver amortization base for a plan year are the amounts necessary to amortize the waiver amortization base in level annual installments over the five-year plan period beginning with the succeeding plan year. The waiver amortization installment with respect to that waiver amortization base for any plan year in the five-year period is the annual installment determined for the shortfall amortization base. Waiver amortization installments are determined using the appropriate segment interest rates (discussed below). The waiver amortization base for a plan year is the amount of the waived funding deficiency (if any) for the plan year.

If a plan's funding shortfall for a plan year is zero (i.e., the value of the plan's assets, reduced by any funding standard carryover balance and prefunding balance, is at least equal to the plan's funding target for the year), any waiver amortization bases for preceding plan years are eliminated. That is, for purposes of determining any waiver amortization charges for that year and succeeding years, the waiver amortization bases for all preceding years (and all waiver amortization installments determined with respect to such bases) are reduced to zero.

Actuarial assumptions used in determining a plan's target normal cost and funding target

Interest rates

The provision specifies the interest rates that must be used in determining a plan's target normal cost and funding target. Under the provision, present value is determined using three interest rates ("segment" rates), each of which applies to benefit payments expected to be made from the plan during a certain period. The first segment rate applies to benefits reasonably determined to be payable during the five-year period beginning on the first day of the plan year; the second segment rate applies to benefits reasonably determined to be payable during the 15-year period following the initial five-year period; and the third segment rate applies to benefits reasonably determined to be payable the end of the 15-year period. Each segment rate is a single interest rate determined monthly by the Secretary of the Treasury on the basis of a corporate bond yield curve, taking into account only the portion of the yield curve based on corporate bonds maturing during the particular segment rate period.

The corporate bond yield curve used for this purpose is to be prescribed on a monthly basis by the Secretary of the Treasury and reflect the average, for the 24-month period ending with the preceding month, of yields on investment grade corporate bonds with varying maturities and that are in the top three quality levels available. The yield curve should reflect the average of the rates on all bonds in the top three quality levels on which the yield curve is based.

The Secretary of the Treasury is directed to publish each month the corporate bond yield curve and each of the segment rates for the month. In addition, such Secretary is directed to publish a description of the methodology used to determine the yield curve and segment rates, which is sufficiently detailed to enable plans to make reasonable projections regarding the yield curve and segment rates for future months, based on a plan's projection of future interest rates.

Under the provision, the present value of liabilities under a plan is determined using the segment rates for the "applicable month" for the plan year. The applicable month is the month that includes the plan's valuation date for the plan year, or, at the election of the plan sponsor, any of the four months preceding the month that includes the valuation date. An election of a preceding month applies to the plan year for which it is made and all succeeding plan years unless revoked with the consent of the Secretary of the Treasury.

Solely for purposes of determining minimum required contributions, in lieu of the segment rates described above, an employer may elect to use interest rates on a yield curve based on the yields on investment grade corporate bonds for the month preceding the month in which the plan year begins (i.e., without regard to the 24-month averaging described above). Such an election may be revoked only with consent of the Secretary of the Treasury.

The provision provides a transition rule for plan years beginning in 2008 and 2009 (other than for plans first effective after December 31, 2007). Under this rule, for plan years beginning in 2008, the first, second, or third segment rate with respect to any month is the sum of: (1) the product of the segment rate otherwise determined for the month, multiplied by 33-1/3 percent; and (2) the product of the applicable long-term corporate bond rate,[28] multiplied by 66-2/3 percent. For plan years beginning in 2009, the first, second, or third segment rate with respect to any month is the sum of: (1) the product of the segment rate otherwise determined for the month, multiplied by 66-2/3 percent; and (2) the product of applicable long-term corporate bond rate multiplied by 33-1/3 percent. An employer may elect not to have the transition rule apply with respect to a plan. Such an election may be revoked only with consent of the Secretary of the Treasury.

Under the provision, certain amounts are determined using the plan's "effective interest rate" for a plan year. The effective interest rate with respect to a plan for a plan year is the single rate of interest which, if used to determine the present value of the benefits taken into account in determining the plan's funding target for the year, would result in an amount equal to the plan's funding target (as determined using the first, second, and third segment rates).

Mortality table

Under the provision, the Secretary of the Treasury is directed to prescribe by regulation the mortality tables to be used in determining present value or making any computation under the funding rules.[29] Such tables are to be based on the actual experience of pension plans and projected trends in such experience. In prescribing tables, the Secretary is to take into account results of available independent studies of mortality of individuals covered by pension plans. In addition, the Secretary is required (at least every 10 years) to revise any table in effect to reflect the actual experience of pension plans and projected trends in such experience.

The provision also provides for the use of a separate mortality table upon request of the plan sponsor and approval by the Secretary of the Treasury in accordance with procedures described below. In order for the table to be used: (1) the table must reflect the actual experience of the pension plans maintained by the plan sponsor and projected trends in general mortality experience, and (2) there must be a sufficient number of plan participants, and the pension plans must have been maintained for a sufficient period of time, to have credible information necessary for that purpose. A separate mortality table can be a mortality table constructed by the plan's enrolled actuary from the plan's own experience or a table that is an adjustment to the table prescribed by the Secretary which sufficiently reflects the plan's experience. Except as provided by the Secretary, a separate table may not be used for any plan unless (1) a separate table is established and used for each other plan maintained by the plan sponsor and, if the plan sponsor is a member of a controlled group, each member of the controlled group,[30] and (2) the requirements for using a separate table are met with respect to the table established for each plan, taking into account only the participants of that plan, the time that plan has been in existence, and the actual experience of that plan. In general, a separate plan may be used during the period of consecutive year plan years (not to exceed 10) specified in the request. However, a separate mortality table ceases to be in effect as of the earlier of (1) the date on which there is a significant change in the participants in the plan by reason of a plan spinoff or merger or otherwise, or (2) the date on which the plan actuary determines that the table does not meet the requirements for being used.

A plan sponsor must submit a separate mortality table to the Secretary for approval at least seven months before the first day of the period for which the table is to be used. A mortality table submitted to the Secretary for approval is treated as in effect as of the first day of the period unless the Secretary, during the 180-day period beginning on the date of the submission, disapproves of the table and provides the reasons that the table fails to meet the applicable criteria. The 180-day period is to be extended upon mutual agreement of the Secretary and the plan sponsor.

Other assumptions

Under the provision, in determining any present value or making any computation, the probability that future benefits will be paid in optional forms of benefit provided under the plan must be taken into account (including the probability of lump-sum distributions determined on the basis of the plan's experience and other related assumptions). The assumptions used to determine optional forms of benefit under a plan may differ from the assumptions used to determine present value for purposes of the funding rules under the provision. Differences in the present value of future benefit payments that result from the different assumptions used to determine optional forms of benefit under a plan must be taken into account in determining any present value or making any computation for purposes of the funding rules.

The provision generally does not require other specified assumptions to be used in determining the plan's target normal cost and funding target except in the case of at-risk plans (discussed below). However, similar to present law, the determination of present value or other computation must be made on the basis of actuarial assumptions and methods, each of which is reasonable (taking into

[27] In the case of single-employer plans, the provision repeals the present-law rules under which the amortization period applicable to an unfunded past service liability or loss may be extended.

[28] The applicable long-term corporate bond rate is a rate that is from 90 to 100 percent of the weighted average of the rates of interest on amounts invested conservatively in long-term investment-grade corporate bonds during the four-year period ending on the last day before the plan year begins as determined by the Secretary under the method in effect for 2007.

[29] As under present law, separate mortality tables are required to be used with respect to disabled participants.

[30] For example, the Secretary may deem it appropriate to provide an exception in the case of a small plan.

account the experience of the plan and reasonable expectations), and which, in combination, offer the actuary's best estimate of anticipated experience under the plan.[31]

Special assumptions for at-risk plans

The provision applies special assumptions ("at-risk" assumptions) in determining the funding target and normal cost of a plan in at-risk status. Whether a plan is in at-risk status for a plan year depends on its funding target attainment percentage for the preceding year. A plan's funding target attainment percentage for a plan year is the ratio, expressed as a percentage, that the value of the plan's assets (reduced by any funding standard carryover balance and prefunding balance) bears to the plan's funding target for the year. For this purpose, the plan's funding target is determined using the actuarial assumptions for plans that are not at-risk.

Under the provision, a plan is in at-risk status for a year if, for the preceding year: (1) the plan's funding target attainment percentage, determined without regard to the at-risk assumptions, was less than 80 percent (with a transition rule discussed below), and (2) the plan's funding target attainment percentage, determined using the at-risk assumptions (without regard to whether the plan was in at-risk status for the preceding year), was less than 70 percent. Under a transition rule applicable for plan years beginning in 2008, 2009, and 2010, instead of 80 percent, the following percentages apply: 65 percent for 2008, 70 percent for 2009, and 75 percent for 2010. In the case of plan years beginning in 2008, the plan's funding target attainment percentage for the preceding plan year may be determined using such methods of estimation as the Secretary of Treasury may provide.

Under the provision, the at-risk rules do not apply if a plan had 500 or fewer participants on each day during the preceding plan year. For this purpose, all defined benefit pension plans (other than multiemployer plans) maintained by the same employer (or a predecessor employer), or by any member of such employer's controlled group, are treated as a single plan, but only participants with respect to such employer or controlled group member are taken into account.

If a plan is in at-risk status, the plan's funding target and normal cost are determined using the assumptions that: (1) all employees who are not otherwise assumed to retire as of the valuation date, but who will be eligible to elect benefits in the current and 10 succeeding years, are assumed to retire at the earliest retirement date under plan, but not before the end of the plan year; and (2) all employees are assumed to elect the retirement benefit available under the plan at the assumed retirement age that results in the highest present value. In some cases, a loading factor also applies.

The at-risk assumptions are not applied to certain employees of specified automobile manufacturers for purposes of determining whether a plan is in at-risk status, i.e., whether the plan's funding target attainment percentage, determined using the at-risk assumptions, was less than 70 percent for the preceding plan year. An employee is disregarded for this purpose if: (1) the employee is employed by a specified automobile manufacturer; (2) the employee is offered, pursuant to a bona fide retirement incentive program, a substantial amount of additional cash compensation, substantially enhanced retirement benefits under the plan, or materially reduced employment duties, on the condition that by a specified date no later than December 31, 2010, the employee retires (as defined under the terms of the plan; (3) the offer is made during 2006 pursuant to a bona fide retirement incentive program and requires that the offer can be accepted no later than a specified date (not later than December 31, 2006); and (4) the employee does not accept the offer before the specified date on which the offer expires. For this purpose, a specified automobile manufacturer is (1) any automobile manufacturer and (2) any manufacturer of automobile parts that supplies parts directly to an automobile manufacturer and which, after a transaction or series of transactions ending in 1999, ceased to be a member of the automobile manufacturer's controlled group.

The funding target of a plan in at-risk status for a plan year is generally the sum of: (1) the present value of all benefits accrued or earned as of the beginning of the plan year, determined using the at-risk assumptions described above, and (2) in the case of a plan that has also been in at-risk status for at least two of the four preceding plans years, a loading factor. The loading factor is the sum of (1) $700 times the number of participants in the plan, plus (2) four percent of the funding target determined without regard to the loading factor.[32] The at-risk funding target is in no event less than the funding target determined without regard to the at-risk rules.

The target normal cost of a plan in at-risk status for a plan year is generally the sum of: (1) the present value of benefits expected to accrue or be earned under the plan during the plan year, determined using the special assumptions described above, and (2) in the case of a plan that has also been in at-risk status for at least two of the four preceding plans years, a loading factor of four percent of the target normal cost determined without regard to the loading factor.[33] The at-risk target normal is in no event less than at-risk normal cost determined without regard to the at-risk rules.

If a plan has been in at-risk status for fewer than five consecutive plan years, the amount of a plan's funding target for a plan year is the sum of: (1) the amount of the funding target determined without regard to the at-risk rules, plus (2) the transition percentage for the plan year of the excess of the amount of the funding target determined under the at-risk rules over the amount determined without regard to the at-risk rules. Similarly, if a plan has been in at-risk status for fewer than five consecutive plan years, the amount of a plan's target normal cost for a plan year is the sum of: (1) the amount of the target normal cost determined without regard to the at-risk rules, plus (2) the transition percentage for the plan year of the excess of the amount of the target normal cost determined under the at-risk rules over the amount determined without regard to the at-risk rules. The transition percentage is the product of 20 percent times the number of consecutive plan years for which the plan has been in at-risk status. In applying this rule, plan years beginning before 2008 are not taken into account.

Funding standard carryover balance or prefunding balance

In general

The provision preserves credit balances that have accumulated under present law (referred to as "funding standard carryover balances"). In addition, for plan years beginning after 2007, new credit balances (referred to as "prefunding balances") result if an employer makes contributions greater than those required under the new funding rules. In general, under the bill, employers may choose whether to count funding standard carryover balances and prefunding balances in determining the value of plan assets or to use the balances to reduce required contributions, but not both. In this regard, the provision provides more favorable rules with respect to the use of funding standard carryover balances.

Under the provision, if the value of a plan's assets (reduced by any prefunding balance) is at least 80 percent of the plan's funding target (determined without regard to the at-risk rules) for the preceding plan year,[34] the plan sponsor may elect to credit all or a portion of the funding standard carryover balance or prefunding balance against the minimum required contribution for the current plan year (determined after any funding waiver), thus reducing the amount that must be contributed for the current plan year.

The value of plan assets is generally reduced by any funding standard carryover balance or prefunding balance for purposes of determining minimum required contributions, including a plan's funding shortfall, and a plan's funding target attainment percentage (discussed above). However, the plan sponsor may elect to permanently reduce a funding standard carryover balance or prefunding balance, so that the value of plan assets is not required to be reduced by that amount in determining the minimum required contribution for the plan year. Any reduction of a funding standard carryover balance or prefunding balance applies before determining the balance that is available for crediting against minimum required contributions for the plan year.

Funding standard carryover balance

In the case of a single-employer plan that is in effect for a plan year beginning in 2007 and, as of the end of the 2007 plan year, has a positive balance in the funding standard account maintained under the funding rules as in effect for 2007, the plan sponsor may elect to maintain a funding standard carryover balance. The funding standard carryover balance consists of a beginning balance in the amount of the positive balance in the funding standard account as of the end of the 2007 plan year, decreased (as described below) and adjusted to reflect the rate of net gain or loss on plan assets.

For subsequent years (i.e., as of the first day of each plan year beginning after 2008), the funding standard carryover balance of a plan is decreased (but not below zero) by the sum of: (1) any amount credited to reduce the minimum required contribution for the preceding plan year, plus (2) any amount elected by the plan sponsor as a reduction in the funding standard carryover balance (thus reducing the amount by which the value of plan assets must be reduced in determining minimum required contributions).

Prefunding balance

The plan sponsor may elect to maintain a prefunding balance, which consists of a beginning balance of zero for the 2008 plan year, increased and decreased (as described below) and adjusted to reflect the rate of net gain or loss on plan assets.

For subsequent years, i.e., as of the first day of plan year beginning after 2008 (the "current" plan year), the plan sponsor may increase the prefunding balance by an amount, not to exceed (1) the excess (if any) of the aggregate total employer contributions for the preceding plan year, over (2) the minimum required contribution for the preceding plan year. For this purpose, any excess contribution for the preceding plan year is adjusted for interest accruing for the periods between the first day of the current plan year and the dates on which the excess contributions were made, determined using the effective interest rate of the plan for the preceding plan year and treating contributions as being first used to satisfy the minimum required contribution.

---

[31] The provision retains the present-law rule under which certain changes in actuarial assumptions that decrease the liabilities of an underfunded single-employer plan must be approved by the Secretary of the Treasury.

[32] This loading factor is intended to reflect the cost of purchasing group annuity contracts in the case of termination of the plan.

[33] Target normal cost for a plan in at-risk status does not include a loading factor of $700 per plan participant.

[34] In the case of plan years beginning in 2008, the percentage for the preceding plan year may be determined using such methods of estimation as the Secretary of Treasury may provide.

The amount by which the aggregate total employer contributions for the preceding plan year exceeds the minimum required contribution for the preceding plan year is reduced (but not below zero) by the amount of contributions an employer would need to make to avoid a benefit limitation that would otherwise be imposed for the preceding plan year under the provisions of the provision relating to benefit limitations for single-employer plans.[35] Thus, contributions needed to avoid a benefit limitation do not result in an increase in the plan's prefunding balance.[36]

As of the first day of each plan year beginning after 2008, the prefunding balance of a plan is decreased (but not below zero) by the sum of: (1) any amount credited to reduce the minimum required contribution for the preceding plan year, plus (2) any amount elected by the plan sponsor as a reduction in the prefunding balance (thus reducing the amount by which the value of plan assets must be reduced in determining minimum required contributions). As discussed above, if any portion of the prefunding balance is used to reduce a minimum required contribution, the value of plan assets must be reduced by the prefunding balance in determining whether a shortfall amortization base must be established for the plan year (i.e., whether the value of plan assets for a plan year is less than the plan's funding target for the plan year). Thus, the prefunding balance may not be included in the value of plan assets in order to avoid a shortfall amortization base for a plan year and also used to reduce the minimum required contribution for the same year.

Other rules

In determining the prefunding balance or funding standard carryover balance as of the first day of a plan year, the plan sponsor must adjust the balance in accordance with regulations prescribed by the Secretary of the Treasury to reflect the rate of return on plan assets for the preceding year. The rate of return is determined on the basis of the fair market value of the plan assets and must properly take into account, in accordance with regulations, all contributions, distributions, and other plan payments made during the period.

To the extent that a plan has a funding standard carryover balance of more than zero for a plan year, none of the plan's prefunding balance may be credited to reduce a minimum required contribution, nor may an election be made to reduce the prefunding balance for purposes of determining the value of plan assets. Thus, the funding standard carryover balance must be used for these purposes before the prefunding balance may be used.

Any election relating to the prefunding balance and funding standard carryover balance is to be made in such form and manner as the Secretary of the Treasury prescribes.

Other rules and definitions

Valuation date

Under the provision, all determinations made with respect to minimum required contributions for a plan year (such as the value of plan assets and liabilities) must be made as of the plan's valuation date for the plan year. In general, the valuation date for a plan year must be the first day of the plan year. However, any day in the plan year may be designated as the plan's valuation date if, on each day during the preceding plan year, the plan had 100 or fewer participants.[37] For this purpose, all defined benefit pension plans (other than multiemployer plans) maintained by the same employer (or a predecessor employer), or by any member of such employer's controlled group, are treated as a single plan, but only participants with respect to such employer or controlled group member are taken into account.

Value of plan assets

Under the provision, the value of plan assets is generally fair market value. However, the value of plan assets may be determined on the basis of the averaging of fair market values, but only if such method: (1) is permitted under regulations; (2) does not provide for averaging of fair market values over more than the period beginning on the last day of the 25th month preceding the month in which the plan's valuation date occurs and ending on the valuation date (or similar period in the case of a valuation date that's not the first day of a month); and (3) does not result in a determination of the value of plan assets that at any time is less than 90 percent or more than 110 percent of the fair market value of the assets at that time. Any averaging must be adjusted for contributions and distributions as provided by the Secretary of the Treasury.

If a required contribution for a preceding plan year is made after the valuation date for the current year, the contribution is taken into account in determining the value of plan assets for the current plan year. For plan years beginning after 2008, only the present value of the contribution is taken into account, determined as of the valuation date for the current plan year, using the plan's effective interest rate for the preceding plan year. In addition, any required contribution for the current plan year is not taken into account in determining the value of plan assets. If any contributions for the current plan year are made before the valuation date, plan assets as of the valuation date does not include (1) the contributions, and (2) interest on the contributions for the period between the date of the contributions and the valuation date, determined using the plan's effective interest rate for the current plan year.

Timing rules for contributions

As under present law, the due date for the payment of a minimum required contribution for a plan year is generally 8½ months after the end of the plan year. Any payment made on a date other than the valuation date for the plan year must be adjusted for interest accruing at the plan's effective interest rate for the plan year for the period between the valuation date and the payment date. Quarterly contributions must be made during a plan year if the plan had a funding shortfall for the preceding plan year (that is, if the value of the plan's assets, reduced by the funding standard carryover balance and prefunding balance, was less than the plan's funding target for the preceding plan year).[38] If a quarterly installment is not made, interest applies for the period of underpayment at the rate of interest otherwise applicable (i.e., the plan's effective interest rate) plus 5 percentage points.

Excise tax on failure to make minimum required contributions

The provision retains the present-law rules under which an employer is generally subject to an excise tax if it fails to make minimum required contributions and fails to obtain a waiver from the IRS.[39] The excise tax is 10 percent of the aggregate unpaid minimum required contributions for all plan years remaining unpaid as of the end of any plan year. In addition, a tax of 100 percent may be imposed if any unpaid minimum required contributions remain unpaid after a certain period.

Conforming changes

The provision makes various technical and conforming changes to reflect the new funding requirements.

Effective Date

The extension of the interest rate applicable in determining current liability for plan years beginning in 2004 and 2005 is effective for plan years beginning after December 31, 2005, and before January 1, 2008. The modifications to the single-employer plan funding rules are effective for plan years beginning after December 31, 2007.

[Extension of replacement of 30-year treasury rates]

The provisions relating to extension of the replacement of the 30-year Treasury rate for purposes of single-employer funding rules are described above, under Title I. The provision relating to extension of the replacement of the 30-year Treasury rate for PBGC premium purposes is described below, under Title IV.

[Special rules for multiple-employer plans of certain cooperatives]

The provision provides a delayed effective date for the new single-employer plan funding rules in the case of a plan that was in existence on July 26, 2005, and was an eligible cooperative plan for the plan year including that date. The new funding rules do not apply with respect to such a plan for plan years beginning before the earlier of: (1) the first plan year for which the plan ceases to be an eligible cooperative plan, or (2) January 1, 2017. In addition, in applying the present-law funding rules to an eligible cooperative plan to such a plan for plan years beginning after December 31, 2007, and before the first plan year for which the new funding rules apply, the interest rate used is the interest rate applicable under the new funding rules with respect to payments expected to be made from the plan after the 20-year period beginning on the first day of the plan year (i.e., the third segment rate under the new funding rules).

A plan is treated as an eligible cooperative plan for a plan year if it is maintained by more than one employer and at least 85 percent of the employers are: (1) certain rural cooperatives;[52] or (2) certain cooperative organizations that are more than 50-percent owned by agricultural producers or by cooperatives owned by agricultural producers, or organizations that are more than 50-percent owned, or controlled by, one or more such cooperative organizations. A plan is also treated as an eligible cooperative plan for any plan year for which it is maintained by more than one employer and is maintained by a rural telephone cooperative association.

Effective Date

The provision is effective on the date of enactment.

---

[35] Any contribution that may be taken into account in satisfying the requirement to make additional contributions with respect to more than one type of benefit limitation is taken into account only once for purposes of this reduction.

[36] The benefit limitations are discussed in Part B below.

[37] In the case of a plan's first plan year, the ability to use a valuation date other than the first day of the plan year is determined by taking into account the number of participants the plan is reasonably expected to have on each day during that first plan year.

[38] The provision retains the present-law rules under which the amount of any quarterly installment must be sufficient to cover any liquidity shortfall.

[39] The provision retains the present-law rules under which a lien in favor of the plan with respect to property of the employer (and members of the employer's controlled group) arises in certain circumstances in which the employer fails to make required contributions.

[52] This is as defined in Code section 401(k)(7)(B) without regard to (iv) thereof and includes (1) organizations engaged primarily in providing electric service on a mutual or cooperative basis, or engaged primarily in providing electric service to the public in its service area and which is exempt from tax or which is a State or local government, other than a municipality; (2) certain civic leagues and business leagues exempt from tax 80 percent of the members of which are described in (1); (3) certain cooperative telephone companies; and (4) any organization that is a national association of organizations described above.

[Temporary relief for certain PBGC settlement plans]

The provision agreement provides a delayed effective date for the new single-employer plan funding rules in the case of a plan that was in existence on July 26, 2005, and was a "PBGC settlement plan" as of that date. The new funding rules do not apply with respect to such a plan for plan years beginning before January 1, 2014. In addition, in applying the present-law funding rules to a such a plan for plan years beginning after December 31, 2007, and before January 1, 2014, the interest rate used is the interest rate applicable under the new funding rules with respect to payments expected to be made from the plan after the 20-year period beginning on the first day of the plan year (i.e., the third segment rate under the new funding rules).

Under the provision, the term "PBGC settlement plan" means a single-employer defined benefit plan: (1) that was sponsored by an employer in bankruptcy proceedings giving rise to a claim by the PBGC of not greater than $150 million, and the sponsorship of which was assumed by another employer (not a member of the same controlled group as the bankrupt sponsor) and the PBGC's claim was settled or withdrawn in connection with the assumption of the sponsorship; or (2) that, by agreement with the PBGC, was spun off from a plan subsequently terminated by the PBGC in an involuntary termination.

Effective Date

The provision is effective on the date of enactment.

[Special rules for plans of certain government contractors]

The provision provides a delayed effective date for the new single-employer plan funding rules in the case of an eligible government contractor plan. The new funding rules do not apply with respect to such a plan for plan years beginning before the earliest of: (1) the first plan year for which the plan ceases to be an eligible government contractor plan, (2) the effective date of the Cost Accounting Standards Pension Harmonization Rule, and (3) the first plan year beginning after December 31, 2010. In addition, in applying the present-law funding rules to a such a plan for plan years beginning after December 31, 2007, and before the first plan year for which the new funding rules apply, the interest rate used is the interest rate applicable under the new funding rules with respect to payments expected to be made from the plan after the 20-year period beginning on the first day of the plan year (i.e., the third segment rate under the new funding rules).

Under the provision, a plan is treated as an eligible government contractor plan if it is maintained by a corporation (or member of the same affiliated group): (1) whose primary source of revenue is derived from business performed under contracts with the United States that are subject to the Federal Acquisition Regulations and also to the Defense Federal Acquisition Regulation Supplement; (2) whose revenue derived from such business in the previous fiscal year exceeded $5 billion; and (3) whose pension plan costs that are assignable under those contracts are subject to certain provisions of the Cost Accounting Standards.

The provision also requires the Cost Accounting Standards Board, not later than January 1, 2010, to review and revise the relevant provisions of the Cost Accounting Standards to harmonize minimum contributions required under ERISA of eligible government contractor plans and government reimbursable pension plan costs. Any final rule adopted by the Cost Accounting Standards Board shall be deemed the Cost Accounting Standards Pension Harmonization Rule.

Effective Date

The provision is effective on the date of enactment.

[Special funding rules for plans maintained by commercial airlines]

In general

The provision provides special funding rules for certain eligible plans. For purposes of the provision, an eligible plan is a single-employer defined benefit pension plan sponsored by an employer that is a commercial passenger airline or the principal business of which is providing catering services to a commercial passenger airline.

The plan sponsor of an eligible plan may make one of two alternative elections. In the case of a plan that meets certain benefit accrual and benefit increase restrictions, an election allowing a 17-year amortization of the plan's unfunded liability is available. A plan that does not meet such requirements may elect to use a 10-year amortization period in amortizing the plan's shortfall amortization base for the first taxable year beginning in 2008.

Election for plans that meet benefit accrual and benefit increase restriction requirements

In general

Under the provision, if an election of a 17-year amortization period is made with respect to an eligible plan for a plan year (an "applicable" plan year), the minimum required contribution is determined under a special method.[97] If minimum required contributions as determined under the provision are made: (1) for an applicable plan year beginning before January 1, 2008 (for which the present-law funding rules apply), the plan does not have an accumulated funding deficiency; and (2) for an applicable plan year beginning on or after January 1, 2008 (for which the funding rules under the provision apply), the minimum required contribution is the contribution determined under the provision.

The employer may select either a plan year beginning in 2006 or 2007 as the first plan year to which the election applies. The election applies to such plan year and all subsequent plan years, unless the election is revoked with the approval of the Secretary of the Treasury. The election must be made (1) no later than December 31, 2006, in the case of an election for a plan year beginning in 2006, or (2) not later than December 31, 2007, in the case of a plan year beginning in 2007. An election under the provision must be made in such manner as prescribed by the Secretary of the Treasury. The employer may change the plan year with respect to the plan by specifying a new plan year in the election. Such a change in plan year does not require approval of the Secretary of the Treasury.

Determination of required contribution

Under the provision, the minimum required contribution for any applicable plan year during the amortization period is the amount required to amortize the plan's unfunded liability, determined as of the first day of the plan year, in equal annual installments over the remaining amortization period. For this purpose, the amortization period is the 17-plan-year period beginning with the first applicable plan year. Thus, the annual amortization amount is redetermined each year, based on the plan's unfunded liability at that time and the remainder of the amortization period. For any plan years beginning after the end of the amortization period, the plan is subject to the generally applicable minimum funding rules (as provided under the bill, including the benefit limitations applicable to underfunded plans). The plan's prefunding balance and funding standard carryover balance as of the first day of the first year beginning after the end of the amortization period is zero.[98]

Any waived funding deficiency as of the day before the first day of the first applicable plan year is deemed satisfied and the amount of such waived funding deficiency must be taken into account in determining the plan's unfunded liability under the provision. Any plan amendment adopted to satisfy the benefit accrual restrictions of the provision (discussed below) or any increase in benefits provided to such plan's participants under a defined contribution or multiemployer plan will not be deemed to violate the prohibition against benefit increases during a waiver period.[99]

For purposes of the provision, a plan's unfunded liability is the unfunded accrued liability under the plan, determined under the unit credit funding method. As under present law, minimum required contributions (including the annual amortization amount) under the provision must be determined using actuarial assumptions and methods, each of which is reasonable (taking into account the experience of the plan and reasonable expectations), or which, in the aggregate, result in a total plan contribution equivalent to a contribution that would be obtained if each assumption and method were reasonable. The assumptions are required also to offer the actuary's best estimate of anticipated experience under the plan. Under the election, a rate of interest of 8.85 percent is used in determining the plan's accrued liability. The value of plan assets used must be the fair market value.

If any applicable plan year with respect to an eligible plan using the special method includes the date of enactment of the provision and a plan was spun off from such eligible plan during the plan year, but before the date of enactment, the minimum required contribution under the special method for the applicable plan year is an aggregate amount determined as if the plans were a single plan for that plan year (based on the full 12-month plan year in effect prior to the spin off). The employer is to designate the allocation of the aggregate amount between the plans for the applicable plan year.

Benefit accrual and benefit increase restrictions

Benefit accrual restrictions.—Under the provision, effective as of the first day of the first applicable plan year and at all times thereafter while an election under the provision is in effect, an eligible plan must include two accrual restrictions. First, the plan must provide that, with respect to each participant: (1) the accrued benefit, any death or disability benefit, and any social security supplement are frozen at the amount of the benefit or supplement immediately before such first day; and (2) all other benefits under the plan are eliminated. However, such freezing or elimination of benefits or supplements is required only to the extent that it would be permitted under the anticutback rule if implemented by a plan amendment adopted immediately before such first day.

Second, if an accrued benefit of a participant has been subject to the limitations on benefits under section 415 of the Code and would otherwise be increased if such limitation is increased, the plan must provide that, effective as of the first day of the first applicable plan year (or, if later, the date of enactment) any such increase will not take effect. The plan does not fail to meet the anticutback rule solely because the plan is amended to meet this requirement.

[97] Any charge or credit in the funding standard account determined under the present-law rules or any prefunding balance or funding standard carryover balance (determined under the funding provisions of the bill) as of the end of the last year preceding the first applicable year is reduced to zero.

[98] If an election to use the special method is revoked before the end of the amortization period, the plan is subject to the generally applicable minimum funding rules beginning with the first plan year for which the election is revoked, and the plan's prefunding balance as of the beginning of that year is zero.

[99] ERISA sec. 304(b); Code sec. 412(f).

Benefit increase restriction.—No applicable benefit increase under an eligible plan may take effect at any time during the period beginning on July 26, 2005, and ending on the day before the first day of the first applicable plan year. For this purpose, an applicable benefit increase is any increase in liabilities of the plan by plan amendment (or otherwise as specified by the Secretary) which would occur by reason of: (1) any increase in benefits; (2) any change in the accrual of benefits; or (3) any change in the rate at which benefits become nonforfeitable under the plan.

Exception for imputed disability service.—The benefit accrual and benefit increase restrictions do not apply to any accrual or increase with respect to imputed serviced provided to a participant during any period of the participant's disability occurring on or after the effective date of the plan amendment providing for the benefit accrual restrictions (on or after July 26, 2005, in the case of benefit increase restrictions) if the participant was: (1) was receiving disability benefits as of such date or (2) was receiving sick pay and subsequently determined to be eligible for disability benefits as of such date.

Rules relating to PBGC guarantee and plan terminations

Under the provision, if a plan to which an election applies is terminated before the end of the 10-year period beginning on the first day of the first applicable plan year, certain aspects of the PBGC guarantee provisions are applied as if the plan terminated on the first day of the first applicable plan year. Specifically, the amount of guaranteed benefits payable by the PBGC is determined based on plan assets and liabilities as of the assumed termination date. The difference between the amount of guaranteed benefits determined as of the assumed termination date and the amount of guaranteed benefits determined as of the actual termination date is to be paid from plan assets before other benefits.

The provision of the bill under which defined benefit plans that are covered by the PBGC insurance program are not taken into account in applying the overall limit on deductions for contributions to combinations of defined benefit and defined contribution plans, does not apply to an eligible plan to which the special method applies. Thus, the overall deduction limit applies.

In the case of notice required with respect to an amendment that is made to an eligible plan maintained pursuant to one or more collective bargaining agreements in order to comply with the benefit accrual and benefit increase restrictions under the provision, the provision allows the notice to be provided 15 days before the effective date of the plan amendment.

Termination premiums

If a plan terminates during the five-year period beginning on the first day of the first applicable plan year, termination premiums are imposed at a rate of $2,500 per participant (in lieu of the present-law $1,250 amount). The increased termination premium applies notwithstanding that a plan was terminated during bankruptcy reorganization proceedings pursuant to a bankruptcy filing before October 18, 2005 (i.e., the present-law grandfather rule does not apply).

The Secretary of Labor may waive the additional termination premium if the Secretary determines that the termination occurred as the result of extraordinary circumstances such as a terrorist attack or other similar event. It is intended that extraordinary circumstances means a substantial, system-wide adverse effect on the airline industry such as the terrorist attack which occurred on September 11, 2001. It is intended that the waiver of the additional premiums occur only in rare and unpredictable events. Extraordinary circumstances would not include a mere economic event such as the high price of oil or fuel, or a downturn in the market.

Alternative election in the case of plans not meeting benefit accrual and benefit increase restrictions

In lieu of the election above, a plan sponsor may elect, for the first taxable year beginning in 2008, to amortize the shortfall amortization base for such taxable year over a period of 10 plan years (rather than seven plan years) beginning with such plan year. Under such election, the benefit accrual, benefit increase and other restrictions discussed above do not apply. This 10-year amortization election must be made by December 31, 2007.

Authority of Treasury to disqualify successor plans

If either election is made under the provision and the eligible plan is maintained by an employer that establishes or maintains one or more other single-employer defined benefit plans, and such other plans in combination provide benefit accruals to any substantial number of successor employees, the Secretary of Treasury may disqualify such successor plans unless all benefit obligations of the eligible plan have been satisfied. Successor employees include any employee who is or was covered by the eligible plan and any employee who performs substantially the same type of work with respect to the same business operations as an employee covered by the eligible plan.

Alternative deficit reduction contribution for certain plans

In the case of an employer which is a commercial passenger airline, the provision extends the alternative deficit reduction contributions rules to plan years beginning before December 28, 2007.

Application of minimum coverage rules

In applying the minimum coverage rules to a plan, management pilots who are not represented in accordance with title II of the Railway Labor Act are treated as covered by a collective bargaining agreement if the management pilots manage the flight operations of air pilots who are so represented and the management pilots are, pursuant to the terms of the agreement, included in the group of employees benefiting under the plan.

The exclusion under the minimum coverage rules for air pilots represented in accordance with title II of the Railway Labor Act does not apply in the case of a plan which provides contributions or benefits for employees whose principal duties are not customarily performed aboard an aircraft in flight (other than management pilots described above).

Effective Date

The provision is effective for plan years ending after the date of enactment except that the modifications to the minimum coverage rules apply to years beginning before, on, or after the date of enactment.

[¶ 12,250.025]

Committee Reports on P.L. 108-218 (Pension Funding Equity Act of 2004)

[Temporary replacement of interest rate used for certain pension plan purposes and alternative deficit reduction contribution for certain plans]

Present Law

In general

Under present law, the interest rate on 30-year Treasury securities is used for several purposes related to defined benefit pension plans. Specifically, the interest rate on 30-year Treasury securities is used: (1) in determining current liability for purposes of the funding and deduction rules; (2) in determining unfunded vested benefits for purposes of Pension Benefit Guaranty Corporation ("PBGC") variable rate premiums; and (3) in determining the minimum required value of lump-sum distributions from a defined benefit pension plan and maximum lump-sum values for purposes of the limits on benefits payable under a defined benefit pension plan.

The IRS publishes the interest rate on 30-year Treasury securities on a monthly basis. The Department of the Treasury does not currently issue 30-year Treasury securities. As of March 2002, the IRS publishes the average yield on the 30-year Treasury bond maturing in February 2031 as a substitute.

Funding rules

In general

The Internal Revenue Code (the "Code") and the Employee Retirement Income Security Act of 1974 ("ERISA") impose minimum funding requirements with respect to defined benefit pension plans.[1] Under the funding rules, the amount of contributions required for a plan year is generally the plan's normal cost for the year (i.e., the cost of benefits allocated to the year under the plan's funding method) plus that year's portion of other liabilities that are amortized over a period of years, such as benefits resulting from a grant of past service credit.

Additional contributions for underfunded plans

Under special funding rules (referred to as the "deficit reduction contribution" rules),[2] an additional contribution to a plan is generally required if the plan's funded current liability percentage is less than 90 percent.[3] A plan's "funded current liability percentage" is the actuarial value of plan assets[4] as a percentage of the plan's current liability. In general, a plan's current liability means all liabilities to employees and their beneficiaries under the plan.

The amount of the additional contribution required under the deficit reduction contribution rules is the sum of two amounts: (1) the excess, if any, of (a) the deficit reduction contribution (as described below), over (b) the contribution required under the normal funding rules; and (2) the amount (if any) required with respect to unpredictable contingent event benefits.[5] The amount of the additional contribution cannot exceed the amount needed to increase the plan's funded current liability percentage to 100 percent.

---

[1] Code sec. 412; ERISA sec. 302. The Code also imposes limits on deductible contributions, as discussed below.

[2] The deficit reduction contribution rules apply to single-employer plans, other than single-employer plans with no more than 100 participants on any day in the preceding plan year. Single-employer plans with more than 100 but not more than 150 participants are generally subject to lower contribution requirements under these rules.

[3] Under an alternative test, a plan is not subject to the deficit reduction contribution rules for a plan year if (1) the plan's funded current liability percentage for the plan year is at least 80 percent, and (2) the plan's funded current liability percentage was at least 90 percent for each of the two immediately preceding plan years or each of the second and third immediately preceding plan years.

[4] The actuarial value of plan assets is the value determined under an actuarial valuation method that takes into account fair market value and meets certain other requirements. The use of an actuarial valuation method allows appreciation or depreciation in the market value of plan assets to be recognized gradually over several plan years. Sec. 412(c)(2); Treas. reg. sec. 1.412(c)(2)-1.

[5] A plan may provide for unpredictable contingent event benefits, which are benefits that depend on contingencies that are not reliably and reasonably predictable, such as facility shutdowns or reductions in workforce. An additional contribution is generally not required with respect to unpredictable contingent event benefits unless the event giving rise to the benefits has occurred.

The deficit reduction contribution is the sum of (1) the "unfunded old liability amount," (2) the "unfunded new liability amount," and (3) the expected increase in current liability due to benefits accruing during the plan year.[6] The "unfunded old liability amount" is the amount needed to amortize certain unfunded liabilities under 1987 and 1994 transition rules. The "unfunded new liability amount" is the applicable percentage of the plan's unfunded new liability. Unfunded new liability generally means the unfunded current liability of the plan (i.e., the amount by which the plan's current liability exceeds the actuarial value of plan assets), but determined without regard to certain liabilities (such as the plan's unfunded old liability and unpredictable contingent event benefits). The applicable percentage is generally 30 percent, but is reduced if the plan's funded current liability percentage. is greater than 60 percent.

Required interest rate and mortality table

Specific interest rate and mortality assumptions must be used in determining a plan's current liability for purposes of the special funding rule. The interest rate used to determine a plan's current liability must be within a permissible range of the weighted average[7] of the interest rates on 30-year Treasury securities for the four-year period ending on the last day before the plan year begins. The permissible range is generally from 90 percent to 105 percent.[8] The interest rate used under the plan must be consistent with the assumptions which reflect the purchase rates which would be used by insurance companies to satisfy the liabilities under the plan.[9]

The Job Creation and Worker Assistance Act of 2002[10] amended the permissible range of the statutory interest rate used in calculating a plan's current liability for purposes of applying the additional contribution requirements. Under this provision, the permissible range is from 90 percent to 120 percent for plan years beginning after December 31, 2001, and before January 1, 2004.

The Secretary of the Treasury is required to prescribe mortality tables and to periodically review (at least every five years) and update such tables to reflect the actuarial experience of pension plans and projected trends in such experience.[11] The Secretary of the Treasury has required the use of the 1983 Group Annuity Mortality Table.[12]

Full funding limitation

No contributions are required under the minimum funding rules in excess of the full funding limitation. In 2004 and thereafter, the full funding limitation is the excess, if any, of (1) the accrued liability under the plan (including normal cost), over (2) the lesser of (a) the market value of plan assets or (b) the actuarial value of plan assets.[13] However, the full funding limitation may not be less than the excess, if any, of 90 percent of the plan's current liability (including the current liability normal cost) over the actuarial value of plan assets. In general, current liability is all liabilities to plan participants and beneficiaries accrued to date, whereas the accrued liability under the full funding limitation may be based on projected future benefits, including future salary increases.

Timing of plan contributions

In general, plan contributions required to satisfy the funding rules must be made within 8 ½ months after the end of the plan year. If the contribution is made by such due date, the contribution is treated as if it were made on the last day of the plan year.

In the case of a plan with a funded current liability percentage of less than 100 percent for the preceding plan year, estimated contributions for the current plan year must be made in quarterly installments during the current plan year.[14] The amount of each required installment is 25 percent of the lesser of (1) 90 percent of the amount required to be contributed for the current plan year or (2) 100 percent of the amount required to be contributed for the preceding plan year.[15]

Funding waivers

Within limits, the IRS is permitted to waive all or a portion of the contributions required under the minimum funding standard for a plan year.[16] A waiver may be granted if the employer (or employers) responsible for the contribution could not make the required contribution without temporary substantial business hardship and if requiring the contribution would be adverse to the interests of plan participants in the aggregate. Generally, no more than three waivers may be granted within any period of 15 consecutive plan years.

If a funding waiver is in effect for a plan, subject to certain exceptions, no plan amendment may be adopted that increases the liabilities of the plan by reason of any increase in benefits, any change in the accrual of benefits, or any change in the rate at which benefits vest under the plan. In addition, the IRS is authorized to require security to be granted as a condition of granting a funding waiver if the sum of the plan's accumulated funding deficiency and the balance of any outstanding waived funding deficiencies exceeds $1 million.

Excise tax

An employer is generally subject to an excise tax if it fails to make minimum required contributions and fails to obtain a waiver from the IRS.[17] The excise tax is generally 10 percent of the amount of the funding deficiency. In addition, a tax of 100 percent may be imposed if the funding deficiency is not corrected within a certain period.

Deductions for contributions

Employer contributions to qualified retirement plans are deductible, subject to certain limits. In the case of a defined benefit pension plan, the employer generally may deduct the greater of: (1) the amount necessary to satisfy the minimum funding requirement of the plan for the year; or (2) the amount of the plan's normal cost for the year plus the amount necessary to amortize certain unfunded liabilities over ten years, but limited to the full funding limitation for the year.[18] However, the maximum amount of deductible contributions is generally not less than the plan's unfunded current liability.[19]

PBGC premiums

Because benefits under a defined benefit pension plan may be funded over a period of years, plan assets may not be sufficient to provide the benefits owed under the plan to employees and their beneficiaries if the plan terminates before all benefits are paid. The PBGC generally insures the benefits owed under defined benefit pension plans (up to certain limits) in the event a plan is terminated with insufficient assets. Employers pay premiums to the PBGC for this insurance coverage.

PBGC premiums include a flat-rate premium and, in the case of an underfunded plan, a variable rate premium based on the amount of unfunded vested benefits.[20] In determining the amount of unfunded vested benefits, the interest rate used is 85 percent of the annual yield on 30-year Treasury securities for the month preceding the month in which the plan year begins.

Under the Job Creation and Worker Assistance Act of 2002, for plan years beginning after December 31, 2001, and before January 1, 2004, the interest rate used in determining the amount of unfunded vested benefits for PBGC variable rate premium purposes is increased to 100 percent of the annual yield on 30-year Treasury securities for the month preceding the month in which the plan year begins.

Lump-sum distributions

Accrued benefits under a defined benefit pension plan generally must be paid in the form of an annuity for the life of the participant unless the participant consents to a distribution in another form. Defined benefit pension plans generally provide that a participant may choose among other forms of benefit offered under the plan, such as a lump-sum distribution. These optional forms of benefit generally must be actuarially equivalent to the life annuity benefit payable to the participant.

A defined benefit pension plan must specify the actuarial assumptions that will be used in determining optional forms of benefit under the plan in a manner that precludes employer discretion in the assumptions to be used. For example, a plan may specify that a variable interest rate will be used in determining actuarial equivalent forms of benefit, but may not give the employer discretion to choose the interest rate.

Statutory assumptions must be used in determining the minimum value of certain optional forms of benefit, such as a lump sum.[21] That is, the lump sum

---

[6] If the Secretary of the Treasury prescribes a new mortality table to be used in determining current liability, as described below, the deficit reduction contribution may include an additional amount.

[7] The weighting used for this purpose is 40 percent, 30 percent, 20 percent and 10 percent, starting with the most recent year in the four-year period. Notice 88-73, 1988-2 C.B. 383.

[8] If the Secretary of the Treasury determines that the lowest permissible interest rate in this range is unreasonably high, the Secretary may prescribe a lower rate, but not less than 80 percent of the weighted average of the 30-year Treasury rate.

[9] Code sec. 412(b)(5)(B)(iii)(II); ERISA sec. 302(b)(5)(B)(iii)(II). Under Notice 90-11, 1990-1 C.B. 319, the interest rates in the permissible range are deemed to be consistent with the assumptions reflecting the purchase rates that would be used by insurance companies to satisfy the liabilities under the plan.

[10] Pub. L. No. 107-147.

[11] Code sec. 412(l)(7)(C)(ii); ERISA sec. 302(d)(7)(C)(ii).

[12] Rev. Rul. 95-28, 1995-1 C.B. 74. The IRS and the Treasury Department have announced that they are undertaking a review of the applicable mortality table and have requested comments on related issues, such as how mortality trends should be reflected. Notice 2003-62, 2003-38 I.R.B. 576; Announcement 2000-7, 2000-1 C.B. 586.

[13] For plan years beginning before 2004, the full funding limitation was generally defined as the excess, if any, of (1) the lesser of (a) the accrued liability under the plan (including normal cost) or (b) a percentage (170 percent for 2003) of the plan's current liability (including the current liability normal cost), over (2) the lesser of (a) the market value of plan assets or (b) the actuarial value of plan assets, but in no case less than the excess, if any, of 90 percent of the plan's current liability over the actuarial value of plan assets. Under the Economic Growth and Tax Relief Reconciliation Act of 2001 ("EGTRRA"), the full funding limitation based on 170 percent of current liability is repealed for plan years beginning in 2004 and thereafter. The provisions of EGTRRA generally do not apply for years beginning after December 31, 2010.

[14] Code sec. 412(m); ERISA sec. 302(e).

[15] In connection with the expanded interest rate range available for 2002 and 2003, special rules apply in determining current liability for the preceding plan year for purposes of applying the quarterly contributions requirements to plan years beginning in 2002 (when the expanded range first applies) and 2004 (when the expanded range no longer applies). In each of those years ("present year"), current liability for the preceding year is redetermined, using the permissible range applicable to the present year. This redetermined current liability will be used for purposes of the plan's funded current liability percentage for the preceding year, which may affect the need to make quarterly contributions, and for purposes of determining the amount of any quarterly contributions in the present year, which is based in part on the preceding year.

[16] Code sec. 412(d); ERISA sec. 303.

[17] Code sec. 4971.

[18] Code sec. 404(a)(1).

[19] Code sec. 404(a)(1)(D). In the case of a plan that terminates during the year, the maximum deductible amount is generally not less than the amount needed to make the plan assets sufficient to fund benefit liabilities as defined for purposes of the PBGC termination insurance program (sometimes referred to as "termination liability").

[20] ERISA sec. 4006.

[21] Code sec. 417(e)(3); ERISA sec. 205(g)(3).

payable under the plan may not be less than the amount of the lump sum that is actuarially equivalent to the life annuity payable to the participant, determined using the statutory assumptions. The statutory assumptions consist of an applicable mortality table (as published by the IRS) and an applicable interest rate.

The applicable interest rate is the annual interest rate on 30-year Treasury securities, determined as of the time that is permitted under regulations. The regulations provide various options for determining the interest rate to be used under the plan, such as the period for which the interest rate will remain constant ("stability period") and the use of averaging.

Limits on benefits

Annual benefits payable under a defined benefit pension plan generally may not exceed the lesser of (1) 100 percent of average compensation, or (2) $165,000 (for 2004).[22] The dollar limit generally applies to a benefit payable in the form of a straight life annuity beginning no earlier than age 62. The limit is reduced if benefits are paid before age 62. In addition, if the benefit is not in the form of a straight life annuity, the benefit generally is adjusted to an equivalent straight life annuity. In making these reductions and adjustments, the interest rate used generally must be not less than the greater of (1) five percent; or (2) the interest rate specified in the plan. However, for purposes of adjusting a benefit in a form that is subject to the minimum value rules (including the use of the interest rate on 30-year Treasury securities), such as a lump-sum benefit, the interest rate used must be not less than the greater of: (1) the interest rate on 30-year Treasury securities; or (2) the interest rate specified in the plan.

House Bill

Interest rate for determining current liability and PBGC premiums

The House bill changes the interest rate used for plan years beginning after December 31, 2003, and before January 1, 2006, in determining current liability for funding and deduction purposes and in determining PBGC variable rate premiums. For these purposes, the House bill replaces the interest rate on 30-year Treasury securities with the rate of interest on amounts conservatively invested in long-term corporate bonds.

For purposes of determining a plan's current liability for plan years beginning after December 31, 2003, and before January 1, 2006, the interest rate used must be within a permissible range of the weighted average of the rates of interest on amounts conservatively invested in long-term corporate bonds during the four-year period ending on the last day before the plan year begins, as determined by the Secretary of the Treasury on the basis of one or more indices selected periodically by the Secretary. The permissible range for these years is from 90 percent to 100 percent. The Secretary of the Treasury is directed to publish the interest rate within the permissible range.

In determining the amount of unfunded vested benefits for PBGC variable rate premium purposes for plan years beginning after December 31, 2003, and before January 1, 2006, the interest rate used is 85 percent of the annual yield on amounts conservatively invested in long-term corporate bonds for the month preceding the month in which the plan year begins, as determined by the Secretary of the Treasury on the basis of one or more indices selected periodically by the Secretary. The Secretary of the Treasury is directed to publish such annual yield.

Interest rate used to apply benefit limits to lump sums

No provision.

Alternative deficit reduction contribution for certain plans

No provision.[23]

Effective date

The House bill is generally effective for plan years beginning after December 31, 2003. For purposes of applying certain rules ("lookback rules") to plan years beginning after December 31, 2003, the amendments made by the provision may be applied as if they had been in effect for all years beginning before the effective date. For purposes of the provision, "lookback rules" means: (1) the rule under which a plan is not subject to the additional funding requirements for a plan year if the plan's funded current liability percentage was at least 90 percent for each of the two immediately preceding plan years or each of the second and third immediately preceding plan years; and (2) the rule under which quarterly contributions are required for a plan year if the plan's funded current liability percentage was less than 100 percent for the preceding plan year.

Senate Amendment

Interest rate for determining current liability and PBGC premiums

The Senate amendment is the same as the House bill, with the following modifications.

The Senate amendment replaces the interest rate on 30-year Treasury securities with a conservative long-term bond rate reflecting the rates of interest on amounts invested conservatively in long term corporate bonds and based on the use of two or more indices that are in the top two quality levels available reflecting average maturities of 20 years or more. The Secretary of the Treasury is directed to prescribe by regulation a method for periodically determining conservative long-term corporate bond rates.[24]

Under the Senate amendment, an employer may elect to disregard the temporary interest rate change for purposes of determining the maximum amount of deductible contributions to a defined benefit pension plan (regardless of whether the plan is subject to the deficit reduction contribution requirements). In such a case, the present-law interest rate rules apply, i.e., the interest rate used in determining current liability for that purpose must be within the permissible range (90 to 105 percent) of the weighted average of the interest rates on 30-year Treasury securities for the preceding four-year period.

Interest rate used to apply benefit limits to lump sums

Under the Senate amendment, in the case of plan years beginning in 2004 or 2005, in adjusting a form of benefit that is subject to the minimum value rules, such as a lump-sum benefit, for purposes of applying the limits on benefits payable under a defined benefit pension plan, the interest rate used must be not less than the greater of: (1) 5.5 percent; or (2) the interest rate specified in the plan.

Alternative deficit reduction contribution for certain plans

In general

The Senate amendment allows certain employers ("applicable employers") to elect a reduced amount of additional required contribution under the deficit reduction contribution rules (an "alternative deficit reduction contribution") with respect to certain plans for applicable plan years. An applicable plan year is a plan year beginning after December 27, 2003, and before December 28, 2005, for which the employer elects a reduced contribution. If an employer so elects, the amount of the additional deficit reduction contribution for an applicable plan year is the greater of: (1) 20 percent (40 percent in the case of a plan year beginning after December 27, 2004) of the amount of the additional contribution that would otherwise be required; or (2) the additional contribution that would be required if the deficit reduction contribution for the plan year were determined as the expected increase in current liability due to benefits accruing during the plan year.

An election of an alternative deficit reduction contribution may be made only with respect to a plan that was not subject to the deficit reduction contribution rules for the plan year beginning in 2000. An election may not be made with respect to more than two plan years. An election is to be made at such time and in such manner as the Secretary of the Treasury prescribes. An election does not invalidate any obligation pursuant to a collective bargaining agreement in effect on the date of the election to provide benefits, to change the accrual of benefits, or to change the rate at which benefits vest under the plan.

An applicable employer is an employer that is: (1) a commercial passenger airline; (2) primarily engaged in the production or manufacture of a steel mill product, or in the mining or processing of iron ore or beneficiated iron ore products; or (3) an organization described in section 501(c)(5) that established the plan for which an alternative deficit reduction contribution is elected on June 30, 1955. In addition, an employer not described in the preceding sentence is treated as an applicable employer if the employer files an application (at such time and in such manner as the Secretary of the Treasury prescribes) to be treated as an applicable employer. However, an employer making such an application is not treated as an applicable employer if, within 90 days of the application, the Secretary determines (taking into account the application of the provision) that there is a reasonable likelihood that the employer will be unable to make required future contributions to the plan in a timely manner.

Restrictions on amendments

Certain plan amendments may not be adopted during an applicable plan year (i.e., a plan year for which an alternative deficit reduction contribution is elected). This restriction applies to an amendment that increases the liabilities of the plan by reason of any increase in benefits, any change in the accrual of benefits, or any change in the rate at which benefits vest under the plan. The restriction applies unless: (1) the plan's funded current liability percentage as of the end of the applicable plan year is projected to be at least 75 percent (taking into account the effect of the amendment); (2) the amendment provides for an increase in benefits under a formula that is not based on a participant's compensation, but only if the rate of the increase does not exceed the contemporaneous rate of increase in average wages of participants covered by the amendment; (3) the amendment is required by a collective bargaining agreement that is in effect on the date of enactment of the provision; (4) the amendment is determined by the Secretary of Labor to be reasonable and provides for only de minimis increases in plan liabilities; or (5) the amendment is required as a condition of qualified retirement plan status.

If a plan is amended during an applicable plan year in violation of the provision, an election of an alternative deficit reduction contribution does not apply to any applicable plan year ending on after the date on which the amendment is adopted.

[22] Code sec. 415(b).

[23] Section 2002 of H.R. 3521, the "Tax Relief Extension Act of 2003," as passed by the House of Representatives on November 20, 2003, provides for a reduced deficit reduction contribution for plan years beginning after December 27, 2003, and before December 28, 2005, in the case of plans maintained by commercial passenger airlines. For each year of these years, the reduced contribution is 20 percent of the otherwise required additional contribution.

[24] The Senate amendment also repeals the present-law rule under which, for purposes of applying the quarterly contributions requirements to plan years beginning in 2004, current liability for the preceding year is redetermined.

Notice requirement

The Senate amendment amends ERISA to provide that, if an employer elects an alternative deficit reduction contribution for any applicable plan year, the employer must provide written notice of the election to participants and beneficiaries within 30 days of filing the election (120 days in the case of an employer that files an application to be treated as an applicable employer). The notice to participants must include: (1) the due date of the alternative deficit reduction contribution; (2) the amount by which the required contribution to the plan was reduced as a result of the election; (3) a description of the benefits under the plan that are eligible for guarantee by the PBGC; and (4) an explanation of the limitations on the PBGC guarantee and the circumstances in which the limitations apply, including the maximum guaranteed monthly benefits that the PBGC would pay if the plan terminated while underfunded. An employer that fails to provide the required notice to a participant or beneficiary may (in the discretion of a court) be liable to the participant or beneficiary in the amount of up to $100 a day from the date of the failure, and the court may in its discretion order such other relief as it deems proper.

The Senate amendment also amends ERISA to require that an employer electing an alternative deficit reduction contribution for any year must provide written notice of the election to the PBGC within 30 days of the election (120 days in the case of an employer that files an application to be treated as an applicable employer). The notice to the PBGC must include: (1) the due date of the alternative deficit reduction contribution; (2) the amount by which the required contribution to the plan was reduced as a result of the election; (3) the number of years it will take to restore the plan to full funding if the employer makes only the required contributions; and (4) information as to how the amount by which the plan is underfunded compares with the capitalization of the employer.

Effective date

Interest rate for determining current liability and PBGC premiums

The Senate amendment is generally effective for plan years beginning after December 31, 2003. For purposes of applying certain rules ("lookback rules") to plan years beginning after December 31, 2003, the amendments made by the provision may be applied as if they had been in effect for all years beginning before the effective date. For purposes of the provision, "lookback rules" means: (1) the rule under which a plan is not subject to the additional funding requirements for a plan year if the plan's funded current liability percentage was at least 90 percent for each of the two immediately preceding plan years or each of the second and third immediately preceding plan years; and (2) the rule under which quarterly contributions are required for a plan year if the plan's funded current liability percentage was less than 100 percent for the preceding plan year.

Interest rate used to apply benefit limits to lump sums

The Senate amendment is generally effective for plan years beginning after December 31, 2003. Under a special rule, in the case of a distribution made to a participant or beneficiary after December 31, 2003, and before January 1, 2005, in a form of benefit that is subject to the minimum value rules, such as a lump-sum benefit, and that is subject to adjustment in applying the limit on benefits payable under a defined benefit pension plan, the amount payable may not, solely by reason of the Senate amendment, be less than the amount that would have been payable if the amount payable had been determined using the applicable interest rate in effect as of the last day of the last plan year beginning before January 31, 2004.

Alternative deficit reduction contribution for certain plans

The Senate amendment is effective on the date of enactment.

Conference Agreement

Interest rate for determining current liability and PBGC premiums

The conference agreement follows the House bill with modifications.

Under the conference agreement, the interest rate used for plan years beginning after December 31, 2003, and before January 1, 2006, in determining current liability for funding and deduction purposes and in determining PBGC variable rate premiums is generally the rate of interest on amounts invested conservatively in long-term investment-grade corporate bonds.[25]

For purposes of determining a plan's current liability for plan years beginning after December 31, 2003, and before January 1, 2006, the interest rate used must be within a permissible range of the weighted average of the rates of interest on amounts invested conservatively in long-term investment-grade corporate bonds during the four-year period ending on the last day before the plan year begins. The permissible range for these years is from 90 percent to 100 percent. The interest rate is to be determined by the Secretary of the Treasury on the basis of two or more indices that are selected periodically by the Secretary and are in the top three quality levels available.

The interest rate on long-term corporate bonds shall be calculated pursuant to a method, prescribed by the Secretary of the Treasury, which relies on publicly available indices of high-quality bonds (i.e., the top three quality levels). The Secretary may use bonds with average maturities of 20 years or more in determining the rate. The Secretary of Treasury may prescribe that two thirds of the rate may be based on two or more indices that are in the top three quality levels, and one third of such rate may be based on two or more indices that are in the third quality level. The Secretary shall have discretion to determine which publicly available indices to use.

The Secretary is directed to make the permissible range of the interest rate, as well as the indices and methodology used to determine the average rate, publicly available. The methodology used by the Secretary to arrive at a single rate shall be publicly available (including for a subscription fee or other charge). The Secretary shall publish the rate on a monthly basis, along with an updated four-year weighted average of the rate and an updated permissible range. The Secretary shall consider and monitor the current marketplace indices to produce the specified rate to ensure that the indices continue to be appropriate for this purpose. Through regulations, the Secretary shall, as appropriate, make prospective changes in the indices used to determine the rate.

For purposes of determining the four-year weighted average of interest rates under the temporary provision, the weighting applicable under present law applies (i.e., 40 percent, 30 percent, 20 percent and 10 percent, starting with the most recent year in the four-year period). In addition, consistent with current IRS guidance, the interest rates in the permissible range under the temporary provision are deemed to be consistent with the assumptions reflecting the purchase rates that would be used by insurance companies to satisfy the liabilities under the plan. Thus, any interest rate in the permissible range may be used in determining current liability while the temporary provision is in effect.

The temporary interest rate generally applies in determining current liability for purposes of determining the maximum amount of deductible contributions to a defined benefit pension plan (regardless of whether the plan is subject to the deficit reduction contribution requirements). However, under the conference agreement, an employer may elect to disregard the temporary interest rate change for purposes of determining the maximum amount of deductible contributions (regardless of whether the plan is subject to the deficit reduction contribution requirements). In such a case, the present-law interest rate rules apply, i.e., the interest rate used in determining current liability for that purpose must be within the permissible range (90 to 105 percent) of the weighted average of the interest rates on 30-year Treasury securities for the preceding four-year period. This is intended solely as a temporary provision to ensure that, pending long-term reform of the funding and deduction rules, the deduction limit is neither increased nor decreased so that employers are not penalized for fully funding their plans. Because the 30-year Treasury rate is an obsolete rate, its use must be revisited promptly in the context of long-term funding and deduction reform. However, the use of the 30-year Treasury rate for the purposes of determining maximum deduction limits should not be considered precedent for the determination of other pension plan calculations. Furthermore, the use of different interest rates for certain pension plan calculations in the context of this temporary bill should not be considered precedent for the use of different discount rates to measure pension plan liabilities.

Under the conference agreement, in determining the amount of unfunded vested benefits for PBGC variable rate premium purposes for plan years beginning after December 31, 2003, and before January 1, 2006, the interest rate used is 85 percent of the annual rate of interest determined by the Secretary of the Treasury on amounts invested conservatively in long-term investment-grade corporate bonds for the month preceding the month in which the plan year begins (subject to the same requirements applicable to the determination of the interest rate used in determining current liability).

Interest rate used to apply benefit limits to lump sums

The conference agreement follows the Senate amendment.

Under the conference agreement, in the case of plan years beginning in 2004 or 2005, in adjusting a form of benefit that is subject to the minimum value rules, such as a lump-sum benefit, for purposes of applying the limits on benefits payable under a defined benefit pension plan, the interest rate used must be not less than the greater of: (1) 5.5 percent; or (2) the interest rate specified in the plan.

Plan amendments

The conference agreement permits certain plan amendments made pursuant to the interest rate provision of the bill to be retroactively effective. If certain requirements are met, the plan will be treated as being operated in accordance with its terms, and the amendment will not violate the anticutback rules (except as provided by the Secretary of the Treasury).[26] In order for this treatment to apply, the plan amendment must be made on or before the last day of the first plan year beginning on or after January 1, 2006. In addition, the amendment must apply retroactively as of the date on which the interest rate provision became effective with respect to the plan and the plan must be operated in compliance with the interest rate provision until the amendment is made.

A plan amendment will not be considered to be pursuant to the interest rate provision of the bill if it has an effective date before the effective date of the interest rate provision. Similarly, relief from the anticutback rules does not apply for periods prior to the effective date of the interest rate provision or the plan amendment.

---

[25] The conference agreement also repeals the present-law rule under which, for purposes of applying the quarterly contributions requirements to plan years beginning in 2004, current liability for the preceding year is redetermined.

[26] Code sec. 411(d)(6); ERISA sec. 204(g).

Alternative deficit reduction contribution for certain plans

In general

The conference agreement follows the Senate amendment with modifications.

The conference agreement allows certain employers ("applicable employers") to elect a reduced amount of additional required contribution under the deficit reduction contribution rules (an "alternative deficit reduction contribution") with respect to certain plans for applicable plan years. An applicable plan year is a plan year beginning after December 27, 2003, and before December 28, 2005, for which the employer elects a reduced contribution. If an employer so elects, the amount of the additional deficit reduction contribution for an applicable plan year is the greater of: (1) 20 percent of the amount of the additional contribution that would otherwise be required; or (2) the additional contribution that would be required if the deficit reduction contribution for the plan year were determined as the expected increase in current liability due to benefits accruing during the plan year.

An election of an alternative deficit reduction contribution may be made only with respect to a plan that was not subject to the deficit reduction contribution rules for the plan year beginning in 2000.[27] An election may not be made with respect to more than two plan years. An election is to be made at such time and in such manner as the Secretary of the Treasury prescribes. Guidance relating to the time and manner in which an election is made is to be issued expeditiously. An election does not invalidate any obligation pursuant to a collective bargaining agreement in effect on the date of the election to provide benefits, to change the accrual of benefits, or to change the rate at which benefits vest under the plan.

An applicable employer is an employer that is: (1) a commercial passenger airline; (2) primarily engaged in the production or manufacture of a steel mill product, or the processing of iron ore pellets; or (3) an organization described in section 501(c)(5) that established the plan for which an alternative deficit reduction contribution is elected on June 30, 1955.

Restrictions on amendments

Certain plan amendments may not be adopted during an applicable plan year (i.e., a plan year for which an alternative deficit reduction contribution is elected). This restriction applies to an amendment that increases the liabilities of the plan by reason of any increase in benefits, any change in the accrual of benefits, or any change in the rate at which benefits vest under the plan. The restriction applies unless: (1) the plan's enrolled actuary certifies (in such form and manner as prescribed by the Secretary of the Treasury) that the amendment provides for an increase in annual contributions that will exceed the increase in annual charges to the funding standard account attributable to such amendment; or (2) the amendment is required by a collective bargaining agreement that is in effect on the date of enactment of the provision.

If a plan is amended during an applicable plan year in violation of the provision, an election of an alternative deficit reduction contribution does not apply to any applicable plan year ending on after the date on which the amendment is adopted.

Notice requirement

The conference agreement amends ERISA to provide that, if an employer elects an alternative deficit reduction contribution for any applicable plan year, the employer must provide written notice of the election to participants and beneficiaries and to the PBGC within 30 days of filing the election. The notice to participants and beneficiaries must include: (1) the due date of the alternative deficit reduction contribution; (2) the amount by which the required contribution to the plan was reduced as a result of the election; (3) a description of the benefits under the plan that are eligible for guarantee by the PBGC; and (4) an explanation of the limitations on the PBGC guarantee and the circumstances in which the limitations apply, including the maximum guaranteed monthly benefits that the PBGC would pay if the plan terminated while underfunded. The notice to the PBGC must include: (1) the due date of the alternative deficit reduction contribution; (2) the amount by which the required contribution to the plan was reduced as a result of the election; (3) the number of years it will take to restore the plan to full funding if the employer makes only the required contributions; and (4) information as to how the amount by which the plan is underfunded compares with the capitalization of the employer.

An employer that fails to provide the required notice to a participant, beneficiary, or the PBGC may (in the discretion of a court) be liable to the participant, beneficiary, or PBGC in the amount of up to $100 a day from the date of the failure, and the court may in its discretion order such other relief as it deems proper.

Effective date

Interest rate for determining current liability and PBGC premiums

The conference agreement is generally effective for plan years beginning after December 31, 2003. For purposes of applying certain rules ("lookback rules") to plan years beginning after December 31, 2003, the amendments made by the provision may be applied as if they had been in effect for all years beginning before the effective date. For purposes of the provision, "lookback rules" means: (1) the rule under which a plan is not subject to the additional funding requirements for a plan year if the plan's funded current liability percentage was at least 90 percent for each of the two immediately preceding plan years or each of the second and third immediately preceding plan years; and (2) the rule under which quarterly contributions are required for a plan year if the plan's funded current liability percentage was less than 100 percent for the preceding plan year. The amendments made by the provision may be applied for purposes of the lookback rules, regardless of the funded current liability percentage reported for the plan on the plan's annual reports (i.e., Form 5500) for preceding years.

Interest rate used to apply benefit limits to lump sums

The conference agreement is generally effective for plan years beginning after December 31, 2003. Under a special rule, in the case of a distribution made to a participant or beneficiary after December 31, 2003, and before January 1, 2005, in a form of benefit that is subject to the minimum value rules, such as a lump-sum benefit, and that is subject to adjustment in applying the limit on benefits payable under a defined benefit pension plan, the amount payable may not, solely by reason of the conference agreement, be less than the amount that would have been payable if the amount payable had been determined using the applicable interest rate in effect as of the last day of the last plan year beginning before January 31, 2004.

Alternative deficit reduction contribution for certain plans

The conference agreement is effective on the date of enactment.

[Election for deferral of charge for portion of net experience loss of multiemployer plans]

Present Law

General funding requirements

The Code and ERISA impose minimum funding requirements with respect to defined benefit plans.[30] Under the minimum funding rules, the amount of contributions required for a plan year is generally the plan's normal cost for the year (i.e., the cost of benefits allocated to the year under the plan's funding method) plus that year's portion of other liabilities that are amortized over a period of years, such as benefits resulting from a grant of past service credit.[31] A plan's normal cost and other liabilities must be determined under an actuarial cost method permissible under the Code and ERISA.

Funding standard account

As an administrative aid in the application of the funding requirements, a defined benefit plan is required to maintain a special account called a "funding standard account" to which specified charges and credits (including credits for contributions to the plan), plus interest, are made for each plan year. If, as of the close of a plan year, the account reflects credits equal to or in excess of charges, the plan is generally treated as meeting the minimum funding standard for the year. Thus, as a general rule, the minimum contribution for a plan year is determined as the amount by which the charges to the account would exceed credits to the account if no contribution were made to the plan. If, as of the close of the plan year, charges to the funding standard account exceed credits to the account, then the excess is referred to as an "accumulated funding deficiency."[32]

Experience gains and losses

In determining plan funding under an actuarial cost method, a plan's actuary generally makes certain assumptions regarding the future experience of a plan. These assumptions typically involve rates of interest, mortality, disability, salary increases, and other factors affecting the value of assets and liabilities, such as increases or decreases in asset values. The actuarial assumptions are required to be reasonable and may be subject to other restrictions. If, on the basis of these assumptions, the contributions made to the plan result in actual unfunded liabilities that are less than those anticipated by the actuary, then the excess is an experience gain. If the actual unfunded liabilities are greater than those anticipated, then the difference is an experience loss.

If a plan has a net experience gain, the funding standard account is credited with the amount needed to amortize the net experience gain over a certain period. If a plan has a net experience loss, the funding standard account is charged with the amount needed to amortize the net experience loss over a certain period. In the case of a multiemployer plan, the amortization period for net experience gains and losses is 15 years.

Funding waivers

Within limits, the IRS is permitted to waive all or a portion of the contributions required under the minimum funding standard for a plan year.[33] A waiver may be

---

[27] Whether a plan was subject to the deficit reduction contribution rules for the plan year beginning in 2000 is determined without regard to the rule that allows the temporary interest rate based on amounts invested conservatively in long-term investment-grade corporate bonds to be used for lookback rule purposes, as discussed below.

[30] Code sec. 412; ERISA sec. 302.

[31] Under special funding rules (referred to as the "deficit reduction contribution" rules), an additional contribution may be required to a single-employer plan if the plan's funded current liability percentage is less than 90 percent. The deficit reduction contribution rules do not apply to multiemployer plans.

[32] In addition to the funding standard account, a reconciliation account is sometimes used to balance certain items for purposes of reporting actuarial information about the plan on the plan's annual report (Schedule B of Form 5500).

[33] Sec. 412(d).

granted if the employer (or employers) responsible for the contribution could not make the required contribution without temporary substantial business hardship and if requiring the contribution would be adverse to the interests of plan participants in the aggregate. In the case of a multiemployer plan, no more than five waivers may be granted within any period of 15 consecutive plan years.

If a funding waiver is in effect for a plan, subject to certain exceptions, no plan amendment may be adopted that increases the liabilities of the plan by reason of any increase in benefits, any change in the accrual of benefits, or any change in the rate at which benefits vest under the plan.

Excise tax

An employer is generally subject to an excise tax if it fails to make minimum required contributions and fails to obtain a waiver from the IRS.[34] The excise tax is 10 percent of the amount of the funding deficiency (five percent in the case of a multiemployer plan). In addition, a tax of 100 percent may be imposed if the funding deficiency is not corrected within a certain period.

House Bill

No provision.

Senate Amendment

The Senate amendment allows certain multiemployer plans to elect to defer the beginning of the amortization of certain net experience losses for up to three plan years. The period during which the amortization of a net experience loss is deferred by reason of such an election is referred to as a "hiatus period." The Senate amendment applies to a multiemployer plan that has a net experience loss for any plan year beginning after June 30, 2002, and before July 1, 2006. Such a plan may elect to begin the 15-year amortization period with respect to such a loss in any of the three immediately succeeding plan years as selected by the plan. A plan may elect to delay the beginning of the amortization of net experience losses with respect to net experience losses occurring for only two plan years beginning after June 30, 2002, and before July 1, 2006 (regardless of the number of plan years in that period for which the plan has net experience losses). An election under the Senate amendment is to be made at such time and in such manner as the Secretary of Labor prescribes, after consultation with the Secretary of the Treasury.

If an election is made, the net experience loss is treated, for purposes of determining any charge to the funding standard account (or interest) with respect to the loss, in the same manner as if the net experience loss occurred in the year selected by the plan for the amortization period to begin (without regard to any net experience loss or gain otherwise determined for such year). Interest accrued on any net experience loss during a hiatus period is charged to a reconciliation account and not to the funding standard account.

Certain plan amendments may not take effect for any plan year in the hiatus period. This restriction applies to an amendment that increases the liabilities of the plan by reason of any increase in benefits, any change in the accrual of benefits, or any change in the rate at which benefits vest under the plan. The restriction applies unless: (1) the plan's funded current liability percentage as of the end of the plan year is projected to be at least 75 percent (taking into account the effect of the amendment); (2) the plan's actuary certifies that, due to an increase in the rates of contributions to the plan, the normal cost attributable to the benefit increase or other change is expected to be fully funded in the year following the year in which the increase or other change takes effect, and any increase in the plan's accrued liabilities attributable to the benefit increase or other change is expected to be fully funded by the end of the third plan year following the end of the plan hiatus period of the plan; (3) the amendment is determined by the Secretary of Labor to be reasonable and provides for only de minimis increases in plan liabilities; or (4) the amendment is required as a condition of qualified retirement plan status. The restriction on amendments does not apply to an increase in benefits for a group of participants resulting solely from a collectively bargained increase in the contributions on their behalf. Failure to comply with this restriction is a violation of ERISA and of the qualification requirements of the Code.

If a plan elects to defer the beginning of an amortization period, the plan administrator must provide written notice of the election within 30 days to participants and beneficiaries, to each labor organization representing participants and beneficiaries, and to each employer that has an obligation to contribute under the plan. The notice must include: (1) the amount of the net experience loss to be deferred under the election and the period of the deferral; and (2) the maximum guaranteed monthly benefits that the PBGC would pay if the plan terminated while underfunded. If a plan administrator fails to comply with the notice requirement, the Secretary of Labor may assess a civil penalty of not more than $1,000 a day for each violation.

Effective date

The Senate amendment is effective on the date of enactment.

Conference Agreement

The conference agreement allows the plan sponsor of an eligible multiemployer plan to elect to defer certain charges to the funding standard account that would otherwise be made to the plan's funding standard account for a plan year beginning after June 30, 2003, and before July 1, 2005. The charges may be deferred to any plan year selected by the plan sponsor from either of the two plan years immediately succeeding the plan year for which the charge would otherwise be made. An election may be made with respect to up to 80 percent of the charge to the funding standard account attributable to the amortization of a net experience loss for the first plan year beginning after December 31, 2001. An election is to be made at such time and in such manner as the Secretary of the Treasury prescribes. For the plan year to which a charge is deferred under the plan sponsor's election, the funding standard account is required to be charged with interest at the short-term Federal rate on the deferred charge for the period of the deferral.

An eligible multiemployer plan is a multiemployer plan: (1) that, for the first plan year beginning after December 31, 2001, had an actual net investment loss of at least 10 percent of the average fair market value of plan assets during the plan year; and (2) with respect to which the plan's enrolled actuary certifies that (not taking into account the deferral of charges under the provision and based on the actuarial assumptions used for the last plan year before date of enactment of the provision), the plan is projected to have an accumulated funding deficiency for any plan year beginning after June 30, 2003, and before July 1, 2006. In addition, a plan is not treated as an eligible multiemployer plan if: (1) for any taxable year beginning during the ten-year period preceding the first plan year for which an election is made under the provision, any employer required to contribute to the plan failed to timely pay an excise tax imposed on the plan for failure to make required contributions; (2) for any plan year beginning after June 30, 1993, and before the first plan year for which an election is made under the provision, the average contribution required to be made to the plan by all employers does not exceed 10 cents per hour, or no employer is required to make contributions to the plan; or (3) with respect to any plan year beginning after June 30, 1993, and before the first plan year for which an election is made under the provision, a funding waiver or extension of an amortization period was granted to the plan.

Certain plan amendments may not be adopted during the period for which a charge is deferred. This restriction applies to an amendment that increases the liabilities of the plan by reason of any increase in benefits, any change in the accrual of benefits, or any change in the rate at which benefits vest under the plan. The restriction applies unless: (1) the plan's enrolled actuary certifies (in such form and manner as prescribed by the Secretary of the Treasury) that the amendment provides for an increase in annual contributions that will exceed the increase in annual charges to the funding standard account attributable to such amendment; or (2) the amendment is required by a collective bargaining agreement that is in effect on the date of enactment of the provision. If a plan is amended in violation of the provision, an election under the provision does not apply to any plan year ending on after the date on which the amendment is adopted.

If a plan sponsor elects to defer charges attributable to a net experience loss, the plan administrator must provide written notice of the election within 30 days to participants and beneficiaries, to each labor organization representing participants and beneficiaries, to each employer that has an obligation to contribute under the plan, and to the PBGC. The notice must include: (1) the amount of the charges to be deferred under the election and the period of the deferral; and (2) the maximum guaranteed monthly benefits that the PBGC would pay if the plan terminated while underfunded. If a plan administrator fails to comply with the notice requirement, the Secretary of Labor may assess a civil penalty of not more than $1,000 a day for each violation.

Effective date

The conference agreement is effective on the date of enactment.

[¶ 12,250.03]

Committee Reports on P.L. 107-16 (Economic Growth and Tax Relief Reconciliation Act)

[House Committee Report]

Modification of timing of plan valuations

The provision incorporates into the statute the proposed regulation regarding the date of valuations. The provision also provides, as an exception to this general rule, that the valuation date with respect to a plan year may be any date within the immediately preceding plan year if, as of such date, plan assets are not less than 125 percent of the plan's current liability. Information determined as of such date is required to be adjusted actuarially, in accordance with Treasury regulations, to reflect significant differences in plan participants. An election to use a prior plan year valuation date, once made, may only be revoked with the consent of the Secretary.

Effective Date

The provision is effective for plan years beginning after December 31, 2001.

[Conference Committee Report]

Senate Amendment

The Senate amendment is the same as the House bill.

[34] Sec. 4971.

Conference Agreement

The conference agreement incorporates into the statute the proposed regulation regarding the date of valuations. The conference agreement also provides, as an exception to this general rule, that the valuation date with respect to a plan year may be any date within the immediately preceding plan year if, as of such date, plan assets are not less than 100 percent of the plan's current liability. Information determined as of such date is required to be adjusted actuarially, in accordance with Treasury regulations, to reflect significant differences in plan participants. A change in funding method to take advantage of the exception to the general rule may not be made unless, as of such date, plan assets are not less than 125 percent of the plan's current liability. The Secretary is directed to automatically approve changes in funding method to use a prior year valuation date if the change is within the first three years that the plan is eligible to make the change.

[¶ 12,250.05]

Committee Reports on P.L. 107-16 (Economic Growth and Tax Relief Reconciliation Act)

[Senate Committee Report]

Repeal of current liability full funding limit

Current liability full funding limit

The provision gradually increases and then repeals the current liability full funding limit. The current liability full funding limit is 160 percent of current liability for plan years beginning in 2002, 165 percent for plan years beginning in 2003, and 170 percent for plan years beginning in 2004. The current liability full funding limit is repealed for plan years beginning in 2005 and thereafter. Thus, in 2005 and thereafter, the full funding limit is the excess, if any, of (1) the accrued liability under the plan (including normal cost), over (2) the value of the plan's assets.

* * *

Effective Date

The provision is effective for plan years beginning after December 31, 2001.

[Conference Committee Report]

The conference agreement follows the Senate amendment, with modifications.

The conference agreement gradually increases and then repeals the current liability full funding limit. Under the conference agreement, the current liability full funding limit is 165 percent of current liability for plan years beginning in 2002, and 170 percent for plan years beginning in 2003. The current liability full funding limit is repealed for plan years beginning in 2004 and thereafter. Thus, in 2004 and thereafter, the full funding limit is the excess, if any, of (1) the accrued liability under the plan (including normal cost), over (2) the value of the plan's assets.

* * *

[¶ 12,250.068]

Committee Reports on P.L. 105-34 (Taxpayer Relief Act)

Senate Committee Report

Increase in full funding limit.—The bill increases the 150-percent of full funding limit as follows: 155 percent for plan years beginning in 1999 or 2000, 160 percent for plan years beginning in 2001 or 2002, 165 percent for plan years beginning in 2003 and 2004, and 170 percent for plan years beginning in 2005 and thereafter.

Effective Date

The provision is effective for plan years beginning after December 31, 1998.

Conference Committee Report

Increase in full funding limit.—

Senate [Floor] Amendment.—* * *

In addition, under the provision, amounts that cannot be contributed due to the current liability full funding limit are amortized over 20 years. Amounts that could not be contributed because of such full funding limit and that have not been amortized as of the last day of the plan year beginning in 1998 are amortized over this 20-year period.

Effective Date

Plan years beginning after December 31, 1998.

Conference Agreement

The conference agreement follows the Senate amendment, with the modification that, with respect to amortization bases remaining at the end of the 1998 plan year, the 20-year amortization period is reduced by the number of years since the amortization base had been established. The conference agreement also clarifies that no amortization is required with respect to funding methods that do not provide for amortization bases.

[¶ 12,250.07]

Committee Report on P.L. 103-465 (General Agreement on Tariffs and Trade (GATT); Retirement Protection Act)

[House Committee Report]

Minimum funding requirements

Special funding rules for underfunded plans

In general.—The bill changes the special funding rules for underfunded single-employer defined benefit plans (other than plans with no more than 100 participants on any day in the preceding plan year) that were adopted in the Pension Protection Act of 1987. In general, the bill (1) provides (a) a permanent rule that exempts from the special funding rules applicable to underfunded plans, plans that have a funded current liability percentage of at least 90 percent and certain plans that have a funded current liability percentage between 80 percent and 90 percent, and (b) transition rules under which certain other plans are exempt, (2) modifies the calculation of the minimum required contribution applicable to underfunded plans, (3) changes the permissible range of interest rates and requires uniform mortality assumptions for the purpose of determining a plan's current liability, (4) accelerates the funding of a plan's "unfunded new liability", (5) changes the calculation of the additional funding contribution required on account of an unpredictable contingent event, (6) provides an elective transition rule for sponsors of underfunded plans to protect against possibly large increases in their minimum required contributions on account of the proposed changes in the special funding rules, and (7) changes the manner in which sponsors of defined benefit pension plans determine the full funding limit of their plans.

Certain underfunded plans exempt from the special funding rules—Permanent rules.—The bill provides two exceptions to the special funding rules for underfunded plans. First, such rules do not apply to a plan which for any plan year has a current funded liability percentage of at least 90 percent. This rule is referred to as the "90-percent exemption."

Second, the special funding rules for underfunded plans do not apply for a plan year if (1) the funded current liability percentage for the plan year is at least 80 percent and (2) the funded current liability percentage for each of the two immediately preceding plan years (or each of the second and third immediately preceding plan years) is at least 90 percent. This rule is referred to as the "volatility rule."

For purposes of these exemptions, the funded current liability percentage is determined using the highest interest rate in the permissible range and the mortality assumptions contained in the bill. In addition, assets are not reduced by credit balances in the funding standard account.

The following example illustrates the exceptions to the special funding rules for underfunded plans.

Example 1: Assume that the funded current liability percentage (determined as specified under the bill) for Plan A for each of the plan years beginning on January 1, 1996, 1997, 1998, and 1999 is as follows: 95%, 95%, 75%, and 80%. For plan years 1996 and 1997, the plan is not subject to the additional funding rules for underfunded plans because the funded current liability percentage is at least 90%. The plan is subject to the additional funding rules for plan year 1998 because the funded current liability percentage is below 80%. The plan is not subject to the additional funding rules for plan year 1999, because it satisfies the volatility rule.

Transition rules.—The bill provides two transition rules under which certain plans are exempt from the new rules for underfunded pension plans.

The first rule applies for purposes of determining whether a plan is subject to the new rules in plan years beginning in 1995 and 1996. A plan is not subject to the new rules for a plan year beginning in 1995 or 1996 if (1) in that year, the plan's funded current liability percentage is at least 80 percent, and (2) the plan meets a transition test in any two of the plan years beginning in 1992, 1993, and 1994. The transition test need not be satisfied by the same method in each year. The transition test is met for a plan year if, for the plan year, the plan met one of the following requirements (under the law as then in effect):

(1) the plan did not have an additional charge under the special funding rules for underfunded plans (or would not have had such a charge if the plan used the highest interest rate within the permissible range and assets are determined by taking into account credit balances in the funding standard account);

(2) the plan's full funding limit was zero; or

(3) the amount required to be contributed under the special rules for underfunded plans (i.e., the amount of the deficit reduction contribution) did not exceed the lesser of .5 percent of current liability or $5 million.

The second rule applies for purposes of determining whether a plan is subject to the new rules for plan years beginning in 1996 and 1997. A plan is not subject to the new rules for a plan year beginning in 1996 or 1997 if (1) in that year, the plan's funded current liability percentage is at least 80 percent, (2) the plan's current liability percentage for the plan year beginning in 1995 was at least 90 percent, and (3) in the plan year beginning in 1994, the plan met one of the three transition requirements described above.

Calculation of minimum required contribution

The bill changes the manner in which underfunded plans calculate their minimum required contribution for a plan year. Under the bill, amounts necessary to amortize experience gains and losses and gains and losses resulting from changes of actuarial assumptions are no longer considered in the calculation of the minimum required contribution for underfunded plans. According to the PBGC, one reason that the minimum required contribution for underfunded plans adopted in the Pension Protection Act of 1987 has not been effective in increasing contributions to underfunded plans is because experience gains or gains from changes in actuarial assumptions are counted twice under present law, i.e., to reduce the minimum required contribution for underfunded plans and as a credit to the funding standard account under the normal funding rules. Thus, under the bill, the minimum required contribution for underfunded plans is, in general, the greater of (1) the amount determined under the normal funding rules, or (2) the deficit reduction contribution plus the amount required with respect to benefits that are contingent on unpredictable events.

Further, the bill adds a third and fourth component to the calculation of the deficit reduction contribution under present law. Under the bill, the deficit reduction contribution is the sum of (1) the unfunded old liability amount, (2) the unfunded new liability amount, (3) the expected increase in current liability due to benefits accruing during the plan year, and (4) the amount needed to amortize the increase in current liability due to certain future changes in the required mortality tables. The third component replaces the normal cost component of the calculation under present law. The fourth component is discussed below.

In addition, the bill provides that the amount of the minimum required contribution for underfunded plans cannot exceed the amount necessary to increase the funded current liability percentage of the plan to 100 percent, taking into account all charges and credits to the funding standard account and the expected increase in current liability attributable to benefits accruing during the plan year.

Changes in interest rates and mortality assumptions

In general.—As under present law, the calculation of the deficit reduction contribution for underfunded plans is based on the plan's current liabilities. Under the bill, a plan's current liability is determined as under present law, except that the bill (1) lowers the maximum interest rate that can be used to determine the current liability, and (2) requires all underfunded plans to use the same mortality table to determine current liability.

Interest rate.—For plan years beginning on or after January 1, 1999, the bill reduces the highest permissible rate that may be used to calculate current liability to 105 percent of the weighted average of the rates of interest on 30-year Treasury securities during the 4-year period ending on the last day before the beginning of the plan year. For years beginning after 1994 and before 1999, the maximum permitted interest rate is the following percentage of such 4-year weighted average rate: plan years beginning in 1995, 109 percent; plan years beginning in 1996, 108 percent; plan years beginning in 1997, 107 percent; and plan years beginning in 1998, 106 percent.

Mortality tables.—Under the bill, in the case of plan years beginning after December 31, 1994, the mortality table used to determine current liability is to be prescribed by the Secretary based upon the 1983 Group Annuity Mortality Table (GAM 83 mortality table). Such mortality table will be effective until the later of plan years beginning in 2000 or such time as the Secretary prescribes new tables by regulations. Any tables prescribed by the Secretary are to reflect the actual experience of pension plans and projected trends in such experience. In prescribing tables, the Secretary is to take into account the results of independent studies on mortality of individuals covered by pension plans. The Secretary is required to review the new tables at least every five years and update them as necessary to reflect changes in pension plan experience and trends. Increases in liability due to changes in mortality assumptions in the first year in which new mortality tables are effective are to be amortized over 10 years in equal installments.

Plans are permitted to use a different mortality table for certain participants who are entitled to benefits on account of disability ("disabled participants"). For plan years beginning in 1995, plans may use their own mortality assumptions for disabled participants (under the plan's definition of disability) provided such assumptions meet the general requirement that actuarial assumptions be reasonable. For plan years beginning on or after January 1, 1996, the Secretary is to prescribe mortality tables for disabled participants. The Secretary is to prescribe two tables: one table for persons who become entitled to disability benefits (under the plan's definition of disability) before the plan year beginning in 1995; and another table for persons who become eligible for disability benefits in a plan year beginning on or after January 1, 1995. The separate disability table may not be used with respect to persons who become entitled to disability benefits under the plan on or after January 1, 1995, unless such persons are disabled within the meaning of Title II of the Social Security Act.

Amortization of increases in current liability under the bill.—Under the bill, increases in current liability attributable to the bill's changes in interest rates and mortality assumptions for the 1995 plan year are treated as an "additional unfunded old liability amount" and are amortized in equal annual installments over 12 years beginning with the 1995 plan year. The additional unfunded old liability amount is the difference between the current liability of the plan as of the beginning of the 1995 plan year using (1) the interest and mortality assumptions contained in the bill and (2) the mortality assumption and relative interest rate used to determine current liability for the 1993 plan year. For example, if the plan used 110 percent of the weighted average in the 1993 plan year, the relative interest rate for this calculation would be 110 percent of the weighted average in the 1995 plan year.

As an alternative to amortization of only the change in current liability due to changes in interest and mortality assumptions, an employer may make an irrevocable election to expand the 12-year amortization to the entire increase in current liability attributable to plan years beginning after December 31, 1987 and before January 1, 1995.

The increase in liability for this optional rule would be measured as the amount by which the plan's unfunded current liability as of the beginning of the 1995 plan year, valued using the new specified interest and mortality assumptions, exceeds the unamortized portion of the unfunded old liability under the plan as of the beginning of the 1995 plan year. This increase would be treated as unfunded old liability and amortized over 12 years beginning with the first plan year beginning on or after January 1, 1995. If an election is made to amortize this amount and the plan would otherwise be subject to the special rules for underfunded plans, the amount charged to the funding standard account under section 302(d) of ERISA and section 412(l) of the Code for plan years beginning after December 31, 1994 and before January 1, 2002, would not be less, for any year, than the amount that would have been required under those sections if current law had remained in effect.

Acceleration of unfunded new liability

* * * The bill increases the 35 percent threshold under present law to 60 percent. Thus, under the bill, if a plan's funded current liability percentage is 60 percent or less, 30 percent of the plan's unfunded new liability for the plan year would be included in the calculation of the deficit reduction contribution for the plan year. Under the bill, the 30 percent amount decreases by .40 of one percentage point for each percentage point by which the plan's funded current liability percentage exceeds 60 percent, to a minimum of 18 percent for a plan that is 90-percent funded.

Unpredictable contingent event benefits

The bill adds a third component to the calculation of the additional funding contribution required on account of an unpredictable contingent event. Under the bill, the amount of the additional funding contribution is equal to the greater of the amounts determined under present law or the additional contribution that would be required if the unpredictable contingent event benefit liabilities were included in the calculation of the plan's unfunded new liability for the plan year. * * *

In addition, the bill limits the present value of the additional funding contribution with respect to one event to the unpredictable contingent event benefit liabilities attributable to that event.

Transition rule

The bill provides an elective transition rule for sponsors of underfunded plans to protect against possibly large increases in their minimum required contributions on account of changes in the special funding rules. Under the transition rule, the minimum required contribution for a plan year cannot be less than the minimum required contribution determined under present law.

Relief under the transition rule depends on the plan's funded current liability percentage. This relief is based upon the amount necessary to increase the plan's funded current liability percentage by a specified percentage by the end of the plan year, including the expected increase in current liability due to benefits accruing and the expected benefit payments during the plan year. The specified percentages and the initial funded current liability percentage are not adjusted to reflect the changes in the maximum permitted interest rate scheduled for plan years beginning before January 1, 2000.

Changes in full funding limit

The bill changes the manner in which sponsors of defined benefit pension plans determine the full funding limit to conform to IRS practice. The bill retains the present-law rules relating to the determination of a defined benefit pension plan's full funding limit but also provides that the expected increase in current liability due to benefits accruing during the plan year be included when determining the employer's current liability. The bill allows plans to determine their 150 percent of current liability limit for full funding limit purposes without regard to the modifications of the interest rate and mortality assumptions set forth in the bill.

The bill also provides that the full funding limit is not less than 90 percent of the plan's current liability (using the modifications to the interest rate and mortality assumptions set forth in the bill). In determining whether a plan is at this 90 percent limit, plan assets are not reduced by credit balances in the funding standard account.

It is intended that reporting requirements will be revised as necessary to implement the revised funding rules, for example, to reflect the volatility rules, the liquidity requirement (discussed below), the revised full funding limitation, and the transition rules.

Plan liquidity requirement.—In general, the bill requires underfunded single-employer defined benefit pension plans to make quarterly contributions sufficient to maintain liquid plan assets, i.e., cash and marketable securities, at an amount approximately equal to three times the total trust disbursements for the preceding 12-month period.

Under the bill, the plan liquidity requirement applies to underfunded single-employer defined benefit pension plans (other than small plans) that (1) are required to make quarterly installments of their estimated minimum funding contribution for the plan year, and (2) have a liquidity shortfall for any quarter during the plan year. A plan has a liquidity shortfall if its liquid assets as of the last day of the quarter are less than the base amount for the quarter. Liquid assets are cash, marketable securities and such other assets as specified by the Secretary of the Treasury. The base amount for the quarter is an amount equal to the product of three times the adjusted disbursements from the plan for the 12 months ending on the last day of the last month preceding the quarterly installment due date. If the base amount exceeds the product of two times the sum of adjusted disbursements for the 36 months ending on the last day of the last month preceding the quarterly installment due date, and an enrolled actuary certifies to the satisfaction of the Secretary of the Treasury that the excess is the result of nonrecurring circumstances, such nonrecurring circumstances are not included in the base amount. For purposes of determining the base amount, adjusted disbursements mean the amount of all disbursements from the plan's trust, including purchases of annuities, payments of single sums, other benefit payments, and administrative expenses reduced by the product of the plan's funded current liability percentage for the plan year and the sum of the purchases of annuities, payments of single sums, and such other disbursements as the Secretary of the Treasury provides in regulations.

Under the bill, the amount of the required quarterly installment for defined benefit pension plans that have a liquidity shortfall for any quarter is the greater of the quarterly installment as determined under present law or the liquidity shortfall. The amount of the liquidity shortfall must be paid in the form of liquid assets. It may not be paid by the application of credit balances in the funding standard account. The amount of any liquidity shortfall payment when added to prior installments for the plan year cannot exceed the amount necessary to increase the funded current liability percentage of the plan to 100 percent, taking into account the expected increase in current liability due to benefits accruing during the plan year.

If a liquidity shortfall payment is not made, then the plan sponsor will be subject to a nondeductible excise tax equal to 10 percent of the amount of the outstanding liquidity shortfall. A liquidity shortfall payment will no longer be considered outstanding on the earlier of (1) the last day of a later quarter for which the plan does not have a liquidity shortfall or (2) the date on which the liquidity shortfall for a later quarter is timely paid. If the liquidity shortfall remains outstanding after four quarters, the excise tax increases to 100 percent.

The bill amends ERISA to prohibit fiduciaries from making certain payments from defined benefit pension plans during the period in which the plan has a liquidity shortfall. Prohibited payments include (1) plan distributions in excess of the monthly amount paid under a single life annuity (plus any social security supplements) to plan participants or beneficiaries whose annuity starting date (as defined under present law) occurs during the period in which there is a liquidity shortfall, (2) purchases of benefit annuities from insurers, or (3) other payments as provided by the Secretary of the Treasury. The bill also amends ERISA to include a civil penalty for violations of the prohibited payment rule. Under the bill, if a fiduciary makes a prohibited distribution from the plan, he or she will be subject to a civil penalty for each prohibited distribution equal to the lesser of the amount of the distribution or $10,000. Finally, the bill amends the Code to provide that compliance with ERISA's prohibited payment rules will not result in plan disqualification for tax purposes.

Effective date

The provision generally applies to plan years beginning after December 31, 1994.

Limitation on changes in current liability assumptions

The bill prohibits certain underfunded plans from changing the actuarial assumptions used to determine current liability for a plan year (other than interest rate and mortality assumptions) unless the new assumptions are approved by the Secretary of the Treasury. Under the bill, approval of changes in actuarial assumptions applies to a single-employer defined benefit pension plan if: (1) the plan is subject to the termination insurance program under Title IV of ERISA; (2) the aggregated unfunded vested benefits of all underfunded plans maintained by the employer and members of the employer's controlled group exceed $50 million; and (3) the change in assumptions decreases the plan's unfunded current liability for the current plan year by (a) more than $50 million or (b) more than $5 million and at least 5 percent of the current liability.

Effective date

The provision is effective with respect to changes in actuarial assumptions for plan years beginning after October 28, 1993. In addition, any changes in actuarial assumptions for plan years beginning after December 31, 1992, and before October 29, 1993, that would have been subject to the approval requirements set forth in the bill will not be effective for plan years beginning after 1994 unless approved by the Secretary of the Treasury.

Anticipation of bargained benefit increases

The bill requires sponsors of collectively bargained plans to recognize any negotiated benefit increases scheduled to take effect in a future plan year in the plan year in which the collective bargaining agreement is entered into for purposes of the normal funding rules but not the special rules for underfunded plans.

Effective date

The provision applies to plan years beginning after December 31, 1994, with respect to collective bargaining agreements in effect on or after January 1, 1995.

Modification of quarterly contribution requirement

Under the bill, single-employer defined benefit plans with at least a 100-percent funded current liability percentage in the preceding plan year are not required to make quarterly estimated contributions during the current plan year.

Effective date

The provision is effective for plan years beginning after the date of enactment [December 8, 1994].

Adjustments to lien for missed minimum funding contributions

The bill (1) eliminates the 60-day waiting period before the lien arises, (2) eliminates the $1 million exclusion on amounts subject to the lien, and (3) provides that the lien applies only to plans covered by the PBGC termination insurance program. Thus, for example, the lien provision does not apply to plans maintained by a professional services employer which do not have more than 25 active participants or to plans maintained exclusively for substantial owners.

Effective date

The provision is effective for required contributions that become due on or after the date of enactment [December 8, 1994].

[¶ 12,250.071]

Committee Report on P.L. 103-465 (General Agreement on Tariffs and Trade (GATT); Retirement Protection Act)

[House Committee Report]

Special funding rule for certain plans

The bill provides that any changes made by the bill to the funding rules of the Code or ERISA do not apply to certain plans. In particular, such changes do not apply to a plan that, on the date of enactment [December 8, 1994], is subject to a restoration payment schedule order issued by the PBGC and that meets the requirements of Treasury regulations.

Such changes do not apply to a plan maintained by an affected air carrier (as defined in section 4001(a) of ERISA) and assumed by a new plan sponsor pursuant to the terms of a written agreement with the PBGC dated January 5, 1993, and approved by the U.S. Bankruptcy Court on December 30, 1992.

The bill also provides that for the first 5 plan years beginning after December 31, 1994, certain amortization amounts are not taken into account in the calculation of offsets under section 412(l)(1)(A)(ii) of the Code (and the corresponding section of ERISA). The amortization amounts that are not taken into account are those established for plan years beginning after December 31, 1987, and before January 1, 1993, by reason of nonelective changes under the frozen entry age actuarial cost method. An example of a nonelective change is a change in the method to redetermine the unfunded liability so as to prevent the calculation of a normal cost under the method that was negative.

Effective date

The provision is effective on the date of enactment [December 8, 1994].

[¶ 12,250.073]

Committee Reports on P.L. 101-239 (Omnibus Budget Reconciliation Act of 1989)

[House Committee Report]

Modifications of minimum funding standard

Deficit reduction contribution.—Under the bill, as under the Act, unfunded existing benefit increase liability is unfunded current liability determined by (1) taking into account only liabilities attributable to the benefit increase, and (2) by reducing plan assets by the plan's current liability determined without regard to the benefit increase. The bill clarifies that the calculation in (2) does not reduce plan assets below zero.

Under the bill, unfunded new liability is the unfunded current liability determined without regard to (1) the unamortized portion of the unfunded old liability, (2) the unamortized portion of the unfunded existing benefit increase liability, and (3) the liability with respect to any unpredictable contingent event benefits (without regard to whether or not the event has occurred). The bill thus conforms the treatment of unamortized existing benefit increase liability to the treatment of unamortized old liability for purposes of determining unfunded new liability.

The bill provides that the new funding rule for unpredictable contingent event benefits applies to such benefits with respect to which the event on which the benefit is contingent occurs in a plan year beginning after December 31, 1988. Benefits with respect to which the contingency occurs in a plan year beginning before January 1, 1989, are subject to the otherwise applicable funding rules, generally as an experience loss. This change in the effective date is made to eliminate issues arising with respect to transition from the pre-Act funding rule to the Act's funding rule for benefits with respect to which the contingency occurs after October 16, 1987, and before a plan year beginning after December 31, 1988.

Current liability.—In accordance with the legislative history, the bill provides that the rule disregarding certain preparticipation service does not apply with respect to a participant who does not, at the time of becoming a participant, have years of service in excess of the years required for plan eligibility.

The bill also provides that the rule disregarding preparticipation service is elective. The rule was intended to provide relief for employers in certain situations, for example, if the employer establishes a new plan that takes into account past service. The rule does not need to be imposed whether the employer does not need such relief. The bill provides that the election not to take advantage of the rule may be revoked only with the consent of the Secretary. Of course, if an employer does disregard preparticipation service, such service is disregarded for all purposes in calculating current liability. Thus, for example, it would be disregarded for purposes of the deduction rules as well as the minimum funding rules.

The bill provides that assets are to be reduced by any credit balance in the funding standard account for purposes of the new funding requirements (sec. 412(l)), and that, in other places where the term "unfunded current liability" is used, the Secretary may provide for such a reduction. Unfunded current liability is relevant not only for purposes of the new minimum funding requirements, but also for a number of other purposes under the Act. In calculating unfunded current liability, it is appropriate to reduce assets by any credit balance in the funding standard account for some purposes (such as the new funding rules) but not for others.

It is anticipated that no reduction will be made for purposes of the rule permitting deductions up to the amount of unfunded current liability (Code sec. 404(a)(1)(D)), the lien on missed contributions (Code sec. 412(n)), the security requirement for certain benefit increases (Code sec. 401(a)(29)), or the additional Pension Benefit Guaranty Corporation (PBGC) premium (ERISA sec. 4006(a)(3)(E)).

Valuations.—The bill provides that plan valuations are to be made not less frequently than annually. Annual valuations are necessary under the Act's minimum funding rules and the new full funding limit because the minimum and maximum contributions for a plan year depend on the plan's funded status for that year.

Steel employee plans.—For purposes of calculating the funded current liability percentage under the steel employee plan rule, the bill provides that unpredictable contingent event benefit liability, contributions relating to such liability, and income on such contributions are disregarded. The exclusion of income on such contributions is consistent with the Act's intent to provide a separate funding rule for unpredictable contingent event benefit liability.

[House Committee Report]

Time for contributions.—The bill clarifies that the installment payment requirement applies only to defined benefit plans (other than multiemployer plans) that are subject to the minimum funding requirements. Thus, under the bill, the installment payment requirement does not apply to money purchase pension plans. This is consistent with the general purpose of the pension provisions of the Act, which is to address problems associated with single employer defined benefit pension plans.

The bill modifies the special installment payment rule with respect to unpredictable contingent event benefits to conform the rule to the funding rule for such benefits. Under the bill, the otherwise required installment (determined without regard to unpredictable contingent event benefits) is increased by the greater of (1) the unfunded percentage (as determined under sec. 412(l)(5)(A)) of unpredictable contingent event benefits paid during the 3-month period preceding the month in which the installment is due, or (2) 25 percent of the amount required to be contributed for the plan year under the amortization rule for such benefits (sec. 412(l)(5)(A)(ii)).

The bill adds a sanction for failure to notify plan participants and beneficiaries of the failure to make required contributions. Under the bill, a court may require an employer who fails to comply to pay the affected participants and beneficiaries up to $100 per day from the date of the failure. This sanction is consistent with the existing sanctions under ERISA for failure to provide participants and beneficiaries with required information.

The bill conforms the Act to the legislative history by providing that the notice requirement with respect to participants and beneficiaries is effective with respect to plan years beginning after December 31, 1987.

The bill clarifies that the interest rate on underpayments of required installments is the greater of (1) 175 percent of the applicable Federal mid-term rate, or (2) the rate of interest used under the plan to determine costs (including any adjustments required for plans subject to the new funding rules under section 412(1)). Thus, under the bill, the interest rate on undeppayments will be at least equal to the interest rate the plan is using under the minimum funding rules.

[House Committee Report]

Limitation on interest rate

Present Law

Under the Act, the interest rate used for certain purposes under the minimum funding rules is required to be (1) within a specific permissible range, and (2) within that range, consistent with the interest rate which would be used by an insurance company to establish the amount it would charge an employer to satisfy the liabilities under the employer's plan. The permissible range under the Code is, in general, not more than 10 percent above and not more than 10 percent below the weighted average of the rates of interest on 30-year Treasury securities during a 4-year period.

Explanation of Provision

To reflect the legislative history, the bill provides that these special interest rate rules apply for purposes of determining current liability and for purposes of determining a plan's required contribution under the funding rules applicable to plans with assets less than current liability. Thus, the bill clarifies that these special rules do not apply for all purposes under the minimum funding rules. For purposes for which these special rules do not apply, the plan's interest rate is required to be reasonable in light of the experience of the plan and reasonable expectations.

The bill conforms the definition of the permissible range in ERISA to the Code definition of the permissible range.

[¶ 12,250.075]

Committee Reports on P.L. 100-203 (Omnibus Budget Reconciliation Act of 1987)

Conference Committee Report

Under the House bill, the full funding limitation generally is defined to mean the excess, if any, of (1) the lesser of (a) the accrued liability (including normal cost) under the plan, or (b) 150 percent of termination liability, over (2) the lesser of (a) the fair market value of the plan's assets, or (b) the value of the plan's assets determined under section 412(c)(2).

The bill does not modify the definition of accrued liability in section 412(c)(7). Also, the requirement that all amortizable amounts be considered fully amortized (sec. 412(c)(6)(B)) is applied without regard to the change in the full funding limitation (adding the 150 percent of termination liability limitation).

It is intended that the full funding limitation (as well as the other limitations on deductions for plan contributions) may not be avoided by the creation of multiple plans with coordination of benefits between the plans. The Secretary is to prescribe rules consistent with this intent.

The Secretary may, under regulations, adjust the 150-percent figure in the full funding limitation to take into account the average age (and length of service, if appropriate) of the participants in the plan (weighted by the value of their benefits under the plan). Any such adjustments are to be prescribed only if, in the aggregate, their effect on Federal budget receipts is substantially identical to the effect of this provision of the bill. For example, the Secretary could, if it satisfies the budget receipts requirement, adjust the 150-percent figure to 175 percent for younger workforces and to 125 percent for older workforces.

This provision is effective for years beginning after December 31, 1987.

The conference agreement follows the House bill (using the term "current liability" rather than "termination liability"), with certain modifications.

In addition to the regulatory authority provided under the House bill, the conference agreement authorizes the Secretary to prescribe regulations that apply, in lieu of the 150 percent of current liability limitation, a different full funding limitation based on factors other than current liability. The Secretary may exercise this authority only in a manner so that, in the aggregate, the effect of the regulations on Federal budget receipts is substantially identical to the effect of the 150-percent limitation.

In addition, under the conference agreement, the Secretary is to prescribe rules with respect to the treatment of contributions that would be required to be made but for the modification of the full funding limitation. The rules are to provide that the amount of such contributions are to be cumulated. In years in which the contributions required to be made to the plan are less than the full funding limitation (without regard to these cumulated amounts), the employer is to be required to contribute a portion of the cumulated amount. In determining the amount of this supplemental contribution, the Secretary may take into account factors such as the remaining working lifetime of the participants over which the entire cumulated amount may be contributed.

The conference agreement requires the Treasury Department to study the effect of the modification of the full funding limitation on benefit security in defined benefit pension plans and to report the results of the study to the House Ways and Means Committee, the Senate Finance Committee, and the Joint Committee on Taxation by August 15, 1988.

In addition, under the conference agreement, the Secretary is to prescribe regulations under this provision no later than August 15, 1988.

Conference Committee Report

[The House bill provides:] A special funding rule applies to plans with a funded ratio less than 100 percent. This special rule does not apply to (1) plans exempt from the funding requirements under present law, or (2) multiemployer plans.

A contribution in excess of the contribution required under the present-law funding rules generally is not required if a plan has a funded ratio of 100 percent.

[The Senate amendment provides:] Same as the Ways and Means Committee bill. In addition, the new funding rules for plans with a funded ratio of less than 100 percent do not apply to (1) plans that are not defined benefit plans and (2) plans with no more than 100 participants on any day in the preceding plan year. In the case of a plan with more than 100 but no more than 150 participants during the preceding year, the amount of the additional contribution is determined by multiplying the otherwise required additional contribution by 2 percent for each participant in excess of 100.

The amendment retains the present-law funding standards, with certain modifications. In addition, with respect to certain plans with a funded ratio less than 100 percent, the minimum required contribution is, in general terms, the greater of (1) the amount determined under section 412 (with the modifications made by the amendment), or (2) the sum of (i) normal cost, (ii) the amount necessary to amortize experience gains and losses and gains and losses resulting from changes in actuarial assumptions over 5 years, and (iii) the deficit reduction contribution. In addition, a special funding rule applies with respect to benefits that are contingent on unpredictable events.

Under the amendment, the deficit reduction contribution is the sum of (1) the unfunded old liability amount, and (2) the unfunded new liability amount. Calculation of these amounts is based upon the plan's "current liability".

Under the amendment, the term "current liability" means all liabilities to employees and their beneficiaries under the plan (Code Sec. 401(a)(2)) determined as if the plan terminated. However, the value of any "unpredictable contingent event benefit" is not taken into account in determining current liability until the event on which the benefit is contingent occurs. An "unpredictable contingent event benefit" is in general any benefit contingent on an event other than (1) age, service, compensation, death, or disability, or (2) an event which is reasonably and reliably predictable as determined by the Secretary.

Current liability is generally determined in accordance with plan assumptions, including the interest rate assumption. However, the amendment provides a special limitation on the interest rate used for purposes of calculating current liability. Under the amendment, if the plan interest rate is not within the permissible range, then the plan must establish a new rate within the permissible range. The permissible range is defined as a rate of interest that is not more than 20 percent above or below the average mid-term applicable Federal rate (AFR) for the 3-year period ending on the last day before the beginning of the plan year for which the interest rate is being used (or, if shorter, the period that the AFR has been computed). The average is determined by averaging the rate in effect for each month during the applicable 3-year period. The Secretary may prescribe one or more indices in lieu of the average mid-term AFR to be used in determining the permissible range.

The amendment provides that certain service may be disregarded at the employer's election in calculating the plan's current liability. In the case of certain participants, the applicable percentage of the years of service before the individual became a participant are taken into account in determining current liability. The applicable percentage is (1) 0, if the individual has 5 or less years of participation, (2) 20, if the individual has 6 years of participation, (3) 40, if the individual has 7 years of participation, (4) 60, if the individual has 8 years of participation, (5) 80, if the individual has 9 years of participation, and (6) 100 if the individual has 10 or more years of participation. Partial years of participation are rounded to the nearest whole year.

The amendment provides that unfunded current liability means, with respect to any plan year, the excess of (1) the current liability under the plan over (2) the value of the plan's assets reduced by any credit balance in the funding standard account. The funded current liability percentage of a plan for a plan year is the percentage that (1) the value of the plan's assets reduced by any credit balance in the funding standard account is of (2) the current liability under the plan.

The unfunded old liability amount is, in general, the amount necessary to amortize the unfunded old liability under the plan in equal annual installments (until fully amortized) over a fixed period of 15 plan years (beginning with the first plan year beginning after December 31, 1987). The "unfunded old liability" with respect to a plan is the unfunded current liability of the plan as of the beginning of the first plan year beginning after December 31, 1987, determined without regard to any plan amendment adopted after October 16, 1987, that increases plan liabilities (other than amendments adopted pursuant to certain collective bargaining agreements).

Under a special rule applicable to collectively bargained plans, increases in liabilities pursuant to a collective bargaining agreement ratified before October 17, 1987, are also amortized over 15 years.

The unfunded new liability amount for a plan year is the applicable percentage of the plan's "unfunded new liability." "Unfunded new liability" means the unfunded current liability of the plan for the plan year, determined without regard to (1) the unamortized portion of the unfunded old liability and (2) the liability with respect to any unpredictable contingent event benefits, without regard to whether or not the event has occurred. Thus, in calculating the unfunded new liability, all unpredictable contingent event benefits are disregarded, even if the event on which that benefit is contingent has occurred.

If the funded current liability percentage is less than 35 percent, then the applicable percentage is 30 percent. The applicable percentage decreases by .25 of one percentage point for each 1 percentage point by which the plan's funded current liability percentage exceeds 35 percent.

If the event on which an unpredictable contingent event benefit is contingent occurs during the plan year and the assets of the plan are less than current liability (calculated after the event has occurred), then an additional funding contribution (over and above the minimum funding contribution otherwise due) is required. The amount of the required additional contribution is generally equal to the greater of (1) the amount of unpredictable contingent event benefits paid during the plan year (regardless of the form in which paid), including (except as provided by the Secretary of the Treasury) any payment for the purchase of an annuity contract with respect to a participant with respect to such benefits, and (2) the amount that would be determined for the year if the unpredictable contingent event benefit liabilities were amortized in equal annual installments over 5 years, beginning with the plan year in which the event occurs. For the year in which the event occurs, an amount equal to 150 percent of the amount determined under (1) above may, at the employer's election, be treated as the unpredictable contingent benefit amount. In no case, however, will the unpredictable contingent event amount exceed the unfunded current liability (including the liability due to the contingent event benefit) of the plan.

A plan's funded ratio is the ratio of plan assets to current liability.

The portion of the regulations permitting asset valuations to be based on a range between 85 percent and 115 percent of average value are to have no force and effect.

In general, the changes in the minimum funding requirements for defined benefit pension plans apply with respect to plan years beginning after December 31, 1988. Unpredictable contingent event benefits with respect to which the event has occurred before October 17, 1987, are not subject to the new funding rule for such benefits. If the event has not occurred before October 17, 1987, such benefits are subject to the new funding rules for such benefits. For the first plan year beginning after December 31, 1987, unpredictable contingent event benefits are subject to the provisions of the amendment relating to gains and losses.

With respect to provisions that cross reference the definition of "current liability", the definition is effective at the time the provision cross referencing it is effective.

The change in the valuation regulations is effective with respect to plan years beginning after December 31, 1987.

The Secretary of the Treasury is to prescribe appropriate adjustments in the unpredictable contingent event amount, the old liability amount, the new liability amount, and the other charges and credits under section 412 as are necessary to avoid inappropriate duplication or omission of any factors in the determination of such amounts, charges and credits (for example, adjustments reflecting asset appreciation or depreciation).

It is also intended that the Secretary will provide special rules for multiple-employer plans where appropriate.

In general, the conference agreement follows the Finance Committee amendment, with certain modifications.

The conference agreement follows the Senate Finance Committee amendment. As under the Senate Finance Committee amendment, for purposes of the rules for plans with no more than 100 participants or plans with 101 to 150 participants, all defined benefit plans (including multiemployer plans) of the employer and the employer's controlled group are treated as a single plan. The definition of a controlled group is the same as the definition in section 414(b)), (c), (m) and (o). With respect to a multiemployer plan, only employees of the employer (or a controlled group member) are taken into account.

The conference agreement follows the Finance Committee amendment, with the following modifications. Gains and losses due to changes in actuarial assumptions are amortized over 10 years, rather than over 5 years. The conferees intend that reporting requirements will be revised as necessary to implement the new funding rules, for example, to reflect current liability, unfunded old liability, unfunded new liability, and the liabilities for unpredictable event contingent benefits.

Current liability is defined as in the Finance Committee amendment, with the following modifications. Thus, current liability is, in general, all liabilities to participants and beneficiaries under the plan (Code sec. 401(a)(2)) determined as if the plan terminated. Under the conference agreement, the permissible range for the interest rate is not more than 10 percent above or below the average rate for 30-year Treasury bonds for the 4-year period ending on the last day before the beginning of the plan year for which the interest rate is being used. Under appropriate circumstances, the Secretary of the Treasury may provide that the permissible range is expanded to include rates between 80 and 90 percent of the average rate described above. For purposes of determining the average rate for the 4-year period, the Secretary may prescribe rules weighting the more recent years more heavily.

No rate outside the permissible range is permitted under any circumstances. Also, the specified corridor is not intended to be a safe harbor with respect to whether an interest rate is reasonable. The Secretary is authorized to adjust a rate within the range to the extent that it is unreasonable under the rules applicable to actuarial assumptions.

The conference agreement modifies the rule disregarding certain preparticipation service. Under the modification, preparticipation years of service are taken into account over 5 years of participation. Partial years of participation are rounded to the nearest whole year.

The rule disregarding preparticipation service is available with respect to any participant who, at the time of becoming a participant, has not accrued any other benefits under any defined benefit pension plan (whether or not terminated) of the employer or a member of the controlled group of the employer, and has years of service before such time in excess of the years of service required for eligibility to participate in the plan. The rule applies only with respect to new participants in years beginning after December 31, 1987. The rule is not elective.

With respect to the definition of unpredictable contingent event benefits, the conferees do not intend that an event will be considered reliably and reasonably predictable solely because an actuarial probability of the event occurring may be determined. It is further intended that the Secretary of the Treasury will prescribe rules defining events that can and cannot be reasonably and reliably predicted and will revise these rules as new benefits are developed.

Unpredictable contingent event benefits are intended to include benefits that depend on contingencies that, like facility shutdowns or reductions or contractions in workforce, are not reliably and reasonably predictable. Such contingencies are not limited to events that are similar to shutdowns or reductions in force. For example, a benefit dependent on the profits of the employer or the value of employer stock dropping below a certain level would be considered a benefit contingent on an event that is not reasonably and reliably predictable (unless the contingency is illusory).

If an employer provides an early retirement window benefit under which employees who have satisfied certain age or service requirements or both are offered a limited period of time during which they may elect to retire, such a window benefit is generally considered to be contingent on an event that can be reasonably and reliably predicted. The Secretary of the Treasury may, in appropriate circumstances, treat such window benefits which are contingent on an event that cannot be reasonably and reliably predicted.

It is intended that a benefit contingent on marital status, such as a qualified joint and survivor annuity, is generally to be considered a benefit that is contingent on an event that can be reasonably and reliably predicted.

It is intended that the Secretary of the Treasury may prescribe rules to prevent employers from avoiding the new minumum funding rules by characterizing contingencies as not reasonably and reliably predictable. For purposes of the definition of current liability, a benefit is generally not to be considered contingent on an event which is not reasonably and reliably predictable if there is substantial certainty that the event on which the benefit depends will occur.

An early retirement subsidy, social security supplement, survivor subsidy or similar benefit in addition to the basic retirement benefit under a plan that is payable only on the satisfaction of certain eligibility conditions (e.g., age and/or years of service eligibility conditions), is included in current liability (provided it is not an unpredictable event contingent benefit) to the extent that the employee has earned the subsidy, supplement, or similar benefit.

For example, assume that a plan provides that an employee is entitled to a basic retirement benefit commencing at age 65 of 1 percent of final average pay times years of service and that, if the employee retires at age 55 with at least 25 years of service, the employee's retirement benefit will not be actuarially reduced for early commencement (i.e., this is an early retirement subsidy). For purposes of calculating the current liability for such plan for a year, an employee age 50 with 20 years of service has a total retirement benefit (i.e., normal retirement benefit plus early retirement subsidy) of 80 percent of the unreduced age 55 benefit (based on final average pay at age 50). That is, there is no actuarial reduction for commencement before age 65. The same analysis applies in determining the extent to which a social security supplement, survivor subsidy, or similar benefit has been earned under the plan.

Current liability is generally determined in accordance with plan assumptions. Thus, in the example described above, because not all employees who have earned a right to some portion of the early retirement benefit will ultimately satisfy the eligibility conditions for the subsidy (e.g., not all such employees will remain with the employer until age 55 or retire at age 55), a plan is to calculate its current liability for the year by using reasonable turnover and mortality factors.

The conference agreement follows the Finance Committee amendment, except that the unfunded old liability amount is amortized over 18 years rather than 15 years. Thus, under the conference agreement, the unfunded old liability amount with respect to a collectively bargained plan is increased by the amount necessary to amortize the unfunded existing benefit increase liabilities in equal annual installments over a fixed period of 18 plan years, beginning with the plan year in which the increase in liabilities occurs pursuant to the bargaining agreement (or, if later, the first plan year beginning after December 31, 1988). For purposes of this rule, the unfunded existing benefit increase liability means the unfunded current liability determined by taking into account ony (1) liabilities attributable to the increase in liabilities pursuant to the agreement, and (2) the value of assets in excess of current liability (determined without regard to the liabiities described in (1)).

For purposes of the special rule applicable to certain benefit increases pursuant to a collective bargaining agreement ratified before October 17, 1987, any extension, amendment, or other modification of a bargaining agreement after October 16, 1987, is not taken into account. In general, the special rule only includes increases in liability pursuant to the bargaining agreement and therefore does not include liability increases with respect to individuals covered by the plan who are not subject to the collective bargaining agreement. However, if more than 75 percent of the employees covered by the plan in October 16, 1987, are subject to the collective bargaining agreement, then the unfunded existing benefit increase liability includes the liability with respect to all employees in the plan whose benefits are determined directly or indirectly by reference to the terms of the bargaining agreement, whether or not such employees are subject to the agreement. Separate plans may not be treated as a single plan for purposes of this rule, even if the benefits under the plans are coordinated.

The conference agreement follows the Finance Committee amendment with respect to the definition and funding of unpredictable contingent event benefits, except that the cash flow rule and amortization period are modified. Under the conference agreement, the amount of the additional contributions is generally equal to the greater of (1) the unfunded portion of the benefits paid during the plan year (regardless of the form in which paid), including (except as provided by the Secretary of the Treasury) and any payment for the purchase of an annuity contract with respect to a participant with respect to contingent event benefits, and (2) the amount that would be determined for the year if the unpredictable contingent event benefit liabilities were amortized in equal annual installments over 7 years, beginning with the plan year in which the event occurs.

The effects of the cash flow rule in (1) are phased in at a rate of 5 percent for plan years beginning in 1989 and 1990, 10 percent for plan years beginning in 1991, 15 percent for plan years beginning in 1992, 20 percent for plan years beginning in 1993, 30 percent for plan years beginning in 1994, 40 percent for plan years beginning in 1995, 50 percent for plan years beginning in 1996, 60 percent for plan years beginning in 1997, 70 percent for plan years beginning in 1998, 80 percent for plan years beginning in 1999, 90 percent for plan years beginning in 2000, and 100 percent for plan years beginning in 2001.

The event on which an unpredictable contingent event benefit is contingent is generally not considered to have occurred until all events on which the benefit is contingent have occurred. If the event on which an unpredictable contingent event benefit is contingent occurs during the plan year and the assets of the plan equal or exceed current liability (calculated after the event has occurred), then the employer may continue to fund the plan's unpredictable contingent event benefits as under present law (i.e., generally as an experience loss), subject to application of the special rule if the plan's funding falls below current liability.

The conference agreement follows the Finance Committee amendment with respect to the value of assets under section 412(c)(2)(A). In addition, the conference agreement repeals section 412(c)(2)(B) (except for multiemployer plans), subjecting bonds and other evidence of indebtedness to the general valuation rules. The Secretary may, however, prescribe regulations under which a dedicated bond portfolio is to be valued by using the interest rate used to determine current liability.

Effective date

The conference agreement generally follows the Finance Committee amendment, except that the modified cash flow rule for unpredictable contingent event benefits is effective for plan years beginning after December 31, 1988.

In addition, the conference agreement adopts the special rule for steel employer plans in the Ways and Means Committee bill, with a modification. Under the modification, liabilities (and contributions) with respect to unpredictable event contingent benefits with respect to which the contingency occurs after December 17, 1987, are not taken into account in calculating current liability under the rule, but are amortized separately over 10 years.

Conference Committee Report

Under the [House] bill, three installments of estimated contributions are required during the plan year, with the total contribution due within 2 ½ months after the end of the plan year. The amount of each installment is ¼ of the lesser of (1) 80 percent of the amount required to be contributed for the current plan year or (2) 90 percent of the amount required to be contributed for the preceding plan year.

An excise tax is imposed if the full amount of any required installment is not paid. The excise tax is determined by applying the interest rate for underpayment of income taxes to the amount of the underpayment for the period of the underpayment. The period of the underpayment begins on the due date of the installment and ends on the earlier of the date on which the underpayment is contributed to the plan or the date the total contribution is due. Each member of the employer's controlled group is jointly and severally liable for the tax.

Each member of the employer's controlled group is jointly and severally liable for the excise tax.

The acceleration of the due date for required plan contributions generally is effective for plan years beginning after December 31, 1988, with a phase-in rule applying for plan years beginning in 1988. The provision requiring plan contributions to be made in installments is effective for plan years beginning after December 31, 1987, with a transition rule applicable for 1988 plan years.

[The Finance Committee amendment provides:] Similar to the Ways and Means Committee bill, except that four installments are required during the plan year, with the total contribution due within 8 ½ months after the end of the plan year. The amount of each required installment is ¼ of the lesser of (1) 90 percent of the amount required to be contributed for the current plan year or (2) 100 percent of the amount required to be contributed for the preceding plan year.

Failure to make installments.—Same as the Ways and Means Committee bill, except that interest is paid to the plan rather than as an excise tax, and the interest rate on missed contributions is the greater of (1) 175 percent of the mid-term applicable Federal interest rate (AFR) or (2) the rate of interest taken into account in determining costs under the plan. In addition, a lien arises if a required installment is not paid in full. The employer is required to notify employees of the failure to make required installments.

Failure to make total contribution for plan year.—Same as the Ways and Means Committee bill. In addition, the 5-percent excise tax is increased to 10 percent, and a lien arises in favor of the plan if the required contribution is not paid in full. The employer is required to notify employees of the failure to make contributions.

The provisions apply for plan years beginning after December 31, 1987.

The conference agreement generally follows the Finance Committee amendment, with modifications.

With respect to the interest rate applicable to a failure to make contributions when due, the conference agreement clarifies that the interest rate continues at the specified rate until the missed contributions are actually paid to the plan.

In the case of a plan with a funded ratio of less than 100 percent, a statutory tax lien arises on all controlled group property in favor of the plan 60 days after the due date of an unpaid contribution (whether or not a waiver application is pending). The amount of the lien is the cumulative missed contributions in excess of $1 million. Missed contributions originally due before the effective date are not subject to this lien provision (but they are taken into account in applying the $1 million rule).

Under the conference agreement, the employer and each member of the controlled group that includes the employer are liable for contributions required under the minimum funding rules. However, this controlled group liability does not alter the rules for determining the extent to which an employer's contributions to a plan are deductible. Thus, in general, a deduction for a contribution is available under section 404 only for the employer who directly employs the participants.

Conference Committee Report

Ways and Means Committee bill: The bill clarifies that a waiver can be granted only if the business hardship is temporary and if the entire controlled group of which the employer is a member, as well as the employer itself, is experiencing the hardship.

A request for a waiver is required to be submitted within 2 ½ months after the end of the plan year.

Funding waivers cannot be granted in more than 3 of any 15 consecutive plan years.

In addition to the notice to employee organizations, an employer is required to demonstrate that it made reasonable efforts to notify current employees that a waiver is being requested.

The interest rate charged on waived contributions is the greater of (1) the rate used in computing costs under the plan, or (2) 150 percent of the mid-term applicable Federal interest rate (AFR) in effect for the first month of the plan year.

The amortization period for waived contributions is the greater of (1) 5 years or (2) 15 years multiplied by the funded termination liability percentage for the plan year, rounded to the nearest whole number of years.

The bill lowers from $2 million to $250,000 the threshold on the accumulated funding deficiency with respect to which the IRS can require security. In the case of a plan with accumulated funding deficiencies in excess of $1 million or a plan that is not more than 70 percent funded, the PBGC is authorized to require that an employer provide security as a condition of granting a funding waiver.

The provision relating to the funding waivers generally is effective with respect to (1) any application for a funding waiver submitted after June 30, 1987, and (2) any waiver granted with respect to an application submitted after June 30, 1987. The provision requiring that applications for funding waivers be filed within 2 ½ months following the close of a plan year is effective for plan years beginning after December 31, 1987, with a transition rule for 1988 plan years.

Education and Labor bill: The present-law notice is to be provided to all affected parties (i.e., participants, beneficiaries, alternate payees, and employee organizations representing employees covered under the plan). In addition, the notice must describe the extent to which the plan is funded with respect to guaranteed benefits and benefit liabilities.

Labor and Human Resources Committee amendment: Notice of waiver requests: Same as the Education and Labor Committee bill, except that no definition of affected party is provided.

Amortization period for waived contributions: The amortization period for waived contributions is 5 plan years.

Conference Agreement: The conference agreement [generally] follows the Ways and Means Committee and Education and Labor Committee bills, and the Labor and Human Resources Committee amendment. In addition, the conference agreement provides that the Secretary may provide that an analysis of the financial hardship of a member of the controlled group of the employer need not be conducted. Such an analysis is not necessary because taking into account the circumstances of the member of the controlled group would not significantly affect the determination of whether a waiver should be granted. Although, with respect to multi-employer plans, the conference agreement does not incorporate in the statute the requirement that the financial hardship be temporary, the conferees do not intend to create an inference with respect to the current IRS practice of granting waivers only in the case of temporary hardship.

Time for requesting waivers: The conference agreement follows the Ways and Means Committee and Education and Labor Committee bills, and the Labor and Human Resources Committee amendment.

Frequency of waivers: The conference agreement follows the Ways and Means Committee and Education and Labor Committee bills, and the Labor and Human Resources Committee amendment, except that employers will not be treated as exceeding the number of permissible waivers due to waivers granted with respect to the plan years beginning before January 1, 1988. Thus, under the conference agreement, employers are provided a fresh start with respect to the frequency limit on waivers. As under present law, where a plan undergoes a transaction pursuant to the Implementation Guidelines, the successor plan shall not be considered a new plan for purposes of the frequency limit on waivers.

Notice of waiver requests: The conference agreement follows the Education and Labor Committee bill and the Labor and Human Resources Committee amendment. The conference agreement does not require that the employer furnish a copy of the waiver request to employees, and does not require that the Secretary furnish (or make available) a copy of the request to employees.

Interest rate charged for waived contributions: The conference report follows the Ways and Means Committee bill and the Finance Committee amendment.

Amortization period for waived contributions: The conference agreement follows the Labor and Human Resources Committee amendment.

Security for waivers: The conference agreement follows the Education and Labor Committee bill, and the Finance Committee and Labor and Human Resources Committee amendments, except that the present-law threshold with respect to which IRS may require security, etc., is reduced from $2 million to $1 million.

Effective date

The conference agreement follows the Ways and Means Committee bill, except that the date after which a submission of a funding waiver request is subject to the funding waiver provisions is December 17, 1987, rather than June 30, 1987. In addition, the provision regarding notice of waiver requests is effective with respect to applications for waivers submitted more than 90 days after the date of enactment.

House bill

Education and Labor Committee bill: The employer is required to notify each affected party that an extension is being requested. The interest rate charged with respect to an extension is the greater of (1) the interest rate used for calculating contributions under the plan or (2) [150] percent of the mid-term AFR in effect on the first day of the plan year for which the extension is requested.

Labor and Human Resources Committee amendment: Same as the Education and Labor Committee bill, except that no definition of affected party is provided.

Conference Agreement: The conference agreement follows the Education and Labor Committee bill and the Labor and Human Resources Committee amendments, with two modifications.

First, the interest rate charged is the greater of (1) the rate used in computing costs under the plan, or (2) 150 percent of the mid-term AFR in effect for the first month of the plan year.

Second, the $2 million threshold on the accumulated funding deficiency with respect to which the IRS can require security is reduced to $1 million, as under the rules of funding waivers.

The effective date of the provision is the same as the effective date of the funding waiver provisions.

[Conference Committee Report]

House bill

Education and Labor Committee bill: The period for amortizing experience gains and losses is reduced to 5 years from 15 years.

Finance Committee amendment: The Finance Committee amendment is the same as the Education and Labor Committee bill, except that the provision is effective for years beginning after December 31, 1987.

Conference Agreement: The conference agreement follows the Finance Committee amendment. The provision does not apply to gains and losses arising in plan years beginning before January 1, 1988.

Finance Committee amendment: Gains and losses due to changes in actuarial assumptions are amortized over [10] years. The provision is effective for years beginning after December 31, 1987.

Conference Agreement: The conference agreement follows the Finance Committee amendment, except that the amortization period is 10 years.

Ways and Means Committee bill: All costs, liabilities, interest rates, and other factors are required to be determined on the basis of actuarial assumptions and methods (1) each of which is reasonable individually or (2) which result, in the aggregate, in a total plan contribution equivalent to the contribution that would be obtained if each assumption were reasonable. The interest rate used in calculating costs generally is required to be within a permissible range, defined as an interest rate not more than 20 percent above or below the average long-term AFR for the 5-year period ending on the last day of preceding plan year. The provision applies to plan years beginning after December 31, 1987.

Finance Committee amendment: The Finance Committee amendment is the same as the Ways and Means bill, except that the amendment does not include the requirement that the plan's interest rate be within the permissible range. The provision applies to years beginning after December 31, 1987.

Conference Agreement: The conference agreement follows the Finance Committee amendment, with certain modifications. The interest rate applicable in determining current liability is required to be used with respect to determining the required contribution under section 412(l).

In addition, with respect to the interest rate that is used to determine current liability and thus is required to be within the permissible range, the determination of whether such interest rate is reasonable depends on the cost of purchasing an annuity sufficient to satisfy current liability. The interest rate is to be a reasonable estimate of the interest rate used to determine the cost of such annuity, assuming that the cost only reflected the present value of the payments under the annuity (i.e., did not reflect the seller's profit, administrative expenses, etc.). For example, if an annuity costs $1,100, the cost of $1,100 is considered to be the present value of the payments under the annuity for purposes of the interest rate rule, even though $100 of the $1,100 represents the seller's administrative expense and profit. Also, in making this determination with respect to the interest rate used to determine the cost of an annuity, other factors and assumptions (e.g., mortality) are to be individually reasonable.

It is further intended that, for purposes of determining the reasonableness of an interest rate under the approach described above, the plan benefit generally is a normal benefit under the plan (without regard to, for example, any provision providing for a lump sum payment).

Ways and Means Committee bill: The bill clarifies that the amortizable base in determining an employer's maximum deduction for past service liability equals only the unfunded costs attributable to such liability. The provision is effective for plan years beginning after December 31, 1987.

Conference Agreement: The conference agreement follows the Ways and Means Committee bill. No inference is intended with respect to present law.

Ways and Means Committee bill: The maximum deduction limit for contributions is not less than the unfunded termination liability of the plan. This rule applies only to a plan subject to the plan termination insurance provisions of ERISA and only if the plan has 100 or more participants during the plan year. The provision is effective for plan years beginning after December 31, 1987.

Finance Committee amendment: The Finance Committee amendment follows the Ways and Means Committee bill (using "current liability" instead of "termination liability," without a substantive change), except that the increased deduction limit applies to all defined benefit pension plans with 100 or more participants. The provision is effective for years beginning after December 31, 1987.

Conference Agreement: The conference agreement follows the Finance Committee agreement, but also provides that, in determining unfunded current liability, assets are not reduced by credit balances.

House Bill: Under the House bill, the full funding limitation generally is defined to mean the excess, if any, of (1) the lesser of (a) the accrued liability (including normal cost) under the plan, or (b) 150 percent of termination liability, over (2) the lesser of (a) the fair market value of the plan's assets, or (b) the value of the plan's assets determined under section 412(c)(2).

The House bill provides a special limitation on the interest rate used for funding purposes (including the full funding limitation). Under the bill, the interest rate is required to be within a permissible range, which is defined as a rate of interest that is not more than 20 percent above or below the average long-term applicable Federal rate (AFR) for the 5-year period ending on the last day before the beginning of the plan year for which the interest rate is being used.

If any interest rate used under the plan is not within the permissible range, then the plan generally is required to establish a new interest rate that is within the permissible range. However, the Secretary may permit a plan to use an interest rate that is not within the permissible range if it is established, to the satisfaction of the Secretary, that the interest rate is reasonable. Further, if the Secretary determines that any interest rate used under the plan is not reasonable (without regard to whether the rate is within the permissible range), then the plan is required to establish a new interest rate that is permitted by the Secretary.

This provision is effective for years beginning after December 31, 1987.

Senate Amendment: The Senate amendment generally follows the House bill, with the following exceptions.

The Senate amendment uses the term "current liability" instead of the term "termination liability" as under the House bill, but the substance of the two terms is the same. For purposes of calculating current liability under the amendment, the interest rate is the rate used for calculating costs under the plan. If such rate is not within the permissible range, however, then for this purpose the plan is required to establish a new interest rate that is within the permissible range. The permissible range is defined as a rate of interest that is not more than 20 percent above or below the average mid-term applicable Federal rate (AFR) for the 3-year period ending on the last day before the beginning of the plan year for which the interest rate is being used (or, if shorter, the period that the AFR has been computed). The average is determined by averaging the rate in effect for each month during the applicable 3-year period. The Secretary may prescribe one or more indices in lieu of the average mid-term AFR to be used in determining the permissible range.

Conference Agreement: The conference agreement follows the House bill (using the term "current liability" rather than "termination liability"), with certain modifications.

The conference agreement follows the rule under the Senate amendment with respect to the interest rate to be used in determining current liability, with certain modifications. Under the conference agreement, for this purpose, the interest rate is generally the rate determined under the plan's assumptions. However, notwithstanding the plan's assumptions, the interest rate is required to be within 10 percent of the average rate for 30-year Treasury bonds for the 4-year period ending on the last day before the beginning of the plan year for which the interest rate is being used. This creates a permissible range of between 90 percent and 110 percent of such average rate. Under appropriate circumstances, the Secretary may also permit interest rates that are between 80 percent and 90 percent of the average rate described above. For purposes of determining the average rate for the 4-year period, the Secretary may prescribe rules weighting the more recent years more heavily.

No rate outside of the specified corridor is permitted under any circumstances. Also, the specified corridor is not intended to be a safe harbor with respect to whether an interest rate is reasonable. The Secretary is authorized to adjust a rate within the corridor to the extent that it is unreasonable under the rules applicable to actuarial assumptions.

The conference agreement requires the Treasury Department to study the effect of the modification of the full funding limitation on benefit security in defined benefit pension plans and to report the results of the study to the House Ways and Means Committee, the Senate Finance Committee, and the Joint Committee on Taxation by August 15, 1988.

In addition, under the conference agreement, the Secretary is to prescribe regulations under this provision no later than August 15, 1988.

[¶ 12,250.08]

Committee Report on P.L. 99-272 (Consolidated Omnibus Budget Reconciliation Act)

[Conference Committee Report]

The conference agreement clarifies that the IRS is authorized to require that security be provided as a condition of granting a waiver of the minimum funding standard, the extension of an amortization period, or modification of a previously granted waiver of the minimum funding standard with respect to a single employer defined benefit plan. The conference agreement requires that, before granting an application for a waiver, extension or modification to a single employer defined benefit plan, the IRS notify the PBGC of the receipt of a completed application for a waiver, extension, or modification, and consider the views of any interested party, including the PBGC, submitted in writing. The PBGC has a 30-day period after the date of receipt of notice to submit to the IRS comments on the application.

The conference agreement provides that the notice of the application and any other information or materials relating to the application that is sent to the PBGC by the IRS constitutes tax return information and is subject to the safeguarding and reporting requirements of section 6103(p) of the Code.

Under the conference agreement, the security, notice, and comment provisions do not apply if, with respect to the plan for which a waiver is requested, the sum of (a) the accumulated funding deficiencies (including the amount of any increase in the accumulated funding deficiency that would result if the request for a waiver were denied); (b) the outstanding balance of any previously waived funding deficiencies; and (c) the outstanding balance of any decreases in the minimum funding standard allowed under section 303 of ERISA, is less than $2 million. As under current law, the mere creation of a security interest at the direction of the Secretary of the Treasury as a condition for granting a waiver does not by itself constitute a prohibited transaction. The provisions of the conference agreement relating to security are intended by the conferees to provide appropriate rules for the future. The conferees intend that no inference is to be drawn from this provision with respect to the application of present law to such transactions.

The conference agreement also contains an amendment to the Code requiring that if the IRS grants a request for a waiver, extension, or modification, the interest on the waived amount must be computed by using a rate prescribed in section 6621(b) of the Code.

Finally, under the conference agreement, an employer that submits an application for a waiver of the minimum funding standard is required to notify any employee organization representing participants in the plan of the application.

See also ¶ 11,900.085 for the Committee Report relating to the repeal of the bond purchase provisions.

[¶ 12,250.085]

Committee Report on P.L. 96-364 (Multiemployer Pension Plan Amendments Act of 1980)

The Senate Committee Report on P.L. 96-364 (Sec. 208(c)) is at ¶ 15,709.10.

[¶ 12,250.09]

Committee Report on P.L. 96-364 (Multiemployer Pension Plan Amendments Act of 1980)

[Senate Committee Report]

Minimum funding requirements.—Explanation of provisions.—1. In general.—The bill modifies the periods over which past service liabilities and experience gains and losses under multiemployer plans would be required to be amortized for the purpose of making charges and credits to the funding standard account. In general, the new amortization periods follow those required of single-employer plans for funding purposes. However, certain transitional rules are provided under which the present-law amortization periods continue to apply to multiemployer plans in certain circumstances.

The bill includes two changes of general applicability in the amortization periods now prescribed by ERISA. Special funding requirements for financially troubled plans are described in the discussion of reorganization below.

For purposes of determining charges to the funding standard account, the bill provides that certain unfunded past service liabilities are amortized over 30 rather than 40 years, and net experience gains or losses are amortized in equal annual installments over 15 rather than 20 years. These changes generally result in the same funding requirements for these items as are now required for single-employer plans.

The Committees believe that 40-year funding of past services liability is too long. In many instances, the promised benefits will have to be paid before the 40-year funding is completed. The change to 30-year funding will help to assure that plan assets are adequate to meet emerging liabilities yet will increase the annual funding cost to employers only modestly.

The bill prescribes transitional rules under which the longer amortization periods of current law would continue to apply to the following: past service liabilities and experience gains and losses that arose before the enactment date of this bill; past service liabilities arising from an amendment adopted before the enactment date and effective by the end of the third plan year after enactment; and past service liabilities arising from movement of participants from lower to higher benefit levels on a schedule of benefits adopted before the enactment date and effective before the first plan year after enactment.

The bill authorizes the Secretary of the Treasury to prescribe regulations requiring additional charges and credits to the funding standard account to prevent withdrawal liability payments from being unduly reflected as advance funding of plan liabilities. The bill also makes conforming amendments of the funding rules to take the account of changes made in other parts of the bill.

2. Modification of charges to funding standard account.—a. Past service liability.—Under the bill, certain amounts of unfunded past service liability are to be amortized in equal annual installments over 30 years for purposes of determining charges to the funding standard account. These charges are (1) unfunded past service liability determined as of the first day of the first plan year of a plan not in existence on enactment, and (2) any net increase in unfunded past service liability arising from plan amendments adopted during a plan year.

b. Experience losses.—Under the bill, a net experience loss is to be amortized in equal annual installments over 15 years for purposes of determining charges to the funding standard account.

3. Modification of credits to funding standard account.—a. Past service liability.—Under the bill, any decrease in unfunded past service liability arising from plan amendments adopted during a plan year is to be amortized in equal annual installments over 30 years for purposes of determining credits to the funding standard account.

b. Experience gains.—Under the bill, a net experience gain is to be amortized in equal annual installments over 15 years for purposes of determining credits to the funding standard account.

c. Withdrawal liability.—Under the bill, any withdrawal liability payment to a plan for a plan year is to be treated as an amount contributed to the plan for the year. Accordingly, it will generate a credit to the funding standard account.

4. Prior amortizable amounts and transitional rules.—Under the bill, any amortizable amounts described above that arose in a plan year beginning before the date the bill was enacted are to continue to be amortized over their respective previously established amortization periods. The bill also provides transitional rules under which the amortization periods of present law apply to certain future changes in past service liability.

5. Application of minimum funding standards to terminated multiemployer plan.—Under the bill, the minimum funding standard applies with respect to a terminated multiemployer plan until the date on which the last remaining employer withdraws from the plan.

Effective Date

These provisions of the bill apply on the date of enactment.

[¶ 12,250.10]

Committee Report on P.L. 93-406 (Employee Retirement Income Security Act of 1974)

[Conference Committee Explanation]

Timing of contributions.—The conference substitute clarifies the intent of both the House bill and Senate amendment, that contributions made after the close of a plan year may relate back to that plan year for purposes of the minimum funding standards. Under the conference substitute, the contribution may relate back to the plan year if it is made within 2 ½ months after the close of that plan year, plus any extension granted by the Internal Revenue Service up to an additional 6 months (for a maximum of 8 ½ months after the end of the year).

Coverage and exemptions from coverage.—

* * *

Under the conference substitute, government plans, including plans financed by contributions required under the Railroad Retirement Act, are to be exempt from the new funding requirement but they must meet the requirements of present law (sec. 401(a)(7) of the Internal Revenue Code). The conferees intended that no changes are to be made in the application of the present funding requirements of the Internal Revenue Code to government plans. Although present law establishes a "safe haven rule" for payment of normal cost plus interest on past service costs, it is not intended that this safe haven rule become a requirement for government plans, but that (as under present Regs. § 1.401-6(c)(1)) the determination on whether a plan has terminated is to be made on "all the facts and circumstances in the particular case." Thus, it is intended that there be no change in the application of present law to government plans.

The conference substitute exempts church plans from the new funding requirement if they meet the requirements of present law. However, church plans which elect to be covered under the participation, vesting, and termination insurance provisions are also to be covered by the new funding requirements.

The conference substitute excludes from the minimum funding rules plans established and maintained outside the United States if they are primarily for the benefit of persons substantially all of whom are nonresident aliens. This is specifically provided in the title I provisions, while under title II, such plans would have no need to seek tax deferral qualification.

The conference substitute excludes from the minimum funding rules of title I unfunded plans maintained by the employer primarily to provide deferred compensation for select management or highly compensated employees (under title II, such plans do not seek tax qualification). The conferees intend that this exemption is to include "consultant contracts" for retired management employees. Additionally, the substitute exempts from the funding rules plans adopted by a partnership exclusively for the benefit of a partner pursuant to section 736 of the Internal Revenue Code.

Under the conference substitute, plans which have not provided for employer contributions at any time after the date of enactment are to be exempt from minimum funding rules (i.e., plans of unions funded exclusively by contributions of the union members).

An exemption is also provided for profit-sharing and stock bonus plans; however, money purchase pension plans and other individual account plans generally are not excluded from the minimum funding rules.

It is intended that plans generally are to be considered money purchase pension plans which meet the "definitely determinable" standard where the employer's contributions are fixed by the plan, even if the employer's obligation to contribute for any individual employee may vary based on the amount contributed to the plan in any year by the employee. For example, it is expected that a matching plan which provides that an employer will annually contribute up to 6 percent of an employee's salary, but that this contribution will be no more than the employee's own (nondeductible) contribution, will meet the "definitely determinable" criteria. In this case, the employer's contributions are set by the plan, will not vary with profits, and cannot be varied by the employer's action (other than by a plan amendment). (Of course, the plan must meet the nondiscrimination and other requirements of the Code to be qualified.)

Plans funded exclusively by the purchase of certain qualified level premium individual insurance contracts also are not to be subject to the minimum funding requirements. Additionally, the conference substitute makes it clear that where, instead of buying a series of such individual contracts, the employer holds a group insurance contract under which each employee's plan benefit is funded in the same manner as if individual contracts were purchased, the situation is to be treated the same as where there are individual insurance contracts. This generally will be available where the employer's premium is based on the sum of the level premiums attributable to each employee, where an employee's accrued benefit at any point in time is comparable to what would be provided under an individual contract, and as otherwise determined by regulations.

Supplemental unfunded plans which provide benefits in excess of limitations on contributions and benefits under the Internal Revenue Code and plans which are for the highly paid are to be excluded from the new funding standard. In addition, plans established by fraternal societies or other organizations described in section 501(c)(8) or (9) of the Internal Revenue Code are to be exempt if no employer contributions are made to the plan. Also, trusts which are part of plans described in section 501(c)(18) of the Code are to be exempt from the funding standards of title I (the standards of title II do not apply because those plans are not qualified plans).

[Code Sec. 413]

[¶ 12,300.095]

Committee Reports on P.L. 100-647 (Technical and Miscellaneous Revenue Act of 1988)

[Senate Committee Report]

* * *

Under present law, certain special rules apply to a plan maintained pursuant to an agreement that the Secretary of Labor finds to be a collective bargaining agreement between employee representatives and 1 or more employers. Under these special rules, the coverage rules (sec. 410 (other than sec. 410(a))) are to be applied as if all employees of each of the employers who are parties to the collective bargaining agreement and who are subject to the same benefit computation formula under the plan were employed by a single employer (sec. 413(b)(1)). In addition, certain other rules (secs. 401(a)(4) and 411(d)(3)) are to be applied as if all participants who are subject to the same benefit computation formula and who are employed by employers who are parties to the collective bargaining agreement were employed by a single employer (sec. 413(b)(2)).

Explanation of Provision

Under the bill, the special rules of section 413(b)(1) (with respect to the coverage rules) and (b)(2) do not apply to a plan that covers any professional employee (e.g., doctor, lawyer, or investment banker). Thus, such plans are to apply sections 401(a)(4), 410 (without regard to sec. 410(a)), and 411(d)(3) under the general rules otherwise applicable with respect to qualified plans.

[Joint Committee Explanation of Senate Consensus Amendment]

Under present law, the minimum funding requirement with respect to a multiple employer plan and the maximum permissible deductible contribution to a multiple employer plan are calculated at the plan level.

The provision would provide that, for purposes of calculating the required or permissible contribution to a pension plan pursuant to the minimum funding rules and the full funding limitation, each employer participating in a multiple employer pension plan is deemed to be maintaining a separate plan. The assets and liabilities of each such plan are deemed to be those that would be transferred to a successor plan if the employer were to withdraw from the multiple employer plan, determined in accordance with section 414(l) and the terms governing the multiple employer plan.

The provision would be effective on the date of enactment, with respect to plans established after December 31, 1988. In the case of a multiple employer plan established on or before December 31, 1988, the plan administrator is permitted to elect to have the new rule apply to the plan. The election is required to be made on or before the last day of the first plan year beginning after the date of enactment and applies to the plan year during which the election is made and all subsequent plan years. The election may be revoked only with the consent of the Secretary.

[Conference Committee Report]

* * *

Conference Agreement

The conference agreement follows the Senate amendment.

As under the Senate amendment, the minimum funding standard is to be determined by treating each employer in a multiple employer plan as maintaining a separate plan, unless the plan's method for determining required contributions assures that each employer will contribute at least the amount that would be required if each employer were maintaining a separate plan. If the plan's method satisfies this requirement, then the multiple employer plan will file only a single Form 5500 and only a single Schedule B for the entire plan will be required to be prepared. Plans are required, however, to be able to demonstrate compliance with the employer-by-employer rule. It may be possible to demonstrate this compliance, for example, by using appropriate plan-wide assumptions for turnover, mortality, future growth in wages, and investment experience such that each employer contributed, at a minimum, the sum of normal cost plus required amortization of any unfunded liabilities, or net experience or other losses reduced by the amortization of any credits for experience or other gains and any contributions the deduction for which would be denied by the full funding limitation. Each employer's normal cost is required to reflect the actual salary and demographics of its employees. In addition, unfunded past service liabilities are to be amortized at least as rapidly as required by the minimum funding rules applicable to qualified plans. Under any acceptable method, no deficiencies arise and no prior year credit balances are permitted with respect to any employer.

Under the conference agreement, the assets and liabilities of each plan treated as a separate plan are the assets and liabilities that would be allocated to a plan maintained by the employer if the employer withdrew from the multiple employer plan, determined under a reasonable and consistent method. It is intended that the Secretary prescribe rules to prevent plan withdrawal mechanisms from being manipulated in order to avoid the deduction limits.

[¶ 12,300.10]

Committee Report on P.L. 93-406 (Employee Retirement Income Security Act of 1974)

[Conference Committee Explanation]

The tax provisions of the substitute provide, in the case of collectively bargained plans, that the vesting requirements are to be applied as if all employers who are parties to the plan are a single employer. Generally, the substitute provides similar rules with respect to the application of the participation, discrimination, exclusive benefit, etc. requirements so that the collectively bargained plan generally will be looked to as a unit to see if these requirements are satisfied, rather than testing the requirements on an employer-by-employer basis.

In addition, the tax provisions of the substitute generally provide that, for purposes of these rules, employees of labor unions and of a collectively bargained plan are to be treated as employees of an employer which is a party to the collective bargaining agreement. However, this rule is to apply only if the union, etc. as an employer additionally meets the nondiscrimination and coverage requirements of the tax laws.

The conferees understand that the rules of the substitute are the same as the rules of present law, and it is intended that the substitute merely confirm the rules of present law.

[Code Sec. 414]

[¶ 12,350.038]

Committee Report on P.L. 109-280 (Pension Protection Act of 2006)

[Joint Committee on Taxation Report]

[Treatment of eligible combined defined benefit plans and qualified cash or deferred arrangements]

In general

The provision provides rules for an "eligible combined plan." An eligible combined plan is a plan: (1) that is maintained by an employer that is a small employer at the time the plan is established; (2) that consists of a defined benefit plan and an "applicable" defined contribution plan; (3) the assets of which are held in a single trust forming part of the plan and are clearly identified and allocated to the defined benefit plan and the applicable defined contribution plan to the extent necessary for the separate application of the Code and ERISA; and (4) that meets certain benefit, contribution, vesting and nondiscrimination requirements as discussed below. For this purpose, an applicable defined contribution plan is a defined contribution plan that includes a qualified cash or deferred arrangement (i.e., a section 401(k) plan). A small employer is an employer that employed an average of at least two, but not more than 500, employees on business days during the preceding calendar year and at least two employees on the first day of the plan year.

Except as specified in the provision, the provisions of the Code and ERISA are applied to any defined benefit plan and any applicable defined contribution plan that are part of an eligible combined plan in the same manner as if each were not part of the eligible combined plan. Thus, for example, the present-law limits on contributions and benefits apply separately to contributions under an applicable defined contribution plan that is part of an eligible combined plan and to benefits under the defined benefit plan that is part of the eligible combined plan. In addition, the spousal protection rules apply to the defined benefit plan, but not to the applicable defined contribution plan except to the extent provided under present law. Moreover, although the assets of an eligible combined plan are held in a single trust, the funding rules apply to a defined benefit plan that is part of an eligible combined plan on the basis of the assets identified and allocated to the defined benefit, and the limits on investing defined benefit plan assets in employer securities or real property apply to such assets. Similarly, separate participant accounts are required to be maintained under the applicable defined contribution plan that is part of the eligible combined plan, and earnings (or losses) on participants' account are based on the earnings (or losses) with respect to the assets of the applicable defined contribution plan.

Requirements with respect to defined benefit plan

A defined benefit plan that is part of an eligible combined plan is required to provide each participant with a benefit of not less than the applicable percentage of the participant's final average pay. The applicable percentage is the lesser of: (1) one percent multiplied by the participant's years of service; or (2) 20 percent. For this purpose, final average pay is determined using the consecutive-year period (not exceeding five years) during which the participant has the greatest aggregate compensation.

If the defined benefit plan is an applicable defined benefit plan,[263] the plan is treated as meeting this benefit requirement if each participant receives a pay credit for each plan year of not less than the percentage of compensation determined in accordance with the following table:

Table 2.—Percentage of Compensation

Participant's age as of the beginning of the plan year:	Percentage:
30 or less	2 percent
Over 30 but less than 40	4 percent
Over 40 but less than 50	6 percent
50 or over	8 percent

A defined benefit that is part of an eligible combined plan must provide the required benefit to each participant, regardless of whether the participant makes elective deferrals to the applicable defined contribution plan that is part of the eligible combined plan.

Any benefits provided under the defined benefit plan (including any benefits provided in addition to required benefits) must be fully vested after three years of service.

Requirements with respect to applicable defined contribution plan

Certain automatic enrollment and matching contribution requirements must be met with respect to an applicable defined contribution plan that is part of an eligible combined plan. First, the qualified cash or deferred arrangement under the plan must constitute an automatic contribution arrangement, under which each employee eligible to participate is treated as having elected to make deferrals of four percent of compensation unless the employee elects otherwise (i.e., elects not to make deferrals or to make deferrals at a different rate). Participants must be given notice of their right to elect otherwise and must be given a reasonable period of time after receiving notice in which to make an election. In addition, participants must be given notice of their rights and obligations within a reasonable period before each year.

Under the applicable defined contribution plan, the employer must be required to make matching contributions on behalf of each employee eligible to participate in the arrangement in an amount equal to 50 percent of the employee's elective deferrals up to four percent of compensation, and the rate of matching contribution with respect to any elective deferrals for highly compensated employees must not be not greater than the rate of match for nonhighly compensated employees.[264] Matching contributions in addition to the required matching contributions may also be made. The employer may also make nonelective contributions under the applicable defined contribution plan, but any nonelective contributions are not taken into account in determining whether the matching contribution requirement is met.

Any matching contributions under the applicable defined contribution plan (including any in excess of required matching contributions) must be fully vested when made. Any nonelective contributions made under the applicable defined contribution plan must be fully vested after three years of service.

Nondiscrimination and other rules

An applicable defined contribution plan satisfies the ADP test on a safe-harbor basis. Matching contributions under an applicable defined contribution plan must satisfy the ACP test or may satisfy the matching contribution safe harbor under present law, as modified to reflect the matching contribution requirements applicable under the provision.

Nonelective contributions under an applicable defined contribution plan and benefits under a defined benefit plan that are part of an eligible combined plan are generally subject to the nondiscrimination rules as under present law. However, neither a defined benefit plan nor an applicable defined contribution plan that is part of an eligible combined plan may be combined with another plan in determining whether the nondiscrimination requirements are met.[265]

An applicable defined contribution plan and a defined benefit plan that are part of an eligible combined plan are treated as meeting the top-heavy requirements.

All contributions, benefits, and other rights and features that are provided under a defined benefit plan or an applicable defined contribution plan that is part of an eligible combined plan must be provided uniformly to all participants. This requirement applies regardless of whether nonuniform contributions, benefits, or other rights or features could be provided without violating the nondiscrimination rules. However, it is intended that a plan will not violate the uniformity requirement merely because benefits accrued for periods before a defined benefit or defined contribution plan became part of an eligible combined plan are protected (as required under the anticutback rules).

Annual reporting

An eligible combined plan is treated as a single plan for purposes of annual reporting. Thus, only a single Form 5500 is required. All of the information required under present law with respect to a defined benefit plan or a defined contribution plan must be provided in the Form 5500 for the eligible combined plan. In addition, only a single summary annual report must be provided to participants.

Other rules

The provision of the bill relating to default investment options and the preemption of State laws with respect to automatic enrollment arrangements are applicable to eligible combined plans. It is intended that in the case that an eligible combined plan terminates, the PBGC guarantee applies only to benefits under the defined benefit portion of the plan.

Effective Date

The provision is effective for plan years beginning after December 31, 2009.

[Revocation of election relating to treatment as multiemployer plan]

The provision allows multiemployer plans to revoke an existing election not to treat the plan as a multiemployer plan if, for each of the three plan years prior to the date of enactment, the plan would have been a multiemployer plan, but for the extension in place. The revocation must be pursuant to procedures prescribed by the PBGC.

The provision also provides that a plan to which more than one employer is required to contribute which is maintained pursuant to one or more collective bargaining agreements between one or more employee organizations and more than one employer (collectively the "criteria") may, pursuant to procedures prescribed by the PBGC, elect to be a multiemployer plan if (1) for each of the three plan years prior to the date of enactment, the plan has met the criteria; (2) substantially all of the plan's employer contributions for each of those plan years were made or required to be made by organizations that were tax-exempt; and (3) the plan was established prior to September 2, 1974. Such election is also available in the case of a plan sponsored by an organization that was established in Chicago, Illinois, on August 12, 1881, and is described in Code section 501(c)(5). There is no inference that a plan that makes an election to be a multiemployer plan was not a multiemployer plan prior to the date of enactment or would not be a multiemployer plan without regard to the election.

An election made under the provision is effective beginning with the first plan year ending after date of enactment and is irrevocable. A plan that elects to be a multiemployer plan under the provision will cease to be a multiemployer plan as of the plan year beginning immediately after the first plan year for which the majority of its employer contributions were made or required to be made by organizations that were not tax-exempt. Elections and revocations under the provision must be made within one year after the date of enactment.

Not later than 30 days before an election is made, the plan administrator must provide notice of the pending election to each plan participant and beneficiary, each labor organization representing such participants or beneficiaries, and to each employer that has an obligation to contribute to the plan. Such notice must include the principal differences between the guarantee programs and benefit restrictions for single employer and multiemployer plans. The Secretary of Labor must prescribe a model notice within 180 days after date of enactment. The plan administrator's failure to provide the notice is treated as a failure to file an annual report. Thus, an ERISA penalty of $1,100 per day applies.

Effective Date

The provision is effective on the date of enactment.

[Treatment of plans maintained by Indian tribes]

Under the provision, the term "governmental plan" for purposes of section 414 of the Code, section 3(32) of ERISA, and the PBGC termination insurance program includes a plan: (1) which is established and maintained by an Indian tribal government (as defined in Code sec. 7701(a)(40)), a subdivision of an Indian tribal government (determined in accordance with Code sec. 7871(d)), or

[263] Applicable defined benefit plan is defined as under the TITLE VII of the bill.

[264] As under present law, matching contributions may be provided at a different rate, provided that: (1) the rate of matching contribution doesn't increase as the rate of elective deferral increases; and (2) the aggregate amount of matching contributions with respect to each rate of elective deferral is not less than the amount that would be provided under the general rule.

[265] The permitted disparity rules do not apply in determining whether an applicable defined contribution plan or a defined benefit plan that is part of an eligible combined plan satisfies (1) the contribution or benefit requirements under the provision or (2) the nondiscrimination requirements.

an agency or instrumentality of either; and (2) all of the participants of which are qualified employees of such entity. A qualified employee is an employee of an entity described in (1) all of whose services for such entity are in the performance of essential governmental services and not in the performance of commercial activities (whether or not such activities are an essential governmental function). Thus, for example, a governmental plan would include a plan of a tribal government all of the participants of which are teachers in tribal schools. On the other hand, a governmental plan would not include a plan covering tribal employees who are employed by a hotel, casino, service station, convenience store, or marina operated by a tribal government.

Under the provision, the special benefit limitations applicable to employees of police and fire departments of a State or political subdivision (Code sec. 415(b)(2)(H)) apply to such employees of an Indian tribe or any political subdivision thereof. In addition, the rules relating to pick up contribution under governmental plans (Code sec. 414(h)) and special benefit limitations for governmental plans (sec. 415(b)(10)) apply to tribal plans treated as governmental plans under the provision.

Effective Date

The provision is effective for plan years beginning on or after the date of enactment.

[Increasing participation through automatic enrollment arrangements]

For the Committee Report on P.L. 109-280 on automatic enrollment arrangements, see ¶ 11,700.02.

[¶ 12,350.04]

Committee Report on P.L. 107-16 (Economic Growth and Tax Relief Reconciliation Act)

[Conference Committee Report]

Additional catch-up contributions

House Bill

The House bill provides that the otherwise applicable dollar limit on elective deferrals under a section 401(k) plan, section 403(b) annuity, SEP, or SIMPLE, or deferrals under a section 457 plan are increased for individuals who have attained age 50 by the end of the year.[1] Additional contributions are permitted by an individual who has attained age 50 before the end of the plan year and with respect to whom no other elective deferrals may otherwise be made to the plan for the year because of the application of any limitation of the Code (e.g., the annual limit on elective deferrals) or of the plan. Under the House bill, the additional amount of elective contributions that are permitted to be made by an eligible individual participating in such a plan is the lesser of (1) $5,000, or (2) the participant's compensation for the year reduced by any other elective deferrals of the participant for the year. This $5,000 amount is indexed for inflation in $500 increments in 2007 and thereafter.[2]

Catch-up contributions made under the House bill are not subject to any other contribution limits and are not taken into account in applying other contribution limits. Such contributions are subject to applicable nondiscrimination rules. Although catch-up contributions are subject to applicable nondiscrimination rules, a plan does not fail to meet the applicable nondiscrimination requirements under section 401(a)(4) with respect to benefits, rights, and features if the plan allows all eligible individuals participating in the plan to make the same election with respect to catch-up contributions. For purposes of this rule, all plans of related employers are treated as a single plan.

An employer is permitted to make matching contributions with respect to catch-up contributions. Any such matching contributions are subject to the normally applicable rules.

Effective Date

The House bill is effective for taxable years beginning after December 31, 2001.

[Senate Committee Report]

The Senate amendment provides that the otherwise applicable dollar limit on elective deferrals under a section 401(k) plan, section 403(b) annuity, SEP, or SIMPLE, or deferrals under a section 457 plan is increased for individuals who have attained age 50 by the end of the year.[3] Additional contributions could be made by an individual who has attained age 50 before the end of the plan year and with respect to whom no other elective deferrals may otherwise be made to the plan for the year because of the application of any limitation of the Code (e.g., the annual limit on elective deferrals) or of the plan. Under the Senate amendment, the additional amount of elective contributions that could be made by an eligible individual participating in such a plan is the lesser of (1) the applicable dollar amount or (2) the participant's compensation for the year reduced by any other elective deferrals of the participant for the year.[4] The applicable dollar amount is $500 for 2002 through 2004, $1,000 for 2005 and 2006, $2,000 for 2007, $3,000 for 2008, $4,000 for 2009, and $7,500 for 2010 and thereafter.

Catch-up contributions made under the Senate amendment are not subject to any other contribution limits and are not taken into account in applying other contribution limits. In addition, such contributions are not subject to applicable nondiscrimination rules.[5]

An employer is permitted to make matching contributions with respect to catch-up contributions. Any such matching contributions are subject to the normally applicable rules.

The following examples illustrate the application of the Senate amendment, after the catch-up is fully phased-in.

Example 1: Employee A is a highly compensated employee who is over 50 and who participates in a section 401(k) plan sponsored by A's employer. The maximum annual deferral limit (without regard to the provision) is $15,000. After application of the special nondiscrimination rules applicable to section 401(k) plans, the maximum elective deferral A may make for the year is $8,000. Under the provision, A is able to make additional catch-up salary reduction contributions of $7,500.

Example 2: Employee B, who is over 50, is a participant in a section 401(k) plan. B's compensation for the year is $30,000. The maximum annual deferral limit (without regard to the provision) is $15,000. Under the terms of the plan, the maximum permitted deferral is 10 percent of compensation or, in B's case, $3,000. Under the provision, B can contribute up to $10,500 for the year ($3,000 under the normal operation of the plan, and an additional $7,500 under the provision).

Effective Date

The Senate amendment is effective for taxable years beginning after December 31, 2001.

[Conference Agreement]

The conference agreement provides that the otherwise applicable dollar limit on elective deferrals under a section 401(k) plan, section 403(b) annuity, SEP, or SIMPLE, or deferrals under a section 457 plan is increased for individuals who have attained age 50 by the end of the year.[6] The catch-up contribution provision does not apply to after-tax employee contributions. Additional contributions may be made by an individual who has attained age 50 before the end of the plan year and with respect to whom no other elective deferrals may otherwise be made to the plan for the year because of the application of any limitation of the Code (e.g., the annual limit on elective deferrals) or of the plan. Under the conference agreement, the additional amount of elective contributions that may be made by an eligible individual participating in such a plan is the lesser of (1) the applicable dollar amount or (2) the participant's compensation for the year reduced by any other elective deferrals of the participant for the year.[7] The applicable dollar amount under a section 401(k) plan, section 403(b) annuity, SEP, or section 457 plan is $1,000 for 2002, $2,000 for 2003, $3,000 for 2004, $4,000 for 2005, and $5,000 for 2006 and thereafter. The applicable dollar amount under a SIMPLE is $500 for 2002, $1,000 for 2003, $1,500 for 2004, $2,000 for 2005, and $2,500 for 2006 and thereafter. The $5,000 and $2,500 amounts are adjusted for inflation in $500 increments in 2007 and thereafter.[8]

Catch-up contributions made under the conference agreement are not subject to any other contribution limits and are not taken into account in applying other contribution limits. In addition, such contributions are not subject to applicable nondiscrimination rules. However, a plan fails to meet the applicable nondiscrimination requirements under section 401(a)(4) with respect to benefits, rights, and features unless the plan allows all eligible individuals participating in the plan to make the same election with respect to catch-up contributions. For purposes of this rule, all plans of related employers are treated as a single plan.

An employer is permitted to make matching contributions with respect to catch-up contributions. Any such matching contributions are subject to the normally applicable rules.

The following examples illustrate the application of the conference agreement, after the catch-up is fully phased-in.

Example 1: Employee A is a highly compensated employee who is over 50 and who participates in a section 401(k) plan sponsored by A's employer. The maximum annual deferral limit (without regard to the provision) is $15,000. After application of the special nondiscrimination rules applicable to section 401(k) plans, the maximum elective deferral A may make for the year is $8,000. Under

[1] Another provision of the House bill increases the dollar limit on elective deferrals under such arrangements.

[2] In the case of a section 457 plans, this catch-up rule does not apply during the participant's last three years before retirement (in those years, the regularly applicable dollar limit is doubled).

[3] Another provision of the Senate amendment increases the dollar limit on elective deferrals under such arrangements.

[4] In the case of a section 457 plan, this catch-up rule does not apply during the participant's last three years before retirement (in those years, the regularly applicable dollar limit is doubled).

[5] Another provision increases the dollar limit on elective deferrals under such arrangements.

[6] Another provision of the conference agreement increases the dollar limit on elective deferrals under such arrangements.

[7] In the case of a section 457 plan, this catch-up rule does not apply during the participant's last three years before retirement (in those years, the regularly applicable dollar limit is doubled).

[8] In the case of a section 457 plans, this catch-up rule does not apply during the participant's last three years before retirement (in those years, the regularly applicable dollar limit is doubled).

the provision, A is able to make additional catch-up salary reduction contributions of $5,000.

Example 2: Employee B, who is over 50, is a participant in a section 401(k) plan. B's compensation for the year is $30,000. The maximum annual deferral limit (without regard to the provision) is $15,000. Under the terms of the plan, the maximum permitted deferral is 10 percent of compensation or, in B's case, $3,000. Under the provision, B can contribute up to $8,000 for the year ($3,000 under the normal operation of the plan, and an additional $5,000 under the provision).

Effective Date

The Senate amendment is effective for taxable years beginning after December 31, 2001.

[¶ 12,350.05]

Committee Report on P.L. 104-188 (Small Business Job Protection Act)

Miscellaneous Pension Simplification

[House Committee Report]

Special vesting rule for multiemployer plans eliminated

The bill conforms the vesting rules for multiemployer plans to the rules applicable to other qualified plans.

Effective Date

The provision is effective for plan years beginning on or after the earlier of (1) the later of January 1, 1997, or the date on which the last of the collective bargaining agreements pursuant to which the plan is maintained terminates, or (2) January 1, 1999, with respect to participants with an hour of service after the effective date.

[Conference Committee Report]

Senate Amendment

The Senate amendment is the same as the House bill.

Conference Agreement

The conference agreement follows the House bill and the Senate amendment.

Nondiscrimination Provisions

[House Committee Report]

Definition of highly compensated employees and repeal of family aggregation rules

Definition of highly compensated employee.—Under the bill, an employee is treated as highly compensated if the employee (1) was a 5-percent owner of the employer at any time during the year or the preceding year or (2) had compensation for the preceding year in excess of $80,000 (indexed for inflation) and the employee was in the top 20 percent of employees by compensation for such year. The bill also repeals the rule requiring the highest paid officer to be treated as a highly compensated employee.

Family aggregation rules.—The bill repeals the family aggregation rules.

Effective Date

The provisions are effective for years beginning after December 31, 1996.

[Conference Committee Report]

Senate Amendment

Definition of highly compensated employee.—The Senate amendment is the same as the House bill, except an employee who had compensation for the preceding year in excess of $80,000 is treated as highly compensated without regard to whether the employee was in the top 20 percent of employees by compensation.

Family aggregation rules.—The Senate amendment is the same as the House bill.

Conference Agreement

Definition of highly compensated employee.—The conference agreement follows the House bill and the Senate amendment. Thus, under the conference agreement, a plan may elect for a plan year to use either the definition of highly compensated employee in the House bill or the Senate amendment.

Family aggregation rules.—The conference agreement follows the House bill and the Senate amendment.

Nondiscrimination Provisions

[House Committee Report]

Compensation for purposes of the limits on contributions and benefits

The bill provides that elective deferrals to section 401(k) plans and similar arrangements, elective contributions to nonqualified deferred compensation plans of tax-exempt employers and State and local governments (sec. 457 plans), and salary reduction contributions to a cafeteria plan are considered compensation for purposes of the limits on contributions and benefits.

Effective Date

The provision is effective for years beginning after December 31, 1997.

[Conference Committee Report]

Senate Amendment

The Senate amendment is the same as the House bill.

Conference Agreement

The conference agreement follows the House bill and the Senate amendment.

Miscellaneous Pension Simplification

[House Committee Report]

Treatment of leased employees

Under the bill, the present-law "historically performed" test is replaced with a new test under which an individual is not considered a leased employee unless the individual's services are performed under primary direction or control by the service recipient. As under present law, the determination of whether someone is a leased employee is made after determining whether the individual is a common-law employee of the recipient. Thus, an individual who is not a common-law employee of the service recipient could nevertheless be a leased employee of the service recipient. Similarly, the fact that a person is or is not found to perform services under primary direction or control of the recipient for purposes of the employee leasing rules is not determinative of whether the person is or is not a common-law employee of the recipient.

Whether services are performed by an individual under primary direction or control by the service recipient depends on the facts and circumstances. In general, primary direction and control means that the service recipient exercises the majority of direction and control over the individual. Factors that are relevant in determining whether primary direction or control exists include whether the individual is required to comply with instructions of the service recipient about when, where, and how he or she is to perform the services, whether the services must be performed by a particular person, whether the individual is subject to the supervision of the service recipient, and whether the individual must perform services in the order or sequence set by the service recipient. Factors that generally are not relevant in determining whether such direction or control exists include whether the service recipient has the right to hire or fire the individual and whether the individual works for others.

For example, an individual who works under the direct supervision of the service recipient would be considered to be subject to primary direction or control of the service recipient even if another company hired and trained the individual, had the ultimate (but unexercised) legal right to control the individual, paid his wages, withheld his employment and income taxes, and had the exclusive right to fire him. Thus, for example, temporary secretaries, receptionists word processing personnel and similar office personnel who are subject to the day-to-day control of the employer in essentially the same manner as a common law employee are treated as leased employees if the period of service threshold is reached.

On the other hand, an individual who is a common-law employee of Company A who performs services for Company B on the business premises of Company B under the supervision of Company A would generally not be considered to be under primary direction or control of Company B. The supervision by Company A must be more than nominal, however, and not merely a mechanism to avoid the literal language of the direction or control test.

An example of the situation in the preceding paragraph might be a work crew that comes into a factory to install, repair, maintain, or modify equipment or machinery at the factory. The work crew includes a supervisor who is an employee of the equipment (or equipment repair) company and who has the authority to direct and control the crew, and who actually does exercise such direction and control. In this situation, the supervisor and his or her crew are required to comply with the safety and environmental precautions of the manufacturer, and the supervisor is in frequent communication with the employees of the manufacturer. As another example, certain professionals (e.g., attorneys, accountants, actuaries, doctors, computer programmers, systems analysts, and engineers) who regularly make use of their own judgement and discretion on matters of importance in the performance of their services and are guided by professional, legal, or industry standards, are not leased employees even though the common law employer does not closely supervise the professional on a continuing basis, and the service recipient requires the services to be performed on site and according to certain stages, techniques, and timetables. In addition to the example above, outside professionals who maintain their own businesses (e.g., attorneys, accountants, actuaries, doctors, computer programmers, systems analysts, and engineers) generally would not be considered to be subject to such primary direction or control.

Under the direction or control test, clerical and similar support staff(e.g., secretaries and nurses in a doctor's office) generally would be considered to be subject to primary direction or control of the service recipient and would be leased employees provided the other requirements of section 414(n) are met.

In many cases, the "historically performed" test is overly broad, and results in the unintended treatment of individuals as leased employees. One of the principal purposes for changing the leased employee rules is to relieve the unnecessary hardship and uncertainty created for employers in these circumstances. However, it is not intended that the direction or control test enable employers to engage in abusive practices. Thus, it is intended that the Secretary interpret and apply the leased employee rules in a manner so as to prevent abuses. This ability to prevent abuses under the leasing rules is in addition to the present-law authority of the Secretary under section 414(o). For example, one potentially abusive situation exists where the benefit arrangements of the service recipient overwhelmingly favor its highly compensated employees, the employer has no or very few nonhighly compensated common-law employees, yet the employer makes substantial use of the services of nonhighly compensated individuals who are not its common-law employees.

Effective Date

The provision is effective for years beginning after December 31, 1996, except that the bill would not apply to relationships that have been previously determined by an IRS ruling not to involve leased employees. In applying the leased employee rules to years beginning before the effective date, it is intended that the Secretary use a reasonable interpretation of the statute to apply the leasing rules to prevent abuse.

[Conference Committee Report]

Senate Amendment

The Senate amendment is the same as the House bill.

Conference Agreement

The conference agreement follows the House bill and the Senate amendment.

Miscellaneous Pension Simplification

[Managers' Amendment to H.R. 3448]

Church pension plan simplification

* * *

Highly compensated church employees defined for pre-ERISA rules for church plans.—The amendment would provide that church plans subject to the pre-ERISA nondiscrimination rules apply the same definition of highly compensated employee as other pension plans, rather than the pre-ERISA rule relating to employees who are officers, shareholders, persons whose principal duties consist of supervising the work of other employees or highly compensated employees.

The amendment would provide that the Secretary of the Treasury may develop safe harbor rules for church plans under the applicable coverage and nondiscrimination rules.

* * *

Effective Date

The amendment would be effective for years beginning after December 31, 1996.

[Conference Committee Report]

The conference agreement follows the Senate amendment with technical modifications.

Other Tax Technical Corrections

[House Committee Report]

Treatment of certain veterans' reemployment rights

The bill provides special rules in the case of certain contributions ("make-up contributions") with respect to a reemployed veteran that are required or authorized under USERRA. The bill applies to contributions made by an employer or employee to an individual account plan or to contributions made by an employee to a defined benefit plan that provides for employee contributions.

Under the bill, if any make-up contribution is made by an employer or employee with respect to a reemployed veteran, then such contributions are not subject to the generally applicable plan contribution limits (i.e., secs. 402(g), 402(h), 403(b), 408, 415, or 457) or the limit on deductible contributions (i.e., secs. 404(a) or 404(h)) as applied with respect to the year in which the contribution is made. In addition, the make-up contribution are not taken into account in applying the plan contribution or deductible contribution limits to any other contribution made during the year. However, the amount of any make-up contribution could not exceed the aggregate amount of contributions that would have been permitted under the plan contribution and deductible contribution limits for the year to which the contribution relates had the individual continued to be employed by the employer during the period of uniformed service.

Under the bill, a plan to which a make-up contribution is made on account of a reemployed veteran is not treated as failing to meet the qualified plan nondiscrimination, coverage, minimum participation, and top heavy rules (i.e., secs. 401(a)(4), 401(a)(26), 401(k)(3), 401(k)(11), 401(k)(12), 401(m), 403(b)(12), 408(k)(3), 408(k)(6), 408(p), 410(b), or 416) by reason of the making of such contribution. Consequently, for purposes of applying the requirements and tests associated with these rules, make-up contributions are not taken into account either for the year in which they are made or for the year to which they relate.

Under the bill, a special rule applies in the case of make-up contributions of salary reduction, employer matching, and after-tax employee amounts. A plan that provides for elective deferrals or employee contributions is treated as meeting the requirements of USERRA if the employer permits reemployed veterans to make additional elective deferrals or employee contributions under the plan during the period which begins on the date of reemployment and has the same length as the lesser of (1) the period of the individual's absence due to uniformed service multiplied by three or (2) five years.

The employer is required to match any additional elective deferrals or employee contributions at the same rate that would have been required had the deferrals or contributions actually been made during the period of uniformed service. Additional elective deferrals, employer matching contributions, and employee contributions is treated as make-up contributions for purposes of the rule exempting such contributions from qualified plan nondiscrimination, coverage, minimum participation, and top heavy rules as described above.

The bill clarifies that USERRA does not require (1) any earnings to be credited to an employee with respect to any contribution before such contribution is actually made or (2) any make-up allocation of any forfeiture that occurred during the period of uniformed service.

The bill also provides that the plan loan, plan qualification, and prohibited transaction rules will not be violated merely because a plan suspends the repayment of a plan loan during a period of uniformed service.

The bill also defines compensation to be used for purposes of determining make-up contributions and would conform the rules contained in the Code with certain rights of reemployed veterans contained in USERRA pertaining to employee benefit plans.

Effective Date

The provision is effective as of December 12, 1994, the effective date of the benefits-related provisions of USERRA.

[Conference Committee Report]

Senate Amendment

The Senate amendment follows the House bill.

Conference Agreement

The conference agreement follows the House bill and the Senate amendment* * *.

[¶ 12,350.051]

Committee Report on P.L. 102-318 (Unemployment Compensation Amendments of 1992)

For Committee Report on Unemployment Compensation Amendments of 1992 (P.L. 102-318), dealing with rollovers and withholding on nonperiodic pension distributions, see ¶ 11,750.036.

[¶ 12,350.053]

Committee Reports on P.L. 101-239 (Omnibus Budget Reconciliation Act of 1989)

[House Committee Report]

Transfer of interests in IRAs and qualified governmental plans

The rule relating to transfers of interests in an IRA incident to a divorce is amended to conform to the treatment generally of such transfers under qualified plans pursuant to the Retirement Equity Act of 1984. The provision permits a transfer of an interest in an IRA to be treated as a nontaxable transfer if the transfer is to a spouse or former spouse under a divorce or separation.

The tax rules relating to transfers of interests in a governmental plan are also amended to conform generally to the tax rules applicable to other qualified plans pursuant to the Retirement Equity Act. Under the provision, the same tax rules applicable to transfers pursuant to a QDRO apply to transfers of interests in a governmental plan pursuant to a domestic relations order as defined in section 414(p)(1), without regard [to] section 414(p)(1)(A).

The provisions are effective for transfers after the date of enactment in taxable years ending after the date of enactment.

[Conference Committee Report]

The conference agreement follows the House bill with the following modifications:

* * *

(6) *Tax treatment of transfers of interests in retirement plans incident to divorce.*—The House bill provides that the tax rules applicable to qualified domestic relations orders with respect to qualified plans also apply in the case of certain transfers of interests in individual retirement accounts and governmental plans incident to divorce or legal separation. The conference agreement also applies to church plans.

[¶ 12,350.055]

Committee Reports on P.L. 100-647 (Technical and Miscellaneous Revenue Act of 1988)

[Senate Committee Report]

The bill clarifies the applicability of the special rule for family members of certain highly compensated employees. The rule generally is to be used in applying any provision that refers to the definition of highly compensated employee (e.g., secs. 89, 401(a)(4), 401(a)(5), 401(k), 401(l) (through sec. 401(a)(5)), 401(m), 403(b)(12) (by reference to 401(a)(4), etc.), 408(k), 410(b)). Thus, the special rule does not apply for purposes of, for example, the limits on contributions or benefits (sec. 415) or the $7,000 (indexed) limit on elective deferrals (sec. 402(g)).

In addition, the bill provides the Secretary with regulatory authority to prevent the application of the special family member rule to inappropriate, clearly unintended situations. This regulatory authority is only to be used, however, in a manner consistent with the general policy underlying the family member rule, i.e., that, for purposes of all rules relating to nondiscrimination (or deductibility), the members of the family constitute one economic unit and thus are to be treated as one employee.

For exemple, assume employees A and B are married and both work for the same employer. A's compensation is $150,000 for the 1990 plan year; she is one of the top 10 highly compensated employees (by compensation). B's compensation is $25,000. Assume further that the employer maintains a money purchase pension plan providing contributions of 10 percent of compensation. The Secretary's regulatory authority could be exercised to prevent the plan from allocating any more than $15,000 to A's account for the 1990 plan year. Thus, the Secretary could preclude the use of compensation paid to one person to be used to provide allocations or accruals to another person.

The bill also clarifies that the special family member rule applies for purposes of the $200,000 limit on the amount of compensation that may be taken into account under a qualified plan (for qualification or deduction purposes) or under an employee benefit plan (secs. 89, 401(a)(17), and 404(l)). (The special family member rule does not apply, however, for purposes of the $200,000 limit that applies under section 416(d), but which was repealed generally for years beginning after December 31, 1988.) However, for this purpose, the definition of a family member is modified to refer only to the employee's spouse and lineal descendants of the employee who do not attain age 19 by the close of the year.

For example, assume that in 1988 employee A of employer X receives compensation (as defined under sec. 414(s)) of $275,000 and is the highly compensated employee with the highest compensation from X. A's spouse (B), adult child (C), and 17-year old child (D) also are employees of X. B, C, and D receive $100,000, $225,000, and $10,000 of compensation (as defined under Sec. 414(s)), respectively. X maintains a qualified cash or deferred arrangement (sec. 401(k)) under which A, B, C, and D are eligible. A, B, and C each defers $7,000 under the arrangement; D makes no deferral.

For purposes of applying the special nondiscrimination test applicable to the arrangement (sec. 401(k)(3)), A, B, C, and D are treated as 1 employee. The compensation of this "1 aggregated employee" is determined as follows: A, B, and D are combined and limited to $200,000 (rather than the $385,000 they actually receive). The $200,000 limit applies separately to C because, under the special definition of a family member for purposes of the $200,000 limit, C is not a family member of A, B, or D. Thus, the compensation taken into account for the aggregated employee is $200,000 (for A, B, and D) plus $200,000 (for C) for a total of $400,000. The total deferrals for this aggregated employee are $21,000. Thus, for purposes of applying the special nondiscrimination test to the cash or deferred arrangement, A, B, C, and D are treated as a single employee with a deferral percentage of $21,000/$400,000 or 5.25 percent. Since the family aggregation rule does not apply for purposes of the $7,313 limit ($7,000 indexed for 1988) on elective deferrals (sec. 402(g)), none of the family members is considered to have exceeded such limit.

The bill further clarifies the application of the special family member rule to the integration rules under section 401(l). Although the special family member rule generally applies for purposes of section (401)(l), it does not apply in determining the amount of compensation below the plan's integration level except that the total of the compensation below the integration level is subject to the $200,000 limit (sec. 401(a)(17)). Thus, for example, assume the same facts described in the above example, except that instead of maintaining a qualified cash or deferred arrangement, X maintains an integrated, nonelective profit-sharing plan with an integration level of $45,000. Again, the compensation of the aggregated employee is $400,000. Of that $400,000, a total of $145,000 is considered to be below the integration level (i.e., $45,000 each attributable to A, B, and C, and $10,000 attributable to D).

[Senate Committee Report]

Indexing

The bill provides that the $50,000 and $75,000 amounts are to be adjusted at the same time and in the same manner as the dollar limit applicable to defined benefit plans (sec. 415(d)). Such adjustments will prevent the definition of "highly compensated employee" from becoming inappropriate by virtue of inflation.

Nonresident aliens

In addition, under the bill, nonresident aliens who receive no United States-source earned income from the employer are to be disregarded for all purposes in determining the identity of the highly compensated employees of the employer. This modification will simplify the application of the rules and will prevent employees who are disregarded for purposes of the nondiscrimination rules from affecting the identity of the highly compensated employees.

Compensation

Although the definition of compensation used for purposes of determining highly compensated employees under section 414(q) generally is based on the definition used under section 415(c)(3), it is intended that the definitions vary in certain ways. First, it is not intended that, for purposes of section 414(q), compensation be required to be determined on the basis of the plan's limitation year under section 415. Second, it is not intended that employers be permitted to use an employee's accrued compensation for purposes of section 414(q).

Officers

The employees who are excluded for purposes of determining the size of the top-paid group are to be excluded for purposes of determining the 10-percent limit on the number of officers. (As with respect to the top-paid group, the excluded employees may be officers; they are only excluded for purposes of determining the limit on the number of officers.) This limit is to apply for purposes of determining highly compensated employees and key employees (sec. 416).

[Senate Committee Report]

Under the bill, the Secretary is to prescribe rules providing certain minimum standards regarding the age and service requirements that are to apply for purposes of determining which employees are taken into account in determining if a line of business or operating unit may be treated as separate. (The standards are to apply, for example, for purposes of determining if a line of business or operating unit has 50 employees.) Under this authority, the Secretary could provide that, for such purpose, section 414(q)(8) is to be applied without regard to the last sentence thereof, i.e., the employer may not elect to reduce the age or service requirements specified in the statute.

The primary purpose for this provision of the bill is to prevent the use of nominal age or service requirements to avoid the effect of the requirement that, to be treated as separate, a line of business or operating unit is required to have 50 employees.

[Senate Committee Report]

Explanation of Provision

The bill provides that if employee contributions (and the incoe attributable thereto) under a defined benefit plan are credited to a separate account that generally is treated as a defined contribution plan (sec. 414(k)), then such separate account is also treated as a defined contribution plan for purposes of the basis recovery rules. The bill clarifies that this separate contract treatment applies without regard to whether the distribution is received as an annuity.

[Senate Committee Report]

The bill modifies the general definition of compensation so that generally it is the same one used (for employees or self-employed individuals, whichever is applicable) for purposes of the limit on contributions under a defined contribution plan (sec. 415(c)(3)). (The bill does not affect the employer's right to elect to include elective deferrals or the Secretary's authorization to provide alternative definitions of compensation.) This provides greater uniformity, and excludes certain items (such as deductible reimbursements of moving expenses) that were not intended to be taken into account. It is not the intent of the bill, however, to restrict future regulatory modifications of the definition of compensation under section 415(c)(3).

Although the general definition of compensation under section 414(s) is to be the same one used under section 415(c)(3), it is intended that the definitions vary in certain ways. First, it is not intended that, for purposes of section 414(s), the general definition of compensation be required to be determined on the basis of the plan's limitation year under section 415. Second, it is not intended that the general definition of compensation under section 414(s) be an employee's accrued compensation. Third, with respect to defined contribution plans, the general definition of compensation for purposes of section 414(s) is not to include amounts received while an employee is not a participant.

The bill also clarifies that the definition of compensation provided in section 414(s) only applies to provisions that specifically refer to it. Thus, for example, the definition does not apply for purposes of the limits on deductions (sec. 404) or on contributions and benefits (sec. 415).

[Senate Committee Report]

Spin-off Involving Defined Benefit Plans

The bill provides, in the case of spin-offs involving defined benefit plans, that assets (in the original plan) in excess of the amount required to be allocated under the present-law rule ("excess assets") are to be allocated to each spun off plan in the proportion that (1) the excess of the full funding limitation for the spun off plan over the value of assets required to be allocated under the present-law rule, bears to (2) the sum of excesses calculated separately under (1) for each of the spun off plans.

If, after a spin-off, one or more of the resulting plans is maintained by an employer that is not a member of the same controlled group as the employer maintaining the original plan, the rule does not apply to excess assets allocated to the plan (or plans) that is maintained by the employer outside such controlled group. However, to the extent that excess assets are allocated to plans remaining within the controlled group, the general rule applies with respect to the allocation of such assets. (For this purpose, controlled group means any group treated as a single employer under section 414(b), (c), (m), or (o).)

The rule also does not apply to any multiemployer plan with respect to any transaction to the extent that participants either before or after the transaction are covered under a multiemployer plan to which title IV of ERISA applies.

Except to the extent provided by the Secretary, rules similar to these rules apply in the case of transactions similar to spin-offs. It is intended that the Secretary is to provide only limited exceptions to the application of the rule.

The application of the rule is illustrated by the following examples.

Example 1. Assume Employer X maintains a single-employer defined benefit plan, Plan A, which covers employees of three divisions (Divisions 1, 2 and 3). Plan A has assets of $200 million and liabilities, on a termination basis, of $150 million. Assume further that the full funding limitation for Plans 1 and 2 is $60 million, and that the full funding limitation for Plan 3 is $75 million. The value of benefits on a termination basis for each of the plans is $50 million. Thus, the value of excess assets is $50 million.

Employer X sells Division 1 to Employer Y. Employer Y is not a member of the controlled group of Employer X. When the sale occurs, Employer X splits Plan A into three plans, one of which covers employees of Division 1 (Plan 1) and which is transferred to Employer Y, one of which covers employees of Division 2 (Plan 2), and the other of which covers employees of Division 3 (Plan 3).

As under present law, the value of assets allocated to each of the spun off plans cannot be less than the present value of the benefits on a termination basis for all participants in the plan. That is, at least $50 million of assets are to be allocated to each of Plan 1, Plan 2, and Plan 3. Employer X may allocate all of the remaining $50 million of plan assets to Plan 1.

However, if Employer X does not allocate all of the excess assets to Plan 1, than the remaining excess must be allocated to Plans 2 and 3 under the general rule. For example, assume that $25 million of the excess assets are allocated to Plan 1. In that case, $7.1 million of the excess is allocated to Plan 2 [($10 million divided by $35 million) × $25 million], and $17.9 million of the excess is allocated to Plan 3 [($25 million divided by $35 million) × $25 million)].

Example 2. Assume the same facts in Example 1, except that Employer X is not selling a division, but is simply splitting Plan A into three plans, one that covers the employees of Division 1 (Plan 1), one that covers the employees of Division 2 (Plan 2), and one that covers the employees of Division (Plan 3). When the spin-off occurs, $11.1 million of the excess assets is to be allocated to Plan 1, $11.1 million of the excess assets is to be allocated to Plan 2, and $27.8 million of the excess assets is to be allocated to Plan 3.

Effective Date

The provision is effective with respect to transactions occurring after July 26, 1988. In addition, the provision does not apply to any transaction occuring after July 26, 1988, if, on or before such date, the board of directors of the employer approved the transaction or the employer took similar binding action.

[Conference Committee Report]

* * *

Senate Amendment

The Senate amendment also provides that the allocation rule applies to a spin off involving a plan maintained by a bank that has been closed by appropriate bank authorities and a plan maintained by a bridge bank (as described in 12 U.S.C. 1821(i)). The amendment also authorizes the bridge bank to cause the plan maintained by the closing bank to spin off assets to a defined benefit plan maintained by the bridge bank in accordance with the allocation rule within 180 days after the closing of the bank.

The provision is effective with respect to transactions occurring after July 26, 1988.

* * *

Conference Agreement

The conference agreement follows the Senate amendment with respect to the provision relating to bridge banks, with the modification that the provision only applies with respect to 50 percent of the excess assets. (The conference agreement follows the Senate amendment with respect to the technical corrections provision.)

[Conference Committee Report]

Definition of Highly Compensated Employee

* * *

House Bill

Under the House bill, employers are entitled to elect to determine their highly compensated employees under a simplified method. Under the simplified method, an electing employer may treat employees who receive more than $50,000 in annual compensation from the employer as highly compensated employees in lieu of applying the $75,000 and $50,000 compensation tests of present law.

Senate Amendment

The Senate amendment follows the House bill, except that the Senate amendment deletes the requirements that an employer operate in at least two geographic areas and not maintain any top-heavy plans in order to use this alternative rule.

Conference Agreement

The conference agreement follows the Senate amendment with respect to the simplified method of determining highly compensated employees, except that the availability of this simplified method is limited to employers that maintain significant business operations in at least two significantly separate geographic areas. For this purpose, the 35-mile safe harbor for operating units under section 89 (discussed below) does not apply.

In addition, the Secretary is given authority to provide for other situations in which the alternative definition cannot be used. It is intended that the Secretary use this authority to prohibit use of the alternative definition where to do so would result in greater discrimination than permitted under the present-law definition. For example, some employees who are nonhighly compensated under the present-law definition will be considered highly compensated under the alternative definition. By excluding such highly compensated employees from the plan, the nonhighly compensated employees may be provided a lower benefit than would otherwise be permitted under the nondiscrimination rules. The conferees intended that any further restrictions would not be effective until the issuance of guidance by the Secretary describing the situations in which the alternative definition is not available.

Employers with No Nonhighly Compensated Employees

House Bill

The House bill clarifies that the nondiscrimination rules do not apply to an employer in a year in which such employer has no nonhighly compensated employees. This rule applies separately with respect to former employees under rules prescribed by the Secretary.

* * *

Conference Agreement

The conference agreement follows the House bill * * *.

Special Rules for Part-Time Employees

* * *

House Bill

Determination of hours worked. The House bill provides a simplified method for determining the number of hours an employee is considered to work normally in a week. Until the end of the applicable testing year in which an employee commences work with the employer, the employee is considered to work normally the average num- ber of hours such employee is scheduled to work during such year (disregarding any time the employee is not employed by the employer). The determination of the average scheduled hours is to be made in good faith and is to take into account periods in which it is expected that hours will be higher due to, for example, seasonal business cycles.

For subsequent testing years, an employee is considered to work normally the average number of hours worked during the preceding testing year (disregarding any time the employee was not employed by the employer). In determining the number of hours an employee has worked or is scheduled to work, rules similar to the qualified plan "hour of service" rules apply.

* * *

Senate Amendment

Determination of hours worked.—The Senate amendment modifies the House bill method for determining the number of hours an employee is considered to work normally in a week. Under the Senate amendment, for a testing year, an employee is considered to work normally the average number of hours worked during the period in the testing year prior to the testing date. If such period is less than 60 days, an employee is considered to work normally (1) the average number of hours worked during the prior testing year, or (2) if the employee did not work at least 60 days during the prior testing year, the average number of hours such employee is scheduled to work, as of the testing date, during the longer of (i) the next 60 days, or (ii) the period between the testing date and the end of the testing year. For purposes of these rules, periods during which an employee does not work are disregarded. The amendment follows the House bill with respect to how scheduled hours are to be determined and the definition of hours worked.

Proportionate reduction.—The Senate amendment allows application of the proportionate reduction rule without regard to the requirement that more than 50 percent of the nonexcludable employees normally work at least 30 hours per week.

Conference Agreement

The conference agreement follows the Senate amendment with respect to the determination of hours worked and the proportionate reduction rule. In addition, the conference agreement clarifies that the same method for determining hours worked applies for purposes of determining whether an employee is a part-time employee under the definition of highly compensated employee (sec. 414(q)(8)(B)).

Excludable Employees

* * *

House Bill

Multiemployer plans.—Under the House bill, the initial service requirement applicable under a multiemployer plan is not taken into account in determining the extent to which the one-year and six-month figures are reduced with respect to other plans of the employer. This special rule for multiemployer plans does not apply to a multiemployer plan that covers any professional (e.g., a doctor, lawyer, or investment banker).

Entry dates.—Under the House bill, an employer may use the first day of a period of less than 31 days specified by a plan as the first day of participation in the plan after satisfaction of the initial service requirement.

Senate Amendment

Multiemployer plans.—The Senate amendment extends the rule in the House bill with respect to the initial waiting period for multiemployer plans to employees excluded based on their age, part-time status, or seasonal status. Thus, the exclusion (or lack thereof) under a multiemployer plan (as defined under the House bill) of employees based on age, part-time status, or seasonal status does not affect the employer's ability to disregard employees based on different age, part-time status, or seasonal status rules.

Entry dates.—The Senate amendment is the same as the House bill.

Conference Agreement

The conference agreement follows the Senate amendment.—In addition, the conference agreement provides that employees of an employer who are also students attending classes at the employer may be disregarded if (1) the students are performing services as described in section 3121(b)(10) (relating to services performed by students that are disregarded for employement tax purposes) and (2) core health coverage is made available to the students by the employer.

Under the conference agreement, an employer contributing to a multiemployer plan is entitled to use the special method for determining excludable employees only if that employer does not contribute to the plan on behalf of an employee who performs professional services. Thus, the determination of eligibility for the special method is applied on a contributing employer by contributing employer basis. For purposes of this provision, professional services include the following services: legal, medical, engineering, architecture, actuarial science, financial, consulting, accounting, and such other services as the Secretary shall determine.

Reporting Requirements for Multiemployer Plans

* * *

Senate Amendment

The Senate amendment provides that, in the case of benefits provided under a multiemployer plan, the Secretary is to allocate the reporting responsibility with respect to the plan under section 6039D between the employer and the multiemployer plan based on the agreement between the parties.

Conference Agreement

The conference agreement follows the Senate amendment.

Line of Business

* * *

House Bill

The House bill allows the safe-harbor rule under section 414(r)(3) to be applied based on the proportion of highly compensated and nonhighly compensated employees in a line of business or operating unit in the preceding plan year if (1) no more than a de minimis number of employees shifted to or from the line of business or operating unit since the end of the prior year; or (2) the employees shifted to or from the line of business or operating unit since the end of the prior year contained a substantially proportional number of highly compensated employees.

The House bill provides that employees who perform at least 75 percent of their services for a particular line of business or operating unit are required to be allocated to such line or unit.

The modifications also apply for qualified plan purposes.

Senate Amendment

The Senate amendment is the same as the House bill, with the following modifications.

Under the Senate amendment, activities are considered geographically separate for purposes of the operating unit rules if they are at least 35 miles apart. In addition, for testing years beginning in 1989, the classification test, passage of which is required to use the separate line of business or operating unit rule, is to be the prior-law section 410(b)(1)(B) test without regard to any modification of such test by the Secretary. These two provisions apply only for purposes of section 89 (and thus do not apply for purposes of the qualified plan coverage and nondiscrimination rules).

Conference Agreement

The conference agreement generally follows the Senate amendment, with the following modifications.

The conferees intend that the rule that operating units are considered to be in significantly separate geographic areas if they are at least 35 miles apart is a safe harbor. Under certain circumstances, the Secretary may provide that operating units that are less than 35 miles apart may be considered to be in significantly separate geographic areas. In addition, the conferees do not intend to create any inference with respect to the appropriate line of business or operating unit rules for qualified pension plan purposes, i.e., no inference is intended that the Secretary is required to adopt similar rules or more or less restrictive rules for purposes of the qualified plan coverage and nondiscrimination rules.

Acquisitions and Dispositions

* * *

Senate Amendment

Under the Senate amendment, the Secretary is authorized to prescribe additional rules with respect to the application of section 89 in the case of business transactions such as acquisitions and dispositions.

Conference Agreement

The conference agreement follows the Senate amendment.

Qualification Requirements

* * *

House Bill

Under the House bill, employers may comply with the written plan requirement (sec. 89(k)(1)(A)) for any plan year beginning in 1989 by completing the required, full written documentation by the end of such plan year. For plan years beginning after 1989, rules prescribed by the Secretary are to permit employers a reasonable period to move from a written plan evidenced by a collection of separate written documents to a written plan evidenced by a stand-alone document. Standard short-term sick pay plans are not subject to the qualification rules of section 89(k) under the House bill.

Senate Amendment

The Senate amendment follows the House bill, but deletes the inference in the House bill that, after a transition period, the writing requirement may only be satisfied by a stand-alone document.

Conference Agreement

The conference agreement follows the Senate amendment. The conferees clarify that there is no intent to imply that the written plan requirement must be satisfied by a single stand-alone document, rather than by a collection of separate written documents.

Group-Term Life Insurance

* * *

Senate Amendment

Under the Senate amendment, the exception permitting group-term life insurance to vary on the basis of age also applies in the same manner to group-term life insurance coverage under which required employee contributions vary according to the age of the employee, but only up to a specified limit (e.g., the employee's cost may not exceed $X per $1,000 of coverage).

The Senate amendment deletes the provision under which an employer that uses the exception for age-related costs or the exception provided above must use the same exception with respect to all group-term life insurance coverage of the employer. Under the Senate amendment, if one of the exceptions is used with respect to a plan, the same exception must be used with respect to all plans aggregated with such plan for purposes of the 50-percent test and the 80-percent test. In addition, for purposes of applying the 90-percent/50-percent test and the 75-percent test, the employer is to elect to apply the tests as if it had used the general rule or one of the two exceptions with respect to all plans being tested.

The Senate amendment also modifies the definition of compensation for purposes of applying section 89 to group-term life insurance. Under the Senate amendment, for testing years beginning in 1989 and 1990, an employer may apply section 89 to group-term life insurance by using, in lieu of compensation as defined under section 414(s), base compensation. Thus, for example, overtime and bonuses could be disregarded. For testing years beginning after December 31, 1990, the employer may use base compensation, or any definition of compensation, provided that such definition of compensation is not discriminatory based on the experience in the prior year. A definition of compensation will be considered nondiscriminatory if the ratio of (1) the average compensation of the nonhighly compensated employees under the alternative definition to (2) the average compensation of the nonhighly compensated employees under section 414(s) is at least 90 percent of the same ratio for highly compensated employees.

Conference Agreement

The conference agreement follows the Senate amendment, but modifies the provision that provides two additional exceptions to the general rule that, if two types of insurance coverage vary in any way, they are considered separate plans.

The conference agreement clarifies that the use of age brackets of up to five years is not inconsistent with the provision under both exceptions that the required employee contributions increase with age. Thus, for example, an employer could establish a series of five-year age brackets and have the required employee contributions only increase when an employee moves from one bracket to another.

The conference agreement clarifies that, for purposes of the 90-percent/50-percent test and the 75-percent test, the employer may use the general definition of a group-term life insurance plan or one of the two exceptions despite the fact that the employer did not use the same definition for purposes of applying the 50-percent test to any particular plan.

The conference agreement modifies the Senate amendment by allowing employers to use any nondiscriminatory definition of compensation, as described above, not only in testing years beginning after December 31, 1990, but also in testing years beginning in 1989 and 1990. The conference agreement also modifies the standard for determining whether a definition of compensation is nondiscriminatory. Under the modified standard, a definition of compensation will be considered nondiscriminatory for purposes of applying section 89 to group-term life insurance only if the ratio of (1) the average compensation of the nonhighly compensated employees under the definition to (2) the average compensation of the nonhighly compensated employees under section 414(s) is at least 100 percent of the same ratio for highly compensated employees (rather than 90 percent as under the Senate amendment).

As under the Senate amendment, in testing years beginning in 1989 and 1990, employers also have the option of using base compensation, which would not be required to satisfy the nondiscrimination standard described above.

Dependent Care Assistance

* * *

House Bill

For purposes of applying the special benefits test to salary reduction amounts under a dependent care assistance program that is not treated as a statutory employee benefit plan under section 89, the House bill provides that an employer may elect to take into account employees with compensation (as defined in sec. 414(q)(7)) below $25,000. Thus, the employer may elect to take into account all employees with compensation below $25,000 or may disregard employees with compensation below any specified amount lower than $25,000.

Senate Amendment

The Senate amendment follows the House bill. In addition, under the Senate amendment, an employer is entitled to elect certain alternative definitions of compensation for purposes of the $25,000 rule under rules prescribed by the Secretary provided that such definition does not overstate the number of employees with less than $25,000 of compensation under section 414(q)(7) by more than five percent based on the experience in the prior year.

Conference Agreement

The conference agreement follows the Senate amendment.

The conference agreement also provides that, for purposes of section 125, a plan will not be treated as failing to be a cafeteria plan solely because a participant elected before January 1, 1989, to receive reimbursements under the plan for dependent care assistance for periods after December 31, 1988, and such assistance is includible in income under the provisions of the Family Support Act of 1988. This rule is intended to provide relief for individuals who have made, or are in the process of making, elections with respect to dependent care assistance and who are affected by the new rules regarding taxation of dependent care assistance under the Family Support Act of 1988. This rule is similar to the rule provided under the technical corrections provisions with respect to overnight camp expenses.

Medical Diagnostic Examinations

* * *

House Bill

The House bill clarifies the valuation of health coverage, including physical examinations.

* * *

Conference Agreement

As under the House bill * * *, normal valuation principles are to be applied to determine the value of a medical diagnostic benefit that is included in income because it is provided on a discriminatory basis.

Legally Required Benefits

* * *

Conference Agreement

The conference agreement broadens the Secretary's authority to disregard State-mandated ancillary (i.e., noncore) benefits under certain circumstances by providing that such authority applies to all ancillary accident or health benefits required by Federal, State, or foreign law. Thus, for example, in comparing the benefits of a class of employees to the benefits of another class of employees, the Secretary may permit ancillary benefits that are required by State law for one of the classes but not for the other to be disregarded. This broadened authority does not apply to benefits provided in connection with continuation coverage (old sec. 162(k); new sec. 4980B) for which different special rules apply under present law.

Health Care Continuation Rules

* * *

House Bill

The technical corrections provisions of the House bill extends the rules aggregating related employers (sec. 414(b), (c), (m), (o), and (t)) and the employee leasing rules (sec. 414(n)) to the health care continuation rules.

Senate Amendment

The Senate amendment is the same as the House bill.

Conference Agreement

The conference agreement follows the House bill and the Senate amendment.

Sanctions

* * *

House Bill

Year of inclusion.—The House bill provides a special rule with respect to plans with a testing year ending after September 30, and on or before December 31. Under this special rule, an employer may elect to have the discriminatory excess included in the incomes of highly compensated employees in their taxable years following the taxable year with or within which the testing year ends. If an employer makes such an election, however, the employer's deduction relating to such discriminatory excess is to be allowable only in the employer's taxable year with or within which ends the testing year following the testing year in which the discriminatory excess occurred.

Discriminatory excess.—For purposes of determining and allocating the discriminatory excess with respect to a group-term life insurance plan, employer-provided coverage over $50,000 is treated as nontaxable. Thus, to the extent that the discriminatory coverage does not exceed the total coverage over $50,000, the effect of a finding of discrimination is simply the inclusion in income of the excess, if any, of the actual cost of the discriminatory coverage over the cost of such coverage under section 79(c).

Qualification rule sanction.—Under the House bill, if a plan to which section 505 applies (generally, a plan part of which is a VEBA or a GLSO) violates the new qualification requirements (sec. 89(k)), the VEBA or GLSO is not to be exempt from tax under section 501(a). A plan failing to satisfy the new qualification requirements is not the type of plan for which the VEBA or GLSO tax exemption was established.

In addition, the House bill provides that, in the case of a group-term life insurance plan that fails the qualification rule, the benefits provided under the plan are to be included in the beneficiary's income rather than the employee's.

The House bill further provides for the coordination of the sanction for failure to satisfy the qualification rules with the sanction for discrimination. Generally, any amount included in the income of a highly compensated employee attributable to discriminatory coverage is to offset the amount includible under section 89(k) with respect to the same highly compensated employee for the same coverage.

If, however, any discriminatory excess would be included in the income of a highly compensated employee for a year subsequent to the year of inclusion under section 89(k) with respect to the same coverage, the coordination described above is to work in reverse, i.e., the section 89(k) inclusion is to offset the inclusion of the discriminatory excess.

* * *

Welfare benefit funds.—The House bill modifies the present-law sanctions with respects to discriminatory VEBAs, GLSOs, and other welfare benefit funds because such sanctions are inconsistent with the general approach under section 89 to apply the sanctions solely with respect to the discriminatory amount.

Under the House bill, if section 89 applies to a plan, a VEBA, or GLSO that is part of the plan does not lose its tax-exempt status under section 501(a) merely because the plan is a discriminatory employee benefit plan (within the meaning of sec. 89(c)). In lieu of this sanction, the bill imposes an excise tax on an employer maintaining a welfare benefit fund if a discriminatory employee benefit plan is part of the fund for the testing year. The tax applies to the taxable year of the employer with or within which the testing year ends.

* * *

The House bill also modifies the 100-percent excise tax applicable to disqualified benefits in the case of a post-retirement medical benefit or life insurance benefit that is subject to section 89. The House bill provides that the amount of the disqualified benefit subject to the tax is not to exceed the aggregate excess benefits (within the meaning of sec. 89(b)) provided under the plan.

Senate Amendment

* * *

Employer sanction.—Under the Senate amendment, the penalty for failure to report income includible under section 89 only applies to the portion of the employee's benefit that bears the same relationship to the total benefit as the unreported amount bears to the entire amount that should have been reported.

* * *

Conference Agreement

Year of inclusion.—The conference agreement follows the House bill and the Senate amendment, except that the conference agreement clarifies that the rule permitting a deduction in the employer's taxable year for amounts paid within 2 ½ months of the taxable year does not apply with respect to amounts includible in income by reason of section 89.

Discriminatory excess.—The conference agreement follows the House bill and the Senate amendment.

Qualification rule sanction.—The conference agreement follows the House bill and the Senate amendment.

Employer sanction.—The conference agreement follows the Senate amendment.

Welfare benefit fund.—The conference agreement modifies the calculation of the excise tax with respect to a discriminatory welfare benefit fund in the following respects. Under the conference agreement, with respect to any employer, the first step described above is revised so that the determination is of the lesser of (1) the aggregate excess benefits (within the meaning of sec. 89(b)) provided by the employer for the testing year under all plans of the same type or types as the plan or plans of the welfare benefit fund; or (2) the taxable income of the fund for the testing year (without regard to sec. 501(c)(9) or (c)(20)) allocable to the employer. In addition, the amount counted under clause 1 with respect to benefits of any type is limited to the excess benefits of such type provided by the employer under the welfare benefit fund, assuming that excess benefits were provided to the maximum extent possible under such welfare benefit fund or another welfare benefit fund. Also, if the welfare benefit fund is maintained by more than one employer, the taxable income of the fund is to be allocated among the employers for purposes of clause (2) above in any reasonable manner that is consistently applied and not inconsistent with rules issued by the Secretary. Further, with respect to any employer, the final step in determining the excise tax, the offset by the income tax imposed on the fund, is limited to the portion of such tax allocable to the employer, determined under rules similar to those applicable in allocating the taxable income of the fund.

The conference agreement provides that the amount of the disqualified benefit subject to the 100-percent excise tax is not to exceed the amount described in clause 1 above, as limited in the same paragraph.

Inclusion in Wages

* * *

House Bill

Under the House bill, amounts that are includible in gross income by reason of section 89 (either directly or indirectly (as in the case of sec. 129(d)(1)(B))) are included in wages (or compensation) as of the time includible in gross income for purposes of the Federal Insurance Contributions Act (sec. 3121), the Railroad Retirement Tax Act (sec. 3231(e)), the Federal Unemployment Tax Act (sec. 3306), income tax withholding (sec. 3401), and the Social Security Act (sec. 209). These provisions of the House bill do not apply to former employees who separate from service prior to January 1, 1989.

* * *

Conference Agreement

The conference agreement follows the House bill * * *.

Self-Employed Individuals

* * *

House Bill

The House bill clarifies that, for purposes of applying the nondiscrimination rules to statutory employee benefit plans, the term "employee" includes any self-employed individual (as defined in sec. 401(c)(1)), and the term "compensation" includes such individual's earned income (as defined in sec. 401(c)(2)).

* * *

Conference Agreement

The conference agreement follows the House bill * * *.

Definition of Plan

* * *

House Bill

Under the House bill, each different option is valued separately, but is not considered a separate plan. A plan is a group of options with comparable values (under the otherwise applicable comparability rules). With respect to the nondiscrimination rules, the effect of these changes is only one of terminology rather than of substance.

Conference Agreement

The conference agreement follows the House bill * * *.

Effective Date

House Bill

Except as otherwise provided, these provisions apply as if included in the Tax Reform Act of 1986.

Under the House bill, an employer may elect to apply the new rules of section 1151 of the Act (including the nondiscrimination rules, qualification rules, reporting rules, and cafeteria plan rules) to certain group-term life insurance plans in plan years beginning after October 22, 1986. The plans for which this election is available are described in section 125(c)(2)(C).

Conference Agreement

The conference agreement follows the House bill * * *. In addition, the conferees have become aware that some employers are considering changing the plan years of their employee benefit plans to delay substantially the effective date of the new nondiscrimination rules. The conferees expect that Treasury rules will disregard such changes for effective date purposes.

Further, the conferees expect that these rules will require the employer to base testing for the first testing year on all plans providing coverage during that period without regard to whether they are effective for purposes of section 89. If a discriminatory excess is calculated based on coverage that is not effective for section 89 purposes, such excess is to be prorated on the basis of the coverage in effect for section 89 purposes as described under rules prescribed by the Secretary.

[¶ 12,350.06]

Committee Reports on P.L. 99-514 (Tax Reform Act of 1986)

[Senate Committee Report]

Tax treatment of divorce distributions

The bill provides that the special rules for determining the taxability of benefits subject to a qualified domestic relations order apply only to distributions made to an alternate payee who is the spouse or the former spouse of the participant. Thus, distributions to a spouse or former spouse generally will be included in the gross income of the spouse or former spouse. Under the bill, however, a distribution to an alternate payee other than a spouse (e.g., a child) is generally to be includible in the gross income of the participant. (For purposes of lump sum treatment, amounts paid to an alternate payee other than a spouse, or former spouse, shall be treated as part of the balance to the credit of the participant).

In addition, under the bill, the rules for allocating an employee's investment in the contract between the employee and an alternate payee apply only if the alternate payee is a spouse or former spouse of the participant.

If the alternate payee is not a spouse or former spouse, then the investment in the contract is not allocated to the alternate payee and is recovered by the participant under the general basis recovery rules applicable to the participant.

Determination by plan administrator

* * *

The bill makes it clear that the 18-month period during which benefits may be deferred begins with the date on which any payments would, but for the deferral, be required to commence. Accordingly, if a payment is deferred pending the resolution of a dispute, then that payment and each other payment that is deferred within the next 18 months because of the dispute are to be segregated. If the dispute is not resolved within 18 months after the first payment is deferred, then all payments deferred during the 18-month period with respect to the dispute are to be paid to the persons who would have received them if the order had not been issued.

If a plan administrator determines that a domestic relations order is defective before the expiration of the 18-month suspension period, the committee intends that the plan administrator may delay payment of a participant's benefit until the expiration of the 18-month period if the plan administrator has notice that the parties are attempting to rectify any deficiencies in the order.

Notice of issuance of a stay during the time an appeal is pending is deemed to be notice that the parties are attempting to cure deficiencies in a domestic relations order. Further, the committee intends that a plan administrator will honor a restraining order prohibiting the disposition of a participant's benefits pending resolution of a dispute with respect to a domestic relations order.

In addition, the bill eliminates the requirement that a defined benefit plan establish an escrow account for amounts that would have otherwise been paid during the 18-month period. Instead, the plan administrator is required only to account separately for such amounts. If the deficiency is not cured or the dispute not resolved within the 18-month period, all payments deferred during the 18-month period are to be paid to the persons who would have received them if the stay or order had not been issued.

* * *

Form of benefit

The bill clarifies that a qualified domestic relations order may not require that payments prior to, or subsequent to, a participant's separation from service be made in the form of a qualified joint and survivor annuity with respect to the alternate payee and his or her subsequent spouse.

Application of domestic relations provisions to plans not subject to assignment or alienation restrictions

* * *

The bill clarifies that the qualified domestic relations provisions do not apply to any plan to which the assignment or alienation restrictions do not apply. For example, a domestic relations order relating to the division of pension benefits of a participant in a plan maintained by a governmental employer is not required to meet the rules relating to qualified domestic relations orders because the payment of benefits to a spouse or former spouse of the participant is not a prohibited assignment or alienation of the participant's benefits.

Coordination of domestic relations provisions with Federal garnishment restrictions

* * *

The bill clarifies that the payment of benefits pursuant to a qualified domestic relations order is not treated as a garnishment of wages for purposes of Federal or State law restrictions on garnishment.

Coordination with qualified plan requirements

* * *

The bill makes it clear that a plan is not treated as failing to satisfy the qualification requirements of section 401(a) or (k) or section 409(d) of the Internal Revenue Code (prohibiting payment of benefits prior to termination of employment or such time as distributions are otherwise permitted) solely because the plan makes payment to the alternate payee, even if the payments are made with respect to a participant who has not separated from service, and they commence before the participant has attained the earliest retirement age under the plan. This exception applies, however, only if the present value of the benefit to be paid to an alternate payee (1) does not exceed $3,500 or (2) exceeds at least $3,500 and the alternate payee consents in writing to such earlier distribution. Further, the exception applies only if the distribution, if paid to the participant, would not contravene the provisions of the plan (except as permitted under section 414(p)(4)). Of course, a plan could not make distributions to an alternate payee at a time not specified in a qualified domestic relations order unless (1) the order also provided for such earlier distributions pursuant to an agreement between the plan and an alternate payee, and (2) the plan authorized such distributions.

In determining whether the present value of the benefit payable to the alternate payee exceeds $3,500, the present value of the participant's accrued benefit or that of any other alternate payee (after reduction for the benefits payable to the alternate payee) is disregarded. Similarly, for purposes of determining whether the present value of a benefit payable to a participant exceeds $3,500, the present value of amounts payable to an alternate payee under a qualified domestic relations order is disregarded.

The bill provides that, to the extent provided in a qualified domestic relations order, a spouse of a participant is not treated as a spouse. For example, a qualified domestic relations order could provide for the division of a participant's accrued benefits under a pension plan as part of a separation agreement and could further provide that the participant's spouse is not entitled to receive any survivor benefits under the usual survivor benefits provisions. Thus, the plan administrator would not be required to secure spousal consent to the participant's election to waive a survivor benefit.

In addition, the bill authorizes the Secretary of the Treasury to issue such regulations as may be necessary to otherwise coordinate the Code provisions affecting qualified domestic relations orders (sections 401(a)(13)(B) and 414(p)), and the regulations issued by the Secretary of Labor thereunder with other Code provisions affecting qualified plans. The Secretary of Labor has authority to issue regulations under the qualified domestic relations order provisions of ERISA, and the Code (secs. 401(a)(13)(B) and 414(p)), and the bill does not affect the authority of the Secretary of Labor to prescribe such regulations.

Earliest retirement age

* * *

[The Conference Committee changed the definition of "earliest retirement age."]

[Conference Committee Report]

The conference agreement follows the Senate amendment except as follows.

* * *

Qualified domestic relations orders.—Under present law, a domestic relations order is not a qualified domestic relations order ("QDRO") if such order requires a plan to provide any type or form of benefit, or any option, not otherwise provided under the plan. Thus, and order generally constitutes a QDRO if it provides that payments attributable to a participant's benefits are to begin before the participant separates from service and becomes eligible for a distribution. As an exception to the rule, present law provides that a QDRO may require that an alternate payee commence receiving payments on or after the date that the participant attains the earliest retirement age under the plan, even if the participant has not yet separated from service.

Under the conference agreement, the definition of "earliest retirement age" for purposes of the QDRO provisions in the case of a defined contribution plan or a defined benefit plan is the earlier of: (1) the earliest date benefits are payable under the plan to the participant, and (2) the later of the date the participant attains age 50 and the date on which the participant could obtain a distribution from the plan if the participant separated from service.

For example, in the case of a plan which provides for payment of benefits upon separation from service (but not before then), the earliest date on which a QDRO can require payments to an alternate payee to begin is the date the participant separates from service. A QDRO could also require such a plan to begin payments to an alternate payee when the participant attains age 50, even if the participant has not then separated from service. The amount payable under a QDRO following the participant's earliest retirement age cannot exceed the amount which the participant is (or would be) entitled to receive at such time. For example, assume that a profit-sharing plan provides that a participant may withdraw some, but not all, of the participant's account balance before separation from service. A QDRO may provide for payment to an alternate payee up to the amount which the participant may withdraw.

A plan may provide for payment to an alternate payee prior to the earliest retirement age as defined under the conference agreement.

The conference agreement adopts the provisons in the Senate amendment with regard to procedures during the 18-month period. If a plan administrator determines that a domestic relations order is defective before the expiration of the 18-month suspension period, the conference committee intends that the plan administrator may delay payment of a participant's benefit until the expiration of the 18-month period if the plan administrator has notice that either party is attempting to rectify any deficiencies in the order.

Similarly, the committee intends that the plan administrator may delay payment of benefits for a reasonable period of time if the plan administrator receives notice that a domestic relations order is being sought. For example, a participant in a profit-sharing plan which is exempt from the survivor benefit rules request a lump sum distribution from the plan. Before the distribution is made, the plan administrator receives notice that the participant's spouse is seeking a domestic relations order. The plan administrator may delay payment of benefits.

[House Committee Report.]

Employee leasing

Present Law

Under the Act, the Secretary of the Treasury is granted regulatory authority to develop rules as may be necessary to prevent the avoidance of any employee benefit requirement to which the employee leasing provisions apply through the use of employee leasing or other arrangements (sec. 414(o)).

Explanation of Provisions

Under the bill, the special regulatory authority provided to the Secretary of the Treasury with respect to abuses through the use of affiliated service groups (sec. 414(m)(7)) is repealed in favor of the broader general authority provided under the Act (sec. 414(o)). In addition, the bill clarifies that the other definitions relating to affiliated service groups (sec. 414(m)(6)) continue to apply.

[¶ 12,350.065]

Committee Reports on P.L. 98-397 (Retirement Equity Act of 1984)

[Senate Committee Report]

In general.—The bill clarifies the spend-thrift provisions by providing new rules for the treatment of certain domestic relations orders. In addition, the bill creates an exception to the ERISA preemption provision with respect to these orders. The bill also provides procedures to be followed by a plan administrator (including the Pension Benefit Guaranty Corporation (PBGC)) and an alternative payee (a child, spouse, former spouse, or other dependent of a participant) with respect to domestic relations orders.

Under the bill, if a domestic relations order requires the distribution of all or a part of a participant's benefits under a qualified plan to an alternative payee, then the creation, recognition, or assignment of the alternative payee's right to the benefits is not considered an assignment or alienation of benefits under the plan if and only if the order is a qualified domestic relations order. Because rights created, recognized, or assigned by a qualified domestic relations order, and benefit payments pursuant to such an order, are specifically permitted under the bill, State law providing for these rights and payments under a qualified domestic relations order will continue to be exempt from Federal preemption under ERISA.

Qualified domestic relations order.—Under the bill, the term "qualified domestic relations order" means a domestic relations order that (1) creates or recognizes the existence of an alternate payee's right to, or assigns to an alternative payee the right to, receive all or a portion of the benefits payable with respect to a participant under a pension plan, and (2) meets certain other requirements. A domestic relations order is any judgment, decree, or order (including approval of a property settlement agreement) that relates to the provision of child support, alimony payments, or marital property rights to a spouse, former spouse, child, or other dependent of the participant, and is made pursuant to a State domestic relations law (including community property law). Under the bill, an alternate payee includes any spouse, former spouse, child, or other dependent of a participant who is recognized by a qualified domestic relations order as having a right to receive all, or a portion of, the benefits payable under a plan with respect to the participant.

To be a qualified order, a domestic relations order must clearly specify (1) the name and last known mailing address (if available) of the participant and the name and mailing address of each alternate payee to which the order relates, (2) the amount or percentage of the participant's benefits to be paid to an alternate payee or the manner in which the amount is to be determined, and (3) the number of payments or period for which payments are required. The committee intends that an order will not be treated as failing to be a qualified order merely because the order does not specify the current mailing address of the participant and alternate payee if the plan administrator has reason to know that address independently of the order. For example, if the plan administrator is aware that the alternate payee is also a participant under the plan and the plan records include a current address for each participant, the plan administrator may not treat the order as failing to qualify.

The committee intends that an order that is qualified is to remain qualified with respect to a successor plan of the same employer or a plan of a successor employer (within the meaning of sec. 414(a)).

A domestic relations order is not a qualified order if it (1) requires a plan to provide any type or form of benefit, or any option, not otherwise provided under the plan, (2) requires the plan to provide increased benefits, or (3) requires payment of benefits to an alternate payee that are required to be paid to another alternate payee under a previously existing qualified domestic relations order. An order does not require a plan to provide increased benefits if the order does not provide for the payment of benefits in excess of the benefits to which the participant would be entitled in the absence of the order.

The bill provides that a domestic relations order is not treated as failing the requirements for a qualified domestic relations order merely because the order provides that payments must begin to the alternate payee on or after the date on which the participant attains the earliest retirement age under the plan whether or not the participant actually retires on that date. If the participant dies before that date, the alternate payee is entitled to benefits only if the qualified domestic relations order requires survivor benefits to be paid. In the case of an order providing for the payment of benefits after the earliest retirement age, the payments to the alternate payee at the time are computed as if the participant had retired on the date on which benefit payments commence under the order.

When payments are made to an alternate payee before the participant retires, the payments are computed by taking into account only benefits actually accrued and not taking into account any employer subsidy for early retirement. The amount to be paid to the alternate payee is to be calculated by using the participant's normal retirement benefit accrued as of the date payout begins and by actuarially reducing such benefit based on the interest rate specified in the plan or 5 percent, if the plan does not specify an interest rate. A plan providing only normal and subsidized early retirement benefits would not specify a rate for determining actuarially equivalent, unsubsidized benefits.

If an alternate payee begins to receive benefits under the order and the participant subsequently retires with subsidized early retirement benefits, the order may specify that the amount payable to the alternate payee is to be recalculated so that the alternate payee also receives a share of the subsidized benefit to which the participant is entitled. The payment of early retirement benefits with respect to a participant who has not yet retired or the increase in benefits payable to the alternate payee after the recalculation is not to be considered to violate the prohibition against a qualified domestic relations order providing for increased benefits.

The payments to the alternate payee after the earliest retirement date may be paid in any form permitted under the plan (other than a joint and survivor annuity with respect to the alternate payee and the alternate payee's spouse). In the case of a defined contribution plan, the earliest retirement date is the date on which the participant attains an age that is 10 years before the normal retirement age.

Under the bill, a plan is not treated as failing to satisfy the requirements of section 401(a), 409(d), or 401(k) of the Internal Revenue Code that prohibit payment of benefits prior to termination of employment solely because the plan makes payments to the alternate payee in accordance with a qualified domestic relations order.

Under the bill, an alternative payee is treated as a beneficiary for all purposes under the plan. In no event, however, will more than one PBGC premium be collected with respect to the participant's benefits (determined as if a qualified domestic relations order had not been issued) even though such benefits, subject to the usual limits, may be guaranteed by the PBGC.

Determination by plan administrator.—Under the bill, the administrator of a plan that receives a domestic relations order is required to notify promptly the participant and any other alternate payee of receipt of the order and the plan's procedures for determining whether the order is qualified. In addition, within a reasonable period after receipt of the order, the plan administrator is to determine whether the order is qualified and notify the participant and alternate payee of the determination. The notices required under these rules are to be sent to the addresses specified in the order or, if the order fails to specify an address, to the last address of the participant or alternate payee known to the plan administrator.

The bill authorizes the Secretary of Labor to prescribe regulations defining the reasonable period during which the plan administrator is to determine whether an order is qualified. In addition, the bill provides that plans are to establish reasonable procedures to determine whether domestic relations orders are qualified and to administer distributions under qualified orders. Ordinarily, a plan need not be amended to implement the domestic relations provisions of the bill.

Deferral of benefit payments.—During any period in which the issue of whether a domestic relations order is a qualified order is being determined (by the plan administrator, by a court of competent jurisdiction, or otherwise), the plan administrator is to defer the payment of any benefits in dispute. These deferred benefits are segregated either in a separate account in the plan or in an escrow account. In the case of a defined benefit plan, the amounts are to be placed in an escrow account. Of course, segregation is not required for amounts that would not otherwise be paid during the period of the dispute.

If the order is determined to be a qualified domestic relations order within 18 months after the deferral of benefits, the plan administrator is to pay the segregated amounts (plus interest) to the persons entitled to receive them. If the plan administrator determines that the order is not a qualified order or, after the 18-month period has expired, has not resolved the issue of whether the order is qualified, the segregated amounts are paid to the persons or persons who would have received the amounts if the order had not been issued.

Any determination that an order is qualified after expiration of the 18-month period is to be applied prospectively. Thus, if the plan administrator determines that the order is qualified after the 18-month period, the plan is not liable for payments to the alternate payee for the period before the order is determined to be qualified.

Of course, the provisions of the bill do not affect any cause of action that an alternate payee may have against the participant. For example, if an order is determined to be qualified after the 18-month period, the alternate payee may have a cause of action under State law against the participant for amounts paid to the participant that should have been paid to the alternate payee.

During any period in which the alternate payee cannot be located, the plan is not permitted to provide for the forfeiture of the amounts that would have been paid unless the plan provides for full reinstatement when the alternate payee is located.

Consultation with the Secretary of the Treasury.—Under the bill, the Secretary of Labor is required to consult with the Secretary of the Treasury in prescribing regulations under these provisions.

Tax treatment of divorce distributions.—The bill provides rules for determining the tax treatment of benefits subject to a qualified domestic relations order. Under the bill, for purposes of determining the taxability of benefits, the alternate payee is treated as a distributee with respect to payments received from or under a plan.

Under the bill, net employee contributions (together with other amounts treated as the participant's investment in the contract) are apportioned between the participant and the alternate payee under regulations prescribed by the Secretary of the Treasury. The apportionment is to be made pro rata, on the basis of the present value of all benefits of the participant under the plan and the present value of all benefits of the alternate payee under the plan (as alternate payee with respect to the participant under a qualified domestic relations order).

Payments to an alternate payee before the participant attains age 59 ½ are not subject to the 10-percent additional income tax that would otherwise apply under certain circumstances if the participant received the amounts.

The bill provides that the interest of the alternate payee is not taken into account in determining whether a distribution to the participant is a lump sum distribution. Under the bill, benefits distributed to an alternate payee under a qualified domestic relations order can be rolled over, tax-free, to an individual retirement account or to an individual retirement annuity. The usual income tax rules apply to benefits not rolled over. The special rules for lump sum distributions from qualified plans will not apply to benefits distributed to an alternate payee.

[¶ 12,350.07]

Committee Reports on P.L. 98-369 (Tax Reform Act of 1984)

[Senate Committee Report]

The committee believes it is necessary to change the attribution rules applicable to the determination of whether a group of employers constitutes an affiliated service group in order to prevent abusive circumvention of the qualified pension plan requirements. In addition, the committee is aware that some individuals have interpreted the present law safe-harbor rule for employee leasing arrangements as overriding traditional common-law employee rules. The committee believes that present law should be clarified to prevent this interpretation.

Under the bill, in determining whether a group of employers constitutes an affiliated service group, the constructive ownership rules of sec. 318(a), rather than those of sec. 267(c), apply.

The bill clarifies the present law definition of a leased employee to include only those individuals who are not otherwise employees of the lessee.

Effective Dates

The provisions relating to affiliated service groups are effective for plan years beginning after December 31, 1984. The employee leasing provisions are effective for plan years beginning after December 31, 1983.

[Conference Committee Report]

The conference agreement follows the Senate amendment. In addition, the conference agreement provides the Secretary of the Treasury with regulatory authority to develop any rules as may be necessary to prevent the avoidance of any employee benefit requirement to which the employee leasing provisions apply through the use of employee leasing or other arrangements. The conferees do not intend to imply that such regulations could only be applied prospectively.

For example, the conferees are aware of situations in which professionals are hired as leased employees of their own professional corporations in order to avoid the nondiscrimination rules applicable to qualified plans. The conferees intend that regulations will prevent the avoidance of the nondiscrimination rules through the use of such employee leasing arrangements.

The conferees do not intend any inference that this example is the sole situation in which employee leasing is used to avoid the qualified plan requirements. However, the conferees do not intend to imply that legitimate uses of employee leasing are necessarily abuses. For example, the conferees recognize that the historical use by businesses of temporary help company employees on temporary projects generally is not an avoidance situation subject to the Secretary's regulatory authority provided under the conference agreement if the project has an ascertainable termination date and it is not customary under the circumstances to hire permanent employees for such a project.

See also ¶ 11,900.085 for the Committee Report relating to the repeal of the bond purchase provisions.

[¶ 12,350.075]

Committee Report on P.L. 97-248 (Tax Equity and Fiscal Responsibility Act of 1982)

The Committee Report on P.L. 97-248 relating to employee leasing and organizations performing management funtions is at ¶ 12,400.06.

[¶ 12,350.085]

Committee Report on P.L. 96-364 (Multiemployer Pension Plan Amendments Act of 1980)

[Senate Committee Report]

The Senate Committee Report on P.L. 96-364, Sec. 207(a) on multiemployer plans and Sec. 407(b) on church plans, is at ¶ 14,130.095 and ¶ 15,310.10.

[¶ 12,350.09]

Testimony of Congressman Ullman of Oregon on P.L. 96-605 (Miscellaneous Revenue Act of 1980)

Testimony of Congressman Ullman of Oregon on P.L. 96-605 during the House debate on December 13, 1980 (Congressional Record of December 15, 1980).

Mr. Speaker, the provision expands the class of controlled groups of employers which are treated as a single employer in testing whether a pension, et cetera, plan, a cafeteria or medical reimbursement plan, or a simplified employee pension meets the nondiscrimination standards and other requirements of the tax law for favorable tax treatment. The provision does not change present law under which aggregation of employers may otherwise be required.

In particular, under the provision, for purposes of the employee benefit requirements,[2] all employees of employers who are members of an affiliated service group are treated as employed by a single employer except as provided by

[2] The employee benefit requirements consist of (1) in the case of qualified pension, etc. plans, the requirements of sec. 401(a) (3), (4), (7), and (16), and secs. 410, 411 and 415 (these provisions related to employee participation and eligibility, discrimination, vesting, and limits on benefits and contributions) and, in the case of a plan adopted by more than one employer, the requirements of sec. 412 relating to funding and the limitations of sec. 404(a) relating to employer deductions, (2) the requirements of sec. 105(h) for medical reimbursement plans, (3) the requirements of section 125 for cafeteria plans, and (4) the requirements of sec. 408(k) for simplified employee pensions.

Treasury regulations. Under the provision, an affiliated service group consists of a service organization (the "first organization") and (1) each other service organization which is related to the first organization, and (2) each other organization which is related to either (a) the first organization, or (b) a service organization which is related to the first organization.

Under the provision, a service organization is an organization the principal business of which is the performance of services. Also, the first organization and another service organization (an "other related service organization") are considered to be related if (1) the other service organization is a share-holder[3] or partner in the first organization, and (2) the other service organization regularly performs services for the first organization or is regularly associated with the first organization in performing services for third persons.

Under the provision, any other organization (an "other related organization") is related to the first organization (or to an other related service organization) if: First, a significant portion of the business of the other organization is the performance of services, for the first organization (or an other related service organization), of a type historically performed in the service field by employees, and second, at least 10 percent of the interests in the other organization is held by persons who are officers, highly compensated employees, or owners of the first organization (or an other related service organization).

In determining whether services in a particular service field are historically performed by employees, it is intended that the general historical practice in the service field be considered, rather than the practice of the particular organizations involved. In this regard, it is also intended that if services in a particular service field are historically performed by partners or proprietors, but are also of a type historically performed by employees in that service field, the services are to be considered of a type historically performed by employees in that service field.

The operation of the provision can be illustrated as follows: If the A corporation and the B corporation form a partnership (the first organization), the principal business of which is the performance of services, A corporation and B corporation (other related service organizations, and the partnership would constitute an affiliated service group under the provision if they regularly provided services to the partnership or are regularly associated with the partnership in performing services for third persons.

Similarly, if C is an individual partner in a partnership (the first organization) the principal business of which is the performance of services, and if, together, C and the other partners own at least 10 percent of a corporation (an other related organization), a significant portion of the business of which is the performance of services for the partnership, of a type historically performed in the service field by employees, the other related organization would be included in an affiliated service group with the partnership.

The provision authorizes the Secretary of the Treasury to prescribe such regulations as may be necessary to prevent the avoidance with respect to service organizations, through the use of separate organizations, of any employee benefit requirement to which the provision applies.

[¶ 12,350.10]

Committee Report on P.L. 93-406 (Employee Retirement Income Security Act of 1974)

[Conference Committee Explanation]

Predecessor employer.—Service with a predecessor employer must be counted for purposes of the plan if the successor employer continues to maintain the plan of the predecessor employer (and, of course, the successor employer cannot evade this requirement by nominally discontinuing the plan). The question of the extent to which such service must be counted in other circumstances is to be determined under regulations.

Multiemployer plans.—Under the conference substitute, service with any employer who is a member of a multiemployer plan is to be counted for purposes of the plan. The term "multiemployer plan" means a plan maintained pursuant to a collective bargaining agreement, to which more than one employer is required to contribute, and to which no one employer makes as much as 50 percent of the contributions. (This percentage test would become a 75-percent test once the plan qualifies as a multiemployer plan.) Also, the plan must provide that benefits will be payable to each participant, even though his employer subsequently ceases to make contributions under the plan. However, the plan would not be required to provide past service benefits, i.e., benefits for periods before the participant's employer entered the plan. Also, service during a period for which the employer was not a member of the plan would not be required to be counted for participation or vesting purposes.

Additional requirements relating to multiemployer plans may be prescribed in Department of Labor regulations. The conferees intend that a plan not be classified as a multiemployer plan unless it is a collectively bargained plan to which a substantial number of unafiliated employers are required to contribute. Also, a plan is not to be classified as a multiemployer plan where there is no substantial business purposes in having a multiemployer plan (except to obtain the advantages of multiemployer plan status under this bill).

In addition to employees of employers making contributions to a multiemployer plan, under the conference substitute such a plan may cover employees of labor unions which negotiated the multiemployer plan and employees of the plan itself. For this purpose, the plan would have to satisfy the general breadth-of-coverage and nondiscrimination requirements of the Internal Revenue Code separately with respect to these union or plan employees and collectively (i.e., with respect to all groups of employees covered under the plan), but would not be required to meet the exclusive benefit rules of the tax law. Instead, the exclusive benefit rules would be applied to the beneficiaries of the multiemployer plan as a whole. (Similar treatment for union employees or plan employees would also be available in the case of a single-employer collectively bargained plan.)

* * *

Amounts designated as employee contributions.—To clarify present law, the substitute provides that amounts contributed to a qualified plan in taxable years beginning after December 31, 1973, are to be treated as employee contributions if they are designated as employee contributions under the plan. This rule does not apply, however, to government "pick-up" plans, where the contribution is paid by the government, with no withholding from the employee's salary, and these amounts would be treated as employer contributions, no matter how designated under the plan.

[¶ 12,350.15]

Committee Report on P.L. 93-406 (Employee Retirement Income Security Act of 1974)

[House Ways and Means Committee Explanation]

Affiliated employers.—The committee bill also provides that in applying the coverage test, as well as the antidiscrimination rules, the vesting requirements, and the limitations on and benefits, employees of all corporations who are members of a "controlled group of corporations" (within the meaning of sec. 1563(a)) are to be treated as if they were employees of the same corporation. Thus, if two or more corporations were members of a parent-subsidiary, brother-sister, or combined controlled group, all of the employees of all of these corporations would have to be taken into account in applying these tests. A comparable rule is provided in the case of partnerships and proprietorships which are under common control (as determined under regulations), and all employees of such organizations are to be treated for purposes of these rules as though they were employed by a single person. The committee, by this provision, intends to make it clear that the coverage and antidiscrimination provisions cannot be avoided by operating through separate corporations instead of separate branches of one corporation. For example, if managerial functions were performed through one corporation employing highly compensated personnel, which has a generous pension plan, and assembly-line functions were performed through one or more other corporations employing lower-paid employees, which have less generous plans or no plans at all, this would generally constitute an impermissible discrimination. By this provision the committee is clarifying this matter for the future. It intends that prior law on this point be determined as if this provision had not been enacted.

At the same time, however, the committee provision is not intended to mean that all pension plans of a controlled group of corporations or partnerships must be exactly alike, or that a controlled group could not have pension plans for some corporations but not others. Thus, where the corporation in question contains a fair cross-section of high- and low-paid employees (compared to the employees of the controlled group as a whole), and where the plan coverage is nondiscriminatory with respect to the employees of the corporation in question, it is anticipated that the Internal Revenue Service would find that the plan met the antidiscrimination tests, even though other corporations in the controlled group had a less favorable retirement plan, or no plan at all. On the other hand, if, looking at the controlled group as a whole, it were found that a disproportionate number of highly compensated employees were covered under the plan of the corporation in question, or that the average compensation of covered employees was substantially higher in that plan than the average compensation of noncovered employees, it would be anticipated that the plan would not be found to be qualified, because the corporation does not contain a fair cross section of the controlled group of employees.

The bill also provides special rules for applying the excise tax to a controlled group of corporations. Under the bill, if corporations that are members of a controlled group (defined by section 1563(a) of the Code without regard to section 1563(e)(e)(C) [sic]) adopt a plan, the excise tax on underfunding is to be determined as if all the corporations were a single employer, and the tax is to be allocated to each corporation in accord with regulations prescribed by the Secretary of the Treasury. It is expected that generally the minimum funding requirements will be allocated proportionately to the relative amount of plan liabilities attributed to the employees of such corporation and any funding tax will be allocated in proportion to failures to make these required minimum contributions.

Under the bill as passed by the House, a plan must provide protection to participants in the case of a merger of the plan with another plan or the transfer of assets or liabilities from a plan. The value of benefits to the participant and the extent to which the benefits have been funded is [*sic*] to be protected by comparing what the participant's benefit would be if the plan had terminated immediately before the merger and what the participant's benefits would be

[3] Under the provision, the principles of sec. 267(c) apply for purposes of determining ownership.

under the merged plan had the merged plan been terminated just after the merger. The postmerger termination benefit may not be less than the premerger termination benefit. Further, a plan could not make a lump-sum distribution to a participant or beneficiary if the distribution exceeded the premerger termination benefit. Further, no merger or transfer of assets or liabilities could occur without an actuarial statement indicating compliance with the requirements being filed with the Secretary of the Treasury at least 30 days before the merger or distribution. The bill as passed by the Senate did not contain comparable provisions.

Under the conference agreement, a trust is not to constitute a qualified tax-exempt trust under the tax law, and also is not to satisfy the requirements of title I, unless it provides that in the case of any merger or consolidation of a plan, or any transfer of assets or liabilities of a plan, to any other plan each participant in the plan would receive post merger termination benefits which are equal to or greater than the premerger termination benefits. In the case of multiemployer plans these rules are to apply only to the extent that the Pension Benefit Guaranty Corporation determines that these rules are necessary for the participant's protection. These rules are to apply to mergers or transfers made after the date of enactment of the bill [September 2, 1974], but the plan provision to this effect does not have to be adopted prior to January 1, 1976.

[Code Sec. 415]

[¶ 12,400.013]

Committee Report on P.L. 109-280 (Pension Protection Act of 2006)

[Joint Committee on Taxation Report]

[Interest rate assumption for applying benefit limitations to lump-sum distributions]

Under the bill, for purposes of adjusting a benefit in a form that is subject to the minimum value rules, such as a lump-sum benefit, the interest rate used generally must be not less than the greater of: (1) 5.5 percent; (2) the rate that provides a benefit of not more than 105 percent of the benefit that would be provided if the rate (or rates) applicable in determining minimum lump sums were used; or (3) the interest rate specified in the plan.[86]

Effective Date

The provision is effective for years beginning after December 31, 2005.

[Purchase of permissive service credit]

Permissive service credit

The provision modifies the definition of permissive service credit by providing that permissive service credit means service credit which relates to benefits to which the participant is not otherwise entitled under such governmental plan, rather than service credit which such participant has not received under the plan. Credit qualifies as permissive service credit if it is purchased to provide an increased benefit for a period of service already credited under the plan (e.g., if a lower level of benefit is converted to a higher benefit level otherwise offered under the same plan) as long as it relates to benefits to which the participant is not otherwise entitled.

The provision allows participants to purchase credit for periods regardless of whether service is performed, subject to the limits on nonqualified service.

Under the provision, service as an employee of an educational organization providing elementary or secondary education can be determined under the law of the jurisdiction in which the service was performed. Thus, for example, permissive service credit can be granted for time spent teaching outside of the United States without being considered nonqualified service credit.

Trustee-to-trustee transfers to purchase permissive service credit

The provision provides that the limits regarding nonqualified service are not applicable in determining whether a trustee-to-trustee transfer from a section 403(b) annuity or a section 457 plan to a governmental defined benefit plan is for the purchase of permissive service credit. Thus, failure of the transferee plan to satisfy the limits does not cause the transferred amounts to be included in the participant's income. As under present law, the transferee plan must satisfy the limits in providing permissive service credit as a result of the transfer.

The provision provides that trustee-to-trustee transfers under sections 457(e)(17) and 403(b)(13) may be made regardless of whether the transfer is made between plans maintained by the same employer. The provision also provides that amounts transferred from a section 403(b) annuity or a section 457 plan to a governmental defined benefit plan to purchase permissive service credit are subject to the distribution rules applicable under the Internal Revenue Code to the defined benefit plan.

Effective Date

The provision is generally effective as if included in the amendments made by section 1526 of the Taxpayer Relief Act of 1997, except that the provision regarding trustee-to-trustee transfers is effective as if included in the amendments made by section 647 of the Economic Growth and Tax Relief Reconciliation Act of 2001.

[Special rule for computing high-three average compensation for benefit limitation purposes]

Under the bill, for purposes of determining average compensation for a participant's high three years, the high three years are the period of consecutive calendar years (not more than three) during which the participant had the greatest aggregate compensation from the employer.

Effective Date

The provision is effective for years beginning after December 31, 2005.

[Church plan rule for benefit limitations]

The provision provides that the 100 percent of compensation limit does not apply to a plan maintained by a church or qualified church controlled organization defined in section 3121(w)(3)(A) except with respect to "highly compensated benefits". The term "highly compensated benefits" means any benefits accrued for an employee in any year on or after the first year in which such employee is a highly compensated employee (as defined in sec. 414(q)) of the organization. For purposes of applying the 100 percent of compensation limit to highly compensated benefits, all the benefits of the employee which would otherwise be taken into account in applying the limit shall be taken into account, i.e., the limit does not apply only to those benefits accrued on or after the first year in which the employee is a highly compensated employee.

Effective Date

The provision is effective for years beginning after December 31, 2006.

[¶ 12,400.015]

Committee Report on P.L. 109-135 (Gulf Opportunity Zone Act of 2005)

[Joint Committee on Taxation]

Technical Corrections

[Amendments Related to the Economic Growth and Tax Relief Reconciliation Act of 2001 (P.L. 107-16)]

Equitable treatment for contributions to defined contribution plans (Act sec. 632).—Under the law as in effect before the Act, a special limit applied to contributions to tax sheltered annuities for foreign missionaries with adjusted gross income not exceeding $17,000. The special limit was inadvertently dropped by the Act. The special limit was restored in a technical correction in the Job Creation and Worker Assistance Act of 2002, but did not accurately reflect the pre-Act rule. The provision revises the special limit to reflect the pre-Act rule.

[¶ 12,400.017]

Committee Report on P.L. 108-311 (Working Families Tax Relief Act of 2004)

[Conference Agreement]

Rounding rule for retirement plan benefit and contribution limits.—Section 611 of EGTRRA increases the dollar limits on qualified retirement plan benefits and contributions under Code section 415, and adds a new rounding rule for cost-of-living adjustments to the dollar limit on annual additions to defined contribution plans. This new rounding rule is in addition to a pre-existing rounding rule that applies to benefits payable under defined benefit plans. The provision clarifies that the pre-existing rounding rule applies for purposes of other Code provisions that refer to Code section 415 and do not contain a specific rounding rule.

[¶ 12,400.02]

Committee Report on P.L. 107-16 (Economic Growth and Tax Relief Reconciliation Act)

[House Committee Report]

Code Sec. 415 limits for multiemployer plans

Under the provision, the 100 percent of compensation defined benefit plan limit would not apply to multiemployer plans. With respect to aggregation of multiemployer plans with other plans, the provision provides that multiemployer plans are not aggregated with single-employer defined benefit plans maintained by an

---

[86] Under the provision of the bill relating to plan amendments, if certain requirements are met, a plan amendment to implement the change made to the interest rate used in adjusting a benefit in a form that is subject to the minimum value rules may be made retroactively and without violating the anticutback rule.

employer contributing to the multiemployer plan for purposes of applying the 100 percent of compensation limit to such single-employer plan.

Effective Date

The provision is effective for years beginning after December 31, 2001.

[Conference Committee Report]

The conference agreement follows the House bill.

[¶ 12,400.03]

Committee Report on P.L. 107-16 (Economic Growth and Tax Relief Reconciliation Act)

[House Committee Report]

Increase in defined contribution plan limit

The provision increases the 25 percent of compensation limitation on annual additions under a defined contribution plan[1] to 100 percent.[2]

* * *

Effective Date

The provision generally is effective for years beginning after December 31, 2001.

* * *

[Conference Committee Report]

The conference agreement follows the House bill, with the following modifications.

With respect to the increase in the defined contribution plan limit, the conferees intend that the Secretary of the Treasury will use the Secretary's existing authority to address situations where qualified nonelective contributions are targeted to certain participants with lower compensation in order to increase the average deferral percentage of nonhighly compensated employees.

For taxable years beginning after December 31, 1999, a plan may disregard the requirement that contributions to a defined benefit plan be treated as previously excluded amounts for purposes of the exclusion allowance.

[¶ 12,400.04]

Committee Report on P.L. 107-16 (Economic Growth and Tax Relief Reconciliation Act)

[House Committee Report]

Increase in benefit and contribution limits

The provision increases the $35,000 limit on annual additions to a defined contribution plan to $40,000. This amount is indexed in $1,000 increments.[1]

The provision increases the $140,000 annual benefit limit under a defined benefit plan to $160,000. The dollar limit is reduced for benefit commencement before age 62 and increased for benefit commencement after age 65.[2] In adopting rules regarding the application of the increase in the defined benefit plan limits under the bill, it is intended that the Secretary will apply rules similar to those adopted in Notice 99-44 regarding benefit increases due to the repeal of the combined plan limit under former section 415(e). Thus, for example, a defined benefit plan could provide for benefit increases to reflect the provisions of the bill for a current or former employee who has commenced benefits under the plan prior to the effective date of the bill if the employee or former employee has an accrued benefit under the plan (other than an accrued benefit resulting from a benefit increase solely as a result of the increases in the section 415 limits under the bill). As under the notice, the maximum amount of permitted increase is generally the amount that could have been provided had the provisions of the bill been in effect at the time of the commencement of benefit. In no case may benefits reflect increases that could not be paid prior to the effective date because of the limits in effect under present law. In addition, in no case may plan amendments providing increased benefits under the relevant provision of the bill be effective prior to the effective date of the provision.

* * *

Effective Date

The provision is effective for years beginning after December 31, 2001.

[Conference Committee Report]

Limits on contributions and benefits.—The conference agreement follows the House bill.

* * *

Effective Date

The conference agreement generally is effective for years beginning after December 31, 2001. The provisions relating to defined benefit plans are effective for years ending after December 31, 2001.

[¶ 12,400.044]

Committee Report on P.L. 102-318 (Unemployment Compensation Amendments of 1992)

For Committee Report on Unemployment Compensation Amendments of 1992 (P.L. 102-318), dealing with rollovers and withholding on nonperiodic pension distributions, see ¶ 11,750.036.

[¶ 12,400.045]

Committee Reports on P.L. 101-239 (Omnibus Budget Reconciliation Act of 1989)

For Committee Reports on Omnibus Budget Reconciliation Act of 1989 (P.L. 101-239), relating to interest exclusion for ESOP loans, see ¶ 12,130.063.

[¶ 12,400.046]

Committee Reports on P.L. 100-647 (Technical and Miscellaneous Revenue Act of 1988)

[Senate Committee Report]

The bill clarifies that the rule requiring separate phaseins for each change in benefit structure under a plan does not apply in the case of the phasein of the 100 percent of compensation limit or the $10,000 limit on de minimis benefits.

The bill further provides that, for purposes of the combined limit on contributions and benefits (sec. 415(e)), the dollar limit on benefits under a defined benefit pension plan is to be phased in over 10 years of service, rather than 10 years of participation. Correspondingly, the rule requiring a separate phasein for each change in benefit structure does not apply for purposes of the combined limit.

[Senate Committee Report]

Limit requirement

The bill clarifies that a plan will not fail to satisfy the limit requirement if it provides for a minimum increase for each year of 3 percent of the retirement benefit (determined without regard to the current year's increase). Thus, the minimum increase may be 3 percent of the retirement benefit as adjusted under the cost-of-living arrangement in prior years.

Election requirement

Under the bill, a plan may permit participants to make an election under the qualified cost-of-living arrangement during any year, as long as the plan permits elections to be made at least in the year in which the participant (1) attains the earliest retirement age under the defined benefit pension plan (determined without regard to any requirement of separation from service), or (2) separates from service.

[Senate Committee Report]

* * *

Under a transition rule of the Act, in the case of a plan that satisfied the requirements of the overall limits on contributions and benefits (sec. 415) for its last year beginning before January 1, 1987, Treasury regulations are to provide for the determination of an amount that is to be subtracted from the numerator of the defined contribution fraction so that the sum of the defined benefit plan fraction and the defined contribution plan fraction (sec. 415(e)(1)) does not exceed 1.0 for such year. This amount to be subtracted is not to exceed the numerator of the fraction.

* * *

The bill clarifies that the adjustment to the sum of the defined benefit plan fraction and the defined contribution fraction so that such sum does not exceed

---

[1] The 25 percent of compensation limitation is increased to 100 percent of compensation under another provision of the bill.

[2] Another provision of the bill modifies the defined benefit pension plan limits for multiemployer plans.

[1] Another provision increases the defined contribution plan dollar limit.

[2] The provision preserves the present-law deduction rules for money purchase pension plans. Thus, for purposes of such rules, the limitation on the amount the employer generally may deduct is an amount equal to 25 percent of compensation of the employees covered by the plan for the year.

1.0 for purposes of this transition rule is determined as if the new rules were in effect for the last year beginning before January 1, 1987.

[Joint Committee on Taxation Explanation of Senate Consensus Amendment]

Under the provision, in the case of a plan maintained by a State or local government, the limitation on benefits under a defined benefit pension plan would be the greater of (1) the normal limit on benefits (sec. 415(b)) or (2) the accrued benefit of a participant determined without regard to any benefit increases adopted after October 14, 1987. The provision would only apply to individuals who are participants before January 1, 1990. In addition, to qualify for this special limitation, the employer maintaining the plan would be required to elect to satisfy the general requirements of section 415 without regard to the special rules for public plans (other than the special rules for police and firefighters). This election could be made indirectly through the modification of the plan maintained by governmental employers.

The provision would be effective with respect to years beginning after December 31, 1982, and the employer's election would be required by the close of the first plan year beginning after December 31, 1989.

[Conference Committee Report]

* * *

Conference Agreement

The conference agreement follows the Senate amendment * * *.

[Conference Committee Report]

* * *

Senate Amendment

Under the Senate amendment, the 20 years of service requirement for eligibility for the special rule for police and firefighters is decreased to 15 years.

The provision is effective as if included in the Tax Reform Act of 1986.

Conference Agreement

The conference agreement follows the Senate amendment.

[¶ 12,400.048]

Committee Reports on P.L. 99-514 (Tax Reform Act of 1986)

Dollar Limits

[Senate Committee Report]

Dollar limits on benefits adjusted to conform to social security retirement age

Under the bill, if retirement benefits under a defined benefit plan begin before the social security retirement age, the $90,000 limit (but not the 100 percent of compensation limit) generally is to be reduced so that it is the actuarial equivalent of an annual benefit of $90,000 beginning at the social security retirement age (65 for 1986). In addition, the bill repeals the special rule for early retirement under which the dollar limit for benefits commencing at or after age 55 is not reduced below $75,000. Thus, the dollar limit for benefits which commence at any age before the social security retirement age will be the actuarial equivalant of the inflation-adjusted dollar limit ($90,000 for 1986) for benefits commencing at the social security retirement age.

Under present law, the social security retirement age is phased up to age 67 from age 65 over 20 years and the social security retirement age with respect to any individual may be age 65 or 66 plus a fraction of a year depending upon when the individual attains the social security early retirement age (age 62). Under the bill, this phase up to age 67 is modified so that employers will not be required to determine the number of months included in the phase up with respect to each plan participant. The bill provides that, in calculating the social security retirement age for participants, the age increase factor is ignored. Thus, the following method is to be used to determine the social security retirement age of a plan participant during the phase up period: (1) in the case of a plan participant who attains age 62 before January 1, 2000, age 65; (2) in the case of a plan participant who attains age 62 after December 31, 1999, and before January 1, 2017, age 66; and (3) in the case of a plan participant who attains age 62 after December 31, 2016, age 67.

Under the bill, the adjustment of the dollar limitation on benefits with respect to a participant who retires at or after age 62 and before the social security retirement age is to be done in a manner consistent with the reduction for early retirement benefits under social security. The reduction for early retirement will equal, under the bill, 5/9 of 1 percent for each month the individual is under age 65 at retirement. This reduction produces a benefit equal, at age 62, to 80 percent of the benefit otherwise payable if the individual had retired at age 65. When the social security retirement age begins to phase up, the reduction will continue to be 5/9 of 1 percent for the first 36 months of early retirement plus 5/12 of 1 percent for each additional month of early retirement at or after age 62. Therefore, if an individual retires at age 62 when the social security retirement age is 67, the benefit at age 62 will equal 70 percent of the benefit otherwise payable at social security retirement age. Benefits commencing prior to age 62 will be reduced to reflect the actuarial equivalent of the benefit payable at age 62. As under present law, the reduction is to be computed using an interest rate assumption not less than the greater of 5 percent or the rate specified in the plan for purposes of determining early retirement benefits.

The provisions of the bill conforming normal retirement age under a plan to the social security retirement age and providing an early retirement reduction consistent with the social security reduction for early retirement applies for purposes of the dollar limit on benefits under a defined benefit plan and for purposes of determining the employer's deduction for funding of such benefits. The provisions do not affect in any way either the time at which plan participants may retire or the employer's assumption (for funding purposes) with respect to the time at which participants will retire. In addition, the provisions apply only to individuals whose benefits exceed the dollar limits on benefits and, thus, do not require an actuarial reduction for early retirement benefits for all participants whose benefits commence before the social security retirement age.

The bill also modifies the present-law rule permitting an increased limit with respect to benefits commencing after attainment of age 65. Accordingly, under the bill, if retirement benefits under a defined benefit plan begin after the social security retirement age, the dollar limit is increased so that it is the actuarial equivalent of an annual benefit of $90,000 beginning at the social security retirement age. As under present law, the increase is to be computed using an interest rate assumption not higher than the lesser of five percent or the rate specified in the plan.

Special rules for airline pilots, police, and firefighters, and correctional officers

The bill provides special rules for commercial airline pilots, participants in a qualified police or firefighters' pension plan, and for certain correctional officers.

Federal regulations require that commercial airline pilots retire after attaining age 60. The committee believes that it is inappropriate to require actuarial reduction in the dollar limit on benefits payable under these circumstances. Accordingly, under the bill, the reduction for early retirement does not apply to airline pilots whose benefit payments commence at or after age 60 and provides that the dollar limit applicable to annual benefits beginning at age 60 is $90,000 (adjusted for cost-of-living increases).

Similarly, the committee believes it is inappropriate to provide full actuarial reduction of the limit on benefits payable to participants in a qualified police or firefighters' pension plan, or benefits provided for certain correctional officers. The bill provides that the dollar limit on benefits payable to participants in a qualified police or firefighters' pension plan or benefits provided to such correctional officers will never be actuarially reduced to an amount less than $50,000, regardless of the age at which the benefits commence. Further, the provisions in the bill conforming the retirement age for purposes of the limits on benefits to the social security retirement age and modifying the actuarial reductions for early retirement do not apply to such plans or to benefits provided to such officers.

For purposes of this provision, a qualified police or firefighters' pension plan is defined as a defined benefit plan maintained by a State (or political subdivision thereof) for the benefit of all full-time employees of any police or fire department organized and operated by such State or political subdivision to provide police protection, fire-fighting services, or emergency medical care. In addition, a qualified police or firefighters' pension plan is required to (1) limit service taken into account to service with a police or fire department (or the armed services of the United States); and (2) require, as a condition to the payment of benefits, at least 20 years of service.

[Conference Committee Report]

The conference agreement generally follows the Senate amendment with respect to the separate limits applicable to defined benefit pension plans and defined contribution plans except that the method of indexing the dollar limits is the same as under the House bill and present law, i.e., by reference to increases in the consumer price index. The conference agreement generally follows the House bill with respect to the imposition of an excise tax on benefit payments in excess of a specified level.

Normal retirement age

The conference agreement follows the Senate amendment, except that the conference agreement exempts plans maintained by tax-exempt or governmental employers and a specified class of merchant seamen from the provisions relating to the normal retirement age and the elimination of the $75,000 floor for benefits beginning at age 55.

The conference agreement generally follows the special rules in the Senate amendment for commercial airline pilots and participants in a qualified police or firefighters' defined benefit pension plan. The conference agreement clarifies the definition of a qualified police or firefighters' plan and provides for indexing of the $50,000 limit applicable under the special rules for those plans. The conference agreement does not adopt the special rules for correctional officers.

In addition, the conference agreement clarifies the application of the special rules for pilots who retire before age 60. Under the conference agreement, in the case of any participant who is a commercial airline pilot, the actuarial reduction for early retirement does not reduce the limitation on benefits below (1) $75,000, if the participant's benefit begins at or after age 55 or (2) the actuarial equivalent of the $75,000 limitation at age 55, if the benefit begins before age 55. In addition, if, as of the time an individual retires, Federal Aviation Administration regulations require an individual to separate from service as a commercial airline pilot after attaining any age occurring on or after age 60 and before the social security retirement age, the age prescribed in such regulations is to be substituted for the social security retirement age, unless the individual separates from service prior to age 60. The conference agreement also clarifies that the special rule for commercial airline pilots is limited to individuals whose services as a pilot constitute substantially all of their services to which the benefit relates.

Cost of Living Adjustments—Defined Benefit Plans

[House Committee Report]

The bill retains the present-law cost-of-living adjustments for the defined benefit plan dollar limit (sec. 415(d)). Thus, beginning in 1988, the $77,000 defined benefit dollar limit will be adjusted to reflect post-1986 cost-of-living increases. However, cost-of-living adjustments to the $25,000 defined contribution plan dollar limit will be temporarily suspended until that limit is equal to 25 percent of the defined benefit dollar limit. Thereafter, cost-of-living adjustments will be provided, effectively ensuring that the defined contribution plan dollar limit will be equal to the greater of $25,000 or 25 percent of the defined benefit plan limit.

As under present law, anticipated cost-of-living adjustments to the overall benefit limits may not be taken into account under the rules relating to the deduction allowed for employer contributions to a qualified plan.

[Senate Committee Report]

The bill retains the present-law cost-of-living adjustments for the defined benefit plan dollar limit (sec. 415(d)), but modifies the manner in which such adjustments are calculated. Under the bill, the dollar limits on benefits are adjusted (beginning in 1988) for the percentage increases in the taxable wage base under social security. Rather than being adjusted for increases in the Consumer Price Index (as under present law), the defined benefit pension dollar limit is adjusted for increases both in wages and in prices, which is projected to result in a greater increase in the dollar limits than the present-law method would produce. However, under the bill, cost-of-living adjustments to the $30,000 defined contribution plan dollar limit will be temporarily suspended until that limit is equal to 25 percent of the defined benefit plan dollar limit. Thereafter, cost-of-living adjustments will be provided, effectively ensuring that the defined contribution plan dollar limit will be equal to the greater of $30,000 or 25 percent of the defined benefit plan limit.

As under present law, anticipated cost-of-living adjustments to the overall benefit limits may not be taken into account under the rules relating to the deduction allowed for employer contributions to a qualified plan.

The committee intends that, if the social security wage base is modified by Congress (e.g., by an amendment halving or doubling the current taxable wage or altering the indexing method), that such independent actions is not to affect the indexing method for qualified plans.

Cost of Living Adjustments—Defined Contribution Plans

[Conference Committee Report]

With respect to defined contribution plans, the conference agreement adopts the rules of the House bill applicable to cost-of-living adjustments and adopts the Senate amendment with respect to the amount of the current dollar limitation ($30,000). Although cost-of-living adjustments will be made to the defined benefit pension plan limit beginning in 1988, no cost-of-living adjustments to the defined contribution plan limit will be made until the $30,000 defined contribution plan limit is equal to 25 percent of the defined benefit dollar limit. The cost-of-living adjustment will be determined by reference to the consumer price index.

Under the agreement, contributions made by retired nonkey employees for retiree medical coverage are not subject to the percentage-of-compensation limit on annual additions.

Less Than 10 Years' Participation

[House Committee Report]

Under the bill, reduced limits apply to participants with fewer than 10 years of participation in the defined benefit plan (sec. 415(b)(5)). The dollar limit on benefits payable from a defined benefit plan (but not the percentage limit) generally is reduced by ten percent per year for each year of participation in the plan less than 10. In no event, however, is the limit reduced to an amount less than one-tenth of the dollar limit (under the bill, [$9,000]). Thus, service with the employer prior to becoming a participant under the plan is disregarded in determining the dollar limit on benefits payable. For example, if a participant who would otherwise be entitled under the terms of the plan to receive the maximum annual benefit (under the bill, [$90,000] for 1986) had only three years of participation in the plan (regardless of the number of years of service), the maximum benefit payable would be the lesser of 100 percent of compensation, or [$27,000] (3/10ths of [$90,000]).

Except as provided in regulations to be issued by the Secretary of the Treasury, a new ten-year period of participation will be required with respect to increases in the otherwise applicable limit made available through changes in the benefit structure (whether made by plan amendment or otherwise). In general, no participant will be entitled to the full amount of the increased limit until they complete ten years of participation after the change in benefit structure. The Secretary of the Treasury is to prescribe regulations defining those changes in benefit structure for which a new ten-year period of participation would not be required. The committee generally does not intend plan provisions that incorporate cost-of-living increases (within the meaning of section 415(d)) to be treated as changes in benefit structure requiring an additional ten years of participation. However, to the extent that cost-of-living increases or post-retirement benefit increases are inconsistent with the purposes of this benefit limit, the committee does intend such increases to be subject to this rule. In addition, the bill authorizes the Secretary of the Treasury to issue regulations for the application of this rule in situations involving plan mergers or spin-offs.

The bill retains the present-law provision that phases in the special $10,000 de minimis benefit based on years of service.

[Conference Committee Report]

The conference agreement adopts the House bill and the Senate amendment provision under which the dollar limit on annual benefits under a qualified defined benefit pension plan is phased in over 10 years of plan participation is adopted.

As under both bills, the conference agreement also provides that, to the extent provided in regulations, the phase-in is to be applied to any benefit increases under a plan as though such increase were a new plan. Thus, for example, an amendment improving the benefit formula may increase benefits by up to one-tenth of the applicable dollar limit under this section 415 for each year of participation after the amendment. A second amendment within 10 years of a prior amendment increasing benefits is subject to the limit under the phase-in triggered by the prior amendment (along with benefit increases under the prior amendment).

In addition, the conferees do not intend the phase-in for benefit increases to apply to benefit improvements due to updating compensation in a career average pay plan, cost-of-living increases for retirees, the beginning of a new collective bargaining cycle, and other reasonable benefit improvements that are not primarily for highly compensated employees. Thus, the conferees expect that the Secretary will apply a concentration test under which the phase-in will not apply to a benefit increase if the resulting increase in benefits is not primarily for highly compensated employees. In addition, the Secretary is to provide rules permitting the tacking of participation under separate plans in circumstances not inconsistent with the purposes of the phase-in.

Incorporation of Limits by Reference

[Conference Committee Report]

Under the conference agreement, a plan does not fail to meet the requirements for qualified status merely because the plan incorporates the benefit and contribution limits of section 415 of the Code by reference. The agreement provides that incorporation by reference is permitted except that, if the limitation may be applied in more than one manner, the plan is to specify the manner in which the limitation is to be applied.

For example, in the case of a defined contribution plan, Treasury regulations provide several methods for establishing a suspense account for excess annual additions and allocating amounts in the suspense account. Thus, the plan must specify which method is to be used.

The agreement does not change the requirements of present law relating to definitely determinable benefits and the requirement that profit-sharing and stock bonus plans must specify a definite allocation formula. Under the conference agreement, however, a plan does not fail to provide definitely determinable benefits merely because it incorporates the limits by reference. For example, if an employee participates in both a defined contribution plan and a defined benefit pension plan maintained by the same employer, the manner in which the employee's benefits will be adjusted to comply with the combined limitation (sec. 415(e)) is to be specified.

Qualified Cost of Living Arrangements

[House Committee Report]

The bill also permits a defined benefit plan to maintain a qualified cost-of-living arrangement under which employer and employee contributions may be applied to provide cost-of-living increases to the primary benefit. A qualified cost-of-living arrangement is defined as an arrangement under a defined benefit plan that complies with the limits, election procedures, and nondiscrimination requirements of the bill, as well as such other requirements as the Secretary of the Treasury may prescribe by regulations.

Of course, a qualified cost-of-living arrangement must satisfy all of the applicable qualification requirements of section 401(a) not specifically altered or made inapplicable by the bill. For example, the right to the employer-provided portion of a cost-of-living benefit under a qualified arrangement is part of the accrued benefit subject to section 411 (including section 411(d)(6)) and thus will accrue and vest as the employee accrues and vests in the normal retirement benefit. Thus, an employer may reduce or eliminate the employer contribution under a qualified cost-of-living arrangement only with respect to benefits not yet accrued.

Similarly, such cost-of-living increases must be available on the same terms for all participants. Thus, a greater subsidy could not be provided for employees who work until retirement than to those who separate from service with vested benefits prior to retirement.

A qualified cost-of-living arrangement satisfies the limit requirement added by the bill if it (1) limits cost-of-living adjustments to those increases occurring after the annuity starting date, and (2) bases the cost-of-living adjustment on average cost-of-living increases determined by reference to one or more indexes prescribed by the Secretary (or three percent).

A cost-of-living arrangement meets the election requirements added by the bill if it provides that participation in the qualified cost-of-living arrangement is elective and permits participants to make an election (1) in the year in which the participant attains the earliest retirement age under the defined benefit plan, or separates from service, or (2) both such years.

A cost-of-living arrangement meets the nondiscrimination rules added by the bill only if the arrangement does not discriminate in favor of highly compensated employees as to eligibility to participate.

Special rule for key employees

Under the bill, key employees generally are precluded from participating in a qualified cost-of-living arrangement. However, in a plan that is not top heavy, officers who are key employees solely by reason of their status as officers may participate. For purposes of this rule, key employee has the same meaning as it does for top-heavy plans (sec. 416(i)).

Treatment of contributions to qualified cost-of-living arrangements

Under the bill, any employee contribution made to a qualified cost-of-living arrangement will not be treated as an annual addition for purposes of the annual limit (sec. 415(c), but will be treated as an annual limit for purposes of applying the combined plan limit (sec. 415(e)). However, the benefit attributable to such employee contribution will be treated as an employer-provided benefit (for purposes of section 415(b)).

[Conference Committee Report]

The conference agreement generally follows the House bill with respect to qualified cost-of-living arrangements. The agreement clarifies the terms under which an employee may obtain an employer-provided cost-of-living subsidy. In addition, the conferees intend that the right to the employer-derived portion of a qualified cost-of-living benefit is part of an employee's accrued benefit subject to the vesting and benefit accrual requirements and the prohibition on a retroactive reduction in accrued benefits and is to be treated under rules similar to the rules applicable to employer-derived early retirement benefits.

For example, the employer-derived portion of the cost-of-living benefit need not be provided to an employee who fails to satisfy the applicable conditions for receipt of the benefit, including any required employee contributions. Further, the cost-of-living benefit need not be provided to an employee who has separated from service and received a distribution of the employee's benefit without making the required contributions for the cost-of-living benefit. The employee could, however, return to service and buy back the benefit by proper repayment of the cashed out benefit.

Effective Dates

[Senate Committee Report]

In general

The provisions generally apply to years beginning after December 31, 1986. Under the bill, a plan will not fail to be qualified for any year beginning before January 1, 1989, merely because the plan is not amended to provide that benefits or contributions will not exceed the limits under the bill. However, employer deductions with respect to years beginning after December 31, 1986, are limited to those amounts required to fund the limits provided by the bill (whether or not contributions required by the plan document exceed those limits). In addition, no later than the first plan year beginning after December 31, 1988, the plan is to be amended to provide that benefits in excess of the limits (other than benefits grandfathered under the transition rule below) are reduced to conform to the limits as amended.

The bill provides a special effective date for plans maintained pursuant to one or more collective bargaining agreements ratified before March 1, 1986, between employee representatives and one or more employers. Under the bill, the new limits on benefits and contributions will not apply to years beginning before the earlier of (i) the date on which the last of the collective bargaining agreements terminates, or (ii) January 1, 1991. For this purpose, any extension of the collective bargaining agreement agreed to after February 28, 1986, will be disregarded. In addition, any plan amendment that amends the plan solely to conform to the amendments made by the bill (with respect to benefit limits and distribution requirements) will not be considered a termination or extention of the collective bargaining agreement.

Transitional rules relating to current accrued benefits

The bill also provides a transition rule to ensure that a participant's previously accrued benefit under a defined benefit pension plan is not reduced merely because the bill reduces the dollar limits on benefits payable under the plan or increases the period of participation required to earn the maximum benefit. This rule applies with respect to an individual who is a participant before January 1, 1987, in a plan that was in existence on May 6, 1986. If such an individual has a current accrued benefit that exceeds the dollar limit permitted under the bill (but does not exceed the dollar limit in effect under prior law), then the applicable dollar limit for the individual is equal to that current accrued benefit. Similarly, in computing the participant's defined benefit fraction, the current accrued benefit would replace the dollar limit otherwise used in the denominator of the fraction.

Under the bill, an individual's current accrued benefit is defined as the individual's accrued benefit as of the close of the last year beginning before January 1, 1987, expressed as an annual benefit determined pursuant to the rules in effect prior to the amendments made by the bill.

For purposes of determining an individual's current accrued benefit, no change in the terms and conditions of the plan after May 6, 1986, is taken into account. Accordingly, if an individual's current accrued benefit is a specified percentage of average pay, rather than a specified amount, the current accrued benefit is the specified percentage of the average pay computed as of the close of the last year beginning before 1987, based upon compensation paid up to that time (without regard to compensation advances). Although subsequent salary increases might increase the benefit to which a participant is entitled under the plan, those increases would not increase the participant's current accrued benefit. Similarly, cost-of-living adjustments occurring after 1986 are not taken into account in computing the current accrued benefit. In addition, with respect to an individual whose annual benefit is treated as not exceeding the annual benefit limit (sec. 415(b)) on account of the transitional rule provided by section 2004(d)(2) of the Employee Retirement Income Security Act of 1974, or section 237(g) of the Tax Equity and Fiscal Responsibility Act of 1982 (TEFRA), the individual's accrued benefit is the individual's annual benefit or the current accrued benefit as defined therein.

The bill does not affect the obligation of a plan to provide the current accrued benefit and the bill does not affect the consequences of an employer's failure to fund an individual's current accrued benefit. However, benefits accruing in years beginning after December 31, 1986, are not protected by this transition rule. Consistent with changes made by the Retirement Equity Act of 1984, the committee intends that the Secretary may prescribe rules under which such reductions to conform the plan to the limits, as amended, will not be considered a violation of the rules precluding a reduction in accrued benefits (sec. 411(d)(6)) as long as the amount of the reduction does not exceed the amount required to bring the plan into compliance with the bill. Thereafter, no further accruals will be permitted for an individual whose current accrued benefit exceeds the bill's usual dollar limit until that dollar limit, as adjusted for cost-of-living increases, exceeds the individual's current accrued benefit.

With respect to a plan maintained pursuant to one or more collective bargaining agreements ratified before May 6, 1986, the current accrued benefit of an individual is the individual's accrued benefit as of the close of the last year beginning before the earlier of (1) the date on which the last of the collective bargaining agreements terminates, or (2) January 1, 1991.

Employee Contributions as Annual Additions

The provision treating all employee contributions as annual additions generally is effective for years beginning after December 31, 1986. However, for purposes of calculating the defined contribution plan fraction and applying the combined plan limit (sec. 415(e)), the present-law rules will still apply in calculating the fraction applicable to years beginning before January 1, 1987. Thus, the defined contribution plan fraction applicable to years beginning before January 1, 1987, need not be recalculated to conform to the new definition of annual additions.

[Conference Committee Report]

The conference agreement follows the Senate amendment except that it does not allow a plan to accrue benefits in excess of the new limits (or the grandfathered current accrued benefit, if higher), even during the period prior to the time the plan must be amended.

A special effective date applies to plans maintained pursuant to a collective bargaining agreement. Under this special rule, in the case of employees covered under a plan maintained pursuant to a collective bargaining agreement between employee representatives and one or more employers ratified before March 1, 1986, the amendments are not effective for plan years beginning before the earlier of (1) January 1, 1989, or (2) the date on which the last of the collective bargaining agreement terminates (determined without regard to any extensions in the collective bargaining agreement).

[Senate Committee Report]

Key Employees

Explanation of Provision

The bill amends the definition of a key employee to exclude any individual who is an officer or employee of an entity described in section 414(d) (relating to governmental plans). The effect of this provision is to clarify that certain separate accounting and nondiscrimination provisions of the Code (e.g., secs. 79, 415(l), and 419A) do not apply to employees of a State or local government or certain other governmental entities. The bill does not repeal the provision that exempts governmental plans from the top-heavy plan requirements.

The bill also provides that the rule disregarding benefits of an employee after 5 plan years applies to employees who have not performed services for the employer maintaining the plan at any time during the 5-year period ending on the determination date. This provision is added to relieve the administrative difficulties associated with determining whether or not amounts an individual might receive after separation from service are in the nature of compensation.

[Conference Committee Report]

The conference agreement follows the Senate amendment * * *.

[¶ 12,400.05]

Committee Reports on P.L. 98-369 (Tax Reform Act of 1984)

[House Committee Report]

Under the provision, the cost-of-living increases to the dollar limits on contributions and benefits under qualified pension plans, tax-sheltered annuity programs, and SEPs would be postponed until 1988.

[Senate Committee Report]

Finally, the bill postpones the cost-of-living increases to the dollar limits on contributions and benefits under qualified pension plans until 1988. Beginning in 1988, the limits will be adjusted for post-1986 cost-of-living increases under the formula then in effect to provide cost-of-living increases in social security benefits.

[House Committee Report]

Explanation of Provision

In applying the overall limits on contributions and benefits under qualified pension plans, the bill provides that any contributions allocated to an individual medical benefit account (sec. 401(h)(2)) of an employee under a qualified defined benefit plan is to be treated as an annual addition under a qualified defined contribution plan. Accordingly, the amount allocated for a year would be included, together with employer contributions and reallocated forfeitures, in determining whether the defined benefit plan and any defined contribution plan of the employer meet the separate limits and the combined limits provided with respect to such plans. To the extent provided by Treasury regulations, an amount allocated to a medical benefit account under a defined benefit plan before the effective date of the provision could be reallocated to the individual medical benefit account of a participant without inclusion in the annual addition.

The bill provides that an account is an individual medical benefit account if it is established for a participant in a defined benefit plan, all medical benefits permitted to be paid under the plan with respect to the participant, the participant's spouse, or their dependents are payable solely from the account, and the account may be used for no other participant.

Under the bill, a defined benefit plan that provides medical benefits for retired employees is required to maintain an individual medical benefit account for any plan participant who [at any time during the plan year or any preceding plan year during which contributions were made on behalf of such employee] is a 5-percent owner (as defined in sec. 416(i)(1)(B)(i)). Of course, the medical benefits provided under a qualified defined benefit plan are required to meet nondiscrimination standards.

Effective Date

The provision applies to years beginning after March 31, 1984.

[House Committee Report]

Present Law

TEFRA permitted an employer to elect to continue deductible contributions to a profit-sharing plan on behalf of an employee who is permanently and totally disabled. The contributions are deductible, however, only if contributions are nonforfeitable when contributed.

Explanation of Provision

The bill clarifies that the election is available for contributions to profit-sharing and stock bonus plans. In addition, the bill clarifies that only those contributions that are the subject of the employer's election must be nonforfeitable when made under the special rule.

See also ¶ 11,900.085 for the Committee Report relating to the repeal of the bond purchase provisions.

[¶ 12,400.06]

Committee Report on P.L. 97-248 (Tax Equity and Fiscal Responsibility Act of 1982)

Overall Limits on Contributions, Benefits, and Exclusions

Senate amendment

The Senate amendment makes several changes to the overall limits on contributions and benefits for an employee under a tax-qualified pension, etc., plan. The amendment (1) reduces the dollar limit for annual additions to profit-sharing plans and other defined contribution plans from $45,475 to $30,000; (2) reduces the dollar limit for annual benefits under defined benefit pension plans from $136,425 to $90,000, and requires that an interest rate assumption of at least 5 percent be used to determine whether alternative benefit forms (e.g., lump sum distributions) are within the annual benefit limit; (3) suspends cost-of-living adjustments to the dollar limits until 1986, at which time the limits will be adjusted for post-1984 cost-of-living increases (as measured by the social security benefit index), and provides that employers cannot deduct contributions to fund anticipated cost-of-living increases, (4) requires that the dollar limit ($90,000 for 1983) be actuarially reduced (using an interest rate assumption of at least 5 percent) if benefits commence before age 62 (increased from age 55); and (5) reduces the aggregate limit for an individual who participates in a defined contribution plan and a defined benefit plan of the same employer from 1.4 (140 percent of the otherwise applicable separate dollar or percentage limit) to the lesser of 1.25, as applied only to the dollar limits, or 1.4, as applied under present law.

In general, these provisions will apply to plan years beginning after December 31, 1982, except that plan amendments are required with respect to plan years beginning after December 31, 1983.

Conference agreement

The conference agreement generally follows the Senate amendment except that the dollar limit for benefits under a defined benefit plan commencing before age 62 is to be actuarially reduced (using an interest rate of not less than the greater of 5 percent or the rate specified in the plan)[1] to the equivalent of the dollar limit for benefits commencing at age 62 (age 55 where the $75,000 minimum applies). Thus, the dollar limit is not less than $75,000 at age 55 or later. For ages below 55 the limit is not less than the actual equivalent of a $75,000 annual benefit commencing at age 55. Also, for benefits commencing after age 65 the dollar limit is increased (using an interest rate not exceeding the lesser of 5 percent or the rate specified in the plan) to the equivalent of the benefit limit as applied to benefits commencing at age 65. In no event, however, could future cost-of-living increases in the dollar limit be assumed in determining actuarial equivalence.

The conference agreement revises the transition rule relating to cases where the sum of the defined benefit plan and defined contribution plan fractions exceeds 1.25 (as applied to the dollar limits). Under the provision, the Secretary of the Treasury is to prescribe regulations under which the defined contribution plan fraction (as determined for the last year ending before January 1, 1983) is reduced, so that the sum of the fractions does not exceed the aggregate limit under the conference agreement.

The conference agreement clarifies present law by providing that the employer's deduction limit for the year under a defined benefit plan may not be based on benefits in excess of the dollar limit applicable for the year (without regard to anticipated cost-of-living increases). Deductions may be based on benefits which take into account anticipated salary increases, subject to limitation described in the preceding sentence.

The conference agreement also places a $100,000 aggregate limit on the estate tax exclusion for certain retirement benefits under qualified pension, etc., plan, tax-sheltered annuities, individual retirement accounts (IRA's) and certain military retirement plans. The limit applies with respect to decedents dying after December 31, 1982.

Loans from Retirement Plans

* * *

Senate amendment

The Senate amendment generally provides that a loan received by a participant under a qualified plan or a tax-sheltered annuity program is treated as a distribution to the extent that the participant's outstanding loan balance under all plans in which the participant participates exceeds $10,000. A higher limit (not to exceed

[1] Rev. Rul. 79-90 1979-1CB 156, requires that a plan specify the actuarial assumptions used by the plan to determine benefit equivalence.

$50,000) is permitted if the loan proceeds are applied towards the purchase, reconstruction, etc., of a personal residence. Loan amounts treated as distributions generally are subject to the usual income tax and withholding rules for plan distributions.

The amendment applies to loans made after July 1, 1982. Loans made before that date are not affected except to the extent that the loan is renegotiated, revised, or extended. A loan is treated as received if the proceeds are paid to or on behalf of a participant or beneficiary or if the loan is extended, etc. The amendment changes the tax treatment of loans but does not change the rules of the Employee Retirement Income Security Act of 1974 limiting the availability of loans.

Conference agreement

In general.—The conference agreement follows the Senate amendment except that a loan from a tax-qualified plan, or, government plan, or tax sheltered annuity which is to be repaid within 5 years is treated as a distribution only to the extent that the amount of the loan, when added to the outstanding loan balance with respect to the employee under all plans of the employer, exceeds the lesser of (1) $50,000, or (2) one-half of the present value of the employee's nonforfeitable accrued benefit under such plans, but not less than $10,000. For this purpose, plans of separate employers which generally are treated as a single employer under the pension, etc., plan rules (sec. 414) are treated as plans of a single employer.

A loan made with respect to an employee under a qualified plan, etc., which is not required to be repaid within 5 years, is treated as a distribution. For this purpose, the period within which a loan is required to be repaid is determined at the time the loan is made. If a repayment period of less than 5 years is subsequently extended beyond 5 years, it is intended that the balance payable under the loan at the time of the extension is to be treated as distributed at the time of the extension. In addition, if payments under a loan with a repayment period of less than 5 years are not in fact made, so that an amount remains payable at the end of 5 years, the amount remaining payable is treated as if distributed at the end of the 5-year period. A loan which is treated as a distribution on account of a repayment period of more than 5 years will not be treated as other than a distribution merely because it is repaid within 5 years (whether by reason of a renegotiation of the payment period or otherwise). Of course, a loan to a beneficiary which is treated as a distribution is included in the income of the participant, if the participant is alive at the time the loan is treated as a distribution.

The conference agreement provides an exception to the 5-year repayment rule to the extent that a loan made with respect to a plan participant is applied toward acquiring, constructing, or substantially rehabilitating any house, apartment, condominium, or mobile home (not used on a transient basis) which is used or is to be used within a reasonable time as the principal residence of the participant or a member of the participant's family. The determination as to whether a dwelling is to be used as a principal residence of the participant or dependent is to be determined at the time the loan is entered into.

Certain mortgage loans

Under the conference agreement, investments (including investments in residential mortgages) which are made in the ordinary course of an investment program will not be considered as loans, if the amount of thr mortgage loan does not exceed the fair market value of the property purchased with the loan proceeds. An investment program exists, for example, when trustees determine that a specific percentage or amount of plan assets will be invested in residential mortgages under specified conditions. However, mortgage loans made as a result of the direction of investments of an individual account will not be considered as made under an investment program and no loan which benefits an officer, director, or owner or his beneficiaries will be treated as an investment. In addition, the agreement makes no changes to the present-law prohibited transaction rules and fiduciary standards for qualified pension, etc., plans and does not restrict the rules of present law under which certain loans are treated as distributions.

Effective dates

The conference agreement applies to loans made after August 13, 1982.

Amounts outstanding on August 13, 1982, under a loan which is renegotiated, extended, revised, or renewed after such date will not be treated as made on the date of the renegotiation, etc., to the extent such amounts are required to be, and are repaid on or before August 13, 1983. Thus, such amounts will continue to be treated as amounts outstanding with respect to the participant on August 13, 1982.

The conferees intend that a scheduled change in the interest rate charged on a loan balance (e.g., a variable rate contract) will not be treated as a revision or renegotiation of the loan.

Parity Under the Qualified Plan Rules for Corporate and Noncorporate Employers; Group-Term Life Insurance

* * *

Senate amendment

The Senate amendment increases the dollar limits applicable to defined contribution H.R. 10 plans, plans of subchapter S corporations, and SEPs, from $15,000 in 1982 to $20,000 in 1983, $25,000 in 1984, and $30,000 in 1985. The 15-percent of earned income limit is not changed. To provide a similar increase in the level of benefits permitted under a defined benefit H.R. 10 plan or subchapter S corporation plan, the compensation taken into account in determining permitted annual benefit accruals is increased from $100,000 to $133,000 in 1983, $167,000 in 1984 and $200,000 in 1985.

Beginning in 1986, the bill adjusts the limits for post-1984 cost-of-living increases.

Conference agreement

In general.—The conference agreement generally eliminates distinctions in the tax law between qualified pension, etc., plans of corporations and those of self-employed individuals (H.R. 10 plans). The agreement (1) repeals certain of the special rules, for H.R. 10 plans, (2) extends other of the special rules to all qualified plans, including those maintained by corporate employers, and (3) generally applies the remainder of the special rules, with appropriate modifications, only to those plans (whether maintained by a corporate or noncorporate employer) which primarily benefit the employer's key employees (top-heavy plans). The top-heavy plan rules are provided in addition to the usual rules for plan qualification.

The special rules for H.R. 10 plans which are repealed include those which (1) set lower limits on contributions and benefits for self-employed individuals, (2) prevent certain H.R. 10 plans from limiting coverage to a fair cross section of employees, and (3) prohibit integration with social security.

The special rules for H.R. 10 plans which are extended to all qualified plans are certain of those rules to (1) distributions made to the employee or to the employee's beneficiaries after the employee's death, and (2) integration of a defined contribution plan with social security.

The special rules for H.R. 10 plans which generally are extended (with modifications) to plans of corporate and noncorporate employers which primarily benefit key employees (top-heavy plans) include those rules relating to (1) includible compensation, (2) vesting (alternative schedules are provided) and (3) distributions. The rules for a top-heavy plan also require that such a plan provide a non-key employee a nonintegrated minimum benefit or a nonintegrated minimum contribution, and in some cases reduce the aggregate limit on contributions and benefits for a key employee who is covered by more than one plan of an employer.

These provisions apply for years beginning after December 31, 1983.

Repeal of rules for H.R. 10 plans

Deductible contributions and permitted benefit accruals.—The conference agreement generally repeals the special deduction limits (sec. 404(e)(1), (2), and (4)) for contributions on behalf of a self-employed individual under an H.R. 10 plan. Conforming amendments are made with respect to simplified employee pensions and plans of subchapter S corporations.

In addition, the conference agreement repeals the special qualification rules for a defined benefit plan which covers a self-employed individual or a shareholder-employee of a subchapter S corporation (sec. 401(j)). Thus, defined benefit plans which cover a self-employed individual or a shareholder-employee of a subchapter S corporation will be subject to the rules applicable to other defined benefit plans.

Earned income.—For purposes of the pension rules, the conference agreement revises the definition of earned income of a self-employed individual so that the amount of earned income corresponds to the amount of compensation of a common-law employee. Under the agreement, earned income is computed after taking into account amounts contributed by the employer to a qualified plan to the extent a deduction is allowed for the contributions. Also, in this regard, no change is made to the present-law rule (sec. 401(d)(11)) for owner-employees which has the effect of limiting the earned income which may be taken into account under the pension rules to that derived from the trade or business with respect to which the plan is established.

In addition, no change is made to the present-law rules under which no deduction is allowed for contributions to an H.R. 10 plan on behalf of a self-employed individual to the extent that the contributions are allocable to the purchase of incidental life, health, or accident insurance (sec. 404(e)(3)), and under which a self-employed individual generally is denied a basis in amounts applied under an H.R. 10 plan to purchase life insurance protection for the individual (sec. 72(m)(2)).

Coverage.—The agreement repeals the additional qualification requirement under which an H.R. 10 plan benefiting an owner-employee generally is required to benefit all employees who have completed at least three years of service with the employer (sec. 401(d)(3)(A)).

The agreement retains the special rules for H.R. 10 plans under which all employees of all unincorporated trades or businesses controlled by an owner-employee (or owner-employees) are treated as if employed by a single trade or business for purposes of the nondiscrimination rules (sec. 401(a)(9) and (10)).

Employee contributions.—The agreement repeals the special rules precluding employer contributions on behalf of an owner-employee under an H.R. 10 plan in excess of the deduction limit (sec. 401(d)(5)), and those rules limiting or precluding mandatory or voluntary employee contributions by an owner-employee (sec.

4972). The agreement also repeals the six-percent excise tax on excess contributions made on behalf of an owner-employee.

Miscellaneous restrictions.—The following special H.R. 10 plan rules are also repealed:

(1) the requirement that a profit-sharing plan provide a definite contribution formula for employees who are not owner-employees (sec. 401(d)(2)(B));

(2) the requirement that an owner-employee must consent to participate (sec. 401(d)(4)(A));

(3) the requirement that the plan trustee be a bank or other approved financial institution (sec. 401(d)(1));

(4) the prohibition against contributions on behalf of an owner-employee for the five taxable years following an early withdrawal by the owner-employee (sec. 401(d)(5)(C)); and

(5) the denial of the $5,000 income exclusion for death benefits paid with respect to a self-employed individual under the plan (sec. 101(b)).

Nothing in the agreement requires that an H.R. 10 plan delete these provisions. For example, an employer may prefer that an H.R.10 plan continue to provide that an owner-employee must consent to participate, thereby permitting an owner-employee to elect against plan participation.

Extension of certain H.R. 10 rule to all plans

Required distributions.—The agreement extends to all qualified plans the requirement that payment of a participant's benefits must commence not later than (1) the taxable year in which the participant attains age 70 ½, or (2) if later, the year in which the participant retires (sec. 401(a)(9)).

In addition, if participant dies before the entire interest is distributed, the entire remaining interest generally must be distributed to the participant's beneficiary or beneficiaries within 5 years. However, this rule does not apply if the distribution has commenced to the participant and is payable over a period which does not exceed the joint life expectancy of the participant and the participant's spouse. A conforming change is made to the IRA distribution rules.

Integration with social security.—The bill extends to all qualified defined contribution plans a rule under which the tax rate applicable to employers for old age, survivors, and disability insurance (OASDI) under social security is the maximum rate at which employer contributions can be reduced under plans that are integrated with social security. This provision is designed to decrease the extent of integration in defined contribution plans without increasing the extent of integration in any plan.

For 1982, the employer's tax rate with respect to OASDI benefits under social security is 5.4 percent, and the taxable wage base is the first $32,400 of an employee's pay. Thus, if the provisions were applicable for 1982, a profit-sharing plan could provide contributions of 5.4 percent of 1982 pay in excess of $32,400 and no contributions for 1982 with respect to the first $32,400 of pay. Similarly, if a plan provided for 1982 contributions of 10 percent of pay in excess of $32,400, it would integrate only if it provided for 1982 contributions of at least 4.6 percent (10% minus 5.4%) with respect to the first $32,400 of pay. The same rules apply to a self-employed individual.

The wage base and tax rates which apply for any plan year are the wage base and tax rates in effect on the first day of the plan year.

The remaining present-law rules which restrict integration with social security under an H.R. 10 defined contribution which benefits an owner-employer are repealed.

Additional qualification requirements for top-heavy plans

In general.—Under the agreement, additional qualification requirements are provided for plans which primarily benefit an employer's key employees (top-heavy plans). These additional requirements (1) limit the amount of a participant's compensation which may be taken into account, (2) provide greater portability of benefits for plan participants who are non-key employees, (3) provide minimum nonintegrated contributions or benefits for plan participants who are non-key employees, and (4) reduce the aggregate limit on contributions and benefits for certain key employees. Further, additional restrictions are placed on distributions to key employees.

Top-heavy plans.—Under the agreement, a defined benefit plan is a top-heavy plan for a plan year if, as of the determination date, (1) the present value of the accumulated accrued benefits for participants who are key employees for the plan year exceeds sixty percent of the present value of the accumulated accrued benefits for all employees under the plan, or (2) the plan is a part of a top-heavy group. A defined contribution plan is a top-heavy plan for a plan year if, as of the determination date, (1) the sum of the account balances of participants who are key employees for the plan year exceeds sixty percent of the sum of the account balances of all employees under the plan, or (2) the plan is a part of a top-heavy group. Under these rules, a simplified employee pension is considered a defined contribution plan, and at the election of the employer, the account balance of any employee covered by a simplified employee pension is deemed to be the sum of the employer contributions made on the employee's behalf.

The determination date for any plan year generally is the last day of the preceding plan year. However, in the case of the first plan year, the determination date is the last day of that year. Further, to the extent provided in regulations, the determination date may be determined on the basis of a year other than a plan year.

Top-heavy groups.—The agreement also provides rules under which two or more plans of a single employer are aggregated to determine whether the plans, as a group, are top-heavy. The aggregation group must include (1) any plan which covers a key employee, and (2) any plan upon which a plan covering a key employee depends for qualification under the Code's coverage or antidiscrimination rules (secs. 401(a)(4) and 410). In addition, in testing for top-heaviness, an employer may elect to expand the aggregation group to take into account any other plan maintained by the employer, if such expanded aggregation group continues to satisfy the coverage and antidiscrimination rules.

An aggregation group is a top-heavy group if, as of the determination date, the sum of (1) the present values of the accumulated accrued benefits for key employees under any defined benefit plans included in the group, and (2) the sum of the account balances of key employees under any defined contribution plans included in the group, exceeds 60 percent of the same amount determined for all participants under all plans included in the group. If an aggregation group is a top-heavy group, each plan required to be included in the group is a top-heavy plan. Of course, no plan included in the aggregation group at the election of the employer is subject to the top-heavy plan rules on account of such election.

The top-heavy group rules apply to all plans of related employers which are treated as a single employer (sec. 414).

Additional rules.—For purposes of determining the present value of accumulated accrued benefits under a defined benfit plan and the sum of the account balances under a defined contribution plan, benefits derived from both employer contributions and employee contributions generally are taken into account. However, accumulated deductible employee contributions under a plan are to be disregarded. In addition, to insure relative stability and to preclude distortions under the top-heavy plan computation, the present value of the accrued benefit of a participant in a defined benefit plan or the account balance of a participant in a defined contribution plan generally includes any amount distributed with respect to the participant under the plan within the five-year period ending on the determination date.

A rollover contribution (or similar transfer) made after December 31, 1983, generally is not taken into account under the transferee plan for purposes of the top-heavy plan computation. The conferees intend that this rule will not apply if the contribution (or transfer) is made incident to a merger or consolidation of two or more plans or the division of a single plan into two or more plans. In addition, the conferees intend that this rule will not apply to rollover contributions (or transfers) between plans of the same employer, including plans of related employers which are treated as a single employer (sec. 414). Of course, in any case in which a rollover contribution (or transfer) is required to be taken into account under the transferee plan, the amount distributed by the transferor or plan is not also taken into account under the transferor plan.

If an employee ceases to be treated as a key employee, the employee's accrued benefit under a defined benefit plan or the employee's account balance under a defined contribution plan is disregarded under the top-heavy plan computation for any plan year following the last plan year for which the employee was treated as a key employee.

Key employees.—Key employees generally include employees who (1) are officers (but in no event will officers of any employer include more than 50 employees or, if lesser, the greater of 3 employees or 10 percent of all employees),[1] (2) are one of the 10 employees owning the largest interests in the employer (there are not 10 employees owning greater interests than the employee), (3) own more than a five-percent interest in the employer, or (4) own more than a one-percent interest in the employer and have annual compensation from the employer in excess of $150,000. An employee is considered an officer, or as owning an interest in the employer, if the employee was an officer, or owned such an interest, at any time during the plan year or the four preceding plan years. In the case of an employer which has more officers than are required to be counted as key employees, the officers to be taken into account are the officers with the highest compensation.

Under the agreement, an employee is considered as owning more than a five-percent interest in a corporate employer if the employee owns more than five percent of the employer's outstanding stock or stock possessing five percent of the total combined voting power of all stock of the employer. An employee is also treated as owning stock owned by certain members of the employee's family or, in certain cases, by partnerships, estates, trusts, or corporations in which the employee has an interest (sec. 318). The same rules apply to determine whether an individual owner is a one-percent owner.

In the case of an employer which is not a corporation, ownership will be determined in accordance with regulations prescribed by the Secretary. The

[1] As under present law, the determination as to whether an employee is an officer is to be determined upon the basis of all the facts and circumstances, including, for example, the source of the employee's authority, the term for which elected or appointed, and the nature and extent of the employee's duties. As generally accepted in connection with corporations, the term "officer" means an administrative executive who is in regular and continued service. It implies continuity of service and excludes those employed for a special and single transaction, or those with only nominal administrative duties. Thus, for example, all the employees of a bank who have the title of vice president or assistant vice president would not automatically be considered to be officers. See, for example, Rev. Rul. 80-314, 1980-2 C.B. 152.

conferees intend that these regulations be based on principles similar to the principles of section 318. In addition, to determine whether a self-employed individual who is a one-percent owner, is a key employee, compensation means earned income from the trade or business with respect to which the plan is maintained.

Qualification rules.—These additional rules for top-heavy plans are tax-qualification requirements. Thus, a top-heavy plan is a qualified plan, and a trust forming part of a top-heavy plan is a qualified trust only if the additional requirements are met. Except as the Secretary of the Treasury may provide by regulations, a plan (whether or not top-heavy in fact) will constitute a qualified plan only if the plan includes provisions which will automatically take effect if the plan becomes a top-heavy plan and which meet the additional qualification requirements for top-heavy plans.

Includible compensation.—For any plan year for which a plan is a top-heavy plan, only the first $200,000 of an employee's compensation may be taken into account in determining contributions or benefits under the plan. Beginning in 1986, this $200,000 limit will be adjusted under the same rules used to adjust the overall limits on contributions and benefits. For a self-employed individual, compensation means earned income as redefined by the conference agreement.

Vesting.—For any plan year for which a plan is a top-heavy plan, an employee's right to the accrued benefit derived from employer contributions must become nonforfeitable (sec. 411(a)) under a vesting schedule which satisfies one of two alternative schedules provided by the agreement. These vesting schedules apply to all accrued benefits, whether or not the accrued benefits are required by the top-heavy plan rules.

A plan will satisfy the first alternative vesting schedule (three-year full vesting) if an employee who has at least three years of service with the employer or employers maintaining the plan has a nonforfeitable right to 100 percent of his accrued benefit derived from employer contributions. As under present law, a plan which provides three-year, 100 percent vesting will satisfy the participation requirements if the plan provides that an employee who is at least 25 years old, with three years of service, is eligible to participate.

A plan will satisfy the second alternative vesting schedule (six-year graded vesting) if an employee has a nonforfeitable right to at least 20 percent of the accrued benefit derived from employer contributions at the end of two years of service, 40 percent at the end of three years of service, 60 percent at the end of four years of service, 80 percent at the end of five years of service with the employer, and 100 percent at the end of six years of service with the employer.

For purposes of determining service under these vesting schedules, the present-law rules (sec. 411) relating to years of service, breaks in service, and certain permitted forfeitures etc., apply. Accordingly, all years of service with the employer generally are to be taken into account, including years of service completed prior to enactment and service during periods for which a plan is not a top-heavy plan.

Minimum nonintegrated benefit for non-key employees.—In addition, a qualified pension, etc., plan which is a top-heavy plan must provide a minimum benefit or contribution for each non-key employee who is a participant in the plan.

Under the conference agreement, any individual excluded from coverage under a defined benefit or defined contribution plan because of compensation below a specified amount, or any individual considered to be a participant for purposes of the coverage requirements (sec. 410) must be provided the applicable minimum contribution or benefit.

For a plan year for which a defined benefit plan is a top-heavy plan, each plan participant who is not a key employee for the year generally must accrue a benefit which, when expressed as an annual retirement benefit is not less than two percent of the employee's average annual compensation from the employer during the employee's testing period, multiplied by the employee's years of service with the employer. However, an employee's minimum benefit is not required to exceed 20 percent of such average annual compensation. All years of an employee's service otherwise required to be taken into account under the plan generally are required to be taken into account under the minimum benefit rules, except a year of service (1) ending before the date of enactment, or (2) within which ends a plan year for which the plan is not a top-heavy plan.

For purposes of the minimum benefit rules, only benefits derived from employer contributions (other than amounts employees have elected to defer (e.g. under a salary reduction cash or deferred arrangement)) to the plan are taken into account, and an employee's social security benefits are disregarded. Thus, the required minimum benefit for an employee may not be eliminated or reduced on account of the employee's social security benefits attributable to contributions by the employer (i.e., the minimum benefit is a "non-integrated" benefit).

The term annual retirement benefit is defined as a benefit payable annually in the form of a life annuity (with no ancillary benefits) beginning at the normal retirement age. An employee's testing period is the period of the employee's consecutive years of service (not exceeding five) during which the employee had the greatest aggregate compensation from the employer. However, a year of service (and compensation paid to the employee during such year) need not be included in the employee's testing period if it ends before the date of enactment or begins within or after the last plan year for which the plan is a top-heavy plan.

Minimum nonintegrated contribution for non-key employees.—For a plan year for which a defined contribution plan is a top-heavy plan, the employer generally must contribute on behalf of each plan participant who is not a key employee for the year an amount not less than three percent of the participant's compensation. However, if the employer's contribution rate for each participant who is a key employee for the plan year is less than three percent, the required minimum contribution rate for each non-key employee generally is limited to not more than the highest contribution rate for any key employee. For example, if, under a profit-sharing plan, no amount is contributed by the employer for any key employee, then under this limitation no contribution is required under the minimum contribution rules for any non-key employee. Under the minimum contribution rules, reallocated forfeitures are taken into account as employer contributions.

However, the limitation to the rate of contributions for key employees does not apply with respect to a defined contribution plan upon which a defined benefit plan depends for qualification under the Code's coverage or anti-discrimination rules, if the defined benefit plan benefits a key employee (or if a plan which benefits a key employee also depends upon the defined benefit plan). Under such circumstances, the required minimum contribution rate for a non-key employee is in every case three percent even if the contribution rate on behalf of a key employee is less than 3 percent. For purposes of the limitation, as well as for purposes of the minimum contribution rules generally, all defined contribution plans of the employer are considered a single plan.

To determine the contribution rate for an employee (including a key employee), the employer contributions and reallocated forfeitures on behalf of the employee for the year are divided by the employee's total compensation (or, with respect to a self-employed individual, the individual's earned income) from the employer for the year, not to exceed $200,000.

Amounts paid by the employer for the year to provide social security benefits for the employee are disregarded. Thus, the required minimum contribution for a non-key employee may not be eliminated or reduced on account of benefits attributable to taxes paid by the employer under social security (i.e., the minimum contribution is a "nonintegrated" contribution). Similarly, the employer contribution rate for a key employee is determined without regard to employer contributions under social security. For example, if a plan is integrated with social security by providing key employees with employer contributions equal to 5 percent of compensation in excess of $32,400, the contribution rate for an employee whose total compensation is $50,000 is 1.76 percent (($0.05 \times \$17,600) \div \$50,000$).

No duplication of minimum benefits for non-key employees under a top-heavy group.—If a non-key employee participates in both a defined benefit plan and a defined contribution plan maintained by an employer, the employer is not required by this section to provide the non-key employee with both the minimum benefit and the minimum contribution.

Rules are also provided to preclude inappropriate omissions or required duplication of minimum benefits or contributions. It is anticipated that these rules would preclude an employee who is covered under more than one plan from receiving lower benefits or contributions than that employee would receive if covered under one plan. Similarly, larger total benefits should not be required merely because an employee is covered under more than one plan (except as required where the limit of 1.0 is exceeded by a top-heavy plan). For example, if an employee participates in a top-heavy money purchase pension plan that provides an annual non-integrated contribution rate of 5 percent of compensation and a defined benefit plan that provides an annual benefit of 1 percent of pay, the employer would not be required to provide an additional 1-percent benefit for non-key employees participating in the defined benefit plan.

Of course, contributions to either plan on behalf of the non-key employee may otherwise be required (for example, by reason of the nondiscrimination rules). In any case in which separate plans are required to be considered together for purposes of the coverage or non-discrimination rules, the required minimum benefit or minimum contribution may of course be taken into account. However, two plans are not necessarily comparable merely because one plan provides the required minimum benefit while the other provides the required minimum contribution. Similarly, the fact that two plans both provide the required minimum benefit, or that two plans both provide the required minimum contribution, does not insure that the two plans, as a whole, are comparable.

Aggregate limit on contributions and benefits for key employees.—The agreement includes additional rules with respect to the aggregate limit on benefits and contributions (sec. 415(e)) for a key employee who participates in both a defined benefit plan and a defined contribution plan which are included in a top-heavy group. Unless certain requirements are met, for any year for which the plans are included in the top-heavy group, the aggregate limit for the key employee is the lesser of 1.0 (as applied only to the dollar limits) or 1.4 (as determined under present law). However, the aggregate limit is increased to the lesser of 1.25 (as applied only to the dollar limits) or 1.4 (as under present law) if the plans of the employer in which the key employee participates (1) meet the requirements of the concentration test, and (2) provide either an extra minimum benefit (in the case of the defined benefit plan) or an extra minimum contribution (in the case of the defined contribution plan) for non-key employees participating in the plans. The extra contribution or benefit is in addition to the minimum contribution or benefit required for all top-heavy plans.

The concentration test is generally satisfied with respect to a key employee for a year if, as of the last determination date before the first day of such year, the sum of (1) the present value of the accumulated accrued benefits for key employees under the defined benefit plans of the employer in which the key employee participates, and (2) the sum of the account balances of key employees under the defined contribution plans of the employer in which the key employee participates is not greater than 90 percent of the same amount determined for all participants under the plans. For purposes of this computation, the rules for determining whether two or more plans constitute a top-heavy group apply.

The requirement for an extra minimum benefit for non-key employees is satisfied for a year if, for the plan year ending with or within such year, each non-key employee who is a participant in a defined benefit plan of the employer in which the key employee is a participant accrues an extra benefit which, when expressed as an annual retirement benefit, is not less than the lesser of (1) one percent of the employee's average annual compensation, multiplied by the employee's years of service with the employer, or (2) 10 percent of such average annual compensation. This extra minimum benefit generally is determined in the same manner as the minimum benefit required under the rules for a top-heavy defined benefit plan. However, for purposes of the extra minimum benefit, a year of service is required to be taken into account only if (1) such year of service includes the last day of a plan year for which the plan is a top-heavy plan (or included in a top-heavy group), and (2) such plan year ends with or within a year for which the aggregate limit of the key employee exceeds 1.0 (as applied to the dollar limits).

The requirement for an extra minimum contribution is satisfied with respect to a key employee for a year if, for the plan year ending with or within such year, the employer contributes on behalf of each non-key employee who is a participant in a defined contribution plan in which the key employee is a participant an extra amount not less than the amount equal to one percent of the employee's compensation for the year. Accordingly, the extra minimum contribution generally is determined under the rules for top-heavy defined contribution plans.

In some cases, the aggregate of a key employee's accrued benefit under an employer's defined benefit plans and annual additions under the employer's defined contribution plans may exceed 1.0 (as applied to the dollar limits) at the time the key employee becomes subject to an aggregate limit of 1.0. In such a case, the key employee is permitted no further benefit accruals under the defined benefit plans and no additional employer contributions under the defined contribution plans until (1) the aggregate of the key employee's accrued benefits and annual additions is less than 1.0 (as applied to the dollar limits), or (2) the aggregate limit for the key employee is increased to 1.25 (as applied to the dollar limits) under the bill. Of course, in no event are further benefit accruals permitted if the aggregate of the employee's accrued benefit and annual additions exceeds 1.25 (as applied to the dollar limit) or 1.4 (as applied under present law).

Distributions to key employees.—The agreement also provides new rules for distributions from top-heavy plans to key employees. If a distribution is made to a key employee before he attains age 59 ½, an additional income tax is imposed equal to 10 percent of the amount includible in income, unless the distribution is made on account of death or disability.

In addition, a top-heavy plan must provide that distributions to a key employee will commence no later than the taxable year in which the key employee attains age 70 ½, whether or not he separates from service in that year. As under present law, the required distributions must be made in such a manner that more than 50 percent of the total benefits for the employee are payable to the employee over the employee's life expectancy (or the joint life expectancy of the employee and the employee's spouse).

Organizations performing management functions

The conference agreement expands the class of employers which, under the present-law rules for affiliated service groups (sec. 414(m)), are to be treated as a single employer for purposes of certain of the tax-law rules for qualified pension, etc., plans (including the rules for top-heavy plans), cafeteria or medical reimbursement plans, or simplified employer pensions (SEPs). Under the provision, if an organization's principal business is performing, on a regular and continuing basis, management functions for another organization, the person performing the functions and the organization for whom the functions are performed are treated as a single employer.

Under the provision, any person related to the organization performing the management functions is also included in the group which is treated as a single employer. An organization related to the organization for whom the functions are performed is included in the group under the management function rules, if the management functions are also performed, on a regular and continuing basis, for such related organization. However, the provision does not change present law under which aggregation of employers is otherwise required.

For purposes of the provision, the term "organization" includes an individual, corporation, partnership, etc. Whether organizations are related is determined under present law (sec. 103(b)(6)(C)).

The conferees intend that the provision is to apply only where the management functions performed by one person for another are functions historically performed by employees, including partners or sole proprietors in the case of unincorporated trades and businesses. For this purpose, the present-law rules relating to affiliated service organizations and to services historically performed by employees in the case of an affiliated service organization are to apply.

Employee leasing

The conference agreement also provides that, for purposes of certain of the tax-law rules for qualified pension, etc., plans (including the rules for top-heavy plans) and SEPs, an individual (a leased employee) who performs services for another person (the recipient) may be treated as the recipient's employee where the services are performed pursuant to an agreement between the recipient and a third person (the leasing organization) who is otherwise treated as the individual's employer. Under the provision, the individual is to be treated as the recipient's employee only if the individual has performed services for the recipient (or for the recipient and persons related to the recipient) on a substantially full-time basis for a period of at least 12 months, and the services are of a type historically performed by employees in the recipient's business field. For this purpose, the present-law rules relating to services historically performed by employees in the case of an affiliated service organization are to apply.

The employee leasing rules do not apply where services in a particular business field historically have been performed by one person for another. For example, some prepaid health care service programs organized on a group practice basis involve two or three components: the health plan, a separate medical group that provides or arranges physicians' services to the health plan members, and often a related hospital. The hospital and the medical group each may employ its own staff (nurses, technicians, etc.), but both sets of employees may be jointly managed. Alternatively, the staff that supports the medical group may be employed by the health plan. These forms of operation are well established in the group practice prepaid health care field. The conferees intend that the "historically performed" exception is to apply in these cases (whether the form of operation is currently in effect or put into effect for existing components of an established group practice prepaid health care service program or for the components of a new program) if the health plan, the hospital, and the medical group provide substantially similar, though not necessarily exactly equivalent retirement benefits through tax qualified plans to salaried nonunion employees and partners.

For purposes of determining whether a pension, etc., plan or a SEP maintained by the recipient satisfies the applicable tax-law requirements, the leased employee is treated as the recipient's employee for periods after the close of the 12-month period described in the preceding paragraph. However, the leased employee's years of service for the recipient are determined by taking into account the entire period for which the leased employee performed services for the recipient (or for a related person).

Under the provision, contributions or benefits for the leased employee which are provided by the leasing organization under a qualified plan or a SEP maintained by the leasing organization are to be treated as if provided by the recipient to the extent such contributions or benefits are attributable to services performed by the leased employee for the recipient.

Under the provision, an individual who otherwise would be treated as a recipient's employee will not be treated as such an employee, if certain requirements are met with respect to contributions and benefits provided for the individual under a qualified money purchase pension plan maintained by the leasing organization. Such a plan qualifies if it provides that (1) an individual is a plan participant on the first day on which the individual becomes an employee of an employer maintaining the plan, (2) each employee's rights to or derived from employer contributions under the plan are nonforfeitable (sec. 411(a)) at the time the contributions are made, and (3) amounts are to be contributed by the employer on behalf of an employee at a rate not less than 7 ½ percent of the employee's compensation for the year (the 7 ½ percent contribution is not to be reduced by integration with social security).

For purposes of the provision, the term person includes individuals and organizations (corporations, partnerships, etc.). Whether persons are related persons is determined under present law (sec. 103(b)(6)(C)).

The provision authorizes the Secretary of the Treasury to prescribe regulations under which a leased employee will not be treated as the recipient's employee notwithstanding that the provision may otherwise apply. Under the conference agreement, the Secretary is to prescribe such regulations where it is determined that to treat a leased employee as the recipient's employee is not appropriate, taking into account the purposes underlying those qualified plan rules with respect to which the provision applies.

Certain corporations performing personal services

Under the conference agreement, if a corporation, the principal activity of which is the performance of personal services substantially all of which are performed by employee-owners for or on behalf of another corporation, partnership, or entity (including related parties), is availed of for the principal purpose of evasion or avoidance of Federal income tax by securing for any employee-owner significant tax benefits which would not otherwise be available, then the Secretary may allocate all income, as well as such deductions, credits, exclusions, etc., as may be allowable, between or among the corporation and employee-owners involved. For this purpose, an employee-owner is defined as any employee who owns (after application of the attribution rules under section 318) more than 10 percent of the outstanding stock of the corporation. The conferees intend that the provisions overturn the results reached in cases like *Keller v. Commissioner,* 77 TC 1014 (1981), where the corporation served no meaningful business purpose other than to secure tax benefits which would not otherwise be available.

The provision applies to taxable years beginning after December 31, 1982.

Disincorporation relief

The conferees understand that a number of personal service corporations may wish to liquidate when the parity provisions of the conference agreement take effect. Therefore, a transitional rule is provided under which personal service corporations may, during 1983 or 1984, complete a one-month liquidation under section 333 of the Code without the risk that the corporation would incur tax on its unrealized receivables. Of course, the income represented by unrealized receivables will retain its character as ordinary income and will be fully recognized by the distributee shareholder upon subsequent collection or other disposition.

Group-term life insurance

The conference agreement also provides that the income exclusion for employer-provided group term life insurance (sec. 79) will apply with respect to a key employee only if the life insurance is provided under a program of the employer which does not discriminate in favor of key employees as to (1) eligibility to participate, or (2) the life insurance benefits provided under the plan.

A program of an employer providing group-term life insurance for employees generally will not be considered to discriminate in favor of key employees as to eligibility to participate if (1) the program benefits at least 70 percent of all employees, (2) at least 85 percent of all participating employees are not key employees, or (3) the program benefits employees who qualify under a classification set up by the employer and found by the Secretary of the Treasury not to discriminate in favor of key employees. Alternatively, a program of an employer providing group-term life insurance which is provided under a cafeteria plan (sec. 125) will not be considered to discriminate in favor of key employees as to eligibility to participate if the eligibility rules for cafeteria plans are satisfied. For purposes of the provision's rules relating to eligibility to participate, employees of certain related employers would generally be treated as if employed by a single employer. However, the following employees could be excluded from consideration: (1) those who have not completed 3 years of service with the employer, (2) part-time and seasonal employees, and (3) nonresident aliens who receive no U.S. source income from the employer. For this purpose, part-time employees are those whose customary employment is for not more than 20 hours in any one week, and seasonal employees are those whose customary employment is for not more than 5 months in any calendar year. In addition, employees not covered by the program but covered by a collective bargaining agreement need not be taken into account if group-term life insurance was the subject of good faith bargaining between the employer and employee representatives.

A program of an employer providing group-term life insurance for employees will not be considered to discriminate in favor of key employees as to the benefits provided, if the program does not discriminate in favor of such employees with regard to the type and amount of the benefits. For this purpose, group-term life insurance benefits will not be considered to discriminate merely because the amount of life insurance provided employees bears a uniform relationship to compensation. Of course, the requirement that group-term life insurance benefits be nondiscriminatory can be satisfied where, under the facts and circumstances, no discrimination in favor of key employees occurs. For example, the requirement would be satisfied when the life insurance benefits are a level dollar amount which is the same for all covered employees.

The conferees intend that the Secretary of the Treasury is to revise the tables for computing the amount includible in an employee's gross income on account of employer-provided group-term life insurance. The conferees further intend that the tables be periodically revised to reflect current group-term life insurance costs.

Effective dates

The agreement's provisions relating to parity between corporate and noncorporate employers, top-heavy plans, organizations performing management functions, employee leasing, and group-term life insurance apply to years beginning after December 31, 1983.

The provisions relating to certain corporations performing personal services applies to taxable years beginning after December 31, 1982.

Retirement Savings for Church Employees

* * *

Senate amendment

The Senate amendment revises the present-law tax-sheltered annuity rules as they apply to church employees by (1) providing a minimum exclusion allowance equal to the lesser of $3,000 or 100 percent of compensation for employees with adjusted gross income of $17,000 or less; (2) providing that all years of service with organizations that are part of a particular church are treated as years with one employer; (3) extending to all church employees the special catchup elections to increase the annual contribution limit; (4) providing an additional election for church employees which increases the contribution limit by up to $10,000 for any year, subject to a $40,000 lifetime cap; (5) permitting churches to maintain segregated defined contributions retirement savings programs pursuant to the tax-sheltered annuity rules; and (6) providing a special retroactive correction period for church plans.

These changes apply to taxable years beginning after December 31, 1981, except that the provision permitting retroactive amendments applies after July 1, 1982.

Conference agreement

The conference agreement follows the Senate amendment with regard to permitted contributions for church employees under the exclusion allowance and annual contribution limit for tax-sheltered annuities.

The conference agreement also follows the Senate amendment by allowing a church which maintains a tax-sheltered annuity, retirement income account, or pension plan, a retroactive amendment period if the annuity, account or plan, is required to be amended by reason of any law, or any regulation, ruling or other action under the tax laws. During the correction period, the annuity, account, or plan would be treated as satisfying the applicable tax-law requirement. To qualify for this treatment, the required amendment or other modification generally must be made not later than at the next earliest church convention. However, the Secretary of the Treasury may prescribe an alternative time period within which the required amendment is to be made. In this regard, the Secretary is to take into account that church governing bodies typically meet at lengthy intervals. Of course, in no event is the permitted correction period for a church to be less than that allowed under present law (sec. 401(b)).

The conference agreement also follows the Senate amendment by providing that the tax rules for tax-sheltered annuities are to apply to church-maintained retirement income accounts that are defined contributions plans (sec. 414(i)). However, the conference agreement further provides that a church-maintained retirement income program in existence on August 13, 1982 will not be considered as failing to satisfy the requirements for a tax-sheltered annuity (sec. 403(b)) merely because the program is a defined benefit plan (sec. 414(j)). For this purpose, a church-maintained retirement income program is considered to be in existence on August 13, 1982, not withstanding that after that date the program is amended, otherwise modified, or extended to benefit other employees. In addition, if a church-maintained retirement income program which is otherwise a defined benefit plan provides a benefit which is based, in part, on the balance of a separate account of an employee, the conferees intend that the separate account can qualify as a defined contribution plan for purposes of the rules relating to retirement income accounts.

The conferees intend that the assets of a retirement income account for the benefit of an employee or his beneficiaries may be commingled in a common fund made up of such accounts. However, that part of the common fund which equitably belongs to any account must be separately accounted for (i.e., it must be possible at all times to determine the account's interest in the fund), and cannot be used for, or diverted to, any purposes other than the exclusive benefit of such employee and beneficiaries. Provided those requirements are met, the assets of a retirement income account also may be commingled with the assets of a tax-qualified plan without adversely affecting the status of the account or the qualification of the plan.

The conferees also intend that the assets of a church plan (sec. 414(e)) may be commingled in a common fund with other amounts devoted exclusively to church purposes (for example, a fund maintained by a church pension board) if that part of the fund which equitably belongs to the plan is separately accounted for and cannot be used for or diverted to purposes other than for the exclusive benefit of employees and their beneficiaries. Of course, the reasonable costs of administering a retirement income account (including an account which is a part of a common fund) may be charged against the account. Such costs include the reasonable costs of administering a retirement income program of which the account is a part, including costs associated with informing employees and employers of the availability of the program.

State Judicial Retirement Plans

* * *

Senate amendment

The Senate amendment provides that participants in a qualified State judicial plan are not required to include benefits in gross income merely because there is no substantial risk that the benefits will be forfeited. The plan must be a mandatory retirement plan for State judges under which each contributes the same percentage of income and receives a retirement benefit based upon compensation paid to judges holding similar positions. The plan must have been continuously in existence since December 31, 1978, and must meet certain additional requirements. The provision applies to taxable years beginning after December 31, 1978.

Conference agreement

The conference agreement follows the Senate amendment.

Contribution for Disabled Employees

* * *

Senate amendment

The Senate amendment permits an employer to continue deductible contributions to a profit-sharing or other defined contribution plan for an employee (other than an officer, owner, or highly compensated individual) who is permanently and totally disabled provided that the contributions are nonforfeitable when made. For this purpose, a disabled employee's compensation is deemed equal to his annualized compensation prior to his becoming disabled. The provision applies to years beginning after December 31, 1981.

Conference agreement

The conference agreement follows the Senate amendment.

Participation in Group Trusts By Governmental Plans

Senate amendment

The Senate amendment provides that the tax-exempt status of a group trust will not be adversely affected merely because a participating trust is part of a governmental plan without regard to whether the governmental trust is a qualified trust or the governmental plan is a qualified plan. The provision applies to taxable years beginning after December 31, 1981.

Conference agreement

The conference agreement modifies the Senate amendment generally to permit all governmental retirement plans to participate in a tax-exempt group trust. Under the conference agreement, the tax-exempt status of a group trust will not be adversely affected merely because the trust accepts monies from (a) a retirement plan of a State or local government, whether or not the plan is a qualified plan and whether or not the assets are held in trust, or (b) any State or local governmental monies intended for use in satisfying an obligation of such State or local government to provide a retirement benefit under a governmental plan. Of course, any group trust in which a plan of a private employer participates will remain subject to the present-law rules relating to unrelated business taxable income (sec. 511 et seq.), notwithstanding that the trust includes a governmental plan.—Conference Committee Report.

Testimony of Senator Dole of Kansas on P.L. 97-248 during the Senate debate in the Congressional Record of August 19, 1982, page 5 10903.

I want to make it clear that under the conference agreement a personal service corporation will not be considered to be formed or availed of for the purpose of evading or avoiding Federal income tax solely because, for 1983, the qualified plan rules will permit higher contributions and other advantages for corporate employees. Thus, in applying section 269A, the Secretary of the Treasury will not take a corporation's retirement plan into account.

[¶ 12,400.07]

Committee Report on P.L. 96-605 (Miscellaneous Revenue Act of 1980)

[Senate Committee Report]

Present law

Under present law, the dollar limitation on annual additions with respect to a participant in a tax credit employee stock ownership plan or an employee stock ownership plan may be increased, provided certain requirements with respect to allocations of employer contributions are met. The amount of such increase is the lesser of (1) the usual dollar limitation on annual additions to a participant's account or (2) the amount of employer securities contributed to the plan.

Reasons for change

The committee has determined that it is necessary to make a clarifying change to the rule of present law which allows an increase in the limitation on contributions with respect to a participant in a tax credit employee stock ownership plan or an employee stock ownership plan. The change will make it clear that cash used to purchase employer securities is included for purposes of determining the increased limitation on annual additions to a participant's account.

Explanation of provision

Under the provision, the increase in the dollar limitation on annual additions with respect to a participant in a tax credit employee stock ownership plan or an employee stock ownership plan (provided certain requirements of present law are met with respect to allocations under the plan) would be the lesser of (1) the usual dollar limitation on annual additions to a participant's account, or (2) the amount of employer securities (or cash used to acquire such securities) contributed to the plan.

Effective date

The provision is effective for limitation years beginning after December 31, 1980.

[¶ 12,400.075]

Committee Report on P.L. 96-222 (Technical Corrections Act of 1979)

[Senate Committee Report]

Secs. 101(a)(10)(I) and 101(b)(1)(G)—Aggregation of SEPs with other plans.

The Code provides limits on the annual addition to the account of a participant in a profit-sharing or other contribution plan. For this purpose, annual additions consist of employer contributions, reallocated forfeitures, and a portion of employee contributions.

The limits are applied to the aggregate of all defined contribution plans maintained by an employer. If the employer is in a controlled group of companies (whether or not incorporated), the limits are applied to the aggregate of all defined contribution plans maintained by the group. Under the rules, employer contributions to the simplified employee pension of an employee are aggregated with other employer contributions to defined contribution plans only if the employee has direct or indirect control of the employer.

The committee believes that, under the limitation provisions, it is appropriate to treat employer contributions to simplified employee pensions as employer contributions to a defined contribution plan maintained by the employer regardless of the ownership of the employer or the employer's trade or business.

Under the bill, if an employer contributes to a simplified employee pension, the contribution is taken into account as an employer contribution to a defined contribution plan regardless of the ownership of the employer or of the employer's trade or business. The bill does not change the rule of present law under which employee contributions to an individual retirement account or annuity, or a retirement bond are treated as employer contributions to a defined contribution plan maintained by an employer where the employee has the requisite control of the employer. The House bill did not include any similar provision.

The amendment applies for years beginning after the date of enactment of the bill.

Sec. 101(a)(11)(A)—Exception to limits on benefits for collectively bargained plans.

Under the Code, limits are provided for benefits and contributions under tax-qualified plans, individual retirement plans, and tax-sheltered annuities. Generally, under those rules, benefits under a defined benefit pension plan may not exceed 100 percent of a participant's average high 3-year compensation. An exception to the 100-percent limit was provided by the Revenue Act of 1978 for participants in certain collectively bargained plans.

The 1978 Act did not provide for situations in which an employee participates in more than one plan maintained by a single employer.

Under the bill, the exception to the 100-percent limit is restricted to an employee who is a participant in a collectively bargained plan where the employee does not participate in any other plan (subject to the limits on benefits or contributions) maintained by an employer who maintains the collectively bargained plan.

This provision applies for years beginning after December 31, 1978. This is the same as the effective date provided by the 1978 Act for the exception to the 100-percent limitation.

Sec. 101(a)(11)(B)—Factors of age and length of service.

Prior to the Revenue Act of 1978, benefits under a qualified defined benefit pension plan generally were limited to the lesser of 100 percent of pay or $75,000 per year, adjusted for inflation since 1974 ($98,100 for 1979). The Act provides that the 100-percent-of-pay limit is disregarded, and the $75,000 limit is reduced to $37,500 (adjusted for inflation since 1974), in the case of certain large collectively bargained plans under which each employee who serves during a particular year earns the same pension credit. Under the 1978 Act, the pension credit for a participant must be determined without regard to age at retirement or date of retirement.

It was intended that the factors of age at retirement and date of retirement be permitted to be taken into account by a plan under the exception to the 100-percent-of-pay limit.

The bill clarifies that the 100-percent-of-pay limit applies in the case of certain large collectively bargained plans where the amount of the pension credit for a particular employee is based solely on one or more of the following factors: (1) the length of service, (2) the particular years during which service was rendered, (3) the age at retirement, and (4) the date of retirement.

The provision applies for years beginning after December 31, 1978. This is the same effective date as was provided by the Revenue Act of 1978 for the exception to the 100-percent-of-pay limit.

[¶ 12,400.08]

Committee Report on P.L. 95-600 (Revenue Act of 1978)

Sec. 141(f)(7)—Employee stock ownership plans—Committee reports on Sec. 141, employee stock ownership plans, are at ¶ 12,130.10.

Sec. 152(g)—Simplified employee pensions.—The Senate Committee Report on Sec. 152 is at ¶ 12,050.09.

Sec. 153—Defined benefit plan limits.

[Senate Committee Report]

In the case of certain participants in certain collectively bargained defined benefit pension plans, the bill would remove the present law requirement that annual benefits under a defined benefit pension plan are limited to 100 percent of a plan participant's average compensation for his or her highest 3 consecutive years of participation. The bill would not apply to a participant whose compensation for each of any 3 of his or her latest 10 years of plan participation is more than the average compensation of all plan participants for each of the same 3 years. Also, the bill would not apply to a participant who is covered by another plan maintained by one or more of the employers maintaining the collectively bargaining plan. The bill would apply only in the case of a plan (1) which is maintained pursuant to a collective bargaining agreement, (2) which covers at least 100 employees, (3) which computes retirement benefits by multiplying a uniform amount by the number of the participant's years of service, (4) which provides for full vesting after a participant has completed 4 years of service, and (5) which provides for employee participation after an employee has completed not more than a 60-day period of service. If the special rule added by the amendment applies to a participant, the dollar limitation ($75,000, adjusted for cost-of-living) is reduced by half.

The amendment applies for years beginning after December 31, 1978.

[¶ 12,400.09]

Committee Report on P.L. 94-455 (Tax Reform Act of 1976)

Other provisions

In situations where the value of employer stock can be expected to increase rapidly, the rule of present law limiting the annual addition to the account of a participant in a defined contribution plan to $25,000 (plus a cost-of-living adjustment) may discourage the establishment of an ESOP designed to acquire employer stock from a present shareholder by causing the shareholder to suffer an unacceptable level of dilution of his interest in the company. In order to remove this barrier to ESOPs, the committee amendment doubles the dollar limitation provided by present law in the case of defined contribution plans but the additional amount may only consist of employer stock. Also, under the committee amendment, the limitation on benefits which may be provided under a defined benefit plan would be reduced where the additional defined contribution limitation is allowed for an ESOP. In order to assure that the doubled allowance is not available to a plan unless rank-and-file employees are the chief beneficiaries of the plan, however, under the amendment, the doubled allowance is not available for a plan if more than one-third of the employer contributions to the plan for a year are allocated to employees who are officers or shareholders, or whose compensation for the year exceeds twice the amount of the dollar limitation ordinarily applicable to the annual addition to the account of a participant in a defined contribution plan. (This is not intended to affect any determination of which employees are considered highly compensated for purposes of the coverage and nondiscrimination requirements applicable to qualified plans generally.) For this purpose, employees who hold 10 percent or less (determined with attribution rules) of the employer's stock (outside of the ESOP) are not considered shareholders.—**Senate Committee Report.**

The amendment permits contributions to be made to an H.R. 10 plan on behalf of an owner-employee under annuity contracts despite the overall 25-percent limitation if no other amounts are added to his account for the year under any other defined contribution plan or tax-sheltered annuity maintained by the employer or a related employer and if the employee is not an active participant for the year in a defined benefit plan maintained by the employer or a related employer. Under the amendment, the overall limitations which apply where an employee participates in both a defined contribution plan and a defined benefit plan are not changed. No comparable provision is included in the House bill.—**Senate Committee Supplemental Report.**

Conference agreement

The conference agreement follows the Senate amendment but adds rules regarding the treatment of contributions under the anti-discrimination rules applicable to pension plans.—**Conference Committee Report.**

[¶ 12,400.10]

Committee Report on P.L. 93-406 (Employee Retirement Income Security Act of 1974)

[Conference Committee Explanation]

Coverage of limitations.—The conference substitute imposes an overall limitation (described below) on the contributions and benefits which are allowable under qualified pension, profit-sharing, ald stock bonus plans and annuities (including H.R. 10 plans in cases where the overall limits are lower than the H.R. 10-plan limits). The overall limitation also applies to annuity contracts or mutual fund arrangements for employees of educational, charitable, etc., organizations or of public schools (i.e., sec. 403(b) annuities), as well as individual retirement accounts, annuities and retirement bonds.

Application to defined benefit plans.—Under the conference substitute, in general, the highest annual benefit which can be paid (in the form of a straight-life annuity) out of a defined benefit plan to a participant is not to exceed the lesser of (a) $75,000, or (b) 100 percent of the participant's average compensation in his high-three-years of employment. (Both of these ceilings are to be adjusted to reflect cost-of-living increases.)

In the event of retirement before age 55, the $75,000 ceiling (but not the 100 percent ceiling) is to be scaled down on an actuarial basis (but not below $10,000). In general, there is no required scale down for preretirement ancillary benefits (such as medical, death and disability), but there would have to be an adjustment for post-retirement ancillary benefits, such as term-certain annuities, post-retirement death benefits, or a guaranteed payment for a period of years.

If a benefit were paid in the form of a joint and survivor annuity for the benefit of the participant and his spouse, the value of this feature would not be taken into account unless the survivor benefit were greater than the joint benefit.

Upward adjustments in the benefit schedule would be permitted to reflect any employee contributions to the plan, including rollover contributions from another qualified plan or from an individual retirement account.

Also the substitute would provide a *de minimus* rule, which would allow a qualified plan to pay an annual retirement benefit of up to $10,000 per annum, notwithstanding the 100-percent limitation, or the required adjustment for certain ancillary benefits, to any employee who had not participated in a qualified defined contribution plan of the employer.

As a further adjustment to the rules described above, the maximum allowable defined benefit would have to be scaled down proportionately for an employee with less than 10 years of service.

Application to defined contribution plans.—In the case of a defined contribution plan, the annual additions for the year are not to exceed the lesser of $25,000 (subject to an annual cost-of-living increase) or 25 percent of the participant's compensation from the employer. The term "annual additions" means the sum of (a) the employer's contributions, (b) the lesser of (i) one-half of all the employee's contributions, or (ii) the employee's contributions in excess of 6 percent of his compensation, and (c) any forfeitures which are added to the employee's account. Annual additions do not include rollovers from a qualified plan or individual retirement account. If forfeitures for a particular year could cause the plan not to meet these requirements with respect to a particular employee, these forfeitures must be reallocated to other participants in the plan (i.e., they may not be held in a suspense account), but regulations are to provide for the situation where none of the employees in the plan are eligible to receive forfeitures.

For purposes of the overall limitation, target benefit plans (i.e., plans where the employer establishes a target benefit for his employees, but where the employee's actual pension is based on the amount in his individual account) are to be treated as defined contribution plans. If the plan is a hybrid, i.e., part target benefit and part defined benefit, the plan will be treated as a defined contribution plan, for purposes of those rules, to the extent that benefits under the plan are based on the individual account of the participant. In the case of other plans which have characteristics both of a defined benefit plan and a defined contribution plan (such as a defined contribution plan with a guaranteed benefit or certain variable annuity plans) the Secretary or his delegate may prescribe the regulations applying the limitations to the defined benefit of the plan, and the part of the plan in which benefits are based on individual account balances.

Application of limitation to combination of plans.—Under the substitute, where an employer has two or more plans, the overall ceiling is to be computed, in general, by aggregating similar plans (defined contribution or defined benefit) to determine if the limitation for that type of plan has been met on an overall basis (i.e., for purposes of this test a 1.0 fraction is used). If an employer maintains a defined benefit plan and a defined contribution plan, each plan would be subject to the limit appropriate to that type of plan ($75,000 or 100 percent benefits for the defined benefit plan, $25,000 or 25 percent contributions for the defined contribution plan); in addition, the two plans must be combined in computing the overall limitation.

To achieve this purpose, the substitute establishes a formula (to be applied each year to each employee) under which a defined benefit plan fraction for the year is added to a defined contribution plan fraction. Each fraction indicates what portion the participant has used of the maximum permitted limit for the kind of plan involved. If the sum of these fractions exceeds 1.4 then one or more of the plans will be disqualified.

The order in which plans are to be disqualified is to be determined under regulations. The regulations are to provide that no terminated plan may be disqualified until all other plans of the employer have been disqualified. However (unlike the House bill), the substitute does not require that plans having the fewest number of participants must be disqualified before plans having more participants because, in some cases, such a rigid rule might result in lower qualified plan benefits for the employees viewed as a whole.

Plans of all corporations, partnerships, or proprietorships which are under common control must be aggregated (using a 50-percent common control test).

Application of limitations to section 403(b) annuities for teachers or employees of tax-exempt organizations.—In general, section 403(b) annuities are to be treated as defined contribution plans for purposes of the limitations. Thus, such plans would be subject to the 25 percent/$25,000 limitations which apply to other defined contribution plans, and also are to be subject to the limitations of present law under section 403(b) (20 percent of includable contributions, times years of service, minus all tax excludable contributions by the employer for annuities for prior taxable years).

However, under present law, certain categories of employees covered under section 403(b), such as teachers, typically have a pattern of low contributions in the early stages of their careers, with relatively high "catch-up" contributions made late in their careers. (Often section 403(b) plans operate on a salary-reduction basis.) In order to make allowance, for this problem, the conference substitute provides teachers, hospital employees, and employees of home health care institutions (which are tax-exempt and which the Secretary of Health, Education and Welfare has classified as a home health agency for purposes of medicare) with a choice of three alternative rules which permit a significant amount of "catch up." The individual may elect the alternative he wishes to use (in a time and manner to be prescribed in regulations) and the election, once made, is to be irrevocable.

Under the first alternative (which may be used only once) at the time an employee separates from service he may use the catch-up rules of section 403(b) for the 10-year period ending on the date of his separation, without regard to the 25-percent limitation of section 415 (in other words, his exclusion allowance would equal 20 percent of current compensation times 10, minus employer contributions already made for annuities for the 10-year period). The $25,000 limitation would apply, however.

Under the second alternative, which could be used each year by the employee, catch-up contributions otherwise permitted under section 403(b), could equal the lesser of 25 percent of current compensation, plus $4,000, or his exclusion allowance computed under section 403(b), but the deductible amount under this alternative could never exceed $15,000 for any one year.

For purposes of the overall limitations (sec. 415) in applying either of these two alternatives, the employee is not to be required to combine contributions to a 403(b) contract (which the participant would be deemed to control) with contributions by his employer to a qualified plan which he does not control (for example, a State wide plan for teachers). (Of course, the combination rules under section 403(b) of present law would not be changed.)

Under the third alternative, however, the employee would be permitted to come under the overall limitation (sec. 415) for all purposes (and the exclusion allowance of sec. 403(b) would not apply). This would mean that the employee would be covered under the overall limitation rules on combination plans, including the 1.4 fraction. For purposes of the combination rules both the employer and the employee would be deemed to have control of the 403(b) contract, but such a contract (which is to be treated as a defined contribution plan) could be combined with a State wide defined benefit plan, and benefits under the two plans, considered together, could equal 1.4 times the amount which could be provided under either plan when viewed separately.

If contributions to provide a section 403(b) annuity exceed the allowable limitations, the excess amounts must be included in income by the employee. Also, the employee's exclusion allowance under section 403(b) is to be reduced by the amount of the excess contribution (even though it was not excludable from the employee's income). If amounts are contributed for the purchase of mutual fund stock (which is permitted under another provision of the conference substitute), these amounts are to be subject to the 6 percent tax on overfunding until the excess is eliminated (see discussion above on individual retirement accounts). This tax is not imposed on contributions for annuity contracts, since earnings on these contracts are not taxed to the individual (until distributed) even when the annuity is not covered under section 403(b).

Treatment of benefits or contributions over the limitations.—The House bill provided that benefits or contributions in addition to those allowable under qualified plans may be paid or accrued under a qualified plan, if the contributions by the employer for the additional benefits were not deductible until they were includible in income by the employee.

The Senate amendment provided, in effect, that no retirement benefits could be paid, except from a qualified plan.

To avoid technical difficulties, the conference substitute omits both provisions. The conferees intend that, for tax purposes, additional benefits may not be paid from a qualified plan. However, for purposes other than tax law, a qualified plan and a plan providing additional benefits may be treated as one plan by the employer.

Applications of limitation where records not available.—Under the conference substitute, the Treasury is authorized to prescribe reasonable assumptions which may be used by the employer in cases where the facts needed to compute the overall limitation are not known.

Application of limitation to existing cases.—The conference substitute contains a provision which provides that an individual who is an active plan participant on or before October 2, 1973, may receive a pension equal to the lesser of (a) 100 percent of his annual compensation on that date (or on the date he separated from service with the employer), or (b) the benefit payable under the terms of the plan as in effect on that date (assuming no later change in compensation). If the regular rules of the (sec. 415) provision result in a higher limit (due to pre-retirement cost-of-living-increases, for example) than that allowable under this transition provision, the individual is to be entitled to the higher limitation. If an individual covered under this feature is also covered under a defined contribution plan, contributions may continue to be made to the defined contribution plan, to the extent that prior contributions to this plan (or other plans of the same employer), plus the defined benefit available under this feature (which may exceed 1.0 for these purposes), do not exceed the 1.4 fraction. In the case of a participant who separated from the service of the employer prior to October 2, 1973, the benefit allowed under this feature cannot exceed the individual's vested benefit on the date when he separated from service.

Aggregate deduction limits in the case of profit-sharing and pension plans, etc.—The conference substitute provides that carry-over deductions of excess contributions in a combination pension and profit-sharing plan may not exceed 25 percent of aggregate compensation for any year (present law allows 30 percent). Also, the carryover of unused aggregate contribution limitations to a profit-sharing plan for any year is not to exceed 25 percent (compared to 30 percent under present law).

Timing of contributions.—Under the substitute, contributions by cash basis taxpayers which are made by the time for filing the tax return for the year in question may be treated as paid in the year in question.

Effective dates

The new rules with respect to limitations on corporate plans are to apply to years beginning after December 31, 1975. (For purposes of this provision the term "year" is to be defined in regulations.) In applying the limitations, contributions or accruals which occur before the effective date must, of course, be taken into account. For example, an employee with an accrued benefit of $60,000 on December 31, 1975, could accrue an additional benefit of $15,000 after that date (for a total benefit of $75,000) assuming that this was not in excess of the 100-percent limitation.

[Code Sec. 416]

[¶ 12,500.08]

Committee Report on P.L. 107-16 (Economic Growth and Tax Relief Reconciliation Act)

[House Committee Report]

Definition of top-heavy plan

The provision provides that a plan consisting of a cash-or-deferred arrangement that satisfies the design-based safe harbor for such plans and matching contributions that satisfy the safe harbor rule for such contributions is not a top-heavy plan. Matching or nonelective contributions provided under such a plan may be taken into account in satisfying the minimum contribution requirements applicable to top-heavy plans.[1]

In determining whether a plan is top-heavy, distributions during the year ending on the date the top-heavy determination is being made are taken into account. The present-law five-year rule would apply with respect to in-service distributions. Similarly, the provision provides that an individual's accrued benefit or account balance is not taken into account if the individual has not performed services for the employer during the one-year period ending on the date the top-heavy determination is being made.

Definition of key employee

The bill (1) provides that an employee is not considered a key employee by reason of officer status unless the employee earns more than $150,000 and (2) repeals the top-10 owner key employee category. The bill repeals the four-year lookback rule for determining key employee status and provide that an employee is a key employee only if he or she is a key employee during the preceding plan year.

Thus, under the bill, an employee is considered a key employee if, during the prior year, the employee was (1) an officer with compensation in excess of $150,000, (2) a five-percent owner, or (3) a one-percent owner with compensation in excess of $150,000. The present-law limits on the number of officers treated as key employees under (1) continue to apply.

The family ownership attribution rule no longer applies in determining whether an individual is a five-percent owner of the employer for purposes of the top-heavy rules only. The family ownership attribution rule continues to apply to other provisions that cross reference the top-heavy rules, such as the definition of highly compensated employee and the definition of one-percent owner under the top-heavy rules.

Minimum benefit for nonkey employees

Under the bill, matching contributions are taken into account in determining whether the minimum benefit requirement has been satisfied.[2]

The bill provides that, in determining the minimum benefit required under a defined benefit plan, a year of service does not include any year in which no key employee or former key employee benefits under the plan (as determined under sec. 410).

Effective Date

The provision is effective for years beginning after December 31, 2001.

[Conference Committee Report]

The conference agreement follows the House bill, with the following modifications.

Under the conference agreement, an employee is considered a key employee if, during the prior year, the employee was (1) an officer with compensation in excess of $130,000 (adjusted for inflation in $5,000 increments), (2) a five-percent owner, or (3) a one-percent owner with compensation in excess of $150,000. The present-law limits on the number of officers treated as key employees under (1) continue to apply.

Under the conference agreement, the family ownership attribution rule continues to apply in determining whether an individual is a five-percent owner of the employer for purposes of the top-heavy rules.

Effective date

The conference agreement is effective for years beginning after December 31, 2001.

[1] This provision is not intended to preclude the use of nonelective contributions that are used to satisfy the safe harbor rules from being used to satisfy other qualified retirement plan nondiscrimination rules, including those involving cross-testing.

[2] Thus, this provision overrides the provision in Treasury regulations that, if matching contributions are used to satisfy the minimum benefit requirement, then they are not treated as matching contributions for purposes of the section 401(m) nondiscrimination rules.

[¶ 12,500.083]

Committee Report on P.L. 100-647 (Technical and Miscellaneous Revenue Act of 1988)

[Senate Committee Report]

Under the bill, for purposes of determining whether an employee is a key employee by virtue of having annual compensation over $150,000, compensation means compensation as defined in section 415(c)(3) plus elective deferrals under sections 125, 402(a)(8), 402(h), and 403(b). This is the same definition used for purposes of determining whether an employee is highly compensated (sec. 414(q)(7)), a determination that is similar to the determination of who is a key employee. This provision of the bill applies to years beginning after December 31, 1988.

[¶ 12,500.085]

Committee Reports on P.L. 99-514 (Tax Reform Act of 1986)

[House Committee Report]

Present Law

* * *

Accrued benefits

In general, a defined benefit pension plan will not be considered a qualified plan unless participants accrue benefits at a rate that meets one of three alternative schedules (sec. 411(b)). The purpose of these schedules generally is to limit the extent to which an employer may defer (i.e., "backload") benefit accruals.

Under the first alternative, known as the "three-percent rule," a plan participant must accrue a benefit during each year of participation (up to 33⅓ years) not less than three percent of the benefit to which an employee who entered the plan at the earliest entry age and participated until the earlier of normal retirement age or age 65 would otherwise be entitled.

Under the second alternative, known as the "133⅓ percent rule," a plan will satisfy the accrued benefit requirements if the accrued benefit of a plan participant, as of his normal retirement age, is equal to the normal retirement benefit under the plan and the annual rate at which any individual who is or could be a plan participant accruing the retirement benefits in any year, is never more than 133⅓ percent of the annual accrual rate for any prior year.

Under the third alternative, known as the "fractional rule," each plan participant's accrued benefit at the end of any year must be at least equal to a fractional portion of the retirement benefit to which the participant would be entitled under the plan's benefit formula if the participant continued to earn annually until normal retirement age the same rate of compensation. The fractional portion is determined by dividing the participant's actual years of participation by the total number of years of participation that would have been completed if the participant had continued in service until normal retirement age.

In determining whether a plan is top-heavy, cumulative accrued benefits are calculated using the benefit accrual method selected by the plan. If the plan is determined to be top-heavy, the plan generally must provide that each participant's minimum benefit is, on a cumulative basis, at least equal to two percent of compensation for each year of service during which the plan is top heavy, not to exceed 20 percent (sec. 416(c)). Under the top-heavy rules, benefits accrued under the plan's benefit formula must be at least equal to the required minimum benefit.

* * *

Explanation of Provisions

Under the bill, a uniform accrual rule is used in testing whether a qualified plan is top heavy (or super top heavy) (sec. 416(g)(4)(F)). Thus, solely for determining whether the present value of cumulative accrued benefits for key employees exceeds 60 percent of the present value of cumulative accrued benefits for all employees (90 percent for purposes of the super top-heavy plan rules), cumulative accrued benefits would be uniformly measured. [If benefits under all plans of an employer accrue at the same rate, then that accrual rate is used in determining whether the plans are top heavy or super top heavy. If there is no single accrual rate used by all plans of an employer, then the plans' top-heavy status is to be determined by treating the benefits of the participants in each plan as accruing no more rapidly than the slowest permitted rate under the fractional rule].

This * * * applies only for purposes of determining whether the plan is top heavy or super top heavy. * * *

Effective Date

The provision applies for plan years beginning after December 31, [1986].

[Senate Committee Report]

* * *

Effective Date

The provision applies for plan years beginning after December 31, 1986.

[Conference Committee Report]

The conference agreement follows the House bill and the Senate amendment except that the conference agreement provides that if benefits under all plans of the employer accrue at the same rate, then that accrual rate is to be used in determining whether the plans are top heavy or super top heavy. If there is no single accrual rate used by all plans of the employer, then the plans' top-heavy status is to be determined by treating the benefits of the participants in each plan as accruing no more rapidly than the slowest permitted rate under the fractional accrual rule.

The provision applies for plan years beginning after December 31, 1986.

[¶ 12,500.09]

Committee Reports on P.L. 98-369 (Tax Reform Act of 1984)

[Senate Committee Report]

Provisions relating to top-heavy plans

* * *

Under the bill, if an individual has not been an employee with respect to any plan of the employer at any time during the 5-year period ending on the determination date, any accrued benefit (or account balance) of the individual is disregarded for purposes of determining whether the plan is top heavy.

The bill provides that amounts contributed to a qualified pension plan pursuant to a salary reduction arrangement are taken into account under the top-heavy provisions. The bill also exempts governmental plans (as defined in sec. 414(d)) from the top-heavy plan requirements.

* * *

Effective Dates

Generally, the provisions are effective for plan years beginning after December 31, 1983. The provisions relating to separated employees and salary reduction arrangements are effective for plan years beginning after December 31, 1984.

[Conference Committee Report]

The conference agreement generally follows the Senate amendment, with two exceptions. First, the conference agreement retains the special combined limit on contributions and benefits under a super top-heavy plan. Second, the conference agreement revises the definition of the term "key employee" to exclude officers who earn less than 1 ½ times the dollar limit on contributions under a defined contribution plan ($45,000 for 1984).

Under the conference agreement (as under the Senate amendment), if the Secretary of the Treasury fails to issue final regulations under the Code rules relating to top-heavy plans before January 1, 1985 (as in effect on the day before the date of enactment of these provisions), the Secretary is required to publish plan amendment provisions that may be incorporated into all qualified plans of an employer. If a plan is amended to incorporate these provisions, then the plan is deemed to have met the top-heavy plan requirements and is not required to be amended further to comply with the top-heavy provisions until the date that is 6 months after the issuance of the final regulations.

Under the conference agreement, if the Secretary fails to publish the required plan amendment provisions by January 1, 1985, then a plan is treated as meeting the top-heavy plan requirements if the plan is amended to incorporate such requirements by reference. In any case in which a plan is so amended and the plan does not specify the particular provisions that apply, the conferees intend that the employer is to be considered, in those situations in which more than one provision may apply, to have elected the provision that maximizes the vested, accrued benefits for each non-key employee. For example, if a plan is amended to incorporate the top-heavy plan requirements by reference and does not specify a vesting schedule, the plan is deemed to provide a vesting schedule that maximizes the vested, accrued benefits of each non-key employee. Thus, if a particular non-key employee separates from service after two years of service, the plan is considered to have incorporated the graduated vesting schedule with respect to that employee and the employee would have a 20-percent vested accrued benefit. On the other hand, if another non-key employee under the same plan has at least three years of service, the plan is considered to have incorporated the three-year, 100-percent vesting schedule with respect to that employee. Similarly, if an employer maintains a top-heavy group of plans and the plans are amended to incorporate the top-heavy plan requirements by reference without specifying the plan or plans under which the minimum benefits or minimum contributions are provided, then a non-key employee in any plan that is a required member of the group must be provided with the minimum contribution or benefit under each plan that is a required member in which the employee participates.

The conference agreement does not change the effective date of the top-heavy plan rules. In addition, the conferees intend that the issuance, as final regulations, of regulations similar to the proposed regulations under section 416 (published on March 15, 1983) will constitute the issuance of final regulations for purposes of this provision.

See also ¶ 12,050.065 for the Committee Report on P.L. 98-369, relating to the definition of key employee.

[¶ 12,500.10]

Committee Report on P.L. 97-248 (Tax Equity and Fiscal Responsibility Act of 1982)

The Committee Report on P.L. 97-248, Sec. 240(a), on top-heavy plans, is at ¶ 12,400.06.

[Code Sec. 417]

[¶ 12,550.07]

Committee Report on P.L. 109-280 (Pension Protection Act of 2006)

[Joint Committee on Taxation Report]

[Interest rate assumption for determination of lump-sum distributions]

The provision changes the interest rate and mortality table used in calculating the minimum value of certain optional forms of benefit, such as lump sums.[83]

Minimum value is calculated using the first, second, and third segment rates as applied under the funding rules, with certain adjustments, for the month before the date of distribution or such other time as prescribed by Treasury regulations. The adjusted first, second, and third segment rates are derived from a corporate bond yield curve prescribed by the Secretary of the Treasury for such month which reflects the yields on investment grade corporate bonds with varying maturities (rather than a 24-month average, as under the minimum funding rules). Thus, the interest rate that applies depends upon how many years in the future a participant's annuity payment will be made. Typically, a higher interest applies for payments made further out in the future.

A transition rule applies for distributions in 2008 through 2011. For distributions in 2008 through 2011, minimum lump-sum values are determined as the weighted average of two values: (1) the value of the lump sum determined under the methodology under present law (the "old" methodology); and (2) the value of the lump sum determined using the methodology applicable for 2008 and thereafter (the "new" methodology). For distributions in 2008, the weighting factor is 80 percent for the lump-sum value determined under the old methodology and 20 percent for the lump-sum determined under the new methodology. For distributions in 2009, the weighting factor is 60 percent for the lump-sum value determined under the old methodology and 40 percent for the lump-sum determined under the new methodology. For distributions in 2010, the weighting factor is 40 percent for the lump-sum value determined under the old methodology and 60 percent for the lump-sum determined under the new methodology. For distributions in 2011, the weighting factor is 20 percent for the lump-sum value determined under the old methodology and 80 percent for the lump-sum determined under the new methodology.

The mortality table that must be used for calculating lump sums under the bill is based on the mortality table required for minimum funding purposes under the bill, modified as appropriate by the Secretary of the Treasury. The Secretary is to prescribe gender-neutral tables for use in determining minimum lump sums.

Effective date

The provision is effective for plan years beginning after December 31, 2007.

[Requirement for additional survivor annuity option]

The provision revises the minimum survivor annuity requirements to require that, at the election of the participant, benefits will be paid in the form of a "qualified optional survivor annuity." A qualified optional survivor annuity means an annuity for the life of the participant with a survivor annuity for the life of the spouse which is equal to the applicable percentage of the amount of the annuity that is: (1) payable during the joint lives of the participant and the spouse; and (2) the actuarial equivalent of a single annuity for the life of the participant.

If the survivor annuity provided by the QJSA under the plan is less than 75 percent of the annuity payable during the joint lives of the participant and spouse, the applicable percentage is 75 percent. If the survivor annuity provided by the QJSA under the plan is greater than or equal to 75 percent of the annuity payable during the joint lives of the participant and spouse, the applicable percentage is 50 percent. Thus, for example, if the survivor annuity provided by the QJSA under the plan is 50 percent, the survivor annuity provided under the qualified optional survivor annuity must be 75 percent.

The written explanation required to be provided to participants explaining the terms and conditions of the qualified joint and survivor annuity must also include the terms and conditions of the qualified optional survivor annuity.

Under the provision of the bill relating to plan amendments, a plan amendment made pursuant to a provision of the bill generally will not violate the anticutback rule if certain requirements are met. Thus, a plan is not treated as having decreased the accrued benefit of a participant solely by reason of the adoption of a plan amendment pursuant to the provision requiring that the plan offer a qualified optional survivor annuity. The elimination of a subsidized QJSA is not protected by the anticutback provision in the bill unless an equivalent or greater subsidy is retained in one of the forms offered under the plan as amended. For example, if a plan that offers a subsidized 50 percent QJSA is amended to provide an unsubsidized 50 percent QJSA and an unsubsidized 75 percent joint and survivor annuity as its qualified optional survivor annuity, the replacement of the subsidized 50 percent QJSA with the unsubsidized 50 percent QJSA is not protected by the anticutback protection.

Effective date

The provision applies generally to plan years beginning after December 31, 2007. In the case of a plan maintained pursuant to one or more collective bargaining agreements, the provision applies to plan years beginning on or after the earlier of (1) the later of January 1, 2008, and the last date on which an applicable collective bargaining agreement terminates (without regard to extensions), and (2) January 1, 2009.

[Notice and consent period regarding distributions]

Under the provision, a qualified retirement plan is required to provide the applicable distribution notice no less than 30 days and no more than 180 days before the date distribution commences. The Secretary of the Treasury is directed to modify the applicable regulations to reflect the extension of the notice period to 180 days and to provide that the description of a participant's right, if any, to defer receipt of a distribution shall also describe the consequences of failing to defer such receipt.

Effective date

The provision and the modifications required to be made under the provision apply to years beginning after December 31, 2006. In the case of a description of the consequences of a participant's failure to defer receipt of a distribution that is made before the date 90 days after the date on which the Secretary of the Treasury makes modifications to the applicable regulations, the plan administrator is required to make a reasonable attempt to comply with the requirements of the provision.

[Benefit accrual standards]

For the Committee Report on P.L. 109-280 on cash balance and other hybrid plans, see ¶ 12,200.035.

[¶ 12,550.08]

Committee Report on P.L. 104-188 (Small Business Job Protection Act)

Miscellaneous Pension Simplification

[House Committee Report]

Waiver of minimum waiting period

The bill provides that the minimum period between the date the explanation of the qualified joint and survivor annuity is provided and the annuity starting date does not apply if it is waived by the participant and, if applicable, the participant's spouse. For example, if the participant has not elected to waive the qualified joint and survivor annuity, only the participant needs to waive the minimum waiting period.

Effective date

The provision is effective with respect to plan years beginning after December 31, 1996.

[Conference Committee Report]

The conference agreement codifies the provision in the temporary Treasury regulations which provides that a plan may permit a participant to elect (with any applicable spousal consent) a distribution with an annuity starting date before 30 days have elapsed since the explanation was provided, as long as the distribution commences more than seven days after the explanation was provided. The conference agreement also provides that a plan is permitted to provide the explanation after the annuity starting date if the distribution commences at least 30 days after such explanation was provided, subject to the same waiver of the 30-day minimum waiting period as described above. This is intended to allow retroactive payments of benefits which are attributable to the period before the explanation was provided.

---

[83] Under the provision of the bill relating to plan amendments, if certain requirements are met, a plan amendment to implement the changes made to the minimum value requirements may be made retroactively and without violating the anticutback rule.

[¶ 12,550.09]

Committee Report on P.L. 103-465 (General Agreement on Tariffs and Trade (GATT); Retirement Protection Act)

[House Committee Report]

Single sum distributions

a. Determination of present value.—Under the bill, present value for purposes of the cash-out rules must be no less than the present value determined by using the mortality table that is to be prescribed by the Secretary of the Treasury based upon the "prevailing commissioners' standard table" used to determine reserves for group annuity contracts issued on the date as of which present value is determined. The prevailing commissioners' standard table means, with respect to any contract, the most recent commissioners' standard tables prescribed by the National Association of Insurance Commissioners which are permitted to be used in computing reserves for that type of contract under the insurance laws of at least 26 States when the contract was issued (sec. 807(d)(5)(A) of the Code). Currently, the prevailing commissioners' standard table used to determine reserves for annuity contracts is the GAM 83 mortality table. Future changes in the prevailing table will only apply to the calculation of present value when the Secretary of the Treasury issues guidance making such changes applicable.

In addition, present value for purposes of the cash-out rules must be no less than the present value determined by using the annual rate of interest on 30-year Treasury securities for the month before the date of distribution or such earlier time as provided in Treasury regulations. The annual rate of interest on 30-year Treasury securities is the rate published by the Board of Governors of the Federal Reserve System.

A plan will not violate the prohibition on the reduction of accrued benefits merely because it calculates benefits in accordance with the provision.

Effective date

The provision is generally effective for plan years beginning after December 31, 1994, except that an employer can elect to treat the provision as being effective on or after the date of enactment [December 8, 1994].

Under a transition rule for distributions from plans in effect on the date of enactment [December 8, 1994] of the bill, until the earlier of the first plan year beginning after 1999 or the later of when a plan amendment applying the provision is adopted or made effective, the bill requires present value to be calculated as under present law, using the interest rate valuation methodology for lump-sum distributions under PBGC regulations in effect on September 1, 1993, the present-law Code and ERISA rules, and the current plan provisions (provided they are consistent with present law).

b. Limitation on maximum benefits.—The bill provides that the mortality table required to be used for purposes of adjusting any benefit or limitation in applying the limit on maximum benefits is to be prescribed by the Secretary of the Treasury based upon the "prevailing commissioners' standard table" used to determine reserves for group annuity contracts issued on the date as of which the adjustments described in this provision are made. The prevailing commissioners' standard table means, with respect to any contract, the most recent commissioners' standard tables prescribed by the National Association of Insurance Commissioners which are permitted to be used in computing reserves for that type of contract under the insurance laws of at least 26 States when the contract was issued (sec. 807(d)(5)(A) of the Code). Currently, the prevailing commissioners' standard table used to determine reserves for annuity contracts is the GAM 83 mortality table. Future changes in the prevailing table will only apply to the adjustments described in this provision when the Secretary of the Treasury issues guidance making such changes applicable. In addition, in adjusting benefits that are payable in a form other than a single life annuity, if the benefit is subject to the joint and survivor annuity rules, the interest rate is the same interest rate used to calculate benefits under those rules (as described above).

A plan will not violate the prohibition on reduction in accrued benefits merely because it calculates benefits in accordance with the provision.

Effective date

The provision is effective for limitation years beginning after December 31, 1994, except that an employer can elect to treat the provision as being defective on or after the date of enactment [December 8, 1994]. Benefits accrued as of the last day of the last plan year beginning before January 1, 1995, will not have to be reduced merely because of the provision. A plan does not have to be amended to comply with the provision until a date to be specified by the Secretary of the Treasury, provided the plan complies with the proposal in operation.

[¶ 12,550.095]

Committee Reports on P.L. 99-514 (Tax Reform Act of 1986)

[House Committee Report]

Notice requirements for participants of preretirement survivor annuity plans

The bill clarifies that the notice period in the case of a participant who separates from service before age 35 overrides any other period during which notice might be required. In such a case, the bill provides that the notification period is a reasonable period after separation without regard to any other required notice periods.

This provision is effective for distributions after the date of enactment of the bill.

[Senate Committee Report]

1. Coordination between qualified joint and survivor annuity and qualified preretirement survivor annuity

* * *

Explanation of Provision

In general

The bill clarifies and coordinates the application of the qualified joint and survivor annuity and qualified preretirement survivor annuity provisions in the case of (1) an individual who dies before or after the annuity starting date, and (2) an individual who receives a disability benefit under a plan.

Coordination of preretirement survivor annuity and joint and survivor annuity

The bill provides that the survivor benefit payable to a participant's spouse is to be provided in the form of a qualified joint and survivor annuity if the participant does not die before the annuity starting date unless the benefit is waived in favor of another benefit and the spouse consents to the waiver. As under present law, the qualified preretirement survivor annuity rules apply in the case of a death before the annuity starting date if the preretirement survivor annuity has not been waived.

Thus, if a participant dies after separation from service or attainment of normal retirement age, but prior to the participant's annuity starting date, the survivor benefit payable to the participant's spouse is to be paid in the form of a qualified preretirement survivor benefit.

Disability benefits

The bill amends the definition of a participant's annuity starting date to exclude the commencement of disability benefits, but only if the disability benefit is an auxiliary benefit. If a participant receiving a disability benefit will, upon attainment of early or normal retirement age, receive a benefit that satisfies the accrual and vesting rules of section 411 (without taking the disability benefit payments up to that date into account), the disability benefit may be characterized as auxiliary.

For example, consider a married participant who becomes disabled at age 45 with a deferred vested accrued benefit of $100 per month commencing at age 65 in the form of a joint and survivor annuity. If the participant is entitled under the plan to a disability benefit and is also entitled to a benefit of not less than $100 per month commencing at age 65, whether or not the participant is still disabled, the payments made to the participant between ages 45 and 65 would be considered auxiliary. Thus, the participant's annuity starting date would not occur until the participant attained age 65. The participant's surviving spouse would be entitled to receive a qualified preretirement survivor annuity if the participant died before age 65, and the survivor portion of a qualified joint and survivor annuity if the participant died after age 65. The value of the qualified preretirement survivor annuity payable upon the participant's death prior to age 65 would be computed by reference to the qualified joint and survivor annuity that would have been payable had the participant survived to age 65.

If, in the above example, the participant's benefit payable at age 65 were reduced to $90 per month as a result of the disability benefits paid to the participant prior to age 65, the disability benefit would not be auxiliary. The benefit of $90 per month payable at age 65 would not, without taking into account the disability benefit payments prior to age 65, satisfy the minimum vesting and accrual rules of section 411 of the Code. Accordingly, the first day of the first period for which the disability payments were made would constitute the participant's annuity starting date, and any benefits paid to the participant would be required to be paid in the form of a qualified joint and survivor annuity (unless waived by the participant with the consent of the spouse).

2. Transferee plan rules

Present Law

* * *

A plan is a transferee of a plan required to provide survivor benefits if the plan (1) receives a direct transfer of assets in connection with a merger, spinoff, or conversion of a plan that is subject to the survivor benefit requirements, or (2) receives a direct transfer of assets solely with respect to the participant. Also, a plan is a transferee plan with respect to a participant if it receives amounts from a plan that is a transferee plan with respect to that participant. A plan is not a transferee plan merely because it receives rollover contributions from another plan. The transferee plan rules do not apply in the case of a rollover contribution because the consent of the participant's spouse had to be obtained in order to make the plan distribution that qualified for rollover treatment.

Explanation of Provision

The bill includes two provisions relating to the transferee plan rules. First, the bill clarifies that a plan is not to be considered a transferee plan on account of a transfer completed before January 1, 1985.

In addition, the bill clarifies that the transferee plan rule is limited to benefits attributable to the transferred assets if separate accounting is provided for the transferred assets and the allocable investment yield from those assets. Under the bill, if separate accounting is not maintained for transferred assets (and any allocable investment yield) with respect to an employee, then the survivor benefit requirements apply to all benefits payable with respect to the employee under the plan.

3. Rules relating to qualified preretirement survivor annuity

* * *

Explanation of Provision

The bill clarifies that, in the case of a participant who separates from service prior to death, the amount of the qualified preretirement survivor annuity, is to be calculated by reference to the actual date of separation from service, rather than the date of death. Thus, for purposes of calculating the qualified preretirement survivor annuity, a participant is not to be considered to accrue benefits after the date of separation from service.

The bill also clarifies that, under the special rule for defined contribution plans, a qualified preretirement survivor annuity payable to a participant's surviving spouse is required to be the actuarial equivalent of not less than 50 percent of [the portion of the account balance of the participant to which the participant had a nonforfeitable right]. For purposes of determining who is a vested participant subject to the survivor benefit provisions, the bill provides that a participant's accrued benefit includes accrued benefits derived from employee contributions.

The bill also clarifies that a plan that is exempt from the survivor benefit [provisions] may provide for the payment of the participant's nonforfeitable accrued benefit (without the consent of the participant's surviving spouse) to a beneficiary other than the participant's spouse if the participant and spouse have been married for less than 1 year as of the death of the participant [or the participant's annuity starting date, whichever is the earliest].

The committee intends that, with respect to a defined benefit or defined contribution plan, the qualified preretirement survivor annuity is to be treated as attributable to employee contributions in the same proportion which the employee contributions are to the total accrued benefit of the participant. Thus, a plan is not permitted to allocate a preretirement survivor annuity only to employee contributions.

* * *

4. Spousal consent requirements

* * *

Explanation of Provision

Designation of nonspouse beneficiary

Under the bill, a spouse's consent to waive a qualified joint and survivor annuity or a qualified preretirement survivor annuity is not valid unless the consent (1) names a designated beneficiary who will receive any survivor benefits under the plan and the form of any benefits paid under the plan (including the form of benefits that the designated beneficiary will receive), or (2) acknowledges that the spouse has the right to limit consent only to a specific beneficiary or a specific form of benefits, and that the spouse voluntarily elects to reliquish one or both of such rights.

The spousal consent form is to contain such information as may be appropriate to disclose to the spouse the rights that are relinquished. If the consent names a designated beneficiary, then any subsequent change to the beneficiary designation (or the form of distribution, if any, specified in the consent) is invalid unless a new consent is obtained from the participant's spouse. Of course, spousal consent is not required if a participant dies and the beneficiary designated (with spousal consent) to receive the participant's death benefit elects to receive the benefit in a form not specified in the waiver.

If a plan is required to permit the waiver of a survivor benefit, the committee intends that the plan may not restrict the spouse's ability to waive a benefit by providing only a general consent to waive under which a spouse relinquishes the right to designate a beneficiary or a form of benefit. Thus, a spouse is always permitted to waive a survivor benefit only in favor of a specific beneficiary or a specific form of benefit. The committee intends that, if a plan permits a general consent, the acknowledgment of the general consent should indicate that the spouse is aware that a more limited consent could be provided.

Similar rules relating to the manner in which spousal consent is obtained apply to a spousal consent obtained to waive a death benefit under a profit-sharing or stock bonus plan that is not otherwise subject to the survivor benefit requirements.

Spousal consent with respect to loans

In addition, under the bill, in the case of a participant's benefit that is not exempt from the survivor benefit requirements, a plan is to provide that no portion of the accrued benefit of the participant may be used as security for any loan unless, at the time the security agreement is entered into, the participant's spouse (determined as of the date the security agreement is entered into) consents to the use of the accrued benefit as security. If the individual who is the participant's spouse at the time that the security agreement is entered into consents, then the plan is not prevented by the spousal consent rules from realizing its security interest in the event of a default on the participant's loan, even if, at the time of the default, the participant is married to a different spouse. Similarly, if a participant is not married at the time the security agreement is executed, then the plan is not prevented from realizing its security interest if a default on the loan subsequently occurs when the participant is married.

For example, assume that a spouse consents to a pledge of the participant's account balance as security for a loan from the plan. Under the plan, the plan administrator is to realize on the security for the loan if it is not repaid by the time the employee separates from service. Because the spouse consented to the loan, the plan is not prevented from using the security (i.e., the account balance) to recover the amount due on the loan. In addition, if the participant had remarried after the loan was made but before the plan realized on its security, then the consent of the first spouse would continue to be effective for purposes of determining the plan's ability to realize its security interest.

In the case of a participant whose accrued benefit is not subject to the survivor benefit provisions at the time the security is provided (e.g., a profit-sharing plan that is not a transferee plan with respect to the participant), the plan will not be treated as failing to meet the survivor benefit requirements if the participant's benefit is used as security for a loan and spousal consent is not obtained for the use of the accrued benefit as security, even if the plan subsequently becomes subject to the survivor benefit requirements with respect to the participant.

The bill further clarifies that for purposes of determining the survivor benefit, if any, to which a participant's surviving spouse is entitled upon the participant's death, any security interest held by the plan by reason of a loan outstanding to the participant is taken into account and, if there is a default on the loan, then the participant's nonforfeitable accrued benefit is first reduced by any security interest held by the plan by reason of a loan outstanding to the participant. The rule applies only if (a) the loan is secured by the participant's accrued benefit and (b) the spousal consent requirements, if any, applicable to the participant's accrued benefit at the time the security arrangement was entered into were satisfied. In addition, the participant's nonforfeitable accrued benefit is adjusted (where appropriate), taking into account the terms of the plan and the terms of the qualified domestic relations order, by the value of amounts payable under any outstanding qualified domestic relations order, for purposes of determining the survivor benefit, if any, to which the participant's surviving spouse is entitled upon the participant's death.

Similarly, upon a married participant's retirement, for purposes of determining the amount of the joint and survivor annuity payable to the participant and spouse, any security held by the plan by reason of a loan outstanding to the participant and the present value of any outstanding qualified domestic relations order are taken into account in the same manner as they are taken into account for purposes of the qualified preretirement survivor annuity.

Determination of amount of preretirement survivor annuity

The bill provides that, in the case of a defined contribution plan subject to the survivor benefit requirements, the participant's vested account balance (including any portion of the account balance attributable to employee contributions) is used for purposes of determining the amount of the qualified preretirement survivor annuity.

Scope of spousal consent requirements

The bill clarifies that certain of the election period and notice requirements with respect to spousal consent also apply in the case of spousal consent (1) to waive a survivor benefit under a plan exempt from the preretirement survivor annuity and joint and survivor annuity requirements, (2) to permit the participant's accrued benefit to be pledged as security for a loan, (3) to permit the election of a cash-out of amounts after the annuity starting date, and (4) to permit the immediate distribution of amounts in excess of $3,500.

In the case of a loan secured by a participant's accrued benefits, the notice and election period requirements apply at the time the security arrangement is entered into. Consequently, the election period for spousal consent with respect to the execution of a security agreement is the 90-day period before the execution of the agreement.

Similarly, in the case of a cash-out subsequent to a participant's annuity starting date, the election period is the 90-day period before the distribution is permitted.

The committee intends that, for purposes of the spousal consent rules, in the case of a participant residing outside of the United States, that spousal consent may be witnessed by the equivalent of a notary public in the jurisdiction in which consent is executed. The committee also intends that an election under section 242(b) of the Tax Equity and Fiscal Responsibility Act of 1982 will not be invalidated because a plan secures spousal consent to the election.

In addition, the committee intends that a participant will be treated as having no spouse, if the participant has been abandoned (within the meaning of local law) by the spouse, even if the participant knows where the spouse is located. The committee intends that the spousal consent requirement may be waived, however, only if the participant has a court order specifying that the participant has been abandoned within the meaning of local law. Of course, a participant could provide a qualified domestic relations [instrument] (such as a separation agreement) rather than a court order specifying that the participant has been abandoned.

Gift tax consequences of waiver

The bill provides that the waiver of a qualified joint and survivor annuity or a qualified preretirement survivor annuity by a nonparticipant spouse prior to the death of the participant does not result in a taxable transfer for purposes of the gift tax provisions.

Effective Dates

The provision relating to spousal consents to beneficiary designations is effective for consents given on or after January 1, 1985. [The provision relating to spousal consent to changes in benefit form is effective for plan years beginning after the date of enactment.] The provision relating to the notice and election period requirements for plans that are exempt from the survivor benefit requirements is effective upon the date of enactment.

The provision relating to accrued benefits pledged as security for a loan is effective for loans made after August 18, 1985. In addition, any accrued benefits pledged as security for a loan prior to August 19, 1985, are exempt from the requirement that spousal consent be obtained. Accordingly, in the case of a pledge made before August 19, 1985, a plan is not required to obtain the consent of any spouse of a participant before it applies the benefit against the loan. Finally, any loan that is revised, extended, renewed, or renegotiated after August 18, 1985, is treated as a loan made (and security pledged) after August 18, 1985.

[Conference Committee Report]

* * * The provision relating to spousal consent to changes in benefit form is effective for plan years beginning after the date of enactment.

[Senate Committee Report]

5. Notice requirement

* * *

Explanation of Provision

The bill provides that the period during which notice is required to be provided to an individual does not end before the latest of (1) the close of the plan year in which a participant attains age 35; (2) a reasonable period of time after the individual becomes a plan participant; (3) a reasonable period of time after the survivor benefit applicable to a participant is no longer subsidized (as defined in Code sec. 417(a)(4)); or (4) a reasonable period of time after the survivor benefit provisions (Code sec. 401(a)(11)) become applicable with respect to a participant.

The bill also provides that if a participant separates from service prior to age 35, the plan must provide the participant with notice, within a reasonable time after separation from service, of the right to decline a qualified preretirement survivor annuity.

6. Clarification of rule for subsidized benefits

Present Law

Under REA, a plan is not required to provide notice of the right to waive the qualified joint and survivor annuity or the qualified preretirement survivor annuity if the plan fully subsidizes the cost of the benefit. A plan fully subsidizes the cost of a benefit only if the failure to waive the benefit by a plan participant does not result in either (1) a decrease in any plan benefits with respect to the participant, or (2) in increased plan contributions by the participant.

Explanation of Provision

The bill clarifies that a plan is not required to provide a participant with a right to waive a qualified joint and survivor annuity or qualified preretirement survivor annuity if the plan fully subsidizes the cost of the benefit.

The bill further clarifies that the present-law exception to the notice requirement only applies if (1) the plan fully subsidizes the benefit, and (2) the plan does not permit a participant to waive the benefit or to designate * * * another beneficiary.

The committee intends that a benefit is not to be considered fully subsidized if the cost of the survivor benefit is spread among all plan participants, including participants who are not married, or among some subgroup of participants, even if the benefits and contributions of those charged with the cost of survivor benefit protection are unaffected by the waiver or failure to waive survivor benefit protection. Of course, if a participant is not entitled to waive a survivor benefit, the participant cannot be charged for the benefit.

7. Clarification of annuity starting date

* * *

Explanation of Provision

Under the bill, the definition of the annuity starting date is amended to provide that, in the case of a benefit not payable in the form of an annuity, the annuity starting date is the date on which [all events have occurred which entitle the participant to a benefit]. [Where benefits are payable as a joint and survivor annuity, the starting date is the first day of the first period for which an amount is payable as an annuity, regardless of when or whether payment is actually made.]

[Conference Committee Report]

* * *

* * * Under the conference agreement, in the case of benefits payable in the form of an annuity, the annuity starting date is the first day of the first period for which an amount is payable as an annuity, regardless of when or whether payment is actually made. For example, a participant is to begin receiving annuity payments on the first day of the month following the participant's sixtieth birthday. After that date, but before any annuity payments are actually made, the participant dies. The annuity starting date is the first day of the month following the participant's sixtieth birthday.

Under the conference agreement, in the case of benefits not payable as an annuity, the annuity starting date is the date on which all events have occurred which entitle the participant to a benefit (e.g., separation from service, applicable consent to payment).

* * *

[Senate Committee Report]

Transitional Rules

* * *

Explanation of Provision

The bill clarifies the application of the transitional rule relating to qualified preretirement survivor benefits in situations in which the participant had designated a beneficiary other than the participant's spouse. Under the bill, the present value of a death benefit payable to any beneficiary with respect to an individual who (1) performs at least one hour of service under the plan on or after August 23, 1984, (2) dies before the annuity starting date, and (3) dies before the effective date of the Act, may be reduced by the present value of the amount payable to the participant's surviving spouse pursuant to the transition rule. If death benefits payable under a plan are divided among more than one beneficiary, the present value of the amount payable to each beneficiary (including benefits, other than survivor benefits payable under the transition rules, payable to the surviving spouse) is reduced proportionately by the amount payable to the surviving spouse pursuant to the transition rule.

However, the bill also permits the surviving spouse to waive the right to receive the qualified preretirement survivor annuity. Under the bill, if it is made on or before the close of the second plan year to which the Act applies, then the waiver is not to be treated as a taxable transfer for purposes of the gift tax or as a prohibited assignment or alienation for purposes of ERISA or the Code. In addition, death benefits waived by the surviving spouse during this period would not be includible in the spouse's income. Such benefits would be includible in the gross income of the recipient.

Finally, the bill clarifies that in the case of a plan that was amended, as of the effective date of REA, to be exempt from the REA survivor benefit requirements, but that (1) was not technically exempt from the survivor benefit requirements during the transition rule period and that (2) failed to satisfy the REA transition rules solely because with respect to a participant who died during the transition period, the plan paid to the surviving spouse the participant's entire vested account balance in a form other than a life annuity, the plan will not be treated as failing to satisfy the survivor benefit requirements of REA.

[Conference Committee Report]

The conference agreement follows the Senate amendment * * *

[¶ 12,550.10]

Committee Report on P.L. 98-397 (Retirement Equity Act of 1984)

[Senate Committee Report]

In general.—Under the bill, a pension plan is to provide automatic survivor benefits (1) in the case of a participant who retires under the plan, in the form of a qualified joint and survivor annuity, and (2) in the case of a vested participant who dies before the annuity starting date (the first period for which an amount is received as an annuity (whether by reason of death or disability) under the plan) and who has a surviving spouse, in the form of a qualified preretirement survivor annuity. A vested participant is any participant (whether or not still employed by the employer) who has a nonforfeitable right to any portion of the accrued benefit derived from employer contributions.

The provisions of the bill requiring automatic survivor benefits apply to any pension plan. An exception is provided, however, for a participant under a profit-sharing or stock bonus plan if (1) the plan provides that the nonforfeitable accrued benefits will be paid to the surviving spouse of the participant (or to another beneficiary if the surviving spouse consents or if there is no surviving spouse) if the participant dies, (2) under a plan that offers a life annuity, the participant does not elect payment of benefits in the form of a life annuity, and (3) with respect to the participant, the plan is not a direct or indirect transferee of a plan required to provide automatic survivor benefits. A plan is a transferee of a plan required to provide automatic survivor benefits if the plan (1) receives a direct transfer of assets in connection with a merger, spinoff or conversion of a plan or (2) receives a direct transfer of assets solely with respect to the participant. Also, a plan is a transferee if it receives amounts from a plan that is a transferee. As under present law, the cost of survivor benefit coverage may be imposed on the participant or beneficiary.

Under the bill, an exception to the application of the rules relating to joint and survivor benefits is provided in the case of certain employee stock ownership plans (ESOPs) for the portion of an employee's accrued benefit that is subject to the requirements of section 409(h) of the Code. This exception applies only if the requirements applicable to profit-sharing and stock bonus plans are also met.

Qualified joint and survivor annuity and qualified preretirement survivor annuity.—Under the bill, a qualified joint and survivor annuity is an annuity for the life of the participant with a survivor annuity for the life of the spouse that is not less than 50 percent (and not greater than 100 percent) of the amount that is (1) payable during the joint lives of the participant and the spouse, and (2) the actuarial equivalent of a single life annuity for the life of the participant. A qualified joint and survivor annuity also includes an annuity having the effect of a qualified joint and survivor annuity, which is defined as a benefit at least the actuarial equivalent of the normal form of life annuity or, if greater, any optional form of life annuity. Equivalence may be determined on the basis of consistently applied reasonable actuarial factors if such determination does not result in discrimination in favor of employees who are officers, shareholders, or highly compensated.

The bill defines a qualified preretirement survivor annuity as an annuity for the life of the surviving spouse of the participant. The amount of the payments under a qualified preretirement survivor annuity is not to be less than the payments that would have been made under the qualified joint and survivor annuity if (1) in the case of a participant who dies after attaining the earliest retirement age under the plan, the participant had retired with an immediate qualified joint and survivor annuity on the day before the participant's death, and (2) in the case of a participant who dies on or before the earliest retirement age under the plan, the participant had separated from service on the date of death, survived until the earliest retirement age, and retired at that time with a qualified joint and survivor annuity. In the case of a defined contribution plan, the payments under a qualified preretirement survivor annuity are not to be less than the payments under a single life annuity, the present value of which is at least equal to 50 percent of the participant's account balance on the date of death. Under the bill, the plan is not to prohibit the commencement of the qualified preretirement survivor annuity to the surviving spouse later than the month in which the participant would have reached the earliest retirement age under the plan. If the surviving spouse wishes to delay commencement of benefit payments until a later date and the present value of the benefit is more than $3,500 at the earliest retirement date, then the plan cannot require that benefit payments commence at the participant's earliest retirement age. Of course, the incidental benefit rule of present law is required to be satisfied with respect to the preretirement survivor benefit.

Election and notice procedures.—Under the bill, a participant is to be given the opportunity to waive the qualified joint and survivor annuity and qualified preretirement survivor annuity during the applicable election period. In addition, the participant is permitted to revoke any waiver during the applicable election period. The bill does not limit the number of times a participant may waive a survivor benefit or revoke a waiver.

The bill provides that the consent of a participant's spouse is required for an election to decline the qualified joint and survivor annuity and the qualified preretirement survivor annuity. This consent is to be given in writing at the time of the participant's election, and the consent is to acknowledge the effect of the election. A consent is not valid unless it is witnessed by a plan representative or a notary public. Any consent obtained is effective only with respect to the spouse who signs it.

The requirement that the consent of the spouse be obtained may be waived if it is established to the satisfaction of a plan representative that the consent required cannot be obtained because there is no spouse, because the spouse cannot be located, or because of other circumstances that the Secretary of the Treasury prescribes by regulation.

If the plan administrator acts in accordance with the fiduciary standards of ERISA in securing spousal consent or in accepting the representations of the participant that the spouse's consent cannot be obtained, then the plan will not be liable for payments to the surviving spouse. For example, if the plan administrator receives a notarized spousal consent, valid on its face, which the administrator has no reason to believe is invalid, the plan would certainly be allowed to rely on the consent even if it is, in fact, invalid. In addition, if a third-party payor relies on a consent obtained or determination made by the plan administrator who acts in accordance with the fiduciary standards, or if a third party payor acting in accordance with such standards (whether or not the payor is a plan fiduciary under ERISA) establishes that consent cannot be obtained, then the payor will be relieved of any liability for payments to the surviving spouse.

As under present law, the plan is required to provide to the participant, within a reasonable period of time before the annuity starting date, a written explanation of (1) the terms and conditions of the qualified joint and survivor annuity, (2) the participant's right to make, and the effect of, an election to waive the qualified joint and survivor annuity, (3) the rights of the participant's spouse, and (4) the right to revoke an election and the effect of such a revocation. In addition, the committee intends that plans will provide to participants notification of their rights to decline a qualified preretirement survivor annuity period before the applicable election period. This notice is to be provided within the period beginning on the first day of the plan year in which the participant attains age 32 and ending with the close of the plan year in which the participant attains age 35. This notice is to be comparable to the notice required with respect to the qualified joint and survivor annuity. Of course, the preretirement survivor benefit coverage may become automatic prior to the time that the participant is entitled to decline such coverage.

Under the bill, a plan is not required to provide notice of the right to waive the qualified joint and survivor annuity or the qualified preretirement survivor annuity if the plan fully subsidizes the cost of the benefit. A plan fully subsidizes the costs of a benefit only if the failure to waive the benefit by a plan participant does not result in either (1) a decrease in any plan benefits with respect to the participant, or (2) in increased plan contributions by the participant. A plan that provides for no employee contributions and does not require employee contributions if the participant does not waive any survivor benefits is treated as not requiring increased plan contributions by the participant. A plan may fully subsidize the cost of the qualified joint and survivor annuity, the qualified preretirement survivor annuity, or both.

The bill defines the applicable election period to mean (1) in the case of a qualified joint and survivor annuity, a period of time not exceeding 90 days before the annuity starting date or (2) in the case of a qualified preretirement survivor annuity, a period beginning on the first day of the plan year in which the participant attains age 35 and ending on the date of the participant's death. If a participant separates from service, the applicable election period begins on that date with respect to benefits accrued before the separation from service. For example, if a participant who is age 30 separates from service with vested, accrued benefits of $4,000, the participant is permitted to waive the qualified preretirement survivor annuity with respect to the benefits of $4,000 at the time of separation from service. If the participant returns to service at age 32, the applicable election period with respect to benefits accrued after the participant returns does not begin until the first day of the plan year in which the participant attains age 35. Thus, the participant will have automatic survivor coverage during the period from age 32 to 35 with respect to the vested benefits accrued during that period, without regard to whether the participant waived the coverage with respect to the pre-separation accrued benefits. At age 35, the participant may waive any preretirement survivor annuity coverage. Of course, a waiver made by a participant or by a participant and spouse is not valid with respect to a future spouse.

Special rules.—The bill provides that a qualified joint and survivor annuity is not required to be provided by a plan unless the participant and spouse have been married throughout the one-year period ending on the earlier of (1) the participant's annuity starting date (the first day of the first period for which an amount is received as an annuity (whether by reason of retirement or disability)), or (2) the date of the participant's death. If a participant dies after the annuity starting date, the spouse to whom the participant was married during the one-year period ending on the annuity starting date is entitled to the survivor annuity under the plan whether or not the participant and spouse are married on the date of the participant's death. This rule does not apply, however if a qualified domestic relations order * * * [¶ 206 below] otherwise provides for the division or payment of the participant's retirement benefits. For example, a qualified domestic relations order could provide that the former spouse is not entitled to any survivor benefits under the plan.

Under the bill, an exception to the one-year marriage requirement is provided if a participant marries within one year before the annuity starting date and the participant has been married to that spouse for at least one year ending on the date of the participant's death. The committee recognizes that this exception may create administrative burdens for a plan in cases in which the participant has not been married for one year before the payment of benefits commence. The committee intends that the plan may require a participant to notify the plan when the participant has been married for one year so that the plan administrator may alter the form of benefit payments to reflect the qualified joint and survivor annuity if the participant and spouse do no waive it.

If a former spouse of a participant is entitled to receive a portion of the participant's benefit under a qualified domestic relations order, the qualified joint and survivor annuity and qualified preretirement survivor annuity requirements do no apply unless they are consistent with the order. A plan is not required to provide a qualified joint and survivor annuity or a qualified preretirement survivor annuity to the spouse of a participant's former spouse.

The bill provides that a plan may immediately distribute the present value of the benefit under either the qualified joint and survivor annuity or the qualified preretirement survivor annuity if the present value of the benefit does not exceed $3,500. No distribution may be made after the annuity starting date unless the participant and the participant's spouse (or the surviving spouse of the participant) consent in writing to the distribution.

In addition, under the bill, if the present value of the benefit under the qualified joint and survivor annuity or the qualified preretirement survivor annuity exceeds $3,500, the participant and spouse (or the surviving spouse if the participant has died) must consent in writing before the plan can immediately distribute the present value. For purposes of calculating the present value of a benefit as of the date of the distribution, the plan is required to use an interest rate no greater than the rate used by the Pension Benefit Guaranty Corporation (PBGC) in valuing a lump sum distribution upon plan termination. The committee intends that the PBGC rate in effect at the beginning of a plan year may be used throughout the plan year if the plan so provides.

The bill repeals the two-year nonaccidental death rule of present law. Thus, a plan may not provide that any election or revocation of an election does not take effect if (1) the participant dies within a period not in excess of two years beginning on the date of the election or revocation, and (2) the death of the participant is not due to an accident that occurred after the election or revocation.

Consultation with the Secretary of Labor.—Under the bill, the Secretary of the Treasury is required to consult with the Secretary of Labor in prescribing regulations under these provisions.

[Code Sec. 418]

[¶ 12,600.10]

Committee Report on P.L. 96-364 (Multiemployer Pension Plan Amendments Act of 1980)

The Senate Committee Report on P.L. 96-364 (Sec. 202(a)) is at ¶ 15,706.10.

[Code Sec. 418A]

[¶ 12,650.10]

Committee Report on P.L. 96-364 (Multiemployer Pension Plan Amendments Act of 1980)

The Senate Committee Report on P.L. 96-364 (Sec. 202(a)) is at ¶ 15,708.10.

[Code Sec. 418B]

[¶ 12,700.10]

Committee Report on P.L. 96-364 (Multiemployer Pension Plan Amendments Act of 1980)

The Senate Committee Report on P.L. 96-364 (Sec. 202(a)) is at ¶ 15,709.10.

[Code Sec. 418C]

[¶ 12,750.10]

Committee Report on P.L. 96-364 (Multiemployer Pension Plan Amendments Act of 1980)

The Senate Committee Report on P.L. 96-364 (Sec. 202(a)) is at ¶ 15,710.10.

[Code Sec. 418D]

[¶ 12,800.10]

Committee Report on P.L. 96-364 (Multiemployer Pension Plan Amendments Act of 1980)

The Senate Committee Report on P.L. 96-364 (Sec. 202(a)) and the House Ways and Means Committee Report on P.L. 96-364 (Sec. 202(a)) are at ¶ 15,712.10.

[Code Sec. 418E]

[¶ 12,850.09]

Committee Report on P.L. 109-280 (Pension Protection Act of 2006)

[Joint Committee on Taxation Report]

The provision modifies the requirements for anticipating future insolvencies of plans in reorganization status. Under the provision, unless the plan sponsor determines that the value of plan assets exceeds three times the total amount of benefit payments, the plan sponsor must determine whether the plan will be insolvent for any of the next five plan years, rather than three plan years as under present law. If the plan sponsor makes a determination that the plan will be insolvent for any of the next five plan years, the plan sponsor must make the comparison of plan assets and benefit payments under the plan at least annually until the plan sponsor makes a determination that the plan will not be insolvent in any of the next five plan years.

Effective Date

The provision is effective with respect to determinations made in plan years beginning after 2007.

[¶ 12,850.10]

Committee Report on P.L. 96-364 (Multiemployer Pension Plan Amendments Act of 1980)

The Senate Committee Report on P.L.96-364 (Sec. 202(a)) is at ¶ 15,713.10.

[Code Sec. 419]

[¶ 12,900.095]

Committee Reports on P.L. 99-514 (Tax Reform Act of 1986)

[House Committee Report]

Funded Welfare Benefit Plans * * *

Under the Act, the amount of the deduction otherwise allowable to an employer for a contribution to a welfare benefit fund for any taxable year is not to exceed the qualified cost of the fund for the year. The Act defines the qualified cost of a welfare benefit fund for a year as the sum of (1) the qualified direct cost of the fund for the year and (2) the addition (within limits) to reserves under the fund for the year (the qualified asset account), reduced by the after-tax income of the fund. The deduction limits do not apply to a 10-or-more employer plan.

a. Definition of fund

Explanation of Provision

The bill amends the definition of a "fund" to exclude amounts held under three different types of insurance arrangements: (1) an insurance contract described at Code sec. 264(a)1); (2) certain "qualified nonguaranteed contracts"; and (3) certain "guaranteed renewal contracts."

First, under the bill, the term "fund" would exclude amounts held by an insurance company pursuant to a life insurance policy on the life of an officer, employee, or person financially interested in the trade or business of the employer, where the employer is the direct or indirect beneficiary of the policy; these are amounts otherwise subject to sec. 264.

The bill also modifies the term "fund" to exclude amounts held by an insurance company under certain "qualified nonguaranteed insurance contracts." [A qualified nonguaranteed, insurance contract is discussed in the Conference Committee Report.] Thus, under the bill, amounts that are held by an insurance company for an employer generally are not to be treated as a fund to the extent that the amounts are subject to a significant current risk of economic loss that is determined, in part, by factors other than the amount of welfare benefits paid to (or on behalf of) the employees of the employer.

In addition, the bill provides that even an arrangement that satisfies the foregoing description will not be excluded from treatment as a fund, unless the amount of any experience rated refund or policy dividend payable with respect to a policy year is treated by the employer as paid or accrued in the taxable year in which the policy year ends. If the actual amount of the refund or dividend is not known by the due date of the employer's tax return for the year, Treasury regulations could permit the use of a reasonable estimate of the amount of such refund or dividend. In addition, Treasury regulations could require insurance companies to submit information (including proprietary information of the insurance company) relating to the basis for the calculation of experience-rated refunds and policy dividends.

To the extent that the general rules for the exclusion of amounts held by an insurance company are satisfied, amounts held by an insurance company for a reasonable premium stabilization reserve for an employer are not treated as a fund. Thus, a premium stabilization reserve, if limited to a reasonable amount, such as 20 percent of premiums for the year, would not be treated as a fund to the extent that (1) such amounts are subject to a significant current risk of economic loss, and (2) experience rated refunds and policy dividends payable by the reserve with respect to a policy year are treated by the employer as paid or accrued in the taxable year in which the policy year ends.

Solely for purposes of these provisions, the amounts released from a premium stabilization reserve to purchase current insurance coverage are to be treated as experience-rated refunds or policy dividends. Thus, the amounts released from the premium stabilization reserve in a given policy year are to be treated by the employer as paid or accrued in the taxable year in which such policy year ends.

Whether amounts are subject to a significant current risk of loss depends upon the facts and circumstances. For example, if an employer does not have a guaranteed right under an insurance contract to policy dividends based solely on the employer's experience but the insurance company has, in practice, consistently paid such dividends based solely on the employer's experience, it is anticipated that Treasury regulations would provide that the amounts held under the contract constitute a fund because they are not subject to a significant current economic risk of loss.

Finally, the bill clarifies that the definition of a "fund" excludes amounts held by an insurance company pursuant to certain "guaranteed renewal contracts," under which, the employer's right to renew the contract is guaranteed, but the level of premiums is not.

[Conference Committee Report]

Welfare benefit plan provisions

The conference agreement follows the Senate amendment with the following exceptions:

a. *Definition of fund.*—The conference agreement follows the House bill with the following modifications:

The conference agreement also modifies the exclusion from the term "fund" for amounts held by an insurance company under certain "qualified, nonguaranteed insurance contracts." A qualified, nonguaranteed insurance contract is defined as an insurance contract (including a reasonable premium stabilization reserve) under which (1) there is not a guarantee of a renewal of the contract at guaranteed premium rates, and (2) other than current insurance protection, the only payments to which the employer or employees are entitled under the contract are refunds or policy dividends that are not guaranteed, that are experience rated and that are determined by factors other than the amount of welfare benefits paid to (or on behalf of) the employees of the employer or their beneficiaries.

Thus, under the conference agreement, amounts that are held by an insurance company for an employer generally are not to be treated as a fund to the extent that the amounts are subject to a significant current risk of economic loss that is determined, in part, by factors other than the amount of welfare benefits paid to (or on behalf of) the employees of the employer. Experience refunds or policy dividends are determined by additional factors where they reflect a charge for pooling of large individual claims, where the insurance company's retention reflects a risk charge related to the insurer's actual or anticipated experience under the class of business to which the contract belongs, or where the claims experience of other policyholders is otherwise taken into account. For example, an additional factor is present where the experience refund or policy dividend is based on the experience of a single employer together with a risk charge that is intended to assess the employer for an appropriate share of the insurance company's anticipated losses under policies where claims and expenses exceed premiums collected. The conferees do not intend, however, that a de minimis risk charge on its own will be sufficient to create a significant risk of economic loss.

The conferees emphasize that, in prescribing regulations relating to the definition of a fund, the Treasury Department is to take into account that the principal purpose of the provision is to prevent employers from taking premature deductions for expenses that have not yet been incurred. To the extent that the temporary and proposed regulations could be interpreted to include in the definition of a fund certain experience-rated insurance arrangements with a significant current risk of economic loss, the conferees do not believe that the regulations implemented this purpose. The conferees believe that significant premature deductions do not occur with respect to experience-rated group insurance because of the element of insurance risk transferred to the insurance company. Thus, by excluding qualified nonguaranteed insurance contracts from the definition of a fund, the conference agreement makes clear that typical group insurance arrangements are not to be made subject to the welfare benefit fund provisions through regulations. In addition, the conferees reiterate that any regulations defining the term "fund" should take into account that the principal purpose of the provision is to prevent premature deductions by employers.

* * *

[Senate Committee Report]

b. Coordination of post-retirement medical benefits with limits on contributions under qualified plans

Present Law

Under the provisions of DEFRA relating to the coordination of net contributions for post-retirement medical benefits with the overall limits on contributions and benefits under qualified pension plans and certain other funded plans deferring compensation (secs. 415(c) and (e)), any amount allocated to a separate account for a key employee is treated as an annual addition to a defined contribution plan. Under the overall limits, the annual addition with respect to an employee under all defined contribution plans of an employer for a year is not to exceed the lesser of $30,000 or 25 percent of compensation.

* * *

Explanation of Provision

The bill provides that the amount treated as an annual addition under the rules for coordinating the post-retirement medical benefits with the overall limits on qualified plans is not subject to the 25-percent-of-compensation limit usually applicable to annual additions. For example, assume the compensation of an employee is $100,000 for a year and $5,000 is treated as an annual addition under the limits for the employee under the rules for post-retirement medical benefits under a qualified plan. Assume further that the employee's annual addition for the year under a qualified defined contribution plan, without regard to the post-retirement medical benefit, is $25,000 (a contribution equal to the maximum percentage of compensation limit). Under the bill, the total annual addition for post-retirement medical benefits does not cause the annual addition to exceed the 25-percent limit on annual additions even though the annual addition would exceed that limit if the amount added for post-retirement medical benefits were taken into account. The annual addition of $30,000 would, however, be subject to the separate dollar limit of section 415(c) for the year and, if the employer also maintains a defined benefit plan for the employee, the full annual addition of $30,000 would be taken into account in determining whether the combined plan limits of section 415(e) are satisfied.

The effect of this rule also is to permit the funding of post-retirement medical benefits on behalf of a key employee during periods when the employee has no compensation from the employer (e.g., after retirement).

c. Separate accounting required for certain amounts

* * *

Explanation of Provision

The bill clarifies the requirement for separate accounting with respect to post-retirement medical benefits and post-retirement life insurance benefits. Under the bill, the requirement does not apply until the first taxable year for which a reserve is computed using the special provisions applicable to these benefits (or assets of a fund held before the effective date are allocated to a separate account). The separate account requirement applies for that first year and for all subsequent taxable years.

d. Reserves for discriminatory post-retirement benefits disregarded

* * *

Explanation of Provision

The bill provides that no reserve generally may be taken into account in determining the account limit for a welfare benefit fund for post-retirement medical benefits or life insurance benefits (including death benefits) unless the plan meets the nondiscrimination requirements with respect to those benefits (sec. 505(b)), whether or not those nondiscrimination requirements apply in determining the tax-exempt status of the fund. The bar against taking post-retirement medical benefits and life insurance benefits into account in determining the account limit does not apply, under the bill, in the case of benefits provided pursuant to a collective bargaining agreement between one or more employee representatives and one or more employers if the Secretary of the Treasury finds that the agreement is a collective bargaining agreement and that post-retirement medical benefits or post-retirement life insurance benefits (as the case may be) were the subject of good faith bargaining between the employee representatives and the employer or employers.

The bill clarifies that certain post-retirement group-term life insurance benefits that fail to satisfy the nondiscrimination requirements of Code section 505(b) may, nevertheless, be taken into account in determining the account limit to the extent that the group-term life insurance benefits are provided under an arrangement with respect to individuals grandfathered under section 223 of the Act.

e. Account limit for life insurance benefits

* * *

Explanation of Provision

The bill clarifies that life insurance benefits are not to be taken into account in determining the account limit under a welfare benefit fund to the extent that the aggregate amount of such benefits to be provided with respect to an employee exceeds $50,000. Accordingly, under the bill, the $50,000 limit applies with respect to the aggregate of self-insured and insured life insurance benefits under all funds maintained by the employer. The bill does not change the rules of DEFRA under which certain post-retirement life insurance benefits in excess of $50,000 may be taken into account in determining the account limit for certain individuals under plans in existence on Janaury 1, 1984 (Act sec. 223(d)(2)).

f. Actuarial certification

Present Law

* * *

Unless there is an actuarial certification with respect to benefits other than (1) post-retirement medical benefits or post-retirement life insurance benefits or (2) supplemental unemployment compensation (SUB) or severance pay benefits, the account limit for a welfare benefit fund is not to exceed certain safe-harbor limits.

* * *

Explanation of Provision

The bill provides that the requirement for an actuarial certification also applies to post-retirement medical benefits and post-retirement life insurance benefits, unless a safe harbor computation is used.

The committee clarifies the application of the account limit rules to short-term disability. Because of a disability that is expected to last more than 5 months, but less than 12 months, is not treated as a long-term disability, the committee intends that the legislative history of DEFRA will not prohibit the funding of up to 12 months of benefit payments for short-term disabilities that are expected to last more than 5 months.

g. Aggregation of funds

* * *

Explanation of Provision

The bill provides that, in computing the dollar limits applicable to the amount of reserves for disability benefits, post-retirement medical benefits, and post-retirement life insurance benefits for which reserves may be accumulated for any participant, all welfare benefit funds of an employer are treated as a single fund.

In the absence of Treasury regulations to the contrary, the limit is allocated proportionately to the amount of the death benefit in each plan.

h. Transition rules

* * *

Explanation of Provision

The bill provides that, under the transition rules for existing excess reserves, the amount of existing excess reserves for any year is the excess (if any) of (1) the amount of assets set aside at the close of the first taxable year ending after July 18, 1984, to provide disability benefits, medical benefits, SUB or severance pay benefits, or life insurance benefits, over (2) the account limit (without regard of the transition rules) for the taxable year for which the excess is being computed. The bill further provides that the transition rule allowing an increase in the account limit because of existing excess reserves applies only to a welfare benefit fund which, on July 18, 1984, had assets set aside to provide the enumerated benefits.

Accordingly, in the case of an employer that maintains a funded plan which had assets set aside to provide disability benefits, medical benefits, SUB or severance pay benefits, or life insurance benefits on July 18, 1984, and to which the deduction limits first apply for the taxable year beginning January 1, 1986, the increase in the account limit for 1986 attributable to existing excess reserves is 80 percent of the excess, if any, of the amount of assets set aside at the close of 1984 (the first taxable year ending after July 18, 1984) over the account limit determined under the general rules for 1986. For 1987, however, the increase attributable to existing excess reserves is 60 percent of the excess, if any, of the amount of assets set aside at the close of 1984 over the account limit determined for 1987.

i. Tax on unrelated business income

* * *

Explanation of Provision

The bill makes it clear that the tax on unrelated business income applies in the case of a 10-or-more employer plan. Under the bill, the account limit is to be determined as if the rules limiting deductions for employer contributions applied.

In addition, the bill provides that the transition rule for pre-existing reserves for post-retirement medical and life insurance benefits applies to the greater of the amount of assets set aside as of (1) July 18, 1984, or (2) the close of the last plan year ending before July 18, 1984, rather than only to assets set aside as of the end of the plan year ending before July 18, 1984.

The bill deletes the provision of the Code barring a set aside for certain assets used in the provision of permissible benefits (facilities). Treasury regulations are to provide that facilities used to provide permissible benefits are disregarded in determining whether fund assets exceed the account limit for a qualified asset account.

In addition, the bill provides that if any amount is included in the gross income of an employer for a taxable year as deemed unrelated income with respect to a welfare benefit fund, then the amount of the income tax imposed on the deemed unrelated income is to be treated as a contribution paid by the employer to the fund on the last day of the taxable year and, thus, is deductible, subject to the limits on deductions for fund contributions. The tax attributable to the deemed unrelated income is to be treated as if it were imposed on the fund for purposes of determining the after-tax income of the fund.

j. Tax on disqualified benefits provided under funded welfare benefit plans

Present Law

Under DEFRA, if a welfare benefit fund (other than an arrangement funded exclusively by employee contributions) provides a disqualified benefit during a taxable year, then an excise tax is imposed for that year on each employer who maintains the fund. The tax is equal to 100 percent of the disqualified benefit.

* * *

Explanation of Provision

With respect to benefits required to be paid from a separate account, the bill defines the term "disqualified benefit" to mean any post-retirement medical benefit or post-retirement life insurance benefit provided with respect to a key employee if a separate account is required to be established for the employee and the payment is not from such an account. Accordingly, pre-retirement benefits would not be considered to be disqualified benefits under the bill merely because they are paid to a key employee from a source other than a separate account.

In addition, under the bill, a post-retirement medical benefit or post-retirement life insurance benefit provided by a fund with respect to an individual in whose favor discrimination is prohibited is a disqualified benefit unless the plan meets the nondiscrimination requirements of DEFRA with respect to the benefit (sec. 505(b)), whether or not the nondiscrimination requirements apply in determining the tax-exempt status of the fund from which the benefit is provided.

Under the bill, if a plan is not exempt from the nondiscrimination rules under the rules for collectively bargained plans, a discriminatory benefit is a disqualified benefit subject to the excise tax even though no discrimination test applies for purposes of determining the exempt status of the fund from which the benefit is provided. A benefit is not subject to the nondiscrimination requirements if it is provided under a plan maintained pursuant to a collective bargaining agreement between one or more employee representatives and one or more employers if the Secretary of the Treasury finds that the agreement is a collective bargaining agreement and that post-retirement medical benefits or post-retirement life insurance benefits (as the case may be) were the subject of good faith bargaining between the employee representatives and the employer or employers.

Further, under the bill, a payment that reverts to the benefit of an employer is not a disqualified benefit to the extent it is attributable to an employer contribution with respect to which no deduction is allowable in the current or any preceding taxable year or to an employee contribution. As under current law, the excise tax on disqualified benefits is inapplicable to welfare benefit contributions funded solely by employees. A reduction is to be made to the amount treated as a carryover (sec. 419(d)) to the extent that any nondeducted contribution reverts to the benefit of an employer. Any amounts reverting to the benefit of an employer are treated as coming first out of nondeducted contributions for purposes of this rule.

Also, the bill provides that a benefit that would otherwise be a disqualified benefit because it does not meet the separate-account rule or because it is discriminatory is not a disqualified benefit if it is a post-retirement benefit that is charged against an existing reserve (or against any income properly allocable to an existing excess reserve) for post-retirement medical or post-retirement life insurance benefits as provided under the transition rules of DEFRA (sec. 512(a)(3)) applicable to the unrelated business income tax.

k. Application of account limits to collectively bargained plans

* * *

Explanation of Provision

The bill permanently exempts collectively bargained VEBAs from the account limits applicable to welfare benefit funds without regard to any Treasury regulations providing special account limits for such funds. Thus, employer contributions to such VEBAs are deductible and earnings on assets of such VEBAs are tax exempt.

l. Application of account limits to welfare benefit plans funded solely with employee contributions

* * *

Explanation of Provision

The bill exempts certain VEBAs funded solely with employee contributions from the account limits applicable to welfare benefit funds. This exemption is available only if (1) the VEBA covers at least 50 employees, and (2) other than current insurance protection, the only amounts payable to employees as experience-rated refunds or policy dividends are not guaranteed and are determined by factors other than the amount of welfare benefits paid to (or on behalf of) the employee or the employee's beneficiaries, the administrative expenses of providing such benefits, or the investment experience of such employee contributions (and earnings thereto). Thus, in order for the exemption to apply, the amounts contributed by an employee are required to be subject to a significant risk of current economic loss.

[Conference Committee Report]

Employee pay-all VEBAs.—The Senate amendment exempts certain employee pay-all VEBAs with at least 50 employees from the welfare benefit fund provisions if the amount of any refund or rebate to an employee is determined by factors other than the employee's experience. Under the conference agreement, an employee pay-all VEBA is not considered to fail to qualify for this exemption merely because an employee's refund or rebate may vary depending upon the number of years the employee contributed to the fund. For example, if a VEBA provides a set employee contribution rate that applies for 3 years, the mere fact that an employee who contributes for 3 years may receive a larger refund or rebate than an employee who contributes for less than 3 years does not cause the fund to fail to meet the requirements for exemption as long as there is a significant current risk of economic loss (i.e., the amount of the refund or rebate is also determined by factors other than any employee's experience).

[Senate Committee Report]

* * *

2. Treatment of Deferred Compensation Arrangements and Deferred Benefits

a. Transition rule for certain taxpayers with fully vested vacation pay plans

Present Law

Under present law, any plan, method, or arrangement providing for deferred benefits for employees, their spouses, or their dependents is treated as a plan deferring the receipt of compensation (deferred benefit plan). DEFRA provided that a deferred benefit plan includes an extended vacation pay plan, i.e., a plan under which employees gradually, over a period of years, earn the right to additional vacation that cannot be taken until the end of the period. Similarly, a vacation pay plan under which employees can delay the vacation (and also the income inclusion) beyond the current taxable year is a deferred benefit plan. However, any vacation benefit to which an election applies under section 463 (relating to accrual of vacation pay) is not considered a deferred benefit.

The provision of DEFRA was effective for amounts paid or incurred after July 18, 1984, in taxable years ending after that date.

Explanation of Provision

The bill provides a transition rule in the case of a fully vested vacation pay plan in which payments are required within one year after the accrual of the vacation (and are, in fact, paid). If the taxpayer makes an election under section 463 for the taxpayer's first taxable year ending after July 18, 1984, then, in lieu of establishing a suspense account under section 463, the election is treated as a change in the taxpayer's method of accounting and the adjustments required under section 481 are taken into account.

Under the bill, the time for making a section 463 election is extended to six months after the date of enactment in the case of a taxpayer otherwise eligible for the transition rule.

[Conference Committee Report]

Accrued vacation pay.—The transition rule for accrued vacation pay applies in the case of a fully vested vacation pay plan under which the vacation pay is expected to be paid (or is in fact paid) within 12 months following the close of the employer's taxable year.

[Senate Committee Report]

b. Clarification of the scope of the deduction-timing rules applicable to deferred compensation arrangements

* * *

The bill clarifies that the deduction-timing rules for deferred compensation arrangements apply to any plan or method of deferring compensation regardless of the section under which the amounts might otherwise be deductible and that the amounts shall be deductible under section 404(a)(5) and shall not otherwise be deductible under any other section. This clarification is necessary to prevent taxpayers from asserting that deferred compensation is attributable to capitalizable compensation expenses and, thereby, accelerate the timing of the deduction for such deferred compensation. Further, this clarification conforms the treatment of deferred compensation with the treatment of losses, expenses, and interest with respect to transactions between related taxpayers (as amended by DEFRA).

[Conference Committee Report]

Unfunded deferred compensation.—The provision in the Senate amendment clarifying that the deductibility of deferred compensation is governed by section 404 if the amounts would, but for section 404, otherwise be deductible under any other provision is modified to apply also for purposes of determining the deductibility of foreign deferred compensation (sec. 404A) and for purposes of the welfare benefit fund provisions.

[¶ 12,900.10]

Committee Reports on P.L. 98-369 (Tax Reform Act of 1984)

[House Committee Report]

Explanation of Provision

In general

The bill provides additional rules for determining the timing and the amount of an employer's deduction for a contribution to a funded welfare benefit plan. Under the bill, a contribution which is otherwise deductible under the Code will be deductible only to the extent that it does not exceed the qualified cost of the plan for the taxable year. The limitation also applies to contributions with respect to independent contractors.

Under the bill, if an employer pays or accrues[1] a contribution to a funded welfare benefit plan during a taxable year, and the usual requirements for deductibility are met,[2] the contribution will be deductible for the taxable year in which paid to the extent that it does not exceed the qualified cost of the plan for the year.[3] The bill provides that the qualified cost of a funded welfare benefit plan for a year is generally the sum of (1) the qualified direct cost of the plan for the year, and (2) the reasonable addition to the qualified asset account maintained by the fund for the year. Under the bill, the qualified cost is reduced by the after-tax income of the fund for the year.

In the case of a sale of property by an employer to a welfare benefit fund for less than fair market value, the excess of fair market value over the selling price is treated as an employer contribution to the plan. Of course, this rule does not change present law with respect to the disallowance of deductions for losses on transactions between related parties (sec. 267).

Qualified direct cost

The bill provides that the qualified direct cost for any taxable year of the employer is the aggregate amount which would have been allowable as a deduction to a cash method taxpayer with respect to benefits provided during the taxable year if that taxpayer had provided the benefits directly on a current basis. This may include properly allocable administrative costs and insurance premiums as well as direct benefit costs. For example, in the case of a self-insured medical reimbursement plan, the qualified direct cost equals the actual benefit payments made to employees for the taxable year, plus a properly allocable share of the administrative costs of providing such benefits.

With respect to the ownership by the fund of recovery property, the qualified direct cost for a year is the deduction that would have been allowed to the employer under sec. 168 for that property for the year if the employer had owned the recovery property. Thus, in the year of a contribution of recovery property by an employer to a fund under a plan, the contribution would be treated as a sale of the property in that year (as under present law) and, if the property is placed in service that year, the employer would be allowed only the deduction with respect to the first year the property is placed in service under the usual rules for determining deductions for recovery property.[4]

Other rules that generally limit deductions are also "passed through" under the bill to limit deductions with respect to fund contributions. Thus, if an employer contributes amounts that the fund uses for the purchase of land used for an employee recreational facility, no deduction is allowed with respect to this contribution because sec. 263 would not have allowed a deduction if the employer had purchased the land directly. Similarly, other expenses of the fund (such as maintenance expenses) with respect to this facility would be qualified direct costs giving rise to employer deductions only if the requirements of sec. 274 are satisfied. As a further example, fund expenditures for insurance that would not have been deductible under sec. 264 if made directly by the employer are not qualified direct costs and, thus, no deductions are available to the employer with respect to such expenditures.

Under the bill, for the purpose of determining the qualified direct cost, a benefit is to be treated as provided when the benefit would be includible in the gross income of the employee (or would be includible in the employee's gross income but for a provision of the Code).[5]

* * *

After-tax income

The bill provides that the qualified cost for a taxable year under a funded welfare benefit plan is to be reduced by the fund's after-tax income for the year. Under the bill, the after-tax income of a fund for a taxable year is the gross income of the fund, reduced by deductions directly connected with the production of that gross income for the year and by the income tax (if any) imposed on the fund for the year. In determining the gross income of a fund, contributions and other amounts received from employees (dues, fees, etc.) are to be taken into account as income but employer contributions are not to be taken into account. Accordingly, employee contributions, etc., will reduce an employer's qualified cost of a plan for a year. The bill provides that no item is to be taken into account more than once in determining the qualified cost for a year.

Carryovers

The bill provides for carryovers of excess contributions from years in which contributions exceed the qualified costs to subsequent years. Under the bill, if the amount contributed (or deemed contributed under the carryover rule) to a funded welfare benefit plan by an employer during a taxable year exceeds the qualified cost of the plan for the year, but is otherwise deductible, then the excess is to be treated as an amount paid by the employer under the plan in the succeeding taxable year. Amounts contributed before the effective date and not previously deducted would be deductible under the rules of present law.

Funded welfare benefit plan

Generally, a plan is a funded welfare benefit plan if it provides welfare benefits to employees (or their beneficiaries) and the plan includes a fund.[6] The bill

[1] If the taxpayer has elected to deduct accrued vacation pay under section 463, the deduction would be limited to the amount properly accrued under that section for a contribution to the fund providing the vacation pay.

[2] Secs. 162 and 212. Of course, in determining whether compensation is reasonable compensation under sec. 162, welfare benefits provided by the employer are taken into account as compensation.

[3] The amount would be deductible for the employer's taxable year in which (or with which) the plan year ends.

[4] Sec. 115 of the bill also extends the rules of the Code relating to sales of property between related parties (sec. 1239) to certain exempt organizations.

[5] For example, if an employer contributes to a fund to pay premiums or considerations for insurance under a plan, then the qualified direct cost for the year would be determined on the basis of the cost of the insurance for the period for which the coverage is provided, without regard to whether any part of that cost is excludable from the gross income of an employee. On the other hand, to the extent the liability is self-insured, the time at which benefits would be included would be based on the time at which benefits are paid, rather than the time of current insurance coverage, because this is the time when the benefits would be included if the self-insured benefits were provided directly by the employer on an unfunded basis.

[6] The bill defines the term "fund" for this purpose as (1) any organization described in paragraph (7), (9), (17), or (20) of section 501(c) (a social club, a voluntary employee beneficiary's association, a supplemental

provides, however, that a plan of deferred compensation is not a funded welfare benefit plan.[7] In addition, the bill provides that a plan is not a funded welfare benefit plan to the extent the special rules for transfers of property in connection with services apply in determining the timing or amount of the employer's deduction.[8] The bill provides that if there is no plan, but a method or arrangement or employer contributions or benefits which has the effect of a plan, the rules of the bill are to apply as if there were a plan. In addition, under the bill, if any plan would be a funded welfare plan (including, of course, a method, etc., having the effect of a plan) but for the fact that there is no employee-employer relationship, then the bill is to apply as if there were such a plan.

Aggregation rules

In applying the rules of the bill relating to funded welfare benefit plans, all funds under all welfare benefit plans of an employer are to be treated as a single fund, and all employees who are treated as employed by a single employer under the rules relating to qualified pension plans[9] are to be treated as employed by a single employer. In addition, as under the rules for qualifed pension plans, an individual is to be considered an employee of an employer if the individual is a common-law employee or if the individual is a leased employee.

* * *

[Conference Committee Report]

a. Contributions to funded welfare benefit plans

The conference agreement generally follows the House bill, with modifications. In general, deductions for contributions to a welfare benefit fund are limited to qualified costs, which is the sum of (i) qualified direct costs, and (ii) additions, within limits, to a qualified asset account. Several changes are made to the definitions of qualified direct cost and welfare benefit and substantial modifications are made to the allowable limit on a qualified asset account.

Child care facilities.—Under the conference agreement, in determining qualified direct costs with respect to a child care facility held by a fund, the adjusted basis of the facility is treated as deductible ratably over a period of 60 months. A child care facility is tangible property of a character subject to depreciation and located in the United States, and must be child care center primarily for children of the employees of the employer. As under the House bill, qualified direct costs with respect to other capital expenditures are those which wold be allowed under the usual Code rules which would be applied if the employer owned the asset.

Definition of welfare benefit fund.—In general, this section of the bill applies to contributions to welfare benefit funds which are organizations, reserves or accounts held by organizations, through which an employer provides welfare benefits to employees or their beneficiaries. In prescribing regulations relating to the definition of the term "fund," the conferees wish to emphasize that the principal purpose of this provision of the bill is to prevent employers from taking premature deductions, for expenses which have not yet been incurred, by interposing an intermediry organization which holds assets which are used to provide benefits to the employees of the employer. Thus, a retired life reserve or premium stabilization account ordinarily is to be considered a fund or part of a fund, since such an account is maintained for an individual employer and that employer has a determinable right to have the amount in such an account applied against that employer's future costs of benefit claims or insurance premiums. A similar situation exists with respect to premium arrangements, under which an employer may, in some case, pay an insurance company more in a year than the benefit costs incurred in that year and the employer has an unconditional right in a later year to a refund or credit of the excess of payments over benefit costs. In contrast, an ordinary disability income policy under which an employer pays a premium so that employees who become disabled in that year may collect benefit payments for the duration of disability is not a fund, since the employer has no right to recover any part of the premium payment and the future benefit payments to an employee whose disability occurs during the period for which the premium is paid is not contingent on any further payments by the employer. While in many cases welfare benefit funds are designed to function in a manner similar to insurance arrangements, the conference is concerned that there are no clear standards or limitations applicable to such funds that prevent their utilization for substantial nonqualified deferred compensation funding outside the general pension plan funding, accrual and vesting rules.

Limitations on qualifed asset account.—The conference agreement includes substantial modifications to the provisions setting forth the limitation on additions to a qualified asset account. Such an account consists of assets set aside for the payment of disability benefits, medical benefits, supplemental unemployment or severance pay benefits, and life insurance or death benefits.

In general, the account limit is the amount estimated to be necessary under actuarial assumptions that are reasonable in the aggregate, to fund the liabilities of the plan for the amount of claims incurred but unpaid, for benefits described in the previous paragraph and administrative costs of such benefits, as of the close of the taxable year. Claims are incurred only when an event entitling the employee to benefits, such as a medical expense, a separation, a disability, or a death actually occurs. The allowable reserve includes amounts or claims estimated to have been incurred but which have not yet been reported, as well as those claims which have been reported but have not yet been paid. An example of an incurred but unpaid claim is the occurrence of the death of an employee during the year under a plan that provides for payments to a survivor of the employee for the survivor's remaining life. Under the conference agreement, the qualified asset account may include the estimated present value of the future stream of benefits payable to this survivor, using reasonable assumptions as to earnings of the fund and mortality experience.

With respect to disability benefits, the conferees expect that Treasury regulations will provide more specific guidance as to the time at which claims are incurred. It is the intention of the conferees that a disability is to be defined as any serious physical or mental impairment which causes an inability to perform a substantial portion of the duties of an individual's ordinary employment. The conferees intend that funding of claims with respect to an indefinite period of time is to be allowed only in connection with disabilities which are determined to be long-term disabilities. Such disabilities are those which (1) a medical evaluation determines is expected to last for more than 12 months and (2) has persisted for at least 5 months. With respect to such disabilities, current deductions are to be allowed for contributions necessary to fund the expected future stream of benefit payments using reasonable assumptions as to morbidity, mortality, and fund earnings. Other disabilities which have persisted for at least 2 weeks are to be considered short-term disabilities; no more than 5 months of benefit payments may be deemed to have been incurred with respect to short-term disabilities.

In general, in addition to requiring that actuarial assumptions are to be reasonable in the aggregate, Treasury regulations may prescribe specific interest rate and mortality assumptions to be used in all actuarial calculations. Such assumptions are to be consistent with requirements provided elsewhere in conference agreement for the computation of tax reserves held by life insurance companies.

Limitation on disability, or SUB, or severance benefits taken into account.—In the case of any disability benefit, a reserve may not be establised with respect to a benefit payment in excess of the lesser of the limit for the year on an annual benefit under a qualified defined benefit pension plan ($90,000 for 1984) or 75 percent of a disabled employee's annual compensation from the employer.

With respect to supplemental unemployment compensation benefits (SUB) and severance pay benefits the portion of an annual benefit in excess of 1.5 times the limit on contributions under a qualified defined contribution plan ($45,000 for 1984) for any employee is not to be taken into account in determining the limit.

Prefunding of life insurance, death benefits, or medical benefits for retirees.—The qualified asset account limits allowed amounts reasonably necessary to accumulate reserves under a welfare benefit plan so that the medical benefit or life insurance (including death benefit) payable to a retired employee during retirement is fully funded upon retirement. These amounts may be accumulated no more rapidly than on a level basis over the working life of the employee, with the employer of each employee. Each year's computation of contributions with respect to retiree medical benefits is limited to the use of assumptions that the medical benefits provided to retirees in the future will have the same cost as medical benefits currently provided to retirees (projected inflation is not to be taken into account). Of course, no advance deduction is to be allowed with regard to a plan which provided medical or life insurance benefits exclusively for retireees, since such a plan would be considered a deferred compensation plan subject to the rules of section 404 rather than the provision applicable to funded welfare benefit plans. The conferees intend that the Treasury Department prescribe rules requiring that the funding of retiree benefits be based on reasonable and consistently applied actuarial cost methods, which take into account experince gains and losses, changes in assumptions, and other similar items, and be no more rapid than on a level basis over the remaining working lifetimes of the current participants (reduced on the basis of reasonable turnover and mortality assumptions).

Further, contributions for any employee who is a key employee are required to be accounted for separately by a welfare benefit fund. The seperate account is to include amounts contributed to the plan with respect to any service after the employee becomes a key employee as well as a reasonable allocation (determined under Treasury regulations) of amounts contributed to the fund on account of the employee before key employee status was attained. Medical and life insurance benefits with respect to such an employee may be only from such account. In addition, in the case of a key employee, the conference agreement provides that post-retirement medical benefits are to be taken into account in applying the limitations on contributions and benefits under qualified plans (sec. 415) under principles similar to those applicable to post-retirement medical benefits provided by qualified pension plans.

(Footnote Continued)

unemploymet benefit trust, or a qualified group legal organization) or (2) any corporation, trust, or other organization that is not exempt from income tax. Such an organization includes a retired lives reserve account maintained by an insurance company. Further, if an employer contributes amounts to an insurance company for benefits that are purely experience-rated (i.e., the employer is entitled to an automatic rebate if the amount paid exceeds benefit claims and is liable if the benefit claims exceed the amount paid), such contributions are considered to have been made to a welfare benefit fund. On the other hand, employer contributions to a separate bank account of the employer or to a subsidiary or other related party would not be considered contributions to a fund.

[7] Section 404 provides deduction rules for domestic plans of deferred compensation. Sec. 404A provides rules for foreign plans of deferred compensation. The bill also provides rules for the treatment of unfunded deferred benefits provided under a plan. Accordingly, except for current, unfunded compensation and current, unfunded benefits, no deduction is to be allowed under sec. 162 or 212 with respect to compensation or benefits except as provided under subchapter D of the Code.

[8] See section 83(h).

[9] Sec. 414(b), (c), and (m).

In addition, under the conference agreement, if the life insurance or medical coverage provided by a plan discriminates in favor of employees who are officers, shareholders, or highly compensated, then the limit on the qualified asset account may not take account of contributions to provide such coverage.

Finally, the amount of life insurance or death benefit that may be taken into account with respect to prefunding of retiree benefits of any employee is not to exceed the amount of the insurance that may be provided to the employee tax-free under section 79. This amount generally is limited to $50,000 but the $50,000 limit may not apply in the case of certain grandfathered employees defined by amendments to section 79 elsewhere in the conference agreement.

SUB and severance pay reserve.—The conference agreement provides an additional reserve for SUB and severance pay benefits equal to 75 percent of the sum of (a) the average annual qualified direct cost of such benefits provided and (b) the administrative costs, during any 2 of the immediately preceding 7 years. Such benefits may include medical or other benefit payable to severed or unemployed workers. The agreement also authorizes Treasury regulations under which an interim limit is to be provided in the case of a new SUB or severance pay plan. The interim reserve is not available, under the agreement, in the case of a plan that provides SUB or severance benefits for any employee who is a key employee.

Safe-harbor.—The conference agreement provides that an actuarial certification by a qualifed actuary (determined under Treasury regulations) justifying the taxpayer's reserve computations is not necessary if the amount in the qualified asset account is below a prescribed safe harbor, equal to the sum of separate safe harbor amounts computed with respect to each benefit. For short-term disability benefits, the safe harbor amount is 17.5 percent of benefit costs plus administrative costs in the prior taxable year; for medical benefits, the safe harbor amount is 35 percent of prior year medical benefits and allocable administrative costs. For SUB or severance benefits, the safe harbor amount is the additional reserve described above. Safe harbor amounts for long-term disability, life insurance and retiree medical benefits may be prescribed by Treasury regulations. For any safe harbor limitation based on prior plan costs, insurance premiums may not be taken into account, because the conferees do not intend that a fund is to be used as a vehicle for prepayment of insurance premiums for current benefits. Even if the safe harbors are satisfied, the taxpayer is to show that the reserves, as allowed under the general standards provided by the bill (e.g., claims incurred but unpaid) are reasonable.

Certain collectively bargained plans.—By July 1, 1985, the Treasury Department is to publish final regulations establishing special reserve limit principles with respect to welfare benefit funds maintained pursuant to an agreement that the Secretary of Labor finds to be a collective bargaining agreement between employee representatives and one or more employers, if there is evidence of good faith bargaining over the benefits provided by the plan between the employee representatives and the employer (or employers).

In establishing these limits, the Treasury is to presume that reserves in such plans are not excessive because of the arm's-length negotiations between adversary parties inherent in the collective bargaining process. Because contributions under such plans are often made on the basis of a defined contribution fixed over a multiyear period on the basis of economic assumptions which prove to be incorrect and because such contributions may be the only source of benefits to be provided during layoffs, strikes, lockouts, and economic recession, these special limits are to allow substantial flexibility in determining the application of these provisions with respect to such plans.

Transitional rule.—Under the conference agreement, in the case of a plan that was in existence on June 22, 1984, special rules are provided for the determination of the limit for each of the first four years to which the provision applies. In particular, the agreement provides that for the first year, the limit for the year is to be the sum of (1) the limit determined without regard to the transitional rule, and (2) 80 percent of the excess reserve amount. The excess reserve amount for any year is the excess of the reserve as of the end of the first plan year ending after the date of enactment over the limit determined without regard to the transitional rule. For the second, third, and fourth succeeding years, 60, 40, and 20 percent, respectively, of the excess reserve amount for such years is to be added to the limit determined under the usual rules.

Elective aggregation.—Under the conference agreement, an employer may elect to aggregate plans and funds in applying the deduction limits and the rules prohibiting discrimination in favor of certain employees. The agreement provides, however, that the election to aggregate must be consistent for deduction and discrimination purposes. For example, if an employer elects to aggregate 2 plans for deduction purposes, those 2 plans must be aggregated for discrimination purposes.

10 or more employer plans.—For a plan year in which no employer (or employers related to an employer) are [is] required to contribute more than 10 percent of the total contributions, the conference agreement provides that the deduction limits do not apply. The exclusion is provided because under such a plan, the relationship of a participating employer to the plan often is similar to the relationship of an insured to an insurer. The agreement authorizes Treasury regulation under which the percentage may be increased in appropriate cases. For example, a higher percentage could be appropriate in the case of a plan maintained by employers in the construction industry if unusual building activity in the geographic area covered by the plan causes temporary and unusual distortions in the contribution pattern under the plan.

The agreement provides, however, that notwithstanding compliance with the 10-percent rule, and consistent with the discussion above on definition of a fund, a plan is not exempt from the deduction limits if the liability of any employer who maintains the plan is determined on the basis of experience rating because the employer's interest with respect to such a plan is more similar to the relationship of an employer to a fund than an insured to an insurer.

Effective date

These provisions generally apply to contributions paid or accrued after December 31, 1985. However, in the case of a plan maintained under a collective bargaining contract in effect on July 1, 1985, or ratified before that date, the provisions do not apply until the termination of the contract, determined without regard to any contract extension agreed to after that date.

In addition, these provisions apply to any contribution of a facility to a welfare benefit fund after June 22, 1984, so that deductions with respect to this contribution are to be determined under usual Code rules applicable to recovery of the cost of assets (but taking account of the special rule for child care facilities described above). Further, these rules apply to other contributions, such as cash, made after that date which are to be used to acquire a facility, so that later acquisition of [a] facility with the use of such funds will limit the deduction for the original contribution. This rules does not apply for any facility acquired under a binding contract in effect on and at all times after that date or any facility under construction on June 22, 1984.

* * *

The agreement also provides for a tax on an employer who maintains a welfare benefit fund that is not exempt from income tax. Under the agreement, in the case of any welfare benefit fund, such as a retired life reserve account, that is not exempt from income tax as a social club, VEBA, SUB, or GLSO, the employer who maintains the fund is to include in gross income for the taxable year an amount equal to the deemed unrelated income of the fund. The agreement provides that deemed unrelated income of such a welfare benefit fund is the amount that would be unrelated business taxable income of the fund if it were a tax exempt social club, VEBA, SUB, or GLSO. In determining deemed unrelated income, at the election of the employer, 2 or more nonexempt welfare benefit funds of the employer may be treated as a single fund. Also, under the rules relating to deemed unrelated income, the aggregation rules applicable to qualified pension plans are to apply.

This provision is effective under the same rules applicable to the provisions relating to deductions for plan contributions.

[Code Sec. 419A]

[¶ 12,950.09]

Committee Report on P.L. 109-280 (Pension Protection Act of 2006)

The bill allows deductions for contributions to fund a reserve for medical benefits (other than retiree medical benefits) for future years provided through a bona fide association as defined in section 2791(d)(3) of the Public Health Service Act. In such case, the account limit may include a reserve not to exceed 35 percent of the sum of (1) qualified direct costs, and (2) the change in claims incurred, but unpaid for such taxable year with respect to medical benefits (other than post-retirement medical benefits).

Effective date

The provision is effective for taxable years ending after December 31, 2006.

[¶ 12,950.10]

Committee Reports on P.L. 98-369 (Tax Reform Act of 1984)

For the Committee Reports on P.L. 98-369, relating to contributions to funded welfare benefit plans, see ¶ 12,900.10.

[Code Sec. 420]

[¶ 13,030.06]

Committee Report on P.L. 109-280 (Pension Protection Act of 2006)

[Joint Committee on Taxation Report]

[Ability to use excess pension assets for future retiree health benefits and collectively bargained retiree health benefits]

In general

If certain requirements are satisfied, the bill permits transfers of excess pension assets under a single-employer plan to retiree medical accounts to fund the expected cost of retiree medical benefits for the current and future years (a "qualified future transfer") and also allows such transfers in the case of benefits provided under a collective bargaining agreement (a "collectively bargained transfer"). Transfers must be made for at least a two-year period. An employer can elect to make a qualified future transfer or a collectively bargained transfer rather than a qualified transfer. A qualified future transfer or collectively bargained transfer must meet the requirements applicable to qualified transfers, except that the provision modifies the rules relating to (1) the determination of excess pension assets; (2) the limitation on the amount transferred; and (3) the minimum cost requirement. Additional requirements apply in the case of collectively bargained transfer.

The general sunset applicable to qualified transfer applies (i.e., transfers can be made only before January 1, 2014).

Rule applicable to qualified future transfers and collectively bargained transfers

Qualified future transfers and collectively bargained transfers can be made to the extent that plan assets exceed the greater of (1) accrued liability, or (2) 120 percent of current liability.[190] The provision requires that, during the transfer period, the plan's funded status must be maintained at the minimum level required to make transfers. If the minimum level is not maintained, the employer must make contributions to the plan to meet the minimum level or an amount required to meet the minimum level must be transferred from the health benefits account. The transfer period is the period not to exceed a total of ten consecutive taxable years beginning with the taxable year of the transfer. As previously discussed, the period must be not less than two consecutive years.

A limit applies on the amount that can be transferred. In the case of a qualified future transfer, the amount of excess pension assets that may be transferred is limited to the sum of (1) the amount that is reasonably estimated to be the amount the employer will pay out of the account during the taxable year of the transfer for current retiree health liabilities, and (2) the sum of the qualified current retiree health liabilities which the plan reasonably estimates, in accordance with guidance issued by the Secretary, will be incurred for each additional year in the transfer period. The amount that can be transferred under a collectively bargained transfer cannot exceed the amount which is reasonably estimated, in accordance with the provisions of the collective bargaining agreement and generally accepted accounting principles, to be the amount the employer maintaining the plan will pay out of such account during the collectively bargained cost maintenance period for collectively bargained retiree health liabilities.

The provision also modifies the minimum cost requirement which requires retiree medical benefits to be maintained at a certain level. In the case of a qualified future transfer, the minimum cost requirement will be satisfied if, during the transfer period and the four subsequent years, the annual average amount of employer costs is not less than applicable employer cost determined with respect to the transfer. An employer may elect to meet this minimum cost requirement by meeting the requirements as in effect before the amendments made by section 535 of the Tax Relief Extension Act of 1999 for each year during the transfer period and the four subsequent years. In the case of a collectively bargained transfer, the minimum cost requirements is satisfied if each collectively bargained group health plan under which collectively bargained health benefits are provided provides that the collectively bargained employer cost for each table year during the collectively bargained cost maintenance period is not less than the amount specified by the collective bargaining agreement. The collectively bargained employer cost is the average cost per covered individual of providing collectively bargained retiree health benefits as determined in accordance with the applicable collective bargaining agreement. Thus, retiree medical benefits must be provided at the level determined under the collective bargaining agreement for the shorter of (1) the remaining lifetime of each covered retiree (and any covered spouse and dependent), or (2) the period of coverage provided under the collectively bargained health plan for such covered retiree (and any covered spouse and dependent).

Additional requirements for collectively bargained transfers

As previously discussed, the bill imposes certain additional requirements in the case of a collectively bargained transfer. Collectively bargained transfers can be made only if (1) for the employer's taxable year ending in 2005, medical benefits are provided to retirees (and spouses and dependents) under all the employer's benefit plans, and (2) the aggregate cost of benefits for such year is at least five percent of the employer's gross receipts. The provision also applies to successors of such employers. Before a collectively bargained transfer, the employer must designate in writing to each employee organization that is a party to the collective bargaining agreement that the transfer is a collectively bargained transfer.

Collectively bargained retiree health liabilities means the present value, as of the beginning of a taxable year and determined in accordance with the applicable collective bargaining agreement, of all collectively bargained health benefits (including administrative expenses) for such taxable year and all subsequent taxable years during the collectively bargained cost maintenance period (with the exclusion of certain key employees) reduced by the value of assets in all health benefits accounts or welfare benefit funds set aside to pay for the collectively bargained retiree health liabilities. Collectively bargained health benefits are health benefits or coverage provided to retired employees who, immediately before the collectively bargained transfer, are entitled to receive such benefits upon retirement and who are entitled to pension benefits under the plan (and their spouses and dependents). If specified by the provisions of the collective bargaining agreement, collectively bargained health benefits also include active employees who, following their retirement, are entitled to receive such benefits and who are entitled to pension benefits under the plan (and their spouse and dependents).

Assets transferred in a collectively bargained transfer can be used to pay collectively bargained retiree health liabilities (other than liabilities of certain key employees not taken into account) for the taxable year of the transfer and for any subsequent taxable year during the collectively bargained cost maintenance period. The collectively bargained cost maintenance period (with respect to a retiree) is the shorter of (1) the remaining lifetime of the covered retiree (and any covered spouse and dependents) or (2) the period of coverage provided by the collectively bargained health plan with respect to such covered retiree (and any covered spouse and dependents).

The limit on deductions in the case of certain amounts paid for qualified current retiree health liabilities other than from the health benefits account does not apply in the case of a collectively bargained transfer.

An employer may contribute additional amounts to a health benefits account or welfare benefit fund with respect to collectively bargained health liabilities for which transferred assets are required to be used. The deductibility of such contributions are subject to the limits that otherwise apply to a welfare benefit fund under a collective bargaining agreements without regard to whether such contributions are made to a health benefits account or a welfare benefit fund and without regard to the limits on deductions for contributions to qualified retirement plans (under Code section 404). The Secretary of the Treasury is directed to provide rules to prevent duplicate deductions for the same contributions or for duplicate contributions to fund the same benefits.

Effective date

The provision is effective for transfers after the date of enactment.

[Transfer of excess pension assets to multiemployer health plans]

The bill allows qualified transfers of excess defined benefit plan assets to be made by multiemployer defined benefit plans.

Effective date

The provision is effective for transfer made in taxable years beginning after December 31, 2006.

[¶ 13,030.07]

Committee Report on P.L. 108-218 (Pension Funding Equity Act of 2004)

Present Law

Defined benefit plan assets generally may not revert to an employer prior to termination of the plan and satisfaction of all plan liabilities. In addition, a reversion may occur only if the plan so provides. A reversion prior to plan termination may constitute a prohibited transaction and may result in plan disqualification. Any assets that revert to the employer upon plan termination are includible in the gross income of the employer and subject to an excise tax. The excise tax rate is 20 percent if the employer maintains a replacement plan or makes certain benefit increases in connection with the termination; if not, the excise tax rate is 50 percent. Upon plan termination, the accrued benefits of all plan participants are required to be 100-percent vested.

A pension plan may provide medical benefits to retired employees through a separate account that is part of such plan. A qualified transfer of excess assets of a defined benefit plan to such a separate account within the plan may be made in order to fund retiree health benefits.[40] A qualified transfer does not result in plan disqualification, is not a prohibited transaction, and is not treated as a reversion. Thus, transferred assets are not includible in the gross income of the employer and are not subject to the excise tax on reversions. No more than one qualified transfer may be made in any taxable year. A qualified transfer can be made only from a single-employer plan.

Excess assets generally means the excess, if any, of the value of the plan's assets[41] over the greater of (1) the accrued liability under the plan (including normal cost) or (2) 125 percent of the plan's current liability.[42] In addition, excess assets transferred in a qualified transfer may not exceed the amount reasonably estimated to be the amount that the employer will pay out of such account during the taxable year of the transfer for qualified current retiree health liabilities. No deduction is allowed to the employer for (1) a qualified transfer or (2) the payment of qualified current retiree health liabilities out of transferred funds (and any income thereon).

Transferred assets (and any income thereon) must be used to pay qualified current retiree health liabilities for the taxable year of the transfer. Transferred amounts generally must benefit pension plan participants, other than key employees, who are entitled upon retirement to receive retiree medical benefits through the separate account. Retiree health benefits of key employees may not be paid out of transferred assets.

Amounts not used to pay qualified current retiree health liabilities for the taxable year of the transfer are to be returned to the general assets of the plan.

---

[190] The single-employer plan funding concepts are updated after 2007 to reflect the changes to the single-employer plan funding rules under the bill.

[40] Sec. 420.

[41] The value of plan assets for this purpose is the lesser of fair market value or actuarial value.

[42] In the case of plan years beginning before January 1, 2004, excess assets generally means the excess, if any, of the value of the plan's assets over the greater of (1) the lesser of (a) the accrued liability under the plan (including normal cost) or (b) 170 percent of the plan's current liability (for 2003), or (2) 125 percent of the plan's current liability. The current liability full funding limit was repealed for years beginning after 2003. Under the general sunset provision of EGTRRA, the limit is reinstated for years after 2010.

These amounts are not includible in the gross income of the employer, but are treated as an employer reversion and are subject to a 20-percent excise tax.

In order for the transfer to be qualified, accrued retirement benefits under the pension plan generally must be 100-percent vested as if the plan terminated immediately before the transfer (or in the case of a participant who separated in the one-year period ending on the date of the transfer, immediately before the separation).

In order for a transfer to be qualified, the employer generally must maintain retiree health benefits at the same level for the taxable year of the transfer and the following four years.

In addition, the ERISA provides that, at least 60 days before the date of a qualified transfer, the employer must notify the Secretary of Labor, the Secretary of the Treasury, employee representatives, and the plan administrator of the transfer, and the plan administrator must notify each plan participant and beneficiary of the transfer.[43]

No qualified transfer may be made after December 31, 2005.

House Bill

No provision.

Senate Amendment

The Senate amendment allows qualified transfers of excess defined benefit plan assets through December 31, 2013.

Effective date

The provision is effective on the date of enactment.

Conference Agreement

The conference agreement follows the Senate amendment. The conference agreement allows qualified transfers of excess defined benefit plan assets through December 31, 2013.

Effective date

The provision is effective on the date of enactment.

[¶ 13,030.08]

Committee Report on P.L. 106-170 (Ticket to Work and Work Incentives Improvement Act)

[Senate Committee Report]

Explanation of Provision

The present-law provision permitting qualified transfers of excess defined benefit pension plan assets to provide retiree health benefits under a section 401(h) account is extended through September 30, 2009. In addition, the present-law minimum benefit requirement is replaced by the minimum cost requirement that applied to qualified transfers before December 9, 1994, to section 401(h) accounts. Therefore, each group health plan or arrangement under which applicable health benefits are provided is required to provide a minimum dollar level of retiree health expenditures for the taxable year of the transfer and the following 4 taxable years. The minimum dollar level is the higher of the applicable employer costs for each of the 2 taxable years immediately preceding the taxable year of the transfer. The applicable employer cost for a taxable year is determined by dividing the employer's qualified current retiree health liabilities by the number of individuals to whom coverage for applicable health benefits was provided during the taxable year.

Effective Date

The provision is effective with respect to qualified transfers of excess defined benefit pension plan assets to section 401(h) accounts after December 31, 2000, and before October 1, 2009. The modification of the minimum benefit requirement is effective with respect to transfers after the date of enactment. An employer is permitted to satisfy the minimum benefit requirement with respect to a qualified transfer that occurs after the date of enactment during the portion of the cost maintenance period of such transfer that overlaps the benefit maintenance period of a qualified transfer that occurs before the date of enactment. For example, suppose an employer (with a calendar year taxable year) made a qualified transfer in 1998. The minimum benefit requirement must be satisfied for calendar years 1998, 1999, 2000, 2001, and 2002. Suppose the employer also makes a qualified transfer in 2000. Then, the employer is permitted to satisfy the minimum benefit requirement in 2000, 2001, and 2002, and is required to satisfy the minimum cost requirement in 2003 and 2004.

[Conference Committee Report]

House Bill

No provision.

Conference Agreement

The conference agreement extends the present-law provision permitting qualified transfers of excess defined benefit pension plan assets to provide retiree health benefits under a section 401(h) account through December 31, 2005.[30] The modification of the minimum benefit requirement is effective with respect to transfers after the date of enactment. The Secretary of the Treasury is directed to prescribe such regulations as may be necessary to prevent an employer who significantly reduces retiree health coverage during the cost maintenance period from being treated as satisfying the minimum cost requirement. In addition, the conference agreement contains a transition rule regarding the minimum cost requirement. Under this rule, an employer must satisfy the minimum benefit requirement with respect to a qualified transfer that occurs after the date of enactment during the portion of the cost maintenance period of such transfer that overlaps the benefit maintenance period of a qualified transfer that occurs on or before the date of enactment. For example, suppose an employer (with a calendar year taxable year) made a qualified transfer in 1998. The minimum benefit requirement must be satisfied for calendar years 1998, 1999, 2000, 2001, and 2002. Suppose the employer also makes a qualified transfer in 2000. Then, the employer is required to satisfy the minimum benefit requirement in 2000, 2001, and 2002, and is required to satisfy the minimum cost requirement in 2003 and 2004.

Effective date

The conference agreement is effective with respect to qualified transfers of excess defined benefit pension plan assets to section 401(h) accounts after December 31, 2000, and before January 1, 2006. The modification of the minimum benefit requirement is effective with respect to transfers after the date of enactment. In addition, the conference agreement contains a transition rule regarding the minimum cost requirement. Under this rule, an employer must satisfy the minimum benefit requirement with respect to a qualified transfer that occurs after the date of enactment during the portion of the cost maintenance period of such transfer that overlaps the benefit maintenance period of a qualified transfer that occurs on or before the date of enactment. For example, suppose an employer (with a calendar year taxable year) made a qualified transfer in 1998. The minimum benefit requirement must be satisfied for calendar years 1998, 1999, 2000, 2001, and 2002. Suppose the employer also makes a qualified transfer in 2000. Then, the employer is required to satisfy the minimum benefit requirement in 2000, 2001, and 2002, and is required to satisfy the minimum cost requirement in 2003 and 2004.

[¶ 13,030.095]

Committee Report on P.L. 103-465 (General Agreement on Tariffs and Trade (GATT); Retirement Protection Act)

[House Committee Report]

***Under the bill, the employer is required to maintain substantially the same level of employer-provided retiree health coverage for the taxable year of the transfer and the following 4 taxable years. The level of coverage that must be maintained will be based on coverage provided in the year immediately preceding the taxable year of the transfer. For purposes of determining whether there are excess assets in a defined benefit pension plan, the interest rates required to be used under the bill for purposes of minimum funding requirements would apply.

The bill clarifies how amounts that can otherwise be transferred are reduced by amounts previously set aside to pay retiree health liabilities. Under the bill, for transfers occurring after December 31, 1995, in determining qualified retiree health liabilities with respect to a taxable year, such liabilities are reduced by the percentage that the amounts previously set aside are the total future qualified retiree health liabilities. For example, assume that on December 31, 1995, an employer has a welfare benefit fund that has $2 million in assets to pay retiree health liabilities, the present value of future qualified retiree health liabilities is $10 million, and qualified retiree health liabilities for 1996 (without regard to any offset) are $1 million. In determining the amount that can be transferred in 1996, the $1 million is reduced by 20 percent. No inference is intended as to the proper reduction in transferred amounts under present law.

Effective date

The provision generally is effective with respect to taxable years beginning after December 31, 1995, and before January 1, 2001. The modification to the maintenance of effort requirement is effective for transfers occurring after the date of enactment [December 8, 1994].

[43] ERISA sec. 101(e). ERISA also provides that a qualified transfer is not a prohibited transaction under ERISA or a prohibited reversion.

[30] The conference agreement modifies the corresponding provisions of ERISA.

[¶ 13,030.10]

Committee Reports on P.L. 101-508 (Omnibus Budget Reconciliation Act of 1990)

[House Committee Report]

Excess pension plan assets

Reversions of excess pension assets

In general.—Under the bill, the rate of the reversion excise tax is either 50 percent or 20 percent. The applicable rate depends, in part, on the actions of the employer in connection with the plan termination. The excise tax rate is 50 percent if the employer (1) does not establish or maintain a qualified replacement plan following the plan termination, or (2) provide certain pro-rata benefit increases in connection with the plan termination. If the employer maintains a qualified replacement plan or provides certain pro-rata benefit increases, the reversion excise tax rate is 20 percent. In addition, the excise tax is 20 percent in the case of an employer who, as of the plan termination date, is in bankruptcy liquidation under chapter 7 of title 11 of the United States Code or in liquidation under similar proceedings under State law.

Qualified replacement plan.—The reversion tax is 20 percent if the employer establishes a qualified replacement plan in connection with the plan termination or maintains a qualified replacement plan following the plan termination. A qualified replacement plan is a qualified plan maintained by the employer which meets (1) a participation requirement, (2) an asset transfer requirement, and (3) in the case of a qualified replacement plan that is a defined contribution plan, certain allocation requirements. A qualified replacement plan can be either a defined contribution plan or a defined benefit pension plan. The Secretary of the Treasury may provide that 2 or more plans may be treated as 1 plan for purposes of determining whether there is a qualified replacement plan.

The participation requirement is satisfied if substantially all of the active participants in the terminated plan who are employees of the employer after the plan termination are active participants in the replacement plan. This requirement is designed to ensure that participants who were accruing benefits under the terminating plan continue to earn benefits under the replacement plan.

The asset transfer requirement is satisfied if, prior to any employer reversion, assets equal to 30 percent of the maximum reversion that could be received are transferred directly from the terminated plan to the replacement plan.

The amount required to be transferred is reduced by the amount of the present value of increases in participants' (including both active and nonactive participants) vested accrued benefits that are made pursuant to a plan amendment adopted during the 60-day period ending on the date of plan termination and which take effect on the termination date. Any such increases in vested benefits must, of course, comply with the normally applicable qualification requirements.

In the case of a replacement plan that is a defined contribution plan, the transferred assets (and income thereon) are required to be (1) allocated to participants and beneficiaries in the plan year in which the transfer occurs, or (2) credited to a suspense account and allocated from that account no less rapidly than ratably over a period not to exceed 7 years (including the year of the transfer). Income credited on assets in the suspense account is to be allocated no less rapidly than ratably over the remainder of the 7-year period.

Transferred assets (and income thereon) are treated as annual additions when allocated to participant accounts for purposes of the limits on contributions and benefits (sec. 415). The 7-year allocation period can be extended only to the extent that such limits prevent the allocation from taking place during such period. In determining whether such limits preclude transferred assets from being allocated, it is intended that transferred assets are treated as the first annual additions allocated to participant accounts for any year. Amounts that cannot be allocated during such period due to the application of the section 415 limits on contributions and benefits are to be reallocated to other plan participants at the end of the period. If all remaining amounts cannot be allocated due to application of the limits on contributions and benefits such amounts are to be allocated as soon as possible consistent with such limits and before any other amounts can be allocated.

In the event that the replacement plan terminates before the assets in the suspense account have been allocated, the remaining amount is to be allocated as of the termination date to participant accounts. Any amount that cannot be so allocated to a participant due to the limitations on contributions and benefits is to be reallocated to other participants. If such limits preclude the allocation of the entire amount remaining in the suspense account, then the amount that cannot be allocated is treated as an employer reversion and subject to the reversion excise tax and includible in gross income. Of course, in the case of a newly established plan, the present-law permanence requirement may in some circumstances adversely affect the qualified status of the plan if it is terminated before the end of the 7-year period.

Amounts transferred to a qualified replacement plan are not includible in the gross income of the employer and are not subject to the excise tax on reversions. The employer is not entitled to a deduction for amounts transferred to a qualified replacement plan.

The following example illustrates the application of the asset transfer rule. Assume that Employer A terminates a defined benefit pension plan and that, after satisfaction of all plan liabilities, the remaining assets in the plan are $100x. $30x is transferred to a defined contribution plan of the employer that qualifies as a qualified replacement plan. No benefit increases are provided in connection with the plan termination. The $30x transferred to the qualified replacement plan is not includible in the gross income of the employer nor subject to the reversion excise tax. The employer is liable for an excise tax of $14x [.20 × ($100x − $30x)], and $70x is includible in the gross income of the employer.

Pro-rata benefit increases.—The reversion excise tax is also 20 percent if the employer provides certain pro-rata benefit increases to plan participants (including both active and nonactive participants) as part of the plan termination transaction. Under this rule, the vested accrued benefits of all participants under the terminating plan must be increased effective as of the termination date so that the total present value of increased benefits (determined on a termination basis) is at least 25 percent of the maximum employer reversion which could be received. The present value of the increase in the nonforfeitable benefit of each participant is to be equal to the amount which bears the same ratio to the total present value of benefit increases as the participant's nonforfeitable accrued benefit bears to the total nonforfeitable accrued benefits under the terminated plan. In no event can the aggregate increase in the nonforfeitable accrued benefits of nonactive participants as of the termination date exceed 40 percent of the minimum benefit increase possible under the provision. Benefit increases that would exceed this 40 percent limitation are to be allocated among the active plan participants on a pro-rata basis.

For purposes of the provision, a nonactive participant is (1) a participant in pay status as of the termination date, (2) a beneficiary who has a vested benefit under the terminated plan as of the termination date, or (3) a participant who has a vested right to a benefit under the plan as of the termination date and who separated from service before the period beginning 3 years before the termination date and ending on the date of final distribution of plan assets.

All benefit increases and allocations of transferred assets made in accordance with the provision are subject to the limitations on contributions and benefits (sec. 415) and the nondiscrimination rules (sec. 401(a)(4)), as well as other generally applicable qualification rules.

Under present law, the limitations on contributions and benefits are phased in over 10 years of plan participation. The Secretary of the Treasury has the authority to provide that this rule applies separately with respect to each change in benefit structure of a plan. The Secretary has provided that this rule generally applies to all changes in benefit structures, including benefit increases on plan termination (I.R.S. Notice 89-45). The bill provides that, except as provided by the Secretary of the Treasury in the future, the 10-year rule does not apply to benefit increases pursuant to the provisions of the bill, if the benefit increases do not discriminate in favor of highly compensated employees. It is intended that the Secretary may apply a more stringent test under this provision than the general nondiscrimination rule (sec. 401(a)(4)).

Fiduciary duties.—The bill provides that certain of the reversion excise tax provisions create specific fiduciary obligations under ERISA if an employer elects to establish or maintain a qualified replacement plan or to increase benefits pursuant to the reversion excise tax rules. These specific duties are in addition to the generally applicable fiduciary obligations. These specific duties apply only if the employer elects to establish or maintain a qualified replacement plan or provide benefit increases under the excise tax rules; the employer may elect to pay the 50-percent excise tax.

Under the bill, if the employer elects to establish a qualified replacement plan, a fiduciary of the terminating plan is required to discharge his or her fiduciary duties under titles I and IV of ERISA in accordance with the asset transfer provisions (with respect to transfer of assets from the terminating plan). If the employer elects to increase benefits under the excise tax provisions, the fiduciary of the terminating plan is required to discharge his or her fiduciary duties in accordance with the benefit increase provisions of the excise tax rules. Similarly, a fiduciary of a qualified replacement plan is required to discharge his or her fiduciary duties under titles I and IV of ERISA in accordance with the participation requirement, the transfer provision with respect to receipt of assets from the terminating plan, and the allocation requirements with respect to participants in the qualified replacement plan. These duties relate to the excise tax provisions as in effect on January 1, 1991.

The bill also amends title IV of ERISA to provide that the ability of the employer to obtain residual assets is subject to the fiduciary requirements described above and the excise tax provisions.

Transfer of excess pension plan assets to retiree health accounts.

In general.—Under the bill, qualified transfers of excess assets are permitted from the pension assets in a defined benefit pension plan (other than a multiemployer plan) to the section 401(h) account that is a part of such plan. The assets transferred are not includible in the gross income of the employer and are not subject to the excise tax on reversions. The defined benefit pension plan does not fail to satisfy the qualification requirements (sec. 401(a)) solely on account of the transfer and does not violate the present-law requirement that medical benefits under a section 401(h) account be subordinate to the retirement benefits under the plan. In addition, the transfer is not a prohibited transaction and does not violate other specific fiduciary requirements of title I of ERISA.

In order to qualify for the treatment described above (i.e., to be a qualified transfer): (1) except with respect to a special rule for 1990 expenses, a transfer of assets to a section 401(h) account may be made only once in any taxable year of the employer and may be made only in taxable years beginning after December

31, 1990, and before January 1, 1996; (2) the transferred assets (and income thereon) are required to be used to pay certain retiree health benefit liabilities; (3) certain vesting requirements must be satisfied; (4) certain minimum benefit requirements must be satisfied; and (5) the amount transferred cannot exceed certain limits. Notice of the transfer must also be provided.

The special rule for 1990 provides that a transfer is treated as a qualified transfer if the transfer (1) is made with respect to current retiree health liabilities for the employer's first taxable year beginning after December 31, 1989, (2) is made before the earlier of (a) the due date (including extensions) of the employer's tax return for such taxable year or (b) the date the return is filed, and (3) does not exceed the employer's expenditures for current retiree health liabilities for such taxable year. The employer may make 2 qualified transfers in the 1991 taxable year if one of the transfers is for 1990 expenses. If an employer transfers assets for 1990 expenses, then additional vesting requirements apply. The employer's otherwise allowable deductions for the 1990 taxable year are reduced by the amount of the qualified transfer made to reimburse 1990 expenses.

Use of transferred assets.—Assets transferred in a qualified transfer (and any income thereon) are required to be used to pay qualified current retiree health liabilities (either directly or through reimbursement) for the taxable year of the transfer. In general, qualified current retiree health liabilities are defined as the amount of retiree health benefits (including administrative expenses) which would have been deductible by the employer with respect to applicable health benefits provided during the taxable year, determined as if the benefits were provided directly by an employer on a cash accounting basis. Transferred amounts are generally required to benefit all participants in the pension plan who are entitled upon retirement to receive retiree medical benefits (other than key employees) through the section 401(h) account. Retiree health benefits of key employees (sec. 416(i)(1)) may not be paid (directly or indirectly) out of transferred assets.

Amounts not used to pay qualified retiree health liabilities for the taxable year of the transfer are to be returned at the end of the taxable year to the general assets of the plan. Amounts so transferred are not includible in the gross income of the employer, but are subject to the 20-percent excise tax on reversions. The 50-percent reversion tax does not apply.

Vesting requirements.—In order for the transfer to be qualified, accrued retirement benefits under the pension plan must be nonforfeitable as if the plan terminated on the date of transfer. In addition, the benefits of plan participants who separated from service before the transfer but during the one-year period preceding the transfer also must be nonforfeitable as if the plan terminated immediately before the separation from service.

In the case of a transfer pursuant to the special rule for 1990, the vesting requirement is satisfied if, with respect to any participant who separated from service during the 1990 taxable year, the participant's vested benefits are recomputed as if the plan had terminated immediately before the participant's separation from service.

Minimum cost requirement.—An employer that makes a transfer to a section 401(h) account under the proposal is to maintain employer-provided retiree health expenditures for covered retirees at a minimum dollar level for the taxable year of the transfer and the following 4 taxable years. The minimum level is equal to the higher of the applicable employer cost for each of the 2 taxable years preceding the year of the transfer. If a taxable year is in 2 or more overlapping minimum cost periods, the requirement is to be applied by taking into account the highest applicable cost.

The applicable employer cost for a year is generally determined by dividing (1) the qualified current retiree health liabilities for the year, by (2) the number of individuals who (immediately before the transfer or, if there was no transfer, as of the end of the taxable year) were entitled to pension benefits under the plan and retiree health benefits. For this purpose qualified current retiree health liabilities are determined without reduction for liabilities previously funded. Each health plan or arrangement under which applicable health benefits are provided are required to contain the minimum cost requirement. An employer is permitted to apply the minimum cost requirement under the bill separately with respect to those covered retirees who are eligible for medicare and those that are not.

The minimum cost requirement is illustrated by the following examples.

Example 1.—Assume Employer A maintains a defined benefit pension plan that contains a section 401(h) account, and the employer makes a qualified transfer to the 401(h) account in taxable year 1991. In taxable years 1989 and 1990, qualified current retiree health liabilities (determined as described above) were $200,000 and $250,000, respectively. In such years, the number of pension plan participants entitled to receive retiree health benefits was 200.

The applicable employer cost is $1,000 ($200,000 divided by 200) for the 1989 taxable year and is $1,250 ($250,000 divided by 200) for 1990. Thus, the minimum employer cost of health benefits that must be provided to covered retirees is $1,250, for taxable years 1991 through 1995 (if no further transfers occur).

Example 2.—Same as Example 1, except that the applicable cost for the 1991 taxable year is $1,500 and the employer makes a qualified transfer in 1992. The minimum benefit requirement for taxable years 1992 through 1996 is therefore $1,500 (unless further transfers occur that result in a higher applicable cost).

Limits on amounts transferable.—The maximum amount of excess assets that may be transferred in a taxable year cannot exceed the amount reasonably estimated to be the amount the employer will pay out of the section 401(h) account during the taxable year for qualified current retiree health liabilities. In determining the amount that may be transferred, the employer is to consider earnings that will be attributable to such assets subsequent to the transfer.

The amount of qualified current retiree health liabilities is generally reduced to the extent that the employer has previously made a contribution to a section 401(h) account or a welfare benefit fund (e.g., voluntary employees' beneficiary association (VEBA)) relating to the same liabilities. The portion of existing reserves in a welfare benefits fund that relate to qualified current retiree health liabilities is determined on a pro-rata basis.

The retired employees who may be taken into account in calculating qualified current retiree health liabilities are limited to those who are eligible for retirement benefits under the defined benefit pension plan containing the separate account and eligible for retiree health benefits (other than key employees).

Definition of excess assets.—Under the proposal, excess assets are defined to be the excess of the value of plan assets (calculated as under the full funding limitation) over the greater of (1) the lesser of (a) 150 percent of current liability or (b) the accrued liability under the plan, or (2) 125 percent of current liability. Thus, for example, in the case of a plan subject to the accrued liability full funding limitation, the value of assets remaining in the pension plan following a transfer must be at least the greater of the plan's accrued liability and 125 percent of current liability. The calculation of excess assets is generally made as of the most recent valuation date preceding the transfer. However, if the fiduciary knows or has reason to know that use of the most recent plan valuation date will not accurately reflect any increased liabilities the plan may experience during the year (e.g., if benefit increases will take effect or early retirement incentives may be offered) a transfer based on the most recent plan valuation date may not be consistent with the fiduciary duties of title I of ERISA.

Other limitations.—The employer is not entitled to a deduction when amounts are transferred into the section 401(h) account or when such amounts (or income on such amounts) are used to pay retiree health benefits. No deduction or contribution is allowed the employer for the provision of retiree health benefits (whether directly, through a 401(h) account, or a welfare benefit fund) except to the extent that the total of such payments for qualified current retiree health liabilities exceed the amount transferred to the section 401(h) account (including any income thereon). An employer may not make after December 31, 1990, any contributions to a health benefits account or a welfare benefit fund with respect to qualified current retiree health liabilities for which transferred assets (and income thereon) are required to be used under the proposal until after such assets (and income) have been totally expended from the account.

Assets transferred after the valuation date for the plan year (and income thereon) are required to be treated, for purposes of the full funding limitation, as plan assets as of the valuation date for the next year. The transfer is to be treated as a net experience loss for funding purposes, except that the amortization period is 10 years rather than 5 years.

Fiduciary rules.—A transfer made in accordance with the provision is not a violation of the fiduciary duties under ERISA.

Notice.—The bill amends title I of ERISA to require that notice of a proposed transfer be provided to the Secretary of Treasury, the Secretary of Labor, plan participants, and employee representatives (if any) at least 60 days prior to the transfer.

Effective Date

The provision permitting the transfer of excess pension assets to pay current retiree health benefits is effective for transfers occurring in taxable years beginning after December 31, 1990, and before January 1, 1996.

The provisions relating to reversions apply to reversions occurring after September 30, 1990, other than (1) in the case of plans subject to title IV of ERISA, reversions pursuant to a termination, notice of which was provided under such title to participants (or if no participants, the Pension Benefit Guaranty Corporation) on or before such date, and (2) in the case of plans not subject to title IV of ERISA, but subject to title I, a notice of intent to reduce future benefit accruals was provided to plan participants on or before such date.

[Senate Committee Report]

Excess pension plan assets

Reversions of excess pension assets

In general.—Under the bill, the rate of the reversion excise tax is either 40 percent or 20 percent. The applicable rate depends, in part, on the actions of the employer in connection with the plan termination. The excise tax rate is 40 percent if the employer (1) does not establish or maintain a qualified replacement plan following the plan termination, or (2) provide certain pro-rata benefit increases in connection with the plan termination. If the employer maintains a qualified replacement plan or provides certain pro-rata benefit increases, the reversion excise tax rate is 20 percent. In addition, the excise tax is 20 percent in the case of an employer who, as of the plan termination date, is in bankruptcy liquidation under chapter 7 of title 11 of the United States Code or in liquidation under similar proceedings under State law.

Qualified replacement plan.—The reversion tax is 20 percent if the employer establishes a qualified replacement plan in connection with the plan termination or maintains a qualified replacement plan following the plan termination. A qualified replacement plan is a qualified plan maintained by the employer which meets (1) a participation requirement, (2) an asset transfer requirement, and (3) in the case of a qualified replacement plan that is a defined contribution plan, certain allocation requirements. A qualified replacement plan can be either a defined contribution plan or a defined benefit pension plan. The Secretary of the Treasury may provide that 2 or more plans may be treated as 1 plan for purposes of determining whether there is a qualified replacement plan.

The participation requirement is satisfied if substantially all of the active participants in the terminated plan who are employees of the employer after the plan termination are active participants in the replacement plan. This requirement is designed to ensure that participants who were accruing benefits under the terminating plan continue to earn benefits under the replacement plan.

The asset transfer requirement is satisfied if, prior to any employer reversion, assets equal to 20 percent of the maximum reversion that could be received are transferred directly from the terminated plan to the replacement plan.

The amount required to be transferred is reduced by the amount of the present value of increases in participants' (including both active and nonactive participants) vested accrued benefits that are made pursuant to a plan amendment adopted during the 60-day period ending on the date of plan termination and which take effect on the termination date. Any such increases in vested benefits must, of course, comply with the normally applicable qualification requirements.

In the case of a replacement plan that is a defined contribution plan, the transferred assets (and income thereon) are required to be (1) allocated to participants and beneficiaries in the plan year in which the transfer occurs, or (2) credited to a suspense account and allocated from that account no less rapidly than ratably over a period not to exceed 7 years (including the year of the transfer). Income credited on assets in the suspense account is to be allocated no less rapidly than ratably over the remainder of the 7-year period.

Transferred assets (and income thereon) are treated as annual additions when allocated to participant accounts for purposes of the limits on contributions and benefits (sec. 415). The 7-year allocation period can be extended only to the extent that such limits prevent the allocation from taking place during such period. In determining whether such limits preclude transferred assets from being allocated, it is intended that transferred assets are treated as the first annual additions allocated to participant accounts for any year. Amounts that cannot be allocated during such period due to the application of the section 415 limits on contributions and benefits are to be reallocated to other plan participants at the end of the period. If all remaining amounts cannot be allocated due to application of the limits on contributions and benefits such amounts are to be allocated as soon as possible consistent with such limits and before any other amounts can be allocated.

In the event that the replacement plan terminates before the assets in the suspense account have been allocated, the remaining amount is to be allocated as of the termination date to participant accounts. Any amount that cannot be so allocated to a participant due to the limitations on contributions and benefits is to be reallocated to other participants. If such limits preclude the allocation of the entire amount remaining in the suspense account, then the amount that cannot be allocated is treated as an employer reversion and subject to the reversion excise tax and includible in gross income. Of course, in the case of a newly established plan, the present-law permanence requirement may in some circumstances adversely affect the qualified status of the plan if it is terminated before the end of the 7-year period.

Amounts transferred to a qualified replacement plan are not includible in the gross income of the employer and are not subject to the excise tax on reversions. The employer is not entitled to a deduction for amounts transferred to a qualified replacement plan.

The following example illustrates the application of the asset transfer rule. Assume that Employer A terminates a defined benefit pension plan and that, after satisfaction of all plan liabilities, the remaining assets in the plan are \$100x. \$20x is transferred to a defined contribution plan of the employer that qualifies as a qualified replacement plan. No benefit increases are provided in connection with the plan termination. The \$20x transferred to the qualified replacement plan is not includible in the gross income of the employer nor subject to the reversion excise tax. The employer is liable for an excise tax of \$16x [.20 × (\$100x – \$20x)], and \$80x is includible in the gross income of the employer.

Pro-rata benefit increases.—The reversion excise tax is also 20 percent if the employer provides certain pro-rata benefit increases to plan participants (including both active and nonactive participants) as part of the plan termination transaction. Under this rule, the vested accrued benefits of all participants under the terminating plan must be increased effective as of the termination date so that the total present value of increased benefits (determined on a termination basis) is at least 15 percent of the maximum employer reversion which could be received. The present value of the increase in the nonforfeitable benefit of each participant is to be equal to the amount which bears the same ratio to the total present value of benefit increases as the participant's nonforfeitable accrued benefit bears to the total nonforfeitable accrued benefits under the terminated plan. In no event can the aggregate increase in the nonforfeitable accrued benefits of nonactive participants as of the termination date exceed 40 percent of the minimum benefit increase possible under the provision. Benefit increases that would exceed this 40 percent limitation are to be allocated among the active plan participants on a pro-rata basis.

For purposes of the provision, a nonactive participant is (1) a participant in pay status as of the termination date, (2) a beneficiary who has a vested benefit under the terminated plan as of the termination date, or (3) a participant who has a vested right to a benefit under the plan as of the termination date and who separated from service during the period beginning 3 years before the termination date and ending on the date of final distribution of plan assets.

All benefit increases and allocations of transferred assets made in accordance with the provision are subject to the limitations on contributions and benefits (sec. 415) and the nondiscrimination rules (sec. 401(a)(4)), as well as other generally applicable qualification rules.

Under present law, the limitations on contributions and benefits are phased in over 10 years of plan participation. The Secretary of the Treasury has the authority to provide that this rule applies separately with respect to each change in benefit structure of a plan. The Secretary has provided that this rule generally applies to all changes in benefit structures, including benefit increases on plan termination (I.R.S. Notice 89-45). The bill provides that, except as provided by the Secretary of the Treasury in the future, the 10-year rule does not apply to benefit increases pursuant to the provisions of the bill, if the benefit increases do not discriminate in favor of highly compensated employees. It is intended that the Secretary may apply a more stringent test under this provision than the general nondiscrimination rule (sec. 401(a)(4)).

Fiduciary duties.—The bill provides that certain of the reversion excise tax provisions create specific fiduciary obligations under ERISA if an employer elects to establish or maintain a qualified replacement plan or to increase benefits pursuant to the reversion excise tax rules. These specific duties are in addition to the generally applicable fiduciary obligations. These specific duties apply only if the employer elects to establish or maintain a qualified replacement plan or provide benefit increases under the excise tax rules; the employer may elect to pay the 40-percent excise tax.

Under the bill, if the employer elects to establish a qualified replacement plan, a fiduciary of the terminating plan is required to discharge his or her fiduciary duties under titles I and IV of ERISA in accordance with the asset transfer provisions (with respect to transfer of assets from the terminating plan). If the employer elects to increase benefits under the excise tax provisions, the fiduciary of the terminating plan is required to discharge his or her fiduciary duties in accordance with the benefit increase provisions of the excise tax rules. Similarly, a fiduciary of a qualified replacement plan is required to discharge his or her fiduciary duties under titles I and IV of ERISA in accordance with the participation requirement, the transfer provision with respect to receipt of assets from the terminating plan, and the allocation requirements with respect to participants in the qualified replacement plan. These duties relate to the excise tax provisions as in effect on January 1, 1991.

The bill also amends title IV of ERISA to provide that the ability of the employer to obtain residual assets is subject to the fiduciary requirements described above and the excise tax provisions.

Transfer of excess pension plan assets to retiree health accounts

In general.—Under the bill, qualified transfers of excess assets are permitted from the pension assets in a defined benefit pension plan (other than a multiemployer plan) to the section 401(h) account that is a part of such plan. The assets transferred are not includible in the gross income of the employer and are not subject to the excise tax on reversions. The defined benefit pension plan does not fail to satisfy the qualification requirements (sec. 401(a)) solely on account of the transfer and does not violate the present-law requirement that medical benefits under a section 401(h) account be subordinate to the retirement benefits under the plan. In addition, the transfer is not a prohibited transaction and does not violate other specific fiduciary requirements of title I of ERISA.

In order to qualify for the treatment described above (i.e., to be a qualified transfer): (1) except with respect to a special rule for 1990 expenses, a transfer of assets to a section 401(h) account may be made only once in any taxable year of the employer and may be made only in taxable years beginning after December 31, 1990, and before January 1, 1996; (2) the transferred assets (and income thereon) are required to be used to pay certain retiree health benefit liabilities; (3) certain vesting requirements must be satisfied; (4) certain minimum benefit requirements must be satisfied; and (5) the amount transferred cannot exceed certain limits. Notice of the transfer must also be provided. The transfer may not contravene any other provision of law.

The special rule for 1990 provides that a transfer is treated as a qualified transfer if the transfer (1) is made with respect to current retiree health liabilities for the employer's first taxable year beginning after December 31, 1989, (2) is made before the earlier of (a) the due date (including extensions) of the employer's tax return for such taxable year or (b) the date the return is filed, and (3) does not exceed the employer's expenditures for current retiree health liabilities for such taxable year. The employer may make 2 qualified transfers in the 1991 taxable year if one of the transfers is for 1990 expenses. If an employer transfers assets for 1990 expenses, then additional vesting requirements apply. The employer's otherwise allowable deductions for the 1990 taxable year are reduced by the amount of the qualified transfer made to reimburse 1990 expenses.

Use of transferred assets.—Assets transferred in a qualified transfer (and any income thereon) are required to be used to pay qualified current retiree health liabilities (either directly or through reimbursement) for the taxable year of the transfer. In general, qualified current retiree health liabilities are defined as the amount of retiree health benefits (including administrative expenses) which would have been deductible by the employer with respect to applicable health benefits provided during the taxable year, determined as if the benefits were provided directly by an employer on a cash accounting basis. Transferred amounts are generally required to benefit all participants in the pension plan who are entitled upon retirement to receive retiree medical benefits (other than key employees) through the section 401(h) account. Retiree health benefits of key employees (sec. 416(i)(1)) may not be paid (directly or indirectly) out of transferred assets.

Amounts not used to pay qualified retiree health liabilities for the taxable year of the transfer are to be returned at the end of the taxable year to the general assets of the plan. Amounts so transferred are not includible in the gross income of the employer, but are subject to the 20-percent excise tax on reversions. The 40-percent reversion tax does not apply.

Vesting requirements.—In order for the transfer to be qualified, accrued retirement benefits under the pension plan must be nonforfeitable as if the plan terminated on the date of transfer. In addition, the benefits of plan participants who separated from service before the transfer but during the one-year period preceding the transfer also must be nonforfeitable as if the plan terminated immediately before the separation from service.

In the case of a transfer pursuant to the special rule for 1990, the vesting requirement is satisfied if, with respect to any participant who separated from service during the 1990 taxable year, the participant's vested benefits are recomputed as if the plan had terminated immediately before the participant's separation from service.

Minimum cost requirement.—An employer that makes a transfer to a section 401(h) account under the proposal is to maintain employer-provided retiree health expenditures for covered retirees at a minimum dollar level for the taxable year of the transfer and the following 4 taxable years. The minimum level is equal to the higher of the applicable employer cost for each of the 2 taxable years preceding the year of the transfer. If a taxable year is in 2 or more overlapping minimum cost periods, the requirement is to be applied by taking into account the highest applicable cost.

The applicable employer cost for a year is generally determined by dividing (1) the qualified current retiree health liabilities for the year, by (2) the number of individuals who (immediately before the transfer or, if there was no transfer, as of the end of the taxable year) were entitled to pension benefits under the plan and retiree health benefits. For this purpose qualified current retiree health liabilities are determined without reduction for liabilities previously funded. Each health plan or arrangement under which applicable health benefits are provided are required to contain the minimum cost requirement. An employer is permitted to apply the minimum cost requirement under the bill separately with respect to those covered retirees who are eligible for medicare and those that are not.

The minimum cost requirement is illustrated by the following examples.

Example 1.—Assume Employer A maintains a defined benefit pension plan that contains a section 401(h) account, and the employer makes a qualified transfer to the 401(h) account in taxable year 1991. In taxable years 1989 and 1990, qualified current retiree health liabilities (determined as described above) were $200,000 and $250,000, respectively. In such years, the number of pension plan participants entitled to receive retiree health benefits was 200.

The applicable employer cost is $1,000 ($200,000 divided by 200) for the 1989 taxable year and is $1,250 ($250,000 divided by 200) for 1990. Thus, the minimum employer cost of health benefits that must be provided to covered retirees is $1,250, for taxable years 1991 through 1995 (if no further transfers occur).

Example 2.—Same as Example 1, except that the applicable cost for the 1991 taxable year is $1,500 and the employer makes a qualified transfer in 1992. The minimum benefit requirement for taxable years 1992 through 1996 is therefore $1,500 (unless further transfers occur that result in a higher applicable cost).

Limits on amounts transferable.—The maximum amount of excess assets that may be transferred in a taxable year cannot exceed the amount reasonably estimated to be the amount the employer will pay out of the section 401(h) account during the taxable year for qualified current retiree health liabilities. In determining the amount that may be transferred, the employer is to consider earnings that will be attributable to such assets subsequent to the transfer.

The amount of qualified current retiree health liabilities is generally reduced to the extent that the employer has previously made a contribution to a section 401(h) account or a welfare benefit fund (e.g., voluntary employees' beneficiary association (VEBA)) relating to the same liabilities. The portion of existing reserves in a welfare benefits fund that relate to qualified current retiree health liabilities is determined on a pro-rata basis or in accordance with such rules as the Secretary of the Treasury may prescribe.

The retired employees who may be taken into account in calculating qualified current retiree health liabilities are limited to those who are eligible for retirement benefits under the defined benefit pension plan containing the separate account and eligible for retiree health benefits (other than key employees).

Definition of excess assets.—Under the proposal, excess assets are defined to be the excess of the value of plan assets (calculated as under the full funding limitation) over the greater of (1) the lesser of (a) 150 percent of current liability or (b) the accrued liability under the plan, or (2) 125 percent of current liability. Thus, for example, in the case of a plan subject to the accrued liability full funding limitation, the value of assets remaining in the pension plan following a transfer must be at least the greater of the plan's accrued liability and 125 percent of current liability. The calculation of excess assets is generally made as of the most recent valuation date preceding the transfer. However, if the fiduciary knows or has reason to know that use of the most recent plan valuation date will not accurately reflect any increased liabilities the plan may experience during the year (e.g., if benefit increases will take effect or early retirement incentives may be offered) a transfer based on the most recent plan valuation date may not be consistent with the fiduciary duties of title I of ERISA.

Other limitations.—The employer is not entitled to a deduction when amounts are transferred into the section 401(h) account or when such amounts (or income on such amounts) are used to pay retiree health benefits. No deduction or contribution is allowed the employer for the provision of retiree health benefits (whether directly, through a 401(h) account, or a welfare benefit fund) except to the extent that the total of such payments for qualified current retiree health liabilities exceed the amount transferred to the section 401(h) account (including any income thereon). An employer may not make after December 31, 1990, any contributions to a health benefits account or a welfare benefit fund with respect to qualified current retiree health liabilities for which transferred assets (and income thereon) are required to be used under the proposal until after such assets (and income) have been totally expended from the account.

Assets transferred after the valuation date for the plan year (and income thereon) are required to be treated, for purposes of the full funding limitation, as plan assets as of the valuation date for the next year. The transfer is to be treated as a net experience loss for funding purposes, except that the amortization period is 10 years rather than 5 years.

Fiduciary rules.—A transfer made in accordance with the provision is not in violation of the fiduciary duties under ERISA.

Notice.—The bill amends title I of ERISA to require that notice of a proposed transfer be provided to the Secretary of Treasury, the Secretary of Labor, plan participants, and employee representatives (if any) at least 60 days prior to the transfer.

Effective Date

The provision permitting the transfer of excess pension assets to pay current retiree health benefits is effective for transfers occurring in taxable years beginning after December 31, 1990, and before January 1, 1996.

The provisions relating to reversions apply to reversions occurring after September 30, 1990, other than (1) in the case of plans subject to title IV of ERISA, reversions pursuant to a termination, notice of which was provided under such title to participants (or if no participants, the Pension Benefit Guaranty Corporation) on or before such date, and (2) in the case of plans not subject to title IV of ERISA, but subject to title I, a notice of intent to reduce future benefit accruals was provided to plan participants on or before such date.

[Conference Committee Report]

Excess pension plan assets

Treatment of employer reversions of qualified plan assets

Reversion excise tax.—The conference agreement follows the House bill and the Senate amendment with the following modifications. Under the conference agreement, the rate of the reversion tax is increased to 50 percent or 20 percent, depending on the circumstances. The excise tax rate is 20 percent if the employer transfers assets equal to 25 percent of the maximum reversion that could be received (reduced by the present value of certain increases in participant's benefits that take effect upon the termination), or (2) provides pro-rata benefit increases in the accrued benefits of qualified participants in connection with the plan termination equal to at least 20 percent of the maximum reversion that could be received. The reversion tax is 50 percent if the employer does not maintain a qualified replacement plan or provide certain pro-rata benefit increases.

The conference agreement clarifies the rules regarding (1) benefit increases that reduce dollar for dollar the 25-percent cushion requirement and (2) pro-rata benefit increases under the 20-percent pro-rata benefit increase provision.

With respect to benefit increases that reduce the 25-percent cushion, the conference agreement clarifies that the increases may be provided to any group of participants and/or beneficiaries under the plan (provided the increases satisfy the generally applicable qualification requirements, such as the nondiscrimination rules). Thus, for example, under this provision benefit increases may be, but are not required to be, provided to participants in pay status.

The conference agreement also clarifies the participants to whom benefit increases must be provided under the pro-rata benefit increase rule. Under this provision, increases must be provided to all qualified participants. Qualified participants include active participants, participants in pay status, certain beneficiaries, or individuals who have a nonforfeitable right to an accrued benefit under the terminated plan as of the termination date (determined without regard to this provision) and whose service terminated during the period beginning 3 years before the termination date and ending with the date on which the final distribution of assets occurs. Thus, for example, individuals who terminated employment before the termination date and received a lump-sum distribution of their benefits would not be qualified participants. Under the conference agreement, as under the House bill and the Senate amendment, the aggregate maximum benefit increase that may be provided under this provision to qualified participants other than active participants is 40 percent of the aggregate minimum required benefit increase.

The conference agreement also clarifies that the increases under both benefit increase provisions are to be made to participants' accrued benefits (rather than nonforfeitable accrued benefits). Total accrued benefits (including the increase in benefits under the provision) will become nonforfeitable upon plan termination.

Under the conference agreement, the participation requirement applicable to qualified replacement plans is modified so that, in order for the requirement to be satisfied, at least 95 percent of the active participants in the terminated plan who remain as employees of the employer after the termination are required to be active participants in the replacement plan. The conference agreement also clarifies that the employer is determined on a controlled group basis.

The conference agreement provides that, as provided by the Secretary of the Treasury, a plan of a successor employer may be taken into account in determining whether there is a qualified replacement plan.

Of course, the present-law permanence requirement which precludes premature plan termination applies to both the terminating plan and the replacement plan.

The conferees intend that the Secretary of the Treasury will prevent avoidance of the reversion tax provisions, for example, in cases involving avoidance of the replacement plan rules through successive plan terminations or abuses of the participation rule.

Transfers to retiree health accounts.—The conference agreement follows the House bill and the Senate amendment with the following modifications: (1) the conference agreement does not adopt the provision of the Senate bill permitting allocation of existing reserves to qualified current retiree health liabilities on other than a pro-rata basis, and (2) the conference agreement provides that no addition to tax shall be made under the estimated tax provisions for the taxable year preceding the taxpayer's first taxable year beginning after December 31, 1990, with respect to any underpayment that occurs by reason of the rule permitting reimbursement of 1990 qualified current retiree health liabilities.

Effective Date

The conference agreement adds an additional transitional rule under the reversion excise tax provisions. Under the conference agreement, in the case of plans not subject to either title I or title IV of ERISA, the provisions relating to the reversion excise tax do not apply to terminations with respect to which a request for a determination letter was filed with the Secretary of the Treasury before October 1, 1990. In addition, in the case of plans that have only one participant, the provisions relating to the reversion tax do not apply if a resolution terminating the plan was adopted before October 1, 1990.

[Code Sec. 421]

[¶ 13,100.05]

Committee Report on P.L. 108-357 (American Jobs Creation Act of 2004)

[House Committee Report]

The provision provides specific exclusions from FICA and FUTA wages for remuneration on account of the transfer of stock pursuant to the exercise of an incentive stock option or under an employee stock purchase plan, or any disposition of such stock. Thus, under the provision, FICA and FUTA taxes do not apply upon the exercise of a statutory stock option.[65] The provision also provides that such remuneration is not taken into account for purposes of determining Social Security benefits.

Additionally, the provision provides that Federal income tax withholding is not required on a disqualifying disposition, nor when compensation is recognized in connection with an employee stock purchase plan discount. Present law reporting requirements continue to apply.

Effective Date

The provision is effective for stock acquired pursuant to options exercised after the date of enactment.

[Conference Agreement]

The conference agreement follows the House bill.

[¶ 13,100.06]

Committee Report on P.L. 108-357 (American Jobs Creation Act of 2004)

[Conference Committee Report]

Present Law

Statutory stock options

Generally, when an employee exercises a compensatory option on employer stock, the difference between the option price and the fair market value of the stock (i.e., the "spread") is includible in income as compensation. Upon such exercise, an employer is allowed a corresponding compensation deduction. In the case of an incentive stock option or an option to purchase stock under an employee stock purchase plan (collectively referred to as "statutory stock options"), the spread is not included in income at the time of exercise.[942]

If an employee disposes of stock acquired upon the exercise of a statutory option, the employee generally is taxed at capital gains rates with respect to the excess of the fair market value of the stock on the date of disposition over the option price, and no compensation expense deduction is allowable to the employer, unless the employee fails to meet a holding period requirement. The employee fails to meet this holding period requirement if the disposition occurs within two years after the date the option is granted or one year after the date the option is exercised. The gain upon a disposition that occurs prior to the expiration of the applicable holding period(s) (a "disqualifying disposition") does not qualify for capital gains treatment. In the event of a disqualifying disposition, the income attributable to the disposition is treated by the employee as income received in the taxable year in which the disposition occurs, and a corresponding deduction is allowable to the employer for the taxable year in which the disposition occurs.

Sale of property to comply with conflict of interest requirements

The Code provides special rules for recognizing gain on sales of property which are required in order to comply with certain conflict of interest requirements imposed by the Federal Government.[943] Certain executive branch Federal employees (and their spouses and minor or dependent children) who are required to divest property in order to comply with conflict of interest requirements may elect to postpone the recognition of resulting gains by investing in certain replacement property within a 60-day period. The basis of the replacement property is reduced by the amount of the gain not recognized. Permitted replacement property is limited to any obligation of the United States or any diversified investment fund approved by regulations issued by the Office of Government Ethics. The rule applies only to sales under certificates of divestiture issued by the President or the Director of the Office of Government Ethics.

House Bill

No provision.

Senate Amendment

Under the Senate amendment, an eligible person who, in order to comply with Federal conflict of interest requirements, is required to sell shares of stock acquired pursuant to the exercise of a statutory stock option is treated as satisfying the statutory holding period requirements, regardless of how long the stock was actually held. An eligible person generally includes an officer or employee of the executive branch of the Federal Government (and any spouse or minor or dependent children whose ownership in property is attributable to the officer or employee). Because the sale is not treated as a disqualifying disposition, the individual is afforded capital gain treatment on any resulting gains. Such gains are eligible for deferral treatment under section 1043.

The employer granting the option is not allowed a deduction upon the sale of the stock by the individual.

Effective Date

The Senate amendment is effective for sales after the date of enactment.

[Conference Agreement]

The conference agreement follows the Senate amendment.

[Code Sec. 422]

[¶ 13,120.09]

Committee Reports on P.L. 94-455 (Tax Reform Act of 1976)

Present Law

An employee stock option is a right, which is limited in time, granted by a coporate employer to one or more employees to purchase a stated amount of stock in the corporation at a stated price. An option is a relatively low risk means of acquiring an equity interest in a corporation, since the option need not be exercised unless the value of the stock increases during the option period. If the value of the stock drops below the price at which the stock may be purchased (i.e., below the option price), the employee can allow the option to lapse (although ordinarily the employee would lose the amount which he may have originally paid for the option, if any).

Under present law, employee stock options fall broadly into two categories: "qualified" and nonqualified options. The former category is governed by statutory rules which set forth conditions which the option must meet in order to receive the favorable tax treatment accorded "qualified" stock options under present law. Employee options which do not satisfy these requirements (often called "non-qualified" or "nonstatutory" options) are governed by rules set forth in the income tax regulations (Reg. § 1.421-6) and by certain statutory rules which apply generally to property transferred to employees in connection with their performance of services (sec. 83).

---

[65] The provision also provides a similar exclusion under the Railroad Retirement Tax Act.

[942] Sec. 421.

[943] Sec. 1043.

Under present law, no income is recognized on the grant to a corporate employee, or on his exercise of, a "qualified" option to receive stock in the employer corporation (sec. 421 of the Code). The stock acquired by the exercise of the option is a capital asset in the hands of the employee and the income realized from the eventual sale of the stock is generally treated as long-term capital gain or loss.[1]

No deduction is available to the employer, as a business expense (under sec. 162) with respect to either the granting of a qualified stock option or the transfer of stock to the employee when he exercises a qualified option.

A qualified option (meeting the requirements in sec. 422) must be granted pursuant to a plan approved by the shareholders of the corporation. The option must, by its terms, be exercised within 5 years from the date it is granted and the purchase price of the shares (option price) may not be less than the fair market value of the company's stock on the date when the option is granted to the employee. In addition, any stock acquired under a qualified option may not be disposed of within 3 years after it is transferred to the employee. The option must also be exercised while the option holder is an employee of the corporation, or within three months after the termination of his employment.

By contrast, nonqualified stock options are generally subject to the rules of section 83 of the Code. Generally, under section 83, the value of a nonqualified stock option constitutes ordinary income to the employee if the option itself had a readily ascertainable fair market value at the time it was granted to the employee. If the option did not have a readily ascertainable value when granted, it would not constitute ordinary income at the time it was granted; when the option is exercised, however, the spread between the option price and the value of the stock at that time constitutes ordinary income to the employee.

As can be seen from the above description, qualified options have the advantage that an executive is not required to pay any ordinary income tax on the value of the option as such when the company grants it to him, or on any "bargain element" which may exist if and when he decides to exercise the option and purchase stock in the company. (The bargain element is the excess of the fair market value of a share of stock over its purchase price.) The employee is only required to pay tax when he sells the shares purchased under the option. Further, if he holds the shares for at least 3 years (as required for the option to remain qualified) he is entitled to pay tax at capital gain rates on the full amount of his gain (if any) over the price which he originally paid to buy the shares.

Although an employee does not have to pay tax under the qualified stock option rules at the time he exercises the option and receives stock worth more than he paid for it, the bargain element is treated as an item of tax preference under present law. This means that the excess of the fair market value of the share at the time of exercise over the purchase price paid by the employee is subject to the 10-percent minimum tax under present law (sec. 57(a)(6)).

General reasons for change

The principal reason for the present tax treatment of qualified stock options is said to be that such treatment allows corporate employers to provide "incentives" to key employees by enabling these employees to obtain an equity interest in the corporation. However, it seems doubtful whether a qualified stock option gives key employees more incentive than does any other form of compensation, especially since the value of compensation in the form of a qualified option is subject to the uncertainties of the stock market. Moreover, even to the extent a qualified option is an incentive, it still represents compensation and your committee believes that as such it should be subject to tax in much the same manner as other compensation. Moreover, to the extent that there is an incentive effect resulting from stock options, it could be argued that present law discriminates in favor of corporations (which are the only kind of employers who can grant qualified options) as opposed to all other forms of business organization.

Explanation of provisions

Under the committee bill, present law will not apply to qualified stock options granted after September 23, 1975 except in the case of an option granted under a written plan adopted and approved on or before that date, or under a plan adopted by a board of directors on or before September 23, 1975 (even if the plan is approved by the shareholders after that date).

Thus, generally, stock options granted after September 23, 1975, whether or not qualified (under the requirements of section 422) will be subject to the rules which apply today in the case of most nonqualified options granted after June 30, 1969 (sec. 83 of the Code). Under these rules, if an employee receives an option which has a readily ascertainable fair market value at the time it is granted, this value (less the price paid for the option, if any) constitutes ordinary income to the employee at that time.[2]

On the other hand, if the option does not have a readily ascertainable fair market value at the time it is granted, the value of the option does not constitute income to the employee at that time, but would be taxable to the employee when the option is exercised. The ordinary income recognized at that time is the spread between the option price and the value of the stock (unless the stock is nontransferable and subject to a substantial risk of forfeiture).

Any option which is subject to the provisions outlined above (sec. 83) is not treated as a tax preference for purposes of the minimum tax.

To illustrate these rules, consider the case of a qualified option granted to a corporate executive to buy 100 shares at $10 per share. The employee exercises the option in full when the shares are selling at $15 per share in the open market. Under the committee bill, this transaction would be treated (under sec. 83) as follows:

(a) At the time that the company grants the option to the executive, if the option as such has a readily ascertainable fair market value, the value of the option (less any amount which he may have been paid for it) is taxable to the executive as ordinary income.

(b) If the option itself does not have a readily ascertainable market value, the executive will be subject to tax when he exercises the option and acquires the share under option to him. In this example, the employee will be taxable on the $5 per share bargain element (or a total of $500) at the time he exercises his option. This income will be treated as compensation taxable at ordinary income rates.[3]

Income recognized by the employee under these rules would generally constitute earned income for purposes of the maximum tax on earned income (sec. 1348).

(c) After the executive pays tax at ordinary income rates on the compensation portion of the transaction, he would be entitled to add the amount of ordinary income recognized to his basis in the shares. Any further gain (realized when the employee sells the shares) would generaly be taxable as a capital gain.

(d) The employer corporation is entitled to a deduction (under sec. 83) in an amount equal to the ordinary income realized by an employee under the above rules. The employer's deduction accrues at the time that the employee is considered to have realized compensation income.

The rules outlined above are not to apply to employee "stock purchase plans" (described in sec. 423 of the Code) under which the rank and file employees of a corporation (as well as the executives) are afforded an opportunity to purchase corporate stock on a nondiscriminatory basis. The present Federal tax treatment of this type of plan is not affected by the committee bill.

The committee bill also provides certain transition rules so as not to disturb arrangements which were entered into in reliance on present law. Under the transition rules, present law will continue to govern qualified stock options granted pursuant to a written qualified stock option plan which was adopted by the board of directors of the corporation before September 24, 1975. For purposes of this rule, it is immaterial whether the shareholders approve the plan before, on, or after that date, although in order to a be a qualified plan the shareholders must approve the plan within 12 months before or after its adoption by the board (sec. 422(b)(1)). In order to retain its qualification the option must be exercised by the employee before September 24, 1980 (i.e., within five years of the September 23, 1975 cut-off date). However, this requirement does not have to be spelled out under the terms of the option; it is sufficient if the option is actually exercised on or before September 23, 1980.

In general, a plan is to be treated as having been "adopted" by the board of directors of the corporation by September 23, 1975, only if all of the action required for adoption has been completed by that date. For example, if the plan had been adopted by the directors of a corporation under procedures which were valid under State law, the plan would generally be treated as having been "adopted" within the meaning of the statute. For purposes of these rules, any amendment of an existing plan to increase the number of shares which may be granted under the plan is to be treated as a new plan. Thus options granted as a result of a plan amendment adopted after September 23, 1975, would not be qualified options. It is not necessary, however, in the case of a plan adopted by September 23, 1975, for options to have been granted under the plan by that date or for the directors or shareholders to have authorized the specific grant of options under the plan to specific individuals.

If qualified options are granted under the transition rule, but the options are not exercised until after September 23, 1980, the committee intends that the option is to be treated as an option which did not have a readily ascertainable fair market value at the time it was granted (within the meaning of sec. 83(e)(3)). Thus, the value of the option in this case would not constitute income to the employee when granted (or at a time the transition rule expires), but if the option subsequently is exercised, and if the fair market value of the stock exceeds the option price, this excess will constitute ordinary income to the employee at the time of exercise.

The committee bill also requires that all outstanding restricted stock options (sec. 424) must be exercised on or before September 23, 1980, in order to receive the Federal tax treatment currently accorded these options.

[1] Generally similar tax treatment is also available in the case of "restricted" stock options which were the predecessors to qualified options, but restricted stock options are no longer being granted, and most restricted options which were granted in the past have now been exercised or have lapsed.

[2] However, if the option was nontransferable and was also subject to a substantial risk of forfeiture, recognition of income would be postponed until one or both of these encumbrances is removed.

[3] As indicated above, recognition of income could be postponed if the stock is not transferable and if it subject to a substantial risk of forfeture. In this case, the tax is imposed (at ordinary income rates) at the time when either of these two restrictions is removed and the tax base is the excess of the fair market value of the shares at the time when either of these two restrictions is removed over the amount which the employee originally paid for the property. However, under section 83, an employee who receives stock (or other property) in his employer corporation burdened by restrictions which would free him from paying a tax at that time may, nevertheless, elect to pay tax on the bargain element existing at that time. If the employee makes this election and pays tax when he exercises the option, any later increase in value of the shares will generally be taxable to him as capital gain (rather than compensation income) when he disposes of the shares.

As under present law, in the event of a corporate merger, consolidation or other reorganization, the employer corporation may substitute a new option for an old option, as long as the new option and the old option are substantially equivalent (sec. 425). Thus the surviving corporation in a corporate merger could substitute options on its stock for options on the stock of the nonsurviving corporation, so long as the options were of equivalent value and the new option did not provide for any additional benefits for the employee which he did not have under the old option. These substitutions can occur after September 23, 1975, on the same basis as before that date. (Of course, "old options" could not be granted after September 23, 1975, by the acquired corporation, except as provided under the transition rules.)

Effective date

The amendments made by these provisions apply to taxable years ending after September 23, 1975.

Revenue effect

It is estimated that this provision will result in an increase in tax liability of *$7 million for calendar year 1976, $22 million for 1977, and* a decrease *in tax liability of $32 million for 1981.*— **House Ways and Means Committee Report.**

House bill

The House bill repeals qualified stock option treatment and subjects qualified stock options to the same rules as presently apply in the case of nonqualified options. The bill generally applies to options granted after September 23, 1973, but contains certain transition rules for options granted after that date under preexisting plans.

Senate amendment

The Senate amendment is generally the same as the House bill, including the transition rules, but applies to options granted after May 20, 1976. In addition, however, the Senate amendment contains a provision which allows an employee to elect early valuation of an option which does not have a readily ascertainable fair market value at the time it is granted. If the election is made, the option is to be valued and be subject to tax at the time it is granted. Otherwise, tax recognition is to be postponed until the option is exercised.

Conference agreement

Under the conference agreement, the qualified stock option provisions are repealed. The additional provision in Senate amendment dealing with an election for early valuation of an option which does not have a readily ascertainable fair market value when granted is not included in the bill (but see discussion below.) The agreement adopts the effective date of the Senate amendment. In interpreting the transition rules, the conferees agree with the statement in the Senate Finance Committee Report (p. 164) that if a corporation adopted an option plan in 1974 and is reorganized in 1977 into a holding company with one or more operating subsidiaries, the holding company may adopt the 1974 option plan and continue to grant qualified stock options to the extent permissible had the reorganization not occurred.

Under the conference agreement, for the future, all options are to be governed under the rules which apply under present law for nonqualified stock options. This means that if the option has a "readily ascertainable fair market value" at the time it is granted, then the value of the option will constitute ordinary income to the employee at that time, but any gain later realized by the employee upon the sale of any stock acquired under the option will generally be treated as capital gain. On the other hand, if the option does not have a readily ascertainable fair market value at the time it is granted, it would not constitute income to the employee at that time, but if the option is subsequently exercised, and if the fair market value of the stock exceeds the option price, this excess will constitute ordinary income to the employee at the time the option is exercised.

The conferees intend that in applying these rules for the future, the Service will make every reasonable effort to determine a fair market value for an option (i.e., in cases where similar property would be valued for estate tax purposes) where the employee irrevocably elects (by reporting the option as income on his tax return or in some other manner to be specified in regulations) to have the option value at the time it is granted (particularly in the case of an option granted for a new business venture). The conferees intend that the Service will promulgate regulations and rulings setting forth as specifically as possible the criteria which will be weighed in valuing an option which the employee elects to value at the time it is granted.

The conferees intend that under these rules, the value of an option would be determined under all the facts and circumstances of a particular case. Among other factors that would be taken into account would be the value of the stock underlying the option (to the extent that this could be ascertained), the length of the option period (the longer the period, the greater the chance the underlying stock might increase in value), the earnings potential of the corporation, and the success (or lack of success) of similar ventures. Corporate assets, including patents, trade secrets and knowhow would also have to be taken into account.

The conferees anticipate that under the Service's rules, certain options, such as those traded publicly, would be treated as having a readily ascertainable fair market value, regardless of whether the employee makes an election. However, the regulations could provide that in certain other cases the option would ordinarily not be valued at the time it is granted unless the employee so elects.— **Conference Committee Report.**

[¶ 13,124.08]

Committee Report on P.L. 100-647 (Technical and Miscellaneous Revenue Act of 1988)

[House Committee Report]

Incentive Stock Options

The bill provides that an option shall not be treated as an incentive stock option if, at the time the option is granted, the terms of the option provide that it will not be treated as an incentive stock option. Thus, an option that otherwise satisfies the requirements of section 422A(b) shall not be treated as an incentive stock option if, at the time of grant, the option is designated as not constituting an incentive stock option. In the case of an option granted after December 31, 1986, and before the date of enactment of this bill, an option will not be treated as an incentive stock option if the terms of the option are so amended before 90 days after the enactment of this bill.

The bill also deletes the $100,000 requirement added by the Act and instead provides that to the extent the aggregate fair market value (determined at the time the option is granted) of stock with respect to which options meeting the requirements of section 422A(b) are exercisable for the first time by any individual during any calendar year (under all plans of the individual's employer corporation and its parent and subsidiary corporations) exceeds $100,000, then such options shall not be treated as incentive stock options. This rule is applied by taking options that meet the requirements of section 422A(b) and are exercisable for the first time in the calendar year into account in the order granted.

[¶ 13,124.085]

Committee Reports on P.L. 98-369 (Tax Reform Act of 1984)

[Senate Committee Report]

Present Law

* * *

In addition, present law provides for "incentive stock options", under which there are no tax consequences when the option is granted or, except for the alternative minimum tax, when the option is exercised, and the employee generally is taxed at capital gains rates when the stock received on exercise of the option is sold. No business expense deduction is allowed to the employer with respect to an incentive stock option (sec. 421(a)).

The option price of an incentive stock option must equal or exceed the fair market value of the stock at the time the option is granted. These options must not be exercisable while an earlier incentive stock option is outstanding. This rule prevents a downward adjustment in the option price by the granting of a new option where the stock has declined in value. These options may not be transferable by the employee other than by reason of death. A special rule provides that the change in terms of an option to meet the nontransferability requirements of section 422A(b)(5) will not be treated as the grant of a new option requiring the option price to be set by reference to the stock's fair market value on the modification date (sec. 425(h)(3)(B)).

Finally, the difference between the fair market value of the stock on the date the option is exercised and the option price of the stock is an item of tax preference for purposes of the individual alternative minimum tax.

* * *

Two amendments are made to the incentive stock option provision to insure that the fair market value requirements of present law may not be avoided. First, the determination of fair market value is to be made without regard to any restriction other than a restriction which, by its terms, will never lapse. Second, a change in the terms of an option to make it nontransferable in order to qualify as an incentive stock option will be treated as the grant of a new option. The option will thus be required to meet the incentive stock option requirements, including the option price requirement, based on the later grant date.

Effective Date

* * *

The provisions relating to incentive stock options will apply to options granted, exercised, or modified (as the case may be) after March 20, 1984.

[Conference Committee Report]

House bill

No provision.

Senate amendment

The Senate amendment disregards "lapse restrictions" in determining the fair market value of the stock. It also treats the modification of an option making it nontransferable as the grant of a new option, thus requiring the fair market value to be determined on the modification date.

The provision generally applies to options granted, exercised or modified (as the case may be) after March 20, 1984. If an option [is] granted after March 20, 1984, pursuant to corporate action taken before that date, the provision will not apply if the option is issued before September 20, 1984 (or, in the case of the minimum tax, if the option is exercised before December 31, 1984).

Conference agreement

The conference agreement generally follows the Senate amendment. The date by which corporate action must be taken under the transitional rule is changed to May 15, 1984.

[¶ 13,124.09]

Committee Report on P.L. 97-448 (Technical Corrections Act of 1982)

The bill allows a good faith valuation to be used in applying the maximum dollar limit and the carryover of any unused limit, under regulations prescribed by the Treasury.

The bill provides that an employee's transfer of stock acquired pursuant to the exercise of a statutory stock option to acquire other stock in connection with the exercise of an incentive stock option will be treated as a recognition transaction if the transferred stock has not met the minimum statutory holding period to receive special tax treatment (under sec. 421(a)).

Thus, such a disposition will result in ordinary income treatment (under section 421(b)) with respect to the stock disposed of, but will not affect the favorable tax treatment for the stock received.

Effective date

The provisions generally apply with respect to incentive stock options granted on or after January 1, 1976, and exercised after 1980. The provision relating to taxable dispositions applies to dispositions made after March 15, 1982.

Present law

ERTA added provisions to allow all income with respect to certain employee stock options ("incentive stock options") to be taxed at capital gains rates when the stock received on the exercise of the option is sold. The amount of stock with respect to which incentive stock options may be granted in any year after 1980 is limited to $100,000 (determined at the time of grant) plus a partial carryover of any previously unused amount.

Explanation of provision

The bill clarifies that if the option stock is sold or exchanged in a recognition transaction prior to the end of the required holding period (two years from the grant of the option and one year from the exercise), the amount of ordinary income to be recognized is limited to the excess of the amount realized over the adjusted basis of the stock.

The bill clarifies that the dollar limit (under sec. 422A(b)(8) with respect to options which may be granted in any year applies only to incentive stock options and that the limit is not affected by non-qualified options.

[¶ 13,124.10]

Committee Reports on P.L. 97-34 (Economic Recovery Act of 1981)

[Senate Committee Report]

In general.—The bill provides for "incentive stock options," which will be taxed in a manner similar to the tax treatment previously applied to restricted and qualified stock options. That is, there will be no tax consequences when an incentive stock option is granted or when the option is exercised, and the employee will be taxed at capital gains rates when the stock received on exercise of the option is sold. Similarly, no business expense deduction will be allowed to the employer with respect to an incentive stock option.

The term "incentive stock option" means an option granted to an individual, for any reason connected with his or her employment, by the employer corporation or by a parent or subsidiary corporation of the employer corporation, to purchase stock of any of such corporations.

Requirements (holding period, etc.).—To receive incentive stock option treatment, the bill provides that the employee must not dispose of the stock within two years after the option is granted, and must hold the stock itself for at least one year. If all requirements other than these holding period rules are met, the tax will be imposed on sale of the stock, but gain will be treated as ordinary income rather than capital gain, and the employer will be allowed a deduction at that time.[1]

In addition, for the entire time from the date of granting the option until three months before the date of exercise, the option holder must be an employee either of the company granting the option, a parent or subsidiary of that corporation, or a corporation (or parent or subsidiary of that corporation) which has assumed the option of another corporation as a result of a corporate reorganization, liquidation, etc. This requirement and the holding period requirements are waived in the case of the death of the employee.[2]

Terms of option.—For an option to qualify as an "incentive stock option," terms of the option itself must meet the following conditions:

1. The option must be granted under a plan specifying the number of shares of stock to be issued and the employees or class of employees to receive the options. This plan must be approved by the stockholders of the corporation within 12 months before or after the plan is adopted.

2. The option must be granted within ten years of the date the plan is adopted or the date the plan is approved by the stockholders, whichever is earlier.

3. The option must by its terms be exercisable only within 20 years of the date it is granted.

4. The option price must equal or exceed the fair market value of the stock at the time the option is granted. This requirement will be deemed satisfied if there has been a good faith attempt to value the stock accurately, even if the option price is less than the stock value.

5. The option by its terms must be nontransferable other than at death and must be exercisable during the employee's lifetime only by the employee.

6. The employee must not, immediately before the option is granted, own stock representing more than ten percent of the voting power or value of all classes of stock of the employer corporation or its parent or subsidiary.[3] However, the stock ownership limitation will be waived if the option price is at least 110 percent of the fair market value (at the time the option is granted) of the stock subject to the option and the option by its terms is not exercisable more than five years from the date it is granted.

7. The option by its terms is not to be exercisable while there is outstanding any incentive stock option which was granted to the employee at an earlier time. For this purpose, an option which has not been exercised in full is outstanding for the period during which under its initial terms it could have been exercised. Thus, the cancellation of an earlier option will not enable a subsequent option to be exercised any sooner. Also, for this purpose an option is considered to retain its original date of grant even if the terms of the option or the plan are later amended to qualify the option as an incentive stock option.

Other rules.—The bill provides that stock acquired on exercise of the option may be paid for with stock of the corporation granting the option.

The difference between the option price and the fair market value of the stock at the exercise of the option will not be an item of tax preference.

Also, under the bill, any option which was a qualified stock option or restricted stock option under prior law will become an incentive stock option, if it was not exercised before January 1, 1981, and if it otherwise satisfies requirements for incentive stock options. Such an option will not be subject to the minimum tax.

An option will not be disqualified because of the inclusion of any condition not inconsistent with the qualification requirements,[4] nor because the corporation may make a cash payment to the employee at the time of exercise.

Effective Date

The bill generally applies to options exercised or granted after December 31, 1980, or outstanding on such date. However, in the case of an option which was granted on or before December 31, 1980, and which was not a qualified option, the corporation granting the option may elect (within six months after enactment of the bill) to have the option not be treated as an incentive stock option.

In the case of an option granted before 1982, the modification or deletion of any stock appreciation right or right to receive cash payments to permit the option to qualify as an incentive stock option can be made within one year of the enactment of the bill without the modification being treated as the grant of a new option.

In addition, the terms of a stock option plan or an option issued before 1982 can be modified to conform to the incentive stock option rules within one year of the date of enactment of the bill, without the modification being considered as giving rise to a new option requiring a new option price.

Conference agreement

The agreement generally follows the Senate amendment except—

(1) the term of the option may not exceed 10 years from the date of grant,

(2) a disabled employee has 12 months after leaving employment to exercise the option,

(3) the amendment clarifies that additional cash or other property may be transferred to the employee at the time the option is exercised, so long as such property is subject to inclusion in income under the provisions of section 83,

[1] In the case of a sale which does not meet the holding period requirements, the amount of ordinary income, and the amount of the employer's deduction, will be limited to the difference between the amount realized on the sale and the option price.

[2] For purposes of the holding period requirements, the bill also provides that certain transfers by an insolvent individual of stock received pursuant to exercise of an incentive stock option are not to be treated as dispositions of such stock. The transfers covered by this rule are transfers to a trustee, receiver, or similar fiduciary, or other transfers for the benefit of the individual's creditors, in a bankruptcy case or similar insolvency proceeding.

[3] For this purpose, the individual is considered to own stock owned directly or indirectly by brothers and sisters, spouse, ancestors, and lineal descendants, and stock owned directly or indirectly by a corporation, partnership, estate, or trust is considered as being owned proportionately by shareholders, partners, or beneficiaries.

[4] For example, the transfer of shares of stock for local law purposes will not disqualify a plan where the arrangement constitutes the grant of an option for Federal tax purposes. Treas. Reg. §§1.83-3(a) and 1.421-7(a) contain rules relating to the definition of "option" and rules setting forth when a "transfer" of property as compensation for services occurs.

(4) the managers wish to clarify that alternative rights may be granted, so long as no alternative options to purchase stock are granted which cause the option to violate the terms of section 422A(b), and

(5) in the case of options granted after 1980, the terms of the plan must limit the amount of aggregate fair market value of the stock (determined at the time of the grant of the option) for which any employee may be granted incentive stock options in any calendar year to not more than $100,000 plus the carryover amount. The carryover amount from any year is one-half of the amount by which $100,000 exceeds the value (at time of grant) of the stock for which incentive stock options were granted in such prior year. Amounts may be carried over 3 years. Options granted in any year use up the $100,000 current year limitation first and then the carryover from earliest year.

The agreement will apply to options granted after January 1, 1976, and exercised after December 31, 1980, or outstanding on such later date.

However, in the case of options granted before January 1, 1981, an option is an incentive stock option only if the employer elects such treatment for an option. The aggregate value (determined at time of grant) of stock for which any employee may be granted incentive stock options prior to 1981 shall not exceed $50,000 per calendar year and $200,000 in the aggregate.

In the case of an option granted after January 1, 1976, and outstanding on the date of enactment, the option terms (or the terms of the plan under which the option was granted or shareholder approval) may be changed, to conform to the incentive stock option rules, within one year of the date of enactment, without the change giving rise to a new option requiring the setting of an option price based on a later valuation date.

All such changes relate back to the time of granting the original option. For example, if the option price of a ten-year option granted in 1978 is increased during the one year after date of enactment to 100 percent (110 percent, if applicable) of the fair market value of the stock on the date the option was granted in 1978, the price requirement will be met. Likewise, if the term of an option held by a 10-percent shareholder is shortened to five years from the date the option was granted, the 10-percent stock ownership limitation will not apply.

[Code Sec. 423]

[¶ 13,130.08]

Committee Report on P.L. 108-357 (American Jobs Creation Act of 2004)

For Committee Reports on P.L. 108-357 relating to stock options, see ¶ 13,100.05.

[¶ 13,132.085]

Committee Report on P.L. 98-369 (Tax Reform Act of 1984)

[Senate Committee Report]

The holding period for determining whether gain or loss on the sale or exchange of a capital asset or certain business property is long-term or short-term is reduced from 1 year to 6 months. Thus, property held for more than 6 months will be eligible for long-term capital gain or loss treatment.

Effective Date

The amendment applies to assets acquired after February 29, 1984.

[Code Sec. 424]

[¶ 13,140.09]

Committee Report on P.L. 94-455 (Tax Reform Act of 1976)

For Committee Reports on P.L. 94-455 covering amendments made to Code Sec. 424, see ¶ 13,120.09.

[¶ 13,150.08]

Committee Report on P.L. 104-188 (Small Business Job Protection Act)

Technical Corrections to the Revenue Reconciliation Act of 1990

[House Committee Report]

Expired or obsolete provisions

The bill makes several amendments to restore the substance of prior law which was inadvertently changed by the deadwood provisions of the 1990 Act. * * *

The bill also makes several nonsubstantive clerical amendments to conform the Code to the amendments made by the deadwood provisions. None of these amendments is intended to change the substance of pre-1990 law.

[Conference Committee Report]

Senate Amendment

The Senate amendment is the same as the House bill.

Conference Agreement

The conference agreement follows the House bill and the Senate amendment * * *.

[¶ 13,150.09]

Committee Report on P.L. 98-369 (Tax Reform Act of 1984)

For the Committee Report on P.L. 98-369, relating to the modifications of the fair market value requirements of incentive stock options, see ¶ 13,124.085.

[Code Sec. 430]

[¶ 13,151L.50]

Committee Report on P.L. 109–280 (Pension Protection Act of 2006)

For the Committee Report on P.L. 109-280 on minimum funding standards for single-employer defined benefit pension plans, see ¶ 12,250.023.

[Code Sec. 431]

[¶ 13,151M.50]

Committee Report on P.L. 109-280 (Pension Protection Act of 2006)

[Joint Committee on Taxation Report]

[Funding rules for multiemployer defined benefit plans]

Amortization periods

The provision modifies the amortization periods applicable to multiemployer plans so that the amortization period for most charges is 15 years. Under the provision, past service liability under the plan is amortized over 15 years (rather than 30); past service liability due to plan amendments is amortized over 15 years (rather than 30); and experience gains and losses resulting from a change in actuarial assumptions are amortized over 15 years (rather than 30). As under present law, experience gains and losses and waived funding deficiencies are amortized over 15 years. The new amortization periods do not apply to amounts being amortized under present-law amortization periods, that is, no recalculation of amortization schedules already in effect is required under the provision. The provision eliminates the alternative funding standard account.

Actuarial assumptions

The provision provides that in applying the funding rules, all costs, liabilities, interest rates, and other factors are required to be determined on the basis of actuarial assumptions and methods, each of which is reasonable (taking into account the experience of the plan and reasonable expectations). In addition, as under present law, the assumptions are required to offer the actuary's best estimate of anticipated experience under the plan.

Extension of amortization periods

The provision provides that, upon application to the Secretary of the Treasury, the Secretary is required to grant an extension of the amortization period for up to five years with respect to any unfunded past service liability, investment loss, or experience loss. Included with the application must be a certification by the plan's actuary that (1) absent the extension, the plan would have an accumulated funding deficiency in the current plan year and any of the nine succeeding plan years, (2) the plan sponsor has adopted a plan to improve the plan's funding status, (3) taking into account the extension, the plan is projected to have sufficient assets to timely pay its expected benefit liabilities and other anticipated expenditures, and (4) that required notice is provided. The automatic extension provision does not apply with respect to any application submitted after December 31, 2014.

The Secretary of the Treasury may also grant an additional extension of such amortization periods for an additional five years. The standards for determining whether such an extension may be granted are the same as under present law. In addition, the provision requires the Secretary of the Treasury to act upon an application for an additional extension within 180 days after submission. If the Secretary rejects the application, the Secretary must provide notice to the plan detailing the specific reasons for the rejection.

As under present law, these extensions do not apply unless the applicant demonstrates to the satisfaction of the Treasury Secretary that notice of the application has been provided to each affected party (as defined in ERISA section 4001(a)(21)).

Interest rate applicable to funding waivers and extension of amortization periods

The provision eliminates the special interest rate rule for funding waivers and extensions of amortization periods so that the plan rate applies.

Additional provisions

Controlled group liability for required contributions

The provision imposes joint and several liability to all members of the employer's controlled group for minimum required contributions to single-employer or multiemployer plans.

Shortfall funding method

The provision provides that, for plan years beginning before January 1, 2015, certain multiemployer plans may adopt, use or cease using the shortfall funding method and such adoption, use, or cessation of use is deemed approved by the Secretary of the Treasury. Plans are eligible if (1) the plan has not used the shortfall funding method during the five-year period ending on the day before the date the plan is to use the shortfall funding method; and (2) the plan is not operating under an amortization period extension and did not operate under such an extension during such five-year period. Benefit restrictions apply during a period that a multiemployer plan is using the shortfall funding method. In general, plan amendments increasing benefits cannot be adopted while the shortfall funding method is in use. The provision is not intended to affect a plan's ability to adopt the shortfall funding method with IRS approval or to affect a plan's right to change funding methods as otherwise permitted.

Effective Date

The provision is effective for plan years beginning after 2007.

[Special rule for certain benefits funded under an agreement approved by the PBGC]

The provision modifies the amortization periods applicable to multiemployer plans so that the amortization period for most charges is 15 years. Under the provision, past service liability under the plan is amortized over 15 years (rather than 30); past service liability due to plan amendments is amortized over 15 years (rather than 30); and experience gains and losses resulting from a change in actuarial assumptions are amortized over 15 years (rather than 30). As under present law, experience gains and losses and waived funding deficiencies are amortized over 15 years. The new amortization periods do not apply to amounts being amortized under present-law amortization periods, that is, no recalculation of amortization schedules already in effect is required under the provision. The provision eliminates the alternative funding standard account.

Effective Date

The provision is effective on the date of enactment

[Sunset of multiemployer plan funding provisions]

The provision directs the Secretary of Labor, the Secretary of Treasury, and the Executive Director of the PBGC, not later than December 31, 2011, to conduct a study of the effect of the changes made by the provision on the operation and funding status of multiemployer plans and report the results of the study, including recommendations for legislation, to Congress. The study must include (1) the effect of funding difficulties, funding rules in effect before the date of enactment, and the changes made by the provision on small businesses participating in multiemployer plans; (2) the effect on the financial status of small employers of funding targets set in funding improvement and rehabilitation plans and associated contribution increases, funding deficiencies, excise taxes, withdrawal liability, the possibility of alternative schedules and procedures for financially-troubled employers, and other aspects of the multiemployer system; and (3) the role of the multiemployer pension plan system in helping small employers to offer pension benefits.

The provision provides that the rules applicable to plans in endangered and critical status and the rules relating to the automatic amortization extension and shortfall funding method under the general funding rules for multiemployer plans do not apply to plan years beginning after December 31, 2014. The present-law rules are reinstated for such years except that funding improvement and rehabilitation plans and amortization schedules in effect at the time of the sunset continue.

Effective Date

The provision is effective on the date of enactment

[Code Sec. 432]

[¶ 13,151N.50]

Committee Report on P.L. 109-280 (Pension Protection Act of 2006)

[Joint Committee on Taxation Report]

In general

The provision provides additional funding rules for multiemployer defined benefit plans in effect on July 16, 2006, that are in endangered or critical status. The provision requires the adoption of and compliance with (1) a funding improvement plan in the case of a multiemployer plan in endangered status, and (2) a rehabilitation plan in the case of a multiemployer plan in critical status.

Under the provision, in the case of a plan in critical status, additional required contributions and benefit reductions apply and employers are relieved of liability for minimum required contributions under the otherwise applicable funding rules, provided that a rehabilitation plan is adopted and followed.

Annual certification of status; notice; annual reports

Not later than the 90th day of each plan year, the plan actuary must certify to the Secretary of the Treasury and to the plan sponsor whether or not the plan is in endangered or critical status for the plan year. In the case of a plan that is in a funding improvement or rehabilitation period, the actuary must certify whether or not the plan is making scheduled progress in meeting the requirements of its funding improvement or rehabilitation plan.

In making the determinations and projections applicable under the endangered and critical status rules, the plan actuary must make projections for the current and succeeding plan years of the current value of the assets of the plan and the present value of all liabilities to participants and beneficiaries under the plan for the current plan year as of the beginning of such year. The actuary's projections must be based on reasonable actuarial estimates, assumptions, and methods that offer the actuary's best estimate of anticipated experience under the plan. An exception to this rule applies in the case of projected industry activity. Any projection of activity in the industry or industries covered by the plan, including future covered employment and contribution levels, must be based on information provided by the plan sponsor, which shall act reasonably and in good faith. The projected present value of liabilities as of the beginning of the year must be based on the most recent actuarial statement required with respect to the most recently filed annual report or the actuarial valuation for the preceding plan year.

Any actuarial projection of plan assets must assume (1) reasonably anticipated employer contributions for the current and succeeding plan years, assuming that the terms of one or more collective bargaining agreements pursuant to which the plan is maintained for the current plan year continue in effect for the succeeding plan years, or (2) that employer contributions for the most recent plan year will continue indefinitely, but only if the plan actuary determines that there have been no significant demographic changes that would make continued application of such terms unreasonable.

Failure of the plan's actuary to certify the status of the plan is treated as a failure to file the annual report (thus, an ERISA penalty of up to $1,100 per day applies).

If a plan is certified to be in endangered or critical status, notification of the endangered or critical status must be provided within 30 days after the date of certification to the participants and beneficiaries, the bargaining parties, the PBGC and the Secretary of Labor.[61] If it is certified that a plan is or will be in critical status, the plan sponsor must included in the notice an explanation of the possibility that (1) adjustable benefits may be reduced and (2) such reductions may apply to participants and beneficiaries whose benefit commencement date is on or after the date such notice is provided for the first plan year in which the plan is in critical status. The Secretary of Labor is required to prescribe a model notice to satisfy these requirements.

The plan sponsor must annually update the funding improvement or rehabilitation plan. Updates are required to be filed with the plan's annual report.

Endangered status

Definition of endangered status

A multiemployer plan is in endangered status if the plan is not in critical status and, as of the beginning of the plan year, (1) the plan's funded percentage for the plan year is less than 80 percent, or (2) the plan has an accumulated funding deficiency for the plan year or is projected to have an accumulated funding deficiency in any of the six succeeding plan years (taking into account amortization extensions). A plan's funded percentage is the percentage of plan assets over accrued liability of the plan. A plan that meets the requirements of both (1) and (2) is treated as in seriously endangered status.

Information to be provided to bargaining parties

Within 30 days of the adoption of a funding improvement plan, the plan sponsor must provide to the bargaining parties schedules showing revised benefit structures, revised contribution structures, or both, which, if adopted, may reasonably be expected to enable the multiemployer plan to meet the applicable benchmarks in accordance with the funding improvement plan, including (1) one proposal for reductions in the amount of future benefit accruals necessary to achieve the applicable benchmarks, assuming no amendments increasing contributions under the plan (other than amendments increasing contributions necessary to achieve the applicable benchmarks after amendments have reduced future benefit accruals to the maximum extent permitted by law) (the "default schedule"), and (2) one proposal for increases in contributions under the plan necessary to achieve the applicable benchmarks, assuming no amendments reducing future benefit accruals under the plan. The applicable benchmarks are the requirements of the funding improvement plan (discussed below). The plan sponsor may provide the bargaining parties with additional information if deemed appropriate.

The plan sponsor must annually update any schedule of contribution rates to reflect the experience of the plan.

[61] If a plan actuary certifies that it is reasonably expected that a plan will be in critical status with respect to the first plan year after 2007, notice may be provided at any time after date of enactment, as long as it is provided on or before the date otherwise required.

Funding improvement plan and funding improvement period

In the case of a multiemployer plan in endangered status, a funding improvement plan must be adopted within 240 days following the deadline for certifying a plan's status.[62] A funding improvement plan is a plan which consists of the actions, including options or a range of options, to be proposed to the bargaining parties, formulated to provide, based on reasonably anticipated experience and reasonable actuarial assumptions, for the attainment by the plan of certain requirements.

The funding improvement plan must provide that during the funding improvement period, the plan will have a certain required increase in the funded percentage and no accumulated funding deficiency for any plan year during the funding improvement period, taking into account amortization extensions (the "applicable benchmarks"). In the case of a plan that is not in seriously endangered status, under the applicable benchmarks, the plan's funded percentage must increase such that the funded percentage as of the close of the funding improvement period equals or exceeds a percentage equal to the sum of (1) the funded percentage at the beginning of the period, plus (2) 33 percent of the difference between 100 percent and the percentage in (1). Thus, the difference between 100 percent and the plan's funded percentage at the beginning of the period must be reduced by at least one-third during the funding improvement period.

The funding improvement period is the 10-year period beginning on the first day of the first plan year beginning after the earlier of (1) the second anniversary of the date of adoption of the funding improvement plan, or (2) the expiration of collective bargaining agreements that were in effect on the due date for the actuarial certification of endangered status for the initial determination year and covering, as of such date, at least 75 percent of the plan's active participants. The period ends if the plan is no longer in endangered status or if the plan enters critical status.

In the case of a plan in seriously endangered status that is funded 70 percent or less, under the applicable benchmarks, the difference between 100 percent and the plan's funded percentage at the beginning of the period must be reduced by at least one-fifth during the funding improvement period. In the case of such plans, a 15-year funding improvement period is used.

In the case of a seriously endangered plan that is more than 70 percent funded as of the beginning of the initial determination year, the same benchmarks apply for plan years beginning on or before the date on which the last collective bargaining agreements in effect on the date for actuarial certification for the initial determination year and covering at least 75 percent of active employees in the multiemployer plan have expired if the plan actuary certifies within 30 days after certification of endangered status that the plan is not projected to attain the funding percentage increase otherwise required by the provision. Thus, for such plans, the difference between 100 percent and the plan's funded percentage at the beginning of the period must be reduced by at least one-fifth during the 15-year funding improvement period. For subsequent years for such plans, if the plan actuary certifies that the plan is not able to attain the increase generally required under the provision, the same benchmarks continue to apply.

As previously discussed, the plan sponsor must annually update the funding improvement plan and must file the update with the plan's annual report.

If, for the first plan year following the close of the funding improvement period, the plan's actuary certifies that the plan is in endangered status, such year is treated as an initial determination year. Thus, a new funding improvement plan must be adopted within 240 days of the required certification date. In such case, the plan may not be amended in a manner inconsistent with the funding improvement plan in effect for the preceding plan year until a new funding improvement plan is adopted.

Requirements pending approval of plan and during funding improvement period

Certain restrictions apply during the period beginning on the date of certification for the initial determination year and ending on the day before the first day of the funding improvement period (the "funding plan adoption period").

During the funding plan adoption period, the plan sponsor may not accept a collective bargaining agreement or participation agreement that provides for (1) a reduction in the level of contributions for any participants; (2) a suspension of contributions with respect to any period of service; or (3) any new or indirect exclusion of younger or newly hired employees from plan participation.

In addition, during the funding plan adoption period, except in the case of amendments required as a condition of qualification under the Internal Revenue Code or to apply with other applicable law, no amendment may be adopted which increases liabilities of the plan by reason of any increase in benefits, any change in accrual of benefits, or any change in the rate at which benefits become nonforfeitable under the plan.

In the case of a plan in seriously endangered status, during the funding plan adoption period, the plan sponsor must take all reasonable actions (consistent with the terms of the plan and present law) which are expected, based on reasonable assumptions, to achieve an increase in the plan's funded percentage and a postponement of an accumulated funding deficiency for at least one additional plan year. These actions include applications for extensions of amortization periods, use of the shortfall funding method in making funding standard account computations, amendments to the plan's benefit structure, reductions in future benefit accruals, and other reasonable actions.

Upon adoption of a funding improvement plan, the plan may not be amended to be inconsistent with the funding improvement plan. During the funding improvement period, a plan sponsor may not accept a collective bargaining agreement or participation agreement with respect to the multiemployer plan that provides for (1) a reduction in the level of contributions for any participants; (2) a suspension of contributions with respect to any period of service, or (3) any new direct or indirect exclusion of younger or newly hired employees from plan participation.

After the adoption of a funding improvement plan, a plan may not be amended to increase benefits, including future benefit accruals, unless the plan actuary certifies that the benefit increase is consistent with the funding improvement plan and is paid for out of contributions not required by the funding improvement plan to meet the applicable benchmark in accordance with the schedule contemplated in the funding improvement plan.

Effect of and penalty for failure to adopt a funding improvement plan

If a collective bargaining agreement providing for contributions under a multiemployer plan that was in effect at the time the plan entered endangered status expires, and after receiving one or more schedules from the plan sponsor, the bargaining parties fail to agree on changes to contribution or benefit schedules necessary to meet the applicable benchmarks, the plan sponsor must implement the default schedule. The schedule must be implemented on the earlier of the date (1) on which the Secretary of Labor certifies that the parties are at an impasse, or (2) which is 180 days after the date on which the collective bargaining agreement expires.

In the case of the failure of a plan sponsor to adopt a funding improvement plan by the end of the 240-day period after the required certification date, an ERISA penalty of up to $1,100 a day applies.

Excise tax on employers failing to meet required contributions

If the funding improvement plan requires an employer to make contributions to the plan, an excise tax applies upon the failure of the employer to make such required contributions within the time required under the plan. The amount of tax is equal to the amount of the required contribution the employer failed to make in a timely manner.

Application of excise tax to plans in endangered status/penalty for failure to achieve benchmarks

In the case of a plan in endangered status, which is not in seriously endangered status, a civil penalty of $1,100 a day applies for the failure of the plan to meet the applicable benchmarks by the end of the funding improvement period.

In the case of a plan in seriously endangered status, an excise tax applies for the failure to meet the benchmarks by the end of the funding improvement period. In such case, an excise tax applies based on the greater of (1) the amount of the contributions necessary to meet such benchmarks or (2) the plan's accumulated funding deficiency. The excise tax applies for each succeeding plan year until the benchmarks are met.

Waiver of excise tax

In the case of a failure which is due to reasonable cause and not to willful neglect, the Secretary of the Treasury may waive all or part of the excise tax on employers failing to make required contributions and the excise tax for failure to achieve the applicable benchmarks. The party against whom the tax is imposed has the burden of establishing that the failure was due to reasonable cause and not willful neglect. Reasonable cause includes unanticipated and material market fluctuations, the loss of a significant contributing employer, or other factors to the extent that the payment of tax would be excessive or otherwise inequitable relative to the failure involved. The determination of reasonable cause is based on the facts and circumstances of each case and requires the parties to act with ordinary business care and prudence. The standard requires the funding improvement plan to be based on reasonably foreseeable events. It is expected that reasonable cause would include instances in which the plan experiences a net equity loss of at least ten percent during the funding improvement period, a change in plan demographics such as the bankruptcy of a significant contributing employer, a legal change (including the outcome of litigation) that unexpectedly increases the plan's benefit obligations, or a strike or lockout for a significant period.

Critical status

Definition of critical status

A multiemployer plan is in critical status for a plan year if as of the beginning of the plan year:

1. The funded percentage of the plan is less than 65 percent and the sum of (A) the market value of plan assets, plus (B) the present value of reasonably anticipated employer and employee contributions for the current plan year and each of the six succeeding plan years (assuming that the terms of the collective bargaining agreements continue in effect) is less than the present value of

[62] This requirement applies for the initial determination year (i.e., the first plan year that the plan is in endangered status).

all benefits projected to be payable under the plan during the current plan year and each of the six succeeding plan years (plus administrative expenses),

2. (A) The plan has an accumulated funding deficiency for the current plan year, not taking into account any amortization extension, or (B) the plan is projected to have an accumulated funding deficiency for any of the three succeeding plan years (four succeeding plan years if the funded percentage of the plan is 65 percent or less), not taking into account any amortization extension,

3. (A) The plan's normal cost for the current plan year, plus interest for the current plan year on the amount of unfunded benefit liabilities under the plan as of the last day of the preceding year, exceeds the present value of the reasonably anticipated employer contributions for the current plan year, (B) the present value of nonforfeitable benefits of inactive participants is greater than the present value of nonforfeitable benefits of active participants, and (C) the plan has an accumulated funding deficiency for the current plan year, or is projected to have an accumulated funding deficiency for any of the four succeeding plan years (not taking into account amortization period extensions), or

4. The sum of (A) the market value of plan assets, plus (B) the present value of the reasonably anticipated employer contributions for the current plan year and each of the four succeeding plan years (assuming that the terms of the collective bargaining agreements continue in effect) is less than the present value of all benefits projected to be payable under the plan during the current plan year and each of the four succeeding plan years (plus administrative expenses).

Additional contributions during critical status

In the case of a plan in critical status, the provision imposes an additional required contribution ("surcharge") on employers otherwise obligated to make a contribution in the initial critical year, i.e., the first plan year for which the plan is in critical status. The amount of the surcharge is five percent of the contribution otherwise required to be made under the applicable collective bargaining agreement. The surcharge is 10 percent of contributions otherwise required in the case of succeeding plan years in which the plan is in critical status. The surcharge applies 30 days after the employer is notified by the plan sponsor that the plan is in critical status and the surcharge is in effect. The surcharges are due and payable on the same schedule as the contributions on which the surcharges are based. Failure to make the surcharge payment is treated as a delinquent contribution. The surcharge is not required with respect to employees covered by a collective bargaining agreement (or other agreement pursuant to which the employer contributes), beginning on the effective date of a collective bargaining agreement (or other agreement) that includes terms consistent with a schedule presented by the plan sponsor. The amount of the surcharge may not be the basis for any benefit accrual under the plan.

Surcharges are disregarded in determining an employer's withdrawal liability except for purposes of determining the unfunded vested benefits attributable to an employer under ERISA section 4211(c)(4) or a comparable method approved under ERISA section 4211(c)(5).[63]

Reductions to previously earned benefits

Notwithstanding the anti-cutback rules, the plan sponsor may make any reductions to adjustable benefits which the plan sponsor deems appropriate, based upon the outcome of collective bargaining over the schedules required to be provided by the plan sponsor as discussed below. Adjustable benefits means (1) benefits, rights, and features under the plan, including post-retirement death benefits, 60-month guarantees, disability benefits not yet in pay status, and similar benefits; (2) any early retirement benefit or retirement-type subsidy and any benefit payment option (other than the qualified joint-and-survivor annuity); and (3) benefit increase that would not be eligible for PBGC guarantee on the first day of the initial critical year because the increases were adopted (or, if later, took effect) less than 60 months before such first day. Except as provided in (3), nothing should be construed to permit a plan to reduce the level of a participant's accrued benefit payable at normal retirement age.

The plan sponsor may not reduce adjustable benefits of any participant or beneficiary whose benefit commencement date is before the date on which the plan provides notice to the participant or beneficiary that the plan is in critical status and that benefits may be reduced. An exception applies in the case of benefit increases that would not be eligible for PBGC guarantee because the increases were adopted less than 60 months before the first day of the initial critical year.

The plan sponsor must include in the schedules provided to the bargaining parties an allowance for funding the benefits of participants with respect to whom contributions are not currently required to be made, and shall reduce their benefits to the extent permitted under the Code and ERISA and considered appropriate by the plan sponsor based on the plan's then current overall funding status.

Notice of any reduction of adjustable benefits must be provided at least 30 days before the general effective date of the reduction for all participants and beneficiaries. Benefits may not be reduced until the notice requirement is satisfied. Notice must be provided to (1) plan participants and beneficiaries; (2) each employer who has an obligation to contribute under the plans; and (3) each employee organization which, for purposes of collective bargaining, represents plan participants employed by such employer. The notice must contain (1) sufficient information to enable participants and beneficiaries to understand the effect of any reduction of their benefits, including an estimate (on an annual or monthly basis) of any affected adjustable benefit that a participant or beneficiary would otherwise have been eligible for as of the general effective date for benefit reductions; and (2) information as to the rights and remedies of plan participants and beneficiaries as well as how to contact the Department of Labor for further information and assistance where appropriate. The notice must be provided in a form and manner prescribed in regulations of the Secretary of Labor. In such regulations, the Secretary of Labor must establish a model notice.

Benefit reduction are disregarded in determining a plan's unfunded vested benefits for purposes of determining an employer's withdrawal liability.[64]

Information to be provided to bargaining parties

Within 30 days after adoption of the rehabilitation plan, the plan sponsor must provide to the bargaining parties schedules showing revised benefit structures, revised contribution structures, or both which, if adopted, may reasonably be expected to enable the multiemployer plan to emerge from critical status in accordance with the rehabilitation plan.[65] The schedules must reflect reductions in future benefit accruals and adjustable benefits and increases in contributions that the plan sponsor determined are reasonably necessary to emerge from critical status. One schedule must be designated as the default schedule and must assume no increases in contributions other than increases necessary to emerge from critical status after future benefit accruals and other benefits (other than benefits the reduction or elimination of which are not permitted under the anti-cutback rules) have been reduced. The plan sponsor may also provide additional information as appropriate.

The plan sponsor must periodically update any schedule of contributions rates to reflect the experience of the plan.

Rehabilitation plan

If a plan is in critical status for a plan year, the plan sponsor must adopt a rehabilitation plan within 240 days following the required date for the actuarial certification of critical status.[66]

A rehabilitation plan is a plan which consists of actions, including options or a range of options to be proposed to the bargaining parties, formulated, based on reasonable anticipated experience and reasonable actuarial assumptions, to enable the plan to cease to be in critical status by the end of the rehabilitation period and may include reductions in plan expenditures (including plan mergers and consolidations), reductions in future benefits accruals or increases in contributions, if agreed to by the bargaining parties, or any combination of such actions.

A rehabilitation plan must provide annual standards for meeting the requirements of the rehabilitation. The plan must also include the schedules required to be provided to the bargaining parties.

If the plan sponsor determines that, based on reasonable actuarial assumptions and upon exhaustion of all reasonable measures, the plan cannot reasonably be expected to emerge from critical status by the end of the rehabilitation period, the plan must include reasonable measures to emerge from critical status at a later time or to forestall possible insolvency. In such case, the plan must set forth alternatives considered, explain why the plan is not reasonable expected to emerge from critical status by the end of the rehabilitation period, and specify when, if ever, the plan is expected to emerge from critical status in accordance with the rehabilitation plan.

As previously discussed, the plan sponsor must annually update the rehabilitation plan and must file the update with the plan's annual report.

Rehabilitation period

The rehabilitation period is the 10-year period beginning on the first day of the first plan year following the earlier of (1) the second anniversary of the date of adoption of the rehabilitation plan or (2) the expiration of collective bargaining agreements that were in effect on the due date for the actuarial certification of critical status for the initial critical year and covering at least 75 percent of the active participants in the plan.

The rehabilitation period ends if the plan emerges from critical status. A plan in critical status remains in critical status until a plan year for which the plan actuary certifies that the plan is not projected to have an accumulated funding deficiency for the plan year or any of the nine succeeding plan years, without regard to the use of the shortfall method and taking into account amortization period extensions.

Rules for reductions in future benefit accrual rates

Any schedule including reductions in future benefit accruals forming part of a rehabilitation plan must not reduce the rate of benefit accruals below (1) a monthly benefit (payable as a single life annuity commencing at the participant's

[63] The PBGC is directed to prescribe simplified methods for determining withdrawal liability in this case.

[64] The PBGC is directed to prescribe simplified methods for determining withdrawal liability in this case.

[65] A schedule of contribution rates provided by the plan sponsor and relied upon by bargaining parties in negotiating a collective bargaining agreement must remain in effect for the duration of the collective bargaining agreement.

[66] The requirement applies with respect to the initial critical year.

normal retirement age) equal to one percent of the contributions required to be made with respect to a participant or the equivalent standard accrual rate for a participant or group of participants under the collective bargaining agreements in effect as of the first day of the initial critical year, or (2) if lower, the accrual rate under the plan on such first day.

The equivalent standard accrual rate is determined by the plan sponsor based on the standard or average contribution base units which the plan sponsor determines to be representative for active participants and such other factors that the plan sponsor determines to be relevant.

Benefit reductions are disregarded in determining an employer's withdrawal liability.

Requirements pending approval and during rehabilitation period

Rehabilitation plan adoption period.—Certain restrictions apply during the period beginning on the date of certification and ending on the day before the first day of the rehabilitation period (defined as the "rehabilitation plan adoption period").

During the rehabilitation plan adoption period, the plan sponsor may not accept a collective bargaining agreement or participation agreement that provides for (1) a reduction in the level of contributions for any participants; (2) a suspension of contributions with respect to any period of service; or (3) any new direct or indirect exclusion of younger or newly hired employees from plan participation. Except in the case of amendments required as a condition of qualification under the Internal Revenue Code or to comply with other applicable law, during the rehabilitation plan adoption period, no amendments that increase the liabilities of the plan by reason of any increase in benefits, any change in the accrual of benefits, or any change in the rate at which benefits become nonforfeitable may be adopted.

During rehabilitation period.—A plan may not be amended after the date of adoption of a rehabilitation plan to be inconsistent with the rehabilitation plan.

A plan may not be amended after the date of adoption of a rehabilitation plan to increase benefits (including future benefit accruals) unless the plan actuary certifies that such increase is paid for out of additional contributions not contemplated by the rehabilitation plan and, after taking into account the benefit increases, the plan is still reasonably expected to emerge from critical status by the end of the rehabilitation period on the schedule contemplated by the rehabilitation plan.

Beginning on the date that notice of certification of the plan's critical status is sent, lump sum and other similar benefits may not be paid. The restriction does not apply if the present value of the participant's accrued benefit does not exceed $5,000. The restriction also does not apply to any makeup payment in the case of a retroactive annuity starting date or any similar payment of benefits owed with respect to a prior period.

The plan sponsor must annually update the plan and must file updates with the plan's annual report. Schedules must be annually updated to reflect experience of the plan.

Effective Date

The provision is effective for plan years beginning after 2007.

[Special rule for certain benefits funded under an agreement approved by the PBGC]

The provision modifies the amortization periods applicable to multiemployer plans so that the amortization period for most charges is 15 years. Under the provision, past service liability under the plan is amortized over 15 years (rather than 30); past service liability due to plan amendments is amortized over 15 years (rather than 30); and experience gains and losses resulting from a change in actuarial assumptions are amortized over 15 years (rather than 30). As under present law, experience gains and losses and waived funding deficiencies are amortized over 15 years. The new amortization periods do not apply to amounts being amortized under present-law amortization periods, that is, no recalculation of amortization schedules already in effect is required under the provision. The provision eliminates the alternative funding standard account.

Effect and penalty for failure to adopt a rehabilitation plan

If a collective bargaining agreement providing for contributions under a multiemployer plan that was in effect at the time the plan entered endangered status expires, and after receiving one of more schedules from the plan sponsor, the bargaining parties fail to adopt a contribution or benefit schedule with terms consistent with the rehabilitation plan and the scheduled from the plan sponsor, the plan sponsor must implement the default schedule. The schedule must be implemented on the earlier of the date (1) on which the Secretary of Labor certifies that the parties are at an impasse, or (2) which is 180 days after the date on which the collective bargaining agreement expires.

Upon the failure of a plan sponsor to adopt a rehabilitation plan within 240 days after the date required for certification, an ERISA penalty of $1,100 a day applies. In addition, upon the failure to timely adopt a rehabilitation plan, an excise tax is imposed on the plan sponsor equal to the greater of (1) the present law excise tax or (2) $1,100 per day. The tax must be paid by the plan sponsor.

Excise tax on employers failing to meet required contributions

If the rehabilitation plan requires an employer to make contributions to the plan, an excise tax applies upon the failure of the employer to make such required contributions within the time required under the plan. The amount of tax is equal to the amount of the required contribution the employer failed to make in a timely manner.

Application of excise tax to plans in critical status/penalty for failure to meet benchmarks or make scheduled progress

In the case of a plan in critical status, if a rehabilitation plan is adopted and complied with, employers are not liable for contributions otherwise required under the general funding rules. In addition, the present-law excise tax does not apply.

If a plan fails to leave critical status at the end of the rehabilitation period or fails to make scheduled progress in meeting its requirements under the rehabilitation plan for three consecutive years, the present law excise tax applies based on the greater of (1) the amount of the contributions necessary to leave critical status or make scheduled progress or (2) the plan's accumulated funding deficiency. The excise tax applies for each succeeding plan year until the requirements are met.

Waiver of excise tax

In the case of a failure which is due to reasonable cause and not to willful neglect, the Secretary of the Treasury may waive all or part of the excise tax on employers failing to make required contributions and the excise tax for failure to meet the rehabilitation plan requirements or make scheduled progress. The standards applicable to waivers of the excise tax for plans in endangered status apply to waivers of plans in critical status.

Additional rules

In general

The actuary's determination with respect to a plan's normal cost, actuarial accrued liability, and improvements in a plan's funded percentage must be based on the unit credit funding method (whether or not that method is used for the plan's actuarial valuation).

The actuary's determination with respect to a plan's normal cost, actuarial accrued liability, and improvements in a plan's funded percentage must be based on the unit credit funding method (whether or not that method is used for the plan's actuarial valuation).

In the case of a plan sponsor described under section 404(c) of the Code, the term "plan sponsor" means the bargaining parties.

Expedited resolution of plan sponsor decisions

If, within 60 days of the due date for the adoption of a funding improvement plan or a rehabilitation plan, the plan sponsor has not agreed on a funding improvement plan or a rehabilitation plan, any member of the board or group that constitutes the plan sponsor may require that the plan sponsor enter into an expedited dispute resolution procedure for the development and adoption of a funding improvement plan or rehabilitation plan.

Nonbargained participation

In the case of an employer who contributes to a multiemployer plan with respect to both employees who are covered by one or more collective bargaining agreements and to employees who are not so covered, if the plan is in endangered or critical status, benefits of and contributions for the nonbargained employees, including surcharges on those contributions, must be determined as if the nonbargained employees were covered under the first to expire of the employer's collective bargaining agreements in effect when the plan entered endangered or critical status.[67] In the case of an employer who contributes to a multiemployer plan only with respect to employees who are not covered by a collective bargaining agreement, the additional funding rules apply as if the employer were the bargaining party, and its participation agreement with the plan was a collective bargaining agreement with a term ending on the first day of the plan year beginning after the employer is provided the schedule requires to be provided by the plan sponsor.

Special rule for certain restored benefits

In the case of benefits which were reduced pursuant to a plan amendment adopted on or after January 1, 2002, and before June 30, 2005, if, pursuant to the plan document, the trust agreement, or a formal written communication from the plan sponsor to participants provided before June 30, 2005, such benefits were restored, the rules under the provision do not apply to such benefit restorations to the extent that any restriction on the providing or accrual of such benefits would otherwise apply by reason of the provision.

[67] Treasury regulations allowing certain noncollectively bargained employees covered by a multiemployer plan to be treated as collectively bargained employees for purposes of the minimum coverage rules of the Code do not apply in making determinations under the provision.

Cause of action to compel adoption of funding improvement or rehabilitation plan

The provision creates a cause of action under ERISA in the case that the plan sponsor of a plan certified to be endangered or critical (1) has not adopted a funding improvement or rehabilitation plan within 240 days of certification of endangered or critical or (2) fails to update or comply with the terms of the funding improvement or rehabilitation plan. In such case, a civil action may be brought by an employer that has an obligation to contribute with respect to the plan, or an employee organization that represents active participants, for an order compelling the plan sponsor to adopt a funding improvement or rehabilitation plan or to update or comply with the terms of the funding improvement or rehabilitation plan.

Effective Date

The provision is effective for plan years beginning after 2007. The additional funding rules for plans in endangered or critical status do not apply to plan years beginning after December 31, 2014.

If a plan is operating under a funding improvement or rehabilitation plan for its last year beginning before January 1, 2015, the plan shall continue to operate under such funding improvement or rehabilitation plan during any period after December 31, 2014, that such funding improvement or rehabilitation plan is in effect.

[Code Sec. 436]

[¶ 13,151O.50]

Committee Report on P.L. 109-280 (Pension Protection Act of 2006)

[Joint Committee on Taxation Report]

Plant shutdown and other unpredictable contingent event benefits

Under the provision, if a participant is entitled to an unpredictable contingent event benefit payable with respect to any event occurring during any plan year, the plan must provide that such benefits may not be provided if the plan's adjusted funding target attainment percentage for that plan year: (1) is less than 60 percent; or (2) would be less than 60 percent taking into account the occurrence of the event. For this purpose, the term unpredictable contingent event benefit means any benefit payable solely by reason of: (1) a plant shutdown (or similar event, as determined by the Secretary of the Treasury); or (2) any event other than attainment of any age, performance of any service, receipt or derivation of any compensation, or the occurrence of death or disability.

The determination of whether the limitation applies is made in the year the unpredictable contingent event occurs. For example, suppose a plan provides for benefits upon the occurrence of a plant shutdown, and a plant shut down occurs in 2010. Taking into account the plan shutdown, the plan's adjusted funding target attainment percentage is less than 60 percent. Thus, the limitation applies, and benefits payable solely by reason of the plant shutdown may not be paid (unless the employer makes contributions to the plan as described below), regardless of whether the benefits will be paid in the 2010 plan year or a later plan year.[47]

The limitation ceases to apply with respect to any plan year, effective as of the first day of the plan year, if the plan sponsor makes a contribution (in addition to any minimum required contribution for the plan year) equal to: (1) if the plan's adjusted funding target attainment percentage is less than 60 percent, the amount of the increase in the plan's funding target for the plan year attributable to the occurrence of the event; or (2) if the plan's adjusted funding target attainment percentage would be less than 60 percent taking into account the occurrence of the event, the amount sufficient to result in a adjusted funding target attainment percentage of 60 percent.

The limitation does not apply for the first five years a plan (or a predecessor plan) is in effect.

Plan amendments increasing benefit liabilities

Certain plan amendments may not take effect during a plan year if the plan's adjusted funding target attainment percentage for the plan year: (1) is less than 80 percent; or (2) would be less than 80 percent taking into account the amendment.[48] In such a case, no amendment may take effect if it has the effect of increasing the liabilities of the plan by reason of any increase in benefits, the establishment of new benefits, any change in the rate of benefit accrual, or any change in the rate at which benefits vest under the plan. The limitation does not apply to an amendment that provides for an increase in benefits under a formula which is not based on compensation, but only if the rate of increase does not exceed the contemporaneous rate of increase in average wages of the participants covered by the amendment.

The limitation ceases to apply with respect to any plan year, effective as of the first day of the plan year (or, if later, the effective date of the amendment), if the plan sponsor makes a contribution (in addition to any minimum required contribution for the plan year) equal to: (1) if the plan's adjusted funding target attainment percentage is less than 80 percent, the amount of the increase in the plan's funding target for the plan year attributable to the amendment; or (2) if the plan's adjusted funding target attainment percentage would be less than 80 percent taking into account the amendment, the amount sufficient to result in a adjusted funding target attainment percentage of 80 percent.

The limitation does not apply for the first five years a plan (or a predecessor plan) is in effect.

Prohibited payments

A plan must provide that, if the plan's adjusted funding target attainment percentage for a plan year is less than 60 percent, the plan will not make any prohibited payments after the valuation date for the plan year.

A plan must also provide that, if the plan's adjusted funding target attainment percentage for a plan year is 60 percent or greater, but less than 80 percent, the plan may not pay any prohibited payments exceeding the lesser of: (1) 50 percent of the amount otherwise payable under the plan, and (2) the present value of the maximum PBGC guarantee with respect to the participant (determined under guidance prescribed by the PBGC, using the interest rates and mortality table applicable in determining minimum lump-sum benefits). The plan must provide that only one payment under this exception may be made with respect to any participant during any period of consecutive plan years to which the limitation applies. For this purpose, a participant and any beneficiary of the participant (including an alternate payee) is treated as one participant. If the participant's accrued benefit is allocated to an alternate payee and one or more other persons, the amount that may be distributed is allocated in the same manner unless the applicable qualified domestic relations order provides otherwise.

In addition, a plan must provide that, during any period in which the plan sponsor is in bankruptcy proceedings, the plan may not pay any prohibited payment. However, this limitation does not apply on or after the date the plan's enrolled actuary certifies that the adjusted funding target attainment percentage of the plan is not less than 100 percent.

For purposes of these limitations, "prohibited payment" is defined as under the present-law rule restricting distributions during a period of a liquidity shortfall and means (1) any payment in excess of the monthly amount paid under a single life annuity (plus any social security supplement provided under the plan) to a participant or beneficiary whose annuity starting date occurs during the period, (2) any payment for the purchase of an irrevocable commitment from an insurer to pay benefits (e.g., an annuity contract), or (3) any other payment specified by the Secretary of the Treasury by regulations.

The prohibited payment limitation does not apply to a plan for any plan year if the terms of the plan (as in effect for the period beginning on September 1, 2005, and ending with the plan year) provide for no benefit accruals with respect to any participant during the period.

Cessation of benefit accruals

A plan must provide that, if the plan's adjusted funding target attainment percentage is less than 60 percent for a plan year, all future benefit accruals under the plan must cease as of the valuation date for the plan year. The limitation applies only for purposes of the accrual of benefits; service during the freeze period is counted for other purposes. For example, if accruals are frozen under the provision, service earned during the freeze period still counts for vesting purposes. Or, as another example, suppose a plan provides that payment of benefits begins when a participant terminates employment after age 55 and with 25 years of service. Under this example, if a participant who is age 55 and has 23 years of service when the freeze on accruals becomes applicable terminates employment two years later, the participant has 25 years of service for this purpose and thus can begin receiving benefits. However (assuming the freeze on accruals is still in effect), the amount of the benefit is based on the benefit accrued before the freeze (i.e., counting only 23 years of service).

The limitation ceases to apply with respect to any plan year, effective as of the first day of the plan year, if the plan sponsor makes a contribution (in addition to any minimum required contribution for the plan year) equal to the amount sufficient to result in an adjusted funding target attainment percentage of 60 percent.

The limitation does not apply for the first five years a plan (or a predecessor plan) is in effect.

Adjusted funding target attainment percentage

In general

The term "funding target attainment percentage" is defined as under the minimum funding rules, i.e., the ratio, expressed as a percentage, that the value of the plan's assets (reduced by any funding standard carryover balance and prefunding balance) bears to the plan's funding target for the year (determined without regard to at-risk status). A plan's adjusted funding target attainment percentage is determined in the same way, except that the value of the plan's assets and the plan's funding target are both increased by the aggregate amount of purchases of annuities for employees other than highly compensated employees made by the plan during the two preceding plan years.

[47] Benefits already being paid as a result of a plant shutdown or other event that occurred in a preceding year are not affected by the limitation.

[48] Under the provision, the present-law rules limiting benefit increases while an employer is in bankruptcy continue to apply.

Special rule for fully funded plans

Under a special rule, if a plan's funding target attainment percentage is at least 100 percent, determined by not reducing the value of the plan's assets by any funding standard carryover balance or prefunding balance, the value of the plan's assets is not so reduced in determining the plan's funding target attainment percentage for purposes of whether the benefit limitations apply. Under a transition rule for a plan year beginning after 2007 and before 2011, the "applicable percentage" for the plan year is substituted for 100 percent in applying the special rule. For this purpose, the applicable percentage is 92 percent for 2007, 94 percent for 2008, 96 percent for 2009, and 98 percent for 2010. However, for any plan year beginning after 2008, the transition rule does not apply unless the plan's funding target attainment percentage (determined by not reducing the value of the plan's assets by any funding standard carryover balance or prefunding balance) for each preceding plan year in the transition period is at least equal to the applicable percentage for the preceding year.

Presumptions as to funded status

Under the provision, certain presumptions apply in determining whether limitations apply with respect to a plan, subject to certification of the plan's adjusted funding target attainment percentage by the plan's enrolled actuary.

If a plan was subject to a limitation for the preceding year, the plan's adjusted funding target attainment percentage for the current year is presumed to be the same as for the preceding year until the plan actuary certifies the plan's actual adjusted funding target attainment percentage for the current year.

If (1) a plan was not subject to a limitation for the preceding year, but its adjusted funding target attainment percentage for the preceding year was not more than 10 percentage points greater than the threshold for a limitation, and (2) as of the first day of the fourth month of the current plan year, the plan actuary has not certified the plan's actual adjusted funding target attainment percentage for the current year, the plan's funding target attainment percentage is presumed to be reduced by 10 percentage points as of that day and that day is deemed to be the plan's valuation date for purposes of applying the benefit limitation. As a result, the limitation applies as of that date until the actuary certifies the plan's actual adjusted funding target attainment percentage.

In any other case, if the plan actuary has not certified the plan's actual adjusted funding target attainment percentage by the first day of the tenth month of the current plan year, for purposes of the limitations, the plan's adjusted funding target attainment percentage is conclusively presumed to be less than 60 percent as of that day and that day is deemed to be the valuation date for purposes of applying the benefit limitations.[49]

Reduction of funding standard carryover and prefunding balances

Election to reduce balances

As discussed above, the value of plan assets is generally reduced by any funding standard carryover or prefunding in determining a plan's funding target attainment percentage. As provided for under the funding rules applicable to single-employer plans, a plan sponsor may elect to reduce a funding standard carryover balance or prefunding balance, so that the value of plan assets is not required to be reduced by that amount in determining the plan's funding target attainment percentage.

Deemed reduction of balances in the case of collectively bargained plans

If a benefit limitation would otherwise apply to a plan maintained pursuant to one or more collective bargaining agreements between employee representatives and one or more employers, the plan sponsor is treated as having made an election to reduce any prefunding balance or funding standard carryover balance by the amount necessary to prevent the benefit limitation from applying. However, the employer is not treated as having made such an election if the election would not prevent the benefit limitation from applying to the plan.

Deemed reduction of balances in the case of other plans

If the prohibited payment limitation would otherwise apply to a plan that is not maintained pursuant to a collective bargaining agreement, the plan sponsor is treated as having made an election to reduce any prefunding balance or funding standard carryover balance by the amount necessary to prevent the benefit limitation from applying. However, the employer is not treated as having made such an election if the election would not prevent the benefit limitation from applying to the plan.

Contributions made to avoid a benefit limitation

Under the provision, an employer may make contributions (in addition to any minimum required contribution) in an amount sufficient to increase the plan's adjusted funding target attainment percentage to a level to avoid a limitation on unpredictable contingent event benefits, a plan amendment increasing benefits, or additional accruals. An employer may not use a prefunding balance or funding standard carryover balance in lieu of such a contribution, and such a contribution does not result in an increase in any prefunding balance.

Instead of making additional contributions to avoid a benefit limitation, an employer may provide security in the form of a surety bond, cash, certain U.S. government obligations, or such other form as is satisfactory to the Secretary of the Treasury and the parties involved. In such a case, the plan's adjusted funding target attainment percentage is determined by treating the security as a plan asset. Any such security may be perfected and enforced at any time after the earlier of: (1) the date on which the plan terminates; (2) if the plan sponsor fails to make a required contribution for any subsequent plan year, the due date for the contribution; or (3) if the plan's adjusted funding target attainment percentage is less than 60 percent for a consecutive period of seven years, the valuation date for the last year in the period. The security will be released (and any related amounts will be refunded with any accrued interest) at such time as the Secretary of the Treasury may prescribe in regulations (including partial releases by reason of increases in the plan's funding target attainment percentage).

Treatment of plan as of close of prohibited or cessation period

Under the provision, if a limitation on prohibited payments or future benefit accruals ceases to apply to a plan, all such payments and benefit accruals resume, effective as of the day following the close of the period for which the limitation applies.[50] Nothing in this rule is to be construed as affecting a plan's treatment of benefits which would have been paid or accrued but for the limitation.

Notice to participants

The plan administrator must provide written notice to participants and beneficiaries within 30 days: (1) after the plan has become subject to the limitation on unpredictable uncontingent event benefits or prohibited payments; (2) in the case of a plan to which the limitation on benefit accruals applies, after the valuation date for the plan year in which the plan's adjusted target attainment percentage is less than 60 percent (or, if earlier, the date the adjusted target attainment percentage is deemed to be less than 60 percent). Notice must also be provided at such other times as may be determined by the Secretary of the Treasury. The notice may be in electronic or other form to the extent such form is reasonably accessible to the recipient.

If the plan administrator fails to provide the required notice, the Secretary of Labor may impose a civil penalty of up to $1,000 a day from the time of the failure.

Effective Date

The provision generally applies with respect to plan years beginning after December 31, 2007.

In the case of a plan maintained pursuant to one or more collective bargaining agreements between employee representatives and one or more employers ratified before January 1, 2008, the provision does not apply to plan years beginning before the earlier of: (1) the later of (a) the date on which the last collective bargaining agreement relating to the plan terminates (determined without regard to any extension thereof agreed to after the date of enactment), or (b) the first day of the first plan year to which the provision would otherwise apply; or (2) January 1, 2010. For this purpose, any plan amendment made pursuant to a collective bargaining agreement relating to the plan that amends the plan solely to conform to any requirement under the provision is not to be treated as a termination of the collective bargaining agreement.

[Code Sec. 457]

[¶ 13,153.018]

Committee Report on P.L. 109-280 (Pension Protection Act of 2006)

[Joint Committee on Taxation Report]

[Eligibility for participation in eligible deferred compensation plans]

Under the provision, an individual is not precluded from participating in an eligible deferred compensation plan by reason of having received a distribution under section 457(e)(9) as in effect before the Small Business Job Protection Act of 1996.

Effective Date

The provision is effective on the date of enactment.

Early retirement incentive plans of local educational agencies and education associations

In general

The provision addresses the treatment of certain voluntary early retirement incentive plans under section 457, ERISA, and ADEA.

Code section 457

Under the provision, special rules apply under section 457 to a voluntary early retirement incentive plan that is maintained by a local educational agency or a tax-exempt education association which principally represents employees of one or more such agencies and that makes payments or supplements as an early retirement benefit, a retirement-type subsidy, or a social security supplement in coordination with a defined benefit pension plan maintained by a State or local government or by such an association. Such a voluntary early retirement incen-

[49] For purposes of applying the presumptions to plan years beginning in 2008, the funding target attainment percentage for the preceding year may be determined using such methods of estimation as the Secretary of Treasury may provide.

[50] This rule does not apply to limitations on unpredictable contingent event benefits and plan amendments increasing liabilities.

tive plan is treated as a bona fide severance plan for purposes of section 457, and therefore is not subject to the limits under section 457, to the extent the payments or supplements could otherwise be provided under the defined benefit pension plan. For purposes of the provision, the payments or supplements that could otherwise be provided under the defined benefit pension plan are to be determined by applying the accrual and vesting rules for defined benefit pension plans.[280]

ERISA

Under the provision, voluntary early retirement incentive plans (as described above) are treated as welfare benefit plans for purposes of ERISA (other than governmental plans that are exempt from ERISA).

ADEA

The provision also addresses the treatment under ADEA of voluntary early retirement incentive plans that are maintained by local educational agencies and tax-exempt education associations which principally represent employees of one or more such agencies, and that make payments or supplements that constitute the subsidized portion of an early retirement benefit or a social security supplement and that are made in coordination with a defined benefit pension plan maintained by a State or local government or by such an association. For purposes of ADEA, such a plan is treated as part of the defined benefit pension plan and the payments or supplements under the plan are not severance pay that may be subject to certain deductions under ADEA.

Employment retention plans of local educational agencies and education associations

The provision addresses the treatment of certain employment retention plans under section 457 and ERISA. The provision applies to employment retention plans that are maintained by local educational agencies or tax-exempt education associations which principally represent employees of one or more such agencies and that provide compensation to an employee (payable on termination of employment) for purposes of retaining the services of the employee or rewarding the employee for service with educational agencies or associations.

Under the provision, special tax treatment applies to the portion of an employment retention plan that provides benefits that do not exceed twice the applicable annual dollar limit on deferrals under section 457 ($14,000 for 2005). The provision provides an exception from the rules under section 457 for ineligible plans with respect to such portion of an employment retention plan. This exception applies for years preceding the year in which benefits under the employment retention plan are paid or otherwise made available to the employee. In addition, such portion of an employment retention plan is not treated as providing for the deferral of compensation for tax purposes.

Under the provision, an employment retention plan is also treated as a welfare benefit plan for purposes of ERISA (other than a governmental plan that is exempt from ERISA).

Effective Date

The provision is generally effective on the date of enactment. The amendments to section 457 apply to taxable years ending after the date of enactment. The amendments to ERISA apply to plan years ending after the date of enactment. Nothing in the provision alters or affects the construction of the Code, ERISA, or ADEA as applied to any plan, arrangement, or conduct to which the provision does not apply.

For the Committee Report on P.L. 109-280 on the purchase of permissive service credit, see ¶ 12,400.013. For the Committee Report on P.L. 109-280 on the modification of rules governing hardships and unforeseen financial emergencies, see ¶ 11,700.02.

[¶ 13,153.02]

Committee Report on P.L. 107-16 (Economic Growth and Tax Relief Reconciliation Act)

[House Committee Report]

Distribution rules

The provision provides that amounts deferred under a section 457 plan of a State or local government are includible in income when paid. The provision also repeals the special minimum distribution rules applicable to section 457 plans. Thus, such plans are subject to the minimum distribution rules applicable to qualified plans.

Effective Date

The provision is effective for distributions after December 31, 2001.

[Conference Committee Report]

The conference agreement follows the House bill.

[¶ 13,153.03]

Committee Report on P.L. 107-16 (Economic Growth and Tax Relief Reconciliation Act)

[House Committee Report]

Purchase of service credit under governmental pension plans

A participant in a State or local governmental plan is not required to include in gross income a direct trustee-to-trustee transfer to a governmental defined benefit plan from a section 403(b) annuity or a section 457 plan if the transferred amount is used (1) to purchase permissive service credits under the plan, or (2) to repay contributions and earnings with respect to an amount previously refunded under a forfeiture of service credit under the plan (or another plan maintained by a State or local government employer within the same State).

Effective Date

The provision is effective for transfers after December 31, 2001.

[Conference Committee Report]

Senate Amendment

The Senate amendment is the same as the House bill.

Conference Agreement

The conference agreement follows the House bill and the Senate amendment.

[¶ 13,153.04]

Committee Report on P.L. 107-16 (Economic Growth and Tax Relief Reconciliation Act)

[House Committee Report]

Tax treatment of 457 plan benefits upon divorce

The provision applies the taxation rules for qualified plan distributions pursuant to a QDRO to distributions made pursuant to a domestic relations order from a section 457 plan. In addition, a section 457 plan does not violate the restrictions on distributions from such plans due to payments to an alternate payee under a QDRO. The special rule applicable to governmental plans and church plans applies for purposes of determining whether a distribution is pursuant to a QDRO.

Effective Date

The provision is effective for transfers, distributions, and payments made after December 31, 2001.

[Conference Committee Report]

The conference agreement follows the House bill.

[¶ 13,153.05]

Committee Report on P.L. 107-16 (Economic Growth and Tax Relief Reconciliation Act)

[House Committee Report]

Code Sec. 457 plans

The provision increases the 33-1/3 percent of compensation limitation on deferrals under a section 457 plan to 100 percent of compensation.

Effective Date

The provision generally is effective for years beginning after December 31, 2001.

* * *

[¶ 13,153.06]

Committee Report on P.L. 107-16 (Economic Growth and Tax Relief Reconciliation Act)

[House Committee Report]

Repeal of coordination requirement

The provision repeals the rules coordinating the section 457 dollar limit with contributions under other types of plans.[1]

---

[280] The accrual and vesting rules have the effect of limiting the social security supplements and early retirement benefits that may be provided under a defined benefit pension plan; however, government plans are exempt from these rules.

[1] The limits on deferrals under a section 457 plan are modified under other provisions of the bill.

Effective Date

The provision is effective for years beginning after December 31, 2001.

[Conference Committee Report]

Senate Amendment

The Senate amendment is the same as the House bill.

Conference Agreement

The conference agreement follows the House bill and the Senate amendment.

[¶ 13,153.07]

Committee Report on P.L. 107-16 (Economic Growth and Tax Relief Reconciliation Act)

[House Committee Report]

Code Sec. 457 plans

The provision increases the dollar limit on deferrals under a section 457 plan to conform to the elective deferral limitation. Thus, the limit is $11,000 in 2002, and is increased in $1,000 annual increments thereafter until the limit reaches $15,000 in 2006. The limit is indexed thereafter in $500 increments. The limit is twice the otherwise applicable dollar limit in the three years prior to retirement.[2]

Effective Date

The provision is effective for years beginning after December 31, 2001.

[Conference Committee Report]

The conference agreement follows the House bill.

* * *

Effective Date

The conference agreement generally is effective for years beginning after December 31, 2001. The provisions relating to defined benefit plans are effective for years ending after December 31, 2001.

[¶ 13,153.076]

Committee Reports on P.L. 104-188 (Small Business Job Protection Act)

Miscellaneous Pension Simplification

[House Committee Report]

Deferred compensation plans—State and local governments and tax-exempt organizations

The bill makes three changes to the rules governing section 457 plans.

The bill: (1) permits in-service distributions of accounts that do not exceed $3,500 under certain circumstances; (2) increases the number of elections that can be made with respect to the time distributions must begin under the plan, and (3) provides for indexing (in $500 increments) of the dollar limit on deferrals.

Effective Date

The provision is effective for taxable years beginning after December 31, 1996.

[Conference Committee Report]

Senate Amendment

The Senate amendment is the same as the House bill.

Conference Agreement

The conference agreement follows the House bill and the Senate amendment.

Miscellaneous Pension Simplification

[House Committee Report]

Trust requirement for deferred compensation plans of state and local governments

Under the bill, all amounts deferred under a section 457 plan maintained by a State and local governmental employer have to be held in trust (or custodial account or annuity contract) for the exclu sive benefit of employees. The trust (or custodial account or annuity contract) is provided tax-exempt status. Amounts will not be considered made available merely because they are held in a trust, custodial account, or annuity contract.

Effective Date

The provision generally is effective with respect to amounts held on or after the date of enactment. In the case of amounts deferred before the date of enactment, a trust will not need to be established by reason of this provision until January 1, 1999.

[Conference Committee Report]

Senate Amendment

The Senate amendment is the same as the House bill.

Effective Date

The Senate amendment is the same as the House bill, except that in the case of plans in existence on the date of enactment, the trust requirement does not have to be satisfied until January 1, 1999. Thus, deferrals prior to and after the date of enactment (and earnings thereon) do not have to be held in trust (or custodial account or annuity contract) until January 1, 1999.

Conference Agreement

The conference agreement follows the House bill and the Senate amendment. The conference agreement clarifies that amounts held in trust (or custodial account or annuity contract), may be loaned to plan participants (or beneficiaries) pursuant to rules applicable to loans from qualified plans (sec. 72(p)).[3] A section 457 plan is not required to permit loans. The conferees intend that the income inclusion rules in the Code (secs. 83 and 402(b), do not apply to amounts deferred under the section 457 plan (and income thereon) merely because such amounts are contributed to the trust (or custodial account or annuity contract).

Effective Date

The conference agreement follows the House bill and the Senate amendment. Under the conference agreement, in the case of plans in existence on the date of enactment, the trust requirement does not have to be satisfied until January 1, 1999. Thus, deferrals prior to and after the date of enactment (and earnings thereon) do not have to be held in trust (or custodial account or annuity contract) until January 1, 1999.

Miscellaneous Pension Simplification

[Senate Committee Report]

Volunteers' length of service awards under section 457

Under the bill, the requirements of section 457 do not apply to any plan paying solely length of service awards to bona fide volunteers (or their beneficiaries) on account of fire fighting and prevention, emergency medical, and ambulance services performed by such volunteers. An individual is considered a "bona fide volunteer" if the only compensation received by such individual for performing such services is reimbursement (or a reasonable allowance) for expenses incurred in the performance of such services or reasonable benefits (including length of service awards) and nominal fees for such services customarily paid by tax-exempt or governmental employers in connection with the performance of such services by volunteers. Under the bill, a length of service award plan will not qualify for this special treatment under section 457 if the aggregate amount of length of service awards accruing with respect to any year of service for any bona fide volunteer exceeds $3,000.

In addition, any amounts exempt from the requirements of section 457 under the bill are not considered wages for purposes of the Federal Insurance Contribution Act ("FICA") taxes.

Effective Date

The provision applies to accruals of length of service awards after December 31, 1996.

[Conference Committee Report]

The conference agreement follows the Senate amendment.

[¶ 13,153.078]

Committee Report on P.L. 101-239 (Omnibus Budget Reconciliation Act of 1989)

[House Committee Report]

Deferred compensation plans for churches

As originally enacted, the 1988 Act provision did not accomplish the intent of exempting church plans from section 457. The provision clarifies the exemption from the application of section 457 for such plans. Under the provision, churches would be exempt from the definition of eligible employer.

---

[2] Another provision increases the 33-1/3 percentage of compensation limit to 100 percent.

[3] Under section 72(p), a loan from a plan is treated as a distribution unless the loan generally (1) does not exceed certain limits (generally, the lesser of $50,000 or one-half of the participant's vested plan benefit; (2) must be repaid within 5 years; and (3) must be amortized on a substantially level basis with payments at least quarterly.

[¶ 13,153.08]

Committee Reports on P.L. 100-647 (Technical and Miscellaneous Revenue Act of 1988)

[Senate Committee Report]

Unfunded Deferred Compensation Arrangements of State and Local Governments and Tax-Exempt Employers

Application to tax-exempt employers; distribution requirements. The bill reconciles the rules under section 457 and section 401(a)(9) relating to the time that distributions are to be made. With respect to the rule prohibiting distributions prior to separation from service or the occurrence of an unforeseen emergency, the bill provides an exception for distributions in or after the year in which the employee attains age 70 ½. Thus, under the bill, amounts may not be available under a section 457 plan earlier than (1) the calendar year in which the participant attains age 70 ½, (2) when the participant separates from service, or (3) when the participant is faced with an unforeseeable emergency.

The bill deletes the rule contained in section 457(d)(2)(B)(i)(I). In lieu of this rule, the bill in structs the Secretary to issue tables that implement the incidental death benefit rule and that are similar to those applicable under section 401(a)(9) but require more rapid distributions.

Generally, the extent to which more rapid distributions are to be required is to be similar to the extent to which the former section 457(d)(2)(B)(i)(I) rule required more rapid distributions than the former version of the incidental death benefit rule.

The bill clarifies that the exception to the constructive receipt rule with respect to an election to receive a lump-sum distribution does not override the distribution restrictions otherwise applicable to eligible deferred compensation plans. Thus, the bill provides that the exception is not available for distributions payable prior to separation from service. This provision applies to years beginning after December 31, 1988.

Amount of deferrals. An employee may participate in a section 457 plan of 1 employer and, for example, a cash or deferred arrangement of another employer. Thus, the employer maintaining the section 457 plan may not know whether an employee is making elective deferrals to a plan that is coordinated with the section 457 plan for purposes of the limit on deferred compensation. Thus, it is not appropriate to disqualify the entire section 457 plan in such cases.

Accordingly, the bill provides that, for purposes of determining whether an unfunded deferred compensation plan is an eligible plan under section 457, the rule requiring coordination of the deferred compensation limit with other plans is disregarded. Of course, if the limit (as so coordinated) is exceeded, the deferral of income inclusion provided by section 457 does not apply to the excess; instead, the rules of section 457(f) apply to such excess.

In order to prevent avoidance of the limit on deferred compensation under a section 457 plan by, for example, the use of affiliated service groups or leasing arrangements, the bill provides that the Secretary's general regulatory authority to prevent avoidance of certain requirements (sec. 414(o)) applies to section 457 plans.

Effective Date

The bill clarifies that the grandfather rule applicable to unfunded deferred compensation arrangements of tax-exempt employers applies to all deferred compensation plans of tax-exempt organizations that otherwise meet the requirements of the grandfather rule, without regard to whether the plans would be eligible deferred compensation plans within the meaning of section 457.

It is intended that with regard to amounts deferred from taxable years beginning before January 1, 1987, the grandfather rule applies without regard to whether the organization maintaining the deferred compensation plan was tax-exempt when the plan was established. For example, assume that a deferred compensation plan is established on January 1, 1985, by a taxable organization with respect to individuals all of whose taxable year is the calendar year. The organization becomes tax-exempt on January 1, 1987. If the amounts deferred under the plan from taxable years beginning before January 1, 1987, otherwise meet the requirements of the grandfather rule, then the application of the grandfather rule to such amounts will not be affected by the fact that the organization was not tax-exempt when the plan was established. This rule is not intended to create any inference with respect to the effect of a change in taxable status for other purposes relating to section 457.

The bill also clarifies that the grandfather rule only applies to individuals who were covered under the plan and agreement on August 16, 1986. Thus, for example, the grandfather rule does not apply to a new employee hired after August 16, 1986, or an employee who was hired on or before such date, but who was not a participant in the deferred compensation plan until after August 16, 1986.

[Conference Committee Report]

* * *

Conference Agreement

The conference agreement follows the Senate amendment with the following modifications.

* * *

The conference agreement does not adopt the provision in the Senate amendment that bona fide vacation pay plans, severance pay plans, and certain other benefit plans are not subject to section 457. The conference agreement modifies section 457, as discussed under part V of Substantive Revenue Provisions.

[House Committee Report]

* * * [T]he position of the IRS in Notice 88-68 is codified and section 457 would not apply to bona fide vacation leave, sick leave, compensatory time, severance pay, disability pay, and death benefits plans.

Further, section 457 also does not apply to nonelective deferred compensation deferred (1) from periods before July 14, 1988, or (2) pursuant to a deferred compensation plan or agreement if (a) the plan or agreement was in writing on July 14, 1988, and (b) on such date the plan or agreement provided for a deferral for each taxable year covered by the agreement of a fixed amount or an amount determined pursuant to a fixed formula, and (c) the individual with respect to whom the deferral was made was covered by the plan or agreement on July 14, 1988.

* * *

In applying the section 457 limits to a deferral not grandfathered, grandfathered amounts are taken into account.

The Treasury Department is directed to perform a study * * * regarding the tax treatment of deferred compensation paid by State and local governments and tax-exempt organizations (including deferred compensation paid to independent contractors). The committee expects that the study will focus on such issues as (1) the amounts of deferred compensation paid by State and local governments and tax-exempt organizations relative to the amounts of deferred compensation provided by private employers, and (2) whether discrimination in favor of highly compensated employees in either coverage or benefits is more prevalent with respect to State and local governments or tax-exempt organizations than with respect to private employers.

[Conference Committee Report]

* * *

Conference Agreement

The conference agreement follows the House bill with respect to the codification of IRS Notice 88-68, the Treasury Department study, and the grandfather rule for nonelective deferred compensation under governmental plans for amounts deferred under agreements in effect on July 14, 1988. In addition, the conference agreement provides that this grandfather rule does not cease to apply merely because of a modification to the agreement prior to January 1, 1989, which does not increase benefits for participants in the plan.

The conference agreement also provides a grandfather rule for nonelective compensation deferred under a plan in effect on December 31, 1987, and maintained pursuant to one or more collective bargaining agreements. This grandfather is the same as the grandfather rule provided in IRS Notice 88-98, except that the grandfather rule does not expire on January 1, 1991. Thus, the same conditions that apply to the grandfather rule in Notice 88-98 apply under the conference agreement.

In addition, the conference agreement provides that section 457 does not apply to nonelective deferred compensation provided to individuals other than in their capacity as employees. For purposes of this rule, a deferred compensation plan is considered nonelective only if all individuals (other than those who have not satisfied any applicable initial service requirement) with the same relationship to the payor are covered under the same plan with no individual variations or options. For example, if a nonemployee doctor receives deferred compensation from a hospital, such deferred compensation is to be considered nonelective only if all nonemployee doctors (who have satisified any applicable initial service requirements) are covered under the same plan. This provision is effective with respect to taxable years beginning after December 31, 1987.

The conference agreement also provides that section 457 does not apply in the case of a plan maintained by a church (as defined for employment tax purposes in sec. 3121(w)(3)(A)), including a qualified church-controlled organization (as defined in sec. 3121(w)(3)(B)). This provision is effective with respect to taxable years beginning after December 31, 1987.

[¶ 13,153.085]

Committee Reports on P.L. 99-514 (Tax Reform Act of 1986)

[House Committee Report]

Overview

The bill applies the limitations and restrictions applicable to eligible and ineligible unfunded deferred compensation plans of State and local governments to unfunded deferred compensation plans maintained by nongovernmental tax-exempt organizations. In addition, the bill (1) requires that amounts deferred by an employee under a qualified cash or deferred arrangement that is grandfathered under the bill be taken into account in determining whether the employee's deferrals under an eligible deferred compensation plan exceed the limits on deferrals under the eligible plan; (2) modifies the distribution requirements applicable to eligible deferred compensation plans; (3) permits rollovers between eligible deferred compensation plans; and (4) modifies the rule that an employee is taxable on deferrals under an eligible plan when such amounts are made available.

Nongovernmental tax-exempt employers

Under the bill, an employee of a nongovernmental tax-exempt organization is not considered to be in constructive receipt of compensation deferred under an eligible deferred compensation plan maintained by the tax-exempt organization if the plan satisfies the requirements applicable to eligible deferred compensation plans of State and local governments. Under the bill, deferrals under an ineligible deferred compensation plan, agreement, or arrangement (other than a qualified State judicial plan, qualified plan, or tax-sheltered annuity) maintained by a nongovernmental tax-exempt entity are to be included in an employee's gross income when the amounts are not subject to a substantial risk of forfeiture.

Offset for deferrals under qualified cash or deferred arrangement

Under the bill, the limits on the amount that a participant may defer under an eligible deferred compensation plan are reduced, dollar for dollar, by a participant's elective deferrals, under a qualified cash or deferred arrangement (except a qualified cash or deferred arrangement maintained by a rural electic cooperative). Of course, the rule has no application except with respect to those employees of State and local governments that maintain a qualified cash or deferred arrangement that is grandfathered under the bill. In addition, as under present law, all amounts deferred under a tax-sheltered annuity are taken into account in calculating whether an employee's deferrals under an unfunded deferred compensation plan exceed the limits on deferrals under an eligible deferred compensation plan.

Minimum distribution requirements

The bill also modifies the distribution requirements for eligible deferred compensation plans maintained by State and local governments and nongovernment tax-exempt entities. As modified, distributions commencing prior to the death of a participant under an eligible deferred compensation plan are required to satisfy a payout schedule under which benefits projected to be paid over the lifetime of the participant are at least 66 ⅔ percent of the total benefits payable with respect to the participant.

If the participant dies prior to the date that the participant's entire interest has been distributed, or if the participant dies prior to commencment of the distribution of benefits, the bill requires that payments to the participant's beneficiary commence within sixty days of the close of the plan year in which the participant's death occurs and that the entire amount deferred be distributed over a period not in excess of 15 years, unless the beneficiary is the participant's surviving spouse. If the beneficiary is the participant's surviving spouse, payments must be made over the life of the surviving spouse or any shorter period.

Whenever distributions (pre- or post-death) are to be made over a period extending beyond one year, the bill requires that the distribution be made in substantially nonincreasing periodic payments not less frequently than annually.

Constructive receipt

The bill provides that benefits are not treated as made available under an eligible deferred compensation plan merely because an employee is allowed to elect to receive a lump sum payment within 60 days of the election. However, the 60-day rule only applies if the employee's total deferred benefit does not exceed $3,500 and no additional amounts may be deferred with respect to the employee.

[*Transfers*]

The bill also amends present law to permit the [transfer] of benefits between eligible deferred compensation plans under certain circumstances.

* * *

State judicial plans

The bill exempts from the new requirements for eligible deferred compensation plans any qualified State judicial plan (as defined in section 131(c)(3)(B) of the Revenue Act of 1978, as amended by section 252 of the Tax Equity and Fiscal Responsibility Act of 1982).

* * *

[Conference Committee Report]

Application to tax-exempt employers

The conference agreement follows the House bill provision extending the rules relating to eligible unfunded deferred compensation plans of State and local governments to tax-exempt organizations. In addition, the conference agreement provides that a plan maintained by a tax-exempt organization that does not meet the requirements of an eligible deferred compensation plan is immediately treated as not meeting such requirements without regard to notification by the Secretary or a grace period. The conference agreement also provides that amounts deferred under an eligible deferred compensation plan are treated as elective contributions under a tax-sheltered annuity for purposes of the special catch-up election.

Distributive requirements

The conference agreement follows the House bill and the Senate amendment, except that the conference agreement provides that employees under an eligible unfunded deferred compensation plan are subject to the required beginning date and minimum required distribution requirements applicable to qualified plans (sec. 401(a)(9)), in addition to the special distribution rules applicable under section 457. The conference agreement permits transfers, rather than rollovers, between eligible plans.

Effective dates

The provision extending the eligible unfunded deferred compensation rules to tax-exempt employers is effective for taxable years beginning after December 31, 1986.

An exception is provided under the conference agreement for amounts deferred under a plan which (1) were deferred from taxable years beginning before January 1, 1987, or (2) are deferred from taxable years beginning after December 31, 1986, pursuant to an agreement that (i) was in writing on August 16, 1986, and (ii) on August 16, 1986, provided for a deferral for each taxable year of a fixed amount or an amount determined pursuant to a fixed formula. This exception does not apply with respect to amounts deferred in a fixed amount or under a fixed formula for any taxable year ending after the date on which the amount or formula is modified after August 16, 1986. Providing the participant with any discretion regarding the amount of the deferral constitutes a modification to this purpose.

For purposes of the grandfather rule, amounts are considered deferred from a taxable year if, but for the deferral, they would have been paid in that year. Also, in applying the limits to a deferral not grandfathered, grandfathered amounts are taken into account.

The modifications to the distribution requirements applicable to eligible unfunded deferred compensation plans generally are effective for taxable years beginning after December 31, 1988. However, the provisions (1) permitting transfers between eligible unfunded deferred compensation plans and (2) permitting cashouts of certain benefits without constructive receipt are effective with respect to transfers or distributions in years beginning after December 31, [1986].

[¶ 13,153.09]

Committee Report on P.L. 96-222 (Technical Corrections Act of 1979)

[Senate Committee Report]

Sec. 101(a)(4)—Rural electric cooperatives.

The Revenue Act of 1978 provided that employees and independent contractors who provide services for a State or local government, a rural electric cooperative (described in section 501(c)(12)), or an association of such cooperatives, that maintains an eligible deferred compensation plan will be able to defer the inclusion in income of compensation so long as such deferral does not exceed certain prescribed annual limitations.

The 1978 Act provision did not apply to certain rural electric cooperatives in the Tennessee Valley Authority ("TVA") area which are exempt from taxation under section 501(c)(4) (but which, generally because of TVA requirements, cannot meet all the requirements for exemption under section 501(c)(12)). In addition, the provision did not apply to certain national and State associations of rural electric cooperatives because some of their members are not domestic rural electric cooperatives and because some of the organizations are exempt from taxation as social welfare organizations (described in sec. 501(c)(4)) rather than as trade associations (described in sec. 501(c)(6)).

The committee believes that these omissions were inadvertent and that the provision should apply to these organizations.

The bill provides that the types of rural electric organizations eligible for the deferred compensation rules include (1) any organization which is exempt from tax under section 501(a) and which is engaged primarily in providing electric service on a mutual or cooperative basis[1] and (2) any organization described in section 501(c)(4) or (6) which is exempt from tax under section 501(a) and at least 80 percent of the members of which are rural electric cooperatives which are eligible for these rules.

This provision is effective as if it had been included in section 457 of the Code by section 131 of the Revenue Act of 1978. Thus, any plan to which section 457 applies by virtue of this provision will have until January 1, 1982, to satisfy the plan requirements for classification as an eligible State deferred compensation plan. However, the limitations on amounts that can be deferred under such a plan will apply for all taxable years beginning after December 31, 1978.

[¶ 13,153.10]

Committee Report on P.L. 95-600 (Revenue Act of 1978)

Sec. 131—State deferred compensation plans.

[House Committee Report]

In general.—Amounts of compensation deferred by a participant in an eligible State deferred compensation plan, plus any income attributable to the investment of such deferred amounts, will be includible in the income of the participant or his beneficiary only when it is paid or otherwise made available. For this purpose, the fair market value of any property (including an annuity contract or a life insurance policy) distributed to the participant from the plan will be includible in income. Amounts will not be considered "made available" merely because the plan allows the participant to choose among various options that the employer may provide for the investment of deferred amounts or to elect, prior to the earliest distribution date provided under the plan, the manner in which deferred amounts are to be paid. Of course, if a participant assigns or alienates his benefit under a plan, the benefit is considered made available to him. If life insurance is purchased with some, or all, of the amounts deferred under the plan, the cost of current life insurance protection will not be considered made available as long as the State or local government (1) retains all of the incidents of ownership of the policy, (2) is the sole beneficiary under the policy, and (3) is under no obligation to transfer the policy or to pass through the proceeds of the policy as such to the participant or a beneficiary of the participant. However, if the plan provides a death benefit, whether or not funded by the employer through the purchase of life insurance on the participant, any such death benefit will not qualify for exclusion from gross income as life insurance proceeds under section 101(a) of the Code. Instead, the committee intends that any death benefit will be treated under the deferred compensation rules by the recipient.

Plan requirements.—To qualify as an eligible State deferred compensation plan, the plan must be maintained by (1) a State, a political subdivision of a State, an agency or instrumentality of a State or one of its political subdivisions, or (2) a rural electric cooperative exempt under section 501(c)(12) of the Code, and any affiliates which are exempt under section 501(c)(6). In addition, the plan by its terms must not allow the deferral of more than $7,500, or 33 ⅓ percent of the participant's includible compensation for the taxable year, whichever is less. For this purpose, includible compensation is determined before any reduction for amounts deferred under a tax-sheltered annuity described in section 403(b) of the Code.

An eligible State deferred compensation plan may provide a limited "catch-up" provision for any, or all, of the last three taxable years of a participant ending before the normal retirement age specified by the plan (or if no normal retirement age is specified by the plan, then either the later of the normal retirement age specified in any other retirement plan maintained by the sponsoring entity for age 65). Under the catch-up provision, in addition to the amount that may be deferred under the usual $7,500 and 33 ⅓-percent-of-includible-compensation limitations, a participant may defer an additional amount equal to any deferral limitations not utilized for prior taxable years in which the participant was eligible to participate in the plan (even if nothing was deferred) and was subject to the deferral limitations imposed by the bill. The maximum that can be deferred in any taxable year through the utilization of both the normal deferral limitation and the catch-up provision is $15,000. (Of course, the deferred amount also cannot exceed the amount of the participant's compensation from the State, etc.) For example, a 62-year-old participant in a plan with a normal retirement age of 65 who is scheduled to receive a salary of $20,000 during the next taxable year, could elect to defer $15,000 of that compensation if prior year's deferral limitations have been underutilized by at least $10,000. (The regular limitation is $5,000 ($20,000 - $5,000 ÷ 3 = $5,000); the catch-up amount is $10,000 ($15,000 - $5,000).)

The underutilized deferral limitation for a taxable year is the difference between compensation actually includible in income for that year and compensation that would have been includible in income if the maximum deferral limitation had been utilized. For example, an individual with a salary of $20,000 who did not elect to defer any compensation would have an underutilized deferral limitation of $5,000 ($20,000 - $15,000 (includible compensation if the 33 ⅓ percent deferral limitation had been utilized)). In calculating the underutilized deferral limitation, the participant must use the actual plan limitations if they are less than the limitations provided by this bill.

In addition to providing limitations on amounts of compensation that can be deferred, the bill provides that the plan must not permit participants to defer compensation for a [month] unless an agreement providing for such deferral has been entered into before the beginning of [such month]. In the case of (1) persons first performing services for the sponsoring entity, and (2) newly implemented deferred compensation plans, employees or independent contractors would have a reasonable period of time from the date participation in the plan is offered to them to effect an election to defer. In such case, the election to defer compensation would become effective for pay periods beginning after the date the participation agreement is filed with the sponsoring entity or the plan administrator. If a plan is amended to provide for participation by a group of employees or independent contractors not previously permitted to participate, or in the case of individuals first meeting any eligibility requirements provided under the plan, it is intended that a reasonable period of time will be allowed for affected individuals to elect to participate as if this were a newly implemented plan or as if these were new employees.

An eligible State deferred compensation plan cannot make benefits available to participants before the earlier of (1) separation from service with the sponsoring entity, (2) retirement in accordance with the terms of any retirement plan maintained by the sponsoring entity, (3) death, or (4) the occurrence of an unforeseeable emergency. While the Secretary of the Treasury is to prescribe regulations defining what constitutes an unforeseeable emergency, it is not intended that such term would include the purchase of a home or the need for funds to send children to college. In addition, it is expected that plans will permit the withdrawal of only the amount of funds reasonably needed to satisfy the emergency needs.

Finally, for the deferred compensation plan to be eligible under the bill, all amounts of compensation deferred under the plan, all property or rights to property (including rights as a beneficiary of life insurance protection) purchased with the amounts deferred, and any income earned on property purchased with amounts deferred must remain assets of the plan sponsor subject to the claims of its general creditors. Thus, while plan participants may select among any optional methods provided under the plan for investing amounts of deferred compensation, they cannot have any secured interest in the assets purchased with their deferred compensation and the assets may not be segregated for their benefit in any manner which would put them beyond the reach of the general creditors of the sponsoring entity.

Any plan which is not administered in accordance with the bill's requirements for eligible State deferred compensation plans will lose its eligible status on the first day of the first plan year beginning more than 180 days after notification by the Secretary of the Treasury that such requirements are not being met, unless satisfactory corrective action is taken by the first day of such plan year. If a plan loses its status as an eligible State deferred compensation plan, amounts subsequently deferred by participants will be includible in income when deferred (unless the amounts are subject to a substantial risk of forfeiture when deferred). However, it is intended that (amounts pre-entity) he must designate how the $7,500 limitation will be allocated in income until paid or otherwise made available.

Participants in more than one eligible plan, or in a section 403(b) annuity.—Except for the limited "catch-up" provision, $7,500 is the maximum compensation that can be deferred in a taxable year by an employee or an independent contractor who is a participant in an eligible State deferred compensation plan. This dollar limitation (as well as the percentage limitation) applies at the individual level as well as at the plan level. Thus, if a person participates in more than one eligible plan (whether or not maintained by the same sponsoring entity) he must designate how the $7,500 limitation will be allocated among the various plans in which he participates. If the $7,500 limitation is exceeded, all excess amounts deferred for the taxable year will be currently includible in income.

If an individual participates in an eligible State deferred compensation plan and also has amounts contributed by an employer for the purchase of a tax-sheltered annuity or mutual fund shares held in a custodial account, and part or all of such contributions are excludable under section 403(b), the contributions excludable under section 403(b) reduce both the $7,500 and the 33 ⅓ percent of includible compensation limitations even though the percent of includible compensation limitation is computed without regard to such exclusion. For example, a public school official with a contract salary of $30,000 in his or her first year of service with the school system could be eligible to participate in both an eligible State deferred compensation plan and a tax-sheltered (section 403(b)) annuity plan (with all contributions assumed to come from salary reductions) sponsored by the employer. If the employee elected to participate in the tax-sheltered annuity plan to the maximum extent possible while still participating in the eligible deferred compensation plan, he or she could elect to defer $4,500 under section 403(b) for contributions used to purchase an annuity contract or mutual fund shares and $3,000 under the eligible State deferred compensation plan.[1]

---

[1] This provision is not intended to have any effect on the issue of whether a rural electric cooperative which is not described in section 501(c)(12) may qualify for tax exempt status under section 501(a) as an organization described in section 501(c)(4).

[1] The applicable limitations would be computed as follows:

(1) Sec. 403(b) exclusion for the tax-sheltered annuity—20% × $22,500 (includible compensation after reduction of contract salary for salary reductions deferred under both plans) × 1 (one year of service) = $4,500. (There is no reduction under sec. 403(b)(2)(A)(ii) for amounts contributed in prior years by the employer and excludable by the employee, since this is assumed to be the first year of service with the school system.)

(2) The sec. 457(b)(2) limitation (limitation on deferral under an eligible State deferred compensation plan) is $3,000, which is the lesser of—

(a) $7,500, or

(b) 33 ⅓% × $27,000 (includible compensation after reduction of contract salary by deferral under the eligible State deferred compensation plan but before reduction for the exclusion under sec. 403(b)) = $9,000.

For purposes of determining the exclusion allowance under section 403(b), any amount deferred in a prior taxable year of the employee under an eligible State deferred compensation plan (without regard to the sponsoring entity) will be treated as an amount contributed by the employer for annuity contracts and excluded by the employee, if the taxable year of deferral counts as a year of service in the computation of the exclusion allowance under section 403(b).[2]

Treatment of participants in an ineligible plan.—If a State or local government deferred compensation plan fails to meet the requirements of an "eligible" plan, then all compensation deferred under the plan is currently includible in income by the participants unless the amounts deferred are subject to a substantial risk of forfeiture. If amounts deferred are subject to a substantial risk of forfeiture, then they are includible in the gross income of participants or beneficiaries in the first taxable year there is no substantial risk of forfeiture.

While amounts deferred under an ineligible State deferred compensation plan generally would be included in income in the year of deferral, earnings credited on such deferred amounts would not be subject to current taxation as long as the participant has no interest in the assets of the State or local government sponsoring the plan which is more secure than that of general creditors. Where the participant has no such interest, earnings on amounts deferred under the plan will not be taxable to the participant until paid or otherwise made available and then will be taxed according to the annuity rules (sec. 72). This is also the treatment that will be accorded any excess deferrals and the earnings thereon.

The treatment provided by the bill for an ineligible State deferred compensation plan extends only to plans which provide an option to defer compensation and is inapplicable to a State's regular retirement system (whether or not such plan is a tax-qualified plan) which does not provide such an option. The bill will not result in double taxation of income in the event that a plan becomes ineligible. For example, if an amount is set aside by the employer for an employee under a plan, and the amount set aside is taxed to the employee under section 83, the employee would not be taxed on that amount again if the plan becomes ineligible. Similarly, under the bill, if an employee is taxed on compensation under an ineligible plan and an amount is subsequently set aside by the employer for the employee under the plan, the amount set aside would not be taxed again under section 83.

Present value of compensation.—The bill provides that compensation shall be taken into account at its present value. This rule was provided for those cases where the amount of deferral for a particular taxable year is not readily ascertainable.

In the case of the normal salary reduction deferral agreement entered into by an employee and a State or local government, the amount withheld by the State or local government will be considered to be the present value of the compensation deferred. This amount will then be compared to the includible compensation for the taxable year to determine if the limitations on deferral have been satisfied for the taxable year. However, in the case of an independent contractor who agrees to perform services during a taxable year in return for some compensation payable currently and additional compensation payable in a later taxable year, it will be necessary, as of the close of the taxable year, to determine the present value of the right to receive the future payment or payments and compare that to the includible compensation for the taxable year to determine if the limitations on deferral have been satisfied.

If future payments are subject to a substantial risk of forfeiture, then they will not be valued until there is no longer a substantial risk of forfeiture. At the close of the first taxable year in which the future payments are no longer subject to a substantial risk of forfeiture, the present value of such payments must be compared to the includible compensation for such year to determine if the deferral limitations have been met.

Effective date

All plans to which this provision applies (whether currently in existence or not) will have until January 1, 1982, to satisfy the plan requirements for classification as an eligible State deferred compensation plan. It is believed that this transitional rule will provide State legislatures with ample time to adopt necessary amendments to their enabling statutes. However, the limitations on amounts that can be deferred under such a plan will apply for all taxable years beginning after December 31, 1978. In addition, the catch-up provisions will apply prior to 1982 only if all State deferred compensation plans in which a participant is participating, or has participated in during taxable years for which there is an underutilized deferral limitation, are "eligible" State deferred compensation plans (i.e., all plans involved actually satisfy the plan requirements of sec. 457(b)).

[Senate Committee Report]

Includible compensation (rather than gross compensation) is used in determining the percentage of an employee's compensation that may be deferred because of the necessity of coordinating with the provisions of section 403(b) which also are based on includible compensation. In addition, there may be contractual deferred compensation arrangements where only includible compensation is readily determinable. For example, if a consultant agrees to provide service to a State agency for one year in return for current payments of $25,000 plus payments of $5,000 per year for an additional five years, such payments to begin after a period of ten years, it is clear that includible compensation is $25,000, but until the present value of the right to receive the additional $5,000 per year for 5 years is determined, compliance with the percentage limitation cannot be determined. (See discussion in *Present value of compensation* below.) Also, from the terms of the contract it generally would not be possible to tell how much compensation the consultant could have received in the year the services were performed ("gross compensation") but for the agreement to take periodic payments beginning at a later date.

[Conference Committee Report]

Conference agreement

The conference agreement generally follows the House bill except that it permits monthly, rather than annual, elections to defer compensation.

[Code Sec. 501]

[¶ 13,160.081]

Committee Report on P.L. 109-280 (Pension Protection Act of 2006)

[Joint Committee on Taxation Report]

[Eliminate aggregate limit for usage of excess funds from black lung disability trusts to pay for retiree health]

The provision eliminates the aggregate limit on the amount of excess black lung benefit trust assets that may be used to pay accident and health benefits or premiums for insurance exclusively covering such benefits (including administrative and other incidental expenses relating to such benefits) for retired coal miners and their spouses and dependents.

Effective Date

The provision is effective for taxable years beginning after December 31, 2006.

[¶ 13,160.083]

Committee Report on P.L. 104-191 (Health Insurance Portability and Accountability Act)

State Insurance Pools

[House Committee Report]

State organizations providing health care

The bill provides tax-exempt status to any membership organization that is established by a State exclusively to provide coverage for medical care on a nonprofit basis to certain high-risk individuals, provided certain criteria are satisfied.[16] The organization may provide coverage for medical care either by issuing insurance itself or by entering into an arrangement with a health maintenance organization ("HMO").

High-risk individuals eligible to receive medical care coverage from the organization must be residents of the State who, due to a pre-existing medical condition, are unable to obtain health coverage for such condition through insurance or an HMO, or are able to acquire such coverage only at a rate that is substantially higher than the rate charged for such coverage by the organization. The State must determine the composition of membership in the organization. For example, a State could mandate that all organizations that are subject to insurance regulation by the State must be members of the organization.

The bill further requires the State or members of the organization to fund the liabilities of the organization to the extent that premiums charged to eligible individuals are insufficient to cover such liabilities. Finally, no part of the net earnings of the organization can inure to the benefit of any private shareholder or individual.

Effective Date

The provision applies to taxable years beginning after December 31, 1996.

[Conference Committee Report]

Senate Amendment

The Senate amendment is the same as the House bill.

(Footnote Continued)

(c) Lesser of $7,500 or $9,000 = $7,500.

(d) $7,500, as determined under (c), reduced by the exclusion of $4,500 under sec. 403(b) = $3,000.

[2] In the example contained in footnote 1, if in year 2 the employee still had a contract salary of $30,000 and elected to defer the maximum amount possible under a tax-sheltered annuity while not taking advantage of the deferral under an eligible State deferred compensation plan, the exclusion allowance under sec. 403(b) would be $3,214.28, computed as follows:

(a) 20% × $26,785.72 (includible compensation) = $5,357.14

(b) × 2 years of service = $10,714.28

(c) less $7,500 ($4,500 excluded under sec. 403(b) in the prior taxable year and $3,000 deferred under an eligible State deferred compensation plan in the prior taxable year)

(d) maximum exclusion allowance = $3,214.28 (assuming no deferral under the eligible State deferred compensation plan in year 2).

[16] No inference is intended as to the tax treatment of other types of State-sponsored organizations.

Conference Agreement

The conference agreement follows the House bill and the Senate amendment.

Effective Date

The provision applies to taxable years ending after the date of enactment.

State Insurance Pools

[Conference Committee Report]

State organizations providing workman's compensation reinsurance

The conference agreement provides tax-exempt status to any membership organization that is established by a State before June 1, 1996, exclusively to reimburse its members for workers' compensation insurance losses, and that satisfies certain other conditions. A State must require that the membership of the organization consist of all persons who issue insurance covering workers' compensation losses in such State, and all persons who issue insurance covering workers' compensation losses in such State, and all persons and governmental entities who self-insure against such losses. In addition, the organization must operate as a nonprofit organization by returning surplus income to members or to workers' compensation policyholders on a periodic basis and by reducing initial premiums in anticipation of investment income.

Effective Date

The provision applies to taxable years ending after the date of enactment.

[¶ 13,160.084]

Committee Report on P.L. 104-188 (Small Business Job Protection Act)

Small Business Provisions

[House Committee Report]

Treatment of certain charitable risk pools

Under the bill, a qualified charitable risk pool is treated as organized and operated exclusively for charitable purposes. The provision makes inapplicable to a qualified charitable risk pool the present-law rule under section 501(m) that a charitable organization described in section 501(c)(3) is exempt from tax only if no substantial part of its activities consists of providing commercial-type insurance.

The bill defines a qualified charitable risk pool as an organization organized and operated solely to pool insurable risks of its members (other than medical malpractice risks) and to provide information to its members with respect to loss control and risk management. Because a qualified charitable risk pool must be organized and operated SOLELY to pool insurable risks of its members and to provide information to members with respect to loss control and risk management, no profit or other benefit may be accorded to any member of the organization other than through providing members with insurance coverage below the cost of comparable commercial coverage and through providing members with loss control and risk management information. Only charitable tax-exempt organizations described in section 501(c)(3) may be members of a qualified charitable risk pool.

The bill further requires that a qualified charitable risk pool is required to (1) be organized as a nonprofit organization under State law authorizing risk pooling for charitable organizations; (2) be exempt from State income tax; (3) obtain at least $1 million in startup capital from nonmember charitable organizations; (4) be controlled by a board of directors elected by its members; and (5) provide in its organizational documents that members must be tax-exempt charitable organizations at all times, and if a member loses that status it must immediately notify the organization, and that no insurance coverage applies to a member after the date of any final determination that the member no longer qualifies as a tax-exempt charitable organization.

To be entitled to tax-exempt status under section 501(c)(3), a qualified charitable risk pool described in the provision also must satisfy the other requirements of that section (i.e., the private inurement test and the prohibition of political campaign activities and substantial lobbying).

Effective Date

The provision applies to taxable years beginning after the date of enactment.

Conference Committee Report

The conference agreement follows the House bill.

[¶ 13,160.085]

Committee Report on P.L. 102-486 (Comprehensive National Energy Policy Act of 1982)

The conference agreement allows excess assets in qualified black lung benefit trusts to be used to pay accident and health benefits or premiums for insurance for such benefits (including administrative and other incidental expenses relating to such benefits) for retired coal miners and their spouses and dependents. The amount of assets available for such purpose is subject to a yearly limit as well as an aggregate limit. The yearly limit is the amount of assets in excess of 110 percent of the present value of the liability for black lung benefits determined as of the close of the preceding taxable year of the trust. The aggregate limit is the amount of assets in excess of 110 percent of the present value of the liability for black lung benefits determined as of the close of the taxable year of the trust ending prior to the effective date, plus earnings thereon. Each of these determinations is required to be made by an independent actuary.

The amounts used to pay retiree accident or health benefits are not includible in the income of the company, nor is a deduction allowed for such amounts.

Effective Date

The provision is effective for taxable years beginning after December 31, 1991. * * * **Conference Committee Report.**

[¶ 13,160.09]

Committee Reports on P.L. 94-455 (Tax Reform Act of 1976)

Group Legal Services Plans.—* * * The amendment also provides that a trust created or organized in the United States, whose exclusive function is to form part of a qualified group legal services plan under section 120, is to be exempt from income tax (new sec. 501(c)(20)). Such a trust shall be subject to the rules governing organizations exempt under section 501(c), including the taxation of any unrelated business income. * * * **Senate Committee Supplemental Report.**

[Code Sec. 505]

[¶ 13,193.085]

Committee Reports on P.L. 103-66 (Omnibus Budget Reconciliation Act of 1993)

For Committee Reports on P.L. 103-66, Sec. 13212, relating to compensation for retirement plan purposes, see ¶ 11,700.040.

[¶ 13,193.10]

Committee Reports on P.L. 98-369 (Tax Reform Act of 1984)

[House Committee Report]

In general

An association that is otherwise exempt from tax as a voluntary employees' beneficiary association (VEBA) or group legal services organization would not continue to be tax exempt unless it meets new standards provided by the bill.

* * *

Nondiscrimination

In general, a VEBA meets the nondiscrimination standards of the bill only if, under the plan of that it is a part, (1) each class of benefits is available to employees under a classification which is set forth in the plan and that is found by the Treasury not to be discriminatory in favor of employees who are highly compensated, and (2) such class of benefits provided does not discriminate in favor of highly compensated employees. In testing whether the benefits are available to a nondiscriminatory classification of employees, employees who decline to make required contributions must be considered.

Under the bill, however, if a plan provides a benefit of a type for which a nondiscrimination standard is provided by the Code as a condition of an exclusion from gross income, that benefit is not subject to the general nondiscrimination standard. Such a benefit will be considered to be nondiscriminatory if and only if it meets the nondiscrimination standard of the applicable provision of the Code. For example, benefits provided under a medical reimbursement plan would meet the nondiscrimination standard under a VEBA if, and only if, they meet the nondiscrimination standard provided for such plans by section 105(h)(3) and (4).

The bill overrides the nondiscrimination rules of present law for those VEBAs subject to the rules of the bill. The nondiscrimination standards of the bill do not apply to a VEBA maintained pursuant to a collective bargaining agreement. Of course, such VEBAs continue to be subject to the nondiscrimination standards of present law.

In determining whether the nondiscrimination standards are satisfied, the committee intends that the Secretary may take into consideration benefits that vary on acount of reasonable and significant geographic disparities.

As under present law, the nondiscrimination standards are applicable with respect to the form of a plan (or exempt organization), its operation, and its termination.

Under the nondiscrimination standard for benefits provided by a VEBA, a life, disability, severance pay, and supplemental unemployment compensation benefit is not considered to be discriminatory merely because the benefit bears a uniform relationship to the total compensation, or to the basic or regular rate of compensation, of covered employees. Generally, such a benefit could not be integrated with social security benefits or benefits under a qualified plan or a simplified employee pension. In the case of a disability benefit, however, integration with the employer-provided portion of social security disability benefits (or contributions) is allowed to the extent employer-provided social security disability benefits (or contributions) are not taken into account under a qualified pension, profit-sharing, or stock bonus plan, or under a simplified employee pension.

* * *

Notice of claim of exempt status

Under the bill, a VEBA or SUB would be required to notify the Internal Revenue Service that it is applying for recognition of its exempt status. The committee believes that such notice is required for efficient administration of the tax law. Organizations that have previously notified the IRS are not required, under the bill, to renotify the IRS.

Under the bill, an organization is not exempt as a VEBA or a SUB unless it has given the notice in the manner required by Treasury regulations. The organization will not be exempt as a VEBA or a SUB for any period before the notice is given if the notice is given after the time prescribed by the regulations. In the case of an organization that is in existence on the date of the enactment of the Tax Reform Act of 1984, the time for giving the notice is not to expire before the end of 1 year after the date of enactment.

[Conference Committee Report]

* * *

With respect to the nondiscrimination rules, certain employees who are not covered by a plan may be excluded from consideration in applying the nondiscrimination standards. These employees are employees who have not attained the age of 21, employees who have not completed 3 years of service with the employer, less than ½-time employees, employees who are included in certain collective bargaining units, and certain nonresident aliens.

The conferees wish to clarify the rules of the House bill relating to integration of benefits under a VEBA with social security. In testing whether a disability plan funded with an exempt trust violates the rules forbidding discrimination in favor of employees who are officers, shareholders, or highly compensated, a part of each employee's Social Security benefit (the part considered to be paid for by the employer) can be taken into account as if it were provided under the employer's plan. Similar integration rules are provided for qualified pension plans.

For example, a pension plan may provide a retirement benefit that is reduced by up to 83 ⅓ percent of the primary insurance amount for the employee under Social Security. This 83 ⅓ percent offset represents the part of the employee's Social Security benefit that the employer is considered to have provided. It includes the value of the employer's Disability Income (DI) contribution, as well as his Old-Age and Survivor's Insurance (OASI) contribution. The Disability Income benefit is considered to make up 10 percent of the value of employer-provided Social Security benefits. Thus, if the employer provides a disability benefit under the pension plan and the disability benefit is reduced by 100 percent of the Social Security benefit, then the employer may "take credit" for only 90 percent of employer-provided Social Security benefits when paying a retirement benefit. Accordingly, only 75 percent (90 percent of 83 ⅓) of Social Security benefits could be subtracted from the retirement benefit.

Thus, under the agreement, if an employer's pension plan is not more than 90 percent integrated—that is, it does not reduce benefits by more than 90 percent of the amount by which they could be reduced (e.g., by more than 75 percent of social security benefits)—then double integration does not occur. In this case, the agreement requires no change in either the pension plan or the disability plan.

On the other hand, if an employee's pension plan is more than 90 percent integrated, the full value of the Disability Income benefit under Social Security could not be used to reduce long-term disability benefits under the employer's plan. For example, if the pension plan is 93 percent integrated (so that 30 percent of the employer's Social Security Disability Income benefit has been used by the pension plan), then no more than 70 percent of the Disability Income benefit could be applied to reduce long-term disability benefits under the employer's plan. Of course, if the pension plan were 100 percent integrated, the long-term disability benefit under the employer's plan could not be integrated with Social Security. The rules relating to integration of long-term disability benefits apply to benefits funded by employer contributions as well as benefits funded by employee contributions.

Of course, the agreement also permits the integration of long-term disability benefits with workers' compensation benefits.

In addition, the agreement does not affect the integration of long-term disability benefits for employees who are disabled before the effective date.

[Code Sec. 817]

[¶ 13,312.03]

Committee Report on P.L. 104-188 (Small Business Job Protection Act)

Revenue Offsets

[Senate Committee Report]

Treatment of certain insurance contracts on retired lives

The bill provides that a variable contract is to include a contract that provides for the funding of group term life or group accident and health insurance on retired lives if: (1) the contract provides for the allocation of all or part of the amounts received under the contract to an account that is segregated from the general asset account of the company; and (2) the amounts paid in, or the amounts paid out, under the contract reflect the investment return and the market value of the segregated asset account underlying the contract.

Thus, the reserve for such a contract is to be adjusted by (1) subtracting any amount that has been added to the reserve by reason of appreciation in the value of assets underlying such contract, and (2) adding any amount that has been subtracted from the reserve by reason of depreciation in the value of assets underlying such contract. In addition, the basis of each asset underlying the contract is to be adjusted for appreciation or depreciation to the extent that the reserve is adjusted.

Effective Date

The provision applies to taxable years beginning after December 31, 1995.

[Conference Committee Report]

The conference agreement follows the Senate amendment.

[Code Sec. 817A]

[¶ 13,313.03]

Committee Reports on P.L. 104-188 (Small Business Job Protection Act)

Revenue Offsets

[Conference Committee Report]

Treatment of modified guaranteed contracts

House Bill

No provision.

Senate Amendment

No provision.

Conference Agreement

The conference agreement generally applies a mark-to-market regime to assets held as part of a segregated account under a modified guaranteed contract issued by a life insurance company. Gain or loss with respect to such assets held as of the close of any taxable year are taken into account for that year (even though the assets have not been sold or exchanged),[58] and are treated as ordinary. If gain or loss is taken into account by reason of the mark-to-market requirement, then the amount of gain or loss subsequently realized as a result of sale, exchange, or other disposition of the asset, or as a result of the application of the mark-to-market requirement is appropriately adjusted to reflect such gain or loss. In addition, the reserve for a modified guaranteed contract is determined by taking into account the market value adjustment required on surrender of the contract.

A modified guaranteed contract is defined as any life insurance contract, annuity contract or pension plan contract[59] that is not a variable contract (within the meaning of Code section 817), and that satisfies the following requirements. All or part of the amounts received under the contract must be allocated to an account which, pursuant to State law or regulation, is segregated from the general asset accounts of the company and is valued from time to time by reference to market values.

The reserves for the contract must be valued at market for annual statement purposes and the Federally prescribed reserve for the contract under section 807(d)(2) must be valued at market. Further, a modified guaranteed contract includes only a contract that provides either for a net surrender value or for a policyholder's fund (within the meaning of section 807(e)(1)). It is intended that a policyholder's fund be more than de minimis. For example, Treasury regulations could provide that a policyholder's fund that represents 15 percent or less of the insurer's reserve for the contract under section 807, and that is attributable to employee contributions, would be considered de minimis.

If only a portion of the contract is not described in section 817, that portion is treated as a separate contract for purposes of the provision.

The Treasury Department is authorized to issue regulations that provide for the application of the mark-to-market requirement at times other than the close of a taxable year or the last business day of a taxable year. The Treasury Department is also authorized to issue such regulations as may be necessary or

[58] The wash sale rules of section 1091 of the Code are not to apply to any loss that is required to be taken into account solely by reason of the mark-to-market requirement.

[59] The provision applies only to a pension plan contract that is not a life, accident or health, property, casualty, or liability contract.

appropriate to carry out the purposes of the provision and to provide for treatment of modified guaranteed contracts under sections 72, 7702, and 7702A. In addition, the Treasury Department is authorized to determine the interest rates applicable under section 807(c)(3), 807(d)(2)(B) and 812 with respect to modified guaranteed contracts annually, calculating such rates as appropriate for modified guaranteed contracts. The Treasury Department has discretion to determine an appropriate rate that is a current market rate, which could be determined, for example, either by using a rate that is appropriate for the obligations under the contract to which the reserve relates, or by taking into account the yield on the assets underlying the contract. The Treasury Department may exercise this authority by issuing a periodic announcement of the appropriate market interest rates or formula for determining such rates. The Treasury Department is also authorized, to the extent appropriate for such a contract, to modify or waive section 811(d).

The Treasury Department is also authorized to provide rules limiting the ordinary treatment provided under the provision to gain or loss on those assets properly taken into account in calculating the reserve for Federal tax purposes (and necessary to support such reserves) for modified guaranteed contracts, and to provide rules for limiting such treatment with respect to other assets (such as assets representing surplus of the company). Particular concern has been expressed about characterization of gain or loss as ordinary under the provision in transactions that would otherwise either (1) have to meet the requirements of the hedging exception to the straddle rules to receive this treatment, or (2) by treated as capital transactions under present law. It is intended that the mark-to-market treatment apply to all assets held as part of a segregated account established under the provision, even though ordinary treatment may not apply (pursuant to Treasury regulatory authority) to assets held as part of the segregated account that are not necessary to support the reserve for modified guaranteed contracts.

The conference agreement authorizes the Treasury Department to prescribe regulations that provide for the treatment of assets transferred to or from a segregated account. This regulatory authority is provided because of concern that taxpayers may exercise selective ordinary loss (or income or gain) recognition by virtue of the ordinary treatment under the provision. One example of selective ordinary loss recognition could arise if assets are always marked to market when transferred out of the segregated account. For example, if at the beginning of the taxable year an asset in the segregated account is worth $1,000, but declines to $900 in July, the taxpayer might choose to recognize $100 of ordinary loss while continuing to own the asset, simply by transferring it out of the segregated account in July and replacing $1,000 of cash (for example) in the segregated account.

It is intended that the regulations relating to asset transfers will forestall opportunities for selective recognition of ordinary items. Prior to the issuance of these regulations, the following rules shall apply.

If an asset is transferred to a segregated account, gain or loss attributable to the period during which the asset was not in the segregated account is taken into account when the asset is actually sold, and retains the character (as ordinary or capital) properly attributable to that period. Appropriate adjustments are made to the basis of the asset to reflect gain or loss attributable to that period.

If an asset is transferred out of a segregated account, the transfer is deemed to occur on the last business day of the taxable year and gain or loss with respect to the transferred asset is taken into account as of that day. Loss with respect to such transferred asset is treated as ordinary to the extent of the lesser of (1) the loss (if any) that would have been recognized if the asset had been sold for its fair market value on the last business day of the taxable year (or the date the asset was actually sold by the taxpayer, if earlier) or (2) the loss (if any) that would have been recognized if the asset had been sold for its fair market value on the date of the transfer. A similar rule applies for gains. Proper adjustment is made in the amount of any gain or loss subsequently realized to reflect gain or loss under the provision.

For example, assume that a capital asset in the segregated account that is worth $1,000 at the beginning of the year is transferred out of the segregated account in July at a value of $900, is retained by the company and is worth $950 on the last business day of the taxable year. A $50 ordinary loss is taken into account with respect to the asset for the taxable year (the difference Between $1,000 and $950). The asset is not marked to market in any subsequent year under the provision, provide that it is not transferred back to the segregated account.

As an additional example, assume that a capital asset in the segregated account that is worth $1,000 at the beginning of the year is transferred out of the segregated accounted in July at a value of $900, is retained by the company and continues to decline in value to $850 on the last business day of the taxable year. A $100 ordinary loss ($1,000 less $900) and a $50 capital loss ($900 less $850) is taken into account with respect to the asset for the taxable year.

Effective Date

The provision applies to taxable years beginning after December 31, 1995. A taxpayer that is required to (1) change its calculation of reserves to take into account market value adjustments and (2) mark to market its segregated assets in order to comply with the requirements of the provision is treated as having initiated changes in methods of accounting and as having received the consent of the Treasury Department to make such changes.

Except as otherwise provided in special rules (described below), the section 481(a) adjustments required by reason of the changes in method of accounting are to be taken into account as ordinary income for the taxpayer's first taxable year beginning after December 31, 1995.

Special rules providing for a seven-year spread apply in the case of certain losses (if any), and in the case of certain reserve increases (if any), in order to limit selective loss recognition or selective minimization of gain recognition. Thus, the seven-year spread rule applies when the taxpayer's section 481(a) adjustment is negative.

First, if, for the taxpayer's first taxable year beginning after December 31, 1995, (1) the aggregate amount of the loss recognized by reason of the change in method of accounting with respect to segregated assets under modified guaranteed contracts (i.e., the switch to a mark-to-market regime for such assets) exceeds (2) the amount include in income by reason of the change in method of accounting with respect to reserves (i.e., the change permitting a market value adjustment to be taken into account with respect to a modified guaranteed contract), then the excess is not allowed as a deduction in the taxpayer's first taxable year beginning after December 31, 1995. Rather, such excess is allowed ratably over the period of seven taxable years beginning with the taxpayer's first taxable year beginning after December 31, 1995. The adjusted basis of each such segregated asset is nevertheless determined as if such losses were realized in the taxpayer's first taxable year beginning after December 31, 1995.

Second, if, for the taxpayer's first taxable year beginning after December 31, 1995, (1) the aggregate amount the taxpayer's deduction that arises by reason of the change in method of accounting with respect to reserves (i.e., the change permitting a market value adjustment to be taken into account with respect to a modified guaranteed contract), exceeds (2) the aggregate amount of the gain recognized by reason of the change in method of accounting with respect to segregated assets under modified guaranteed contracts (i.e., the switch to a mark-to-market regime for such assets), then the excess is not allowed as a deduction in the taxpayer's first taxable year beginning after December 31, 1995. Rather, such excess is allowed ratably over the period of seven taxable years beginning with the taxpayer's first taxable year beginning after December 31, 1995.

[Code Sec. 818]

[¶ 13,314.10]

Committee Report on P.L. 104-191 (Health Insurance Portability and Accountability Act)

Accelerated Death Benefits

[House Committee Report]

Accelerated death benefits companies

For life insurance company tax purposes, the bill provides that a life insurance contract is treated as including a reference to a qualified accelerated death benefit rider to a life insurance contract (except in the case of any rider that is treated as a long-term care insurance contract under section 7702B, as added by the bill). A qualified accelerated death benefit rider is any rider on a life insurance contract that provides only for payments of a type that are excludable under this provision.

Effective Date

The provision treating a qualified accelerated death benefit rider as life insurance for life insurance company tax purposes takes effect on January 1, 1997. The issuance of qualified accelerated death benefit rider to a life insurance contract, or the addition of any provision required to conform an accelerated death benefit rider to these provisions, is not treated as a modification or material change of the contract (and is not intended to affect the issue date of any contract under section 101(f)).

[Conference Committee Report]

Senate Amendment

The Senate amendment is the same as the House bill * * *[.]

Conference Agreement

The conference agreement follows the House bill and the Senate amendment * * *[.]

[Code Sec. 856]

[¶ 13,327.095]

Committee Reports on P.L. 103-66 (Omnibus Budget Reconciliation Act of 1993)

Pension funds—Relaxation of limitations on investments in REITs

[House Committee Report]

Qualification as a REIT.—The bill provides that a pension trust generally is not treated as a single individual for purposes of the five-or-fewer rule. Rather, the bill treats beneficiaries of the pension trust as holding stock in the REIT in proportion to their actuarial interests in the trust. This rule does not apply if disqualified persons, within the meaning of section 4975(e)(2) (other than by reason of subparagraphs (B) and (I)), together own five percent or more of the value of the REIT stock and the REIT has earnings and profits attributable to a period during which it did not qualify as a REIT.[10]

In addition, the bill provides that a REIT cannot be a personal holding company and, therefore, is not subject to the personal holding company tax on its undistributed income.

Unrelated business taxable income.—Under the bill, certain pension trusts owning more than 10 percent of a REIT must treat a percentage of dividends from the REIT as UBTI. This percentage is the gross income derived from an unrelated trade or business (determined as if the REIT were a pension trust) divided by the gross income of the REIT for the year in which the dividends are paid. Dividends are not treated as UBTI, however, unless this percentage is at least five percent.

The UBTI rule applies only if the REIT qualifies as a REIT by reason of the above modification of the five or fewer rule. Moreover, the UBTI rule applies only if (1) one pension trust owns more than 25 percent of the value of the REIT, or (2) a group of pension trusts individually holding more than 10 percent of the value of the REIT collectively own more than 50 percent of the value of the REIT.

Effective Date

The provision applies to taxable years beginning on or after January 1, 1994.

[Conference Committee Report]

Senate Amendment

The Senate amendment is the same as the House bill.

Conference Agreement

The Conference agreement follows the House bill and the Senate amendment.

[Code Sec. 1042]

[¶ 13,382.10]

Committee Report on P.L. 101-239 (Omnibus Budget Reconciliation Act of 1989)

For Committee Reports on P.L. 101-239, relating to interest exclusion for ESOP loans, see ¶ 12,130.063.

[Code Sec. 1372]

[¶ 13,463.10]

Committee Report on P.L. 97-354 (Subchapter S Act)

[House Committee Report]

Present law

Under present law, the statutory exemptions for fringe benefits applicable to shareholder-employees of regular corporations also apply in the case of subchapter C corporations. The benefits include the following:

(1) the $5,000 death benefit exclusion (sec. 101(b));

(2) the exclusion from income of amounts paid for an accident and health plan (secs. 105(b), (c) and (d));

(3) the exclusion from income of amounts paid by an employer to an accident and health plan (sec. 106);

(4) the exclusion of the cost of up to $50,000 of group-term life insurance on an employee's life (sec. 79); and

(5) the exclusion from income of meals or lodging furnished for the convenience of the employer (sec. 119).

Explanation of Provision (sec. 1372)

Under the bill, the treatment of fringe benefits of any person owning more than two percent of the stock of the corporation will be treated in the same manner as a partner in a partnership. Thus, for example, amounts paid for the medical care of a shareholder-employee will not be deductible by the corporation (by reason of secs. 1363(b)(2) and 703(a)(2)(E)), will be deductible by that individual only to the extent personal medical expenses will be allowed as an itemized deduction under section 213. However, similar amounts paid by the corporation on behalf of shareholders owning two percent or less of the corporation may be deducted as a business expense.

[Code Sec. 1400M]

[¶ 13,473.020]

Committee Report on P.L. 109-135 (Gulf Opportunity Zone Act of 2005)

[Joint Committee on Taxation]

[Definitions of "Gulf Opportunity Zone," "Rita GO Zone," "Wilma GO Zone," and other definitions]

Gulf Opportunity Zone

For purposes of the bill, the "Gulf Opportunity Zone" is defined as that portion of the Hurricane Katrina Disaster Area determined by the President to warrant individual or individual and public assistance from the Federal Government under the Robert T. Stafford Disaster Relief and Emergency Assistance Act by reason of Hurricane Katrina.

Hurricane Katrina disaster area

The term "Hurricane Katrina disaster area" means an area with respect to which a major disaster has been declared by the President before September 14, 2005, under section 401 of the Robert T. Stafford Disaster Relief and Emergency Assistance Act by reason of Hurricane Katrina.

Rita GO Zone

The term "Rita GO Zone" means that portion of the Hurricane Rita disaster area determined by the President to warrant individual or individual and public assistance from the Federal Government under section 401 of the Robert T. Stafford Disaster Relief and Emergency Assistance Act by reason of Hurricane Rita.

Hurricane Rita disaster area

The term "Hurricane Rita disaster area" means an area with respect to which a major disaster has been declared by the President before October 6, 2005, under section 401 of the Robert T. Stafford Disaster Relief and Emergency Assistance Act, by reason of Hurricane Rita.

Wilma GO Zone

The term "Wilma GO Zone" means that portion of the Hurricane Wilma disaster area determined by the President to warrant individual or individual and public assistance from the Federal Government under section 401 of the Robert T. Stafford Disaster Relief and Emergency Assistance Act by reason of Hurricane Wilma.

Hurricane Wilma disaster area

The term "Hurricane Wilma disaster area" means an area with respect to which a major disaster has been declared by the President before November 14, 2005, under section 401 of the Robert T. Stafford Disaster Relief and Emergency Assistance Act, by reason of Hurricane Wilma.

[Code Sec. 1400P]

[¶ 13,474.020]

Committee Report on P.L. 109-135 (Gulf Opportunity Zone Act of 2005)

[Joint Committee on Taxation]

[Housing Relief for Individuals Affected by Hurricane Katrina]

Explanation of Provision

The provision provides a temporary income exclusion for the value of in-kind lodging provided for a month to a qualified employee (and the employee's spouse or dependents) by or on behalf of a qualified employer. The amount of the exclusion for any month for which lodging is furnished cannot exceed $600. The exclusion does not apply for purposes of social security and Medicare taxes or unemployment tax.

The provision also provides a temporary credit to a qualified employer of 30 percent of the value of lodging excluded from the income of a qualified employee under the provision. The amount taken as a credit is not deductible by the employer.

Qualified employee means, with respect to a month, an individual who: (1) on August 28, 2005, had a principal residence in the Gulf Opportunity ("GO") Zone; and (2) performs substantially all of his or her employment services in the GO Zone for the qualified employer furnishing the lodging. Qualified employer means any employer with a trade or business located in the GO Zone.

Effective Date

The provision applies to lodging provided during the period beginning on the first day of the first month beginning after the date of enactment and ending on the date that is six months after such first day.

[10] Moreover, as under present law, any investment by a pension trust must be in accordance with the fiduciary rules of the Employee Retirement Security Act ("ERISA") and the prohibited transaction rules of the Code and ERISA.

[Code Sec. 1400Q]

[¶ 13,475.020]

Committee Report on P.L. 109-135 (Gulf Opportunity Zone Act of 2005)

[Joint Committee on Taxation]

[Tax-Favored Withdrawals from Retirement Plans Relating to Hurricanes Rita and Wilma]

Explanation of Provision

The provision codifies and expands the relief provided under the Katrina Emergency Tax Relief Act of 2005 in the case of qualified Hurricane Katrina distributions to any "qualified hurricane distribution," which is defined to include distributions relating to Hurricanes Rita and Wilma. Under the provision, a qualified hurricane distribution includes distributions that meet the definition of qualified Hurricane Katrina distribution under the Katrina Emergency Tax Relief Act of 2005, as well as any other distribution from an eligible retirement plan made on or after September 23, 2005, and before January 1, 2007, to an individual whose principal place of abode on September 23, 2005, is located in the Hurricane Rita disaster area and who has sustained an economic loss by reason of Hurricane Rita. A qualified hurricane distribution also includes a distribution from an eligible retirement plan made on or after October 23, 2005, and before January 1, 2007, to an individual whose principal place of abode on October 23, 2005, is located in the Hurricane Wilma disaster area and who has sustained an economic loss by reason of Hurricane Wilma.

The total amount of qualified hurricane distributions that an individual can receive from all plans, annuities, or IRAs is $100,000.

Effective Date

The provision is effective on the date of enactment.

[¶ 13,475.022]

Committee Report on P.L. 109-135 (Gulf Opportunity Zone Act of 2005)

[Joint Committee on Taxation]

[Recontributions of Withdrawals for Home Purchases Cancelled Due to Hurricanes Rita and Wilma]

Explanation of Provision

The provision codifies and expands the provision under the Katrina Emergency Tax Relief Act of 2005 allowing recontribution of certain distributions from a 401(k) plan, 403(b) annuity, or IRA to qualified Hurricane Rita distributions and to qualified Hurricane Wilma distributions.

A qualified Hurricane Rita distribution is a hardship distribution from a 401(k) plan or 403(b) annuity, or a qualified first-time homebuyer distribution from an IRA: (1) that is received after February 28, 2005, and before September 24, 2005; and (2) that was to be used to purchase or construct a principal residence in the Hurricane Rita disaster area, but the residence is not purchased or constructed on account of Hurricane Rita. Any portion of a qualified Hurricane Rita distribution may, during the period beginning on September 23, 2005, and ending on February 28, 2006, be recontributed to a plan, annuity or IRA to which a rollover is permitted.

A qualified Hurricane Wilma distribution is a hardship distribution from a 401(k) plan or 403(b) annuity, or a qualified first-time homebuyer distribution from an IRA: (1) that is received after February 28, 2005, and before October 24, 2005; and (2) that was to be used to purchase or construct a principal residence in the Hurricane Wilma disaster area, but the residence is not purchased or constructed on account of Hurricane Wilma. Any portion of a qualified Hurricane Wilma distribution may, during the period beginning on October 23, 2005, and ending on February 28, 2006, be recontributed to a plan, annuity or IRA to which a rollover is permitted.

Effective Date

The provision is effective on the date of enactment.

[¶ 13,475.024]

Committee Report on P.L. 109-135 (Gulf Opportunity Zone Act of 2005)

[Joint Committee on Taxation]

[Loans from Qualified Plans to Individuals Sustaining an Economic Loss Due to Hurricanes Rita and Wilma]

Explanation of Provision

The provision codifies and expands the special rules for loans from a qualified employer plan provided under the Katrina Emergency Tax Relief Act of 2005 to loans from a qualified employer plan to a qualified Hurricane Rita or Hurricane Wilma individual made on or after the date of enactment and before January 1, 2007.

A qualified Hurricane Rita individual includes an individual whose principal place of abode on September 23, 2005, is located in a Hurricane Rita disaster area and who has sustained an economic loss by reason of Hurricane Rita. In the case of a qualified Hurricane Rita individual with an outstanding loan on or after September 23, 2005, from a qualified employer plan, if the due date for any repayment with respect to such loan occurs during the period beginning on September 23, 2005, and ending on December 31, 2006, such due date is delayed for one year.

A qualified Hurricane Wilma individual includes an individual whose principal place of abode on October 23, 2005, is located in a Hurricane Wilma disaster area and who has sustained an economic loss by reason of Hurricane Wilma. In the case of a qualified Hurricane Wilma individual with an outstanding loan on or after October 23, 2005, from a qualified employer plan, if the due date for any repayment with respect to such loan occurs during the period beginning on October 23, 2005, and ending on December 31, 2006, such due date is delayed for one year.

An individual cannot be a qualified individual with respect to more than one hurricane.

Effective Date

The provision is effective on the date of enactment.

[¶ 13,475.026]

Committee Report on P.L. 109-135 (Gulf Opportunity Zone Act of 2005)

[Joint Committee on Taxation]

[Plan Amendments Relating to Hurricane Rita and Hurricane Wilma Relief]

Explanation of Provision

The provision codifies and expands the ability to make retroactive plan amendments under the Katrina Emergency Tax Relief Act of 2005 to apply to changes made pursuant to new section 1400Q of the Code, or regulations issued thereunder.

Effective Date

The provision is effective on the date of enactment.

[Code Sec. 1402]

[¶ 13,480.09]

Committee Reports on P.L. 104-188 (Small Business Job Protection Act)

Miscellaneous Pension Simplification

[House Committee Report]

No self-employment tax on retirement benefits of ministers

The bill provides that retirement benefits received from a church plan after a minister retires, and the rental value of a parsonage (including utilities) furnished to a minister after retirement, are not subject to self-employment taxes.

Effective Date

The provision is effective for years beginning before, on, or after December 31, 1994.

[Conference Committee Report]

Senate Amendment

The Senate amendment is the same as the House bill.

Conference Agreement

The conference agreement follows the House bill and the Senate amendment.

[Code Sec. 2039]

[¶ 13,500.06]

Committee Report on P.L. 97-248 (Tax Equity and Fiscal Responsibility Act of 1982)

For Committee Reports on P.L. 97-248, relating to exclusion limits, see ¶ 12,400.06.

[¶ 13,500.062]

Committee Report on P.L. 97-34 (Economic Recovery Tax Act of 1981)

For Commitee Reports on P.L. 97-34, Sec. 311, relating to individual retirement plans and taxation of distributions of voluntary employee distributions, see ¶ 11,330.02.

[¶ 13,500.065]

Committee Report on P.L. 96-222 (Technical Corrections Act of 1979)

[Senate Committee Report]

Sec. 101(a)(8)(B)— Unrealized appreciation in employer securities.

Under the Revenue Act of 1978, it is not clear whether the recipient of a lump sum death benefit distribution from a tax-qualified pension, etc., plan, who elects to forego favorable income tax treatment of the distribution in order for the distribution to be excludible from the deceased plan participant's gross estate for Federal estate tax purposes, may exclude from gross income the net unrealized appreciation on any employer securities distributed from the plan.

The bill makes it clear that, if an individual receives a lump sum death benefit distribution from a tax-qualified pension, etc., plan and elects to forego favorable income tax treatment of the distribution in order for the distribution to be excluded from the deceased plan participant's gross estate for Federal estate tax purposes, the election will not preclude the recipient from excluding from gross income the net unrealized appreciation on any employer securities distributed from the plan.

The amendment made by this section is effective as if it had been included in section 142 of the Revenue Act of 1978.

[¶ 13,500.07]

Committee Report on P.L. 95-600 (Revenue Act of 1978)

Secs. 142(a) and 142(b)— Employee stock ownership plans—The Senate Committee Report on Secs. 141—143 is at ¶ 12,130.10.

Sec. 156(c)(4)— Tax sheltered annuity rollover—The Conference Committee Report on Sec. 156 is at ¶ 11,800.06.

Sec. 702(j)(1)— Annuities from IRA's for non-working spouse.

Senate Committee Report (H.R. 67.15.)—* * * Under present law as amended by the 1976 Act, in general, the value of an annuity receivable by a beneficiary (other than the executor) under an individual retirement account is excluded from a decedent's gross estate. The exclusion applies only to the portion of the account attributable to contributions which were allowable as a deduction for income tax purposes or attributable to rollover contributions from a tax-qualified plan.[1]

This exclusion specifically refers to indivdual retirement accounts, individual retirement annuities, and retirement bonds for which a deduction was allowable under section 219 of the Code but does not refer to the new spouse-covered plans for which a deduction is allowable under § 220.

The committee believes an individual retirement account for an individual and his spouse should be treated in the same way as other individual retirement accounts for purposes of the estate tax exclusions.

The bill, as passed by the House and reported by the commitee, makes it clear that annuities receivable by a beneficiary (other than the exector) under a spouse-covered individual retirement account (§ 220) may qualify for the estate tax exclusion.

[¶ 13,500.08]

Committee Report on P.L. 94-455 (Tax Reform Act of 1976)

[Conference Committee Report]

H.R. 14844.—Under present law, the value of a survivor's interest in an annuity purchased by the decedent is included in the decedent's gross estate. However, an exclusion for estate and gift tax purposes is provided for the value of the portion of a survivor's annuity attributable to employer contributions to a qualified retirement plan.

H.R. 14844 excludes from the gross estate a survivor's interest in an H.R. 10 plan and an individual retirement account This bill removes the exclusion for all lump-sum distributions of the survivor's interest. This provision applies to decedents dying and gifts made after December 31, 1976.

Senate amendment

No provision.

Conference agreement

The conference agreement generally follows H.R. 14844.

The conference agreement modifies the provisions of H.R. 14844 to make it clear that a distribution from an individual retirement account to a beneficiary does not have to be in the form of a typical commercial annuity contract to qualify for the exclusion. Generally, the exclusion is to be available in situations where a liquidity problem might exist because the schedule of payments to be made from the account will not provide current funds to pay the estate tax. Under the conference agreement, the exclusion will be available if the distribution from an individual retirement account to the beneficiary consists of an annuity contract or other arrangement providing for a series of substantially equal periodic payments to be made to a beneficiary (other than the executor) for his life or over a period extending for at least 36 months after the date of the decedent's death. For this purpose, payments under an annuity contract are to be considered to be "substantially equal" under a variable annuity if the variance in payments are not solely attributable to tax avoidance motives. Of course, the annuity or other arrangement need not provide payments for the life of the beneficiary. Generally, satisfaction of the 3-year payment standard will be based on the payment provisions of the account or the settlement options, if any, elected no later than the earlier of the date the estate tax return is filed or the date on which the return is required to be filed (including extension of time to file).

[¶ 13,500.09]

Committee Report on P.L. 92-580 (No popular name designated)

[Senate Finance Committee Report]

[The amendment relating to the estate tax treatment of annuities in community property states] removes a discrimination in existing estate tax law against spouses of employees in community property states who die before the employee spouse. Generally, an estate tax exclusion is provided for the proportion of the value of a survivor annuity to the extent it is attributable to the contributions of the employer. In a common law state where the nonemployee (often the wife) dies first, no value representing the employer's contribution is included in her estate tax base. However, in a community property state, as a result of the operation of community property laws, half of the value of the annuity in such a case is included in the estate tax base of the nonemployee spouse, even though attributable to employer contributions. This amendment overcomes this discrimination against employee spouses in community property states.

* * *

This provision does not, in the case of the spouse in the community property state, provide any exclusion for her property interest in the plan to the extent it is attributable to the contributions of the employee spouse.

[Code Sec. 3121]

[¶ 13,530.07]

Committee Report on P.L. 104-188 (Small Business Job Protection Act)

Miscellaneous Pension Simplification

[House Committee Report]

Uniform penalty provisions for certain pension reporting requirements

The bill incorporates into the general penalty structure the penalties for failure to provide information reports relating to pension payments to the IRS and to recipients.

Effective Date

The provision is effective with respect to returns and statements the due date for which is after December 31, 1996.

[Conference Committee Report]

Senate Amendment

The Senate amendment is the same as the House bill.

Conference Agreement

The conference agreement follows the House bill and the Senate amendment.

[¶ 13,530.075]

Committee Report on P.L. 104-188 (Small Business Job Protection Act)

Committee Report on P.L. 104-188 [Increased Access to Retirement Savings see ¶ 12,050.056.

[¶ 13,530.08]

Committee Report on P.L. 100-647 (Technical and Miscellaneous Revenue Act of 1988)

[Conference Committee Report]

Employer Pension Contributions Not Included in FICA Wage Base

* * *

Senate Amendment

The Senate amendment would relieve State or local governments from FICA tax liability for employer "pickups" subsequent to the effective date of the 1984 Act to the extent that the State did not pay the FICA taxes in good faith reliance on a letter ruling of the Internal Revenue Service.

The relief would apply only to pickups for which FICA taxes were not paid and only for the period ending with the earlier of the date of enactment of this provision or the receipt by the State or local government from the IRS of a notice of revocation of the letter ruling.

Conference Agreement

The conference agreement follows the Senate amendment, with technical modifications.

---

[1] However, the estate tax exclusion is limited to an annuity receivable under a qualifying program.

[¶ 13,530.085]

Committee Reports on P.L. 100-203 (Omnibus Budget Reconciliation Act of 1987)

[House Committee Report]

The provision treats the cost of employer-provided group-term life insurance as wages for FICA tax purposes to the extent such cost is includible in gross income for income tax purposes.

[Conference Committee Report]

The conference agreement follows the House bill * * *.

[¶ 13,530.09]

Committee Reports on P.L. 98-21 (Social Security Act Amendments of 1983)

[House Committee Report]

Under present law (Code sec. 3121(b)), social security tax under the Federal Insurance Contributions Act (FICA tax) is imposed on wages paid to U.S. citizens for service performed for American employers inside and outside the United States. The term "American employer" is defined to include an individual who is a U.S. resident, a partnership in which two-thirds or more of the partners are U.S. residents, a trust of which all of the trustees are U.S. residents, and a corporation organized under the laws of the United States or of any State (sec. 3121(h)). The FICA tax is also imposed on wages paid to resident aliens for services performed for American employers inside the United States. However, no FICA tax is imposed on wages paid to resident aliens for services performed for American employers outside the United States.

Your Committee believes that the disparate treatment of U.S. citizens and resident aliens who work for American employers abroad should be eliminated. Your Committee recognizes that resident aliens working for American employers outside the United States are likely to have same economic and personal ties with the United States, and the same expectation of returning to the United States, as do U.S. citizens. Your Committee believes that the coverage of these resident aliens will prevent the gaps in coverage which would otherwise occur when resident aliens who ordinarily work in covered employment outside the United States temporarily work abroad for an American employer.

Your Committee's bill provides that FICA tax will be imposed on wages for service performed outside the United States by a resident alien as an employee for an American employer, to the same extent that FICA tax is imposed on wages paid to a U.S. citizen for such service. Thus, FICA tax will be imposed on wages paid to a resident alien working for an American employer only if the services performed would constitute covered employment if performed in the United States. A conforming amendment is made for purposes of benefits paid under the Social Security Act.

The provisions will be effective for remuneration paid after December 31, 1983.

[Senate Committee Report]

* * *

Non-qualified deferred compensation plans

Under present law (sec. 3121(a)), standby pay or payments made to an employee on account of retirement, either on an individual basis or under a plan or system of the employer providing for employees generally, may be excluded from the social security wage base without regard to whether the payments are under a tax-qualified retirement plan (sec. 401(a) or 403(a)) or other tax-favored retirement savings program (e.g., a tax-sheltered annuity (sec. 403(b)).

Under the bill, nonqualified deferred compensation generally is includible in the social security wage base when it becomes available to the employee. For this purpose, nonqualified deferred compensation generally includes payments under a deferred compensation arrangement which is not (1) a tax-qualified plan, (2) an individual retirement arrangement (IRA), (3) a simplified employee pension (SEP), (4) a tax-sheltered annuity, or (5) a governmental plan. A governmental plan is one established and maintained for its employees by the Government of the United States, by any State or political subdivision thereof, or by any agency or instrumentality of any of the foregoing. However, elective deferrals under an eligible State deferred compensation plan (sec. 457(a)) are includible in the wage base as described in the preceding paragraph, and amounts payable under a deferred compensation plan of a State or local government which is not an eligible plan (sec. 457(e)(1) and (e)(2)(D) and (E)) are includible in the wage base when there is no substantial risk of forfeiture by the employee.

[House Committee Report]

Under the Code, amounts which constitute wages for income tax withholding purposes (sec. 3306) and amounts which constitute wages for social security tax purposes (sec. 3121) are separately defined. However, in *Rowan Companies, Inc. v. United States,* 452 U.S. 247 (1981), the Supreme Court held that the definition of wages for social security tax purposes and the definition of wages for income tax withholding purposes must be interpreted in regulations in the same manner in the absence of statutory provisions to the contrary.

At issue in *Rowan* was whether the value of meals and lodgings provided employees at the convenience of the employer were wages for social security tax purposes (i.e., were includible in the social security wage base). The value of such employer-provided meals and lodging may be excluded from the income of an employee (sec. 119). Treasury regulations required that the value of the meals and lodging be included in the social security wage base, but excluded such value from the definition of wages subject to income tax withholding. The Supreme Court decision invalidated those Treasury regulations which required that the value of the meals and lodging be included in the social security wage base.

The social security program aims to replace the income of beneficiaries when that income is reduced on account of retirement and disability. Thus, the amount of "wages" is the measure used both to define income which should be replaced and to compute FICA tax liability. Since the social security system has objectives which are significantly different from the objectives underlying the income tax withholding rules, your Committee believes that amounts exempt from income tax withholding should not be exempt from FICA unless Congress provides an explicit FICA tax exclusion.

Your Committee's bill provides that, with the exception of the value of meals and lodging provided for the convenience of the employer, the determination whether or not amounts are includible in the social security wages base is to be made without regard to whether such amounts are treated as wages from income tax withholding purposes. Accordingly, an employee's "wages" for social security tax purposes may be different from the employee's "wages" for income tax withholding purposes. In addition, the bill provides that definition of wages for social security tax and benefit purposes is revised to exclude the value of employer-provided meals and lodging to the extent such value is also excluded from the employee's gross income.

This provision applies to remuneration paid after December 31, 1983.

[Senate Committee Report]

Present law

Under present law, the Internal Revenue Code excludes from the social security wage base employer payments to or on behalf of an employee under a simplified employee pension (SEP). However, such employer contributions are treated as covered wages for social security benefit purposes.

Reasons for change

The committee believes that it is inappropriate to treat employer payments to a SEP as covered wages for benefit purposes where such amounts are excluded from the social security wage base for tax purposes.

Explanation of provision

The bill amends the Social Security Act to exclude from the definition of covered wages for social security coverage purposes employer contributions to a SEP that are deductible as such by the employer. The bill makes clear that the exclusion applies, for both tax and coverage purposes, only with respect to the employer's contribution to a SEP, not with respect to the amount equivalent to the employee's contribution to an individual retirement arrangement (IRA).

Effective date

This provision applies to remuneration paid after December 31, 1983.

See also Committee Reports at ¶ 13,540.06.

[¶ 13,530.10]

Committee Report on P.L. 96-222 (Technical Corrections Act of 1979)

[Senate Committee Report]

Sec. 101(a)(10)(B)—Exemption from FICA and FUTA taxes.

The Revenue Act of 1978 created a new type of individual retirement plan, known as a simplified employee pension. Under present law, employer contributions to an IRA (individual retirement account, annuity, or retirement bond) of an employee are considered remuneration subject to FICA and FUTA taxes, but employer contributions with respect to an employee to a tax-qualified plan are not subject to these taxes. The 1978 Act did not specify whether employer contributions to a simplified employee pension were subject to FICA or FUTA taxes.

Employer contributions to a tax-qualified pension plan on behalf of an employee are exempt from FICA and FUTA taxes. The absence of a corresponding exemption for employer contributions to simplified employee pensions is an unintended barrier to the establishment of simplified employee pensions.

Under the bill, an amount paid by an employer to an employee's individual retirement account or annuity is not subject to FICA or FUTA taxes if the account or annuity is a simplified employee pension and it is reasonable to believe that the employee will be entitled to deduct the payments under the IRA rules applicable to simplified employee pensions.

This provision applies for payments made on or after January 1, 1979. This is the same effective date as was provided by the 1978 Act with respect to simplified employee pensions.

[Code Sec. 3306]

[¶ 13,540.06]

Committee Reports on P.L. 98-21 (Social Security Act Amendments of 1983)

[Conference Committee Report]

Present law

(1) Cash or deferred arrangements (Code section 401(k)).—Under a cash or deferred arrangement forming a part of a qualified profit-sharing or stock bonus plan, a covered employee may elect to have the employer contribute an amount to the plan on the employee's behalf or to receive such amount directly in cash. Amounts contributed to the plan pursuant to the election are treated as employer contributions and are excluded from the employee's taxable income and social security wage base.

(2) Cafeteria plans (Code section 125).—Under a cafeteria plan of an employer, an employee may choose among various benefits including cash, taxable benefits and nontaxable benefits (including a cash or deferred arrangement) offered under the plan. If certain requirements are met, amounts applied toward nontaxable benefits are excluded from the employee's taxable income and generally from the social security wage base.

(3) Tax-sheltered annuities (Code section 403(b)).—Subject to certain limitations, amounts paid by the employer for the purchase of a tax-sheltered annuity for an eligible employee are excluded from the employee's taxable income and social security wage base. Tax-sheltered annuities may be purchased for employees of educational institutions and certain tax-exempt organizations. Tax-sheltered annuities may be purchased pursuant to a salary reduction agreement.

(4) Nonqualified deferred compensation plans.— Amounts deferred under a nonqualified deferred compensation plan generally are taxable when they are paid or when there is no substantial risk of forfeiture, depending upon whether or not the plan is unfunded or funded. However, if the plan is a retirement plan or the amounts are paid on account of retirement, the amounts are generally excludible from FICA and FUTA. These plans may be utilized by (1) taxable employers to provide retirement benefits in excess of those permitted under tax-qualified retirement plans or coverage limited primarily to highly compensated or management employees, (2) tax-exempt employers, and (3) State and local governments.

House bill

(1) An employer's plan contributions on behalf of an employee under a qualified cash or deferred arrangement would be includible in the social security wage base for tax and coverage purposes to the extent that the employee could have elected to receive cash in lieu of the contribution, effective for remuneration paid after Dec. 31, 1983.

(2) Amounts subject to an employee's designation under a cafeteria plan would be includible in the social security wage base to the extent that such amounts may be paid to the employee in cash or property or applied to provide a benefit for the employee not excluded from the FICA wage base effective for remuneration paid after Dec. 31, 1983.

(3) Amounts paid by an employer for a tax-sheltered annuity for an employee will be includible in the social security wage base.

(4) No provision.

Senate amendment

(1) Same as House bill.

(2) Same as House bill, except applies only to cafeteria plans which include a cash-or-deferred arrangement as one of the optional fringe benefits.

(3) Any amounts paid by an employer to a tax-sheltered annuity by reason of a salary reduction agreement between the employer and the employee would be includible in the social security wage base.

(4) The amount deferred under a (non-qualified) compensation plan will be includible in the social security wage base as of the later of (1) when the services are performed or (2) when there is no substantial risk of forfeiture of the rights to the amounts. In the case of a governmental plan, a deferred compensation plan will only include certain nonqualified plans of State and local governments.

Conference agreement

(1) The conference agreement generally follows the House bill and the Senate amendment with respect to qualified cash or deferred arrangements. Employer contributions to these arrangements will be taxable for FICA and FUTA purposes whether or not the cash or deferred arrangement is part of a cafeteria plan. A transition rule is provided to exclude certain remuneration paid after the effective date of this provision if paid pursuant to certain elective deferrals made before January 1, 1984 (January 1, 1985, with respect to FUTA taxes).

(2) The conference agreement contains no other provision concerning the inclusion of amounts applied toward nontaxable (for FICA purposes) benefits in a cafeteria plan.

(3) The conference agreement generally follows the Senate amendment by providing that employer contributions to a section 403(b) annuity contract would be included in the wage base if made by reason of a salary reduction agreement (whether evidenced by a written agreement or otherwise). For this purpose, the conferees intend that employment arrangements, which under the facts and circumstances are determined to be individually negotiated, would be treated as salary reduction agreements. Of course, the mere fact that only one individual is receiving employer contributions (*e.g.,* where the employer has only a few employees, only one of whom is a member of a class eligible for such contributions) is not, by itself, to be considered proof of individual negotiation.

(4) With respect to nonqualified deferred compensation plans, the conference agreement generally follows the Senate amendment that includes amounts deferred in the employee's FICA and FUTA wage base when services are performed or, if later, when there is a lapse of a substantial risk of forfeiture (within the meaning of sec. 83) of the employee's right to those amounts. As under present law, amounts treated as employer contributions under a State pick-up plan (sec. 414(h)(2)) or amounts deferred under eligible State and local deferred compensation arrangements are includible in the wage base when deferred. The conference agreement provides that any payment to, or on behalf of, an employee or his beneficiary under certain supplemental retirement plans, which provide cost-of-living adjustments to the pension benefits under tax-qualified plans, will not be included in the wage base. Finally, under the conference agreement, in the case of certain agreements, in existence on March 24, 1983, between a nonqualified deferred compensation plan and an individual, the provision would only apply to services performed after December 31, 1983 (December 31, 1984, for FUTA purposes).

[Senate Committee Report]

* * * The bill also includes conforming changes to the provisions (sec. 3306) defining "wages" for purposes of the Federal Unemployment Tax Act (FUTA). Deferred compensation includible in the social security wage base under the bill would also be treated as wages for FUTA purposes. In addition, the bill provides that certain sick pay which is includible in the social security wage base under provisions enacted in 1978 would also be treated as wages for FUTA purposes.

[¶ 13,540.07]

Committee Report on P.L. 97-248 (Tax Equity and Fiscal Responsibility Act of 1982)

[Conference Committee Report]

*FUTA tax rate.— * * * Senate amendment.*—Effective January 1, 1983, the Senate amendment would increase the Federal unemployment tax wage base from $6,000 to $7,000. (This will require States, in order for employers to qualify for the 2.7 credit against the gross Federal tax rate, to have a State unemployment tax wage base of a least $7,000.)

The gross Federal unemployment tax rate would be increased from 3.4 to 3.5. Employers in States with approved State programs will continue to receive the 2.7 offset credit, so the standard net Federal tax would be 0.8 percent. This provision also is effective January 1, 1983.

Effective January 1, 1985, the Senate amendment would increase the gross Federal tax rate to 6.2 percent. This includes a permanent tax of 6.0 percent plus a temporary 0.2 percent that would remain in effect until all outstanding general revenue loans to the Federal Extended Unemployment Compensation Account (EUCA) have been repaid. The offset credit would increase to 5.4, so the net Federal tax rate would remain at 0.8 percent until the EUCA account has paid off all general revenue loans, when it would drop to 0.6 percent. The wage base remains at $7,000.

[¶ 13,540.08]

Committee Report on P.L. 96-222 (Technical Corrections Act of 1979)

[Senate Committee Report]

Sec. 101(a)(10)(B)—Exemption from FICA and FUTA taxes—The Senate Report on Sec. 101(a)(10)(B) of P.L. 96-222 is at ¶ 13,530.10.

[¶ 13,540.09]

Committee Reports on P.L. 95-600 (Revenue Act of 1978)

Sec. 164—Educational assistance plans—The committee reports on Sec. 164 are at ¶ 11,289.10.

[Code Sec. 3401]

[¶ 13,550.078]

Committee Report on P.L. 100-647 (Technical and Miscellaneous Revenue Act of 1988)

[Senate Committee Report]

The bill coordinates the effective date of the new integration rules with respect to qualified plans and SEPs. Thus, the bill provides that the integration rules applicable to SEPs (sec. 408(k)(3)(D) and (E)) prior to the Act will continue to apply to years beginning before January 1, 1989, when the new integration rules are effective. However, no integration is permitted under the 125-percent nondiscrimination test for salary reduction SEPs.

[¶ 13,550.08]

Committee Report on P.L. 96-222 (Technical Corrections Act of 1979)

[Senate Committee Report]

Sec. 103(a)(13)(A)—Withholding on medical reimbursements.

In some cases, it may not be possible to make a determination under the medical reimbursement plan rules as to the amount which is includible in gross income until after the year has ended. Consequently, the committee concluded that it is inappropriate for these amounts to be subject to withholding tax.

The bill provides an exclusion from withholding tax for amounts paid under a self-insured medical reimbursement plan for an employee. The bill also corrects a clerical error by redesignating one of two paragraphs numbered (18) of Code section 3401(a) as paragraph (19). (The House bill provides an exclusion from withholding tax where it is reasonable to believe that a reimbursement will be excludible from the employee's gross income under section 105.)

The amendment applies to amounts reimbursed after December 31, 1979.

[¶ 13,550.09]

Committee Reports on P.L. 95-600 (Revenue Act of 1978)

Sec. 164—Educational assistance plans.—The committee reports on Sec. 164 are at ¶ 11,289.10.

[Code Sec. 3405]

[¶ 13,566.095]

Committee Report on P.L. 100-647 (Technical and Miscellaneous Revenue Act of 1988)

[House Committee Report]

Withholding on pensions, annuities and certain other deferred income

The bill clarifies that the Act's automatic withholding rule does not apply if the recipient certifies to the payor that he or she is not a U.S. citizen or a resident alien of the United States, and not a tax avoidance expatriate. Thus under the bill the automatic withholding rule generally applies to foreign-delivered pension benefits and similar payments to individuals subject to U.S. income taxation on their worldwide income.

In addition, the bill restricts automatic withholding under the Act to those benefits and payments that are delivered outside both the United States and its possessions. Thus, recipients of benefits and payments delivered in any U.S. possession would continue to be eligible to elect to forego withholding on the same terms available to taxpayers whose payments or benefits are delivered in the United States. These amendments would apply to distributions made after the date of the bill's enactment.

[¶ 13,566.10]

Committee Report on P.L. 97-248 (Tax Equity and Fiscal Responsibility Act of 1982)

[Senate Amendment]

The Senate amendment provides that payors generally will be required to withhold tax from all designated distributions (the taxable part of payments made from or under a pension, profit-sharing, stock bonus, or annuity plan, a deferred compensation plan where the payments are not otherwise considered wages, an IRA, or a commercial annuity contract (whether or not the contract was purchased under an employer's plan for employees)). A partial surrender of an annuity contract and certain loans from employee plans and IRAs will also be considered a distribution subject to withholding. The withholding rate is determined by the nature of the distribution. Tax will be withheld on periodic payments in excess of $5,400, under the wage withholding tables. Tax on certain total distributions will be withheld under a schedule designed to reflect the special tax treatment accorded to lump sum distributions, and tax on other non-periodic distributions will be withheld at a flat 10-percent rate. Withholding will be required with respect to payments made after December 31, 1982, unless the recipient elects not to have tax withheld.

In general, a recipient may elect (for any reason) not to have tax withheld, except that a recipient of a total distribution may elect out only to the extent that the distribution is rolled over to another eligibleretirement plan. An election is generally effective for the distribution for which the election is made, except that an election with respect to periodic payments is generally effective for a calendar year. Thus, an election not to have tax withheld from periodic payments must be renewed annually.

In addition, the amendment generally requires that payors notify recipients of the withholding rules and their rights to elect out. With respect to periodic payments, notice must be provided (1) no earlier than 6 months and not later than 2 months before making the first payment, and (2) annually, within the third quarter of the calendar year. With respect to other payments, notice must be provided no later than the time of distribution.

[Conference Agreement]

The conference agreement generally follows the Senate amendment except that (1) a recipient may elect (for any reason) not to have tax withheld from any distribution (including total distributions which are not rolled over to another eligible retirement plan); (2) an election with respect to a periodic payment is effective until revoked, although a payor would still be required to provide annual notice of a participant's right to make, renew, or revoke an election, and (3) a payor of a periodic payment is required to provide initial notice of a recipient's right to make, renew, or revoke an election no earlier than six months before and no later than the date of the first payment. It is expected that the notice will also advise recipients that penalties may be incurred under the estimated tax payment rules if the payments of estimated tax are not adequate and sufficient tax is not withheld from any designated distributions.

As under the Senate amendment, tax would generally be withheld on periodic payments pursuant to the recipient's withholding certificate. For example, a married recipient whose spouse is not a wage earner would not be subject to tax on periodic distributions payable at an annual rate of up to $7,400 if both the wage earner and his spouse were at least age 65 and a withholding certificate were filed. If no certificate is filed, the amount withheld will be determined by treating the payee as a married individual claiming three withholding exemptions. Thus, in effect, there would be no withholding on pensions payable at an annual rate of $5,400 or less.

Annuity payments and other distributions under the Civil Service Retirement System are subject to the income tax withholding rules. The conferees intend that the cost of administering the withholding rules will be borne by the Civil Service Retirement System.

The conferees recognize the difficulty some payors may have in immediately complying with the new withholding requirements for annuity payments. Accordingly, the civil and criminal penalties for failure to withhold tax will not apply to any failure before July 1, 1983, if the payor made a good faith effort to withhold, and actually withholds from any subsequent 1983 payments sufficient amounts to satisfy the pre-July 1983 requirements. No relief is provided for any failure to timely pay over any amounts that are in fact withheld. Also, the Secretary is authorized, on a case-by-case basis, to exempt payors from any obligation to withhold with respect to pre-July 1983 payments if the payor has attempted to comply in good faith, has a plan to assure its ability to comply by July 1, 1983, and cannot comply on January 1, 1983, without unduehardship. If such a waiver of the withholding obligations is granted, the payor will not be required to make up the withholding obligation out of post-June 1983 payments.—Conference Committee Report.

[Code Sec. 4965]

[¶ 13,598.05]

Committee Report on P.L. 109-222 (Tax Increase Prevention and Reconciliation Act of 2005)

[Conference Committee Report]

Tax involvement of accommodation parties in tax shelter transactions—

In general, under the provision, certain tax-exempt entities are subject to penalties for being a party to a prohibited tax shelter transaction. A prohibited tax shelter transaction is a transaction that the Secretary determines is a listed transaction (as defined in section 6707A(c)(2)) or a prohibited transaction. A prohibited reportable transaction is a confidential transaction or a transaction with contractual protection (as defined by the Secretary in regulations) which is a reportable transaction as defined in sec. 6707A(c)(1). Under the provision, a tax-exempt entity is an entity that is described in section 501(c), 501(d), or 170(c) (not including the United States), Indian tribal governments, and tax qualified pension plans, individual retirement arrangements ("IRAs"), and similar tax-favored savings arrangements (such as Coverdell education savings accounts, health savings accounts, and qualified tuition plans).

Entity tax level

Under the provision, if a tax-exempt entity is a party at any time to a transaction during a taxable year and knows or has reason to know that the transaction is a prohibited tax shelter transaction, the entity is subject to a tax for such year equal to the greater of (1) 100 percent of the entity's net income (after taking into account any tax imposed with respect to the transaction) for such year that is attributable to the transaction or (2) 75 percent of the proceeds received by the entity that are attributable to the transaction.

In addition, if a transaction is not a listed transaction at the time a tax-exempt entity enters into the transaction (and is not otherwise a prohibited tax shelter transaction), but the transaction subsequently is determined by the Secretary to be a listed transaction (a "subsequently listed transaction"), the entity must pay each taxable year an excise tax at the highest unrelated business taxable income rate times the greater of (1) the entity's net income (after taking into account any tax imposed) that is attributable to the subsequently listed transaction and that is properly allocable to the period beginning on the later of the date such transaction is listed by the Secretary or the first day of the taxable year or (2) 75 percent of the proceeds received by the entity that are attributable to the subsequently listed transaction and that are properly allocable to the period beginning on the later of the date such transaction is listed by the Secretary or the first day of the taxable year. The Secretary has the authority to promulgate regulations that provide guidance regarding the determination of the allocation of net income of a tax-exempt entity that is attributable to a transaction to various periods, including before and after the listing of the transaction or the date which is 90 days after the date of enactment of the provision.

The entity level tax does not apply if the entity's participation is not willful and is due to reasonable cause, except that the willful and reasonable cause exception does not apply to the tax imposed for subsequently listed transactions. The entity level taxes do not apply to tax qualified pension plans, IRAs, and similar tax-favored savings arrangements (such as Coverdell education savings accounts, health savings accounts, and qualified tuition plans).

***

Conference Agreement

The conference agreement includes the Senate amendment provision, with modifications.

The conference agreement does not include the provision that the entity level or entity manager tax does not apply if the entity's participation is not willful and is due to reasonable cause.

In addition, the conference agreement adds a tax in the event that a tax-exempt entity becomes a party to a prohibited tax shelter transaction without knowing or having reason to know that the transaction is a prohibited tax shelter transaction. In that case, the tax-exempt entity is subject to a tax in the taxable year the entity becomes a party and any subsequent taxable year of the highest unrelated business taxable income rate times the greater of (1) the entity's net income (after taking into account any tax imposed with respect to the transaction) for such year that is attributable to the transaction or (2) 75 percent of the proceeds received by the entity that are attributable to the transaction for such year.[110]

The conference agreement clarifies that the entity level tax rate that applies if the entity knows or has reason to know that a transaction is a prohibited tax shelter transaction does not apply to subsequently listed transactions.

The conference agreement modifies the definition of an entity manager to provide that: (1) in the case of tax qualified pension plans, IRAs, and similar tax-favored savings arrangements (such as Coverdell education savings accounts, health savings accounts, and qualified tuition plans) an entity manager is the person that approves or otherwise causes the entity to be a party to a prohibited tax shelter transaction, and (2) in all other cases the entity manager is the person with authority or responsibility similar to that exercised by an officer, director, or trustee of an organization, and with respect to any act, the person having authority or responsibility with respect to such act.

In the case of a qualified pension plan, IRA, or similar tax-favored savings arrangement (such as a Coverdell education savings account, health savings account, or qualified tuition plan), the conferees intend that, in general, a person who decides that assets of the plan, IRA, or other savings arrangement are to be invested in a prohibited tax shelter transaction is the entity manager under the provision. Except in the case of a fully self-directed plan or other savings arrangement with respect to which a participant or beneficiary decides to invest in the prohibited tax shelter transaction, a participant or beneficiary generally is not an entity manager under the provision. Thus, for example, a participant or beneficiary is not an entity manager merely by reason of choosing among pre-selected investment options (as is typically the case if a qualified retirement plan provides for participant-directed investments).[111] Similarly, if an individual has an IRA and may choose among various mutual funds offered by the IRA trustee, but has no control over the investments held in the mutual funds, the individual is not an entity manager under the provision.

Under the provision, certain taxes are imposed if the entity or entity manager knows or has reason to know that a transaction is a prohibited tax shelter transaction. In general, the conferees intend that in order for an entity or entity manager to have reason to know that a transaction is a prohibited tax shelter transaction, the entity or entity manager must have knowledge of sufficient facts that would lead a reasonable person to conclude that the transaction is a prohibited tax shelter transaction. If there is justifiable reliance on a reasoned written opinion of legal counsel (including in-house counsel) or of an independent accountant with expertise in tax matters, after making full disclosure of relevant facts about a transaction to such counsel or accountant, that a transaction is not a prohibited tax shelter transaction, then absent knowledge of facts not considered in the reasoned written opinion that would lead a reasonable person to conclude that the transaction is a prohibited tax shelter transaction, the reason to know standard is not met.

Not obtaining a reasoned written opinion of legal counsel does not alone indicate whether a person has reason to know. However, if a transaction is extraordinary for the entity, promises a return for the organization that is exceptional considering the amount invested by, the participation of, or the absence of risk to the organization, or the transaction is of significant size, either in an absolute sense or relative to the receipts of the entity, then, in general, the presence of such factors may indicate that the entity or entity manager has a responsibility to inquire further about whether a transaction is a prohibited tax shelter transaction, or, absent such inquiry, that the reason to know standard is satisfied. For example, if a tax-exempt entity's investment in a transaction is $1,000, and the entity is promised or expects to receive $10,000 in the near term, in general, the rate of return would be considered exceptional and the entity should make inquiries with respect to the transaction. As another example, if a tax-exempt entity's expected income from a transaction is greater than five percent of the entity's annual receipts, or is in excess of $1,000,000, and the entity fails to make appropriate inquiries with respect to its participation in such transaction, such failure is a factor tending to show that the reason to know standard is met. Appropriate inquiries need not involve obtaining a reasoned written opinion. In general, if a transaction does not present the factors described above and the organization is small (measured by receipts and assets) and described in section 501(c)(3), it is expected that the reason to know standard will not be met.

***

Effective Date

In general, the provision is effective for taxable years ending after the date of enactment, with respect to transactions before, on, or after such date, except that no tax shall apply with respect to income or proceeds that are properly allocable to any period ending on or before the date that is 90 days after the date of enactment. The tax on certain knowing transactions does not apply to any prohibited tax shelter transaction to which a tax-exempt entity became a party on or before the date of enactment. The disclosure provisions apply to disclosures the due date for which are after the date of enactment.—**Conference Committee Report (H.R. CONF REP. NO. 109-455).**

[Code Sec. 4971]

[¶ 13,600.07]

Committee Report on P.L. 109-280 (Pension Protection Act of 2006)

[Joint Committee on Taxation Report]

Under the provision, the present-law excise tax does not apply with respect to any accumulated funding deficiency of a multiemployer plan (1) with less than 100 participants; (2) with respect to which the contributing employers participated in a Federal fishery capacity reduction program; (3) with respect to which employers under the plan participated in the Northeast Fisheries Assistance Program; and (4) with respect to which the annual normal cost is less than $100,000 and the plan is experiencing a funding deficiency on the date of enactment. The tax does not apply to any taxable year beginning before the earlier of (1) the taxable year in which the plan sponsor adopts a rehabilitation plan, or (2) the taxable year that contains January 1, 2009.

Effective Date

The provision is effective for any taxable year beginning before the earlier of (1) the taxable year in which the plan sponsor adopts a rehabilitation plan, or (2) the taxable year that contains January 1, 2009.

[¶ 13,600.08]

Committee Report on P.L. 104-188 (Small Business Job Protection Act)

Miscellaneous Pension Simplification

[Managers' Amendment to H.R. 3448]

Waiver of excise tax on failure to pay liquidity shortfall

The amendment would give the Secretary authority to waive all or part of the excise tax imposed for a failure to make a liquidity shortfall payment if the plan sponsor establishes to the satisfaction of the Secretary that the liquidity shortfall was due to reasonable cause and not willful neglect and reasonable steps have been taken to remedy such shortfall.

Effective Date

The amendment would be effective as if included in GATT.

[Conference Committee Report]

The conference agreement follows the Senate amendment.

[¶ 13,600.09]

Committee Report on P.L. 96-364 (Multiemployer Pension Plan Amendments Act of 1980)

[Senate Committee Report]

Excise taxes

Present law

Under present law, an employer who maintains a plan to which the ERISA minimum funding standard applies is subject to a two-tier annual nondeductible excise tax on any accumulated funding deficiency under the plan. The initial tax

[110] The conference agreement clarifies that in all cases the 75 percent of proceeds received by the entity that are attributable to the transaction are with respect to the taxable year.

[111] Depending on the circumstances, the person who is responsible for determining the pre-selected investment options may be an entity manager under the provision.

is 5 percent of the deficiency. If the deficiency is not corrected within a correction period, an additional excise tax equal to 100 percent of the deficiency is imposed.

Before issuing a notice of deficiency under this provision, the Internal Revenue Service is required to notify the Secretary of Labor and afford to the Secretary of Labor an opportunity to (1) require the responsible employer to eliminate the deficiency and (2) to comment on the imposition of the tax.

Reason for change

Under the bill, a required contribution to a multiemployer plan may, under certain circumstances (e.g., reorganization) differ from the amount required to satisfy the minimum funding standard of ERISA.

Explanation of provisions

The bill conforms the penalty excise tax provisions relating to the ERISA funding standard to the plan reorganization provisions of the bill by changing the accumulated funding deficiency of a plan in reorganization (the amount to which the excise tax applies) to the reorganization deficiency computed under the bill. The bill also provides that in the case of a multiemployer plan in reorganization, the notice issued by the Internal Revenue Service to the Secretary of Labor with respect to a notice of deficiency for a tax on an accumulated funding deficiency, and the opportunity to comment on the imposition of the tax, are to be provided to the PBGC.

Effective date

These provisions of the bill apply on the date of enactment.

[¶ 13,600.10]

Committee Report on P.L. 93-406 (Employee Retirement Income Security Act of 1974)

[House Ways and Means Committee]

Enforcement

The sanctions under present law on the failure to meet the minimum funding requirements appear to have little effect on an employer's decision to fund a plan at the required minimum levels. To resolve this problem the bill imposes an excise tax on the employer if he fails to fund the plan at the minimum required amounts (only if a waiver has not been obtained).

The tax initially is to be 5 percent of the accumulated funding deficiency—the excess of charges over credits in the funding standard account—at the end of the plan year. If a plan year ends with an aggregate funding deficiency, the employer will owe a 5 percent excise tax on the deficiency and that tax may be due for the taxable year of the employer with or within which the plan year ends. Furthermore, a deficiency in a prior year will continue in later years (and will be increased with interest), until paid. The 5 percent tax will apply to each year (of the employer) in which there is a funding deficiency at the end of the plan year. For example, if there is a funding deficiency in 1978 that is not corrected until 1980, there will be a 5 percent tax on the 1978 deficiency and a 5 percent tax on the 1979 deficiency (which will be the same as the 1978 deficiency plus interest).[9] If the deficiency is corrected within the time allowed for contributions for the year 1980, there would be no 5 percent tax for 1980.

In any case in which the 5 percent tax is imposed and the accumulated funding deficiency is not corrected within the correction period allowed after notice by the Internal Revenue Service, a 100 percent tax equal to the accumulated funding deficiency (to the extent not corrected) is to be imposed on the employer. In accord with present law respecting the excise taxes with regard to private foundations, neither the 5 percent nor the 100 percent taxes are to be deductible.

As discussed above, the bill provides that an employer's contributions to a plan that are made by the time for filing its tax return can relate back to the year of that return. Consequently, generally an employer will have a period of time after the close of the plan year to contribute to the plan and avoid the excise tax on underfunding. In addition, the bill provides that for purposes of the minimum funding requirements, a plan can be amended to a limited extent without the approval of the Secretary of Labor after the close of the plan year, but by the time for filing the employer's return for the taxable year with or within which the plan year ends (in the case of multiemployer plans, the amendment may be within two years of the close of the plan year). This allows limited retroactive decreases in plan benefits so liabilities for the excise tax can be reduced or eliminated when there has been a mistake in estimating the amount of benefits that an employer could properly fund.

* * *

The minimum period allowed for correcting any funding deficiency after notice from the Service is 90 days from the date of mailing a notice of deficiency with respect to the 5 percent tax. However, this period may be extended for the time that the Internal Revenue Service determines is reasonable and necessary to eliminate the accumulated funding deficiency (and is automatically extended for any period in which a deficiency cannot be assessed under section 6213(a) relating to petitions to the Tax Court). It is intended that the Secretary require significant reasons before granting an extension under this provision.

In the usual case, the excise taxes will be owed when a deficiency is showing in the plan's funding standard account. However, as under present law, where the actuarial assumptions used in determining the minimum funding requirements are unreasonable in the aggregate, the Service may on audit retroactively (for open years) require a change in these assumptions. Such a change may result in a change in the plan's funding standard account. If a funding deficiency occurs as a result of such change, an excise tax may be levied. It is expected that retroactive changes of actuarial assumptions would occur only where the initial assumptions used were substantially unreasonable.

The bill provides special rules for applying the excise tax to collectively bargained plans. Generally, the "plan year" for a collectively bargained plan will be considered to be the contract period. If, at the beginning of that contract period, the actuarial assumptions used in setting the plan contributions are reasonable in the aggregate, and the actuarial calculations are correct, then generally no excise tax will be owned [sic] by employers who timely pay their appropriate share of the plan contributions during the contract period. However, to the extent that plan contributions are not timely paid, the funding standard account may show a deficiency and an excise tax would be owed. (The excise tax would be owed on the basis of the employer's taxable year and not on the basis of the plan year which runs for the period of the contract.) When a plan has such an accumulated funding deficiency, generally the tax will be imposed only on the employers who do not timely contribute, since the underfunding is the result of their failure to contribute.

At the end of a contract period, even assuming that all contributions were timely made, a collectively bargained plan can have experience losses. In that event, the next contract must provide for the experience loss. This generally will be by higher contributions, though it could also be by amending the plan to decrease benefits. If appropriate adjustments in contributions or benefits do not occur, then the plan will have a funding deficiency and an excise tax will be owed. Liability for this tax is to be determined first on the basis of failure to meet the required employer contributions under the plan, and then on the basis of respective liabilities for contributions under the plan.

[Code Sec. 4972]

[¶ 13,610.025]

Committee Report on P.L. 109-280 (Pension Protection Act of 2006)

For the Committee Report on P.L. 109-280 on updated deduction rules for combinations of plans, see ¶ 11,850.039.

[¶ 13,610.03]

Committee Report on P.L. 108-311 (Working Families Tax Relief Act of 2004)

[Conference Agreement]

Excise tax on nondeductible contributions.—Under section 614 of EGTRRA, the limits on deductions for employer contributions to qualified retirement plans do not apply to elective deferrals, and elective deferrals are not taken into account in applying the deduction limits to other contributions. The provision makes a conforming change to the Code provision that applies an excise tax to nondeductible contributions.

[¶ 13,610.04]

Committee Report on P.L. 107-16 (Economic Growth and Tax Relief Reconciliation Act)

[House Committee Report]

Excise tax relief for sound pension funding

In determining the amount of nondeductible contributions, the employer is permitted to elect not to take into account contributions to a defined benefit pension plan except to the extent they exceed the accrued liability full funding limit. Thus, if an employer elects, contributions in excess of the current liability full funding limit would not be subject to the excise tax on nondeductible contributions. An employer making such an election for a year would not be permitted to take advantage of the present-law exceptions for certain terminating plans and certain contributions to defined contribution plans. The provision applies to terminated plans as well as ongoing plans.

Effective Date

The provision is effective for years beginning after December 31, 2001.

[Conference Committee Report]

Senate Amendment

The Senate amendment is the same as the House bill.

---

[9] Of course, if an employer fails to contribute a plan's normal cost in any year, that amount will not thereafter become a past service cost (or experience loss to be charged in amortized amounts). The funding standard accounts will show as a deficiency subject to tax each year until corrected the unpaid normal cost plus interest (as well as any unpaid past service cost, plus interest).

Conference Agreement

The conference agreement follows the House bill and the Senate amendment.

[¶ 13,610.05]

Committee Report on P.L. 107-16 (Economic Growth and Tax Relief Reconciliation Act)

[Senate Committee Report]

Pension coverage for domestic and similar workers

The 10-percent excise tax on nondeductible contributions does not apply to contributions to a SIMPLE plan or a SIMPLE IRA that are nondeductible solely because the contributions are not a trade or business expense under section 162 because they are not made in connection with a trade or business of the employer. Thus, for example, employers of household workers are able to make contributions to such plans without imposition of the excise tax. As under present law, the contributions are not deductible. The present-law rules applicable to such plans, e.g., contribution limits and nondiscrimination rules, continue to apply. The provision does not apply with respect to contributions on behalf of the individual and members of his or her family.

No inference is intended with respect to the application of the excise tax under present law to contributions that are not deductible because they are not made in connection with a trade or business of the employer.

As under present law, a plan covering domestic workers is not qualified unless the coverage rules are satisfied by aggregating all employees of family members taken into account under the attribution rules in section 414(c), but disregarding employees employed by a controlled group of corporations or a trade or business.

It is intended that the provision is restricted to contributions made by employers of household workers with respect to whom all applicable employment taxes have been and are being paid.

Effective Date

The provision is effective for taxable years beginning after December 31, 2001.

[Conference Committee Report]

The conference agreement follows the House bill.

[¶ 13,610.06]

Committee Report on P.L. 105-34 (Taxpayer Relief Act)

Senate Committee Report

Modification of 10-percent tax on nondeductible contributions

The bill adds an additional exception to the 10-percent excise tax on nondeductible contributions. Under the provision, the excise tax does not apply to contributions to one or more defined contribution plans that are not deductible because they exceed the combined plan deduction limit to the extent such contributions do not exceed the amount of the employer's matching contributions plus the elective deferral contributions to a section 401(k) plan.

Effective date

The provision is effective with respect to taxable years beginning after December 31, 1997.

[¶ 13,610.08]

Committee Report on P.L. 103-465 (General Agreement on Tariffs and Trade (GATT); Retirement Protection Act)

[House Committee Report]

Exceptions to excise tax on nondeductible contributions

Under the bill, nondeductible contributions to a terminating single-employer defined benefit pension plan subject to Title IV of ERISA with less than 101 participants for the year are not subject to the excise tax on nondeductible contributions to the extent such nondeductible contributions do not exceed the plan's unfunded current liability as determined under the minimum funding rules.

In addition, employer contributions to one or more defined contribution plans that are nondeductible because they exceed the combined plan deduction limits are not subject to the 10-percent nondeductible excise tax to the extent such contributions do not exceed 6 percent of compensation in the year for which the contributions are made. The 6-percent of compensation limit is determined on an aggregate basis. For example, if an employer makes contributions to two defined contribution plans under the rule, the excise tax does not apply as long as the contributions are less than 6 percent of the aggregate compensation of participants in both plans. For purposes of this rule, the combined plan deduction limits are first applied to contributions to the defined benefit pension plan. If contributions exceed the 6-percent limit, only those in excess of 6 percent are subject to the excise tax. This provision applies only if the defined benefit pension plan is a single-employer defined benefit pension plan that has more than 100 participants. Amounts that are not subject to the excise tax in the year contributed shall not be taken into account for purposes of applying the 6-percent limit in any future year.

Effective date

The provision waiving the excise tax for nondeductible contributions to a terminating single-employer defined benefit pension plan is effective for taxable years ending on or after the date of enactment [December 8, 1994]. The provision waiving the excise tax for nondeductible contributions to certain defined contribution plans is effective for taxable years ending on or after December 31, 1992.

[¶ 13,610.083]

Committee Reports on P.L. 100-647 (Technical and Miscellaneous Revenue Act of 1988)

[Senate Committee Report]

Deduction Limits for Qualified Plans

Amount of nondeductible contributions. Under the bill, the definition of nondeductible contributions includes, for purposes of the excise tax, contributions allocable to the purchase of life, accident, health, or other insurance on behalf of a self-employed individual, but only to the extent that the contributions would be nondeductible without regard to the special rule limiting deductions for such contributions (sec. 404(e)).

The bill clarifies that the amount allowable as a deduction (without regard to sec. 404(e)) for any taxable year is treated as coming first from carryforwards to the taxable year from preceding taxable years (in order of time) and then from employer contributions made during the taxable year.

Further, under the bill, the unapplied amounts in the preceding taxable year do not include nondeductible contributions made for years prior to the effective date of the excise tax on nondeductible contributions. However, carryforwards from pre-effective date years are applied first against the deduction limit (without regard to sec. 404(e)) in determining whether contributions after the effective date are subject to the excise tax.

Time for determination of nondeductible contributions. Because the determination of nondeductible contributions as of the end of a taxable year includes contributions made after the close of the taxable year with respect to the year, the bill provides that contributions that are returned (together with the income allocable thereto) to an employer (to the extent permitted under sec. 401(a)(2)) by the due date of plan contributions for the year (sec. 404(a)(6)) are not treated as nondeductible contributions subject to the excise tax.

Nondeductible contributions to underfunded plans. Under the bill, the excise tax on nondeductible contributions does not apply in the case of a plan that is underfunded and to which Title IV of ERISA applies. A plan is underfunded if, as of the close of the plan year with or within which the taxable year begins, (1) the liabilities of the plan (determined as if the plan were terminated on that date) exceed (2) the assets of the plan. In the case of such an underfunded plan, contributions for a plan year up to the excess calculated under the preceding sentence are not subject to the excise tax even if such contributions are not deductible by the employer. This provision does not apply to years beginning after December 31, 1987. In such years, section 404(a)(1)(D), added by the Omnibus Budget Reconciliation Act of 1987, generally permits certain employers to deduct contributions to defined benefit pension plans that raise the level of plan assets up to current liability.

Definition of employer. The bill provides that the excise tax on nondeductible contributions does not apply in the case of an employer that has been exempt from income tax at all times. Under rules to be prescribed by the Secretary, this exception does not apply to the extent that the employer has been subject to unrelated business income tax or has otherwise derived a tax benefit from the qualified plan.

The original rationale for the excise tax was that, by making nondeductible contributions to qualified plans, often the benefit of tax-free growth on the amounts contributed outweighed the delay in the employer's deduction for plan contributions. Such an incentive to make nondeductible contributions increased the likelihood that employers would use qualified plans as a tax-favored savings vehicle, particularly in the case of small plans that primarily benefit the owners of the employer. The excise tax on reversions may not offset the value of the deferral of tax on earnings on nondeductible contributions to qualified plans.

Such a rationale does not apply in the case of contributions to plans maintained by governments or tax-exempt organizations. In the case of such plans, the employer generally has no incentive to make plan contributions solely to receive the benefit of tax-free growth because the employer could hold the funds directly without incurring current income tax. Thus, an incentive to use a qualified plan as a tax-favored savings vehicle generally does not exist in the case of a qualified plan maintained by a government or tax-exempt employer.

Combinations of pension and other plans. The bill clarifies that the limit on an employer's deduction for contributions to a combination of qualified plans (sec. 404(a)(7)) also applies in the case of (1) a combination of a profit-sharing or stock bonus plan and a money purchase pension plan or an annuity plan (sec. 404(a)(2)), and (2) a money purchase pension plan and an annuity plan. In addition, for purposes of section 404(a)(7), the bill treats a simplified employee pension (SEP) as a separate profit-sharing or stock bonus plan. Thus, a combination of a SEP and certain qualified plans is subject to section 404(a)(7).

Effective date

The bill provides a delayed effective date for the changes in the deduction rules for plans maintained pursuant to a collective bargaining agreement.

[Senate Committee Report]

Contributions to Meet Minimum Funding Rules

The bill provides that contributions required to meet the minimum funding rules are not subject to the 10-percent excise tax on nondeductible contributions, even if the contributions exceed the earned income of the self-employed individual. The bill does not change the deduction rule with respect to contributions on behalf of such individuals.

[¶ 13,610.085]

Committee Reports on P.L. 99-514 (Tax Reform Act of 1986)

[Conference Committee Report]

Present Law

In general

The contributions of an employer to a qualified plan are deductible in the year for which the contributions are paid, within limits. No deduction is allowed, however, for a contribution that is not an ordinary and necessary business expense or an expense for the production of income. The deduction limits applicable to an employer's contribution depend on the type of plan to which the contribution is made and may depend on whether an employee covered by the plan is also covered by another plan of the employer. Under the Code, if a contribution for a year exceeds the deduction limits, then the excess generally may be deducted in succeeding years as a carryover. Deductions are not allowed with respect to contributions or benefits in excess of the overall limits on contributions or benefits.

Profit-sharing and stock bonus plans

In the case of a qualified profit-sharing or stock bonus plan, employer contributions for a year not in excess of 15 percent of the aggregate compensation of covered employees are generally deductible for the year paid. Under the Code, if employer contributions for a group of employees for a particular year exceed the deduction limits, then the excess may be carried over and deducted in later years. On the other hand, if the contribution for a particular year is lower than the deduction limit, then the unused limitation may be carried over and used in later years. In the case of a limitation carryover, the amount deducted in a later year is not to exceed 25 percent of the aggregate compensation of employees covered by the plan during that year.

Defined benefit pension plans

In general

Employer contributions under a defined benefit pension plan are required to meet a minimum funding standard. The deduction allowed by the Code for an employer's contribution to a defined benefit pension plan is limited to the greatest of the following amounts:

(1) The amount necessary to meet the minimum funding standard for plan years ending with or within the taxable year.

(2) The level amount (or percentage of compensation) necessary to provide for the remaining unfunded cost of the past and current service credits of all employees under the plan over the remaining future service of each employee. Under the Code, however, if the remaining unfunded cost with respect to any three individuals is more than 50 percent of the cost for all employees, then the cost attributable to each of those employees is spread over at least five taxable years.

(3) An amount equal to the normal cost of the plan plus, if past service or certain other credits are provided, an amount necessary to amortize those credits in equal annual payments over 10 years. Generally, this rule permits contributions in excess of the contributions required by the minimum funding standard.

Certain excess contributions

The minimum funding standard includes provisions (the full funding limitation) designed to eliminate the requirement that additional employer contributions be made for a period during which it is fully funded. The funding standard, however, does not prohibit employers from making contributions in excess of the full funding limitation.

Employer contributions in excess of the deduction limits provided by the Code are not currently deductible. A deduction carryover is generally allowed, however, for employer contributions to a qualified plan in excess of the deductible limits.

A pension, profit-sharing, or stock bonus plan does not meet the requirements of the Code for qualified status unless it is for the exclusive benefit of employees and their beneficiaries. Under some circumstances, employer contributions in excess of the level for which a deduction is allowed may indicate that the plan is not being maintained for the exclusive benefit of employees.

Money purchase pension plans

Employer contributions to a money purchase plan are generally deductible under the same rules that apply to defined benefit pension plans. Under a qualified money purchase pension plan, the amount required under the minimum funding standard is the contribution rate specified by the plan.

Combination of pension and other plans

If an employer maintains a pension plan (defined benefit or money purchase) and either a profit-sharing or a stock bonus plan for the same employee for the same year, then the employer's deduction for contributions for that year is generally limited to the greater of the contribution necessary to meet the minimum funding requirements of the pension plan for the year or 25 percent of the aggregate compensation of employees covered by the plans for the year. Deduction and limitation carryovers are provided.

House Bill

The House bill repeals the limit carryforward applicable to profit-sharing and stock bonus plans, extends the combined plan deduction limit to a combination of a defined benefit and a money purchase pension plan, requires that certain social security taxes be taken into account in applying the 15 percent and 25 percent of compensation deduction limits, and imposes a 10-percent excise tax on nondeductible contributions to qualified plans.

The provisions of the House bill relating to deduction limits generally apply to employer taxable years beginning after December 31, 1985. However, certain unused pre-1986 limit carryforwards are not affected by the provision generally repealing limit carryforwards.

Senate Amendment

The Senate amendment is the same as the House bill except that (1) the Senate amendment does not require that certain social security taxes be taken into account in applying the 15 percent and 25 percent of compensation deduction limits, and (2) the Senate amendment does not impose an excise tax on nondeductible contributions to qualified plans. The Senate amendment also clarifies that a fully insured plan (sec. 412(i)) is treated as a defined benefit pension plan for purposes of the combined plan deduction limit.

The Senate amendment is effective for employer taxable years beginning after December 31, 1986.

Conference Agreement

In general

The conference agreement generally follows the Senate amendment with modifications. The conference agreement adopts the House bill applying a 10-percent excise tax to nondeductible employer contributions. The conferees clarify that, with respect to an employer that is exempt from tax, the 10-percent excise tax is to apply to contributions that would, if the employer were not exempt, be nondeductible. The conference agreement also imposes a limit of $200,000 on the amount of compensation that may be taken into account in computing deductions for plan contributions. The limit is to be adjusted for cost-of-living increases at the time and in the manner provided for adjusting the overall limits on annual benefits under a qualified defined benefit pension plan (sec. 415(d)).

Fully insured plans

The conference agreement includes a technical modification relating to fully insured plans which provides that the annual premium payments are deemed to be the amount required to meet the minimum funding requirements in the case of a fully insured plan.

Effective date

The provisions are effective for taxable years beginning after December 31, 1986.

[¶ 13,610.089]

Committee Reports on P.L. 97-248 (Tax Equity and Fiscal Responsibility Act of 1982)

For Committee Reports on P.L. 97-248, relating to the repeal of Keogh plan rules, see ¶ 12,400.06.

[¶ 13,610.09]

Committee Report on P.L. 97-34 (Economic Recovery Tax Act of 1981)

For Committee Report on P.L. 97-34, Sec. 312, relating to self-employed retirement plans, see ¶ 11,850.062.

[¶ 13,610.10]

Committee Report on P.L. 93-406 (Employee Retirement Income Security Act of 1974)

[Conference Committee Explanation]

Excess contributions

Present law provides that excess contributions to an H.R. 10-plan on behalf of an owner-employee must be repaid from the plan and provides, in the case of a willful excess contribution, that the owner-employee is barred from participating in a qualified plan for 5 years. The conference substitute repeals these provisions and, in lieu thereof, the substitute imposes an excise tax of 6 percent on excess contributions to plans for the self-employed. The tax is payable by the employer who maintains the plan.

In the case of a defined contribution plan (for example, a money purchase pension plan) excess contributions include amounts contributed for the self-employed person in excess of the 15-percent/$7,500 limitations. (However, the tax would never exceed 6% of the assets of the account.) In the case of a defined benefit plan, the tax is imposed where the plan is fully funded at the close of the employer's taxable year, and is imposed on the amount that has not been deductible for the taxable year or any prior taxable year. Also, in the case of either type of plan, excess contributions include voluntary contributions by owner-employees in excess of the allowable amount of such contributions.

The tax applies for the year in which the excess contribution is made and for every subsequent year that the excess contribution is outstanding. The excess contribution may be eliminated (so as to stop the running of the tax) in one of two ways—either by repayment of the excess contribution from the plan (which would reduce or eliminate the tax for subsequent years), or by a carryover of the excess payment and applying it against the amount allowable in the next year (or subsequent year).

In the case of a defined benefit plan, the repayment would have to be made to the employer. In the case of a defined contribution plan, the repayment could be made either to the employer or to the employee (but, as under present law, a distribution could generally not be made to the employee from a money purchase plan until he attained retirement age). An excess voluntary contribution would be repaid to the owner-employee who made it. Of course, any distribution made to eliminate an excess contribution would not be in violation of the exclusive benefit rules of present law, or the fiduciary standards imposed under this bill.

The excess contribution could also be eliminated through means of a carryover. For example, if contributions of $10,000 were made to a plan (where voluntary contributions were not permitted) on behalf of a self-employed person (who was entitled to the full $7,500 deduction) the $2,500 excess contribution could be purged in the next year if the contribution made on behalf of the individual in that year were limited to $5,000. In this case, the 6-percent tax would be imposed, but only once, because the excess contribution had been eliminated in the second year. Also, in the second year the individual would be entitled to a deduction of $7,500 ($5,000 of contributions in that year, plus the $2,500 carryover). Of course, there would be no tax on underfunding under these circumstances even if the plan were a money purchase plan, the terms of which required a $7,500 contribution for the individual in the second year.

[Code Sec. 4973]

[¶ 13,620.05]

Committee Report on P.L. 105-34 (Taxpayer Relief Act)

For Committee Report on P.L. 105-34, dealing with Roth IRAs, see ¶ 12,097.10.

[¶ 13,620.08]

Committee Report on P.L. 96-222 (Technical Corrections Act of 1979)

[Senate Committee Report]

Sec. 101(a)(13)—Tax sheltered annuity rollover—The Senate Committee Report on Sec. 101(a)(13) of P.L. 96-222 is at ¶ 11,800.055.

[¶ 13,620.095]

Committee Report on P.L. 95-600 (Revenue Act of 1978)

[House Committee Report 95-1739]

Under the committee bill, the dollar limitation would be removed. Thus, an individual who makes an excess contribution to an IRA but withdraws the full amount of the excess contributed and any earnings thereon on or before the date prescribed by law for filing his or her tax return for the year (including extensions), will be treated as not having made an excess contribution for the year. Accordingly, no 6-percent excise tax would be imposed for the year with respect to the excess contributed. The earnings on the excess contributed up to the date of withdrawal would be includible in the gross income of the individual for the year for which the excess contribution was made.

The amendments made by this section will apply to contributions made for taxable years beginning after December 31, 1977.

[¶ 13,620.10]

Committee Report on P.L. 93-406 (Employee Retirement Income Security Act of 1974)

[Conference Committee Explanation]

Excess contributions

In general where contributions in excess of the deductible limits are made to an individual retirement account, no deduction is allowed for the excess amount, and this amount will be subject to a 6 percent tax for the year in which it is made, and each year thereafter, until there is no excess. The distribution is not to be includible in income if the excess is distributed to the individual on or before the due date for filing the employee's tax return for the year in question (including extensions). If the distribution occurs after that date, however, the distribution is to constitute taxable income to the employee (because his basis in his account is always zero) and will also give rise to a 10-percent additional tax if the distribution occurs before the employee is 59 ½.

The excess contribution may be removed by a distribution, or by underutilizing the allowable deduction limits for a later year. For example, if an employee contributed $3,000 in one year, and nothing the second year, then a 6 percent tax on $1,500 would be imposed only once (assuming the employee was entitled to a full $1,500 contribution for both years). (Similarly, if the participant withdrew the $1,500 excess contribution in the year in which the contribution was made, the 6 percent excise tax would be imposed only for that year.) Also (to prevent undue hardship resulting from bad investment experience), the tax may never exceed 6 percent of the assets in the account (but a decline in the asset value of the account does not remove the excess contribution and the 6 percent tax will be imposed until the excess contribution has been distributed or eliminated by underutilization of allowable contributions in a subsequent year).

A similar tax is to be imposed on excess contributions for section 403(b) plan investments in mutual fund stock (which are permitted under the conference substitute). (Section 403(b) allows deductions of up to 20 percent of salary, without regard to discrimination requirements, in the case of employees of educational and certain other types of exempt organizations.) However, the 6 percent tax is not imposed on section 403(b) annuity contracts, since earnings on annuity contracts are not taxable until distributed, even when the annuities are purchased outside the scope of a qualified plan.

No retirement savings deduction is to be allowed for contributions made during or after the year in which the individual attains age 70 ½, and contributions of an individual after attaining this age are to be treated as excess contributions.

[Code Sec. 4975]

[¶ 13,640.018]

Committee Report on P.L. 109-280 (Pension Protection Act of 2006)

[Joint Committee on Taxation Report]

[Investment advice]

In general

The provision adds a new category of prohibited transaction exemption under ERISA and the Code in connection with the provision of investment advice through an "eligible investment advice arrangement" to participants and beneficiaries of a defined contribution plan who direct the investment of their accounts under the plan and to beneficiaries of IRAs.[129] If the requirements under the provision are met, the following are exempt from prohibited transaction treatment: (1) the provision of investment advice; (2) an investment transaction (i.e., a sale, acquisition, or holding of a security or other property) pursuant to the advice; and (3) the direct or indirect receipt of fees or other compensation in connection with the provision of the advice or an investment transaction pursuant to the advice. The prohibited transaction exemptions provided under the provision do not in any manner alter existing individual or class exemptions provided by statute or administrative action.

The provision also directs the Secretary of Labor, in consultation with the Secretary of the Treasury, to determine, based on certain information to be solicited by the Secretary of Labor, whether there is any computer model investment advice program that meets the requirements of the provision and may be used by IRAs. The determination is to be made by December 31, 2007. If the Secretary of Labor determines there is such a program, the exemptions described above apply in connection with the use of the program with respect to IRA beneficiaries. If the Secretary of Labor determines that there is not such a program, such Secretary is directed to grant a class exemption from prohibited transaction treatment (as discussed below) for the provision of investment advice, investment transactions pursuant to such advice, and related fees to beneficiaries of such arrangements.

Eligible investment advice arrangements

In general

The exemptions provided under the provision apply in connection with the provision of investment advice by a fiduciary adviser under an eligible investment advice arrangement. An eligible investment advice arrangement is an arrangement (1) meeting certain requirements (discussed below) and (2) which either (a) provides that any fees (including any commission or compensation) received by the fiduciary adviser for investment advice or with respect to an investment transaction with respect to plan assets do not vary depending on the basis of any investment option selected, or (b) uses a computer model under an investment advice program as described below in connection with the provision of invest-

[129] The portions of the provision relating to IRAs apply to HSAs, Archer MSAs, and Coverdell education savings accounts. References here to IRAs include such other arrangements as well.

ment advice to a participant or beneficiary. In the case of an eligible investment advice arrangement with respect to a defined contribution plan, the arrangement must be expressly authorized by a plan fiduciary other than (1) the person offering the investment advice program, (2) any person providing investment options under the plan, or (3) any affiliate of (1) or (2).

Investment advice program using computer model

If an eligible investment advice arrangement provides investment advice pursuant to a computer model, the model must (1) apply generally accepted investment theories that take into account the historic returns of different asset classes over defined periods of time, (2) use relevant information about the participant or beneficiary, (3) use prescribed objective criteria to provide asset allocation portfolios comprised of investment options under the plan, (4) operate in a manner that is not biased in favor of any investment options offered by the fiduciary adviser or related person, and (5) take into account all the investment options under the plan in specifying how a participant's or beneficiary's account should be invested without inappropriate weighting of any investment option. An eligible investment expert must certify, before the model is used and in accordance with rules prescribed by the Secretary, that the model meets these requirements. The certification must be renewed if there are material changes to the model as determined under regulations. For this purpose, an eligible investment expert is a person who meets requirements prescribed by the Secretary and who does not bear any material affiliation or contractual relationship with any investment adviser or related person.

In addition, if a computer model is used, the only investment advice that may be provided under the arrangement is the advice generated by the computer model, and any investment transaction pursuant the advice must occur solely at the direction of the participant or beneficiary. This requirement does not preclude the participant or beneficiary from requesting other investment advice, but only if the request has not been solicited by any person connected with carrying out the investment advice arrangement.

Audit requirements

In the case of an eligible investment advice arrangement with respect to a defined contribution plan, an annual audit of the arrangement for compliance with applicable requirements must be conducted by an independent auditor (i.e., unrelated to the person offering the investment advice arrangement or any person providing investment options under the plan) who has appropriate technical training or experience and proficiency and who so represents in writing. The auditor must issue a report of the audit results to the fiduciary that authorized use of the arrangement. In the case of an eligible investment advice arrangement with respect to IRAs, an audit is required at such times and in such manner as prescribed by the Secretary of Labor.

Notice requirements

Before the initial provision of investment advice, the fiduciary adviser must provide written notice (which may be in electronic form) containing various information to the recipient of the advice, including information relating to: (1) the role of any related party in the development of the investment advice program or the selection of investment options under the plan; (2) past performance and rates of return for each investment option offered under the plan; (3) any fees or other compensation to be received by the fiduciary adviser or affiliate; (4) any material affiliation or contractual relationship of the fiduciary adviser or affiliates in the security or other property involved in the investment transaction; (5) the manner and under what circumstances any participant or beneficiary information will be used or disclosed; (6) the types of services provided by the fiduciary adviser in connection with the provision of investment advice; (7) the adviser's status as a fiduciary of the plan in connection with the provision of the advice; and (8) the ability of the recipient of the advice separately to arrange for the provision of advice by another adviser that could have no material affiliation with and receive no fees or other compensation in connection with the security or other property. This information must be maintained in accurate form and must be provided to the recipient of the investment advice, without charge, on an annual basis, on request, or in the case of any material change.

Any notification must be written in a clear and conspicuous manner, calculated to be understood by the average plan participant, and sufficiently accurate and comprehensive so as to reasonably apprise participants and beneficiaries of the required information. The Secretary is directed to issue a model form for the disclosure of fees and other compensation as required by the provision. The fiduciary adviser must maintain for at least six years any records necessary for determining whether the requirements for the prohibited transaction exemption were met. A prohibited transaction will not be considered to have occurred solely because records were lost or destroyed before the end of six years due to circumstances beyond the adviser's control.

Other requirements

In order for the exemption to apply, the following additional requirements must be satisfied: (1) the fiduciary adviser must provide disclosures applicable under securities laws; (2) an investment transaction must occur solely at the direction of the recipient of the advice; (3) compensation received by the fiduciary adviser or affiliates in connection with an investment transaction must be reasonable; and (4) the terms of the investment transaction must be at least as favorable to the plan as an arm's length transaction would be.

Fiduciary adviser

For purposes of the provision, "fiduciary adviser" is defined as a person who is a fiduciary of the plan by reason of the provision of investment advice to a participant or beneficiary and who is also: (1) registered as an investment adviser under the Investment Advisers Act of 1940 or under State laws; (2) a bank, a similar financial institution supervised by the United States or a State, or a savings association (as defined under the Federal Deposit Insurance Act), but only if the advice is provided through a trust department that is subject to periodic examination and review by Federal or State banking authorities; (3) an insurance company qualified to do business under State law; (4) registered as a broker or dealer under the Securities Exchange Act of 1934; (5) an affiliate of any of the preceding; or (6) an employee, agent or registered representative of any of the preceding who satisfies the requirements of applicable insurance, banking and securities laws relating to the provision of advice. A person who develops the computer model or markets the investment advice program or computer model is treated as a person who is a plan fiduciary by reason of the provision of investment advice and is treated as a fiduciary adviser, except that the Secretary may prescribe rules under which only one fiduciary adviser may elect treatment as a plan fiduciary. "Affiliate" means an affiliated person as defined under section 2(a)(3) of the Investment Company Act of 1940. "Registered representative" means a person described in section 3(a)(18) of the Securities Exchange Act of 1934 or a person described in section 202(a)(17) of the Investment Advisers Act of 1940.

Fiduciary rules

Subject to certain requirements, an employer or other person who is a plan fiduciary, other than a fiduciary adviser, is not treated as failing to meet the fiduciary requirements of ERISA, solely by reason of the provision of investment advice as permitted under the provision or of contracting for or otherwise arranging for the provision of the advice. This rule applies if: (1) the advice is provided under an arrangement between the employer or plan fiduciary and the fiduciary adviser for the provision of investment advice by the fiduciary adviser as permitted under the provision; (2) the terms of the arrangement require compliance by the fiduciary adviser with the requirements of the provision; and (3) the terms of the arrangement include a written acknowledgement by the fiduciary adviser that the fiduciary adviser is a plan fiduciary with respect to the provision of the advice.

The provision does not exempt the employer or a plan fiduciary from fiduciary responsibility under ERISA for the prudent selection and periodic review of a fiduciary adviser with whom the employer or plan fiduciary has arranged for the provision of investment advice. The employer or plan fiduciary does not have the duty to monitor the specific investment advice given by a fiduciary adviser. The provision also provides that nothing in the fiduciary responsibility provisions of ERISA is to be construed to preclude the use of plan assets to pay for reasonable expenses in providing investment advice.

Study and determination by the Secretary of Labor; class exemption

Under the provision, the Secretary of Labor must determine, in consultation with the Secretary of the Treasury, whether there is any computer model investment advice program that can be used by IRAs and that meets the requirements of the provision. The determination is to be made on the basis of information to be solicited by the Secretary of Labor as described below. Under the provision, a computer model investment advice program must (1) use relevant information about the beneficiary, (2) take into account the full range of investments, including equities and bonds, in determining the options for the investment portfolio of the beneficiary, and (3) allow the account beneficiary, in directing the investment of assets, sufficient flexibility in obtaining advice to evaluate and select options. The Secretary of Labor must report the results of this determination to the House Committees on Ways and Means and Education and the Workforce and the Senate Committees on Finance and Health, Education, Labor, and Pensions no later than December 31, 2007.

As soon as practicable after the date of enactment, the Secretary of Labor, in consultation with the Secretary of the Treasury, must solicit information as to the feasibility of the application of computer model investment advice programs for IRAs, including from (1) at least the top 50 trustees of IRAs, determined on the basis of assets held by such trustees, and (2) other persons offering such programs based on nonproprietary products. The information solicited by the Secretary of Labor from such trustees and other persons is to include information on their computer modeling capabilities with respect to the current year and the preceding year, including their capabilities for investment accounts they maintain. If a person from whom the Secretary of Labor solicits information does not provide such information within 60 days after the solicitation, the person is not entitled to use any class exemption granted by the Secretary of Labor as required under the provision (as discussed below) unless such failure is due to reasonable cause and not willful neglect.

The exemptions provided under the provision with respect to an eligible investment advice arrangement involving a computer model do not apply to IRAs. If the Secretary of Labor determines that there is a computer model investment advice program that can be used by IRAs, the exemptions provided under the provision with respect to an eligible investment advice arrangement involving a computer model can apply to IRAs.

If, as a result of the study of this issue as directed by the provision, the Secretary of Labor determines that there is not such a program, the Secretary of Labor must grant a class exemption from prohibited transaction treatment for (1) the provision of investment advice by a fiduciary adviser to beneficiaries of IRAs; (2) investment transactions pursuant to the advice; and (3) the direct or indirect receipt of fees or other compensation in connection with the provision of the advice or an investment transaction pursuant to the advice. Application of the exemptions are to be subject to conditions as are set forth in the class exemption and as are (1) in the interests of the IRA and its beneficiary and protective of the rights of the beneficiary, and (2) necessary to ensure the requirements of the applicable exemptions and the investment advice provided utilizes prescribed objective criteria to provide asset allocation portfolios comprised of securities or other property available as investments under the IRA. Such conditions could require that the fiduciary adviser providing the advice (1) adopt written policies and procedures that ensure the advice provided is not biased in favor of investments offered by the fiduciary adviser or a related person, and (2) appoint an individual responsible for annually reviewing the advice provided to determine that the advice is provided in accordance with the policies and procedures in (1).

If the Secretary of Labor later determines that there is any computer model investment advice program that can be used by IRAs, the class exemption ceases to apply after the later of (1) the date two years after the Secretary's later determination, or (2) the date three years after the date the exemption first took effect.

Any person may request the Secretary of Labor to make a determination with respect to any computer model investment advice program as to whether it can be used by IRAs, and the Secretary must make such determination within 90 days of the request. If the Secretary determines that the program cannot be so used, within 10 days of the determination, the Secretary must notify the House Committees on Ways and Means and Education and the Workforce and the Senate Committees on Finance and Health, Education, Labor, and Pensions thereof and the reasons for the determination.

Effective Date

The provisions are effective with respect to investment advice provided after December 31, 2006. The provision relating to the study by the Secretary of Labor is effective on the date of enactment.

[Exemption for block trading]

The provision provides prohibited transaction exemptions under ERISA and the Code for a purchase or sale of securities or other property (as determined by the Secretary of Labor) between a plan and a disqualified person (other than a fiduciary) involving a block trade if: (1) the transaction involves a block trade; (2) at the time of the transaction, the interest of the plan (together with the interests of any other plans maintained by the same plan sponsor) does not exceed 10 percent of the aggregate size of the block trade; (3) the terms of the transaction, including the price, are at least as favorable to the plan as an arm's length transaction with an unrelated party; and (4) the compensation associated with the transaction must be no greater than the compensation associated with an arm's length transaction with an unrelated party. For purposes of the provision, block trade is defined as any trade of at least 10,000 shares or with a market value of at least $200,000 that will be allocated across two or more unrelated client accounts of a fiduciary. Examples of property other than securities that the Secretary of labor may apply the exemption to include (but are not limited to) future contracts and currency.

Effective Date

The provision is effective with respect to transactions occurring after the date of enactment.

[Bonding relief]

The provision provides an exception to the ERISA bonding requirement for an entity registered as a broker or a dealer under the Securities Exchange Act of 1934 if the broker or dealer is subject to the fidelity bond requirements of a self-regulatory organization (within the meaning of the Securities Exchange Act of 1934).

Effective Date

The provision is effective for plan years beginning after the date of enactment.

[Exemption for electronic communication network]

The provision provides a prohibited transaction exemption under ERISA and the Code for a transaction involving the purchase or sale of securities (or other property as determined under regulations) between a plan and a party in interest if: (1) the transaction is executed through an electronic communication network, alternative trading system, or similar execution system or trading venue that is subject to regulation and oversight by (a) the applicable Federal regulating entity or (b) a foreign regulatory entity as the Secretary may determine under regulations; (2) either (a) neither the execution system nor the parties to the transaction take into account the identity of the parties in the execution of trades, or (b) the transaction is effected under rules designed to match purchases and sales at the best price available through the execution system in accordance with applicable rules of the SEC or other relevant governmental authority; (3) the price and compensation associated with the purchase and sale are not greater than an arm's length transaction with an unrelated party; (4) if the disqualified person has an ownership interest in the system or venue, the system or venue has been authorized by the plan sponsor or other independent fiduciary for this type of transaction; and (5) not less than 30 days before the first transaction of this type executed through any such system or venue, a plan fiduciary is provided written notice of the execution of the transaction through the system or venue.

Examples of other property for purposes of the exemption include (but are not limited to) futures contracts and currency.

Effective Date

The provision is effective with respect to transactions occurring after the date of enactment.

[Exemption for service providers]

The provision provides a prohibited transaction exemption under ERISA for certain transactions (such as sales of property, loans, and transfers or use of plan assets) between a plan and a person that is a party in interest solely by reason of providing services (or solely by reason of having certain relationships with a service provider), but only if, in connection with the transaction, the plan receives no less, nor pays no more, than adequate consideration. For this purpose, adequate consideration means: (1) in the case of a security for which there is a generally recognized market, the price of the security prevailing on a national securities exchange registered under the Securities Exchange Act of 1934, taking into account factors such as the size of the transaction and marketability of the security, or, if the security is not traded on such a national securities exchange, a price not less favorable to the plan than the offering price for the security as established by the current bid and asked prices quoted by persons independent of the issuer and of any disqualified person, taking into account factors such as the size of the transaction and marketability of the security; and (2) in the case of an asset other than a security for which there is a generally recognized market, the fair market value of the asset as determined in good faith by a fiduciary or named fiduciaries in accordance with regulations. The exemption does not apply to a fiduciary (or an affiliate) who has or exercises any discretionary authority or control with respect to the investment of the assets involved in the transaction or provides investment advice with respect to the assets.

Effective Date

The provision is effective with respect to transactions occurring after the date of enactment.

[Relief for foreign exchange transactions]

The provision provides a prohibited transaction exemption under ERISA and the Code for foreign exchange transactions between a bank or broker-dealer (or an affiliate of either) and a plan in connection with the sale, purchase, or holding of securities or other investment assets (other than a foreign exchange transaction unrelated to any other investment in securities or other investment assets) if: (1) at the time the foreign exchange transaction is entered into, the terms of the transaction are not less favorable to the plan than the terms generally available in comparable arm's length foreign exchange transactions between unrelated parties or the terms afforded by the bank or the broker-dealer (or any affiliate thereof) in comparable arm's-length foreign exchange transactions involving unrelated parties; (2) the exchange rate used for a particular foreign exchange transaction may not deviate by more than three percent from the interbank bid and asked rates at the time of the transaction for transactions of comparable size and maturity as displayed on an independent service that reports rates of exchange in the foreign currency market for such currency; and (3) the bank, broker-dealer (and any affiliate of either) does not have investment discretion or provide investment advice with respect to the transaction.

Effective Date

The provision is effective with respect to transactions occurring after the date of enactment.

[Definition of plan asset vehicle]

Under the provision, the term "plan assets" means plan assets as defined under regulations prescribed by the Secretary of Labor. Under the regulations, the assets of any entity are not to be treated as plan assets if, immediately after the most recent acquisition of any equity interest in the entity, less than 25 percent of the total value of each class of equity interest in the entity (disregarding certain interests) is held by benefit plan investors. For this purpose, an entity is considered to hold plan assets only to the extent of the percentage of the equity interest held by benefit plan investors, which means an employee benefit plan subject to the fiduciary rules of ERISA, any plan to which the prohibited transaction rules of the Code applies, and any entity whose underlying assets include plan assets by reason of a plan's investment in such entity.

Effective Date

The provision is effective with respect to transactions occurring after the date of enactment.

[Exemption for cross trading]

The provision provides prohibited transaction exemptions under ERISA and the Code for a transaction involving the purchase and sale of a security between a plan and any other account managed by the same investment manager if certain requirements are met. These requirements are—

- the transaction is a purchase or sale, for no consideration other than cash payment against prompt delivery of a security for which market quotations are readily available;
- the transaction is effected at the independent current market price of the security;
- no brokerage commission fee (except for customary transfer fees, the fact of which is disclosed) or other remuneration is paid in connection with the transaction;
- a fiduciary (other than the investment manager engaging in the cross trades or any affiliate) for each plan participating in the transaction authorizes in advance of any cross-trades (in a document that is separate from any other written agreement of the parties) the investment manager to engage in cross trades at the investment manager's discretion, after the fiduciary has received disclosure regarding the conditions under which cross trades may take place (but only if the disclosure is separate from any other agreement or disclosure involving the asset management relationship), including the written policies and procedures of the investment manager;
- each plan participating in the transaction has assets of at least $100,000,000, except that, if the assets of a plan are invested in a master trust containing the assets of plans maintained by employers in the same controlled group, the master trust has assets of at least $100,000,000;
- the investment manager provides to the plan fiduciary who has authorized cross trading a quarterly report detailing all cross trades executed by the investment manager in which the plan participated during such quarter, including the following information as applicable: the identity of each security bought or sold, the number of shares or units traded, the parties involved in the cross trade, and the trade price and the method used to establish the trade price;
- the investment manager does not base its fee schedule on the plan's consent to cross trading and no other service (other than the investment opportunities and cost savings available through a cross trade) is conditioned on the plan's consent to cross trading;
- the investment manager has adopted, and cross trades are effected in accordance with, written cross-trading policies and procedures that are fair and equitable to all accounts participating in the cross-trading program and that include a description of the manager's pricing policies and procedures, and the manager's policies and procedures for allocating cross trades in an objective manner among accounts participating in the cross-trading program; and
- the investment manager has designated an individual responsible for periodically reviewing purchases and sales to ensure compliance with the written policies and procedures and, following such review, the individual must issue an annual written report no later than 90 days following the period to which it relates, signed under penalty of perjury, to the plan fiduciary who authorized the cross trading, describing the steps performed during the course of the review, the level of compliance, and any specific instances of noncompliance.

The written report must also notify the plan fiduciary of the plan's right to terminate participation in the investment manager's cross-trading program at any time.

No later than 180 days after the date of enactment, the Secretary of Labor, after consultation with the Securities and Exchange Commission, is directed to issue regulations regarding the content of policies and procedures required to be adopted by an investment manager under the requirements for the exemption.

Effective Date

The provision is effective with respect to transactions occurring after the date of enactment.

[Correction period for certain transactions involving securities and commodities]

The bill provides a prohibited transaction exemption under ERISA and the Code for a transaction in connection with the acquisition, holding, or disposition of any security or commodity if the transaction is corrected within a certain period, generally within 14 days of the date the disqualified person (or other person knowingly participating in the transaction) discovers, or reasonably should have discovered, the transaction was a prohibited transaction. For this purpose, the term "correct" means, with respect to a transaction: (1) to undo the transaction to the extent possible and in any case to make good to the plan or affected account any losses resulting from the transaction; and (2) to restore to the plan or affected account any profits made through the use of assets of the plan. If the exemption applies, no excise tax is to be assessed with the transaction, any tax assessed is to be abated, and any tax collected is to be credited or refunded as a tax overpayment.

The exemption does not apply to any transaction between a plan and a plan sponsor or its affiliates that involves the acquisition or sale of an employer security or the acquisition, sale, or lease of employer real property. In addition, in the case of a disqualified person (or other person knowingly participating in the transaction), the exemption does not apply if, at the time of the transaction, the person knew (or reasonably should have known) that the transaction would constitute a prohibited transaction.

Effective Date

The provision is effective with respect to any transaction that a fiduciary or other person discovers, or reasonably should have discovered, after the date of enactment constitutes a prohibited transaction.

[¶ 13,640.02]

Committee Report on P.L. 108-357 (American Jobs Creation Act of 2004)

[House Committee Report]

The bill allows an IRA (including a Roth IRA) to be a shareholder of a bank that is an S corporation, but only to the extent of bank stock held by the IRA on the date of enactment of the provision.[33]

The bill also provides an exemption from prohibited transaction treatment for the sale by an IRA to the IRA beneficiary of bank stock held by the IRA on the date of enactment of the provision. Under the bill, a sale is not a prohibited transaction if: (1) the sale is pursuant to an S corporation election by the bank; (2) the sale is for fair market value (as established by an independent appraiser) and is on terms at least as favorable to the IRA as the terms would be on a sale to an unrelated party; (3) the IRA incurs no commissions, costs, or other expenses in connection with the sale; and (4) the stock is sold in a single transaction for cash not later than 120 days after the S corporation election is made.

Effective Date

The provision takes effect on the date of enactment of the bill.

[Conference Agreement]

The conference agreement includes the provision in the House bill.

[¶ 13,640.03]

Committee Report on P.L. 105-34 (Taxpayer Relief Act)

[House Committee Report]

Prohibited transaction provisions involving plan loans

The provision generally eliminates the special present-law rules relating to plan loans made to an owner-employee (other than the owner of an IRA). Thus, the general statutory exemption applies to such transactions. Present law continues to apply with respect to IRAs.

Effective Date

The provision is effective with respect to years beginning after December 31, 2001.

[Conference Committee Report]

Senate Amendment

The Senate amendment is the same as the House bill.

Conference Agreement

The conference agreement follows the House bill and the Senate amendment. The conferees intend that the Secretary of the Treasury and the Secretary of Labor will waive any penalty or excise tax in situations where a loan made prior to the effective date of the provision was exempt when initially made (treating any refinancing as a new loan) and the loan would have been exempt throughout the period of the loan if the provision had been in effect during the period of the loan.

[¶ 13,640.04]

Committee Report on P.L. 105-34 (Taxpayer Relief Act)

[Senate Committee Report]

Tax on prohibited transactions

The bill increases the initial-level prohibited transaction tax from 10-percent to 15-percent. No changes were made to the prohibited transaction provisions of title I of the Employee Retirement Income Security Act of 1974, as amended ("ERISA").

Effective date

The provision is effective with respect to prohibited transactions occurring after the date of enactment.

---

[33] Under the bill, the present-law rules treating S corporation stock held by a qualified retirement plan (other than an employee stock ownership plan) or a charity as an interest in an unrelated trade or business apply to an IRA holding S corporation stock of a bank.

[¶ 13,640.06]

Committee Reports on P.L. 104-188 (Small Business Job Protection Act)

Technical Corrections to the Revenue Reconciliation Act of 1990

[House Committee Report]

Prohibited transaction rules

The bill conforms the statutory language to legislative intent by providing that transactions that are exempt from the prohibited transaction rules of ERISA by reason of ERISA section 408(b)(12) are also exempt from the prohibited transaction rules of the Code.

[Conference Committee Report]

Senate Amendment

The Senate amendment is the same as the House bill * * *.

Conference Agreement

The conference agreement follows the House bill and the Senate amendment * * *.

[¶ 13,640.07]

Committee Reports on P.L. 101-508 (Omnibus Budget Reconciliation Act of 1990)

[House Committee Report]

Prohibited transactions

H.R. 5822 provides that transactions that are exempt from the prohibited transaction rules of the Employee Retirement Income Security Act (ERISA) under section 408(b)(12) of ERISA (relating to dispositions of certain employer securities) are also exempt from the prohibited transaction rules of the Code.

[Conference Committee Report]

The conference agreement contains the tax technical correction provisions of H.R. 5822 as reported by the House Ways and Means Committee.

[¶ 13,640.08]

Committee Report on P.L. 96-222 (Technical Corrections Act of 1979)

[Senate Committee Report]

Sec. 101(a)(7)(C)—Qualifying employer securities.

The Revenue Act of 1978 made certain changes in the rules governing employee stock ownership plans. Because of these changes, the definition of qualifying employer securities, as it relates to such plans, is unclear.

The bill clarifies that, for purposes of the rules governing employee stock ownership plans, the term "qualifying employer securities" is defined in the same manner as the term "employer securities" in the case of tax credit employee stock ownership plans. This definition generally includes readily tradable common stock of the employer and preferred stock convertible into such readily tradable common stock.

This provision applies to stock acquired after December 31, 1979.

Sec. 101(a)(7)(K)—Voting rights pass through.

Under the Revenue Act of 1978, an employee stock ownership plan is required to pass through to plan participants voting rights with respect to qualifying employer securities held by the plan. If the plan is maintained by an employer which has a registration-type class of securities, the vote pass-through requirement applies generally. If the plan is maintained by an employer which does not have a registration-type class of securities, the vote pass-through requirement applies only with respect to major corporate issues (e.g., mergers, consolidations, sales of substantially all of a corporation's assets).

Also, under the Revenue Act of 1978, a defined contribution plan which is established by an employer the stock of which is not publicly traded is required to pass through to plan participants voting rights on major corporate issues. This vote pass-through applies only if, after December 31, 1979, the plan acquires securities of the employer and, after the acquisition, more than 10 percent of the plan's assets are invested in such securities.

Under the Revenue Act of 1978, an employee stock ownership plan maintained by an employer the stock of which is not publicly traded may be subject to vote pass-through rules with respect to employer securities under two separate provisions of the Code. The committee believes that this duplication should be eliminated by deleting the special vote pass-through rule for employee stock ownership plans maintained by an employer which does not have a registration-type class of securities.

Under the bill, an employee stock ownership plan maintained by an employer which does not have a registration-type class of securities will be required to pass through voting rights to plan participants only under the vote pass-through rule generally applicable to defined contribution plans. Thus, the vote pass-through will be required only (1) with respect to major corporate issues, (2) if the plan is maintained by an employer the stock of which is not publicly traded, and (3) if after acquiring securities of the employer, more than 10 percent of the plan's assets are in such securities.

The amendment made by this section is effective as if it had been included in section 141 of the Revenue Act of 1978.

Sec. 101(a)(7)(L)—Nomenclature—The Senate Committee Report on Sec. 101(a)(7)(L) of P.L. 96-222 is at ¶ 12,130.09.

[¶ 13,640.09]

Committee Report on P.L. 95-600 (Revenue Act of 1978)

Committee Reports on P.L. 95-600 are at ¶ 12,130.10.

[¶ 13,640.10]

Committee Report on P.L. 93-406 (Employee Retirement Income Security Act of 1974)

[Conference Committee Explanation]

Excise tax on prohibited transactions

In general.—* * * the substitute establishes an excise tax on disqualified persons who participate in specific prohibited transactions respecting a pension plan. The tax applies with rspect to a plan which has qualified after the effective date of the prohibited transaction provisions (or has been determined to qualify by the Secretary of the Treasury under section 401, 403(a), or 405(a) of the Code) and with respect to a qualified individual retirement account, bond or annuity (under sections 408 or 409). The prohibited transaction rules and excise tax sanctions are to continue to apply even if the plan, etc., should later lose its tax qualification.

This excise tax generally follows the same procedures as the tax on self-dealing enacted in 1969 Tax Reform Act with respect to private foundations. The tax is at two levels; initially, disqualified persons who participate in a prohibited transaction are to be subject to a tax of 5 percent of the amount involved in the transaction per year. A second tax of 100 percent is imposed if the transaction is not corrected after notice from the Internal Revenue Service that the 5-percent tax is due.

Following present law with respect to private foundations, under the substitute where a fiduciary participates in a prohibited transaction in a capacity other than that, or in addition to that, of a fiduciary, he is to be treated as other disqualified persons and subject to tax. Otherwise, a fiduciary is not to be subject to the excise tax.

The first-level tax is owned for each taxable year (or part of a year) in the period that begins with the date when the prohibited transaction occurs and ends on the earlier of the date of collection or the date of mailing of a deficiency notice for the first-level tax (under section 6212 of the Internal Revenue Code). The first-level tax is imposed automatically without regard to whether the violation was inadvertent.

If more than one person is liable for the excise tax as a result of a particular prohibited transaction, they all are to be jointly and severally liable. For example, if the prohibited transaction involves $100,000, all disqualified persons who participated in the transaction will be jointly and severally liable for the first-level tax of $5,000 (per year in the taxable period) and also jointly and severally liable for the second-level tax of $100,000.

The excise tax on a prohibited transaction is dependent upon the amount involved in the transaction. The substitute provides that the amount involved is the greater of the fair market value of the property (including money) given or received in a transaction. However, with regard to services which are necessary to the operation of the plan and which generally may be paid for if the compensation is not excessive, the amount involved generally is the excess compensation. For the first-level tax, the amount involved in a prohibited transaction is valued as of the date of the transaction. However, for the second-level tax, the amount involved is valued at the highest fair market value during the correction period. The higher valuation is used for the second-level tax so the person subject to tax will not delay returning the amount involved to the trust in order to earn income with this amount.

A prohibited transaction may be corrected to avoid a second-level tax at any time before the 90th day after the Internal Revenue Service mails a notice of deficiency with respect to the second-level tax. However, the 90-day period may be extended by any period within which a deficiency cannot be assessed (because of petitions to the Tax Court), and may also be extended for a period which the Internal Revenue Service determines is both reasonable and necessary to correct the prohibited transaction.

To correct a prohibited transaction, the transaction must be undone to the extent possible, but in any case the final position of the plan must be no worse than it would have been if the disqualified person were acting under the highest fiduciary standards. The higher valuation to be used in computing any second-level tax that might be applicable is also the valuation to be used in correcting the transaction. In other words, correction requires that the plan receive the benefit of whatever bargain turns out to have been involved in the transaction.

Before sending a notice of deficiency with respect to the first level and second level taxes, the Internal Revenue Service is to notify the Secretary of Labor and provide him a reasonable opportunity to obtain a correction of the prohibited transaction or to comment on the imposition of these taxes. However, the Service will be able to waive (or abate) only the second level tax (and not the first level tax) upon a correction that is obtained by the Secretary of Labor.

Voluntary retroactive application.—Under present law, if a prohibited transaction occurs, a plan (and trust) loses its exemption from taxation. If a trust is disqualified because of an act of the trustee and the employer, then the income tax imposed on the trust may be paid out of funds otherwise available to provide employees' retirement benefits and the sanction may then fall on innocent employees. To correct this problem in the future, the substitute eliminates disqualification and instead would impose an excise tax sanction for a violation of the prohibited transaction provisions.

The substitute also makes the excise tax sanction available—on a wholly voluntary basis—instead of the disqualification sanction in the cse of plans which have engaged in prohibited transactions in (open) years before the effective date of the new prohibited transactions. Therefore, if a disqualified person with respect to a plan elects to be subject to and pays the excise tax, the plan and trust are not to be disqualified. For purposes of this application of the excise tax, the prohibited transactions are to be defined by present section 503(b) or (g) of the Code and the amount involved is to be the amount that would be determined under new section 4975 of the Code. Since the tax is to be wholly voluntary, the joint and several liability provisions of new section 4975 are not to apply (unless there is an election by several disqualified persons to this effect). Also, the first-level tax that is to be paid under this provision will be owed for taxable periods calculated under new section 4975. Thus, if the prohibited transaction (under present section 503) occurred in 1972 and is corrected in 1974, the first-level tax will be owed for 1972, 1973, and 1974. As under new section 4975, the second-level tax will be owed only if the transaction is not corrected within the time allowed by that section.

Since this is to be a relief provision, no liability is to be imposed under the labor provisions of the substitute on a person who may be a plan fiduciary after January 1, 1975, if he fails to pay the tax and the plan is disqualified. Consequently, any decision to pay or not to pay this optional tax is to be deemed to have been made before January 1, 1975, and, therefore, to be made before the substitute would establish any duties on plan fiduciaries.

Definitions.—The substitute defines "fiduciary" as any person who exercises any discretionary authority or control respecting management of a plan, exercises any authority or control respecting the management or disposition of its assets or has any discretionary authority or responsibility in the administration of the plan. Under this definition, fiduciaries include officers and directors of a plan, members of a plan's investment committee and persons who select these individuals. Consequently, the definition includes persons who have authority and responsibility with respect to the matter in question, regardless of their formal title. The term "fiduciary" also includes any person who renders investment advice for a fee and includes persons to whom "discretionary" duties have been delegated by named fiduciaries.

While the ordinary functions of consultants and advisers to employee benefit plans (other than investment advisers) may not be considered as fiduciary functions, it must be recognized that there will be situations where such consultants and advisers may because of their special expertise, in effect, be exercising discretionary authority or control with respect to the management or administration of such plan or some authority or control regarding its assets. In such cases, they are to be regarded as having assumed fiduciary obligations within the meaning of the applicable definition.

The labor definition of a "party-in-interest" includes the following general categories. (1) Plan administrators, officers, fiduciaries, trustees, custodians, counsel and employees. (2) Persons providing services to a plan. (3) The employer, its employees, officers, directors, or 10-percent shareholders. (4) Controlling or controlled parties or parties under common control (and their employees, officers, directors, or 10-percent shareholders). (Under the substitute, "control" is generally defined at 50-percent ownership. However, the Secretary of Labor and Secretary of Treasury may, by regulation, reduce this percentage.) (5) Employee organizations with members covered by the plan, its employees, its officers and directors and its affiliates. (6) Certain relatives and partners of parties-in-interest are also treated as parties-in-interest.

Under the tax provisions, the same general categories of persons are disqualified persons, with some differences. Although fiduciaries are disqualified persons under the tax provisions, they are to be subject to the excise tax only if they act in a prohibited transaction in a capacity other than that of a fiduciary. Also, only highly-compensated employees are to be treated as disqualified persons, not all employees of an employer, etc.

Application of prohibited transaction and other taxes to IRA's.—Generally, an individual retirement account is to be exempt from Federal tax, but the unrelated business income of the account, if any, is to be subject to tax (under sec. 511).

Under the House bill, individual retirement accounts generally would be subject to the prohibited transaction rules of present law. However, with respect to prohibited transactions, the conference substitute (generally following the Senate amendment) replaces present law with an excise tax on prohibited transactions (instead of using disqualification as a sanction) and changes the existing prohibited transaction rules. Consequently, the conference substitute applies the new prohibited transaction rules applicable to an owner-employee (e.g., no borrowing from the account is permitted) to individual retirement accounts, with respect to transactions involving the employer or union sponsor of the account, or other parties in interest.

However, if an individual participant engages in an unauthorized transaction with his individual retirement account then, as indicated previously, the sanction, in general, is disqualification of the account. In this case the assets of the account are to be deemed to be distributed, and the appropriate taxes, including the 10 percent additional tax on premature distributions, are to apply. However, the individual is not to be subject to the prohibited transaction excise taxes (of sec. 4975).

Thus, where there is a union or employer-sponsored account, and there is an individual retirement account trust covering more than one employee, only the employee who engages in the prohibited transaction is to be subject to disqualification of his separate account. However, if the employer (or union) sponsoring the account is the party engaging in a prohibited transaction, then the employer (or other party) will be liable for the excise tax, but the individual participants will not.

The labor prohibitions affect "parties-in-interest", and the tax prohibitions affect "disqualified persons." The two terms are substantially the same in most respects, but the labor term includes a somewhat broader range of persons, as described below.

Coverage.—The prohibited transaction rules under the labor provisions apply to all plans to which the general labor fiduciary rules apply, as described above. The tax law prohibited transaction rules apply to all qualified retirement plans (under secs. 401, 403(a), and 405(a) of the Internal Revenue Code) and to all qualified individual retirement accounts, individual retirement annuities, and individual retirement bonds (under secs. 408 and 409 of the Code). In addition, the tax rules are to continue to apply even if the plan, etc., should later lose its tax qualification.

The tax law prohibited transaction provisions follow the labor provisions with respect to whether the assets of an insurance company or mutual funds are to be considered the assets of a plan. Also, the tax provisions exclude from the new prohibited transaction rules government plans, and church plans which have not elected coverage under the new participation, vesting, funding, and insurance provisions. (The latter plans, if they are qualified plans, will be subject to present law.)

* * *

[Code Sec. 4977]

[¶ 13,648D.10]

Committee Reports on P.L. 98-369 (Tax Reform Act of 1984)

For Committee Reports on P.L. 98-369, relating to fringe benefits, see ¶ 11,289M.10.

[Code Sec. 4978]

[¶ 13,648F.10]

Committee Reports on P.L. 104-188 (Small Business Job Protection Act)

Revenue Offsets

[Senate Committee Report]

Repeal 50-percent interest income exclusion for financial institution loans to ESOPs

The provision repeals the 50-percent interest exclusion with respect to ESOP loans.

Effective Date

The provision is effective with respect to loans made after the date of enactment, other than loans made pursuant to a written binding contract in effect before June 10, 1996, and at all times thereafter before such loan is made. The repeal of the 50-percent interest exclusion does not apply to the refinancing of an ESOP loan originally made on or before the date of enactment or pursuant to a binding contract in effect before June 10, 1996, provided: (1) such refinancing loan otherwise meets the requirements of section 133 in effect on the day before the date of enactment; (2) the outstanding principal amount of the loan is not increased; and (3) the term of the refinancing loan does not extend beyond the term of the original ESOP loan.

[Conference Committee Report]

Conference Agreement

The conference agreement follows the Senate amendment.

[Code Sec. 4978B]

[¶ 13,648I.10]

Committee Reports on P.L. 101-508 (Omnibus Budget Reconciliation Act of 1990)

[House Committee Report]

Excise tax on disposition of employer securities

The bill clarifies that the tax on securities acquired in a transaction to which section 133 applies does not apply to securities to which a tax is imposed under the provisions relating to dispositions of securities acquired in a section 1042 or section 2057 transaction. This clarification conforms the statute to Congressional intent that only one excise should be imposed with respect to the disposition of any employer securities and eliminates an unintended inference that the excise tax does not apply in the case of nonpublicly traded securities.

[Conference Committee Report]

The conference agreement contains the tax technical correction provisions of H.R. 5822 as reported by the House Ways and Means Committee.

[¶ 13,648I.17]

Committee Report on P.L. 101-239 (Omnibus Budget Reconciliation Act of 1989)

For Committee Reports on P.L. 101-239, relating to interest exclusion for ESOP loans, see ¶ 12,130.063.

[Code Sec. 4979]

[¶ 13,648J.09]

Committee Report on P.L. 109-280 (Pension Protection Act of 2006)

For the Committee Report on P.L. 109-280 on automatic enrollment arrangements, see ¶ 11,700.02.

[¶ 13,648J.10]

Committee Reports on P.L. 100-647 (Technical and Miscellaneous Revenue Act of 1988)

[Senate Committee Report]

Under the bill, the special nondiscrimination test applicable to matching contributions and employee contributions only applies to contributions to defined contribution plans within the meaning of sec. 414(k). Also under the bill, the definition of "matching contributions" includes any contribution to a defined contribution plan made on account of an employee contribution or an elective deferral under a qualified cash or deferred arrangement, whether such contributions are made to the same plan or a different plan. Contributions to a defined benefit pension plan may be employee contributions or matching contributions to the extent treated as contributions to a defined contribution plan (sec. 414(k)).

In accordance with the Statement of Managers with respect to the Act, the bill provides that contributions to tax-sheltered annuities that are treated as elective deferrals for purposes of the dollar limit on elective deferrals (sec. 402(g)) are also to be treated as elective deferrals for purposes of the nondiscrimination rules applicable to employer matching contributions and employee contributions (sec. 401(m)). Under the bill, this provision is subject to the effective date provisions in the Act, as amended, with respect to the application of nondiscrimination rules to tax-sheltered annuities (Act sec. 1120(c)). Thus, for example, employer contributions to any type of plan that match an elective deferral to a tax-sheltered annuity are subject to the nondiscrimination requirements of section 401(m) in years beginning after December 31, 1988 (or later under the special effective date applicable to plans maintained pursuant to a collective bargaining agreement).

As under the rules applicable to elective deferrals under a cash or deferred arrangement, elective deferrals under a tax-sheltered annuity may be used to help satisfy the nondiscrimination test applicable to matching contributions with respect to a tax-sheltered annuity. (Similarly, consistent with the rules applicable to cash or deferred arrangements, elective deferrals to a tax-sheltered annuity may not be used to help a tax-sheltered annuity program satisfy the applicable coverage tests (sec. 410(b) without regard to sec. 410(c)) except for purposes of the average benefits test.)

Under the bill, matching contributions that are treated as elective deferrals for purposes of the special nondiscrimination test applicable to cash or deferred arrangements are not subject to the special test applicable to matching contributions and employee contributions.

Required aggregation

The bill modifies the requirement with respect to aggregation of plans in which a highly compensated employee participates. Under the bill, if a highly compensated employee participates in 2 or more plans of an employer to which contributions subject to the special nondiscrimination test (sec. 401(m)) are made, then all such contributions are aggregated for purposes of the test. For example, assume an employer maintains a plan with a cash or deferred arrangement under which matching contributions are made, and a thrift plan providing for after-tax employee contributions and matching contributions. Highly compensated employees participate in both plans. Under the bill, matching contributions that are not treated as elective deferrals in applying the special section 401(k) nondiscrimination test and after-tax contributions under the plans are aggregated for purposes of the special nondiscrimination test. The elective deferrals, however, are not required to be aggregated with the matching contributions and employee contributions.

Treatment of excess aggregate contributions

The bill provides that excess aggregate contributions for a plan year that are distributed before the end of the following plan year are not subject to the 15-percent excise tax on excess distributions (sec. 4980A).

In addition, to be consistent with the rules applicable to excess deferrals and excess contributions, the bill provides that generally such distributions may be made without regard to the terms of the plan until the close of the first plan year for which an amendment is required (Act sec. 1140). The bill similarly provides that the Secretary is to prescribe a model amendment that allows a plan to distribute excess aggregate contributions and that a plan distribution in accordance with such amendment is to be treated as in accordance with the terms of the plan. It is understood that the Secretary has already prescribed model amendments under the Act; accordingly, it is not intended that the Secretary be required to prescribe a new amendment regarding excess aggregate contributions.

The Act provides that excess contributions and excess aggregate contributions that are distributed within 2 ½ months after the end of the plan year are treated as received and earned by the recipient in the taxable year to which the contribution relates in order to prevent deferral of income. Such deferral is not of major concern, however, where the amount involved is not significant. Accordingly, the bill provides an exception to the general rule. Under this exception, if the total distributions of excess contributions and excess aggregate contributions under a plan for a plan year with respect to an individual are less than $100, then the distributions are treated as earned and received by the individual in the taxable year in which the distributions were made.

[Conference Committee Report]

* * *

The conference agreement follows the Senate amendment, with the clarification that the provision is effective as if included in section 1120(b) of the Reform Act. The conferees intend that the institution maintaining the plan is generally to be interpreted as not including any employer (or portion thereof) that may not maintain a section 403(b) annuity program.

[Code Sec. 4980]

[¶ 13,648P.08]

Committee Report on P.L. 101-508 (Omnibus Budget Reconciliation Act of 1990)

For Committee Reports on P.L. 101-508, relating to the revision of excess pension plan assets, see ¶ 13,030.10.

[¶ 13,648P.095]

Committee Reports on P.L. 100-647 (Technical and Miscellaneous Revenue Act of 1988)

[Senate Committee Report]

Excise Tax on Reversion of Qualified Plan Assets to Employer

The bill clarifies that the exception to the excise tax on reversions in the case of transfers of tax-credit ESOPs (sec. 409) as well as ESOPs described in section 4975(e)(7). Absent this clarification, a tax-credit ESOP would be required, in order to qualify for the ESOP exception, to add plan language applicable to leveraged ESOPs even if the ESOP did not have any outstanding loans.

The bill provides an exception to the rule that the employer securities acquired with transferred assets are to be held under the plan until distributed to plan participants. Under this exception, the transferred amounts are not required to be held in employer securities if a plan participant elects to diversify a portion of the participant's account balance (under the rules of sec. 401(a)(28)) that includes such employer securities and diversification cannot be accomplished through the use of nontransferred assets.

The bill also clarifies that amounts attributable to the employer securities acquired with the transferred assets are also subject to the requirements that (1) such amounts, within 90 days, be invested in employer securities (as defined in sec. 409(l)) or used to repay loans used to acquire such securities, and (2) subject to the exception discussed above, such employer securities remain in the plan until distribution to participants in accordance with the provisions of the plan.

In addition, the bill provides that, with respect to the allocation of employer securities acquired with transferred amounts (and amounts attributable thereto), the minimum amount required to be allocated to participants' accounts in the ESOP in the year in which the transfer occurs is not to be less than the lesser of (1) the maximum amount that could be allocated without violating the requirements of section 415, or (2) 1/8 of the shares acquired with the amounts transferred (and amounts attributable to such amounts). Thus, the requirement in the Act that stock acquired with amounts transferred to an ESOP is required to be allocated in the year of transfer up to the maximum amount permitted to be allocated under the limits on contributions (sec. 415) is repealed.

If employer securities are held in a suspense account pending allocation under the foregoing rule, the bill clarifies that dividends on such securities are to be (1) allocated to the accounts of participants and beneficiaries in proportion to their account balances, (2) paid to participants and beneficiaries in proportion to their account balances, or (3) used to repay any loans the proceeds of which were used to purchase employer securities.

The bill clarifies the exception for transfers to ESOPs to the general rule that the employer is required to include the amount of any reversion in income. Under the bill, the exception to the income inclusion requirement applies to any reversion occurring after March 31, 1985, if the reversion is transferred to an ESOP, subject to the January 1, 1989, termination of the ESOP exception.

Finally, the bill clarifies, by statute, that an employer is not entitled to any deduction or credit for any amount transferred to an ESOP to the extent that the special exception to the reversion tax applies to the transfer. This rule is added to prevent an employer from gaining a double tax benefit (i.e., granting a deduction or credit for previously deductible contributions) by transferring assets to an ESOP.

[Joint Committee Explanation of Senate Consensus Amendment]

The increase in the excise tax would apply with respect to reversions received after [October 20, 1988, if notice of the intent to terminate the plan was not provided before October 21, 1988.] * * * The acceleration of time for payment of the tax would apply to reversions received * * * after [December 31, 1988.]

[Conference Committee Report]

The conference agreement follows the Senate amendment with respect to the acceleration of the time for payment of the excise tax, except that the provision applies to reversions received after December 31, 1988. The conference agreement modifies the temporary increase in the excise tax in the Senate amendment to provide for a permanent increase in the excise tax from 10 to 15 percent. The increase is effective for reversions received after October 20, 1988, if notice of the intent to terminate the plan was not provided before October 21, 1988. The conferees do not intend any inference with respect to the issue of when a reversion is received for income and excise tax purposes.

The conferees intend that an employer is to be treated as providing notice of intent to terminate to employees if the employer has provided notice to substantially all employees by a specific date (such as through a mass mailing to employees by such date), even if some employees are not notified through an inadvertent failure of the employer. The conferees do not intend any inference with respect to whether notice has been provided for any other purpose.

[¶ 13,648P.10]

Committee Reports on P.L. 99-514 (Tax Reform Act of 1986)

[Senate Committee Report]

In general

The bill imposes a 10-percent nondeductible excise tax on a reversion from a qualified plan. The tax is imposed on the person who receives the reversion.

Under the bill, the excise tax applies to a reversion from a plan (or from a trust under a plan) if the plan met the requirements of the Code for qualified status (sec. 401(a) or sec. 403(a)) at any time or if the plan was, at any time, determined to have met those requirements by the Internal Revenue Service.

Amount of reversion

The bill defines a reversion as the amount of cash and the fair market value of other property received (directly or indirectly) from a qualified plan. No inference is to be drawn from the definition of a reversion in the bill as to the income tax consequences and the effect on a plan's qualified status of a transfer of assets from a qualified plan that has not been terminated to another qualified plan.

The amount of a reversion does not include any amount distributed to any employee (or beneficiary) if such amount could have been distributed before the termination of the plan without violating the plan qualification requirements (secs. 401(a) and 403(a)). However, the provision of a benefit or other obligation that causes the disqualification of a plan (or would cause the disqualification of the plan if it were otherwise qualified) is to be taken into account as a reversion if it is provided pursuant to the termination of the plan. For example, if benefits under a plan are increased to a level in excess of the overall limits on contributions and benefits, and if the increase is related to or in contemplation of the termination of the plan, then the value of the excess benefits is to be treated as a reversion.

Special rule for assets transferred to ESOPs

The bill provides an exception to the excise tax on reversions in the case of transfers of assets from a defined benefit pension plan upon plan termination to an employee stock ownership plan (ESOP). The amount transferred is not includible in the income of the employer.

In addition, under the bill, the amount transferred may be allocated under the plan to ESOP participants immediately subject to the dollar limits on annual additions under section 415(c). Alternatively, as provided under the plan, the amount transferred may be held in a suspense account pending allocation (provided allocations are made no more slowly than ratably over a 7-year period) or may be used to repay an acquisition loan (as described in section 404(a)(9)). Such allocations, the establishment of a suspense account, or the repayment of a loan is to occur within 90 days after the transfer. Amounts must be used either to acquire employer securities or to repay an acquisition loan and are to be allocated to the accounts of participants (as long as the allocations do not violate sec. 415(a)). If the plan is terminated prior to such amounts being fully allocated to participants' accounts, the employer will be subject to the 10 percent excise tax on such reversion amounts that have not been allocated.

Dividends paid on employer securities held in the suspense account must be either (a) applied to repay an acquisition loan, or (b) paid out currently to plan participants and beneficiaries proportionate to their account balances (attributable to such amounts) on the date such dividends are distributed.

The amounts held in the suspense account are required to be allocated to participants' accounts before any other employer contributions are allocated. In other words, during the period that reversion amounts are held in a suspense account, the employer is not permitted to make additional contributions to the ESOP to the extent that the contributions, when added to the amount held in a suspense account, would exceed the overall limits on annual additions under a defined contribution plan if allocated to participants' accounts.

Amounts transferred to a suspense account that (due to the limitations on contributions and benefits under section 415) cannot be allocated to participants' accounts within seven plan years (including the years in which such amounts were transferred to the plan) must revert to the employer and will be subject to the 10% excise tax in the taxable years in which such reversion occurs.

The waiver of the excise tax is to apply only if at least 50 percent of the employees who are participants in the terminated defined benefit pension plan (as of the date the notice of intent to terminate is filed with the PBGC) are also eligible to particpate in the ESOP to which the the excess assets are transferred. For this purpose, an employer may disregard those participants in the terminated defined benefit pension plan who are not employed by the employer on the date of the first allocation of such reversion amounts under the ESOP. All employees participating in the ESOP as of the close of the plan year in which the employer receives a notice of sufficiency of assets from the Pension Benefit Guaranty Corporation with respect to the termination of the defined benefit pension plan are to be entitled to share in that year's allocation of the excess assets in the ESOP.

The bill permits the ESOP to be maintained by any member of a controlled group of corporations, including a corporation other than the corporation that maintained the terminated defined benefit pension plan as long as the 50 percent test is met with respect to the employees participating in the ESOP.

For those employees receiving allocations under the ESOP, the committee intends that the employer provide the employees with a written notice describing the source of the funds attributable to the allocations (i.e., that the amounts represent excess assets determined upon termination of a defined benefit pension plan).

[Conference Committee Report]

The conference agreement follows the Senate amendment under which a 10-percent nondeductible excise tax is imposed on a reversion from a qualified plan. In addition, the tax is imposed on reversions from programs described in section 403(a). The tax is imposed on the employer maintaining the plan. In the case of a partnership that is treated as the employer maintaining the plan under section 401(a), the partners are liable for the tax. The agreement provides that the excise tax does not apply to a reversion to an employer that has at all times been tax-exempt. Of course, this exception does not apply to the extent that such employer has been subject to unrelated business income tax or has otherwise derived a tax benefit from the qualified plan.

In addition, the conference agreement clarifies that a return of mistaken contributions within section 401(a)(2) is not a reversion subject to the excise tax. Similarly, amounts which may be returned under section 403(c)(2) of the Employee Retirement Income Security Act of 1974, as amended, are not considered reversions subject to the tax. A payment to an employer under a participating annuity purchased upon plan termination is treated as a reversion subject to the tax.

* * *

The conferees are aware that the Secretary is currently considering the circumstances in which asset transfers between ongoing plans, plan mergers and spinoffs, and transfers of plan sponsorship in connection with the sale of a business may result in income tax consequences to the employer. The conferees stress that no inference is to be drawn from the agreement as to either the income or reversion tax consequences of such transactions.

The provision generally applies to reversions received after December 31, 1985 but does not apply to a reversion received after December 31, 1985, if the termination date of the plan is before January 1, 1986. * * * Under the conference agreement, the date of termination of a plan is the dates of termination under section 411(d)(3).

The conference agreement adopts the provision in the Senate amendment waiving the excise tax with respect to the portion of a reversion that is transferred to an employee stock ownership plan (ESOP) under certain circumstances. No inference is to be drawn from this exception as to the circumstances in which asset transfers will or will not satisfy the exclusive benefit rule and any other applicable qualification requirements (e.g., sec. 414(1)).

* * * For purposes of determining which plan participants in the defined benefit plan from which assets where transferred to the ESOP are required to be participants in the ESOP, the conferees intend that only active employees, as opposed to retirees, who are participants in the plan need be included.

The conferees clarify that the prohibition against employer contributions (including elective deferrals) to an ESOP in receipt of a transfer from a terminated defined benefit plan is not intended to prohibit contributions to an ESOP to the extent that the amount of the suspense account required to be allocated for a year, when combined with additional contributions, does not exceed the limits under section 415.

The provision generally applies to reversions received after December 31, 1985 but does not apply to a reversion received after December 31, 1985, if the termination date of the plan is before January 1, 1986. Under the agreement, the special provision for transfers to an ESOP applies with respect to reversions occurring after December 31, 1985, and before January 1, 1989, and reversions received pursuant to terminations occurring after December 31, 1985, and before January 1, 1989. Under the conference agreement, the date of termination of a plan is the dates of termination under section 411(d)(3).

[Code Sec. 4980B]

[¶ 13,648W.07]

Committee Reports on P.L. 104-188 (Small Business Job Protection Act)

Other Tax Technical Corrections

[House Committee Report]

Health care continuation rules (ERISA)

The bill amends the Code (sec. 4980B), title I of the Employee Retirement Income Security Act (sec. 602), and the Public Health Service Act (sec. 2202(2)(A)) to limit the continuation coverage in such cases to no more than 36 months.

Effective Date

The provision is effective for plan years beginning after December 31, 1989.

[Conference Committee Report]

Senate Amendment

The Senate amendment is the same as the House bill.

Conference Agreement

The conference agreement follows the House bill and the Senate amendment * * *.

[¶ 13,648W.08]

Committee Reports on P.L. 104-191 (Health Insurance Portability and Accountability Act)

Long-Term Care Services and Contracts

* * *

[Conference Committee Report]

* * *

Health care continuation rules.—The health care continuation rules do not apply to coverage under a plan, substantially all of the coverage under which is for qualified long-term care services.

[¶ 13,648W.09]

Committee Reports on P.L. 103-66 (Omnibus Budget Reconciliation Act of 1993)

Excise tax on vaccines

[House Committee Report]

Childhood immunization program trust fund.—

* * *

Maintenance-of-effort requirement in childhood immunization program.—The bill makes the failure of health plans that provide coverage for the cost of pediatric vaccines as of May 1, 1993, to continue to provide that coverage subject to the excise tax penalty (under sec. 4980B(f)) applicable to plans that fail to provide COBRA continuation coverage.

Effective Date

The extension of coverage under the National Vaccine Injury Compensation Program is effective for vaccines administered on or after October 1, 1992. The extension of the vaccine excise taxes is effective on the date of enactment, with a floor stocks tax imposed on vaccines purchased after December 31, 1992, that are being held for sale or use on the date of enactment.

The maintenance-of-effort requirement applies to plan years beginning after the date of enactment.

[Conference Committee Report]

Senate Amendment

Maintenance-of-effort requirement for pediatric vaccine health care coverage.—No tax provision.

Conference Agreement

Maintenance-of-effort requirement for pediatric vaccine health care coverage.—The conference agreement follows the House bill.

[¶ 13,648W.095]

Committee Reports on P.L. 101-239 (Omnibus Budget Reconciliation Act of 1989)

[Conference Committee Report]

The conference agreement follows the House bill with the following modifications:

* * *

(2) *Continuation health care coverage rules.*—The conference agreement also makes modifications to the continuation coverage rules in the case of individuals who are entitled to Medicare coverage. The conferees intend that if a covered employee has a qualifying event that results in 18 months of continuation coverage and the covered employee becomes entitled to Medicare coverage before the expiration of the 18 months, a qualified beneficiary (other than the covered employee) who is at that time covered under the group health plan is entitled to continuation coverage for a total of 36 months from the date of the original qualifying event. Thus, this rule is the same as if, for example, a reduction in hours were followed by the death of the employee. Failure to comply with this rule is not a good faith interpretation of the continuation coverage rules.

The conference agreement adopts the provision in the Ways and Means Committee bill regarding termination of continuation coverage in the case of preexisting conditions, with a modification to the effective date.

[House Committee Report]

(a) In general.—Amends section 4980(B)(f) of the Internal Revenue Code (providing for continuation coverage requirements of group health plans). Provides that in the case of a qualified beneficiary who is determined under title II (OASDI) or XVI (SSI) of the Social Security Act to have been disabled at the time of the qualifying event of termination of employment or reduction in hours of employment, the beneficiary is entitled to 29 (as opposed to 18) months of continuation coverage, but only if the qualified beneficiary has provided notice of such determination before the end of the 18 months. Provides that the extended continuation of coverage can be terminated in the month that begins more than 30 days after the date of the final determination under title II or title XVI of the Social Security Act that the qualified beneficiary is no longer disabled.

(b) Increased premium permitted.—Amends the law to allow employers to charge 150 percent of the applicable premium for the eleven additional months of coverage provided to disabled beneficiaries provided by this section.

(c) Notices required.—Amends the notice requirements of Title X of COBRA to require that each qualified beneficiary who is determined under title II or title XVI of the Social Security Act to have been disabled at the time of a qualifying event (termination of employment or reduction in hours of employment) is responsible for notifying the plan administrator of such determination within 60 days after the date of the determination and for notifying the plan administrator

within 30 days of the date of any final determination that the qualified beneficiary is no longer disabled.

Effective date

Effective for plan years beginning on or after the date of enactment, regardless of whether the qualifying event occurred before, on, or after such date.

[¶ 13,648W.10]

Committee Report on P.L. 100-647 (Technical and Miscellaneous Revenue Act of 1988)

[Conference Committee Report]

* * *

House Bill

In general. The House bill replaces the present-law sanctions for failures to satisfy the health care continuation rules with an excise tax.

Amount of excise tax. The amount of the excise tax is $100 per day during the noncompliance period with respect to a failure to satisfy the health care continuation rules. The tax applies separately with respect to each qualified beneficiary for whom a failure occurs.

Noncompliance period. The noncompliance period generally begins on the date a failure first occurs and ends on the earlier of (1) the date the failure is corrected, or (2) the date that is one year after the last date on which the employer could have been required to provide continuation coverage to the qualified beneficiary (without regard to payment of premiums). Subject to special rules described below, the noncompliance period does not start on the date the failure first occurred if it can be established that none of the persons who could be liable for the tax knew, or should have known, that the failure existed. In such a case, the noncompliance period does not begin until any of such persons knew or should have known of the failure. (This rule is referred to below as the inadvertent failure rule.)

Grace period. The excise tax generally does not apply to any failure if such failure was due to reasonable cause and not to willful neglect and the failure is corrected within the first 30 days of the noncompliance period.

Audit rule. A special audit rule overrides the inadvertent-failure and grace-period rules. Under the audit rule, if a failure with respect to a qualified beneficiary is not corrected by the date a notice of examination of income tax liability is sent to the employer and the failure occurred or continued during the period under examination, the excise tax is not to be less than the lesser of (1) $2,500, or (2) the excise tax determined without regard to the inadvertent-failure and grace-period rules. If failures for any year are more than de minimis with respect to the employer (or multiemployer plan) and any other person liable with respect to the failure.

Correction. A failure to satisfy the continuation coverage rules is considered corrected if (1) the rules are retroactively satisfied to the extent possible, and (2) the qualified beneficiary (or his or her estate) is placed in a financial position that is as good as it would have been had the failure not occurred.

Maximum liability. In the case of failures with respect to plans other than multiemployer plans, the maximum excise tax for failures during an employer's taxable year is the lesser of (1) 10 percent of the total amount paid or incurred by the employer during the preceding taxable year for the employer's group health plans, or (2) $500,000. In the case of failures with respect to a multiemployer plan, the maximum excise tax for failures during the taxable year of the trust that is part of the plan is the lesser of (1) 10 percent of the total amount paid or incurred by the trust to provide medical care, or (2) $500,000. These caps on the amount of the excise tax do not apply if the failure is due to willful neglect.

Liable persons. In the case of a failure with respect to coverage provided by a plan other than a multiemployer plan, the employer is liable for the excise tax. In addition, any other person is liable for the tax if the person (1) is responsible for administering or providing benefits under the plan pursuant to a legally enforceable written agreement, and (2) failed to perform one or more of such responsibilities and thereby caused (in whole or in part) the failure. In addition, another person may be liable for the excise tax if the person fails to comply with a written request of the employer (or qualified beneficiary or plan administrator) to make available to qualified beneficiaries the same benefits that the person provides to similarly situated active employees. In the case of a multiemployer plan, the rules described above apply, except that "multiemployer plan" is substituted for "employer."

Waiver. In the case of a failure to comply with the continuation coverage rules that is due to reasonable cause and not to willful neglect, the Secretary may waive all or a part of the excise tax to the extent that the payment of the tax would be unduly burdensome relative to the failure involved.

Effective Date

The House bill provisions are effective for taxable years beginning after December 31, 1988.

* * *

Conference Agreement

The conference agreement follows the House bill, with the following exceptions.

Amount of excise tax. The conference agreement provides that the amount of the excise tax is $100 per day during the noncompliance period with respect to each qualified beneficiary. However, under the conference agreement, if a failure occurs with respect to more than one qualified beneficiary who are members of the same family, then the amount of the excise tax is no more than $200 per day for the failure with respect to such qualified beneficiaries in the same family.

Noncompliance period. Under the conference agreement, the noncompliance period ends on the earlier of (1) the date the failure is corrected, or (2) the date that is 6 months after the last date on which the employer could have been required to provide continuation coverage to the qualified beneficiary (without regard to payment of premiums).

Maximum liability. The conference agreement follows the House bill and the Senate amendment, except that the maximum excise tax for failures (not due to willful neglect) during a taxable year by a person other than an employer (or multiemployer plan in case of coverage under such a plan) is limited to $2 million.

Liable persons. The conference agreement follows the House bill with respect to the determination of who is liable for the excise tax, with the following clarifications. First, the conference agreement clarifies that the liability for the excise tax applies to a person if the person fails to "make continuation coverage available to" a qualified beneficiary, rather than if the person fails to "provide continuation coverage to" the qualified beneficiary.

As under the House bill, the conferees intend that a failure to make continuation coverage available does not automatically make a person liable for all other continuation coverage violations (such as a failure to provide written notice) without regard to the written agreement requirement. In other words, such a person is liable for a failure other than the failure to make continuation coverage available only pursuant to the written agreement provision. Also, as under the House bill, a person is not liable for the excise tax to the extent that an employer's act or failure to act made the person unable to comply with its responsibilities under the health care continuation rules.

The conference agreement clarifies the rule under which a person other than the employer is liable for the excise tax if such person fails to comply with a written request of a qualified beneficiary to make continuation coverage available to such qualified beneficiary. The conference agreement conforms the rule to the situations in which, under present law, the qualified beneficiary would provide notice to such person. Thus, under the conference agreement, liability may be triggered by a written request from a qualified beneficiary to a person other than the employer to provide continuation coverage only if such person is the plan administrator and the individual becomes a qualified beneficiary by reason of (1) the divorce or legal separation of the covered employee from the employee's spouse or (2) ceasing to be a dependent child under the generally applicable requirements of the plan. In all other cases, liability of a person other than the employer may be triggered only by a written request made by the employer or plan administrator.

Under the conference agreement, a person other than an employer (or multiemployer plan in the case of coverage under such a plan) is not liable for the excise tax for failure to make continuation coverage available pursuant to a written request until the date that is 45 days following the date that notice was provided to such person. The conferees anticipate that this rule will create an incentive for employers to provide adequate advance notice to a person (such as an insurance company) of the person's obligation to make continuation coverage available to qualified beneficiaries if such person had not previously been providing such coverage. For example, if the coverage was provided by another insurance carrier, or the employer self insured the coverage. The conferees do not intend this rule to relieve insurers, the employer, or other parties of their responsibility to provide continuation coverage during this 45-day period if they are so responsible. The provision is intended only to relieve third parties of liability for the excise tax for failure to make continuation coverage available in cases in which the employer fails to notify the third party of its responsibility to make continuation coverage available, but does not override a written agreement between the employer and the third party that the third party is to provide continuation coverage.

Waiver. The conference agreement follows the Senate amendment. As under the Senate amendment, the conferees intend that the determination of whether imposition of the excise tax would be excessive is to be made based on the seriousness of the failure and not on a particular taxpayer's ability to pay the tax.

[Code Sec. 4980F]

[¶ 13,648W-75.045]

Committee Report on P.L. 109-280 (Pension Protection Act of 2006)

[Joint Committee on Taxation Report]

[Access to multiemployer pension plan information]

Under the provision, a plan administrator of a multiemployer plan must, within 30 days of a written request, provide a plan participant or beneficiary, employee organization or employer that has an obligation to contribute to the plan with a copy of: (1) any periodic actuarial report (including any sensitivity testing) for any plan year that has been in the plan's possession for at least 30 days; (2) a copy of any quarterly, semi-annual, or annual financial report prepared for the plan by any plan investment manager or advisor or other person who is a plan fiduciary that has been in the plan's possession for at least 30 days; and (3) a copy of any application for an amortization extension filed with the Secretary of the Treasury. Any actuarial report or financial report provided to a participant, beneficiary, or employer must not include any individually identifiable information regarding any participant, beneficiary, employee, fiduciary, or contributing employer, or reveal any proprietary information regarding the plan, any contributing employer, or any entity providing services to the plan. Regulations relating to the requirement to provide actuarial or financial reports on request must be issued within one year after the date of enactment.

In addition, the plan sponsor or administrator of a multiemployer plan must provide to any employer having an obligation to contribute to the plan, within 180 days of a written request, notice of: (1) the estimated amount that would be the employer's withdrawal liability with respect to the plan if the employer withdrew from the plan on the last day of the year preceding the date of the request; and (2) an explanation of how the estimated liability amount was determined, including the actuarial assumptions and methods used to determine the value of plan liabilities and assets, the data regarding employer contributions, unfunded vested benefits, annual changes in the plan's unfunded vested benefits, and the application of any relevant limitations on the estimated withdrawal liability. Regulations may permit a longer time than 180 days as may be necessary in the case of a plan that determines withdrawal liability using certain methods.

A person is not entitled to receive more than one copy of any actuary or financial report or more than one notice of withdrawal liability during any 12-month period. The plan administrator may make a reasonable charge to cover copying, mailing, and other costs of furnishing copies or notices, subject to a maximum amount that may be prescribed by regulations. Any information required to be provided under the provision may be provided in written, electronic, or other appropriate form to the extent such form is reasonably available to the persons to whom the information is required to be provided.

In the case of a failure to comply with these requirements, the Secretary of Labor may assess a civil penalty of up to $1,000 per day for each failure to provide a notice.

Under the provision, notice of an amendment that provides for a significant reduction in the rate of future benefit accrual must be provided also to each employer that has an obligation to contribute to the plan.

Effective Date

The provision is effective for plan years beginning after December 31, 2007.

[¶ 13,648W-75.05]

Committee Report on P.L. 107-16 (Economic Growth and Tax Relief Reconciliation Act)

[House Committee Report]

Notice of significant reduction in plan benefit accruals

The provision adds to the Internal Revenue Code a requirement that the plan administrator of a defined benefit pension plan or a money purchase pension plan furnish a written notice concerning a plan amendment that provides for a significant reduction in the rate of future benefit accrual, including any elimination or reduction of an early retirement benefit or retirement-type subsidy. The plan administrator is required to provide in this notice, in a manner calculated to be understood by the average plan participant, sufficient information (as defined in Treasury regulations) to allow participants to understand the effect of the amendment.

The notice requirement does not apply to governmental plans or church plans with respect to which an election to have the qualified plan participation, vesting, and funding rules apply has not been made (sec. 410(d)). The provision authorizes the Secretary of the Treasury to provide a simplified notice requirement or an exemption from the notice requirement for plans with less than 100 participants and to allow any notice required under the provision to be provided by using new technologies. The provision also authorizes the Secretary to provide a simplified notice requirement or an exemption from the notice requirement if participants are given the option to choose between benefits under the new plan formula and the old plan formula. In such cases, the provision would have no effect on the fiduciary rules applicable to pension plans that may require appropriate disclosure to participants, even if no disclosure is required under the provision.

The plan administrator is required to provide this notice to each affected participant, each affected alternate payee, and each employee organization representing affected participants. For purposes of the provision, an affected participant or alternate payee is a participant or alternate payee whose rate of future benefit accrual may reasonably be expected to be significantly reduced by the plan amendment.

Except to the extent provided by Treasury regulations, the plan administrator is required to provide the notice within a reasonable time before the effective date of the plan amendment. The provision permits a plan administrator to provide any notice required under the provision to a person designated in writing by the individual to whom it would otherwise be provided.

The provision imposes on a plan administrator that fails to comply with the notice requirement an excise tax equal to $100 per day per omitted participant and alternate payee. No excise tax is imposed during any period during which any person subject to liability for the tax did not know that the failure existed and exercised reasonable diligence to meet the notice requirement. In addition, no excise tax is imposed on any failure if any person subject to liability for the tax exercised reasonable diligence to meet the notice requirement and such person provides the required notice during the 30-day period beginning on the first date such person knew, or exercising reasonable diligence would have known, that the failure existed. Also, if the person subject to liability for the excise tax exercised reasonable diligence to meet the notice requirement, the total excise tax imposed during a taxable year of the employer would not exceed $500,000. Furthermore, in the case of a failure due to reasonable cause and not to willful neglect, the Secretary of the Treasury is authorized to waive the excise tax to the extent that the payment of the tax would be excessive relative to the failure involved.

It is intended under the provision that the Secretary issue the necessary regulations with respect to disclosure within 90 days of enactment. It is also intended that such guidance may be relatively detailed because of the need to provide for alternative disclosures rather than a single disclosure methodology that may not fit all situations, and the need to consider the complex actuarial calculations and assumptions involved in providing necessary disclosures.

In addition, the provision directs the Secretary of the Treasury to prepare a report on the effects of conversions of traditional defined benefit plans to cash balance or hybrid formula plans. Such study is to examine the effect of such conversions on longer service participants, including the incidence and effects of "wear away" provisions under which participants earn no additional benefits for a period of time after the conversion. The Secretary is directed to submit such report, together with recommendations thereon, to the Committee on Ways and Means and the Committee on Education and the Workforce of the House of Representatives and the Committee on Finance and the Committee on Health, Education, Labor, and Pensions of the Senate as soon as practicable, but not later than 60 days after the date of enactment.

Effective Date

The provision is effective for plan amendments taking effect on or after the date of enactment. The period for providing any notice required under the provision would not end before the last day of the 3-month period following the date of enactment. Prior to the issuance of Treasury regulations, a plan is treated as meeting the requirements of the provision if the plan makes a good faith effort to comply with such requirements. The notice requirement under the provision does not apply to any plan amendment taking effect on or after the date of enactment if, before April 25, 2001, notice is provided to participants and beneficiaries adversely affected by the plan amendment (or their representatives) that is reasonably expected to notify them of the nature and effective date of the plan amendment.

[Conference Committee Report]

The conference agreement follows the House bill, with the following modifications. The conference agreement also modifies the present-law notice requirement contained in section 204(h) of Title I of ERISA to provide that an applicable pension plan may not be amended to provide for a significant reduction in the rate of future benefit accrual in the event of an egregious failure by the plan administrator to comply with a notice requirement similar to the notice requirement that the conference agreement adds to the Internal Revenue Code. In addition, the conference agreement expands the current ERISA notice requirement regarding significant reductions in normal retirement benefit accrual rates to early retirement benefits and retirement-type subsidies.

[Code Sec. 4980G]

[¶ 13,648W-92.085]

Committee Report on P.L. 109-432 (Tax Relief and Health Care Act of 2006)

For the Committee Report on P.L. 109-432 on Health Savings Accounts, see ¶ 11,335.085.

[Code Sec. 6039I]

[¶ 13,678.50]

Committee Report on P.L. 109-280 (Pension Protection Act of 2006)

[Joint Committee on Taxation Report]

The provision provides generally that, in the case of an employer-owned life insurance contract, the amount excluded from the applicable policyholder's income as a death benefit cannot exceed the premiums and other amounts paid by such applicable policyholder for the contract. The excess death benefit is included in income.

Exceptions to this income inclusion rule are provided. In the case of an employer-owned life insurance contract with respect to which the notice and consent requirements of the provision are met, the income inclusion rule does not apply to an amount received by reason of the death of an insured individual who, with respect to the applicable policyholder, was an employee at any time during the 12-month period before the insured's death, or who, at the time the contract was issued, was a director or highly compensated employee or highly compensated individual. For this purpose, such a person is one who is either: (1) a highly compensated employee as defined under the rules relating to qualified retirement plans, determined without regard to the election regarding the top-paid 20 percent of employees; or (2) a highly compensated individual as defined under the rules relating to self-insured medical reimbursement plans, determined by substituting the highest-paid 35 percent of employees for the highest-paid 25 percent of employees.[233]

In the case of an employer-owned life insurance contract with respect to which the notice and consent requirements of the provision are met, the income inclusion rule does not apply to an amount received by reason of the death of an insured, to the extent the amount is (1) paid to a member of the family[234] of the insured, to an individual who is the designated beneficiary of the insured under the contract (other than an applicable policyholder), to a trust established for the benefit of any such member of the family or designated beneficiary, or to the estate of the insured; or (2) used to purchase an equity (or partnership capital or profits) interest in the applicable policyholder from such a family member, beneficiary, trust or estate. It is intended that such amounts be so paid or used by the due date of the tax return for the taxable year of the applicable policyholder in which they are received as a death benefit under the insurance contract, so that the payment of the amount to such a person or persons, or the use of the amount to make such a purchase, is known in the taxable year for which the exception from the income inclusion rule is claimed.

An employer-owned life insurance contract is defined for purposes of the provision as a life insurance contract which (1) is owned by a person engaged in a trade or business and under which such person (or a related person) is directly or indirectly a beneficiary, and (2) covers the life of an individual who is an employee with respect to the trade or business of the applicable policyholder on the date the contract is issued.

An applicable policyholder means, with respect to an employer-owned life insurance contract, the person (including related persons) that owns the contract, if the person is engaged in a trade or business, and if the person (or a related person) is directly or indirectly a beneficiary under the contract.

For purposes of the provision, a related person includes any person that bears a relationship specified in section 267(b) or 707(b)(1)[235] or is engaged in trades or businesses that are under common control (within the meaning of section 52(a) or (b)).

The notice and consent requirements of the provision are met if, before the issuance of the contract, (1) the employee is notified in writing that the applicable policyholder intends to insure the employee's life, and is notified of the maximum face amount at issue of the life insurance contract that the employer might take out on the life of the employee, (2) the employee provides written consent to being insured under the contract and that such coverage may continue after the insured terminates employment, and (3) the employee is informed in writing that an applicable policyholder will be a beneficiary of any proceeds payable on the death of the employee.

For purposes of the provision, an employee includes an officer, a director, and a highly compensated employee; an insured means, with respect to an employer-owned life insurance contract, an individual covered by the contract who is a U.S. citizen or resident. In the case of a contract covering the joint lives of two individuals, references to an insured include both of the individuals.

The provision requires annual reporting and recordkeeping by applicable policyholders that own one or more employer-owned life insurance contracts. The information to be reported is (1) the number of employees of the applicable policyholder at the end of the year, (2) the number of employees insured under employer-owned life insurance contracts at the end of the year, (3) the total amount of insurance in force at the end of the year under such contracts, (4) the name, address, and taxpayer identification number of the applicable policyholder and the type of business in which it is engaged, and (5) a statement that the applicable policyholder has a valid consent (in accordance with the consent requirements under the provision) for each insured employee and, if all such consents were not obtained, the total number of insured employees for whom such consent was not obtained. The applicable policyholder is required to keep records necessary to determine whether the requirements of the reporting rule and the income inclusion rule of new section 101(j) are met.

Effective Date

The provision generally applies to contracts issued after the date of enactment, except for contracts issued after such date pursuant to an exchange described in section 1035 of the Code. In addition, certain material increases in the death benefit or other material changes will generally cause a contract to be treated as a new contract, with an exception for existing lives under a master contract. Increases in the death benefit that occur as a result of the operation of section 7702 of the Code or the terms of the existing contract, provided that the insurer's consent to the increase is not required, will not cause a contract to be treated as a new contract. In addition, certain changes to a contract will not be considered material changes so as to cause a contract to be treated as a new contract. These changes include administrative changes, changes from general to separate account, or changes as a result of the exercise of an option or right granted under the contract as originally issued.

Examples of situations in which death benefit increases would not cause a contract to be treated as a new contract include the following:

1. Section 7702 provides that life insurance contracts need to either meet the cash value accumulation test of section 7702(b) or the guideline premium requirements of section 7702(c) and the cash value corridor of section 7702(d). Under the corridor test, the amount of the death benefit may not be less than the applicable percentage of the cash surrender value. Contracts may be written to comply with the corridor requirement by providing for automatic increases in the death benefit based on the cash surrender value. Death benefit increases required by the corridor test or the cash value accumulation test do not require the insurer's consent at the time of increase and occur in order to keep the contact in compliance with section 7702.

2. Death benefits may also increase due to normal operation of the contract. For example, for some contracts, policyholder dividends paid under the contract may be applied to purchase paid-up additions, which increase the death benefits. The insurer's consent is not required for these death benefit increases.

3. For variable contacts and universal life contracts, the death benefit may increase as a result of market performance or the contract design. For example, some contracts provide that the death benefit will equal the cash value plus a specified amount at risk. With these contracts, the amount of the death benefit at any time will vary depending on changes in the cash value of the contract. The insurance company's consent is not required for these death benefit increases.

[Code Sec. 6047]

[¶ 13,690.05]

Committee Reports on P.L. 104-188 (Small Business Job Protection Act)

For Committee Reports on P.L. 104-188, see ¶ 12,050.056.

[¶ 13,690.08]

Committee Reports on P.L. 101-239 (Omnibus Budget Reconciliation Act of 1989)

For Committee Reports on P.L. 101-239, relating to interest exclusion for ESOP loans, see ¶ 12,130.063.

[¶ 13,690.09]

Committee Reports on P.L. 97-248 (Tax Equity and Fiscal Responsibility Act of 1982)

[Senate Amendment]

The Senate amendment provides for reporting of necesary information by employers and plan administrators of plans from which designated distributions can be made and issuers of insurance or annuity contracts from which designated distributions can be made. The form and manner of reporting will be determined under forms or regulations prescribed by the Secretary of the Treasury. These reports are to be made to the Secretary, to the participants and beneficiaries, and to such other persons as the Secretary may prescribe. As under present law, penalties apply to any person failing to file any required report.

The provision is effective for calendar years beginning after December 31, 1982.

[Conference Agreement]

The conference agreement generally follows the Senate amendment. In addition, the conference agreement makes it clear that an exchange of insurance contracts under which any designated distribution may be made (including a section 1035 tax-free exchange) is intended to be a reportable event even though no designated distribution occurs in the particular transaction. Thus, to insure proper reporting of any designated distributions under the new contract, it is anticipated that, under regulations to be issued by the Secretary, the issuer of the contract to be exchanged will be required to provide information to the policyholder, the issuer of the new contract, and such other persons as the Secretary may require.—Conference Committee Report.

---

[233] As under present law, certain employees are disregarded in making the determinations regarding the top-paid groups.

[234] For this purpose, a member of the family is defined in section 267(c)(4) to include only the individual's brothers and sisters (whether by the whole or half blood), spouse, ancestors, and lineal descendants.

[235] The relationships include specified relationships among family members, shareholders and corporations, corporations that are members of a controlled group, trust grantors and fiduciaries, tax-exempt organizations and persons that control such organizations, commonly controlled S corporations, partnerships and C corporations, estates and beneficiaries, commonly controlled partnerships, and partners and partnerships. Detailed rules apply to determine the specific relationships.

[Code Sec. 6050U]

[¶ 13,706.50]

Committee Report on P.L. 109-280 (Pension Protection Act of 2006)

[Joint Committee on Taxation Report]

The provision provides tax rules for long-term care insurance that is provided by a rider on or as part of an annuity contract, and modifies the tax rules for long-term care insurance coverage provided by a rider on or as part of a life insurance contract.

Under the provision, any charge against the cash value of an annuity contract or the cash surrender value of a life insurance contract made as payment for coverage under a qualified long-term care insurance contract that is part of or a rider on the annuity or life insurance contract is not includable in income. The investment in the contract is reduced (but not below zero) by the charge.

The provision expands the rules for tax-free exchanges of certain insurance contracts. The provision provides that no gain or loss is recognized on the exchange of a life insurance contract, an endowment contract, an annuity contract, or a qualified long-term care insurance contract for a qualified long-term care insurance contract. The provision provides that a contract does not fail to be treated as an annuity contract, or as a life insurance contract, solely because a qualified long-term care insurance contract is a part of or a rider on such contract, for purposes of the rules for tax-free exchanges of certain insurance contracts.

The provision provides that, except as otherwise provided in regulations, for Federal tax purposes, in the case of a long-term care insurance contract (whether or not qualified) provided by a rider on or as part of a life insurance contract or an annuity contract, the portion of the contract providing long-term care insurance coverage is treated as a separate contract. The term "portion" means only the terms and benefits under a life insurance contract or annuity contract that are in addition to the terms and benefits under the contract without regard to long-term care coverage. As a result, if the applicable requirements are met by the long-term care portion of the contract, amounts received under the contract as provided by the rider are treated in the same manner as long-term care insurance benefits, whether or not the payment of such amounts causes a reduction in the life insurance contract's death benefit or cash surrender value or in the annuity contract's cash value.

No deduction as a medical expense is allowed for any payment made for coverage under a qualified long-term care insurance contract if the payment is made as a charge against the cash value of an annuity contract or the cash surrender value of a life insurance contract.

The provision provides that, for taxable years beginning after December 31, 2009, the guideline premium limitation is not directly increased by charges against a life insurance contract's cash surrender value for coverage under the qualified long-term care insurance portion of the contract. Rather, because such charges are not included in the holder's income by reason of new section 72(e)(11),[196] the charges reduce premiums paid under section 7702(f)(1), for purposes of the guideline premium limitation of section 7702. The amount by which premiums paid (under 7702(f)(1)) are reduced under this rule is intended to be the sum of any charges (but not premium payments) against the life insurance contract's cash surrender value (within the meaning of section 7702(f)(2)(a)) for long-term care coverage made to that date under the contract. For taxable years beginning before January 1, 2010, the present-law rule of section 7702B(e)(2) before amendment by the bill (the so-called "pay-as-you-go" rule) increases the guideline premium limitation by this same amount, reduced by charges the imposition of which reduces the premiums paid under the contract. Thus, the provision of the bill recreates the result of the "pay-as-you-go" rule (which is repealed by the provision) as a reduction in premiums paid rather than as an increase in the guideline premium limitation.

The provision provides that certain retirement-related arrangements are not treated as annuity contracts, for purposes of the provision.

The provision requires information reporting by any person who makes a charge against the cash value of an annuity contract, or the cash surrender value of a life insurance contract, that is excludible from gross income under the provision. The information required to be reported includes the amount of the aggregate of such charges against each such contract for the calendar year, the amount of the reduction in the investment in the contract by reason of the charges, and the name, address, and taxpayer identification number of the holder of the contract. A statement is required to be furnished to each individual identified in the information report. Penalties apply for failure to file the information report or furnish the statement required under the provision.

The provision modifies the application of the rules relating to capitalization of policy acquisition expenses of insurance companies. In the case of an annuity or life insurance contract that includes a qualified long-term care insurance contract as a part of or rider on the annuity or life insurance contract, the specified policy acquisition expenses that must be capitalized is determined using 7.7 percent of the net premiums for the taxable year on such contracts.

The provision clarifies that, effective as if included in the Health Insurance Portability and Accountability Act of 1996 (when section 7702B was enacted), except as otherwise provided in regulations, for Federal tax purposes (not just for purposes of section 7702B), in the case of a long-term care insurance contract (whether or not qualified) provided by a rider on or as part of a life insurance contract, the portion of the contract providing long-term care insurance coverage is treated as a separate contract.

Effective Date

The provisions are effective generally for contracts issued after December 31, 1996, but only with respect to taxable years beginning after December 31, 2009. The provisions relating to tax-free exchanges apply with respect to exchanges occurring after December 31, 2009. The provision relating to information reporting applies to charges made after December 31, 2009. The provision relating to policy acquisition expenses applies to specified policy acquisition expenses determined for taxable years beginning after December 31, 2009. The technical amendment relating to long-term care insurance coverage under section 7702B(e) is effective as if included with the underlying provisions of the Health Insurance Portability and Accountability Act of 1996.

[Code Sec. 6057]

[¶ 13,730.095]

Committee Report on P.L. 98-397 (Retirement Equity Act of 1984)

Under the bill, any statement provided to a plan participant of total accrued benefits and nonforfeitable accrued benefits, or any statement provided to a separated plan participant who has a vested deferred benefit, must include a notice to the participant that certain benefits may be forfeited if the participant dies before a particular date. The notice that certain benefits may be forfeited if a participant dies before a particular date need not include the amount of the benefits that are forfeitable.

[¶ 13,730.10]

Committee Report on P.L. 93-406 (Employee Retirement Income Security Act of 1974)

[Conference Committee Explanation]

The substitute generally follows the House bill with respect to registration with Social Security. However, the House bill includes requirements for registration under both the labor and tax provisions. Under the substitute, the registration procedure is included only in the tax provisions, but this procedure applies to all plans to which the vesting standards of the labor provisions apply. In addition, under the substitute the labor provisions as well as the tax provisions require the plan administrator to furnish each person an individual statement giving him the information reported to the government; this is included so the individual may enforce his rights to receive this statement by civil action in the courts.

Under the substitute, each plan which is covered by the vesting requirements of the labor provisions is to file with the Internal Revenue Service an annual statement regarding individuals who have terminated employment in the year in question and who have a right to a deferred vested benefit in the plan. Also, the plan administrator is to furnish each person an individual statement giving him the same information which is reported to the Government.

The Social Security Administration is to maintain records of the retirement plans in which individuals have vested benefits, and is to provide this information to participants and beneficiaries on their request and also on their application for Social Security benefits.

The provisions governing registration with Social Security are to apply to a multiemployer plan to the extent provided in regulations.

The provisions requiring registration with Social Security are to apply to plan years beginning after December 31, 1975, except that reports need not be made by Social Security for 3 years after that date.

[Code Sec. 6058]

[¶ 13,740.10]

Committee Report on P.L. 95-600 (Revenue Act of 1978)

House Committee Report on 95-1739.—Under the committee bill, an individual would not have to file a tax return for an IRA for any taxable year (1) for which no penalty tax is imposed with respect to the IRA, and (2) for which no activity is engaged in with respect to the IRA other than making deductible contributions to and permissible distributions from the IRA. (Under the committee bill, separate reporting could still be required with respect to rollover contributions.) Information with respect to the deductible contribution or permissible distribution would be included on the regular Form 1040. (Presently this information is reported both on the Form 1040 and on a separate form.)

The amendments made by this section will apply to taxable years beginning after December 31, 1977.

---

[196] Because such charges are not included in the holder's income under new section 72(e)(11), the effect would be to increase the guideline premium limitation under present-law section 7702B(e)(2)(A) by the amount of the charges and simultaneously to reduce it by the same charges under section 7702B(e)(2)(B). Such charges that are not included in income serve to reduce premiums paid under section 7702(f)(1), and therefore would cancel each other out under 7702B(e)(2)(A) and (B).

[Code Sec. 6059]

[¶ 13,750.10]

Committee Report on P.L. 93-406 (Employee Retirement Income Security Act of 1974)

[Conference Committee Explanation]

—Every plan subject to the funding requirements of title I must retain an enrolled actuary who is to prepare an actuarial statement on an annual basis. This statement is to show the present value of all plan liabilities for nonforfeitable pension benefits allocated by the termination priority categories. The actuary is to supply a statement to be filed with the annual report as to his opinion as to whether the actuarial statements of the plan are reasonably related to the experience of the plan and to the reasonable expectations of the plan. The actuary is to use assumptions and techniques as are necessary to form an opinion as to whether the contents of the matters upon which the reports are in the aggregate reasonable related to the experience of the plan and to reasonable expectations, and represent his best estimate of anticipated experience under plan. The actuarial statement is not required for plans which need not file annual reports, and may be waived by the Secretary of Labor for plans for which simplified annual reports are allowed.

[¶ 13,750A.10]

Committee Report on P.L. 93-406 (Employee Retirement Income Security Act of 1974)

[Conference Committee Explanation]

Reports—Both the House bill and the Senate amendment provide that actuarial reports are to be made separately to the Department of Labor and the Internal Revenue Sevice. The conference substitute largely follows the provisions of the House bill in the technical aspects. In keeping with the general principle of eliminating, to the maximum extent feasible, duplication of effort in reporting, the conference substitute also requires the Secretaries of Labor and Treasury to take such steps as may be necessary to assure coordination, to the maximum extent feasible, between the actuarial reports they file with the Secretary of Labor and the Internal Revenue Service.

[Code Sec. 6109]

[¶ 13,780.09]

Committee Reports on P.L. 94-455 (Tax Reform Act of 1976)

Present law

Under present law, a person required to file an income tax return must include an identifying number in his return (sec. 6109). In general, individuals use their social security numbers for this purpose (regs. sec. 301.6109-1).

The Social Security Act currently provides criminal penalties for the willful, knowing and deceitful use of a social security number for purposes relating to obtaining, or increasing the amount of, benefits under Social Security and certain other programs (sec. 208(g) of the Social Security Act).

Under present law, it is unlawful for any Federal, State or local government agency to deny to any individual any right, benefit, or privilege provided by law because of such individuals's refusal to disclose his social security account number, except where disclosure is required by Federal statute or is required by a Federal, State or local agency under statute or regulation adopted prior to January 1, 1975.[1]

Reasons for change

Section 6104 of the Code requires taxpayers to use identifying numbers as prescribed by regulations. Although the social security number has in fact been used as the identifying number since that section was enacted in 1961, there is no provision in the Code requiring or specifically authorizing use of the social security number as the identifying number on tax returns. The Secretary of the Treasury has stated that the ability of the IRS to use social security numbers as identifying numbers for tax purposes is essential to Federal tax administration. The committee believes that this provision is necessary to eliminate any question as to the authority of the Secretary to use these numbers.

While the Social Security Act currently provides criminal penalties for the wrongful use of a social security number for the purpose of obtaining or increasing certain benefit payments, including social security benefits, there is no provision in the Code or in the Social Security Act relating to the use of a social security number for purposes unrelated to benefit payments. The committee believes that social security numbers should not be wrongfully used for any purpose.

The Privacy Act of 1974 provides that Federal, State and local agencies may not deny any individual any rights, benefit or privilege provided by law because such individual refuses to disclose his social security number. An exemption is provided for disclosures required by Federal statute or by a statute or regulation adopted before January 1, 1975, in regard to a Federal, State or local agency operating a system of records before that date.

The committee has been told that State and local governments consider the use of social security numbers to be needed as a means of positively identifying taxpayers and as a means of comparing information on State income tax returns with Federal tax returns. The adoption of separate State systems of identifying numbers would be costly, duplicative and confusing to taxpayers. The committee believes that State and local governments should have the authority to use social security numbers for identification purposes when they consider it necessary for administrative reasons.

Explanation of provision

The committee amendment amends section 6109 to require that, except as otherwise specified under regulations, an individual shall use his social security number as his identifying number for tax purposes.

The committee amendment also amends section 208(g) of the Social Security Act to make the willful, knowing and deceitful use of a social security number a misdemeanor for all purposes, rather than only for purposes related to benefit payments.

The committee amendment amends section 205(c)(7) of the Social Security Act to establish as the policy of the United States that any State or political subdivision thereof may use social security numbers for the purpose of establishing the identification of individuals affected by any law or program within its jurisdiction. The State or local government may, in addition, require any such individual to furnish his social security number (or numbers; if he has more than one such number) to the State (or its political subdivision). This amendment further provides that, to the extent that any existing provision of Federal law is inconsistent with the policy set forth above, such provision shall be null, void and of no effect.

Effective date

The provisions of this section are effective on the date of enactment.

Revenue effect

This provision has no effect on Federal revenues.—**Senate Committee Report.**

[Code Sec. 6652]

[¶ 13,800.06]

Committee Report on P.L. 109-280 (Pension Protection Act of 2006)

For the Committee Report on P.L. 109-280 on tax-free distributions from individual retirement plans for charitable purposes, see ¶ 12,050.031.

[¶ 13,800.07]

Committee Reports on P.L.104-188 (Small Business Job Protection Act)

For the Committee Reports P.L. 104-188, see ¶ 12,050.056.

[¶ 13,800.08]

Committee Report on P.L. 98-397 (Retirement Equity Act of 1984)

Under the bill, when the administrator of a qualified plan makes a qualifying rollover distribution, the administrator is to provide notice to the recipient that (1) the distribution will not be taxed currently to the extent transferred to another qualified pension plan or an IRA, and (2) the transfer must be made within 60 days of receipt in order to qualify for this tax-free rollover treatment. In the case of a series of distributions that may constitute a lump sum distribution, the committee intends that this notice will explain that the 60-day period does not begin to run until the last distribution is made. In addition, this notice is to provide a written explanation of the 10-year income averaging and capital gains provisions if applicable.

The committee intends that the Secretary of the Treasury will provide an officially approved notice that plan administrators may use to satisfy this notice requirement.

The committee recognizes that, under certain circumstances, it may be difficult for a plan administrator to determine whether a particular distribution is a qualifying rollover distribution. Thus, your committee intends that a plan administrator satisfies the notice requirement if notice is provided with every payment from or under the plan so long as the notice, in addition to satisfying the other requirements, includes a statement describing how a recipient may determine whether the particular distribution is a qualifying rollover distribution.

Failure of the plan administrator to give the required notice of rollover treatment results in imposition of a $10 penalty for each failure up to $5,000 for each calendar year. This penalty does not apply if the failure is shown to be due to reasonable cause and not to willful neglect.

[1] Section 7(a) of the Privacy Act of 1974, P.L. 93-579.

[¶ 13,800.085]

Committee Reports on P.L. 97-248 (Tax Equity and Fiscal Responsibility Act of 1982)

[Senate Amendment]

The category of information returns subject to the general penalty for failure to timely file information returns is expanded to include broker returns and direct seller returns. The bill also increases the penalty for failure to file most information returns to $50 per failure, not to exceed $50,000 in any calendar year. When the failure to file information returns is due to intentional disregard of the filing requirements, the penalty will not be less than 10 percent of the aggregate amount of the amounts not properly reported (5 percent in the case of returns to be filed by brokers and $100 in the case of direct sellers) and the $50,000 limitation will not apply.

The provision applies to returns the due date of which (without extensions) is after December 31, 1982.

[Conference Agreement]

The conference agreement follows the Senate amendment except that (1) the penalty for failure to file information returns or statements with respect to certain deferred compensation plans (sec. 6058), and certain term, annuity and bond purchase plans (sec. 6047) is increased to $25 per day during which the failure continues, but not more than $15,000, and (2) the penalty for failure to provide information statements to taxpayers (sec. 6678) is increased from $10 per statement to $50 per statement up to $50,000 per calendar year (from $25,000). These amendments are effective for returns and statements, the due date of which (without regard to extensions) is after December 31, 1982.

The conference agreement also makes certain technical and conforming amendments.

[Code Sec. 6693]

[¶ 13,850.09]

Committee Report on P.L. 104-188 (Small Business Job Protection Act)

For the Committee Reports on Small Business Job Protection Act of 1989 (P.L. 104-188), see ¶ 12,050.056.

[¶ 13,850.095]

Committee Report on P.L. 100-647 (Technical and Miscellaneous Revenue Act of 1988)

Nondeductible IRA contributions. Under present law, there is no separate penalty with respect to an individual who fails to file the form prescribed by the Secretary with respect to nondeductible IRA contributions. Accordingly, under the bill, a taxpayer who fails to file the form required by the Secretary is subject to a penalty of $50 for each such failure unless the taxpayer shows that the failure is due to reasonable cause.

In order to take into account taxpayers with fiscal year taxable years, the bill provides that the information that the Secretary may require to be included on the form or return includes the aggregate balance of all IRAs of the individual as of the close of the calendar year in which the taxable year begins (rather than the calendar year with or within which the taxable year ends).

[¶ 13,850.10]

Committee Report on P.L. 96-222 (Technical Corrections Act of 1979)

[Senate Committee Report]

Sec. 101(a)(10)(H)—Reporting requirements on IRAs.

The rules relating to simplified employee pensions provide that if an employer contributes to a simplified employee pension, the employer may be required by Treasury regulations to file simplified reports with the Internal Revenue Service and to furnish reports to employees.

It is not clear that present law provides a penalty for an employer's failure to file or furnish the reports with respect to simplified employee pensions.

The bill provides that a penalty of $10 per report applies to each failure to furnish a report required under the rules for simplified employee pensions, unless the failure is due to reasonable cause. This is the same penalty that is applicable under present law for a trustee's failure to provide certain reports with respect to individual retirement accounts or annuities. The House bill did not include any similar provision.

The amendment applies with respect to failures occurring after the date of enactment of the bill.

[Code Sec. 7476]

[¶ 13,910.09]

Committee Report on P.L. 95-600 (Revenue Act of 1978)

Sec. 701(dd)—Jurisdiction of Tax Court expanded.

[Senate Finance Committee Report (H.R. 6715)]

The legislative history of ERISA and of the Tax Reform Act of 1976 clearly indicate that Congress intended the Tax Court to have jurisdiction over cases involving revocation of prior favorable determination by the IRS. However, in light of the recent *Sheppard & Myers Inc.* case, it appears that this intent should be expressed explicitly in the statute.

The bill makes clear that the declaratory judgment provisions relating to the qualification of retirement plans and relating to the status and classification of charitable organizations are to apply for revocations of any IRS determination in these areas.

Under the bill, as passed by the House and reported by the committee, the provisions are to take effect as if included in the separate declaratory judgment provisions at the time those provisions were added to the Internal Revenue Code.

[Conference Committee Report]

Conference agreement

The conference agreement follows the Senate amendment.

[¶ 13,910.10]

Committee Report on P.L. 93-406 (Employee Retirement Income Security Act of 1974)

[Conference Committee Explanation]

Tax Court declaratory judgment proceedings.—Both the House bill and the Senate amendment provide a procedure for obtaining a declaratory judgment with respect to the tax-qualified status of an employee benefit plan. Under both the House and Senate versions of the bill, jurisdiction to issue a declaratory judgment is given to the United States Tax Court. This remedy is available only if the Internal Revenue Service has issued a determination as to the status of the plan which is adverse to the party petitioning in the Tax Court, or has failed to issue a determination but the petitioner has exhausted his administrative remedies inside the Internal Revenue Service.

The differences between the bill as passed by both the House and the Senate are technical in nature. For example, the Senate amendment provides that the burden of proof is to be on the petitioner (the employer, plan administrator, or employee) as to those grounds set forth in the Internal Revenue Service determination; the burden of proof is to be on the Service as to any other grounds that the Service relies upon in the court proceeding (e.g., if the Service does not issue a determination as to the plan, then the Service is to have the burden of proof as to every ground as to which it relies). On the other hand, the House bill does not make specific provisions for burden of proof.

Under the conference agreement, the House provision is accepted with a number of amendments. The Pension Benefit Guaranty Corporation is permitted to be a petitioner, on the same basis as other petitioners. Employees are permitted to be petitioners if they qualify as interested parties under Treasury regulations and have exhausted their administrative remedies. It is contemplated that only those employees who are entitled to petition the Secretary of Labor under section 3001 of this Act are to be treated as interested parties. It is contemplated that the question as to who bears the burden of proof will be determined by the Tax Court under its existing rule-making authority. Under the existing Tax Court rules the taxpayer has the burden of proof as to matters in the notice of deficiency. As to matters raised by the Service at the time of the Tax Court hearing, the Service has the burden. It is expected that rules similar to these will be adopted by the Tax Court.

Under the House bill, the declaratory judgment provisions are to take effect on January 1, 1978. The bill as passed by the Senate provides that the declaratory judgment provisions are to take effect on January 1, 1975.

Both the House and Senate bills authorize the assignment of the declaratory judgment proceedings provided in this bill to be heard by commissioners of the Tax Court. They also authorize a commissioner to enter a decision of the court in these proceedings. The conference substitute provides for this same procedure, but in doing so the conferees wish to make clear that it is not intended that this be construed as indicating that all of these proceedings should be heard by commissioners and decisions entered by them rather than by the judges of the court. Instead, it is intended to provide more flexibility to the Tax Court in the use of commissioners in these types of cases. It is anticipated, for example, that if the volume of these cases should be large, that the Tax Court will expedite the resolution of these cases by authorizing commissioners to hear and enter decisions in cases where similar issues have already been heard and decided by the judges of the court or in other cases where, in the discretion of the court, it is appropriate for the commissioners to hear and decide cases.

Under the conference agreement, the declaratory judgment provisions are to take effect with respect to petitions filed more than one year after the date of enactment [September 2, 1974].

[Code Sec. 7701]

[¶ 13,920.085]

Committee Report on P.L. 98-369 (Tax Reform Act of 1984)

[House Committee Report]

Explanation of Provision

The bill clarifies present law by providing that, under the Code, in determining whether there is a collective bargaining agreement between employee representatives and one or more employers, an organization is not to be considered an employee representative if more than one-half of its members are employees (including a self-employed individual who is considered to be an employee under the rules for qualified pension plans) who are owners, officers, or executives of the employer.

Effective Date

The provision takes effect on April 1, 1984.

[¶ 13,920.09]

Committee Report on P.L. 95-600 (Revenue Act of 1978)

Sec. 157(k)—The House Committee Report on Sec. 157(k) is at ¶ 13,740.10.

[¶ 13,920.10]

Committee Report on P.L. 93-406 (Employee Retirement Income Security Act of 1974)

[Conference Committee Explanation]

Enrollment of Actuaries.— Standards.— * * *

The conference substitute largely follows the provisions of the House bill. With respect to persons applying for enrollment before January 1, 1976, the substitute provides that the standards and qualifications are to include a requirement for "responsible actuarial experience relating to pension plans," and deletes the requirement for experience in the "administration" of pension plans. This change is intended only to clarify the application of the standards before January 1, 1976, so that persons who apply for enrollment before that date have responsible actuarial experience (and not only administrative experience) relating to pension plans. With respect to persons who perform actuarial services for smaller and simpler plans, the conferees anticipate that, to the extent feasible, the standards for enrollment will make it possible to use standard actuarial tables and standard earnings assumptions whether or not the actuary's training includes the highest level of actuarial skills. The limited number of persons with a high level of actuarial skills makes it desirable that the standards acceptable for persons examining smaller and simpler plans need not be as restrictive as in the case of those examining the larger plans.

The conference substitute also provides that actuaries may be enrolled on a temporary basis for a limited period. This makes it clear that actuaries can be enrolled almost immediately after enactment of the bill in order that enrolled actuaries will be available to help plans meet the requirements of the new law. The conferees intend that such temporary enrollment is not to be in lieu of any special enrollment standards for persons who apply for enrollment before January 1, 1976, but is only to allow immediate enrollment before the final standards are established.

Procedures.—

* * *

Under the conference substitute, a single standard for enrollment is achieved by directing the Secretary of Labor and the Secretary of the Treasury to establish a joint board which will set standards for enrollment and enroll actuaries to practice before the Department of Labor and Internal Revenue Service. In order that enrollment might begin as soon as possible, it is provided than an interim joint board is to be established no later than the last day of the first month following the date of enactment.

The joint board also is to administer the standards for disenrollment of actuaries and is to write the regulations on enrollment (to be approved by the two Secretaries or their delegates). As under the House bill, an actuary can be disenrolled only after notice and hearing, and if there is a finding that he does not comply with the governing rules or regulations, or is shown not to be competent in actuarial matters.

[Code Sec. 7702B]

[¶ 13,945.90]

Committee Report on P.L. 109-280 (Pension Protection Act of 2006)

For the Committee Report on P.L. 109-280 on the tax treatment of combined annuity or life insurance contracts with a long-term care insurance feature, see ¶ 13,706.50.

[Code Sec. 7802]

[¶ 13,950.10]

Committee Report on P.L. 93-406 (Employee Retirement Income Security Act of 1974)

[Conference Committee Explanation]

Administering office in Internal Revenue Service.—Under the bill as passed by both the House and the Senate, there is established an Office of Employee Plans and Exempt Organizations, in the Internal Revenue Service, headed by an Assistant Commissioner of Internal Revenue, to administer the tax provisions with regard to employee benefit plans and other exempt organizations.

The House bill does not provide a compensation schedule for the employees of the new Office of Employee Plans and Exempt Organizations. The bill as passed by the House authorizes appropriations for this office in the amount of $20 million for fiscal year 1974 and $70 million for each fiscal year thereafter. However, the bill as passed by the House neither imposes nor earmarks any specific revenue source for this authorization of appropriations.

The bill as passed by the Senate provides for the Assistant Commissioner in charge of this office to be classified as GS-18 and that this is to be in addition to the number of positions at that level otherwise authorized for the Internal Revenue Service. Also the bill as passed by the Senate authorizes for the Service an additional 20 positions at the level of GS-17 and 16. The Senate amendment authorizes appropriations for each of the fiscal years 1974, 1975, and 1976 in the amount of $35 million plus one-half of the revenue of the private foundation investment income tax (under section 4940 of the Code). For each fiscal year thereafter the bill as passed by the Senate authorizes appropriations of amounts equal to the collections of a new excise tax on employee benefit plans ($1 per participant per plan per calendar year, beginning with 1974) plus one-half of the private foundation investment income tax collections.

The conference agreement accepts the Senate provision authorizing the Assistant Commissioner Office of Employee Plans and Exempt Organizations to be classified as a GS-18 and providing to the Service an additional 20 positions in the level of GS-16 and 17. However, the conference agreement does not accept the Senate provision authorizing a new tax on employee benefit plans of $1 per participant. In place of the authorization of the new excise tax on participants, the conference provides a permanent authorization for fiscal year 1975 and for each fiscal year thereafter of an amount equal to the revenues from the private foundation investment income taxes if the rate of such tax was 2 percent plus an amount equal to that 2-percentage-point figure or $30,000,000, whichever is the larger.

Under the House bill, the provisions regarding the new office are to take effect 90 days after the date of enactment. Under the bill as passed by the Senate, no specified effective date is provided. The conference agreement accepts the House provision.

[¶ 13,950.15]

Committee Report on P.L. 93-406 (Employee Retirement Income Security Act of 1974)

[House Ways and Means Committee Explanation]

Office of Assistant Commissioner, Employee Plans and Exempt Organizations.—The bill establishes within the Internal Revenue Service a new office of Assistant Commissioner to be known as the Office of Assistant Commissioner, Employee Plans and Exempt Organizations. This office is to have the supervision and direction of the basic activities of the Internal Revenue Service in connection with pension, etc. plans (governed by secs. 401 through 415 of the code) and tax exempt organizations (exempt from tax under sec. 501(a) of the code). The bill authorizes the prescribing of the activities this office is to be responsible for in connection with organizations exempt from tax (under sec. 501(a) of the code) and plans which receive the special tax benefits of the qualified deferred compensation provisions of the tax laws (secs. 401 through 415 of the code).

In connection with deferred compensation plans it is intended that this office will be made responsible for, among other things, the question as to the qualification of the plan and the related trust and the exemption from tax of the trust. It also is intended that question[s] as to the deductibility of contributions to a plan, the taxability of a beneficiary of an employees' trust and the taxation of employee annuities be included in the jurisdiction of this office. * * *

* * *

In connection with organizations exempt from tax (under sec. 501(a) of the code) it is intended that this office have the responsibilities to an organization's exempt qualification, the taxes on unrelated business income of an organization exempt from tax, and the rules relating to the private foundation provisions of the Internal Revenue Code.

To carry out the provisions of this bill, it is intended that the principal activities referred to above will be transferred from the various Assistant Commissioners' offices to the new Office of the Assistant Commissioner (Employees Plans and Exempt Organizations). With these transfers it is intended that the Assistant Commissioner (Employee Plans and Exempt Organizations), under the direction and supervision of the Secretary, or his delegate, will have the authority to direct national and field office policy in connection with the basic activities of the Service relating to employee plans and exempt organizations.

[Code Sec. 9812]

[¶ 13,968U-8.045]

Committee Report on P.L. 109-432 (Tax Relief and Health Care Act of 2006)

For the Committee Report on P.L. 109-432 on mental health parity, see ¶ 15,050K.045.

[¶ 13,968U-8.05]

Committee Reports on P.L. 108-311 (Working Families Tax Relief Act)

See ¶ 15,050K.05.

[¶ 13,968U-8.10]

Committee Reports on P.L. 104-204 (Mental Health Parity Act of 1996)

See ¶ 15,050K.10.

ERISA Committee Reports

[ERISA Sec. 2]

[¶ 14,120.10]

Committee Report on P.L. 93-406 (Employee Retirement Income Security Act of 1974)

[House Education and Labor Committee Report]

Purposes.—* * * (1) to establish minimum standards of fiduciary conduct for Trustees, Administrators and others dealing with retirement plans, to provide for their enforcement through civil and criminal sanctions, to require adequate public disclosure of the plans' administrative and financial affairs, and (2) to improve the equitable character and soundness of private pension plans by requiring them to: (a) vest the accrued benefits of employees with significant periods of service with an employer, (b) meet minimum standards of funding and (c) guarantee the adequacy of the plan's assets against the risk of plan termination prior to completion of the normal funding cycle by insuring the unfunded portion of the benefits promised.

[ERISA Sec. 3]

[¶ 14,130.08]

Committee Report on P.L. 109-280 (Pension Protection Act of 2006)

For the Committee Report on P.L. 109-280 on prohibited transaction rules relating to financial investments, see ¶ 13,640.018.

For the Committee Report on P.L. 109-280 on distributions during working retirement, see ¶ 11,700.02.

For the Committee Report on P.L. 109-280 on the treatment of plans maintained by Indian tribes, see ¶ 12,350.038.

For the Committee Report on P.L. 109-280 on voluntary early retirement incentive and employment retention plans maintained by local educational agencies, see ¶ 13,153.018.

For the Committee Report on P.L. 109-280 on the revocation of elections relating to treatment as multiemployer plan, see ¶ 12,350.038.

[¶ 14,130.085]

Committee Report on P.L. 102-89 (Rural Telephone Cooperative Association Amendments, ERISA Act Amendments of 1991)

This section amends section 3(40) of Title I of the Employee Retirement Income Security Act of 1974 to exclude rural telephone cooperative associations from the definition of a multiple employer welfare arrangement (MEWA). Under section 514, ERISA's preemption provision, a MEWA may be subject to some or all provisions of state insurance law. Thus, the effect of this amendment is to treat rural telephone cooperative associations in the same manner as rural electric cooperative associations are currently treated under ERISA, i.e., both would be exempt from state insurance laws.

[¶ 14,130.09]

Committee Reports on P.L. 100-202 (Long-Term Continuing Appropriations Act)

Conference Committee Report

Amendment No. 79: Inserts section as proposed by the Senate amending the Employee Retirement Income Security Act of 1974 for the purpose of defining "qualified football coaches plan" to mean a defined contribution plan established and maintained by a tax-exempt organization whose membership consists of full-time football coaches at four-year colleges and universities. The House resolution contained no similar provision.

Statement of Sen. Hatch (R-Utah).—* * * This amendment modifies the Employee Retirement Security Act to allow a "qualified football coaches plan" to be treated as a multiemployer plan. Under this amendment, college football coaches will be able to contribute to a retirement plan that would be portable. Both the coach and employer could make tax-favored deposits, and the coach would own the assets and advantageous tax treatment at the time of distribution. (Congressional Record, December 11, 1987, p. S 17815).

[¶ 14,130.092]

Committee Report on P.L. 97-473 (Periodic Payments Settlement Act of 1982)

For Conference Committee Report on P.L. 97-473, see ¶ 15,040.09.

[¶ 14,130.093]

Committee Report on P.L. 96-364 (Multiemployer Pension Plan Amendments Act of 1980)

For Senate Committee Report (P.L. 96-364) on the multiemployer plan definition, see the committee report at ¶ 15,310.10.

[¶ 14,130.095]

Committee Report on P.L. 96-364 (Multiemployer Pension Plan Amendments Act of 1980)

[Senate Committee Reports]

Under present law, the standards provided by the labor law provisions of ERISA generally do not apply to the pension plan of a church for its employees. Church plans are also generally exempt from the tax qualification standards which correspond to the labor standards.

Under present law, a church plan may cover employees of a tax-exempt agency related to a church only if the plan was in existence on January 1, 1974. For taxable years beginning after December 31, 1982, a church plan no longer will be able to cover such employees.

Reason for change

The Committees believe that plans maintained by churches should be allowed to cover all employees of related tax-exempt agencies.

Explanation of the bill

The bill would permit a church plan to cover employees of a tax-exempt agency controlled by or affiliated with a church or a convention or association of churches. This would include ministers and other clerical employees as well as lay employees of the church agency. Thus, for plans in existence on January 1, 1974, present law would be continued after December 31, 1982, and for other plans present law would be modified. Also, the bill would provide a period of time during which a plan intended to qualify as a church plan but failing to do so could be amended to so qualify without penalty.

Effective date

The provisions of the bill would be effective as of January 1, 1974.

* * *

The bill would allow the Department of Labor to prescribe rules, consistent with the standards and purposes of title I of ERISA, under which certain categories of (1) severance pay arrangements, and (2) supplemental retirement income payments, would be treated as welfare plans rather than pension plans.

For example, as supplemental income payments, an employer might provide for the payment of monthly supplemental amounts to retirees based on a formula amounting to 3 percent, multiplied by the retiree's monthly pension benefit, multiplied by the number of years that such retirees' pension benefit has been in pay status.

The Committees expect that in prescribing regulations applicable to such supplemental payments, the Secretary of Labor will take into account the overall percentage of retirees' total retirement benefits represented by such payments.

Also, in order to protect plan participants and beneficiaries against an erosion of ERISA's standards, supplemental retirement income payments or a severance pay arrangement, a principal effect of which is the evasion of the standards or purpose of title I of ERISA is treated under the bill as a pension plan rather than a welfare plan. Thus, it is subject to the ERISA standards (e.g., vesting, funding) applicable to pension plans.

Effective date

The provisions would be effective upon the date of enactment.

[¶ 14,130.10]

Committee Report on P.L. 93-406 (Employee Retirement Income Security Act of 1974)

[House Education and Labor Committee Report]

Definitions.—* * * The definition of "employee" is intended to encompass any person who has the status of an "employee" under a collective bargaining agreement.

The exclusion of assets of investment companies regulated under the Investment Company Act of 1940 from the definition of "fund" is not intended to exclude participating shares in an investment company held by the fund.

With respect to the term "profit-sharing retirement" plan, it is intended that stock bonus, thrift and savings or similar plans with retirement features be treated as the equivalent of profit-sharing retirement plans for purposes of this Act unless expressly indicated otherwise.

With respect to the term "non-forfeitable right" or "vested right", it is not contemplated that vesting be required in benefits such as death benefits, disability benefits, or other forms of ancillary benefits provided by the plan. The plan may, of course, at its option, provide for vesting in such benefits.

With respect to "adequate consideration," it is intended that this term be read to include the fair market value of the use of leased property.

* * *

[¶ 14,130.15]

Committee Report on P.L. 93-406 (Employee Retirement Income Security Act of 1974)

[Conference Committee Joint Explanation]

Definitions.—The substitute defines "fiduciary" as any person who exercises any discretionary authority or control respecting management of a plan, exercises any authority or control respecting the management or disposition of its assets or has any discretionary authority or responsibility in the administration of the plan. Under this definition, fiduciaries include officers and directors of a plan, members of a plan's investment committee and persons who select these individuals. Consequently, the definition includes persons who have authority and responsibility with respect to the matter in question, regardless of their formal title. The term "fiduciary" also includes any person who renders investment advice for a fee and includes persons to whom "discretionary" duties have been delegated by named fiduciaries.

While the ordinary functions of consultants and advisers to employee benefit plans (other than investment advisers) may not be considered as fiduciary functions, it must be recognized that there will be situations where such consultants and advisers may because of their special expertise, in effect, be exercising discretionary authority or control with respect to the management or administration of such plan or some authority or control regarding its assets. In such cases, they are to be regarded as having assumed fiduciary obligations within the meaning of the applicable definition.

The labor definition of a "party-in-interest" includes the following general categories. (1) Plan administrators, officers, fiduciaries, trustees, custodians, counsel and employees. (2) Persons providing services to a plan. (3) The employer, its employees, officers, directors, or 10-percent shareholders. (4) Controlling or controlled parties or parties under common control (and their employees, officers, directors, or 10-percent shareholders). (Under the substitute, "control" is generally defined as 50-percent ownership. However, the Secretary of Labor and Secretary of Treasury may, by regulation, reduce this percentage.) (5) Employee organizations with members covered by the plan, its employees, its officers and directors and its affiliates. (6) Certain relatives and partners of parties-in-interest are also treated as parties-in-interest.

Under the tax provisions, the same general categories of persons are disqualified persons, with some differences. Although fiduciaries are disqualified persons under the tax provisions, they are to be subject to the excise tax only if they act in a prohibited transaction in a capacity other than that of a fiduciary. Also, only highly-compensated employees are to be treated as disqualified persons, not all employees of an employer, etc.

[ERISA Sec. 4]

[¶ 14,140.08]

Committee Report on P.L. 107-16 (Economic Growth and Tax Relief Reconciliation Act)

For the Committee Report on P.L. 107-16 on deemed IRAs under employer plans, see ¶ 12,050.045.

[¶ 14,140.10]

Committee Reports on P.L. 93-406 (Employee Retirement Income Security Act of 1974)

See Committee Reports at ¶ 14,240.10, ¶ 14,410.10, ¶ 14,610.10, and ¶ 14,710.10.

[ERISA Sec. 101]

[¶ 14,210.07]

Committee Report on P.L. 109-280 (Pension Protection Act of 2006)

[Joint Committee on Taxation Report]

[Defined benefit plan funding notice]

The provision expands the annual funding notice requirement that applies under present law to multiemployer plans, so that it applies also to single-employer plans and, in the case of a single-employer plan, includes a summary of the PBGC rules governing plan termination. The provision also changes the information that must be provided in the notice and accelerates the time when the notice must be provided.

In addition to the information required under present law, an annual funding notice with respect to either a single-employer or multiemployer plan must include the following additional information, as of the end of the plan year to which the notice relates: (1) a statement of the number of participants who are retired or separated from service and receiving benefits, retired or separated participants who are entitled to future benefits, and active participants); (2) a statement setting forth the funding policy of the plan and the asset allocation of investments under the plan (expressed as percentages of total assets); (3) an explanation containing specific information of any plan amendment, scheduled benefit increase or reduction, or other known event taking effect in the current plan year and having a material effect on plan liabilities or assets for the year (as defined in regulations by the Secretary); and (4) a statement that a person may obtain a copy of the plan's annual report upon request, through the Department of Labor Internet website, or through an Intranet website maintained by the applicable plan sponsor.

In the case of a single-employer plan, the notice must provide: (1) a statement as to whether the plan's funding target attainment percentage (as defined under the minimum funding rules for single-employer plans) for the plan year to which the notice relates and the two preceding plan years, is at least 100 percent (and, if not, the actual percentages); (2) a statement of (a) the total assets (separately stating any funding standard carryover or prefunding balance) and the plan's liabilities for the plan year and the two preceding years, determined in the same manner as under the funding rules, and (b) the value of the plan's assets and liabilities as of the last day of the plan year to which the notice relates, determined using fair market value and the interest rate used in determining variable rate premiums; and (3) if applicable, a statement that each contributing sponsor, and each member of the sponsor's controlled group, was required to provide the information under section 4010 for the plan year to which the notice relates.

In the case of a multiemployer plan, the notice must provide: (1) a statement as to whether the plan's funded percentage (as defined under the minimum funding rules for multiemployer plans) for the plan year to which the notice relates and the two preceding plan years, is at least 100 percent (and, if not, the actual percentages); (2) a statement of the value of the plan's assets and liabilities for the plan year to which the notice relates and the two preceding plan years; (3) whether the plan was in endangered or critical status and, if so, a summary of the plan's funding improvement or rehabilitation plan and a statement describing how a person can obtain a copy of the plan's funding improvement or rehabilitation plan and the actuarial or financial data that demonstrate any action taken by the plan toward fiscal improvement; and (4) a statement that the plan administrator will provide, on written request, a copy of the plan's annual report to any labor organization representing participants and beneficiaries and any employer that has an obligation to contribute to the plan.

The annual funding notice must be provided within 120 days after the end of the plan year to which it relates. In the case of a plan covering not more than 100 employees for the preceding year, the annual funding notice must be provided upon filing of the annual report with respect to the plan (i.e., within seven months after the end of the plan year unless the due date for the annual report is extended).

The Secretary of Labor is required to publish a model notice not later than one year after the date of enactment. In addition, the Secretary of Labor is given the authority to promulgate any interim final rules as appropriate to carry out the requirement that a model notice be published.

Under the provision, the annual funding notice includes the information provided in the notice required under present law in the case of a single-employer plan that is subject to PBGC variable rate premiums. Accordingly, that present-law notice requirement is repealed under the provision.

Effective date

The provision is effective for plan years beginning after December 31, 2007, except that the repeal of the notice required under present law in the case of a single-employer plan that is subject to PBGC variable rate premiums is effective for plan years beginning after December 31, 2006. Under a transition rule, any requirement to report a plan's funding target attainment percentage or funded percentage for a plan year beginning before January 1, 2008, is met if (1) in the case of a plan year beginning in 2006, the plan's funded current liability percentage is reported, and (2) in the case of a plan year beginning in 2007, the funding target attainment percentage or funded percentage as determined using such methods of estimation as the Secretary of the Treasury may provide is reported.

[Notice of freedom to divest employer securities]

The provision requires a new notice in connection with the right of an applicable individual to divest his or her account under an applicable defined contribution plan of employer securities, as required under the provision of the provision relating to diversification rights with respect to amounts invested in employer securities. Not later than 30 days before the first date on which an applicable individual is eligible to exercise such right with respect to any type of contribution, the administrator of the plan must provide the individual with a notice setting forth such right and describing the importance of diversifying the investment of retirement account assets. Under the diversification provision, an applicable individual's right to divest his or her account of employer securities attributable to elective deferrals and employee after-tax contributions and the right to divest his or her account of employer securities attributable to other contributions (i.e., nonelective employer contributions and employer matching contributions) may become exercisable at different times. Thus, to the extent the applicable individual is first eligible to exercise such rights at different times, separate notices are required.

The notice must be written in a manner calculated to be understood by the average plan participant and may be delivered in written, electronic, or other appropriate form to the extent such form is reasonably accessible to the applicable individual. The Secretary of Treasury has regulatory authority over the required notice and is directed to prescribe a model notice to be used for this purpose within 180 days of the date of enactment of the provision. It is expected that the Secretary of Treasury will consult with the Secretary of Labor on the description of the importance of diversifying the investment of retirement account assets. In addition, it is intended that the Secretary of Treasury will prescribe rules to enable the notice to be provided at reduced administrative expense, such as allowing the notice to be provided with the summary plan description, with a reminder of these rights within a reasonable period before they become exercisable.

In the case of a failure to provide a required notice of diversification rights, the Secretary of Labor may assess a civil penalty against the plan administrator of up to $100 a day from the date of the failure. For this purpose, each violation with respect to any single applicable individual is treated as a separate violation.

Effective date

The provision generally applies to plan years beginning after December 31, 2006. Under a transition rule, if notice would otherwise be required to be provided before 90 days after the date of enactment, notice is not required until 90 days after the date of enactment.

[Notice to participants or beneficiaries of blackout periods]

The provision modifies the definition of a one-participant retirement plan to be consistent with Department of Labor regulations under which certain business owners and their spouses are not treated as employees.[126] As modified, a one-participant retirement plan is a plan that: (1) on the first day of the plan year, either covered only one individual (or the individual and his or her spouse) and the individual owned 100 percent of the plan sponsor, whether or not incorporated, or covered only one or more partners (or partners and their spouses) in the plan sponsor; and (2) does not cover a business that leases employees.

Effective date

The provision is effective as if included in section 306 of the Sarbanes-Oxley Act of 2002.

[Benefit limitations under single-employer defined benefit pension plans]

For the Committee Report on P.L. 109-280 on minimum funding rules, see ¶ 13,151O.50.

[Access to multiemployer pension plan information]

For the Committee Report on P.L. 109-280 on multiemployer plan reporting, see ¶ 13,648W-75.045.

[Pension plan reporting simplification]

For the Committee Report on P.L. 109-280 on filing rules for one-participant plans, see ¶ 14,230.085.

[¶ 14,210.075]

Committee Reports on P.L. 108-218 (Pension Funding Equity Act of 2004)

Present Law

Under present law, defined benefit plans are generally required to meet certain minimum funding rules. These rules are designed to help ensure that such plans are adequately funded. Both single-employer plans and multiemployer plans are subject to minimum funding requirements; however, the requirements are different for each type of plan.

Similarly, the Pension Benefit Guaranty Corporation ("PBGC") insures certain benefits under both single-employer and multiemployer defined benefit plans, but the rules relating to the guarantee vary for each type of plan. In the case of multiemployer plans, the PBGC guarantees against plan insolvency. Under its multiemployer program, PBGC provides financial assistance through loans to plans that are insolvent (that is, plans that are unable to pay basic PBGC-guaranteed benefits when due).

Employers maintaining single-employer defined benefit plans are required to provide certain notices to plan participants relating to the funding status of the plan. For example, ERISA requires an employer of a single-employer defined benefit plan to notify plan participants if the employer fails to make required contributions (unless a request for a funding waiver is pending).[28] In addition, in the case of an underfunded plan for which variable rate PBGC premiums are required, the plan administrator generally must notify plan participants of the plan's funding status and the limits on the PBGC benefit guarantee if the plan terminates while underfunded.[29]

House Bill

No provision.

Senate Amendment

In general

The Senate amendment requires the administrator of a defined benefit plan which is a multiemployer plan to provide an annual funding notice to: (1) each participant and beneficiary; (2) each labor organization representing such participants or beneficiaries; and (3) each employer that has an obligation to contribute under the plan.

Such a notice must include: (1) identifying information, including the name of the plan, the address and phone number of the plan administrator and the plan's principal administrative officer, each plan sponsor's employer identification number, and the plan identification number; (2) a statement as to whether the plan's funded current liability percentage for the plan year to which the notice relates is at least 100 percent (and if not, a statement of the percentage); (3) a statement of the value of the plan's assets, the amount of benefit payments, and the ratio of the assets to the payments for the plan year to which the report relates; (4) a summary of the rules governing insolvent multiemployer plans, including the limitations on benefit payments and any potential benefit reductions and suspensions (and the potential effects of such limitations, reductions, and suspensions on the plan); (5) a general description of the benefits under the plan which are eligible to be guaranteed by the PBGC and the limitations of the guarantee and circumstances in which such limitations apply; and (6) any additional information which the plan administrator elects to include to the extent it is not inconsistent with regulations prescribed by the Secretary of Labor.

The annual funding notice must be provided no later than two months after the deadline (including extensions) for filing the plan's annual report for the plan year to which the notice relates. The funding notice must be provided in a form and manner prescribed in regulations by the Secretary of Labor. Additionally, it must be written so as to be understood by the average plan participant and may be provided in written, electronic, or some other appropriate form to the extent that it is reasonably accessible to persons to whom the notice is required to be provided.

The Secretary of Labor is directed to issue regulations (including a model notice) necessary to implement the provision no later than one year after the date of enactment.

Sanction for failure to provide notice

In the case of a failure to provide the annual multiemployer plan funding notice, the Secretary of Labor may assess a civil penalty against a plan administrator of up to $100 per day for each failure to provide a notice. For this purpose, each violation with respect to a single participant or beneficiary is treated as a separate violation.

Effective date

The Senate amendment is effective for plan years beginning after December 31, 2004.

Conference Agreement

In general

The conference agreement follows the Senate amendment, with the following modification. The administrator of a defined benefit plan which is a multiemployer plan is also required to provide an annual funding notice to the PBGC.

The conference agreement requires the administrator of a defined benefit plan which is a multiemployer plan to provide an annual funding notice to: (1) each participant and beneficiary; (2) each labor organization representing such participants or beneficiaries; (3) each employer that has an obligation to contribute under the plan; and (4) the PBGC.

Such a notice must include: (1) identifying information, including the name of the plan, the address and phone number of the plan administrator and the plan's principal administrative officer, each plan sponsor's employer identification number, and the plan identification number; (2) a statement as to whether the plan's funded current liability percentage for the plan year to which the notice relates is at least 100 percent (and if not, a statement of the percentage); (3) a statement of the value of the plan's assets, the amount of benefit payments, and the ratio of the assets to the payments for the plan year to which the report relates; (4) a summary of the rules governing insolvent multiemployer plans, including the limitations on benefit payments and any potential benefit reductions and suspensions (and the potential effects of such limitations, reductions, and suspensions on the plan); (5) a general description of the benefits under the plan which are eligible to be guaranteed by the PBGC and the limitations of the guarantee and circumstances in which such limitations apply; and (6) any additional information which the plan administrator elects to include to the extent it is not inconsistent with regulations prescribed by the Secretary of Labor.

The annual funding notice must be provided no later than two months after the deadline (including extensions) for filing the plan's annual report for the plan year to which the notice relates. The funding notice must be provided in a form and manner prescribed in regulations by the Secretary of Labor. Additionally, it must be written so as to be understood by the average plan participant and may be provided in written, electronic, or some other appropriate form to the extent that it is reasonably accessible to persons to whom the notice is required to be provided.

The Secretary of Labor is directed to issue regulations (including a model notice) necessary to implement the provision no later than one year after the date of enactment.

[126] 29 C.F.R. sec. 2510.3-3(c) (2006).

[28] ERISA sec. 101(d).

[29] ERISA sec. 4011. Multiemployer plans are not required to pay variable rate premiums.

Sanction for failure to provide notice

In the case of a failure to provide the annual multiemployer plan funding notice, the Secretary of Labor may assess a civil penalty against a plan administrator of up to $100 per day for each failure to provide a notice. For this purpose, each violation with respect to a single participant or beneficiary is treated as a separate violation.

Effective date

The conference agreement is effective for plan years beginning after December 31, 2004.

[¶ 14,210.080]

Committee Reports on P.L. 105-34 (Taxpayer Relief Act)

For Committee Reports on P.L. 105-34, relating to filing plan descriptions, see ¶ 14,240.096.

[¶ 14,210.090]

Committee Report on P.L. 104-188 (Small Business Job Protection Act)

[Senate Committee Report]

The bill also amend[s] parts 1 and 4, Subtitle B, Title 1 of ERISA so that only simplified reporting requirements apply to SIMPLE plans and so that the employer (and any other plan fiduciary) will not be subject to fiduciary liability resulting from the employee (or beneficiary) exercising control over the assets in the SIMPLE account. For this purpose an employee (or beneficiary) will be treated as exercising control over the assets in his or her account upon the earlier of (1) an affirmative election with respect to the initial investment of any contributions, (2) a rollover contribution (including a trustee-to-trustee transfer) to another SIMPLE account or IRA, or (3) one year after the SIMPLE account is established. The Committee intends that once an employee (or beneficiary) is treated as exercising control over his or her SIMPLE account, the relief from fiduciary liability would extend to the period prior to when the employee (or beneficiary) was deemed to exercise control.

Reporting requirements.—

Trustee requirements.—The trustee of a SIMPLE account is required each year to prepare, and provide to the employer maintaining the SIMPLE plan, a summary description containing the following basic information about the plan; the name and address of the employer and the trustee; the requirements for eligibility; the benefits provided under the plan; the time and method of making salary reduction elections; and the procedures for and effects of, withdrawals (including rollovers) from the SIMPLE account. At least once a year, the trustee is also required to furnish an account statement to each individual maintaining a SIMPLE account. In addition, the trustee is required to file an annual report with the Secretary. A trustee who fails to provide any of such reports or descriptions will be subject to a penalty of $50 per day until such failure is corrected, unless the failure is due to reasonable cause.

Employer reports.—The employer maintaining a SIMPLE plan is required to notify each employee of the employee's opportunity to make salary reduction contributions under the plan as well as the contribution alternative chosen by the employer immediately before the employee becomes eligible to make such election. This notice must include a copy of the summary description prepared by the trustee. An employer who fails to provide such notice will be subject to a penalty of $30 per day on which such failure continues, unless the failure is due to reasonable cause.

* * *

[Conference Committee Report]

The conference agreement follows the Senate amendment.

[¶ 14,210.095]

Committee Report on P.L. 100-203 (Omnibus Budget Reconciliation Act of 1987)

[Conference Committee Report]

Under the [House] bill, three installments of estimated contributions are required during the plan year, with the total contribution due within 2 ½ months after the end of the plan year. The amount of each installment is ¼ of the lesser of (1) 80 percent of the amount required to be contributed for the current plan year or (2) 90 percent of the amount required to be contributed for the preceding plan year.

An excise tax is imposed if the full amount of any required installment is not paid. The excise tax is determined by applying the interest rate for underpayment of income taxes to the amount of the underpayment for the period of the underpayment. The period of the underpayment begins on the due date of the installment and ends on the earlier of the date on which the underpayment is contributed to the plan or the date the total contribution is due. Each member of the employer's controlled group is jointly and severally liable for the tax.

Each member of the employer's controlled group is jointly and severally liable for the excise tax.

The acceleration of the due date for required plan contributions generally is effective for plan years beginning after December 31, 1988, with a phase-in rule applying for plan years beginning in 1988. The provision requiring plan contributions to be made in installments is effective for plan years beginning after December 31, 1987, with a transition rule applicable for 1988 plan years.

[The Finance Committee amendment provides:] Similar to the Ways and Means Committee bill, except that four installments are required during the plan year, with the total contribution due within 8 ½ months after the end of the plan year. The amount of each required installment is ¼ of the lesser of (1) 90 percent of the amount required to be contributed for the current plan year or (2) 100 percent of the amount required to be contributed for the preceding plan year.

Failure to make installments.—Same as the Ways and Means Committee bill, except that interest is paid to the plan rather than as an excise tax, and the interest rate on missed contributions is the greater of (1) 175 percent of the mid-term applicable Federal interest rate (AFR) or (2) the rate of interest taken into account in determining costs under the plan. In addition, a lien arises if a required installment is not paid in full. The employer is required to notify employees of the failure to make required installments.

Failure to make total contribution for plan year.—Same as the Ways and Means Committee bill. In addition, the 5-percent excise tax is increased to 10 percent, and a lien arises in favor of the plan if the required contribution is not paid in full. The employer is required to notify employees of the failure to make contributions.

The provisions apply for plan years beginning after December 31, 1987.

The conference agreement generally follows the Finance Committee amendment, with modifications.

With respect to the interest rate applicable to a failure to make contributions when due, the conference agreement clarifies that the interest rate continues at the specified rate until the missed contributions are actually paid to the plan.

In the case of a plan with a funded ratio of less than 100 percent, a statutory tax lien arises on all controlled group property in favor of the plan 60 days after the due date of an unpaid contribution (whether or not a waiver application is pending). The amount of the lien is the cumulative missed contributions in excess of $1 million. Missed contributions originally due before the effective date are not subject to this lien provision (but they are taken into account in applying the $1 million rule).

Under the conference agreement, the employer and each member of the controlled group that includes the employer are liable for contributions required under the minimum funding rules. However, this controlled group liability does not alter the rules for determining the extent to which an employer's contributions to a plan are deductible. Thus, in general, a deduction for a contribution is available under section 404 only for the employer who directly employs the participants.

[¶ 14,210.10]

Committee Report on P.L. 93-406 (Employee Retirement Income Security Act of 1974)

[Conference Committee Explanation]

Plans subject to the provisions and exemptions.—Under the conference substitute, the new reporting and disclosure requirements are to be administered by the Secretary of Labor and are to be applied to all pension and welfare plans established or maintained by an employer or employee organization engaged in, or affecting, interstate commerce. Governmental plans, certain church plans, workmen's compensation and unemployment compensation plans, plans maintained outside the United States for the benefit of persons substantially all of whom are nonresident aliens, and so-called excess benefit plans, which provide benefits in addition to those for which deductions may be taken under the tax laws, are exempted from the requirements. The Secretary of Labor also is authorized to waive and modify certain of these requirements for employee benefit plans.

All plans of the types subject to the reporting and disclosure provisions are to be required to file an annual report with the Secretary of Labor regardless of the number of participants involved. However, simplified reports may be authorized for plans with fewer than 100 participants.

Reports on termination.—In addition to the annual reports which must be filed with the Secretary of Labor, special terminal reports are required to be filed for pension plans that are winding up their affairs. These terminal reports may also be required by the Secretary of Labor for welfare plans. Also in the year a plan is terminated the Secretary may require the supplementary information to be filed with the annual report.

[ERISA Sec. 102]

[¶ 14,220.07]

Committee Reports on P.L. 105-34 (Taxpayer Relief Act)

For Committee Reports on P.L. 105-34, relating to filing plan descriptions, see ¶ 14,240.096.

[¶ 14,220.10]

Committee Report on P.L. 93-406 (Employee Retirement Income Security Act of 1974)

For Committee Reports on P.L. 93-406, see ¶ 14,240.10.

[ERISA Sec. 103]

[¶ 14,230.085]

Committee Report on P.L. 109–280 (Pension Protection Act of 2006) [Joint Committee on Taxation Report]

Annual report

The provision requires additional information to be provided in the annual report filed with respect to a defined benefit pension plan. In a case in which the liabilities under the plan as of the end of a plan year consist (in whole or in part) of liabilities under two or more other pension plans as of immediately before the plan year, the annual report must include the plan's funded percentage as of the last day of the plan year and the funded percentage of each of such other plans. Funded percentage is defined as: (1) in the case of a single-employer plan, the plan's funded target attainment percentage (as defined under the minimum funding rules for single-employer plans); and (2) in the case of a multiemployer plan, the plan's funded percentage (as defined under the minimum funding rules for multiemployer plans).

An annual report filed with respect to a multiemployer plan must include, as of the end of the plan year, the following additional information: (1) the number of employers obligated to contribute to the plan; (2) a list of the employers that contributed more than five percent of the total contributions to the plan during the plan year; (3) the number of participants on whose behalf no contributions were made by an employer as an employer of the participant for the plan year and two preceding years; (4) the ratio of the number of participants under the plan on whose behalf no employer had an obligation to make an employer contribution during the plan year, to the number of participants under the plan on whose behalf no employer had an obligation to make an employer contribution during each of the two preceding plan years; (5) whether the plan received an amortization extension for the plan year and, if so, the amount by which it changed the minimum required contribution for the year, what minimum contribution would have been required without the extension, and the period of the extension; (6) whether the plan used the shortfall funding method and, if so, the amount by which it changed the minimum required contribution for the year, what minimum contribution would have been required without the use of this method, and the period for which the method is used; (7) whether the plan was in critical or endangered status for the plan year, and if so, a summary of any funding improvement or rehabilitation plan (or modification thereto) adopted during the plan year, and the funding percentage of the plan; (8) the number of employers that withdrew from the plan during the preceding plan year and the aggregate amount of withdrawal liability assessed, or estimated to be assessed, against the withdrawn employers; (9) if the plan that has merged with another plan or if assets and liabilities have been transferred to the plan, the actuarial valuation of the assets and liabilities of each affected plan during the year preceding the effective date of the merger or transfer, based upon the most recent data available as of the day before the first day of the plan year, or other valuation method performed under standards and procedures as prescribed by regulation.

The Secretary of Labor is required, not later than one year after the date of enactment, to publish guidance to assist multiemployer plans to identify and enumerate plan participants for whom there is no employer with an obligation to make an employer contribution under the plan and report such information in the annual report. The Secretary may provide rules as needed to apply this requirement with respect to contributions made on a basis other than hours worked, such as on the basis of units of production.

The actuarial statement filed with the annual return must include a statement explaining the actuarial assumptions and methods used in projecting future retirements and asset distributions under the plan.

Electronic display of annual report

Identification and basic plan information and actuarial information included in the annual report must be filed with the Secretary of Labor in an electronic format that accommodates display on the Internet (in accordance with regulations). The Secretary of Labor is to provide for the display of such information, within 90 days after the filing of the annual report, on a website maintained by the Secretary of Labor on the Internet and other appropriate media. Such information is also required to be displayed on any Intranet website maintained by the plan sponsor (or by the plan administrator on behalf of the plan sponsor) in accordance with regulations.

Summary annual report

Under the provision, the requirement to provide a summary annual report to participants applies does not apply to defined benefit pension plans.[116]

Multiemployer plan summary report

The provision requires the plan administrator of a multiemployer plan to provide a report containing certain summary plan information to each employee organization and each employer with an obligation to contribute to the plan within 30 days after the due date of the plan's annual report. The report must contain: (1) a description of the contribution schedules and benefit formulas under the plan, and any modification to such schedules and formulas, during such plan year; (2) the number of employers obligated to contribute to the plan; (3) a list of the employers that contributed more than 5 percent of the total contributions to the plan during such plan year; (4) the number of participants under the plan on whose behalf no employer contributions have been made to the plan for such plan year and for each of the two preceding plan years; (5) whether the plan was in critical or endangered status for the plan year and, if so, a list of the actions taken by the plan to improve its funding status and a statement describing how to obtain a copy of the plan's improvement or rehabilitation plan, as appropriate, and the actuarial and financial data that demonstrate any action taken by the plan toward fiscal improvement; (6) the number of employers that withdrew from the plan during the preceding plan year and the aggregate amount of withdrawal liability assessed, or estimated to be assessed, against such withdrawn employers, as reported on the annual report for the plan year; (7) if the plan that has merged with another plan or if assets and liabilities have been transferred to the plan, the actuarial valuation of the assets and liabilities of each affected plan during the year preceding the effective date of the merger or transfer, based upon the most recent data available as of the day before the first day of the plan year, or other valuation method performed under standards and procedures as prescribed by regulation; (8) a description as to whether the plan sought or received an amortization extension or used the shortfall funding method for the plan year; and (9) notification of the right to obtain upon written request a copy of the annual report filed with respect to the plan, the summary annual report, the summary plan description, and the summary of any material modification of the plan, subject to a limitation of one copy of any such document in any 12-month period and any reasonable charge to cover copying, mailing, and other costs of furnishing the document. Nothing in this report requirement waives any other ERISA provision requiring plan administrators to provide, upon request, information to employers that have an obligation to contribute under the plan.

Effective Date

The provisions are effective for plan years beginning after December 31, 2007.

[Pension plan reporting simplification]

The Secretary of the Treasury is directed to modify the annual return filing requirements with respect to a one-participant plan to provide that if the total value of the plan assets of such a plan as of the end of the plan year does not exceed $250,000, the plan administrator is not required to file a return. In addition, the Secretary of the Treasury and the Secretary of Labor are directed to provide simplified reporting requirements for plan years beginning after December 31, 2006, for certain plans with fewer than 25 participants.

Effective Date

The provision relating to one-participant retirement plans is effective for plan years beginning on or after January 1, 2007. The provision relating to simplified reporting for plans with fewer than 25 participants is effective on the date of enactment.

[¶ 14,230.09]

Committee Report on P.L. 100-203 (Omnibus Budget Reconciliation Act of 1987)

[Conference Committee Report]

Ways and Means Committee bill: The report that employees are required to receive annually is required to include a statement of the extent to which the plan is funded. This provision applies to plan years beginning after December 31, 1987.

Conference Agreement: The conference agreement follows the Ways and Means Committee bill, except that the requirement only applies to plans that are funded below 70 percent of current liability.

Education and Labor Committee bill: The bill deletes the provision under which the statute of limitations begins to run on the date a report is filed from which the plaintiff could reasonably be expected to have obtained knowledge of a breach of fiduciary liability.

Conference Agreement: The conference agreement follows the Education and Labor Committee bill. This provision applies to reports filed after December 31, 1987.

Education and Labor Committee bill: The bill provides that the Secretary of Labor may assess a civil penalty of up to $1,000 a day from the date of a plan administrator's failure or refusal to file an annual report. In addition, an annual report that has been rejected is not to be treated as having been filed for purposes of this penalty.

---

[116] As discussed in Part A above, detailed information about a defined benefit pension plan must be provided to participants in an annual funding notice.

Conference Agreement: The conference agreement follows the Education and Labor Committee bill, with the clarification that the penalty is to reflect the materiality of the failure. This provision applies for reports due after December 31, 1987.

[¶ 14,230.095]

Committee Report on P.L. 96-364 (Multiemployer Pension Plan Amendments Act of 1980)

[Senate Committee Report]

Under the bill, an actuary performing a plan valuation will be required to disclose events which could have a material adverse effect on the plan. Where such events occur after the date of the valuation but before the valuation is published so that they are not reflected in the valuation, the actuary would nevertheless be required to disclose their occurrence in an attachment or footnote to the valuation. The bill would also require the actuary to disclose trends which have occurred in the past but which he is assuming will not continue in the future. The Committees intend that in fulfilling these requirements, an enrolled actuary will make appropriate inquiries of plan sponsors but will not be required to make further inquiry unless, under the circumstances, further inquiry is considered necessary because of information already known to the actuary. The Committees expect that material failure to comply with the provision could be an important factor to be considered by the Joint Board for the Enrollment of Actuaries in a disenrollment proceeding. The Committees do not intend the provision to cause an actuary to assume the role of an auditor.

[¶ 14,230.10]

Committee Report on P.L. 93-406 (Employee Retirement Income Security Act of 1974)

[Conference Committee Explanation]

Contents of annual report

The annual report generally is to include audited financial statements for both welfare plans and pensions plans. With respect to welfare plans the statement is to include a statement of assets and liabilities, a statement of changes in fund balance, and a statement of changes in financial position. With respect to employee pension plans the statement is to include a statement of assets and liabilities and a statement of changes in net assets available for plan benefits, including details as to revenues and expenses and other changes aggregated by general source and application.

In the notes to the annual financial statement, the accountant is to disclose any significant changes in the plan, material lease commitments and contingent liabilities, any agreements and transactions with persons known to be parties-in-interest, information as to whether a tax ruling or determination letter has been obtained, and any other relevant matters necessary to fairly present the financial status of the plan. In addition, in the case of employee pension plans the notes should also deal with funding policy (including policy with respect to prior service costs and changes in such policies during the year). An accountant may rely on the correctness of any actuarial matter certified by any enrolled actuary if the accountant indicates his reliance on such certification.

In addition to the audited financial statement, the annual report is to include for all employee benefit plans a statement on separate schedules showing among other things, a statement of plan assets and liabilities aggregated by categories, a statement of receipts and disbursements, a schedule of all assets held for investment purposes aggregated and identified by issuer, borrower, or lessee and a schedule of each transaction involving a person known to be a party-in-interest. Also, a schedule of all loans and leases in default at the end of the year or which are classified during the year as uncollectible is to be included in the annual report.

There is also to be supplied with the annual report a schedule listing each transaction which exceeds 3 percent of the value of the fund. If some or all of the assets of a plan are held in a common or collective trust maintained by a bank or similar institution the annual report is to include the most recent annual statement of assets and liabilities of the common or collective trust. (The Secretary of Labor will have authority to prescribe for the filing of a master copy of the annual statement of this common or collective trust in order to avoid duplicative filings of this statement by plans participating in this common or collective trust.)

With respect to persons employed by the plan the annual report is to include the name and address of each fiduciary, the name of each person who receives more than minimal compensation from the plan for services rendered, along with the amount of compensation (or who performs duties which are not ministerial), the nature of the services, and the relationship to the employer or any other party in interest to the plan. Also, the reasons for any changes in trustees, accountant, actuary, investment manager, or administrator are to be provided in the annual report.

As indicated in the discussion of the funding provisions, under the conference agreement, the annual report is to include an actuarial statement for all pension plans which are subject to the funding requirements of title I. If plan benefits are purchased from, and guaranteed by, an insurance company, the annual report is to include the premiums paid, benefits paid, charges for administrative expenses, commissions and other information. The insurance carrier is to certify to the plan administrator the information needed to comply with the annual reporting requirements within 120 days after the close of the plan year, or within such other period as is prescribed by the Secretary of Labor.

The annual report for a plan is to be filed within 210 days after the close of the plan year or within such period of time as the Secretary of Labor may require in order to reduce the necessity for duplicate filing with the Internal Revenue Service. The Secretary of Labor may reject the filing of an annual report if he finds that it is incomplete or there is a material qualification in the accountant's or actuary's opinion. If a revised report is not submitted within 45 days after rejection, the Secretary may retain an accountant to perform an audit, or retain an actuary, whichever is appropriate, or bring a civil action for legal or equitable relief. The plan is to bear the costs of any expenses of an audit or actuarial report.

Accountant and actuary reports

Every plan is to retain on behalf of its participants an independent qualified public accountant who annually is to prepare an audited financial statement of the plan's operations. The accountant is to give an opinion as to whether the financial statements of the plan conform with generally accepted accounting principles and the statement is to be based upon an examination in accordance with generally accepted auditing standards. An accountant's opinion is not to be required for statements prepared by banks or similar institutions or an insurance carrier if the statements of the bank or insurance carrier are certified by the bank and are made part of an annual report. For purposes of this provision a qualified public accountant includes certified public accountants, licensed public accountants and any person certified by the Secretary as a qualified public accountant in accordance with regulations published by him for a person who practices in a State where there is no certification or licensing procedure for accountants. Further, to the extent a plan is not required to make an annual report to the Secretary of Labor an annual audit is not required (and an independent, qualified public accountant need not be retained). Also the Secretary of Labor may waive the requirement of a audited financial statement in cases where simplified annual reports are permitted to be filed.

Every plan subject to the funding requirements of title I must retain an enrolled actuary who is to prepare an actuarial statement on an annual basis. This statement is to show the present value of all plan liabilities for nonforfeitable pension benefits allocated by the termination priority categories. The actuary is to supply a statement to be filed with the annual report as to his opinion as to whether the actuarial statements of the plan are reasonably related to the experience of the plan and to the reasonable expectations of the plan. The actuary is to use assumptions and techniques as are necessary to form an opinion as to whether the contents of the matters upon which he reports are in the aggregate reasonably related to the experience of the plan and to reasonable expectations, and represent his best estimate of anticipated experience under the plan. The actuarial statement is not required for plans which need not file annual reports, and may be waived by the Secretary of Labor for plans for which simplified annual reports are allowed.

[ERISA Sec. 104]

[¶ 14,240.065]

Conference Committee Report on P.L. 109-280 (Pension Protection Act of 2006)

For the Committee Report on P.L. 109-280 on annual reports, see ¶ 14,230.085.

[¶ 14,240.096]

Committee Report on P.L. 105-34 (Taxpayer Relief Act)

[Conference Committee Report]

[Senate Committee Report]

Elimination of paperwork burdens on plans.—The bill eliminates the requirement that SPDs and SMMs be filed with the Secretary of Labor. Employers would be required to furnish these documents to the Secretary of Labor upon request. A civil penalty could be imposed by the Secretary of Labor on the plan administrator for failure to comply with such requests. The penalty would be up to $100 per day of failure, up to a maximum of $1,000 per request. No penalty would be imposed if the failure was due to matters reasonably outside the control of the plan administrator.

Effective date

The provision is effective on the date of enactment.

[Conference Committee Report]

The Conference Agreement follows the Senate Amendment.

[¶ 14,240.07]

Committe Report on P.L.100-203 (Omnibus Budget Relief Reconciliation Act of 1987)

For the committee report on P.L. 100-203, relating to reporting requirements for underfunded plans, see ¶ 14,230.09.

[¶ 14,240.10]

Committee Report on P.L. 93-406 (Employee Retirement Income Security Act of 1974)

[Conference Committee Explanation]

Disclosure to participants.—Each administrator of an employee benefit plan is to furnish to each participant and to each beneficiary a summary plan description written in a manner calculated to be understood by the average plan participant or beneficiary. The summary is to include important plan provisions, names and addresses of persons responsible for plan investment or management, a description of benefits, the circumstances that may result in disqualification or ineligibility and the procedures to be followed in presenting claims for benefits under the plan.

Summary plan descriptions are to be furnished to participants within the later of 120 days after the plan is established or 90 days after an individual becomes a participant. Updated plan descriptions are also to be provided to participants every five years thereafter where there have been plan amendments in the interim; in any case, a new description is to be provided every ten years. Also, participants are to receive descriptions of material changes in a plan within 210 days after the end of any plan year in which a material change occurs. Also, the annual report and plan documents are to be available for examination by participants or beneficiaries at the principal office of the plan administrator and such other places as is necessary to provide reasonable access to these reports and documents. Thus, if the participants covered under the plan are employed in more than one geographic area, each geographic area is to have available for examination the required documents. Each participant is also to be furnished a copy within 210 days after the close of the plan year of the schedule of plan assets and liabilities and receipts and disbursements as submitted with the annual report, including any other material which is necessary to thoroughly summarize the latest annual report. Upon a written request, a plan administrator is to furnish a participant or beneficiary a complete copy of the comprehensive plan description, the latest annual report and other instruments under which the plan is established and operated. The plan administrator may charge a reasonable amount for fulfilling such a request.

Upon the request of a plan participant or beneficiary, a plan administrator is to furnish on the basis of the latest available information the total benefits accrued and the nonforfeitable pension benefit rights, if any, which have accrued. No more than one request may be made by any participant or beneficiary for this information during any one 12-month period.

A copy of the statement of the deferred vested benefits in the plan for individuals who have terminated employment during a plan year which is furnished to the Social Security Administration also is to be furnished to the individual participant.

[ERISA Sec. 105]

[¶ 14,250.08]

Committee Report on P.L. 109-280 (Pension Protection Act of 2006)

[Joint Committee on Taxation Report]

In general

The provision revises the benefit statement requirements under ERISA. The new requirements depend in part on the type of plan and the individual to whom the statement is provided. The benefit statement requirements do not apply to a one-participant retirement plan.[120]

A benefit statement is required to indicate, on the basis of the latest available information: (1) the total benefits accrued; (2) the vested accrued benefit or the earliest date on which the accrued benefit will become vested; and (3) an explanation of any permitted disparity or floor-offset arrangement that may be applied in determining accrued benefits under the plan.[121] With respect to information on vested benefits, the Secretary of Labor is required to provide that the requirements are met if, at least annually, the plan: (1) updates the information on vested benefits that is provided in the benefit statement; or (2) provides in a separate statement information as is necessary to enable participants and beneficiaries to determine their vested benefits.

If a plan administrator fails to provide a required benefit statement to a participant or beneficiary, the participant or beneficiary may bring a civil action to recover from the plan administrator $100 a day, within the court's discretion, or other relief that the court deems proper.

Requirements for defined contribution plans

The administrator of a defined contribution plan is required to provide a benefit statement (1) to a participant or beneficiary who has the right to direct the investment of the assets in his or her account, at least quarterly, (2) to any other participant or other beneficiary who has his or her own account under the plan, at least annually, and (3) to other beneficiaries, upon written request, but limited to one request during any 12-month period.

A benefit statement provided with respect to a defined contribution plan must include the value of each investment to which assets in the individual's account are allocated (determined as of the plan's most recent valuation date), including the value of any assets held in the form of employer securities (without regard to whether the securities were contributed by the employer or acquired at the direction of the individual). A quarterly benefit statement provided to a participant or beneficiary who has the right to direct investments must also provide: (1) an explanation of any limitations or restrictions on any right of the individual to direct an investment; (2) an explanation, written in a manner calculated to be understood by the average plan participant, of the importance, for the long-term retirement security of participants and beneficiaries, of a well-balanced and diversified investment portfolio, including a statement of the risk that holding more than 20 percent of a portfolio in the security of one entity (such as employer securities) may not be adequately diversified; and (3) a notice directing the participant or beneficiary to the Internet website of the Department of Labor for sources of information on individual investing and diversification.

Requirements for defined benefit plans

The administrator of a defined benefit plan is required either: (1) to furnish a benefit statement at least once every three years to each participant who has a vested accrued benefit under the plan and who is employed by the employer at the time the benefit statements are furnished to participants; or (2) to furnish at least annually to each such participant notice of the availability of a benefit statement and the manner in which the participant can obtain it. The Secretary of Labor is authorized to provide that years in which no employee or former employee benefits under the plan need not be taken into account in determining the three-year period. It is intended that the annual notice of the availability of a benefit statement may be included with other communications to the participant if done in a manner reasonably designed to attract the attention of the participant.

The administrator of a defined benefit pension plan is also required to furnish a benefit statement to a participant or beneficiary upon written request, limited to one request during any 12-month period.

In the case of a statement provided to a participant with respect to a defined benefit plan (other than at the participant's request), information may be based on reasonable estimates determined under regulations prescribed by the Secretary of Labor in consultation with the Pension Benefit Guaranty Corporation.

Form of benefit statement

A benefit statement must be written in a manner calculated to be understood by the average plan participant. It may be delivered in written, electronic, or other appropriate form to the extent such form is reasonably accessible to the recipient. For example, regulations could permit current benefit statements to be provided on a continuous basis through a secure plan website for a participant or beneficiary who has access to the website.

The Secretary of Labor is directed, within one year after the date of enactment, to develop one or more model benefit statements that may be used by plan administrators in complying with the benefit statement requirements. The use of the model statement is optional. It is intended that the model statement include items such as the amount of vested accrued benefits as of the statement date that are payable at normal retirement age under the plan, the amount of accrued benefits that are forfeitable but that may become vested under the terms of the plan, information on how to contact the Social Security Administration to obtain a participant's personal earnings and benefit estimate statement, and other information that may be important to understanding benefits earned under the plan. The Secretary of Labor is also given the authority to promulgate any interim final rules as determined appropriate to carry out the benefit statement requirements.

Effective date

The provision is generally effective for plan years beginning after December 31, 2006. In the case of a plan maintained pursuant to one or more collective bargaining agreements, the provision is effective for plan years beginning after the earlier of (1) the later of December 31, 2007, or the date on which the last of such collective bargaining agreements terminates (determined without regard to any extension thereof after the date of enactment), or (2) December 31, 2008.

[¶ 14,250.09]

Committee Report on P.L. 98-397 (Retirement Equity Act of 1984)

[Senate Committee Report]

Under the bill, any statement provided to a plan participant of total accrued benefits and nonforfeitable accrued benefits, or any statement provided to a separated plan participant who has a vested deferred benefit, must include a notice to the participant that certain benefits may be forfeited if the participant dies before a particular date. The notice that certain benefits may be forfeited if a participant dies before a particular date need not include the amount of the benefits that are forfeitable.

---

[120] A one-participant retirement plan is defined as under the provision of ERISA that requires advance notice of a blackout period to be provided to participants and beneficiaries affected by the blackout period, as discussed in Part H below.

[121] Under the permitted disparity rules, contributions or benefits may be provided at a higher rate with respect to compensation above a specified level and at a lower rate with respect to compensation up to the specified level. In addition, benefits under a defined benefit plan may be offset by a portion of a participant's expected social security benefits. Under a floor-offset arrangement, benefits under a defined benefit pension plan are reduced by benefits under a defined contribution plan.

[¶ 14,250.10]

Committee Reports on P.L. 93-406 (Employee Retirement Income Security Act of 1974)

See Committee Reports at ¶ 14,240.10.

[ERISA Sec. 106]

[¶ 14,260.10]

Committee Report on P.L. 93-406 (Employee Retirement Income Security Act of 1974)

[Conference Committee Explanation]

Reports made public information.—The contents of the description of plans and reports filed with the Secretary of Labor are to be public information and are to be available for inspection in the Department of Labor. In addition, the Secretary of Labor may use the information and data for statistical and research purposes and for the compiling and publishing of studies as he may deem appropriate. However, information with respect to a plan participant's accrued benefits and nonforfeitable pension rights is to be disclosed only to the extent that information respecting a participant's benefits for old age retirement insurance may be disclosed under the Social Security Act.

[ERISA Sec. 107]

[¶ 14,270.10]

Committee Report on P.L. 93-406 (Employee Retirement Income Security Act of 1974)

See Committee Reports at ¶ 14,220.10, ¶ 14,230.10, and ¶ 14,240.10.

[ERISA Sec. 108]

[¶ 14,280.10]

Committee Report on P.L. 93-406 (Employee Retirement Income Security Act of 1974)

[House Education and Labor Committee Report]

Proven reliance upon a regulation or interpretation by the Secretary of Labor would constitute a defense in a criminal or civil proceeding under certain sections of the act.

[ERISA Sec. 109]

[¶ 14,290.10]

Committee Report on P.L. 93-406 (Employee Retirement Income Security Act of 1974)

[Conference Committee Explanation]

Forms to be provided.—The Secretary of Labor may require that any information required to be filed with the Labor Department, including statements and schedules attached to the annual report, must be submitted on forms that he may prescribe. The financial statement prepared by the independent qualified accountant and the actuarial statement prepared by the enrolled actuary and the summary of the plan description are not required to be submitted on forms. However, the Secretary may prescribe the format and content of the accountant's and actuary's statements and of the summary plan description, the summary annual report, and other statements or reports required under title I to be furnished or made available to participants and beneficiaries.

* * * The two Secretaries [Labor and Treasury] are to unify, to the extent feasible, the reports made to them and it is expected that all of the material subject to the form authority of either Secretary, comprising the annual reports to be made by a plan, can and should be reported on a single form.

[ERISA Sec. 110]

[¶ 14,300.10]

Committee Reports on P.L. 93-406 (Employee Retirement Income Security Act of 1974)

See Committee Report at ¶ 14,210.10.

[ERISA Sec. 111]

[¶ 14,310.10]

Committee Report on P.L. 93-406 (Employee Retirement Income Security Act of 1974)

[Conference Committee Explanation]

Effective dates

The conference agreement provides that the reporting and disclosure provisions generally are to take effect on January 1, 1975. However, in the case of a fiscal year plan year which begins before January 1, 1975, and ends after December 31, 1974, the Secretary of Labor may by regulation postpone the effective date until the beginning of the first plan year of the plan which begins after January 1, 1975.

[ERISA Sec. 201]

[¶ 14,410.09]

Committee Report on P.L. 96-364 (Multiemployer Pension Plan Amendments Act of 1980)

[Senate testimony on floor amendment]

—Mr. LONG. Mr. President, the amendment I am proposing to this bill will correct a terrible injustice which has been done to the employees of South Bend Lathe regarding their loss of pension benefits.

In 1975, I was pleased to help the South Bend Lathe employees purchase ownership of their company through an employee stock ownership plan by encouraging the Department of Commerce to make a grant to the city of South Bend, which in turn loaned the money to the ESOP. Since the parent company was planning to liquidate South Bend Lathe, this saved over 500 jobs. The president of that company has testified about the success of their employee stock ownership plan before several congressional committees over the past few years.

However, at the time the employees bought the company, through no fault of their own and no fault on the part of South Bend Lathe, they lost their pension benefits from the pension plan maintained by the parent company. Even though this happened after we passed ERISA, it occurred in a plan year which began prior to ERISA and therefore this law could not protect these employees' pension benefits. The parent company obtained an IRS ruling that the sale of the South Bend Lathe division was not a "termination" of the plan and therefore the employees were not automatically vested; in short, they lost these pension benefits.

Mr. President, many of these same employees worked in the 1960s for Studebaker in the same building where South Bend Lathe is now located. They lost their pension benefits at that time, too. In fact, as most Senators know, it was the Studebaker closing, and the resulting loss of pension benefits by its employees, that ultimately led to the enactment of ERISA.

The employees of South Bend Lathe, who are the sole owners of the company, now propose that each employee who retired since they bought the company or who retires in the future will receive a letter from the company promising that, if the company can afford it, the lost pension benefits will be made up. I repeat: This is agreeable to the employees, who are the sole shareholders of the company and who elect its board of directors.

The terrible irony is that ERISA, which has twice failed to protect these employees, now prevents them from setting up a plan to compensate themselves for these lost pension benefits. Under a strict reading of ERISA, this would constitute a "pension plan" or an "employee pension benefit plan," and would therefore have to be currently funded and meet other ERISA requirements. Until the employees finish paying for the company they bought, they cannot afford the cost of a permanent, funded pension plan.

Mr. President, we have let these employees down twice before regarding their pension benefits. I do not propose to do it again. All they want to do is pay themselves their lost pension benefits and I am determined that ERISA not leave them without these beneifts a third time.

The amendment (UP No. 1465) was agreed to.

[¶ 14,410.10]

Committee Report on P.L. 93-406 (Employee Retirement Income Security Act of 1974)

[Conference Committee Explanation]

Plans subject to the provisions.—Under title I of the conference substitute (the labor law provisions) the new participation and coverage rules are to be enforced by the Secretary of Labor when participants bring violations to his attention or when cases come to his attention which initially were under consideration by the Secretary of Treasury on which he has previously initiated action. The rules are to apply to employee pension benefit plans of employers or employee organizations established in or affecting interstate commerce. Under this title II (the tax law provisions), the participation and coverage rules are to be administered by the Secretary of the Treasury or his delegate, and the rules apply to tax-qualified pension, profit-sharing, and stock bonus plans.[1]

[1] The division of administrative responsibility between Labor and Treasury is discussed in Part XII, below "General Provisions Relating to Jurisdiction, Administration, Enforcement: Joint Pension Task Force, Etc." [CCH ¶ 15,110]. Except where otherwise noted, the regulations with respect to participation, vesting and funding are to be written by the Secretary of the Treasury or his delegate.

Exceptions to coverage.—The participation and coverage requirements of title I (the labor law provisions) do not apply to governmental plans (including Railroad Retirement Act plans), church plans (except those electing coverage), plans maintained solely to comply with workmen's unemployment, disability, or compensation laws, plans maintained outside the United States primarily for the benefit of nonresident aliens, employee welfare plans, excess plans (which provide for benefits or contributions in excess of those allowable for tax-qualified plans), unfunded deferred compensation arrangements, plans established by labor organizations (those referred to in sec. 501(c)(5) of the Internal Revenue Code) which do not provide for employer contributions after the date of enactment, and fraternal or other plans of organizations (described in sec. 501(c)(8), 501(c)(9)) which do not receive employer contributions, or trusts described in 501(c)(18) of the Internal Revenue Code. Title I does not apply to buy-out agreements involving retiring or deceased partners (under sec. 736 of the Internal Revenue Code). In addition, title I does not apply to employer or union-sponsored individual retirement accounts (see "Employee Savings for Retirement").

The participation requirements of title II apply only to plans which qualify for certain tax deferral privileges by meeting the standards as to participation and other matters set forth in the Internal Revenue laws. However, governmental plans and church plans which do not elect to come under the new provisions will nevertheless be treated as qualified for purposes of the tax deferral privileges for the employees, if they meet the requirements of present law. Also the rules do not apply to plans of labor organizations (described in sec. 501(c)(5)) or fraternal or other organizations (described in sec. 501(c)(8) or (9)) which do not provide for employer contributions.

Exemption for church plans.—As indicated above, both title I and title II exempt church plans from the participation and coverage requirements of the conference substitute (although title II requires these plans to comply with present law in order to be qualified). This exemption does not apply to a plan which is primarily for the benefit of employees engaged in an unrelated trade or business, or (except as noted below) to a multiemployer plan unless all of the participating employers are churches or conventions or associations of churches (rather than merely church-related agencies). However, a multiemployer plan which was in existence on January 1, 1974, and which covers church-related agencies (such as schools and hospitals) is to be treated as a church plan for purposes of the exemption (even though it continues to cover those agencies) for plan years beginning before January 1, 1983, but not for subsequent plan years.

A church plan may make an irrevocable election to be covered under title I and title II (in a form and manner to be prescribed in regulations). A plan which makes this election is to be covered under the bill for purposes of the new participation, vesting, funding and form of benefit rules, as well as the fiduciary and disclosure rules and will also be covered under the plan termination insurance provisions.

[ERISA Sec. 202]

[¶ 14,420.07]

Committee Reports on P.L.99-514 (Tax Reform Act of 1986)

For Committee Reports on P.L. 99-514, see ¶ 14,430.085.

[¶ 14,420.09]

Committee Reports on P.L. 98-397 (Retirement Equity Act of 1984)

[Senate Committee Report]

Maximum age conditions.—The bill provides that a pension plan may not require, as a condition of participation, completion of more than one year of service or attainment of an age greater than 21 (whichever occurs later). The reduction in the maximum participation age further limits the extent of backloading of benefit accruals.

Under the bill, a plan is not permitted to ignore, for purposes of the minimum vesting requirements, an employee's years of service completed after the employee has attained age 18.

[Senate Committee Report]

Break in service rules.—The bill provides that, in the case of a nonvested participant, years of service with the employer or employers maintaining the plan before any period of consecutive 1-year breaks in service are required to be taken into account after a break in service unless the number of consecutive 1-year breaks in service equals or exceeds the greater of (1) 5 years or (2) the aggregate number of years of service before the consecutive 1-year breaks in service. * * * This "rule of parity" is applicable for participation and vesting purposes.

For example, if a nonvested participant with 3 years of service under a plan terminates employment and incurs 4 consecutive 1-year breaks in service, the plan generally is not permitted to disregard the participant's 3 years of service for either participation or vesting purposes upon the participant's resumption of employment with the employer. On the other hand, if the participant incurs 5 consecutive 1-year breaks in service under this example, the plan could disregard the years of service prior to the break in service.

In addition, the bill provides that, in the case of a participant in a defined contribution plan or in a defined benefit pension plan funded solely by insurance contracts, years of service after a break in service are counted for purposes of determining the vested percentage of the participant's accrued benefit derived from employer contributions before the break in service unless the participant incurs at least 5 consecutive 1-year breaks in service. Under the bill, a conforming change is made to the rules relating to the cash out of accrued benefits.

[¶ 14,420.10]

Committee Report on P.L. 93-406 (Employee Retirement Income Security Act of 1974)

[Conference Committee Explanation]

General rule as to participation.—Generally, under title I and title II of the conference substitute, an employee cannot be excluded from a plan on account of age or service if he is at least 25 years old and has had at least one year of service. However, if the plan provides full and immediate vesting for all participants, it may require employees to be age 25, with 3 years of service, in order to participate. As an alternative, any plan which is maintained exclusively for employees of a governmental or tax-exempt educational organization which provides full and immediate vesting for all participants may have a participation requirement of age 30, with 1 year of service.

Maximum age requirement.—Under the conference substitute, in general, a plan may not exclude an employee because he is too old. However, because of cost factors, it was decided that in a defined benefit plan it would be appropriate to permit the exclusion of an employee who is within 5 years of attaining normal retirement age under the plan (or older) when he is first employed. (These employees would be counted as part of the employer's work force, however, for purposes of determining whether or not his plan satisfied the breadth-of-coverage requirements.) Of course, if a plan defines normal retirement age as the later of age 65, or the tenth anniversary of the employee's participation in the plan, the plan could not impose a maximum age requirement (because no employee would be within 5 years of normal retirement age when first employed). A "target benefit" plan, as defined in Treasury regulations, could also impose a maximum age requirement (even though it is not a defined benefit plan), because in many respects the pattern of costs and benefits of target benefit plans closely resembles the pattern of costs and benefits of defined benefit plans.

Year of service defined.—Under the conference substitute, in general, for purposes of the participation requirements, the term "year of service" means a 12-month period during which the employee has worked at least 1,000 hours. This 12-month period is measured from the date when the employee enters service. Thus, the employee has fulfilled his 1,000-hour-requirement if he has 1,000 hours of work by the first anniversary date of his employment. Under the substitute, the employee (if age 25 or older) would then be admitted to the plan within 6 months or his anniversary date of employment or by the beginning of the first plan year following his first anniversary date, whichever occurred earlier. (Of course, this does not mean that an employee would have to be admitted to the plan if he were lawfully excluded for reasons other than age or service.)

The plan would not be required to admit the employee if he had "separated from the service" before the otherwise applicable admission date. In general, "separated from the service" means the employee was discharged or quit; it does not mean temporary absence due to vacation, sickness, strike, seasonal layoff, etc.

If the employee did not complete 1,000 hours of service by his first anniversary date, but is still employed, he would start over toward meeting his 1,000 hour requirement. For this purpose, the plan could provide (on a consistent basis) that the relevant 12-month period is either (a) the year between his first anniversary date and his second anniversary date, or (b) the first plan year which began after the individual was first employed. For example, assume the plan is on a calendar year basis, and that an employee begins work on July 1, 1976. Between July 1, 1976, and June 30, 1977, the employee has less than 1,000 hours of service. The plan could provide that the employee would be tested the second time for purposes of participation based on the year from July 1, 1977 through June 30, 1978, or based on the year from January 1, 1977 through December 31, 1977 (but not January 1, 1978 through December 31, 1978).

The regulations with respect to "year of service" are to be written by the Secretary of Labor for purposes of participation and vesting. The term "hour of service" will also be defined in Labor Department regulations.

For purposes of participation (and vesting), in the case of any maritime industry (as defined in Labor Department regulations), 125 days of service are to be treated as the equivalent of 1,000 hours of service, but this rule will not apply to other industries.

Seasonal and part-time workers.—In general, the 1,000 hour standard is to apply for purposes of determining whether or not an employee may be excluded from the plan as a seasonal or part-time employee (replacing the 5-month year, 20-hour week standard now in the Internal Revenue Code). However, in the case of seasonal industries where the customary period of employment is less than 1,000 hours, the term "year of service" is to be determined in accordance with Labor Department regulations.

Breaks in service.—Under the conference substitute, a 1-year break in service occurs in any calendar year, plan year, or other consecutive 12-month period designated by the plan on a consistent basis (and not prohibited under Labor Department regulations) in which the employee has 500 hours of service or less.

The general rule is that all service with the employer (pre-break and post-break) is to be taken into account for purposes of determining whether the employee has met the participation requirements. However, if an employee has a 1-year break in service, the plan may require a 1-year waiting period before reentry, at which point the employee's pre-break and post-break service are [sic] to be aggregated, and the employee is to receive full credit for the waiting period service. For example, if the plan is on a calendar year basis, and an employee who has a 1-year break in service reenters employment on November 1, 1976, works 200 hours in 1976, and 1700 hours by November 1, 1977, the employee under this provision would be considered as reentering the plan for 1977. As a result, his pre-break and post-break service would be aggregated, and he would advance one year on the vesting schedule for 1977. He would also accrue benefits for that year. (Other rules with respect to break-in-service are explained below in connection with vesting and benefit accrual.)

In the case of a plan which has a 3-year service requirement for participation (because the plan provides 100 percent immediate vesting), the plan may provide that employees who have a 1-year break in service before completing their 3-year service requirement must start over toward fulfilling that requirement after the break in service.

H.R. 10 plans.—In general, the provisions of present law which allow a 3-year service requirement for participation (but do not allow the plan to impose an age requirement), and require 100 percent immediate vesting, would continue to govern owner-employee H.R. 10 plans (those for sole proprietors and 10 percent owners and their employees). However, certain provisions of this bill, such as the rules with respect to year of service and breaks in service are also to apply for purposes of the H.R. 10 plans.

[ERISA Sec. 203]

[¶ 14,430.075]

Committee Report on P.L. 109-280 (Pension Protection Act of 2006)

For the Committee Report on P.L. 109-280 on cash balance and other hybrid plans, see ¶ 12,200.035.

For the Committee Report on P.L. 109-280 on vesting schedules for matching contributions, see ¶ 12,200.035.

[¶ 14,430.077]

Committee Report on P.L. 107-16 (Economic Growth and Tax Relief Reconciliation Act)

For the Committee Report on P.L. 107-16 on disregarding rollovers for purposes of cash-out rules, see ¶ 12,200.04.

[¶ 14,430.079]

Committee Report on P.L. 107-16 (Economic Growth and Tax Relief Reconciliation Act)

For the Committee Report on P.L. 107-16 on faster vesting of employer matching contributions, see ¶ 12,200.06.

[¶ 14,430.081]

Committee Reports on P.L. 105-34 (Taxpayer Relief Act)

[House Committee Report]

Cash out of accrued benefits

Cash out of certain accrued benefits.—The bill increases the limit on involuntary cash-outs to $5,000 from $3,500. The $5,000 amount is adjusted annually for inflation beginning after 1997 (in $50 increments).

Effective date

The provision is effective for plan years beginning on and after the date of enactment.

[Conference Committee Report]

Senate Amendment

The Senate amendment is the same as the House bill, except the Senate amendment also makes a corresponding change to title I of ERISA and provides that the $5,000 amount is adjusted for inflation beginning after 1997 in $50 increments.

Conference Agreement

The conference agreement follows the House bill and the Senate amendment, except that the conference agreement does not increase the $5,000 limit for inflation.

[¶ 14,430.083]

Committee Reports on P.L. 104-188 (Small Business Job Protection Act)

[House Committee Report]

Special vesting rule for multiemployer plans eliminated

The bill conforms the vesting rules for multiemployer plans to the rules applicable to other qualified plans.

Effective Date

The provision is effective for plan years beginning on or after the earlier of (1) the later of January 1, 1997, or the date on which the last of the collective bargaining agreements pursuant to which the plan is maintained terminates, or (2) January 1, 1999, with respect to participants with an hour of service after the effective date.

[Conference Committee Report]

Senate Amendment

The Senate amendment is the same as the House bill.

Conference Agreement

The conference agreement follows the House bill and the Senate amendment.

[¶ 14,430.084]

Committee Report on P.L. 103-465 (General Agreement on Tariffs and Trade (GATT); Retirement Protection Act)

— . . . relating to single sum distributions—see ¶ 12,550.09.

[¶ 14,430.085]

Committee Reports on P.L. 99-514 (Tax Reform Act of 1986)

[Senate Committee Report]

Explanation of Provision

In general

The bill provides that a plan is not a qualified plan (except in the case of a multiemployer plan), unless a participant's employer-provided benefit vest[s] at least as rapidly as under one of 2 alternative minimum vesting schedules.

A plan satisfies the first schedule if a participant has a nonforfeitable right to 100 percent of the participant's accrued benefit derived from employer contributions upon the participant's completion of 5 years of service. A plan satisfies the second alternative schedule if a participant has a nonforfeitable right to at least 20 percent of the participant's accrued benefit derived from employer contributions after 3 years of service, 40 percent at the end of 4 years of service, 60 percent at the end of 5 years of service, 80 percent at the end of 6 years of service, and 100 percent at the end of 7 years of service.

Top-heavy plans

The provisions of the bill relating to vesting do not alter the requirements applicable to plans that become top heavy. Thus, a plan that becomes top heavy is required to satisfy one of the two alternative vesting schedules applicable under present law to top-heavy plans.

Class year plans

Under the bill, a plan with class year vesting will not meet the qualification standards of the Code unless, under the plan's vesting schedule, a participant's total accrued benefit becomes nonforfeitable at least as rapidly as under one of the two alternative vesting schedules specified in the bill.

Changes in vesting schedule

Under the bill, if a plan's vesting schedule is modified by plan amendment, the plan will not be qualified unless each participant with no less than 3 years of service is permitted to elect, within a reasonable period after the adoption of the amendment, to have the nonforfeitable percentage of the participant's accrued benefit computed without regard to the amendment.

Multiemployer plans

As an exception to the general vesting requirements, the bill requires that, in the case of a multiemployer plan, a participant's accrued benefit derived from employer contributions be 100 percent vested no later than upon the participant's completion of 10 years of service.

Effective Date

The provisions are generally applicable for years beginning after December 31, 1988, with [respect] to participants who perform at least one hour of service in a plan year to which the new provision applies.

A special effective date applies to plans maintained pursuant to a collective bargaining agreement. Under this special rule, in the case of a plan maintained pursuant to a collective bargaining agreement between employee representatives and one or more employers ratified before March 1, 1986, the amendments are not effective for plan years beginning before the earlier of (1) the later of (i) January 1, 1989, or (ii) the date on which the last of the collective bargaining agreements terminates, or (2) January 1, 1991. Extensions or renegotiations of the collective bargaining agreement, if ratified after February 28, 1986, are disregarded.

[Conference Committee Report]

The conference agreement follows the Senate amendment. In addition, the conference agreement modifies the rule permitting an employer to condition participation in a plan with 3 years of service. Under the conference agreement a plan may require, as a condition of participation, that an employee complete a period of service with the employer of no more than two years. A plan that requires that an employee complete more than one year of service as a condition of participation must also provide that each participant in the plan has a nonforfeitable right to 100 percent of the accrued benefit under the plan when the benefit is accrued.

In addition, the conference agreement limits the special rule for multiemployer plans to employees covered by a collective bargaining agreement.

Also, benefits that become vested due to the provisions are to be immediately guaranteed by the PBGC (without regard to the phase-in rule).

The conference agreement also modifies the effective date so that the provision applies to all employees who have one hour of service after the effective date. This revised effective date also applies to the conference agreement modifications regarding years of service required for participation.

In addition, the conference agreement limits the delayed effective date for plans maintained pursuant to a collective bargaining agreement to employees covered by such agreements.

[Senate Committee Report]

The bill generally conforms the break-in-service rules applicable to class-year plans to the break-in-service rules provided for other types of plans. Under the bill, a class-year plan generally is to provide that 100 percent of each participating employee's right to benefits derived from employer contributions for a plan year (the contribution year) is to be nonforfeitable as of the close of the fifth plan year of service (whether or not consecutive) with the employer following the contribution year. A plan year is a plan year of service with the employer if the participant has not separated from service with the employer as of the close of the year.

The bill provides that, if a participant incurs five consecutive one-year breaks in service before the completion of five plan years of service with respect to a contribution year, then the plan may provide that the participant forfeits any right to or derived from the employer contributions for the contribution year.

The provision is effective for contributions made for plan years beginning after the date of enactment, except that the provision is not effective with respect to a collectively bargained plan until the applicable effective date of the Act for that plan.

* * *

[¶ 14,430.09]

Committee Report on P.L. 98-397 (Retirement Equity Act of 1984)

[Senate Committee Report]

Maternity or paternity leave.—Under the bill, for purposes of determining whether a break in service has occurred for participation and vesting purposes, an individual is deemed to have completed hours of service during certain periods of absence from work. This rule applies to an individual who is absent from work (1) by reason of the pregnancy of the individual, (2) by reason of the birth of a child of the individual, (3) by reason of the placement of a child in connection with the adoption of the child by the individual, or (4) for purposes of caring for the child during the period immediately following the birth or placement for adoption.

The committee intends that an individual will qualify for this maternity or paternity leave credit if a child is placed with the individual for a trial period prior to adoption. No credit need be given, however, merely by reason of the placement of a child in a foster home.

During the period of absence, the individual is treated as having completed (1) the number of hours that normally would have been credited but for the absence, or (2) if the normal work hours are unknown, eight hours of service for each normal workday during the leave (whether or not approved). The total number of hours of service required to be treated as completed under the bill is 501 hours.

The hours of service required to be credited under the bill must be credited only (1) in the year in which the absence begins for one of the permitted reasons if the crediting is necessary to prevent a break in service in that year, or (2) in the following year. For example, an individual who completes at least 501 hours during a year before leaving employment by reason of pregnancy or who is otherwise entitled to credit for up to 501 hours during the year is entitled to credit of up to 501 hours in the next year, because such credit is not needed in the year in which the absence begins.

Under the bill, an individual is not entitled to credit for maternity or paternity leaves unless the absence from work is for one of the permitted reasons. For example, suppose that an individual was absent from work on account of a layoff, gave birth to a child two years after the layoff began, and was not recalled to work. Under these circumstances, the individual is not entitled to credit for maternity or paternity leave because the absence from work was not for one of the permitted reasons. On the other hand, if the employer had recalled the individual immediately prior to the birth of the child, the individual would be entitled to credit for maternity or paternity leave.

An employer may require, as a condition of providing credit for the hours required under this rule, that the individual certify to the employer that the leave was taken for the permitted reasons. This certification could be required to include, for example, a statement from a doctor that the leave was taken by reason of the birth of a child of the individual. In addition, the employer may require that the individual supply information relating to the number of normal workdays for which there was an absence. The committee intends that credit will not be denied for failure to supply any required information if the plan administrator has access to the relevant information without regard to whether the participant submits it.

Under the bill, hours credited under these rules for maternity or paternity leave are not required to be taken into account for purposes of determining a participant's year of participation under the benefit accrual rules.

[¶ 14,430.095]

Committee Report on P.L. 96-364 (Multiemployer Pension Plan Amendments Act of 1980)

For Senate Committee Report on P.L. 96-364, see Committee Report at ¶ 12,200.09.

[¶ 14,430.10]

Committee Report on P.L. 93-406 (Employee Retirement Income Security Act of 1974)

[Conference Committee Explanation]

Plans subject to the provisions; exceptions from coverage; exemption for church plans.—The rules in these areas are the same as the corresponding rules discussed above under Participation and Coverage [CCH ¶ 14,410.10].

General rules.—Under the conference substitute[1] plans must provide full and immediate vesting in benefits derived from employee contributions.

With respect to employer contributions, the plan (except class year plans) must meet one of three alternative standards. Two of those, the 5-to 15-year graded standard and the 10-year/100-percent standard are the same as provided in the House bill (and briefly described above). The third standard under the conference substitute is a modification of the House-bill "rule of 45". As under the House rule, under the modified rule of 45, an employee with 5 or more years of covered service must be at least 50 percent vested when the sum of his age and years of coverd service total 45, and there must be provision for at least 10 percent additional vesting for each year of covered service thereafter. Unlike the House bill, however, each employee with 10 years of covered service (regardless of his age) must be at least 50 percent vested and there must be provision for 10 percent additional vesting for each year of service thereafter.

In addition, all plans would have to meet the requirement of present law that an employee must be 100 percent vested in his accrued benefit when he attains the normal or stated retirement age (or actually retires).

Service credited for vesting purposes.—Generally, under the conference substitute, once an employee becomes eligible to participate in a pension plan, all his years of service with an employer (including pre-participation service, and service performed before the effective date of the Act) are to be taken into account for purposes of determining his place on the vesting schedule. However, the plan may ignore periods for which the employee declined to make mandatory contributions, and periods for which the employer did not maintain the plan or a predecessor plan, as defined in Treasury regulations (i.e., if the plan provides past service credits for purposes of benefit accrual, it must also provide past service credits for purposes of participation and vesting).

Generally, the plan may also ignore service performed before age 22; however, if a plan elects to use the rule of 45, service before age 22 may be ignored only if the employee was not a participant in the plan during the years before age 22.

The plan may also exclude part-time or seasonal service (i.e., generally years when the employee had less than 1,000 hours of service).

Also, if the employee has had a "break in service", his service performed prior to the break may be ignored to the extent permitted under the "break in service" rules (discussed below).

Service performed prior to January 1, 1971, may be ignored by the plan, unless (and until) the employee has at least 3 years of service after December 31, 1970.

[1] Unless otherwise indicated, the rules with respect to vesting appear in both title I and title II of the conference substitute. Unless otherwise indicated, the regulations with respect to vesting are to be written by the Secretary of the Treasury, or his delegate.

Year of service defined.—In general, under the conference substitute, the rules with respect to "year of service", seasonal and part-time employees, etc., are the same for purposes of the vesting schedule as they are for purposes of participation (i.e., generally 1,000 hours of service except for seasonal industries, where the customary work year is less than 1,000 hours). However, the relevant year for purposes of applying the vesting schedule may be any 12-month period provided under the plan (plan year, calendar year, etc.) regardless of the anniversary date of the participant's employment (even though the anniversary date is the measuring point for purposes of the participation requirements for an employee's first year).

For purposes of benefit accrual, in general, the plan may use any definition of the term "year of service" which the plan applies on a reasonable and consistent basis (subject to Department of Labor regulations). (Of course, the "year" for benefit accrual purposes cannot exceed the customary work year for the industry involved.) However, the plan must accrue benefits for less than full-time service on at least a pro rata basis. For example, if a plan requires 2,000 hours of service for a full benefit accrual (50 weeks of 40 hours each) then the plan would have to accrue at least 75 percent of a full benefit for a participant with 1,500 hours of service. Generally, a plan would not be required to accrue any benefit for years in which the participant had less than 1,000 hours of service. In the case of industries or occupations where the customary year is less than 1,000 hours (for example, the tuna fishing industry, or the winter season employees of a ski lodge), the rules with respect to benefit accrual would be determined under Department of Labor regulations. As previously indicated a special rule is provided for the maritime industries.

Breaks in service.—Under the conference substitute, a 1-year break in service occurs in any calendar year, plan, or other consecutive 12-month period designated by the plan and applied on a consistent basis (and not prohibited under Labor Department regulations) in which the employee has no more than 500 hours of service. For example, if the plan is on a calendar year basis, and the employee works 1,000 hours in 1976, 501 hours in 1977, 501 hours in 1978, and 1,000 hours or more in 1979, the employee would not have a break in service (although the plan would not be required to accrue benefits or give vesting schedule credit for 1977 or 1978).

The rules with respect to breaks in service for vesting and benefit accrual purposes may be summarized as follows:

(1) If an employee has a 1-year break in service, the plan may require (for administrative reasons) a 1-year waiting period before his pre-break and post-break service must be aggregated under the plan. However, once the employee has completed this waiting period, he must receive credit for that year (for purposes of vesting and accrued benefit).

(2) In the case of an individual account plan (including a plan funded solely by individual insurance contracts, as well as a "target benefit plan") if any employee has a 1-year break in service, his vesting percentage in pre-break benefit accruals does not have to be increased as a result of post-break service.

(3) Subject to rules (1) and (2), once an employee has achieved any percentage of vesting, then all of his pre-break and post-break service must be aggregated for all purposes.

(4) For all nonvested employees (and subject to rules (1) and (2)), the employee would not lose credits for pre-break service until his period of absence equaled his years of covered service. Under this "rule of parity" for example, if a nonvested employee had three years of service with the employer, and then had a break in service of 2 years, he could return, and after fulfilling his 1-year reentry requirement, he would have 4 years of covered service, because his pre-break and post-break service would be aggregated.[2]

For years beginning prior to the effective date of the vesting provisions, a plan may apply the break-in-service rules provided under the plan, as in effect from time to time. However, no plan amendment made after January 1, 1974, may provide for break-in-service rules which are less beneficial to any employee than the rules in effect under the plan on that date, unless the amendment complies with the break-in-service rules established under this bill.

The principles of some of the rules outlined above may be illustrated as follows: For example, assume a plan is on a calendar year basis, and an employee with a 1-year break in service reenters employment on November 1, 1976, works 200 hours in 1976, and 1,700 hours by November 1, 1977. In this case, the employee would be eligible to reenter the plan on November 1, 1977, his pre-break and post-break service would be aggregated, he would advance one year on the vesting schedule for 1977, and he would also accrue benefits for 1977. On the other hand, if the employee reentered employment on March 1, 1976, worked 1,700 hours before December 31, 1976, and was not separated from service by March 1, 1977, he would be eligible to reenter the plan on March 1, 1977, advance one year on the vesting schedule for his 1976 service, and the plan would have to provide at least a partial accrual for 1976.

Predecessor employer.—The rules concerning service with a predecessor employer are the same for purposes of vesting and benefit accrual as the rules for purposes of participation, discussed above.

Multiemployer plans.—Under the conference substitute, service with any employer, for any year in which the employer is a member of the plan, is to be counted for purposes of vesting as if all employers who are parties to the plan were a single employer.

Permitted forfeitures of vested rights.—Under the conference substitute, except as outlined below, an employee's rights, once vested, are not to be forfeitable for any reason. An employee's rights to benefits attributable to his own contributions may never be forfeited.

(1) The plan may provide that an employee's vested rights to benefits attributable to employer contributions may be forfeited on account of the employee's death (unless a "joint and survivor" annuity is to be provided).

(2) Also, the plan may provide that payment of benefits attributable to employer contributions may be suspended for any period in which the employee is reemployed by the same employer under whose plan the benefits are being paid (in the case of a single employer plan). In the case of a multiemployer plan, however, a suspension of benefit payments is permitted when the employee is employed in the same industry, in the same trade or craft and also in the same geographical area covered under the contract, as was the case immediately before he retired. Regulations with respect to the suspension of benefits are to be prescribed by the Department of Labor.

(3) A plan amendment may reduce an employee's vested or nonvested accrued benefit attributable to employer contributions, but only for the current year, and only if the amendment is adopted within 2 ½ months from the close of the plan year in question (without regard to any extensions). In the case of a multiemployer plan, the retroactive amendment may effect [sic] the current year, and the two immediately preceding years (thus, a multiemployer plan amendment adopted by December 31, 1978, could effect [sic] plan benefits for 1976, if the plan was on a calendar year). However, no plan amendment which reduces accrued benefits is permitted unless the Secretary of Labor has 90 days prior notice of the proposed amendment, and approves it (or fails to disapprove it). No such approval is to be granted, except to prevent substantial economic hardship, including a serious danger that the plan will be terminated unless the amendment is allowed. In addition, it must be found that the economic hardship cannot be overcome by means of a funding variance. Subject to these rules, no plan amendment may retroactively reduce the accrued benefit of any participant (whether or not that benefit is vested).

(4) A plan may provide that an employee's rights to benefits from employer contributions may be forfeited where the employee is less than 50 percent vested in these benefits and withdraws all or any part of his own mandatory contributions to the plan. However, the plan must also provide a "buy back" rule, i.e., that the employee's forfeited benefits will be fully restored if the employee repays the withdrawn contributions (with interest of 5-percent per annum, compounded annually) to the plan.

In the case of a plan which does not provide for mandatory contributions after the date of enactment [September 2, 1974], the plan may provide, in this case, that the employee will forfeit a proportionate part of his pre-date-of-enactment accrued benefits derived from employer contributions even if he is 50 percent or more vested in these benefits. Also, the plan is not required to have a "buy back" clause with respect to the withdrawal of preenactment contributions. Additional regulations in this area are to be prescribed by the Secretary of the Treasury, or his delegate.

Changes in vesting schedule.—The conference substitute provides that if, at any time in the future, the plan changes its vesting schedule, the vesting percentage for each participant in his accrued benefit accumulated to the date when the plan amendment is adopted (or the date the amendment becomes effective, if later) cannot be reduced as a result of the amendment. In addition, as a further protection for long service employees, any participant with at least 5 years of service may elect to remain under the pre-amendment vesting schedule with respect to all of his benefits accrued both before and after the plan amendment.

Discrimination.—Under the conference substitute the rules of the House bill are adopted with respect to the relationship of the minimum vesting standards of the bill to the antidiscrimination rules of present law (sec. 401(a)(4) of the Internal Revenue Code). In general, a plan which meets the vesting requirements provided in this substitute is not to be considered as discriminatory, insofar as its vesting provisions are concerned, unless there is a pattern of abuse under the plan (such as the firing of employees before their accrued benefits vest) or there has been (or there is reason to believe there will be) an accrual of benefits or forfeitures tending to discriminate in favor of employees who are officers, shareholders or who are highly compensated.

In the past, however, the law in this area has been administered on a case-by-case basis, without uniform results in fact situations of a similar nature. As a result, except in cases where actual misuse of the plan occurs in operation, the Internal Revenue Service is directed not to require a vesting schedule more stringent than 40 percent vesting after 4 years of employment with 5 percent additional vesting for each for each of the next 2 years, and 10 percent additional vesting for each of the following five years. Also, this more rapid vesting would generally not be required except in a case where the rate of likely turnover for officers, shareholders, or highly compensated employees was substantially less

[2] Also, in the case of a defined benefit plan, the employee would have at least 3 years of accrued benefits under the plan (2 years of accrued benefits due to his pre-break participation and 1 year of benefits accrued with respect to the 1-year reentry period).

(perhaps as much as 50 percent less) than the rate of likely turnover for rank-and-file employees. Of course, where there is a pattern of firing employees to avoid vesting, the limitations described above would not apply. Also, it generally is not intended that any plan (or successor plan of a now existing plan) which is presently under a more rapid vesting schedule should be permitted to cut back its vesting schedule as a result of this statement.

In addition, the conferees have directed the joint pension task force study group to examine problems of the interrelationship of the vesting and the antidiscrimination rules carefully. The conferees also expect the Treasury or the Internal Revenue Service to supply information with respect to patterns of benefit loss for different categories of plans (as designated by the task force) under the minimum vesting schedules prescribed under this legislation, and such other information as the task force study group may require. In other words, the experimental rules outlined above (40 percent vesting after 4 years, etc.) are intended to apply only until the responsible congressional committees can review the situation after receiving the report of the task force study group.

Moreover, the conferees intend that the antidiscrimination rules of present law in areas other than the vesting schedule are not to be changed. Thus, the present antidiscrimination rules with respect to coverage, and with respect to contributions and benefits are to remain in effect. Also, the antidiscrimination rules may be applied with respect to benefit accruals.

The conference substitute contains a technical rule to be applied in the case of target benefit plans (and other defined contribution plans), which provides that regulations may establish reasonable earnings assumptions and other factors for these plans in order to prevent discrimination.

Class year plans.—Under the substitute, the minimum vesting requirements are satisfied in the case of a class year plan if the plan provides for 100 percent vesting of the benefits derived from employer contributions within 5 years after the end of the plan year for which the contributions were made. Also, under the substitute, forfeitures with respect to employer contributions would be permitted on a class-year-by-class-year basis, for any year for which the employee withdraws his own mandatory contributions to the plan, if he is less than 50 percent vested with respect to that year. For purposes of these rules, withdrawals will be applied to the earliest year for which the employee has made contributions which have not yet been withdrawn.

[ERISA Sec. 204]

[¶ 14,440.038]

Committee Report on P.L. 109-280 (Pension Protection Act of 2006)

For the Committee Report on P.L. 109-280 on access to multiemployer pension plan information, see ¶ 13,648W-75.045.

For the Committee Report on P.L. 109-280 on cash balance and other hybrid plans, see ¶ 12,200.035.

For the Committee Report on P.L. 109-280 on investment diversification, see ¶ 11,700.02.

For the Committee Report on P.L. 109-280 on plan amendments, see ¶ 12,200.035.

[¶ 14,440.04]

Committee Report on P.L. 107-16 (Economic Growth and Tax Relief Reconciliation Act)

For the Committee Report on P.L. 107-16 on forms of distribution see ¶ 12,200.05.

[¶ 14,440.06]

Committee Report on P.L. 107-16 (Economic Growth and Tax Relief Reconciliation Act)

For the Committee Report on P.L. 107-16 on the notice of significant reduction in plan benefit accruals, see ¶ 13,648W-75.05.

[¶ 14,440.08]

Committee Report on P.L. 100-203 (Omnibus Budget Reconciliation Act of 1987)

[Conference Committee Report]

Under the [Labor and Human Resources Committee amendment], the 5-percent rate is replaced by a rate equal to 120 percent of the mid-term applicable Federal rate (AFR) (as in effect for the first [month] of the plan year). The Secretary of the Treasury does not have the authority to alter this rate. The provision is effective on the date of enactment.

The conference agreement follows the Labor and Human Resources Committee amendment, effective for years beginning after December 31, 1987.

[¶ 14,440.085]

Committee Report on P.L. 99-272 (Consolidated Omnibus Budget Reconciliation Act)

[Conference Committee Report]

The conference agreement provides that an amendment to reduce significantly future benefit accruals under a plan is not effective unless, subsequent to the adoption of the amendment and at least 15 days prior to the effective date of the amendment, the plan administrator gives written notice of the reduction to each participant in the plan, * * * each beneficiary who is an alternate payee under a qualified domestic relations order, and each employee organization representing participants in the plan. This notice does not apply to any amendment (or portion thereof) to retroactively reduce plan benefits (Sec. 412(c)(8) of the Code and Section 302(c)(8) of ERISA).

The conference agreement does not affect the requirements for qualifications of a plan under the Code. For example, the agreement does not change the requirement of minimum benefit accruals under a frozen top-heavy plan.

[¶ 14,440.09]

Committee Reports on P.L. 98-397 (Retirement Equity Act of 1984)

[Senate Committee Report]

The bill provides that, if the present value of an accrued benefit exceeds $3,500, then the benefit is not to be considered nonforfeitable if the plan provides that the present value of the benefit can be immediately distributed without the consent of the participant (and, if applicable, the participant's spouse). Under the bill, the interest rate to be used in determining whether the present value of a benefit exceeds $3,500 is not to be greater than the interest rate that would be used (as of the date of the distribution) by the Pension Benefit Guaranty Corporation (PBGC) for purposes of determining the present value of a lump sum distribution upon termination of the plan. The committee intends that the PBGC rate in effect at the beginning of a plan year may be used throughout the plan year if the plan so provides.

[Senate Committee Report]

[The bill provides, as under present law that] if any years of service are not required to be taken into account by reason of a period of breaks in service under [the parity] rule, then those years of service are not required to be taken into account * * * if there is a subsequent break in service.

[¶ 14,440.10]

Committee Report on P.L. 93-406 (Employee Retirement Income Security Act of 1974)

[Conference Committee Explanation]

* * *

(5) A plan may provide for the "cash out" of an employee's accrued benefit. In other words, the plan may pay out, in a lump sum, the entire value of an employee's vested accrued benefit. (However, portability is available to the employee because other provisions of the bill permit the employee to reinvest in an individual retirement account on a tax-sheltered basis.) If the plan does make such a cash-out, then the plan would not be required to vest the employee in his accrued benefits which are not vested at the time he separates from the service, if the employee is later reemployed. (However, the employee's prebreak service would have to be taken into account for all other purposes, subject to the break-in-service rules, e.g., for purposes of his place on the vesting schedule.)

A cash-out could be made from the plan without the employee's consent only if the payment (a) was made due to the termination of the employee's participation in the plan, (b) constituted the value of the employee's entire interest in the plan, and (c) did not exceed an amount (to be prescribed in regulations by the Secretary of the Treasury or his delegate) based on the reasonable administrative needs of the plan, and, in any event, not in excess of $1,750 (with respect to the value of the benefit attributable to the employer's contributions). Despite the foregoing provision, generally, the conferees prefer that all amounts contributed for retirement purposes be retained and used for those purposes. Thus, a plan could provide for no cash-out, or the employee's collective bargaining unit might wish to bargain for such a provision.

A higher cash-out could be made with the employee's consent. However, even these voluntary cash-outs could only be made if the employee terminated his participation in the plan, or under other circumstances to be prescribed in regulations.

Moreover, the plan must provide, in all cases (except where a distribution equal to the value of the full accrued benefit is made), that all accrued benefits must be fully restored (except to the extent provided under the break-in-service rules) if the employee repays the amount of the cash-out, with interest. Repayment of an involuntary cash-out would have to be allowed under the plan at any time after the employee reentered employment under the plan, and repayment of voluntary cash-outs would have to be allowed under circumstances to be prescribed in regulations. However, an individual account plan would not be required to permit repayment after the employee had a one year break in service.

Accrued benefit.—Under the conference substitute, the term "accrued benefit" refers to pension or retirement benefits. The term does not apply to ancillary benefits, such as payment of medical expenses (or insurance premiums for such expenses), or disability benefits which do not exceed the normal retirement benefit payable at age 65 to an employee with comparable service under the plan, or to life insurance benefits payable as a lump sum.

Also, the accrued benefit does not include the value of the right to receive early retirement benefits, or the value of social security supplements or other benefits under the plan which are not continued for any employee after he has attained normal retirement age. However, an accrued benefit may not be reduced on account of increasing age or service (except to the extent of social security supplements or their equivalents).

In the case of a plan other than a defined benefit plan, the accrued benefit is to be the balance in the employee's individual account.

In the case of a defined benefit plan, the accrued benefit is to be determined under the plan, subject to certain requirements. In general, the accrued benefit is to be defined in terms of the benefit payable at normal retirement age. Normal retirement age generally is to be the age specified under the plan. However, it may not be later than age 65 or the tenth anniversary of the time the participant commenced participation, whichever last occurs. No actuarial adjustment of the accrued benefit would be required, however, if an employer voluntarily postponed his own retirement. For example, if the plan provided a benefit of $400 a month payable at age 65, this same $400 a month benefit (with no upward adjustment) could also be paid by the plan to an individual who voluntarily retired at age 68.

Each defined benefit plan is to be required to satisfy one of the three accrued benefit tests (which limit the extent of "back-loading" permitted under the plan).

The three percent test.—Under this alternative each participant must accrue, for each year of participation, at least 3 percent of the benefit which is payable under the plan to a participant who begins participation at the earliest possible entry age and serves continuously until age 65, or normal retirement age under the plan, whichever is earlier. This test is to be applied on a cumulative basis (i.e., any amount of "front loading" is permitted). Also, in the case of a plan amendment, the test would be cumulative. For example, assume that a plan provided a flat benefit of $200 a month payable at age 65 during the first 10 years of an individual's participation, then [was] amended to provide a flat benefit of $400 a month; the participant's accrued benefit at the end of his 11th year of participation would equal $132 (3 percent of $400, times 11 years of service).

In addition, if a plan elects this alternative, and if the plan provides a given benefit to a person who is employed when he attains retirement age, who has a given amount of service, then any employee who has that amount of service, even though he leaves before retirement age, would be entitled to this same benefit when he reached retirement age. For example, if the plan is based on compensation and provides a 40 percent of salary benefit for an employee who served at least 20 years and is still employed at age 65, then the plan must provide that an employee who served 20 years from age 35 to age 55 would be entitled to that same 40 percent of compensation benefit (beginning at normal retirement age or age 65).

133 ⅓ percent test.—Under this alternative, the plan is to qualify if the accrual rate for any participant for any later year is not more than 133 ⅓ percent of his accrual rate for the current year. Thus, (unlike the House Bill) the conference substitute permits an unlimited amount of "front loading" under this test. The accrual rate can be based on either a dollar or percentage rate. In applying these rules, a plan amendment in effect for the current year is to be treated as though it were in effect for all plan years. (For example, if a plan provides a one percent rate of accrual for all participants in 1976, and is amended to provide a 2 percent rate of accrual for all participants in 1977, the plan will meet this test, even though 2 is more than 1 ⅓ times 1.) Also, if the plan has a scheduled increase in the rate of accruals, which will not be in effect for any participant until future years, this scheduled increase will not be taken into account for purposes of the backloading rules until it actually takes effect. Also, in applying the 133 ⅓ percent test, social security benefits and all other factors used to compute benefits under the plan will be treated as remaining constant, at current year levels, for all future years.

Pro rata rule.—As a third alternative, the conference substitute contains a modified version of the rule contained in the Senate amendment. Under this test, for purposes of determining the accrued benefit, the retirement benefit is to be computed as though the employee continued to earn the same rate of compensation annually that he had earned during the years which would have been taken into account under the plan (but not in excess of 10), had the employee retired on the date in question. This amount is then to be multiplied by a fraction, the numerator of which is the employee's total years of active participation in the plan up to the date when the computation is being made, and the denominator of which is the total number of years of active participation he would have had if he continued his employment until normal retirement age. This test is cumulative in the sense that unlimited front loading is permitted. For purposes of this test, social security benefits and all other relevant factors used to compute benefits shall be treated as remaining constant at current year levels for all future years. Also for purposes of this rule the term "normal retirement age" would be defined as set forth above, and the test would apply only to the benefit payable at, or after, normal retirement age (i.e., it would not take account of subsidized early retirement (to the extent such a benefit does not exceed the benefit payable at normal retirement age) and social security supplements).[2]

A plan is not to be treated as failing to meet the tests solely because the accrual of benefits under the plan does not become effective until the employee has two continuous years of service, measured from the anniversary date of employment.

In the case of a plan funded exclusively through the purchase of insurance contracts, the accrued benefit is to be the cash surrender value of the contract (determined as though the funding requirements with respect to the plan had been fully satisfied).

In the case of a variable annuity plan, the accrued benefit is to be determined in accordance with regulations to be prescribed by the Secretary of the Treasury or his delegate.

Benefits accrued in the past.—Generally, the vesting rules of the conference substitute are to apply to all accrued benefits, including those which accrued before the effective date of the provisions (subject, however, to the break-in-service rules discussed above). However, many plans now in existence have no accrued benefit formula for the past, thus making it impossible in these cases to determine what the employee is vested in. To deal with this situation, the conference substitute provides that the accrued benefit under a plan for years prior to the effective date of the vesting provisions for any participant is to be not less than the greater of (1) the accrued benefit under the provisions of the plan (as in effect from time to time), or (2) an accrued benefit which is not less than one-half of the benefit which would have accrued under one of the three back-loading tests described above.

The plan may choose which of the 3 standards it wishes to apply for the past (subject to the antidiscrimination rules); however, the same standard must be applied to all the plan's participants on a consistent basis. The plan is not required to choose, for the past, the same test which it applies in the future.

Allocations between employee and employer contributions.—The House bill and the Senate amendment are quite similar in the rules they apply in allocating contributions between those made by the employee and the employer and the conference substitute follows the House bill as to technical matters in the case of this provision. In addition, the substitute makes a clarifying amendment which provides (in the case of a defined benefit plan), that the accrued benefit attributable to employee contributions can never be less than the sum of those contributions (computed without interest). This assures that the employee will at least be vested in his own contributions to the plan, on a dollar-for-dollar basis. Thus, for example, in the case of an individual insurance contract, employer contributions to the plan must at least absorb the load factor, but, of course, payment of the load factor by the employer would not cause the plan to be treated as a plan which was not funded solely through the purchase of insurance contracts.

[ERISA Sec. 205]

[¶ 14,450.083]

Committee Reports on P.L. 109-280 (Pension Protection Act of 2006).

For the Committee Report on P.L. 109-280 on interest rate assumption for determining lump-sum distributions, see ¶ 12,550.07.

For the Committee Report on P.L. 109-280 on cash balance and other hybrid plans, see ¶ 12,200.035.

For the Committee Report on P.L. 109-280 on minimum survivor annuity requirements, see ¶ 12,550.07.

For the Committee Report on P.L. 109-280 on notice and consent periods for distributions, see ¶ 12,550.07.

[¶ 14,450.084]

Committee Reports on P.L. 104-188 (Small Business Job Protection Act)

[House Committee Report]

Waiver of minimum waiting period

The bill provides that the minimum period between the date the explanation of the qualified joint and survivor annuity is provided and the annuity starting date does not apply if it is waived by the participant and, if applicable, the participant's

---

[2] For example, assume a social security offset plan providing a benefit equal to 2 percent of high-3 years compensation per year of service with the employer, minus 30 percent of the primary social security benefit, with a normal retirement age of 65. Assume also an employee who began employment at age 25, and terminated employment at age 45, 100 percent vested, with high-3 years pay of $19,000, $20,000, and $21,000. At the time the employee separates from service the primary social security benefit payable to him at age 65 (under the social security law as [sic] effect when he terminates) would be $6,000 if he continued to work with the employer at his same annual rate of compensation until normal retirement age. His accrued benefit under the plan would equal $7,100. (If the employee had remained in service until age 65, he would have 40 years service, times 2 percent per year (80 percent), times $20,000 average high-3-years compensation ($16,000), minus 30 percent of the $6,000 primary social security benefit payable to the employee at age 65 under then current law ($16,000 minus $1,800 equals $14,200) times $^{20}/_{40}$ths (20 years of service over 40 total years from age 25 to age 65) equals $7,100.)

In the case of a plan amendment, the rule would work as follows. Assume an individual begins participation at age 25 in a plan which provides 1 percent of high-three-years pay during his first 10 years of service. In the 11th year the plan amends to provide 2 percent of pay for all future years of service. The employee separates from service at the end of the 11th year (and is 100 percent vested). His accrued benefit would equal 19.25 percent of average high-three-years pay (10 (years of participation) times 1 percent per year, 30 (years of projected participation) times 2 percent per year, times $^{11}/_{40}$ths (11 years of participation over 40 total years between age 25 and age 65)).

spouse. For example, if the participant has not elected to waive the qualified joint and survivor annuity, only the participant needs to waive the minimum waiting period.

Effective Date

The provision is effective with respect to plan years beginning after December 31, 1996.

[Conference Committee Report]

The conference agreement codifies the provision in the temporary Treasury regulations which provides that a plan may permit a participant to elect (with any applicable spousal consent) a distribution with an annuity starting date before 30 days have elapsed since the explanation was provided, as long as the distribution commences more than seven days after the explanation was provided. The conference agreement also provides that a plan is permitted to provide the explanation after the annuity starting date if the distribution commences at least 30 days after such explanation was provided, subject to the same waiver of the 30-day minimum waiting period as described above. This is intended to allow retroactive payments of benefits which are attributable to the period before the explanation was provided.

[¶ 14,450.085]

Committee Reports on P.L. 99-514 (Tax Reform Act of 1986)

[Senate Committee Report]

1. Coordination between qualified joint and survivor annuity and qualified preretirement survivor annuity

* * *

Explanation of Provision

In general

The bill clarifies and coordinates the application of the qualified joint and survivor annuity and qualified preretirement survivor annuity provisions in the case of (1) an individual who dies before or after the annuity starting date, and (2) an individual who receives a disability benefit under a plan.

Coordination of preretirement survivor annuity and joint and survivor annuity

The bill provides that the survivor benefit payable to a participant's spouse is to be provided in the form of a qualified joint and survivor annuity if the participant does not die before the annuity starting date unless the benefits is waived in favor of another benefit and the spouse consents to the waiver. As under present law, the qualified preretirement survivor annuity rules apply in the case of a death before the annuity starting date if the preretirement survivor annuity has not been waived.

Thus, if a participant dies after separation from service or attainment of normal retirement age, but prior to the participant's annuity starting date, the survivor benefit payable to the participant's spouse is to be paid in the form of a qualified preretirement survivor benefit.

Disability benefits

The bill amends the definition of a participant's annuity starting date to exclude the commencement of disability benefits, but only if the disability benefit is an auxiliary benefit. If a participant receiving a disability benefit will, upon attainment of early or normal retirement age, receive a benefit that satisfies the accrual and vesting rules of section 411 (without taking the disability benefit payments up to that date into account), the disability benefit may be characterized as auxiliary.

For example, consider a married participant who becomes disabled at age 45 with a deferred vested accrued benefit of $100 per month commencing at age 65 in the form of a joint and survivor annuity. If the participant is entitled under the plan to a disability benefit and is also entitled to a benefit not less than $100 per month commencing at age 65, whether or not the participant is still disabled, the payments made to the participant between ages 45 and 65 would be considered auxiliary. Thus, the participant's annuity starting date would not occur until the participant attained age 65. The participant's surviving spouse would be entitled to receive a qualified preretirement survivor annuity if the participant died before age 65, and the survivor portion of a qualified joint and survivor annuity if the participant died after age 65. The value of the qualified preretirement survivor annuity payable upon the participant's death prior to age 65 would be computed by reference to the qualified joint and survivor annuity that would have been payable had the participant survived to age 65.

If, in the above example, the participant's benefit payable at age 65 were reduced to $90 per month as a result of the disability benefits paid to the participant prior to age 65, the disability benefit would not be auxiliary. The benefit of $90 per month payable at age 65 would not, without taking into account the disability benefit payments prior to age 65, satisfy the minimum vesting and accrual rules of section 411 of the Code. Accordingly, the first day of the first period for which the disability payments were made would constitute the participant's annuity starting date, and any benefits paid to the participant would be required to be paid in the form of a qualified joint and survivor annuity (unless waived by the participant with the consent of the spouse).

2. Transferee plan rules

Present Law

* * *

A plan is a transferee of a plan required to provide survivor benefits if the plan (1) receives a direct transfer of assets in connection with a merger, spinoff, or conversion of a plan that is subject to the survivor benefit requirements, or (2) receives a direct transfer of assets solely with respect to the participant. Also, a plan is a transferee plan with respect to a participant if it receives amounts from a plan that is a transferee plan with respect to that participant. A plan is not a transferee plan merely because it receives rollover contributions from another plan. The transferee plan rules do not apply in the case of a rollover contribution because the consent of the participant's spouse had to be obtained in order to make the plan distribution that qualified for rollover treatment.

Explanation of Provision

The bill includes two provisions relating to the transferee plan rules. First, the bill clarifies that a plan is not to be considered a transferee plan on account of a transfer completed before January 1, 1985.

In addition, the bill clarifies that the transferee plan rule is limited to benefits attributable to the transferred assets if separate accounting is provided for the transferred assets and the allocable investment yield from those assets. Under the bill, if separate accounting is not maintained for transferred assets (and any allocable investment yield) with respect to an employee, then the survivor benefit requirements apply to all benefits payable with respect to the employee under the plan.

3. Rules relating to qualified preretirement survivor annuity

* * *

Explanation of Provision

The bill clarifies that, in the case of a participant who separates from service prior to death, the amount of the qualified preretirement survivor annuity, is to be calculated by reference to the actual date of separation from service, rather than the date of death. Thus, for purposes of calculating the qualified preretirement survivor annuity, a participant is not to be considered to accrue benefits after the date of separation from service.

The bill also clarifies that, under the special rule for defined contribution plans, a qualified preretirement survivor annuity payable to a participant's surviving spouse is required to be the actuarial equivalent of not less than 50 percent of [the portion of the account balance of the participant to which the participant had a nonforfeitable right]. For purposes of determining who is a vested participant subject to the survivor benefit provisions, the bill provides that a participant's accrued benefit includes accrued benefits derived from employee contributions.

The bill also clarifies that a plan that is exempt from the survivor benefit [provisions] may provide for the payment of the participant's nonforfeitable accrued benefit (without the consent of the participant's surviving spouse) to a beneficiary other than the participant's spouse if the participant and spouse have been married for less than 1 year as of the death of the participant [or the participant's annuity starting date, whichever is the earliest].

The committee intends that, with respect to a defined benefit or defined contribution plan, the qualified preretirement survivor annuity is to be treated as attributable to employee contributions in the same proportion which the employee contributions are to the total accrued benefit of the participant. Thus, a plan is not permitted to allocate a preretirement survivor annuity only to employee contributions.

* * *

4. Spousal consent requirements

* * *

Explanation of Provision

Designation of nonspouse beneficiary

Under the bill, a spouse's consent to waive a qualified joint and survivor annuity or a qualified preretirement survivor annuity is not valid unless the consent (1) names a designated beneficiary who will receive any survivor benefits under the plan and the form of any benefits paid under the plan (including the form of benefits that the designated beneficiary will receive), or (2) acknowledges that the spouse has the right to limit consent only to a specific beneficiary or a specific form of benefits, and that the spouse voluntarily elects to relinquish one or both of such rights.

The spousal consent form is to contain such information as may be appropriate to disclose to the spouse the rights that are relinquished. If the consent names a designated beneficiary, then any subsequent change to the beneficiary designation (or the form of distribution, if any, specified in the consent) is invalid unless a new consent is obtained from the participant's spouse. Of course, spousal consent is not required if a participant dies and the beneficiary designated (with spousal consent) to receive the participant's death benefit elects to receive the benefit in a form not specified in the waiver.

If a plan is required to permit the waiver of a survivor benefit, the committee intends that the plan may not restrict the spouse's ability to waive a benefit by providing only a general consent to waive under which a spouse relinquishes the right to designate a beneficiary or a form of benefit. Thus, a spouse is always permitted to waive a survivor benefit only in favor of a specific beneficiary or a specific form of benefit. The committee intends that, if a plan permits a general consent, the acknowledgment of the general consent should indicate that the spouse is aware that a more limited consent could be provided.

Similar rules relating to the manner in which spousal consent is obtained apply to a spousal consent obtained to waive a death benefit under a profit-sharing or stock bonus plan that is not otherwise subject to the survivor benefit requirements.

Spousal consent with respect to loans

In addition, under the bill, in the case of a participant's benefit that is not exempt from the survivor benefit requirements, a plan is to provide that no portion of the accrued benefit of the participant may be used as security for any loan unless, at the time the security agreement is entered into, the participant's spouse (determined as of the date the security agreement is entered into) consents to the use of the accrued benefit as security. If the individual who is the participant's spouse at the time that the security agreement is entered into consents, then the plan is not prevented by the spousal consent rules from realizing its security interest in the event of a default on the participant's loan, even if, at the time of the default, the participant is married to a different spouse. Similarly, if a participant is not married at the time the security agreement is executed, then the plan is not prevented from realizing its security interest if a default on the loan subsequently occurs when the participant is married.

For example, assume that a spouse consents to a pledge of the participant's account balance as security for a loan from the plan. Under the plan, the plan administrator is to realize on the security for the loan if it is not repaid by the time the employee separates from service. Because the spouse consented to the loan, the plan is not prevented from using the security (i.e., the account balance) to recover the amount due on the loan. In addition, if the participant had remarried after the loan was made but before the plan realized on its security, then the consent of the first spouse would continue to be effective for purposes of determining the plan's ability to realize its security interest.

In the case of a participant whose accrued benefit is not subject to the survivor benefit provisions at the time the security is provided (e.g., a profit-sharing plan that is not a transferee plan with respect to the participant), the plan will not be treated as failing to meet the survivor benefit requirements if the participant's benefit is used as security for a loan and spousal consent is not obtained for the use of the accrued benefit as security, even if the plan subsequently becomes subject to the survivor benefit requirements with respect to the participant.

The bill further clarifies that for purposes of determining the survivor benefit, if any, to which a participant's surviving spouse is entitled upon the participant's death, any security interest held by the plan by reason of a loan outstanding to the participant is taken into account and, if there is a default on the loan, then the participant's nonforfeitable accrued benefit is first reduced by any security interest held by the plan by reason of a loan outstanding to the participant. The rule applies only if (a) the loan is secured by the participant's accrued benefit and (b) the spousal consent requirements, if any, applicable to the participant's accrued benefit at the time the security arrangement was entered into were satisfied. In addition, the participant's nonforfeitable accrued benefit is adjusted (where appropriate), taking into account the terms of the plan and the terms of the qualified domestic relations order, by the value of amounts payable under any outstanding qualified domestic relations order, for purposes of determining the survivor benefit, if any, to which the participant's surviving spouse is entitled upon the participant's death.

Similarly, upon a married participant's retirement, for purposes of determining the amount of the joint and survivor annuity payable to the participant and spouse, any security held by the plan by reason of a loan outstanding to the participant and the present value of any outstanding qualified domestic relations order are taken into account in the same manner as they are taken into account for purposes of the qualified preretirement survivor annuity.

Determination of amount of preretirement survivor annuity

The bill provides that, in the case of a defined contribution plan subject to the survivor benefit requirements, the participant's vested account balance (including any portion of the account balance attributable to employee contributions) is used for purposes of determining the amount of the qualified preretirement survivor annuity.

Scope of spousal consent requirements

The bill clarifies that certain of the election period and notice requirements with respect to spousal consent also apply in the case of spousal consent (1) to waive a survivor benefit under a plan exempt from the preretirement survivor annuity and joint and survivor annuity requirements, (2) to permit the participant's accrued benefit to be pledged as security for a loan, (3) to permit the election of a cash-out of amounts after the annuity starting date, and (4) to permit the immediate distribution of amounts in excess of $3,500.

In the case of a loan secured by a participant's accrued benefits, the notice and election period requirements apply at the time the security arrangement is entered into. Consequently, the election period for spousal consent with respect to the execution of a security agreement is the 90-day period before the execution of the agreement.

Similarly, in the case of a cash-out subsequent to a participant's annuity starting date, the election period is the 90-day period before the distribution is permitted.

The committee intends that, for purposes of the spousal consent rules, in the case of a participant residing outside of the United States, that spousal consent may be witnessed by the equivalent of a notary public in the jurisdiction in which consent is executed. The committee also intends that an election under section 242(b) of the Tax Equity and Fiscal Responsibility Act of 1982 will not be invalidated because a plan secures spousal consent to the election.

In addition, the committee intends that a participant will be treated as having no spouse, if the participant has been abandoned (within the meaning of local law) by the spouse, even if the participant knows where the spouse is located. The committee intends that the spousal consent requirement may be waived, however, only if the participant has a court order specifying that the participant has been abandoned within the meaning of local law. Of course, a participant could provide a qualified domestic relations [instrument] (such as a separation agreement) rather than a court order specifying that the participant has been abandoned.

Gift tax consequences of waiver

The bill provides that the waiver of a qualified joint and survivor annuity or a qualified preretirement survivor annuity by a nonparticipant spouse prior to the death of the participant does not result in a taxable transfer for purposes of the gift tax provisions.

Effective Dates

The provision relating to spousal consents to beneficiary designations is effective for consents given on or after January 1, 1985. [The provision relating to spousal consent to changes in benefit form is effective for plan years beginning after the date of enactment.] The provision relating to the notice and election period requirements for plans that are exempt from the survivor benefit requirements is effective upon the date of enactment.

The provision relating to accrued benefits pledged as security for a loan is effective for loans made after August 18, 1985. In addition, any accrued benefits pledged as security for a loan prior to August 19, 1985, are exempt from the requirement that spousal consent be obtained. Accordingly, in the case of a pledge made before August 19, 1985, a plan is not required to obtain the consent of any spouse of a participant before it applies the benefit against the loan. Finally, any loan that is revised, extended, renewed, or renegotiated after August 18, 1985, is treated as a loan made (and security pledged) after August 18, 1985.

[Conference Committee Report]

* * * The provision relating to spousal consent to changes in benefit form is effective for plan years beginning after the date of enactment.

[¶ 14,450.09]

Committee Reports on P.L. 98-397 (Retirement Equity Act of 1984)

[Senate Committee Report]

In general.—Under the bill, a pension plan is to provide automatic survivor benefits (1) in the case of a participant who retires under the plan, in the form of a qualified joint and survivor annuity, and (2) in the case of a vested participant who dies before the annuity starting date (the first period for which an amount is received as an annuity (whether by reason of death or disability) under the plan) and who has a surviving spouse, in the form of a qualified preretirement survivor annuity. A vested participant is any participant (whether or not still employed by the employer) who has a nonforfeitable right to any portion of the accrued benefit derived from employer contributions.

The provisions of the bill requiring automatic survivor benefits apply to any pension plan. An exception is provided, however, for a participant under a profit-sharing or stock bonus plan if (1) the plan provides that the nonforfeitable accrued benefits will be paid to the surviving spouse of the participant (or to another beneficiary if the surviving spouse consents or if there is no surviving spouse) if the participant dies, (2) under a plan that offers a life annuity, the participant does not elect payment of benefits in the form of a life annuity, and (3) with respect to the participant, the plan is not a direct or indirect transferee of a plan required to provide automatic survivor benefits. A plan is a transferee of a plan required to provide automatic survivor benefits if the plan (1) receives a direct transfer of assets in connection with a merger, spinoff or conversion of a plan or (2) receives a direct transfer of assets solely with respect to the participant. Also, a plan is a transferee if it receives amounts from a plan that is a transferee. As under present law, the cost of survivor benefit coverage may be imposed on the participant or beneficiary.

Under the bill, an exception to the application of the rules relating to joint and survivor benefits is provided in the case of certain employee stock ownership plans (ESOPs) for the portion of an employee's accrued benefit that is subject to the requirements of section 409(h) of the Code. This exception applies only if the requirements applicable to profit-sharing and stock bonus plans are also met.

Qualified joint and survivor annuity and qualified preretirement survivor annuity.—Under the bill, a qualified joint and survivor annuity is an annuity for the life of the participant with a survivor annuity for the life of the spouse that is not less than 50 percent (and not greater than 100 percent) of the amount that is (1) payable during the joint lives of the participant and the spouse, and (2) the actuarial equivalent of a single life annuity for the life of the participant. A qualified joint and survivor annuity also includes an annuity having the effect of a qualified joint and survivor annuity, which is defined as a benefit at least the actuarial equivalent of the normal form of life annuity or, if greater, any optional form of life annuity. Equivalence may be determined on the basis of consistently applied reasonable actuarial factors if such determination does not result in discrimination in favor of employees who are officers, shareholders, or highly compensated.

The bill defines a qualified preretirement survivor annuity as an annuity for the life of the surviving spouse of the participant. The amount of the payments under a qualified preretirement survivor annuity is not to be less than the payments that would have been made under the qualified joint and survivor annuity if (1) in the case of a participant who dies after attaining the earliest retirement age under the plan, the participant had retired with an immediate qualified joint and survivor annuity on the day before the participant's death, and (2) in the case of a participant who dies on or before the earliest retirement age under the plan, the participant had separated from service on the date of death, survived until the earliest retirement age, and retired at that time with a qualified joint and survivor annuity. In the case of a defined contribution plan, the payments under a qualified preretirement survivor annuity are not to be less than the payments under a single life annuity, the present value of which is at least equal to 50 percent of the participant's account balance on the date of death. Under the bill, the plan is not to prohibit the commencement of the qualified preretirement survivor annuity to the surviving spouse later than the month in which the participant would have reached the earliest retirement age under the plan. If the surviving spouse wishes to delay commencement of benefit payments until a later date and the present value of the benefit is more than $3,500 at the earliest retirement date, then the plan cannot require that benefit payments commence at the participant's earliest retirement age. Of course, the incidental benefit rule of present law is required to be satisfied with respect to the preretirement survivor benefit.

Election and notice procedures.—Under the bill, a participant is to be given the opportunity to waive the qualified joint and survivor annuity and qualified preretirement survivor annuity during the applicable election period. In addition, the participant is permitted to revoke any waiver during the applicable election period. The bill does not limit the number of times a participant may waive a survivor benefit or revoke a waiver.

The bill provides that the consent of a participant's spouse is required for an election to decline the qualified joint and survivor annuity and the qualified preretirement survivor annuity. This consent is to be given in writing at the time of the participant's election, and the consent is to acknowledge the effect of the election. A consent is not valid unless it is witnessed by a plan representative or a notary public. Any consent obtained is effective only with respect to the spouse who signs it.

The requirement that the consent of the spouse be obtained may be waived if it is established to the satisfaction of a plan representative that the consent required cannot be obtained because there is no spouse, because the spouse cannot be located, or because of other circumstances that the Secretary of the Treasury prescribes by regulation.

If the plan administrator acts in accordance with the fiduciary standards of ERISA in securing spousal consent or in accepting the representations of the participant that the spouse's consent cannot be obtained, then the plan will not be liable for payments to the surviving spouse. For example, if the plan administrator receives a notarized spousal consent, valid on its face, which the administrator has no reason to believe is invalid, the plan would certainly be allowed to rely on the consent even if it is, in fact, invalid. In addition, if a third-party payor relies on a consent obtained or determination made by the plan administrator who acts in accordance with the fiduciary standards, or if a third party payor acting in accordance with such standards (whether or not the payor is a plan fiduciary under ERISA) establishes that consent cannot be obtained, then the payor will be relieved of any liability for payments to the surviving spouse.

As under present law, the plan is required to provide to the participant, within a reasonable period of time before the annuity starting date, a written explanation of (1) the terms and conditions of the qualified joint and survivor annuity, (2) the participant's right to make, and the effect of, an election to waive the qualified joint and survivor annuity, (3) the rights of the participant's spouse, and (4) the right to revoke an election and the effect of such a revocation. In addition, the committee intends that plans will provide to participants notification of their rights to decline a qualified preretirement survivor annuity period before the applicable election period. This notice is to be provided within the period beginning on the first day of the plan year in which the participant attains age 32 and ending with the close of the plan year in which the participant attains age 35. This notice is to be comparable to the notice required with respect to the qualified joint and survivor annuity. Of course, the preretirement survivor benefit coverage may become automatic prior to the time that the participant is entitled to decline such coverage.

Under the bill, a plan is not required to provide notice of the right to waive the qualified joint and survivor annuity or the qualified preretirement survivor annuity if the plan fully subsidizes the cost of the benefit. A plan fully subsidizes the costs of a benefit only if the failure to waive the benefit by a plan participant does not result in either (1) a decrease in any plan benefits with respect to the participant, or (2) in increased plan contributions by the participant. A plan that provides for no employee contributions and does not require employee contributions if the participant does not waive any survivor benefits is treated as not requiring increased plan contributions by the participant. A plan may fully subsidize the cost of the qualified joint and survivor annuity, the qualified preretirement survivor annuity, or both.

The bill defines the applicable election period to mean (1) in the case of a qualified joint and survivor annuity, a period of time not exceeding 90 days before the annuity starting date or (2) in the case of a qualified preretirement survivor annuity, a period beginning on the first day of the plan year in which the participant attains age 35 and ending on the date of the participant's death. If a participant separates from service, the applicable election period begins on that date with respect to benefits accrued before the separation from service. For example, if a participant who is age 30 separates from service with vested, accrued benefits of $4,000, the participant is permitted to waive the qualified preretirement survivor annuity with respect to the benefits of $4,000 at the time of separation from service. If the participant returns to service at age 32, the applicable election period with respect to benefits accrued after the participant returns does not begin until the first day of the plan year in which the participant attains age 35. Thus, the participant will have automatic survivor coverage during the period from age 32 to 35 with respect to the vested benefits accrued during that period, without regard to whether the participant waived the coverage with respect to the pre-separation accrued benefits. At age 35, the participant may waive any preretirement survivor annuity coverage. Of course, a waiver made by a participant or by a participant and spouse is not valid with respect to a future spouse.

Special rules.—The bill provides that a qualified joint and survivor annuity is not required to be provided by a plan unless the participant and spouse have been married throughout the one-year period ending on the earlier of (1) the participant's annuity starting date (the first day of the first period for which an amount is received as an annuity (whether by reason of retirement or disability)), or (2) the date of the participant's death. If a participant dies after the annuity starting date, the spouse to whom the participant was married during the one-year period ending on the annuity starting date is entitled to the survivor annuity under the plan whether or not the participant and spouse are married on the date of the participant's death. This rule does not apply, however, if a qualified domestic relations order * * * [¶ 206 below] otherwise provides for the division or payment of the participant's retirement benefits. For example, a qualified domestic relations order could provide that the former spouse is not entitled to any survivor benefits under the plan.

Under the bill, an exception to the one-year marriage requirement is provided if a participant marries within one year before the annuity starting date and the participant has been married to that spouse for at least one year ending on the date of the participant's death. The committee recognizes that this exception may create administrative burdens for a plan in cases in which the participant has not been married for one year before the payment of benefits commence. The committee intends that the plan may require a participant to notify the plan when the participant has been married for one year so that the plan administrator may alter the form of benefit payments to reflect the qualified joint and survivor annuity if the participant and spouse do not waive it.

If a former spouse of a participant is entitled to receive a portion of the participant's benefit under a qualified domestic relations order, the qualified joint and survivor annuity and qualified preretirement survivor annuity requirements do not apply unless they are consistent with the order. A plan is not required to provide a qualified joint and survivor annuity or a qualified preretirement survivor annuity to the spouse of a participant's former spouse.

The bill provides that a plan may immediately distribute the present value of the benefit under either the qualified joint and survivor annuity or the qualified preretirement survivor annuity if the present value of the benefit does not exceed $3,500. No distribution may be made after the annuity starting date unless the participant and the participant's spouse (or the surviving spouse of the participant) consent in writing to the distribution.

In addition, under the bill, if the present value of the benefit under the qualified joint and survivor annuity or the qualified preretirement survivor annuity exceeds $3,500, the participant and spouse (or the surviving spouse if the participant has died) must consent in writing before the plan can immediately distribute the present value. For purposes of calculating the present value of a benefit as of the date of the distribution, the plan is required to use an interest rate no greater than the rate used by the Pension Benefit Guaranty Corporation (PBGC) in valuing a lump sum distribution upon plan termination. The committee intends that the PBGC rate in effect at the beginning of a plan year may be used throughout the plan year if the plan so provides.

The bill repeals the two-year nonaccidental death rule of present law. Thus, a plan may not provide that any election or revocation of an election does not take effect if (1) the participant dies within a period not in excess of two years beginning on the date of the election or revocation, and (2) the death of the participant is not due to an accident that occurred after the election or revocation.

Consultation with the Secretary of Labor.—Under the bill, the Secretary of the Treasury is required to consult with the Secretary of Labor in prescribing regulations under these provisions.

[¶ 14,450.10]

Committee Report on P.L. 93-406 (Employee Retirement Income Security Act of 1974)

[Conference Committee Explanation]

Joint and survivor annuities.—Under the conference substitute, when a plan provides for a retirement benefit in the form of an annuity, and the participant has been married for the one-year period ending on the annuity starting date, the plan must provide for a joint and survivor annuity. The survivor annuity must be not less than half of the annuity payable to the participant during the joint lives of the participant and his spouse.

In the case of an employee who retires, or who attains the normal retirement age, the joint and survivor provision is to apply unless the employee elected otherwise.

In the case of an employee who is eligible to retire prior to the normal retirement age under the plan, and who does not retire, the joint and survivor provisions need not be applicable under the plan, unless the employee made an affirmative election. Moreover, the plan need not make this option available until the employee is within 10 years of normal retirement age. (Of course, a plan may provide that a joint and survivor annuity is to be the only form of benefit payable under the plan, and in this case, no election need be provided.)

These rules should help to avoid the situation where an employee who had not yet retired might have his own retirement benefit reduced as a result of inaction on his part and should also help to prevent adverse selection as against the plan.

The employee is to be afforded a reasonable opportunity, in accordance with regulations, to exercise his election out of (or, before normal retirement age, possibly into) the joint and survivor provision before the annuity starting date (or before he becomes eligible for early retirement). The employee is to be supplied with a written explanation of the joint and survivor provision, explained in layman's language, as well as the practical (dollar and cents) effect on him (and his or her spouse) of making an election either to take or not to take the provision. At the same time, regulations in this area should take cognizance of the practical difficulties which certain industries (particularly those having multiemployer plans) may have in contacting all of their participants.

To prevent adverse selection the plan may provide that any election, or revocation of an election, is not to become effective if the participant dies within some period of time (not in excess of two years) of the election or revocation (except in the case of accidental death where the accident which causes death occurs after the election).

[¶ 14,450.15]

Committee Report on P.L. 93-406 (Employee Retirement Income Security Act of 1974)

[House Ways and Means Committee Explanation]

* * * The bill does not require the plan to "subsidize" the joint and survivor annuity. Consequently, such a joint and survivor annuity could be less (in terms of dollars per annuity payment) than the single life annuity. Also, the bill does not forbid plans from making reasonable actuarial adjustments to take appropriate account of the possibility that otherwise total costs would be increased because of adverse selection.

[ERISA Sec. 206]

[¶ 14,460.085]

Committee Report on P.L. 109-280 (Pension Protection Act of 2006)

[Joint Committee on Taxation Report]

[*Regulations on time and order of issuance of domestic relations orders*]

The Secretary of Labor is directed to issue, not later than one year after the date of enactment of the provision, regulations to clarify the status of certain domestic relations orders. In particular, the regulations are to clarify that a domestic relations order otherwise meeting the QDRO requirements will not fail to be treated as a QDRO solely because of the time it is issued or because it is issued after or revises another domestic relations order or QDRO. The regulations are also to clarify that such a domestic relations order is in all respects subject to the same requirements and protections that apply to QDROs. For example, as under present law, such a domestic relations order may not require the payment of benefits to an alternate payee that are required to be paid to another alternate payee under an earlier QDRO. In addition, the present-law rules regarding segregated amounts that apply while the status of a domestic relations order as a QDRO is being determined continue to apply.

Effective date

The provision is effective on the date of enactment.

For the Committee Report on P.L. 109-280 on benefit limitations under single-employer defined benefit pension plans, see ¶ 13,151O.50.

[¶ 14,460.09]

Committee Report on P.L. 105-34 (Taxpayer Relief Act)

[Senate Committee Report]

Modify assignment or alienation prohibition

Modification of prohibition on assignment or alienation.—The bill permits a participant's benefit in a qualified plan to be reduced to satisfy liabilities of the participant to the plan due to (1) the participant being convicted of committing a crime involving the plan, (2) a civil judgment (or consent order or decree) entered by a court in an action brought in connection with a violation of the fiduciary provisions of ERISA, or (3) a settlement agreement between the Secretary of Labor or the Pension Benefit Guaranty Corporation and the participant in connection with a violation of the fiduciary provisions of ERISA. The court order establishing such liability must require that the participant's benefit in the plan be applied to satisfy the liability. If the participant is married at the time his or her benefit under the plan is offset to satisfy the liability, spousal consent to such offset is required unless the spouse is also required to pay an amount to the plan in the judgment, order, decree or settlement or the judgment, order, decree or settlement provides a 50-percent survivor annuity for the spouse. The bill will make the corresponding changes to ERISA.

Effective date

The provision is effective for judgments, orders, and degrees issued, and settlement agreements entered into, on or after the date of enactment.

[Conference Committee Report]

The conference agreement follows the Senate amendment. The conference agreement clarifies that an offset is includible in income on the date of the offset.

[¶ 14,460.095]

Committee Report on P.L. 98-397 (Retirement Equity Act of 1984)

[Senate Committee Report]

In general.—The bill clarifies the spendthrift provisions by providing new rules for the treatment of certain domestic relations orders. In addition, the bill creates an exception to the ERISA preemption provision with respect to these orders. The bill also provides procedures to be followed by a plan administrator (including the Pension Benefit Guaranty Corporation (PBGC)) and an alternate payee (a child, spouse, former spouse, or other dependent of a participant) with respect to domestic relations orders.

* * *

Qualified domestic relations order.—Under the bill, the term "qualified domestic relations order" means a domestic relations order that (1) creates or recognizes the existence of an alternate payee's right to, or assigns to an alternate payee the right to, receive all of a portion of the benefits payable with respect to a participant under a pension plan, and (2) meets certain other requirements. A domestic relations order is any judgment, decree, or order (including approval of a property settlement agreement) that relates to the provision of child support, alimony payments, or marital property rights to a spouse, former spouse, child, or other dependent of the participant, and is made pursuant to a State domestic relations law (including community property law). Under the bill, an alternate payee includes any spouse, former spouse, child, or other dependent of a participant who is recognized by a qualified domestic relations order as having a right to receive all, or a portion of, the benefits payable under a plan with respect to the participant.

To be a qualified order, a domestic relations order must clearly specify (1) the name and last known mailing address (if available) of the participant and the name and mailing address of each alternate payee to which the order relates, (2) the amount or percentage of the participant's benefits to be paid to an alternate payee or the manner in which the amount is to be determined, and (3) the number of payments or period for which payments are required. The committee intends that an order will not be treated as failing to be a qualified order merely because the order does not specify the current mailing address of the participant and alternate payee if the plan administrator has reason to know that address independently of the order. For example, if the plan administrator is aware that the alternate payee is also a participant under the plan and the plan records include a current address for each participant, the plan administrator may not treat the order as failing to qualify.

The committee intends that an order that is qualified is to remain qualified with respect to a successor plan of the same employer or a plan of a successor employer (within the meaning of sec. 414(a)).

A domestic relations order is not a qualified order if it (1) requires a plan to provide any type or form of benefit, or any option, not otherwise provided under the plan, (2) requires the plan to provide increased benefits, or (3) requires payment of benefits to an alternate payee that are required to be paid to another alternate payee under a previously existing qualified domestic relations order. An order does not require a plan to provide increased benefits if the order does not provide for the payment of benefits in excess of the benefits to which the participant would be entitled in the absence of the order.

The bill provides that a domestic relations order is not treated as failing the requirements for a qualified domestic relations order merely because the order provides that payments must begin to the alternate payee on or after the date on which the participant attains the earliest retirement age under the plan whether or not the participant actually retires on that date. If the participant dies before that date, the alternate payee is entitled to benefits only if the qualified domestic relations order requires survivor benefits to be paid. In the case of an order providing for the payment of benefits after the earliest retirement age, the payments to the alternate payee at the time are computed as if the participant had retired on the date on which benefit payments commence under the order.

When payments are made to an alternate payee before the participant retires, the payments are computed by taking into account only benefits actually accrued and not taking into account any employer subsidy for early retirement. The amount to be paid to the alternate payee is to be calculated by using the participant's normal retirement benefit accrued as of the date payout begins and by actuarially reducing such benefit based on the interest rate specified in the plan or 5 percent, if the plan does not specify an interest rate. A plan providing only normal and subsidized early retirement benefits would not specify a rate for determining actuarially equivalent, unsubsidized benefits.

If an alternate payee begins to receive benefits under the order and the participant subsequently retires with subsidized early retirement benefits, the order may specify that the amount payable to the alternate payee is to be recalculated so that the alternate payee also receives a share of the subsidized benefit to which the participant is entitled. The payment of early retirement benefits with respect to a participant who has not yet retired or the increase in benefits payable to the alternate payee after the recalculation is not to be considered to violate the prohibition against a qualified domestic relations order providing for increased benefits.

The payments to the alternate payee after the earliest retirement date may be paid in any form permitted under the plan (other than a joint and survivor annuity with respect to the alternate payee and the alternate payee's spouse). In the case of a defined contribution plan, the earliest retirement date is the date on which the participant attains an age that is 10 years before the normal retirement age.

Under the bill, a plan is not treated as failing to satisfy the requirements of section 401(a), 409(d), or 401(k) of the Internal Revenue Code that prohibit payment of benefits prior to termination of employment solely because the plan makes payments to the alternate payee in accordance with a qualified domestic relations order.

Under the bill, an alternate payee is treated as a beneficiary for all purposes under the plan. In no event, however, will more than one PBGC premium be collected with respect to the participant's benefits (determined as if a qualified domestic relations order had not been issued) even though such benefits, subject to the usual limits, may be guaranteed by the PBGC.

Determination by plan administrator.—Under the bill, the administrator of a plan that receives a domestic relations order is required to notify promptly the participant and any other alternate payee of receipt of the order and the plan's procedures for determining whether the order is qualified. In addition, within a reasonable period after receipt of the order, the plan administrator is to determine whether the order is qualified and notify the participant and alternate payee of the determination. The notices required under these rules are to be sent to the addresses specified in the order or, if the order fails to specify an address, to the last address of the participant or alternate payee known to the plan administrator.

The bill authorizes the Secretary of Labor to prescribe regulations defining the reasonable period during which the plan administrator is to determine whether an order is qualified. In addition, the bill provides that plans are to establish reasonable procedures to determine whether domestic relations orders are qualified and to administer distributions under qualified orders. Ordinarily, a plan need not be amended to implement the domestic relations provisions of the bill.

Deferral of benefit payments.—During any period in which the issue of whether a domestic relations order is a qualified order is being determined (by the plan administrator, by a court of competent jurisdiction, or otherwise), the plan administrator is to defer the payment of any benefits in dispute. These deferred benefits are segregated either in a separate account in the plan or in an escrow account. In the case of a defined benefit plan, the amounts are to be placed in an escrow account. Of course, segregation is not required for amounts that would not otherwise be paid during the period of the dispute.

If the order is determined to be a qualified domestic relations order within 18 months after the deferral of benefits, the plan administrator is to pay the segregated amount (plus interest) to the persons entitled to receive them. If the plan administrator determines that the order is not a qualified order or, after the 18-month period has expired, has not resolved the issue of whether the order is qualified, the segregated amounts are paid to the person or persons who would have received the amounts if the order had not been issued.

Any determination that an order is qualified after expiration of the 18-month period is to be applied prospectively. Thus, if the plan administrator determines that the order is qualified after the 18-month period, the plan is not liable for payments to the alternate payee for the period before the order is determined to be qualified.

Of course, the provisions of the bill do not affect any cause of action that an alternate payee may have against the participant. For example, if an order is determined to be qualified after the 18-month period, the alternate payee may have a cause of action under State law against the participant for amounts paid to the participant that should have been paid to the alternate payee.

During any period in which the alternate payee cannot be located, the plan is not permitted to provide for the forfeiture of the amounts that would have been paid unless the plan provides for full reinstatement when the alternate payee is located.

Consultation with the Secretary of the Treasury.—Under the bill, the Secretary of Labor is required to consult with the Secretary of the Treasury in prescribing regulations under these provisions.

Tax treatment of divorce distributions.—The bill provides rules for determining the tax treatment of benefits subject to a qualified domestic relations order. Under the bill, for purposes of determining the taxability of benefits, the alternate payee is treated as a distributee with respect to payments received from or under a plan.

Under the bill, net employee contributions (together with other amounts treated as the participant's investment in the contract) are apportioned between the participant and the alternate payee under regulations prescribed by the Secretary of the Treasury. The apportionment is to be made pro rata, on the basis of the present value of all benefits of the participant under the plan and the present value of all benefits of the alternate payee under the plan (as alternate payee with respect to the participant under a qualified domestic relations order).

Payments to an alternate payee before the participant attains age 59 ½ are not subject to the 10-percent additional income tax that would otherwise apply under certain circumstances if the participant received the amounts.

The bill provides that the interest of the alternate payee is not taken into account in determining whether a distribution to the participant is a lump sum distribution. Under the bill, benefits distributed to an alternate payee under a qualified domestic relations order can be rolled over, tax-free, to an individual retirement account or to an individual retirement annuity. The usual income tax rules apply to benefits not rolled over. The special rules for lump sum distributions from qualified plans will not apply to benefits distributed to an alternate payee.

[¶ 14,460.10]

Committee Report on P.L. 93-406 (Employee Retirement Income Security Act of 1974)

[Conference Committee Explanation]

Alienation.—Under the conference substitute, a plan must provide that benefits under the plan may not be assigned or alienated. However, the plan may provide that after a benefit is in pay status, there may be a voluntary revocable assignment (not to exceed 10 percent of any benefit payment) by an employee which is not for purposes of defraying the administrative costs of the plan. For purposes of this rule, a garnishment or levy is not to be considered a voluntary assignment. Vested benefits may be used as collateral for reasonable loans from a plan, where the fiduciary requirements of the law are not violated.*

Social security benefits of terminated participants.—The conference substitute codifies the current administrative practice which provides that qualified plans may not use increases in social security benefits or wage base levels to reduce employee plan benefits that are already in pay status. A similar protection is also extended against reductions in plan benefits where social security benefit levels (or wage base levels) are increased after the individuals concerned are separated from service prior to retirement. This requirement also applies to plans covered under title I (even if the plan is not qualified). A similar principle will apply in the case of an individual receiving disability benefits under social security and also under an employee plan.

Payment of benefits.—Under the conference substitute, a plan is generally required to commence benefit payments (unless the participant otherwise elects) not later than the 60th day after the close of the plan year in which the latest of the following events occurs:

(1) the participant attains age 65 (or any earlier normal retirement age specified under the plan),

(2) ten years have elapsed from the time the participant commenced participation in the plan, or

(3) the participant terminates his service with the employer.

Also, if the plan permits an employee who has not separated from service to receive a subsidized early retirement benefit if he meets certain age and service requirements, the plan must also permit an employee who fulfills the service

* This rule will not apply to irrevocable assignments made before the date of enactment and the plan provision required under this rule need not be adopted prior to January 1, 1976 (so long as the plan complies with the substance of this rule after enactment).

requirement, but separates from service before he meets the age requirement, to receive benefit payments, on an actuarially reduced basis, when the separated employee meets the age requirement. For example, if the plan provides a benefit of $100 a month at age 65, or at age 55 for employees with 30 years of service who are still employed on their 55th birthday, then an employee who separates from service at age 50 with 30 years of service would have the right to draw down an actuarially reduced benefit (perhaps $50 a month) at age 55. The actuarial adjustments are to be made in accordance with regulations to be prescribed by the Secretary of the Treasury, or his delegate.

[ERISA Sec. 207]

[¶ 14,470.10]

Committee Report on P.L. 93-406 (Employee Retirement Income Security Act of 1974)

[Conference Committee Explanation]

Variations.—Under the conference substitute, a variation is to be available with respect to the vesting schedule (for benefits attributable to employer contributions) and the accrued benefit rules for plans in existence on January 1, 1974. Under this procedure, a variation is to be allowed only if it is found by the Secretary of Labor that application of the rules of the bill would increase the cost of the plan to such an extent that there would be a substantial danger that the plan would be terminated, or that there would be a substantial reduction in benefits provided under the plan, or in the compensation of the employees. Also, it would have to be determined that the application of the vesting schedule requirements, or accrued benefit requirements, or discontinuance of the plan, would be adverse to the interest of the plan participants as a whole. Finally, it would have to be determined that the hardship described above could not be sufficiently mitigated by the granting of a funding variance.

The variation with respect to benefit accruals is not to apply for any year except years (not in excess of 7) during which the variation is in effect. (For example, there could be no variation with respect to the rules for benefits accrued in the past.)

No plan may receive a vesting variation unless application is made (in accordance with regulations to be prescribed by the Secretary of Labor or his delegate) within two years after the date of enactment of this bill [September 2, 1974]. The variation would be granted for an initial period not to exceed 4 years. Plans can receive one additional variation (for a period not to exceed 3 years), but application for the additional variation would have to be made at least one year prior to the expiration of the initial variation period.

During the period when a variation is in effect, there can be no plan amendment which has the effect of increasing plan liabilities because of benefit increases, changes in accruals, or changes in the rate of vesting, except to a de minimis extent (in accordance with regulations to be prescribed by the Secretary of Labor).

[ERISA Sec. 208]

[¶ 14,480.10]

Committee Report on P.L. 93-406 (Employee Retirement Income Security Act of 1974)

[Conference Committee Explanation]

* * * Under the conference agreement, a trust is not to constitute a qualified tax-exempt trust under the tax law, and also is not to satisfy the requirements of title I, unless it provides that in the case of any merger or consolidation of a plan, or any transfer of assets or liabilities of a plan, to any other plan each participant in the plan would receive post-merger termination benefits which are equal to or greater than the premerger termination benefits. In the case of multiemployer plans these rules are to apply only to the extent that the Pension Benefit Guaranty Corporation determines that these rules are necessary for the participant's protection. These rules are to apply to mergers or transfers made after the date of enactment of the bill [September 2, 1974], but the plan provision to this effect does not have to be adopted prior to January 1, 1976.

[ERISA Sec. 209]

[¶ 14,490.10]

Committee Report on P.L. 93-406 (Employee Retirement Income Security Act of 1974)

[Conference Committee Explanation]

Recordkeeping requirements.—Under the conference substitute, in the case of a single employer plan, the employee, once each year, is to be entitled to request his plan administrator to furnish a statement as to his vesting and accrued benefit status. A similar statement is to be supplied automatically when a vested employee terminates his coverage under the plan. In the case of multiemployer plans, the recordkeeping and information supplying duties are to be performed by the plan administrator and, to the maximum extent practicable (in light of their different circumstances), multiemployer plans are to meet the same standards in this area as single employer plans (in accordance with regulations to be prescribed by the Secretary of Labor or his delegate).

[ERISA Sec. 210]

[¶ 14,500.09]

Committee Report on P.L. 109-280 (Pension Protection Act of 2006)

For the Committee Report on P.L. 109-280 on the treatment of eligible combined plans, see ¶ 12,350.038.

[¶ 14,500.10]

Committee Report on P.L. 93-406 (Employee Retirement Income Security Act of 1974)

[Conference Committee Explanation]

Predecessor employer.—Service with a predecessor employer must be counted for purposes of the plan if the successor employer continues to maintain the plan of the predecessor employer (and, of course, the successor employer cannot evade this requirement by nominally discontinuing the plan). The question of the extent to which such service must be counted in other circumstances is to be determined under regulations.

[ERISA Sec. 211]

[¶ 14,510.10]

Committee Report on P.L. 93-406 (Employee Retirement Income Security Act of 1974)

[Conference Committee Explanation]

***Effective date*[1]**

Under the conference substitute the changes made in the bill with respect to participation and vesting are to apply to new plans in plan years beginning after the date of enactment [September 2, 1974]. For plans in existence on January 1, 1974, the general effective date of these provisions is to be plan years beginning after December 31, 1975.

The general effective date of plan years beginning after December 31, 1975 applies in the case of collectively bargained plans in the same manner as in the case of other plans. However, in order that the opening up of the contract to comply with the requirements of this bill will not require negotiations with respect to other matters, the conference substitute provides that a collective bargaining contract, in existence on January 1, 1974, which does not expire until after the general effective date for existing plans, may be reopened solely for the purpose of allowing the plan to meet the requirements of this bill, without having to be opened for any other purpose. Where it is necessary, as a result of this bill, to modify an employee benefit plan, it is the conferees' understanding that it is not an unfair labor practice under the National Labor Relations Act for a party to a collective bargaining agreement to refuse to bargain regarding matters unrelated to the modification required by this bill, provided this refusal is not otherwise an unfair labor practice. In addition, the changes required to be made in a plan are not themselves to be treated as constituting the expiration of a contract for purposes of any other provisions of this bill which depend on the date of the expiration of a contract.

Finally, the conference substitute provides that if a plan, adopted pursuant to a collective bargaining agreement in effect on January 1, 1974, contains a clause: (1) which provides supplementary benefits which are in the form of a lifetime annuity and refer to not more than one-third of the basic benefit to which the employees generally are entitled; or (2) which provides that a 25-year service employee is to be treated as a 30-year service employee, if that right is granted by a contractual agreement which is based on medical evidence as to the effects of working in an adverse environment for an extended period of time (such as workers in foundries or workers in asbestos plants), then the application of the accrued benefit provision of this bill to those benefits is to be delayed until the expiration of the collective bargaining agreement (but no later than plan years beginning after December 31, 1980). * * *

An existing plan which would be entitled to a delayed participation vesting, funding, etc. provision is to be permitted to elect to have all those provisions apply sooner. Any such election is to be made under regulations, must apply with respect to all the provisions of the Act, and is to be irrevocable.

[ERISA Sec. 301]

[¶ 14,610.08]

Committee Report on P.L. 109-280 (Pension Protection Act of 2006)

For the Committee Report on P.L. 109-280 on funding rules for multiemployer plans, see ¶ 13,151M.50.

---

[1] Because of the interrelationship of the effective date provisions for participation and vesting, this discussion deals with the effective dates for both.

[¶ 14,610.09]

Committee Report on P.L. 96-364 (Multiemployer Pension Plan Amendments Act of 1980)

[Senate testimony on floor amendment]

. . . see ¶ 14,410.09.

[¶ 14,610.10]

Committee Report on P.L. 93-406 (Employee Retirement Income Security Act of 1974)

[Conference Committee Explanation]

Coverage and exemptions from coverage.—

* * *

Under the conference substitute, government plans, including plans financed by contributions required under the Railroad Retirement Act, are to be exempt from the new funding requirement but they must meet the requirements of present law (sec. 401(a)(7) of the Internal Revenue Code). The conferees intend that no changes are to be made in the application of the present funding requirements of the Internal Revenue Code to government plans. Although present law establishes a "safe haven rule" for payment of normal cost plus interest on past service costs, it is not intended that this safe haven rule become a requirement for government plans, but that (as under present Regs. § 1.401-6(c)(1)) the determination on whether a plan has terminated is to be made on "all the facts and circumstances in the particular case." Thus, it is intended that there be no change in the application of present law to government plans.

The conference substitute exempts church plans from the new funding requirement if they meet the requirements of present law. However, church plans which elect to be covered under the participation, vesting, and termination insurance provisions are also to be covered by the new funding requirements.

The conference substitute excludes from the minimum funding rules plans established and maintained outside the United States if they are primarily for the benefit of persons substantially all of whom are nonresident aliens. This is specifically provided in the title I provisions, while under title II, such plans would have no need to seek tax deferral qualification.

The conference substitute excludes from the minimum funding rules of title I unfunded plans maintained by the employer primarily to provide deferred compensation for select management or highly compensated employees (under title II, such plans do not seek tax qualification). The conferees intend that this exemption is to include "consultant contracts" for retired management employees. Additionally, the substitute exempts from the funding rules plans adopted by a partnership exclusively for the benefit of a partner pursuant to section 736 of the Internal Revenue Code.

Under the conference substitute, plans which have not provided for employer contributions at any time after the date of enactment are to be exempt from the minimum funding rules (i.e., plans of unions funded exclusively by contributions of the union members).

An exemption is also provided for profit-sharing and stock bonus plans; however, money purchase pension plans and other individual account plans generally are not excluded from the minimum funding rules.

It is intended that plans generally are to be considered money purchase pension plans which meet the "definitely determinable" standard where the employer's contributions are fixed by the plan, even if the employer's obligation to contribute for any individual employee may vary based on the amount contributed to the plan in any year by the employee. For example, it is expected that a matching plan which provides that an employer will annually contribute up to 6 percent of an employee's salary, but that this contribution will be no more than the employee's own (nondeductible) contribution, will meet the "definitely determinable" criteria. In this case, the employer's contributions are set by the plan, will not vary with profits, and cannot be varied by the employer's action (other than by a plan amendment). (Of course, the plan must meet the nondiscrimination and other requirements of the Code to be qualified.)

Plans funded exclusively by the purchase of certain qualified level premium individual insurance contracts also are not to be subject to the minimum funding requirements. Additionally, the conference substitute makes it clear that where, instead of buying a series of such individual contracts, the employer holds a group insurance contract under which each employee's plan benefit is funded in the same manner as if individual contracts were purchased, the situation is to be treated the same as where there are individual insurance contracts. This generally will be available where the employer's premium is based on the sum of the level premiums attributable to each employee, where an employee's accrued benefit at any point in time is comparable to what would be provided under an individual contract, and as otherwise determined by regulations.

Supplemental unfunded plans which provide benefits in excess of limitations on contributions and benefits under the Internal Revenue Code and plans which are for the highly paid are to be excluded from the new funding standard. In addition, plans established by fraternal societies or other organizations described in section 501(c)(8) or (9) of the Internal Revenue Code are to be exempt if no employer contributions are made to the plan. Also, trusts which are part of plans described in section 501(c)(18) of the Code are to be exempt from the funding standards of title I (the standards of title II do not apply because those plans are not qualified plans).

With respect to the civil enforcement of the funding requirements, see "Labor and Tax Administration and Enforcement," "*Labor Department*" (Part VII, below) [CCH ¶ 14,910.10]. The excise tax provisions on underfunding in the conference substitute are the same as those in the House bill. However, before sending a notice of deficiency with respect to the first level (and second level) tax, the Internal Revenue Service is to notify the Secretary of Labor and provide him reasonable opportunity to obtain a correction of the funding deficiency, or to comment on the imposition of these taxes. The Service will be able to waive (or abate) the second level, but not the first level, tax upon a correction of underfunding that is obtained by the Secretary of Labor.

[The text of ERISA Sec. 1013(d) is reproduced at ¶ 12,250A (Committee Report at ¶ 12,250A.10) in the "Internal Revenue Code & Regulations" division.—CCH.]

[ERISA Sec. 302]

[¶ 14,620.082]

Committee Report on P.L. 109-280 (Pension Protection Act of 2006)

For the Committee Report on P.L. 109-280 on single-employer plan minimum funding standards, see ¶ 12,250.023.

For the Committee Report on P.L. 109-280 on special rules for multiple-employer plans of certain cooperatives, see ¶ 12,250.023.

For the Committee Report on P.L. 109-280 on temporary relief for certain PBGC settlement plans, see ¶ 12,250.023.

For the Committee Report on P.L. 109-280 on special rules for plans of certain government contractors, see ¶ 12,250.023.

For the Committee Report on P.L. 109-280 on extension of replacement of 30-year treasury rates, see ¶ 12,250.023.

[¶ 14,620.084]

Committee Report on P.L. 107-16 (Economic Growth and Tax Relief Reconciliation Act)

For the Committee Report on P.L. 107-16 on the phase-in repeal of 160 percent of current liability funding limit, see ¶ 12,250.05.

[¶ 14,620.086]

Committee Report on P.L. 107-16 (Economic Growth and Tax Relief Reconciliation Act)

For the Committee Report on P.L. 107-16 on the modification of the timing of plan valuations, see ¶ 12,250.03.

[¶ 14,620.088]

Committee Reports on P.L. 105-34 (Taxpayer Relief Act)

[Senate Committee Report]

Full funding limit

Increase in full funding limit.—The bill increases the 150-percent of full funding limit as follows: 155 percent for plan years beginning in 1999 or 2000, 160 percent for plan years beginning in 2001 or 2002, 165 percent for plan years beginning in 2003 and 2004, and 170 percent for plan years beginning in 2005 and thereafter.

Effective date

The provision is effective for plan years beginning after December 31, 1998.

[Conference Committee Report]

The conference agreement follows the Senate amendment * * *.

[Conference Committee Report]

Code Sec. 412(b)(2) amortization

Increase in full funding limit.—

Senate [Floor] Amendment.—* * *

In addition, under the provision, amounts that cannot be contributed due to the current liability full funding limit are amortized over 20 years. Amounts that could not be contributed because of such full funding limit and that have not been amortized as of the last day of the plan year beginning in 1998 are amortized over this 20-year period.

Effective date

Plan years beginning after December 31, 1998.

Conference Agreement

The conference agreement follows the Senate amendment, with the modification that, with respect to amortization bases remaining at the end of the 1998 plan year, the 20-year amortization period is reduced by the number of years since the amortization base had been established. The conference agreement also clarifies that no amortization is required with respect to funding methods that do not provide for amortization bases.

[¶ 14,620.07]

Committee Report on P.L. 103-465 (General Agreement on Tariffs and Trade (GATT); Retirement Protection Act)

. . . relating to minimum funding requirements, see ¶ 12,250.07.

[¶ 14,620.08]

Committee Report on P.L. 103-465 (General Agreement on Tariffs and Trade (GATT); Retirement Protection Act)

. . . relating to special funding rule for certain plans, see ¶ 12,250.071.

[¶ 14,620.09]

Committee Reports on P.L. 100-203 (Omnibus Budget Reconciliation Act of 1987)

[Conference Committee Report]

House Committee Report

Full funding limition.—Under the House bill, the full funding limitation generally is defined to mean the excess, if any, of (1) the lesser of (a) the accrued liability (including normal cost) under the plan, or (b) 150 percent of termination liability, over (2) the lesser of (a) the fair market value of the plan's assets, or (b) the value of the plan's assets determined under section 412(c)(2).

The bill does not modify the definition of accrued liability in section 412(c)(7). Also, the requirement that all amortizable amounts be considered fully amortized (sec. 412(c)(6)(B)) is applied without regard to the change in the full funding limitation (adding the 150 percent of termination liability limitation).

It is intended that the full funding limitation (as well as the other limitations on deductions for plan contributions) may not be avoided by the creation of multiple plans with coordination of benefits between the plans. The Secretary is to prescribe rules consistent with this intent.

The Secretary may, under regulations, adjust the 150-percent figure in the full funding limitation to take into account the average age (and length of service, if appropriate) of the participants in the plan (weighted by the value of their benefits under the plan). Any such adjustments are to be prescribed only if, in the aggregate, their effect on Federal budget receipts is substantially identical to the effect of this provision of the bill. For example, the Secretary could, if it satisfies the budget receipts requirement, adjust the 150-percent figure to 175 percent for younger workforces and to 125 percent for older workforces.

This provision is effective for years beginning after December 31, 1987.

The conference agreement follows the House bill (using the term "current liability" rather than "termination liability"), with certain modifications.

In addition to the regulatory authority provided under the House bill, the conference agreement authorizes the Secretary to prescribe regulations that apply, in lieu of the 150 percent of current liability limitation, a different full funding limitation based on factors other than current liability. The Secretary may exercise this authority only in a manner so that, in the aggregate, the effect of the regulations on Federal budget receipts is substantially identical to the effect of the 150-percent limitation.

In addition, under the conference agreement, the Secretary is to prescribe rules with respect to the treatment of contributions that would be required to be made but for the modification of the full funding limitation. The rules are to provide that the amount of such contributions are to be cumulated. In years in which the contributions required to be made to the plan are less than the full funding limitation (without regard to these cumulated amounts), the employer is to be required to contribute a portion of the cumulated amount. In determining the amount of this supplemental contribution, the Secretary may take into account factors such as the remaining working lifetime of the participants over which the entire cumulated amount may be contributed.

The conference agreement requires the Treasury Department to study the effect of the modification of the full funding limitation on benefit security in defined benefit pension plans and to report the results of the study to the House Ways and Means Committee, the Senate Finance Committee, and the Joint Committee on Taxation by August 15, 1988.

In addition, under the conference agreement, the Secretary is to prescribe regulations under this provision no later than August 15, 1988.

[Conference Committee Report]

Funding requirements.—[The House bill provides:] A special funding rule applies to plans with a funded ratio less than 100 percent. This special rule does not apply to (1) plans exempt from the funding requirements under present law, or (2) multiemployer plans.

A contribution in excess of the contribution required under the present-law funding rules generally is not required if a plan has a funded ratio of 100 percent.

[The Senate amendment provides:] Same as the Ways and Means Committee bill. In addition, the new funding rules for plans with a funded ratio of less than 100 percent do not apply to (1) plans that are not defined benefit plans and (2) plans with no more than 100 participants on any day in the preceding plan year. In the case of a plan with more than 100 but no more than 150 participants during the preceding year, the amount of the additional contribution is determined by multiplying the otherwise required additional contribution by 2 percent for each participant in excess of 100.

The amendment retains the present-law funding standards, with certain modifications. In addition, with respect to certain plans with a funded ratio less than 100 percent, the minimum required contribution is, in general terms, the greater of (1) the amount determined under section 412 (with the modifications made by the amendment), or (2) the sum of (i) normal cost, (ii) the amount necessary to amortize experience gains and losses and gains and losses resulting from changes in actuarial assumptions over 5 years, and (iii) the deficit reduction contribution. In addition, a special funding rule applies with respect to benefits that are contingent on unpredictable events.

Under the amendment, the deficit reduction contribution is the sum of (1) the unfunded old liability amount, and (2) the unfunded new liability amount. Calculation of these amounts is based upon the plan's "current liability".

Under the amendment, the term "current liability" means all liabilities to employees and their beneficiaries under the plan (Code Sec. 401(a)(2)) determined as if the plan terminated. However, the value of any "unpredictable contingent event benefit" is not taken into account in determining current liability until the event on which the benefit is contingent occurs. An "unpredictable contingent event benefit" is in general any benefit contingent on an event other than (1) age, service, compensation, death, or disability, or (2) an event which is reasonably and reliably predictable as determined by the Secretary.

Current liability is generally determined in accordance with plan assumptions, including the interest rate assumption. However, the amendment provides a special limitation on the interest rate used for purposes of calculating current liability. Under the amendment, if the plan interest rate is not within the permissible range, then the plan must establish a new rate within the permissible range. The permissible range is defined as a rate of interest that is not more than 20 percent above or below the average mid-term applicaboederal rate (AFR) for the 3-year period ending on the last day before the beginning of the plan year for which the interest rate is being used (or, if shorter, the period that the AFR has been computed). The average is determined by averaging the rate in effect for each month during the applicable 3-year period. The Secretary may prescribe one or more indices in lieu of the average mid-term AFR to be used in determining the permissible range.

The amendment provides that certain service may be disregarded at the employer's election in calculating the plan's current liability. In the case of certain participants, the applicable percentage of the years of service before the individual became a participant are taken into account in determining current liability. The applicable percentage is (1) 0, if the individual has 5 or less years of participation, (2) 20, if the individual has 6 years of participation, (3) 40, if the individual has 7 years of participation, (4) 60, if the individual has 8 years of participation, (5) 80, if the individual has 9 years of participation, and (6) 100 if the individual has 10 or more years of participation. Partial years of participation are rounded to the nearest whole year.

The amendment provides that unfunded current liability means, with respect to any plan year, the excess of (1) the current liability under the plan over (2) the value of the plan's assets reduced by any credit balance in the funding standard account. The funded current liability percentage of a plan for a plan year is the percentage that (1) the value of the plan's assets reduced by any credit balance in the funding standard account is of (2) the current liability under the plan.

The unfunded old liability amount is, in general, the amount necessary to amortize the unfunded old liability under the plan in equal annual installments (until fully amortized) over a fixed period of 15 plan years (beginning with the first plan year beginning after December 31, 1987). The "unfunded old liability" with respect to a plan is the unfunded current liability of the plan as of the beginning of the first plan year beginning after December 31, 1987, determined without regard to any plan amendment adopted after October 16, 1987, that increases plan liabilities (other than amendments adopted pursuant to certain bargaining agreements).

Under a special rule applicable to collectively bargained pleas, increases in liabilities pursuant to a collective bargaining agreement ratified before October 17, 1987, are also amortized over 15 years.

The unfunded new liability amount for a plan year is the applicable percentage of the plan's "unfunded new liability." "Unfunded new liability" means the unfunded current liability of the plan for the plan year, determined without regard to (1) the unamortized portion of the unfunded old liability and (2) the liability with respect to any unpredictable contingent event benefits, without regard to whether or not the event has occurred. Thus, in calculating the unfunded new liability, all unpredictable contingent event benefits are disregarded, even if the event on which that benefit is contingent has occurred.

If the funded current liability percentage is less than 35 percent, then the applicable percentage is 30 percent. The applicable percentage decreases by .25 of one percentage point for each 1 percentage point by which the plan's funded current liability percentage exceeds 35 percent.

If the event on which an unpredictable contingent event benefit is contingent occurs during the plan year and the assets of the plan year are less than current liability (calculated after the event has occurred), then an additional funding contribution (over and above the minimum funding contribution otherwise due) is required. The amount of the required additional contribution is generally equal to the greater of (1) the amount of unpredictable contingent event benefits paid during the plan year (regardless of the form in which paid), including (except as provided by the Secretary of the Treasury) any payment for the purchase of an annuity contract with respect to a participant with respect to such benefits, and (2) the amount that would be determined for the year if the unpredictable contingent event benefit liabilities were amortized in equal annual installments over 5 years, beginning with the plan year in which the event occurs. For the year in which the event occurs, an amount equal to 150 percent of the amount determined under (1) above may, at the employer's election, be treated as the unpredictable contingent benefit amount. In no case, however, will the unpredictable contingent event amount exceed the unfunded current liability (including the liability due to the contingent event benefit) of the plan.

A plan's funded ratio is the ratio of plan assets to current liability.

The portion of the regulations permitting asset valuations to be based on a range between 85 percent and 115 percent of average value are to have no force and effect.

In general, the changes in the minimum funding requirements for defined benefit pension plans apply with respect to plan years beginning after December 31, 1988. Unpredictable contingent event benefits with respect to which the event has occurred before October 17, 1987, are not subject to the new funding rule for such benefits. If the event has not occurred before October 17, 1987, such benefits are subject to the new funding rules for such benefits. For the first plan year beginning after December 31, 1987, unpredictable contingent event benefits are subject to the provisions of the amendment relating to gains and losses.

With respect to provisions that cross reference the definition of "current liability", the definition is effective at the time the provision cross referencing it is effective.

The change in the valuation regulations is effective with respect to plan years beginning after December 31, 1987.

The Secretary of the Treasury is to prescribe appropriate adjustments in the unpredictable contingent event amount, the old liability amount, the new liability amount, and the other charges and credits under section 412 as are necessary to avoid inappropriate duplication or omission of any factors in the determination of such amounts, charges and credits (for example, adjustments reflecting asset appreciation or depreciation).

It is also intended that the Secretary will provide special rules for multiple-employer plans where appropriate.

In general, the conference agreement follows the Finance Committee amendment, with certain modifications.

The conference agreement follows the Senate Finance Committee amendment. As under the Senate Finance Committee amendment, for purposes of the rules for plans with no more than 100 participants or plans with 101 to 150 participants, all defined benefit plans (including multiemployer plans) of the employer and the employer's controlled group are treated as a single plan. The definition of a controlled group is the same as the definition in section 414(b), (c), (m) and (o). With respect to a multiemployer plan, only employees of the employer (or a controlled group member) are taken into account.

The conference agreement follows the Finance Committee amendment, with the following modifications. Gains and losses due to changes in actuarial assumptions are amortized over 10 years, rather than over 5 years. The conferees intend that reporting requirements will be revised as necessary to implement the new funding rules, for example, to reflect current liability, unfunded old liability, unfunded new liability, and the liabilities for unpredictable event contingent benefits.

Current liability is defined as in the Finance Committee amendment, with the following modifications. Thus, current liability is, in general, all liabilities to participants and beneficiaries under the plan (Code sec. 401(a)(2)) determined as if the plan terminated. Under the conference agreement, the permissible range for the interest rate is not more than 10 percent above or below the average rate for 30-year Treasury bonds for the 4-year period ending on the last day before the beginning of the plan year for which the interest rate is being used. Under appropriate circumstances, the Secretary of the Treasury may provide that the permissible range is expanded to include rates between 80 and 90 percent of the average rate described above. For purposes of determining the average rate for the 4-year period, the Secretary may prescribe rules weighting the more recent years more heavily.

No rate outside the permissible range is permitted under any circumstances. Also, the specific corridor is not intended to be a safe harbor with respect to whether an interest rate is reasonable. The Secretary is authorized to adjust a rate within the range to the extent that it is unreasonable under the rules applicable to actuarial assumptions.

The conference agreement modifies the rule disregarding certain preparticipation service. Under the modification, preparticipation years of service are taken into account over 5 years of participation. Partial years of participation are rounded to the nearest whole year.

The rule disregarding preparticipation service is available with respect to any participant who, at the time of becoming a participant, has not accrued any other benefits under any defined benefit pension plan (whether or not terminated) of the employer or a member of the controlled group of the employer, and has years of service before such time in excess of the years of service required for eligibility to participate in the plan. The rules applies only with respect to new participants in years beginning after December 31, 1987. The rule is not elective.

With respect to the definition of unpredictable contingent event benefits, the conferees do not intend that an event will be considered reliably and reasonably predictable solely because an actuarial probability of the event occurring may be determined. It is further intended that the Secretary of the Treasury will prescribe rules defining events that can and cannot be reasonably and reliably predicted and will revise these rules as new benefits are developed.

Unpredictable contingent event benefits are intended to include benefits that depend on contingencies that, like facility shutdowns or reductions or contractions in workforce, are not reliably and reasonably predictable. Such contingencies are not limited to events that are similar to shutdowns or reductions in force. For example, a benefit dependent on the profits of the employer or the value of employer stock dropping below a certain level would be contingent on an event that is not reasonably and reliably predictable (unless the contingency is illusory).

If an employer provides an early retirement window benefit under which employees who have satisfied certain age or service requirements or both are offered a limited period of time during which they may elect to retire, such a window benefit is generally considered to be contingent on an event that can be reasonably and reliably predicted. The Secretary of the Treasury may, in appropriate circumstances, treat such window benefits as benefits which are contingent on an event that cannot be reasonably and reliably predicted.

It is intended that a benefit contingent on marital status, such as qualified joint and survivor annuity, is generally to be considered a benefit that is contingent on an event that can be reasonably and reliably predicted.

It is intended that the Secretary of the Treasury may prescribe rules to prevent employers from avoiding the new minimum funding rules by characterizing contingencies as not reasonably and reliably predictable. For purposes of the definition of current liability, a benefit is generally not to be considered contingent on an event which is not reasonably and reliably predictable if there is substantial certainty that the event on which the benefit depends will occur.

An early retirement subsidy, social security supplement, survivor subsidy or similar benefit in addition to the basic retirement benefit under a plan that is payable only on the satisfaction of certain eligibility conditions (e.g., age and/or years of service eligibility conditions), is included in current liability (provided it is not an unpredictable event contingent benefit) to the extent that the employee has earned the subsidy, supplement, or similar benefit.

For example, assume that a plan provides that an employee is entitled to a basic retirement benefit commencing at age 65 of 1 percent of final average pay times years of service and that, if the employee retires at age 55 with at least 25 years of service, the employee's retirement benefit will not be actuarially reduced for early commencement (i.e., this is an early retirement subsidy). For purposes of calculating the current liability for such plan for a year, an employee age 50 with 20 years of service has a total retirement benefit (i.e., normal retirement benefit plus early retirement subsidy) of 80 percent of the unreduced age 55 benefit (based on final average pay at age 50). That is, there is no actuarial reduction for commencement before age 65. The same analysis applies in determining the extent to which a social security supplement, survivor subsidy, or similar benefit has been earned under the plan.

Current liability is generally determined in accordance with plan assumptions. Thus, in the example described above, because not all employees who have earned a right to some portion of the early retirement benefit will ultimately satisfy the eligibility conditions for the subsidy (e.g., not all such employees will remain with the employer until age 55 or retire at age 55), a plan is to calculate its current liability for the year by using reasonable turnover and mortality factors.

The conference agreement follows the Finance Committee amendment except that the unfunded old liability amount is amortized over 18 years rather than 15 years. Thus, under the conference agreement, the unfunded old liability amount with respect to a collectively bargained plan is increased by the amount necessary to amortize the unfunded existing benefit increase liabilities in equal annual installments over a fixed period of 18 plan years, beginning with the plan year in which the increase in liabilities occurs pursuant to the bargaining agreement (or, if later, the first plan year beginning after December 31, 1988). For purposes of this rule, the unfunded existing benefit increase liability means the unfunded current liability determined by taking into account only (1) liabilities attributable to the increase in liabilities pursuant to the agreement, and (2) the value of assets in excess of current liability (determined without regard to the liabilities described in (1)).

For purposes of the special rule applicable to certain benefit increases pursuant to a collective bargaining agreement ratified before October 17, 1987, any extension, amendment, or other modification of a bargaining agreement after October 16, 1987, is not taken into account. In general, the special rule only includes increases in liability pursuant to the bargaining agreement and therefore does not include liability increases with respect to individuals covered by the plan who are not subject to the collective bargaining agreement. However if more than 75 percent of the employees covered by the plan on October 16, 1987, are subject to the collective bargaining agreement, then the unfunded existing benefit increase liability includes the liability with respect to all employees in the plan whose benefits are determined directly or indirectly by reference to the terms of the bargaining agreement, whether or not such employees are subject to the agreement. Separate plans may not be treated as a single plan for purposes of this rule, even if the benefits under the plans are coordinated.

The conference agreement follows the Finance Committee amendments with respect to the definition and funding of unpredictable contingent event benefits, except that the cash flow rule and amortization period are modified. Under the conference agreement, the amount of the additional contributions is generally equal to the greater of (1) the unfunded portion of the benefits paid during the plan year (regardless of the form in which paid), including (except as provided by the Secretary of the Treasury) and any payment for the purchase of an annuity contract with respect to a participant with respect to contingent event benefits, and (2) the amount that would be determined for the year if the unpredictable contingent event benefit liabilities were amortized in equal annual installments over 7 years, beginning with the plan year in which the event occurs.

The effects of the cash flow rule in (1) are phased in at a rate of 5 percent for plan years beginning in 1989 and 1990, 10 percent for plan years beginning in 1991, 15 percent for plan years beginning in 1992, 20 percent for plan years beginning in 1993, 30 percent for plan years beginning in 1994, 40 percent for plan years beginning in 1995, 50 percent for plan years beginning in 1996, 60 percent for plan years beginning in 1997, 70 percent for plan years beginning in 1998, 80 percent for plan years beginning in 1999, 90 percent for plan years beginning in 2000, and 100 percent for plan years beginning in 2001.

The event on which an unpredictable contingent event benefit is contingent is generally not considered to have occurred until all events on which the benefit is contingent have occurred. If the event on which an unpredictable contingent event benefit if contingent occurs during the plan year and the assets of the plan equal or exceed current liability (calculated after the event has occurred), then the employer may continue to fund the plan's unpredictable contingent event benefit as under present law (i.e., generally as an experience loss), subject to application of the special rule if the plan's funding falls below current liability.

The conference agreement follows the Finance Committee amendment with respect to the value of assets under section 412(c)(2)(A). In addition, the conference agreement repeals section 412(c)(2)(B) (except for multiemployer plans), subjecting bonds and other evidence of indebtedness to the general valuation rules. The Secretary may, however, prescribe regulations under which a dedicated bond portfolio is to be valued by using the interest rate used to determine current liability.

Effective date

The conference agreement generally follows the Finance Committee amendment, except that the modified cash flow rule for unpredictable contingent event benefits is effective for plan years beginning after December 31, 1988.

In addition, the conference agreement adopts the special rule for steel employer plans in the Ways and Means Committee bill, with a modification. Under the modification, liabilities (and contributions) with respect to unpredictable event contingent benefits with respect to which the contingency occurs after December 17, 1987, are not taken into account in calculating current liability under the rule, but are amortized separately over 10 years.

[Conference Committee Report]

[*Funding requirements.*]. —*House Bill.* Education and Labor Committee bill: The period for amortizing experience gains and losses is reduced to 5 years from 15 years.

Finance Committee amendment: The Finance Committee amendment is the same as the Education and Labor Committee bill, except that the provision is effective for years beginning after December 31, 1987.

Conference Agreement: The conference agreement follows the Finance Committee amendment. The provision does not apply to gains and losses arising in plan years beginning before January 1, 1988.

Finance Committee amendment: Gains and losses due to changes in actuarial assumptions are amortized over [10] years. The provision is effective for years beginning after December 31, 1987.

Conference Agreement: The conference agreement follows the Finance Committee amendment, except that the amortization period is 10 years.

Ways and Means Committee bill: All costs, liabilities, interest rates, and other factors are required to be determined on the basis of actuarial assumptions and methods (1) each of which is reasonable individually or (2) which result, in the aggregate, in a total plan contribution equivalent to the contribution that would be obtained if each assumption were reasonable. The interest rate used in calculating costs generally is required to be within a permissible range, defined as an interest rate not more than 20 percent above or below the average long-term AFR for the 5-year period ending on the last day of the preceding plan year. The provision applies to plan years beginning after December 31, 1987.

Finance Committee amendment: The Finance Committee amendment is the same as the Ways and Means bill, except that the amendment does not include the requirement that the plan's interest rate be within the permissible range. The provision applies to years beginning after December 31, 1987.

Conference Agreement: The conference agreement follows the Finance Committee amendment, with certain modifications. The interest rate applicable in determining current liability is required to be used with respect to determining the required contribution under section 412(l).

In addition, with respect to the interest rate that is used to determine current liability and thus is required to be within the permissible range, the determination of whether such interest rate is reasonable depends on the cost of purchasing an annuity sufficient to satisfy current liability. The interest rate is to be a reasonable estimate of the interest rate used to determine the cost of such annuity, assuming that the cost only reflected the present value of the payments under the annuity (i.e., did not reflect the seller's profit, administrative expenses, etc.). For example, if an annuity costs $1,100, the cost of $1,100 is considered to be the present value of the payments under the annuity for purposes of the interest rate rule, even though $100 of the $1,100 represents the seller's administrative expense and profit. Also, in making this determination with respect to the interest rate used to determine the cost of an annuity, other factors and assumptions (e.g., mortality) are to be individually reasonable.

It is further intended that, for purposes of determining the reasonableness of an interest rate under the approach described above, the plan benefit generally is the normal benefit under the plan (without regard to, for example, any provision providing for a lump sum payment).

Ways and Means Committee bill: The bill clarifies that the amortizable base in determining an employer's maximum deduction for past service liability equals only the unfunded costs attributable to such liability. The provision is effective for plan years beginning after December 31, 1987.

Conference Agreement: The conference agreement follows the Ways and Means Committee bill. No inference is intended with respect to present law.

Ways and Means Committee bill: The maximum deduction limit for contributions is not less than the unfunded termination liability of the plan. This rule applies only to a plan subject to the plan termination insurance provisions of ERISA and only if the plan has 100 or more participants during the plan year. The provision is effective for plan years beginning after December 31, 1987.

Finance Committee amendment: The Finance Committee amendment follows the Ways and Means Committee bill (using "current liability" instead of "termination liability," without a substantive change), except that the increased deduction limit applies to all defined benefit pension plans with 100 or more participants. The provision is effective for years beginning after December 31, 1987.

Conference Agreement: The conference agreement follows the Finance Committee agreement, but also provides that, in determining unfunded current liability, assets are not reduced by credit balances.

House Bill: Under the House bill, the full funding limitation generally is defined to mean the excess, if any, of (1) the lesser of (a) the accrued liability (including normal cost) under the plan, or (b) 150 percent of termination liability, over (2) the lesser of (a) the fair market value of the plan's assets, or (b) the value of the plan's assets determined under section 412(c)(2).

The House bill provides a special limitation on the interest rate used for funding purposes (including the full funding limitation). Under the bill, the interest rate is required to be within a permissible range, which is defined as a rate of interest that is not more than 20 percent above or below the average long-term applicable Federal rate (AFR) for the 5-year period ending on the last day before the beginning of the plan year for which the interest rate is being used.

If any interest rate used under the plan is not within the permissible range, then the plan generally is required to establish a new interest rate that is within the permissible range. However, the Secretary may permit a plan to use an interest rate that is not within the permissible range if it is established, to the satisfaction of the Secretary, that the interest rate is reasonable. Further, if the Secretary determines that any interest rate used under the plan is not reasonable (without regard to whether the rate is within the permissible range), then the plan is required to establish a new interest rate that is permitted by the Secretary.

This provision is effective for years beginning after December 31, 1987.

Senate Amendment: The Senate amendment generally follows the House bill, with the following exceptions.

The Senate amendment uses the term "current liability" instead of the term "termination liability" as under the House bill, but the substance of the two terms is the same. For purposes of calculating current liability under the amendment, the interest rate is the rate used for calculating costs under the plan. If such rate is not within the permissible range, however, then for this purpose the plan is required to establish a new interest rate that is within the permissible range. The permissible range is defined as a rate of interest that is not more than 20 percent above or below the average mid-term applicable Federal rate (AFR) for the 3-year period ending on the last day before the beginning of the plan year for which the interest rate is being used (or, if shorter, the period that the AFR has been computed). The average is determined by averaging the rate in effect for each month during the applicable 3-year period. The Secretary may prescribe one or more indices in lieu of the average mid-term AFR to be used in determining the permissible range.

Conference Agreement: The conference agreement follows the House bill (using the term "current liability" rather than "termination liability"), with certain modifications.

The conference agreement follows the rule under the Senate amendment with respect to the interest rate to be used in determining current liability, with certain modifications. Under the conference agreement, for this purpose, the interest rate is generally the rate determined under the plan's assumptions. However, notwithstanding the plan's assumptions, the interest rate is required to be within 10 percent of the average rate for 30-year Treasury bonds for the 4-year period ending on the last day before the beginning of the plan year for which the interest rate is being used. This creates a permissible range of between 90 percent and 110 percent of such average rate. Under appropriate circumstances, the Secretary may also permit interest rates that are between 80 percent and 90 percent of the average rate described above. For purposes of determining the average rate for the 4-year period, the Secretary may prescribe rules weighting the more recent years more heavily.

No rate outside of the specified corridor is permitted under any circumstances. Also, the specified corridor is not intended to be a safe harbor with respect to whether an interest rate is reasonable. The Secretary is authorized to adjust a rate within the corridor to the extent that it is unreasonable under the rules applicable to actuarial assumptions.

The conference agreement requires the Treasury Department to study the effect of the modification of the full funding limitation on benefit security in defined benefit security in defined benefit pension plans and to report the results of the study to the House Ways and Means Committee, the Senate Finance Committee, and the Joint Committee on Taxation by August 15, 1988.

In addition, under the conference agreement, the Secretary is to prescribe regulations under this provision no later than August 15, 1988.

[¶ 14,620.095]

Committee Report on P.L. 96-364 (Multiemployer Pension Plan Amendments Act of 1980)

[Senate Committee Explanation]

. . . see the Committee Report at ¶ 12,250.09.

[¶ 14,620.10]

Committee Report on P.L. 93-406 (Employee Retirement Income Security Act of 1974)

[Conference Committee Explanation]

* * *

General rule as to funding.—The conference substitute establishes new minimum funding requirements for plans of employers and unions in or affecting interstate commerce (title I) and qualified plans (title II) so these plans will accumulate sufficient assets within a reasonable time to pay benefits to covered employees when they retire. Of course, contributions generally may be greater than these minimum requirements if the employer so desires. (However, there may be limits on the ability to currently deduct these larger contributions, under the tax laws.) The new requirements generally are not to apply to profit-sharing or stock bonus plans, governmental plans, certain church plans, plans with no employer contributions, and certain insured plans. Under the tax provisions, once a plan or trust has been tax qualified, the minimum funding requirements will apply, and they are to continue to apply to the plan or trust, even if it later loses its qualified status. If a plan loses its qualified status, the deduction rules for nonqualified plans are to apply even though the minimum funding standard continues to apply to the plan.

Generally, under the new funding requirements, the minimum amount that an employer is to contribute annually to a defined benefit pension plan includes the normal costs of the plan plus amortization of past service liabilities, experience losses, etc. Except as described below (under "Variances—alternative funding methods"), minimum amortization payments required by the conference substitute are calculated on a level payment basis—including interest and principal—over stated periods of time and are based on all accrued liabilities. Generally, initial past service liabilities and past service liabilities arising under plan amendments are to be amortized over no more than 30 years (40 years for the unfunded past service liabilities on the effective date of these new funding rules, in the case of existing plans), and experience gains and losses are to be amortized over no more than 15 years. However, generally experience gains and losses need not be calculated more often than every three years. With respect to multiemployer plans, past service liabilities generally may be amortized over no more than 40 years, and experience losses over no more than 20 years. Following the Senate amendment, the conference substitute does not include a second general minimum funding standard based only on "vested" liabilities.

If an employer would otherwise incur substantial business hardship, and if application of the minimum funding requirements would be adverse to plan participants in the aggregate, the Internal Revenue Service may waive the requirement of current payment of part or all of a year's contributions of normal costs, and amounts needed to amortize past service liabilities and experience losses. This waiver is to be available for single employer and multiemployer plans. The amount waived (plus interest) is to be amortized not less rapidly than ratably (including interest) over 15 years, and no more than 5 waivers may be granted for any 15 consecutive years. Also, the Secretary of Labor may extend the amortization period for amortization of past service costs up to an additional 10 years, on a showing of economic hardship.

For money purchase pension plans, the minimum amount that an employer is to annually contribute to the plan generally is the amount that must be contributed for the year under the plan formula. For purposes of this rule, a plan (for example, a so-called Taft-Hartley plan) which provides an agreed level of benefits and a specified level of contributions during the contract period is not to be considered a money purchase plan if the employer or his representative participated in the determination of the benefits. On the other hand, a "target benefit plan" is to be treated as a money purchase plan for purposes of the minimum funding rules.

Under the new funding rules, generally each covered plan is to maintain a new account called a "funding standard account." This account is to aid both the taxpayer-employer and the Government in administering the minimum funding rules. The account also is used to assure that a taxpayer who has funded more than the minimum amount required is properly credited for that excess and for the interest earned on the excess. Similarly, where a taxpayer has paid too little, the account is to assist in enforcing the minimum funding standard, and to assure that the taxpayer is charged with interest on the amount of underfunding.

Each year the funding standard account is to be charged with the liabilities which must be paid to meet the minimum funding standard. Also, each year the funding standard account is to be credited with contributions under the plan and with any other decrease in liabilities (such as amortized experience gains). If the plan meets the minimum funding requirements as of the end of each year, the funding standard account will show a zero balance (or a positive balance, if the employer has contributed more than the minimum required). If the minimum contributions have not been made, the funding standard account will show a deficiency (called an "accumulated funding deficiency"). If there is an accumulated funding deficiency, an excise tax is to be imposed on the employer who is responsible for making contributions to the plan. Also, the responsible employer may be subject to civil action in the courts on failure to meet the minimum funding standards.

* * *

[¶ 14,620.15]

Committee Report on P.L. 93-406 (Employee Retirement Income Security Act of 1974)

[House Ways and Means Committee Explanation]

The funding standard accounts—special rules—combining and offsetting amounts to be amortized.—Your committee recognizes that the amortization rules may require a plan to keep accounts for amortizing a number of different items. While the amortization charges and credits to be entered in the funding standard account for any one year will net out to a single figure, some may prefer not to maintain a number of different amortization accounts. Therefore, the bill provides that amounts required to be amortized may, at the taxpayer's discretion, be combined into a single amount to be amortized.

The bill provides, pursuant to regulations to be issued by the Secretary of Treasury, that amounts which are amortizable credits and charges may be offset against each other with the balance to be amortized over a period determined on the basis of the remaining amortization periods for all items entering into the credits or charges, whichever is greater. Also, pursuant to regulations, amortizable credits (or amortizable charges) may be combined into one credit or one charge to be amortized over a period determined on the basis of the remaining amortization periods for all items entering into the combined amount. It is expected that if a taxpayer elects to offfset or combine amounts to be amortized, this election will apply to all amounts (both charges and credits) required to be amortized for the year of election.

* * *

[¶ 14,620.20]

Committee Report on P.L. 93-406 (Employee Retirement Income Security Act of 1974)

[Conference Committee Explanation]

Reasonable actuarial assumptions.—The conference substitute combines the rules relating to actuarial assumptions of the House bill and of the Senate amendment and requires that, for purposes of the minimum funding standard, all plan costs, liabilities, rates of interest, and other factors under the plan are to be determined on the basis of actuarial assumptions and methods which, in the aggregate, are reasonable. Actuarial assumptions are to take into account the experience of the plan and reasonable expectations. These assumptions are expected to take into consideration past experience as well as other relevant factors.

In addition, under the conference substitute, the actuarial assumptions in combination are to offer the actuary's best estimate of anticipated experience under the plan. The conferees intend that under this provision a single set of actuarial assumptions will be required for all purposes (e.g., for the minimum funding standard, reporting to the Department of Labor and to participants and beneficiaries, financial reporting to stockholders, etc.)

Treatment of certain changes as experience gains or losses.—* * * Under the conference substitute, changes in plan liabilities resulting from changes in actuarial assumptions are to be amortized over a 30-year period.

[¶ 14,620.25]

Committee Report on P.L. 93-406 (Employee Retirement Income Security Act of 1974)

[House Ways and Means Committee Explanation]

Experience losses and gains.—During the course of a pension plan, actual plan experience may turn out to be poorer than anticipated. For example, the value of plan assets may turn out to be less than expected. Where this occurs, there generally will be an "experience loss" which must be funded if the plan is to be able to pay the benefits owed.[5] Since experience losses relate to previously established plan liability, they may indicate that the plan has become underfunded in relation to the required minimum for funding normal costs and past service liabilities. Consequently, your committee believes it is reasonable to require faster funding for these amounts than for newly established past service liabilities. The bill provides that under the minimum funding rules these losses are to be amortized (with level annual payments, including principal and interest) over not more than 15 years (20 years for multiemployer plans) from the date the loss is determined. Your committee believes that a 15-year amortization period generally will provide adequate funding of experience losses, while at the same time protecting employers from potentially severe financial burdens arising from experience losses created by uncontrollable events.

Your committee understands that the 15-year period, while protecting the financial security of plans, generally will not discourage pension plans such as "final average pay plans" which increase accrued benefits as pay increases, and thus are generally desirable from the employee's view. Additionally, it is believed that under the 15-year requirement employers will not be subject to unnecessary financial burdens where they have experience losses beyond their control.

A pension plan also may have experience gains during the course of its operation. These gains would occur because experience is more favorable than anticipated. For example, the value of plan assets may be greater than expected. The bill treats experience gains symmetrically with experience losses, so that gains are spread over 15 years (20 years for multiemployer plans) from the date they are determined.

The bill provides that changes in plan cost that result from changes in the Social Security Act (or other retirement benefits created by State or Federal law), from changes in the definition of wages under section 3121 of the Code, or from changes in the amount of such wages taken into account for purposes of section 401(a)(5) (relating to integration with Social Security, etc.) are treated as experience losses (or gains). It is expected that the actuarial assumptions for plans affected by Social Security, etc. now generally will allow for such changes since to a substantial extent these changes may be anticipated. In this circumstance, if changes in plan cost from changes in social security were not treated as experience gains to be amortized, employers with plans that did not properly allow for social changes might be able to, upon increases in social security payments, substantially decrease current contributions and thereupon plan participants would receive correspondingly less protection.

[¶ 14,620.30]

Committee Report on P.L. 93-406 (Employee Retirement Income Security Act of 1974)

[Conference Committee Explanation]

Definition of experience gain or loss.—Under the conference substitute (following title II of the House bill and the Senate amendment) experience gain or loss is the difference between the anticipated experience of the plan and the actual experience.

The conferees understand that certain plans are maintained pursuant to collectively bargained agreements which provide for a predetermined level of contributions over a period longer than 12 months, such as a specified dollar amount per hour of covered service by an employee or a specified dollar amount per ton of coal mined. It is intended that, for the funding requirements to be workable in these cases, employers generally must be allowed to base their contributions on the bargained and agreed upon basis during the period to which the collective bargaining agreement relates (but generally for not more than three years). Under such a plan, if the actuarial assumptions were reasonable and the actuarial calculations were correct as of the beginning of the term of the agreement, and the agreed upon contributions were made when required during the term of the agreement, it is intended that there would be no deficiency in the funding standard account for the term of the collectively bargained agreement (limited as indicated above). This would be the case even if the amount of contributions were less than what was reasonably expected at the beginning of the term of the agreement (for example, because the hours worked or the tons of coal mined were less than reasonably anticipated). In this case, it is expected that any difference between the reasonably anticipated contributions and actual contributions would be treated as an experience loss which could be made up under the next agreement by adjustment of the contribution rate (or by adjustment of the level of benefits).

Change in funding method or plan year.—The conference substitute (following the House bill and Senate amendment) provides that a change in a plan's funding method (or plan year) can be used to determine plan costs and liabilities only if the change is approved by the administering Secretary. (Note that this requirement of prior approval does not apply to use of the alternative minimum funding standard, described below.) The conferees intend that a change in funding method or plan year also is to be reported to the Pension Benefit Guaranty Corporation in order that the Corporation may be fully apprised of events which may adversely affect the funding status of a plan.

[¶ 14,620.35]

Committee Report on P.L. 93-406 (Employee Retirement Income Security Act of 1974)

[House Ways and Means Committee Explanation]

Special rules—the full funding limitation.—In some cases, the difference between the total liabilities of the plan (all accrued liabilities including normal cost) and the total value of the plan assets may be smaller than the minimum funding requirement for the year. For example, this could occur where the plan assets had increased substantially and unexpectedly in value. Where the excess of total plan liabilities over assets is less than the minimum funding requirement otherwise determined, your committee believes that an employer should not have to contribute more than the amount of this excess liability, for upon contribution of this amount the plan will become fully funded. As a result, in this case the bill provides that the amount to be charged to the funding standard account (and to be contributed), is to be limited to the difference between the total liabilities of the plan and the fair market value of the plan assets. Since the full funding limitation reduces the amount otherwise required to be contributed to a plan, it appears appropriate to use the lower of fair market value or the value of plan assets as normally determined. (As discussed below, the value of plan assets as normally determined may be greater than fair market value in certain cases and in such situations use of the normal valuation method could inappropriately limit contributions to a plan.)

When the full funding limit applies, the amortization schedule for charges and credits to the funding standard account are to be considered as fully amortized, and these schedules generally are to be eliminated from the calculations under the funding standard account. However, if the plan is amended in later years to increase plan liabilities, a new amortization schedule would be established with respect to this increase in liabilities. For years after the full funding level is reached, the funding standard account will continue to be charged with the normal cost of the plan. Consequently, unless asset values increase correspondingly with the increase in plan liabilities, eventually the full funding limitation will not be applicable and the employer will have to make contributions to the plan to meet the minimum funding requirements.

If the employer fails to make the required contributions in a year in which the full funding limitation is applicable, the excise tax (described below) on underfunding in that year is to be based only on the amount that should have been contributed, given the full funding limitation.

For the purpose of calculating the full funding limitation, the bill provides that plan liabilities (including normal cost) are to be determined under the funding method used by the plan to determine costs for the year, if the liabilities can be directly calculated under this funding method. However, if this cannot be done under the plan's funding method, in order to allow the full funding limitation to apply, the bill provides that the accrued liabilities are to be calculated under the entry age normal method, solely for the purpose of determining the application of the full funding limitation.

Whether the full funding limitation applies generally is to be determined at the end of the plan year, after all plan liabilities for that year have accrued. For purposes of the full funding limitation, the value of plan assets generally is to be determined as of the usual valuation date for the plan. Since, as discussed above, contributions generally can be made to a plan after the end of a plan year and yet relate back to the previous plan year, there should be no timing problem with respect to such year-end calculations.

[¶ 14,620.40]

Committee Report on P.L. 93-406 (Employee Retirement Income Security Act of 1974)

[Conference Committee Explanation]

Full funding limitation.—Both the House bill and the Senate amendment include special provisions establishing the minimum amount to be funded where the difference between plan liabilities and plan assets is smaller than the amount otherwise required to be contributed under the minimum funding requirement for the year. Generally, these provisions are substantially the same; the conference substitute follows the House bill in the technical aspects. However, the conferees wish to clarify statements in the House report with respect to the time at which plan liabilities and plan assets are to be valued for purposes of determining the full funding standard. Generally, the conferees intend that assets and liabilities are to be valued at the usual time used by the plan for such valuations, if done on a consistent basis and in accordance with regulations.

Retroactive plan amendments.—

[5] However, the bill provides that experience gains and losses are to be determined under the funding method used to determine costs under the plan. It is understood that some funding methods, such as the "aggregate method", do not provide experience gains or losses, but differences between anticipated and actual experience are subsumed in the basic funding requirements of the method. If a plan were to use such a funding method, it is anticipated that the plan would not need to separately amortize experience gains or losses.

* * *

The conference substitute generally allows limited retroactive plan amendments, but only with the approval of the Secretary of Labor.

Under the conference substitute, plan amendments that reduce plan benefits may be made after the close of the plan year, and yet apply to that year if they are made within 2 ½ months after the end of the plan year. However, since a single plan year is not a workable standard for multiemployer plans, with respect to multiemployer plans, an amendment may be made under the conference substitute within 2 years of the close of the plan year.

To protect participants, amendments made under this provision are not to decrease vested benefits of any participant determined as of the time the amendment is adopted. In addition, such a retroactive amendment cannot reduce the accrued benefit (whether or not vested) of any participant determined as of the beginning of the first plan year to which the amendment applies. Moreover, such an amendment is not to retroactively reduce the accrued benefit to any participant, unless there would otherwise be an accumulated funding deficiency for all or part of the plan year in question, the funding deficiency could not be avoided through the implementation of any other reasonably available alternative (including amortization of experience losses or a waiver of the funding requirement), and the funding deficiency was not primarily attributable to the failure by employers to discharge contractual obligations to make contributions under the plan (e.g., failing to contribute a required amount per hour of work of plan participants).

Under the conference substitute, the plan administrator is to notify the Secretary of Labor of any amendment which retroactively decreases plan liabilities, before the amendment goes into effect. The amendment can then go into effect only if the Secretary has approved it, or if the Secretary does not disapprove it within 90 days after notice is filed. It is expected that within the 90-day period the Secretary may notify the plan [administrator] of a tentative disapproval, if he needs more information or more time before making a final determination. The Secretary of Labor is not to approve any retroactive amendment unless he determines that it meets the requirements discussed above and determines that it is necessary because of substantial business hardship.

Three-year determination of gains and losses.—Under the House bill, experience gains and losses would be determined every three years (more frequently in particular cases as required by regulations). * * *

The conference substitute follows the rules of the House bill. The conferees intend that regulations may be issued to require a determination of gains and losses and valuation of a plan's liabilities more frequently than every three years with respect to situations where there is a need for more frequent review. For example, the regulations might provide that a determination of experience gains and losses would be made more frequently than every three years by plans which have sustained substantial experience gains or losses for several periods in succession.

[ERISA Sec. 303]

[¶ 14,630.09]

Committee Report on P.L. 109-280 (Pension Protection Act of 2006)

For the Committee Report on P.L. 109-280 on single-employer plan minimum funding standards, see ¶ 12,250.023.

[¶ 14,630.10]

Committee Report on P.L. 93-406 (Employee Retirement Income Security Act of 1974)

[House Ways and Means Committee Explanation]

Variance from funding requirements.—At times an employer's financial circumstances may prevent him from meeting the minimum funding requirements. Your committee does not believe that in such a situation an employer should be forced to abandon his plan. To deal with cases of this type the bill provides that upon a demonstration by the employer of substantial business hardship and a showing that application of the minimum funding requirements would be adverse to the interests of the plan participants in the aggregate, the Internal Revenue Service may waive all or part of the minimum funding requirements for a year, including normal costs, amortization of past service costs and amortization of experience losses. However, to limit the underfunding which may occur in cases of this type, the bill provides that the Service may not waive all or part of the funding requirements for more than five years (whether or not consecutive) in any fifteen-year period. Also, the Service may not waive amortization of previously waived contributions.

* * *

[¶ 14,630.15]

Committee Report on P.L. 93-406 (Employee Retirement Income Security Act of 1974)

[Conference Committee Explanation]

Year-by-year waivers.—Title II of the House bill and the Senate amendment both provide that the Secretary of the Treasury may waive all or part of the minimum funding requirement for a plan year if an employer is unable to satisfy this requirement without incurring substantial business hardship.

The conference substitute follows the House bill with respect to the technical aspects and with respect to the number of variances that may be granted in any consecutive period of years. In addition, under the conference substitute, it is made clear that this waiver is to be available for employers contributing to a multiemployer plan. For multiemployer plans, the Secretary of Treasury may waive part or all of the funding requirements if at least 10 percent of the employers contributing to the plan demonstrate that they would experience substantial business hardship without the waiver, and if applying the minimum funding standard would be adverse to the interests of plan participants as a whole.

[ERISA Sec. 304]

[¶ 14,640.09]

Committee Report on P.L. 109-280 (Pension Protection Act of 2006)

For the Committee Report on P.L. 109-280 on single-employer plan minimum funding standards, see ¶ 12,250.023.

For the Committee Report on P.L. 109-280 on multiemployer plan funding rules, see ¶ 13,151M.50.

For the Committee Report on P.L. 109-280 on special rules for certain benefits funded under an agreement approved by the PBGC, see ¶ 13,151M.50.

For the Committee Report on P.L. 109-280 on sunset of multiemployer plan funding provisions, see ¶ 13,151M.50.

For the Committee Report on P.L. 109-280 on special funding rules for plans maintained by commercial airlines, see ¶ 12,250.023.

[¶ 14,640.095]

Committee Report on P.L. 100-203 (Omnibus Budget Reconciliation Act of 1987)

[Conference Committee Report]

Ways and Means Committee bill: The bill clarifies that a waiver can be granted only if the business hardship is temporary and if the entire controlled group of which the employer is a member, as well as the employer itself, is experiencing the hardship.

A request for a waiver is required to be submitted within 2 ½ months after the end of the plan year.

Funding waivers cannot be granted in more than 3 of any 15 consecutive plan years.

In addition to the notice to employee organizations, an employer is required to demonstrate that it made reasonable efforts to notify current employees that a waiver is being requested.

The interest rate charged on waived contributions is the greater of (1) the rate used in computing costs under the plan, or (2) 150 percent of the mid-term applicable Federal interest rate (AFR) in effect for the first month of the plan year.

The amortization period for waived contributions is the greater of (1) 5 years or (2) 15 years multiplied by the funded termination liability percentage for the plan year, rounded to the nearest whole number of years.

The bill lowers from $2 million to $250,000 the threshold on the accumulated funding deficiency with respect to which the IRS can require security. In the case of a plan with accumulated funding deficiencies in excess of $1 million or a plan that is not more than 70 percent funded, the PBGC is authorized to require that an employer provide security as a condition of granting a funding waiver.

The provision relating to the funding waivers generally is effective with respect to (1) any application for a funding waiver submitted after June 30, 1987, and (2) any waiver granted with respect to an application submitted after June 30, 1987. The provision requiring that applications for funding waivers be filed within 2 ½ months following the close of a plan year is effective for plan years beginning after December 31, 1987, with a transition rule for 1988 plan years.

Education and Labor bill: The present-law notice is to be provided to all affected parties (i.e., participants, beneficiaries, alternate payees, and employee organizations representing employees covered under the plan). In addition, the notice must describe the extent to which the plan is funded with respect to guaranteed benefits and benefit liabilities.

Labor and Human Resources Committee amendment: Notice of waiver requests: Same as the Education and Labor Committee bill, except that no definition of affected party is provided.

Amortization period for waived contributions: The amortization period for waived contributions is 5 plan years.

Conference Agreement: The conference agreement [generally] follows the Ways and Means Committee and Education and Labor Committee bills, and the Labor and Human Resources Committee amendment. In addition, the conference agreement provides that the Secretary may provide that an analysis of the financial hardship of a member of the controlled group of the employer need not be conducted. Such an analysis is not necessary because taking into account the circumstances of the member of the controlled group would not significantly affect the determination of whether a waiver should be granted. Although, with respect to multiemployer plans, the conference agreement does not incorporate in the statute the requirement that the financial hardship be temporary, the conferees do not intend to create an inference with respect to the current IRS practice of granting waivers only in the case of temporary hardship.

Time for requesting waivers: The conference agreement follows the Ways and Means Committee and Education and Labor Committee bills, and the Labor and Human Resources Committee amendment.

Frequency of waivers: The conference agreement follows the Ways and Means Committee and Education and Labor Committee bills, and the Labor and Human Resources Committee amendment, except that employers will not be treated as exceeding the number of permissible waivers due to waivers granted with respect to the plan years beginning before January 1, 1988. Thus, under the conference agreement, employers are provided a fresh start with respect to the frequency limit on waivers. As under present law, where a plan undergoes a transaction pursuant to the Implementation Guidelines, the successor plan shall not be considered a new plan for purposes of the frequency limit on waivers.

Notice of waiver requests: The conference agreement follows the Education and Labor Committee bill and the Labor and Human Resources Committee amendment. The conference agreement does not require that the employer furnish a copy of the waiver request to employees, and does not require that the Secretary furnish (or make available) a copy of the request to employees.

Interest rate charged for waived contributions: The conference report follows the Ways and Means Committee bill and the Finance Committee amendment.

Amortization period for waived contributions: The conference agreement follows the Labor and Human Resources Committee amendment.

Security for waivers: The conference agreement follows the Education and Labor Committee bill, and the Finance Committee and Labor and Human Resources Committee amendments, except that the present-law threshold with respect to which IRS may require security, etc., is reduced from $2 million to $1 million.

Effective date: The conference agreement follows the Ways and Means Committee bill, except that the date after which a submission of a funding waiver request is subject to the funding waiver provisions is December 17, 1987, rather than June 30, 1987. In addition, the provision regarding notice of waiver requests is effective with respect to application for waivers submitted more than 90 days after the date of enactment.

House bill.—Education and Labor Committee bill: The employer is required to notify each affected party that an extension is being requested. The interest rate charged with respect to an extension is the greater of (1) the interest rate used for calculating contributions under the plan or (2) [150] percent of the mid-term AFR in effect on the first day of the plan year for which the extension is requested.

Labor and Human Resources Committee amendment: Same as the Education and Labor Committee bill, except that no definition of affected party is provided.

Conference Agreement: The conference agreement follows the Education and Labor Committee bill and the Labor and Human Resources Committee amendments, with two modifications.

First, the interest rate charged is the greater of (1) the rate used in computing costs under the plan, and (2) 150 percent of the mid-term AFR in effect for the first month of the plan year.

Second, the $2 million threshold on the accumulated funding deficiency with respect to which the IRS can require security is reduced to $1 million, as under the rules for funding waivers.

The effective date of the provision is the same as the effective date of the funding waiver provisions.

[¶ 14,640.10]

Committee Report on P.L. 93-406 (Employee Retirement Income Security Act of 1974)

[Conference Committee Explanation]

Variances—extension of amortization periods.—

* * *

Under the conference substitute, the Secretary of Labor may extend the amortization period for unfunded past service liabilities and experience gains and losses for both multiemployer and single employer plans. These periods may be extended up to an additional ten years where there would otherwise be a substantial risk that the plan might be terminated or a substantial risk that pension benefit levels or employee compensation might be limited. Additionally, to grant an extension of time the Secretary must find that (1) the extension would carry out the purposes of the Act, (2) the extension would provide adequate protection for participants and beneficiaries, and (3) not granting the extension would be adverse to the interests of plan participants and beneficiaries as a whole.

Limit on increase in benefits during variance.—

* * *

The conference substitute generally follows the House bill in its technical aspects and limits plan amendments which increase liabilities where there has been a year-by-year waiver, or an extension of time to amortize past service costs or experience gains and losses. This limitation is to apply until the waived amount has been fully amortized or until the extension of time for amortization is not longer in effect. Also, under the conference substitute, benefits may not be increased if there has been a plan amendment which retroactively decreased plan benefits within the preceding 12 months (24 months in the case of multiemployer plans). However, the conference substitute makes it clear that reasonable, *de minimis* increases in plan liabilities are to be allowed, under regulations of the Secretary of Labor. (It is expected that the regulations will indicate the types of plan amendments considered *de minimis* for this purpose.) Also, amendments are to be allowed even though they increase plan liabilities if they are required as a condition of tax qualification. Further, amendments which merely repeal (in whole or in part) a previous retroactive decrease in benefits are to be allowed.

[ERISA Sec. 305]

[¶ 14,650.09]

Committee Report on P.L. 109-280 (Pension Protection Act of 2006)

For the Committee Report on P.L. 109-280 on single-employer plan minimum funding standards, see ¶ 12,250.023.

For the Committee Report on P.L. 109-280 on additional funding rules for multiemployer plans in endangered or critical status, see ¶ 13,151N.50.

[¶ 14,650.10]

Committee Report on P.L. 93-406 (Employee Retirement Income Security Act of 1974)

[Conference Committee Explanation]

Alternative minimum funding standard.—Under Title II of the House bill, the same funding method and assumptions would be used for determining the minimum amount that must be contributed to a plan and for determining the maximum amount for which a current tax deduction is available. The Senate amendment does not include a similar requirement.

The conference substitute generally follows the rules of the House bill in requiring the funding method used by a plan to be the same for purposes of determining the minimum amount to be contributed and the maximum deduction for contributions. However, the conference substitute also would allow the use of an alternative minimum funding standard in order that there may be some leeway between the minimum required contributions and the maximum deductible contributions.

Under the alternative funding standard, generally the minimum amount to be contributed to a plan is (1) the excess (if any) of the value of accrued benefits over the value of plan assets, plus (2) normal cost. Under this standard, plan assets are to be annually valued at fair market value and plan liabilities are to be valued on the same basis as the Pension Benefit Guaranty Corporation would have computed them if the plan terminated. These valuation methods are used because this minimum funding standard is similar to a "termination test" funding standard. When the financial status of a plan is examined on a termination basis, it is considered appropriate to use fair market valuations rather than valuations which tend to spread out fluctuations in value. In addition, under this standard normal cost is to be the lesser of normal cost as determined under the method used by the plan or normal cost under the unit credit method.

The alternative standard generally is to be available only for plans using funding methods which provide contributions which are no less than the contributions required under the entry age normal method. In this case, plan participants and beneficiaries will have the protection of a relatively faster build-up of plan assets in the early years of the plan than under, *e.g.,* the unit credit method.

On electing to use the alternative method, a plan must maintain an alternate funding standard account. The account will be charged with normal costs plus the excess of accrued benefits over assets (but not less than zero), and will be credited with contributions. There is to be no carryover of contributions over the minimum required from one year to another, because this amount automatically will become part of the next year's calculation in determining whether liabilities are greater than assets (that is, excess contributions will become part of plan assets for purposes of the next year's calculation). On the other hand, any shortfall of contributions less than the amount required will be carried over from year to year (with interest added) and an excise tax will be payable on these amounts (or on the funding deficiency as shown by the basic funding standard account, if smaller).

A plan that chooses to use the alternative funding method is to maintain both an alternative funding standard account and the basic funding standard account. The basic funding standard account will be charged and credited under the usual rules, but an excise tax generally will not be owed on any "deficiency" shown in that basic account. A plan making this choice is required to maintain both accounts because the minimum funding requirement will be the minimum required contribution under either account, whichever is the lesser.

The requirement under the alternative method could become higher than under the basic method if there was a substantial decrease in the market value of the assets, or if there was a substantial increase in plan liabilities (as through a plan amendment). If the minimum required contributions are lower under the basic standard than under the alternative funding standard has been the plan will switch back to the basic funding method.

If a plan switches back from the alternate funding standard to the basic funding standard, generally there is to be a 5-year amortization of the excess of charges over credits that have built up in the basic funding standard account over the years in which the alternative standard has been used. This will give the employer a reasonable period of time to fund the amounts that otherwise would have been contributed under the basic funding method, but were not contributed while the alternative funding method was being used. However, to the extent that excess charges (over contributions) have been previously built up in the alternate funding standard account, these are not to be amortized over 5 years, but instead are to be contributed immediately if the excise tax on underfunding is to be avoided. When an employer switches back from the alternative funding standard to the basic funding standard, the employer ceases to maintain the alternate minimum funding standard account. If the employer in some subsequent year returns to the alternate standard, a new account with a zero balance is to be established.

[ERISA Sec. 306]

[¶ 14,655.09]

Committee Report on P.L. 109-280 (Pension Protection Act of 2006)

—For the Committee Report on P.L. 109-280 on single-employer plan minimum funding standards, see ¶ 12,250.023.

[¶ 14,655.10]

Committee Report on P.L. 99-272 (Consolidated Omnibus Budget Reconciliation Act)

[Conference Committee Report]

The conference agreement clarifies that the IRS is authorized to require that security be provided as a condition of granting a waiver of the minimum funding standard, the extension of an amortization period, or modification of a previously granted waiver of the minimum funding standard with respect to a single employer defined benefit plan. The conference agreement requires that, before granting an application for a waiver, extension or modification to a single employer defined benefit plan, the IRS notify the PBGC of the receipt of a completed application for a waiver, extension, or modification, and consider the views of any interested party, including the PBGC, submitted in writing. The PBGC has a 30-day period after the date of receipt of notice to submit to the IRS comments on the application.

The conference agreement provides that the notice of the application and any other information or materials relating to the application that is sent to the PBGC by the IRS constitutes tax return information and is subject to the safeguarding and reporting requirements of section 6103(p) of the Code.

Under the conference agreement, the security, notice, and comment provisions do not apply if, with respect to the plan for which a waiver is requested, the sum of (a) the accumulated funding deficiencies (including the amount of any increase in the accumulated funding deficiency that would result if the request for a waiver were denied); (b) the outstanding balance of any previously waived funding deficiencies; and (c) the outstanding balance of any decreases in the minimum funding standard allowed under section 303 of ERISA, is less that $2 million. As under current law, the mere creation of a security interest at the direction of the Secretary of the Treasury as a condition for granting a waiver does not by itself constitute a prohibited transaction. The provisions of the conference agreement relating to security are intended by the conferees to provide appropriate rules for the future. The conferees intend that no inference is to be drawn from this provision with respect to the application of present law to such transactions.

* * *

Finally, under the conference agreement, an employer that submits an application for a waiver of the minimum funding standard is required to notify any employee organization representing participants in the plan of the application.

[ERISA Sec. 307]

[¶ 14,657.09]

Committee Report on P.L. 109-280 (Pension Protection Act of 2006)

For the Committee Report on P.L. 109-280 on single-employer plan minimum funding standards, see ¶ 12,250.023.

[¶ 14,657.10]

Committee Report on P.L. 100-203 (Omnibus Budget Reconciliation Act of 1987)

[Conference Committee Report]

The conference agreement generally follows the Finance Committee amendment, with certain modifications. Under the conference agreement, if a plan amendment increasing current liability is adopted, the contributing sponsor and members of the controlled group of the contributing sponsor must provide security in favor of the plan (e.g., a bond) equal to the excess of (1) the lesser of (i) the amount by which the plan's assets are less than 60 percent of current liability, taking into account the benefit increase and the unfunded current liability attributable to prior plan amendments, or (ii) the amount of the benefit increase, over (2) $10 million. The employer must notify the PBGC of the benefit increase before it is effective. As under the Finance Committee amendment, current liability is calculated by disregarding the unamortized portion of unfunded old liability.

[ERISA Sec. 308]

[¶ 14,660.09]

Committee Report on P.L. 109-280 (Pension Protection Act of 2006)

—For the Committee Report on P.L. 109-280 on single-employer plan minimum funding standards, see ¶ 12,250.023.

[¶ 14,660.10]

Committee Report on P.L. 93-406 (Employee Retirement Income Security Act of 1974)

[Conference Committee Explanation]

Effective dates

In the case of new plans, the funding provisions are to apply to the first full plan year beginning after the date of enactment [September 2, 1974] of the bill. For example, if a plan was established on October 1, 1974, but its plan year is a calendar year, the new provisions are to apply to the plan year beginning January 1, 1975.

Generally, in the case of plans existing on January 1, 1974, the new funding provisions are to become applicable for plan years beginning after December 31, 1975. In the case of collectively bargained plans (both single employer and multiemployer plans) existing on January 1, 1974, the effective date would be delayed until the termination of the contract existing on January 1, 1974, but not later than plan years beginning after December 31, 1980. Where an employer has plans which involve both collective bargaining unit employees and other employees, the effective dates applicable to collectively bargained plans are to govern if (on January 1, 1974) at least 25 percent of the plan participants are members of the employee unit covered by the collectively bargained agreement. (This is described more fully in connection with the effective dates for participation.)

Where a qualified plan does not meet the funding requirements of existing law because of vesting or participation requirements made applicable by the substitute and where the funding requirements of the conference substitute do not become applicable until a later time than the vesting or participation requirements, then to the extent that failure to meet the funding requirements of existing law is attributable to these non-vesting or participation requirements, no plan is to be disqualified in this interim period on the grounds of underfunding.

The effective date for the rules with respect to maximum deduction limits is the same as the effective date for the funding rules generally.

[ERISA Sec. 401]

[¶ 14,710.095]

Committee Reports on P.L. 104-188 (Small Business Job Protection Act)

[Managers' Amendment to H.R. 3448]

Application of ERISA to insurance company general accounts clarified

Under the amendment, not later than December 31, 1996, the Secretary of Labor would be required to issue proposed regulations providing guidance for the purpose of determining, in cases where an insurer issues 1 or more policies (supported by the assets of the insurer's general account) to or for the benefit of an employee benefit plan, which assets of the insurer (other than plan assets held in its separate account) constitute plan assets for purposes of ERISA and the Code. Such proposed regulations would be subject to public notice and comment until March 31, 1997, and the Secretary of Labor would be required to issue final regulations by June 30, 1997. Any regulations issued by the Secretary of Labor in accordance with the amendment could not take effect before the date on which such regulations became final.

In issuing regulations, the Secretary of Labor would have to ensure that such regulations are administratively feasible and are designed to protect the interests and rights of the plan and of the plan's participants and beneficiaries. In so doing, the Secretary of Labor may exclude any assets of the insurer with respect to its operations, products, or services from treatment as plan assets. Further, the regulations would have to provide that plan assets do not include assets which are not treated as plan assets under present-law ERISA by reason of being (1) assets of an investment company registered under the Investment Company Act of 1940, and (2) assets of an insurer with respect to a guaranteed benefit policy issued by such insurer.

Under the amendment, no person would be liable under ERISA or the Code for conduct which occurred prior to the date which is 18 months following the effective date of the final regulations on the basis of a claim that the assets of the insurer (other than plan assets held in a separate account) constituted plan assets, except as otherwise provided by the Secretary of Labor in order to prevent avoidance of the guidance in the regulations or as provided in an action brought by the Secretary of Labor under ERISA's enforcement provisions for a breach of fiduciary responsibility which would also constitute a violation of Federal criminal law or constitute a felony under applicable State law.[17]

The amendment would not preclude the application of any Federal criminal law.

Effective Date

The amendment generally would be effective on January 1, 1975. However, the amendment would not apply to any civil action commenced before November 7, 1995.

[Conference Committee Report]

The conference agreement follows the Senate amendment with the following modifications.

Proposed regulations need not be issued by the Secretary of Labor until June 30, 1997. Such proposed regulations will be subject to public notice and comment until September 30, 1997. Final regulations need not be issued until December 31, 1997.

Such regulations will only apply with respect to a policy issued by an insurer on or before December 31, 1998. In the case of such a policy, the regulations will take effect at the end of the 18 month period following the date such regulations become final. New policies issued after December 31, 1998, will be subject to the fiduciary obligations under ERISA.

In issuing regulations, the Secretary of Labor must ensure that such regulations protect the interests and rights of the plan and of its participants and beneficiaries as opposed to ensuring that such regulations are designed to protect the interests and rights of the plan and of its participants and beneficiaries.

Under the conference agreement, in connection with any policy (other than a guaranteed benefit policy) issued by an insurer to or for the benefit of an employee benefit plan, the regulations issued by the Secretary of Labor must require (1) that a plan fiduciary totally independent of the insurer authorize the purchase of such policy (unless it is the purchase of a life insurance, health insurance, or annuity contract exempt from ERISA's prohibited transaction rules); (2) that after the date final regulations are issued the insurer provide periodic reports to the policyholder disclosing the method by which any income or expenses of the insurer's general account are allocated to the policy and disclosing the actual return to the plan under the policy and such other financial information the Secretary may deem appropriate; and (3) that the insurer disclose to the plan fiduciary the extent to which alternative arrangements supported by assets of separate accounts of the insurer are available, whether there is a right under the policy to transfer funds to a separate account and the terms governing any such right, and the extent to which support by assets of the insurer's general account and support by assets of separate accounts of the insurer might pose differing risks to the plan; and (4) that the insurer must manage general account assets with the level of care, skill, prudence and diligence under the circumstances then prevailing that a prudent man acting in a like capacity and familiar with such matters would use in the conduct of an enterprise of a like character and with like aims, taking into account all obligations supported by such enterprise.

Under the Conference agreement, compliance by the insurer with all the requirements of the regulations issued by the Secretary of Labor will be deemed compliance by such insurer with ERISA's fiduciary duties, prohibited transactions, and limitations on holding employer securities and employer real property provisions (ERISA secs. 404, 406, and 407).

[¶ 14,710.10]

Committee Report on P.L. 93-406 (Employee Retirement Income Security Act of 1974)

[Conference Committee Explanation]

Coverage of the labor provisions.—The labor fiduciary responsibility rules generally apply to all employee benefit plans (both retirement plans and welfare plans) in or affecting interstate commerce. The usual exceptions for government plans, church plans (which do not elect to have the participation, vesting, funding, and insurance rules apply), workmen's compensation plans, and nonresident alien plans apply here as well as to the other parts of the labor provisions. In addition, the labor fiduciary rules do not apply to an unfunded plan primarily devoted to providing deferred compensation for a select group of management or highly compensated employees. For example, if a "phantom stock" or "shadow stock" plan were to be established solely for the officers of a corporation, it would not be covered by the labor fiduciary rules. Also, a deferred compensation arrangement solely for retiring partners (under sec. 736 of the Internal Revenue Code) is to be exempt from the fiduciary responsibility rules. Additionally, the fiduciary responsibility rules do not apply to a so-called excess benefit plan which is unfunded.

Since mutual funds are regulated by the Investment Company Act of 1940 and, since (under the Internal Revenue Code) mutual funds must be broadly held, it is not considered necessary to apply the fiduciary rules to mutual funds merely because plans invest in their shares. Therefore, the substitute provides that the mere investment by a plan in the shares of a mutual fund is not to be sufficient to cause the assets of the fund to be considered the assets of the plan. (However, a plan's assets will include the shares of a mutual fund held by the plan.)

The substitute also provides that a mutual fund is not to be considered a fiduciary or a party-in-interest merely because a plan invests in its shares, except that the mutual fund may be a fiduciary or party-in-interest if it acts in connection with a plan covering the employees of the investment company, the investment adviser, or its principal underwriter.

An insurance company also is not considered to hold plan assets if a plan purchases an insurance policy from it, to the extent that the policy provides payments guaranteed by the company. If the policy guarantees basic payments but other payments may vary with, *e.g.,* investment performance, then the variable part of the policy and assets attributable thereto are not to be considered as guaranteed, and are to be considered as plan assets subject to the fiduciary rules. (However, such assets need not be held in trust under the fiduciary responsibility rule.)

Additionally, it is understood that assets placed in a separate account managed by an insurance company are separately managed and the insurance company's payments generally are based on the investment performance of these particular assets. Consequently, insurance companies are to be responsible under the general fiduciary rules with respect to assets held under separate account contracts, and the assets of these contracts are to be considered as plan assets (but need not be held in trust). However, to the extent that insurance companies place some of their own funds in these separate accounts to provide for contingencies, this separate account "surplus" is not to be subject to the fiduciary responsibility rules.

These rules are to apply with respect to insurance policies issued by an insurance company, or by an insurance service or insurance organization. The conferees understand that some companies that provide, *e.g.,* health insurance, are not technically considered as "insurance companies." It is intended that these companies are to be included within the terms "insurance service or insurance organization."

[ERISA Sec. 402]

[¶ 14,720.10]

Committee Report on P.L. 93-406 (Employee Retirement Income Security Act of 1974)

[Conference Committee Explanation]

Structure of plan administration—Establishment of plan.—Under the labor provisions of the conference substitute, every covered employee benefit plan (both retirement and welfare plan) is to be established and maintained in writing. A written plan is to be required in order that every employee may, on examining the plan documents, determine exactly what his rights and obligations are under the plan. Also, a written plan is required so the employees may know who is responsible for operating the plan. Therefore, the plan document is to provide for the "named fiduciaries" who have authority to control and manage the plan operations and administration. A named fiduciary may be a person whose name actually appears in the document, or may be a person who holds an office specified in the document, such as the company president. A named fiduciary also may be a person who is identified by the employer or union, under a procedure set out in the document. For example, the plan may provide that the employer's board of directors is to choose the person who manages or controls the plan. In addition, a named fiduciary may be a person identified by the employers and union acting jointly. For example, the members of a joint board of trustees of a Taft-Hartley plan would usually be named fiduciaries.

Plan contents.—Under the labor provisions of the substitute, each plan is to provide a procedure of establishing a funding policy and method to carry out the plan objectives. This procedure is to enable the plan fiduciaries to determine the plan's short- and long-run financial needs and communicate these requirements to the appropriate persons. For example, with a retirement plan it is expected that under this procedure the persons who manage the plan will determine whether the plan has a short-run need for liquidity, (*e.g.,* to pay benefits) or whether liquidity is a long-run goal and investment growth is a more current need. This in turn is to be communicated to the persons responsible for investments, so that investment policy can be appropriately coordinated with plan needs. Also, the plan documents are to set out the basis for contributions to and payments from the plan. Thus, the plan is to specify what part (if any) of contributions are to come from employees and what part from employers. Also, it is to specify the basis on which payments are to be made to participants and beneficiaries.

It is customary for those who manage and control the plan to allocate their responsibilities and, within limits, designate others to carry out the daily management of the plan. The conference substitute establishes special rules which will enable fiduciaries to continue to allocate and delegate their responsibilities. However, allocation or delegation is to be allowed only if the plan provides for it (or provides procedures for it) in accordance with the terms of the substitute, as discussed below.

Each plan also is to provide a procedure for amendments and for identifying who can amend the plan. Additionally, following common practice, a plan may

[17] The amendment would provide that the term policy includes a contract.

provide that a person may serve in more than one fiduciary capacity under the plan, including service both as administrator and trustee. As described below, the plan may also provide for the hiring of investment (and other) advisers and investment managers.

[ERISA Sec. 403]

[¶ 14,730.085]

Committee Report on P.L. 100-203 (Omnibus Budget Reconciliation Act of 1987)

[Conference Committee Report]

The [House] bill would provide that, except to the extent specifically provided in the Code, the Code is to be interpreted as if the provisions of Titles I and IV of ERISA had not been enacted. In addition, the bill specifically rejects the holding in *Calfee, Halter & Griswold.* The bill does not override or otherwise affect the provisions of Reorganization Plan No. 4.

The Education and Labor Committee bill is similar to the Ways and Means Committee bill, except that Title I of ERISA is amended to permit a return of contributions to an employer if the contribution is conditioned on initial qualification of the plan, if the plan does not qualify initially, and if the application for determination relating to initial qualification is filed by the due date of the employer's return for the taxable year in which the plan was adopted. The bill clarifies that a determination by the Secretary of the Treasury under the Code is not prima facie evidence on issues relating to certain parts of Title I of ERISA. The provision is effective on the date of enactment.

The conference agreement follows the Ways and Means Committee bill with respect to the rejection of the holding in *Calfee, Halter & Griswold.* The conference agreement also provides that, except to the extent provided by the Code or determined by the Secretary of the Treasury, Titles I and IV of ERISA are not applicable in interpreting the Code. As under the Ways and Means Committee bill, the conference agreement does not override or otherwise affect the provisions of Reorganization No. 4. Nor is it intended that the bill preclude coordination between the Department of Labor, the PBGC, and the Treasury Department on issues of mutual jurisdiction. These provisions are a clarification of present law.

The conference agreement follows the Education and Labor Committee bill with respect to the effect on Title I of ERISA of a determination by the Secretary of the Treasury under the Code (a clarification of present law) and with respect to conditioning contributions only on initial qualification, effective on the date of enactment.

[¶ 14,730.09]

Committee Report on P.L. 96-364 (Multiemployer Pension Plan Amendments Act of 1980)

For Senate testimony on floor amendment (P.L. 96-364), see ¶ 14,410.09.

[¶ 14,730.095]

Committee Report on P.L. 96-364 (Multiemployer Pension Plan Amendments Act of 1980)

[Senate Committee Report]

Under the bill, in the case of a contribution to a multiemployer plan which was made because of a mistake of law or fact, the contribution may be returned without penalty within six months after the date the plan administrator determines that the contribution resulted from a mistake of law or fact. For this purpose, a mistake of law relating to plan qualification under the Code is not considered a mistake of law.

The bill provision is retroactive with respect to its application to multiemployer plans. For such plans the date the plan administrator determines that the contribution resulted from a mistake of law or fact is deemed to be the later of (1) the date of the actual determination, or (2) the date of enactment.

For Senate testimony on floor amendment (P.L. 96-364), see ¶ 14,410.09.

[¶ 14,730.10]

Committee Report on P.L. 93-406 (Employee Retirement Income Security Act of 1974)

[Conference Committee Explanation]

Establishment of trust.—The labor provisions of the substitute generally provide that all plan assets are to be held in trust by trustees and also provide that the trustees are to manage and control the plan assets. Also, the plan trustees are to be appointed in the plan or trust documents or appointed by a named fiduciary. However, in order that persons who act as trustees recognize their special responsibilities with respect to plan assets, trustees are to accept appointment before they act in this capacity.

If the plan provides that the trustees are subject to the direction of named fiduciaries, then the trustees are not to have the exclusive management and control over the plan assets, but generally are to follow the directions of the named fiduciary. Therefore, if the plan sponsor wants an investment committee to direct plan investments, he may provide for such an arrangement in the plan. In addition, since investment decisions are basic to plan operations, members of such an investment committee are to be named fiduciaries. (For example, the plan could provide that the investment committee is to consist of the persons who serve as the president, vice-president for finance, and comptroller of the employer.) If the plan so provides, the trustee who is directed by an investment committee is to follow that committee's directions unless it is clear on their face that the actions to be taken under those directions would be prohibited by the fiduciary responsibility rules of the bill or would be contrary to the terms of the plan or trust.

In addition (as discussed below), to the extent that the management of plan assets is delegated to a special category of persons called "investment managers", the trustee is not to have exclusive discretion to manage and control the plan assets, nor would the trustee be liable for any act of such investment manager.

A trust is not to be required in the case of plan assets which consist of insurance (including annuity) contracts or policies issued by an insurance company qualified to do business in a State (or the District of Columbia). The same exemption will apply to the new section 403(b) custodial account arrangement involving investment in mutual funds, since these are treated as amounts contributed for an annuity contract under the tax law. Although these contracts need not be held in trust, nevertheless, the person who holds the contract is to be a fiduciary and is to act in accordance with the fiduciary rules of the substitute with respect to these contracts. For example, this person is to prudently take and keep exclusive control of the contracts, and is to use prudent care and skill to preserve this property.

To the extent that plan assets are held by an insurance company they need not be held in trust. However, to the extent the substitute treats assets held by an insurance company as "plan assets", the insurance company is to be treated as a fiduciary with respect to the plan, and is to meet the fiduciary standards of the conference substitute.

The labor provisions of the substitute also provide that the assets of H.R. 10 plans (plans for the self-employed and their employees) and individual retirement accounts need not be held in trust to the extent they are held in custodial accounts qualified under the Internal Revenue Code. It is recognized that the substitute generally amends the Internal Revenue Code to make use of custodial accounts more available for all plans, and that this is expected to decrease the cost of asset administration for many plans. Custodial accounts also may be used by all plans under the labor provisions. However, a plan (which is not exempt from the trust requirements) that uses a custodial account also will have to have a trustee (who can be the plan administrator or sponsor). The plan trustee will have the responsibility for investment decisions with regard to the assets and the custodian will (as under present practice) merely retain custody of these assets. Since the plan sponsor could be the trustee, the costs of plan administration will remain as low as with the present custodial account arrangements, but the plan also would have a responsible person in charge of investment decisions.

A trust also is not to be required for a plan not subject to the participation, vesting and funding provisions of title I, and the plan termination insurance provisions, to the extent provided by the Secretary of Labor.

Exclusive benefit for employees.—Under the conference substitute each fiduciary of a plan must act solely in the interests of the plan's participants and beneficiaries and exclusively to provide benefits to these participants and beneficiaries (or to pay reasonable plan administrative costs).

Since the assets of the employee benefit plan are to be held for the exclusive benefit of participants and beneficiaries, plan assets generally are not to inure to the benefit of the employer. However, the conference substitute allows an employer's contributions to be returned to him in certain limited situations.

An employer's contributions can be returned within one year after they are made to the plan, if made as a mistake of fact. (For example, an employer may have made an arithmetical error in calculating the amounts that were to be contributed to the plan.) Also, if an employer contributes to a plan on the condition that the plan is tax-qualified or on the condition that a current tax deduction is allowed for the contribution, and it is later determined that the plan is not qualified (or the deduction is not allowed), the contribution can be returned if the plan provides for it. In this case, the contribution can be returned within one year after the disallowance of qualification or deduction. With regard to a disallowance of deductions, contributions can be returned only to the extent of the amount for which a deduction is denied. (For example, if $100 is contributed on the condition it is deductible and $20 is later determined not to be deductible, only $20 could be returned, and not $100.) Also with respect to qualification, contributions can be returned on the denial of initial or of continuing qualification (in the case of contributions made after *e.g.*, a plan amendment).

An employer's contributions under an H.R. 10 plan also can be returned to the employer to the extent permitted to avoid payment of an excise tax on excess contributions.

Under the labor (but not the tax) provisions of the substitute, the transfer or distribution of the assets of a welfare plan on termination of the plan is to be in accordance with the terms of the plan except as otherwise prescribed by regulations of the Secretary of Labor. It is intended that the Secretary of Labor would allow the terms of the plan (or in the case of a plan subject to collective bargaining, the collective bargaining agreement) to govern such distribution or transfer of assets except to the extent that implementation of the terms of the plan or agreement would unduly impair the accrued benefits of the plan participants or would not be in the best interests of the plan participants. Where such distribution or transfer is incidental to the merger of one multiemployer plan with another, it is expected that the Secretary of Labor would disallow the distribution or transfer only where the merger would reasonably be expected to jeopardize the ability of the plan to meet its obligations or would otherwise not be in the best interests of the plan participants.

Also, under the labor (but not the tax) provisions of the substitute, on termination of a pension plan to which the plan termination insurance provisions do not apply, the assets of the plan are to be allocated in accordance with the provisions under the plan termination insurance title of the Act governing such allocation (as if the plan were covered by termination insurance), except as otherwise provided in regulations prescribed by the Secretary of Labor. It is intended that regulations by the Secretary of Labor in this case would be similar to the regulations governing the distribution of assets on termination of a welfare plan as described above.

[ERISA Sec. 404]

[¶ 14,740.091]

Committee Report on P.L. 109-280 (Pension Protection Act of 2006)

[Joint Committee on Taxation Report]

[Inapplicability of relief from fiduciary liability during suspension of ability of participant or beneficiary to direct investments]

The bill amends the special rule applicable if a participant exercises control over the assets in his or her account with respect to a case in which a qualified change in investment options offered under the defined contribution plan occurs. In such a case, for purposes of the special rule, a participant or beneficiary who has exercised control over the assets in his or her account before a change in investment options is not treated as not exercising control over such assets in connection with the change if certain requirements are met.

For this purpose, a qualified change in investment options means a change in the investment options offered to a participant or beneficiary under the terms of the plan, under which: (1) the participant's account is reallocated among one or more new investment options offered instead of one or more investment options that were offered immediately before the effective date of the change; and (2) the characteristics of the new investment options, including characteristics relating to risk and rate of return, are, immediately after the change, reasonably similar to the characteristics of the investment options offered immediately before the change.

The following requirements must be met in order for the rule to apply: (1) at least 30 but not more than 60 days before the effective date of the change in investment options, the plan administrator furnishes written notice of the change to participants and beneficiaries, including information comparing the existing and new investment options and an explanation that, in the absence of affirmative investment instructions from the participant or beneficiary to the contrary, the account of the participant or beneficiary will be invested in new options with characteristics reasonably similar to the characteristics of the existing investment options; (2) the participant or beneficiary has not provided to the plan administrator, in advance of the effective date of the change, affirmative investment instructions contrary to the proposed reinvestment of the participant's or beneficiary's account; and (3) the investment of the participant's or beneficiary's account as in effect immediately before the effective date of the change was the product of the exercise by such participant or beneficiary of control over the assets of the account.

In addition, the provision amends the special rule applicable if a participant or beneficiary exercises control over the assets in his or her account so that the provision under which no person who is otherwise a fiduciary is liable for any loss, or by reason of any breach, that results from the participant's or beneficiary's exercise of control does not apply in connection with a blackout period[140] in which the participant's or beneficiary's ability to direct the assets in his or her account is suspended by a plan sponsor or fiduciary. However, if a plan sponsor or fiduciary meets the requirements of ERISA in connection with authorizing and implementing a blackout period, any person who is otherwise a fiduciary is not liable under ERISA for any loss occurring during the blackout period.

[Treatment of investment of assets by plan where participant fails to exercise investment election]

Under the bill, a participant is treated as exercising control with respect to assets in an individual account plan if such amounts are invested in a default arrangement in accordance with Department of Labor regulations until the participant makes an affirmative election regarding investments. Such regulations must provide guidance on the appropriateness of certain investments for designation as default investments under the arrangement, including guidance regarding appropriate mixes of default investments and asset classes which the Secretary considers consistent with long-term capital appreciation or long-term capital preservation (or both), and the designation of other default investments. The Secretary of Labor is directed to issue regulations under the provision within six months of the date of enactment.

In order for this treatment to apply, notice of the participant's rights and obligations under the arrangement must be provided. Under the notice requirement, within a reasonable period before the plan year, the plan administrator must give each participant notice of the rights and obligations under the arrangement which is sufficiently accurate and comprehensive to apprise the participant of such rights and obligations and is written in a manner to be understood by the average participant. The notice must include an explanation of the participant's rights under the arrangement to specifically elect to exercise control over the assets in the participant's account. In addition, the participant must have a reasonable period of time after receipt of the notice and before the assets are first invested to make such an election. The notice must also explain how contributions made under the arrangement will be invested in the absence of any investment election by the employee.

Effective Date

The provision is effective for plan years beginning after December 31, 2006.

[Clarification of fiduciary rules]

The bill directs the Secretary of Labor to issue final regulations within one year of the date of enactment, clarifying that the selection of an annuity contract as an optional form of distribution from a defined contribution plan is not subject to the safest available annuity requirement under the ERISA interpretive bulletin and is subject to all otherwise applicable fiduciary standards.

The regulations to be issued by the Secretary of Labor are intended to clarify that the plan sponsor or other applicable plan fiduciary is required to act in accordance with the prudence standards of ERISA section 404(a). It is not intended that there be a single safest available annuity contract since the plan fiduciary must select the most prudent option specific to its plan and its participants and beneficiaries. Furthermore, it is not intended that the regulations restate all of the factors contained in the interpretive bulletin.

Effective Date

The provision is effective on the date of enactment.

[Automatic enrollment features]

For the Committee Report on P.L. 109-280 on automatic enrollment arrangements, see ¶ 13,648J.09.

[¶ 14,740.093]

Committee Report on P.L. 107-16 (Economic Growth and Tax Relief Reconciliation Act)

For the Committee Report on P.L. 107-16 on automatic rollovers of certain mandatory distributions, see ¶ 11,700.024.

[¶ 14,740.095]

Committee Report on P.L. 104-188 (Small Business Job Protection Act)

[Senate Committee Report]

Reporting requirements

Trustee requirements.—The trustee of a SIMPLE account is required each year to prepare, and provide to the employer maintaining the SIMPLE plan, a summary description containing the following basic information about the plan; the name and address of the employer and the trustee; the requirements for eligibility; the benefits provided under the plan; the time and method of making salary reduction elections; and the procedures for and effects of, withdrawals (including rollovers) from the SIMPLE account. At least once a year, the trustee is also required to furnish an account statement to each individual maintaining a SIMPLE account. In addition, the trustee is required to file an annual report with the Secretary. A trustee who fails to provide any of such reports or descriptions will be subject to a penalty of $50 per day until such failure is corrected, unless the failure is due to reasonable cause.

* * *

[Conference Committee Report]

Conference Agreement

The conference agreement follows the Senate amendment.

[¶ 14,740.10]

Committee Report on P.L. 93-406 (Employee Retirement Income Security Act of 1974)

[Conference Committee Explanation]

Basic fiduciary rules—Prudent man standard.—The substitute requires that each fiduciary of a plan act with the care, skill, prudence, and diligence under the circumstances then prevailing that a prudent man acting in a like capacity and familiar with such matters would use in conducting an enterprise of like character and with like aims. The conferees expect that the courts will interpret this

[140] For this purpose, blackout period is defined as under the present-law provision requiring advance notice of a blackout period.

prudent man rule (and the other fiduciary standards) bearing in mind the special nature and purpose of employee benefit plans.

Under the Internal Revenue Code, qualified retirement plans must be for the exclusive benefit of the employees and their beneficiaries. Following this requirement, the Internal Revenue Service has developed general rules that govern the investment of plan assets, including a requirement that cost must not exceed fair market value at the time of purchase, there must be a fair return commensurate with the prevailing rate, sufficient liquidity must be maintained to permit distributions, and the safeguards and diversity that a prudent investor would adhere to must be present. The conferees intend that to the extent that a fiduciary meets the prudent man rule of the labor provisions, he will be deemed to meet these aspects of the exclusive benefit requirements under the Internal Revenue Code.

Under the conference substitute, plan fiduciaries also must act in accordance with plan documents and instruments to the extent that they are consistent with the requirements established in the bill.

Diversification requirement.—The substitute requires fiduciaries to diversify plan assets to minimize the risk of large losses, unless under the circumstances it is clearly prudent not to do so. It is not intended that a more stringent standard of prudence be established with the use of the term "clearly prudent." Instead, by using this term it is intended that in an action for plan losses based on breach of the diversification requirement, the plaintiff's initial burden will be to demonstrate that there has been a failure to diversify. The defendant then is to have the burden of demonstrating that this failure to diversify was prudent. The substitute places these relative burdens on the parties in this matter, because the basic policy is to require diversification, and if diversification on its face does not exist, then the burden of justifying failure to follow this general policy should be on the fiduciary who engages in this conduct.

The degree of investment concentration that would violate this requirement to diversify cannot be stated as a fixed percentage, because a prudent fiduciary must consider the facts and circumstances of each case. The factors to be considered include (1) the purposes of the plan; (2) the amount of the plan assets; (3) financial and industrial conditions; (4) the type of investment, whether mortgages, bonds or shares of stock or otherwise; (5) distribution as to geographical location; (6) distribution as to industries; (7) the dates of maturity.

A fiduciary usually should not invest the whole or an unreasonably large proportion of the trust property in a single security. Ordinarily the fiduciary should not invest the whole or an unduly large proportion of the trust property in one type of security or in various types of securities dependent upon the success of one enterprise or upon conditions in one locality, since the effect is to increase the risk of large losses. Thus, although the fiduciary may be authorized to invest in industrial stocks, he should not invest a disproportionate amount of the plan assets in the shares of corporations engaged in a particular industry. If he is investing in mortgages on real property he should not invest a disproportionate amount of the trust in mortgages in a particular district or on a particular class of property so that a decline in property values in that district or of that class might cause a large loss.

The assets of many pension plans are managed by one or more investment managers. For example, one investment manager, A, may be responsible for 10 percent of the assets of a plan and instructed by the named fiduciary or trustee to invest solely in bonds; another investment manager, B, may be responsible for a different 10 percent of the assets of the same plan and instructed to invest solely in equities. Such arrangements often result in investment returns which are quite favorable to the plan, its participants, and its beneficiaries. In these circumstances, A would invest solely in bonds in accordance with his instructions and would diversify the bond investments in accordance with the diversification standard, the prudent man standard, and all other provisions applicable to A as a fiduciary. Similarly, B would invest solely in equities in accordance with his instructions and these standards. Neither A nor B would incur any liability for diversifying assets subject to their management in accordance with their instructions.

The conferees intend that, in general, whether the plan assets are sufficiently diversified is to be determined by examining the ultimate investment of the plan assets. For example, the conferees understand that for efficiency and economy plans may invest all their assets in a single bank or other pooled investment fund, but that the pooled fund itself could have diversified investments. It is intended that, in this case, the diversification rule is to be applied to the plan by examining the diversification of the investments in the pooled fund. The same is true with respect to investments in a mutual fund. Also, generally a plan may be invested wholly in insurance or annuity contracts without violating the diversification rules, since generally an insurance company's assets are to be invested in a diversified manner.

(With respect to special rules regarding diversification of assets and investment in employer securities, etc., by certain individual account plans, see "Employer securities and employer real property," below) [CCH ¶ 14,770.10].

Certain individual account plans.—Under the substitute, a special rule is provided for individual account plans where the participant is permitted to, and in fact does, exercise independent control over the assets in his individual account. In this case, the individual is not to be regarded as a fiduciary and other persons who are fiduciaries with respect to the plan are not to be liable for any loss that results from the exercise and control by the participant or beneficiary. Therefore, if the participant instructs the plan trustee to invest the full balance of his account in, *e.g.,* a single stock, the trustee is not to be liable for any loss because of a failure to diversify or because the investment does not meet the prudent man standards. However, the investment must not contradict the terms of the plan, and if the plan on its face prohibits such investments, the trustee could not follow the instructions and avoid liability.

The conferees recognize that there may be difficulties in determining whether the participant in fact exercises independent control over his account. Consequently, whether participants and beneficiaries exercise independent control is to be determined pursuant to regulations prescribed by the Secretary of Labor. The conferees expect that the regulations will provide more stringent standards with respect to determining whether there is an independent exercise of control where the investments may inure to the direct or indirect benefit of the plan sponsor since, in this case participants might be subject to pressure with respect to investment decisions. (Because of the difficulty of ensuring that there is independence of choice in an employer established individual retirement account, it is expected that the regulations will generally provide that sufficient independent control will not exist with respect to the acquisition of employer securities by participants and beneficiaries under this type of plan.) In addition, the conferees expect that the regulations generally will require that for there to be independent control by participants, a broad range of investments must be available to the individual participants and beneficiaries.

Transfer of assets outside of the United States.—In order to prevent "runaway assets," the labor provisions of the substitute generally prohibit a fiduciary from transferring or maintaining the indicia of ownership of any plan assets outside the jurisdiction of the district courts of the United States. However, such a transaction may be permitted under regulations issued by the Secretary of Labor.

* * *

[ERISA Sec. 405]

[¶ 14,750.10]

Committee Report on P.L. 93-406 (Employee Retirement Income Security Act of 1974)

[Conference Committee Explanation]

Liability for breach of co-fiduciary responsibility, in general.—Under the labor provisions of the conference substitute, a fiduciary of a plan is to be liable for the breach of fiduciary responsibility by another fiduciary of the plan if he knowingly participates in a breach of duty committed by the other fiduciary. Under this rule, the fiduciary must know the other person is a fiduciary with respect to the plan, must know that he participated in the act that constituted a breach, and must know that it was a breach. For example, A and B are co-trustees, and the terms of the trust provide that they are not to invest in, *e.g.,* commodity futures. If A suggests to B that B invest part of the plan assets in commodity futures, and if B does so, A, as well as B, is to be liable for the breach.

In addition, a fiduciary is to be liable for the breach of fiduciary responsibility by another fiduciary of the plan, if he knowingly undertakes to conceal a breach committed by the other. For the first fiduciary to be liable, he must know that the other is a fiduciary with regard to the plan, must know of the act, and must know that it is a breach. For example, A and B are co-trustees, and B invests in commodity futures in violation of the trust instrument. If B tells his co-trustee A of this investment, A would be liable with B for breach of fiduciary responsibility if he concealed this investment.

Also, if a fiduciary knows that another fiduciary of the plan has committed a breach, and the first fiduciary knows that this is a breach, the first fiduciary must take reasonable steps under the circumstances to remedy the breach. In the second example above, if A has the authority to do so, and if it is prudent under the circumstances, A may be required to dispose of the commodity futures acquired by B. Alternatively, the most appropriate steps in the circumstances may be to notify the plan sponsor of the breach, or to proceed to an appropriate Federal court for instructions, or bring the matter to the attention of the Secretary of Labor. The proper remedy is to be determined by the facts and circumstances of the particular case, and it may be affected by the relationship of the fiduciary to the plan and to the co-fiduciary, the duties and responsibilities of the fiduciary in question, and the nature of the breach.

A fiduciary also is to be liable for the loss caused by the breach of fiduciary responsibility by another fiduciary of the plan if he enables the other fiduciary to commit a breach through his failure to exercise prudence (or otherwise comply with the basic fiduciary rules of the bill) in carrying out his specific responsibilities. For example, A and B are co-trustees and are to jointly manage the plan assets. A improperly allows B to have the sole custody of the plan assets and makes no inquiry as to his conduct. B is thereby enabled to sell the property and to embezzle the proceeds. A is to be liable for a breach of fiduciary responsibility.

Allocation of duties of co-trustees.—Under the conference substitute, if the plan assets are held by co-trustees, then each trustee has the duty to manage and control those assets. For example, shares of stock held in trust by several trustees generally should be registered in the name of all the trustees, or in the name of the trust. In addition, each trustee is to use reasonable care to prevent his co-trustee from committing a breach of fiduciary duty.

Although generally each trustee must manage and control the plan assets, nevertheless, under the substitute specific duties and responsibilities with respect to the management of plan assets may be allocated among co-trustees by the trust instrument. For example, the trust instrument may provide that trustee A is to manage and control one-half of the plan assets, and trustee B is to manage and control the other half of the plan assets.

Also, the trust instrument may provide that specific duties may be allocated by agreement among the co-trustees. In this case, however, the conferees intend that the trust instrument is to specifically delineate the duties that may be allocated by agreement of the co-trustees and is to specify a procedure for such allocation. Also, the trustees must act prudently in implementing such an allocation procedure.

If duties are allocated among co-trustees in accordance with the substitute, a trustee to whom duties have not been allocated is not to be liable for any loss that arises from acts or omissions of the co-trustee to whom such responsibilities have been allocated.

However, a co-trustee will be liable notwithstanding allocation if he individually fails to comply with the other fiduciary standards. For example, a co-trustee would be liable on account of his own acts if he did not act in accordance with the prudent man standard and thereby caused the plan to suffer a loss. In addition, the general rules of co-fiduciary liability are to apply. Therefore, for example, if a trustee had knowledge of a breach by a co-trustee, he would be liable unless he made reasonable efforts to remedy the breach.

Under the substitute, it is made clear that if plan assets are held in separate trusts a trustee of one trust is not responsible as a co-trustee of the other trust.

The conferees understand that under certain circumstances, trustees (and other fiduciaries) in discharging their responsibilities in accordance with the prudent man rule will hire agents to perform ministerial acts. In this case, the liability of the trustees (and other fiduciaries) for acts of their agents is to be established in accordance with the prudent man rule.

Allocation and delegation of duties other than the management of plan assets.—The substitute also provides for the allocation and delegation by fiduciaries of duties that do not involve the management and control of plan assets.[1] However, in order that participants and beneficiaries, etc., may readily determine who is responsible for managing a plan, the substitute generally provides that only "named fiduciaries" will be able to allocate or delegate their responsibilities.

Under the substitute, if the plan so provides, named co-fiduciaries may allocate their specific responsibilities among themselves, and named fiduciaries may delegate all or part of their duties (which do not involve asset management) to others. The substitute also provides that upon proper allocation or delegation fiduciaries will not be liable for the acts or omissions of the persons to whom duties have been allocated or delegated.

Allocation or delegation (and the consequent elimination of liability) can only occur under specific circumstances. The plan must specifically allow such allocation or delegation, and the plan must expressly provide a procedure for it. For example, the plan may provide that delegation may occur only with respect to specified duties, and only on the approval of the plan sponsor or on the approval of the joint board of trustees of a Taft-Hartley plan. Also, in implementing the procedures of the plan, plan fiduciaries must act prudently and in the interests of participants and beneficiaries. The fiduciaries also must act in this manner in choosing the person to whom they allocate or delegate their duties. Additionally, they must act in this manner in continuing the allocation or delegation of their duties.

In order to act prudently in retaining a person to whom duties have been delegated, it is expected that the fiduciary will periodically review this person's performance. Depending upon the circumstances, this requirement may be satisfied by formal periodic review (which may be by all the named fiduciaries who have participated in the delegation or by a specially designated review committee), or it may be met through day-to-day contact and evaluation, or in other appropriate ways. Since effective review requires that a person's services can be terminated, it may be necessary to enter into arrangements which the fiduciary can promptly terminate (within the limits of the circumstances).

Even though a named fiduciary has properly delegated his duties in accordance with the substitute, he may still be liable for the acts of a co-fiduciary if he breaches the general rules of co-fiduciary liability by *e.g.,* knowingly concealing a breach of a co-fiduciary.

Investment managers, investment committees, etc.—Under the substitute, if the plan so provides, a person who is a named fiduciary with respect to the control or management of plan assets may appoint a qualified investment manager to manage all or part of the plan assets. (However, in choosing an investment manager, the named fiduciary must act prudently and in the interests of participants and beneficiaries, and also must act in this manner in continuing the use of an investment manager.) In this case, the plan trustee would no longer have responsibility for managing the assets controlled by the qualified investment manager, and the trustee would not be liable for the acts or omissions of the investment manager. Also, as long as the named fiduciary had chosen and retained the investment manager prudentially, the named fiduciary would not be liable for the acts or omissions of the manager. Under the substitute, a qualified investment manager may be an investment adviser registered under the Investment Advisers Act of 1940, a bank (as defined in that Act), or an insurance company qualified to perform investment management services under State law in more than one State. To be qualified, the investment manager also must acknowledge in writing that he is a plan fiduciary.

As described above *(Establishment of trust)* [CCH ¶ 14,730.10] the plan may also provide that the trustee is to be subject to the direction of named fiduciaries with respect to investment decisions. In this case, if the trustee properly follows the instructions of the named fiduciaries, the trustee generally is not to be liable for losses which arise out of following these instructions. (The named fiduciaries, however, would be subject to the usual fiduciary responsibility rules and would be subject to liability on breach of these rules.)

In addition, a plan may provide that named fiduciaries (or fiduciaries to whom duties have been properly delegated) may employ investment and other advisers. However, a fiduciary cannot be relieved of his own responsibilities merely because he follows the advice of such a person. (Also, investment advisers would be fiduciaries under the substitute.)

[ERISA Sec. 406]

[¶ 14,760.10]

Committee Report on P.L. 93-406 (Employee Retirement Income Security Act of 1974)

[Conference Committee Explanation]

—Prohibited transactions.— * **

Under the labor provisions a fiduciary will be liable for losses to a plan from a prohibited transaction in which he engaged if he would have known the transaction involving the particular party-in-interest was prohibited if he had acted as a prudent man. * * *

In general, it is expected that a transaction will not be a prohibited transaction (under either the labor or tax provisions) if the transaction is an ordinary "blind" purchase or sale of securities through an exchange where neither buyer nor seller (nor the agent of either) knows the identity of the other party involved. In this case, there is no reason to impose a sanction on a fiduciary (or party-in-interest) merely because, by chance, the other party turns out to be a party-in-interest (or plan).

The labor prohibitions affect "parties-in-interest", and the tax prohibitions affect "disqualified persons." The two terms are substantially the same in most respects, but the labor term includes a somewhat broader range of persons, as described below.

Coverage.—The prohibited transaction rules under the labor provisions apply to all plans to which the general labor fiduciary rules apply, as described above. The tax law prohibited transaction rules apply to all qualified retirement plans (under secs. 401, 403(a), and 405(a) of the Internal Revenue Code) and to all qualified individual retirement accounts, individual retirement annuities, and individual retirement bonds (under secs. 408 and 409 of the Code). In addition, the tax law rules are to continue to apply even if the plan, etc., should later lose its tax qualifications.

The tax law prohibited transaction provisions follow the labor provisions with respect to whether the assets of an insurance company or mutual fund are to be considered the assets of a plan. Also, the tax provisions exclude from the new prohibited transaction rules government plans, and church plans which have not elected coverage under the new participation, vesting, funding and insurance provisions. (The latter plans, if they are qualified plans, will be subject to present law.)

Party-in-interest transaction.—Under the substitute, the direct or indirect sale, exchange, or leasing of any property between the plan and a party-in-interest[3] (with exceptions subsequently noted) is a prohibited transaction. Under this rule, the transaction is prohibited whether or not the property involved is owned by the plan or party-in-interest, and the prohibited transaction includes sales, etc., from the party-in-interest to the plan, and also from the plan to the party-in-interest. Also, following the private foundation rules of the tax law, a transfer of property by a party-in-interest to a plan is treated as a sale or exchange if the property is subject to a mortgage or a similar lien which the party-in-interest placed on the property within 10 years prior to the transfer to the plan or if the plan assumes a mortgage or similar lien placed on the property by a party in interest within 10 years prior to the transfer. This rule prevents circumvention of the prohibition on sale by mortgaging the property before transfer to the plan.

The conference substitute also generally prohibits the direct or indirect lending of money or other extension of credit between a plan and parties-in-interest. For example, a prohibited transaction generally will occur if a loan to a plan is guaranteed by a party-in-interest, unless it comes within the special exemption for employee stock ownership plans.

It is intended that prohibited loans include the acquisition by the plan of a debt instrument (such as a bond or note) which is an obligation of a party-in-interest. (However, the transition rules described below establish special rules for certain debt instruments held by a plan before July 1, 1974.) Similarly, it is intended that it would be a prohibited transaction (in effect a loan by the plan to the employer) if the employer funds his contributions to the plan with his own debt obligations.

[1] For example, these rules would govern the allocation or delegation of duties with respect to payment of benefits.

[3] Hereafter, the term "party-in-interest" will include the term "disqualified person" unless otherwise indicated.

With certain exceptions described below, the direct or indirect furnishing of goods or services or facilities between a plan and a party-in-interest also is prohibited. This would apply, for example, to the furnishing of personal living quarters to a party-in-interest.

The substitute prohibits the direct or indirect transfer of any plan income or assets to or for the benefit of a party-in-interest. It also prohibits the use of plan income or assets by or for the benefit of any party-in-interest. As in other situations, this prohibited transaction may occur even though there has not been a transfer of money or property between the plan and a party-in-interest. For example, securities purchases or sales by a plan to manipulate the price of the security to the advantage of a party-in-interest constitutes a use by or for the benefit of a party-in-interest of any assets of the plan.

The labor provisions and the tax provisions differ slightly on the wording with respect to this latter prohibition. The labor provision prohibits such use of the plan's "assets", and the tax provision prohibits use of the plan's "income or assets". (This same difference appears with respect to other prohibited transactions, as well.) The conferees intend that the labor and tax provisions are to be interpreted in the same way and both are to apply to income and assets. The different wordings are used merely because of different usages in the labor and tax laws. In addition, even though the term "income" is used in the tax law, it is intended that this is not to imply in any way that investment in growth assets (which may provide little current income) is to be prohibited where such investment would otherwise meet the prudent man and other rules of the substitute.

Since the substitute prohibits both direct and indirect transactions, it is expected that where a mutual fund, *e.g.*, acquires property from a party-in-interest as part of the arrangement under which the plan invests or retains its investment in the mutual fund, this is to be a prohibited transaction.

Employer securities and employer real property.—The labor provisions also generally prohibit the direct or indirect acquisition by the plan (or holding by the plan) of securities of the employer or real property leased to the employer, except if otherwise allowed. This prohibition (and the exceptions to it) is described in detail below.

Additional prohibitions.—The substitute generally prohibits a fiduciary from dealing with the income or assets of a plan in his own interest or for his own account. However, this does not prohibit the fiduciary from dealings where he has an account in the plan and the dealings apply to all plan accounts without discrimination.

The substitute also prohibits a fiduciary from receiving consideration for his own personal account from any party dealing with the plan in connection with the transaction involving the income or assets of the plan. This prevents, *e.g.*, "kickbacks" to a fiduciary.

In addition, the labor provisions (but not the tax provisions) prohibit a fiduciary from acting in any transaction involving the plan on behalf of a person (or representing a party) whose interests are adverse to the interests of the plan or of its participants or beneficiaries. This prevents a fiduciary from being put in a position where he has dual loyalties, and, therefore, he cannot act exclusively for the benefit of a plan's participants and beneficiaries. (This prohibition is not included in the tax provisions, because of the difficulty in determining an appropriate measure for an excise tax.)

[ERISA Sec. 407]

[¶ 14,770.093]

Committee Report on P.L. 105-34 (Taxpayer Relief Act)

[Conference Committee Report]

401(k) plan investments: Diversification

Senate [Floor] Amendment

The Senate amendment provides that the term "eligible individual account plan" does not include the portion of a plan that consists of elective deferrals (and earnings on the elective deferrals) made under section 401(k) if elective deferrals equal to more than 1 percent of a participant's compensation are required to be invested in employer securities at the direction of a person other than the participant. Such portion of the plan is treated as a separate plan subject to the 10-percent limitation on investment in employer securities and real property.

The Senate amendment does not apply to an individual account plan if the value of the assets of all individual account plans maintained by the employer does not exceed 10 percent of the value of the assets of all pension plans maintained by the employer. The Senate amendment does not apply to an employee stock ownership plan as defined in sections 409(a) and 4975(e)(7) of the Internal Revenue Code.

Effective date

The provision is effective with respect to employer securities and employer real property acquired after the beginning of the first plan year beginning after the 90th day after the date of enactment. The provision does not apply to employer securities or real property acquired pursuant to a binding written contract to acquire such securities or real property in effect on the date of enactment and at all times thereafter.

Conference agreement

The conference agreement follows the Senate amendment, with modifications. The conference agreement clarifies that the provision applies if elective deferrals equal to more than 1 percent of an employee's eligible compensation are required to be invested in employer securities and employer real property. Eligible compensation is compensation that is eligible to be deferred. As under the Senate amendment, if the 1 percent threshold is exceeded, then the portion of the plan that consists of elective deferrals (and earnings thereon) is still treated as an individual account plan as long as elective deferrals (and earnings thereon) are not required to be invested in employer securities and employer real property.

The conference agreement provides that multiemployer plans are not taken into account in determining whether the value of the assets of all individual account plans maintained by the employer does not exceed 10 percent of the value of the assets of all pension plans maintained by the employer. The conference agreement provides that the provision does not apply to an employee stock ownership plan as defined in section 4975(e)(7) of the Internal Revenue Code.

Effective date

Under the conference agreement, the provision is effective with respect to elective deferrals in plan years beginning after December 31, 1998 (and earnings thereon). This provision does not apply with respect to earnings on elective deferrals for years beginning before January 1, 1999.

[¶ 14,770.095]

Committee Report on P.L. 100-203 (Omnibus Budget Reconciliation Act of 1987)

[Conference Committee Report]

Education and Labor Committee Bill: The term "eligible individual account plan" does not include a plan that would otherwise be an individual account plan if the plan is taken into account in determining the benefits payable to a participant under any defined benefit plan. An arrangement consisting of a defined benefit plan and a plan that would otherwise be an individual account plan but for the fact that the plan is taken into account in determining the benefits payable to a participant under the defined benefit plan (a "floor-offset arrangement") is treated as a single plan for purposes of the 10-percent limit.

In the case of a plan other than an individual account plan, stock is considered a qualifying employer security only if (1) not more than 25 percent of the aggregate amount of stock of the same class issued and outstanding at the time of acquisition by the plan is held by the plan, and (2) at least 50 percent of the aggregate amount of such stock is held by persons independent of the issuer.

Effective Date: Acquisitions of employer securities after February 19, 1987, other than pursuant to a binding contract in effect on such date. Plans that, on February 19, 1987, hold employer securities that do not meet the new requirements or that acquire such securities pursuant to a binding contract in effect on such date have until January 1, 1993, to divest themselves of such securities.

* * *

The Conference Agreement follows the Education and Labor Committee Bill, with modifications of the effective dates. The provision regarding the ten-percent limit on employer securities is effective with respect to arrangements established after December 17, 1987. The rule does not apply to arrangements established on or before December 17, 1987. The effective date of the provision regarding the definition of qualifying employer security, except that December 17, 1987, is substituted for February 19, 1987.

[¶ 14,770.10]

Committee Report on P.L. 93-406 (Employee Retirement Income Security Act of 1974)

[Conference Committee Explanation]

Employer securities and employer real property

Eligible individual account plans.—The labor provisions of the substitute generally limit the acquisition and holding by a plan of employer securities and of employer real property (combined) to 10 percent of plan assets. (Employer securities are securities issued by an employer with employees covered by the plan or its affiliates. Employer real property is real property which is leased by a plan to an employer (or its affiliates) with employees covered by the plan.)

However, a special rule is provided for individual account plans which are profit-sharing plans, stock bonus plans, employee stock ownership plans, or thrift or savings plans, since these plans commonly provide for substantial investments in employer securities or real property. Also, money purchase plans which were in existence on the date of enactment, and which invested primarily in employer securities on that date are to be treated the same way as profit-sharing, etc., plans. (However, employer-established individual retirement accounts are not to be eligible individual account plans.)

In recognition of the special purpose of these individual account plans, the 10 percent limitation with respect to the acquisition or holding of employer securities or employer real property does not apply to such plans if they explicitly provide for greater investment in these assets. In addition, the diversification requirements of the substitute and any diversification principle that may develop in the application of the prudent man rule is not to restrict investments by eligible individual account plans in qualifying employer securities or qualifying employer real property.

These exceptions apply only if the plan explicitly provides for the relevant amount of acquisition or holding of qualifying employer securities or qualifying real property. For example, if a profit-sharing plan is to be able to invest half of its assets in qualifying employer securities, the plan must specifically provide that up to 50 percent of plan assets may be so invested. In this way, the persons responsible for asset management, as well as participants and beneficiaries, will clearly know the extent to which the plan can acquire and hold these assets. Plans in existence on the date of enactment will have one year from January 1, 1975, to be amended to comply with this requirement. If the plan does not comply within one year (but, *e.g.,* complies 2 years after January 1, 1975), then during the interim period, the plan will be subject to the 10 percent rule as well as the diversification requirement. This means, generally, that the plan will not be able to acquire any additional employer securities or employer real property during this period (and preparation should be made for divestiture of half of the excess of employer securities and real property by January 1, 1980.)

Under the substitute, only "qualifying" employer securities may be acquired and held by individual account plans under the rules described above. Stock of the employer will constitute qualifying securities. Also, certain debt will be qualifying employer securities if it is traded on a national securities exchange or has a price otherwise established by independent persons, and if the plan holds no more than a quarter of the issue and independent persons hold at least one-half of the issue. (Qualifying employer debt securities essentially are debt securities that meet the present rules of section 503(e) of the Internal Revenue Code.)

Also, under the substitute only "qualifying" employer real property may be acquired and held by eligible individual account plans under the rules described above. Real property which is leased to an employer is qualifying employer real property if a substantial number of the parcels are distributed geographically and if each parcel of real property and the improvements on it are suitable (or adaptable without excessive cost) for more than one use.[4] For example, the plan might acquire and lease to the employer multipurpose buildings which are located in different geographical areas. It is intended that the geographic dispersion be sufficient so that adverse economic conditions peculiar to one area would not significantly affect the economic status of the plan as a whole. All of the qualifying real property may be leased to one lessee, which may be the employer or an affiliate of the employer.

To the extent that an eligible individual account plan can acquire qualifying employer securities, it may acquire these securities from parties-in-interest if the acquisition is for adequate consideration and no commission is charged in the transaction. (The conferees intend that if a purchase is made from an underwriter who assumes the risks of market fluctuations after the award date, the underwriter's margin is not to be regarded as a "commission.") A similar exception from the prohibited transaction rules (in both the labor and tax provisions) is available for the acquisition from an employer of qualifying employer real property, the leasing of such property to the employer (or its affiliate) and the sale of such real property back to the employer on termination of the lease for adequate consideration. However, real property is not qualifying employer real property unless it is leased to the employer. Therefore, except for qualifying leasebacks, a plan generally is prohibited from acquiring real property from the employer.

Other plans.—Under the substitute, a plan other than an eligible individual account plan cannot acquire any employer securities or real property if immediately after doing so the plan would hold more than 10 percent of the fair market value of its assets in employer securities or real property. The acquisition rules apply not only to the purchase of employer securities, etc., but also to acquisition in other ways such as by exercise of warrants or by acquisition on default of a loan where the stock was made security for the loan. Also, these plans (as eligible individual account plans) are not to acquire any employer securities or employer real property other than qualifying employer securities or qualifying employer real property.

In addition, if a plan holds more than 10 percent of the fair market value of its assets in employer securities and real property on January 1, 1975, it is to dispose of enough of these assets to bring its holdings of employer securities, etc. to no more than 10 percent of plan assets on or before December 31, 1984.

In general, the 10 percent holding rule will be met on the first date after January 1, 1975 (and on or before December 31, 1984) that a plan holds no more than 10 percent of the fair market value of its assets in employer securities or employer real property. Thus, if a plan on January 1, 1975, holds qualifying employer securities and qualifying employer real property worth $200,000 and has total assets worth $1,000,000, the plan must bring its employer securities, etc., down to 10 percent of plan assets. If, *e.g.,* there is a substantial market rise in the value of the plan's other assets in the year 1976, so all plan assets are now worth $2,000,000, but employer securities are still worth $200,000, then the holding requirement has been met and from that time on, only the acquisition rule will affect the plan. (Under the acquisition rule, the plan could not acquire any more qualifying employer securities in 1976, since immediately after the acquisition more than 10 percent of plan assets would be invested in employer securities.) Also, if the fair market value of other plan assets decreases to $1,500,000 in 1977, so the plan has $200,000 of employer securities and $1,500,000 total assets, the plan will not violate the holding (or acquisition) rules, since it met the holding rules in 1976.

Under the substitute, a plan is not required to dispose of more qualifying employer securities than would bring its holdings down to 10 percent of the fair market value of assets on the date of enactment. Thus, if a plan had $200,000 of employer securities and $1,000,000 total assets on date of enactment, it would satisfy the 10 percent holding rule when it had employer securities of $100,000, even if its total assets had dropped to $900,000.

The substitute allows a special election for calculating the 10 percent holding rule (but not the 10 percent acquisition rule). Under this election, the 10 percent holdings rule is met if on or before December 31, 1984, the value of employer securities which are held on January 1, 1975, is no greater than 10 percent of the fair market value of plan assets on January 1, 1975, plus employer contributions to the plan made after December 31, 1974, and prior to January 1, 1985. For this purpose, employer contributions are to be included only to the extent of the growth in the value of plan assets (other than employer securities) from January 1, 1975, through December 31, 1984. Election to make this provision applicable must be made prior to January 1, 1976, and the election is irrevocable once it is made. For purposes of this rule, employer securities held on January 1, 1975, are to include employer securities the ownership of which is derived solely from the employer securities held on January 1, 1975, or from the exercise of rights derived from such ownership under regulations to be prescribed by the Secretary of Labor. This election is to be available only for a plan which holds no employer real property, and does not acquire employer real property until after December 31, 1984.

A plan must be half-way toward meeting the 10-percent rule by December 31, 1979. The maximum percentage of assets that a plan may have in employer securities and employer real property on that date is to be established by regulations (which are to be issued by December 31, 1976). Generally, it is expected that the regulations will provide that the maximum percentage of assets that a plan may have in employer securities and real property on (or before) December 31, 1979, is to be determined by adding 10 percent to half of the percentage of employer securities, etc., held by the plan on January 1, 1975 in excess of 10 percent. For example, if 15 percent of the plan's assets are in employer securities on January 1, 1975, generally it is expected that the plan must have reduced its percentage of employer securities to 12 ½ percent on or before December 31, 1979. (That is,

$$10 + \frac{(15 - 10)}{2} = 12\tfrac{1}{2}.)$$

If securities are qualifying employer securities they generally can be acquired or held notwithstanding the prohibited transaction rules, if acquisition is for adequate consideration and no commission is charged and if acquisition is allowed by the employer securities rules. However (except as noted above for eligible individual account plans), acquisition and holding of these assets must also meet the rules of prudence, diversification, etc. Therefore, if the diversification and prudence rules require that less than 10 percent of plan assets are to be held in employer securities and employer real property, the lower limit is to govern. Furthermore, the exclusive benefit rule also may apply. Thus, while a plan may be able to acquire employer securities or real property under the employer securities rules, the acquisition must be for the exclusive benefit of participants and beneficiaries. Consequently, if the real property is acquired primarily to finance the employer, this would not meet the exclusive benefit requirements.

Generally these rules apply only to the holding (or acquiring) of qualified employer securities or qualified employer real property. Under the general prohibited transaction rules, a plan is not to hold (or acquire) any other employer securities or employer real property (since this would be a prohibited loan or lease, respectively). Of course, the general transition rules discussed below will apply to employer securities or real property held on July 1, 1974.

[ERISA Sec. 408]

[¶ 14,780.092]

Committee Report on P.L. 109-280 (Pension Protection Act of 2006)

For the Committee Report on P.L. 109-280 on investment advice, see ¶ 13,640.018.

For the Committee Report on P.L. 109-280 on prohibited transaction rules relating to financial investments, see ¶ 13,640.018.

For the Committee Report on P.L. 109-280 on the correction period for certain transactions involving securities and commodities, see ¶ 13,640.018.

[¶ 14,780.094]

Committee Report on P.L. 107-16 (Economic Growth and Tax Relief Reconciliation Act)

For the Committee Report on P.L. 107-16 on plan loans for S corporation shareholders, partners and sole proprietors, see ¶ 13,640.03.

---

4 Qualifying employer real property includes the real property and related personal property.

[¶ 14,780.096]

Committee Reports on P.L. 105-34 (Taxpayer Relief Act)

[House Committee Report]

S corporation ESOPs

ESOPs maintained by S corporations.—The bill provides that ESOPs of S corporations may distribute cash to plan participants. In addition, the bill extends the exception to certain prohibited transactions rules to S corporations.

Effective date

The provisions are effective for taxable years beginning after December 31, 1997.

[Conference Committee Report]

Senate Amendment

The Senate amendment is the same as the House bill with respect to the provision that permits ESOPs of S corporations to distribute stock in certain cases.

The Senate amendment provides that the sale of stock by a shareholder employee of an S corporation is not a prohibited transaction under the Code or ERISA.

Effective date

Same as the House bill.

Conference Agreement

The conference agreement follows the House bill and the Senate amendment with respect to the provision permitting ESOPs maintained by S corporations to distribute employer securities in certain circumstances. The conference agreement follows the Senate amendment with respect to the provision relating to prohibited transaction rules, as modified. Under the conference agreement, the statutory exceptions do not fail to apply merely because a transaction involves the sale of employer securities to an ESOP maintained by an S corporation by a shareholder employee, a family member of the shareholder employee, or a corporation controlled by the shareholder employee. Thus, the statutory exemptions for such a transaction (including the exemption for a loan to the ESOP to acquire employer securities in connection with such a sale or a guarantee of such a loan) apply.

Effective date

Same as the House bill and the Senate amendment.

[¶ 14,780.098]

Committee Reports on P.L. 104-188 (Small Business Job Protection Act)

[House Committee Report]

* * *

The bill also provides that the plan loan, plan qualification, and prohibited transaction rules will not be violated merely because a plan suspends the repayment of a plan loan during a period of uniformed service.

* * *

[Conference Committee Report]

Senate Amendment

The Senate amendment follows the House bill.

Conference Agreement

The conference agreement follows the House bill and the Senate amendment* * *.

[¶ 14,780.10]

Committee Report on P.L. 93-406 (Employee Retirement Income Security Act of 1974)

[Conference Committee Explanation]

Administrative exemptions or variances.—The conferees recognize that some transactions which are prohibited (and for which there are no statutory exemptions) nevertheless should be allowed in order not to disrupt the established business practices of financial institutions which often performs fiduciary functions in connection with these plans consistent with adequate safeguards to protect employee benefit plans. For example, while brokerage houses generally would be prohibited from providing, either directly or through affiliates, both discretionary investment management and brokerage services to the same plan, the conferees expect that the Secretary of Labor and Secretary of the Treasury would grant a variance with respect to these services (and other services traditionally rendered by such institutions), provided that they can show that such a variance will be administratively feasible and that the type of transaction for which an exemption is sought is in the interest of and protective of the rights of plan participants and beneficiaries. Thus, variances might be granted to brokers or their affiliates to act as investment managers if the Secretary determines that such arrangements are in the interests of plan participants and beneficiaries and that satisfactory safeguards are provided, including *e.g.,* such protections as the monitoring of the investment manager's decisions by a person with appropriate investment experience, as specified by the Secretaries, who is not affiliated with the broker. The conferees did not grant a statutory exemption to brokers for this type of multiple service because of the difficulty of establishing precise statutory standards for protecting against potential abuses. The conferees note that the general issue of institutional investment management by brokers is under consideration in separate legislation, and expect that any action taken by the Secretaries on requests for variances under this Act will be consistent with the outcome of such legislation.

In addition, the conferees recognize that some individual transactions between a plan and party-in-interest may provide substantial independent safeguards for the plan participants and beneficiaries and may provide substantial benefit to the community as a whole, so that the transaction should be allowed under a variance. For example, it is understood that the pension plan of a major corporation with its principal office in Dayton, Ohio, has become committed to invest in a joint venture that will own an office building in a downtown redevelopment area in Dayton. This building is to be a key element of the redevelopment project. The joint venture will lease a portion of this building to the employer that established and maintained this pension plan. Under the general rules, this would be a prohibited indirect lease between the plan and a party-in-interest. However, it is understood that the transaction has substantial safeguards that ensure that the transaction will inure to the benefit of the plan participants and beneficiaries. For example, there are other major investors in the joint venture at this time so the joint venture will seek an adequate rate of return. Additionally, it is understood that the building has another major tenant and the terms of the lease for this tenant and for the employer are substantially identical. Furthermore, it is understood that the rental under these leases is generally higher than the rental for similar space now available in the area. Also, the City of Dayton will have a major investment in the land (and in a superstructure), so that the City will have an independent financial interest in ensuring that the transaction is financially sound.

Under this transaction, each party in the joint venture is to share in profits and losses in proportion to its capital contribution. Therefore, this is not a "tax shelter" transaction with an attempted shift of early period losses away from a tax-exempt entity to taxable entities. Also, it is understood that while the joint venture will borrow to finance the acquisition of the building, neither the joint venture nor the plan (nor any other joint venturer) is to be "personally liable" on the mortgage debt. Therefore, if the transaction were to fail, the plan's liability would be limited to the funds advanced to the joint venture.

It is expected that in this situation, because of the substantial safeguards for the plan and its participants and beneficiaries, because of the lack of "tax abuse" aspects, because the transaction became binding before the conferees' decisions were announced, and because of the importance of the project to the entire community of Dayton, Ohio, that the Secretary of the Treasury and Secretary of Labor will grant a variance to the transaction for its whole term.

Under the substitute, variances may be conditional or unconditional and may exempt a transaction from all or part of the prohibited transaction rules. In addition, variances may be for a particular transaction or for a class of transactions, and may be allowed pursuant to rulings or regulations. A variance from the prohibited transaction rules is to have no effect with respect to the basic fiduciary responsibility rules requiring prudent action, diversification of investments, actions exclusively for the benefit of participants and beneficiaries, etc. (This is the case with respect to all statutory exemptions from the prohibited transaction rules as well.)

Under ths substitute, the Secretary of Labor and the Secretary of the Treasury each must establish a procedure for allowing variances, but neither the Secretary of Labor nor the Secretary of the Treasury is to be required to grant a variance. Variances are to be granted only when each Secretary separately determines that the transaction in question is an appropriate case for a variance. Thus, for example, the Secretary of Labor may refuse to grant a variance if the transaction would constitute an abuse of the labor laws, even though the Secretary of the Treasury may be willing to grant a variance in the particular situation. Similarly, the Secretary of the Treasury may, for example, refuse to grant a variance if the transaction would constitute a tax abuse even though the Secretary of Labor may be willing to grant a variance in the same situation.

In addition, variances are not to be allowed unless each Secretary finds that the transaction is in the interests of the plan and its participants and beneficiaries, that it does not present administrative problems, and that adequate safeguards are provided for participants and beneficiaries.

Although the Secretary of Labor and the Secretary of the Treasury are to separately determine whether a variance is to be provided, they are to coordinate their activities. It is expected that the Secretaries of Labor and Treasury will develop an administrative procedure to allow one application for a variance and that the two departments will coordinate their activities with respect to this single application to prevent unneeded delays and duplication of effort by the applicant.

Before allowing a variance, adequate notice (including publication in the Federal Register) is to be given interested persons, who are to have an opportunity to present their views. In the case of a variance from the prohibitions against a fiduciary dealing with plan assets for his own account, acting on behalf of an adverse party to the plan, or receiving consideration for his personal account, there is to be a hearing and a determination on the record that the conditions required for granting a variance are met. (However, the Secretary of the Treasury may accept the record of a Department of Labor hearing, if he wishes, and make his determination with respect to the variance on the facts presented in that record.)

Exemption for loans to participants and beneficiaries.—Following current practice, the substitute does not probihit a loan by a plan to a participant or beneficiary in certain circumstances. To be permitted, such loans must be made in accord with specific provisions in the plan governing such loans. In addition, a reasonable interest rate must be charged and the loan must be adequately secured. Such loans must be made available to all participants on a reasonably equivalent basis. Consequently, the plan could not unreasonably discriminate between applicants on the basis of, e.g., age or sex; but the plan could make distinctions on the basis of e.g., credit worthiness or financial need. Also, such loans cannot be made available to highly-compensated employees in an amount greater than the amount available to other employees. The conferees intend that this will allow a plan to lend the same percentage of a person's vested benefits to participants with both large and small amounts of accrued vested benefits. (However, the percentage is to be consistent with the requirements of adequate security.) The conferees also intend that a plan may provide that the same dollar amounts may be loaned to participants and beneficiaries without regard to the amount of their vested benefits if adequate security is otherwise provided. For example, a plan could provide for loans to participants and beneficiaries in an amount up to, *e.g.,* $30,000 to buy a house (even if the $30,000 is greater than the amount of the participant's or beneficiary's vested benefits) if the loan is adequately secured by, *e.g.,* a first mortgage on the house.

Exemption for services, etc.—The substitute allows a party-in-interest to furnish to a plan office space, legal services, accounting services, or other similar services necessary for the establishment or operation of the plan, if no more than reasonable compensation is paid for these services, etc. It is expected that such arrangements will allow the plan to terminate the services, etc., on a reasonably short notice under the circumstances so the plan will not become locked into an arrangement that may become disadvantageous. It is also expected that the compensation arrangements will allow for changes so the plan will not be locked into a disadvantageous price.

The substitute also specifically allows the plan to pay a fiduciary or other party-in-interest reasonable compensation (or reimbursement of expenses) for services rendered to the plan if the services are reasonable and necessary. However, to prevent double payment, this does not apply with regard to a fiduciary who is receiving full-time pay from an employer or association of employers (with employees covered by the plan) or from a union (with members covered by the plan), except for the reimbursement of expenses properly and actually incurred and not otherwise reimbursed.

The substitute also makes it clear that a party-in-interest may serve as a fiduciary in addition to being an officer, employee, agent or other representative of a party-in-interest.

Exemption for loans to employee stock ownership plans.—Under the substitute, certain loans or extensions of credit from a party-in-interest to an employee stock ownership plan are not to be prohibited. The conferees understand that it is common practice for these plans to purchase the employer's stock from major shareholders (or from the employer). The proceeds to pay for the purchase often are obtained by the plan from an unrelated lender with a guarantee of repayment by the shareholder. In this case, the substitute does not prohibit the party-in-interest from guaranteeing the loan (or from providing his assets as collateral for the loan). In addition, the conferees understand that it is common practice for a party-in-interest to sell his stock in the employer to these plans and take back a purchase money note from the plan. The substitute also does not prohibit such a loan if the only collateral given by the plan for the loan consists of qualifying employer's securities.

These exceptions to the prohibited transaction rules are to be allowed if the transaction is for the benefit of the plan participants and beneficiaries (and, not, e.g., primarily to benefit the party-in-interest who is selling the stock), and if the interest rate charged on the loan to the plan remains at not more than a reasonable interest rate.

Although these transactions normally are for the benefit of plan participants and beneficiaries, the conferees recognize that there may be potential problems. For example, the interest rate should not be too high and the purchase price of the stock from the party-in-interest should not be too high, so that plan assets might be drained off. Also, the terms of the note between the party-in-interest and the plan should not allow the party-in-interest to call the note at his convenience, which might put undue financial strain on the plan. Because of such potential problems, the conferees intend that all aspects of these transactions will be subject to special scrutiny by the Department of Labor and Internal Revenue Service to ensure that they are primarily for the benefit of plan participants and beneficiaries.

This exception from the prohibited transaction rules is to be available only for employee stock ownership plans and not for other plans. The conferees understand that the basic element common to all employee stock ownership plans is that they are qualified stock bonus plans designed to invest primarily in qualifying securities of the employer whose employees are covered by the plan. In addition it is understood that a qualified money purchase pension plan designed to invest primarily in such securities of the employer may be coupled with such a qualified stock bonus plan (and that a profit-sharing plan sometimes may be used). Furthermore, it is understood that a frequent characteristic of some employee stock ownership plans is that they leverage their purchase of qualifying employer securities as a way to achieve transfers in the ownership of corporate stock and other capital requirements of a corporation and that such a plan is designed to build equity ownership of shares of the employer corporation of its employees in a nondiscriminatory manner.

The conferees intend that the exemption from the prohibited transaction rules with respect to loans to employee stock ownership plans is to apply only in the case of loans (and guarantees) used to leverage the purchase of qualifying employer securities (and related business interests).

Exemption for bank deposits.—In certain cases the prohibited transaction rules of the substitute do not prevent a bank or similar institution (e.g., a savings and loan association or credit union) which is a plan fiduciary from investing all or part of the plan's assets in deposits with the bank, etc., if the deposits bear a reasonable interest rate. This exemption is allowed if the plan covers only employees of the bank, etc., or employees of its affiliates. In this case, it would be contrary to normal business practice for a bank to invest its plan assets in another bank.

A deposit with a bank, etc., fiduciary also is not prohibited if it is expressly authorized by the plan or is specifically authorized by a fiduciary (other than the bank or an affiliate of the bank) who is expressly empowered by the plan to direct that this investment be made. In this case, there is no conflict of interest involving the bank fiduciary upon a deposit with the bank, etc.

This exception, as all other exceptions to the prohibited transaction rules, is not to affect the applicability of the prudent man, diversification, etc., rules. However, it is expected that generally these rules will not be violated if all plan assets in an individual account plan are invested in a federally-insured account, so long as the investments are fully insured. (If an individual's account balance is greater than the amount covered by Federal insurance, this will not violate the prudence and diversification requirements if the individual participant or beneficiary has control over his account and determines, for himself, that the assets should be so invested.)

Exemptions for purchase of insurance.—The substitute does not prohibit a plan from purchasing life insurance, health insurance, or annuities from the employer that maintains the plan if the employer is an insurer qualified to do business in a State (or the District of Columbia). In this case, it would be contrary to normal business practice to require the plan of an insurance company to purchase its insurance from another insurance company. This exemption is available only if no more than adequate consideration is paid for the insurance by the plan.

This exemption also applies to the purchase of life insurance, health insurance, and annuities from an insurer that is wholly-owned, directly or indirectly, by the employer establishing the plan (or is wholly owned by a party-in-interest with respect to the employer establishing a plan). This rule applies if the total premiums and annuity considerations written by all such wholly-owned insurers for life insurance, health insurance, and annuity premiums purchased by all employers which are parties-in-interest and their plans are not more than 5 percent of the total premiums and annuity considerations written for all lines of insurance by these insurers. (In computing this 5 percent figure, all premiums and annuity considerations written by an insurance company for a plan which it maintains are to be excluded from both the numerator and the denominator of the fraction.) This exception also is allowed only if no more than adequate consideration is paid for the insurance.

The conferees understand that for some purposes, certain insurance contracts may be considered as securities. However, the substitute provides that insurance contracts are not to be considered as "employer securities" to the extent that the exception described above from the prohibited transaction requirements would apply to the purchase of insurance contracts by a plan. (Otherwise, the rules with respect to employer securities might, as a practical matter, prevent this exemption from operating as it is intended.)

Exemption for ancillary bank services.—Unless otherwise specifically allowed by statutory or administrative exemption, generally a fiduciary is not to be able to provide "multiple services" to a plan. (However, the prohibition against providing multiple services is not to apply to parties-in-interest, who are not fiduciaries.) This rule was adopted because of the potential problems inherent in situations where persons who can act on behalf of a plan also are in a position to personally benefit at the expense of the plan in exercising that authority. However, as indicated above, it is expected that administrative exemptions will be established for sound commercial and financial practices where there are adequate safeguards. Also, the substitute provides some limited statutory exemptions from the general rule.

Under the substitute, a bank or similar financial institution (such as a savings and loan association or credit union) which is supervised by Federal or State authorities, is not prohibited from providing multiple ancillary services in certain limited circumstances. First, no more than reasonable compensation can be charged by the bank, etc., for these services. Also the bank, etc., must have established adequate internal safeguards to assure that its provision of ancillary services is in accord with sound banking and financial practice, as determined by Federal and State banking authorities. In addition, the bank's action must be in accordance with binding specific guidelines issued by the bank that will prevent the bank from providing ancillary services in an unreasonable or excessive manner or in a manner that would be inconsistent with the best interests of the plan's participants and beneficiaries. Such guidelines are to be subject to, and not inconsistent with, coordinated regulations of the Secretaries of Labor and Treasury, which are to be issued after consultation with State and Federal banking authorities. The bank's guidelines must be reported to the Department of Labor and Internal Revenue Service, and must be reported to each plan to which multiple services are provided. Of course, if the bank does not follow the guidelines, the exemption will not be available.

Placing plan funds in noninterest bearing checking accounts is an example of the type of an [*sic*] ancillary service that might be provided by a bank that is a plan fiduciary. However, a number of short-term investment vehicles have been developed recently so that such cash balances should be kept to the very minimum necessary for the current operations of the plan. Therefore, it is expected that adequate guidelines and procedures to prevent unreasonable cash balances will require the bank to invest plan funds in such vehicles to the maximum extent feasible. Also, in determining whether a plan pays more than reasonable compensation for its checking account services, the interest available on an alternate use of the funds is to be considered. It is also expected that proper procedures and guidelines will keep to a minimum the amount of discretion on the part of the bank, etc., in determining the amount of cash balances. The conferees intend that such limitation of discretion is to be included in guidelines that govern other ancillary services that may be provided by banks, etc.

Exemption for conversion of securities.—Under the substitute a plan may hold or acquire certain employer securities. Since some of these securities may be convertible (*e.g.,* from bonds to stock) the substitute would not prohibit such a conversion to the extent provided in regulations if the plan receives at least fair market value under the conversion. It is expected that a conversion will be permitted if all the securities of the class held by the plan are subject to the same terms and such terms were determined in an arm's-length transaction, so that conversions cannot be tailored to apply only to a particular plan. Similarly, it is intended that a conversion generally will not be permitted if all but an insignificant percentage of unrelated holders of such securities do not exercise such conversion privileges. Also, it is intended that any acquisition of employer securities pursuant to a conversion privilege must be within the limits established by the general rules governing the acquisition and holding of employer securities, discussed below.

Exemption for certain pooled investment funds.—The conferees understand that it is common practice for banks, trust companies and insurance companies to maintain pooled investment funds for plans. If the bank, etc., is the plan trustee and invests the plan assets in its pooled fund (rather than managing the assets individually) this would be considered a purchase of investment units in the fund and would be prohibited under the general rules. However, since generally the net effect of pooling plan assets is to achieve more efficient investment management, in certain circumstances the substitute allows the purchase and sale of interests in a pooled fund maintained by a bank, etc., which is a plan fiduciary.

To be allowed, no more than reasonable compensation may be paid by the plan in the purchase (or sale) and no more than reasonable compensation may be paid by the plan for investment management by the pooled fund. In addition, it generally is inappropriate for the bank, etc., to make the decisions with respect to investment in a pooled fund because of a potential conflict of interest. Therefore, this exception is allowed only if the transaction is specifically permitted by the plan or if a plan fiduciary (other than the bank, etc., or its affiliates) who has authority to manage and control the plan assets specifically permits such investment.

Banks, etc., that operate such pooled investment funds are, of course, plan fiduciaries. As fiduciaries they must act, *e.g.,* for the exclusive benefit of participants and beneficiaries. Therefore, a bank, etc., cannot use pooled funds as a place to dump unwanted investments which were initially made on its own (or another's) behalf.

Exemptions for owner-employees, etc.—The substitute retains the prohibited transaction rules (but not the disqualification sanction) of present law (sec. 503(g) of the Internal Revenue Code) with respect to owner-employees. Consequently, under the substitute the exemptions from the prohibited transaction rules described above generally will not apply with respect to sales, loans, payments for services, etc., between a plan and an owner-employee with regard to that plan. Also, since shareholder employees of subchapter S corporations are generally treated as owner-employees, the same limitations apply with respect to shareholder-employees. Additionally, these limitations apply to participants and beneficiaries of (and employers who establish and maintain) individual retirement accounts, individual retirement annuities, and individual retirement bonds, since these persons generally have the same type of control with respect to a plan as to owner-employees.

Exemptions for distribution of plan assets.—It is not a prohibited transaction for a plan to distribute its assets in accordance with the provisions of the plan and in the case of a pension plan if the distribution is in accord with the allocation of assets rules under the termination insurance provisions of the substitute.

Also, a distribution of assets from a welfare (or pension) plan, as described above in "Basic fiduciary rules" [CCH ¶ 14,740.10] is exempt from the labor provisions as to prohibited transactions.

[ERISA Sec. 409]

[¶ 14,790.10]

Committee Report on P.L. 93-406 (Employee Retirement Income Security Act of 1974)

[Conference Committee Explanation]

Civil liability

Fiduciaries.—Under the labor provisions (but not the tax provisions) of the substitute, a fiduciary who breaches the fiduciary requirements of the bill is to be personally liable for any losses to the plan resulting from this breach. Such a fiduciary is also to be liable for restoring to the plan any profits which he has made through the use of any plan asset. In addition, such a fiduciary is to be subject to other appropriate relief (including removal) as ordered by a court. The place and manner of bringing civil actions against a fiduciary is [*sic*] described below [CCH ¶ 14,920.10].

Generally, a plan fiduciary is not to be liable for any breach of fiduciary duty if it occurred before he became a fiduciary or after he was no longer a fiduciary.

[ERISA Sec. 410]

[¶ 14,800.10]

Committee Report on P.L. 93-406 (Employee Retirement Income Security Act of 1974)

[Conference Committee Explanation]

Exculpatory provisions and liability insurance.—Under the substitute, exculpatory provisions which relieve a fiduciary from liability for breach of the fiduciary responsibility rules are to be void and of no effect. (However, this is not to affect the fiduciary's ability to allocate or delegate his responsibilities, as described above.)

The substitute also provides, however, that a plan may purchase insurance for itself and for its fiduciaries to cover liability or loss resulting from their acts or omissions if the insurance permits recourse by the insurer against the fiduciaries in case of a breach of fiduciary responsibility. Also, under the substitute, a fiduciary may purchase insurance to cover his own liability, and an employer or union may purchase liability insurance for plan fiduciaries (and these policies need not provide for recourse).

[ERISA Sec. 411]

[¶ 14,810.09]

Committee Report on P.L. 98-473 (Continuing Appropriations, 1985—Comprehensive Crime Control Act of 1984)

[Senate Committee Report on Comprehensive Crime Control Act]

Following is material from the Senate Committee Report (No. 98-225) on S. 1762. Most of the substance of this bill was eventually incorporated into P.L. 98-473. In addition, testimony of Senator Nunn on an amendment is included.

"*Section 802* amends section 411(a) of ERISA, which prohibits persons convicted of certain crimes from serving in listed positions with an employee benefit plan. Added to this list of crimes are those offenses relating to abuse or misuse of such person's employee benefit plan position. The categories of positions affected by the disbarment provisions also are enlarged. Section 802 also extends the disbarment period to [13] years, unless, on the convicted individual's motion, the sentencing court sets a lesser period of at least 5 [3] years."

"*Section 802* also amends section 411(b) of ERISA by increasing the penalties for intentional violations of this section from 1 year to 5 years."

"*Section 802* amends section 411(c) of ERISA to change the definition of the word 'convicted.' Current law defines this as the date of the trial court judgment or the final appeal thereof, whichever is later. This title changes the date of disqualification to the date of the trial court judgment, regardless of appeals."

"*Section 802* also adds a new section 411(d) to ERISA which provides that any salary for a position in an employee benefit plan otherwise payable to a person convicted by a trial court shall be placed in escrow pending final disposition of any appeal."

Following is testimony of Senator Nunn (October 4, 1984, Congressional Record, page 5, 13082) concerning an amendment that was adopted to H.J. Res. 648, which was eventually enacted as part of P.L. 98-473.

"Our proposal also attempts to rid labor organizations and employee benefit plans of the influence of persons convicted of criminal offenses. Current disbarment provisions—29 U.S.C. 504 and 29 U.S.C. 1111—are expanded in several significant ways: enlarging the categories of persons affected by the disbarment provisions; increasing the maximum time barred from office or position from 3 to a possible 13 years; and providing for disbarment immediately upon conviction rather than after appeal.

"I point out that it is within the judge's discretion to set the exact term of disbarment, from a minimum of 3 years to a maximum of 13. * * *

[¶ 14,810.10]

Committee Report on P.L. 93-406 (Employee Retirement Income Security Act of 1974)

[Conference Committee Explanation]

Prohibition against certain persons holding office.—The labor provisions of the substitute prohibit a person who is convicted of certain specified crimes from serving as a plan administrator, fiduciary, officer, trustee, custodian, counsel, agent, employee or consultant of a plan for five years after conviction or five years after the end of imprisonment, whichever is later. However, such a person may serve as an administrator, etc., of a plan if his citizenship rights have been fully restored or if the United States Board of Parole determines that his service would not be contrary to the purposes of the labor provisions of the substitute.

Corporations and partnerships are not to be barred from acting as plan administrators, etc., without a determination from the Board of Parole that such service would be inconsistent with the labor provisions of the substitute.

No one is to knowingly permit another to serve as a plan administrator, etc., in violation of this provision. Those who violate this provision may be fined up to $10,000 and also may be imprisoned for up to one year. This provision is to apply to crimes committed before the date of enactment.

[ERISA Sec. 412]

[¶ 14,820.09]

Committee Report on P.L. 109-280 (Pension Protection Act of 2006)

[Joint Committee on Taxation Report]

The provision raises the maximum bond amount to $1 million in the case of a plan that holds employer securities. The provision raises the maximum bond amount to $1 million in the case of a plan that holds employer securities. A plan would not be considered to hold employer securities within the meaning of this section where the only securities held by the plan are part of a broadly diversified fund of assets, such as mutual or index funds.

Effective Date

The provision is effective for plan years beginning after December 31, 2007.

For the Committee Report on P.L. 109-280 on prohibited transaction rules relating to financial investments, see ¶ 13,640.018.

[¶ 14,820.10]

Committee Report on P.L. 93-406 (Employee Retirement Income Security Act of 1974)

[Conference Committee Explanation]

Bonding.—The labor provisions of the substitute generally require every fiduciary of an employee benefit plan (and every person who handles funds or other property of a plan) to be bonded. This provision generally is identical to present section 13 of the Welfare and Pension Plans Disclosure Act and it is intended that the construction given to the bonding requirements before enactment of the substitute would continue. Generally, the amount of the bond is to be not less than 10 percent of the funds handled and not less than $1,000 (nor more than $500,000, except as otherwise required by the 10 percent rule or as prescribed by the Secretary of Labor). The substitute would not require a bond if plan benefits are paid only from the general assets of a union or employer. A bond also is not to be required for a domestic trust or insurance corporation subject to State or Federal supervision or examination if it has capital and surplus combined in excess of $1 million (or such other higher amount determined by the Secretary of Labor). However, a special rule is provided for banks or other financial institutions exercising trust powers if their deposits are not insured by the Federal Deposit Insurance Corporation. In this case a bond will not be required if the corporation meets bonding (or similar requirements) of State law which the Secretary of Labor determines are at least equivalent to bonding requirements imposed on banks under Federal law.

It is expected that regulations to be prescribed by the Secretary of Labor under this provision would include procedures for exempting plans where other bonding arrangements of the employer, employee organization, investment manager or other fiduciaries or the overall financial condition of the plan or the fiduciaries meet specified standards deemed adequate to protect the interests of the beneficiaries and participants, including bonds subject to a reasonable maximum for professional investment managers supervising large aggregations of clients' funds.

[ERISA Sec. 413]

[¶ 14,830.08]

Committee Report on P.L. 100-203 (Omnibus Budget Reconciliation Act of 1987)

For the Committee Report on P.L. 100-203, relating to reporting requirements, see ¶ 14,230.09.

[¶ 14,830.10]

Committee Report on P.L. 93-406 (Employee Retirement Income Security Act of 1974)

See Committee Report at ¶ 14,920.10.

[ERISA Sec. 414]

[¶ 14,840.10]

Committee Report on P.L. 93-406 (Employee Retirement Income Security Act of 1974)

[Conference Committee Explanation]

Effective date and transition rules.—Generally, the new fiduciary responsibility rules are to take effect on January 1, 1975. However, with respect to any plan which is covered by plan termination insurance and which terminates before January 1, 1975, the fiduciary rules are to take effect on the date of enactment of the bill.

Under the labor provisions, the Secretary of Labor may postpone until January 1, 1976, the effective date with respect to the requirements for establishing a plan and establishing a trust, the rules regarding liability for breach by a co-fiduciary (other than the rules allowing delegation of asset management functions to an investment manager) and the rules prohibiting exculpatory clauses. The Secretary of Labor may allow such a delay only for plans in existence on the date of enactment and only if he determines (on application of the plan) that the delay is (1) necessary to amend the plan instrument, and (2) not adverse to the plan participants and beneficiaries.

To prevent undue hardship, the substitute also provides transition rules for situations where employee benefit plans are now engaging in activities which do not violate current law, but would be prohibited transactions under the substitute.

One of the transition rules permits the leasing or joint use of property involving a plan and a party in interest under a binding contract in effect on July 1, 1974 (or pursuant to renewals of the contract), to continue for 10 years beyond that date until June 30, 1984. For this transition rule to apply, the lease or joint use must remain at least as favorable to the plan as an arm's-length transaction with an unrelated party and must not otherwise be a prohibited transaction under present law. A similar 10-year transition rule applies to loans or other extensions of credit under a binding contract in effect on July 1, 1974 (and renewals thereof), where the loan remains as favorable as an arm's-length transaction with an unrelated party and is not prohibited under present law.

The substitute allows a plan to sell property, at arm's-length terms, to a party in interest where the property is now under a lease or joint use which qualifies for the 10-year transition rule described above. Sales of this type must occur before July 1, 1984. This transition rule is provided because it appears that such leases are not uncommon and in such cases often a party in interest is the best available buyer.

The substitute allows a fiduciary to provide multiple services to a plan until June 30, 1977, if he ordinarily and customarily furnishes services on June 30, 1974. Under this provision, such a fiduciary would not be limited to providing these services to plans which he served on that date, but he could take on new customers after that date. Under the substitute, multiple services also can be provided until June 30, 1977, if they were being provided under a binding contract in effect on July 1, 1974 (or under renewals of such a contract). It is intended that under this provision fiduciaries can continue to provide such services for the next three years in order that they might continue their business during the pendency of and application for a variance from the prohibited transaction rules. However, these services can only be provided under the transition rules if the price is at least an arm's-length price during the whole transition period and if they would not constitute a prohibited transaction under current section 503 of the Internal Revenue Code.

The substitute permits a plan to dispose of excess employer securities or employer real property owned by the plan on June 30, 1974, and at all times thereafter to a party-in-interest if the holding of such property would violate the rules governing holding of employer securities and real property, and if the sales, etc., is at fair market value.

[ERISA Sec. 501]

[¶ 14,910.10]

Committee Report on P.L. 93-406 (Employee Retirement Income Security Act of 1974)

[Conference Committee Explanation]

Labor Department—Criminal penalty.—

* * *

Under the conference agreement, any person who willfully violates any provisions in title I of the bill relating to reporting and disclosure may be fined not more than $5,000 or imprisoned for more than 1 year, or both, except that in the case of a violation by a person other than an individual the fine may not exceed $100,000. The conference agreement retains present criminal provisions of Title 18, U.S.C. relating to false statements, bribery, kickbacks, embezzlement, etc., in connection with employee benefit plans.

[ERISA Sec. 502]

[¶ 14,920.081]

Committee Report on P.L. 109-280 (Pension Protection Act of 2006)

For the Committee Report on P.L. 109-280 on access to multiemployer pension plan information, see ¶ 13,648W-75.045.

For the Committee Report on P.L. 109-280 on periodic pension benefit statements, see ¶ 14,250.08.

For the Committee Report on P.L. 109-280 on prohibited transaction rules relating to financial investments, see ¶ 13,640.018.

[¶ 14,920.083]

Conference Committee Report on P.L. 105-34 (Taxpayer Relief Act)

[Senate Committee Report]

Elimination of paperwork burdens on plans.—The bill eliminates the requirement that SPDs and SMMs be filed with the Secretary of Labor. Employers would be required to furnish these documents to the Secretary of Labor upon request. A civil penalty could be imposed by the Secretary of Labor on the plan administrator for failure to comply with such requests. The penalty would be up to $100 per day of failure, up to a maximum of $1,000 per request. No penalty would be imposed if the failure was due to matters reasonably outside the control of the plan administrator.

Effective Date

The provision is effective on the date of enactment.

[Conference Committee Report]

The Conference Agreement follows the Senate Amendment.

[¶ 14,920.085]

Committee Report on P.L. 104-191 (Health Insurance Portability and Accountability Act)

[House Bill]

The House bill would provide that ERISA sanctions apply to group health plans by deeming the provisions of subtitle A and subtitle D (insofar as it is applicable to this subtitle) to be provisions of title I of ERISA. Such sanctions also would apply to an insurer or HMO that was subject to state law in the event that the Secretary of Labor determined that the state had not provided for enforcement of the above provisions of this Act. Sanctions would not apply in the event that the Secretary of Labor established that none of the persons against whom the liability would be imposed knew, or exercising reasonable diligence, would have known that a failure existed, or if the noncomplying entity acted within 30 days to correct the failure. In no case would a civil money penalty be imposed under ERISA for a violation for which an excise tax under the COBRA enforcement provisions was imposed or for which a civil money penalty was imposed by the Secretary of HHS.

[Senate Amendment]

The Senate Amendment would provide that for employee health benefit plans, the Secretary would be required to enforce the reform standards established by the bill in the same manner as provided under sections 502, 504, 506, and 510 of ERISA. (See item IV(I) below for enforcement provisions relating to health plan issuers and group health plans sold to employers and others.)

[Conference Agreement]

The conference agreement provides that provisions with respect to group health plans would be enforced under Title I of ERISA as under current law. The Secretary of Labor would not enforce the provisions of Title I applicable to health insurance issuers. However, private right of action under part V of ERISA would apply to such issuers. Enforcement of provisions with respect to health insurance issuers generally would be limited to civil remedies established under the PHS Act amendments (as described in the following subsection).

The conference agreement provides that a state may enter into an agreement with the Secretary for delegation to the state of some or all of the Secretary's authority under sections 502 and 504 of ERISA to enforce the requirements of this part in connection with MEWAs providing medical care which are not group health plans.

[¶ 14,920.09]

Committee Report on P.L. 100-203 (Omnibus Budget Reconciliation Act of 1987)

[Conference Committee Report]

The [Education and Labor Committee] bill clarifies that the penalty imposed with respect to a prohibited transaction in 5 percent of the amount involved in each prohibited transaction and, if the transaction is not corrected within a certain period of time, 100 percent of the amount involved in each prohibited transaction.

The conference agreement follows the Education and Labor Committee bill. The provision is a clarification of present law.

[¶ 14,920.095]

Committee Report on P.L. 96-364 (Multiemployer Pension Plan Amendments Act of 1980)

[Senate Committee Report]

Under the bill, in the case of a civil action by any person to collect delinquent multiemployer plan contributions, regardless of otherwise applicable law, in which a judgment in favor of the plan is awarded, the court before which the action is brought must award the plan (1) the unpaid contributions, (2) interest on the unpaid contributions, (3) an amount equal to the greater of interest on the unpaid contributions or liquidated damages provided for under the plan not to exceed 20 percent of the amount of delinquent contributions as determined by the court. The bill preempts any State or other law which would prevent the award of reasonable attorney's fees, court costs or liquidated damages or which would limit liquidated damages to an amount below the 20 percent level.

However, the bill does not preclude the award of liquidated damages in excess of the 20 percent level where an award of such a higher level of liquidated damages is permitted under applicable State or other law. This does not change any other type of remedy permitted under State or Federal law with respect to delinquent multiemployer plan contributions.

[¶ 14,920.10]

Committee Report on P.L. 93-406 (Employee Retirement Income Security Act of 1974)

[Conference Committee Explanation]

Civil penalty for failure to disclose.— Under the bill as passed by the House, if a plan administrator fails or refuses to furnish a participant or a beneficiary with a copy of the latest annual report (or such other information that is required to be furnished under the Act) within 30 days after a request for it, the administrator may be personally liable to the participant or beneficiary for up to $50 a day from the date of the failure and a court, in its discretion, may grant such other relief as it deems proper. * * * Under the conference agreement the administrator may be personally liable to the participant or beneficiary for up to $100 per day from the date of the failure and the court may in its discretion order such other relief as it deems proper.

Civil actions by participants and beneficiaries.— * * *

Under the conference agreement, civil actions may be brought by a participant or beneficiary to recover benefits due under the plan, to clarify rights to receive future benefits under the plan, and for relief from breach of fiduciary responsibility. The U.S. district courts are to have exclusive jurisdiction with respect to actions involving breach of fiduciary responsibility as well as exclusive jurisdiction over other actions to enforce or clarify benefit rights provided under title I. However, with respect to suits to enforce benefit rights under the plan or to recover benefits under the plan which do not involve application of the title I provisions, they may be brought not only in U.S. district courts but also in State courts of competent jurisdiction. All such actions in Federal or State courts are to be regarded as arising under the laws of the United States in similar fashion to those brought under section 301 of the Labor-Management Relations Act of 1947. The U.S. district courts are to have jurisdiction of these actions without regard to the amount in controversy and without regard to the citizenship of the parties. In any action brought by a participant or beneficiary, the court may allow reasonable attorney's fees or costs to either party. An action in the U.S. district court may be brought in the district where the plan is administered or where the breach of fiduciary duty took place, or where the plan is administered or where the breach of fiduciary duty took place, or where a defendant resides or may be found. Process may be served in any other district where a defendant resides or may be found. If a participant or beneficiary brings an action in Federal court to enforce rights under title I, he is to provide a copy of the complaint to the Secretary of Labor and the Secretary of Treasury by certified mail. A copy is not required to be provided in any action which is solely for the purpose of recovering benefits under the plan. The Secretary of Labor or the Secretary of Treasury, or both, are to have the right to intervene in any action at their discretion.

Civil actions by the Secretary of Labor.—* * *

* * * The Secretary of Labor may bring an action for breach of a fiduciary duty or to enjoin any act or practice which violates the provision of title I of the Act or to obtain any other appropriate relief to enforce any provision of that title. In the case of a transaction by a party in interest with respect to a plan which is not qualifed under the Internal Revenue Code, the Secretary of Labor may assess a civil penalty not to exceed 5 percent of the amount of the transaction. If not corrected, an additional penalty of not more than 100 percent of the transaction may be imposed.

In the case of any plan which has been found by the Internal Revenue Service to be a qualified employee benefit plan under the Internal Revenue Code (or with respect to any plan which has a pending application for a determination to be so qualified), the Secretary of Labor is not to bring an action for equitable relief with respect to a violation of the participation, vesting and funding standards of title I unless he is requested to do so either by the Secretary of the Treasury or by one or more participants, beneficiaries, or fiduciaries of the plan.

* * *

Service of process.—Under the bill as passed by the House, subpoena or other legal process of a court upon a trustee of plan administrator constitutes service on the plan. In addition, a plan may sue or be sued as an entity. The bill as passed by the Senate does not contain comparable provisions. The conference agreement basically adopts the provisions as passed by the House but provides that where a plan does not designate in its plan description an individual as agent for service of legal process, service upon the Secretary of Labor is to constitute adequate service. In that case the Secretary upon receipt of service of process is to notify the administrator or any trustee of the pending action within 15 days after he is served.

Enforcement of judgment.—The bill as passed by the House provides that a money judgment under title I of the Act against the plan is to be enforceable only against the plan as an entity and not against any other person unless that person's liability is established in his individual capacity. The bill as passed by the Senate did not contain a comparable provision. Under the conference agreement the House provisions are adopted.

Government representation.—Both the House bill and the Senate amendment provide for the Secretary of Labor to be represented by attorneys appointed by him in civil actions arising under the Act, except for litigation before the Supreme Court and the Court of Claims. The conference agreement adds the qualification that "all such litigation shall be subject to the direction and control of the Attorney General." The new language was added in order to make clear that even though litigation is conducted by Labor Department attorneys, there is to be authority in the Attorney General to resolve those situations where two or more agencies of the Federal government have varying positions with respect to issues in litigation and, in such situations, to assure that the government takes uniform positions before the courts. In addition, the Attorney General is to have authority concerning the presentation to the courts of the government's position with respect to such issues of general importance as the constitutionality of Federal laws. Under the conference agreement, it is intended that in civil litigation involving the Secretary of Labor under this bill, the Secretary, in the normal course, will be represented in court by the Solicitor of Labor and his attorneys, with appropriate arrangements being made between the Secretary of Labor and the Attorney General with respect to the active involvement of the Justice Department in the types of situations discussed above.

[ERISA Sec. 503]

[¶ 14,930.10]

Committee Report on P.L. 93-406 (Employee Retirement Income Security Act of 1974)

[Conference Committee Explanation]

Benefit claim procedure.—* * *. Under the conference agreement every employee benefit plan is required to provide adequate notice in writing to any participant or beneficiary whose claim for benefits under the plan has been denied, setting forth the specific reasons for denial written in a manner calculated to be understood by the participant. In addition, the plan administrator is required to afford a reasonable opportunity to any participant or beneficiary whose claim for benefits has been denied for a full and fair review of this decision by the plan administrator.

[ERISA Sec. 504]

[¶ 14,940.10]

Committee Report on P.L. 93-406 (Employee Retirement Income Security Act of 1974)

[Conference Committee Explanation]

Investigatory authority.—* * * Under the conference agreement, the Secretary of Labor is to have the power in order to determine whether there have been violations or there are about to be violations of any provision of title I to make an investigation. In connection with the investigation, he may require the submission of reports, books and records, and the filing of supporting data, but no plan may be required to submit such books, records or supporting data more than once annually unless the Secretary has reasonable cause to believe there may exist a violation under title I. The Secretary also may enter places and inspect records and accounts and question those persons he deems necessary to enable him to determine the facts relative to the investigation if he has reasonable cause to believe there may exist a violation under title I. The Secretary is authorized to make available to persons covered by the plan and to any department or agency of the United States information concerning any matter which has been the subject of the investigation.

Subpoena power.—Under the bill as passed by the House, the Secretary of Labor is given the same powers of subpeona as are given to the Federal Trade Commission. The bill as passed by the Senate contains the same provisions as that passed by the House and in addition provides that the Secretary of Labor may delegate his auditing and investigation functions with respect to insured banks acting as fiduciaries to appropriate Federal banking agencies. The conference agreement adopts the provisions of the bill as passed by the Senate.

[ERISA Sec. 505]

[¶ 14,950.10]

Committee Report on P.L. 93-406 (Employee Retirement Income Security Act of 1974)

See Committee Reports at ¶ 14,280.10 and 14,940.10.

[ERISA Sec. 506]

[¶ 14,960.085]

Committee Report on P.L. 104-191 (Health Insurance Portability and Accountability Act)

[Conference Agreement]

The conference agreement provides that the Secretaries of Treasury, Labor, and HHS would ensure, through execution of an interagency memorandum of understanding, that regulations, rulings, and interpretations are administered so as to have the same effect at all times. It requires the Secretaries to coordinate enforcement policies for the same requirements to avoid duplication of enforcement efforts and assign priorities in enforcement.

It is the intent of the conferees that the committees of jurisdiction should work together to assure the coordination of policies under this Act. Such coordination is considered necessary to maintain consistency in the IRC, ERISA, and the PHS Act.

[¶ 14,960.09]

Committee Testimony on P.L. 98-473 (Continuing Appropriations, 1985—Comprehensive Crime Control Act of 1984)

Following is testimony of Senator Nunn (January 20, 1984 Congressional Record, page S 463) in making an amendment to S. 1762. The provision was eventually incorporated into P.L. 98-473.

"This amendment clearly delineates the responsibility and authority of the Department of Labor to actively and effectively investigate and refer for prosecution criminal activities relating to union or employee benefit plan corruption. This provision responds to the evidence which we found in our investigations that, although the Labor Department is often active in proceeding with civil actions to enforce Federal law, there has been in the past a great deal of confusion as to whether it should or even could engage in criminal investigations and referrals."

[¶ 14,960.10]

Committee Report on P.L. 93-406 (Employee Retirement Income Security Act of 1974)

[Conference Committee Explanation]

Cooperation between agencies.—Under the bill as passed by both the House and the Senate, the Secretary of Labor is authorized to cooperate with other agencies and make agreements for mutual assistance. In addition, under the bill as passed by the House, the Attorney General is authorized to receive from the Secretary of Labor for appropriate action evidence which has been developed that warrants consideration for criminal prosecution under Federal law. Under the conference agreement, the provisions for cooperation of other agencies including the authorization for the Attorney General to receive matters relating to criminal prosecution is [*sic*] adopted.

[ERISA Sec. 507]

[¶ 14,970.10]

Committee Report on P.L. 93-406 (Employee Retirement Income Security Act of 1974)

[Conference Committee Explanation]

Administrative matters.—Under the bill as passed by the House, the Administrative Procedure Act is applicable to the provisions of title I. In addition, no employee of the Department of Labor is to administer or enforce title I with respect to any employee organization of which he is a member or employer organization in which he has an interest. The bill as passed by the Senate does not add any comparable provisions. Under the conference agreement, the provisions of the bill as passed by the House are adopted.

* * *

[ERISA Sec. 508]

[¶ 14,980.10]

Committee Report on P.L. 93-406 (Employee Retirement Income Security Act of 1974)

[Conference Committee Explanation]

Appropriations authorized, etc.—Under the bill as passed by the House and the Senate, there is [*sic*] authorized appropriations of such sums as may be necessary to enable the Secretary of Labor to carry out his functions and duties under the bill. In addition, under the bill as passed by the Senate, the Secretary of Labor is authorized to increase the number of supergrade positions in the Department of Labor. Under the conference agreement the Secretary of Labor is authorized to add one additional position in the GS-18 level in the Department of Labor and to place 20 additional positions in the GS-16 and 17 level in the Department of Labor.

[ERISA Sec. 510]

[¶ 15,000.09]

Committee Report on P.L. 109-280 (Pension Protection Act of 2006)

[Joint Committee on Taxation Report]

The provision provides that in the case of a multiemployer plan, it is unlawful for the plan sponsor or any other person to discriminate against any contributing employer for exercising rights under ERISA or for giving information or testifying in an inquiry or proceedings relating to ERISA before Congress. The provision amends the anti-retaliation section of ERISA to provide protection for employers who contribute to multiemployer plans and others. The provision is intended to close a loophole in the existing whistleblower protections. In June 2005, a witness who appeared on behalf of several other companies testified before the Retirement Security & Aging Subcommittee of the Senate Health, Education, Labor & Pensions Committee. Subsequent to that testimony there was an allegation that some of these companies may have been targeted for possible audits.

It is intended that retaliation against any employer who has an obligation to contribute to a plan due to testifying before Congress or exercising his or her rights to petition for redress of grievances would amount to unlawful retaliation under ERISA as amended by the provision. Exercising rights under ERISA, testifying before Congress, and giving information in any inquiry or proceeding relating to this Act are intended to be protected under the provision.

Effective Date

The provision is effective on the date of enactment.

[¶ 15,000.10]

Committee Report on P.L. 93-406 (Employee Retirement Income Security Act of 1974)

[Conference Committee Explanation]

Interference with rights.—Under the bill as passed by both the House and the Senate, it is unlawful to interfere with the attainment of any rights to which a participant or beneficiary may become entitled or to coercively interfere through the use of fraud, force, or violence with any participant or beneficiary for the purpose of preventing him from exercising any right to which he is or may become entitled to under the plan or title I. The penalties and degrees of proof for violations of the provisions are somewhat different. Under the conference agreement, the participant or beneficiary may bring a civil action against any person who interferes with his rights which are protected under the Act. In addition, any person who willfully uses fraud, force, violence or threatens to restrain, coerce or intimidate any participant or beneficiary for purposes of interfering with the participant's or beneficiary's rights under the plan or title I of the Act is to be fined $10,000 or imprisoned for not more than 1 year, or both.

[ERISA Sec. 511]

[¶ 15,010.09]

Committee Report on P.L. 109-280 (Pension Protection Act of 2006)

[Joint Committee on Taxation Report]

The provision increases the penalties for willful acts of coercive interference with participants' rights under a plan, ERISA, or the WPPDA. The amount of the fine is increased to $100,000, and the maximum term of imprisonment is increased to 10 years.

Effective Date

The provision is effective for violations occurring on and after the date of enactment.

[¶ 15,010.10]

Committee Report on P.L. 93-406 (Employee Retirement Income Security Act of 1974)

See Committee Report at ¶ 15,000.10.

[ERISA Sec. 512]

[¶ 15,020.10]

Committee Report on P.L. 93-406 (Employee Retirement Income Security Act of 1974)

[Conference Committee Explanation]

Advisory Council.—Under the bill as passed by both the House and the Senate, there is established an Advisory Council on Employee Welfare and Pension Benefit Plans. Under the conference agreement, the Council is to consist of 15 members appointed by the Secretary of Labor. Not more than 8 members are to be of the same political party. The Council is to be made up of members who are to be representatives of employee organizations and employers, and members from the fields of insurance, corporate trusts, actuarial counseling, investment counseling, investment management, and accounting, and from the general public. Members are generally to serve for terms of 3 years, are to advise the Secretary of Labor with respect to the carrying out of his functions under the bill and are to submit to the Secretary recommendations as to the administration of the provisions of the bill.

[ERISA Sec. 513]

[¶ 15,030.10]

Committee Report on P.L. 93-406 (Employee Retirement Income Security Act of 1974)

[Conference Committee Explanation]

Reports to Congress.—Under the bill as passed by the House, the Secretary of Labor is to report annually to the Congress regarding the administration of title I. This report is to include an explanation of the variances granted, a status report on any plan operating with a variance and its progress in achieving compliance with the Act, the projected date for terminating the variance and information, and recommendations for further legislation in connection with matters covered by title I. Under the conference agreement, the provisions of the bill as passed by the House generally are adopted.

[ERISA Sec. 514]

[¶ 15,040.075]

Committee Report on P.L. 109-280 (Pension Protection Act of 2006)

For the Committee Report on P.L. 109-280 on automatic enrollment arrangements, see ¶ 13,648J.09.

[¶ 15,040.08]

Committee Report on P.L. 103-66 (Omnibus Budget Reconciliation Act of 1993)

[Conference Committee Report]

* * *

Coordination of ERISA Preemption Rules

House Bill

Section 4201 of the House bill amended section 514(b)(8) of ERISA to exempt from preemption certain additional provisions of state laws.

In 1986, ERISA was amended to add subsection (b)(8) in order to facilitate the ability of the states to assure that Medicaid was the secondary payor for all eligible individuals also covered under group health plans. Under the amendments to title XIX of the Social Security Act contained in title V of the House bill, additional requirements relating to third-party payors are imposed on the states as a condition of receiving Federal matching Medicaid funds. The amendments to ERISA under section 4201 permit states to enforce laws enacted as a result of these additional Medicaid requirements.

Senate Amendment

Similar to House bill.

Conference Agreement

The Senate receded with an amendment.

Under the conference agreement, group health plans are required to pay benefits in accordance with any assignments of rights on behalf of participants and beneficiaries that is [sic] required by Title XIX of the Social Security Act. In enrolling individuals under group health plans, plans are precluded from taking into account the fact that an individual is eligible for or provided assistance under Title XIX.

In addition, under the conference agreement and consistent with provisions [of] title V of this Act, to the extent that payment has been made under Title XIX, states would acquire the right of any other party to payment. State laws enforcing these rights must be honored by group health plans since those laws could be exempt from ERISA's preemption.

Medical Child Support Orders

House Bill

No provision.

Senate Amendment

Section 12301(a) of the Senate amendment amends section 514(b)(8) of ERISA to require group health plans to comply with state laws relating to assignment of rights of payment and child health insurance report[s].

Conference Agreement

The House recedes with an amendment.

Under the conference agreement, group health plans are required to honor "qualified medical child support orders." The term "medical child support order" means generally any judgment, decree, or order (including approval of a settlement agreement) issued by a court of competent jurisdiction providing for child support or health benefit coverage for a child of a participant. The child on whose behalf such an order is issued is an "alternative recipient" and will be treated as a participant under the plans. An order is "qualified" and must be honored by the plan if it meets certain specified requirements.

In addition, group health plans that provide for coverage for dependent children must treat dependent children placed for adoption in the home of participants under the plan the same as dependent children who are the natural children of participants, irrespective of whether that adoption has become final. For purposes of these provisions, a child is defined as an individual who has not attained age 18 as of the date of adoption or placement for adoption.

* * *

[¶ 15,040.085]

Committee Report on P.L. 98-397 (Retirement Equity Act of 1984)

[Senate Committee Report]

In general.—The bill clarifies the spendthrift provisions by providing new rules for the treatment of certain domestic relations orders. In addition, the bill creates an exception to the ERISA preemption provision with respect to these orders. * * *

Under the bill, if a domestic relations order requires the distribution of all or a part of a participant's benefits under a qualified plan to an alternate payee, then the creation, recognition, or assignment of the alternate payee's right to the benefits is not considered an assignment or alienation of benefits under the plan if and only if the order is a qualified domestic relations order. Because rights created, recognized, or assigned by a qualified domestic relations order, and benefit payments pursuant to such an order, are specifically permitted under the bill, State law providing for these rights and payments under a qualified domestic relations order will continue to be exempt from Federal preemption under ERISA.

[¶ 15,040.09]

Committee Report on P.L. 97-473 (Periodic Payments Settlement Act of 1982)

[Conference Committee Report]

Waiver of Preemption in Case of Hawaiian Prepaid Health Care Act

Present law

The Employee Retirement Income Security Act of 1974 (ERISA) provides comprehensive rules relating to employee benefit plans, including plans providing health benefits to employees. The Act (sec. 514(a)) generally supersedes State laws insofar as they relate to employee benefit plans.

The Hawaii Act (Haw.Rev.Stat. §§393-1 through 391-51), provides for a program of health insurance for employees. As a result of litigation, it was determined that the Hawaiian Act was preempted by ERISA (*Standard Oil Company of California v. Agsalud,* 633 F.2d 760 (9th Cir. 1980), aff'd, 454 U.S. 801 (1981)).

House bill

The provision generally exempts the Hawaii Prepaid Health Care Act from preemption by ERISA. Under the provision, however, preemption is continued with respect to (1) any State tax law relating to employee benefit plans, or (2) any amendment of the Hawaii Act enacted after September 2, 1974, to the extent the amendment provides for more than the effective administration of that Act as in effect on September 2, 1974. The provision continues Federal preemption of State law with respect to matters governed by the reporting and disclosure and the fiduciary responsibility provisions of ERISA, as well as certain of the provisions of the administration and enforcement rules of ERISA (Title I, part 1, part 4, and secs. 501 through 514(b)). The provision also permits the Secretary of Labor to enter into cooperative arrangements with the officials of the State of Hawaii to assist them in effectuating the policies of the provisions of the Hawaii Act that are superseded by ERISA.

The provision states that it is not to be considered a prcedent for extending non-preemption to any other State law.

The provision is effective on the date of enactment.

Senate amendment

The Senate amendment generally follows the House bill except that the exemption from the ERISA preemption provision applies to the Hawaii Prepaid Health Care Act, as in effect on January 1, 1976. Additionally, the amendment requires that the Secretary of Labor conduct a study of the feasibility of extending the exemption to include other State laws which establish health care plans and report to the Congress on his findings within two years.

Conference agreement

The conference agreement follows the House bill.

Waiver of Preemption in Case of Multiple Employer Welfare Arrangements

Present law

The Employee Retirement Income Security Act of 1974 (ERISA) provides comprehensive rules relating to employee benefit plans, including plans providing health benefits to employees. The Act (sec. 514(a)) generally supersedes State laws insofar as they relate to employee benefit plans.

House bill

The provision generally exempts certain multiple employer welfare arrangements from the ERISA preemption provision. Under the provision, a multiple employer welfare arrangement is any plan or other arrangement established to offer welfare benefits, such as health insurance, to the employees of two or more employers. However, it continues preemption with respect to State law applying to any plan maintained pursuant to a collective bargaining agreement or maintained by a tax exempt rural electric cooperative.

In the case of a fully insured multiple employer welfare arrangement, the provision exempts from ERISA preemption any State laws that require the maintenance of specified levels of reserves and contributions in order for such an arrangement to be considered adequately funded.

In the case of a multiple employer welfare arrangement that is not fully insured, the provision exempts from ERISA preemption any State laws that regulate insurance. Notwithstanding this provision, the Secretary is authorized to determine the extent to which the ERISA preemption provision will be applied to a multiple employer welfare arrangement that is not fully insured. The Secretary's determination may be made on a case-by-case basis or a class basis.

The provision is effective on the date of enactment.

Senate amendment

No provision.

Conference agreement

The conference agreement follows the House bill.

[¶ 15,040.10]

Committee Report on P.L. 93-406 (Employee Retirement Income Security Act of 1974)

[Conference Committee Explanation]

Under the substitute, the provisions of title I are to supersede all State laws that relate to any employee benefit plan that is established by an employer engaged in or affecting interstate commerce or by an employee organization that represents employees engaged in or affecting interstate commerce. (However, following title I generally, preemption will not apply to government plans, church plans not electing under the vesting, etc., provisions, workmen's compensation plans, non-U.S. plans primarily for nonresident aliens, and so-called "excess benefit plans.")

The preemption provision will take effect on January 1, 1975, except that preemption with respect to plan termination insurance will take effect on the date of enactment of this bill [September 2, 1974]. However, it will not affect any causes of action that have arisen before January 1, 1975, and it will not affect any act or omission which occurred before that date. In addition, the preemption provisions will not apply to any criminal law of general application of a State.

The preemption provisions of title I are not to exempt any person from any State law that regulates insurance, banking or securities. However, the substitute generally provides that an employee benefit plan is not to be considered as an insurance company, bank, trust company, or investment company (and is not to be considered as engaged in the business of insurance or banking) for purposes of any State law that regulates insurance companies, insurance contracts, banks, trust companies, or investment companies. This rule does not apply to a plan which is established primarily to provide death benefits; such plans, or course, may be regulated under the State insurance, etc., laws.

The substitute provides that the congressional Pension Task Force is to study this provision and report back to the labor committees of the Congress on the results of its study. It is expected that the Pension Task Force will consult closely with State insurance, etc., authorities in the course of this study.

[ERISA Sec. 515]

[¶ 15,043.10]

Committee Report on P.L. 96-364 (Multiemployer Pension Plan Amendments Act of 1980)

For Senate Committee Report (P.L. 96-364), see Committee Report at ¶ 15,310.10.

[ERISA Sec. 601]

[¶ 15,045.10]

Committee Reports on P.L. 99-272 (Consolidated Omnibus Budget Reconciliation Act)

[House Committee Report]

In an effort to provide continued access to affordable private health insurance for some of these individuals, the Committee has adopted . . . provisions which would require a five-year continuation option to be offered to certain groups of individuals: (1) widowed spouses and dependent children, (2) a divorced or separated spouse and dependent children, and (3) a Medicare-ineligible spouse and dependent children.

* * *. Under [the bill], employers sponsoring group health plans must extend an option for continued participation in the plan to spouses and dependent children previously covered under the plan if coverage was lost because of a change in family status.

This option would be offered during a period beginning when the individual would otherwise lose coverage and ending not earlier than 60 days after the individual is notified of his or her continuation of coverage rights. "Qualified beneficiaries" (i.e., individuals who fall into the three categories described above) could elect continuation of group coverage on their own behalf. . . . [E]vidence of insurability [would not be required] and the coverage provided would generally be identical in scope to that provided to similarly situated spouses and dependent children who had not undergone a change in family status. * * *. A qualified beneficiary who was a covered dependent child would lose coverage as soon as the person no longer met the group health plan's definition of a dependent child.

Various notice requirements are imposed on the group health plan in order to assure that individuals understand their continuation rights under the bill. In addition, the covered employee would be required to notify the administrator of the group health plan of any change in family status and the employer must notify the administrator in the case of the death of the covered employee.

[Senate Committee Report]

Under the bill, generally effective for plan years beginning after June 30, 1986, no deduction is permitted for employer contributions to any group health plan if that plan or any other plan of the employer fails to provide qualified beneficiaries a continuation coverage election. The election must be provided for previously covered family members of deceased, divorced, or Medicare-eligible workers, employees who have separated from service (and their dependents), and certain children who would otherwise lose coverage under the terms of the plan upon attainment of majority.

In addition, no income exclusion is permitted under the bill for any highly compensated individual if the plan in which the individual participates or any other group health plan maintained by the employer fails to provide continuation coverage.

As under present law, a group health plan is any employer-provided plan to provide medical care to employees, former employees, or the families of such employees or former employees directly or through insurance reimbursement or otherwise.

Under the bill, no employer will be permitted to deduct contributions to any insured or self-insured group health plan (sec. 106) if that plan or any other group health plan maintained by the employer fails to provide qualified beneficiaries a continuation coverage election.

The bill generally requires that continuation coverage be provided under any employer-provided group health plan. However, no continuation coverage would be required in a plan established and maintained by (1) an employer that normally employed 25 or fewer employees during the preceding calendar year, (2) the Government of the United States, the government of any State or political subdivision thereof, or any agency or instrumentality of any the foregoing entities, or (3) a church or convention or association of churches, or a tax-exempt organization that is operated, supervised, or controlled by any of the foregoing.

Under the bill, any highly compensated individual covered by any insured or self-insured group health plan would be denied the income exclusion for employer contributions to the plan (sec. 106) if that plan, or any other group health plan maintained by the employer, fails to provide qualified beneficiaries a continuation coverage election.

The bill defines a highly compensated individual as any employee who is among the five highest-paid officers, a 10-percent shareholder, or among the 25-percent highest-paid employees.

Under the bill, all qualified beneficiaries who would otherwise lose coverage as a result of a qualifying event must have the right to elect, within the 60-day period beginning on the date of the qualifying event, to continue coverage. Qualifying events include (1) the death of the covered employee; (2) the separation from service of the covered employee (whether voluntary or involuntary); (3) the divorce or legal separation of the covered employee from the employee's spouse; (4) the covered employees's commencement of Medicare coverage; or (5) the cessation of dependent child coverage under the terms of the plan (e.g., upon attainment of majority).

* * * The committee intends that the employer should be required to provide notice of the election to all covered employees no later than the date on which the employee becomes entitled to coverage under the plan.

In addition, a qualified beneficiary must, under the bill, elect continuation coverage no later than 60 days after the date of the qualifying event. Provided the qualified beneficiary elects to continue coverage within the 60-day period, the continuation coverage must be effective as of the date of the qualifying event.

In general, the continuation coverage for which a qualified beneficiary must be offered an election is coverage identical to the coverage provided immediately before the qualifying event. For example, if, under the plan, the covered employee had the right to select among several levels of coverage, the qualified beneficiary generally would be entitled to continue whatever level of coverage the employee had selected for the beneficiary prior to the qualifying event.

That coverage could be modified by the employer if such coverage is modified for all similarly situated beneficiaries for whom a qualifying event has not occurred. In addition, if the plan otherwise permits employees and beneficiaries to modify coverage, the qualified beneficiary must be entitled to modify coverage at the same time and in the same manner as other similarly situated beneficiaries.

The applicable level of continuation coverage generally must be provided for a period not less than (1) 18 months immediately following the qualifying event, or (2) such shorter period elected by the qualified beneficiary. However, if the qualified beneficiary initially elects to continue coverage for less than 18 months, the beneficiary need not be granted a subsequent election to extend the coverage for the remainder of the 18-month period. This 18-month period includes, and is not in addition to, any continuation period presently permitted by the plan or required under local law. Thus, for example, if the plan presently provides that dependent coverage ceases one month after the date of an employee's death, the bill would require that beneficiaries be entitled to elect continuation coverage for up to 18 months following the date of death, not the 18-month period beginning with the actual cessation of coverage one month after the employee's death.

Similarly, if there are multiple "qualifying events," the 18-month period begins on the date of the earliest event. For example, if a covered employee terminates employment and is subsequently divorced one month later, the 18-month continuation period applicable to the divorced spouse commences on the date of termination rather than the divorce.

However, coverage need not be provided beyond the date on which the employer ceases to provide any group health plan to employees. If the employer maintains more than one plan, continuation must be provided so long as any plan is offered by the employer.

The bill authorizes the Secretary of the Treasury to prescribe rules defining the appropriate continuation coverage for qualified beneficiaries under a plan terminated in connection with a plant closing. The commitee intends that continuation coverage be required notwithstanding the plant closing if the employer continues to maintain any other health plan. The required continuation coverage generally would be that coverage in effect immediately prior to the closing. However, the regulations are to include rules precluding an employer from reducing or eliminating coverage in anticipation of the plant closing.

Under the bill, some or all of the cost of continuation coverage (including reasonable administrative costs of processing the election) could be charged to the qualified beneficiary. The entire premium could be charged to the qualified beneficiary whether or not the employer otherwise subsidizes some or all of the premiums for covered employees. However, in no event may the cost charged to the qualified beneficiary exceed 102 percent of the applicable premium. The applicable premium is defined as the cost to the plan for the period of coverage for a similarly situated beneficiary with respect to whom a qualifying event has not occurred (without regard to whether such cost is paid by the employer or employee).

In the case of a self-insured plan, the bill defines the applicable premium for any year as the cost for a similarly situated beneficiary for the preceding calendar year, adjusted to reflect cost-of-living increases as measured by the GNP deflator. If there has been a significant change affecting a self-insured plan (e.g., a modification of covered benefits, a significant change in the number or composition of the covered workforce, etc.), the employer must determine the cost under regulations to be prescribed by the Secretary of the Treasury, on the basis of a reasonable actuarial estimate.

If the qualified beneficiary elects to continue coverage within 60 days of the qualifying event, the coverage is effective as of the date of the qualifying event. A qualifying beneficiary who elects coverage may be charged for the cost of coverage during the 60-day period.

In addition, the employer may require the qualified beneficiary to pay the applicable premium either directly to the insurer, if any, or to the employer. However, at the election of the qualified beneficiary, premiums may be payable in monthly installments. Of course, a qualified beneficiary who fails to make required premium payments could be denied continuation coverage.

The bill also provides that continuation coverage may not be conditioned directly or indirectly upon insurability of the designated beneficiary.

The bill generally defines qualified beneficiaries to include the spouse and dependent children of an employee entitled to coverage under the terms of the group health plan. In addition, the covered employee is a qualified beneficiary entitled to elect continuation coverage upon termination of employment.

However, the provision intends to extend prior coverage rather than create new classes of covered employees. Thus, no employee, spouse, or child will be considered a qualified beneficiary unless, on the date before the qualifying event, that individual was a beneficiary under the plan. Thus, for example, no employee who had opted not to be covered by a contributory group health plan could elect continuation coverage upon termination of employment. Similarly, if a covered employee had elected not to receive dependent coverage, no spouse or child subsequently is entitled to elect continuation coverage upon the occurrence of a qualifying event.

If there are multiple "qualifying events," the status of an individual as a qualified beneficiary is determined on the day before the occurrence of the earliest qualifying event. For example, if a covered participant terminates employment without electing continuation coverage, no beneficiary could subsequently elect continuation coverage, e.g., upon the participant's death.

If there are multiple "qualified beneficiaries," only one election generally is required. Where the covered employee terminates employment, for example, no spouse or child would receive continuation coverage unless the employee elects to continue coverage. Similarly, upon the employee's death, divorce, or becoming eligible for Medicare, continuation coverage is to be provided only if the spouse so elects. In that instance, the spouse effectively decides whether coverage will be continued for the children.

The only exceptions to this rule occur where the child is the only qualified beneficiary (e.g., where the spouse is not entitled to coverage under the plan, or with respect to children attaining majority).

Effective date

The bill generally applies for plan years beginning after June 30, 1986. In the case of a group health plan maintained pursuant to one or more collective bargaining agreements, the bill does not apply to plan years beginning before the earlier of (1) the date the last of the collective bargaining agreements terminate, or (2) January 1, 1987.

[Conference Committee Report]

The conference agreement generally follows the House bill and the Senate amendment, by amending ERISA, the Code, and the Public Health Service Act. Under the agreement, the changes to the Code and ERISA do not apply to churches, Federal, State and local governments, and small employers. Small employers are defined as those with fewer than 20 employees. In addition, the amendments to the Public Health Service Act apply only with respect to State and local governments (other than those with fewer than 20 employees.)

To avoid the issuance of duplicate and perhaps inconsistent regulations, the conferees authorized the Secretary of Labor to promulgate regulations implementing the disclosure and reporting requirements, and the Secretary of Treasury to issue regulations defining required coverage, deductions, and income inclusions. The Secretary of Health and Human Services is to issue regulations regarding the requirement that State and local governments provide continuation coverage for qualified beneficiaries. The conferees intend that any regulations issued by the Secretary of Health and Human Services will conform (in terms of actual requirements) with those regulations issued by the Secretary of Treasury and Labor. Under the agreement, enforcement of the requirements imposed through the Public Health Service Act will be through suits for equitable relief filed by qualified beneficiaries. Of course, as under present law, all affected agencies will have the opportunity to comment before regulations are issued.

Sanctions for Noncompliance.—Any regulations issued pursuant to these changes are to be effective after the date of issuance. However, pending the promulgation of regulations, employers are required to operate in good faith compliance with a reasonable interpretation of these substantive rules, notice requirements, etc.

The conference agreement generally follows H.R. 3500 and the Senate amendment except that the only sanction imposed on covered State and local governments under the Public Health Service Act are suits for equitable relief.

Qualified Beneficiaries.—The conference agreement generally follows the House bill and the Senate amendment except that no continuation coverage is required for terminated employees if the termination occurs by reason of the employee's gross misconduct.

Type of Benefit Coverage.—The conference agreement generally follows the House bill with a modification so that the type of benefit coverage is identical, as of the time the coverage is being provided, to the coverage provided under the plan to similarly situated beneficiaries under the plan with regard to whom a qualifying event has not occurred.

Duration of Coverage.—The conference agreement generally follows Title IX of the Senate amendment, requiring that continuation coverage provided to widows, divorced spouses, spouses of Medicare-eligible employees, and dependent children who become ineligible for coverage under the plan be provided for 3 years, while coverage for terminated employees and employees with reduced hours must be provided for 16 months. The agreement provides that the coverage period begins with the date of the qualifying event. As under the House bill and Title IX of the Senate amendment, no coverage need be provided after (1) failure to make timely payment under the plan, (2) the qualified beneficiary is covered under another group health plan as a result of employment, reemployment, or remarriage, and (3) the qualified beneficiary becomes entitled to Medicare benefits. In addition, as under the House bill and Title VII of the Senate amendment, no coverage need be provided after the employer ceases to maintain any group health plan.

Cost of Coverage.—The conference agreement generally follows Title VII of the Senate amendment. For a self-insured plan, the conferees agreed that the "applicable" premium for any year generally is equal to a reasonable estimate of the cost of providing coverage for such period for a similarly situated beneficiary. The cost is to be determined on an actuarial basis and takes into account such factors as the Secretary may prescribe in regulations. Alternately, unless there has been a significant change affecting a self-insured plan (e.g., a modification of covered benefits, a significant change in the number or composition of the covered workforce, etc.), the employer may elect to use as the applicable premium, the cost for a similarly situated beneficiary for the preceding year, adjusted to reflect cost-of-living increases as measured by the GNP deflator.

In general, similarly situated individuals are those individuals defined by the plan (consistent with Treasury regulations) to be similarly situated and with respect to which no qualifying event has occurred. The Secretary of the Treasury is to define similarly situated individuals by taking into account the plan under which the coverage is provided (e.g., high or low option), the type of coverage (single or family coverage) and, if appropriate, regional differences in health costs. The conferees do not intend that similarly situated mean medically identical (for example, all employees with heart problems); nor do the conferees intend that plans can define similarly situated beneficiaries by reference to classifications that are in violation of Title VII of the Equal Pay Act.

In addition, the conferees intend that Treasury regulations defining a plan should preclude an employer from grouping employees to inappropriately increase the cost of continuation coverage for qualified beneficiaries who are rank-and-file employees (or their beneficiaries).

Notice Requirements.—The conference agreement generally follows the House bill. Thus, notice of the option to continue health coverage must be provided in the summary plan description. In addition, in the event of an employee's death, separation from service, or Medicare eligibility, the employer is required to notify the plan administrator within 30 days of the qualifying event who will in turn notify the qualified beneficiary within 14 days.

In the event of other qualifying events (e.g., divorce, legal separation, or the child's becoming ineligible) the employee or qualified beneficiary affected by that event is required to notify the plan administrator. Unless the qualified beneficiary is the party providing notice, the plan administrator is in turn required to notify the qualified beneficiary. The election period begins not later than the later of (1) the date on which coverage terminates, or (2) the date on which the qualified beneficiary receives notice of the right to elect continuation coverage. Any election by a qualified beneficiary is considered an election by other qualified beneficiaries who would otherwise lose coverage by reason of the same qualifying event.

The conferees intend that the Secretary of Labor will issue regulations defining what notice will be adequate for this provision. The conferees intend that notice by mail to the qualified beneficiary's last known address is to be adequate; however, mere posting is not to be adequate. In addition, in applying these requirements to multiemployer plans, the conferees intend that the Secretary of Labor should take into account the special problems faced by those plans.

Conversion Option.—The conference agreement generally follows the House bill and Title IX of the Senate amendment. Under the agreement, a qualified beneficiary must be offered a conversion option from any plan (including a self-insured plan) only if such an option is otherwise available under the plan to other participants.

Effective date

These provisions are effective for plan years beginning after June 30, 1986. In the case of a group health plan maintained pursuant to one or more collective bargaining agreements, the bill does not apply to plan years beginning before the later of (1) the date the last of the collective bargaining agreements terminate, or (2) January 1, 1987.

[ERISA Sec. 602]

[¶ 15,045F.098]

Committee Reports on P.L. 104-188 (Small Business Job Protection Act)

[House Committee Report]

Health care continuation rules (ERISA)

The bill amends the Code (sec. 4980B), title I of the Employee Retirement Income Security Act (sec. 602), and the Public Health Service Act (sec.

2202(2)(A)) to limit the continuation coverage in such cases to no more than 36 months.

Effective date

The provision is effective for plan years beginning after December 31, 1989.

[Conference Committee Report]

Senate Amendment

The Senate amendment is the same as the House bill.

Conference Agreement

The conference agreement follows the House bill and the Senate amendment * * *.

[¶ 15,045F.099]

Committee Reports on P.L. 104-191 (Health Insurance Portability Act)

[Senate Amendment]

The Senate amendment modifies the COBRA rules by clarifying that the extended maxium COBRA coverage period of 29 months in cases of disability also applies to the disabled qualified beneficiary of the covered employee. * * *

The Senate amendment also modified the definition of qualified beneficiary to include a child born to or placed for adoption with the covered employee during the period of COBRA coverage. Consequently, since the health care availability provisions in the Senate amendment require group health plans to allow participants to change their coverage status (i.e., to change from individual coverage to family coverage, or to add on the new child) upon the birth or adoption of a new child, COBRA participants would also be allowed to change their coverage status upon the birth or adoption of a new child.

[Conference Committee Report]

The conference agreement follows the Senate amendment, except the extended period of COBRA coverage in cases of disability applies if the disability exists at any time during the first 60 days of COBRA coverage.

[Senate Labor Committee Report]

Modifications improving access for disabled individuals.—Under current rules, individuals who have coverage through firms with 20 or more workers and lose their coverage because they leave their job, or for certain other reasons, may extend their coverage for an additional 18 months by paying 102 percent of the normal premium. Disabled workers may extend their coverage for an additional 11 months if they pay up to 150 percent of the premium for coverage beyond the initial 18 months. The modification contained in section 121 would allow individuals who have disabled family members or who became disabled at any time during their coverage under an initial COBRA extension period to extend their coverage for the additional 11-month period currently granted only to workers who are disabled at the time they lose their coverage.

[Conference Committee Report]

[No conference report found.]

[¶ 15,045F.10]

Committee Report on P.L. 99-514 (Tax Reform Act of 1986)

[Conference Committee Report]

The conference agreements adopts the following technical corrections to the continuing health care provisions of COBRA.

a. Notification requirement.—The conference agreement establishes a 60-day notification period for divorced or legally separated spouses of covered employees, or dependent children ceasing to be dependent children under the generally applicable requirements of the plan, to notify the plan administrator of a qualifying event entitling the spouse or dependent children to continuation health coverage.

b. Maximum period of continuation coverage.—The conference agreement clarifies that a qualified beneficiary may have more than one qualifying event which entitles the beneficiary to continuation coverage, but in no event may the coverage period with respect to such events generally exceed a 36-month period. The second qualifying event must take place during the period of coverage of the first qualifying event to be eligible for a total of 36 months continuation coverage beginning from the date of the first qualifying event.

c. Election of coverage.—The conference agreement clarifies that each qualified beneficiary is entitled to a separate election of continuation coverage. For example, if a covered employee does not elect continuation coverage, the conferees intend that the spouse or dependent children are entitled to elect such coverage. Moreover, even if the employee elects certain coverage, the spouse or dependents may elect different coverage.

d. Failure to pay premium.—The conference agreement provides that the grace period for the failure to pay premiums is the longest of (1) 30 days, (2) the period the plan allows employees for failure to pay premiums, or (3) the period the insurance company allows the plan or the employer for failure to pay premiums.

e. Type of coverage.—The conference agreement provides that, for all purposes, qualified beneficiaries are to be treated under the plan in the same manner as similarly situated beneficiaries for whom a qualifying event has not taken place. For example, if the plan provides for an open enrollment period, then qualified beneficiaries are to be permitted to make elections during the open enrollment period in the same manner as active employees. Thus, an individual who is a qualified beneficiary by reason of being a spouse of a covered employee would have the same rights as active employees during an open enrollment period and would not be limited to the rights of spouses of covered employees.

The conference agreement defines health benefits to mean health benefit plans, including dental and vision care (within the meaning of sec. 213 of the Code). The conferees do not intend that an employer could compel a qualified beneficiary to pay for noncore benefits (such as dental and vision care) even if active employees are required to purchase coverage for such benefits under the plan.

[ERISA Sec. 607]

[¶ 15,046F.10]

Committee Reports on P.L. 104-191 (Health Insurance Portability and Accountability Act)

[House Committee Report]

* * *

Effective Date

The provisions defining long-term care insurance contracts and qualified long-term care services apply to contracts issued after December 31, 1996. Any contract issued before January 1, 1997, that met the long-term care insurance requirements in the State in which the policy was sitused at the time it was issued is treated as a long-term care insurance contract, and services provided under or reimbursed by the contract are treated as qualified long-term care services.

* * *

[Conference Committee Report]

* * *

Health care continuation rules.—The health care continuation rules do not apply to coverage under a plan, substantially all of the coverage under which is for qualified long-term care services.

* * *

[Senate Amendment]

* * *

The Senate amendment also modifies the definition of qualified beneficiary to include a child born to or placed for adoption with the covered employee during the period of COBRA coverage. Consequently, since the health care availability provisions in the Senate amendment require group health plans to allow participants to change their coverage status (i.e., to change from individual coverage to family coverage, or to add on the new child) upon the birth or adoption of a new child, COBRA participants would also be allowed to change their coverage status upon the birth or adoption of a new child.

* * *

[Conference Committee Report]

The conference agreement follows the Senate amendment, * * *

[ERISA Sec. 609]

[¶ 15,046M.098]

Committee Reports on P.L. 104-193 (Personal Responsibility and Work Opportunity Reconciliation Act)

[House Bill]

This provision expands the definition of medical child support order in ERISA to clarify that any judgement [sic], decree, or order that is issued by a court of competent jurisdiction or by an administrative process has the force and effect of law.

[Senate Amendment]

Same.

[Conference Amendment]

The conference agreement follows the House bill and the Senate amendment.

[¶ 15,046M.10]

Conference Committee Report on P.L. 103-66 (Omnibus Budget Reconciliation Act of 1993)

. . . relating to medical child support orders—see ¶ 15,040.08.

[ERISA Sec. 711]

[¶ 15,050J.10]

Committee Reports on P.L. 104-204 (Mental Health Parity Act of 1996)

[Conference Committee Report]

Conference Agreement

The conference agreement includes the Senate amendment with modifications, including the deletion of offsets. It incorporates the requirements of the provision and the authority to enforce the requirements into the new part 7 of subtitle B of ERISA and the new title XXVII of the Public Health Service Act as established by P.L. 104-191. It does not include the exception to the requirement for the 48-hour or 96-hour minimum stay in the case that the plan provides for post-delivery follow-up care. It adds a prohibition that a health plan cannot restrict benefits for any portion of the required minimum 48-hour or 96-hour stay in a manner which is less favorable than the benefits providing for any preceding portion of such stay. In addition, the conference agreement provides that nothing in this provision is intended to be construed as preventing a group health plan or issuer from imposing coinsurance, deductibles, or other cost-sharing in relation to benefits for hospital lengths of stay in connection with childbirth for a mother or newborn child under the plan (or under health insurance coverage offered in connection with a group health plan), except that such coinsurance or other cost-sharing for any portion of a period within a hospital length of stay required under subsection (a) may not be greater than such coinsurance or cost-sharing for any preceding portion of such stay. It is the intent of the conferees that cost-sharing not be used in a manner that circumvents the objectives of this title. It provides for a modification to the notice requirements by conforming them to the summary of material modifications under ERISA. In general, it conforms the provision relating to preemption to State laws to the Health Insurance Portability and Accountability Act of 1996. Notwithstanding section 731(a)(1) of ERISA and sections 2723(a)(1) and 2762 of the Public Health Service Act, the new provisions shall not preempt a State law that requires health insurance coverage to include coverage for maternity and pediatric care in accordance with guidelines established by the American College of Obstetricians and Gynecologists, the American Academy of Pediatrics, or other established professional medical associations. In addition, those sections shall not be construed as superseding a State law that leaves decisions regarding the appropriate hospital length of stay in connection with childbirth entirely to the attending provider in consultation with the mother. In addition, it is the intent of the conferees that, consistent with section 704 (redesignated as section 731) of ERISA and section 2723 of the Public Health Service Act, the application of the preemption provision should permit the operation of any State law or provision which requires more favorable treatment of maternity coverage under health insurance coverage than that required under this title.

It is the intent of the conferees that health plans have sufficient flexibility to encourage or specify that attending providers follow nationally recognized guidelines for maternal and perinatal care in determining when early discharge is medically appropriate.

Throughout the title, the conferees have used the term "hospital length of stay" to indicate that a requirement for coverage of a 48-hour stay following vaginal delivery and a 96-hour length of stay following a cesarean section delivery is triggered by any delivery in connection with hospital care, regardless of whether the delivery is in a hospital inpatient or outpatient setting.

It is the intent of the conferees that a detailed series of conforming changes shall be made as soon as possible to the Internal Revenue Code, specifically subtitle K of the Internal Revenue Code of 1986 (as added by section 401(a) of the Health Insurance Portability Accountability Act of 1996), in order to fully implement these provisions as part of chapter 100 of the Code.

[ERISA Sec. 712]

[¶ 15,050K.045]

Committee Report on P.L. 109-432 (Tax Relief and Health Care Act of 2006)

[Joint Committee on Taxation Report]

[Parity in the application of certain limits to mental health benefits]

The provision extends the present-law Code excise tax for failure to comply with the mental health parity requirements through December 31, 2007. It also extends the ERISA and PHSA requirements through December 31, 2007.

Effective Date

The provision is effective on the date of enactment.

[¶ 15,050K.05]

Committee Reports on P.L. 108-357 (American Jobs Creation Act of 2004)

The conference agreement extends the ERISA and PHSA provisions relating to mental health parity to benefits for services furnished before January 1, 2006. The conference agreement also extends the Code provisions relating to mental health parity to benefits for services furnished on or after the date of enactment and before January 1, 2006. Thus, the excise tax on failures to meet the requirements imposed by the Code provisions does not apply after December 31, 2003, and before the date of enactment.

Effective Date

The provision is effective on the date of enactment.—**Conference Committee Report (H.R. CONF. REP. NO. 108-696).**

[¶ 15,050K.10]

Committee Reports on P.L. 104-204 (Mental Health Parity Act of 1996)

[Conference Committee Report]

Conference Agreement

The conference agreement includes the Senate amendment with modifications. It incorporates the requirement into the new part 7 of subtitle B of title I of ERISA and the new title XXVII of the Public Health Service Act as established by Public Law 104-191. The construction clause has been modified to state that nothing in this section shall be construed as—

(1) requiring a group health plan (or health insurance coverage offered in connection with such a plan) to provide any mental health benefits; or

(2) in the case of such a plan or coverage that provides such mental health benefits, as affecting the terms and conditions (including cost sharing, the limits on numbers of visits or days of coverage, and requirements relating to medical necessity) relating to the amount, duration, or scope of mental health benefits under the plan or coverage, except as specifically provided in regard to parity in the imposition of aggregate lifetime limits and annual limits for mental health benefits.

This language affirms the intent of conferees that group health plans and issuers retain the flexibility, consistent with the requirements of the Act, to define the scope of benefits, establish cost-sharing requirements, and to impose limits on hospital days and out-patient visits. Parity of mental health services with medical and surgical services defined under a group health plan is limited solely to any aggregate dollar life-time limit and any annual dollar limit under such a plan. The conference agreement clarifies that the requirements apply to each group health plan, and, in the case of a group health plan that offers two or more benefit packages, the parity requirements shall be applied separately with respect to each such option. In addition, the conference agreement applies an exemption to small employers as defined in the Health Insurance Portability and Accountability Act; adds certain definitions; and applies the requirements of the provision to group health plan years beginning on or after January 1, 1998. The agreement does not include the Senate language relating to effective dates for the Federal Employee Health Benefit Plan.

It is the intent of the conferees that a detailed series of conforming changes shall be made as soon as possible to the Internal Revenue Code, specifically subtitle K of the Internal Revenue Code of 1986 (as added by section 401(a) of the Health Insurance Portability and Accountability Act of 1996), in order to fully implement these provisions as part of chapter 100 of the Code.

The conferees intend that a limit be considered to apply to "substantially all medical and surgical benefits" if it applies to at least two-thirds of all the medical and surgical benefits covered under the group health plan's benefit package.

It is the intent of the conferees that, consistent with section 704 (redesignated as section 731) of ERISA and section 2723 of the Public Health Service Act, the application of the preemption provision should permit the operation of any State law or provision which requires more favorable treatment of mental health benefits under health insurance coverage than that required under this section.

[ERISA Sec. 1012]

[¶ 15,060.10]

Committee Report on P.L. 93-406 (Employee Retirement Income Security Act of 1974)

[Conference Committee Explanation]

Variations.—Under the conference substitute, a variation is to be available with respect to the vesting schedule (for benefits attributable to employer contributions) and the accrued benefit rules for plans in existence on January 1, 1974. Under this procedure, a variation is to be allowed only if it is found by the Secretary of Labor that application of the rules of the bill would increase the cost of the plan to such an extent that there would be a substantial danger that the plan would be terminated, or that there would be a substantial reduction in benefits provided under the plan, or in the compensation of the employees. Also, it would have to be determined that the application of the vesting schedule requirements, or accrued benefit requirements, or discontinuance of the plan, would be adverse to the interest of the plan participants as a whole. Finally, it would have to be determined that the hardship described above could not be sufficiently mitigated by the granting of a funding variance.

The variation with respect to benefit accruals is not to apply for any year except years (not in excess of 7) during which the variation is in effect. (For example, there could be no variation with respect to the rules for benefits accrued in the past.)

No plan may receive a vesting variation unless application is made (in accordance with regulations to be prescribed by the Secretary of Labor or his delegate) within two years after the date of enactment of this bill. The variation would be granted for an initial period not to exceed 4 years. Plans can receive one additional variation (for a period not to exceed 3 years), but application for the additional variation would have to be made at least one year prior to the expiration of the initial variation period.

During the period when a variation is in effect, there can be no plan amendment which has the effect of increasing plan liabilities because of benefit increases, changes in accruals, or changes in the rate of vesting, except to a de minimis extent (in accordance with regulations to be prescribed by the Secretary of Labor).

* * *

[ERISA Sec. 1032]

[¶ 15,070.10]

Committee Report on P.L. 93-406 (Employee Retirement Income Security Act of 1974)

[Conference Committee Explanation]

—* * * The Social Security Administration is to maintain records of the retirement plans in which individuals have vested benefits, and is to provide this information to participants and beneficiaries on their request and also on their application for Social Security benefits.

[ERISA Sec. 3001]

[¶ 15,110.08]

Committee Report on P.L. 100-203 (Omnibus Budget Reconciliation Act of 1987)

For the Committee Report on P.L. 100-203, relating to the coordination of the IRC and ERISA, see ¶ 14,730.085.

[¶ 15,110.10]

Committee Report on P.L. 93-406 (Employee Retirement Income Security Act of 1974)

[Conference Committee Explanation]

The administration of qualified plans is separated into two stages: first, the stage when the plan seeks from the Internal Revenue Service initial qualification of entitlement to special tax benefits under the Internal Revenue Code; second, the operational stage with respect to the continued eligibility of the plan for the special tax benefits.

Initial stage jurisdiction.—In determining whether a pension, profit-sharing, or stock bonus plan or a trust which is a part of such a plan, is initially entitled to the special tax benefits provided under the tax law, the Secretary of the Treasury is to require that the person applying for the initial qualification of the plan is to provide, in addition to any materials and information which would generally be necessary for the administration of the tax laws, such other forms and information as may reasonably be made available at the time of the determination as the Secretary of Labor may require. The Secretary of the Treasury is also to require that the applicant for a determination provide evidence that any employee who is an interested party with respect to the plan has been notified of the request for a determination. Also the Secretary of the Treasury is to notify the Secretary of Labor and the Pension Benefit Guaranty Corporation when he receives an application for a determination as to the tax status of a plan.

The Secretary of the Treasury when he makes a determination with respect to a plan or trust is to notify the Secretary of Labor of his determination and furnish to the Secretary of Labor the forms and information submitted for the Secretary of Labor. For this purpose a determination includes a determination that a plan is, or is not, qualified for the special tax benefits under the Internal Revenue Code. The Secretary of the Treasury is also to notify the Secretary of Labor if a request for a determination is withdrawn.

Under the conference substitute, the Secretary of the Treasury is to afford the Secretary of Labor an opportunity to comment on the initial determination in any case involving the participation or vesting standards in which the Secretary of Labor requests such an opportunity. It is expected that the two departments will set up procedures implementing this procedure in a manner which affords the Secretary of Labor an ample opportunity to comment but which does not cause undue delay in the granting of initial determinations. A request by the Secretary of Labor to comment upon an application for an initial determination is to be made only upon the request (in writing) of the Pension Benefit Guaranty Corporation or on the request of 10 employees (or 10 percent of the employees if lesser) who would be viewed as interested parties under the plan. A copy of the request submitted to the Secretary of Labor is to be transmitted by him to the Secretary of the Treasury within 5 business days of its receipt.

If the Secretary of Labor does not submit comments on behalf of such groups of employees within 30 days after receiving a petition from the necessary number of interested employees, the Secretary of the Treasury is to afford these interested employees a reasonable opportunity to comment upon the initial request for a determination. The above procedure for enabling employees to comment upon an application for a determination is not the exclusive means by which employees may participate in the determination proceedings. Employees may of course proceed on their own through the declaratory judgment provisions which are provided in the bill. The Pension Benefit Guaranty Corporation and the Secretary of Labor (upon petition by the required number of employees) may intervene in any declaratory judgment proceedings in the Tax Court whether the proceedings are brought on behalf of the employer or interested employees. In addition, the Pension Benefit Guaranty Corporation is to be entitled to bring a suit for a declaratory judgment under rules to be prescribed by the Tax Court.

If a plan is qualified by the Secretary of the Treasury, the plan is to be treated as meeting the initial requirements of the Secretary of Labor with respect to participation and vesting.

The above outlined procedures apply not only to the initial qualification of a plan which seeks the special tax benefits provided under the Internal Revenue Code but apply to a request for an IRS determination with respect to any amendment to the terms of a plan or a trust which seeks a favorable determination from the Internal Revenue Service.

[ERISA Sec. 3002]

[¶ 15,120.10]

Committee Report on P.L. 93-406 (Employee Retirement Income Security Act of 1974)

[Conference Committee Explanation]

Operational stage jurisdiction.—The conference substitute also provides procedures for the exercise of the respective jurisdictional authority of the departments with respect to plans qualified for special tax treatment under the Internal Revenue Code during their operation. The Secretary of the Treasury in carrying out the administration of the Internal Revenue Code with respect to any plan or trust is to examine the plan to determine whether the plan satisfies the requirements relating to minimum participation standards and minimum vesting standards (in secs. 410(a) and 411 of the Code).

The Secretary of the Treasury is to notify the Secretary of Labor before commencing any proceedings to determine whether the plan or trust is in compliance with the minimum vesting and participation standards. While the notice need not be made prior to the time the Internal Revenue Service begins an audit or a review of a plan to verify that the minimum standards have been satisfied, it is expected that if in the course of a review or audit doubts or questions are raised by the Internal Revenue Service as to whether the plan has met the minimum standards, the Secretary of the Treasury is to notify the Secretary of Labor. Notification is to be made prior to the time the Internal Revenue Service issues a 30-day letter of an intention to disqualify the plan or trust. Except in cases of jeopardy the Secretary of the Treasury is not to issue a determination that the trust or plan does not satisfy the minimum standards until the expiration of a period of 60 days after the date on which he notifies the Secretary of Labor. This period of time is provided for the Secretary of Labor so that, if he chooses to do so, he may examine the plan to determine whether he should begin to take any action to compel compliance under those portions of the participation and vesting provisions of the bill in which he has jurisdiction or to coordinate any action he may be required to take by reason of a complaint from a participant or beneficiary. This 60-day period may be extended by the Secretary of the Treasury if he determines that an extension of this period would enable the Secretary of Labor to obtain compliance with the requirements of the law during this extended period. In order to assist the Secretary of Labor in deciding whether he should seek compliance with the requirements of the law the Secretary of the Treasury is to provide the Secretary of Labor with copies of any notices which he issues to the plan administrator with respect to the minimum participation and vesting standards.

The Secretary of the Treasury in administering the provisions relating to taxes on the failure to meet minimum funding standards (sec. 4971 of the Internal Revenue Code) is to notify the Secretary of Labor before imposing any tax on an employer. In addition, prior to the imposition of the tax, in other than jeopardy situations, the Secretary of the Treasury is to afford the Secretary of Labor an opportunity to comment on the appropriateness of imposing the tax. After consultation with the Secretary of Labor, the Secretary of the Treasury may in appropriate cases waive or abate the 100 percent excise tax on failure to satisfy the minimum funding standards. In order to coordinate their respective responsibilities under the funding standards, it is anticipated that both Secretaries will consult with each other as is needed with respect to the provisions relating to minimum funding standards, both those provided in the Internal Revenue Code and the funding standards provided by title I. As part of this coordination, at the request of the Secretary of Labor or the Pension Benefit Guaranty Corporation, the Internal Revenue Service is to initiate an immediate investigation with respect to any liability for the tax on failure to meet the minimum funding standards.

If the Secretary of Labor or the Pension Benefit Guaranty Corporation seek compliance on any case involving the construction or application of the minimum participation, vesting or funding standards, a reasonable opportunity is to be afforded to the Secretary of the Treasury to review and comment upon any proposed pleadings or briefs before they are filed. Of course, the Secretary of Labor need not obtain the approval of the Secretary of the Treasury and the Secretary of the Treasury may intervene and file his own pleadings or briefs in any case.

The Secretary of the Treasury in carrying out the provisions relating to tax on prohibited transactions (sec. 4975 of the Internal Revenue Code) is to inform the Secretary of Labor before imposing the tax under that section. In addition, the Secretary of Labor is to be afforded an opportunity, in other than jeopardy situations to comment on the appropriateness of imposing the tax. After consultation with the Secretary of Labor, the Secretary of the Treasury may in appropriate cases waive or abate the 100 percent excise tax on failure to correct a self-dealing violation. It also is anticipated that both Secretaries will consult as is needed with respect to the provisions relating to prohibited transactions (including the exemptions which may be provided therefrom) in order to coordinate the rules applicable under these standards.To best coordinate these rules the two Secretaries may want to set up a board to review and coordinate these rules. As part of this coordination, the Internal Revenue Service at the request of the Secretary of Labor or the Pension Benefit Guaranty Corporation is to initiate an immediate investigation with respect to the liability of any person for the tax on prohibited transactions.

[ERISA Sec. 3003]

[¶ 15,130.10]

Committee Report on P.L. 93-406 (Employee Retirement Income Security Act of 1974)

See Committee Report at ¶ 15,120.10.

[ERISA Sec. 3004]

[¶ 15,140.10]

Committee Report on P.L. 93-406 (Employee Retirement Income Security Act of 1974)

See Committee Reports at ¶ 15,110.10 and 15,120.10.

[ERISA Sec. 3021]

[¶ 15,150.10]

Committee Report on P.L. 93-406 (Employee Retirement Income Security Act of 1974)

[Conference Committee Explanation]

Joint task force and studies.—* * *

Under the conference substitute the staffs of the Committee on Ways and Means and the Committee on Education and Labor of the House, the Joint Committee on Internal Revenue Taxation, and the Committee on Finance and the Committee on Labor and Public Welfare of the Senate are to carry out duties assigned to the Joint Pension Task Force. By agreement among the Chairmen of these committees, the Joint Pension Task Force is to be furnished with office space, clerical personnel, actuarial and other consultants, and the supplies and equipment which are necessary for the Task Force to carry out its duties. The Joint Pension Task Force is authorized to engage in specified studies and make a report to the abovementioned committees within 24 months after the date of enactment of the bill. In addition, the Joint Pension Task Force is to study any other matter which any of the committees referred to above may refer to it.

[ERISA Sec. 3022]

[¶ 15,160.09]

Committee Report on P.L. 94-455 (Tax Reform Act of 1976)

[Conference Committee Report]

House Bill

No provision.

Senate amendment

The Senate amendment establishes a 15-member Commission on Expanded Stock Ownership to study broadening stock ownership through employee stock ownership plans (ESOPs) and other means. A final report is to be made to the President and the Congress not later than March 30, 1978.

Conference agreement

The conference agreement omits the Senate amendment; however the conference agreement changes the name of the existing Joint Pension Task Force to the Joint Pension, Profit-Sharing, and Employee Stock Ownership Plan Task Force, and provides that the Task Force is to study employee stock ownership plans. The Task Force, which may consult others who have information concerning employee stock ownership plans, is to report its findings to the House Committee on Ways and Means and the Senate Committee on Finance by March 31, 1978.

[¶ 15,160.10]

Committee Report on P.L. 93-406 (Employee Retirement Income Security Act of 1974)

[Conference Committee Explanation]

Joint task force and studies.—* * *

The Joint Pension Task Force is specifically authorized to engage in four studies. First, it is to study and review the three vesting alternatives in the bill to determine the extent of discrimination, if any, among employees in various age groups resulting from the application of these provisions. (The results of this study are to be reported only to the tax committees.) Second, it is to study the means of providing for the portability of pension rights among different pension plans. Third, it is to study the appropriate treatment under the termination insurance provisions of the Act for plans established and maintained by small employers. Fourth, it is to study the effects and desirability of the pre-emption of State law provisions of the bill. In addition elsewhere in this statement it is indicated that the Joint Pension Task Force is to study the effect of the rules in this bill limiting the extent to which antidiscrimination rules may be enforced through additional requirements as to early vesting and the effect on benefits and costs of integrating social security benefits with the benefits payable under retirement plans.

[ERISA Sec. 3031]

[¶ 15,170.10]

Committee Report on P.L. 93-406 (Employee Retirement Income Security Act of 1974)

[Conference Committee Explanation]

Joint task force and studies.—* * * The substitute agreed to by the conferees also provides for a congressional study of retirement plans established and maintained, or financed, by the Government of the United States, by any State (including the District of Columbia), or any political subdivision thereof. The study is to include an analysis of the adequacy of existing levels of participation, vesting, and financing arrangements; existing fiduciary standards; and the unique circumstances affecting mobility of government employees and individuals employed under Federal procurement contracts. In considering whether plans are adequately financed consideration shall be given to the necessity for minimum funding standards as well as the taxing power of the government maintaining the plan. This study is to be submitted not later than December 31, 1976, by the Committee on Education and Labor and the Committee on Ways and Means to the House of Representatives and by the Committee on Finance and the Committee on Labor and Public Welfare to the Senate.

[ERISA Sec. 3032]

[¶ 15,180.10]

Committee Report on P.L. 93-406 (Employee Retirement Income Security Act of 1974)

[Conference Committee Explanation]

Protection of pension rights under Government contracts.—Under the conference substitute, the Secretary of Labor is to undertake a study of steps which can be taken to ensure that professional, scientific, technical, and other personnel employed under Federal contracts are protected against loss of their pensions resulting from job transfers or loss of employment. The Secretary of Labor is to report to Congress on this subject within two years after the date of enactment [September 2, 1974] of the bill and is, if feasible, to develop recommendations for Federal procurement regulations to safeguard pension rights in the situations in question within one year after filing his report. These regulations are to become effective unless either House of Congress adopts a resolution of disapproval within 120 days after the proposed regulations are submitted to the Congress.

Any such disapproval is to be referred to the Labor Committee of the relevant House.

[ERISA Sec. 3041]

[¶ 15,210.10]

Committee Report on P.L. 93-406 (Employee Retirement Income Security Act of 1974)

[Conference Committee Explanation]

Enrollment of Actuaries

Standards.—* * *

The conference substitute largely follows the provisions of the House bill. With respect to persons applying for enrollment before January 1, 1976, the substitute provides that the standards and qualifications are to include a requirement for "responsible actuarial experience relating to pension plans," and deletes the requirement for experience in the "administration" of pension plans. This change is intended only to clarify the application of the standards before January 1, 1976, so that persons who apply for enrollment before that date have responsible actuarial experience (and not only administrative experience) relating to pension plans. With respect to persons who perform actuarial services for smaller and simpler plans, the conferees anticipate that, to the extent feasible, the standards for enrollment will make it possible to use standard actuarial tables and standard earnings assumptions whether or not the actuary's training includes the highest level of actuarial skills. The limited number of persons with a high level of actuarial skills makes it desirable that the standards acceptable for persons examining smaller and simpler plans need not be as restrictive as in the case of those examining the larger plans.

The conference substitute also provides that actuaries may be enrolled on a temporary basis for a limited period. This makes it clear that actuaries can be enrolled almost immediately after enactment of the bill in order that enrolled actuaries will be available to help plans meet the requirements of the new law. The conferees intend that such temporary enrollment is not to be in lieu of any special enrollment standards for persons who apply for enrollment before January 1, 1976, but is only to allow immediate enrollment before the final standards are established.

Procedures.—* * *

The joint board also is to administer the standards for disenrollment of actuaries and is to write the regulations on enrollment (to be approved by the two Secretaries or their delegates). As under the House bill, an actuary can be disenrolled only after notice and hearing, and if there is a finding that he does not comply with the governing rules or regulations, or is shown not to be competent in actuarial matters.

[ERISA Sec. 3042]

[¶ 15,220.10]

Committee Report on P.L. 93-406 (Employee Retirement Income Security Act of 1974)

[Conference Committee Explanation]

Procedures.—* * *

Under the conference substitute, a single standard for enrollment is achieved by directing the Secretary of Labor and the Secretary of the Treasury to establish a joint board which will set standards for enrollment and enroll actuaries to practice before the Department of Labor and Internal Revenue Service. In order that enrollment might begin as soon as possible, it is provided that an interim joint board is to be established no later than the last day of the first month following the date of enactment [i.e., no later than October 31, 1974].

[ERISA Sec. 4001]

[¶ 15,310.07]

Committee Report on P.L. 100-203 (Omnibus Budget Reconciliation Act of 1987)

For the Committee Report on P.L. 100-203 relating to reporting requirements, see ¶ 15,440.085.

[¶ 15,310.09]

Committee Report on P.L. 103-465 (General Agreement on Tariffs and Trade (GATT); Retirement Protection Act)

[House Committee Report]

Contributing sponsor

The bill defines contributing sponsor for purposes of title IV of ERISA to mean the person responsible for making minimum funding contributions to the plan under section 302 of ERISA or section 412 of the Code, without regard to the controlled group rules. All members of a contributing sponsor's controlled group remain liable for making the minimum funding contribution.

Effective date

The provision is effective as if included in the Pension Protection Act of 1987.

[¶ 15,310.095]

Committee Reports on P.L. 99-272 (Consolidated Omnibus Budget Reconciliation Act)

[House Committee Report]

"Substantial employer" means, with respect to a single-employer plan year, contributing sponsors who are members of the same affiliated [controlled] (H. Cong. Res. 305) group and whose required contributions equal or exceed ten percent of all required contributions.

"Contributing sponsor" means, with respect to a single-employer plan, a person who is responsible for meeting the minimum funding requirements * * * or a member of such person's controlled group that has employed a significant number of plan participants while such person was so responsible for funding.

"Controlled group" means a group consisting of a person and all other persons under common control with such person under regulations consistent and coextensive with regulations prescribed under section 414 [(b) and] (H. Cong. Res. 305) (c) of the Internal Revenue Code.

"Single-employer plan" means any plan which is not a multiemployer plan.

* * *

"Amount of unfunded guaranteed benefits" means the excess of (A) the actuarial present value of benefits guaranteed under this title based on assumptions prescribed by the PBGC for purposes of section 4044, over (B) the current value of the assets of the plan which are allocated to those benefits in accordance with section 4044.

"Amount of unfunded benefit entitlements [commitments]" means the excess of (A) the actuarial present value of benefit entitlements [commitments] based on assumptions prescribed by the Corporation for purposes of section 4044 over (B) the current value of the assets of the plan which are allocated to those benefits in accordance with section 4044.

"Outstanding amount of benefit entitlements [commitments]" means the excess of (A) the actuarial present value of benefit entitlements [commitments] over (B) the actuarial present value of benefits guaranteed under Title IV of ERISA or to which assets of the plan are allocated in accordance with section 4044.

"Person" has the same meaning as under title I of ERISA.

"Affected party" means the PBGC, a participant, beneficiary of a deceased participant, beneficiary who is an alternate payee under a qualified domestic relations order, employee organization representing participants and any person designated to receive notice on behalf of an affected party.

Benefit commitments are defined under the conference agreement as all guaranteed benefits (including qualified preretirement survivor annuities) and all benefits that would be guaranteed but for the insurance limits on the amounts or value of the benefit, or the length of time that the benefit has been in effect. In addition, benefit commitments include certain additional benefits for which a participant has satisfied all conditions of entitlement prior to termination. These additional benefits, irrespective of whether they are guaranteed, are (1) early retirement supplements or subsidies, and (2) plant closing benefits.

[¶ 15,310.10]

Committee Report on P.L. 96-364 (Multiemployer Pension Plan Amendments Act of 1980)

[Senate Committee Report]

Definition of multiemployer plan.—Present law.—Under present law, a plan is a multiemployer plan for a year if (1) more than one employer is required to contribute to the plan, (2) the plan is maintained pursuant to a collective bargaining agreement between employee representatives and more than one employer, (3) the amount of contributions made under the plan for the year by each employer is less than 50 percent of the aggregate employer contributions for that year (unless a special rule is satisfied), (4) benefits under the plan are payable to each participant without regard to the cessation of contributions by the employer of the participant except to the extent the benefits accrued because of service with the employer before the employer was required to contribute to the plan, and (5) the plan satisfies other requirements imposed by Labor Department regulations.[1]

All corporations, which are members of a controlled group of corporations, are treated as a single employer in determining the status of a plan as a multiemployer plan for purposes of the tax law.

Reasons for change.—The Committees believe that the definition of a multiemployer plan under ERISA which is limited to a plan in which (1) no employer contributes more than 50 percent of the total employer contributions for the year

[1] See DOL Regs. § 2510.3-37.

and (2) employers share liability for participants' benefits accrued for service while the employer maintained the plan creates two major problems. First, not all plans that share the basic characteristics of multiemployer plans (i.e., plans to which more than one employer is required to contribute and which are maintained pursuant to a collective bargaining agreement) are considered multiemployer plans under the definition presently in ERISA. Second, a plan could move in and out of multiemployer plan status from year to year. The Committees have determined to remove these limitations from the definition of multiemployer plan so that generally plans which share the basic characteristics of multiemployer plans are treated consistently under the law.

Explanation of provisions

Under the bill, the test relating to proportionate employer contributions (the 50-percent test) is deleted, and the test relating to continuity of benefits in the event of a cessation of employer contributions is preserved in the minimum vesting standard of ERISA. The bill provides that all trades and businesses (whether or not incorporated) under common control are considered a single employer for purposes of testing the status of a plan as a multiemployer plan. In addition, the bill provides that a plan continues to be a multiemployer plan after its termination if it was a multiemployer plan for the plan year ending before its termination date.

A plan which is a single-employer plan under present law (even though more than one employer maintains the plan) and which has paid PBGC premiums for the three plan years preceding the date of enactment as a single-employer plan is permitted to irrevocably elect to be considered a single-employer plan where the plan would otherwise be a multiemployer plan under the bill.

Effective date

The provision will apply upon enactment, except that the present law definition will continue for plan years beginning before enactment.

[ERISA Sec. 4002]

[¶ 15,320.07]

Committee Report on P.L. 109-280 (Pension Protection Act of 2006)

[Joint Committee on Taxation Report]

The bill provides that, in carrying out its functions, the PBGC will be administered by a Director, who is appointed by the President by and with the advice and consent of the Senate. The Director is to act in accordance with the policies established by the PBGC board. The Senate Committees on Finance and on Health, Education, Labor, and Pensions are given joint jurisdiction over the nomination of a person nominated by the President to be Director of the PBGC. If one of such Committees votes to order reported such a nomination, the other such Committee is to report on the nomination within 30 calendar days, or it is automatically discharged.[112]

The Director, and any officer designated by the chairman, is given the authority with respect to investigations that is provided under present law to members of the PBGC board and officers designated by the chairman of the board.

The Director is to be compensated at the rate of compensation provided under Level III of the Executive Schedule.[113] Effective January 1, 2006, such annual rate of pay is $152,000.

Effective date

The provision is effective on the date of enactment. The term of the individual serving as Executive Director of the PBGC on the date of enactment expires on the date of enactment. Such individual, or any other individual, may serve as interim Director of the PBGC until an individual is appointed as Director in accordance with the provision.

[¶ 15,320.08]

Committee Report on P.L. 96-364 (Multiemployer Pension Plan Amendments Act of 1980)

[Senate Committee Report]

The Committee's amendment requires that the revenues and expenditures of the PBGC in the discharge of its functions are to be included as part of the annual budget of the United States Government. The amendment continues present law under which the United States is not authorized to pay any expenses of the PBGC and is not liable for payment of any claims arising under guarantee programs administered by the PBGC.

The amendment is effective for fiscal years beginning after September 30, 1980.

[¶ 15,320.09]

Committee Report on P.L. 94-455 (Tax Reform Act of 1976)

[Conference Committee Report]

House bill

No provision.

Senate amendment

Under present law a corporation organized under an Act of Congress is not generally exempt from Federal taxation unless that Act so provides. The Pension Benefit Guaranty Corporation was not specifically exempted from Federal taxation by ERISA (the Employee Retirement Income Security Act of 1974). The Senate amendment amends ERISA to clarify the intent of Congress that the Pension Benefit Guaranty Corporation is to be exempt from all Federal taxation except taxes imposed under the Federal Insurance Contributions Act (social security taxes) and the Federal Unemployment Tax Act (unemployment taxes). The exemption applies from September 2, 1974 (the date of enactment of ERISA).

Conference agreement

The conference agreement follows the Senate amendment.

[¶ 15,320.10]

Committee Report on P.L. 93-406 (Employee Retirement Income Security Act of 1974)

[Conference Committee Explanation]

Administering corporation and its organization.—* * *

The conferees decided, following the Senate amendment, to place the corporation within the Department of Labor under a board consisting of the Secretaries of Labor, Commerce, and the Treasury, with the Secretary of Labor to be chairman of the board. The corporation is to be "within" the Department of Labor in that it is to be quartered there and it is to receive such housekeeping services as it may request from the Labor Department. The board of directors is to establish policy, while the chairman is to be responsible for the overall supervision of the corporation's personnel, organization, and budget practices. The corporation's personnel will be appropriately classified in the usual categories, and they are to be nonpolitical. The conferees contemplate that the corporation may make contractual arrangements for the performance of some of its functions by other agencies, and, in particular, it is anticipated that it may arrange for such functions as recordkeeping to be performed by the Department of Labor insofar as those activities are analogous to the regular duties of the Labor Department. Generally, the other functions of the corporation are to be performed by its own employees, as well as by private parties contracting to perform special duties.

During the temporary start-up period following the date of enactment, the corporation may, in its discretion, make arrangements for performance of any of its functions by other agencies, and, in particular, the Department of Labor.

The conferees also established a seven-man Advisory Committee to advise the corporation on such issues as the investment of funds, appointment of trustees for terminating plans, whether plans should be liquidated immediately through purchase of annuities or continued in operation under a trustee, and on other problems with regard to which the corporation requests advice. The seven members are to be appointed by the President upon the recommendation of the board of directors. Employee organizations and employers are each to have two representatives on the Advisory Committee, with the general public to have three. The President is to designate one of the appointees as chairman.

The Advisory Committee members are to serve staggered, three-year terms, and are to meet at least six times a year. The members may select employees for the Advisory Committee, but its employees, as well as those of the corporation, are to be appointed in accordance with Civil Service regulations.

Investments, borrowing authority, and tax exemption.—Both the House and the Senate versions authorize the corporation to borrow up to $100 million from the Federal Treasury. The conferees expect the program, ultimately, to be self-financing.

The Senate amendment exempts the corporation from Federal taxation (except for social security and unemployment taxes) and from State and local taxation (except that the corporation's real and tangible personal property, other than cash and securities, may be taxed to the same extent according to value as other such property is taxed).

The conferees accepted both the borrowing authority and the tax exemption.

The assets in the corporation's funds representing collections of premiums may be invested in obligations issued or guaranteed by the United States. The assets representing terminated plans in the process of liquidation are to be invested by the trustees of the liquidating plans consistently with investment policies suggested to the corporation by the Advisory Committee.

---

[112] The provision relating to the Senate committees is treated as an exercise of rulemaking power of the Senate and is deemed a part of the rules of the Senate. It is applicable only with respect to the procedure to be followed in the case of a nomination of the Director of the PBGC and it supersedes other Senate rules only to the extent that it is inconsistent with such rules. The provision does not change the constitutional right of the Senate to change its rules (so far as relating to the procedure of the Senate) at any time, in the same manner and to the same extent as in the case of any other rule of the Senate.

[113] 5 U.S.C. sec. 5314.

[ERISA Sec. 4003]

[¶ 15,330.09]

Committee Report on P.L. 109-280 (Pension Protection Act of 2006)

For the Committee Report on P.L. 109-280 on the director of the PBGC, see ¶ 15,320.07.

[¶ 15,330.095]

Committee Report on P.L. 103-465 (General Agreement on Tariffs and Trade (GATT); Retirement Protection Act)

[House Committee Report]

Enforcement of minimum funding requirements

The bill gives the PBGC the authority to bring suit to enforce the minimum funding standards if the amount of missed required contributions exceeds $1 million. The bill does not change existing authority of the Department of the Treasury or the Department of Labor.

Effective date

The provision is effective for minimum funding contributions that become due on or after the date of enactment [December 8, 1994].

[¶ 15,330.10]

Committee Reports on P.L. 93-406 (Employee Retirement Income Security Act of 1974)

See ¶ 14,940.10 and ¶ 14,960.10.

[ERISA Sec. 4004]

[¶ 15,340.10]

Committee Report on P.L. 93-406 (Employee Retirement Income Security Act of 1974)

[Conference Committee Explanation]

Temporary authority for initial period.— Under the conference substitute, the corporation may appoint a receiver during the first 270 days after enactment [the period before May 31, 1975] for a plan if (1) the corporation receives notice that a plan is to be terminated, or (2) the corporation determines the plan should be terminated. Within 20 days after the appointment, the corporation must apply to the court for a decree approving the appointment.

If the court rejects the application or the corporation fails to apply within the 20 days, the plan assets are to be transferred back to the plan administrator within three days.

As an alternative to this procedure, the corporation may request the plan administrator to apply to the district court for the appointment of a receiver until the plan can be terminated.

The receiver is to determine whether the plan assets are sufficient to discharge the plan obligations. If the receiver's determination is approved by the corporation and the court, the receiver is to terminate the plan in accordance with the insurance provisions.

The corporation is also to have special temporary powers during the first 270 days after enactment [the period before May 31, 1975] to—

(1) contract for printing without regard to the provisions of chapter 5 of title 44, United States Code,

(2) waive any notice,

(3) extend the 90-day termination notice period (during which the plan administrator who has filed a notice of termination may not terminate the plan unless he receives a notice of sufficiency of plan assets from the corporation) for an additional 90-day period without the agreement of the plan administrator or approval of the court, and

(4) waive or reduce contingent employer liability for plan terminations, the requirements respecting withdrawals of substantial owners from plans, and the requirements respecting the liability of employers or termination of plans maintained by more than one employer if this appears necessary to avoid unreasonable hardship for an employer who was unable, as a practical matter, to continue its plan.

[ERISA Sec. 4005]

[¶ 15,350.07]

Committee Report on P.L. 100-203 (Omnibus Budget Reconciliation Act of 1987)

... relating to PBGC premiums, see ¶ 15,360.08.

[¶ 15,350.09]

Committee Report on P.L.96-364 (Multiemployer Pension Plan Amendments Act of 1980)

[House Ways and Means Committee Report]

Prohibition against use of amounts held in a particular PBGC fund other than for the purpose for which the fund is maintained.— The Committee has determined that it should be made clear that amounts held in the different PBGC funds, including amounts borrowed from the Treasury, are to be kept separate. The amendment provides that amounts borrowed by the PBGC from the United States Treasury for purposes of its funds established for guaranteeing basic benefits under single-employer and multiemployer pension plans may not be loaned to another fund maintained by the PBGC. In addition, the amendment makes clear that an amount in any fund maintained by the PBGC may be used only for the purpose for which that fund was established (including the payment of appropriate expenses and charges) and may not be used to make loans to any other fund or to finance any other PBGC activity.

The amendment also makes it clear that amounts held by the PBGC under its fund for guaranteed nonbasic benefits may not be applied for the payment of benefits which are nonbasic solely because they are in excess of the guaranteed limitations although such benefits are guaranteed under a supplemental program established in accordance with PBGC regulations.

[¶ 15,350.10]

Committee Report on P.L. 93-406 (Employee Retirement Income Security Act of 1974)

[Conference Committee Explanation]

Establishment of pension benefit guaranty funds.—

* * *

Under the conference substitute, four separate revolving funds are specifically established. They are for the basic retirement benefits of single-employer and multiemployer plans and for such nonbasic benefits of single employer and multiemployer plans that the corporation chooses to insure. It is intended that separate accounts will be maintained in the two basic retirement funds for employer liability payments and for premiums paid for employer liability coverage.

The resources of each fund are not to be used to pay the losses or expenses of another fund, and the funds may draw upon the general funds of the Treasury only to the extent of their borrowing authority. The funds are to be self-sufficient and are not to be a charge on the Federal budget.

Among the receipts to be included in each fund are the appropriate portions of premiums, penalties, interest, and other charges; employer liability payments; amounts borrowed from the Treasury; and interest earned by fund assets.

Disbursements are to be made from each fund for payments of insured benefits (including employer contingent liability coverage), repayment to the Treasury of borrowed amounts, operational and administrative expenses, and payments for assets being purchased under certain circumstances from a plan being terminated.

[ERISA Sec. 4006]

[¶ 15,360.07]

Committee Report on P.L. 109-280 (Pension Protection Act of 2006).

[Joint Committee on Taxation Report]

Variable rate premium

For 2006 and 2007, the bill extends the present-law rule under which, in determining the amount of unfunded vested benefits for variable rate premium purposes, the interest rate used is 85 percent of the annual rate of interest determined by the Secretary of the Treasury on amounts invested conservatively in long term investment-grade corporate bonds for the month preceding the month in which the plan year begins.

Beginning in 2008, the determination of unfunded vested benefits for purposes of the variable rate premium is modified to reflect the changes to the funding rules of the provision. Thus, under the provision, unfunded vested benefits are equal to the excess (if any) of (1) the plan's funding target[92] for the year determined as under the minimum funding rules, but taking into account only vested benefits over (2) the fair market value of plan assets. In valuing unfunded vested benefits the interest rate is the first, second, and third segment rates which would be determined under the funding rules of the provision, if the segment rates were based on the yields of corporate bond rates, rather than a 24-month average of such rates. Under the bill, deductible contributions are no longer limited by the full funding limit; thus, the rule providing that no variable rate premium is required if contributions for the prior plan year were at least equal to the full funding limit no longer applies under the provision.

---

92 The assumptions used in determining funded target are the same as under the minimum funding rules. Thus, for a plan in at-risk status, the at-risk assumptions are used.

Termination premium

The bill makes permanent the termination premium enacted in the Deficit Reduction Act of 2005.

Effective date

The extension of the present-law interest rate for purposes of calculating the variable rate premium is effective for plan years beginning in 2006 and 2007. The modifications to the variable rate premium are effective for plan years beginning after December 31, 2007. The provision extending the termination premium is effective on the date of enactment.

[PBGC premiums for small plans]

In the case of a plan of a small employer, the per participant variable-rate premium is no more than $5 multiplied by the number of plan participants in the plan at the end of the preceding plan year. For purposes of the provision, a small employer is a contributing sponsor that, on the first day of the plan year, has 25 or fewer employees. For this purpose, all employees of the members of the controlled group of the contributing sponsor are to be taken into account. In the case of a plan to which more than one unrelated contributing sponsor contributed, employees of all contributing sponsors (and their controlled group members) are to be taken into account in determining whether the plan was a plan of a small employer. For example, under the provision, in the case of a plan with 20 participants, the total variable rate premium is not more than $2,000, that is, (20 × $5) × 20.

Effective date

The provision applies to plan years beginning after December 31, 2006.

[Modification of transition rule to pension funding requirements for interstate bus company]

The provision revises the special rule for a plan that is sponsored by a company engaged primarily in interurban or interstate passenger bus service and that meets the other requirements for the special rule under present law. The provision extends the application of the special rule under present law for plan years beginning in 2004 and 2005 to plan years beginning in 2006 and 2007. The provision also provides several special rules relating to determining minimum required contributions and variable rate premiums for plan years beginning after 2007 when the new funding rules for single-employer plans apply.

Under the provision, for the plan year beginning in 2006 or 2007, a plan's funded current liability percentage of a plan is treated as at least 90 percent for purposes of determining the amount of required contributions (100 percent for purposes of determining whether quarterly contributions are required). As a result, for the 2006 and 2007 plan years, additional contributions under the deficit reduction contribution rules and quarterly contributions are not required with respect to the plan. In addition, the mortality table used under the plan is used in calculating PBGC variable rate premiums.

Under the provision, for plan years beginning after 2007, the mortality table used under the plan is used in: (1) determining any present value or making any computation under the minimum funding rules applicable to the plan; and (2) calculating PBGC variable rate premiums. Under a special phase-in (in lieu of the phase-in otherwise applicable under the provision relating to funding rules for single-employer plans), for purposes of determining whether a shortfall amortization base is required for plan years beginning after 2007 and before 2012, the applicable percentage of the plan's funding shortfall is the following: 90 percent for 2008, 92 percent for 2009, 94 percent for 2010, and 96 percent for 2011. In addition, for purposes of the quarterly contributions requirement, the plan is treated as not having a funding shortfall for any plan year. As a result, quarterly contributions are not required with respect to the plan.

Effective date

The provision is effective for plan years beginning after December 31, 2005.

For the Committee Report on P.L. 109-280 on the extension of replacement of the 30-year Treasury Rates, see ¶ 12,250.023.

[¶ 15,360.075]

Committee Report on P.L. 103-465 (General Agreement on Tariffs and Trade (GATT); Retirement Protection Act)

[House Committee Report]

Phase-out of variable rate premium cap

The bill phases out the cap on the additional premium for underfunded plans over three years, beginning with plan years beginning on or after July 1, 1994. For plan years beginning on or after July 1, 1994, but before July 1, 1995, the maximum additional premium is $53 per participant, plus 20 percent of the amount of the total premium (determined without regard to the cap) in excess of $53. For plan years beginning on or after July 1, 1995, but before July 1, 1996, the maximum additional premium is $53 per participant, plus 60 percent of the amount of the total premium (determined without regard to the cap) in excess of $53.

The bill also modifies the interest rate and asset valuation method to be used for purposes of determining the additional premium. For plan years beginning on and after July 1, 1997, the interest rate is 85 percent of the 30-year Treasury rate. For plan years beginning during or after the first year in which the successor mortality tables to GAM 83 as prescribed by the Secretary are first effective, the interest rate is 100 percent of the 30-year Treasury rate and assets are valued at market value.

Effective date

The provision is generally effective as described above. In the case of regulated public utilities engaged in providing electric energy, gas, water, or sewerage disposal services (as defined in Code sec. 7701(a)(33)(A)(i)), no premiums in excess of those under present law are payable until the first plan year beginning on or after the earlier of January 1, 1998, or the date that the regulated utility begins to collect from customers rates that reflect the cost incurred for additional premiums pursuant to a final and nonappealable determination by all public utility commissions that the increased premium costs are recoverable from customers of the utility.

[¶ 15,360.08]

Committee Reports on P.L. 100-203 (Omnibus Budget Reconciliation Act of 1987)

[Senate Finance Committee Report]

The amendment also provides that, with respect to a single-employer plan, and contributing sponsor, as well as the plan administrator, is liable for payment of the premium and that each member of the contributing sponsor's controlled group is jointly and severally liable for such payment.

Under the amendment, all amounts related to the exposure-related premium and the increase in the flat-rate premium are to be deposited in a separate revolving fund. Amounts in this fund may not be used to pay administrative costs of the PBGC or benefits under any plan terminated before January 1, 1988, unless no other amounts are available.

[Conference Committee Report]

The conference agreement follows the Ways and Means Committee and Finance Committee bills, with certain modifications.

The conference agreement increases the flat-rate per-participant premium to $16.

Under the conference agreement, the additional premium is $6 per $1,000 of unfunded vested benefits, with a maximum per-participant additional premium of $34. For purposes of determining the value of vested benefits, the interest rate is equal to 80 percent of the yield per annum on 30-year Treasury securities for the month period preceding the plan year.

In addition, if an employer made the maximum deductible contributions to the plan for 1 or more of the 5 plan years preceding the first plan year beginning after December 31, 1987 (i.e., for a calendar year plan, 1983-1987), then the cap on the additional premium is reduced by $3 for each plan year for which such contributions were made. This special rule only applies for the first 5 plan years the premium is in effect.

The conference agreement follows the Finance Committee amendment, effective for fiscal year 1989.

Effective date

Except as provided above, the provisions apply to plan years beginning after December 31, 1987.

[¶ 15,360.085]

Committee Reports on P.L. 99-272 (Consolidated Omnibus Budget Reconciliation Act)

[House Committee Report]

Subtitle B increases the annual per capita premium from $2.60 to $8.50, effective January 1, 1986, in order to allow the PBGC to retire its unacceptably high deficit over a reasonable period of time and to provide for future claims at a realistic level. * * *

In addition, the process by which Congress may adopt any future premium increases is changed from a concurrent to a joint resolution procedure, in response to the decision of the U.S. Supreme Court in *Immigration and Naturalization Service v. Chadha,* 462 U.S. 919 (1983).

The bill also incorporates certain former provisions in section 4006(a) in lieu of the cross reference thereto. This provision is simply a technical correction and is not intended to make any substantive change.

[Conference Committee Report]

The conference agreement follows [the House Committee Report above] except that the conferees agreed generally to require the PBGC to study the premium structure (including the feasibility of a risk-related premium) and make recommendations for change, if necessary. An advisory group appointed by the Chairmen of the House Committees on Education and Labor and Ways and Means and the Senate Committees on Labor and Human Resources and Finance is required to analyze and critique the study. The study is to be filed with the Congress no later than one year from the date of enactment and the advisory group's report is due no later than six months affter the PBGC submits its report to the Advisory Council.

[¶ 15,360.09]

Committee Report on P.L. 96-364 (Multiemployer Pension Plan Amendments Act of 1980)

[Senate Committee Report]

* * * The bill continues the authority of the PBGC to prescribe (subject to approval by the Congress) such schedules of premium rates in excess of $2.60 per year per participant and bases for the application of those rates as may be necessary to provide sufficient revenue to enable the PBGC to carry out its functions.

Premium rates.—Under the bill, as under present law, the PBGC will maintain separate schedules of premium rates and bases for multiemployer plans and for single-employer plans. The bill clarifies present law by providing for separate rates and bases for nonbasic benefits under (1) multiemployer plans and (2) single-employer plans. The bill also continues the authority of the PBGC to revise the premium rate and base schedules for basic benefits (under multiemployer or single-employer plans) whenever the PBGC determines that revision is necessary, subject to approval by Congress (where the annual rate exceeds $2.60 per participant).

Basic benefit rates.—The bill continues the present annual per-participant premium of $2.60 for single-employer plans and provides that the annual per-participant premium for multiemployer plans will increase from the present $.50 rate to $2.60 over a nine-year period. For the first four plan years beginning after enactment of the bill the annual per-participant premium is $1.40. The premium will rise to $1.80 for the fifth and sixth years, to $2.20 for the seventh and eighth years, and to $2.60 for the ninth and succeeding years. For plan years in which the date of enactment of this bill falls, the annual per-participant permium will be the sum of (1) the pro rata portion of the current 50 cent premium for the number of months in the plan year ending on or before the date of enactment and (2) the pro rata portion of a $1.00 premium for the number of months in the plan year ending after such date. However, the PBGC is required to increase the premium automatically before the ninth year if for any year it projects that its assets will be less than twice what it paid out in the prior year to plans as financial assistance or to plan participants or beneficiaries. In such a case, the annual per-participant premium would increase to the lowest specified level (not in excess of $2.60, unless approved by the Congress) necessary to insure that the test will be satisfied in the succeeding calendar year.

* * *

[¶ 15,360.10]

Committee Report on P.L. 93-406 (Employee Retirement Income Security Act of 1974)

[Conference Committee Explanation]

Premiums.—

* * *

The conferees decided to require the corporation to establish separate uniform premium rates for single-employer and for multiemployer plans for retirement benefits. Single-employer plans are to pay $1 per plan participant during the first full plan year following enactment [September 2, 1974] (and a prorated amount for any part of a plan year preceding that first full plan year). Multiemployer plans are to pay 50 cents per plan participant during these periods.

For the first fractional part of a year (after enactment) and the first full plan year after the date of enactment, premiums are to be paid within 30 days after the beginning of the period of coverage. The corporation may follow this or another system thereafter.

In the case of participants in multiemployer plans, no participant is to be counted more than once in computing the per capita ($1 or 50 cents per person) premium. Thus, if, during the course of a plan year, an employee leaves one employer in the multiemployer plan to work for another employer in the plan, the plan need nevertheless pay only one 50-cent premium on account of his participation.

The corporation is directed to establish by regulation appropriate procedures for determining the amount of the premium where there are practical problems such as rapid turnover of participants during a plan year.

During the second full plan year, both single-employer and multiemployer plans may elect to pay a premium determined under the formula of the House bill but not less than one-half of what they would have to pay under the per capita rates. (This rate base for multiemployer plans continues until 1978.) One-half of the premium referred to above is to be determined according to the plan's unfunded insured benefits (but with the premium not to exceed 0.1 percent of unfunded vested benefits for single-employer plans and .025 percent of multiemployer plans). The other half of the premium is to be based on the total insured benefits. In this case the premium is to be fixed at a uniform rate (determined separately for single-employer and multiemployer plans) which is calculated by the corporation to produce the same total yearly revenue as is produced by the premiums on unfunded insured benefits.

In subsequent years the corporation may set premiums using the per capita rate base, the unfunded insured benefits rate base, or the total insured benefits rate base, or any combination of these (subject to the rate limitations above described). If the corporation should want to combine any two or more of these three rate bases, it is to design the bases to produce approximately equal amounts of aggregate premium revenue yearly from each.

The corporation may exceed the rate limitations, produce unequal amounts of aggregate premium income from the different rate bases, or use other rate bases, but only as to plan years beginning after Congress approves these revisions through a special procedure set forth in the conference substitute.

The conferees also decided that the corporation should establish by regulations equitable methods of valuing a plan's assets and benefits for the purpose of setting premium rates.

The basic enforcement mechanism is to be a civil action brought by the corporation for the collection of unpaid premiums past due. There is to be a civil penalty of up to 100 percent of the amount of unpaid premiums to be assessed after 60 days following the due date of the premiums, but application of this penalty may be postponed in cases in which payment of the premiums entails hardship to the plan. The plan is to be liable for both the premiums for coverage of benefits and for any penalty assessed for failure to pay premiums. Besides the penalty, the corporation may also charge interest (at the rate imposed at the time under section 6601(a) of the Internal Revenue Code, or its successor, upon tax underpayments) for unpaid premiums that are past due. Additionally, a court, in any action brought to enforce the insurance provisions, including an action to collect unpaid premiums, may award the corporation all or any part of its costs of litigation.

The corporation may elect to insure nonbasic benefits in covered plans and do this through separate funds. If it does so, uniform premium rates are to be established by the corporation for the risk insured in each category. The term "nonbasic benefits" may include both what are sometimes called ancillary benefits and what are sometimes called supplemental benefits.

As to basic retirement benefits, coverage is to continue although premiums are not paid when due.

As explained subsequently, the corporation is also to provide insurance protection for employer liability upon the termination of plans [CCH ¶ 15,430.10]. In this case the corporation is free to determine the rates in a manner it determines as appropriate. These premiums are to be set at rates sufficient to fund the contingent liability covered. This coverage is not to remain in effect if premiums due are unpaid. For coverage of employer liability, the corporation is to provide regulations to set the appropriate period for which the premiums (which are to be paid by the employer) should be paid. Employers electing this coverage may give notice of their election prior to the coverage period, and the five-year waiting period during which the premiums must be paid before contingent employer liability is covered is to begin with that notification.

[ERISA Sec. 4007]

[¶ 15,370.07]

Committee report on P.L. 109-280 (Pension Protection Act of 2006)

[Joint Committee on Taxation Report]

The provision allows the PBGC to pay interest on overpayments made by premium payors. Interest paid on overpayments is to be calculated at the same rate and in the same manner as interest charged on premium underpayments.

Effective date

The provision is effective with respect to interest accruing for periods beginning not earlier than the date of enactment.

[¶ 15,370.08]

Committee Report on P.L. 100-203 (Omnibus Budget Reconciliation Act of 1987)

... relating to PBGC premiums, see ¶ 15,360.08.

[¶ 15,370.09]

Committee Report on P.L. 93-406 (Employee Retirement Income Security Act of 1974)

See ¶ 15,360.10.

[ERISA Sec. 4008]

[¶ 15,380.10]

Committee report on P.L. 109-280 (Pension Protection Act of 2006)

[Joint Committee on Taxation Report]

Under the bill, additional information is required to be provided in the PBGC's annual report. The report must include (1) a summary of the Pension Insurance Modeling System microsimulation model, including the specific simulation parameters, specific initial values, temporal parameters, and policy parameters used to calculate the PBGC's financial statements; (2) a comparison of (a) the average return on investments earned with respect to assets invested by the PBGC for the year to which the report relates and (b) an amount equal to 60 percent of the average return on investment for the year in the Standard & Poor's 500 Index, plus 40 percent of the average return on investment for such year in the Lehman Aggregate Bond Index (or in a similar fixed income index), and (3) a statement regarding the deficit or surplus for the year that the PBGC would have had if it had earned the return described in (2) with respect to its invested assets.

Effective date

The provision is effective on the date of enactment.

[ERISA Sec. 4009]

[¶ 15,390.10]

Committee Report on P.L. 93-406 (Employee Retirement Income Security Act of 1974)

[Conference Committee Explanation]

Portability assistance.—The Pension Benefit Guaranty Corporation is to provide advice and assistance, upon request, to individuals regarding establishing individual retirement accounts or other forms of deductible individual retirement savings, and also regarding the desirability, in particular cases, of transferring an employee's interest in a qualified plan to a form of individual retirement savings upon that employee's separation from service.

[ERISA Sec. 4010]

[¶ 15,395.09]

Committee Report on P.L. 109-280 (Pension Protection Act of 2006)

[Joint Committee on Taxation Report]

Under the provision, the requirement of section 4010 reporting applicable under present law if aggregate unfunded vested benefits exceed $50 million is replaced with a requirement of section 4010 reporting if: (1) the funding target attainment percentage at the end of the preceding plan year of a plan maintained by a contributing sponsor or any member of its controlled group is less than 80 percent. It is intended that the PBGC may waive the requirement in appropriate circumstances, such as in the case of small plans.

The provision also requires the information provided to the PBGC to include the following: (1) the amount of benefit liabilities under the plan determined using the assumptions used by the PBGC in determining liabilities; (2) the funding target of the plan determined as if the plan has been in at-risk status for at least 5 plan years; and (3) the funding target attainment percentage of the plan.

The value of plan assets, a plan's funding target, a plan's funding target attainment percentage, and at-risk status are determined under the provision relating to funding rules applicable to single-employer plans under the provision. Thus, a plan's funding target for a plan year is the present value of the benefits earned or accrued under the plan as of the beginning of the plan year. A plan's "funding target attainment percentage" means the ratio, expressed as a percentage, that the value of the plan's assets (reduced by any funding standard carryover balance and prefunding balance) bears to the plan's funding target for the year (determined without regard to the special assumptions that apply to at-risk plans). A plan is in at-risk status for a plan year if the plan's funding target attainment percentage for the preceding year was less than (1) 80 percent, determined without regard to the special at-risk assumptions, and (2) 70 percent, determined using the special at-risk assumptions.

The provision requires the PBGC to provide the Senate Committees on Health, Education, Labor, and Pensions and Finance and the House Committees on Education and the Workforce and Ways and Means with a summary report in the aggregate of the information submitted to the PBGC under section 4010.

Effective date

The provision is effective for filings for years beginning after December 31, 2007.

[¶ 15,395.10]

Committee Report on P.L. 103-465 (General Agreement on Tariffs and Trade (GATT); Retirement Protection Act)

[House Committee Report]

Certain information required to be furnished to the PBGC

The bill authorizes the PBGC to require certain contributing sponsors and controlled group members to submit to the PBGC such information as the PBGC may specify by regulation. The required information may include information that the PBGC determines is necessary to determine plan assets and liabilities and copies of audited financial statements. A contributing sponsor or controlled group member is subject to these information requirements if: (1) the total unfunded vested benefits of all underfunded plans sponsored by the controlled group exceed $50 million; (2) missed funding contributions exceed $1 million and the conditions for imposing a lien for missed contributions have been met; or (3) there are outstanding minimum funding waivers in an amount exceeding $1 million, any portion of which remains unpaid. Any information required to be provided to the PBGC under the provision would be exempt from public disclosure.

Effective date

The provision is effective on the date of enactment [December 8, 1994].

[ERISA Sec. 4011]

[¶ 15,400.09]

Committee Report on P.L. 109-280 (Pension Protection Act of 2006)

For the Committee Report on P.L. 109-280 on the defined benefit plan funding notice, see ¶ 14,210.07.

[¶ 15,400.10]

Committee Report on P.L. 103-465 (General Agreement on Tariffs and Trade (GATT); Retirement Protection Act)

[House Committee Report]

Disclosure to participants

The bill amends title IV of ERISA to require that the plan administrator of a plan that must pay the additional premium applicable to underfunded plans must notify plan participants of the plan's funded status and the limits on the PBGC's guarantee should the plan terminate while underfunded, unless the plan is exempt from the special funding rules for underfunded plans (other than on account of the number of plan participants). For purposes of this exception to the disclosure requirement, a plan's funded current liability percentage is determined without subtracting any credit balance in the plan's funding standard account from assets. The notice will have to be provided in the time and manner prescribed by the PBGC.

Effective date

The provision is effective for plan years beginning after the date of enactment [December 8, 1994].

[ERISA Sec. 4021]

[¶ 15,410.09]

Committee Report on P.L. 109-280 (Pension Protection Act of 2006)

For the Committee Report on P.L. 109-280 on rules for substantial owner benefits in terminated plans, see ¶ 15,420.08.

[¶ 15,410.10]

Committee Report on P.L. 93-406 (Employee Retirement Income Security Act of 1974)

[Conference Committee Explanation]

Plans covered.—

* * *

Subject to specific exceptions, the conference substitute requires mandatory coverage of employee pension benefit plans that either affect interstate commerce (and, in the case of nonqualified plans, have for five years met the standards for qualified plans) or that are qualified under the Internal Revenue Code, the so-called 403(b) plans of certain educational and other tax-exempt organizations, and some so-called H.R. 10 plans for the self-employed and their employees. Covered plans must pay the appropriate premium for coverage. As to whether any particular benefit receives insurance coverage, see "Benefits guaranteed," below.

A plan once determined to be a qualified plan by the Internal Revenue Service is a covered plan even if the determination is subsequently deemed erroneous. However, once a qualified plan loses its qualification, benefits thereafter accruing are not insured.

Plans specifically excluded from coverage are:

(1) individual account plans (such as money-purchase pension plans, profit-sharing plans, thrift and savings plans, and stock bonus plans),

(2) governmental plans (including plans set up under the Railroad Retirement Act of 1935 or 1937),

(3) a church plan which has not volunteered for coverage, is not for employees in an unrelated trade or business, and is not a multiemployer plan in which one or more of the employers are not churches or a convention or association of churches,

(4) plans established by fraternal societies or other organizations described in section 501(c)(8), (9), or (18) of the Internal Revenue Code which receive no employer contributions and which cover only members (not employees),

(5) a plan that has not after the date of enactment provided for employer contributions,

(6) nonqualified deferred compensation plans established for a select group of management or highly compensated employees,

(7) a plan outside the United States for nonresident aliens,

(8) a plan primarily for a limited group of highly paid employees, where the benefits to be paid (or contributions received) are in excess of the limitations set forth in section 415 of the Internal Revenue Code (as added by the conference substitute),

(9) a qualified plan established exclusively for "substantial owners" (defined below),

(10) a plan of an international organization exempt from tax under the International Organizations Immunities Act,

(11) a plan maintained only to comply with workmen's compensation, unemployment compensation, or disability insurance laws,

(12) a plan established and maintained by a labor organization described in section 501(c)(5) of the Internal Revenue Code that does not after the date of enactment provide for employer contributions,

(13) a plan which is a defined benefit plan to the extent it is treated as an individual account plan under section 3(35)(B) of the Act, or

(14) a plan established and maintained by one or more professional service employers that has from the date of enactment not had more than 25 active participants. Once one of these plans has more than 25 active participants, it remains covered although the number of such employees drops to 25 or less.

[ERISA Sec. 4022]

[¶ 15,420.08]

Committee Report on P.L. 109-280 (Pension Protection Act of 2006)

[Joint Committee on Taxation Report]

[Limitations on PBGC guarantee of shutdown and other benefits]

Under the bill, the PBGC guarantee applies to unpredictable contingent event benefits as if a plan amendment had been adopted on the date the event giving rise to the benefits occurred. An unpredictable contingent event benefit is defined as under the benefit limitations applicable to single-employer plans (described above) and means a benefit payable solely by reason of (1) a plant shutdown (or similar event as determined by the Secretary of the Treasury), or (2) an event other than the attainment of any age, performance of any service, receipt or derivation of any compensation, or occurrence of death or disability.

Effective date

The provision applies to benefits that become payable as a result of an event which occurs after July 26, 2005.

[Rules for substantial owner benefits in terminated plans]

Under the bill, the PBGC guarantee applies to unpredictable contingent event benefits as if a plan amendment had been adopted on the date the event giving rise to the benefits occurred. An unpredictable contingent event benefit is defined as under the benefit limitations applicable to single-employer plans (described above) and means a benefit payable solely by reason of (1) a plant shutdown (or similar event as determined by the Secretary of the Treasury), or (2) an event other than the attainment of any age, performance of any service, receipt or derivation of any compensation, or occurrence of death or disability.

Effective date

The provision applies to benefits that become payable as a result of an event which occurs after July 26, 2005.

[Rules relating to bankruptcy of the employer]

Under the bill, the amount of guaranteed benefits payable by the PBGC is frozen when a contributing sponsor enters bankruptcy or a similar proceeding.[107] If the plan terminates during the contributing sponsor's bankruptcy, the amount of guaranteed benefits payable by the PBGC is determined based on plan provisions, salary, service, and the guarantee in effect on the date the employer entered bankruptcy. The priority among participants for purposes of allocating plan assets and employer recoveries to non-guaranteed benefits in the event of plan termination is determined as of the date the sponsor enters bankruptcy or a similar proceeding.

A contributing sponsor of a single-employer plan is required to notify the plan administrator when the sponsor enters bankruptcy or a similar proceeding. Within a reasonable time after a plan administrator knows or has reason to know that a contributing sponsor has entered bankruptcy (or similar proceeding), the administrator is required to notify plan participants and beneficiaries of the bankruptcy and the limitations on benefit guarantees if the plan is terminated while underfunded, taking into account the bankruptcy.

The Secretary of Labor is to prescribe the form and manner of notices required under this provision. The notice is to be written in a manner calculated to be understood by the average plan participant and may be delivered in written, electronic, or other appropriate form to the extent that such form is reasonably accessible to the applicable individual.

The Secretary of Labor may assess a civil penalty of up to $100 a day for each failure to provide the notice required by the provision. Each violation with respect to any single participant or beneficiary is treated as a separate violation.

Effective date

The provision is effective with respect to Federal bankruptcy or similar proceedings or arrangements for the benefit of creditors which are initiated on or after the date that is 30 days after enactment.

[Acceleration of PBGC computation of benefits attributable to recoveries from employers]

The bill changes the five-year period used to determine the recovery ratio for unfunded benefit liabilities so that the period begins two years earlier. Thus, under the bill, the recovery ratio that applies to a plan includes the PBGC's actual recovery experience for plan terminations in the five-Federal fiscal year period ending with the third fiscal year preceding the fiscal year in which falls the notice of intent to terminate for the particular plan.

In addition, the provision creates a recovery ratio for determining amounts recovered for contributions owed to the plan, based on the PBGC's recovery experience over the same five-year period.

The provision does not apply to very large plans (i.e., plans for which participants' benefit losses exceed $20 million). As under present law, in the case of a very large plan, actual amounts recovered for unfunded benefit liabilities and for contributions owed to the plan are used to determine the amount available to provide additional benefits to participants.

Effective date

The provision is effective for any plan termination for which notices of intent to terminate are provided (or, in the case of a termination by the PBGC, a notice of determination that the plan must be terminated is issued) on or after the date that is 30 days after the date of enactment.

[¶ 15,420.09]

Committee Report on P.L. 103-465 (General Agreement on Tariffs and Trade (GATT); Retirement Protection Act)

[House Committee Report]

Modification of maximum guaranty for disability benefits

Disability benefits are exempted from the age reduction in the maximum PBGC insurance amount, if the participant has been determined to be entitled to social security benefits on account of disability.

Effective date

The provision is effective for terminations for which a notice of intent to terminate is filed or for which the PBGC institutes termination proceedings on or after the date of enactment [December 8, 1994].

[¶ 15,420.095]

Committee Report on P.L. 100-203 (Omnibus Budget Reconciliation Act of 1987)

[Conference Committee Report]

The conference agreement follows the Ways and Means Committee and Education and Labor Committee bills and the Finance Committee and Labor and Human Resources Committee amendments by increasing the employer's liability to the full amount of termination liability (sec. 401(a)(2) of the Code.). Under the conference agreement, the term "benefit liabilities" is used instead of termination liability.

The conference agreement also repeals the termination trust mechanism for payment of benefits above guaranteed levels. Instead, under the conference agreement, the total amount of the employer's liability is paid to the PBGC. The PBGC pays out a portion of unfunded benefit liabilities in excess of unfunded guaranteed benefits based on the total value of the PBGC's recovery with respect to the total liability of the employer. Amounts paid to participants are allocated in accordance with section 4044.

The conference agreement follows the Ways and Means Committee and Education and Labor Committee bills, and the Finance Committee and Labor and Human Resources Committee amendments.

---

[107] For purposes of the provision, a contributing sponsor is considered to have entered bankruptcy if the sponsor files or has had filed against it a petition seeking liquidation or reorganization in a case under title 11 of the United States Code or under any similar Federal law or law of a State or political subdivision.

[¶ 15,420.10]

Committee Report on P.L. 93-406 (Employee Retirement Income Security Act of 1974)

[Conference Committee Explanation]

Benefits guaranteed.—

* * *

Under the conference substitute, vested retirement benefits guaranteed by the plan (other than benefits vesting only because of the termination) are to be covered to the extent of the insurance limitations except to the extent indicated below. (Nonbasic benefits the corporation had chosen to guarantee are also to be covered. These nonbasic benefits may include that part of annuities in excess of $750 monthly, medical benefits, etc. This coverage is not necessarily to be subject to the phase-in rule limiting coverage of basic retirement benefits.)

One of the principal limitations on the coverage is that it is to be phased in at the rate of 20 percent per year until the plan or benefit is fully covered after it has been in effect for five years. (For this purpose, the period of existence of a successor plan covering substantially the same employees and providing substantially the same benefits is to be added to the period of existence of its predecessor plan in determining how long a benefit has been in effect.)

In determining how long a plan or amendment has been in effect for purposes of the phase-in schedule, the first year following the end of the plan year in which the plan or amendment first becomes effective constitutes the first year (after which 20 percent of the benefit is covered).

The phase-in rule applies to all benefits provided by qualified plans from the date the benefit was provided. In the case of nonqualified plans that affect commerce, the phase-in rule applies only to benefit increases since the original plan benefits must have been in existence for five years when the plan is first covered (after at least five years of meeting all the standards applicable to qualified plans).

In the case of a plan not covered the day after enactment, the five-year phase-in rule is to commence only when the plan is covered.

The benefit coverage of "substantial owners" is not to be phased in. Resultingly, the benefits of substantial owners may be covered only after their plans have been in effect for 5 years, but at that time their benefits may be covered entirely (up to the basic insurance limitation).

In the case of a termination after the date of enactment (after December 31, 1977, in the case of a termination of a multiemployer plan), the phase-in rule is not to apply unless the corporation finds substantial evidence that the plan was terminated for a reasonable business purpose and not for the purpose of obtaining the payment of benefits by the corporation under the bill. For example, if guaranteed benefits had been increased by one or more amendments made during the 5 years before the termination (or if the plan was created during those 5 years), and the employer's financial condition at the time of termination had not deteriorated significantly from his employer's financial condition immediately after the amendment, then no part of the benefit increase attributable to the amendment is to be insured.

If such a termination was for any purpose other than a reasonable business purpose (whether or not the primary purpose) of obtaining insurance benefits, benefits established or increased during the five years prior to termination are to receive no coverage. For the purpose of this provision, a termination to avoid the liability or responsibility imposed under Title IV on an employer is to be considered a termination for a purpose other than a reasonable business purpose.

Guarantee of benefits is not to extend to benefits accrued after the Secretary of the Treasury or his delegate issues a notice of determination that any trust in the plan is no longer tax-qualified (unless the determination is later held erroneous) or after a plan amendment is adopted that causes the Secretary or his delegate to issue a notice of determination that any trust in the plan is not tax-qualified (unless the determination is later held erroneous or unless the amendment is retroactively revoked to comply with the amendment).

Insurance limitations.—

* * *

In general, the conferees followed the outline of the Senate amendment. However, the limitation is set as the actuarial equivalent of the lesser of 100 percent of the employee's wages during his highest-paid five consecutive years (without regard to temporary absences from participation during that period), or $750 monthly. This amount is adjusted to reflect changes in the social security contribution and benefit base.

In computing the limitation, the guarantee of nonbasic benefits is to be disregarded. In other words, employees are entitled to receive insurance payments for nonbasic benefits although those insured benefits, together with the payment of guaranteed retirement benefits, exceeds the maximum limitation.

The maximum benefit for an "owner-employee" as to each benefit or benefit increase is also limited by a fraction representing the number of years in the 30 years (the period for amortizing an unfunded past service liability for single-employer plans created after January 1, 1974) preceding termination in which the owner-employee was an active plan participant. An owner-employee is defined as a person owning 10 percent of an enterprise, whether a corporation or a partnership, or a sole proprietorship, at any time in the five years preceding the termination.

[¶ 15,420.20]

Committee Reports on P.L. 95-216 (Social Security Amendments of 1977)

Section 103(c)(1) of P.L. 95-216, approved December 20, 1977, amended Section 230 of the Social Security Act by adding at the end thereof the following new subsection:

"(d) Notwithstanding any other provision of law, the contribution and benefit base determined under this section for any calendar year after 1976 for purposes of section 4022(b)(3)(B) of Public Law 93-406, with respect to any plan, shall be the contribution and benefit base that would have been determined for such year if this section as in effect immediately prior to the enactment of the Social Security Amendments of 1977 had remained in effect without change."

Section 103(c)(2) states: "The amendment made by paragraph (1) shall apply with respect to plan terminations occurring after the date of the enactment of this Act."

[Summary of Conference Agreement Report on P.L. 95-216]

H.R. 9346.—

Railroad retirement system and Pension Benefit Guaranty Corporation.—The bill contains a provision to guarantee that the new social security financing provisions that increase the taxable earnings base would not increase the employer tax liability to finance tier-II benefits under the railroad retirement system. Tier-II benefits are those paid to supplement the tier-I payments which correspond to basic social security benefits. Similarly, the bill provides that the increases in earnings base would not increase the maximum amount of pension insured by the Pension Benefit Guaranty Corporation established under the Employee Retirement Income Security Act of 1974.

[House Ways and Means Committee Report on P.L. 95-216]

H.R. 9346.—4. Relationship of the taxable earnings base under the railroad retirement program (Tier II) and the Pension Benefit Guaranty Corporation (PBGC).

The Railroad Retirement Act of 1974 restructured the railroad retirement program so that the benefits paid were divided into two parts—tier-I and tier-II. * * *

* * *

Although the tier-II program is authorized by Federal law, financed by Federal taxes and administered by a Federal agency, the present program is the result of industry-wide negotiations between railway management and railway labor organizations. Your committee has been informed that railway labor and management are now engaged in industry-wide negotiations regarding wages, conditions of work and fringe benefits (including railroad retirement benefits), and that these negotiations could be prejudiced if the increases in the social security tax base included in the amendments reported by your committee were also to go into effect for purposes of tier-II of the Railroad Retirement Act. Your committee has no intention of affecting in any way these negotiations and the bill provides that the tier-II tax base and benefit computation base will be at the same levels they would have been under the automatic increase provision of the Social Security Act had your committee's bill not been enacted.

A somewhat similar situation exists with respect to the Pension Benefit Guaranty Corporation (PBGC) under the Employee Retirement Income Security Act of 1974 which provides for the insurance of pensions up to a certain maximum monthly amount. Initially, this was $750. The intent was that this amount should be automatically adjusted annually to reflect increases in the general level of wages. The mechanism was to increase the amount according to the increases in the Social Security maximum taxable earnings base, which under present law rises in accordance with increases in the general level of earnings. However, the ad hoc increases in the earnings base in the bill would have the unintended effect of increasing the maximum amount of pension insured under ERISA more than was the intention of the initial legislation. Accordingly, your committee's bill would rectify this situation by a technical change, so as to maintain the original intent. This would be done by tying the indexing of the insured pension amount under ERISA to the current Social Security earnings base as it would increase under current law had your committee's bill not been enacted.

* * *

[ERISA Sec. 4022A]

[¶ 15,429H.05]

Committee Reports on P.L. 99-272 (Consolidated Omnibus Budget Reconciliation Act)

. . . relating to the increase in PBGC premiums, see ¶ 15,360.085.

[¶ 15,429H.10]

Committee Report on P.L. 96-364 (Multiemployer Pension Plan Amendments Act of 1980)

[Senate Committee Reports]

Multiemployer guarantees; aggregate limit on guarantees.— Present law.—Since ERISA was enacted in 1974, the insurance of employee benefits under terminated multiemployer plans has been discretionary with the PBGC. Under present law, such insurance by the PBGC will become mandatory after July 31, 1980. Only basic benefits are presently eligible for the PBGC insurance. The basic benefits under a plan are the participant's monthly nonforfeitable retirement benefits (excluding supplementary benefits such as temporary early retirement supplements) under the multiemployer plan determined before the plan terminates. Basic benefits may be guaranteed by the PBGC only to the extent of the lesser of (1) a participant's average monthly gross income from the employer during the five consecutive years for which the participant's gross earnings from the employer are the highest, or (2) $750, adjusted for inflation since 1974 ($1,159.09 for 1980).[1]

The guarantee of benefits which have been in effect for fewer than 60 months at the time of plan termination, and of benefit increases within 60 months before plan termination, is generally phased in at the rate of 20 percent per year or $20 per month (if greater) for each year (not in excess of 5) that the plan or benefit increase has been in effect. No guarantee is provided for benefits established or increased during the 60-month period unless the PBGC finds substantial evidence that the plan was terminated for a reasonable business purpose and not for the purpose of obtaining payments under the termination insurance program.[2]

As indicated, in the case of a multiemployer plan which terminates after the effective date of the insurance program but before August 1, 1980, benefits are insured (up to the usual limits) only in the discretion of the PBGC. In order for the PBGC to pay benefits under such a plan, (1) the plan must have been maintained during the full 60-month period preceding termination, and (2) the PBGC must determine that payment of the benefits will not jeopardize the payment of guaranteed benefits under plans which may terminate after July 31, 1980.[3]

Benefits under single-employer plans are insured by the PBGC subject to the same benefit limits that apply to multiemployer plans. For single-employer plans, however, the insurance is automatic and does not depend upon the exercise of discretion by the PBGC as to whether plan benefits should be insured.[4]

The insurance for basic benefits under multiemployer plans is mandatory for the PBGC beginning August 1, 1980, and is provided whether or not premiums are paid.

Reasons for change.—The Committees recognize that it is necessary to guarantee basic benefits under multiemployer plans. However, the Committees believe that lower guarantees create an incentive to avoid insolvency because insolvency would result in benefit reductions. In addition, lower guarantees would reduce the risk of excessive costs and provide a trial period for nondiscretionary coverage under the program. The Committees understand that the lower guarantees are consistent with the level of premiums set by the bill for multiemployer plans.

Explanation of provisions

Insurable event.— Under the bill, the PBGC is to guarantee certain nonforfeitable benefits under a multiemployer plan covered by the program. This guarantee is implemented only if the plan becomes insolvent.

Duration of benefit.—Under the bill, benefits (or benefit increases) in effect under a plan for fewer than 60 months are not guaranteed. For purposes of the 60-month test, (1) the date a benefit (or benefit increase) is first in effect is the later of the date the relevant documents are executed or the effective date of the benefit or benefit increase); (2) the time a benefit (or benefit increase) is in effect under a successful plan includes the time the benefit (or benefit increase) was in effect under a previously established plan; and (3) the 60-month period does not begin before the date the benefit guarantee provisions of ERISA first applied to the plan (September 2, 1974, for plans in existence on that date). Also, the 60-month period does not include any month of a plan year during which the plan is insolvent or any month after the plan is terminated by mass withdrawal of employers.

Level of guarantee.—Generally, for each year of credited service (including years of past service credited by a plan) under a multiemployer plan, the bill limits the maximum for monthly basic benefits to 100 percent of the first $5 of the benefit accrual rate plus 75 percent[5] of the lesser of $15 or the employee's accrual rate for monthly base benefits in excess of $5. The bill includes a full guarantee of the first $5 of the accrual rate in order to protect participants in the lowest benefit plans from suspensions. The bill limits base benefits to retirement benefits which are otherwise subject to guarantee and which (1) are not greater than the plan benefit payable at normal retirement age as a life annuity (determined under PBGC regulations), and (2) are determined without regard to accrued benefit reductions permitted by the bill to be made on account of the cessation of contributions by an employer (See Q. Minimum Vesting Requirements). Also, the bill provides that the accrual rate for base benefits is computed by dividing a participant's base benefit by the number of full and fractional years of service credited to the participant under the plan for benefit accrual purposes (including full and fractional years of pre-plan service taken into account).

For example, if an employee participated in a multiemployer plan for 25 years and had earned a monthly retirement benefit of $175 beginning at age 65 (the normal retirement age under the plan), the employee's accrual rate would be $7 ($175/25 years). Under the bill, the employee's base benefit would be $162.50 per month (($5 + .75 × $2) × 25). If the plan did not meet the funding requirement, the base benefit would be $157.50 per month (($5 + .65 × $2) × 25).

Where a benefit has been reduced because of the cessation of employer contributions, as permitted by the bill, the guaranteed level of benefit is either the benefit determined as described above or the reduced benefit, whichever is less. In addition, the bill provides that benefits for a substantial owner under a multiemployer plan are not guaranteed if they would not be guaranteed under a single-employer plan.

The bill adds a new procedure for periodic Congressional review of premiums and guarantee levels.

In partiicular, the bill provides that not later than five years after enactment, and every fifth year thereafter, the PBGC is to report to the Congress on the level of premiums under multiemployer plans needed to maintain the basic benefit guarantees then in effect and whether those guarantees can be increased without increasing multiemployer plan premiums for basic benefits. If the report indicates that increased premiums are necessary to support the guarantee levels in effect, the PBGC is required to submit to the Congress (1) a revised guarantee schedule that would be necessary if an increased premium is not adopted, (2) a revised schedule of basic-benefit premiums required if basic-benefit guarantees are not revised, and (2) a revised schedule of premiums and a revised schedule of guarantees under which the premium rates are higher than the existing rates but lower than the rates needed to support the existing schedule of guarantees. The report and any proposed revised premium and guarantee schedules would be submitted to the Committee on Ways and Means and the Committee on Education and Labor of the House, and to the Committee on Finance and the Committee on Labor and Human Resources of the Senate by March 31 of any calendar year in which Congressional action is requested. Whichever of the revised schedules in approved by the Congress goes into effect.

If a report indicates that a higher level of guarantees can be supported by the premium level in effect, the PBGC is required to prepare an analysis showing (1) reduced premiums consistent with existing guarantees, and (2) increased guarantees consistent with existing premiums, and to submit both revised schedules as proposals to the specified committees. If the Congress approves one of the proposed schedules by a concurrent resolution, that schedule goes into effect. The bill continues the rules of the House and Senate for consideration of a concurrent resolution approving a change in the premiums for basic benefits and applies that procedure to concurrent resolutions relating to guarantee levels.

Other benefits.—The PBGC is authorized to guarantee benefits under multiemployer plans other than basic benefits, if feasible, subject to terms and conditions specified by the PBGC. Under the bill, within 18 months after enactment, the PBGC is also required to propose regulations to guarantee benefits (referred to as supplemental benefits) that would be basic benefits except for the dollar or percentage limits provided by the bill, subject to terms and conditions specified in PBGC regulations. Under the bill, a plan's election of supplemental guarantees would generally be irrevocable. The supplemental guarantee program is to be established by January 1, 1983. Supplemental benefits (i.e., retirement benefits in excess of basic benefits) under a plan would be guaranteed only if the plan elected to have such benefits guaranteed. The bill mandates a supplemental program because the Committees intend that participants and beneficiaries in multiemployer plans be afforded the fullest feasible benefit guarantee. In particular, the Committees expect the PBGC to monitor whether, and to what extent, the limitation on basic benefit guarantees the bill is necessary and to provide the fullest possible benefit guarantee to multiemployer plan participants consistent with its experience in administering the program.

Aggregate limit on benefits guaranteed.—The bill limits the aggregate present value of benefits provided by the PBGC with respect to any participant to the same level provided by present law except that, under PBGC regulations, financial assistance provided by the PBGC to a plan would be taken into account as a benefit provided by the PBGC to plan participants.

Effective date

Generally, these provisions of the bill apply as of the date of enactment. The bill provides, however, that the level of benefits guaranteed under the termination insurance program for multiemployer plans which have already terminated and which are guaranteed by the PBGC under present law are not to be less than the levels provided by present law.

---

[1] See ERISA sec. 4022(b)(3).

[2] See ERISA sec. 4022(b)(8).

[3] See ERISA sec. 4082(c)(2).

[4] See ERISA secs. 4022 and 4082(a) and (b).

[5] The percentage is reduced to 65 percent in the case of a multiemployer plan which becomes insolvent before the year 2000 if the plan sponsor does not establish to the satisfaction of the PBGC that, for the last plan year beginning before 1976 and for each of the nine preceding plan years during which the plan was maintained, the total contributions required under the plan for each plan year were at least equal to the sum of (1) the normal cost for the plan year, and (2) interest on the amount of the unfunded past service liability as of the beginning of the plan year. The reduction to 65 percent would not apply where contributions meet the minimum requirements during each year of the 10-year period and certain other standards are met.

Insolvent plans.—Under the bill, if a multi-employer plan is insolvent for a plan year, the plan is required to suspend the payment of benefits, other than basic benefits, which exceed the "resource benefit level." The suspension rule does not apply, however, if the PBGC prescribes a procedure for the guarantee of supplemental benefits (retirement benefits exceeding basic benefits) to the extent supplemental benefits are guaranteed by the PBGC. A multiemployer plan is considered insolvent for a plan year if the plan's available resources are not sufficient to pay benefits under the plan when due for the plan year. The term "resource benefit level" means the highest level of monthly benefits which the plan could pay out of its available resources.

For each year for which a multiemployer plan is insolvent, the plan sponsor is required to determine and certify the resource benefit level of the plan, based on its reasonable projection of available resources and benefits payable. Where the suspension of benefits above the resource benefit level takes place, benefits must be suspended in substantially uniform proportions with respect to all persons whose benefits are in pay status under the plan. The proportionate suspension must be done in a manner consistent with regulations prescribed by the Secretary of the Treasury. In addition, the Secretary of the Treasury is authorized to prescribe rules under which the benefits of different participant groups could be suspended in disproportionate fashion if varied equitably to reflect variations in contribution rates and other relevant factors reflecting differences in bargained-for levels of financial support for plan benefit obligations.

A plan sponsor which determines a resource benefit level which is below the level of guaranteed benefits for a plan year must suspend payment of all benefits other than guaranteed benefits.

If, by the end of a plan year for which a plan is insolvent, the plan sponsor determines that benefits can be paid above the resource benefit level, the plan sponsor must distribute such additional benefits in accordance with regulations prescribed by the Secretary of the Treasury. Where by the end of the year, benefits up to the resource benefit level have not been paid, the amount necessary to bring benefits up to that level must be distributed in accordance with regulations prescribed by the Secretary of the Treasury, to the extent possible, considering the plan's available resources.

Every three years during the period when a plan is in reorganization, beginning with the end of the first such plan year, the plan sponsor must compare the value of plan assets with the total amount of benefit payment for the year. Unless plan assets exceed three times the total amount of benefit payments, the plan sponsor must determine whether the plan will be insolvent during any of the next three plan years. In addition, if at any time the plan sponsor of a plan in reorganization determines, on the basis of experience, that available resources are not sufficient to pay benefits when due for the forthcoming plan year, the sponsor must make such determination available to interested parties.

If the plan sponsor determines that the plan may be insolvent any time in the next three plan years, the sponsor is required to so notify (1) the Secretary of the Treasury, (2) the PBGC, (3) plan participants and beneficiaries, (4) each employer required to contribute to the plan, and (5) each affected employee organization. In addition, the above parties other than the Secretary of the Treasury and the PBGC are to be informed that, in the event of insolvency, payments in excess of basic benefits must be suspended (unless guaranteed as supplemental benefits). No later than two months before the first day of a year for which a plan which is in reorganization is insolvent, the plan sponsor must notify each of the above parties of the plan's resource benefit level.

Where the plan sponsor believes that the resource benefit level for a plan year for which a plan is insolvent may not exceed the level of basic benefits, the plan sponsor must notify the PBGC.

Where a plan sponsor determines a resource benefit level below the level of basic benefits, the sponsor must apply to the PBGC for financial assistance. Where the plan sponsor determines a resource benefit level above the level of basic benefits but anticipates that for any month during a year for which the plan is insolvent the plan will not have sufficient assets to pay basic benefits, the plan sponsor is permitted to apply to the PBGC for financial assistance.

Termination insurance premiums

Present Law

Under present law, a multiemployer plan which is subject to the termination insurance program is required to pay annual premiums to the PBGC at the rate of $.50 per plan participant (the annual premium for single employer plans if $2.60 per plan participant). The premium rate may be raised by the PBGC with the approval of the Congress by a concurrent resolution. Such a resolution is referred to the Committee on Ways and Means and the Committee on Education and Labor of the House, and the Committee on Finance and the Committee on Labor and Human Resources of the Senate. Also, the PBGC is authorized to set premium rates for insurance of nonbasic benefits and to develop a risk-related premium schedule.[1]

Reason for change

The Committees believe that an increased premium (over the current 50-cent rate) is needed to support the mandatory insurance program under the bill.

Explanation of provisions

Schedules. The bill continues the authority of the PBGC to prescribe (subject to approval by the Congress) such schedules of premium rates in excess of $2.60 per year per participant and bases for the application of those rates as may be necessary to provide sufficient revenue to enable the PBGC to carry out its functions.

Premium rates.—Under the bill, as under present law, the PBGC will maintain separate schedules of premium rates and bases for multiemployer plans and for single-employer plans. The bill clarifies present law by providing for separate rates and bases for nonbasic benefits under (1) multiemployer plans and (2) single-employer plans. The bill also continues the authority of the PBGC to revise the premium rate and base schedules for basic benefits (under multiemployer or single-employer plans) whenever the PBGC determines that revision is necessary, subject to approval by Congress (where the annual rate exceeds $2.60 per participant).

Basic benefit rates.—The bill continues the present annual per-participant premium of $2.60 for single-employer plans and provides that the annual per-participant premium for multiemployer plans will increase from the present $.50 rate to $2.60 over a nine-year period. For the first four plan years beginning after enactment of the bill the annual per-participant premium is $1.40. The premium will rise to $1.80 for the fifth and sixth years, to $2.20 for the seventh and eighth years, and to $2.60 for the ninth and succeeding years. For plan years in which the date of enactment of this bill falls, the annual per-participant premium will be the sum of (1) the pro rata portion of the current 50 cent premium for the number of months in the plan year ending on or before the date of enactment and (2) the pro rata portion of a $1.00 premium for the number of months in the plan year ending after such date. However, the PBGC is required to increase the premium automatically before the ninth year if for any year it projects that its assets will be less than twice what it paid out in the prior year to plans as financial assistance or to plan participants or beneficiaries. In such a case, the annual per-participant premium would increase to the lowest specified level (not in excess of $2.60, unless approved by the Congress) necessary to insure that the test will be satisfied in the succeeding calendar year.

Additionally, the Board of Directors of the PBGC may require an increase in the annual per-participant premium (not in excess of $2.60, unless approved by the Congress) where the Board determines that the increase is necessary to provide financial assistance to plans which are then receiving assistance from the PBGC or which the Board finds are reasonably expected to receive such assistance in the future.

Under the bill, the PBGC is authorized to prescribe regulations under which the single-employer premium is not required to be paid more than once per plan year where an individual participates in more than one plan maintained by the same employer. Also, the bill continues the authority of the PBGC to prescribe regulations under which the premium rate for multiemployer plans will not apply to the same participant in a multiemployer plan more than once for any plan year.

In addition, the bill modifies the authority of the PBGC to establish alternative premium rates and bases for basic benefits (subject to Congressional approval) by deleting specific restrictions on the computation of such premiums. The bill permits, but does not require, the development of risk-related premiums. The Committees believe that there is sufficient interest in the development of a risk-related premium for single-employer plans and multiemployer plans to justify a study of this matter by the PBGC. Accordingly, the PBGC is directed to report its findings and recommendations as to risk-related premiums to the Congress within two years after the enactment of the bill.

Nonbasic benefits.—The bill generally continues the authority of the PBGC to prescribe schedules of premium rates and bases for nonbasic benefits. With respect to nonbasic benefits in the form of supplemental benefits under a multiemployer plan, the bill provides that premium rates prescribed for nonbasic benefits by the PBGC may reflect any reasonable consideration that the PBGC determines to be relevant. Supplemental benefits would be guaranteed by the PBGC only at the election of a plan. Such guarantees are to be financed only from premiums collected for this program.

Single-employer premiums.—The bill continues the present-law authority of the PBGC to prescribe a risk-related premium for the guarantee of basic benefits under single-employer plans. The bill also continues present law under which premium rates prescribed by the PBGC must be uniform for all single-employer plans with respect to guaranteed basic benefits, and under which the premium rates prescribed by the PBGC must be uniform for all multiemployer plans with respect to guaranteed basic benefits. In addition, the bill provides that in establishing annual premiums with respect to single-employer plans, certain rules in effect before the enactment of the bill are to remain in effect.

Supplemental benefits—PBGC setting of premiums subject to Congressional disapproval; establishment of separate fund.—The bill provides for Congressional review of premiums for coverage under the supplemental withdrawal liability program. Under the bill, no revision of the premium schedule for this coverage could be adopted by the PBGC unless the revised schedule has been submitted to the Congress. (The bill does not provide for Congressional review of the initial premiums set by the PBGC for coverage of supplemental benefits. However, the PBGC is directed to set such premiums at a reasonable level which will not be so

[1] See ERISA sec. 4006. At the present time, the PBGC does not insure nonbasic benefits and has not developed a risk-related premium.

low as to induce plans to subscribe to the coverage and will not be so high as to be prohibitive.) The PBGC can adopt a revised schedule unless, within 60 days after the submission, the Congress disapproves of the revised schedule by a concurrent resolution which has been referred to the Committee on Ways and Means and the Committee on Education and Labor of the house, and to the Committee on Finance and the Committee on Labor and Human Resources of the Senate. The Committees expect that if the Congress disapproves of a revised premium schedule recommended by the PBGC for guarantees of supplemental benefits, the PBGC will exercise its authority to make appropriate adjustments as to the terms and conditions of such guarantees. Of course, the authority to make adjustments is not limited to such disapproval cases.

In addition, the bill provides that the PBGC is to establish a separate fund for the purpose of guaranteeing supplemental benefits. The bill provides that amounts borrowed by the PBGC from the United States Treasury for purposes of its funds established for guaranteeing basic benefits under single-employer may not be loaned to another fund maintained by the PBGC. In addition, the amendment makes clear that an amount in any fund maintained by the PBGC may be used only for the purpose for which that fund was established (including the payment of appropriate expenses and charges) and may not be used to make loans to any other fund or to finance any other PBGC activity.

The bill also makes it clear that amounts held by the PBGC under its fund for guaranteed nonbasic vehicles may not be applied for the payment of benefits which are nonbasic solely because they are in excess of the guarantee limitations although such benefits are guaranteed under a supplemental program established in accordance with PBGC regulations.

Effective Date

These provisions of the bill will apply on the date of enactment.

[ERISA Sec. 4022B]

[¶ 15,429L.10]

Committee Report on P.L. 96-364 (Multiemployer Pension Plan Amendments Act of 1980)

[Senate Committee Report]

* * *

The bill also makes it clear that amounts held by the PBGC under its fund for guaranteed nonbasic benefits may not be applied for the payment of benefits which are nonbasic solely because they are in excess of the guarantee limitations although such benefits are guaranteed under a supplemental program established in accordance with PBGC regulations.

* * *

[ERISA Sec. 4023]

[¶ 15,430.095]

Committee Report on P.L. 96-364 (Multiemployer Pension Plan Amendments Act of 1980)

[Senate Committee Explanation]

Contingent employer liability insurance

Present Law

ERISA provides for a program designed to permit an employer to insure against the contingent employer liability (up to 30 percent of the employer's net worth) arising out of the termination of a plan with insufficient assets to provide benefits at the insured level. Under ERISA, the contingent employer liability insurance (CELI) may be developed by the PBGC in conjunction with private insurors. The PBGC is authorized to provide premium rates and collect premiums under the CELI program.[1]

Reason for Change

The Committees have determined that the provision in present law which authorizes the PBGC to develop a program to insure contingent liability should be repealed because it could threaten the soundness of the termination insurance program.

Explanation of Provisions

The bill repeals the contingent employer liability insurance provisions of ERISA for multiemployer plans and single-employer plans.

Effective Date

This provision of the bill is effective upon enactment.

[¶ 15,430.10]

Committee Report on P.L. 93-406 (Employee Retirement Income Security Act of 1974)

[Conference Committee Explanation]

Employee's contingent liability coverage.—

* * *

Under the conference substitute, coverage of contingent employer liability is mandatory for single and multiemployer plans, but the corporation is instructed to attempt with private insurers to devise within a 36-month period a system under which risks are equitably distributed by the corporation and the private insurers with respect to classes of employers insured by each. The corporation may thereafter require all employers to obtain coverage from the private insurers, the corporation, or both, depending upon the system devised. The corporation is to fix the premiums at a rate sufficient to fund any payment by the corporation required by the coverage. Private insurers are left free to fix the rates of their own premiums, and other terms and conditions of insurance, but the corporation may level any charge upon employers obtaining private insurance that may be necessary to assure that the costs to all employers are reasonable and equitable and to assure the liquidity and adequacy of the corporation's funds used for this purpose. The corporation may not make any coverage payment with respect to contingent liability until the insurance has been in effect, and the premiums have been paid, for more than five years.

The corporation may set the premium levels and collect the premiums (in arrears) for this coverage during any time up to, but not later than, three years after the date of enactment [i.e., the period before September 3, 1977]. An employer may then pay premiums for the period since the date of enactment [September 2, 1974], and this period is to be counted toward completion of the five-year payment of premiums requirement. Once obtained, coverage is to be prospective only, not retroactive.

In making arrangements with private insurers, the corporation is also to consider using private industry guarantees, indemnities, or letters of credit as an alternative or supplement to private insurance.

[ERISA Sec. 4041]

[¶ 15,440.075]

Committee Report on P.L. 109-280 (Pension Protection Act of 2006)

[Joint Committee on Taxation Report]

[Disclosure of plan termination information to plan participants]

The provision revises the rules applicable in the case of a distress termination to require a plan administrator to provide an affected party with any information provided to the PBGC in connection with the proposed plan termination. The plan administrator must provide the information not later than 15 days after: (1) the receipt of a request for the information from the affected party; or (2) the provision of new information to the PBGC relating to a previous request.

The provision also requires the plan sponsor or plan administrator of a plan that has received notice from the PBGC of a determination that the plan should be involuntarily terminated to provide an affected party with any information provided to the PBGC in connection with the plan termination. In addition, the PBGC is required to provide a copy of the administrative record, including the trusteeship decision record in connection with a plan termination. The plan sponsor, plan administrator, or PBGC must provide the required information not later than 15 days after: (1) the receipt of a request for the information from the affected party; or (2) in the case of information provided to the PBGC, the provision of new information to the PBGC relating to a previous request.

The PBGC may prescribe the form and manner in which information is to be provided, which is to include delivery in written, electronic, or other appropriate form to the extent such form is reasonably accessible to individuals to whom the information is required to be provided. A plan administrator or plan sponsor may charge a reasonable fee for any information provided under this subparagraph in other than electronic form.

A plan administrator or plan sponsor may not provide the relevant information in a form that includes any information that may directly or indirectly be associated with, or otherwise identify, an individual participant or beneficiary. In addition, a court may limit disclosure of confidential information (as described under the Freedom of Information Act) to any authorized representative of the participants or beneficiaries that agrees to ensure the confidentiality of such information. For this purposes, an authorized representative means any employee organization representing participants in the pension plan.

Effective Date

The provision generally applies with respect to any plan termination, with respect to which the notice of intent to terminate, or notice that the PBGC has determined that the requirements for an involuntary plan termination are met, occurs after the date of enactment. Under a transition rule, if notice under the

---

[1] See ERISA sec. 4023. Because of concerns over adverse selection, premium levels, and the possibility of abuse, no CELI program has been initiated by the PBGC. (Private insurors have not shown an interest in developing a CELI program.

provision would otherwise be required before the 90th day after the date of enactment, such notice is not required to be provided until the 90th day.

[Treatment of certain plans where there is a cessation or change in membership of a controlled group]

Under the bill, if: (1) there is a transaction or series of transactions which result in a person ceasing to be a member of a controlled group; (2) such person, immediately before the transaction or series of transactions maintained a single-employer defined benefit plan which is fully funded then the interest rate used in determining whether the plan is sufficient for benefit liabilities or to otherwise assess plan liabilities for purposes of section 4041(b) or section 4042(a)(4) shall not be less than the interest rate used in determining whether the plan is fully funded.

The provision does not apply to any transaction or series of transactions unless (1) any employer maintaining the plan immediately before or after such transactions or series of transactions (a) has a outstanding senior unsecured debt instrument which is rated investment grade by each of the nationally recognized statistical rating organizations for corporate bonds that has issued a credit rating for such instrument, or (b) if no such debt instrument of such employer has been rated by such an organization but one or more of such organizations has made an issuer credit rating for such employer, all such organizations which have so rated the employer have rated such employer investment grade and (2) the employer maintaining the plan after the transaction or series of transaction employs at least 20 percent of the employees located within United States who were employed by such employer immediately before the transaction or series of transactions.

The provision does not apply in the case of determinations of liabilities by the PBGC or a court if the plan is terminated within two years of the transaction (or first transaction in a series of transactions).

For purposes of the provision, a plan is considered fully funded with respect to a transaction or series of transactions if (1) in the case of a transaction or series of transactions which occur in a plan year beginning before January 1, 2008, the funded current liability percentage for the plan year (determined under the minimum funding rules) is at least 100 percent, or (2) in the case of a transaction or series of transactions which occur on or after January 1, 2008, the funding target attainment percentage (as determined under the minimum funding rules) as of the valuation date for the plan year is at least 100 percent.

Effective Date

The provision applies to transactions or series of transactions occurring on or after the date of enactment.

[¶ 15,440.08]

Committee Report on P.L. 103-465 (General Agreement on Tariffs and Trade (GATT); Retirement Protection Act)

[House Committee Report]

Procedures to facilitate the distribution of termination benefits

a. Remedies for noncompliance with requirements for standard terminations.—The bill provides that the PBGC is not required to issue a notice of noncompliance (and nullify a termination) in the case of failure to meet procedural requirements with respect to the termination if it determines that it would be inconsistent with the interests of participants and beneficiaries to issue the notice.

Effective date

The provision applies with respect to standard terminations for which the PBGC has not, as of the date of enactment [December 8, 1994], issued a notice of noncompliance that has become final, or otherwise issued a final determination that the plan termination is nullified.

b. Distress termination criteria for banking institutions.—The bill provides that a proceeding under title 11 of the United States Code or any similar Federal law qualifies as a standard for distress criteria. This standard applies, for example, to bank insolvency receivership actions.

Effective date

The provision is effective as if included in the SEPPAA. Thus, it is effective with respect to notices of intent to terminate filed with the PBGC on or after January 1, 1986.

[¶ 15,440.085]

Committee Report on P.L. 100-203 (Omnibus Budget Reconciliation Act of 1987)

[Conference Committee Report]

[Standards for termination] The conference agreement generally follows the Finance Committee amendment. Under the conference agreement, in the case of a reorganization, a distress termination is not available unless the bankruptcy court (or other appropriate court) determines that, unless the plan is terminated the person will be unable to pay all its debts pursuant to a plan of reorganization and will be unable to continue in business outside the Chapter 11 reorganization process.

The conference agreement follows the Education and Labor Committee bill with respect to the provisions relating to a reorganization that has been converted to a liquidation, notification to the PBGC, and the date of determination of whether the distress criteria have been satisfied.

[House Labor and Education Committee Report]

[*Information requirements*].—Information related to the certification by the enrolled actuary in the case of a termination need not be provided in the case of the termination of certain plans funded exclusively by the individual insurance contracts * * * The information required to be provided in a standard or distress termination must be provided in the case of a termination by the PBGC at the request of the PBGC.

A penalty of up to $1,000 per day is payable to the PBGC for failure to provide required information.

[Conference Committee Report]

The conference agreement follows the Education and Labor Committee bill, except that the amount of the penalty is to reflect the materiality of the failure to provide the required information.

Effective dates

The provisions are generally effective in the case of terminations notice of which is provided to participants after December 17, 1987, and terminations instituted by the PBGC after December 17, 1987, and terminations instituted by the security in the case of certain plan amendments is effective with respect to plan years beginning after the date of enactment.

[¶ 15,440.09]

Committee Reports on P.L. 99-272 (Consolidated Omnibus Budget Reconciliation Act)

[Conference Committee Report]

Under the agreement, as under H.R. 3500, an employer may only terminate a single-employer defined benefit pension plan under which benefits are guaranteed by the PBGC in a standard termination or in a distress termination. An employer is permitted to terminate a plan in a standard termination only if the plan holds sufficient assets to pay all "benefit commitments" under the plan.

Not less than 60 days prior to a proposed plan termination date, a plan administrator is required to give written notice of the proposed termination to the PBGC, plan participants and beneficiaries, and unions representing the participants.

[House Committee Report]

Under a standard termination, the plan must contain sufficient assets to pay for the benefit entitlements [commitments] of all participants and beneficiaries. That is, the plan must be made sufficient not only for all benefits guaranteed by the PBGC under section 4022, but also for the other nonguaranteed benefits encompassed within the definition of benefit entitleme¶ [commitments]. * * * Since the plan must be sufficient for all benefit entitlements [commitments], the PBGC will not be required to trustee the plan or to guarantee the payment of any benefits. Furthermore, participants and beneficiaries will receive all benefits to which they are entitled under the terms of the plan.

Because the PBGC and the participants and beneficiaries are protected under a standard termination, the procedures for entering into such a termination are streamlined so as to allow most of the procedures to be handled by private parties, with minimal involvement by the PBGC. This is intended to reduce the administrative burdens on the PBGC and plan sponsors. At the same time, various safeguards are included in the procedures in order to insure that the requirements for a standard termination are met, and that the interests of the PBGC and the participants and beneficiaries are, in fact, fully protected.

In order to terminate a single-employer plan under a standard termination, certain requirements must be met. The plan administrator must notify affected parties 60 days before the proposed termination date. The plan must be made sufficient for benefit entitlements [commitments] before assets can be distributed.

Under the streamlined procedures, the plan administrator is required to send the PBGC a certification by an enrolled actuary of the estimated amount of assets in the plan as of the proposed date of final distribution of assets, the estimated present value of benefit entitlements [commitments] of participants and beneficiaries under the plan as of such date, and a statement that the plan will be sufficient for benefit entitlements [commitments] as of such proposed date of final distribution of assets based on such estimates. The Committee expects that these estimates will be based on reasonable expectations representing the actuary's best estimate of anticipated experience under the plan. The plan administrator must also send the PBGC any additional information required in regulations of the PBGC, as well as certification that all of the information on which the actuarial certification and information provided to the PBGC was based is accurate and complete.

[Conference Committee Report]

(Senate amendment—Title IX).—At the same time as the plan administrator notifies each participant or beneficiary of the benefits to which the participant or beneficiary is entitled, the plan administrator must also notify the participant or beneficiary of the information used in computing the amount of such benefits, including (1) the length of service, (2) the age of the participant or beneficiary, (3) wages, and (4) such other information as the PBGC may require.

The conference agreement generally follows Title IX of the Senate amendment except that, in addition to the other information specified in the Senate amendment, the plan administrator must supply to participants and beneficiaries the actuarial assumptions used in computing plan benefits (including, but not limited to, the interest rate assumption).

[Conference Committee Report]

(H.R. 3500).—As soon as practicable after the proposed termination date [after the date on which notice of intent to terminate is provided] (H. Cong. R. 305), the plan administrator is required to provide the PBGC with certification by an enrolled actuary of the plan's sufficiency as of the plan's proposed date of distribution.

The plan administrator is permitted to distribute plan assets upon the expiration of the 60-day period following the date the certification of sufficiency is filed with the PBGC, provided that the PBGC has not issued a notice of noncompliance with respect to the plan, and the parties have not agreed to extend that period. The plan administrator is also required to notify each participant and beneficiary of such person's benefit entitlement at least 60 days prior to the plan's proposed date of distribution.

* * * The plan administrator is required, within 30 days after the final distribution of assets, to file a notice with the PBGC certifying that assets have been allocated and distributed in accordance with the requirements of ERISA.

The conference agreement generally follows H.R. 3500. As under H.R. 3500, the conference agreement provides that the assets of a terminated plan may be distributed if the PBGC fails to issue a notice of noncompliance within 60 days after receipt of a NOIT [Notice of Intent to Terminate]. As under H.R. 3500, the conference agreement provides that the 60-day period may be extended by PBGC and the plan administrator and that the extension may be subject to conditions to which they have agreed. The conference agreement does not change the rules of the Code for determining the qualified status of a plan (or of a trust forming a part of a plan), or the application of the minimum funding standard to a plan. Accordingly, the conference agreement does not authorize the PBGC to waive, or otherwise modify, the requirements of the Code.

[Conference Committee Report]

(Senate amendment—Title IX).—In order to terminate a plan in a distress termination, a plan administrator is required to demonstrate that (1) a petition in bankruptcy or other State insolvency proceedings has been filed seeking liquidation of each contributing sponsor (as defined in the bill) of the plan and each substantial member (as defined in the bill) of the contributing sponsors' controlled groups, and that the petition has not been dismissed or converted to one seeking reorganization; (2) a petition in a bankruptcy or State insolvency proceeding has been filed seeking reorganization of each contributing sponsor of the plan and each substantial member of their controlled groups, and the bankruptcy court has approved the plan termination; or (3) unless a distress termination occurs, each of the contributing sponsors and the substantial members of their controlled groups will be unable to pay its debts when due, and will be unable to continue in business.

With respect to the circumstances under which an employer may terminate a plan in a distress termination, the bill generally follows Title IX of the Senate amendment except that it provides an additional criteria permitting "distress" termination if pension costs become unreasonably burdensome due to a declining workforce. In addition, the conference agreement makes it clear that different members of a controlled group may separately satisfy different criteria for distress termination.

As under present law, to the extent a pension plan is an executory contract included within the scope of Section 365 (11 USC 365) or is included within the scope of Section 1113 of the Bankruptcy Code (11 USC 1113), these Bankruptcy Code Provisions are applicable to the court's decision on whether to approve the termination of the pension plan. The distress termination criteria are not intended to make any substantive changes in the bankruptcy laws. The conferees take no position on when or whether a pension plan is an executory contract.

[House Committee Report]

For purposes of the distress tests, the term "substantial member of a controlled group" means a person whose assets comprise 5 percent or more of the total assets of the controlled group as a whole. * * * The Committee believes that the financial condition of a controlled group member whose assets comprise 5 percent or more of the group's total assets has a substantial impact on the financial strength of the group as a whole.

* * *

Once the plan administrator notifies the PBGC of a proposed distress termination, the plan shall pay employer-funded benefits (except death benefits) only in annuity form, shall not purchase annuities from an insurer, and shall continue to pay when due all benefit entitlements [commitments] under the plan, except that, commencing on the proposed date of termination, the plan administrator shall limit the payment of benefits to guaranteed or funded amounts. In the event the plan is later determined not to have terminated in a distress termination, any benefits not paid due to this restriction shall be due and payable immediately (with interest).

* * *

In order to terminate a single-employer plan under a distress termination, certain requirements must be met. The plan administrator must give 60-day advance notice to affected parties and must provide pertinent information and certifications to the PBGC. Most importantly, the contributing sponsors and the members of their controlled groups must satisfy certain tests indicative of a financial inability to continue the funding of a plan.

[¶ 15,440.10]

Committee Report on P.L. 93-406 (Employee Retirement Income Security Act of 1974)

[Conference Committee Explanation]

Termination by plan administrator.—The House bill requires an employer or employee organization planning to terminate a plan to first notify the corporation. The Senate amendment requires a 90-day notification period that may be extended by agreement. A notification by the corporation during one of these periods that the plan assets are insufficient is to cause a termination by the corporation under the provisions for a termination by the corporation. If, in the course of an authorized voluntary termination, a plan administrator determines that the plan assets are insufficient, he is required to so notify the corporation, which is then to terminate the plan under the regular proceedings for a termination by the corporation.

The Senate amendment also provides that a change from an insured plan into a money purchase plan, a profit-sharing plan, or a stock bonus plan (none of which may be covered) is to be treated as a voluntary termination (for which authorization from the corporation must first be obtained).

Under the conference substitute, the plan administrator must file notice with the corporation at least 10 days before the date of the proposed termination, and he may pay no benefit under termination procedures of the plan for 90 days after the proposed termination date, unless, in the interim, he receives a notice of determination from the corporation that the plan assets are sufficient to discharge the plan obligations as they fall due. The plan administrator of the corporation is authorized to petition the court for appointment of a trustee to manage the plan under the same procedure by which a trustee may be appointed in the case of an involuntary termination, if the best interest of the participants and beneficiaries would be served by the appointment. In other respects the conferees accepted the substance of the Senate admendment.

A plan termination in the sense that benefits stop accruing (as provided in section 411(d)(3) of the Internal Revenue Code) is not to be termination under the insurance provisions so long as the employer continues to meet the funding standards provided by the substitute.

[ERISA Sec. 4041A]

[¶ 15,449F.10]

Committee Report on P.L. 96-364 (Multiemployer Pension Plan Amendments Act of 1980)

[Senate Committee Report]

The bill provides that a plan termination occurs as the result of (1) the adoption of a plan amendment providing that participants will receive no credit for any purpose under the plan for service with any employer (termination by "freezing"); (2) the adoption of a plan amendment that causes the plan to become a defined contribution plan (termination by "change of plan type"); and (3) the withdrawal of every employer from the plan (termination by "mass withdrawal"). Except for a termination by mass withdrawal, the minimum funding standards continue to apply to a terminated plan.

The PBGC is authorized by the bill to prescribe reporting requirements or standards (not in derogation of any other applicable requirement or standard under ERISA) for the administration of terminated plans as it deems necessary to protect the interests of plan participants or to prevent unreasonable losses to the PBGC.

Termination by plan amendment.—Termination by freezing and termination by change of plan type as opposed to termination by mass withdrawal, are accomplished through plan amendment. These terminations by amendment are effective on the later of the date on which the amendment is adopted or the date on which the amendment takes effect.

If a plan is terminated by amendment, each employer's contribution rate after the termination must at least equal that employer's highest contribution rate in the five preceding plan years ending before the plan termination date. The corporation may, however, approve a reduction in the rate if it finds that the plan is or soon will be fully funded. Plans terminated by amendment remain ongoing plans for purposes of reorganization funding.

The Committees recognize that a plan may terminate by amendment and later become a plan from which every employer has withdrawn. In such a case, the termination by mass withdrawal rules become applicable once every employer has withdrawn.

The date on which a plan terminates by mass withdrawal is the earlier of the dates on which (1) the last employer withdraws or (2) the beginning of the first plan year for which no employer contributions were required under the plan.

In addition to the general rules on limiting payments to nonforfeitable benefits in the form of an annuity, the plan sponsor of a plan terminated by mass withdrawal must observe additional rules concerning the suspension of benefit payments.

If the present value of nonforfeitable benefits exceeds the value of the plan's assets, the plan sponsor must suspend benefits to the extent necessary to ensure that the plan's assets are sufficient to pay benefits (as reduced).

The sponsor of a plan terminated by mass withdrawal must limit the payment of benefits to nonforfeitable benefits under the plan as of the termination date. The sponsor of such a plan must also cause benefits attributable to employer contributions, other than death benefits, to be paid only in the form of an annuity, unless the plan distributes its assets in satisfaction of all nonforfeitable benefits under the plan. Notwithstanding the preceding, (1) the plan sponsor may authorize a distribution of the present value of a participant's entire nonforfeitable benefit attributable to employer contributions, other than a death benefit, in a form other than an annuity if the distribution does not exceed $1,750, and (2) the PBGC may authorize the payment of benefits other than nonforfeitable benefits or in lump sum amounts greater than $1,750 if it makes certain determinations.

Effective date

These provisions of the bill apply on the date of enactment.

[ERISA Sec. 4042]

[¶ 15,450.075]

Committee Report on P.L. 109-280 (Pension Protection Act of 2006)

For the Committee Report on P.L. 109-280 on disclosure of plan termination information to participants, see ¶ 15,440.075.

[¶ 15,450.08]

Committee Report on P.L. 103-465 (General Agreement on Tariffs and Trade (GATT); Retirement Protection Act)

See ¶ 15,461.095.

[¶ 15,450.085]

Committee Report on P.L. 100-203 (Omnibus Budget Reconciliation Act of 1987)

. . . relating to plan terminations see ¶ 15,420.095. For the committee report on P.L. 100-203, relating to reporting requirements, see ¶ 15,440.085.

[¶ 15,450.095]

Committee Report on P.L. 99-272 (Consolidated Omnibus Budget Reconciliation Act)

[House Committee Report]

The PBGC's authority to terminate a plan involuntarily under section 4042 is generally unchanged, except that the PBGC is required to institute proceedings to involuntarily terminate a plan that does not have enough assets to pay benefits that are currently due.

[¶ 15,450.10]

Committee Report on P.L. 93-406 (Employee Retirement Income Security Act of 1974)

[Conference Committee Explanation]

Termination by Pension Benefit Guaranty Corporation.—* * *

Under the conference substitute, the corporation may institute termination proceedings in court if it finds that:

(1) minimum funding standards have not been met,

(2) the plan is unable to pay benefits when due,

(3) a distribution is made to an owner-employee of $10,000 in any 24-month period if not paid by reason of death and if, after the distribution, there are unfunded vested liabilities, or

(4) the possible long-run liability to the corporation with respect to the plan may reasonably be expected to increase unreasonably if the plan is not terminated.

In seeking a termination, the corporation is to apply to the appropriate United States District Court, with notice to the plan, for appointment of a trustee to administer the plan pending issuance of a termination decree. Unless cause is shown within three days thereafter why a trustee should not be appointed, the appointment is to be made and the trustee is to administer the plan until the corporation decides whether the plan should be terminated. The court may appoint the trustee from a list furnished to the court by the corporation, or it may appoint the existing plan administrator or the corporation itself. Even without the appointment of a trustee, however, the corporation may, with notice to the plan, apply for a termination decree.

If it grants the decree, the court is to order the trustee (after first appointing a trustee, if none has yet been appointed) to terminate the plan.

A trustee with the discretion to commence the final liquidation of the trust must first give the corporation at least 10 days' notice. If the corporation should oppose the trustee's proposal, the court is to resolve the dispute.

In the case of small plans, the corporation may prescribe a simplified procedure and may pool assets of small plans so long as the rights of the participants and employers (including the right to a court decree of termination) are preserved. Furthermore, the corporation may agree with any plan administrator to designate a trustee who, without court appointment, is to have the usual powers of trustees appointed by the court.

If the application for a trustee is rejected by the court, the trustee is to transfer all assets and records of the plan back to the plan administrator within three days. If the corporation fails to apply within 30 days after appointment of the trustee for a termination decree, the trustee is to transfer the assets and records back to the plan administrator. This 30-day period may be extended by agreement or court order.

The compensation of the trustee is to be despite the pendency in any court of bankruptcy, mortgage foreclosure, or equity receivership proceeding, or any proceeding to reorganize, conserve, or liquidate such plan or its property, or any proceeding to enforce a lien against property of the plan. The court may also stay any of these proceedings. In the termination proceedings, the court is to have the exclusive jurisdiction of the plan and its assets with powers of a court in bankruptcy and of a court in a Chapter X proceeding.

The corporation may file for termination approved by the corporation, and, in the case of a trustee appointed by the court, with the consent of the court. Trustees are in accordance with regulations to be issued authorized to employ professional assistance by the corporation.

* * *

Management functions.—* * *

Under the conference substitute, the trustee is to take over general management of the assets. The Advisory Committtee is to make timely recommendations to the corporation regarding investment policy relating to funds of terminated plans and on whether terminating plans, at the time, should be operated as liquidating trusts or liquidated (with the proceeds used to purchase annuities for the participants and beneficiaries). The corporation is to make recommendations to trustees of terminated plans regarding investments and is to direct each trustee whether to operate his plan as a wasting trust or to liquidate it and purchase annuities. If the trustee disagrees with the directive of the corporation, he is authorized to apply to the court for a resolution of the dispute.

[ERISA Sec. 4043]

[¶ 15,460.09]

Committee Report on P.L. 109-280 (Pension Protection Act of 2006)

For the Committee Report on P.L. 109-280 on rules for substantial owner benefits in terminated plans, see ¶ 15,420.08.

[¶ 15,460.095]

Committee Report on P.L. 103-465 (General Agreement on Tariffs and Trade (GATT); Retirement Protection Act)

[House Committee Report]

Reportable events

The bill provides that a contributing sponsor that knows or has reason to know that a reportable event has occurred (as well as the plan administrator) is responsible for reporting the event to the PBGC, and repeals the requirement that an employer notify the plan administrator of reportable events.

The bill adds a number of new events to the list of reportable events. Under the bill, a reportable event occurs: (1) when a person ceases to be a member of the controlled group; (2) when a contributing sponsor or a member of a contributing sponsor's controlled group liquidates in a case under title 11, United States Code, or under any similar Federal law or law of a State or political subdivision of a State; (3) when a contributing sponsor or a member of a contributing sponsor's controlled group declares an extraordinary dividend or redeems, in any 12-month period, an aggregate of 10 percent or more of the total combined voting power of all classes of stock entitled to vote, or an aggregate of 10 percent or more of the total value of shares of all classes of stock, of a contributing sponsor and all members of its controlled group; (4) when, in any 12-month period, an aggregate of 3 percent or more of the benefit liabilities of a plan covered by the PBGC insurance program are transferred to a person that is not a member of the contributing sponsor's controlled group or to a plan maintained by a person that is not a member of the contributing sponsor's controlled group.

A contributing sponsor is required to notify the PBGC of the occurrence of one of the new reportable events at least 30 days in advance of the effective date of the event if (1) as of the close of the preceding plan year, aggregate unfunded vested benefits of plans maintained by the contributing sponsor (or controlled group members) exceed $50 million, and (2) the funded vested benefit percentage of the plans is less than 90 percent. This advance notice requirement does not apply to an event if the contributing sponsor or the member of the contributing sponsor's controlled group to which the event relates is a person subject to the reporting requirements of section 13 or section 15(d) of the Securities Exchange Act of 1934 or is a subsidiary (as defined for purposes of such Act) of a person subject to such reporting requirements.

Any information provided to the PBGC with respect to a reportable event generally is exempt from public disclosure.

Effective date

The provision is effective for events occurring 60 days or more after the date of enactment [December 8, 1994].

[¶ 15,460.10]

Committee Report on P.L. 93-406 (Employee Retirement Income Security Act of 1974)

[Conference Committee Explanation]

Reportable events.—Under the House bill, certain events indicating possible danger of plan termination must be reported by the plan administrator to the corporation. These events are:

(a) a tax disqualification;

(b) a benefit decrease by plan amendment;

(c) a decrease in active participants to 80 percent of the number at the beginning of the plan year, or 75 percent of the number at the beginning of the previous plan year;

(d) an IRS determination that there has been a plan termination or partial termination for tax purposes;

(e) a failure to meet the minimum funding standards;

(f) inability to pay benefits when due;

(g) a distribution of $10,000 or more in a 24-month period to a "substantial owner," if the plan has unfunded nonforfeitable benefits after the distribution (unless the distribution was made on account of death);

(h) filing of a report preliminary to a merger, consolidation, transfer of assets or liabilities, or a distribution in excess of $25,000 to a participant in any plan year, or the granting by the Secretary of Labor of a hearing in regard to a variation on the bill's standards; or

(i) the occurrence of any other event which the corporation determines may be indicative of a need to terminate the plan.

* * *

The conference substitute requires the plan administrator to inform the corporation with respect to the same listing or reportable events as listed in the House bill. However, the corporation is authorized to waive the requirement and to require any of the events referred to above to be included in the annual report made by the plan. In addition, any employer in a covered plan who knows, or has reason to know, that a reportable event has occurred is immediately to notify the plan administrator of this event.

[ERISA Sec. 4044]

[¶ 15,470.09]

Committee Report on 109-280 (Pension Protection Act of 2006)

For the Committee Report on P.L. 109-280 on rules for substantial owner benefits in terminated plans, on rules relating to the acceleration of PBGC computation of benefits attributable to recoveries from employers, and on rules relating to the bankruptcy of the employer, see ¶ 15,420.08.

[¶ 15,470.095]

Committee Report on P.L 100-203 (Omnibus Budget Reconciliation Act of 1987)

[Conference Committee Report]

Education and Labor Committee bill: Assets in excess of "benefit liabilities" are allocated to mandatory employee contributions in the ratio that the present value of accrued benefits attributable to mandatory employee contributions bears to the present value of total benefits. Such excess is allocated among participants, beneficiaries, alternate payees, and persons who received a total distribution of plan benefits during the 3-year period before plan termination, based on the amount of employee contributions they are entitled to. The term "benefit liabilities" has the same meaning as termination liability under present law.

[Conference Agreement]

The conference agreement follows the Ways and Means Committee bill, with one modification. The conference agreement follows the Education and Labor Committee bill with respect to the allocation of excess assets to employee contributions, except that the effective date is for plan terminations for which notice of termination is sent to participants after December 17, 1987.

[House Bill]

Education and Labor Committee bill: An employer may receive a reversion of assets in excess of those required to be allocated under the rule described above, but only if the plan so provides. In determining the extent to which a plan provides for the reversion of excess assets, any provision providing for a reversion or increasing the amount that may revert is not effective before the end of the 5th calendar year following the date of the adoption of the provision. A special rule applies with respect to a plan that has been in existence less than 5 years. Additional rules apply to prevent avoidance of this requirement through transactions such as plan mergers.

Any assets that may not be distributed to the employer because of the above rule are to be distributed to participants, beneficiaries, etc., subject to the applicable limits on benefits (sec., 415) and to the nondiscrimination rules (sec. 401(a)(4)).

[Conference Agreement]

The conference agreement follows the Education and Labor Committee bill, with a modification of the effective date.

[¶ 15,470.10]

Committee Report on P.L. 93-406 (Employee Retirement Income Security Act of 1974)

[Conference Committee Explanation]

Allocation of assets as termination.—

* * *

Under the conference substitute, assets are to be allocated among plan benefits in the levels of priorities stated below:

(1) Voluntary employee contributions,

(2) Mandatory employee contributions,

(3) Equally among individuals in the following two subcategories:

(i) in the case of benefits in pay status three years prior to termination (at the lowest pay level in that period and at the lowest benefit level under the plan during the five years prior to termination) and

(ii) in the case of benefits which would have been in pay status three years prior to termination had the participant been retired (and had his benefits commenced then, at the lowest benefit level under the plan during the five years prior to termination),

(4) All other guaranteed benefits up to the insurance limitations (but irrespective of the limitation to one $750 monthly benefit regardless of the number of plans in which the employee participated) and (on an equal level of priority) benefits that would be so guaranteed except for the special limitation on coverage of a "substantial owner,"

(5) All other (meaning uninsured) vested benefits, and

(6) All other benefits under the plan.

The plan may, under regulations, establish subclasses and categories within these six classes.

[ERISA Sec. 4045]

[¶ 15,480.10]

Committee Report on P.L. 93-406 (Employee Retirement Income Security Act of 1974)

[Conference Committee Explanation]

Recapture of plan payments.—Under the Senate amendment, certain payments of a terminated plan affecting interstate commerce made during a three-year period prior to termination may be recovered. Payments made on account of death or disability were not to be subject to recovery, and the corporation was authorized to waive recovery of certain amounts when the recovery would have caused substantial hardship.

In the case of a distribution to an owner-employee that exceeds $10,000 and creates or increases unfunded vested liabilities, the three-year lookback period would not begin until the corporation is informed of the distribution (which is a reportable event under both the Senate amendment and the conference substitute).

Under the conference substitute, the trustee may recover all payments to a participant in excess of $10,000 (or the amount he would have received as a monthly benefit under a lifetime annuity commencing at age 65, if greater) made during any twelve-month period within the three years prior to termination.

As under the Senate amendment, the conference substitute provides that there is to be no recovery of payments for after death or death or disability, that the three-year period is not to end, in the case of a distribution to a substantial owner (after which the plan has unfunded vested liabilities), until the corporation is notified of the distribution, and that the corporation is authorized to waive any recovery that would cause substantial economic hardship.

[ERISA Sec. 4046]

[¶ 15,490.10]

Committee Report on P.L. 93-406 (Employee Retirement Income Security Act of 1974)

See ¶ 15,420.10, ¶ 15,450.10 and ¶ 15,470.10.

[ERISA Sec. 4047]

[¶ 15,500.10]

Committee Report on P.L. 93-406 (Employee Retirement Income Security Act of 1974)

[Conference Committee Explanation]

Restoration of plans.—

* * *

Under the conference substitute, the corporation may cease any termination activities and do what it can to restore the plan to its former status. As a result, a terminated plan being operated by a trustee as a wasting trust may be restored if, during the period of its operation by the trustee, experience gains or increased funding make it sufficiently solvent. The corporation may, when appropriate, transfer to the employer or plan administrator part of all of the remaining assets and liabilities.

[ERISA Sec. 4048]

[¶ 15,510.095]

Committee Report on P.L. 96-364 (Multiemployer Pension Plan Amendments Act of 1980)

[Senate Committee Report]

. . . see ¶ 15,449F.

[¶ 15,510.10]

Committee Report on P.L. 93-406 (Employee Retirement Income Security Act of 1974)

[Conference Committee Explanation]

Date of termination.—The termination date of a plan is to be determined by the plan administrator or the corporation, depending upon which terminates the plan and also depending upon whether this date is agreed to by the other party. If there is not agreement between the corporation and the plan administrator, the termination date is to be established by the court. However, in the case of terminations of plans which occur before the date of enactment, the date of termination is to be set by the corporation on the basis of the date on which benefits ceased to accrue or on any other appropriate basis.

[ERISA Sec. 4049]

[¶ 15,520.09]

Committee Report on P.L. 100-203 (Omnibus Budget Reconciliation Act of 1987)

. . . relating to plan terminations, see ¶ 15,420.095.

[¶ 15,520.10]

Committee Report on P.L. 99-272 (Consolidated Omnibus Budget Reconciliation Act)

. . . relating to new termination rules, see ¶ 15,620.09.

[ERISA Sec. 4050]

[¶ 15,530.07]

Committee Report on P.L. 109-280 (Pension Protection Act of 2006)

[Joint Committee on Taxation Report]

Under the bill, the PBGC is directed to prescribe rules for terminating multiemployer plans similar to the present-law missing participant rules applicable to terminating single-employer plans that are subject to Title IV of ERISA.

In addition, under the bill, plan administrators of certain types of plans not subject to the PBGC termination insurance program under present law are permitted, but not required, to elect to transfer missing participants' benefits to the PBGC upon plan termination. Specifically, the provision extends the missing participants program (in accordance with regulations) to defined contribution plans, defined benefit pension plans that have no more than 25 active participants and are maintained by professional service employers, and the portion of defined benefit pension plans that provide benefits based upon the separate accounts of participants and therefore are treated as defined contribution plans under ERISA.

Effective Date

The provision is effective for distributions made after final regulations implementing the provision are prescribed.

[¶ 15,530.08]

Committee Report on P.L. 103-465 (General Agreement on Tariffs and Trade (GATT); Retirement Protection Act)

[House Committee Report]

Procedures to facilitate the distribution of termination benefits

a. Remedies for noncompliance with requirements for standard terminations.— The bill provides that the PBGC is not required to issue a notice of noncompliance (and nullify a termination) in the case of failure to meet procedural requirements with respect to the termination if it determines that it would be inconsistent with the interests of participants and beneficiaries to issue the notice.

Effective date

The provision applies with respect to standard terminations for which the PBGC has not, as of the date of enactment [December 8, 1994], issued a notice of noncompliance that has become final, or otherwise issued a final determination that the plan termination is nullified.

b. Distress termination criteria for banking institutions.—The bill provides that a proceeding under title 11 of the United States Code or any similar Federal law qualifies as a standard for distress criteria. This standard applies, for example, to bank insolvency receivership actions.

Effective date

The provision is effective as if included in the SEPPAA. Thus, it is effective with respect to notices of intent to terminate filed with the PBGC on or after January 1, 1986.

[ERISA Sec. 4061]

[¶ 15,610.10]

Committee Report on P.L. 93-406 (Employee Retirement Income Security Act of 1974)

See ¶ 15,420.10.

[ERISA Sec. 4062]

[¶ 15,620.08]

Committee Report on P.L. 100-203 (Omnibus Budget Reconciliation Act of 1987)

. . . relating to plan terminations, see ¶ 15,420.095.

[¶ 15,620.09]

Committee Report on P.L. 99-272 (Consolidated Omnibus Budget Reconciliation Act)

[Conference Committee Report]

Employer liability under a terminated plan.—Upon the termination of a plan, pursuant to a standard termination in which all benefit commitments are fully funded, the employer has no further liability to the PBGC or to plan participants.

Liability to PBGC.—Upon the termination of a plan pursuant to a distress termination, if the PBGC determines that plan assets are insufficient to fund guaranteed benefits, the PBGC is required to institute trusteeship proceedings for the plan. Each contributing sponsor of the plan and each member of the controlled group of each contributing sponsor is jointly and severally liable to the PBGC for the sum of (1) the total amount of all unfunded guaranteed benefits, up to 30 percent of the collective net worth of those persons liable to the PBGC; (2) an amount equal to the excess (if any) of (a) 75 percent of the total amount of all unfunded guaranteed benefits over (b) the amount described in (1); and (3) interest on the amount due calculated from the termination date. The total amount of unfunded guaranteed benefits is computed by treating any accumulated funding deficiency and the balance of any waived funding deficiency as a receivable of the plan and, thus, as a plan asset.

The full amount of the liability to the PBGC is generally due and payable as of the date of plan termination. However, if the liability to the PBGC for unfunded guaranteed benefits exceeds 30 percent of the collective net worth of the parties that are liable to the PBGC, the payment of that excess amount is to be made under commercially reasonable terms prescribed by the PBGC. The parties are to make a reasonable effort to reach agreement on such terms. Under the conference agreement, any terms prescribed by the PBGC must provide for the deferral of 50 percent of any amount of liability otherwise payable for any year if the PBGC determines that no person subject to such liability has individual pretax profits for the fiscal year ending during such year.

If a plan terminates pursuant to a distress termination and is subject to PBGC trusteeship proceedings, then each contributing sponsor and each member of their controlled groups is liable to the PBGC for the sum of (1) the outstanding balance of any accumulated funding deficiency, and (2) the balance of the amount of any waived funding deficiencies. The full amount of such liability is due and payable to the PBGC as of the date of plan termination.

The conferees take no position with respect to the treatment in bankruptcy of PBGC claims and liens. Deletion of the amendments to section 4068 that appeared in S. 1730 is not intended to express any view on the meaning of the present language in section 4068. Section 4068 has been amended, however, to assure that it applies only to the liability that was covered by section 4068 prior to these amendments, i.e., the value of unfunded guaranteed benefits up to 30 percent of the employer's net worth. Section 4068 does not apply to liability being added to section 4062 by these amendments for amounts in excess of the 30 percent of net worth cap.

Liability to participants.—If the PBGC determines that there is an outstanding amount of benefit commitments, the PBGC is required to appoint a fiduciary with respect to the termination trust. The fiduciary must be independent of the contributing sponsors (and members of a controlled group including sponsors) and generally is subject to the fiduciary requirements of ERISA (other than the prohibited transaction rules). The "outstanding amount of benefit commitments" under a plan is defined as the excess of (1) the actuarial present value of the benefit commitments of each participant and beneficiary over (2) the actuarial present value of the benefits of each participant and beneficiary that are guaranteed by the PBGC or to which assets of the plan have been allocated under the distribution procedures of section 4044 of ERISA. Each contributing sponsor of the plan and each member of the controlled group of a contributing sponsor is jointly and severally liable to the termination trust for the lesser of (1) 75 percent of the total amount of outstanding benefit commitments under the plan, or (2) 15 percent of the total amount of benefit commitments under the plan. The termination trust generally will be administered by the PBGC except in cases in which PBGC determines that delegation of this responsibility is cost effective.

Under the conference agreement, payment of liability is to be made under commercially reasonable terms prescribed by the fiduciary of the termination trust. The parties are required to make a reasonable effort to reach agreement on such terms. In addition, the conference agreement provides that if liability to the termination trust is less than $100,000, the payment of liability to the trust over 10 years in equal annual installments (with interest at the applicable rate determined under sec. 6621(b) of the Code) will satisfy this requirement even if the terms are not commercially reasonable. The PBGC is permitted to increase, by regulation, the $100,000 ceiling. To phase in this $100,000 rule, the conference agreement provides that no payment under this provision is required before January 1, 1989.

The conference agreement also provides that any payment schedule is to provide for the deferral of 75 percent of the liability otherwise payable to the termination trust for any year if no person subject to liability to the termination trust has any individual pre-tax profits for such person's fiscal year ending during such year. However, the conferees intend that the fact that one person has minimal profits should not make the benefits of deferral totally unavailable. * * * The amount of liability so deferred is payable only after payment of any liability to the PBGC arising in connection with the terminated plan.

The conference agreement provides rules governing the allocation and distribution of assets of the termination trust to participants and beneficiaries.

Under the conference agreement, a participant or beneficiary who receives distributions from a termination trust is, subject to certain requirements, permitted to roll over the distribution to an IRA * * *.

[¶ 15,620.10]

Committee Report on P.L. 93-406 (Employee Retirement Income Security Act of 1974)

[Conference Committee Explanation]

Employer liability.—

* * *

Under the conference substitute, employer liability is required for employers in both single-employer and multiemployer plans. The employer liability is limited to 30 percent of net worth, with net worth valued as of a date chosen by the corporation, but not more than 120 days prior to the termination.

Net worth is to be computed without taking the contingent employer liability into the calculation. It is determined on the basis chosen by the corporation to reflect best the operating value of the employer, and it is to be increased by any transfers made by the employer prior to the termination that the corporation finds improper.

In determining the employer who may be liable for insurance coverage losses of the corporation, all trades or businesses (whether or not incorporated) under common control are to be treated as a single employer. Trades or businesses under common control may, for this purpose, include partnerships and proprietorships as well as corporations.

If, as a result of the cessation of operations at any facility, more than 20 percent of the participants in a plan are separated from their employment, the employer is to be treated as an employer in a terminating plan that is maintained by more than one employer. Furthermore, in the case of withdrawals of employers in multiemployer plans resulting in substantial reductions of contributions, the corporation may treat the withdrawal as constituting a termination with respect to employees of such employers.

In determining the amount of the corporation's liability, the amount of employer liability (but not the employer's net worth), the application of the lien arising out of employer liability, the appropriate allocation of assets in the event of a termination, the value of the plan's assets, the amount of benefits payable with respect to each participant, the amount of benefits guaranteed with respect to each participant, the present value of the aggregate amount of benefits potentially payable by the corporation, and the fair market value of the plan's assets, the date of determination is to be the date of termination.

In determining the fair market value of a plan's assets, unrealized gain is to be taken into account.

[ERISA Sec. 4063]

[¶ 15,630.10]

Committee Report on P.L. 93-406 (Employee Retirement Income Security Act of 1974)

[Conference Committee Explanation]

Liability of substantial employer for withdrawal.—

* * *

Under the conference substitute, the plan administrator is required to notify the corporation within 60 days after the withdrawal of a substantial employer from a plan under which more than one employer makes contributions.

The corporation may require the substantial owner either to pay the potential liability (as determined by the corporation) into escrow or to post a bond in 150 percent of the amount of the liability. The liability is normally to be determined as the substantial employer's share (with the substantial employer's share computed according to that employer's proportion of the total employer contributions to the plan within the past five years) of the total plan liability that would have existed if the plan had terminated when the substantial owner withdrew. However, the corporation is also authorized to determine the liability according to any other equitable basis prescribed by it in regulations.

If the plan terminates within five years, the payment or bond is forfeited for the benefit of the plan, but the employer may be refunded any amount not needed to meet the plan's liabilities. If there is no termination, the payment or bond is to be returned to the substantial employer or cancelled.

As alternatives to the bond or escrow payment requirement, the corporation may, if the withdrawal causes a significant reduction in the amount of plan contributions, require the plan fund to be allocated between those participants no longer under the plan because of the withdrawal and those participants still covered. That portion of the fund allocable to participants no longer in the plan is to be treated as a termination, while the remainder is to be a new plan.

The corporation is entitled to waive the use of either of these procedures if there is an indemnity agreement between all the other employers in the plan sufficient to satisfy all plan liabilities.

[ERISA Sec. 4064]

[¶ 15,640.07]

Committee Report on P.L. 100-203 (Omnibus Budget Reconciliation Act of 1987)

For the Committee Report on P.L. 100-203, relating to plan terminations, see ¶ 15,420.095.

[¶ 15,640.08]

Committee Report on P.L. 96-364 (Multiemployer Pension Plan Amendments Act of 1980)

. . . see Committee Report at ¶ 15,663.10.

[¶ 15,640.10]

Committee Report on P.L. 93-406 (Employee Retirement Income Security Act of 1974)

[Conference Committee Explanation]

Liability of employers on termination of plan maintained by more than one employer.—* * * Under the Senate amendment, the employer liability on termination of a multiemployer plan was to be allocated among the employers who had contributed to the plan during the five years before termination, in proportion to their contributions. The 30-percent of net worth limit on employer liability was to be applied separately to each employer.

Under the conference substitute, the general rule of the Senate amendment is accepted with the three modifications:

1. This particular computation of employer liability is to apply to all plans having more than one employer making contributions at the time of the termination, or at any time within the five plan years preceding the date of termination.

2. The allocation is not to be in accordance with the actual contributions made by employers during the last five plan years ending prior to the termination, but according to the amounts *required* to be contributed by each employer during that period.

3. The corporation is authorized to determine the liability of each employer on any other equitable basis prescribed in the corporation's regulations.

This regulatory authority extends in two directions. That is, the corporation is authorized to permit other equitable methods of allocation to be used by the employers in the plan, where such other method of allocation would not increase the likelihood that the entire plan would terminate. Also, the corporation is authorized to require the use of other equitable methods where allocation in proportion to contributions would produce inequitable results. For example, the corporation is authorized to require a different allocation basis if the employers in a plan have agreed on a contribution formula that would have the effect of shifting employer liability from those employers that had net assets to those employers that had little or no net assets.

In this regard, it should be noted that the affiliated employer rules are to apply in this area. That is, if one member of an affiliated group has employer liability, then that liability is to extend to the entire affiliated group. Also, the 30-percent-of-net-assets limit is to apply with respect to the net assets of the entire group.

[ERISA Sec. 4065]

[¶ 15,650.095]

Committee Report on P.L. 96-364 (Multiemployer Pension Plan Amendments Act of 1980)

[Senate Committee Explanation]

Annual report of plan administrator.—The bill adds a requirement that the annual report of a plan administrator, with respect to a plan subject to termination insurance, include such information with respect to the plan as the PBGC determines is necessary for enforcement purposes and that is required by PBGC regulations. The bill provides that the information required may include (1) a statement by the plan's enrolled actuary of (a) the present value of all benefit entitlements under the plan as of the end of the plan year, and (b) the value of plan assets as of that time; and (2) a statement certified by the plan administrator of the value of each outstanding claim for withdrawal liability as of the close of the plan year and as of the close of the preceding plan year.

[¶ 15,650.10]

Committee Report on P.L. 93-406 (Employee Retirement Income Security Act of 1974)

. . . see ¶ 15,460.10 and ¶ 15,630.10.

[ERISA Sec. 4067]

[¶ 15,661.08]

Committee Report on P.L. 100-203 (Omnibus Budget Reconciliation Act of 1987)

. . . see ¶ 15,420.095.

[¶ 15,661.09]

Committee Report on P.L. 99-272 (Consolidated Omnibus Budget Reconciliation Act)

. . . relating to new termination liability rules, see ¶ 15,620.09.

[¶ 15,661.10]

Committee Report on P.L. 93-406 (Employee Retirement Income Security Act of 1974)

See ¶ 15,620.10, ¶ 15,630.10, and ¶ 15,640.10.

[ERISA Sec. 4068]

[¶ 15,662.09]

Committee Report on P.L. 100-203 (Omnibus Budget Reconciliation Act of 1987)

. . . relating to plan terminations, see ¶ 15,420.095.

[¶ 15,662.10]

Committee Report on P.L. 93-406 (Employee Retirement Income Security Act of 1974)

[Conference Committee Explanation]

Lien for employer liability.—The House bill provides for the imposition of a lien upon all property and rights in property belonging to an employer who is liable to the corporation as a result of a plan termination. Under this provision, the lien would arise if payment were not made after demand for payment was made by the corporation and would be in the amount of the liability including interest. Further, the lien would not be valid against the general Federal tax lien.

The Senate amendment provided that the lien would also be inferior to the special estate and gift tax lien imposed under the Internal Revenue Code and, if arising from an obligation incurred by the employer prior to termination of the plan, a lien or other security interest which is perfected not later than 30 days after termination. The amendment further modifies the House bill by authorizing the corporation to subordinate the lien under certain circumstances.

The conference substitute in general follows the lien imposition provisions of both bills but provides (1) additional rules relating to the period during which the lien will be in existence; (2) that the priority of the lien is to be determined in the same manner as under the Federal tax lien rules to minimize circular priority problems; (3) rules relating to the civil action to foreclose the lien, including the period during which an action must be commenced; and (4) authority for the corporation to release or subordinate the lien under certain circumstances.

More specifically, the revised and added provisions may be explained as follows:

(1) The conference substitute adopts the lien priority rules of the Internal Revenue Code. Generally, these rules provide protection against the lien for a purchaser, holder of a security interest, mechanic's lienor, or judgment lien creditor if any such person's title or interest is acquired or perfected before notice of the lien is filed. Protection is also provided for certain other interests even if acquired or perfected after notice of the lien is filed. Generally, if the purchaser or creditor does not have actual notice or knowledge of the lien, this status is provided for a purchaser or a holder of a security interest in a security (stocks, bonds, negotiable instruments, etc.), a purchaser of a motor vehicle, a purchaser of certain household goods or personal effects in a casual sale for less than $250, an insurer which makes a loan secured by a policy issued by it, and a financial institution which makes a passbook loan secured by an account with the institution. This status is also provided for certain retail purchases, possessory liens, real property tax assessments, liens for repairs to a residence, and attorney's liens.

Protection against the lien is also provided with respect to certain advances which are made, after notice of the lien is filed, pursuant to a commercial transaction financing agreement, a real property construction or improvement financing agreement, or an obligatory disbursement agreement.

In the case of bankruptcy or insolvency proceedings, the lien is to be treated in the same manner as a tax due and owing to the United States.

The conference substitute provides that, for purposes of determining the priority between a Federal tax lien and the employer liability lien each lien is to be treated as a judgment lien arising when notice of that lien is filed. The effect of this is to adopt a "first to file" priority rule with respect to the employer liability lien and the Federal tax lien imposed under section 6321 of the Internal Revenue Code.

(2) The conference substitute provides that the corporation may bring a civil action in a district court of the United States to enforce the employer liability lien or to subject any property belonging to an employer to the payment of the employer's liability to the corporation. Generally, this action must be commenced within 6 years after the date upon which the plan is terminated or prior to the expiration of any period for collection agreed upon in writing by the corporation and the employer before the expiration of the 6-year period.

(3) The conference substitute provides for both the release and subordination of the lien. The lien may be released or subordinated if the corporation determines, with the consent of the board of directors, that release or subordination of the lien would not adversely affect the collection of liability to the corporation. Under these conditions, the corporation may issue a certificate of release or subordination of the lien with respect to the employer's property or any part thereof.

[ERISA Sec. 4069]

[¶ 15,662L.10]

Committee Reports on P.L. 99-272 (Consolidated Omnibus Budget Reconciliation Act)

[House Committee Report]

Currently there is no express provision in title IV of ERISA regarding transactions intended to avoid liability in the single-employer program. The bill incorporates court decisions under current law by adding explicit statutory language to make clear that transactions, a principal purpose of which is to evade liability under the statute, are to be ignored in determining liability.

In the case of *Solar v. PBGC,* 504 F.Supp. 116 (D.C.N.Y 1981), *Aff'd,* 666 F.2d 28 (2d Cir. 1981), the court correctly ruled that a transaction intended to avoid liability should be disregarded for title IV liability purposes. It has always been the intent of the law that solvent employers who benefit from work performed in return for pension promises, pay for those pension benefits rather than shift that cost to other companies which fund plans that pay PBGC premiums.

The absence of an express provision has perhaps increased the likelihood that abusive schemes would be attempted. The bill's evasion rule is intended to deter such attempts, which can lead to complex, costly litigation. The rule in the Committee's bill is written in general terms. In the last Congress, H.R. 3930, the predecessor single-employer reform bill in the House, attempted to specify abusive transfers of liability transactions. There was some concern expressed by employer groups and others that such a detailed provision might result in unintended imposition of liability in some cases and fail to impose intended liability in others. Therefore, a more general rule has been adopted by the Committee in this bill.

The Committee hopes that the existence of this explicit statutory provision will deter shifting of pension obligations to very weak companies. It is the Committee's intention that the PBGC carefully scrutinize transfers of unfunded pension liabilities from stronger to weaker companies, especially where a financial connection exists or has existed between the companies.

In addition to transactions designed to evade liability to the PBGC, this provision also applies to any situations in which a principal purpose of a transaction is to evade liability to participants and beneficiaries for benefit [commitments]. For example, if a principal purpose behind a spinoff transaction is to enable a person to evade responsibility for paying certain benefit entitlements that are not guaranteed by the PBGC, such as early retirement supplements, the person shall continue to be subject to liability for those benefits as if the person was a contributing sponsor of the plan as of the termination date. In the event the person and the members of its controlled group would not have been able to satisfy the criteria for a distress termination, they shall be directly responsible for making the plan sufficient for all benefit entitlements, just as under a standard termination. * * *

The bill contains a 5-year lookback limit for purposes of this provision. Thus if a distress termination occurs more than 5 years after a transaction to evade liability, there will be no liability under this section with respect to such transaction.

The bill also makes it clear that a transferor controlled group shall never be held liable for any benefit increases or improvements that were adopted after the date the transaction became effective.

Notwithstanding this provision, the transferor controlled group may still be held liable for all benefits which were adopted prior to the date of the transaction, even though participants and beneficiaries did not grow into eligibility for such benefits until after the date of the transaction. Thus, for example, if it is determined that a principal purpose of the transaction was to evade liability for certain previously negotiated early retirement or shutdown benefits which participants were going to "grow into" in the next several years, the transferor controlled group may still be held liable for the full value of those benefits.

* * *

[Conference Committee Report]

The conference agreement generally follows H.R. 3500, except that the conference agreement provision is effective only with respect to transactions occurring on or after the earlier [of] January 1, 1986, or the date of enactment. The provisions of the conference agreement relating to evasive transactions are intended by the conferees to provide appropriate rules for the future. The conferees intend that no inference is to be drawn from these provisions with respect to the application of present law to such transactions. In addition, the conference agreement makes it clear that only contributing sponsors (and members of a controlled group including the contributing sponsors) are affected by this provision.

* * *

[ERISA Sec. 4070]

[¶ 15,662R.10]

Committee Report on P.L. 99-272 (Consolidated Omnibus Budget Reconciliation Act)

[House Committee Report]

This section adds a new section 4070 which permits a fiduciary, * * * contributing sponsor, controlled group member, participant, beneficiary, or employee organization representing participants, adversely affected by an act that violates any provision under this subtitle relating to plan terminations and liability, to bring an action to enjoin such act or obtain other appropriate equitable relief.

A single-employer plan may be sued as an entity. * * * Any money judgment against a plan is not enforceable against any other person unless liability is established in that person's individual capacity.

Federal district courts shall have exclusive jurisdiction of civil actions under this section. The PBGC shall receive a copy of the complaint and has the right to intervene in any action.

In any action brought under this section, the courts may award all or a portion of the costs of such action, including reasonable attorney's fees, to any party who prevails or substantially prevails. However, no plan shall be required to pay any such costs.

* * *

Actions under new section 4070 may not be brought after the later of (1) 6 years after the cause of action arose or (2) 3 years after the earliest date the plaintiff acquired or should have acquired actual knowledge of the cause of action (or 6 years after discovery in the case of fraud or concealment).

[ERISA Sec. 4071]

[¶ 15,662U.10]

Committee Report on P.L. 100-203 (Omnibus Budget Reconciliation Act of 1987)

For the Committee Report on P.L. 100-203, dealing with the penalty for not providing timely information, see ¶ 15,440.085.

[ERISA Sec. 4201]

[¶ 15,663.10]

Committee Report on P.L. 96-364 (Multiemployer Pension Plan Amendments Act of 1980)

[Senate Committee Report]

Complete withdrawal.—The bill treats an employer as withdrawing from a multiemployer plan when the employer (1) permanently ceases to have an obligation to contribute under the plan, or (2) permanently ceases all covered operations under the plan. A withdrawal does not occur, however, where an employer ceases to exist merely by reason of a change in form or structure, as long as the employer is replaced by a successor employer and there is no interruption in the successor employer's contributions to the plan or obligation to contribute under the plan. A group of trades or businesses under common control is treated as a single employer. For example, if P Corporation owns 100 percent of the stock of S Corporation, a subsidiary that has an obligation to contribute to a multiemployer plan on behalf of its employees, the controlled group consisting of P and S would be considered an employer with an obligation to contribute to the plan. If P sells all of its interest in S to an unrelated party, the controlled group consisting of P and S would cease to exist. However, if S continues to have an obligation to contribute to the plan, no withdrawal would be considered to have taken place merely because of the change in ownership of S.

In addition, a withdrawal does not take place merely because an employer suspends making plan contributions during a labor dispute which involves its employees.

With respect to an employer who has completely withdrawn from a multiemployer plan and who subsequently resumes covered operations under the plan or renews an obligation to contribute to the plan, the PBGC is to prescribe regulations regarding the reduction or waiver of the employer's withdrawal liability to the extent consistent with the policy of protecting remaining employers, beneficiaries, and other participants. In addition, the PBGC is to prescribe regulations or a procedure under which a plan can provide rules for the reduction or waiver of withdrawal liability with respect to such an employer in appropriate circumstances.

Partial withdrawal.—Under the bill, an employer becomes subject to withdrawal liability in some cases in the event of a partial withdrawal, that is, where the employer neither completely ceases to have an obligation to contribute under the plan nor permanently ceases all covered operations under the plan. Under the bill, a partial withdrawal arises because of the occurrence of any of three specified events which could significantly decrease the employer's obligations for contributions under the plan. Under the bill, a partial withdrawal occurs—

(1) if the number of contribution base units (e.g., hours worked) with respect to which the employer is required to contribute for each of three consecutive plan years (the three-year testing period) does not exceed 30 percent (25 percent in the case of an employer contributing to a plan for employees in the Great Lakes maritime industry) of the number of contribution base units with respect to which the employer was obligated to contribute under the plan for the average of the two highest years in the five plan years preceding the three-year period (a 70-percent decline in contribution base units);

(2) if an employer who is required to contribute to a plan under two or more collective bargaining agreements ceases to have an obligation to contribute under at least one but not all of the agreements, but continues work in the jurisdiction of the agreement of the type for which contributions were previously required or transfers such work to another location; or

(3) if an employer permanently ceases to have an obligation to contribute under the plan for work performed at one or more but fewer than all of its facilities covered under the plan, but continues to perform work at the facility.

A more restrictive partial withdrawal rule is provided for the retail food industry at the request of representatives of both labor and management in that industry. This rule would treat as a partial withdrawal a diminution of the contribution base of 35 percent, rather than 70 percent, computed in the same manner as under the general rule. Because this rule would impose partial withdrawal liability more frequently than the general rule in the bill, the Committees require that it be accompanied by plan rules providing for proportional reduction of liability if the plan's contribution base does not decline by as many base units as the partially withdrawn employer's. A 70-percent decline in the contribution base units is illustrated by the following example:

Assume a determination is to be made as to whether a partial withdrawal takes place for the plan year which is the calendar year 1987. Assume that the employer's contribution base units for 1985, 1986 and 1987 are 25,000 hours, 26,000 hours, and 27,000 hours respectively, and that the employer's contribution base units for 1980, 1981, 1982, 1983 and 1984 are 102,000 hours, 98,000 hours, 95,000 hours, 91,000 hours, and 85,000 hours respectively.

Contribution base units are the highest in 1980 and 1981 when such units are 102,000 hours and 98,000 hours, respectively. Accordingly, to determine if a partial withdrawal occurs in 1987, it must be determined whether the number of contribution base units in each of 1985, 1986 and 1987 are at least 30 percent of the average number of contribution base units in 1980 and 1981. Because such average contribution base units are 100,000 hours, a withdrawal does not occur unless contribution base units are fewer than 30,000 hours in each of 1985, 1986, and 1987. In this case, contribution base units are fewer than 30,000 hours in each year during the three-year testing period. Accordingly, a partial withdrawal in this case would be considered to take place as of the close of 1987.

A cessation of an employer's obligation to contribute to a plan under one but not all the collective bargaining agreements obligating the employer to contribute to the plan will not be considered to take place in any case where there is a mere substitution of an agreement with one collective bargaining agent for an agreement with another collective bargaining agent under the same plan.

Once it has been determined that a partial withdrawal has occurred, the amount of withdrawal liability is determined by multiplying the amount of withdrawal liability which would have applied in the case of a complete withdrawal (determined after application of the de minimis rules but before the application of the 20-year payment cap or the dollar limitations on withdrawal liability) by (1) one minus (2) a fraction. The numerator of the fraction is the employer's contribution base units for the plan year following the plan year of the partial withdrawal. The denominator of the fraction is the average of the employer's contribution base units for the five plan years immediately preceding the plan year for the partial withdrawal. However, in the case of a partial withdrawal because of a 70-percent decline in contributions the denominator of the fraction is the average of the employer's contribution base units for the five plan years immediately preceding the three-year testing period.

Under the bill, if withdrawal liability is determined on account of a partial withdrawal, the amount of the liability (adjusted for any abatement or other reduction) is applied as an offset against withdrawal liability for any future withdrawal from the plan, whether partial or complete. In addition, the future withdrawal will not relieve the employer from continuing to make its payments for withdrawal liability with respect to the earlier partial withdrawal. The PBGC is authorized to prescribe regulations necessary to make appropriate adjustments in the offset for future events so that withdrawal liability in the event of a future withdrawal properly reflects the employer's proper share of the plan's unfunded vested benefits.

The bill provides for abatement of all or part of an employer's partial withdrawal liability in the event of (1) a two-year 90 percent restoration of contributions, (2) a one-year complete restoration of contributions, (3) a "two-year reversal" of the reduction of contributions which triggered the liability, or (4) a ten percent contribution increase. In addition, the PBGC is authorized to prescribe regulations providing for the reduction or elimination of partial withdrawal liability under conditions where the PBGC determines that such an abatement is consistent with the policy of protecting remaining employers. Also, under a PBGC regulatory procedure, a plan may adopt rules for abatement of partial withdrawal liability under any other conditions, subject to PBGC approval to be based on a determination that the rules are consistent with the policy of protecting remaining employers.

An abatement under a 90-percent restoration of contributions rule completely eliminates the employer's partial withdrawal liability for plan years following the two consecutive plan years in which the 90 percent restoration of contributions takes place.

A one-year complete restoration of contributions occurs where the number of contribution base units used to determine the employer's required contributions for a plan year equals or exceeds the number of such units for a specified testing period. Where such a restoration takes place, the employer may, in lieu of continuing to pay partial withdrawal liability, post a bond to the plan for an amount determined by the plan sponsor not exceeding 50 percent of the otherwise required annual partial withdrawal liability payment. If the plan sponsor determines that the employer has no further partial withdrawal liability, the liability is completely eliminated and the bond is cancelled. If the plan sponsor determines that the employer continues to have partial withdrawal liability, (1) the plan may realize on the bond, (2) the employer remains liable for the amount of the year's liability not covered by the bond, and (3) no abatement takes place.

An abatement under a "two-year reversal" completely eliminates the employer's partial withdrawal liability for plan years following the two consecutive years in which the reversal of the reduction in contributions takes place.

A 10-percent contribution increase occurs where, for a plan year following the partial withdrawal, the number of contribution base units applied to determine the employer's required plan contributions exceeds the number of such units for the year of the partial withdrawal by at least 10 percent. In case of an abatement under this rule, the employer's partial withdrawal liability payment for the year of the abatement is reduced pro rata under PBGC regulations. A plan may use a percentage other than 10 percent in applying this rule, except for a percentage prohibited by PBGC regulations.

The bill provides that the PBGC, by regulation, shall promulgate abatement rules for partial withdrawal liability arising from a partial withdrawal other than a 70-percent decline in contributions. These abatement rules are to be based upon principles similar to those governing abatement of partial withdrawal liability in the case of a 70-percent decline in contributions. However, the tests prescribed are to be applied not with respect to an employer's entire contribution base, but only with respect to that portion of the contribution base (e.g., the facility) with respect to which the partial withdrawal occurred. If partial withdrawal liability arises both under the 70-percent decline rule and under another partial withdrawal rule, the abatement rules for the 70-percent decline in contributions are to apply.

The bill provides a special partial withdrawal rule for the building and construction industry. Under this rule, partial withdrawal occurs only where an employer continues its obligation to contribute for only an insubstantial amount of the work it does that is of the type that would otherwise be covered work and is performed in the jurisdiction of the collective bargaining agreement. It is the intent of the Committees that a partial withdrawal occurs only when an employer has substantially shifted its work mix (in the jurisdiction) so that only an insubstantial portion of such work in the jurisdiction is covered. The Committees intend that this be the exclusive partial withdrawal rule for the building and construction industry. Employers in certain segments of the entertainment industry will have liability for a partial withdrawal only to the extent provided in PBGC regulations.

Construction, etc., industry exception.—The bill includes a special definition of withdrawal for the building and construction industry. The Committees believe that this special definition is warranted because, in view of the nature of the industry, it provides substantial protection for the affected plans. For instance, an employer's leaving the jurisdiction of the plan or going out of business does not typically reduce the plan's contribution base. Rather, an employer reduces the plan's contribution base only if it continues to do what would have been covered work but does not have an obligation to contribute to the plan for that work. In order to protect the plan, that continuation of work without contributions is treated as a withdrawal in these industries. Other characteristics of the industries, including the mobility of both employers and employees and the intermittent nature of employment also persuade the Committees that this special rule is needed.

In the case of certain plans under which an employer has an obligation to contribute for work performed in the building and construction industry, a withdrawal is considered to take place only if an employer ceases to have an obligation to contribute under the plan, and (1) continues to perform work in the jurisdiction of the collective bargaining agreement, of the type for which contributions were previously required, or (2) resumes work in the jurisdiction within five years after the date the employer's obligation to contribute under the plan ceased and certain other conditions are satisfied.

An employer contributing to a plan is subject to these special rules only if substantially all of the employees for whom the employer has an obligation to contribute perform work in the building and construction industry, and (1) the plan covers primarily employees in the building and construction industry, or (2) the plan is amended to provide that the rules apply to employers with an obligation to contribute for work performed in the building and construction industry.

The Committees intend that an employer not be treated at [as] having withdrawn simply because the jurisdiction of the plan expands after the employer has ceased its obligation to contribute to the plan.

In the case of plans that terminate through mass withdrawal, an employer who returns to the area covered under the plan within 3 years after its cessation will incur withdrawal liability.

The Committees understand that certain segments of the entertainment industry have characteristics similar to the building and construction industry in that work is performed on a project basis with little continuity of employment or employers. For example, the theatrical production companies typically exist only for the duration of the play. The bill provides that the construction industry definition of withdrawal applies to certain segments of the entertainment industry. Of course, it is not intended that the construction industry exception apply to plans covering segments of the entertainment industry which do not have the characteristics of the construction industry. Thus, for example, a plan covering stable companies would not be eligible for the exception. Further, the PBGC could prescribe definitional regulations extending the special rule, if appropriate, to certain other segments of the entertainment industry.

The Committees have adopted special rules governing withdrawals from plans under which substantially all the contributions are made by employers in the long- and short-haul trucking industry, the household moving industry, or the public warehousing industry. Under the bill, an employer primarily engaged in such work that ceases to perform work within the geographical area coverd by the plan is considered to have withdrawn only if the PBGC determines that the cessation has caused substantial damage to the contribution base of the plan, or if, absent such a determination, the employer fails to post a bond or put an amount in escrow equal to 50 percent of its potential withdrawal liability.

If the employer posts the bond or escrow and the PBGC subsequently determines that the employer's cessation has substantially damaged the plan, the entire bond or escrow shall be paid to the plan, and the employer is liable for the remainder of the withdrawal liability in accordance with the usual withdrawal rules. In making the determination, the PBGC shall consider the cumulative or aggregate effect of all employer withdrawals from the plan.

The bond or escrow requirement will normally remain in effect for 60 months. After that time, the bond will be cancelled or the escrow returned, and the employer will have no further liability. However, the Committees emphasize that the employer will remain subject to a PBGC determination during the entire 60-month period. In addition, the bill provides the PBGC with authority to order the bond cancelled or the escrow returned at any time within the 60-month period upon a determination that the employer's cessation of contributions (considered with such cessations of other employers) has not damaged the plan in a substantial manner, and is not likely to so damage the plan in the future. Because the bond or escrow requirement is designed to protect plan participants and remaining employers, the Committees intended that the PBGC use this power sparingly.

In addition the bill authorizes the PBGC to extend the construction industry definition of withdrawal to other industries or parts of industries where there are clearly displayed the characteristics that would make use of such rules appropriate and where the extension would not pose an appreciable risk to the insurance system.

[ERISA Sec. 4202]

[¶ 15,664.10]

Committee Report on P.L. 96-364 (Multiemployer Pension Plan Amendments Act of 1980)

[Senate Committee Report]

The Senate Committee Report on Act Sec. 4202 is reproduced at ¶ 15,663.10.

[ERISA Sec. 4203]

[¶ 15,665.10]

Committee Report on P.L. 96-364 (Multiemployer Pension Plan Amendments Act of 1980)

[Senate Committee Report]

The Senate Committee Report on Act Sec. 4203 is reproduced at ¶ 15,663.10.

[ERISA Sec. 4204]

[¶ 15,667.10]

Committee Report on P.L. 96-364 (Multiemployer Pension Plan Amendments Act of 1980)

[Senate Committee Report]

Liability of transferor in case of transfer of corporate assets.—Under the bill, an employer would not have partial or complete withdrawal liability solely because covered operations of the employer have been transferred to another employer in connection with a sale of the employer's assets, if certain specified conditions are satisfied.

The Corporation is given the authority to vary these rules by regulation either if it should become necessary to protect plans or if the Corporation determines that lesser safeguards are adequate. In addition, the Corporation is given the authority to grant individual or class exemptions from the sale rules in the bill, in whole or in part, for the period before it issues regulations. The Corporation may grant any such exemption or variance only after a notice of the proposed exemption or variance is published in the *Federal Register,* separate steps adequate to provide notice to plan participants, the joint board of trustees, and the employers and unions sponsoring the plan have been taken, and the Corporation has afforded such interested persons the opportunity to present their views as to the appropriateness and effect of the proposed exemption or variance.

To prevent the sale rule from being used to escape withdrawal liability simply by substituting one employer for another, the bill only extends the rule to bona fide, arm's-length transactions between unrelated parties.

[ERISA Sec. 4205]

[¶ 15,669.09]

Committee Report on P.L. 109-280 (Pension Protection Act of 2006)

[Joint Committee on Taxation Report]

Under the provision, a partial withdrawal also occurs if the employer permanently ceases to have an obligation to contribute under one or more, but fewer than all collective bargaining agreements under which obligated to contribute, but the employer transfers such work to an entity or entities owned or controlled by the employer.

Effective Date

The provision is effective with respect to work transferred on or after the date of enactment.

For the Committee Report on P.L. 109-280 on repeal of limitation on withdrawal liability in certain cases, see ¶ 15,696.09.

For the Committee Report on P.L. 109-280 on application of forgiveness rule to plans primarily covering employees in building and construction, see ¶ 15,676.08.

For the Committee Report on P.L. 109-280 on procedures applicable to disputes involving withdrawal liability, see ¶ 15,689.08.

[¶ 15,669.10]

Committee Report on P.L. 96-364 (Multiemployer Pension Plan Amendments Act of 1980)

[Senate Committee Report]

The Senate Committee Report on Act Sec. 4205 is reproduced at ¶ 15,663.10.

[ERISA Sec. 4206]

[¶ 15,670.10]

Committee Report on P.L. 96-364 (Multiemployer Pension Plan Amendments Act of 1980)

[Senate Committee Report]

The Senate Committee Report on Act Sec. 4206 is reproduced at ¶ 15,663.10.

[ERISA Sec. 4207]

[¶ 15,671.10]

Committee Report on P.L. 96-364 (Multiemployer Pension Plan Amendments Act of 1980)

[Senate Committee Report]

The Senate Committee Report on Act Sec. 4207 is reproduced at ¶ 15,663.10.

[ERISA Sec. 4208]

[¶ 15,673.10]

Committee Report on P.L. 96-364 (Multiemployer Pension Plan Amendments Act of 1980)

[Senate Committee Report]

The Senate Committee Report on Act Sec. 4208 is reproduced at ¶ 15,663.10.

[ERISA Sec. 4209]

[¶ 15,674.10]

Committee Report on P.L. 96-364 (Multiemployer Pension Plan Amendments Act of 1980)

[Senate Committee Report]

Mandatory de minimis rule.—Under the bill, an employer's withdrawal liability would be reduced but not below zero by an amount computed under a mandatory de minimis rule. The mandatory amount would be the lesser of (a) $50,000 or (b) .75 percent of the plan's unfunded vested benefits determined as of the close of the plan year immediately preceding the withdrawal. The de minimis amount would be phased out dollar-for-dollar to the extent that the employer's withdrawal liability (computed without regard to the de minimis rule) exceeds $100,000. The mandatory de minimis rule is to be applied to withdrawal liability determined before the application of any pro rata reduction on account of a partial withdrawal, any reduction as a result of the 20-year payment cap and any reduction because of the dollar limitations on withdrawal liability.

Discretionary de minimis rule.—Under the bill, plans may provide for a reduction but not below zero in liability equal to the greater of (1) the amount of the reduction determined under the mandatory rule, or (2) the lesser of .75 percent of the plan's unfunded vested benefits determined as of the close of the plan year immediately preceding the withdrawal, or $100,000. The de minimis amount would be phased out dollar-for-dollar to the extent that the employer's withdrawal liability (computed without regard to the de minimis rule) exceeds $150,000. The discretionary de minimis rule is to be applied to withdrawal liability determined before the application of any pro rata reduction on account of a partial withdrawal, any reduction as a result of the 20-year payment cap and any reduction because of the dollar limitations on withdrawal liability. Because the discretionary de minimis rule contains the amount determined under the mandatory de minimis rule as an alternative within its formula, the actual de minimis amount applied against withdrawal liability in the case of a plan using the discretionary rule would be only the discretionary de minimis amount and the mandatory rule would not be separately applied.

De minimis rules not applicable in the case of a mass withdrawal.—The de minimis rules under the bill do not apply in the case of a mass withdrawal from a plan. Thus, the rules do not apply to an employer who withdraws from a plan in a plan year in which substantially all employers withdraw, or to an employer who withdraws under an agreement or arrangement under which substantially all employers withdraw from the plan in one or more plan years. Where substantially all employers withdraw from a plan within a period of three plan years, it is presumed that such an agreement or arrangement exists unless the contrary is shown by a preponderance of the evidence.

[ERISA Sec. 4210]

[¶ 15,675.09]

Committee Report on P.L. 109-280 (Pension Protection Act of 2006)

For the Committee Report on P.L. 109-280 on repeal of limitation on withdrawal liability in certain cases, see ¶ 15,696.09.

For the Committee Report on P.L. 109-280 on withdrawal liability where work is contracted out, see ¶ 15,669.09.

For the Committee Report on P.L. 109-280 on application of forgiveness rule to plans primarily covering employees in building and construction, see ¶ 15,676.08.

For the Committee Report on P.L. 109-280 on procedures applicable to disputes involving withdrawal liability, see ¶ 15,689.08.

[¶ 15,675.10]

Committee Report on P.L. 96-364 (Multiemployer Pension Plan Amendments Act of 1980)

[Senate Committee Report]

Exception for new employers.—The bill provides a rule under which an employer first entering a plan would not be subject to withdrawal liability, either in the case of a complete withdrawal or of a partial withdrawal, if certain conditions are met. The applicable conditions are as follows:

(a) the employer was first obligated to make plan contributions after the date of enactment of the bill;

(b) the employer was not required to make plan contributions for more than the lesser of (1) six consecutive plan years preceding the date of withdrawal or (2) the number of years required for vesting under the plan;

(c) for each plan year for which contributions by the employer were required, the employer's contributions were less than 2 percent for all employer contributions to the plan for the plan year;

(d) the plan does not primarily cover employees in the building and construction industry; and

(e) the employer did not previously have the benefit of this exception with respect to the plan.

In addition, the exception applies only if (1) the plan provides for its application; (2) the plan provides that benefits of participants accrued on the basis of service for the employer before the employer was required to contribute to the plan may not be payable if the employer ceases contributions to the plan and (3) the ratio of plan assets to benefit payments during the plan year preceding the first plan year for which the employer was required to make plan contributions was at least 8 to 1. Of course, the rule requiring that a plan provide for cancellation of benefits where the employer ceases contributions to the plan would not require any reduction of benefits to participants or beneficiaries whose benefits are in pay-status at the time of the cessation and who are not working in employment covered by the plan.

This "free look" rule does not apply in the case of a mass withdrawal from the multiemployer plan, as defined in the bill.

[ERISA Sec. 4211]

[¶ 15,676.08]

Committee Report on P.L. 109-280 (Pension Protection Act of 2006)

[Joint Committee on Taxation Report]

The provision extends the rule allowing plans to exempt certain employers from withdrawal liability to plans primarily covering employees in the building and construction industries. In addition, the provision also provides that a plan (including a plan which primarily covers employees in the building and construction industry) may be amended to provide that the withdrawal liability method otherwise applicable shall be applied by substituting the plan year which is specified in the amendment and for which the plan has no unfunded vested benefits for the plan year ending before September 26, 1980.

Effective Date

The provision is effective with respect to plan withdrawals occurring on or after January 1, 2007.

For the Committee Report on P.L. 109-280 on repeal of limitation on withdrawal liability in certain cases, see ¶ 15,696.09.

For the Committee Report on P.L. 109-280 on withdrawal liability where work is contracted out, see ¶ 15,669.09.

For the Committee Report on P.L. 109-280 on procedures applicable to disputes involving withdrawal liability, see ¶ 15,689.08.

[¶ 15,676.09]

Committee Report on P.L. 98-369 (Tax Reform Act of 1984)

[Senate Committee Report]

Generally, under the bill, any liability incurred by an employer under the withdrawal liability provisions of MPPAA, as a result of the complete or partial withdrawal from a multiemployer plan before September 26, 1980, is void. The bill provides for refunds of amounts paid by an employer to a plan sponsor as a result of such withdrawal liability, reduced by a reasonable amount for administrative expenses incurred by the plan sponsor in calculating, assessing, and refunding the payments.

The bill provides that it is not to increase the liability incurred by any employer under the withdrawal liability rules. Accordingly, the amounts payable with respect to withdrawals after September 25, 1980, are not to be increased merely because of the refunds provided by the bill.

Under the bill, in the case of an employer who, on September 26, 1980, had a binding sale agreement to withdraw from a multiemployer plan, the effective date for withdrawal liability is changed to December 31, 1980.

[¶ 15,676.10]

Committee Report on P.L. 96-364 (Multiemployer Pension Plan Amendments Act of 1980)

[Senate Committee Report]

The Senate Committee Report on Act Sec. 4211(b)(4) is reproduced at ¶ 15,663.10.

Computation of withdrawal liability—Presumptive method.—The bill, in its presumptive method for computing withdrawal liability, draws a distinction between employers who contributed to a plan for a plan year ending before April 29, 1980, and employers who did not contribute to the plan for such a year. As to employers who contributed to a plan for such a year, the computation of withdrawal liability is based on (1) the unfunded vested benefits of the plan attributable to those years, as well as on (2) changes in the unfunded vested benefits of the plan for plan years ending on or after April 29, 1980, in which the employer was required to contribute to the plan. In the case of an employer who was not required to contribute to the plan for a plan year ending before April 29, 1980, the employer's withdrawal liability is computed solely with reference to changes in the unfunded vested benefits under the plan for plan years ending on or after April 29, 1980, in which the employer was required to contribute to the plan. Under the bill, the presumptive method generally applies unless a plan adopts one of the alternative methods.

In particular, withdrawal liability under the presumptive method is divided into three parts, as follows:

(1) liability with respect to changes in unfunded vested benefits for plan years ending on or after April 29, 1980, but not after the date of withdrawal, in which the employer was obligated to contribute under the plan;

(2) liability with respect to unfunded vested benefits for plan years ending before April 29, 1980; and

(3) liability with respect to unfunded vested benefits which are reallocated under the plan because they are uncollectible or not assigned to an employer under one of the bill's relief provisions.

In the case of an employer who was not required to contribute to a plan until a plan year ending on or after April 29, 1980, the second component of withdrawal liability does not apply.

The portion of an employer's withdrawal liability attributable to plan years ending after April 29, 1980, is computed in four steps, as follows:

(1) The first step is to determine what is known as the "change in a plan's unfunded vested benefits" for each plan year ending on or after April 28, 1980. Under the bill, this amount is calculated for each plan year as the difference between (a) the unfunded vested benefits as of the end of the plan year, and (b) the sum of (i) the unfunded vested benefits on the last day of the last plan year ending before April 28, 1980, reduced by five percent for each succeeding plan year which precedes the plan year, and (ii) the sum of the changes in unfunded vested benefits for each plan year ending on or after April 29, 1980, and preceding the plan year (computed with each such change reduced by five percent for each succeeding plan year preceding the plan year).

(2) The second step is to determine what is known as "the unamortized amount of the change in a plan's unfunded vested benefits with respect to a plan year". This amount is determined by reducing the change in a plan's unfunded vested benefits for a plan year (determined under step (1)) by five percent for each succeeding plan year.

(3) The third step is to calculate the employer's "proportional share" of the unamortized amount of the change in the plan's unfunded vested benefits for each plan year involved. This is accomplished by multiplying the unamortized amount of the change for each plan year, determined as of the end of the plan year in which the employer withdraws from the plan, by a fraction. The numerator of the fraction is the sum of contributions which the employer was required to make to the plan for the year of the change and for the preceding four plan years. The denominator of the fraction is the sum of contributions which all employers made to the plan for the year of the change and for the preceding four plan years.

(4) The final step is to add up the employer's proportional share of the unamortized amount of the change in the plan's unfunded vested benefits for each of the plan years. This total is the employer's proportional share of the unamortized amount of the change in the plan's unfunded vested benefits for all plan years ending on or after April 29, 1980.

The portion of an employer's withdrawal liability with respect to plan years ending before April 29, 1980, is determined by multiplying (1) the amount of the unfunded vested benefits under the plan at the close of the last plan year ending before April 29, 1980 (reduced by five percent for each succeeding plan year), by

(2) a fraction. The numerator of the fraction is the sum of contributions which the employer was required to make to the plan for the last five plan years ending before April 29, 1980. The denominator of the fraction is the sum, for the same five years, of plan contributions made by all employers who (a) had an obligation to contribute under the plan for the first plan year ending on or after April 29, 1980, and (b) had not withdrawn from the plan before April 29, 1980.

First alternative method.—The first alternative method also draws a distinction between employers who contributed to a plan for plan years ending before April 29, 1980, and employers who did not contribute to the plan for such years. As in the case of the presumptive method, only employers who contributed for years ending before April 29, 1980, are to have their withdrawal liability computed wth reference to unfunded vested benefits under the plan attributable to such years. Other employers are to have their withdrawal liability computed solely with reference to the plan's unfunded vested benefits attributable to plan years ending on or after April 29, 1980. However, unlike the presumptive method, under the first alternative method, an employer's withdrawal liability is to be based on the aggregate change in unfunded vested benefits with respect to all plan years ending on or after April 29, 1980, rather than on the changes in unfunded vested benefits for each separate plan year for which the employer was required to contribute to the plan.

In particular, the first component of withdrawal liability under the first alternative method is to be obtained by multiplying (1) the plan's unfunded vested benefits as of the end of the last plan year ending before April 29, 1980, reduced as if that amount were being amortized thereafter in level annual installments over 15 years, by (2) a fraction. The numerator of the fraction is the sum of the plan contributions required of the employer for the last plan year ending before April 29, 1980, and for the preceding four plan years. The denominator of the fraction is the sum of the contributions made by included employers for that period of five plan years. An employer is included if (1) the employer was required to contribute to the plan for the first plan year ending on or after April 28, 1980 (April 29, 1980), and (2) the employer had not withdrawn from the plan before that date.

The second component of withdrawal liability under the first alternative method is to be obtained by computing the excess of the plan's unfunded vested benefits (as of the last day of the plan year preceding the plan year in which the employer withdraws) over the sum of (1) the value on such date of all outstanding claims for withdrawal liability (with respect to employers withdrawing before the plan year) which can reasonably be expected to be collected and (2) the portion of the plan's unfunded vested benefits as of the last day of the last plan year ending before April 29, 1980 (as reduced by 15-year amortization), which is allocable to remaining included employers and multiplying such excess by a fraction. The numerator of the fraction is the total amount required to be contributed by the employer for the last plan year ending before withdrawal and for the four preceding four plan years. The denominator of the fraction is the total amount contributed by all employers for those five plan years, increased by employer contribution[s] for earlier periods that are collected during the five plan years, and reduced by the contributions made by any employer who withdrew from the plan during any of the five plan years. An employer is included in this case if the employer was required to contribute to the plan for the first plan year ending on or after April 29, 1980, as well as for the plan year preceding the withdrawal.

Second alternative method.—The second alternative method for computing withdrawal liability draws no distinction between employers who were required to contribute to a plan for plan years ending before April 29, 1980, and employers who were required to contribute only for plan years ending on or after April 29, 1980. Accordingly, employers in both categories are to have their withdrawal liability computed with reference to all of a plan's unfunded vested benefits.

Under this method, withdrawal liability is to be determined by multiplying (1) the plan's unfunded vested benefits as of the end of the plan year preceding the withdrawal, reduced by the value as of such date of outstanding claims for withdrawal liability (with respect to employers withdrawing before the plan year) which can reasonably be expected to be collected by (2) a fraction. The numerator of the fraction is the amount which the employer was required to contribute to the plan for the five plan years preceding the plan year of the withdrawal. The denominator of the fraction is the total amount contributed by all employers for those five plan years, increased by employer contributions for earlier periods that are collected during the five plan years, and reduced by the contributions made by any employer who withdrew from the plan during any of the five plan years.

Third alternative method.—The (third) alternative method takes a substantially different approach to computing withdrawal liability. Rather than determining the liability based upon the employer's share of plan contributions during a five-year period, the method is intended to compute the portion of the plan's unfunded vested benefits which are attributable to service of plan participants with the employer. This is generally to be done by attributing portions of the unfunded vested benefits to each employer in accordance with specified rules. In addition, the plan's unfunded vested benefits which are not attributable to any present employer is also to be computed. A portion of those "unattributable benefits" is then to be allocated to the employer. An employer's withdrawal liability is then to be determined as the sum of (1) the portion of the plan's unfunded vested benefits which are attributable to plan participants' service with the employer, and (2) the portion of "unattributable benefits" which is allocated to the employer. All determinations are to be made as of the end of the plan year preceding the plan year of the withdrawal.

Other methods.—The bill authorizes the PBGC to prescribe by regulations a procedure by which a plan may adopt other methods for determining withdrawal liability. The PBGC, before approving any such method, is to be required to determine that the method would not significantly increase the risk of loss to plan participants, beneficiaries, or the PBGC. In addition, the PBGC is to be authorized to prescribe standard approaches for alternative methods for which approval would either not be necessary or would be necessary only under a modified procedure. Any such alternative method is to be required to allocate to employers all of the plan's unfunded vested benefits.

In determining an employer's withdrawal liability under the presumptive method or any of the alternative methods if the method specifies the use of a five plan year period in the numerator or denominator of a fraction, the plan could provide instead for the use of a period of more than five, but not more than 10, plan years, unless PBGC regulations provide otherwise.

Other rules.—The PBGC is authorized by regulation to permit adjustments in any denominator used in a fraction for calculating withdrawal liability where the adjustment would (1) be consistent with the purposes of title IV of ERISA and (2) be appropriate to ease administrative burdens of plan sponsors in making their calculations. Under the bill, in the event of a transfer of liabilities from the plan from which a withdrawal takes place to another plan in connection with a withdrawal, withdrawal liability is to be reduced by an amount equal to the value, determined at the end of the last plan year ending on or before the date of the withdrawal, of the transferred unfunded vested benefits.

In the case of a withdrawal by an employer following a merger of multiemployer plans, withdrawal liability is to be computed under the applicable method in accordance with PBGC regulations. However, in the case of a withdrawal in the first year beginning after the merger, withdrawal liability is determined as if the plans had remained separate.

In the case of certain plans established prior to January 1, 1954, as a result of an agreement between employee representatives and the Government of the United States during a period of government operation, under seizure powers, of a major part of the productive facilities of an industry (Code Sec. 404(c)), the presumptive method for determining withdrawal liability is the second alternative method for computing such liability. In addition, the exception for new employers, and other relief provisions, do not apply to such plan unless the plan is amended to provide for their application.

[ERISA Sec. 4212]

[¶ 15,679.10]

Committee Report on P.L. 96-364 (Multiemployer Pension Plan Amendments Act of 1980)

[Senate Committee Report]

Relationship to other rules.—Actions taken under the bill pursuant to the withdrawal liability rules are not to be considered prohibited self-dealing transactions.

In addition, payments of withdrawal liability are not to be considered employer contributions for purposes of calculating withdrawal liability.

Definition of obligation to contribute.—For purposes of the withdrawal liability rules, an employer has an obligation to contribute if its obligation arises under one or more collective bargaining (or related) agreements or as a result of a duty under applicable, labor-management relations law. An obligation to pay withdrawal liability or delinquent contributions is not considered an obligation to contribute.

Disregard of certain transactions.—The bill provides specific rules governing the imposition of employer liability under multiemployer plans. However, the Committees expect that effective enforcement of these rules will require plan sponsors, employers, and courts to disregard sham transactions, or transactions structured to avoid or evade liability, just as the PBGC is expected to disregard sham transactions in the enforcement of current law. Accordingly, the bill provides that where a principal purpose of any transaction (or series of transactions) is to evade or avoid employer liability, the transaction will be disregarded, and employer liability will be assessed and collected according to the substance of the transaction. The Committees believe that this provision will help plans to disregard transactions that were structured to avoid possible withdrawal liability.

[ERISA Sec. 4213]

[¶ 15,680.10]

Committee Report on P.L. 96-364 (Multiemployer Pension Plan Amendments Act of 1980)

[Senate Committee Report]

Determination of actuarial assumptions, etc.—The PBGC is authorized to prescribe regulations setting forth actuarial assumptions which a plan may use in calculating withdrawal liability. However, a plan may provide instead that its own assumptions will be used to determine withdrawal liability rather than those developed by the PBGC provided such assumptions are reasonable in the aggregate.

In determining the unfunded vested benefits under a plan, the plan's actuary is permitted to rely on data available or on data secured by certain sampling techniques in situations where complete and definite data is absent, provided such data can reasonably be expected to be representative of the status of the entire plan. In addition, the actuary is permitted to rely on the most recent actuarial valuation used for funding purposes and to make reasonable estimates for interim years of unfunded vested benefits. However, the bill continues the authority of the Internal Revenue Service to require more frequent valuations in appropriate cases.

[ERISA Sec. 4214]

[¶ 15,681.10]

Committee Report on P.L. 96-364 (Multiemployer Pension Plan Amendments Act of 1980)

[Senate Committee Report]

Plan rules and amendments.—There are several situations where plans, in the application of their own rules, either initially or by amendment, are permitted a wide degree of latitude in allocating and calculating withdrawal liability. In order to protect an employer from certain retroactive changes in a plan's rules, the bill prohibits the retroactive application of a plan rule or amendment relating to withdrawal liability, that is adopted after January 31, 1981, from applying to a withdrawal occurring before its date of adoption, unless the employer consents to its earlier application.

The bill also requires that plan rules and amendments operate and be applied uniformly with respect to all employers except to the extent that lack of uniformity would be required to take into account employers' credit ratings.

Under the bill, when a plan rule or amendment affects withdrawal liability, the plan sponsor is required to give notice of the adoption of the rule or amendment to all employers required to contribute to the plan and to all employee organizations representing employees covered by the plan.

[ERISA Sec. 4215]

[¶ 15,682.10]

Committee Report on P.L. 96-364 (Multiemployer Pension Plan Amendments Act of 1980)

[Senate Committee Report]

Notice to the PBGC.—Under regulations the PBGC is permitted to require a plan sponsor to notify the PBGC in any case where the withdrawal from a plan of an employer has resulted, or will result, in a significant reduction in total contributions to the plan.

[ERISA Sec. 4217]

[¶ 15,684.09]

Committee Report on P.L. 98-369 (Tax Reform Act of 1984)

. . . relating to the effective date of the Multiemployer Pension Plan Amendments Act of 1980, see ¶ 15,676.09.

[¶ 15,684.10]

Committee Report on P.L. 96-364 (Multiemployer Pension Plan Amendments Act of 1980)

[Senate Committee Report]

Phase-in of withdrawal liability.—The bill provides a special rule which prevents certain events which occurred before April 29, 1980, from triggering withdrawals, and from increasing the liability for a partial withdrawal, on or after that date. Under the bill, for the purpose of determining withdrawal liability, for a complete or a partial withdrawal after April 28, 1980, and for the purpose of determining whether a partial withdrawal has occurred after that date, the amount of contributions and the number of contribution base units of the affected employer which are properly allocable to (1) work performed under a collective bargaining agreement for which there was a cessation of contributions before April 29, 1980, or (2) work performed at a facility for which there was a cessation of contributions before April 29, 1980, are not to be taken into account.

The PBGC is authorized to prescribe regulations setting forth the method by which the withdrawal liability of other employers in a plan is to be adjusted where an employer receives the relief provided by this rule.

Withdrawal liability payment fund.—The bill permits plan sponsors of multiemployer plans to establish and participate in private funds for the purpose of paying withdrawal liabilities under certain circumstances. Any such fund which meets the applicable requirements is to be a tax-exempt organization. The fund would be required to maintain agreements for collection of premiums and payment of withdrawal liability with respect to a substantial portion of the participants in the multiemployer plan eligible to participate in the fund. The fund is to be administered by a board of trustees on which there is equal representation of employers and employees.

The fund would receive contributions from participating plans. Contributions by a plan to the fund during a plan year are to reduce the amount considered contributed to the plan for the year for purposes of the minimum funding standard and the minimum contribution requirement. The Committees expect that, in considering whether to approve a waiver of the funding requirements for a plan under section 412(d) of the Code for a plan year during which the plan has made a contribution to a withdrawal liability payment fund, the amount and nature of the payment will be taken into account.

The eligibility of a plan to participate in a fund is to be determined by the rules of the fund. Where an employer has withdrawn from a participating multiemployer plan and has incurred withdrawal liability, the fund, subject to strict statutory conditions, could pay to the plan certain specified amounts.

The PBGC is authorized to prescribe regulations with respect to withdrawal liability payment funds. The Committees expect that such regulations will assure that the funds do not have the effect of undermining the purposes of the withdrawal liability rules. For example, the Committees expect that PBGC regulations will assure that payments by a fund with respect to unattributable liability are not in excess of appropriate levels. Of course, PBGC rules with respect to the withdrawal liability payment fund and with respect to the PBGC-administered fund are not to be designed or administered for the purpose of providing either of the arrangements a competitive advantage over the other.

The bill provides fiduciary standards with respect to withdrawal liability payment funds and supersedes all State laws providing for such standards.

[ERISA Sec. 4218]

[¶ 15,685.10]

Committee Report on P.L. 96-364 (Multiemployer Pension Plan Amendments Act of 1980)

[Senate Committee Report]

The Senate Committee Report on Act Sec. 4218 is reproduced at ¶ 15,663.10.

[ERISA Sec. 4219]

[¶ 15,686.08]

Committee Report on P.L. 108-218 (Pension Funding Equity Act of 2004)

For Committee Reports relating to the Pension Funding Equity Act of 2004, see ¶ 15,689.09.

[¶ 15,686.09]

Committee Report on P.L. 98-369 (Tax Reform Act of 1984)

For Committee Reports relating to the effective date on the Multiemployer Pension Plan Amendments Act of 1980, see ¶ 15,676.09.

[¶ 15,686.10]

Committee Reports on P.L. 96-364 (Multiemployer Pension Plan Amendments Act of 1980)

The Senate Committee Report (Act Sec. 4219(d) is reproduced at ¶ 15,679.10. * * *— *Payment of withdrawal liability.—In general.*—An employer who withdraws from a multiemployer plan is to be required to pay its withdrawal liability to the plan in accordance with a payment schedule to be determined by the plan sponsor under standards set forth in the bill. As soon as practicable after a withdrawal, the plan sponsor is to be required to notify the employer of (1) the amount of withdrawal liability, and (2) the payment schedule. In addition, the plan sponsor is to be required to demand that the employer make payment of withdrawal liability in accordance with the payment schedule.

In calculating the payment schedule, the plan is to compute the annual payment under a formula set forth in the bill. The employer is generally to be required to make this payment to the plan for the lesser of (1) the number of years it would take to amortize its withdrawal liability (determined under the assumptions used for the most recent actuarial valuation for the plan) or (2) 20 years. The amount of each annual payment under the formula is to be determined as the product of two amounts. * * * (See House Report below.)

House Ways and Means Committee Report (P.L. 96-364).—* * * The first amount is the average number of contribution base units (*e.g.,* hours worked, tons of coal mined) for the three consecutive plan years, during the period of 10 plan years ending with (the plan year preceding) the plan year in which withdrawal occurs, in which the number of units was the highest. The second amount is the highest contribution rate (*e.g.,* cents per hour) which the employer had an obligation to contribute under the plan during the period of 10 plan years ending with the year of withdrawal.

For example, assume that an employer's withdrawal liability is $1 million and that the plan's valuation rate of interest is 6 percent. Assume that in the 3 years for which the contribution base units were the highest during the 10 most recent plan years during which the employer was obligated to contribute to the plan, the number of such units were 80,000 hours, 85,000 hours and 90,000 hours respectively, and that during the last ten plan years the highest contribution rate applicable to the employer under the plan was 75 cents an hour. The product of 85,000 hours (the average of 80,000, 85,000, and 90,000) and 75 cents an hour is $63,750. This would result in the amortization of the liability over approximately 49 years. * * * (See Senate Report below.)

Senate Committee Report (P.L. 96-364).—* * * Because the 49-year schedule is longer than 20 years, the employer would be liable to the plan for 20 annual payments of $63,750.

As an alternative, a plan could provide that for any plan year ending before 1986, the amount of an employer's annual withdrawal liability payment would be the average of the required employer contributions under the plan for the period of two consecutive plan years for which such contributions were the highest during the period of five consecutive plan years ending with the plan year preceding the plan year in which the withdrawal occurs. This method may not be used by a plan for determining withdrawal liability payments in any case in which the plan terminates because of mass withdrawal. If a plan provides for this computation method and then is amended to provide for use of the regular method provided under the bill, the plan must use the regular method thereafter.

In the event that a multiemployer plan terminates upon (1) withdrawal of all employers in the plan or (2) withdrawal of substantially all employers in the plan pursuant to an agreement or arrangement to withdraw (a "mass withdrawal"), the annual amount of withdrawal liability payable by each employer is to be computed without regard to the 20-year limit and total unfunded vested benefits of the plan are allocated to all employers under PBGC regulations. Thus in the above example, if all employers were to withdraw, the liability of the employer would be $63,750 a year for approximately 49 years, unless the amount or payment period were to differ because of PBGC regulations which allocate unfunded vested benefits. The 20-year cap is one of several employer relief provisions contained in the bill. The cap is to be applied to withdrawal liability determined after application of the *de minimis* rules and after any pro rata reduction on account of a partial withdrawal, but before the application of the dollar limitations on withdrawal liability. * * * In the case of a partial withdrawal, the annual payment is to be a pro rata portion of the annual payment which would apply for a complete withdrawal.

Time for payment.—Payment of withdrawal liability is to begin no later than 60 days after the date on which a demand for payment is made by the plan sponsor. Under the bill, payments are generally to be made in four equal quarterly installments unless a particular plan provides for payment at other intervals. In any case where payment is not made when due, the bill requires interest to accrue with respect to the unpaid amount based on the prevailing market rate.

An employer is to be permitted to prepay its withdrawal liability obligations plus accrued interest, if any, in whole or in part without penalty.

In the event of default by an employer in payment of its withdrawal liability, other than a default occurring while an employer is challenging a plan's determination of withdrawal liability, the plan sponsor is to be permitted to require immediate payment of the balance of the employer's withdrawal liability plus an accrued interest thereon. Default is generally considered to occur where an employer fails to make any payment with respect to withdrawal liability when due, and further fails to make payment within 60 days after receiving written notice from the plan sponsor that payment of withdrawal liability is due but unpaid. In addition, the plan is to be permitted to adopt rules which would provide for other instances of default where it is indicated that there is a substantial likelihood that an employer will be unable to pay its withdrawal liability.

A multiemployer plan may adopt rules consistent with the bill which set forth other terms and conditions for the satisfaction of an employer's withdrawal liability.

In the case of a multiemployer plan which terminates, each employer's obligation to make withdrawal liability payments for the future is to cease at the end of the plan year in which the plan's assets, exclusive of outstanding withdrawal liability claims, are sufficient to meet all of its obligations. This determination of sufficiency is to be made by the PBGC.

Notice requirements and furnishing of information.—* * * Withdrawal liability is to be collectible upon notice and demand to the withdrawn employer by the plan sponsor. In order for the plan sponsor to be in a position to accurately determine liability, the bill requires the employer to furnish information to the plan sponsor. After an employer withdraws from a plan, the plan sponsor is to request in writing that the employer furnish such information as the plan sponsor reasonably considers necessary for it to fulfill its duties in computing and collecting withdrawal liability. The bill requires an employer to furnish the requested information within 30 days after such a written request from the plan sponsor.

The actual demand for payment of liability in accordance with the payment schedule is to be made by the plan sponsor. The bill requires that when the plan sponsor demands payment the plan must afford the employer 90 days (1) to identify errors and review specific matters in the determination of withdrawal liability, (2) to identify errors in the payment schedule, and (3) to furnish to the plan sponsor any additional pertinent information. The plan sponsor also is required, if requested, to make relevant plan records reasonably available to the employer for review and duplication. In response to a request by an employer, the plan sponsor is required to conduct a reasonable review of any matter questioned and to notify the employer of (1) its decision, (2) the grounds for its decision, and (3) the reason for any modification in the employer's withdrawal liability or of the payments schedule.

[ERISA Sec. 4220]

[¶ 15,688.10]

Committee Report on P.L. 96-364 (Multiemployer Pension Plan Amendments Act of 1980)

[Senate Committee Report]

Approval of amendments.—If an amendment to a multiemployer plan authorized under the withdrawal liability provisions is adopted more than 36 months after the effective date of the bill, the amendment wil be effective only if (1) the PBGC approves the amendment, or (2) within 90 days after it receives notice of the amendment from the plan sponsor, the PBGC fails to disapprove the amendment. However, certain amendments regarding methods for computing withdrawal liability could be adopted only in accordance with the section of the bill authorizing the amendments. The PBGC is to disapprove of a plan amendment only where it determines that the amendment creates an unreasonable risk of loss to plan participants, beneficiaries, or the PBGC.

[ERISA Sec. 4221]

[¶ 15,689.08]

Committee Report on P.L. 109-280 (Pension Protection Act of 2006).

[Joint Committee on Taxation Report]

Under the provision, if (1) a plan sponsor determines that a complete or partial withdrawal of an employer has occurred or an employer is liable for withdrawal liability payments with respect to the complete or partial withdrawal from the plan and (2) such determination is based in whole or in part on a finding by the plan sponsor that a principal purpose of any transaction that occurred after December 31, 1998, and at least five years (two years in the case of a small employer) before the date of complete or partial withdrawal was to evade or avoid withdrawal liability, the person against which the withdrawal liability is assessed may elect to use a special rule relating to required payments. Under the special rule, if the electing person contests the plan sponsor's determination with respect to withdrawal liability payments through an arbitration proceeding, through a claim brought in a court of competent jurisdiction, or as otherwise permitted by law, the electing person is not obligated to make the withdrawal liability payments until a final decision in the arbitration proceeding, or in court, upholds the plan sponsor's determination. The special rule applies only if the electing person (1) provides notice to the plan sponsor of its election to apply the special rule within 90 days after the plan sponsor notifies the electing person of its liability, and (2) if a final decision on the arbitration proceeding, or in court, of the withdrawal liability dispute has not been rendered within 12 months from the date of such notice, the electing person provides to the plan, effective as of the first day following the 12-month period, a bond issued by a corporate surety, or an amount held on escrow by a bank or similar financial institution satisfactory to the plan, in an amount equal to the sum of the withdrawal liability payments that would otherwise be due for the 12-month period beginning with the first anniversary of such notice. The bond or escrow must remain in effect until there is a final decision in the arbitration proceeding, or on court, of the withdrawal liability dispute. At such time, the bond or escrow must be paid to the plan if the final decision upholds the plan sponsor's determination. If the withdrawal liability dispute is not concluded by 12 months after the electing person posts the bond or escrow, the electing person must, at the start of each succeeding 12-month period, provide an additional bond or amount held in escrow equal to the sum of the withdrawal liability payments that would otherwise be payable to the plan during that period.

A small employer is an employer which, for the calendar year in which the transaction occurred, and for each of the three preceding years, on average (1) employs no more than 500 employees, and (2) is required to make contributions to the plan on behalf of not more than 250 employees.

Effective Date

The provision is effective for any person that receives a notification of withdrawal liability and demand for payment on or after the date of enactment with respect to a transaction that occurred after December 31, 1998.

For the Committee Report on P.L. 109-280 on repeal of limitation on withdrawal liability in certain cases, see ¶ 15,696.09.

For the Committee Report on P.L. 109-280 on withdrawal liability where work is contracted out, see ¶ 15,669.09.

For the Committee Report on P.L. 109-280 on application of forgiveness rule to plans primarily covering employees in building and construction, see ¶ 15,676.08.

[¶ 15,689.09]

Committee Reports on P.L. 108-218 (Pension Funding Equity Act of 2004)

Present Law

Under ERISA, when an employer withdraws from a multiemployer plan, the employer is generally liable for its share of unfunded vested benefits, determined as of the date of withdrawal (generally referred to as the "withdrawal liability"). Whether and when a withdrawal has occurred and the amount of the withdrawal liability is determined by the plan sponsor. The plan sponsor's assessment of withdrawal liability is presumed correct unless the employer shows by a preponderance of the evidence that the plan sponsor's determination of withdrawal liability was unreasonable or clearly erroneous. A similar standard applies in the event the amount of the plan's unfunded vested benefits is challenged.

The first payment of withdrawal liability determined by the plan sponsor is due no later than 60 days after demand, even if the employer contests the determination of liability. Disputes between an employer and plan sponsor concerning withdrawal liability are resolved through arbitration, which can be initiated by either party. Even if the employer contests the determination, payments of withdrawal liability must be made by the employer until the arbitrator issues a final decision with respect to the determination submitted for arbitration.

For purposes of withdrawal liability, all trades or businesses under common control are treated as a single employer. In addition, the plan sponsor may disregard a transaction in order to assess withdrawal liability if the sponsor determines that the principal purpose of the transaction was to avoid or evade withdrawal liability. For example, if a subsidiary of a parent company is sold and the subsidiary then withdraws from a multiemployer plan, the plan sponsor may assess withdrawal liability as if the subsidiary were still part of the parent company's controlled group if the sponsor determines that a principal purpose of the sale of the subsidiary was to evade or avoid withdrawal liability.

[House Bill]

No provision.

[Senate Amendment]

Under the Senate amendment, a special rule may apply if a transaction is disregarded by a plan sponsor in determining that a withdrawal has occurred or that an employer is liable for withdrawal liability. If the transaction that is disregarded by the plan sponsor occurred before January 1, 1999, and at least five years before the date of the withdrawal, then (1) the determination by the plan sponsor that a principal purpose of the transaction was to evade or avoid withdrawal liability is not presumed to be correct, (2) the plan sponsor, rather than the employer, has the burden to establish, by a preponderance of the evidence, the elements of the claim that a principal purpose of the transaction was to evade or avoid withdrawal liability, and (3) if an employer contests the plan sponsor's determination through an arbitration proceeding, or through a claim brought in a court of competent jurisdiction, the employer is not obligated to make any withdrawal liability payments until a final decision in the arbitration proceeding, or in court, upholds the plan sponsor's determination. The provision does not modify the burden of establishing other elements of a claim for withdrawal liability other than whether the purpose of the transaction was to evade or avoid withdrawal liability.

Effective date

The provision applies to an employer that receives a notification of withdrawal liability and demand for payment under ERISA section 4219(b)(1) after October 31, 2003.

[Conference Agreement]

The conference agreement follows the Senate amendment.

Under the conference agreement, a special rule may apply if a transaction is disregarded by a plan sponsor in determining that a withdrawal has occurred or that an employer is liable for withdrawal liability. If the transaction that is disregarded by the plan sponsor occurred before January 1, 1999, and at least five years before the date of the withdrawal, then (1) the determination by the plan sponsor that a principal purpose of the transaction was to evade or avoid withdrawal liability is not presumed to be correct, (2) the plan sponsor, rather than the employer, has the burden to establish, by a preponderance of the evidence, the elements of the claim that a principal purpose of the transaction was to evade or avoid withdrawal liability, and (3) if an employer contests the plan sponsor's determination through an arbitration proceeding, or through a claim brought in a court of competent jurisdiction, the employer is not obligated to make any withdrawal liability payments until a final decision in the arbitration proceeding, or in court, upholds the plan sponsor's determination. The provision does not modify the burden of establishing other elements of a claim for withdrawal liability other than whether the purpose of the transaction was to evade or avoid withdrawal liability.

Effective date

The provision applies to an employer that receives a notification of withdrawal liability and demand for payment under ERISA section 4219(b)(1) after October 31, 2003.

[¶ 15,689.10]

Committee Report on P.L. 96-364 (Multiemployer Pension Plan Amendments Act of 1980)

[Senate Committee Report]

Employer challenge to a plan's determination of withdrawal liability or unfunded vested benefits.— Under the bill, an employer is permitted to challenge a plan's determination of withdrawal liability or of unfunded vested benefits. Such disputes are subject to compulsory arbitration. In the resolution of the dispute, the plan is treated as having met its burden of proof with respect to its unfunded vested benefits if certain standards are satisfied. Pending the resolution of the dispute, the employer is required to pay withdrawal liability as originally determined by the plan, but the failure to pay an installment before the arbitration is concluded would not accelerate payment of future installments. Any party to the arbitration may bring an action in the United States district court to enforce, vacate, or modify the arbitrator's award. In the court proceeding, there is to be a rebuttable presumption that the arbitrator's findings of fact were correct.

[ERISA Sec. 4222]

[¶ 15,690.10]

Committee Report on P.L. 96-364 (Multiemployer Pension Plan Amendments Act of 1980)

[Senate Committee Report]

Supplemental fund for reimbursement for uncollectible withdrawal liability.— Under the bill, the PBGC is required to establish a supplemental program by May 1, 1982, to reimburse multiemployer plans for withdrawal liability payments which are uncollectible because of bankruptcy or similar proceedings involving the employer. Under the program, the PBGC could also provide for the reimbursement of a plan for withdrawal liability which is uncollectible for any other appropriate reason. A plan could elect coverage under the supplemental program and, if it did so, would be charged a premium for such coverage. The cost of the program (including appropriate administrative and legal costs) could be paid only out of premiums collected under the program. The PBGC could carry out the program in whole or in part under an arrangement with private insurers.

[ERISA Sec. 4223]

[¶ 15,691.10]

Committee Report on P.L. 96-364 (Multiemployer Pension Plan Amendments Act of 1980)

[Senate Committee Report]

The Senate Committee Report on Act Sec. 4223 is reported at ¶ 15,684.10.

[ERISA Sec. 4224]

[¶ 15,692.10]

Committee Report on P.L. 96-364 (Multiemployer Pension Plan Amendments Act of 1980)

[Senate Committee Report]

The Senate Committee Report on Act Sec. 4224 is reported at ¶ 15,676.10.

[ERISA Sec. 4225]

[¶ 15,696.09]

Committee Report on P.L. 109-280 (Pension Protection Act of 2006)

[Joint Committee on Taxation Report]

The provision prescribes a new table under ERISA section 4225(a)(2) to be used in determining the portion of the liquidation or dissolution value of the employer for the calculation of the limitation of unfunded vested benefits allocable to an employer in the case of a bona fide sale of all or substantially all of the employer's assets in an arm's length transaction to an unrelated party. The provision also modifies the calculation of the limit so that the unfunded vested benefits allocable to an employer do not exceed the greater of (1) a portion of the liquidation or dissolution value of the employer (determined after the sale or exchange of such assets), or (2) in the case of a plan using the attributable method of allocating withdrawal liability, the unfunded vested benefits attributable to the employees of the employer. Present law ERISA section 4225(b) is not amended by the provision.

Effective Date

The provisions are effective for sales occurring on or after January 1, 2007.

For the Committee Report on P.L. 109-280 on withdrawal liability where work is contracted out, see ¶ 15,669.09.

For the Committee Report on P.L. 109-280 on application of forgiveness rule to plans primarily covering employees in building and construction, see ¶ 15,676.08.

For the Committee Report on P.L. 109-280 on procedures applicable to disputes involving withdrawal liability, see ¶ 15,689.08.

[¶ 15,696.10]

Committee Report on P.L. 96-364 (Multiemployer Pension Plan Amendments Act of 1980)

[Senate Committee Report]

Limitations on withdrawal liability.—* * * special relief rules are provided for (1) insolvency, (2) individual employers, and (3) asset sales. These relief provisions are applied to withdrawal liability determined after the application of (1) the de minimis rules, (2) any pro rata reduction of liability on account of a partial withdrawal, and (3) the 20-year payment cap.

Insolvency.—Under the bill, an insolvent employer undergoing a liquidation or dissolution is always liable for an amount equal to 50 percent of his normal withdrawal liability. However, the employer's exposure for the next 50 percent of his normal withdrawal liability is limited to the employer's liquidation or dissolution value. His value is determined by taking the employer's value as of the beginning of the liquidation or dissolution, and reducing that value by an amount equal to the first 50 percent of the employer's normal withdrawal liability. To qualify for this rule, an insolvent employer need not undergo a formal liquidation or dissolution. It must, however, be insolvent and wind up its business affairs. The insolvency limitation applies in the aggregate to total withdrawal liability at the time of insolvency. Thus, where liabilities arise because of withdrawals from several plans, the 50-percent insolvency rule would be applicable to each such liability.

Individual employers.—The Committees recognize that some employers that are obligated to contribute to multiemployer plans are individuals, i.e., sole proprietors, or partners. The Committees believe that if such an employer withdraws from a multiemployer plan, some of the employer's personal assets, such as his residence, should be shielded from employer liability. A special rule provides that where the withdrawn employer is an individual, the employer's personal assets that would be exempt under bankruptcy law will be protected from employer liability.

Asset sales.—In addition, certain rules apply if an employer withdraws in connection with the sale of all or substantially all of its business assets. In this case, if the liquidation value of the employer (determined without regard to withdrawal liability) does not exceed $2 million, the employer's liability is limited to the greater of (1) 30 percent of liquidation value, or (2) the liability attributable to the employer. For employers with liquidation values which exceed $2 million, this rule applies, except that the 30-percent limit (in (1) above) is gradually increased. Thus, to the extent liquidation value exceeds $10 million, 80 percent of the excess liquidation value may be used to determine withdrawal liability. The percentage limitation applies in the aggregate to all withdrawals in connection with a sale of assets. Thus, where withdrawals from several plans take place, the limitation must be apportioned among the plans.

[ERISA Sec. 4231]

[¶ 15,700.10]

Committee Report on P.L. 96-364 (Multiemployer Pension Plan Amendments Act of 1980)

[Senate Committee Report]

Mergers and transfers involving only multiemployer plans.—The bill establishes four requirements that a multiemployer plan must meet before it can merge with, or engage in a transfer of assets or liabilities to, another multiemployer plan. These four requirements are: (1) the plan sponsor must notify the PBGC of the merger or transfer at least 120 days before the effective date of the merger or transfer; (2) no participant's or beneficiary's accrued benefit may be lower immediately after the effective date of the merger or transfer than immediately before the date; (3) the benefits of participants and beneficiaries are not reasonably expected to be subject to suspension under the insolvency provisions of the bill; and (4) an actuarial valuation of the assets and liabilities of the affected plans must have been performed during the plan year preceding the effective date of the merger or transfer.

A plan to which liabilities are transferred is treated as a successor plan for benefit guarantee purposes.

Transfers between a multiemployer plan and a single-employer plan.—The bill provides that, in the case of a transfer of assets or liabilities between, or a merger, of a multiemployer plan and a single-employer plan, the accrued benefit of any participant may not be lower immediately after the transfer or merger than it was immediately before the transfer or merger.

As a general rule, the bill requires that, where a multiemployer plan transfers liabilities to a single-employer plan, the multiemployer plan is liable to the PBGC in the event of the termination of the single-employer plan within 60 months after the transfer. The amount of the liability is the lesser of (1) the excess of the insufficiency of plan assets of the terminated single-employer plan over 30 percent of the net worth of the employer maintaining the single-employer plan, or (2) the value of the unfunded benefits transferred to the single-employer plan and guaranteed by the PBGC (such value to be determined at the time of the transfer). The multiemployer plan is liable to the PBGC unless the PBGC determines that the interests of the participants and the PBGC are otherwise adequately protected. Where the PBGC makes such determination, it must do so within 180 days after receipt of a complete application from the plan sponsor of the multiemployer plan.

A multiemployer plan is not liable under the bill because of the transfer of liabilities to a single-employer plan where (1) the liabilities had previously accrued under a single-employer plan that merged with the multiemployer plan, (2) the present value of the liabilities transferred to the single-employer plan is not greater than the present value of liabilities for benefits which accrued before the single-employer plan merged with the multiemployer plan, and (3) the value of the assets transferred to the single-employer plan with the liabilities is substantially equal to the value of the assets which would have been in the single-employer plan if the employer had maintained and funded it as a separate plan under which no benefits accrued after the merger. This exception to the liability provision is sometimes referred to as the "in and out rule" because it is designed to protect multi-employer plans which merge with, but later spin off single-employer plans.

In any case where a multiemployer plan is liable under the bill because of a merger or transfer, the PBGC is authorized to make arrangements for satisfaction of the liability.

Where benefits are transferred to a single-employer plan under the merger or transfer rules, the benefits are thereafter to be governed by the termination insurance rules applicable to single-employer plans.

As a general rule, a multiemployer plan is not permitted to transfer assets to a single-employer plan unless the plan sponsor of the single-employer plan agrees to the transfer. In the case of a transfer under the "in and out" rule, however, the plan sponsor need not so consent if advance agreement is obtained from the employer who, after the transfer, will be obligated to contribute to the single-employer plan.

In addition, the bill limits or restricts transfers made from plans that are in reorganization, or that have terminated because of mass withdrawal.

[ERISA Sec. 4232]

[¶ 15,701.10]

Committee Report on P.L. 96-364 (Multiemployer Pension Plan Amendments Act of 1980)

[Senate Committee Report]

The Senate Committee Report on Act Sec. 4232 is reported at ¶ 15,700.10.

[ERISA Sec. 4233]

[¶ 15,702.10]

Committee Report on P.L. 96-364 (Multiemployer Pension Plan Amendments Act of 1980)

[Senate Committee Report]

Partition.—With respect to multiemployer plans, the PBGC may, on its own initiative or upon the application of a plan sponsor, order the partition of a plan. The PBGC may order the partition of a plan only if notice has been given to the plan sponsor and the participants and beneficiaries whose vested benefits will be affected and if the PBGC has made the finding that: (1) a substantial reduction in the amount of aggregate contributions has resulted or will result from a proceeding under Federal bankruptcy law; (2) the plan is likely to become insolvent; (3) contributions will have to be increased significantly in reorganization to meet the minimum contribution requirement and prevent insolvency; and (4) partition would significantly reduce the likelihood that the plan will become insolvent.

The corporation's partition order must provide for a transfer of no more than the nonforfeitable benefits directly attributable to service with the employer involved in the bankruptcy proceeding and an equitable share of plan assets. The new plan to which the benefits attributable to the bankrupt employer are transferred is treated as a successor plan for multiemployer benefit guarantee purposes and as a plan terminated by mass withdrawal. The bankrupt employer will be treated as the only employer to have withdrawal liability with respect to the new plan.

In lieu of ordering the partition of a plan, the PBGC may seek a court decree partitioning the plan and appointing a trustee for the new terminated plan.

The Committees believe that partitions should be ordered only when it is very clear that the failure to partition will result in the insolvency of the multiemployer plan. In deciding whether to order a partition under such circumstances, the PBGC and the courts should fairly balance the interests of participants and beneficiaries in the plan to be terminated and the interests of the participants and beneficiaries who would continue to be covered by the original multiemployer plan.

[ERISA Sec. 4234]

[¶ 15,703.10]

Committee Report on P.L. 96-364 (Multiemployer Pension Plan Amendments Act of 1980)

[Senate Committee Report]

Assets transferable.—Under the bill, multiemployer plans are required to provide rules regarding the transfer of assets to another plan. The rules may not unreasonably restrict the transfer of plan assets in connection with a transfer of plan liabilities and must operate and be applied uniformly with respect to all transfers, except that reasonable variations are permitted to take into account the potential financial impact of a particular transfer on a multiemployer plan.

This requirement is for plan rules, not necessarily plan amendments. These rules, however, will be "documents and instruments governing the plan" pursuant to ERISA, and ERISA's fiduciary provisions are decisions and actions regarding the design as well as the operation of these asset-transfer rules.

Under the bill, the PBGC is required to prescribe regulations exempting de minimis transfers of assets from the merger, etc. rules. In addition, the merger, etc. rules do not apply to transfers of assets pursuant to written reciprocity agreements except to the extent provided in PBGC regulations.

[ERISA Sec. 4235]

[¶ 15,704.09]

Committee Report on P.L. 98-369 (Tax Reform Act of 1984)

. . . relating to the effective date of the Multiemployer Pension Plan Amendments Act of 1980, see ¶ 15,676.09.

[¶ 15,704.10]

Committee Report on P.L. 96-364 (Multiemployer Pension Plan Amendments Act of 1980)

[Senate Committee Report]

Transfers pursuant to change in collective bargaining representative.—In a case where an employer incurs a complete or partial withdrawal from a plan because of a certified change in the employee's collective bargaining representative, assets and liabilities from the old plan attributable to the nonforfeitable benefits of employees no longer working in covered service under the old plan as a result of the change must be transferred to the new multiemployer plan under certain circumstances. Within 180 days after the effective date of the change in collective bargaining representative, the old plan must notify the employer in writing of (1) the amount of the employer's withdrawal liability if no transfer of assets and liability is made to the new plan, and (2) the amount of assets and liabilities which the old plan intends to transfer to the new plan. The notice must also be sent to the new plan.

Unless the employer objects to the transfer or the new plan files an appeal with the PBGC, then within 60 days after the notice is given, the plan sponsor of the old plan must promptly transfer the appropriate amount of assets and liabilities to the new plan. [If] The new plan appeals to the PBGC, the PBGC may prevent the transfer if the transfer would result in substantial financial harm to the new plan. The transfer must be made unless the PBGC makes such a finding of substantial harm within 180 days after the appeal is filed.

If the transfer is made, the employer's withdrawal liability with respect to the old plan is reduced by the value of the unfunded vested benefits transferred to the new plan less the value of the assets transferred.

[ERISA Sec. 4241]

[¶ 15,706.10]

Committee Report on P.L. 96-364 (Multiemployer Pension Plan Amendments Act of 1980)

[Senate Committee Report]

Reorganization status.—A multiemployer plan is in reorganization for a year if the plan's reorganization index is greater than zero. The reorganization index is calculated anew for each plan year. The reorganization index is the excess of the plan's "vested benefits charge" over the contribution necessary to balance charges and credits in the plan's funding standard account without taking into account certain credits. The vested benefits charge is the amount necessary to amortize, in equal annual installments, the unfunded vested benefits of the plan (1) over 10 years in the case of obligations attributable to persons whose benefits are in pay status, and (2) over 25 years in the case of unfunded benefit obligations for other participants. The amortization period for obligations attributable to pay status participants is shorter because the plan will have to pay these obligations over a shorter term than the obligations to other participants.

Under the bill, a plan sponsor can determine whether a plan will be in reorganization before the beginning of a plan year. The determination of the vested benefits charge is based on a valuation of the plan performed as of the last day of the "base plan year". The "base plan year" is the last plan year ending at least six months before the earliest effective date of any "relevant collective bargaining agreement". A "relevant collective bargaining agreement" is a collective bargaining agreement that has been in effect for more than six months during the plan year but has not been in effect for more than three years as of the end of the plan year. In any case where there is no relevant collective bargaining agreement, the base plan year is the plan year ending at least 12 months before the beginning of the plan year for which the vested benefits charge is determined. Of course the Secretary of the Treasury has the authority to require that the vested benefits charge and charges and credits to the funding standard account be computed on a consistent basis.

The reason for using a valuation performed as of the end of the base plan year is to avoid plans going into reorganization unexpectedly during the term of a collective bargaining agreement. The valuation must be adjusted to take into account any decrease of five percent or more in the value of plan assets or increase of five percent or more in the number of persons in pay status between the first day of the plan year following the base plan year and the day which is 90 days before the effective date of the relevant collective bargaining agreement. In addition, the valuation must be adjusted to reflect (1) any later plan valuation, (2) any change in benefits not otherwise taken into account, and (3) any other event which would substantially increase the plan's vested benefits charge (determined in accordance with regulations). For this purpose, "other event" may include a plan amendment effective in the future. This is an exception to the present-law prohibition against funding based on certain types of future events.

Prohibition of certain payments.—Under the bill, while a plan is in reorganization, the present value of a participant's vested benefits derived from employer contributions may not be distributed faster than in the form of substantially level pension payments for the life of the participant if the present value distribution exceeds $1,750. This prohibition does not apply (1) in the case of a death benefit distribution, or (2) as provided in PBGC regulations.

Termination of reorganization status.—A terminated multiemployer plan is not considered to be in reorganization after the date on which the last employer maintaining the plan withdraws from the plan. For this purpose, the determination of whether a withdrawal takes place is made in accordance with the definition of withdrawal contained in the bill's withdrawal liability provisions. Partial withdrawals are not taken into account.

[ERISA Sec. 4242]

[¶ 15,708.10]

Committee Report on P.L. 96-364 (Multiemployer Pension Plan Amendments Act of 1980)

[Senate Committee Report]

Notice of reorganization.—Under the bill when a multiemployer plan is in reorganization and would require an increase in contributions (before taking into account the credit for overburdened plans permitted under the reorganization provisions), the plan sponsor is required to notify employers contributing to the plan and employee organizations representing participants in the plan that the plan is in reorganization. In addition the notice must state that if contributions to the plan are not increased an excise tax may be imposed on employers.

In addition, the PBGC is authorized to issue regulations prescribing additional or alternative requirements for assuring that the interested persons receive appropriate notice that the plan is in reorganization, are adequately informed of the implications of reorganization status, and have reasonable access to relevant information.

[ERISA Sec. 4243]

[¶ 15,709.10]

Committee Report on P.L. 96-364 (Multiemployer Pension Plan Amendments Act of 1980)

[Senate Committee Report]

Minimum contribution requirements—In general.— Under the bill, a plan in reorganization must continue to maintain its funding standard account, but such a plan is also required to meet special minimum funding requirements. These requirements apply to each year separately. If contributions are not sufficient to satisfy the requirements for a plan year, the plan has a funding deficiency, and employers are subject to the current excise taxes on accumulated funding deficiencies (or subject to the current conditions for having such deficiencies waived by the Internal Revenue Service). An "accumulated funding deficiency" for a plan in reorganization is defined as the excess of the "minimum contribution requirement" plus the accumulated funding deficiency for the preceding plan year less amounts contributed by employers to the plan for the plan year, including certain amounts contributed to meet withdrawal liability obligations and a waived funding deficiency.

The bill defines the minimum contribution requirement as the sum of (1) the plan's vested benefits charge, and (2) where the plan has been amended to increase benefits while the plan is in reorganization, the normal cost (determined under the entry age normal funding method) attributable to such plan amendment less the amount of the "overburden credit." The minimum contribution requirement is reduced proportionately where the plan's current contribution base (e.g., hours of service) for which employer contributions are required for the plan year is less than the plan's valuation contribution base. A plan's "valuation contribution base" is generally equal to the plan's contribution base for the plan year for which the actuarial valuation used to determine unfunded vested benefits under the plan was made, with certain adjustments for upward or downward trends. Special rules apply for determining a plan's valuation contribution base for a plan year in which the plan is insolvent.

In the case of a plan in reorganization, if the plan's vested benefits charge is less than the plan's "cash flow amount" for a plan year, the minimum contribution requirement is determined by substituting the cash flow amount for the vested benefits charge. For this purpose, cash flow amount means the aggregate amount of benefits payable under the plan increased by the plan's administrative expenses for the plan year and decreased by the value of available plan assets, as determined under regulations prescribed by the Secretary of the Treasury. Also, in determining a plan's minimum contribution requirement for a plan year, the vested benefits charge may be adjusted to reflect a subsequent plan amendment which reduces benefits under the plan termination provisions of the bill or under the funding standard. This adjustment would only take place, however, if the amendment is adopted and effective not later than 2 ½ months after the close of the plan year, or within an extended period for making the amendment as prescribed in regulations issued by the Secretary of the Treasury.

In addition, during the period that a plan is required to meet the "minimum contribution requirement," a credit or charge balance may build up in the plan's funding standard account. The bill provides that if a plan is not required to meet the "minimum contribution requirement" for a plan year but was required to meet such requirement for the preceding plan year, any balance in the funding standard account is eliminated by an offsetting credit or charge (as appropriate) which is amortized over 30 years.

Under the bill, the minimum contribution requirement applicable to a plan for a plan year cannot exceed an amount which requires a rate of employer contributions in excess of the rate which would be required to meet the greater of (1) the funding standard requirement, i.e., the net charges under the plan's funding standard account as if it were not in reorganization (without regard to any credit balance in the funding standard account) or (2) 107 percent of the amount required for the preceding year. This limitation is further increased with respect to benefit increases while the plan is in reorganization.

The Committees have included a special provision applicable to the 1950 United Mine Workers Pension Plan ("1950 Plan"). Under the provision, employers in that plan have the benefit of the limitation on increases in the minimum contribution requirement (without regard to the increase in the limitation for benefit increases), as long as when an increase is effective, the plan's funding complies with a special funding standard that substantially exceeds the minimum contribution requirement.

Participation in the 1950 Plan is limited solely to retirees and inactive separated participants. The plan has a strong contribution base, and will be fully funded by 1986 at current funding levels. Under these circumstances, it is desirable to permit a benefit increase without removing the protection afforded against unanticipated declines in the contribution base. The PBGC has advised the Committees that the exception made in this case should not increase the risk of loss to the PBGC or participants with respect to the 1950 Plan.

In order for the 1950 Plan to qualify for this special exception several conditions must be met. The amortization schedule for existing benefits must be maintained. This would require completion of the funding for March 1, 1978 benefit levels by July 1, 1986 and for the July 1978 benefit improvements by 1990. In addition, the funding level for any benefit increase must be set so that funding is projected to be completed in no more than 12 years, or if less, the average number of years remaining in the expected lives of persons receiving benefits. Finally in any year following a benefit increase, the contribution rate must be increased at least five percent, or, if less, the amount necessary to maintain the required accelerated funding schedules. The Committees note that in order for the plan to continue to qualify for this exception, whenever benefits are increased, the amortization schedules that apply to prior benefit levels must be fully satisfied and the funding completed within the required period.

[ERISA Sec. 4244]

[¶ 15,710.10]

Committee Report on P.L. 96-364 (Multiemployer Pension Plan Amendments Act of 1980)

[Senate Committee Report]

Credit for overburdened plans.—Where a plan is considered to be financially overburdened for a plan year (determined under standards set forth in the bill), the plan must apply an "overburden credit" against its minimum contribution requirement for the plan year. Accordingly, the overburden credit reduces the additional funding needed to satisfy the minimum contribution requirement. The overburden credit is computed and applied separately for each year that a plan is overburdened. The plan cannot accumulate unused credits to apply against future accumulated funding deficiencies.

A plan is considered overburdened for a plan year under the bill if (1) the average number of participants in pay status in the year exceeds the average of the average number of active participants in that year and in the preceding two plan years, and (2) the rate of employer contributions to the plan is at least equal to the greater of the rate of contributions for the preceding plan year or the rate of contributions for the year before the first plan year in which the plan was in reorganization. For purposes of this rule: "pay status participant" means a participant receiving retirement benefits under the plan and "active participant" means (1) any plan participant who has not failed to accrue a benefit for the year because of insufficient active employment, (2) any active employee who is not a plan participant but who is in an employment unit covered by a collective bargaining agreement requiring the employee's employer to contribute to the plan, and (3) any active employee considered an employee of the employer under a special formula in the bill which treats certain employees as the employer's employees on the basis of the employer's withdrawal liability contributions to the plan.

The amount of overburden credit for a plan year is the product of two amounts. The first amount is one-half of the "average guaranteed benefit paid" in the base plan year and the second amount is the "overburden factor" for the plan year. The "average guaranteed benefit paid" is 12 times the average monthly pension payment guaranteed under the bill, computed by dividing (1) the total guaranteed annuity pension payment under the plan by (2) the number of pay status participants in the plan for the plan year. The "overburden factor" for a plan for a plan year is the excess of (1) the average number of pay status participants for the base plan year over (2) the average of the average number of active participants in the plan in that plan year and the two preceding plan years. The minimum contribution requirement can never be reduced below zero by the application of the overburden credit.

Under the bill, the Secretary of the Treasury could deny a plan of overburden credit for a plan year upon a finding that (1) the plan's current contribution base was reduced without a corresponding reduction in the plan's unfunded vested benefits attributable to pay status participants, and (2) such reduction resulted from a change in an agreement providing for employer contributions to the plan. Accordingly, a plan that has excluded active employees is not eligible for the overburden credit. However, an employer withdrawal from a plan does not prevent the plan from being eligible for the overburden credit, unless the Secretary of the Treasury finds that in connection with the withdrawal a contribution base reduction resulted from a transfer of plan liabilities to another plan.

Under the bill, in the case of the merger of plans involving one or more multiemployer plans, which are in reorganization, there is a limit on the amount of overburden credit which can be applied to the minimum contribution requirement of the plan resulting from the merger. The maximum credit for any of the first three plan years ending after the merger could not exceed the sum of the overburden credits applied by each of the plans to avoid a reorganization deficiency for the last plan year ending before the merger. Of course, the rules relating to mergers also apply in computing the overburden credit in the case of a consolidation of plans. The Committees wish to clarify that the overburden credit does not represent a permanent forgiveness of a portion of a plan's underfunding. Rather, it eliminates that portion of a plan's underfunding for that year for purposes of determining whether the funding standards have been violated. The underfunding will be reflected in subsequent computations of the vested benefits charge.

[ERISA Sec. 4244A]

[¶ 15,712.10]

Committee Report on P.L. 96-364 (Multiemployer Pension Plan Amendments Act of 1980)

[Senate Committee Report]

The Senate Committee Report on Act Sec. 4244A(a) (2) is reported at ¶ 15,709.

[House Ways and Means Committee Report]

Adjustments in accrued benefits.—With very limited exceptions, under present law, plan amendments are not permitted to reduce benefits already accrued by an employee. However, in the case of a multiemployer plan in reorganization, the bill permits plan amendments to reduce accrued benefits attributable to employer contributions under specified circumstances. The accrued benefits which are subject to reduction are those which have been in effect under the plan for less than 60 months and are not eligible for guarantee by the PBGC.

The conditions which must be met in order for a plan's accrued benefits to be reduced are as follows:

a. A notice must be given, at least six months in advance of the first day of the plan year in which the amendment reducing accrued benefits is adopted, to plan participants and beneficiaries, to each employer with an obligation to contribute to the plan, and to each affected employee organization. The notice must state that the plan is in reorganization and that if contributions to the plan are required to be increased and the increase is not made, accrued benefits under the plan are required to be reduced or the failure to increase employer contributions to the plan may result in an excise tax for failure to meet the minimum funding standard.

b. Under regulations to be issued by the Secretary of the Treasury—

(i) accrued benefits of inactive participants are not to be reduced to a greater extent proportionally than accrued benefits for active participants are reduced:

(ii) benefits attributable to employer contributions other than accrued benefits (such as death benefits or health benefits) and the rate of future benefit accruals are to be decreased at least as much as accrued benefits of active participants are decreased; and

(iii) if the reduction in accrued benefits takes the form of a change in the mode of benefit or the requirements for benefit entitlements, the reduction may not affect benefits in pay status on the effective date of the amendment or benefits of any participants who has [sic] reached, or is [sic] within five years of reaching, normal retirement age on the effective date of the amendment.

c. The rate of employer contributions for the plan year in which the amendment becomes effective and for all future years while the plan is in reorganization must at least equal the greater of (i) the rate of employer contributions (without regard to the amendment) for the plan year in which the amendment becomes effective, or (ii) the rate of employer contributions for the preceding plan year.

Where accrued benefits are decreased by a plan amendment, a plan is not to be permitted to recapture a benefit payment which has already been made under the plan's accrued benefit provisions determined before the amendment is adopted.

Once a plan has been amended to decrease accrued benefits, a future plan amendment is not to be permitted to increase (1) accrued benefits, or (2) the rate of future benefit accrual, only if the plan is first amended to restore previously eliminated accrued benefits of inactive participants and participants within five years of normal retirement age at least to the extent of the amount or rate by which the plan amendment increases benefit accruals. Moreover, where a plan is amended so that it partially restores previously accrued benefit levels or the previous rate of accrual, the benefits of inactive participants must be restored in at least the same proportion as accrued benefits are restored overall.

Under the bill, no increase in benefits under a plan is to be permitted to take effect in a plan year in which an amendment reducing accrued benefits is adopted or first becomes effective.

Where a benefit is reduced and later restored, a plan is not required to make retroactive benefit payments to participants who received payment under the reduced accrued benefit levels.

For purposes of applying the benefit reduction rules, an inactive participant is an individual whose benefits are in pay status under the plan or an individual not currently in service under the plan but who nevertheless has a vested plan benefit.

The Secretary of the Treasury is authorized to prescribe regulations permitting benefit reductions or increases for different groups of participants on an equitable basis to reflect variations in contribution rates and other relevant factors reflecting differences in bargained for levels of financial support for plan benefit obligations.

[ERISA Sec. 4245]

[¶ 15,713.09]

Committee Report on P.L. 109-280 (Pension Protection Act of 2006)

For the Committee Report on P.L. 109-280 on measures to forestall insolvency of multiemployer plans, see ¶ 12,850.09.

[¶ 15,713.10]

Committee Report on P.L. 96-364 (Multiemployer Pension Plan Amendments Act of 1980)

[Senate Committee Report]

Insolvent plans.—Under the bill, if a multiemployer plan is insolvent for a plan year, the plan is required to suspend the payment of benefits, other than basic benefits, which exceed the "resource benefit level." The suspension rule does not apply, however, if the PBGC prescribes a procedure for the guarantee of supplemental benefits (retirement benefits exceeding basic benefits) to the extent supplemental benefits are guaranteed by the PBGC. A multiemployer plan is considered insolvent for a plan year if the plan's available resources are not sufficient to pay benefits under the plan when due for the plan year. The term "resource benefit level" means the highest level of monthly benefits which the plan could pay out of its available resources.

For each year for which a multiemployer plan is insolvent, the plan sponsor is required to determine and certify the resource benefit level of the plan, based on its reasonable projection of available resources and benefits payable. Where the suspension of benefits above the resource benefit level takes place, benefits must be suspended in substantially uniform proportions with respect to all persons whose benefits are in pay status under the plan. The proportionate suspension must be done in a manner consistent with regulations prescribed by the Secretary of the Treasury. In addition, the Secretary of the Treasury is authorized to prescribe rules under which the benefits of different participant groups could be suspended in disproportionate fashion if varied equitably to reflect variations in contribution rates and other relevant factors reflecting differences in bargained-for levels of financial support for plan benefit obligations.

A plan sponsor which determines a resource benefit level which is below the level of guaranteed benefits for a plan year must suspend payment of all benefits other than guaranteed benefits.

If, by the end of a plan year for which a plan is insolvent, the plan sponsor determines that benefits can be paid above the resource benefit level, the plan sponsor must distribute such additional benefits in accordance with regulations prescribed by the Secretary of the Treasury. Where by the end of the year, benefits up to the resource benefit level have not been paid, the amount necessary to bring benefits up to that level must be distributed in accordance with regulations prescribed by the Secretary of the Treasury, to the extent possible, considering the plan's available resources.

Every three years during the period when a plan is in reorganization, beginning with the end of the first such plan year, the plan sponsor must compare the value of plan assets with the total amount of benefit payment for the year. Unless plan assets exceed three times the total amount of benefit payments, the plan sponsor must determine whether the plan will be insolvent during any of the next three plan years. In addition, if at any time the plan sponsor of a plan in reorganization determines, on the basis of experience, that available resources are not sufficient to pay benefits when due for the forthcoming plan year, the sponsor must make such determination available to interested parties.

If the plan sponsor determines that the plan may be insolvent any time in the next three plan years, the sponsor is required to so notify (1) the Secretary of the Treasury, (2) the PBGC, (3) plan participants and beneficiaries, (4) each employer required to contribute to the plan, and (5) each affected employee organization. In addition, the above parties other than the Secretary of the Treasury and the PBGC are to be informed that, in the event of insolvency, payments in excess of basic benefits must be suspended (unless guaranteed as supplemental benefits). No later than two months before the first day of a year for which a plan which is in reorganization is insolvent, the plan sponsor must notify each of the above parties of the plan's resource benefit level.

Where the plan sponsor believes that the resource benefit level for a plan year for which a plan is insolvent may not exceed the level of basic benefits, the plan sponsor must notify the PBGC.

Where a plan sponsor determines a resource benefit level below the level of basic benefits, the sponsor must apply to the PBGC for financial assistance. Where the plan sponsor determines a resource benefit level above the level of basic benefits but anticipates that for any month during a year for which the plan is insolvent the plan will not have sufficient assets to pay basic benefits, the plan sponsor is permitted to apply to the PBGC for financial assistance.

Financial assistance.—Under the bill, if the PBGC receives an application for financial assistance from a plan and verifies that the plan will be insolvent and unable to pay basic benefits when due, the PBGC must provide financial assistance to the plan in an amount sufficient to permit the plan to pay its basic benefits. Such financial assistance is provided under such conditions as the PBGC determines to be equitable and appropriate to prevent unreasonable loss to the PBGC with respect to the plan. Where a plan receives financial assistance from the PBGC, it must repay the PBGC on reasonable terms which are consistent with regulations to be issued by the PBGC.

While the PBGC is determining the amount of assistance necessary to permit a plan to pay basic benefits, the PBGC is permitted to provide interim financial assistance to avoid undue hardship to plan participants and beneficiaries.

[ERISA Sec. 4261]

[¶ 15,714.10]

Committee Report on P.L. 96-364 (Multiemployer Pension Plan Amendments Act of 1980)

[Senate Committee Report]

The Senate Committee Report on Act Sec. 4261 is reported at ¶ 15,713.

[ERISA Sec. 4281]

[¶ 15,715.10]

Committee Report on P.L. 96-364 (Multiemployer Pension Plan Amendments Act of 1980)

[Senate Committee Report]

For the Senate Committee Report on Act Sec. 4281(d), see ¶ 15,713.

See, also, Committee Report (on complete and partial withdrawals) at ¶ 15,663.10.

Termination of multiemployer plans

Present law

Under present law, the date of plan termination for purposes of termination insurance, is generally determined by the actions of responsible officials of the plan.[1] However, ERISA provides a procedure under which the PBGC may institute proceedings to terminate a plan.[2]

Reasons for change

The Committees believe that it is desirable to have more appropriate rules to determine the time of termination of a multiemployer plan. In addition, the Committees believe that it is necessary to have limitations on the benefit payments which can be made by certain terminated plans and requirements with respect to continued employer contributions to such a plan.

Explanation of provisions

In general.—The bill provides that a plan termination occurs as the result of (1) the adoption of a plan amendment providing that participants will receive no credit for any purpose under the plan for service with any employer (termination by "freezing"); (2) the adoption of a plan amendment that causes the plan to become a defined contribution plan (termination by "change of plan type"); and (3) the withdrawal of every employer from the plan (termination by "mass withdrawal"). Except for a termination by mass withdrawal, the minimum funding standards continue to apply to a terminated plan.

The PBGC is authorized by the bill to prescribe reporting requirements or standards (not in derogation of any other applicable requirement or standard under ERISA) for the administration of terminated plans as it deems necessary to protect the interests of plan participants or to prevent unreasonable losses to the PBGC.

Termination by plan amendment.—Termination by freezing and termination by change of plan type as opposed to termination by mass withdrawal, are accomplished through plan amendment. These terminations by amendment are effective on the later of the date on which the amendment is adopted or the date on which the amendment takes effect.

---

[1] See ERISA secs. 4041 and 4048.

[2] See ERISA secs. 4042 and 4048.

If a plan is terminated by amendment, each employer's contribution rate after the termination must at least equal that employer's highest contribution rate in the five preceding plan years ending before the plan termination date. The corporation may, however, approve a reduction in the rate if it finds that the plan is or soon will be fully funded. Plans terminated by amendment remain ongoing plans for purposes of reorganization funding.

The Committees recognize that a plan may terminate by amendment and later become a plan from which every employer has withdrawn. In such a case, the termination by mass withdrawal rules become applicable once every employer has withdrawn.

The date on which a plan terminates by mass withdrawal is the earlier of the dates on which (1) the last employer withdraws or (2) the beginning of the first plan year for which no employer contributions were required under the plan.

In addition to the general rules on limiting payments to nonforfeitable benefits in the form of an annuity, the plan sponsor of a plan terminated by mass withdrawal must observe additional rules concerning the suspension of benefit payments.

If the present value of nonforfeitable benefits exceeds the value of the plan's assets, the plan sponsor must suspend benefits to the extent necessary to ensure that the plan's assets are sufficient to pay benefits (as reduced).

The sponsor of a plan terminated by mass withdrawal must limit the payment of benefits to nonforfeitable benefits under the plan as of the termination date. The sponsor of such a plan must also cause benefits attributable to employer contributions, other than death benefits, to be paid only in the form of an annuity, unless the plan distributes its assets in satisfaction of all nonforfeitable benefits under the plan. Notwithstanding the preceding, (1) the plan sponsor may authorize a distribution of the present value of a participant's entire nonforfeitable benefit attributable to employer contributions, other than a death benefit, in a form other than an annuity if the distribution does not exceed $1,750, and (2) the PBGC may authorize the payment of benefits other than nonforfeitable benefits or in lump sum amounts greater than $1,750 if it makes certain determinations.

Effective date

These provisions of the bill apply on the date of enactment.

Benefits under certain terminated plans.—Under the bill, where a plan terminates by a mass withdrawal of employers the plan sponsor is required to amend the plan (1) to reduce benefits, and (2) to suspend certain benefit payments. The reduction in benefits must be to a level at which plan assets will be sufficient to discharge the plan's obligations when due, but not to a level of benefits below the level eligible for guarantee. In making the determination of this level, the present value of vested benefits under the plan and the value of plan assets must be determined as of the end of the plan year in which the plan terminates, and as of the end of every plan year thereafter. For this purpose, plan assets include the value of outstanding claims for withdrawal liability.

Any plan amendment reducing benefits must (1) limit the reduction to the extent necessary to permit the payment of vested benefits, (2) eliminate or reduce only those accrued benefits which are not guaranteed by the PBGC and (3) become effective no later than six months after the plan year in which it was determined that the present value of vested benefits exceed[s] plan assets. The Committees expect that a reduction of benefits for a participant or beneficiary to a greater extent than is permitted under the bill will be considered a violation of the minimum standards of ERISA (*e.g.,* the vesting and fiduciary standards) and that fiduciaries will act prudently in discharging their duties to retirees and other participants and beneficiaries.

Under the bill special rules apply in the case of the termination of an insolvent plan.

[ERISA Sec. 4301]

[¶ 15,716.10]

Committee Report on P.L. 96-364 (Multiemployer Pension Plan Amendments Act of 1980)

[Senate Committee Report]

Civil actions.—Existing law does not provide private parties adequate remedies for resolution of disputes that may arise under certain provisions of the bill. Under the bill, certain parties could bring a civil action for appropriate legal relief, equitable relief, or both. These parties are (1) a plan fiduciary, an employer, a plan participant, or a plan beneficiary, any of whom are adversely affected by an act or omission of any party under the provisions of the bill with respect to multiemployer plans, as well as (2) an employee organization which represents an affected plan participant. However, no such action could be brought against the Secretary of the Treasury, the Commissioner of Internal Revenue, the Secretary of Labor, or the PBGC.

In any case where a civil action is brought to compel an employer to pay withdrawal liability, the court must award (1) the unpaid liability plus interest and (2) the greater of an equal amount of interest or liquidated damages payable to the plan. In general, the district courts of the United States have exclusive jurisdiction for civil actions under the bill without regard to the amount in controversy. In the case of an action brought by a plan fiduciary to collect withdrawal liability, State courts of competent authority are also to have jurisdiction.

The proper venues in Federal district court for bringing an action under the bill are to be (1) the district where the plan is administered, (2) the district where a defendant resides, or (3) the district where a defendant does business. Service of process must be permitted in any district where a defendant (1) resides, (2) does business, or (3) may be found. In addition, a copy of the complaint in any action brought under the bill must be served on the PBGC by certified mail. The PBGC may intervene in any action brought under the bill.

In the case of an action under the bill, the court is permitted to award to the prevailing party all or a portion of costs and expenses in connection with the action, including reasonable attorney's fees.

The period of limitations for the commencement of an action under the bill expires on the later of (1) six years after the date on which the cause of action arose or (2) 3 years after the earliest date on which the moving party acquired or should have acquired actual knowledge of the existence of the cause of action (generally 6 years after the date of discovery in the case of fraud or concealment).

Liquidated damages, etc., in an action to collect delinquent plan contributions.—Under the bill, in the case of a civil action by any person to collect delinquent multiemployer plan contributions, regardless of otherwise applicable law, in which a judgment in favor of the plan is awarded, the court before which the action is brought must award the plan (1) the unpaid contributions, (2) interest on the unpaid contributions, (3) an amount equal to the greater of interest on the unpaid contributions or liquidated damages provided for under the plan not to exceed 20 percent of the amount of delinquent contributions as determined by the court. The bill preempts any state or other law which would prevent the award of reasonable attorneys fees, court costs or liquidated damages or which would limit liquidated damages to an amount below the 20 percent level.

However, the bill does not preclude the award of liquidated damages in excess of the 20 percent level where an award of such a higher level of liquidated damages is permitted under applicable State or other law. This does not change any other type of remedy permitted under State or Federal law with respect to delinquent multiemployer plan contributions.

[ERISA Sec. 4302]

[¶ 15,717.10]

Committee Report on P.L. 96-364 (Multiemployer Pension Plan Amendments Act of 1980)

[Senate Committee Report]

Penalty for failure to provide notice.—If any person fails without reasonable cause to provide any notice required under the termination insurance program for multiemployer plans or under implementing regulations the bill provides that the person is liable to the PBGC in an amount up to $100 for each day that the failure continues. The PBGC is authorized to bring a civil action against the person failing to give notice. The action could be brought in the United States District Court for the District of Columbia or in any United States district court within the jurisdiction where (1) the plan assets are located, (2) the plan is administered, or (3) a defendant resides or does business. Service of process for such an action may take place in any district where a defendant (1) resides, (2) does business, or (3) may be found.

[ERISA Sec. 4303]

[¶ 15,718.10]

Committee Report on P.L. 96-364 (Multiemployer Pension Plan Amendments Act of 1980)

[Senate Committee Report]

Under the bill, the test relating to proportionate employer contributions (the 50-percent test) is deleted, and the test relating to continuity of benefits in the event of a cessation of employer contributions is preserved in the minimum vesting standard of ERISA. The bill provides that all trades and businesses (whether or not incorporated) under common control are considered a single employer for purposes of testing the status of a plan as a multiemployer plan. In addition, the bill provides that a plan continues to be a multiemployer plan after its termination if it was a multiemployer plan for the plan year ending before its termination date.

A plan which is a single-employer plan under present law (even though more than one employer maintains the plan) and which has paid PBGC premiums for the three plan years preceding the date of enactment as a single-employer plan is permitted to irrevocably elect to be considered a single-employer plan where the plan would otherwise be a multiemployer plan under the bill.

Effective date

The provision will apply upon enactment, except that the present law definition will continue for plan years beginning before enactment.

[ERISA Sec. 4402]

[¶ 15,720.085]

Committee Reports on P.L. 99-514 (Tax Reform Act of 1986)

[Senate Committee Report]

The Multi-employer Pension Plan Amendments Act of 1980 (MPPAA) was enacted on September 26, 1980. * * * The withdrawal liability provisions of the MPPAA generally applied retroactively to withdrawals after April 28, 1980.

The Deficit Reduction Act of 1984 (DEFRA) eliminated the retroactive aspect of MPPAA so that, in general, any liability incurred by an employer under the withdrawal liability provisions of ERISA, as a result of the complete or partial withdrawal from a multiemployer plan before September 26, 1980, is void.

Explanation of Provision

The bill modifies the effective date of the withdrawal liability provisions of MPPAA in two instances. First, in the case of an employer who entered into a collective bargaining agreement that was effective on January 12, 1979, and that remained in effect through May 15, 1982, and under which contributions to a multiemployer plan were to cease on January 12, 1982, the bill changes the effective date of the withdrawal liability provision of MPPAA from September 26, 1980 to January 12, 1982.

Second, in the case of an employer engaged in the grocery wholesaling business that had ceased all covered operations under the plan before June 30, 1981, and had relocated its operations to a new facility in another State and that meets certain other conditions listed in the bill, the bill modifies the effective date of the withdrawal liability provisions of MPPAA from September 26, 1980 to June 30, 1981.

[Conference Committee Report]

The conference agreement follows the Senate amendment with the following exceptions.

* * *

c. Multiemployer Pension Plan Amendments Act effective date.—The change in the effective date of the Multiemployer Pension Plan Amendments Act of 1980 with respect to a certain employer is modified to change the effective date from January 12, 1982, to January 16, 1982, and from May 16, 1980, to May 14, 1980, in the case of another employer.

[¶ 15,720.087]

Committee Report on P.L. 98-369 (Tax Reform Act of 1984)

. . . relating to the effective date of the Multiemployer Pension Plan Amendments Act of 1980, see ¶ 15,676.09.

[¶ 15,720.09]

Committee Report on P.L. 96-364 (Multiemployer Pension Plan Amendments Act of 1980)

[Senate Committee Report]

General effective date

The provisions of the bill generally apply on the date of enactment. One exception is that the withdrawal liability rules take effect as of April 29, 1980. For purposes of determining whether an employer has withdrawn from a multiemployer plan, the definition of multiemployer plan in effect at the time of the withdrawal is to be applied. Another exception is that the reorganization provisions take effect on the first day of the first plan year beginning after the earlier of (1) the expiration date of the last collective bargaining agreement in effect on the date of enactment of the bill or (2) 3 years after the date of enactment of the bill.

Under the bill, in the case of employers that withdraw from multiemployer plans covering employees in the seagoing industry on the Pacific Coast of the United States, the withdrawal liability provisions become effective May 3, 1979. In this case all of the provisions of the bill relating to withdrawal liability (including the rules which allocate the liability and which reduce the liability) are to be modified by the PBGC to reflect the earlier effective date. This retroactive application of the withdrawal liability effective date is applied only in the case of the seagoing industry because of specific problems in that industry.

Also, the bill provides that where an employer has withdrawn from a multiemployer plan before the date of enactment of the bill, and a bond or escrow has been provided by the employer under present law, the PBGC is to pay the bond or escrow to the plan if, because of the withdrawal of all employers from the plan, the plan terminates before April 28, 1984 (April 28, 1985). In any case in which the plan is not terminated before April 28, 1984 (April 28, 1985), the liability of the employer is abated and any payment held in escrow is to be refunded without interest to the employer or the employer's bond is to be cancelled.

Partition of plans before effective date

The bill provides the PBGC with continued discretion to partition multiemployer plans from which an employer or employees withdrew before the effective date of the bill. It also makes it clear that where the PBGC decides to partition such a plan and is thereby forced to take on responsibility for the insolvent part of the plan, the benefits of retirees at the time of partition would be guaranteed to the extent provided under the law in effect before enactment of the bill with respect to single-employer plans.

[¶ 15,720.091]

Committee Report on P.L. 96-364 (Multiemployer Pension Plan Amendments Act of 1980)

[House Ways and Means Committee General Explanation]

Certain partial withdrawals announced before December 13, 1979.—* * * The Committee's amendment creates an exception to the general effective date for partial withdrawal liability. Under the amendment, if an employer (1) publicly announced the total cessation of covered operations at a facility before December 13, 1979, and such cessation occurs within 12 months after the announcement; (2) had not been obligated to make contributions to the multiemployer plan on behalf of the employees at such facility for more than eight years; and (3) after the cessation, does not commence operations which would be covered by the plan within the same State for one year, then the employer's partial withdrawal liability attributable to such facility could not exceed the amount determined under a special formula. The special formula generally would limit partial withdrawal liability to the excess of the present value of vested benefits under the plan considered to be attributable to the withdrawing employer (determined on the basis of actual employee data for the period preceding the date of the partial withdrawal and on the basis of actuarial estimates thereafter) less an amount deemed to be an accumulation of employers' contributions to the plan.

[¶ 15,720.10]

Committee Report on P.L. 93-406 (Employee Retirement Income Security Act of 1974)

[Conference Committee Explanation]

Effective Dates

* * *

Under the conference substitute, benefits payable by single-employer plans are covered with respect to plans terminated after June 30, 1974, provided the usual requirements for coverage are met. Employers do not, however, incur contingent liability coverage for plans terminating between June 30, 1974, and the date of enactment [September 2, 1974].

These plans are not covered, however, unless they send the Secretary of Labor a notice received by him not later than 10 days after enactment. If reasonable cause is shown for failure to meet this requirement, notice can be received as late as October 31, 1974.

The opportunity to give notice as late as October 31, 1974 (where good cause is shown), is not intended to apply to situations where the failure to give timely notice was the result of inconvenience or inadvertence. In determining where there is reasonable cause shown for not having given notice within the 10-day period, it is intended that the showing be by clear and convincing evidence that it was not reasonably possible to have given the notice within the time allowed.

With respect to multiemployer plans, benefits generally are not covered for plans terminating before January 1, 1978. However, the corporation may, in its discretion, cover the benefits of multiemployer plans that had been maintained for five years prior to a termination after the date of enactment, if the corporation determines that this coverage will not jeopardize the coverage of multiemployer plans terminating after December 31, 1977.

Notwithstanding the usual requirements for coverage (discussed above with respect to coverage of plans and coverage of benefits), the corporation may exercise its discretion to cover multiemployer plans which terminate after the date of enactment [September 2, 1974] and before January 1, 1978, if these plans were maintained for five years prior to termination and if the plans—

(A) have been in substantial compliance with the funding requirements for a qualified plan with respect to the employees and former employees in those employment units on the basis of which the participating employers have contributed to the plan for the preceding five years, and

(B) if the participating employers and employee organization or organizations had no reasonable recourse other than termination.

* * *

If the corporation decides to exercise its discretion with respect to a multiemployer plan, the corporation—

(A) may establish requirements for the continuation of payments which commenced before January 2, 1974, with respect to retired participants under the plan,

(B) may not make payments with respect to any participant who, on January 1, 1974, was receiving payment of retirement benefits, in excess of the amounts and rates payable with respect to that participant on that date,

(C) may not make payments which are derived, directly or indirectly, from amounts borrowed from the Treasury, and

(D) is to review from time to time these discretionary payments and reduce or terminate them to the extent necessary to allow the corporation to guarantee benefits of multiemployer plans terminating after December 31, 1977, without increasing premium rates.

The premiums for both single-employer and multiemployer plans are to be payable for fractional years beginning with the date of enactment [September 2, 1974].

If the Pension Benefit Guaranty Corporation finds that a plan (other than a multiemployer plan) has terminated after June 30, 1974, and before the date of enactment [September 2, 1974] (and therefore would be eligible for coverage of benefits under the plan termination insurance provisions, but the employer would not be subject to employer liability under those provisions) then the guarantee of benefits is not to apply unless the corporation finds substantial evidence that the plan was terminated for a reasonable business purpose and not for the purpose of obtaining the payment of benefits by the corporation under this bill or of avoiding employer liability.

Topical Index

References are to paragraph (¶) numbers.